W9-CNP-488

Putting the Ill At Ease

Putting the Ill At Ease

Evelyn Wilde Mayerson, Ed. D.

Assistant Professor in Psychiatry
Department of Psychiatry
Temple University School of Medicine
Visiting Assistant Professor
Hahnemann Medical College
Philadelphia, Pennsylvania

LYNN F. BRUMM, DO
M.S.U., C.O.M.
DEPT. FAMILY MEDICINE
WEST FEE HALL
EAST LANSING, MICH.   48824

Medical Department
Harper & Row, Publishers
Hagerstown, Maryland
New York, San Francisco, London

76 77 78 79 80 10 9 8 7 6 5 4 3 2 1

PUTTING THE ILL AT EASE. Copyright © 1976 by Harper & Row, Publishers, Inc. All rights reserved. No part of this book may be used or reproduced in any manner whatsoever without written permission except in the case of brief quotations embodied in critical articles and reviews. Printed in the United States of America. For information address Medical Department, Harper & Row, Publishers, Inc., 2350 Virginia Avenue, Hagerstown, Maryland 21740

Library of Congress Cataloging in Publication Data

Mayerson, Evelyn Wilde
   Putting the ill at ease.

   Bibliography: p.
   Includes index.
   1. Physician and patient. 2. Interpersonal communication. 3. Medicine and psychology. I. Title. [DNLM: 1. Communication. 2. Physician-patient relations. W62 M468p]
   R727.3.M39   610.69'6   75–43550
   ISBN 0–06–141710–6

*To my husband Don and sons Gary and Bobby
who brought me coffee, fresh typewriter ribbons,
and their love.*

Contents

Foreword

The quality of medical care rendered by an individual physician must depend on his knowledge and skill in scientific medical matters. The number of patients seeking his services is largely a function of the physician's personality. The results achieved by a physician in terms of success in both diagnosis and treatment are directly dependent upon his ability to communicate with his patients, perceive their problems and deliver his message. To paraphrase the Apostle Paul we can say that in all medical practice three areas are of basic importance: Scientific knowledge, personality of the practitioner, and communication. The greatest of these is communication.

The practice of medicine is essentially two-way communication between patient and physician. In western medicine the patient initiates this dialogue by seeking out a physician and delivering "problems" to be solved. This—the transmission of medical problems from patient to physician—requires that the physician understand all the modalities of communication—verbal and nonverbal. He must also know something about his patients: what is easy for them to communicate and what will be difficult, where they will be embarrassed or reluctant to verbalize problems and information. The Logos of medical practice dictates that the physician "gets the message." The patient's difficulties in expressing his problems do not justify the physician's failure to perceive the problems.

A diagnosis is impossible unless the patient's problem is communicated in some manner to the physician. However, communication is more than the perception of a patient's problem; it is also the physician's communicating back to the patient such things as a genuine interest in the patient's specific problems and general "welfare." The patient's cooperation in his treatment and its therapeutic effectiveness depends in large part upon the "message" the physician conveys to the patient. This "message" may be both verbal and nonverbal; sometimes expressions, gestures, and tone of voice are better perceived than the actual words. In fact, nonverbal communication often is more significant than its verbal counterpart. The "laying on of the hands" is an important part of the physical examination. The physician checks for masses, rigidity, or fremitus, and the patient gains confidence by experiencing the skillful, palpating fingers of an accomplished clinican. Essentially, the more thorough and probing the physical examination, the sounder the diagnosis and the greater the confidence instilled in the patient by the physician.

The quality of the physician-patient communication varies greatly. Physicians tend to complain that patients don't follow advice, when in many cases the patient does not understand the physician's orders and instructions nor the reason for them. Not infrequently malpractice suits result from this communications gap. Although this situation may not happen to every physician every day, it certainly accounts for much of malpractice litigation, and the rising costs of and concern for this problem attests to its frequency. The malpractice concept of "lack of informed consent" is a blatant communication failure. Clinicians frequently are heard to say that a major cause for the failure of medical treatment is the failure of the patient to take medication as directed. Surgeons also complain that early therapy for malignancy is often frustrated by failure of the patient to consent to surgical intervention.

These phenomena are the end result of nothing more nor less than a basic communication failure. Those who would treat the sick must learn first to communicate with them, and communication to be more effective must be a two way process. The physician must perceive the patient's symptoms in order to achieve the "brilliant diagnosis." In order to successfully treat the patient on whom the brilliant diagnosis was made, it is imperative to communicate the necessity to follow instructions, whether medical or surgical. These phases of communication are inseparable—simply two aspects of the same process. A most undesirable but all too prevalent form of medical communication is the "computer communication concept." When carried to extremes, the physician practitioner relies solely on the results of various ancillary laboratory tests. In the name of objectivity the radiologist or clinical laboratory pathologist confines his examination to the precise test ordered. The chest x-ray or the blood chemistry test can indeed communicate information about the patient but only as a "one-way" message. Thus the abnormal pulmonary disease within the patient's chest casts a shadow when exposed to x-rays and the blood sample removed from the patient's arm contains an abnormal concentration of a certain constituent. The radiologist or pathologist measures in a very precise and exact manner this information from the patient. Since these specialists are trained to be "objective," they interpret this specific information against a narrow established "normal range" of values and deliver a neatly typed report to the physician.

The "two-way" communication process should be completed by the physician in his evaluation of these clinical laboratory reports and in the light of the total knowledge he possesses about that patient. The inadequate medical practitioner ignores this last step and delivers to the patient the results of the test procedures only. If the physician's only function is to deliver the reports of others to the patient, there is an inherent danger of his being replaced by a computer which would probably perform that job much more efficiently.

A very major defect of contemporary medical practice is precisely the failure of patient-physician communication. It may commence when the physician does not "listen" to the patient's complaints and fails to notice the nonverbal communication. It is further compounded by clinical laboratory procedures and the failure of the physician to communicate the results and implications of such procedures and tests to the patient. Even though the patient remains frightened and unenlightened, he seldom fully complies with the physician's recommendations and as a result only partially participates in the therapy. As can be expected, both patient and physician are disappointed and dissatisfied with the end results. In turn there is a never-ending escalation of the cost of medical care and a mounting army of dissatisfied patients who are tempted to seek relief elsewhere. Final solution lies only in the improvement of communication between patient and physician.

One medical school of my acquaintance has a course for first-year students titled "The Doctor-Patient Relationship." The class-room approach to the problem of developing communication skills in physicians has been successful, but communication skills must be put into use in all phases of patient management. It is not enough to teach a course in the doctor-patient relationship; it is also necessary to teach doctor-patient relationship in all courses throughout the entire medical school curriculum and clinical practice.

PUTTING THE ILL AT EASE critically analyzes medical communication in all its varied aspects. After first considering carefully the process of communication throughout the animal kingdom, particularly as it is achieved by man, Dr. Mayerson carefully details the components of clinical communication. Techniques and details of verbal and nonverbal communication, including kinesic signals, somatic signals and lexical signals, are described. The author details the process of inviting and encouraging the patient to communicate his problems to the physician, thus facilitating the communication processes. The fine points of information gathering in the medical interview are carefully analyzed and presented most thoroughly.

One section is devoted to the very critical aspect of giving information. Examples are presented with thorough and detailed analysis of the process by which the physician may communicate his recommendations to patients.

Succeeding portions of the text deal in detail with specialized clinical situations, including communicating with the elderly, the alcoholic, the addict, the child and the dying patient.

The chapter on communicating with the dying should be required reading for all practicing physicians.

This text stresses the "two-way street" aspect of physician-patient communication. The dual process of sending and receiving signals of all types is carefully analyzed and thoroughly presented in a most lucid manner with familiar examples from every-day life. Students and practitioners of medicine who have read and thoroughly digested the contents of this book need not complain about patients failing to follow their advice through a lack of understanding. May this volume add a much needed dimension to the delivery of quality medical care.

William B. Buckingham, MD
Associate Professor of Medicine
Department of Medicine
Northwestern University Medical School
Chicago, Illinois

Preface

I taught my first medical class in a room that doubled as a repository for surplus organs —an aquarium of leftovers from countless anatomy labs. I remember thinking with grim humor characteristic of one who has never dissected a cadaver that sharing a room with livers and brains swimming lazily in formadehyde was some sort of test of my suitability for teaching. While our enforced cohabitation was not a rite of passage designed by the curriculum committee, it represented something far more simple, far more significant: The necessity of teaching a great deal of information to a great many students had caused all available space to be pressed into double service.

Medical Science is not only extensive, but overwhelming in a way Hippocrates never dreamt of. Microbiology, neurophysiology, biochemistry, and pharmacology, among other fields, have increased medical knowledge in exponential proportions, yielding more information in the last 30 years than had been learned in the past 300. Sensors that track, scan, and monitor minutae of body function without violating the integrity of the whole; drugs compounded for exquisite purposes; lasers, ultrasonic scalpels, radioactive isotopes, hemoglobin electrophoresis, and transplantation of body parts from one person to another are part of the legacy to those who will go forth armed with this amazing technology to prolong life and enhance its quality.

This incredible avalanche of hard data had nudged aside the affective part of medicine —its Art. Recent changes in medical education, however, are recalling the affective from background status, and curricula are beginning once again to give more weight to the art of medicine.

In response to this rekindled attention to the compassionate part of the patient-physician contract, I have written this book. Like Melville, I believe it is easier to be compassionate when one is able to do something about the object of one's concern. And to be able to "do something," you must understand the problem. I believe that the patient communicates more specifically when made to feel a partner in the clinical interaction. The resulting clarity in exchange of information between patient and physician enhances the quality of patient care.

PUTTING THE ILL AT EASE treats all communication between physician and patient as a potentially therapeutic act. It includes specific information that the physician can use in understanding his patient and in making himself understood in any clinical situation. The first five chapters address all aspects of clinical interaction, including history-taking, obtaining an informed decision, genetic and environmental counseling, preventive education, and instructions in self-care given in the interview. The last six chapters cover such specialized situations as communication with infants and children, the elderly, the terminally ill, the drug-dependent patient, the emergency-room and hospitalized patient, and the patient's family.

As the title might indicate, the approach is light and sympathetic. Written specifically for medical personnel, PUTTING THE ILL AT EASE is a comprehensive guide to the problem of patient-physician communication. I have attempted to clarify and simplify vague concepts of communication and to spell out the criteria and dynamics of effective patient-physician interaction.

Although PUTTING THE ILL AT EASE was written primarily for the physician, any health care professional—dentists, physician's assistants, nurses, etc.—who comes in contact with the patient should find the information both interesting and clinically applicable.

Acknowledgments

Many have given me encouragement in my work, particularly with regard to this book. For general and specific advice and information, and especially for reading and critiquing the various chapters, I wish particularly to thank Max C. Pepernik, M.D., University of Southern California; George E. Gittens, M.D., Office of Medical Programming, The State of Pennsylvania; Dean Hugo D. Smith, M.D., Anthony F. Panzetta, M.D., Lester Karafin, M.D., Louis C. Harris, M.D., Elizabeth Sieling, R.N., Barry Shmavonian, Ph.D., Lyle Miller, Ph.D., Ben E. Price, M.D., John C. Ball, Ph.D., Philip E. Rosenberg, Ph.D., John R. Benson, M.D., Allan H. Cristol, M.D., Temple University School of Medicine; Ms. Karen Connell and Jean Alberti, Ph.D., University of Illinois College of Medicine, Center for Educational Development; Dean W. Roberts, M.D., and Melvin A. Benarde, Ph.D., Hahnemann Medical College; Mr. E. A. Vastyan, The Milton S. Hershey Medical Center; and Perry Bechtel, Esq. I also wish to extend my thanks to Dr. William B. Buckingham for his keen insight into the problems involved in physician-patient communication.

I wish to express my appreciation to Elizabeth Graff for illustrating the book.

I want also to thank Leslie Blumenthal for her energy and devotion in preparing the manuscript. Most especially I wish to express my appreciation to the countless patients who have given me an understanding of their experience and to my students — the dedicated young men and women tearing around the corridors, their stethoscopes popping out of their pockets, or trooping sedately behind the chief at rounds, their stethoscopes neatly tucked in — who have allowed me to teach them what I know about people.

Putting the Ill At Ease

1
Communication and Its Meaning to the Physician

All sciences are connected; they lend each other material aid as parts of one great whole, each doing its own work not for itself alone but for the other parts, as the eye guides the whole body and the foot sustains it and leads it from place to place.

Roger Bacon

SNAGS IN THE DESIGN

Crabs signal sexual readiness by clicking their claws in the air while gliding across the sand. No one else on the beach gets the message of these crustacean castanets except other crabs. For all his virtuosity, however, the crab is limited. He may manage a more sophisticated message like "hurry up and make the sand bar before the tide runs out," but his repertoire is circumscribed by the relatively few actions and sounds he can successfully produce, by his intellect, which occupies a less than distinguished spot somewhere between the intellect of the shark and that of the crocodile, and by innate prescription determined by the necessities of the survival of his species.

MULTIPLICITY OF SIGNALS

Man is more fortunate. His intricate arrangement of larynx, lip, tongue, palate, diaphragm, and nasal chamber orchestrate in multiple sound effects. A face made mobile by the frontalis muscles with which he shields his eyes and transversalis nasi with which he can flare his nares (a signal which Duchenne suggested was of lascivious intent), a jointed torso, and an opposing thumb and forefinger proliferate soundless signals (2). An autonomic nervous system capable of altering his skin color, odor, external moisture, and respiration gives his efforts the added feature of special effects. The complexity of his social order dictates an equally complex means by which that order is regulated and maintained, necessitating a system of intricate social cues in order to determine behavior and render it predictable. The result is an elaborate system for sending and receiving messages, which makes human communication, like Shakespeare's Cleopatra, capable of "infinite variety."

Infinite variety has its dark side. While it enriches human communication, it is potentially a stumbling block. The capacity for a multiplicity of signals carries with it awesome responsibility. For communication to be successful, there must be agreement on the meaning of the signals. Free style language, no matter how artful, does not lend itself to mutual understanding, as illustrated by the schizophrenic who tosses syntax like smoke bombs, leaving a trail of confusion behind

1

him. The first requirement of communication is consensual validation.

Multiplicity of signals dictate an equally vast appreciation of both the encoder and the decoder although the latter seems to be stuck with the responsibility. Apart from consensual validation, the decoder must be familiar with all the forms a message might take. The skill and accuracy of the sender are only as effective as the decoder's ability to interpret. Finally, the decoder must be able to perceive the signals, lest they share the fate of the spruce crashing unheard in the forest.

The process by which messages are sent is continual; it flashes with the constancy of a neon sign. However infinite its variety, a unit of communication must contain essential components: transmission, perception, and interpretation. The sender, or the encoder, motivated by internal states and external stimuli, emits a signal—lexical, kinesic, or autonomic—which is perceived by another. The signal, perceived by any or all of the senses, is then filtered through a unique prism, the individual understanding of the receiver or the decoder. The receiver then interprets the signal, a decoding process that considers and evaluates all the cues in the light of his past experience. This summary analysis of information leads to prediction and decision making by the receiver, a procedure similar to plotting chess moves. A single unit of communication may contain so many diverse and subtle signals that its graphic depiction would resemble a Comanche attack.

INTERMITTENT FEEDBACK

If the receiver encodes a return message which is in turn perceived and interpreted, it completes the circuit. This feedback tells the original sender whether or not his message got through as intended. Feedback, the fourth possible component, is not always a factor of communication.

The vague status of feedback is the second block to communication, compounding problems caused by the multiplicity of signals. When feedback is present, it acts as a corrective device. The one who provides feedback holds a mirror to the transmittor who then gets a chance to see how he looks. If his tie is crooked he can straighten it. Feedback gives him an opportunity to avoid misunderstanding by restating the message.

"Are you mad at me?"

"No."

"That's funny, I thought you were mad at me."

"What makes you say that?"

"You're glowering at me."

"It's these glasses. I can't get used to them."

When feedback is absent, corrective action cannot occur. The sender is never sure that his message stayed on course. The receiver may respond to a completely different message than the one intended. ("She's got no right to be mad at me. I'll show her.")

The use of feedback may be culturally determined. The Japanese telephone listener provides something every few seconds to let the one who is talking know that he is there, he is listening, he understands, and he is interested. Since most of the words used are *yes, of course, right, very good,* this feedback is more reassuring than corrective, although it fulfills much of the function of response.

Animal communication is largely instinctive; it is composed of a coded signal system that is triggered by specific events. Animal signals may be limited and inflexible, but they are precise and can not be misunderstood. If a mallard drake lifts his chin, slightly turns his head, and says very quickly, "Rabrab, rabrab" to a female, it means he accepts her offer to mate (7). It is the mallard equivalent of "I do." There is no possibility that she misunderstood him and that he won't show up; unless he has his tail feathers gnawed by another mallard drake, he'll be there.

Man has traded most of the instinctive reactions in his behavior for complex problem-solving activity that requires the utilization of both adaptive communication and complex symbols, many of which are imprecise. Consequently, individual interpretation is not only possible, but inevitable.

INDIVIDUAL INTERPRETATION

The third block to effective communication is the filter of individual interpretation. As messages pass through personal prisms, they are reshaped by diffusion and distortion, the error varying from slight to gross depending on the disparity of understanding between the individuals involved. The disparity is determined by differences in life experiences and in levels of awareness, by the expectations of the receiver, and by the manner in which communication was first learned.

Individual understanding is built largely upon an infant's involuntary participation in the communication between him and his mother. An infant needs appropriate and well-timed stimulation according to his individual requirements (9). Additionally, he must receive feedback for his own efforts. If stimulation is over or undersupplied, if his mother's messages are ill-timed, or if his responses are not acknowledged, his future communication is disturbed or, at the very least, inadequate. Since mothers do not meet their infants' needs in precisely the same way, communication skills vary. Additional environmental factors further shape the individual's ability to communicate. Our vastly different experiences make our understanding of one another's signals pervasive and variable.

One's self-concept contributes to unique perception. Interpretation of terms will be affected by personal norms. For example, the concepts short and tall, big and little, beautiful and ugly, young and old, or cowardly and brave will be subjectively colored by the individual. While he may be aware of their objective definitions, his interpretation of any such terms will be shaded according to his perception of himself in relation to them.

Interpretation is also influenced by a predesigned framework. The individual uses a set, an intellectual structure which helps him interpret information. The framework changes as the person changes, but it is the prism through which he processes communications. It involves location, age, education, sex, occupation, race, and culture. It is the background of the attitudes that affect an individual's grasp of information and his ability to interpret it and make sense of a complex world. The communication problem occurs when two persons view the same issue from the vantage points of different frameworks. For example, a discussion of drugs between a middle-aged father and his adolescent son, a discussion of the definition of perception between a Gestaltist and a behaviorist, or a discussion of birth control between a mother from a minority culture and a physician from the majority culture all seem irreconcilable and doomed from the start.

Limitations of the decoder's capacity to retain significant words contribute to individual interpretation. Since he cannot process every single word he hears he tries to compensate for the loss by extrapolating from the cues that he does process (6). In this way, he adds to what he receives, although sometimes incorrectly. Interaction between short and long-term memory is responsible for processing information through extrapolation. The intake of information corresponds to a single pulse of attention. When information continues to be taken in, the result is a series of pulses, each competing with the other for attention. Each pulse, which admits a selection of sensory cues, is linked to the next by short-term memory. Making sense of the cues depends on previous information stored in long-term memory. Extrapolation, then, depends on the pulse capacity of short-term memory and on the evaluation made possible by long-term memory. An individual's interpretation varies with the quality of his neurological equipment.

The problem of individual interpretation is made worse by confused presentation. Words with ambiguous meaning make an additional demand upon the receiver. He must place them in a temporary hold position until he has enough other cues to decode them. If he gets enough of them, they create a cargo overload. Speaking in the negative, using qualifiers, or speaking in complicated terms can confound communication. Listeners have a tendency to translate negative or qualified statements into the affirmative, and complicated terms are often translated through context. Translation simply increases the risk of misinterpretation.

COMMUNICATION AS BARTER

Communication is a layered event, much like an onion. At first glance, the top layer, the easy peel, is a physical act of self-expression, that relieves the tension

from some inner drive of the sender. Self-expression, sometimes called affect expression, is a display of feeling. The most basic communication, the expression of feeling can be either the early warning of a need or the signal of a need fulfilled.

Biological needs for survival of the individual and of the species exist in all species. Oxygen, water, food, maintenance of body temperature, and avoidance of tissue damage are necessary from birth. The early vocalizations of the infant are essentially signals of distress regarding these needs, and like a cash register, they ring loud and clear under conditions of deficits and surfeits. Learned needs, such as those for status or needs activated by maturation, such as those to procreate and care for the young, lead to competitive sexual, care-giving, and exploratory behaviors that serve to fulfill them. All of these behaviors involve communication.

When a human being attempts to fill a need, subtle changes in muscular tension occur as a result of energy arousal. The arousal is at first general, then begins to assume specificity as effort is directed to a particular goal. This may take the shape of vocalization and/or movement. A psychologic reorganization follows in which there is a shift in emphasis from subject to object. Imagined in slow motion, it is like a ballet. A movement plan, already present in nuclear form, begins to unfold and enlarge, influenced in its mitosis by sensations from within and without. The condition of unrest resulting from a need, called the drive state, is responsible for and gives impetus to this evolving movement (10).

The act of communicative expression derives partly from drive and partly from volitional movement. It has been compared to an iceberg in that the gross bulk below the water's surface is the equivalent of the unconscious automatic information processing system essential to the formulation of a message. The remaining tip has been compared to conscious formulation, in which deliberate selection and choice are involved in the precise rendition of an idea.

In becoming expressive, conscious movement is influenced by cultural inhibitions, which are not always successful in hiding true meaning. We will see later how subtle cues often belie the ostensible expression and reveal to the practiced observer the most significant message. Ruesch defines communication as "all behaviors that one employs consciously or unconsciously to affect another. Not only spoken words but gestures, body movements, and somatic signals" (9). Duncan concurs; his definition of communication is an attempt to "persuade others to certain courses of action that we believe necessary to create a given social order" (3). In this sense, communication is propaganda. There is an appeal to the recipient to behave in a certain way, to speak in a certain way, or to believe in some idea.

Peeling the onion deeper, we see that communication, besides offering self-expression to the individual has an important function in human systems. As individuals seek others of their own kind to whom they can express their feelings, communication becomes a market place, an exchange where people express their needs to one another in a kind of barter. The recipient of the expression is in a position to grant or deny affect or status. With that consideration, both transmission and response are potentially rewarding or punitive.

The concept of communication as social barter is an additional element that militates against its success. Everyone is not always satisfied in the market place. There is always someone who feels cheated or shortchanged or who thinks that he bought the wrong merchandise. When someone stands to win or lose, anxiety and frustration accompany the barter; the severity of each feeling depends on how much is expected from the interchange and how much is at stake.

DISTRACTION

A practical consideration that interferes with communication is distraction. Any competing stimulus may disrupt communication. Nearby conversation on a similar theme; other noises; environmental stress of temperature, humidity, ventilation, vibration, and glare; and internal states of sleeplessness, ill health, drug effects, mood variation, or sensory deprivations all affect the understanding between communicators.

Multiplicity of signals, lack of feedback, individual interpretation, inequities inherent in barter, and distraction are troublesome components of all communication. Unlike other species whose mastery of their communication signals has neatly forestalled serious conflcts among their kind, man must contend with the conflct and misunderstanding built into the human experience. Man has trouble with the ground rules. He confuses his signals, and he mixes his cues. When the mix-up is slight, he has a misunderstanding, possibly a confrontation. If he happens to mix his signals in medicine, the results can be more serious, affecting his safety, his well-being, his life. The doctor–patient interaction compounds difficulties inherent in all communication and has additional problems peculiar to medicine.

PHYSICIAN–PATIENT SNAGS

Each of us learns various communication forms and meanings, and we learn to discriminate in their use in accordance with their context (1). Handled by the central nervous system with great efficiency, context involves such variables as the immediate past of the participants in a communication, their total life histories, their ages, sex, socioeconomic status, place of meeting, purpose of meeting, and what each had for breakfast that morning.

A set of socially learned operating rules determines how we formulate and how we interpret messages within a given context. If the context is serious, flip or frivolous responses may be considered violations of the rules (4). Likewise, if the context is casual, serious pronouncements are seen as violations. When two ac-

quaintances of equal status greet one another on the sidewalk, their interchange may go something like this:

"Hi."

"Hi."

"What's happening?"

"Can't complain."

"Don't work too hard."

"See ya." etc.

No information has been exchanged, and no feeling has been expressed. Instead, each response has been a stereotypic formulation according to carefully prescribed social rules of language which determine how relationships are maintained. What has been conveyed is *I continue to hold you in regard.* If one of the two were preoccupied and failed to enter into the exchange, he might cause the other serious concern. Malinowski called conversation that is empty of content but functions as social cement *phatic communication* from words that mean "verbal togetherness" (8).

If "What's happening?" is followed by "I have terrible problems. My mother-in-law is coming to stay for a month, I can't pay my bills, and my car was totaled last week," the context is violated. The recipient of such an answer is probably a little surprised that his question elicited a real response. That wasn't supposed to happen. He may even be annoyed with his acquaintance for not following the rules. Suppose now that the two who greet one another have different status; one is the employer of the other. If the one of greater status were to answer "How goes it?" by saying, "Terrible, the water cooler just broke," the one of lesser status is obliged to adapt to the new mode—one of serious and problem-solving intent—and the context changes. He must make a response appropriate to the new style, so he might say, "That's too bad." or "Maybe I can fix it."

Context functions as a paraphrase of the message, which explains why an identical statement is processed differently in different situations. "I want to see you again next week," said by a physician to a patient carries a different meaning than the same words said by one friend to another. In the first context the statement can be paraphrased as, "Our meetings have been inconclusive. I need more information before I can help you." Even within the clinical experience, "I want to see you again next week" would be processed differently according to the place of the interchange. If made in the cancer clinic the statement would convey more urgency and threat than if made at a first aid station. In the second context the meaning changes to "I enjoy being with you. I want to repeat the pleasure."

The patient–physician interaction occurs in the context of care-giving behavior. Primates grooming each other's coats, elephants gently nuzzling a dying elder, mammalian mothers suckling their young, and physicians treating their patients all share the mutual bond between giver and receiver that is a part of care-giving behavior. Each giver has a responsibility to the receiver. Each receiver learns to trust the giver, unless the giver made the experience unpleasant, like the baboon who sits on the stomach of another in order to pick nits out of his fur.

CONTEXT

The context of the patient–physician interaction, which includes age, sex, socioeconomic status, place and nature of interaction, immediate past of participants, and their total life histories, expands to include stress. Most patients face medical interaction with anxiety. First, this response is conditioned. As children, they

learned to associate the physician's office with bodily insults and indignities. Second, most patients, even those with a fair sophistication in medical matters, regard their bodies and its works as an enigma. They have known others in apparent good health or with minor complaints who suddenly and inexplicably became victims of serious illness.

Patients go to their physician with some sense of vulnerability. The physician may find something wrong. He may assign a label to fleeting sensations, thereby endowing them with reality and forever removing from the patient the privilege of deciding whether they exist or not. The physician may order unpleasant tests that require time lost from work or time spent hitching up socks under a brief and breezy x-ray gown in a waiting room. He may prescribe medication, uncomfortable procedures, or hospitalization. If the patient is to be hospitalized, he may perceive that he abrogates his freedom and his independence. Once inside the hospital, he trades independence for care. He leaves behind his power base in the exchange. His support, found in family, friends, and job, and his status, reflected in his car, his clothes, and his home, remain outside. The moment he checks into the hospital, he surrenders his most precious possession, himself, to strangers. From then on he is at the mercy of an impartial army of people who slap a name tag on his wrist, confine him impotent and helpless in a bed, sample his blood, decide when and if he sleeps, monitor his body fluids, and post on the door, in a kind of box score for all the world to see, his output and input. If he is to undergo surgery, he fears possible loss of virility, body parts, function, or life.

The physician–patient context varies according to the clinical setting. There's a difference between the intimate, familiar private office and the impersonal, unfamiliar hospital. There is also a difference between the small suburban hospital and the blood-and-guts hospital of the inner city. Whatever the setting, stress is inherent in the interaction.

Stress with its resultant anxiety can alter any expression mode, interfering with the patient's message to the physician. Words, postures, gestures, and visceral manifestations are all affected by stress. The result is often ambivalent or contradictory messages, confounding the signal from the patient to the physician.

Just as stress alters the patient's message to his physician, it changes the way he receives a message from his physician. Anxiety has a neat way of blocking perception. The patient under stress will not process all the physician is telling him. The message will skirt the periphery of his understanding. For the moment it is surplus baggage, kept in abeyance by the source of his discomfort that must get the major part of his attention. When an individual is intensely preoccupied with his own distress, the machinery of homeostasis—the tendency of the body to maintain equilibrium—forces him to jettison everything not related to its relief.

TIME LIMITATIONS

Stress militates against effective patient–physician communication. This stumbling block impedes the natural flow of information that must occur for mutual understanding and for successful medical treatment. Exacerbating the problem is lack of time, a commodity the practicing physician has in short supply.

The pace of the private office, the hospital clinic, and the heavy patient load that faces most physicians mandate his speedy and efficient performance. An optimum condition would be one in which the physician has all the time he needs for each patient or could schedule those that require more time at a specific time of day when he is unlikely to be interrupted. Emergencies, phone calls, consultations, and routine administrative problems interrupt the most flexible schedule. The pressure of time requires efficient physician–patient communication. The physician has to say what he means and hopes his patients do likewise. The last thing he has time for is the unravelling of poor or faulty communication resulting from the patient's anxiety.

THE PHYSICIAN'S REACTION TO THE PATIENT'S EMOTION

Even if time were not a factor, the physician's own feelings and experience often determine how he deals with anxiety. Assuming it is identified, someone who is uncomfortable with emotional states in others will rely entirely on the verbal interchange and never address the emotion at all. This dismissal is a protective device; it fends off the threat of what is considered an uncomfortable situation.

Some physicians believe that acknowledging intense emotional states in patients is opening a can of worms. The patient may cry, rage, or seek help that the physician may feel he is unable to give. Since his domain is the body, anything to do with the head, other than ENT, it is not his bailiwick.

Medical school often gives the student a skewed orientation to medicine. Most freshmen spend their first year associating primarily with a cadaver. After a second year of pathology, students rotate through specialties getting keyhole peeks at live patients, the shape of the keyhole changing with the specialty. It is usually a surprise for students who spend time with practicing physicians to discover that much of the physician's work deals with a complete live human being with ordinary complaints. What's even more surprising is that the culprit responsible for the origin, nature, or exacerbation of these complaints is less likely to be a rare spirochete and more likely factors that are psychologic or sociologic in origin. Medicine becomes even more person oriented when one includes the entire range of living problems about which a patient consults his physician—including how to lose weight, what to do about an aging and infirm relative, and how he can be treated for gonorrhea without telling his wife.

Seen globally, psychologic and sociologic factors are responsible for most of the ball game. It is they that determine whether an individual recognizes illness as a threat to his health, whether he can enter in a health care system, whether he can collaborate in the treatment of his problem, and how he hangs in there if it cannot be resolved. Unresolved problems, whatever their origin, are a source of emotional distress and often evoke physical symptoms. Only the alert physician is likely to appreciate the degree to which such presenting complaints reflect these unresolved problems.

There is compelling evidence that the psychologic condition of the patient may significantly contribute to the onset of somatic diseases and also to the restorative and healing process. The power of the patient's state of mind to affect his body, as seen in psychophysiologic illness, should confirm the need for a complete approach to the patient. Those in medicine, unlike the magician who has contentedly sawed off the lady's head, seek to put it back.

HALO EFFECT

There are other factors inherent in the physician–patient relationship that, while supplying the physician with leverage, interfere to some degree with the efficient communication between him and his patient. The first of these is known as the halo effect, a phenomenon in which one person infers from one or a few traits the totality of another (his intentions, behavior, motivation). The halo can be one of either total good or total evil and can operate in any human interaction. In a patient–physician interaction, most patients perceive the physician to be totally good and omniscient, a function of the mystique of the medicine man.

Healers, who constitute the oldest professional class in the evolution of society (contrary to popular opinion), have always enjoyed great prestige. In primitive cultures, the shaman is regarded with awe (5). Historically, the healer was the intercessionary agent, the one barrier between those in his charge and all the malevolent powers in the world that threatened their existence.

Although the idea of the medicine man as a magical being is no longer officially promulgated in Western society, the mystique is maintained by custom. First, the physician's experience still stands between his patients and all threats to their well-being. Second, there are educational and social disparities between the physician and most of his patients. This disparity causes the patient to see the physician as one of high rank and status. Lastly, the physician's trappings sustain the mystique. Although he no longer operates in formal dress (a garb that he exchanged for the amulets of his predecessors), he wears a white coat, is surrounded by an entourage of nurses, interns, and residents who follow him at a respectful distance, and carries a black bag which in some societies enjoys magic status all its own.

The halo effect is in many ways beneficial in the patient–physician interaction, but the belief that the physician is omniscient can cause problems. The patient will leave unsaid that which he assumes the physician knows. "You know what I mean, Doctor," more often originates from presumption than embarrassment. If the physician behaves in a manner which to the patient is brusque, discourteous, or otherwise unfriendly, the patient, because of his frozen image of the physician as a good guy, will consider himself *ipso facto* the bad guy. If the good guy sees fit to be brusque, the bad guy must have something about him which invites brusqueness. The bad guy then must watch carefully what he says and supply answers that will put him back in the graces of the good guy.

TRANSFERENCE

A second factor inherent in the patient–physician relationship contradicts both leverage and interference. Borrowed from psychoanalytical thinking, *transference* is the unconscious attribution of characteristics of important people in the patient's past to the physician. Predetermined feelings of affection or dislike directed toward the physician are recapitulations of earlier infantile and childish relations to a parental figure. These feelings have nothing to do with the physician himself. They represent instead the patient's perception of the physician's high status within the care-giving context and his own reexperiencing of the helplessness of a small child. This perception triggers the process of transference.

Transference, when it occurs, largely determines the patient's behavior toward the physician. His behavior will resemble earlier behavior patterns learned in his relationship with parental or other significant figures in early life. If the transference is positive, the patient will feel love and admiration, but if it is negative, he will feel hostility or envy. Positive transference creates minor difficulties in patient–physician communication. While the patient will still be motivated to reveal the nature of his problems and their sources, he might bring to the relationship feelings of inadequacy and dependency. If the transference is negative, more serious problems occur. For example, if the patient is reminded by the physician of his demanding and irrascible father, he may respond as he did with his father, perhaps with half-references and circumlocutions, the only comfortable way to interact with such a parent. Obviously, in medicine, circumlocutions and half-references are not helpful.

Either of these phenomena, halo effect or transference, that cause the patient to conceive of the physician as one of high status may impair communication. When someone of high status asks "Any questions?" it is often interpreted as "Any complaints?" Even if the questioner were seriously interested in the viewpoint or ideas of the other, he would be unlikely to hear them.

While the halo effect and transference are factors to be considered, they have been and continue to be mitigated. The role of the physician is changing in a way that brings him closer to those within his care by narrowing the gulf that traditionally has separated them.

CHANGES IN PHYSICIAN–PATIENT RELATIONSHIP

MEDIA DISSEMINATION

First, the media disseminates more medical information to the lay public than ever before. Television, radio, magazines, newspapers, and books cover the newest research findings, surgical techniques, and medical procedures. There is a story around about a cardiologist whose patient asked him about a new valve repair procedure. The physician, who knew nothing about it, replied, "I'm sorry. I don't subscribe to *Newsweek.*" As a consequence of this dissemination, the lay public has become more sophisticated in medical terminology and in their understanding of their own bodies. Although medical science is still largely an enigma, there are now some pieces that the lay public can understand. Medical information is no longer seen as esoteric, privy only to the physician.

RAPID ACCUMULATION OF MEDICAL KNOWLEDGE

Second, the formidable accumulation of information in the general body of medicine limits the physician. No physician can hope to become conversant in all areas of medicine. There is simply too much information, and it compounds itself too rapidly. The physician is forced to become proficient in a part rather than the whole of medicine. In the past he stood within the circle of medicine, heir to its entirety; now he, too, stands on the perimeter. While Mercury may be closer to the sun, it shares the solar system with Pluto.

MOBILITY

Third, our population is highly mobile. Statistics show that we have become a nation of back packers; in which each nuclear family moves every 4–5 years. This mobility means that the patient will be subject to multiple medical practitioners.

Each time he settles he must seek a new source of medical aid. Add to this multiplicity the specialization within medicine, and the result is an increasing number of medical professionals who share the role of family physician. The patient sees a diversity of skills as well as a diversity of personal styles. He makes comparisons. Some are better, in his experience, than others. This variability caused by proliferation helps the patient to perceive the physician as less omniscient and more as a human being with foibles and weaknesses similar to his own.

SELF-DETERMINATION

The doctrine of informed consent and recent court rulings on abortion and the artificial maintenance of life, predicated on the patient's right to decide what happens to his body, have also helped to narrow the gulf between the patient and the physician.

The increased concern about the patient–physician relationship and the quality of care within that relationship, the growing public interest in consumer rights, and the phenomenal growth of litigation involving physician and hospital have all affected the patient–physician relationship. Not only must the physician inform his patient about the care he is to receive and the reasons for it, but he must inform the patient in such a way that he understands clearly. This means that the physician has the task of translating organ systems, medical procedures, statistics, and risk into layman's terms, imparting information and sharing the responsibility for decisions that were formerly the exclusive domain of the physician.

THE NEW PHYSICIAN

The last aspect of the medical interaction that has helped to bridge the gap between physician and patient is the fact that the physician himself is changing. The new medical student, a product of his times, reflects the rapid and accelerating cultural and sociologic changes of his society. He is more representative of divergent social elements within the culture. There are more Blacks, women, Puerto Ricans, American Indians, Orientals, and other minority groups in medicine than ever before. Their different socioeconomic backgrounds and attitudes enrich the medical profession with their diversity as they erode class lines and remove the social distinction between physician and patient.

The new physician reflects the new thinking of his post World War II generation, which is not really new thinking at all. It is old thinking that he not only believes now but lives. He has freed himself from the automatic acceptance of social imperatives, bringing new freedom to medicine. As a student he is more questioning, more doubtful, more likely to determine the answer for himself, and more likely to raise hell with the cavalier treatment shown a demonstration patient who is wheeled into the amphitheater of the lecture hall.

While he remains competitive and welcomes favorable assessments from his preceptors, he does not seek distinction from his fellows. He is more aware of equality of status and neither pays attention to nor adopts as many of the trappings that distinguish his predecessors from one another.

Lastly, he demands more honesty in personal relationships. He is more interested in relating to and understanding his patients. He particularly wants to learn to communicate with his patients so that each hears the message of the other.

He has stood before this writer in faded Levi's, textbooks slung over his shoulder in a khaki knapsack, and said with great seriousness, "I know all about anatomy and biochem. Teach me about people."

SUMMARY

PATIENT DIFFICULTIES

Every clinician has dealt with the patient who has difficulty with self-management even after tedious and careful explanation; the patient who does not respond to treatment as well as statistics and data indicate he should, the patient whose presenting complaint turned out to be secondary to a more urgent medical problem, the patient whose complaint could have been prevented, and the patient whose message was somehow lopped off like the legs of the guests in the Procrustean bed. Some patients beleaguer their physicians with constant calls, asking assistance for apparent trifles; others with more legitimate reason offer their complaints with reluctance or do not offer them at all.

PHYSICIAN DIFFICULTIES

On the other side of the desk, many patients are familiar with the physician, who, whereas quite comfortable with the molecular and technological diagnostic procedures of the laboratory, finds it difficult and tedious to counsel a patient in genetics, to teach his family how to care for a diabetic child, to deal with his dying father, or to help him accept difficult medical or surgical procedures.

In all these cases, both patient and physician are responding to what appears to be an intangible in the physician–patient interaction. What seems intangible is not intangible at all but as palpable as a liver. It is communication. A message sent from one person to another was lost, distorted, or discarded in each of these cases. Communication appears to be a clear-cut process: someone sends a message;

someone else receives it. Yet we see again and again miscommunication interfering with clinical reasoning, clinical judgment, and clinical response, all vital components of the physician–patient compact. The simple process is not so simple.

PHYSICIAN'S GOAL

The physician does not dispense indiscriminate treatment like a gumball machine, popping out remedies to anyone who puts in a penny or a health insurance card. He seeks to determine and serve individual needs, but this is more easily said than done. Some patients come into his office equipped to supply history and information as if they had fluorescent print-outs on their foreheads, others supply symtomatology in bits and pieces. The physician finds himself in the role of detective, latching on to those clues that seem significant, discarding those which appear expendable, obliged to go it on his own—a persistent, but slightly hamstrung Sherlock. Other patients supply history as if they were inventing it on the spot, and the physician soon concludes that something else is going on although he's not sure what. Pain or discomfort, not necessarily physical, bring a patient to the physician. Since the physician relies on the patient's description of this discomfort, the patient's ability to describe it is significant.

PROBLEMS IN ACHIEVING GOAL

Some patients have difficulty in locating or describing symptoms. Their presenting complaint is an amorphous "I'm not feeling so good." Under some conditions there are no subjective symptoms. Some patients have difficulty remembering significant data and others become so innured to symptoms, they consider them normal. Even if the patient is quite able in description, other factors intrude.

Many patients like to localize their symptoms by matching bodily sensations to specific spots. They may be so intent on presenting a good case for the spot that they have difficulty considering contradictory information even though the physician may suspect he is dealing with the wrong spot. Many symptoms are typical of more than one condition, and there is often a poor correlation between subjective and objective aspects of symptoms. One man with a high pain threshold and low perception may feel little discomfort, while another, experiencing the same somatic manifestations, suffers acutely.

While the laboratory is an important ally of the physician, clinical observation remains his basic and most important method of determining the relative importance of those symptoms reported, of learning about those that are not reported, and correlating subjective symptoms with objective signs. His selection of laboratory and diagnostic tests is determined by the clinical observations in which he translates verbal, postural, and somatic cues into the conceptual framework of the physical sciences.

ACCURATE COMMUNICATION—THE REMEDY

Since clinical judgments are based largely upon the assessment of the patient, much of which is provided by the patient himself, accurate communication is vital to the validity of the assessment.

It is equally essential then that the physician have as a tool not only his medical expertise to help him distinguish a lub from a dub, but also an adequate idea of patient–physician communication: how it becomes aborted, its relevance to him, its particular adaptation in all services and situations, and how he can help his patients use it skillfully. Precision communication is something the physician does *with* rather than *to* his patient.

Perceiving and interpreting the signals sent by a patient requires that the physician monitor another kind of pulse. It also requires a conscious attention to a life-long transaction in which he engages with all his fellows.

REFERENCES

1. Carswell EA, Rommetveit R (eds): Social Contexts of Messages. New York, Academic Press, 1971
2. Duchenne GBA: Album de Photographie Pathologiques Complementarie du Libre Intitule: de Lectrisation Locolisee. Paris, J B Balliere, 1862
3. Duncan HD: Symbols in Society. London, Oxford University Press, 1968
4. Goffman E: Relations in Public. New York, Basic Books, 1971
5. Jung C: Man and His Symbols. Garden City, Doubleday, 1964
6. Lass NJ, Prater CE: A comparative study of listening rate for preferences for oral reading and impromptu speaking tasks. J Commun 23:95–102, 1973
7. Lorenz K: Habit, Ritual, & Magic. In Lorenz K (ed): On Aggression. New York, Bantam, 1963, pp 54–80
8. Malinowski B: The problem of meaning in primitive languages. In Ogden CK, Richards IA (eds): The Meaning of Meaning. New York, Harcourt Brace, 1923, pp 296–336
9. Ruesch J: Therapeutic Communication. New York, W W Norton, 1961
10. Schilder, Paul: Medical psychology. New York, International Universities Press, 1953

2
Critical Observation

Creatures in general do a great deal of gabbling, and it requires long patience and observation to edit out the parts lacking in syntax and sense.

Lewis Thomas
The Lives of a Cell

CLINICAL COMMUNICATION

The physician must be competent in three basic areas in order to become skilled in clinical communication: critical observation, facilitation, and active intervention. The fundamental skill of critical observation requires that the physician fine tune his habits of watching and listening as he learns to see past his alloted peripheral vision with swiveling eyestalks and listen with what has been called the "third ear" (42). Since it is doubtful that any prospective medical student so endowed would have made it past the interview, successful practice depends upon the heightened sensitivity those appendages suggests. Critical observation begins when the physician focuses on his patient, zeroing in with all his senses and narrowing his attention range in order to minimize the interferences of competing stimuli. In order to process his sensory data, the physician must have some understanding of the way in which signals are sent. Focusing on the patient helps to answer two questions: Who is this patient? What is he saying?

People communicate with one another all the time. It is our most prolific behavior, superseding even that of sex. If we were to engage in the latter to the same degree, we would soon be felled by the billions, littering sidewalks and gullies with exhausted but happy bodies.

CONSTELLATIONS OF EXPRESSIVE BEHAVIOR

When individuals signal to one another, they do so in constellations of expressive behavior. The constellations include three signaling systems: the lexical, which has to do with all speech activities; the kinesic, which includes all body movements; and the somatic, which considers all observable manifestations of the autonomic nervous system.

Searching for meaning in isolated clues of expression from only one of these systems must lead to a dead end. *First,* individual signals occur in constellation. Other signals, while not necessarily simultaneous, are contiguous. Attempting to assign individual meaning would be like trying to identify Betelgeuse without Orion's other stars. It is the full stellar orchestration which yields meaning. *Second,* no single signal or even a constellation of signals ripped from context has absolute value. Unlike the more definitive seismograph, human signals are an indication of,

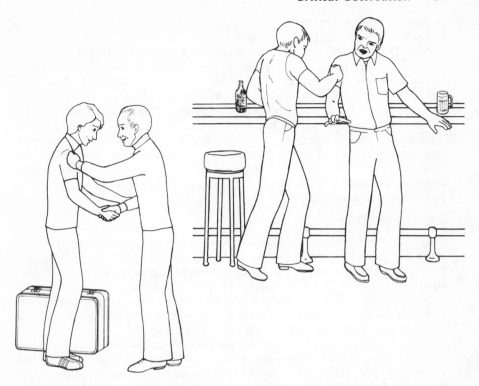

and not the sign for, meaning. Ultimate meaning is determined by context. The odor of burning wood in a campfire and the odor of burning wood in a tenement have totally different meanings. Similarly, one man punching the shoulder of another changes from a friendly greeting to an act of aggression, depending on the context.

CONTEXT

While an understanding of the context of a message requires knowledge of the situation, of any preceding communication within it, and of the relationship between the receiver and the sender, appropriate context is usually observed through a stimulus event. In the previous illustration, the stimulus event may be the punchee's arrival at an airport. *Third,* the act of a painstaking search is self-defeating. In order to observe each nuance of expression and to catch each movement, we would have to watch human behavior in stop frame motion, and the human eye is ill equipped for this feat. We might find ourselves arrested by an intriguing movement, such as a vestigial ear fan, and miss the main message; and finally, we would create the effect of a giant Petri dish, with our patient swimming alone in his new medium and our own participation diminished by the glass. Instead, each signal must be evaluated in the light of sister signals and in the context in which it occurred.

In most cultures, there are restraints placed on communication of affect, evaluation, or preference, particularly when they are negative. If a person experiencing any of these cannot describe it to another, a curious component is added to the event. It is show but not tell, at least not in explicit language. Other systems of communication or their subsidiaries take over the responsibility. The result is ambiguous and contradictory messages.

While communication is enhanced when all systems agree, that is seldom the case unless there is no anxiety or unless the participants have already learned to communicate directly with one another. One of the physician's tasks is to ascertain the degree to which his patient's signals complement one another. He must intervene in the communication process if they do not and resolve any inconsistencies by helping his patient articulate what he feels. He looks for the hidden meaning strangling under the seaweed of circumlocutions and encourages it to surface. The elicitation of vital clinical data, determined by such factors as what, how much, and when information is revealed will depend on how well the physician attends his patient's signals and how effectively he can clear away communicative debris.

IDENTIFICATION

Before he can determine complementariness or disparity among signals or read those that are subtle, the physician has to see and distinguish them from their surroundings; he has to be able to identify them. Identification requires strict attention to process. It requires listening to what his patient says and the manner in which he says it. It requires observation of his patient's kinesic and somatic activities. Lastly, it requires attention to the way in that the three modes of communication complement or contradict one another.

Animals and insects have a neat way of squirting out pheromones, odor signals with precise and obvious meaning. While human language may be somewhat analogous to the pheromone in that it too is a signal, it is seldom squirted with such precision. Additionally, an absent minded sniff is all that is needed to decode a pheromone. Decoding language is more complicated.

LEXICAL SIGNALS

The assessment of lexical signals requires active listening. If the physician asks questions he will usually get an answer but little more. For a more accurate evaluation of what is going on with his patient, he has to listen without interruption, without flipping through his chart, without arguing, and without telling his patient what to do. The physician listens not only for words but for paralanguage, the way in which the words are delivered or not delivered. Active listening also requires the discipline of not evaluating or challenging his patient's statements even to himself until he hears the whole story and of not engaging in a mental chess game by plotting response moves ahead of his patient.

ORIGIN

In ancient cultures, tearing out the victim's tongue was the ultimate punishment, worse than death (11). Even today, despite substitute measures, the loss of speech is a significant handicap. Operated by cables of nerve fiber that, among other things, automatically coordinate breathing with movements of the lips and tongue, speech is used to convey most of our messages. There are many advanced theories concerning the origin of speech. The one that currently enjoys the greatest favor, the Tally Ho theory, postulates that speech originated to regulate the hunt.

When man left the vegetarian life of the forest and took to the open plain, he became a hunter. Hunting was a dangerous occupation. As man's skills earned him a reputation on the savanna, the defenses and wariness of his prey increased. The ability to interpret and imitate the meaningful cries of one's companions therefore became important to survival. It was necessary that all members of the hunting party be able not only to adapt on the spot to changing hunting conditions but also to communicate changing intentions and strategies to one another. Further, one would communicate differently to different members of the party. To the hunter on our flank who was strong but a little stupid, we might say, "Rogo, don't get too close," while to the leader we might say, "Don't worry, Al, we have his flank covered."

Perhaps man simply has a Schwatzbedürfnis, a need to chatter (37). However speech came into being, it is now a vital part of human communication. The stranger is instantly identified by his alien accent, his dialect. Sometimes the question, "Where were you born?" is rhetorical; the information has already been revealed by the accent of the speaker. Spoken language is the primary way a physician obtains information from his patient. It is as important to the physician that he and his patient understand one another as it was to prehistoric hunting parties.

It is with language that the patient tells where it hurts. Spoken words become stand-ins for his body parts and their functions, and it is with vocal combinations and recombinations that he translates subjective feeling. It is language to which we address our primary attention.

SELECTIVE EMPHASIS

The content of speech, besides contributing the specifics of history taking, provides other significant clues. The first of these is an approximate idea of education and intelligence. The ability to select language with precision and the general level of one's vocabulary is an indication of his intellectual function. The second significant clue is syntax, the order and design of the words as they relate to one another. While order is sometimes dictated by custom, its varied use may indicate individual bias. A patient can, by selective emphasis, convey his priorities. If asked, "Who lives with you?", there is a subtle difference between "My wife and daughter," and "My daughter and wife." To the question, "How do you get along with your coworkers?" "It's a hassle." and "They hassle me." represent significantly different responses Selective emphasis can be seen in a symptomatic catalogue. The patient has indicated his priorities when he complains, "I have to hold everything far away to see, I can't breath after I walk upstairs, and sometimes I get this pain that goes into my neck." They may not be the priorities of triage, but they are the patient's priorities.

A passive attitude is another means of selective emphasis. If the physician asks, "What brought you here?", and receives the very literal "My husband brought me to the clinic," as opposed to "I came to the clinic with my husband." the patient has conveyed something of her attitude toward the event by indicating the degree of her active participation.

When there is a shift from a consensual topic to a single component of that topic, disliked attributes are deemphasized through exclusion. For example, if a physician told his patient that he was referring him once more to an orthopedic colleague for an x-ray, and the patient replied, "He's got quite a waiting room," the physician may well wonder what the patient is excluding about his previous experience and how his colleague can afford a noteworthy waiting room. The use of subject is another illustration of selective emphasis. "We said" implies mutuality.

"Remember *you* said" denotes partial separation. *"It* was said" conveys complete objectivity.

The use of demonstrative pronouns can, by selective emphasis, indicate the degree of alienation felt between the speaker and his listener (40). Inconsistence in the use of those, that, these, there, and this which denote spatial relations, may arise from negative feelings or a reluctance to relay this particular information to the listener. For example, "I don't understand those people," said about someone in the same room indicates a separation between the speaker and the other person. "These doctors," "That hospital," and "This job of mine" also signify possible feelings of alienation.

QUALIFIERS

Qualifiers carry the speaker's ostensible attitude. *Just, only, simply, incidentally, by the way,* are intended to minimize the importance of the event or the responsibility of the speaker: "I *only* skipped my pills on Tuesday," "It *simply* does not matter to me," "It was *just* a little piece of cake," *"Incidentally,* I got your bill the other day," *"By the way,* I hear there's a guy in Czechoslovakia who's invented a youth pill."

Some qualifiers are brought in as big guns. They are used to strengthen communication when the speaker may feel a little defensive. "It should be *obvious/evident* to you that its my glands." "It's *true* that I'm happy with my job."

PATTERN

Man speaks in patterns, the music of his speech depending on the man and the moment (13). The content of speech is sometimes expressed in a clear pattern with a recurring theme. Like a red thread running through the weave of a grey suit, the pattern, seen frequently in clinical interactions, can be traced from beginning to end. Singular in its intrusion, the pattern signals an area of importance to the patient. For example, a patient complaining of chest pains may weave into his story the thread of his father's cardiovascular difficulties and subsequent death, or he may simply make many references to his father. Only the physician's attention to the repetition will yield the fact that his father died of a heart attack.

A woman who has just had a colostomy might weave in and out of her speech constant expressions such as "I'm all washed up," "It's finished," and "It's all over." Even if the subject under discussion is the care of her stoma, the red thread of an impairment to her self-image is visible. If the physician were to ask, "What's finished?", he might get in response, "I am." If he were to press this further, "How are you finished?", the answer might be, "I'm nothing anymore. I'm not a woman. I don't know what I am." The patient with an overriding persistent thought has little room to consider anything else. In this case, the patient's concern over what she considers a negative alteration of self will preclude her complete processing of information related to stoma irrigation.

Sometimes the pattern has holes in it. In many interviews, the physician may note a lack of information that he would normally expect. If the patient has been articulate and forthright in other areas, the omission of one area may be an indication of stress or importance. A patient who has colitis and goes into details of eating, sleeping, sex, work, and recreation but omits drinking habits may be indicating by the omission that the subject of drinking is a touchy one.

Pattern looping, a lexical activity responsible for confounding clinical communication, can be seen in a repetitive series of responses (46). An example of pattern looping may occur as follows:

    a. "Why must I go into the hospital?"
    b. "There are tests I would like you to have."
    c. "Why must I have them?"
    d. "Your physical examination is only part of my information. I need further tests to complete my diagnosis."
    e. "When must I go in?"
    f. "Miss Jones will make arrangements for you as you leave the office."
    g. "Will that be all, Dr.?"
    h. "Yes, you can dress."
    a. "Why must I go into the hospital?"
    b. "As I said, there are tests I would like you to have." etc.

Clinicians are often involved in such circular dialogue, an experience similar to sitting through a movie a second time. Pattern looping in the clinical setting is a signal of anxiety, of stress that is unresolved.

CONTENT DISRUPTION

Stress is also responsible for content disruption. Often an irrelevant comment can turn out to be clinically significant. An example of an irrelevant comment is that made by a pregnant woman discussing weight gain with her physician who suddenly inquired if her stay in the hospital could be shortened. The physician remembered what he considered a non sequitur, and in a subsequent interview it was learned that the patient was a heavy user of barbiturates and was afraid that she would go into withdrawal unaware that her baby faced the same possibility. Intrusive comments which appear to have little bearing on the current topic are often accompanied by restless movements or changes in skin color, change in vocal pitch, increased sweating, or tears.

While some hesitation may result from a person's care in choosing words, studies made by Mahl show a correlation between speech error rate and the communicator's discomfort (36). "Ah," and its less frequent variants of "eh" "uh" and "uhm", sentence changes, repetitions, stutters, and tongue slips signal anxiety. Even the most careful speaker cannot completely control his tongue. It is estimated that tongue slips average about one in three consecutive sentences. The following illustrates some of this disruption of fluency. "I'm sorry I missed my appointment last week so you could. . . . . ah. . . . . my car broke down." (ah, and sentence change.) "Because they. . . . . they yell all the time." (repetition) "I couldn't possibly have physillis." (tongue slip)

Some content disruptions are lexical acts of conciliation or pleas for affirmation. "Am I right?" "You know," "O.K.?" and "All right?" can be paraphrased as "You are informed, Tell me I am, too." The speaker may use the listener as a "yes man." When yes is not forthcoming, he goes after it himself.

PARALANGUAGE

Exclusive reliance on content provided by the spoken word means that other significant information may be missed. Lexical activities include not only content of speech but the manner in which the content is expressed. The vocal phenomena of rate of speech, volume, inflection, intensity, timbre, pitch, pausing, and vocalizations are as valuable to the physician as the words themselves. Sometimes referred to as paralanguage (7, 47), the manner of expression creates a "tone of voice" and often yields clues to the patient that are not provided in the ostensible message. They help provide the hidden message of more covert expression upon which the physician can place greater reliance and which determines how literally the overt message may be taken.

Subjects of emotional emphasis or of significance are often accompanied by changes in speech rate, timbre (seen in the cracked voice of tension), or pitch. Additionally, a patient's voice tells a great deal about his sex, his approximate age, his physical health, and his mental health.

Speech is the least trustworthy expression mode. The articulate patient has no difficulty in presenting to the physician that information which for him carries the least threat. This is not a conscious effort to defraud but a simple protective device. Deliberate delivery is more difficult to monitor and sustain than well chosen words. Slow, evenly paced, controlled speech is in itself a clue to the physician listening attentively (43). Recent studies of deliberate misinformation showed characteristic pattern. Among other things they found that these communicators talked less, talked slower, and made more speech errors.

Paralanguage provides cues to patients' emotional states. A depressed patient might speak in a flat tone, with little inflection or stress, and at a slow rate. An anxious patient might run his words together breathlessly, taking few pauses. An angry patient, while using words contradictory to that effect, may offer them in hissing sibilants. In cases of severe depression some patients may be seen formulating words on their lips while appearing to lack the energy to catapult them out.

Speech volume is affected when the individual perceives a threat and feels he must defend himself. Vocal folds, which must blow further apart for increased speech volume, contribute to his figurative "blow up" in the face of a perceived act of aggression. Probably having its roots in man yelling at the wolf to keep it from his kill, increased speech volume signals the response of defense or anger.

Critical language listening depends on inflection for meaning and syntax recognition. When actors simulate a foreign language, they invent nonsense words from the predominant sounds of the language. For authenticity, their greatest reliance is on the inflection peculiar to that language. Two performers simulating a Swedish film got by for 20 minutes with a carefully inflected "Hurdy Gurdy" as the only dialogue. The value of inflection to the physician lies both in the meaning provided by the musical stress of significant words and phrases as well as the possible pathology indicated by its absence.

Pitch, that is largely determined by the rate at which vocal folds vibrate, can flavor content. The tension required to control speech during moments of stress can produce a sharp, high, almost tinny sound. "My neighbors have been wonderful since my husband died," said by a recent widow who is literally attempting to keep her chin up, will produce a pitch that is different in quality from that which accompanies "I seem to be having these terrible headaches."

Pitch and volume combine to create what Birdwhistell calls the interpersonal, intrapersonal, and extrapersonal modes (9). Two associates most likely will adopt the interpersonal mode, a kind of everyday way of speaking. Two close friends speaking on an intimate subject will adopt the intrapersonal mode, one with a lower softer sound. Someone addressing a large group will use the extrapersonal mode, projecting his voice up and out over the heads of his audience. In a later chapter, we will learn how the physician's use of modes can facilitate his patient's expression.

While active listening is used to critically assess lexical signals, focus and attention are also necessary for the assessment of nonverbal kinesic and somatic signals. Everyone believes that he is a keen observer. The truth is similar to that discovered in Orwell's *Animal Farm*, that some observers are keener than others. The many cases of mistaken identity in the law courts testify to the variability of the eyewitness. If a group of observers behind a one-way mirror, all with similar visual acuity and vantage points, seek to evaluate a transaction between a patient and a physician, they will disagree on many events in the transaction. Only a video playback will settle the argument, although not always. Some will continue to argue fine points such as "You call that a quiver? I call that trembling."

In order to observe critically all that can be seen, the physician must pay attention to sight and sound simultaneously. Both modalities should share equal weight. When primary emphasis is placed on what is heard, all contradictory nonverbal manifestations are dismissed, sometimes they are never seen at all. Although it is a little like patting the top of one's head while rubbing one's abdomen, with practice, it can be done.

KINESIC SIGNALS

Kinesic signals, the second system in the constellation of human communication behavior, includes facial expressions, body postures, gestures, and spatial distancing (6). The earliest kinesic communication was probably a ferocious facial display in which lips were drawn back to expose the teeth and eyebrows were lowered; it was a signal to frighten an enemy or to advise a friend, "Get up the tree, the bison's coming back" (2). What became a deliberate signal most likely originated in movements having a function of their own. The exposure of teeth was a preparation for biting; the lowering of eyebrows, a protrusive protection of the eyes in an aggressive encounter.

FACIAL EXPRESSION

Darwin's inquiry into facial expression, a major work even to this day, caused him to believe that emotional expression was innate (17). Cross-cultural research conducted by Ekman, Sorenson, and Friesen on the recognition of facial expression among five disparate cultures began with the assumption that certain situations evoked universally recognizable expressions of a basic set of emotions (21). Subjects were shown photographs expressing one emotion and asked to select a word in their own language that described the emotion portrayed. One culture had no word for disgust—contempt, it was translated into "looking at something that stinks." There was a high percentage of agreement among all cultures, although the investigators took into account the network of communication that is part of our world and the intracultural learning that is part of that network.

In another cross-cultural study conducted by Eibl-Eibesfeldt and Haas, naturally occurring facial expressions of people in nonwestern cultures were photographed (20). This was accomplished with a camera that took pictures at right angles to the direction it points, a technique which eliminated the "on" face people adopt when they know they are being watched or photographed. These photographs revealed similarities between cultures in the basic expressions of smiling, laughing, crying, or anger. Both studies concluded that facial expression of basic emotions is innate.

While the expression of emotion may be innate, Harlow's studies with rhesus monkeys indicate that the proper usage may be dependent upon learning (28).

After separating male and female infants from their mothers and from each other a few hours after birth and rearing them with surrogate mothers fashioned of either wire or cloth, it was found that on maturity they suffered a serious impairment of sexual and social development. They had not learned the proper cues and signals of their society; consequently, most social interaction was a disaster. When placed together, the young primates did not know how to copulate. Males when aroused mounted the bars of the cage; females ran and sometimes attacked the males. When the females became impregnated with the help of a facilitative machine Harlow called the "rape rack," and then only by an experienced feral male who was sent in as a competent shock trooper, they had little if any feeling for their resultant offspring (29,30). When placed among other adult monkeys not reared in a parentless society, the newcomers responded inappropriately, baring their teeth at the wrong time, displaying their rears at the wrong time, and generally disrupting things and causing havoc within the society.

Birdwhistell, in his studies of kinesics, concludes that no expression has the same meaning in all societies (9). In one culture laughter is an appropriate accompaniment to a projection of love. In another, to laugh at such a moment would be insulting. The meaning of a smile may vary from friendliness to embarrassment to threat. The degree of expression is subject to culture. In India and Japan, where self-control is highly regarded, Eibl-Eibsfeldt found that facial expressions were less intense than in other cultures. The converse was found in Southern Europe, where intense facial expressions were more acceptable. Similarly, expressions vary within a culture. No two people express anger in exactly the same way. Their mode may be similar, their posture almost identical, but each one brings to the scene a mannerism that is peculiarly his own. One clenches his fist with his thumb inside, the other who has probably never punched anyone, with his thumb outside. One speaks in a growl, the other vocalizes his rage with a voice that quakes. Yet both expressions are familiar; no recipient would have any trouble understanding the message.

Cumulative evidence seems to support the hypothesis that kinesic signals are a result of innate expression, development, and learning. Although facial mobility is well developed at birth, there is no clear repertoire of expressions linked to specific emotions. Such a link appears to depend on the maturation of affectional processes. Perhaps as Ekman, Sorenson, and Friesen postulate, there are innate subcortical programs linking specific stimuli to distinguishable universal facial displays for each of the primary affects: interest, joy, surprise, fear, anger, distress, disgust, contempt, and shame. These subcortical linkings, subject to cultural alteration and sometimes personal innovation, indicate the manner in which emotion is expressed.

Recent studies have isolated scores of variations of facial expression, including such subtleties as position of the tongue. For our purposes in clarifying the communication of clinical medicine, we will look to total facial impression and to the cohesion (or lack of it) between the eyes and the mouth (25). We have only to study the effects of qualifiers such as the wink, smile, sneer, or a subtle eyebrow lift to see how a deliberate lack of cohesion can alter the meaning of the spoken word (4).

Every clinician who has entered an examining room unannounced or who has turned his back and then looked back unexpectedly has seen the "off" and "on" face of his patient. The "off" face is the private face. The "on" face is the public face, usually the less revealing. Human beings display the proper face, a socially acceptable face, when they are aware of being observed. A controlled expression of high tonus, the "on" face is a learned configuration of the *right* way to look. The "off" face, in contrast, is loosely held, with the mouth slightly open and the tonus low. The significance of the "off" and "on" face is in the disparity between them. Because the face can be controlled, it is not reliable as the only cue in assessing the condition of its owner.

The Smile

We have all seen the brilliant social smile that displays just the right amount of teeth, like the artfully contrived grin of the Empress Josephine who learned to cover a bad case of pyorrhea. The response to such a smile is usually suspicion. It is somehow incomplete and out of place, as if it were superimposed over another expression. What might be missing is the display of both upper and lower teeth, the upward crinkling around the eyes, narrowed eyeslits, and the tilted-back head that is characteristic of the more open spontaneous smile of the child or the relaxed adult.

Our culture reinforces positive attitudes (1, 4). Implicit and more subtle channels of expression have assumed the function of expressing negative attitudes. Positive attitudes are conveyed with a smile. Not just any smile, not the smile of slight upward movement at the corners of the mouth that suggests inner bemusement, not the full smile of one who is ready to break into laughter, but a middle-of-the road smile, a medium grin that says, "I'm happy. There will be no conflict here. You be happy, too."

The human adult smile serves several functions. Its resemblance to the bared teeth face of other primates suggest that it is homologous to appeasement and reassurance. Its appearance in the blind and the deaf-blind indicate that it is a species specific expression of positive emotions; and since one of its most frequent contexts is in greeting behavior, it is an invitation to approach (2, 24, 46).

Studies show that the rate of smiling in an interpersonal activity correlates with the degree of submission felt and the desire to please (18). Someone anxious to create a positive impression will punctuate the conversation with many more quick appropriate smiles and nods of the head than someone less anxious to please.

Expressive activity in adults is often an attempt to mask honest feeling, since the expression of these feelings is considered inappropriate to mature behavior. Sometimes the smile is jettisoned as excess baggage; and one who is especially sad or angry will purse his lips together, sometimes thrusting the lower lip over the upper as if sealing the flap on an envelope. The difference between the two affects is usually seen in the eyebrows. In sadness, the inner corners of the eyebrows fan upward; in anger, they drop lower over the frontal bone. If one is frustrated in his anger, he may direct it toward himself and bite his hand or lower lip. Fatigue diminishes the ability to maintain discipline over facial expression. If masking sadness becomes too difficult, the first line of defense that falls apart is the lower lip, which begins to tremble. When the mask slips away completely, the lower lip becomes squared and lowered, the shoulders sag, the eyelids press tightly together, and the person is prepared for crying.

Looking Behavior

Looking behavior serves as an information seeking monitor, a signal, and a communication coordinator. In reading the face of another person, we give most of our attention to the eyes. It is there that we attempt to judge one another although not steadfastly. Eye contact is carefully regulated behavior (33, 34). Our culture mandates that we avert our gaze from time to time in order not to violate the proscription against the stare which is perceived as hostile, invasive, or coercive. For this reason, eye contact is relieved by roving and scanning. Strangers drop their eyes as they pass one another, people in elevators usually divert their gaze to the floor numbers over the door, and people in subways read signs, sometimes over and over again, all in an effort to avoid the uncivilized act of gazing upon one another too long.

It is possible that looking behavior is also regulated by another more primitive aspect of human society (16). The eye is not only the "window of the soul," but its representation may be the universal mandala. Most cultures conceive both an evil eye and an all-seeing eye of God. The great seal of the United States, found on every dollar bill, depicts an eye in the apex of a pyramid, and Mediterranean fishermen still decorate their boats with eye spots to ward off evil spirits. The power of the eye configuration to evoke mystical associations may be responsible for the dislike of unwavering eye contact.

Eye contact between people who know one another is also subject to social and mechanical regulation. The fleeting look, the insistent look, the loving look, the glower, and the penetrating look depend not only on the way in which eyelids and eyebrows are managed and on the duration of the look, but on total posture. There is a complementarity between eye contact and body orientation. If one is directly in front of another person, he is more likely to engage in direct eye contact than if he were at an angle.

The degree to which eye contact remains more or less steadfast depends, like the rate of smiling, on the relative status between the individuals and the degree to which the one who considers himself of lesser status seeks approval (3, 18, 22). Eye contact will be maintained longer by the subservient member of the pair. In Western culture, attention and respect are conveyed by direct eye contact, with the exception of the Latin peoples, whose young people lower their eyes when talking to an older person. A study of eye movements in the context of sexual encounter concluded that the difference between the sexual eye movements of a man and a woman is that the man's eye will narrow and the woman's eyes will flutter, slide, or roll. A woman's eyes will change after blinks, whereas a man's eyes can be counted on to stay in the same position (12, 23). So much for constancy.

Convention dictates that participants speak in an alternating rhythm, probably because the human being cannot handle encoding and decoding at the same time. When simultaneous speech occurs, someone has missed a cue, changed his mind, or decided to ignore the rules.

Eye contact is one of the major cues used to regulate discourse. In a lengthy monologue, a speaker who has been looking at his listener will break eye contact at the end of each phrase. This is his way of signaling his intention to continue speaking. If at the end of one of these phrases he were to look at his listener in a sustained gaze, his listener might attempt to interrupt. It is roughly analogous to dribbling a basketball and taking your hand away. Someone else rushes in and grabs the ball.

Although eye contact is paramount, there are other cues to regulate discourse. The sound of the speaker's voice signals his intent. If he asks a question, drawls a final syllable, or raises or lowers his pitch, he also indicates that he is finished. If he relaxes his hand on his chair after gesturing during speech, that too is a signal that says, "It's all yours."

In the clinical setting there is a correlation between comfort and eye contact. The length of time one is comfortable looking at another is influenced by the kinds of questions being asked or statements being made (23). Topics related to desires, fears, drugs, sexual, and excretory habits may cause a patient to avert his gaze more frequently, or altogether. Physicians who are uncomfortable with intimacies other than the specifics of corporeal information will also avert their eyes more frequently when discussing these subjects and look instead at the chart in front of them. Distrust or suspicion may make a patient who anticipates distressing topics observe his physician through narrowed eyelids. If his wariness increases, he may lean back and look sideways, not allowing a full view of his face. One's personality and relative comfort with other people will affect his eye contact (35a).

When we search one another's eyes, we look at the size of the pupils, although not necessarily on a conscious level. That is the reason we are distressed when we want to communicate with someone wearing sunglasses. Not only is that person giving us a super stare, but we are unable to guess what lies behind the polaroid. There is evidence that pupillary dilation is a sensitive measure of attention and arousal associated with information processing (10). The more difficult the task, the greater the dilation. There is also evidence that when the perceptual stimulus is considered taboo, the listener's pupils will constrict (32).

Facial expressions are only part of the kinesic signal system. Since they are the easiest to control, they are an unreliable barometer of expression. Like speech and paralanguage, they must be included in the total picture of communication.

POSTURE

Posture is the second category of kinesic signals. We can glance at the occupants in a waiting room and see patients who look like stone figures from Easter Island, or who follow the contour of the furniture. From their posture we immediately have an idea of tension, alertness, relative comfort, and grace which gives us a fair indication of the general state of each of these patients before we see his chart or hear his complaint. Postures can be open, closed, or a little of both. In the clinical setting they should be viewed first for overall appearance, correlating to Mehrabian's Immediacy Principle, which states that we are drawn toward what we like and away from what we don't like. The relative openness or closedness of posture indicates the degree to which one person is receptive to another person and what he represents (40).

Whether a patient adopts an open or closed posture is determined by the degree to which he is comfortable in the clinical setting. In the closed posture, the pa-

tient sits on the edge of his chair, leans backward, and is turned at an angle from the physician. Either his arms and legs or both are tightly crossed, his movements are hesitant, his eye contact is limited, and he clutches a raincoat, purse, or hat in his lap as if he were shielding his genitals. Closed posture is characterized by heightened muscle tension and rigidity and is marked by a defensive attitude (39, 44, 45).

The reverse is seen in the open posture. If arms and legs are crossed at all, they are loosely placed. The patient will sit further back in her seat in a relaxed manner, or she will lean forward. The hands and feet are naturally placed; movements are calm and relaxed or firm and deliberate. She will assume a more direct position vis-a-vis the physician, eye contact is increased, and personal articles rest at her side or on the floor. An open posture conveys an attitude of receptivity.

The position of the patient's head when he is seated also conveys a message. Generally, a head held erect communicates self-confidence and an appropriate level of self-esteem. A head that is bowed communicates shame, guilt, discomfort, or depression. A head tilted back with the nose and chin angled up, while intended to convey defiance and resolution, is a more defensive head position. To a skilled observer it more often indicates fear and uncertainty. A head that is tilted to one side is often seen in courting behavior. It is also seen in patients with a hearing loss or those having a hallucination.

The body sends messages with individual movements of facial expression, posture, and gesture. There is also meaning in the way one body relates to another. One of these ways is the space that it puts between itself and the other body.

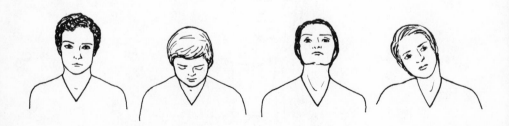

SPATIAL DISTANCING

All species have evolved signals to insure their social order, to maintain their numbers, and to make life a little easier. No species who displayed unchecked aggression towards each other could survive long without enormous spawning potential. When we sit next to someone in a theater and accidentally brush his arm, we hasten to add, "Excuse me," lest he interpret this as an act of aggression. In a crowded elevator we hug our arms and possessions close to our bodies, trying, like Alice, to shrink a little. A really crowded elevator can evoke a host of "Excuse me's" and "Sorry's." We assure the others in the elevator that no harm was meant. We ask for pardon. What code did we violate? We invaded another's space.

One of the signals designed to prevent conflict is spatial distancing, an invisible air bubble around each individual that is uniquely his own (27, 31). An example of this can be seen in starlings who sit on a telephone wire like a string of pearls. The distance between them is specific and amounts to the space they need to face each other and not touch beaks.

Man has specific designations for spatial integrity which alter with culture and with the degree that the participants in an interchange are intimate. Keeping one's distance is complicated business. Four have been described. The first of these is called intimate space and ranges from skin on skin to 18 inches. Within intimate space there is thermal space, where perception is through epidermic and olfactory sensors. With all hospitalized patients and with most ambulatory patients, this intimate space is invaded. In a subsequent chapter, we will see how invasion is made easier and how thermal space can be used to communicate when other signals are absent or minimal.

Intimate space is used in clustering. A group defense, it is often observed in concerned and anxious families of patients as they sit or stand in a waiting room, closing their ranks to bring everyone into intimate space with one another. Intimate space cannot be forced. When very close distances are imposed upon unwilling subjects, they will turn away their upper bodies or avert their eyes.

Personal space may be considered from 18 inches to about 2 feet. We share personal space with someone to whom we feel very close. Personal space varies with culture and with one's relationship to the water cooler; someone with a pendulous belly has a slightly larger personal space. A cocktail party, where people are squeezed together, is an example of a socially engineered design to blur spatial distancing. It is an attempt to create personal feelings through the enforced use of personal space.

Social space, approximately two to four feet, is the distance we keep people with whom we are engaged interpersonally and yet are not intimate. This varies according to the culture and sex of the participants. Teutonic folks opt for three feet, while southern Europeans find two feet very comfortable. The problem can be seen in international gatherings where the Austrian envoys are constantly backing away from the Italian ambassador.

Public space is usually considered any space beyond four feet. It is the greater space between orator and audience, jury and spectator, teacher and student, minister and congregation. Public space, together with the extrapersonal mode of speech necessary to vault its distance, is designed to keep the listener anonymous.

An experiment in spatial integrity is to invade the space of another deliberately at a dinner table by surreptitiously moving one's utensils and service into his space until he makes a response. His first reaction will be slight annoyance, although it is unlikely he will know exactly why he is annoyed. Eventually he may even become angry, challenging the invader on an issue that has nothing to do with the fork in his soup.

ORIENTATION

There is a relationship between rapport and postural congruence (44). The way in which bodies are oriented to one another is another criterion of interaction. The degree of mutual involvement corresponds to the degree the heads, shoulders, and hips are aligned. The degree of alignment also depends on the space between the bodies. There would likely be closer alignment at a greater distance between nonintimates than in a closer space.

In gatherings where there is a seating choice, those with mutual interest more often sit side by side or diagonally from each other while competing pairs choose to sit opposite one another. It is very common in consultative interactions for the participants to sit at right angles to one another with their heads at a 45° angle, allowing each one to turn his head without shifting his whole body (38).

SYNCHRONY

Synchrony is a postural phenomenon sometimes seen in families or between people who have developed warm relationships. Body movements can be seen in tandem, with two or more people assuming identical postures and moving synchronously. Work done by Condon and Ogston has shown that people in rapport show a microsynchrony of many movements in a second, visible only with special photography (14, 15). Synchronized movements suggest identification, cohesiveness, and the effects of modeling. If the model is highly regarded or if there is rapport, posture will be mimicked by the one who holds the high regard. If the physician moves a certain way and if his patient is at ease and likes him, he may find his patient moving in synchrony with him.

The comic Jimmy Durante used to sing a song about postural conflict called, "Did you ever have the feeling that you wanted to stay, and then you had the feeling that you wanted to go", while twisting his body into a pretzel. He demonstrated ambivalence through postural opposition to other signals.

In the mixed message of postural opposition, different modes of communication send contradictory messages. For example, the face can present an open invitation but the body contradicts it with closed rigidity. Sweet purring words and clenched fists represent another postural contradiction. The patient who smiles and says, "I'm not the least bit concerned about surgery," while white-knuckling a chair is presenting postural contradiction. So is the patient who promises to follow a regimen faithfully while making confetti out of the instructions. Postural contradiction reveals conflict or ambivalence to the attentive physician. They lead him to the hidden message by altering the meaning of the spoken word or the "on" face.

Postural contradiction may be the result of passive protest. The ostensible message either verbally or kinesically appears to be in agreement, but it is belied by an opposing signal. For example, a pleasant face and verbal accord accompanied by finger drumming, foot tapping, or furious rocking might indicate passive protest against the physician who refused to prescribe an antibiotic for a bad cold.

There are other contradictions of gesture and facial expression that are deliberate whose function it is to modify the spoken word or other actions. A back slap, a smile, a sneer, and a wink are examples of these modifiers whose message essentially is, "I was only kidding around"(4).

GESTURES

Gestures are the third category of kinesic signals. They stand in place of speech, they qualify speech, and they complement speech. They are so integral to language that it is difficult to speak without them. Someone on the telephone, for example, usually punctuates the air with gestures, even if they are doomed to blush unseen in the booth. Helen Keller related that she used finger language in thinking and speaking to herself. Any attempt to suppress gestural language is doomed to failure. Motor discharge crops up elsewhere: pencils fly, faces twitch, and feet stumble into wastebaskets. Television newscasters, aware of the distracting messages hands wave out, clasp them, fold them, hold papers with them, or put them under a desk. They are simply too unreliable to be let loose in front of a camera.

If through cerebral paresis gestural movements are disturbed, the patient's expression and ability to communicate are also disturbed. Even in temporary immobilizations patients experience limitations in fluency.

Gestures are subject to cultural alteration (19). In some cultures, gestural language is rich and flamboyant; in others, it is inhibited and played closer to the vest. Even so, gestural expressions are common to all cultures and offer alternative cues to a message, like the two-flagged system of the semaphore.

If someone were presented with a chart to read which he took, and then passed his hand over his eyes and rubbed them, the odds are that he doesn't want to read the chart and less likely that he's trying to create phosphenes for retinal stimulation. The gesture of covering his eyes is an alternative cue.

Gestures can refer as when one points to the site of pain; demonstrate by approximating size or shape; and emphasize, such as clutching the left breast in a near miss grab for the heart in a heated discussion. Abstract gestures reinforce words, for example, saying, "I've had it up to here," and then placing a hand to one's neck to indicate that somewhere around the scalene triangle a tolerance level has been reached. There are gestures that are tactile attempts to engage the listener more closely. There can be subtle touchings as gentle as a brush with a butterfly or not so subtle lapel grabbing the aim of which is not to engage but to pinion.

Patients under stress will engage in a host of anxious and defensive gestures. The former may be seen in the polishing movements of hand rubbing, hand clutching, face rubbing, lip pulling, cutical picking, lint rolling, and finger tapping. Defensive gestures appear as movements of the hand to the back of the neck, to the throat, mouth, and head as if to protect the exposed and vulnerable body parts. Stress additionally might cause a patient to look away, letting his eyes go out of focus, appearing further and further out of touch as he begins to disassociate himself from his surroundings. When speaking, particularly about himself, he may address his remarks to the ceiling, the floor, or the window.

SWITCHES

Some signals act as railroad switches. Scheflin calls them terminal markers. They either maintain the interaction on its course or change its direction and the speed of its progression.

Everyone who has ever attended any gathering and engaged another person in conversation knows at which point he has overstayed his allotted time. When the other person begins to comb the room like a radar scanner, it is time to move on. The act of scanning is to effect a switch, either to terminate or divert the current topic. It says, "I have spent enough time talking to you." Other signals that have the effect of ending or changing a topic are eyebrow shifts, crossing or uncrossing legs, restless activity like lip pulling, trailing off one's voice like running with a kite, or asking a question. This last must be distinguished from the behavior of the patient seeking support in the context of an information exchange. A switch is usually an intrusive action made in the middle of an ongoing topic. It's effect is diversionary, similar to dangling shiny beads in the face of hostile natives. The following is an example. The physician is angrily scolding his patient for not following his diet.

Physician: There is no way that you're going to feel better unless you eat exactly what's on the list. Now there's nothing else to tell you. We've talked about this many times and still you have trouble following what is essentially a simple . . .

Patient: Why do you think I'm seeing double?

Signals that end or change a current topic indicate anxiety, boredom, a perceived threat, anger, resolution, or an attempt on the part of the listener to sneak in a word on its edge. Videotaped conversations reveal observable points in which moods, speakers, or topics are changed by an unconscious signal made by one of the participants (45). It is interesting to note that when the recipient of the signal is slow to respond, signaling escalates. The sender emits another often stronger signal until the message is clear. A good example is an interchange in which a physician was trying to get a history. The patient related how the last three physicians he had, all junior staff members who he identified as "novices," did nothing for his arthritis. The physician never verbally addressed this running commentary but simply continued to ask questions related to a review of systems. His nonverbal activity was another matter. He crossed his legs, shifted his note pad around in his lap, folded his arms, and wound up silently counting acoustic tiles.

SOMATIC SIGNALS

A FUNCTION OF THE AUTONOMIC NERVOUS SYSTEM

Lexical and kinesic activities are, to a large degree, subject to individual control. The third signal system in the constellation of human behavior is the somatic, which is a product of the autonomic nervous system. Somatic signals are, by definition, automatic and independent of conscious effort. Recent studies in biofeedback, however, indicate that control of many of the processes can be learned.

An infant first learns to use somatic signals. His increased rate of breathing and reddened skin represent some of his earliest communication efforts. As his mother responds, the reduction of distress she is able to produce acts in some measure as feedback to the infant, completing the circuit of communication. The most accepted theory of the genesis of psychophysiologic illness postulates that the manner in which the mother reinforces those signals lays a foundation for later life peptic ulcer or migraine headache. Thus early classical conditioning may be the basis of most psychosomatic symptom formation (41), even though not the whole picture. Organ predisposition and the frustrations of later life may be necessary to complete response.

Pulse, respiration, motility of the gastrointestinal tract and of the salivary, sweat, and digestive glands, and vascular activity accompany drive attitudes. Since they are functions of the autonomic system that control all internal and many external signs of emotional arousal, they are reliable signals of affect.

CHANGES IN AROUSAL OF FEELINGS

Changes in the level of arousal of certain feelings are usually described in three measures. These are visceral reaction (heart rate, stomach motility etc.), somatic reactions (muscle tension), and neural reactions (cerebral activity). For efficiency, we will use *somatic* to describe all observable manifestations of the vasovegatative system. The somatic signals with which we concern ourselves are those that can be observed without diagnostic tools. These are flushed or blanched skin, sweating, trembling, tears, dry lips, odors, moist palms, rumbling stomachs, respiratory changes, pupil contraction or dilation, eyeblinks, and changes in muscular tension.

RECOGNITION

The process of recognizing emotions in others is one Bindra (5) calls multidimensional categorization. When we experience emotion and consciously check our autonomic activities, the feedback provided by our own feelings validates the label we have assigned to these feelings. "I feel happy" (conscious thought) may produce an awareness of especial well-being. When we attempt to recognize emotion in another, we get no internal feedback as we do from our own emotions. We have only the external cues which we must process through our own perception filter. Thus, our own experience will determine how we label another's feelings. Identifying another's feelings may involve several separate sensory events, of which somatic manifestation might be only one.

AMBIGUOUS AFFECT

Most physiologists believe that emotions must be interpreted in situational reference. Since people do not express emotion in pure form but express complex feeling, the result is often ambiguous affect. Many people, when emotionally aroused, are capable of laughing and crying at the same time. The context of the situation determines the interpretation. For example, an actor clutching the prized Oscar who faced his audience with tears streaming down his cheeks would be recognized as a very happy person. A woman with tears streaming down her cheeks clutching a statuette in the rubble of a tornado would be recognized as a very sad person.

Studies of emotional arousal have revealed no distinct observable patterns onto which they can tie a name tag. This creates problems when one attempts to identify specific emotions as a result of changes in the vasovegative system. Fear, anger, and love produce no unique characteristic patterns (26). Add to this lack of exclusivity the individual variances found in responses to emotional stimuli and the result is a communal arrangement where certain autonomic expressions are the property of all but are subject to slight alterations as they pass from hand to hand.

The data based on somatic manifestations alone is not sufficient to identify a specific emotional state in an individual. As in all clinical judgment, other factors must be weighed. In communication, such variables as speech, body movement, and the context of the situation are necessary to complete a diagnostic picture. If one's patient greets him with a moist palm, there are two possibilities. The first is that autonomic arousal has occurred, and the second is that there were no towels in the wash room. Other cues need to be obtained before an interpretation can be made. If this patient were to sit on the edge of his chair, twist his fingers, and ask for the results of his lab report, a clear picture of anxiety has been completed.

EVENTS COLORED BY SOMATIC SIGNALS

The value of somatic signals to the physician lies in the coloring they lend to ongoing events (35). If all else (speech, facial expression, posture, etc.) is present in controlled neutrality, somatic signals can be counted on to turn the black and white picture into blazing technicolor. One of the things a physician looks for are statements or topics that appear to be tinged with emotion. For example, a routine question concerning urinary function might be answered by a patient who, while lexically and kinesically quite calm, is observed to be sweating and breathing more heavily. Although the physician has made no suggestion of pathology, the question is nevertheless significant to the patient, who might fear waning sexual powers, the presence of an enlarged prostate, or the possibility of surgery.

No isolated signal from any system, either lexical, kinesic, or somatic, should bear exclusive responsibility for the meaning of any expressive behavior that occurs in the clinical encounter. Each cue should be assessed in concert with other cues, according to the context in which they were observed. Unlike molecular studies, these cues do not provide hard data but, instead, an awareness of the clinical interaction as a complicated perceptual event of which hard data is only a part.

REFERENCES

1. Ambrose JA: The development of the smiling response in early infancy. In Foss BM (ed): Determinants of Infant Behaviour, Vol 1. London, Methuen, 1961, pp 179–196

2. Andrew RJ: The origin and evolution of the calls and facial expressions of the primates. Behaviour 20:1–109, 1963

3. Argyle M, Dean J: Eye contact, distance, and affiliation. Sociometry 28:289–304, 1965

4. Bateson G: The message: this is play. In Schaffner B (ed): Group Processes, Vol 2. Madison, Madison Printing, 1955

5. Bindra DA: Unified interpretation of emotion and motivation. Ann NY Acad Sci 159:-1071–1083, 1969

6. Birdwhistell RL: Introduction to Kinesics. Louisville, University of Louisville Press, 1952

7. Birdwhistell RL: Paralanguage: Twenty-Five Years After Sapir. Lectures on Experimental Psychiatry. Pittsburgh, University of Pittsburgh Press, 1961

8. Birdwhistell RL: Communicative signals and their clinical assessment. Voices: The art and science of psychotherapy 1(2):37–42, 1965

9. Birdwhistell RL: Kinesics and Context. Philadelphia, University of Pennsylvania Press, 1970

10. Bradshaw JL: Load and pupillary changes in continuous processing tasks. Br J Psychol 59:265–271, 1968

11. Brown CT, Van Riper C: Speech and Man. Englewood Cliffs, Prentice Hall, 1966

12. Bugetal DE et al.: Perfidious feminine faces. J Pers Soc Psychol 17:314–318, 1971

13. Chomsky N, Halle M: The Sound Pattern of English. New York, Harper & Row, 1968

14. Condon WS, Ogston WD: Sound film analysis of normal and pathological behavior patterns. J Nerv Ment Dis 143:338–347, 1967

15. Condon WS, Ogston WD: A segmentation of behavior. J Psychiatr Res 5:221–235, 1967

16. Coss RG: The perceptual effect of eye-spot patterns and their relevance to gaze behaviour. In Hutt SJ, Hutt C (eds): Behaviour Studies in Psychiatry. Oxford, Pergamon Press, 1970, pp 121–147

17. Darwin C: The Expression of the Emotions in Man and Animals. London, Murray, 1872

18. Efran JS: Looking for approval: effect on visual behavior of approbation from persons differing in importance. J Pers Soc Psychol 10:21–25, 1968

19. Efron D: Gesture and Environment. New York, King's Crown Press, 1941

20. Eibl-Eibesfeldt I, Hass H: Film studies in human ethology. Current Anthropology 8:477–480, 1967

21. Ekman P, Sorenson E, Friesen WU: Pancultural elements in facial displays of emotion. Science 164:86–88, 1969

22. Exline RV: Explorations in the process of person perception: visual interaction in relation to competition, sex, and need for affiliation. J Pers 31:1–20, 1963

23. Exline R, Gray D, Schuette D: Visual behavior in a dyad as affected by interview content, and sex of respondent. J Pers Soc Psychol 1:201–209, 1965

24. Freedman DG: Smiling in blind infants and the issue of innate versus acquired. J Child Psychol Psychiatry 5:171–184, 1964

25. Fridja NH: Recognition of emotion. In Berkowitz L (ed): Advances in Experimental Social Psychology, Vol 4. New York and London, Academic Press, 1969, pp 167–223

26. Funkenstein DH: The physiology of fear and anger. Sci Am 192 (5): 74–80, 1955

27. Hall ET: A system for the notation of proxemic behavior. American Anthropologist 65 (5):1003–1026, 1963

28. Harlow HF: The maternal affectional system. In Foss BM (ed): Determinants of Infant Behaviour, Vol 2. London, Methuen, 1963, pp 3–33

29. Harlow HF: The development of learning in the rhesus monkey. Am Sci 47:459–479, 1959

30. Harlow HF, Harlow MK, Suomi SJ: From thought to therapy: lessons from a primate laboratory. Am Sci 59:538–548, 1971

31. Hediger H: Evolution of territorial behavior. In Washburn SL (ed): The Social Life of Early Man. New York, Wenner-Gren Foundation for Anthropological Research, 1961

32. Hess EH: Attitude and pupil size. Sci Am 212:46–54, 1965

33. Kendon A: Some functions of gaze direction in social interaction. Acta Psychol (Amst) 26:22–63, 1967

34. Kendon A, Cook M: The consistency of gaze patterns in social interaction. Br J Psychol 60:481–494, 1969

35. Lacey JI: An evaluation of autonomic responses: toward a general solution. Ann NY Acad Sci 67:123–164, 1956

35a. Libby WL Jr, et al.: Personality determinants of eye contact and direction of gaze aversion. J Pers Soc Psychol 27(2):197–206, 1973

36. Mahl G: Relationship of disturbances and hesitations in spontaneous speech to anxiety. J Pers Soc Psychol 1:425–433, 1965

37. Meerloo JA: Conversation and Communication. New York, International University Press, 1952

38. Mehrabian A: Relationship of attitude to seated posture orientation and distance. J Pers Soc Psychol 10:26–30, 1968

39. Mehrabian A: Significance of posture and position in the communication of attitude and status relationships. Psychol Bull 71:359–372, 1969

40. Mehrabian A, Wiener M: Nonimmediacy between communicator and object of communication in a verbal message: application to the inference of attitudes. J Consult Clin Psychol 30:420–425, 1966

41. Miller NE: Learning of visceral and glandular responses. Science 163:434–445, 1969

42. Reik T: Listening with the Third Ear. New York, Grove Press, 1948
43. Rochester SR: The significance of pauses in spontaneous speech. J Psycholing Res 2:51–81, 1973
44. Scheflen AE: Some Relationships between American Kinesics and Spoken American English. Presented before Section H, AAAS (Cleveland), 1963, in mimeo pp 27–38
45. Scheflen AE: The significance of posture in communication systems. Psychiatry 27:-316–331, 1964
46. Scheflen AE: Body Language and the Social Order. Englewood Cliffs, Prentice Hall, 1972
47. Trager GL: Paralanguage: a first approximation. Studies in Linguistics 13(1): 1–13, 1958

3
Facilitation

"Name one means of transportation," the professor said to him. No light came into the big tackle's eyes. "Just any means of transportation," said the professor. Bolenciecwcz . . . had the look of a man being led into a trap. "You may choose among steam, horse-drawn, or electrically propelled vehicles," said the instructor . . . All of us, of course, shared Mr. Bassum's desire that Bolenciecwcz should stay ahead of the class in economics, for the Illinois game . . . was only a week off.

"How did you come to college this year Mr. Bolenciecwcz?" asked the professor. "Chuffa chuffa, chuffa chuffa."

James Thurber
The Thurber Carnival

Critical observation may be the only skill needed for studying baboons in Tanzania, when the other necessities are as simple as a big clump of weeds for cover and a nearby land rover if the weeds fail. In communicating successfully with another person, however, critical observation is only a component.

Besides being able to identify significant cues, the physician must be able to facilitate his patient's expression. Facilitation is the process by which a physician creates a climate of warmth and safety in which the possibility of his patient's spontaneous and direct expression is maximized.

COMFORT

There is a taboo in our society against free verbal expression. Children are taught early to restrain their speech, especially if it's honest. The young who have not yet been properly harnessed, the psychotics who are free from socially imposed restraints, and the elderly who either from senescence or the privilege of age refuse to say anything but what they feel are a constant source of embarrassment to the adult majority. Usually when one of these miscreants blurts the painful truth, the socially conscious adult will cover up the error with a surreptitious pinch in the armpit to the offender followed by a wink, a knowing smile, or a hurried translation to the injured party—"What he really meant to say was. . . ." It is interesting that many primitive groups who do not have this taboo against free expression also have no stutterers. Because of this prohibition against direct expression and because of the anxiety of the patient that is part of the clinical interaction, the physician has to provide an atmosphere in which his patient can speak freely.

The principle of facilitation is no different from that of making a guest comfortable in one's home. This applies whether the interaction is in a hallway, in a hospital room, in a waiting room, in an office, or to a limited degree, on the telephone.

TELEPHONE INTERACTION

Comfort often begins on the telephone. Since a patient is usually introduced to his physician through a telephone call to the office, it is important that the actions of the physician's staff reflect his attitudes (2). Being a receptionist is a tricky business. The patient wants to speak to the physician and sees anyone who answers the phone as an interloper standing between him and the relief he seeks. Much of the irritation the receptionist seen is not directed to her personally but to the barrier she represents. When the patient calls and asks if the physician is in, the receptionist establishes better feeling when she responds, "Of course." or "Yes." rather than "Who's calling?" or "What's it about?" which is interpreted (often correctly) as a parry that will let the right person or the right disease pass through. If the receptionist follows this positive response with a pause, the caller will usually give his name.

The patient may state his name but not his business. If the receptionist then asks, "What's the trouble?", the response will usually be nonproductive. The patient believes that there is no point in relating his medical problems to the receptionist when he is going to have to repeat them to the physician; and besides, the receptionist cannot help him, or so he thinks. A more facilitating question is, "How can the doctor help you?" Not all calls require the physician's attention, and the receptionist can field many of them. If the caller then retorts, "I want to discuss that with the doctor personally," the receptionist has one ace that is played this way: "I need to have some idea in case I have to get your chart or schedule an appointment for you."

If the physician cannot be called to the telephone, and that is usually the case, it is helpful if the receptionist makes such statements as, "I understand that you are worried, Mr. G.," or "I know that you are upset, Miss C." this acknowledges the patient's distress, despite the fact that such statements preface "But the doctor will not be able to call you until four o'clock (or five or six)." A definite time commitment sounds better than *a few hours* or *later*. It has an official ring. The receptionist has made a commitment, that, because it is a number rather than a general, unspecified amount of time, does not seem so distant.

OFFICE INTERACTION

The Problem of Time

Once the patient gets to the office, he knows he is going to have to wait. How long he must wait depends on the philosophy of the physician. If patients are prepared in stages so that everyone is in action all the time—a room for changing, a room for blood and urine tests, a room for checking weight and blood pressure—the wait doesn't seem quite as long, and the physician is able to see many more patients.

Unfortunately, the expeditious assembly line route is often one that leaves a few patients unsatisfied. The patient feels that he must state his business quickly before he is moved to another room. Sometimes his only contact with the physician is in the hall when a blurry figure passes him and says, "Miss Jones tells me that you're doing fine. Keep taking your pills." A really efficient office staff can hustle a patient out before he realizes that he hasn't seen the physician at all.

For the problem of time there is no easy answer. Few physicians, unless they are newly in practice or semiretired, have schedules in which there is adequate time for all patients. Even though most schedules are on a first-come, first-served

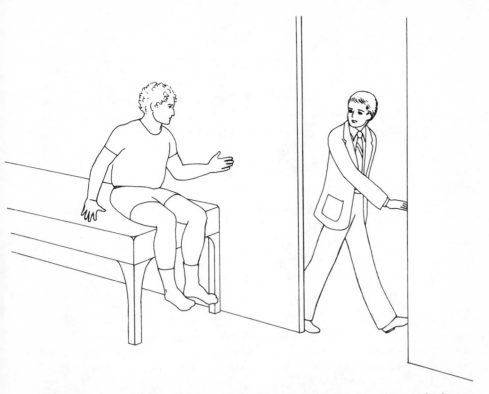

basis, there are always patients with hacking coughs, diarrhea, foreign bodies in the eye, chills and fever, or severe pain who need to be seen immediately. The solution lies somewhere in the physician's expectations for his practice, his own limits, competition for his time, and his skill in obtaining as quickly as possible what he needs for effective diagnosis and what his patient needs in the way of effective treatment.

Office Atmosphere

The sights, sounds, and smells of the office, that are familiar to the physician may be frightening to the patient. If the patient is familiar with the sensory experiences of the clinical situation, they function as differential cues, distinguishing the setting from all others. They bring back a host of associations, often unpleasant, which color the present event.

Plastic seat covers, posters warning against smoking, three-year-old *National Geographics,* and rose-scented Lysol do not create the right atmosphere. Warm, soft colors, good lighting, soundproofing, pictures, carpeting, stuffed furniture upholstered in cloth, a quantity of current reading materials, live plants, objects unrelated to medicine that express the doctor's personality, and soothing music do help to make the clinical setting less threatening (2). Ambience, however, may not be entirely within the physician's control.

Furnishing an office costs money. Sometimes the physician practices from a clinic whose office furnishings have been selected by hospital administrators who favor grey and green army surplus paint or white enamel and chrome furniture. These are conditions he has no control over. There are other things that are within

his control, however, that can help change the atmosphere and make it more facilitative. If he works in one room, he can usually put a colorful poster on the wall that doesn't warn anybody about anything, keep a live plant on his desk, and run a soft and easy sound tape.

In the absence of or in addition to these personal touches, the physician has other means he can use to create an atmosphere of warmth and safety. One of these is to create a sense of privacy. This can be achieved by using a single room, a screen if no single room is available, or two chairs pulled close enough together so that the physician and his patient can speak in an intrapersonal mode without being

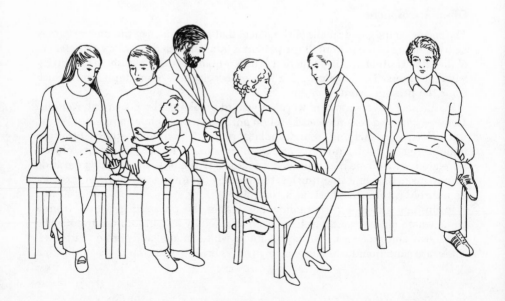

overheard. Sometimes the general noise level of a waiting room provides an adequate auditory shield so that privacy is created in the midst of a mob.

Not all clinical interviews begin the same way. In some, the patient is led to the inner office by a staff member. When this is the case, the physician introduces himself, may or may not shake hands depending on the cues he receives from the patient, indicates where they both might sit, and may spend the first few moments checking demographic data, such as age, race, religion, marital status, or education. This is particularly helpful if the patient is anxious. Other interviews begin when the physician, with chart in hand, seeks the patient in the waiting room. In this instance it is helpful if the physician sits beside the patient and introduces himself before they go off to the examining room. A relaxed introduction in which there is postural parity yields dividends in creating rapport and ease more quickly.

Once inside the examining room, the physician indicates where he and the patient will sit, offering the patient the more comfortable chair if there is such an option and making sure the patient does not face the direct light of a window or a lamp. This removes from an interview, whether casual or structured, the aspect of interrogation. ("I was sick on February 13." "Can you prove it?")

Although the physician may be more comfortable seated at his own desk, it acts as a barrier between him and the patient. Initially it is better not to be separated by the wooden partition that it creates. If later during the interview the physician finds it necessary to write at his desk, it is helpful to arrange for the patient to be seated at its side.

Desks and chairs in some places are luxuries. The interaction may take place in a clinic cubicle, a room large enough for the patient to lie down on an examining table, but small enough so that the physician has to open the door to write on the chart. The patient who sits waiting in one of these cells usually has no idea of who will enter the door. His imaginings are often worse than any lady or tiger. The physician who enters can alleviate anxiety with the use of a basic signal of nonaggressive intent, the smile, that says, "Look, I have no canines to bite you with."

He can then give the patient an opportunity to size him up while he asks an innocuous question such as "Is this your address?"

Many patients clutch coats and handbags over their viscera like a shield or wear their outer jackets like a suit of armor. The effect is that of a combatant prepared for the onslaught. This type of patient needs to be literally disarmed. A more relaxed state can be achieved simply by helping him rid himself of encumbrances and hanging them up for him.

In any setting, it is helpful for the physician to maintain direct eye contact, although he should avert his eyes occasionally to avoid the aspect of observer/ specimen that the patient senses in prolonged staring. The physician should adopt a pleasant expression and an open, relaxed posture. After he has checked any preliminary statistical data, which may be confined to a few lines, he puts aside forms and writing tools and asks in an easy and unhurried manner, "What brought you to the hospital/office?" or "How may I help you?" "What's the matter with you?" or "What seems to be the trouble?" may elicit such defensive responses as "Nothing at all." "Why did you come in?" "I really didn't want to: it was my husband's idea."

If the physician were to demolish the logic of this statement, he would create an even more defensive response. Placing responsibility for her actions on another is a way of abrogating concern. It is a form of defense called denial. She is in effect saying, "I see no reason for my visit. Therefore I am fine." The best approach to a reluctant patient is a tangential one. In this instance, it might be done this way: "Why does he feel that way?" "He's a health crank." "What about your health gives him reason for concern?" "He thinks I shouldn't be tired."

When the patient is more familiar with and more trusting of the physician, confrontation feedback such as "I find it odd that you agreed to come in for an examination that you believe is unnecessary," can be used. If used too soon, or indiscriminately, such confrontation feedback can create a very short interview.

EQUALITY

Implicit in all helping relationships is the idea that the person to be helped, because he needs the services of another, is somehow inadequate. The feeling of inadequacy triggers defensive responses (16, 31). When the one to be helped also perceives the helper as superior in status, power, and intellectual ability, his defensiveness increases. He reacts by not hearing the message, by forgetting it, or by competing with the sender.

The feeling of inadequacy is especially intense for the patient of lower socioeconomic status, who has a keen social awareness of the status discrepancy between him and his physician (32). He is more likely to be embarrassed and uncomfortable in the clinical setting than the middle-class patient who is closer in rank, or the upper-class patient who may outrank the physician in prestige. The basic disparity in medical knowledge between the health care professional and the patient is emphasized by social class distinctions.

Taking the appropriate sick role is part of a middle-class value pattern that emphasizes the merits of individual responsibility and active striving toward health (35). Even the display of pain is regulated by middle-class values. According to these values, a patient is expected to control his pain reaction so that he can *cooperate* with the medical staff by describing his pain as an emotionally detached observer (36).

The disadvantaged patient does not take the prescribed health role. He has a greater chance of contracting illness and yet is less likely to seek health care, thus earning the dislike of health care professionals who view his illness as evidence of his inadequacy. (If he had cared for himself properly, he wouldn't be sick.) The high health penalties suffered by this patient because he is not aware of what promotes good health, such as prenatal care, and because he does not have access to that which might cushion ill health, such as housing, proper nutrition, vacations, good air, etc. result in a deficit that is cumulative and circular. He is often sick as a result of his status, his sickness brings displeasure from health professionals, the displeasure reinforces his apprehension at being seen, thus he delays subsequent visits which hinders the quality of care.

DEFENSIVE COMMUNICATION/NEUTRALITY OF EXPRESSION

The patient's defensive communication is further compounded by the physician's neutrality of expression (16). The detached clinician who looks down an empirical nose on a problem to be solved, rather than a person to be heard, conveys a lack of personal concern. If he speaks and behaves with minimal affect, his neutrality is often interpreted as disinterest.

Sometimes the physician's neutrality of expression is born of his own uncertainties, begun when he was a medical student who had been thrust into a white coat, hung with a stethoscope, and introduced to a patient as a doctor (12). The moment makes the man. Summoning all his ideas on what makes a professional, the student-physician concludes that professional behavior must be the antithesis of what he feels as a layman. He cloaks himself with objectivity and hopes that it covers for his lack of clinical expertise. Changes in attitudes of medical students between first and fourth year as they exchange wide-eyed idealism for cynicism are the result of a mental mechanism, adopted by the students to ward off the intense feelings that can be generated by caring for other people who do not always get well (11, 25).

Whatever the reason, the patient takes detachment a step further and somehow manages to use it against himself. If the physician is not interested in him, he must be uninteresting. If the physician is only interested in the clinical picture, the patient may embellish that picture in an effort to please the physician and gain his acceptance. In some hospitals the ward patient has to convince the staff that he is ill enough or in pain enough to warrant admission. This may mean that those admitted to the wards are not the sickest but the best con artists (9). No physician who is trying to track down disease needs extra symptoms or symptoms that have been rhetorically altered.

Defensive responses could impede such vital communication as teaching a hypertensive patient to record his own pressure or a diabetic to manage his insulin. In order to minimize this defensiveness, the physician should try to convey a sense of equality. Successful communication requires that the participants share an equal footing in the interchange. It means that physician and patient enter into a partnership in which confidence and trust flourish (26). Although the physician's medical background grants him expertise that is not shared by his patient, they try to solve the problem together. One supplies the information, the other interprets. Clinical judgment and clinical management are dependent upon patient cooperation in the sharing of this information.

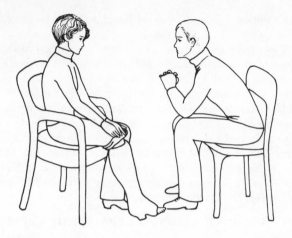

PROBLEM SOLVING AS A JOINT VENTURE

A physician can signal his willingness to enter into a joint venture by showing his patient respect, by paying attention to his responses, by not imposing himself on the conversation, by showing an interest in the patient's problems, by giving credence to his symptoms, and by encouraging questions.

RESPECT

With most mammals, respect involves the perception of another's power to retaliate or instigate aggression. Among humans, the manner in which one person signals respect for another is often very subtle. Generally, it is conveyed in one's tone of voice, in the spatial distance between two people, by the degree in which one's body is inclined to the other, by the number of times one's head nods in agreement, and by the frequency with which he interrupts. In the clinical interaction, respect springs from an attitude toward the patient that he is a unique and worthy being, individual among billions of his species, as corroborated by those who seek to match his tissue.

Respect may be shown initially by addressing the patient as Mr. or Ms. Unless the patient is very young, very sick, or very familiar, calling him by his first name may be perceived as demeaning. Sometimes first names are at the patient's request ("Call me Joe") or a mutual event in which both parties feel comfortable in their use. The patient always cues his preference. When he uses Doctor or Doc much of the time, he signals his need for the purely clinical relationship. If, however, he makes no special use of *doctor* and seems otherwise comfortable, he is more likely to enjoy a first name basis.

The simple procedure of apologizing for keeping him waiting ("I'm sorry you had to wait as long as you did.") or warning him that he may have a longer wait than he expected ("I'll be with you in about 10 minutes. We're running a little late.") acknowledges that the physician considers the patient's time as valuable as his own. Finally, respect is conveyed by the physician's willingness to listen.

Attention

Attention is signalled by postural and facial cues on the part of the physician which indicate that he sees and hears his patient, and by his own verbal responses which corroborate his interest. To convey attention it may be necessary for the physician

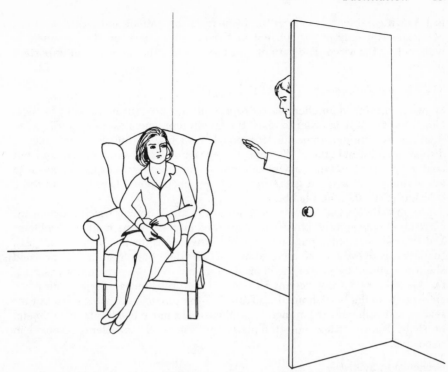

consciously to block out competing thoughts, such as how he is going to get his car back from the mechanic or who will cover for him on Friday night. There is a story about a psychiatrist who was asked by a friend, "How can you stand to listen to people talking to you all day long?" He responded, "Who listens?" Most patients are very sensitive to the physician who does not listen to them. A few convert this sensitivity to other behavior, such as withdrawal or anger, that militates against rewarding clinical communication.

The Physician's Minimal Imposition

The most significant nonverbal action the physician can take to display attentive ness is a minimal imposition of himself. By limiting fidgety movements, expressions of haste, boredom, discomfort, or excessive note-taking, he avoids competing or distracting gestures. Tapping a pencil, slamming an appointment book shut, glancing at a watch, or picking lint off one's clothes, add to the patient's discomfort. Intrusive movements such as these remove the focus from the patient and signal him to hurry up or shut up. They often act as a switch, diverting or stopping an ongoing topic. Limiting his movements does not mean that the physician sits immobile like an icebound mastadon. It means that he should be aware of the extent to which his actions can interfere with his patient's comfort. Anyone interested in experimenting may make deliberate movements when in conversation with another and see how often the topic changes or stops with the movement.

The physician who wishes to minimize imposing himself eliminates the interjection of nonmedical opinion when it is not requested, such as "That was a stupid thing to do." or symptom-matching statements like "I had a condition quite similar to yours." The latter might sound like a good thing to say, but directing attention to his own experience removes the focus from the patient and places it on the physician. Not only is the ball not in the patient's court, but his opponent is withholding the serve. The patient gets the message that he is not an important player.

The Physician's Interest

Showing interest in another person represents a significant investment of time, effort, and self (13). In order to make the investment, one must temporarily withdraw his own immediate needs. Most people respond expansively when someone displays an interest in them. Watching their reaction is like watching someone put cold hands over a warm fire. One of the best ways to observe expansiveness is to ask a stranger at a social gathering questions about himself, particularly those directed to his skills and hobbies.

Korsch's studies, conducted in a children's hospital, demonstrated a significant correlation between the physician's expressed interest in the mother's problems and the mother's willingness to carry out instructions for her baby (13, 20, 21). Interest is conveyed in the medical interaction when the physician is concerned about his patient outside of the clinical interview. Will the patient, for example, be able to carry out instructions for bed rest with relative ease, or will this place an overwhelming burden upon his family? If the physician treating a patient for severe heat rash must recommend that the patient move to a less humid climate, he shows interest when he attempts to understand the problems involved in relocating.

Credence to Symtoms

Many patients will list every somatic experience they can think of in the off chance that it might have some bearing on their present problems. Embellishing his symptoms may be the patient's method of coping with troublesome events in his environment. If he finds the sick role rewarding, it may become a viable alternative to solving problems directly; he stands to gain from making sure the physician is armed with enough medically significant data to find something wrong somewhere. It is not always possible to hear the story of each symptom. What is important is that the patient's subjective evaluation, no matter how inconsequential, be treated with the same attention as a laboratory report. When a lab report is received, the physician assigns it validity until disproved. The same validity should accrue to the patient's descriptions of body sensations, no matter how insignificant they may seem. If he is to share equal partnership, the patient's evaluation of himself, from the vantage point of the best seat in the house, must surely carry the same weight as an objective evaluation from another source. The physician does not have to hear out a chronicle of pathology but can acknowledge subjective complaints by saying, "I know this is important to you, but right now I need to know more about . . ." (5).

Encouraging Questions

The feeling of equality is fostered in an interchange when both parties are free to question one another. For both there must be no censure, no reprisal, and no loss of status. "Do you have any questions?" does not create that effect. The context of the clinical setting will usually elicit a negative response. The physician can facilitate a positive response by saying, "There may be things you are not clear about. Take a few moments to think about what they might be, and then we can discuss them." One way the physician can create a climate in which the patient feels free to ask questions is to allow pauses and hesitations, to space out information, and to look as if he expects a response by using direct eye contact, all in a relaxed, unhurried manner.

This may seem an unnecessary and wasteful procedure, especially when other patients are stacked up like cordwood in the waiting room. Paradoxically, extra time given in this instance is a time saver in the long run. A patient who has felt free to express himself is less likely to call on the telephone, is more able to manage his own care between visits, and will remain cooperative in the clinical interaction.

There will always be questions that the physician is not equipped to answer. When that happens, his best response is to say simply and directly, "I don't know but I will try to find out." Patients respond well to the physician's open and honest admission that he doesn't always have all the answers.

EMPATHY

The physician facilitates his patient's spontaneous and direct expression by conveying empathy (33). Empathy has been called the ability to take the role of another person. The act of slipping on someone else's skin depends on one's ability to see, feel, and understand his perspective (6). The more one is able to tune in to another, to take his role, the fewer interchanges are needed to exchange information between them. In other words, the greater the degree of empathy between participants in an interaction, the more short–circuited is their communication. In the clinical setting, expressed empathy increases the likelihood that a patient will feel comfortable supplying information to his physician. Disclosing information to one's physician involves the risk of being misunderstood, judged, rejected, or in some way harmed (31). A patient concerned about these risks is more guarded against revealing himself, and his defensive preoccupations may cause him to distort the information he receives from his physician.

EMPATHY AS TREATMENT

Besides its other functions, empathy is treatment in its own right. Many physicians report significant changes in the demanding behavior of their chronically ill patients after an empathic expression. Many of those who haunt physician's offices and clinics with endless complaints, in limbo between health and disease, respond to a statement of concern, often by seeking less medical attention.

To convey empathy the physician must make it clear that he understands his patient, shares his feelings, and accepts his emotional reactions at face value. Slipping on another person's skin while keeping one's head intact is quite a trick. To do this, the physician shares his patient's feelings but retains the professional judgment necessary to understand that his patient's reactions are not always the only possible response to a situation. This does not remove the quality of caring from the interaction but is instead a greater guarantee that it will occur at all.

The physician can feel empathy for any patient if it is seen as a function of the clinical relationship. The physician tries to see the problem through his patient's eyes by asking himself this question: If I were this person, with his life experiences and abilities, how would I feel in this present situation? He can convey empathy by allowing his own body, face, and voice to reflect his feelings of commisseration. Medicine and emotional response are not mutually exclusive. Some physicians, moved to tears by a patient's story, make no effort to restrain those tears. If it is all right to laugh with a patient, it is all right to cry with him.

SIGNALING EMPATHY

Empathy is conveyed through both lexical and kinesic signals, although the latter are probably more effective (3). Of all the behavioral cues for warmth, the best single indicator is the smile. It is the smile that issues the invitation to approach and is a pledge of nonhostile intention. Another important indication is the degree of animation. Varied hand movements, head movements, and facial expressions indicate a personal involvement, while their absence is perceived as a lack of interest and warmth.

Touch is another significant statement of empathy (14, 17, 18, 24). For the obstetrician who must tell his patient that her baby has died, touch may be the only viable message of empathy he can give. Wordless touch is not only reminiscent of maternal strokings and pettings but also basic to primate gestural language of affection and support (23, 27). In care-giving behavior, physical contact is a necessary maneuver to signal and establish the care-giving bond. Many doctors routinely shake hands with all their patients while others consider taking a pulse as important for contact as it is for information. Certainly physical examination and treatment allow ample opportunity for touch. It is during this often wordless period of palpating, probing, dressing, and thumping that the care-giving bond of the patient-physician relationship becomes established.

Lexical activities which convey empathy are the tone of the physician's voice, and the fluency with which he speaks. Fluency suggests spontaneity. Carefully monitored speech seems inhibited and suggests guarded content. Fluency gives an impression of openness, which leads to greater trust.

Verbal responses such as "I know," "I understand," or "I can see how being in a cast would make you feel helpless." are empathic statements of shared human experience. The physician does not need a broken leg to understand how confinement and immobility might affect his patient.

If the physician finds it difficult to signal empathy even though he feels it strongly, there are certain additional actions he can take to express his feelings. The intrapersonal mode of speech, which employs the voice that is audible only for the two who speak, direct eye contact, a facial expression of concern, a vis-a-vis posture, a lean forward, a move closer to the patient, the absence of any competing movement while the patient speaks, and the occasional adoption of synchronous posture or movement will all help carry the message.

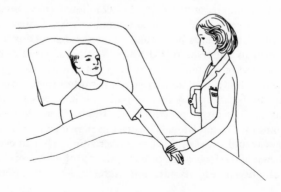

Supportive restatements of his expressed feelings will do the rest. For example, if the patient were to say, "I'm so tired of not feeling good," a supportive restatement of his feeling would be "I can understand that feeling sick would discourage you."

Empathy is not always an easy task. It may be difficult for the emergency room physician treating a drunken driver for leg contusions to feel any empathy for him when he knows the driver has caused the death of another person. However, by focusing on this patient's immediate needs and by the intellectual exercise of asking himself how he would feel if he were this person, sober and faced with the consequences of his actions, the physician will find empathizing less difficult.

Experience in caring for patients helps the physician empathize even under difficult circumstances. With each contact the physician's understanding and insight into human behavior increases. He may not always like the behavior, and there will be times that he will not like the patient. Still he will learn to step into his patient's shoes and understand his feelings by asking himself, "What would it be like to be him?"

ACCEPTANCE

The physician facilitates a comfortable climate for his patient by conveying complete acceptance. Some of the patient's statements will cause the physician to feel disgust, anxiety, and embarrassment, but a negative expression on the part of the physician can quickly dispel an accepting climate. Even a hastily averted glance can be considered a nonverbal statement of negative feeling (31).

It is impossible to exclude the doctor's feelings from the interaction. By recognizing his own feelings, however, he is less likely to act on them. For example, if the patient has made his physician angry by continually referring to other physicians in whom he appears to have more confidence, the physician may respond by lengthening the time between this patient's appointments or by referring him out of the office altogether. Both actions, while unconsciously motivated, are retaliatory, engendered out of anger, and not necessarily in the patient's best interest. The physician is unlikely to act out his hostile feelings when he is aware of them.

The patient needs to feel that her physician is a person in whom she can invest her confidence and trust. If a woman tells an attending physician that her knife wound was inflicted by her lover after she returned to her husband and the physician responds with a disdainfully curled upper lip, she will quickly get the message that if she wants him to like and accept her, she had better censor her material to something like "I backed up into this guy holding a knife 37 times." When a patient must watch what he says in order to avoid offending the physician, the entire clinical interaction, including nonrelated topics, suffers inhibition.

If the physician initially avoids challenging or evaluating statements—even to himself—he will demonstrate an attitude of acceptance in the face of the most startling information. This does not mean that at some later point in the interaction he will not address the issue. It only means that in the beginning, when the patient is learning to trust the physician, nothing interferes with the process. By maintaining an open, relaxed posture, direct eye contact, and a nonjudgmental facial expression, he shows the patient that he need not guard his words.

The physician's easy manner helps in another way. There is a phenomenon of human behavior that resembles the actions of the chameleon who changes color

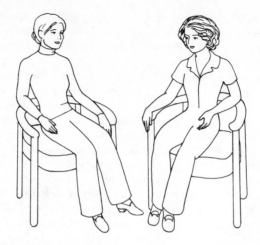

with his surroundings. Called emotional resonance, it functions when one person unknowingly picks up and adopts the feelings of another. After spending some time with another person, one suddenly realizes that for no reason that he can think of he is feeling anxious, angry, or elated. Reflection will usually determine that the feeling and the other person arrived together. Emotional resonance is the reason a funny movie is funnier with more people in the audience. The greater the number, the greater the corroboration and reinforcement. Emotional resonance is also the reason most people don't like being around those who are depressed: it's catching. Laughter is contagious, too, but it's more fun.

When the physician wants to create a feeling of comfort for his patient, he can use emotional resonance to his and his patient's advantage. If he affects ease, slow and even speech, and few hurried or anxious gestures of his own, he increases the likelihood that his patient will adopt a similar attitude.

MODELING

Besides conveying attitudes of equality, empathy, and acceptance, the physician can facilitate the patient's comfort and expression by specific communication techniques. The first of these is example. In his own use of direct and honest language, he acts as a model whose style the patient can imitate (1, 8). False heartiness, clichés, and inappropriate reassurances are eliminated, and in their place are real words and real feelings.

Big talk leads to medical decisions, but small talk makes them possible. The patient is initially facilitated if some mutual expression of small talk is used to ease his entry into the clinical interaction. Like digitalis, small talk has a narrow therapeutic range.

Unless the patient made his way to the office through a blizzard, continued comments on the weather only maintain the wall. They seem to say, "I don't know what to say to you; and I really don't care if you think it will rain, but I'll ask you anyway because making sounds is more comfortable than silence." No comment at all is more honest. A smile and a pleasant expression replace mountains of small talk if they are intended to create good feeling. Talk, even in the clinical setting, need not be constant. The physician teaches honest communication by communicating honestly.

A patient who is sick is not cheered by a physician who stands by his bedside and greets him with an effusive "Well, John, and how are we today?" First, implicit in a Santa Claus message ("Have you been a good boy?") is the hidden message that nothing short of a positive response will be tolerated. Second, the *we* is imperious since there is only one sick person. Third, a sick patient does not feel like keeping up appearances. A more facilitative question would be a very direct "How are you feeling?"

Inappropriate reassurance may make the patient and the physician feel better temporarily, but in the long run it will work against the physician. If asked for a report on a patient's condition, the physician who is not sure can say so with such noncommittal remarks as "What I know presently does not give me cause for concern," or "I do not have enough information yet to make a judgment." Giving a blanket "You're fine," to a patient when the physician has some question about his condition will have a decidedly negative effect if the patient must be informed later that he is not so fine after all. ("Remember when I told you everything was O.K.? Well, I was wrong.") The element of trust that is essential in the clinical relationship will be destroyed and only with the greatest effort can it be reinstated. Informing a gravely ill patient of his condition will be discussed in a subsequent chapter.

AFFIRMATIVE LEADS

The patient needs to be assured from time to time that his contributions are adequate and that he should continue. The doctor can facilitate his continuation by offering affirmative leads, another technique of communication which aids the patient's expression.

Affirmative leads encourage the anxious or inarticulate patient to express himself. They might be such statements as "Go on," "You're doing fine," "I understand," "Please continue," "You were saying . . . ," "What happened next?", "Uh huh," "Tell me more about . . . ," or "Yes." If the patient says, "All of this doesn't mean very much," a facilitative response may be "You're doing very well. Go on." The physician may deliver nonverbal affirmative leads by nodding his head or touching his patient on the arm, hand, head, shoulder, or back. Soft tissue protruberances are clinically taboo for touching. The physician's task is to get hold of an approved part and touch it.

Timing is crucial in the use of affirmative leads. If they are offered too sparingly, the patient founders and feels as he did when he dreamt he walked through town in his underwear. If they are offered too frequently, the patient feels the nervous expectancy of someone who is waiting for the other shoe to fall in the upstairs apartment.

FEEDBACK

The most significant facilitative communication technique that can be used by the physician is feedback (34). Although not a constant component to communication, feedback fulfills many functions when added to the clinical interaction: it acts as a tracking device; it can be a corrective device; it projects empathy; it helps to resolve conflicting messages; it terminates silence; and it stimulates the association.

TRACKING

The first function of feedback, that of tracking, is simply a means of staying in touch. It is a way of acknowledging the patient's expressions and reflecting them to him. "You say you have pain?" tells the patient that his message is getting through. If the interaction is to be a quick one, for example, while the physician is pushing to his next appointment, the physician can still facilitate future communication with his patient by stating firmly, "I can't speak to you now, but I can see that you have something important on your mind. When we meet we can discuss it." This acknowledgment to the patient that his physician sees and hears that he's troubled will not only hold him until their next meeting, but the likelihood of a positive relationship between them for future interations has been enhanced by the commitment.

Clarifying

Feedback also helps to clarify. Perhaps the physician did not hear or misinterpreted what he heard. Feedback gives the patient an opportunity to clarify his words and prevents his responses from being ignored. The physician uses feedback to clarify the patient's responses by asking questions such as "What I have just heard you say is . . . Is that what you mean?"

For convenience patients are sometimes lumped into neat categories. This makes it easier to deal with them. Perhaps the physician has heard so many similar stories that he feels no need to process each one completely. Perhaps one patient shows so many characteristics of another that they appear cast from the same template. Stereotypings is why some physicians expect backache and constipation from all middle-aged women and needle tracks on all inner-city adolescents. The problem with stereotyping is that those responses that do not fit the initial image are often eliminated, even though they may be significant.

Delivery

Feedback may be a restatement of an entire sentence, a crucial phrase, or a single word. It may be a summary of what the patient has already said followed by a

request for more information. "When I lift my arm, my shoulder hurts." *"Your shoulder hurts when you lift your arm* (restatement of sentence). "For some reason the stiffness is *worse in the morning"* (crucial phrase). "I only get these headaches on *Saturdays"* (single word). "Now let me see if I have everything straight; you have had difficulty urinating for the past few days, you have a headache, you've lost your appetite, and you have trouble keeping your food down . . ." *(summary).*

Explanation and clarification may be obtained by such phrases as "I do not understand," "Would, you explain that to me?" "In what way?" "What do you mean?" "Can you describe it?" "Tell me more about . . . ," and "Would you go over that again, please, it was not clear."

There must be consensual validation of terms used between physician and patient. Feedback helps establish general agreement on the meaning of terms. The patient may say, "I get this pain in my gut." Guts can vary from thorax to pubis. "You say your gut. Show me where you mean." When the patient says "My nerves are bad," the physician needs to know what the patient means by *bad nerves.* He is not likely to get helpful synonyms and so instead seeks a descriptive evaluation of the feeling. That is obtained by asking "What happens when your nerves are bad?" or "Tell me what it's like to have bad nerves." One patient may respond, "I get jittery, my heart flops around, and my hands get sweaty." Another may say, "I get a tingling like pin pricks all over my skin."

Sometimes the patient, thinking the physician is all knowing, will say cryptically, "You know what I mean, Doctor." Unless the physician is receiving psychic messages, he should assume that he does not know. It is safer and more accurate to say directly, "No I don't. Would you explain?"

It is helpful to the clinical interaction if the patient is encouraged to use feedback. The patient's use of feedback performs three functions. It keeps the physician informed as to whether or not there is mutual understanding of terms, it makes the patient feel he is an equal partner in the interaction, and it tells the physician whether or not his message has been received. "Now let's see if I have this straight, you're going to inject a purple dye into my kidneys?" Feedback may show discrepancies which the physician can correct.

Few people willingly admit they don't understand something. Asking the patient "Did you understand what I just said?" will usually elicit an affirmative response. Instead of a request for feedback, it is almost a challenge. A more rewarding question is "It is important that you and I understand each other. Would you repeat to me in your own words what I just told you?" Usually the patient will comply. If he responds "Doctor, I understand perfectly," the physician can either insist on feedback ("I'm sure you did. I would still like to hear how I sounded.") or try to find out why the patient is reluctant to comply. "Why do you think I asked you to repeat to me what I said?" "Well, if you must know, because you think that I'm stupid." Feedback is a two-way street. If it is important that the physician use it, it is equally important that the patient use it; it is to the advantage of both.

The patient, like the physician, needs a clarification of terms (29, 30). Those in medicine who deal routinely with medical terminology sometimes forget that it is not the common language of everyone else. Even a single expression such as "workup" should be explained to a medically unsophisticated layman.

The following is an example of clarifying terms.

Physician: There's a gland, right here, kind of butterfly–shaped. It's called the thyroid, and it produces hormones that regulate your body. I think it might be producing more than you need. I want you to have some tests to see if it's functioning properly.

Patient: What kind of tests?

Physician: Two kinds—the first are blood studies, the second is a scan—a cross between an x-ray and a geiger counter. It looks something like this.

Patient: A geiger counter checks radioactivity, doesn't it?

Physician: Yes, you'll drink a very insignificant amount of radioactive iodine, which will go to your thyroid like a homing pigeon. The scan will track the iodine and give us a picture of your thyroid's size and how it's working. While I'm writing the request, why don't you think about what we just discussed and see if there's anything you would like to clarify.

Patient: What happens if it's not working right?

Physician: Your thyroid?

Patient: No, the scan. It looks like a big son-of-a-gun! If it falls on me, I've had it!

EMPATHIC FEEDBACK

Earlier in this chapter expressing empathy was described as a way the physician can comfort his patient. Feedback is another way to express it. In empathic feedback the physician names and reflects, in a supportive manner, a feeling that has been expressed by a patient. ("When you tell me how *frightening* this is for you, I know what you mean." "I can understand your feeling *discouraged* when you have been trying so hard to walk.")

When a patient says, "I can't see why I have to have another blood test just because that stupid laboratory lost my sample!", he is not looking for a reason. He knows that he needs another test. He is angry. He needs a chance to ventilate his anger. The expression of feeling to an interested party, especially if that interested party is one's physician, is a therapeutic act. The physician does not encourage this therapeutic ventilation by saying "Now look, you need another test, and there is nothing I can do about it." He says instead "I can see that such a laboratory error would make you angry." He may get in response "You're damn right I'm angry!"

If the physician can bring such feelings out in the open, he has successfully accomplished some goals of empathy. Ventilation works like a valve on a steam pipe; it allows intense feeling to dissipate. The patient begins to feel better after he has had a chance to express himself. He has also learned that his physician, who has encouraged such expression, understands and cares about him.

The patient who says, "I can't go into the hospital now. I have too many responsibilities," does not need to be told that he is dispensable and that life will somehow go on without him. This kind of response will cause a patient to keep his feelings to himself. His expressed feeling about hospitalization may not be what is really bothering him. Perhaps he is afraid of surgery or its aftereffects. Even if he expresses his real concern directly—for example, "I worry about what will happen to my family when I am not there."—he needs to hear a supportive restatement that indicates the physician understands—"I understand your concern about leaving your family." Sometimes patients will reply, "No you don't, Doctor. You don't understand what it is like." A woman who faces a mastectomy might make such a statement to her male physician. In any case when the patient responds to empathy with "You don't understand," the physician can directly reply, "Maybe I don't. Tell me what it's like."

The act of ventilation and the opportunity to engage in it work against anxiety. Distress is alleviated when the patient is able to discuss his discomfort. It is easier for a patient to discuss his distress when his physician appears to understand and seems willing to hear more about it (28).

Anxiety comes cloaked in many disguises. Among the most frequent is depression, seen in the patient whose despondence masks tension. Anxiety may come disguised as denial, when the patient misleads his physician by omitting significant symtomatology in order to lead him off the scent of pathologic implication. This

patient changes just enough details so that what the physician hears isn't really that bad, he volunteers little, or he will hide his symptoms like Easter eggs to see how much the physician can determine by himself, reasoning that whatever he can find he can have. An extreme of denial is seen in the patient who has been cautioned to take it easy but goes off in a canoe looking for white water.

Irritable and demanding behavior may be a mask for anxiety. The patient may make innumerable requests, telephone calls, or bargains, such as offering to trade frequent office visits for surgery; he may grumble and complain at every diagnostic procedure. This patient is anxious and needs help in articulating his anxiety.

Another way that anxiety may be seen is in the patient who is extremely cooperative. Like the child in school who strains to present a picture of the good student, sitting bolt upright, hands folded on his desk, anxious to please, this patient may be so anxious to please this physician that he will do nothing to burden him. If he fears disapproval because he has waited so long to see a physician, he may lie about when he first became aware of symptoms. To justify the physician's concern, he may exaggerate the severity of the symptoms or the length of time he has had them.

CONFRONTATION

Identification of a contradictory or nonverbalized message is an important step in expediting patient–physician communication. Freud said that "Betrayal oozes from every pore." In Chapter 2 the lexical, kinesic, and somatic forms that the exudate might take have been described. Most of them are fairly easy to identify. Once identification has been made, the next step for the physician is to confront his patient with his findings.

Feedback in the form of confrontation is not a head-on collision. It is a direct way of sharing perception. Used correctly, it may stimulate a patient to verbalize something that he expressed nonverbally as well as pointing out any disparity between what he says and what he does. The success of confrontation lies in its delivery. Timing is crucial. It is not ordinarily a technique used too early in the relationship, since some rapport should have been established. Usually it is necessary for the physician to resolve the spatial difference between him and his patient. He might find it helpful to lean forward on his chair, putting aside paper and pencil, eliminating all of his own competing gestures, maintaining direct eye

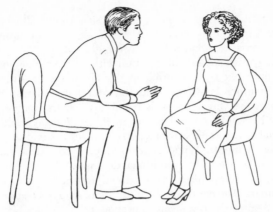

contact, and using the intrapersonal voice, soft and subdued tones only loud enough to be heard by the two who interact. The postural and facial cues are similar to the nonverbal techniques of projecting empathy.

The physician should make his statements of confrontation matter-of-fact and brief, limiting them to one or two sentences. He should state the discrepancy or nonverbalized expression without explanation or apology. Confrontation is telling the patient what the physician sees, hears, and feels. "You are doing a lot of pulling on your lip whenever I explain your tests," "I notice that discussing your father's illness brings tears to your eyes," "I feel that you are angry," "I feel that you are upset."

Even the physician's statement that he is unable to hear the patient can be confrontation. If the patient has been speaking inaudibly, that too is a conflicting message that must be resolved. Since he came to reveal his troubles to his physician, the physician must find out why he is revealing and concealing at the same time. It is more helpful to qualify confrontation with "I feel" rather than "You are . . ." The latter can be perceived as a judgment. It is also didactic with little room for correction. In equal communication the one who confronts the other considers the possibility of error. The physician may have been wrong in his identification. It is not as important for him to be right as it is for him to share his perceptions. If the patient says, "You're wrong," it is better to accept the statement at face value.

Confrontation is used to resolve the circular message of pattern looping. When the physician hears a familiar sequence, he can stop it by attacking the cause.

"You've asked about your medicine several times."

"Well, I want to be sure I understand."

"It seems to me that you're worried about it."

". . . . Yes."

"Can you tell me why?"

"You've told me things about it that can go wrong, like with my skin . . ."

"Yes, there may be some side effects, go on."

"Suppose the gold doesn't work and you have to stop it."

"I have a few aces up my sleeve. There are other treatments. Meanwhile, we'll have to wait together. I know that must be difficult for you."

Confrontation is also used to point out the red thread when it is necessary— "You've mentioned several times that you're not the man you used to be," and the ommission, "I wonder why you haven't mentioned your previous hospitalization."

After confrontation has been made, the physician must allow his patient time to evaluate and think things through. After all, he has been unmasked when he may not have been aware that he was wearing a mask.

The patient may respond to confrontation with "What makes you say that?" The physician will find that by answering to this challenge in a matter-of-fact and nonjudgmental manner, he will facilitate the interchange. Thus, "What makes you say that?" "From the way your lip is trembling." If the patient responds with denial, such as "I am not feeling that way at all," or "I always hold my mouth that way," the physician's most effective response is to let the matter drop and remain silent for a few moments. When confrontation is repeated immediately after denial, the patient may marshall additional defenses. Silence affords the physician an opportunity, by maintaining a relaxed and accepting posture, to reinforce a comfortable climate. The confronted patient then, who has responded with denial will often corroborate the physician's perceptions.

Another example of the way confrontation feedback might go is like this:

"I don't see why you can't find out what's wrong with me. I've been here often enough!"

"You seem to be angry."

"What makes you say that?"

"You look angry, your jaw is clenched, you're gripping your chair."

"O.K., now that you mention it, I'm quite angry."

"Go on."

"Well, that's it! I'm angry!"

"With anyone in particular?"

"Well, if you must know, with you."

"Can you tell me why?"

"It seems to me if you knew what you were doing you could have helped me by now."

"You're feeling angry because I haven't helped you."

"Yes. I could be dying or something and no one would know."

"Are you afraid that you are dying?"

"Who knows, you sure don't."

"Your answer confuses me."

"Could I be?"

"I can tell you right now that I have examined you thoroughly and find nothing to indicate serious illness. Of that I am quite sure."

Shared and corroborated perceptions are necessary for the physician and the patient to transmit and perceive one another's real message. They lead to clear and unimpeded communication to the benefit of both physician and patient.

TERMINATING SILENCE

The active use of feedback functions to acknowledge, clarify, convey empathy, and resolve conflicting messages. Feedback has a fifth function in the physician–patient relationship and that is to terminate silence.

Some cultures put a premium on silence. The Paliyans of Southern India hold speech abstinence in high esteem, and by the time a member of that community approaches 40, he is nearly always silent (19). Since silence is the absence of speech, it is thought to be the negation of speech. Silence is not antithetical to speech but is an important part of the speech process (4). Absolute silence is impossible. Even when not speaking aloud, man carries on a continuous interior monologue, rehearsing for expected interaction, rehashing past interaction, or debating, like Hamlet, the merits of existence. Everyone talks to himself. The distinction between those who are found and those who remain undetected is one of camouflage. In the clinical interaction silence is a necessary part of communication and it is best to let it happen. Many patients need a few moments to sift through new ideas and thoughts, particularly if these thoughts relate to their bodies. The clinical interaction always contains information which the patient must process. Even if all that results from the interaction is a prescription for Podophyllin, the medicine is for *him*, and he needs time to think about it.

Many health care professionals feel anxious during silence. They rush to fill in the gap, plopping down small talk like pontoons or reviewing demographic data until the patient can think of something to say. Rushing to fill silence interferes with the patient's spontaneous expression, however. He may be formulating something. He may be resolving some feeling. Silence gives him a moment to decide what to do or say next. If the physician does not permit a brief period of silence the patient may feel that he does not have the privilege of productive respite, that the physician is uncomfortable with silence, and that the physician is probably uncomfortable with the emotional expressions of the patient. Sometimes the patient is silent because he is embarrassed, angry, fearful, or does not know what is expected of him. Since these silences are usually not productive, few physicians allow them to continue for any length of time. To end them, the physician can provide feedback after he feels that enough time has elapsed. What is enough time is an arbitrary designation that varies with the patient and with the physician. A general rule of thumb is less than a minute. Sixty seconds of silence is a long time.

Feedback to end silence can be a), a summary of what was said before, b), a statement of confrontation, c), a reflection of a significant statement made earlier by the patient, d), something the patient emphasized a great deal, e), or something that he omitted.

a. "Let's see if I've got it straight. A few months ago you began to get pains in your legs, and in the last two or three weeks you noticed that your knees won't always lock when you walk. Is there anything you would like to add?"

b. "I get the feeling that something is really worrying you."

c. "So you work with a jackhammer. I SAID. . . ."

    d. "You mentioned your wife many times. How do you think she will feel about coming in for treatment with you."

    e. "You haven't told me anything about how you spend your time when when you're not working."

In an embarrassed or fearful silence, the patient may display somatic signals of discomfort such as skin color changes, breathing changes, dry lips, or kinesic signals such as looking down at the floor, adopting a closed body posutre, or picking at his cuticles. If the physician maintains an open posture, keeps all competing gestures to a minimum, and averts his gaze instead of engaging in direct eye contact, he will create a climate of acceptance in which the patient will feel free to talk.

If these nonverbal signals do not terminate a silence, a statement of empathic feedback may help. "You seem to be troubled about something." "I think it is hard for you to talk about sex." "I feel that we are close to something important." If this still brings no results, the physician can retreat to neutral ground with a summary of all that was discussed before, similar to a surgical bypass in which he circumvents the blockage by traveling down another route.

The blank or empty silence of the patient who does not know what is expected of him may be signaled by direct eye contact combined with a receptive posture. Someone who is attentive but puzzled may raise his head and brows. If further interaction only adds to his confusion, those same brows will knit. If he suddenly understands, he might look away in reflective contemplation or nod his head. We know that silence will increase in duration and frequency as the physician's distance from the patient decreases. There is something in proximity that encourages silence. One way to break or inhibit a nonproductive silence is to increase spatial distance if it can be done easily. The physician cannot abruptly move his chair backward, but he can move to another seat in order to jot down notes. The patient often creates the feeling of expectancy as if he were waiting for something to happen in such a silence. All that may be needed to terminate a blank silence is an affirmative lead such as "And then what happened?"

Anger and irritation are often the cause of the stubborn, resistant silence. In this silence the patient may maintain direct eye contact but close his posture, perhaps with arms folded, legs crossed, and body angled away from the physician. His general body tone, including his facial expression, will usually be rigid. The physician's best approach is to remain interested but nondemanding. He can ask, "Are you angry?" in a casual and nonjudgmental tone or "What are you thinking?" If he gets no response, he can use feedback of a significant statement made earlier

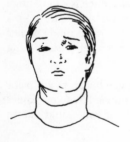 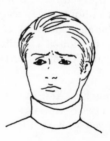 

by the patient. Repeating any previous remark which was made with emotional overtones is helpful in terminating silence. "You mentioned before that you'd like to live on your own, but you can't afford it."

STIMULATING ASSOCIATIONS

The final value of feedback lies in the fact that repeating key words or phrases to the patient can stimulate further association. Statements repeated often, omitted, spoken with emotional overtones, or interjected as apparently irrelevant comments may evoke additional information when fed back to the patient. The effective use of feedback of key phrases or words depends on the accuracy of delivery. If the patient's voice was tremulous when he said, "My food doesn't taste good to me anymore," the statement is probably a significant one. The physician stimulates better association when he feeds back, "A while ago you said that your food doesn't taste good to you anymore," than if he were to say "A while ago you said you lost your appetite."

TOUCH

All mammals enjoy stroking (24). Tactile stimulation can be soothing or erotic; its absence can be pathogenic. Among certain species there is a high mortality due to organ function failure in those young deprived of maternal licking (23). In the past human infants who did not get enough handling died of a wasting disease called marasmus, and the death rate of institutionalized infants under one year was close to 100 percent until the second decade of this century. Although cutaneous stimulation is an important biological need for the physical and behavioral development of the young, it remains an essential mode of communication through adulthood.

As communication, touch is well regulated. Spatial distancing is a protective device partly to insure against injudicious touch. Society has many proscriptions against its indiscriminate use, all governed by age, sex, ethnic, and socioeconomic determinations. These proscriptions govern the occasion, the degree, the loci, and the participants. The physician, as a care giver, is among the few agents of society with full license to make tactile contact with another person (10). This is a fairly recent liberty. A few centuries back he could touch his obstetrical patients only after creeping into a darkened room on his hands and knees. His eastern counterpart could not touch the female patient at all and had to content himself with an examination conducted through a doll surrogate. Today's physician, practicing by contrast a licentious medicine, can put his hands anywhere on any patient. It is a freedom which is underused.

Reassurance is conveyed in tactile stimulation (5). Based on early conditioning, man associates being touched with being wanted, cared for, and valued. The manner in which he is handled determines how well the feelings of reassurance and concern are communicated to him. Cutaneous sensation is not only a matter of pressure but also of temperature. Thus the patient is able to discern the nature of the touch through more than one parameter. If the physician touched him gently but with cold hands, the subjective feeling is quite different from being touched gently with warm hands. It is the quality of cutaneous stimulation that conveys the message.

There are many actions which the physician can take before touching the patient to increase the likelihood of the touch being perceived as reassurance. These include warming one's hands and instruments first; touching the patient gently, slowly, and firmly; drawing the curtains if the examination takes place in an open ward; allowing him to undress and dress in privacy; and seeing that he doesn't have to sit naked on a strip of waxed paper like a tomato waiting to be wrapped.

STUMBLING BLOCKS

Just as there are purposeful actions the physician can take to facilitate communication, there are inadvertent actions that can block communication. While none of these are irrevocable, it is important for the physician to know what they are so that he does not have to leap unnecessary hurdles.

There will be times when the content of the patient's confidences will be embarrassing or annoying to the physician. Changing the subject signals his rejection of the patient and closes him off, however. It is saying, "I don't want to hear that." There will be occasions in the clinical interview when the physician will have to change the subject in order to get the information he needs. This will be discussed in the next chapter. If the physician changes the subject because he is uncomfort-

able, it has a negative effect in communication with his patient. ("You wouldn't believe the fantasies I have, Doctor." "Let's see, you were referred by Dr. Fogle.")

Belittling, ridiculing, or arguing with the patient's feelings creates other stumbling blocks. When the patient expresses fear, it is not reassuring to tell him that his fears are groundless or that he shares them with a host of others. If he reports that he is afraid of a scheduled hernia repair and is told "Everyone is afraid of surgery; but you'll be sleepy when the time comes, and you won't know a thing," he has been belittled. He is not everyone. He is he, very individual, and wanting to be recognized as such. His fears may not be the same as everyone else's. He needs to express just what it is about his operation that frightens him. It might be that his heart will stop beating, that the surgeon's hands will slip, that his sexual powers will be impaired, that his health insurance will not pay enough, that he'll have pain, or that they'll mistake him for someone else and remove his lung.

If the physician jumps to a conclusion before the patient has an opportunity to express himself fully, a third stumbling block is created. Forming a clinical judgment before all the returns are in minimizes the importance of the patient's contribution. It is also contrary to the concept of differential diagnosis, which can best be summed up by Osler's famous line, "All that wheezes is not asthma."

A fourth stumbling block is raised if the physician and the patient do not carefully define the meaning of the terms they use. When there is no common language ground and no mutual clarification, there is too much room for individual interpretation. "Do you drink a lot of fluids?" is a vague question. What is a lot? The physician's *lot* and the patient's *lot* may vary by a six-pack. "When you go home, I want you to rest" is a vague instruction. For one woman rest may mean holing up in bed like a polar bear in hibernation; for a woman with seven children and no one to lend a hand, it may mean sitting down when she folds the diapers.

The remaining stumbling blocks of stereotyping, clichés, false reassurances, and imposing oneself with unsolicited, nonmedical opinions and symptom matching, have been discussed previously. All stumbling blocks impede communication between physician and patient. The physician must be able to identify them when they occur so that he can correct their effects.

COMMUNICATION CRITERIA

There are four criteria which one can apply to determine if communication in the clinical setting has been facilitative. The first is the presence of feedback. Effective communication involves a system of mutual feedback in which messages are relayed back and forth, like clay bowls passed between two potters so that their final shape is the result of constant refinement (27a).

The second criterion is responsiveness. In good clinical communication the physician is responsive to his patient's cues and acknowledges both verbal and nonverbal signals. In order to be responsive, the physician focuses on the patient as an individual whose thoughts, problems, and feelings are unique.

Efficiency is the third criterion. The language that is used is simple; terms have been clarified; instructions are clear, agreed upon, and understood.

Lastly, good clinical communication is flexible. The physician follows the patient's lead, moving with him into areas of significance while temporarily placing his own ideas on a back burner. Flexibility requires the agility of a heron zigzagging after the lead bird, willing to relinquish one avenue of pursuit for another.

This is difficult to do when one is flush with the success of blazing a symtometologic trail. The pull is strong to follow leads to their conclusion so that the loose ends of an interview can be tied in a neat bow. The problem with compulsive and headstrong pursuit of leads is that the patient is thinking and feeling at the same time, and it is equally important that the physician be responsive to his immediate needs.

While it is possible to evaluate the presence of facilitative skills, it is difficult for any physician to evaluate the results of their use in any single clinical interaction. The effects of interactions are usually cumulative, and it is their totality that determines the quality of the therapeutic relationship between physician and patient.

REFERENCES

1. Bandura A, Barab PG: Conditions governing nonreinforced Imitation. Developmental Psychology. 5:244–255, 1971
2. Bates RC: The Fine Art of Understanding Patients. Oradell, Medical Economics Book Division, 1968, pp 54–61
3. Bayes MA: Behavioral cues of interpersonal warmth. J Consult Clin Psychol 39:333–339, 1972
4. Bruneau TJ: Communicative silences: forms and functions. J Commun 23(1):17–46, 1973
5. Carter AB: Reassurance. Br Med J 2:671, 1955
6. Cupchik GC: Expression and impression: the decoding of nonverbal affect. Dissertation. Abstract International 33:5536B, 1973
7. Danish SJ, Kagan N: Measurement of affective sensitivity: toward a valid measure of interpersonal perception. J Counsel Psychol 18(1):51–54, 1971
8. Doster FA et al.: Effect of modeling and model status on verbal behavior in an interview. J Consult Clin Psychol 40:240–243, 1973
9. Duff RS, Hollingshead AB: Sickness and Society. New York, Harper & Row, 1968
10. Engebretson DE: Human territorial behavior: the role of interaction distance in therapeutic interventions. Am J Orthopsychiatry 43:108–116, 1973
11. Eron LD: Effects of medical education on medical students' attitudes. J Med Educ 30(10):559–566, 1955
12. Fox RC: Training for uncertainty—the student–physician. In Merton RK, Reader GG, Kendall PL (eds): Introductory Studies in the Sociology of Medical Education. Cambridge, Harvard University Press, 1957 pp. 207–241
13. Francis V, Korsch BM, Morris MJ: Gaps in doctor–patient communication: patients' response to medical advice. N Engl J Med 280:535–540, 1969
14. Frank LK: Tactile communication. Genet Psychol Monogr 56:227, 1957
15. Fromm E: The Art of Loving. New York, Harper & Row, 1956
16. Gibb JR: Defensive communication. ETC 22(2): 221–229, 1965
17. Gilmer, B. von Haller, Gregg LW: The skin as a channel of communication. ETC. 18:199–209, 1961
18. Hennessy JR: Cutaneous sensitivity communications. Hum Factors 8:463–469, 1966
19. Hymes DH: Models of the interaction of language and social life. In Gumperz J, Hymes

D (eds): Directions in Sociolinguistics. New York, Holt, Rinehart, & Winston, 1972, pp 35–71

20. Korsch BM, Aley EF: Pediatric interviewing techniques. Curr Probl Pediatr 3(7):1–42, 1973

21. Korsch BM, Negrete VF: Doctor–patient communication. Sci Am 227:66–74, 1972

22. Lewis JM: Practicum in attention to affect: course for beginning psychotherapists. Psychiatry 37:109–113, 1974

23. McCance RA, Otley M: Course of the blood urea in newborn rats, pigs, and kittens. J Physiol 113:18–22, 1951

24. Montagu A: Touching: The Human Significance of the Skin. New York, Columbia University Press, 1971

25. Perricone PJ: Social concern in medical students: reconsideration of the eron assumption. J Med Educ 49:541–546, 1974

26. Rogers CR: On Becoming a Person. Boston, Houghton Mifflin, 1961, pp 50–55

27. Rubin R: Maternal touch. Child and Family 4:8, 1965

27a. Ruesch J: Disturbed Communication. New York, WW Norton, 1972

28. Salzinger K, Pisoni S: Reinforcement of verbal affect responses of normal subjects during the interview. J Abnorm Soc Psychol 60:127–130, 1960

29. Samora J, Saunders L, Larson RF: Medical vocabulary knowledge among hospital patients. J Health Soc Behav 2:83–92, 1961

30. Seligmann AW, McGrath NE, Pratt L: Level of medical information among clinical patients. J Chronic Dis 6:497–509, 1957

31. Sermat V, Smyth M: Content analysis of verbal communication in the development of a relationship: conditions influencing self-disclosure. J Pers Soc Psychol 26:332–346, 1973

32. Suchman EA: Social patterns of illness and medical care. In Jaco EG (ed): Patients, Physicians, and Illness. New York, Free Press, 1972, pp 262–279

33. Weinstein E, Feldman KA, Goodman N, Markowitz M: Empathy and communication efficiency. J Soc Psychol 88:247–254, 1972

34. Weisenberg M: Informative and affective feedback: implications for interviewing. Psychol Rep 33:527–534, 1973

35. Wilson RA: The Sociology of Health: An Introduction. New York, Random House, 1970

36. Zborowski M: Cultural components in responses to pain. In Folta JR, Dick ES (authors): A Sociological Framework for Patient Care. New York, John Wiley & Sons, Inc. 1966. pp. 258–271.

4
Information
Gathering
—The Interview

It is the disease of not listening, the malady of not marking that I am troubled withal.

King Henry IV Part II
Wm. Shakespeare

Spontaneous expression is seldom an adequate source from which to obtain complete subjective data. Complete spontaneity can result, like Scheherazade's story, in a tale that takes 1000 and 1 nights to tell, when only one night's story is relevant. Extracting relevant information in a diagnostic interview is a distillation process which requires the physician's knowledge of symptoms and physical signs, a moonshining orientation, and his skill in active intervention.

PURPOSE OF QUESTIONING

In Chapter 3, techniques of facilitation such as affirmative leads, the use of silence, and feedback were discussed. This chapter will add the deliberate use of questioning as a tool the physician can use to obtain and impart information. *Questions* shall be defined here as all active intervention by the physician to pinpoint the patient's problem, whether they are interrogative queries or imperative requests such as *describe to me, tell me, explain to me.*

SHARPENING THE FOCUS

The technique of questioning in an interview is similar to that of sharpening the focus on a camera. For a complete and accurate history, the physician needs to bring the overall picture into sharp focus or perhaps shift the angle of the visual field in his clinical viewfinder.

The physician is confronted by an array of data, including descriptive specifications of the patient's sensations and significant information not volunteered. The process by which he sifts, rejects, and supplements this array with additional data is clinical problem solving which eventually leads to an etiologic formulation, a taxonomic classification of the problem, a course of action, and an idea of which symptoms or signs will serve as a clinical index of response. The diagnosis is usually a decision made under uncertainty (2, 4).

REDUCING MULTIPLE HYPOTHESES

Although the physician flies with limited visibility, he has a knowledge of pattern recognition which allows him to focus quickly on a group of possible diseases in a screening process which forms a differential diagnosis. For example, the pattern of intention tremor, nystagmus, and scanning speech (Charcot's triad) are characteristic of multiple sclerosis. The problem arises when different illnesses share a part of the same pattern, as for example, pneumonia, tuberculosis, and salicilate intoxication, which have in common fever, increased respiratory rate, cough, and lethargy.

Recognition and screening of clinical subgroups must be based on reliable data. Before tests or combinations of tests are ordered to reduce multiple hypotheses, the physician must rely on what his patient tells him. In few other cases of scientific research does the observed object talk. For this reason, the manner and technique the physician questions his patient in focusing down from spontaneous expression to more specific information is crucial (2, 4).

OBTAINING VITAL INFORMATION

Questioning in the clinical interview is designed to obtain reliable data by focusing on significant topics, bringing out specific information, eliciting information that has been overlooked, and limiting extraneous information (35).

PATIENT'S PERCEPTIONS

Before the patient decides that something is wrong, he has a physical experience of pain, discomfort, change of appearance, or debility which he may initially ascribe to the weather, aggravation, or something he ate (34).

When the symptoms persist and cannot be laid to rest in the isobar of a temperature inversion, he may try home remedies for their alleviation, but sooner or later the Maalox doesn't work as well, and he begins to realize that he has a problem. He then seeks reassurance and advice by testing his symptoms out on family or friends. Acting as a preliminary sounding board, they will either confirm that his symptoms are worthy of medical attention or they will reassure him that they are "probably nothing." His own interpretation of his symptoms is made according to how much they impede his function.

The more his symptoms interfere with his usual activities, the more likely he will begin to think about getting medical advice. His concern is generated not so much by the underlying organic disease as by the painful and incapacitating qualities of his symptoms. Contacting the physician does not mean that the patient is willing to enter into a cooperative arrangement, however, only that he is worried. If what he is experiencing is the beginning of chronic diseases which usually have a relatively long period of preclinical development with little incapacitating initial symptoms, he is less likely to seek early medical care.

Recognition of disease is sometimes provided entirely by subjective complaints. Often in the early stages of a disease such as angina pectoris or gastritis, physical examination and laboratory testing will yield results that are normal. Diagnosis of such illness depends entirely upon information supplied by the patient. Conversely, some diseases may be asymptomatic, and recognition may not be due to subjective complaints. Streptococcal infections can occur without a sore throat, hepatitis without jaundice, and rheumatic fever without joint pain.

Symptoms are processed in five phases. The patient must perceive the symptoms, the patient must describe the symptoms, the physician must perceive the description, he must interpret his perception, and he must translate his interpretation into recorded data. Inaccurate communication in any of these five phases may distort the accuracy of the final result. Questions may be well designed and properly asked, but the patient may be unreliable. Questions may be properly framed but poorly asked. Finally, the questions may be good, the responses offered by the patient reliable; but the physician may distort the evidence as he records it.

The purpose of observation, facilitation, and active intervention in the diagnostic interview is to learn from the patient what troubles him by attempting to answer the questions: what has occurred in the patient's life that is sufficiently different to be considered an illness; when did this occur; over what period of time, and in what part or parts of his body.

IDENTIFYING THE PROBLEM

Before the physician can identify the problem, he must be able to communicate with the patient well enough to be able to understand in what way he feels different from how he felt before (17). There is a distinction between learning how he doesn't feel well and attempting to garner enough clues to make a medical diagnosis. The stress in the former is on the patient, and in the latter the stress is on the disease process. In order to understand what is troubling the patient, the physician must know what bothers him about his symptoms, why he comes in at this time, and what he thinks he has.

Some patients seek medical assistance routinely for periodic checkups and have no specific symptom to relate. Anxiety in others has been triggered by an advertisement in the subway that spelled out the warning signs of cancer, a disease from which a parent died. When an asymptomatic patient suddenly appears and asks for a routine checkup, the physician must determine whether he came in because of a sign in the subway or because he experiences fearful symptoms which he denies. ("If you can find it, you can have it.") Another who has had symptoms of long standing may come in because his wife insisted he see a doctor or because his symptoms have changed in character. Most often, patients seek the aid of a doctor because something is not working properly. They may not even acknowledge this to themselves but are uneasy because they are experiencing new bodily manifestations and come in for reassurance. Reassurance fills the need for homeostasis, the organism's requirements for stability.

Knowing the exact reason the patient comes in is important not only for clinical classification but for the clinical relationship. The physician must know precisely why the patient came to see him before he can adequately explain diagnosis and care. For example, a patient complaining of palpitations who is told that he shows a normal EKG may be unsatisfied because his reason for coming was the recent heart attack of an older brother, and he wants reassurance that he is not next in line.

TELEPHONE

DIFFICULTIES

Telephone diagnosis and treatment, may be timesaving in some instances, but usually is not satisfactory. Language and meaning suffer electronic distortion as words and pauses are garbled by cables, terminals, static, and mouths pressing on the speaker. Important kinesic and somatic cues are absent, and corrective feedback is usually limited to an occasional, "What's that?" The physician's perception is usually altered by competing stimuli such as a busy waiting room and a list of other calls to make. The patient's perception is altered by a sense of urgency to

state his business quickly and by the anxiety that caused him to call in the first place.

WHEN NECESSARY

There are times when the physician must speak to his patient on the telephone (pediatricians more so than any other specialist). Patients will call for reassurance that the postsurgical symptoms they experience are minor and to be expected; for answers to questions such as if the baby urinated in the bath water, must the water be changed; and for emergencies. A time-limited illness may also be dealt with by telephone; the physician gives a blanket list of expectations and procedures for the patient to follow along with further instructions to call back if anything unusual develops or if the illness lasts longer than he anticipates. The physician, on the other hand, will call the patient when he is not satisfied with the diagnosis and wishes to examine or test him further, to give normal reports, and where appropriate, to indicate continued concern.

Most physicians adhere to some sort of telephone procedure. Some establish a specific time when patients can call them; others bill for telephone time or insist that their patients come in for treatment, a gambit that eliminates the caller with nothing ostensibly serious. Whatever the individual protocol, it helps to realize the serious limitations of attempting to communicate physician–patient business by telephone. Frequent feedback ("Do you mean . . . , Are you saying . . ."), simply stated questions, and a calm and unhurried voice help the process achieve some clarity.

REFERRED PATIENT

If the patient is referred, he is often under the impression that the referred physician is well informed about significant details and has probably reached some conclusion. While it is true that there has been some discussion between the two physicians, the referring physician has not always shared all significant details with his colleague. In some cases, all that might have been said was "Listen, Fred, I'd like you to take a look at a guy on the 8th floor." In any case, conclusions are never drawn without the referred physician's own investigation of the patient and his illness.

Because of differing communication styles, there can be significant variance between what is told one physician and what is told another (15). A technique-oriented physician who regards the clinical interaction as a scientific challenge and the person-oriented physician who regards the interaction as an opportunity to alleviate suffering would focus on different material in the interview. The primary concern of the first might be determining the need for metabolic, histologic, and radiologic investigations, and the emphasis of the second might be on the living environment that contributes to his patient's complaint.

Because of the variance in what the same patient tells different medical professionals, it is necessary for the referred physician to take his own history. It is not unusual for two different examiners to obtain variations in a history.

A helpful opening question under this circumstance is, "Tell me why Dr. Allen sent you to me." or "Why do you think Dr. Allen sent you to me?" The patient might answer "Well, you have all my charts, don't you?" or "Why do I have to tell everything again?" Empathic feedback would be appropriate here. "You feel annoyed that you have to tell the story all over again?" "Yes. I told it to Dr. Allen." The physician's answer might then be, "While it's true that I spoke to Dr. Allen about you, I would like to hear the story from you in your own words." This recognizes the patient as a responsible individual and as such, is an irresistible request which few people refuse.

BLOCKS TO INFORMATION GATHERING

No patient is equipped to supply data with the sterile efficiency of a computer print-out. He is limited first by his memory, then by his ability to discriminate and describe. The chronologic appearance of clinical manifestations, a significant factor in the classification of many diseases, may be related out of order. Extraneous thoughts and feelings intervene in the information gathering process between human beings. Competing stimuli such as fear of what the physician will think of him, fear of what the physician will recommend for him, personal prejudices, and misinformation impede the giving of accurate information.

Ego is built upon concepts of self-image. Illness is seen as a detractor of that image. For that reason, many patients are reluctant to supply information detrimental to their own image. It is similar in principle to the witness being forced to testify against himself. A patient who is ashamed or afraid to disclose information damaging to his image will consciously or unconsciously neglect it, soft-pedal it, mislead by modifying or omitting significant information, or deny its existence —something like the manner in which the U.N. used to regard Red China.

The man whose personal status is built upon physical prowess may deny waning powers even after the physician calls them to his attention. For example, "You seem to be short of breath," may be met with, "I've been rushing around all day." This response does not acknowledge the physician's observation directly but suggests an unusual amount of activity as an excuse. The effect of this circumlocution is denial.

Some medical problems may be seen as bigger image detractors than others. The young man who believes that hemmorhoids is an old man's disease, a mother who is hesitant to report pinworms or head lice because it may reflect on her standards of hygiene, or the family reluctant to ask if their child is retarded are examples of problems a patient may be embarrassed to discuss because they reflect on image.

Dependency inherent in entering into a health care system may be seen as weakness and contrary to learned concepts of stalwart self–reliance. If a patient subscribes heavily to such concepts, his beliefs may prevent him from entering easily into the system. He may have been pressured into the visit by a concerned relative, while he personally feels that it is up to him to pull himself up by his own restorative bootstraps. This patient, like the others mentioned, will not easily supply the information necessary for an accurate diagnosis.

Illness is a lonely affair (18). It is one of the few times in life when one cannot share the experience. When one's well-being is threatened by pain, discomfort, and disease, he must fight it alone. While he is helped by his physician through diagnosis and treatment, it is his own resources that he must marshall in order to combat the threat, and it is his own bodily integrity that is at stake. The lonely quality of illness makes the patient vulnerable. Asking him to relate directly damaging testimony that increases his sense of personal helplessness is asking him to strip his defenses further.

Few patients voluntarily surrender their protective armor. Fear of what the physician will find and of his recommendations subsequent to such findings may alter significant information. A patient may use an impersonal mode of speech to obscure the physician's understanding. For example, he may say "When the headaches come" instead of "When I get a headache" or "When the bleeding starts" rather than "When I bleed." The information is offered, but the patient, who has become a narrator, is one step removed.

Subjects such as body parts and habits related to sexual or eliminatory functions, information relating to the use of alcohol or other drugs, or explanations of personal feelings do not figure prominently in spontaneous expression. These subjects are restricted by cultural inhibition, which prevents such material from being openly expressed. In some primitive tribes it is customary to refrain from speaking a person's name aloud, often his name is not even known. In our culture free discussion of body function and personal feelings are subject to the same taboo. Body parts and functions particularly are shrouded with protective euphemisms to make their mention more palatable. While many people feel free to discuss these topics with their physician, differences such as subculture, age, and sex of the persons involved can inhibit the clinical interaction. An older man, for example, might feel quite uncomfortable relating details of urinary dysfunction to a young female physician.

Magical thinking which often ascribes physical illness to just retribution for moral wrongs may make the patient believe his personal deficiency is responsible for the illness. Judeo–Christian concepts of reward and punishment for one's deeds neatly supply the rationale which supports physical illness as being either a test or a punishment. Many cases of conversion hysteria are examples of magical thinking. One who has seen something "wicked" may manifest visual impairment. One who has used his hand for "evil purposes" such as masturbation may experience glove paralysis.

Symptoms may not be addressed at all because the patient has forgotten them or because he has grown so used to them that he considers them to be the normal state of affairs. A woman with young children who is fatigued may come in asking for tonic or vitamins to counteract her weariness while neglecting to mention excessive menstrual bleeding, only because she assumes it is normal after childbirth. Description depends on one's ability to translate nuances of body feeling into language. There is a difference between the patient who says "Everything hurts me" and the one who relates "I have a dull, steady ache in my joints." The patient may be unable to discriminate between healthy and pathological body feelings because of a general inattention to self or because of a lack of basic medical information.

The Koos study showed a difference between socioeconomic classes in their awareness of life-threatening symptoms (23). When presented with a list of 17 readily recognized symptoms, members of a designated lower, middle, and upper class saw the symptom as a significant reason to obtain medical assistance in varying degrees. The lower class considered bleeding a medically significant symptom but not other listed symptoms such as coughing or swelling. In this study, four-fifths of the most successful people considered symptoms of chronic cough, blood in the stool, loss of weight, and a lump in the abdomen to indicate a need for medical attention. Two-thirds of the more highly skilled wage earners and one-third of those holding the jobs requiring the least skill thought that these symptoms required medical care. Plato also noted the influence of economic and social factors in recognizing the need for medical aid, as well as tolerating that aid. In the *Republic,* Socrates says to Galucon

"When a carpenter falls ill, he asks the physician for a rough and ready cure, an emetic, a purge, a cautery, or the knife . . . But if someone prescribes for him a course of dietetics or tells him to wrap his head up and keep himself warm, he replies at once that he has no time to be ill, . . . he therefore bids the doctor goodbye . . ."

A couple of milennia have not erased the disparity in the dissemination of basic health information, as well as the disparity in time to be ill (19).

Sometime during the interview, preferably at the beginning after the patient has stated why he is there, he should be praised for the good judgment he has shown in seeking medical advice. Verbal reinforcement acts not only to encourage the patient's future participation in his medical needs, but helps to generalize good feeling to the entire present interaction.

TECHNIQUES OF QUESTIONING

The skillful use of all questions is dependent upon attitude, timing, and phrasing.

PHYSICIAN'S ATTITUDE

The attitude of the physician as he asks a question can determine the answer. For example, "You don't smoke excessively, do you?" has a built-in answer. If the patient is anxious to please or if he is at all intimidated, his response will likely be, "No, not too much." If his illness is likely to be exacerbated by excessive smoking, such a question can be damaging to the information gathering process as well as to the patient. Even "Do you smoke?" accompanied by a facial or vocal cue of disapproval indicate that a negative response is expected.

Before the physician obtains information, it is important that he be aware of his own feelings and perceptions and be alert to how his displeasure or, conversely, bias may alter his patient's response. The permeable membrane that is human interaction may cause his patient's feelings to influence him. If the physician

begins to feel elated, angry, or depressed, he may be reflecting his patient's feelings. The patient's effect on the physician is probably the same as on other people; and the physician can use his own responses as a personal barometer of how the patient affects other people.

His power to influence suggests that the physician should be aware of his own responses. The physician will process information through his own experiences. A negative attitude may cause him to tune out the patient who relates a tale similar to one in his own life that is painful or uncomfortable to consider. A negative attitude toward the patient may reflect in his questions. If the physician finds obesity repellent, an overweight patient seeking medical relief from chronically swollen ankles may be questioned in a cursory manner. The unstated assumption which predisposes the physician's negative response is that the patient brought it on himself and is therefore not deserving of too much assistance.

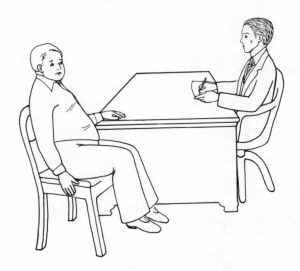

Whatever their cause, neglected or misleading responses may be minimized by the attitude, timing, and phrasing of questions, beginning with the opening question in the history gathering interview.

TIMING

To obtain all the information he needs, the doctor will rely on his own questions. If questions are used too frequently or too soon after the patient has begun to tell something of significance, they have a punitive effect and result in his withdrawal. If he is questioned too frequently with little opportunity for spontaneous expression, the probability of uninhibited spontaneous information is diminished. An ill-timed interruption can cause the patient to lose his train of thought.

Furthermore, frequent questions may channel the interview too tightly into places where the physician thinks they have to go. Narrowing clinical possibilities prematurely is often the result of limited information and more often of a stereotypic response to the patient. For example, a Black patient complaining of headaches and the physical signs of elevated blood pressure may be viewed stereotypically as hypertensive. If the conclusion is foregone, further investigation into other possible etiology, in which symptoms such as headache and elevated blood pressure are less significant than other more serious clues, is precluded. When a premature conclusion is drawn from a stereotypic response, subsequent information is not heard. The communication is filtered through the perceptors of decision, which having been made, stands to reject nonconfirming data.

PHRASING

The phrasing of the physician's questions, particularly the opening questions of the diagnostic interview, (29) can be crucial. Knowing that his patient's self-esteem is involved, such questions as "What's wrong with you?" and "What seems to be the matter?" can connote defectiveness on the patient's part. It may even connote negligence. Many of us learned as children that we were the direct cause of most of the illnesses that befell us. ("No wonder you're sick—you went out without a sweater, got your feet wet, didn't drink your milk, stayed up too late, spit your vitamins in the sink, etc.") A more facile opening would be "What brings you to see me?" or "There is a note here that your stomach has been giving you trouble."

SIMPLICITY

All questions should be brief and simple. Perception, identification, and interpretation of language mandates simplicity in any verbal communication. In the clinical situation it is imperative. The patient's anxiety will interfere with the decoding process by which significant words are extrapolated from context and reorganized into meaning. A long and complicated sentence will then lose its intended meaning.

"Is the nature of your occupation one in which you are likely to inhale fumes during the course of the day?" is too long. "Do you smell any odors at work?" carries the same message and is more likely to retain meaning. Questions should use language that is understandable to the patient. The physician does not have to adopt slang, cadence, or dialect in order to create rapport; in some instances, it may be regarded with suspicion as intent to infiltrate the enemy's lines. He does best to speak in his own language style, aware of the need to clarify all that goes between him and his patient.

TRANSLATION

Medical terminology and complex terms which are commonplace to professionals are a foreign language to many patients and should be avoided. Even if the patient appears conversant with medical terminology, the physician needs to determine if he understands their meaning before using them. A patient may use words or syntax that he does not normally use, misleading the physician about his comprehension of medical terminology. If the patient says, "I'm afraid I'm heading for respiratory alkalosis," the physician needs to find out precisely what he means, that is, if he can get him to answer. A term such as *ambulatory,* referring to an outpatient or someone who is able to get up and walk, often confuses a patient who may think it has something to do with the ambulance. Some patients believe that radical surgery means a wildly revolutionary procedure.

In one study *lumbar puncture* has been translated by a patient as an operation to drain the lungs, and *incubation period* was translated as the amount of time a sick child must be kept in bed. The doctor's reference to *explore* was not connected in any way to surgery (22). In a partial transcript of an interview with a mother a physician mentions SBE (subacute bacterial endocarditis). Later he advises the mother, "Watch your Coombs and things." When she questions, "Watch my what?", he answers, "Your titres, Coombs titres."

Translation is a conscious effort, and the physician must always remind himself of the time when medical terms were not part of his vocabulary. It is a great temptation to use proper terminology at all times. The terms are often so precise that, once learned, it is difficult to imagine or construct alternatives that are more appropriate. While these terms are necessary for common understanding between health care professionals, they only confuse the patient in the clinical interchange.

The following are random examples of medical terminology translated into layman's terms:

edema/swelling due to fluid
sublingual/under the tongue
expectorate/spit
prognosis/forecast
radiates/travels
thrombus/clot in blood vessel
embolism/blood clot that travels
ingest/swallow
catheter/tube (hollow)
subcutaneous/under the skin
heart murmur/extra sound in heart
dyspepsia/heart burn/acid stomach
benign/local
malignant/spread
incontinence/no urinary control
local anesthesia/limited area
general anesthesia/unconscious
hemostasis/control bleeding
intravenous/through the vein
lumbar puncture/spinal tap

low sodium/low salt
aneurysm/like bulging tire wall
work up/series of tests
electrocardiagram/tracing heart contraction
prn/as needed
lavage/wash
sedation/something to relax you
glucose/sugar
vertigo/whirling dizziness
nasal congestion/stuffy nose
phlebitis/inflammation of blood vessel
nares/nostrils
peristalsis/movement of food through intestine
injection/shot

PATIENT'S TERMS

The physician can facilitate mutual understanding by using the patient's own terms, particularly in the initial phases of the interview. When the patient refers to *spells* or *blackouts,* the physician who might be translating into possible epilepsy or cerebrovascular accident, will elicit more pertinent information if he doesn't change the initial referent into *incident, loss of consciousness,* or *episode.* The term *spells* has particular meaning and connotation for the patient who uses it. It evokes a host of associative cues and memories, it acts as a stimulus for recall, and it can produce such additional information as a sick-to-the-stomach feeling, dancing spots before the eyes, a funny taste, etc. Its use as feedback to the patient triggers additional information, which a new referent can not. Thus the physician may further question, "Where are you when these spells come on?" or "How long have you had these spells?"

Likewise, *bad nerves, no pep, moody, short of breath, the runs, insides,* and *pass water,* while not terms the physician might use, may convey a wealth of imagery to the patient and should be used mutually until all information regarding them has been clearly established. The physician must be absolutely clear as to the meaning of the patient's referents, however. "I've been feeling weak," demands clarification which may be obtained by asking, "You say you've been feeling weak. What do you mean by feeling weak?" "Describe the feeling to me." or "What happens when you are feeling weak?" The physician never assumes the meaning of an idiom or terminology which is vague or nonspecific. This is particularly applicable to the patient from another culture. All comments not absolutely clear should be explored. "When you say you're feeling funny, what do you mean?"

Further questions used to obtain clarification are: Is heartburn a pressure or a gnawing sensation?; Is palpitation a slow pounding, a rapid pounding, an awareness of heartbeat, the sensation of a skipped beat, or a fluttery abdominal feeling?; When you get dizzy does the room spin or are you light headed?

Sometimes the patient finds it difficult to substantiate a term with descriptive adjectives but can relate it adequately to function. How it has affected the things he normally does might be simpler for him to answer. "What does it feel like to be weak?" may be better changed to "What do you do differently when you are weak?" "How have things changed since you have become weak?" or "What can you not do or do as well when you are weak?" Such questions might elicit responses such as, "I used to be able to go all day long, but now it seems I'm so tired I have to lay down every afternoon." He may deny pain and be marked negative for angina pectoris, but on further questioning admit to *discomfort* or a *funny feeling*.

When a patient says, "You know what I mean, Doctor?", there is great temptation to nod the head sagely. Everyone would like to think of himself as being prescient, but no one can possibly know for sure what another means or is thinking unless he has special qualities of perception not addressed in this book. The best response to presumptions of omniscience is "No, I don't. Would you explain?"

DIRECT AND INDIRECT QUESTIONS

There are two categories of questions used in the clinical interview, direct or indirect. Both direct and indirect questions are used to obtain data based on the doctor's knowledge of disease manifestations. Besides completing a clinical picture, questions are necessary because the patient forgets, alters information depending on the degree of his anxiety, or fills in gaps creatively or inaccurately to meet the physician's expectations. Most important, questions are necessary because the patient's chief complaint is not necessarily what is medically most harmful to him.

Indirect questions may be broad with no focus; such as "What difficulties are you having?" or general, with the choice of one topic, such as "Tell me about your life at home." Indirect questions are always used to open proceedings. They are generally used at the beginning of each major topic of the clinical interview and their design encourages the patient to tell his story in his own way.

While indirect questions encourage the patient's spontaneity and free expression, they can also be used to focus on important topics, to reduce irrelevance, to reduce the patient's anxiety, and to elicit information that has been overlooked. If the patient has been meticulously listing every grievance he has against his previous physician, his present physician can guide the interview toward more relevant information in this way: "I think I have an understanding about that now. Why don't you tell me how you spend your time when you are not working?" This opens up the specific topic of leisure time but in a general, open–ended way. The patient is quite free to begin anywhere he likes and address the subject in any mode he wishes. It is less direct than "Tell me about your hobbies." If the patient has no hobbies, he might feel constrained to supply one quickly in order to satisfy the physician.

The anxious patient may regard relentless and incisive direct questions as an act of aggression and may become increasingly agitated or plead a medical "Fifth," which means he will give little useful information. The options inherent in the indirect questions give him a chance to relax and unwind. The physician selects what he considers a nonthreatening or neutral area. "I would be interested in hearing something about your past medical experiences." will yield at the same time some personal history and some information on attitudes toward medicine in general. Another example would be "Tell me about your responsibilities at work/home."

Indirect questions do not communicate an expected answer nor do they suggest the way in which a patient is expected to answer. A response may be inaccurate if it is a reflection of the suggestion made by the physician in his question. A patient who complains of nausea and a pain in the upper right quadrant of his abdomen should be asked to describe the pain. The character of the pain can make a significant difference in how the physician tracks down other cues. If the patient has a history of heavy drinking, a physician hot on the trail of cirrhosis may ask in his zeal the direct question, "Is the pain dull?"; and the patient may respond in the affirmative, when in truth his pain was not dull at all but severe and crampy, more typical of gall bladder disturbance. The physician may offer more than suggestion and lead his witness. It may go something like this:

Physician: You say you get throbbing headaches on the right side of your head?
Patient: Yes.
Physician: How often?
Patient: Once every few months, I guess.
Physician: Do you see spots before your eyes before you get these headaches?
Patient: No.
Physician: Do you get nauseated?
Patient: No.
Physician: How long do they last?
Patient: A long time.
Physician: Are you sure you don't get spots in front of your eyes?

In some interviews, the patient may be quite comfortable and articulate in relating all relevant symtomatology. ("Doctor, I have this pain in my stomach, I've been constipated, and I've lost my appetite.") After the doctor has explored all the information he needs regarding these symptoms, indirect questioning opens the door to other symptomatology. The danger of neat symptoms served on a clinical platter lies in their seductiveness. If this patient were a 53–year–old it is a great temptation immediately to consider intestinal obstruction, suggested by the constellation of subjective complaints. An indirect question might yield the fact that the constellation is really symptomatic of psychic depression. Indirect questions such as "How have you been sleeping?" "Tell me more about what's been going on in your life?" or "Take your time and describe how all this came about." will be valuable in eliciting additional information.

Indirect questions are used to keep things moving if the patient finds articulation difficult or if the physician wishes to break a long period of silence. "Tell me more about . . ." "I am interested in hearing how you felt when your mother was hospitalized . . ." "What happened next?" or "You mentioned before some financial difficulties. Tell me about them." are indirect questions that facilitate the story.

Indirect questions are also used to indicate the physician's interest. If the patient can describe his symptoms easily, it can be disconcerting to him to relate his story to a doctor who asks few questions. Lack of questions may be perceived as a lack of interest. The occasional use of the less demanding indirect question interspersed in the spontaneous story indicate the physician's interest. Timing is crucial. Questions to indicate interest must come at a natural pause in the conversation. They cannot interrupt a silence in which it is clear that the patient is gathering his thoughts. On the other hand, the physician often gets clues which indicate to him that his active intervention is sought, the patient may pause and look at him directly with an expectant attitude conveyed by eyebrows slightly elevated and a seated position in which he is inclined forward.

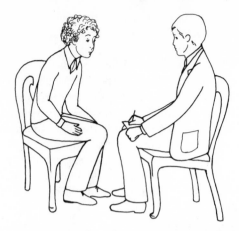

While indirect questions are used to elicit topics, direct questions tie up the loose ends as neatly as the continuous Lembert stitch of the surgeon. Direct questions may be answered in one word or in a short phrase. Some aspects of history are best explored by direct and simple questions. They fill in all the missing details by answering such questions as how, when, where, who, and why. The *why* is usually directed to the patient's understanding of the nature and cause of his illness; the *who*, to his genetic, sociologic, and psychologic composition. "When did your pain start?" "Does your entire body itch?" "What are you doing when your ankles begin to swell?" "Does the pain seem to travel to other parts of your body?" "Why do you think you have no pep?" "Do you share anything else besides the bathroom with the people on the first floor?"

Direct questions are used to help the less than articulate patient, although their indiscriminate use can be counterproductive. Too much direction interferes with the patient's autonomy and sense of responsibility. It is no longer *his* story to tell but the physician's.

If the patient is faced with the continuous use of direct questions, his contribution becomes further minimized. Even if the physician thinks he has a good idea of where he is going, he prevents individual response by the exclusive use of the direct question. Were the physician to rely only upon the use of direct questions, he might then need only a survey that the patient could answer by mail, augmented by a check of physical signs at the time of the visit. This is seldom effective, however, since human beings are not subject to identical stress nor do they function in an identical manner. For the distinct variables that separate one person's disease manifestations from another's, the physician must arrange in his interview for the patient's free expression and reserve the use of direct questions to fill in the gaps, to elaborate, and to clarify.

Direct questions are often parried with denials. It is much easier to modify response with a simple *yes* or *no* than with an elaborate or spontaneous statement. Questions directed to sensitive areas which can be answered with one word or a short phrase are more likely to be denied than indirect questions which seek to elicit peripheral material.

If the physician charges in with direct questions before the patient has had a chance to size him up, he may trump up a complaint to throw the physician off the scent. For example, a patient may complain to his physician of stomach pains when he is really concerned about impotence but isn't quite sure yet if he can bring up the subject.

A helpful variant of the direct question for patients who have difficulty expressing themselves is the laundry list, the question with built-in options. Alternative descriptions may be offered in this way: "Is your pain burning, dull, knifelike, steady, pressing, wavelike, traveling?" For example, if a patient who is not expressive and who believes that getting up during the night to urinate is normal were asked, "How do you sleep?", he might reply, "All right." "All right" is vague. It needs further clarification. The physician can explore the subject with such a patient in this manner:

Physician: Do you sleep heavily, lightly, on and off?
Patient: I guess on and off.
Physician: Would you explain?
Patient: I go to sleep all right at night, but then I wake up around two.
Physician: What do you do when you wake up around two?
Patient: I go to the bathroom.
Physician: And then what happens?
Patient: I can't go to sleep right away, but then I go to sleep around four.
Physician: How do you know it's four?
Patient: I hear the milkman coming down the block.
Physician: And then?
Patient: I get up around six.
Physician: What do you do then?
Patient: I go to the bathroom again.

Only one question should be used at a time. "How long have you been coughing, and do you bring anything up with it?" are two ideas. Each one needs special attention. Listeners attend to what they heard first or what they heard last, with preference usually for the latter. If given a list to remember, one will usually have no trouble recalling the last item. In the two questions used as examples, the respondent would probably have been more concerned with supplying an answer to the second question, "Do you bring anything up with it?" The patient would then have to gloss over the first question in order not to forget the second and hastily supply an answer not necessarily of his best recollection. There is a significant difference between "Let's see, I started coughing last month, and I remember that I was worried about catching a cold the first week of a new job" and "Not too long." There is a suggestion in the first answer of possible industrial poisoning that is lacking in the second.

Two questions at a time or one question following on the heel of the other make the questioner appear impatient and suggest that the answer is expected to be brief. Those who are used to speaking publicly are alert to the challenge of two questions loaded into one sentence. Experienced speakers will always respond, "I see two questions there. May I have them one at a time?"

The direct question, like the indirect question, requires absolute clarification. "Do you drink?" followed by "Yes" requires quantification.

"A little now and then" is vague. The physician runs this down like a hare with the further question, "How much is a little now and then?" "A few drinks in the evening, a couple of beers on Saturday night." The physician may further his questioning with a laundry list: "You say a few drinks, two, three, four, or more?" or elaboration—"A couple of beers on Saturday night, how many is a couple? Are they nine or twelve-ounce bottles?"

"I have trouble breathing" demands qualification and quantification. The physician hones in on when, where, why, under what circumstances, and to what degree. He needs to know if breathing is labored, if it is accompanied by pain, wheezing, or coughing, does the patient feel the need to take deep breaths, and does he need a lot of pillows in order to sleep comfortably at night.

"I can't swallow" requires clarification. The physician must find out if the patient gags, if he regurgitates liquid through his nose, if he experiences discomfort only after the food has passed into his esophagus, whether he can swallow liquid but not solids, and what part of his throat or esophagus gives him trouble (35).

The use of direct and indirect questions is discretionary and will vary within the interview. The physician generally opens topics with indirect questions and closes them with direct. Both are helpful, and he will usually spend an interview alternating their use. Graphically, their relationship with direct questions regarding significant topics would resemble an earthworm.

The following examples illustrate the difference between direct and indirect questions related to the same subject.

What are you doing to your skin to make it so inflamed? (direct)
Tell me something about your bathing habits. (indirect)

Have you gained or lost weight? (direct)
Have you noticed any difference in the way your clothes fit? (indirect)

Do you follow a proper diet? (direct)
Tell me something about your eating habits. (indirect)

Are you happily married? (direct)
How are things at home? (indirect)

Have you ever had any heart trouble? (direct)
Have you noticed any change in your breathing? (indirect)

Any unusual stress in your work? (direct)
Describe your work. (indirect)

Are you using any sedatives? (direct)
Tell me about your sleeping habits. (indirect)

Frequently a significant question is embedded in the middle of a sequence of routine and neutral questions. It might go this way:

Physician: You said that you're eating pretty much as you always have.
Patient: Yes.
Physician: Would you describe what you mean?
Patient: Well, on the fly, you know. I grab whatever's handy, open a can or two . . .
Physician: It seems that you don't make a fuss over eating.
Patient: No.
Physician: Do you have any trouble swallowing what you grab?

A variant of this technique is the loaded question. "How long have you had trouble swallowing?" This second example can only be asked if the physician has some evidence to back up his shot in the dark. The embedding technique is similar to popping a mickey in someone's drink. If not done well and at the appropriate time, it can backfire; and the physician may wind up with the wrong glass. A particularly wary, suspicious, or alert patient may respond negatively to a less than open approach.

Questions not only elicit answers but their design determines what kind of answer. Their skillful variation makes the best use of clinical time by accomodating the needs of both patient and physician. Indirect questions make the patient comfortable, encourage his spontaneity, and allow for idiosyncratic disease manifestation. Direct questions clarify, elaborate, and summarize. Both types seek information that will lead to diagnosis and remedy. To get this information, the physician formulates his interview around the following topics: the patient's immediate concerns, his environmental stresses, his family history, his personal history, a review of systems, and a physical examination. These topics need not be taken in order, and often information obtained in one serves another.

TAKING THE HISTORY

IMMEDIATE CONCERNS

The symptoms that the patient presents fall under the rubric of chief complaint, that may been seen as the headline of the present illness. The label for this subdivision of the clinical interview, which implies a single complaint, is misleading, for often the patient has a constellation of manifestations. It also suggests that the physician concentrate on a single theme which causes him to work prematurely on finding a significant clue. History taking may then become an interrogation in which the physician fires a battery of questions in order to emerge from the foray with a substantiated chief complaint.

Sometimes the patient is so attuned to what is called the chief complaint that he sees as irrelevant any other topic which the doctor seeks to investigate. For example, a patient with back pain who is convinced that he has strained a muscle might be annoyed by the doctor who may be tracking down renal infection and who questions him about his urinary habits. When the physician observes this happening, either by the patient's cursory response to questions or by facial and body cues, he can explain that the chief complaint may be an incidental symptom for an illness not necessarily related to the patient's concept of anatomy. What troubles the patient may not be the most significant clinical complaint. He may, for example, seek remedy for ocular complaints that are secondary to the broader findings of sarcoidosis.

The patient will understand the purpose of the doctor's questions better if he sees his symptoms as clues and the doctor as a detective, who needs to know several things about the case before he can begin to make any judgment. Before the physician can explain his methods effectively, he may first need to empathize with his patient, and, if empathy does not work, confront this patient in order to resolve his conflicting messages. It may go like this: "It must be very frustrating for you to come for relief about your back and have to answer questions about everything else," followed by, if necessary, "You seem very upset. The more we go into other details, the angrier you look."

The patient considers the presenting complaint the most important piece of information he shares. It may be the first symptom he relates in a process of selective emphasis, it may be the symptom he is most concerned about and whispers to the physician at the end of the interview, or it can be the symptom that is the most annoying and the one he wishes the physician to alleviate. It may be what he exchanges for the red herring he had admissions write on his chart in the first place. "Remember I said my stomach itches? Actually, it's a little lower."

Symptoms are warning signs of illness. Each organ system produces characteristic symptoms in the presence of disease. The absence of an exact description may be in itself a property of that particular disease. When the patient relates symptoms, the physician attempts to quantify and qualify them. Every sensation which translates into medicine as a symptom has unique characteristics pertaining to general description, target area, spread, perimeter, radiation, time and events of onset, progress and fluctuations, frequency, and duration of each episode, and events which might make it better or worse, such as weather, movement, specific food intake, or the unwanted advice of a brother-in-law.

The physician wants to know what the symptoms are like, where they are located, where the patient is when they occur, what he is doing, how severe they are, when they were first noticed, how frequent they are, what makes them better or worse, if they are continuous or episodic, if they are getting better or worse, how they affect function, if they are associated with any other symptoms, and if they radiate to any other organs or parts of the body. This formidable listing of qualifying statements can usually be boiled down to three dimensions: *quality, location, and duration.* Since symptoms may not occur in the presence of the physician, his information is dependent upon the patient's description. The sequence of symptoms is important. A difference of even several days or hours in the sequence of such events as angina pectoris and dyspnea might be crucial in considering the prognosis of myocardial infarction. Timing is also crucial although more difficult when the symptom has an insidious onset or when it is discovered by the physician. The duration or occurence of an insidious symptom may be brought to mind by questions related to holidays, public events, or birthdays and anniversaries (14). The patient may not recall the date, but he may recall that it was at the Labor Day picnic that he first became dizzy. The symptom discovered may be checked against other known medical records. The patient can be encouraged to become a partner in the clinical relationships by keeping a medical diary complete with records of x–rays, immunizations, operations, illnesses, electrocardiograms, etc., and his responses to those events. This, together with the physician's record of his patient's reactions to symptoms, will help determine the degree to which his patient's verbal reporting of symptoms is accurate. If the physician knows that his patient tends to minimize symptoms, he is prepared to interpret or edit his story like a space engineer compensating for error.

A word of caution about patients and their diaries. There are very few people who do not believe that their life stories, especially their medical experiences, are worthy of publication. "I could write a book" is often heard, as well as, "My doctor never saw a case like mine." or "They're printing it in a medical journal." To discourage the vast accumulation of subjective experience that might be dumped on the clinician or on publishing houses, it is prudent for any physician who suggests a diary to stress its brevity and its relative unimportance to the world at large.

While there are printed forms that expedite the clinical interaction, their use causes the interview to become structured around the form rather than around the patient, whose story must be squeezed into its formula. It may be impossible to learn what is troubling the patient by using the formula. In order to find out what bothers him about his symptoms, it is more helpful to conduct a free-wheeling interview, using some moderate guidelines.

ENVIRONMENTAL STRESSES

One's physical status is determined not only by the condition of his tissues but by his physical environment and by his interactions with all who make up his social environment (24, 32). The variances in the environment of the human being are limitless, each one composed of a multitude of factors which may predispose him to illness, precipitate illness, or aggravate illness. For example, congenital malformation might predispose one to pulmonary disease, heavy pollution might precipitate it, and four-flight walk-up apartment will surely aggravate it.

These environmental factors, called stressors, have come to include such factors as noxious agents; deprivation, both biologic and psychologic; meterologic changes such as temperature, barometric pressure, and pollution; interpersonal relationships; job demands; and life changes, including those that are considered pleasant, such as marriage or promotion. There is evidence that the greater the change total, the greater the likelihood of somatic disease (20). Other investigators consider the preparedness and personality of the individual more important factors in stress than their cumulative effect (6).

Selye describes the response to stress in three stages: an alarm reaction that produces measurable biochemical changes; resistance to the stressor; and following prolonged exposure to the stressor, exhaustion (31). Changes in body function and structure may occur in any of these stages. The result may be organ dysfunction, seen in reactions such as tachycardia, syncope, muscular or vasomotor pain, hyperventilation, and disruption of gastrointestinal peristalsis, or diseases such as cardiac disorders, hypertension, and peptic ulcer. More globally, stress produces wear and tear on the organism.

To relate environmental stresses to the patient's symptoms, the physician needs to learn as much as he can about his patient's environment; what changes, if any, including illness have occurred; the intensity, duration, cumulative effect, and demands of any stressors; what their temporal relationship is to the symptoms; and most important, what their significance is to the patient. What constitutes stress for one patient may be of minimal importance to another (8).

The patient's current life situation requires an investigation of the significant other people in his life. In a study of routine throat swabs of families in Boston, more streptocci was found at time of family crisis (27). The important information in an inquiry of current life situation reveals who has the power to affect him one way or another, whom he cares about, who cares about him, or if no one cares about him (26a). There is some evidence that living alone is a worse health hazard than overcrowding and that those who live alone are more vulnerable to hypertension, asthma, ulcers, neuroses, drinking, and drugs (7, 9, 37). An investigation of his current life situation covers his living conditions and circumstances, including such topics as housing, neighborhood, dietary habits, the intensity of light in his quarters, population density (40 radios can make anyone jumpy), the quality of sanitation, proximity to industry, and endemic factors of his geography.

Investigation of the patient's occupational environment focuses on where he works, what he does, and his working conditions (24). It considers not only hazards, but such questions as does he commute, must he keep pace with a machine, how heavy are his responsibilities, how many decibels is the noise level, and is he threatened by job loss.

Mobility is a factor that underscores personal, living, and occupational environments. How easily can the patient change his situation? To what extent can he manipulate his environment? Change in itself may not be the goal since the ill effects of stressful living are often outweighed by economic, social, or psychologic advantages for the individual. What is crucial is whether he considers his position irrevocably determined by forces other than himself or whether he believes he has any say in what happens to him (30). It makes a difference if he is the shaper or the shaped.

FAMILY HISTORY

In order to evaluate the effects of stressors on the patient, it is necessary to have an idea of his endowments, both acquired and genetic. A concept of inherited and developed strengths and weaknesses will give the physician an indication of his patient's potential resistance, resilience, and adaptability. His family history is not a museum but a rich and relevant source of information on his genetic and early environmental factors, including development, racial, cultural, and religious influences, diet, habits, family dynamics, and attitudes.

Attitude significantly influences the way one behaves in a medical situation (10, 33). It affects the way one monitors time, vital in taking medication, keeping appointments, or engaging in future-oriented tasks such as exercising to regain muscle tone. Many people do not schedule future-oriented activities because their life experience has taught them that schedules are unworkable in the face of hazardous daily living.

More and more investigations of organic and degenerative diseases suggest that there is likely to be some genetic component in the etiology of nearly every disease (11). The genetic approach to pathogenesis involves a careful study of the entire family group of a diseased individual to search for precursory signs of metabolic peculiarities which predispose the individual to the disease. For example, there is strong evidence that close relatives of those suffering pulmonary tuberculosis are three or four times as likely to contract the disease as unrelated persons comparable in sex, socioeconomic status, and exposure. A detailed family history may reveal unsuspected consanguinity, a factor in predicting genetic disorders. By taking into account family history, the physician who is aware of genetic implications may make an otherwise difficult diagnosis more quickly. A case in point is that of a child with fever, dry skin, sparse hair, and fewer teeth than expected who was treated for hypothyroidism. Extensive examination of the family subsequently revealed several relatives, including the mother, with defective tooth development and other anomalies. These findings invalidated the earlier diagnosis and led to the diagnosis of a rare genetic disease called anhidrotic ectodermal dysplasis, for which thyroid administration would be harmful (21a).

The patient often considers his family history irrelevant to his present concerns.

He wants help for what troubles him, he wants it now, and he doesn't want to waste time discussing his family. When the patient relates details of his current problems, he will usually refer at some point to his family or other significant people in his life. When he feels it is appropriate, the physician can seize these references and use them as a starting point.

Patient: I didn't tell anyone I was coming in about my headaches, especially my mother.

Physician: Why not your mother?

Patient: She worries so about every little thing, it affects her pressure.

Physician: Has she ever been treated for her pressure?

Patient: I don't think so.

Physician: How do you know she has it?

Patient: Oh you know, don't worry. She always tells us when it's going up.

The information here reveals a significant family member with possible hypertension who models a disease picture which may or may not be imitated by the patient.

Family history, which seeks more broad environmental and genetic factors, may flow more easily from an indirect question such as "Tell me about your life at home." or "What was your family like?" If the physician has inadvertently opened up a *Forsythe's Saga,* he can use questions that are more direct and specific, such as "You mentioned your father died when you were 14. Do you recall how you felt then?" or "You haven't mentioned your mother. Can you tell me about her?" The most basic and cursory family medical history is one in which the health and number of near relatives and the presence of such diseases as diabetes, tuberculosis, cancer, heart disease, mental illness, and illness similar to the patient's are noted.

In obtaining a more detailed family history, the physician lists everyone in the patient's immediate family, their ages (if deceased, their ages at death, the nature and duration of their illness, the patient's response to their death), their physical characteristics, psychologic characteristics, socioeconomic status, structure, social habits, and health habits.

In addition to genetic and environmental information, two important facets of the patient will be revealed by family history. The first is an understanding of how his early needs were met, a significant criteria against which to measure his current responses and his ability to cope (12). The second is his relationships to those in his family and the patterns of interaction, which will influence his present style of interaction, his expectations of other people, and his ability to establish and maintain intimate relationships. The importance of the family history is shown by the fact that some medical schools are encouraging students to visit the patient's home in order to obtain information from appropriate relatives (26).

PERSONAL HISTORY

Personal history includes many topics that have already been covered in environmental stresses, in family history, and in the review of systems. A brief personal history includes medications, drug reactions, previous illnesses, surgical operations, vital functions, and personal habits. A more detailed personal history includes previous routine or periodic checks such as other visits to physicians, examinations before entrance to military service, or a casual stop at a sidewalk mobile chest x-ray unit; the patient's childhood, going as far back as he can remember; his physical functions and health; his relations with other people; his learning experiences; and major events in his life and his reaction to them. On some patients it is possible to plot a profile of individual predisposition to certain types of illnesses, based on the psychic parameter of reaction to significant events.

Before engaging the patient in questions related to previous serious illness, vital functions, or personal problems, it may be helpful to begin with neutral questions about his job or hobbies, since most patients consider these areas the least threatening. The physician does this while continuing to be accepting, nonjudgmental facilitating, and consistent. Asking the patient what he does for a living may be perceived as judgmental, since not every one works. A better question is "What do you do with your time?" If some sort of work is the answer, the physician can ask for more information with such questions as "What is your job like?" "What are your responsibilities?" and "How about the other people you work with?" It is easy to move from the vocational to the social with such questions as "What do you do after work?" or if he is unemployed, "What do you do for fun?" His social behavior will give the physician not only an idea of his interests and level of function but also of the way in which he interacts with others.

Questions related to the use of alcohol or drugs should be matter-of-fact and nonjudgmental. All questions related to the use of drugs or alcohol should determine what is taken, over what period of time, under what circumstances, with whom, how much, and the effects. (See Chapter 10 on alcoholism and drugs for more details.) The use of questions will depend on the age of the patient and on the nature of the physician–patient relationship. A young patient may be asked simply "Do you use?" or "What do you take to get high?" or "Do you take anything to get high?" An older patient who may freely volunteer information about alcohol usage may bristle at the word *drug*. This patient may respond more favorably to questions related to the purpose of drugs, such as the use of medication to sleep, lose weight, stay calm, keep awake: "Are you taking anything to lose weight?" or "You have described a rough day to me. Do you feel the need for anything to pep you up or to calm you down?"

Since his sexual activity is a barometer of his general state, it is important for the physician to know if the patient is sexually active and if he enjoys it. People use each other, themselves, and their orifices in artful sexual combinations. Some are less artful than others, but the general guidelines are that if consenting adults are involved and nobody gets badly hurt, variances are merely matters of preference. Frequency is a relative criterion. What is too much for one person is not enough for another. The physician can determine if the patient functions sexually in a manner pleasing to him by asking, "In what ways is sex most pleasing for you?" This acknowledges that there are many ways, all acceptable to the physician. It also acknowledges that some are, for this patient, better than others. It is also more likely to elicit dysfunction than the blanket, "How's your sex life?" or "You have sex?" Unless the patient is articulate and comfortable with the discussion, asking him to describe his sexual activities in a general way such as "Tell me something about your sex life." is more likely to get a response such as "It's o.k."

Questions related to sexual activity are more revealing if they are indirect. "How did you first learn about sex?" will lead to early attitudes. The physician can then respond, "Is there any relationship between the way you felt then and the way you feel now about sex?", which usually elicits a good picture of the patient's current habits. If the physician is interested in determining recent change, he can ask, "Has it always been the way you describe now?" If the answer is *no*, he can ask, "In what way?" or "Tell me how it is different." Sexual function has high status on society's totem pole, somewhere alongside looks, youth, vitality, and success. Unless the patient is candid or quite comfortable in relating all aspects of history to his doctor, it is unlikely that he will voluntarily reveal that his sexual function is less than anyone else's.

SYSTEMS REVIEW

If the patient seems really uncomfortable or if he has difficulty with articulation, the physician can switch to a systems review. A systems review can flow quite naturally out of inquiry into previous health, the physical examination, and the story of the patient's immediate concerns. If the physician has not obtained information related to the patient's vital functions from personal history, he might find the subject easier to approach through the back door of organ function.

The subject of sexual habits, for example, may evolve more easily out of a survey of genitourinary function, which just followed a series of questions reviewing gastrointestinal function. Some physicians tackle a review of systems from the patient's head down ("Ever have headaches?") like a medical salaam; others proceed from his feet up ("Ever have difficulty walking?"). Some shop around, grabbing what they missed while gathering information in other areas. Whatever the direction of inquiry, the review of systems is meant as a survey, a general overview of the past and present state of the patient's organs. In a survey of organ function, it is appropriate to use direct questions. For this reason, a systems review may be relegated to a printed form which is composed of a list of direct questions and used when time is short. Care must be taken to be sure that the patient has no difficulty in reading the form or understanding the terms.

MENTAL STATUS

Out of the interview will emerge the patient's patterns of illness and their usual course, his goals, attitudes, general level of intelligence, skills, resources, and fears; in short, the manner in which his personality contributes to the total disability (16,38). The interview will also reveal his mental status, his present state of psychologic functioning which will affect his ability to handle matters pertaining to his health, and the reliance which the physician can place upon him as a partner in a mutual venture. The physician will consider such things as how his patient's mind works, what he thinks about, his behavior, his mood, his reaction to his environment, and how he handles his feelings. While presuming that the patient is playing with a full deck, the physician needs to be alerted to the symptoms which indicate that he may be missing a few cards.

Not all psychiatric dysfunction interferes in the same degree with the practice of medicine. More frequently encountered and/or more likely to interfere are organic brain syndrome and depression. The former interferes because of a memory deficit, the latter, because of a lack of motivation and the likelihood of mistaking depressive illness for that which is purely somatic. Certainly organic brain syndromes and depression are the most common psychiatric disorders of the 20 million American elderly, a population which will occupy an increasingly larger percentage of medical practice.

Organic Brain Syndrome

The stuperous or delirious patient suffering acute brain syndrome is more commonly encountered on medical and surgical hospital wards. For that reason, discussion here will be limited to the chronic brain syndrome patient.

Symptoms of neurologic disorders such as headaches, convulsions, lapses of consciousness, disorders of gait, coordination, vision, or speech should make the physician suspect organic brain syndrome.

Chronic brain syndrome patients typically manifest intellectual deterioration, including disorders of orientation, memory, concentration, abstraction, calculation, judgment, and fluctuations in their grasp of reality.

Orientation involves the patient's concept of who he is, who others are, in what time, and in what place. By the time the physician has finished with demographic data, he has a pretty good idea of the patient's orientation. Memory disturbances may be seen in the patient who is unable to recall events and place them in proper sequence.

In the early stages of chronic brain sydnrome, the patient may be aware that his memory is deficient and appear puzzled and bewildered over his inability to recall. A few patients with chronic memory deficit will confabulate, inventing missing data on the spot. If events do not correlate or appear in conflict, as he tells them, the patient may be further tested by being given data to recall at a later moment such as the name of a medication, its purpose, and when he is to take it. The integrity of his responses may be tested by such questions as "Do you ever get angry?" "Do you ever tell an untruth?" or "Do you ever laugh at a dirty joke?" If answered in firmly asserted negatives, the physician may become alerted to possible exaggerations or inaccuracies in other responses.

A patient with disturbed concentration may appear lost in thought, then will look up in surprise and ask, "What were we saying?" or make no reference at all to a sentence or thought that has been left hanging. He will find events hard to follow and may often ask the physician to repeat (25).

The responses of the chronic brain syndrome patient are usually literal and concrete. He is unable to evaporate his thoughts into the higher order of cognition that is abstraction. A frequently used test of a patient's ability to abstract is to ask him to interpret proverbs. The meaning of proverbs, however, is often dependent upon cultural learning and bias. One patient, when asked why people in glass houses shouldn't throw stones, replied, "Man, people in glass houses shouldn't do anything."

An idea of the patient's ability to calculate and concentrate may be obtained by requesting him to count backwards from 100 by 7s. A more relevant way is to request that he calculate carfare for successive visits or to ask how he plans to fit the doctor's bill he's going to get into his budget. It is an act of good faith to state, "I'm going to give you a small test." Most patients do not question this. If they do, the physician answers, "To help me understand your difficulties." or "To help me understand you better."

Patients are sometimes asked why traffic lights are needed in order to test their judgment. This kind of question, out of left field, may be confusing, especially for the patient who is having trouble enough making sense out of his world. His judgment can be assessed by determining how he handles his life. If he seems unable to plan, consistently makes wrong choices, or gives his stereo to the mailman, his judgment may be suspect.

If the patient can discuss his symptoms one moment and in the next state that he leaves to assume the presidency the following week, his grasp of reality has fluctuated. While delusions or hallucinations are seen less frequently in the chronic brain syndrome patient, delusional material will usually be revealed during the interview. A persistant irrational idea, a delusion often occurs like a discordant note in an otherwise cohesive story. A patient who is able to relate the chronology of his symptoms with ease may make an occasional reference to other people controlling his mind, not a helpful situation in any case to the physician. Evidence of hallucinations may not come out of the content of the interview but may be obtained by asking, "Do you ever see or hear things other people don't?"

In severe intellectual deterioration, the patient cannot distinguish relevant from irrelevant material. If asked to list his family members, he may include other people, such as his neighbor or the man who owns the drug store.

The chronic brain syndrome patient may display a decline in personal standards. If he once walked a mile to dispose of a gum wrapper, he may now toss used paper cups out of his window with reckless abandon. His affect, the manner in which he presents himself, is more often flattened and he displays little variation in his lexical and kinesic activity. In some cases, the chronic brain syndrome patient shows labile affect, crying or laughing easily with little provocation and at inappropriate moments. Often his speech is disturbed in some way. It may be slurred, as if dipthongs were fused together, or he may speak in a scanning sing–song, emphasizing the wrong syllable.

Depression

Epidemiologic studies show a widely disparate incidence of depression as seen in office practice. The variance in frequency may be the result of differences in vocabulary, systems of classification, patient populations, and the ability to recognize depression (5). Since the depressive state not only produces negative effects on the soma but is life threatening (about 75 percent of depressed patients have suicidal ideas and at least 10 percent carry them out, although not necessarily to completion), its recognition is imperative (1).

Although the state of depression has been teased into separate entities, it may be seen as a continuum, ranging from simple to severe depression. Simple depression may be seen in the breakup of a love affair when the patient feels "lousy" whereas in cases of severe depression the patient may sit all day in the same chair in the same clothes, or pace the floor aimlessly, wringing his hands, and even tearing his hair while moaning that he doesn't deserve to live (which may be echoed by others in his home if he has been doing it long enough). Somewhere between the two, although not necessarily in the middle, is the anxious depression in which one experiences a specific fear or a vague apprehension.

In most cases of depression, everything is down, including the patient's head, voice, face, and mood. As one's eye advances along the continuum, there is generally a corresponding slowdown in the patient's motor activity although agitated motor activity may be a component of depression.

The depressed patient is likely to display poor eye contact and may be entirely turned away from the physician. He may speak in a monotone with little change in pitch or volume and even appear uninterested in speaking. For the more severely depressed patient, speech is an effort, made as if he cannot propel the words past his lips. He doesn't seem to concentrate well, may choke up, change the subject, or cry. He may be unenthusiastic and unresponsive, he may have an air of helplessness, or he may become agitated and irritable. In any degree of depression, anger is also likely to be present. Depression is considered by some to be anger turned inward. It may be that the potential suicide on the ledge would rather push a particular someone over in his place if he could.

Often depression is first noticed in the patient's sighing respiration, an expression of his psychic pain and the harsh judgments of his conscience, which the patient offers as a front runner, usually while the physician is filling in his notes. If the physician looks up and acknowledges it with "That was some sigh." or "You seem to have the world on your shoulders," he will find that the patient is ready to reveal something of his feelings. If no comment is made the patient will keep on sighing and wind up hyperventilating or feeling more depressed.

He may make statements that reflect pessimism ("What's the difference." "It doesn't matter."), failure ("I'm no good."), dissatisfaction ("Nothing is going right."), guilt, often over trivial mattes ("Mea culpa"), self-harm ("I'd be better off dead."), and other statements indicating social withdrawal, indecisiveness, and a change in his self-image. He may state openly that he is feeling *down* or *low* or *blue* (3).

The depressed patient has trouble thinking clearly. He will often select an isolated item and generalize it, always negatively. "No one likes me." "How do you know that?" "When I walked down the street this morning, nobody said hello to me." "Did you know anyone who passed you?" "No."

The history will usually reveal that the patient has suffered some loss, a change in life role such as that brought about by retirement or menopause, loss of employment, loss of status, loss of function or of body parts, or loss of a loved one.

A significant cue to depression is emotional resonance, the way the physician feels in the patient's presence. While depression and ebulliance are contagious, ebulliance is a happier infection. One of the reasons that the depressed patient is unpopular on psychiatric wards is that he makes everyone else feel bad, and the staff will usually avoid him until the Tofranil takes.

Jones and Hall report that the depressed patient is unduly sensitive to minor pains and shows a tendency to be concerned about minor disturbances (21). The chief emphasis in his presenting complaints may be physical symptoms such as aching muscles, constipation, dysuria or frequency, disturbances of appetite or sleep, and loss of weight. Seventy–five percent of those with depressive illness in a general hospital had such physical complaints (31a). This patient more often does not manifest the despairing mood. A great number never mention depression at all, which is why organic illness can mask it and why diagnosis is often missed (13).

The patient who comes in with a variety of vague complaints may respond well to treatment and then return in a few weeks with a new complaint without ever admitting he is depressed. The best clue is that his symptoms don't seem to justify coming in for a visit. (Even though he may be depressed, he may also be physically ill; it is for that reason that a complete physical and appropriate lab tests are given.)

Fatigue is a classic physical symptom of depression, especially when it is accompanied by other symptoms such as vague or specific pain, unrelieved muscular tension, daily headaches which are most severe in the morning, dryness and a bad taste in the mouth, and impairment of the vital functions of eating, digestion, sex, and sleeping.

Often he will complain only of feeling "run down". For this reason, all patients with somatic complaints should be asked how they feel and if the way they feel represents a change in mood.

Besides the information he obtains from questions directed to vital functions and from observation and active listening, the physician attempting to uncover depression will find helpful questions directed to the *future* and *fun*. The depressed patient can think of neither. "What are your plans for this summer?" asked of a depressed patient is likely to elicit a shrug of the shoulders or "Who cares?" The nondepressed patient might answer, "I don't know yet," but the depressed patient indicates no interest in future plans. Joy has gone out of his life, and he cannot even imagine having fun. If asked, "What do you enjoy doing?", he will answer negatively, or he will say, "I used to go riding, but I don't do that anymore."

In dealing with the patient who has not threatened suicide but is depressed, the physician must determine whether or not the patient is a potential suicide. The questioning may begin with "How is it that you are here?" Questions related to disturbances of vital functions such as eating, sleeping, sexual activity, conditions at work and at home will elicit some problems. The physician can follow these with "How long have you had these problems?", acknowledging that they are problems. They may be petty to the physician, but if the patient presents them as major problems, that's what they are. The answer to "What has happened recently to make them worse for you?" gives the physician an idea of what this patient's rock bottom is. He can ask, "Everyone has their ups and downs apparently you're down now.What is it like for you?" followed by "Have you ever thought about doing anything to end it all?" If the answer is yes, the physician continues. "Think how you might do it?" If preparations have been made, if the patient has a stash of pills, a rope made with knots, and a will, if he asks questions with lethal overtones, "Where is my heart?", "How many pills do you have to swallow so that you don't just wake up with brain damage?", he is a suicide risk. The more imminent the planned act, its temporal coincidence with an anniversary of loss, and the availability and lethality of the method increase risk. If he is thinking about injecting himself with curare, it is not as great a risk as planning to jump from a very high bridge to which he has access. Additionally his impression of lethality is significant.

Many health professionals feel uncomfortable asking a depressed patient if he has thoughts about killing himself and view with particular distaste discussing the finer points of how he would go about it. Some are afraid that they will put the idea into his head, but if he is depressed, the idea is there. It may not have concluded in formal plans but it is skirting the periphery of his thoughts. It is far more important to determine clearly suicide potential than to be remiss. Rather than giving him an "idea," questions directed to suicide show the patient that his interviewer is taking him seriously.

Thoughts of suicide are not all direct. Some are more subtle and create the impression of casting off one's moorings. Increased risk taking, giving away valuable possessions, disengagement from close relationships and work, and increasing dependence on alcohol and sleep medication are the actions of someone severing his connections (28).

Severing his connections can also be seen in his emotional movement towards or away from other people. The physician will want to determine how he views the reactions of others. His question in this case might be, "What will everyone think?" If the patient answers, "I don't know," or shrugs his shoulders instead of "They'll be sorry", it's more serious. A statement of unconcern in his response to the physician's interest is also an indication of a movement away from people.

Once the physician has evidence that the patient is a potential suicide, his next step is to estimate risk. (36) Statistically the suicide is more likely to be a white male of advancing age, divorced or widowed, and living alone, although recent evidence show the young black urban male who has a suicide rate almost twice that of the white male as an exception. The risk increases in the presence of serious medical illness, especially if the patient perceives it so. If he has a history of psychiatric illness, if he has made a previous attempt, if it was a violent one, and if it altered anything like making someone else sit up and take notice, the likelihood increases. In assessing potential, the degree of psychomotor retardation is another clue. Paradoxically, the more severely retarded patient is at less risk than the activated depressed patient who has the energy to carry out his plans (28).

The physician then weighs all of the evidence he is able to gather of risk against the patient's social, financial, health, and intellectual resources to determine if they are sufficient to discourage suicide. The means he has at his disposal to alleviate his distress, the people who might give him support, his ability to have insight into his problems, and the way he has handled crises in the past will contribute to an understanding of his resources.

The protocol of treatment will vary with the facility. Most physicians hospitalize the patient of high suicide risk who has no supportive relationships in order to separate him from the means and provide greater control. If he is to be hospitalized the physician conveys empathy and the idea that time cures many things including depression. He may say, "I know you feel that way now, and that is because you are ill. You need care and for that reason I'm going want to hospitalize you."

For the patient that is not to be hospitalized see Chapter 6, section on suicide.

TERMINATION

The clinical interview includes gathering information on symptoms, environmental factors, history, assessment of mental status, and physical signs. It is not always possible to obtain all of the information on these subjects in a single interview. This is particularly difficult when the interview is twenty minutes or less, which seems to be the more common event in a teaching facility. When the physician is caught in a time crunch, he can place his major emphasis on symptoms, current stresses, and the physical examination and skirt lightly other topics which he will tackle at a later session. His immediate concern should be on those topics that will help to identify the patient's most acute problem. Tangential or chronic problems and underlying symptoms and causes may be identified as soon as possible after the acute condition is resolved.

While gathering information to form a clinical judgment is the name of the game, it is equally important to form a therapeutic relationship that will help patient and doctor in subsequent interactions, or which will carry over into other medical situations. If a shortage of time prohibits the full gathering of information, it is important that the physician take the last few moments to signal to the patient that the interview is coming to a close. This facilitates the patient's continued comfort in the clinical situation. A few minutes before the conclusion of the interview, the physician can ask, "Is there anything else you would like to tell me?" or "I have asked a lot of questions, perhaps there is something you would like to ask me?" If the patient is deeply involved in relating a matter of importance to him, the physician can acknowledge his need to express it by saying, "I see this subject is very important to you. Unfortunately, we only have a few more minutes." or "You look as if you have something else on your mind. Let's take a few minutes to discuss it."

Sometimes it is possible to say, "Look, we don't have time to go into that now, but we can discuss it at your next visit." The physician has to remember that he made such a promise, however, so it is a good idea to jot it down somewhere. The chances are good that the patient will have forgotten all about it, but, when the physician brings it up, it pleases the patient to know that his physician is concerned enough to remember.

The abrupt termination of an interview has a negative effect on most patients. When the physician looks at his watch, slams shut his book, or stands up without warning, he causes additional anxiety in his patient. The patient begins to worry about what he did not tell the physician or that he is somehow deficient. This results in the patient who calls on the telephone to obtain continuous reassurance or who haunts the office in person. Patients may also feel angry because their doctor did not think enough of them to allow a few moments for a satisfactory conclusion.

The patient may ask for a prognosis at the conclusion of the interview. It is important not to give hasty or premature assurances that may need retraction at a later time. The physician can reply, "I know too little at this point to form a definite opinion." "I will know more after I get the lab studies back." or "Nothing you have told me or that I have seen so far has given me any cause to worry about the outcome." To alleviate anxiety, the physician can allude to their next appointment or request the patient to call him if he notices certain symptoms.

The physician who would not tolerate a lab report that was scratched out, inked over, or otherwise confusing will often settle for ambiguity in recording the details of the clinical interview. Although recorders differ in their command of language, the fault of imprecision does not rest entirely on the recorder. The problem lies with words. No matter how descriptive, they do not have the accuracy of numerical values. There is a difference between "6 mg" and "a little extra uric acid." Abdominal mass while a clear term, is inadequate. Details on turgidity, size, precise location, etc. are absent, making the statement as vague as describing a number as a "low one".

Feinstein suggests converting verbal description into code numbers by placing each attribute in an individual column and giving it a specific value for absence, presence, or some other distinction (14). The more attributes the physician records, the closer he comes to a precise description of major symptoms.

There is another problem in recording. The physician finds himself in the bind of lexicographer who is also a trained interpreter. What distinguishes him from the policeman who carefully notes all injuries at the scene of an accident is that one of his skills is the ability to translate observations into hypothesis. He may see pallor and record anemia, not only because he may have made a tentative diagnosis, but also because he uses the disease entity interchangebaly with an adjective qualifier.

Instead of describing the pallor, he has made a diagnostic jump. Pallor may be due not to anemia but to shock. For clarity is is necessary for the physician to separate description from interpretation.

REFERRAL OUT

It may become apparent that the physician's services are not appropriate to the needs of the patient and that the patient should be referred to another physician. Referral may connote rejection which may, on occasion, be the case. In a seminar discussion centered around what to do with the unpleasant patient, one medical student offered the quick solution of referring him elsewhere. Referral may also connote serious illness or stigma. The physician should discuss the referral not as if it were the last resort, but rather as his own need for expert corroboration. The physician can say that the patient's problem requires specialized attention and that expert opinion will probably shorten the period of diagnosis and hasten treatment, since the referred physician has greater familiarity with the problem. Saying that two heads are better than one, or comparing it to taking a broken muffler to a shop that specializes in muffler repair (while you wait) help ease the referral process.

The referral may be on the basis of a one–shot consultation. If longer association is necessary, the physician can state that he expects to keep in touch with the referred physician and that the patient should still feel free to contact him with any questions. If the referral is psychiatric, the physician can assure the patient that he is not alone and that, if he cares to check, he will find many friends and acquaintances who have used psychiatric counsel.

REFERENCES

1. Arieti S (ed): American Handbook of Psychiatry. New York, Basic Books, 1959
2. Bain DJ et al.: Difficulties encountered in classifying illness in general practice. J R Coll Gen Pract 23:474–479, 1973
3. Beck AT: Depression. New York, Harper & Row, 1967
4. Bennett G: Scientific Medicine? Lancet 2:453–456, 1974
5. Berkow R et al.: Depression. Patient Care VIII, No. 6, 1974
6. Birley JL: Stress and disease J. Psychosom Res 16:235–40, 1972
7. Booth A, Cowell J: The Effects of Crowding Upon Health. Lincoln, University of Nebraska Press, 1974
8. Cassell J: Psychosocial factors in the genesis of disease. In Kane R (ed): The Challenges of Community Medicine. New York, Springer, 1974, pp 287–300
9. Collette J, Webb SD: Urban density, crowding and stress reactions. Presented at Pacific Sociological Association Meetings, 1974
10. Duff RS, Hollingshead AB: Sickness and Society. New York, Harper & Row, 1968
11. Elandt JRC: Age-at-onset distribution in chronic diseases: a life table approach to analysis of family data. J Chronic Dis 26, 8:529–545, 1973
12. Erikson E: Identity and the life cycle. Psychol Issues I, No. 1, 1959
13. Fawcett J: Suicidal depression and physical illness. JAMA 219:1303–1306, 1972
14. Feinstein AR: Clinical Judgment. Baltimore, Williams & Wilkins, 1967
15. Goldman–Eisler F: Individual differences between interviewers and their effect on interviewee's conversational behaviour. Ment Sci 98:660–671, 1952

16. Gottlieb ME: Mental status examination. Am Fam Physician 9:109–113, 1974

17. Henderson LJ: Physician and patient as a social system. N Engl J Med 212:819–823, 1935

18. Herlich C: Health and Illness. New York, Academic Press, 1973

19. Hollingshead AB, Redlich FC: Social Class and Mental Illness. New York, John Wiley & Sons, 1958

20. Holmes TH, Rahe RH: The social readjustment rating scale. J Psychosom Res 11:-213–218, 1967

21. Jones D, Hall S B: Significance of somatic complaints in patients suffering from psychotic depression. Acta Psychother et Psychosom 11: 193–199, 1963

21a. Kallman FJ: Psychiatric aspects of genetic counseling. Am J Human Genetics 8:97–101, 1956

22. Korsch B, Aley ES: Pediatric interviewing techniques. Curr Probl Pediatr: 1–42, 1973

23. Koos E: The Health of Regionsville: What the People Thought and Did About It. New York, Columbia University Press, 1954

24. Levi L: Stress, distress, and psychosocial stimuli. In McLean A (ed): Occupational Stress. Springfield, Charles C Thomas, 1974

25. Lipowski ZJ: Delirium, clouding of consciousness and confusion. J Nerv Ment Dis 145, 3:227–255, 1967

26. MacNamara M: Teaching interpersonal skills: the use of role playing with sixth year medical students. Med J Aust 2:918–925, 1971

26a Mettlin C, Woelfel J: Interpersonal Influence and symptoms of Stress. J Health Soc Behav 15 (4):311–19 Dec. 74

27. Meyer MG, Haggerty, RG: Streptococcal infections in families. Paediatr 29:539–549, 1962

28. Patterson CW: Suicide. Unpublished text of University of Southern California Department of Psychiatry, May, 1975

29. Payne, S. L. The Art of Asking Questions. Princeton, Princeton Univ. press, 1951

30. Seligman MEP, Maier SF: Alleviation of learned helplessness in the dog. J Abnorm Psychol 73:256–263, 1968

31. Selye H: The Stress of Life. New York, McGraw–Hill, 1956

31a. Sloane RB: Personal Communication. Los Angeles, University of Southern California, 1975

32. Society, Stress, and Disease. WHO Chronicle 25, No. 4, World Health Organization, 168–178, 1971

33. Suchman EA: Social patterns of illness and medical care. J Health Hum Behav 6:2–16, 1965

34. Suchman EA: Stages of illness and medical care. Health Soc Behav 6:114–128, 1965

35. Stevenson I: The Diagnostic Interview. New York, Harper & Row, 1971

36. Tuckman J, Youngman WF: A scale for assessing suicide risk of attempted suicides. J Clin Psychol 24:17–19, 1968

37. Webb SD, Collette J: Urban ecological and household correlates of stress-alleviative drug use. American Behavioral Scientist. In press

38. Weitzel WD et al.: Toward a more effective mental status exam. Arch Gen Psychiatry 28: 215–218, 1973

5
Information Giving

Tis no idle challenge which we physicians throw out to the world when we claim that our mission is . . . not alone in curing disease but in educating people in the laws of health.

Sir William Osler

CLINICAL LEARNING

Gathering information is only one side of the clinical coin. Much of what the physician does in his practice involves giving information. He educates his patients about health maintenance and disease prevention by teaching them self-care, by providing genetic, family, and environmental counseling, and by explaining the risks and alternatives in procedures and treatments as part of the process of obtaining informed consent.

MOTIVATION

When the physician gives medical information, he functions as a teacher. The word *doctor* derives from the Latin *docere*, meaning to teach. Learning doesn't happen because someone decides to teach but is a by–product of an organism's attempt to meet its needs (34). Before anyone learns, he must first be motivated to learn. Various facets of an individual's environment compete for his attention. It is motivation that determines what issue earns his focus.

In the clinical context, it would seem that motivation is inherent when the alternative to accepting medical information is continued ill health or death. Logical considerations about one's health seldom enter into the act of receiving information. Investigation into patient compliance has shown no relationship between patient education and the actual seriousness of the disease or the patient's knowledge of disease (5).

Two major kinds of motivation relate to interactions with other people and control over one's environment. The following is an example of the latter. A hospitalized tuberculous patient was the source of great frustration to staff because he did not take his medication as instructed. A resident who was concerned with the patient's seeming lack of interest in his own welfare complained, "I just don't understand why he can't follow instructions. He's got to know he has TB. I even showed him the spot on the x-ray." When the patient was interviewed at great length, he finally revealed that if he took his medicine, he knew that someone else would "get his place." He was asked, "What do you mean by this place?" and answered, "This room. Here." (pointing to the bed). He was then asked if he preferred the hospital to the outside, and he answered, "Sure! A lot of people are laid off right now." The patient was clearly motivated not to take the medication because he knew that if he got better, he would have to trade the real comforts of the hospital for an uncertain and unknown living situation on the outside.

GOALS AND BEHAVIORAL OBJECTIVES

With all learning, there first must be a clear idea of the goal. Whether trying to establish a response pattern of popping a pill every morning or helping a patient understand birth control methods, both physician and patient need a clear idea of the goals of the information (6). Goals can be broken down into behavioral objectives (29). Whether the goal is continued good health, maintenance of the status quo, relative comfort or function, it can be described as an observable behavior or attitude on the part of the patient. For example, the *goal* might be continued relief from low back pain. The *behavioral objectives* to achieve the goal may include attention to diet, maintaining an erect posture, and performing conditioning exercises.

Patient and physician may not always have the same goals. For example, a patient with primary syphilis may look forward to the resumption of sexual activity while the physician looks to a negative serology. For learning to take place, it is necessary for the physician to have an understanding of the patient's goals and for both goals to be clearly stated and, if possible, reconciled.

RELEVANCE

A patient becomes motivated to accept and process information when he perceives its relevance to him (16). School children are more receptive to arithmetic when they see the relevance of numbers to their daily lives. One of the ways speakers use relevance when addressing an amorphous audience is to learn the name of a well-known member and occasionally address remarks to him. The member becomes a surrogate for the group, who thereafter perceive the speaker's remarks as addressed to them personally rather than to a vague public of which they are a part.

Telling a 20-year-old patient who may not be future-oriented that inadequate oral hygiene will cause him to lose his teeth by the time he is 35 has little relevance. Telling him that inadequate oral hygiene causes an unpleasant mouth odor that discourages kissing does. Making clinical material relevant requires the use of the effective educational principle of individualized instruction, but the physician must have some understanding of the patient before he can individualize his message.

Principles are an abstraction with little relevance. Most people are aware that they should watch their weight or learn to relax, but few do little more about these dictums other than a reminder to themselves that they need to do something about that sometime. Like law and order its a good idea over which few have quarrel. Bradshaw et al. found that patients recalled specific instructions better than general rules (11). Thus, *learn to relax becomes,* "Take 10 minutes every morning and afternoon, prop your feet up and close your eyes." The principle is translated into specific instruction.

EXPECTATION

The physician's attitude of positive expectation can have a beneficial effect on the way in which the patient complies with the regimen. The results of studies of differences in expectation with animals and human beings confirm that subjects who were given subtle cues of facial expression, gestures, posture, and even touch changed their ideas about themselves, their behavior, their motivations, and their learning capacities (41, 45, 46).

The significant variable in these studies was that the teacher really believed that this subject would learn well. This would seem to force the physician to clap for Tinker Bell, whether he believed in her or not. It is difficult to convey positive expectation successfully without feeling it. Nonverbal cues give away the most carefully guarded secret. One of the reasons card sharks do so well is not that they cheat but that they can read those subtle messages and know when someone is trying to fake them out. It helps the physician convey sincere expectation if he considers the patient a human being possessed of integrity and remarkable adaptation. That construct laid across even the retarded, the schizophrenic, or a six-month-old child has been, in this writer's experience, of great benefit in eliciting potential.

FEEDBACK AS REINFORCEMENT AND EVALUATION

The patient as learner responds well to the reinforcement and evaluation that feedback provides (22, 23, 54). Attention paid to his concerns, empathic responses that indicate the physician understands it is a tough regimen for the patient, and praise for his cooperation help to maintain his compliance (51, 52). Initially the patient may require more strongly the extrinsic reward of praise for his learning actions. This reinforcement encourages him to continue his efforts. Later, as the medication relieves his symptoms, the intrinsic rewards of feeling better will take over, and he can coast on an occasional and random back pat, which statistically is a more effective reinforcer anyway.

Evaluation is also a function of feedback. The physician and his patient may make periodic observations of the patient's behavior and its results in terms of their goals. Some criteria of performance levels may be formulated like a medical report card beforehand, which the patient may use to assess himself or which the physician may use. The following is an example.

	INEFFECTIVE	MARGINAL	EFFECTIVE
1. Medication	seldom takes medication, forgets refill	occasionally misses	takes all medication exactly as prescribed
2. Diet	neglects diet, seldom adheres, takes meals at inappropriate times, eats between meals	generally follows diet but occasionally lapses into any of the disapproved eating behaviors	follows diet and all rules pertaining to eating as stated
3. Contact with clinic	problem is developed and patient is ill when seen	waits a few days before calling, may miss an appointment	calls for appt. at first sign of any problem, shows up when expected

Sometimes the patient may choose a monitor who can make the evaluation for him. Most often the monitor is someone in his own family. This monitor must be instructed that his role is not that of informer but of a colleague in a mutual enterprise; otherwise the physician's phone is busy with such calls as "This is Mrs. Adams. Guess Who is not taking his medicine."

The physician and the patient evaluate the behavioral objectives in terms of their goals. The patient contributes subjective observations such as feeling worse, feeling the same, or feeling better, to the physician's clinical observations. The data they gather together measured against their goals may cause them to change objectives by adding a behavior pattern or deleting one, or restating a behavioral objective.

SELF-CARE

EXPECTATION

Many patients must be instructed in self-care for chronic or episodic illnesses. Although most instructions will also be written down, the physician seeks to educate these patients in terms of simple anatomy and function, effects of treatment, and expectations. Inherent in teaching self-management is the idea that the patient is a capable person who is well able to discharge the responsibilities given to him. In this instance, conveying a sense of equality is especially important. The patient who feels a sense of equality does a better job of handling his own care than one who feels inadequate. The concept of fulfilled prophecy, which proposes that one becomes what he is expected to become, derives from studies in which learners responded according to how they perceived that their teacher expected them to respond (45, 46). The same dynamics apply to the clinical situation in which the patient is in the position of learner. If he is made to feel inadequate, he will handle his own care inadequately. If he is made to feel responsible and capable, he will more likely discharge his responsibilities in a capable manner.

ESTABLISHING A CONTRACT

The physician conveys the message that the patient's welfare depends on their working closely together. The message has a dual impact. First, responsibility is shared. The implication is shared responsibility is that the patient's own actions can further his self-interest, a concept as invigorating to a patient as an injection of B-12. Second, the message indicates that the effort will be one of collaboration (4). If illness is a lonely affair, it is especially so for the chronically ill who face medical care that is not designed for recovery but as a holding action. Collaboration as shared problem solving makes illness a little less lonely.

Instructions to all patients should be short, simple, and translated into layman's terms. They should be followed with questions which function to provide response, feedback, and check comprehension. For example, the pregnant patient may be told to come in if she notices any swelling of her hands and feet. Evaluation of edema for some patients may be difficult. The physician must know that the patient has a criterion against which to measure. A checking question to this instruction might be "How would you tell?" If the patient answered, "I could see the difference" or "My shoes would be tight," the physician has a good indication of her comprehension and ability to distinguish between normal and clinically significant signs.

All efforts the patient makes to comply with instructions should be reinforced —"You've done very well this month." Even if he didn't follow instructions exactly, he should be praised for the attempt at the same time the physician renegotiates his responsibilities. "I can see that you really tried to follow the plan, but you need to cough more. Let's review everything once again. First, it will help you to cough more if you drink something hot as soon as you get up in the morning." Crucial information needs to be reinforced. This may be done with repetition, restatement, or a request for patient feedback.

THE CHRONICALLY ILL

The chronically ill patient who has made a career of going from physician to physician seeking relief may know more about his disease than his physician. At the very least he'll know which page of the Merck manual to refer him to. His shopping is born of the exasperation of an unsatisfied customer. If his illness is chronic, he faces a restrictive covenant, for the commodity he seeks is not for sale to him. The physician who undertakes his care faces a medical dropout who, because of a history of dissatisfaction, is likely to be easily annoyed, impatient, and difficult to instruct (50). Before any good working relationship can develop, the physician needs to talk with this patient, to discuss openly why he changed physicians so frequently, and to find out what he expects from his present choice. Empathic statements such as "It must be hard for you—going from doctor to doctor and not feeling that you are getting any help," work like the pop of a champagne cork.

   The physician can expect a catalog of grievances, a seemingly endless harangue of the deficiencies of the medical profession and its practioners. It is essential that this is brought out in a direct interchange so that the patient does not have any unrealistic expectations which the present physician cannot possibly meet. It also helps the physician get some idea of the patient's problems. For example: "Why do you think I can help you when several doctors before me have not succeeded?" "What do you expect that I will be able to do for you?" "How can I help you?"

EXAMPLES

The primary goal of a tuberculosis treatment program is to have the patient complete an effective regimen of chemotherapy (2, 3, 55). Because the tuberculosis patient receives most or all of his treatment as an outpatient, the success of that treatment depends upon his acceptance of his role as a cooperative partner in a long-term venture. It is a mutually binding contract between patient and physician which requires a clear delineation of respective responsibilities. Before the patient can make a firm commitment to two years of self-administered drug therapy, he must understand the objectives, and perceive their relevance to him. He honors the commitment if he has positive expectations, if he perceives his partner's positive expectations, when his efforts are reinforced, and when he gets feedback in the way of periodic review and evaluation.

   The objectives for the tuberculous patient are to cure him of his disease, to avoid his hospitalization, and to prevent him from contaminating his immediate environment. As all educational objectives, they need to be spelled out clearly in his terms and at his individual pace. For example, "Contaminating your environment" may need to be translated into "infecting others," "spreading germs," or "giving your family TB." It then must be related to the process which prevents it such as "Each time you sneeze, cough, spit, or laugh, you must cover your mouth with a tissue so you don't spray germs into the air."

It is helpful if the behavior is offered as a preferred choice. "If you will be careful about covering your mouth, you won't have to use a face mask." Some patients will understand quickly; others will require more time, slower paced information, simpler language, or repeated instruction. Most patients do better when the information is supplemented by audiovisual aids. When bits of information from additional sense modalities are linked together, they enhance one another.

Since understanding in the clinical situation is not always a function of intelligence but of comfort, the physician may need first to alleviate the patient's anxiety. The physician must rely upon his understanding of his patient in order to individualize his instruction. In any case, clear communication between physician and patient are crucial to understanding.

By relating the information to something of particular significance to the patient, the physician makes the information significant. For example, if the patient were a salesman, the physician might say, "I know how important it is for you to make personal contact with your clients. If you take your medication faithfully exactly as I prescribe it, there is no reason why you cannot continue to do so." A homebound housewife may be told, "I know how much time you spend caring for your family. When you follow the program exactly, you will not have to do any special dishwashing or laundering."

The patient's understanding of a meticulous adherence to a medication schedule can be evaluated by observation, urine tests, and medication monitors; but one of the best sources is the feedback obtained from him by questions such as "How has it been since I last saw you?" "How do you manage to follow your medication schedule?" "Do you always remember?" and "Does anything interfere with it?"

Periodic review serves to inform and correct. The physician may uncover the fact that someone in the patient's house is spraying all the doorknobs with carbolic acid, and he may need to redefine just how and under what circumstances the patient can be infectious.

In teaching the diabetic how to administer insulin, the physician must be sure that the patient understands the techniques of injection and must stay in touch with the patient's feelings concerning his new regimen (14a, 44).

Physician: Don't let anything touch the needle.

Patient: That's to keep everything sterile.

Physician: That's right. It's a good idea to rest the syringe on a table edge. Then you will take the bottle and with a little cotton dipped in alcohol wipe the rubber cap, set the plunger at the level of the dose, like this, and insert the needle. Why don't you try it.

Patient: Oh, that's all right. I can see how you do it.

Physician: Try it. It will give you a better feel for what you are doing.

Patient: It seems very complicated.

Physician: It only seems so because this is the first time. It's like learning to drive a car. I'm sure you will soon feel that this is second nature to you.

Patient: Now what?

Physician: Push the air out of the syringe. Good, just like that.

Turn the bottle upside down, pull the plunger back to dose level. Now you are ready to administer the insulin yourself. Wipe your skin with the cotton. You can inject into your thighs here or on the sides of your abdomen. Lift the skin up to make a pocket for the insulin, then quickly push the needle in all the way. You

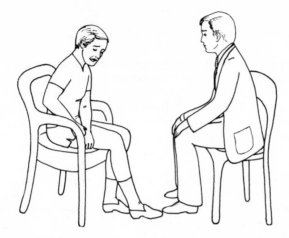

have to pull on the plunger slightly to make sure you haven't hit a blood vessel. If blood shows, the needle must be inserted in another place.

Patient: Is that bad?

Physician: No, but you're aiming for the fatty tissue under the skin.

Patient: Why?

Physician: The body absorbs the insulin more slowly . . . it works better that way. Why don't you repeat it to me so that I can make sure I've covered everything.

Patient: I rest the needle on the edge while I fix the bottle. Then I wipe the bottle top with cotton dipped in alcohol, I set the plunger here, and I put in the needle.

Physician: (nods) Go on.

Patient: I push the measured air out of the syringe into the bottle. I turn the bottle upside down, I pull the plunger back. Here's the part I don't think I can do.

Physician: What part?

Patient: Injecting myself.

Physician: Tell me why you think you can't do it.

Patient: I don't like deliberately sticking a needle into myself.

Physician: I can understand that injecting yourself makes you anxious. (empathy) What worries you about it?

Patient: It will hurt.

Physician: Yes, it may hurt a little; but if you hold the needle close to the skin and inject it with a jab, it will hurt less. (acknowledging)

silence.

Patient: Did I get it right?

Physician: You did very well. I'm very pleased to see that you are able to take care of yourself so well.

When educating a patient in self-care it may be necessary to involve other members of his family. The diabetic needs instructions on diet and food preparation. The specifics of diet are essential, and it is equally important that a discussion of food preparation include those who normally prepare the food in his household. The following is a conversation among the patient, his wife, and the physician.

Physician: I'm glad that you clearly understand about the diet that Mr. Howard must follow.

Wife: It seems to me it would be easier to buy those special diabetic foods that I see in the stores.

Physician: Specially labelled diabetic foods are expensive. Most of the foods that Mr. Howard can have are the same as what the rest of the family will have. His portions are just taken out before any extra fat, flour, or sugar is added. You will only have to measure in the beginning, until you learn to estimate the proper amount.

Wife: That means we can't have cake or cookies or Coca-Cola or have any sugar at the table, any of us?

Physician: Why not?

Wife: Well, he can't. How can we sit there eating those things when we know he can't?

Physician: You will feel bad about eating those things when you know your husband can't. (feedback)

Wife: Yes. Not only bad—guilty.

Husband: I never told you that you couldn't eat what I can't eat.

Physician: There is no question that you will be asked to change many of the things you do. You will have to be extra careful for a while and provide foods that your husband can have. I can understand that the extra work can be burdensome for a woman who already has so much responsibility. (empathy)

Husband: How about me? I'm the one who can't eat like he wants to anymore.

Physician: You're feeling angry about not being able to eat as you like? (feedback)

Husband: Yes. My whole life will change.

Wife: Let's concentrate on what you can eat. Here on the list it says you can have bouillon, which you like, all the coffee and tea you want . . .

PREVENTION

Self-care is not only directed to an existing disorder but to preventing its recurrence. Preventive medicine is not just the administration of antibiotics or the surgical removal of gallstones before they have passed into the duct. Optimally, it is a global monitor of physicochemical, biological, and social environment; a first punch which wards off specific diseases through immunization; a health surveillance which maintains a watchful eye in such programs as well-baby and prenatal clinics; an early detector of disease through the periodic physical examination; and patient education, which attempts to channel the patient's behavior in the interests of his own health and welfare (17).

Preventive patient education is concerned with such specifics as encouraging individuals prone to migraine to avoid occupations where there is likely to be excessive stress, fatigue, or sensory stimulation; explaining to parents that an energetic baby learning to crawl will be at increased risk from accidents; or teaching industrial workers that refreshment pauses and changes of activity reduce accidents.

Preventive education also identifies interpersonal sources of stress and helps patients deal effectively with them. The old phylogentic fight or flight directive is no longer effective in response to the predominantly psychologic and socioeconomic stressors in today's world. Modern man doesn't eat his enemies. His sabre tooth is of a more symbolic nature. When he seeks prestige, love, and satisfaction from his work, he is challenged and maybe thwarted by other people. It is as important to monitor the effects of other people on a patient as it is to monitor mercury level in his food.

If a patient whose arthritis has been under control for years suddenly becomes worse and the physician learns that he is angry because his mother-in-law has come to live in his house, it is part of preventive education to teach him to express his anger more directly.

One aspect of preventive education is environmental counseling, in which the physician is concerned with where and under what conditions his patient lives and works. He advises his patient on what living under certain circumstances means for his health and how he can make his living conditions more healthful. Often this requires improvisation. Not all patients can afford a humidifier, but a pan of water over a radiator will serve as a substitute. The patient suffering from bronchial asthma has alternatives to repeated injections of allergens, if the cause of his condition is an allergy to pollen. He can leave his environment during the time of pollen fallout, he can leave permanently, he can minimize his condition by removing ragweed from the vicinity of his home, or he can air-condition his home (14a, 47).

Physician: Your hay fever is really bad this time, isn't it?

Patient: No worse than usual. The medicine didn't seem to help my eyes much though; they keep running all the time.

Physician: You seem to be breathing a little better.

Patient: Not too bad. I'm not gasping like I did before.

Physician: How do you feel about having to take medication all the time for your hay fever?

Patient: Fine.

Physician: You don't look like you mean fine.

Patient: What else can I do?

Physician: I showed you a map some time ago. It showed the density of pollen fallout—where it's heavy and where it's light.

Patient: I remember seeing something like that.

Physician: Well, there are other places where the pollen is much less concentrated than here. You might give some thought to moving.

Patient: You mean leave here?

Physician: That's only one alternative. There are others. You could leave during late summer and early fall. I take it you don't want to leave.

Patient: Right. I can't leave my job like that.

Physician: There are still other alternatives. If you must stay here, then you should try to make your life here as free from pollen as possible. If you don't have air conditioning or filtering in your home, I recommend it. Do you know what ragweed looks like?

Patient: I'm not sure.

Physician: Here is a picture . . . ever seen this before?

Patient: I think so, in the lot up the street.

Physician: You might consider ways to get it cleaned up. That will be a big help to you.

Environmental education also involves identifying things in the environment that are potentially hazardous, such as toxic substances. A physician alert to the dangers of lead poisoning that might result from pica, the activity of eating dirt or nonfood objects, might counsel a mother in this manner:

Physician: You mentioned that there is a lot of noise in your street.

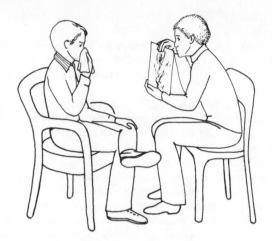

Patient: They're tearing down some of the old buildings on the block.
Physician: Are there empty lots on your block?
Patient: Just one. Next door on the other side. They cleared that away last summer. The kids play there.
Physician: Do they take the baby with them when they go to play?
Patient: I don't think so. They're not supposed to take her from the yard.
Physician: It is important that you find out. Many of these old buildings were painted with leaded paint.
Patient: What's that?
Physician: Paint made with a lead base. Lead is poisonous to human beings.
Patient: What does that have to do with Carol?
Physician: If they take Carol there, there may be some pieces of that old paint lying around, on pieces of walls or just peeled off. Some children like to eat it because it has a sweet taste.
Patient: Is it dangerous?
Physician: Very.
Patient: What can it do?
Physician: If a child eats enough of it, it can cause brain damage.

Preventive medicine requires that the physician alert his patient not only to the cause of disease but its signs. In this way, the patient is alert to danger signals and will seek earlier treatment. Many patients do not report early warnings because of either fear or ignorance. An example of alerting a patient to danger signals would be teaching a woman how to examine her breasts for lumps (14a, 47). This woman is not only taught how to palpate her breasts, but she becomes an ally of the physician with whom she now has a contract of mutual responsibility.

Physician: Stand before a mirror first with your arms at your sides, like this, then with your arms raised. You're looking for dimpling. The presence of a lump will cause the skin to pucker. You're looking for any change in the shape of your breasts or change in the nipples. Then take your hand like this and feel for lumps with your fingers flat.
Patient: Like this?
Physician: No, flat, like this.
Patient: Why flat?
Physician: If there is a lump, it is best not to move it, which you would do with your

fingers curved. Now can you imagine your breast divided in quarters?

Patient: No.

Physician: I'll draw a picture for you. Lie on your back and feel each of these quarters; then you also feel in your armpit.

Patient: I don't understand what my armpit has to do with it.

Physician: There are glands in your armpit that relate to your breast tissue—that's why they're examined together.

This patient made clear that she understands in the feedback provided by the questions she asked. If the same scene were played without patient response, the physician would have to elicit it actively.

Physician: How do you feel about examining your breasts?

Patient: All right.

Physician: Do you feel strange handling your breasts?

Patient: A little.

Physician: Tell me about it.

Patient: Well, it doesn't seem right somehow. I know that's silly but I can't help it.

Physician: I have examined your breasts many times. Did you ever feel that it wasn't right on those occasions?

Patient: No.

Physician: Why not?

Patient: Well, you're the doctor.

Physician: Let me see if I understand what you are saying. It seems all right if I as a doctor examine your breasts but somehow odd if you do it yourself? (feedback)

Patient: I guess that's it.

Physician: Tell me about that.

Silence.

Physician: You seem to be very uncomfortable.

Patient: What do you mean?

Physician: For one thing you're not looking at me, and your face is red. You look like someone who is very embarrassed.

Patient: Look, this whole business is hard for me. I know it sounds stupid, but I was taught not to handle my body.

Physician: I don't think it's stupid at all. It's hard to change your feelings about such things.

Patient: Uh huh.

Physician: Do you think you could check your breasts now in the way that I showed you?

Patient: I'll try.

COUNSELING

Often the physician finds himself in the role of problem solver. As a counselor, the physician should provide his patient with viable alternatives to situations, explore the patient's options with him, and help him arrive at some conclusion (30). True counseling is not giving advice unless advice is specifically requested. It is laying out all the possibilities in front of the patient, like a peddler spreading the contents of a sack, and helping the patient to see the benefits and consequences of each choice. It sometimes involves helping a patient to gain insight into his own actions and behavior.

TECHNIQUES

There are times when courses of action are apparent to an objective bystander but somehow unclear to the person directly involved. It has something to do with not being able to see the forest for the trees. For example, the care of an infirm and aging relative is a problem for most families. It is within the physician's bailiwick to state various courses of action. "You could care for your mother yourself, you can investigate the services of visiting homemakers, you can alternate responsibility with your brothers and sisters, or you can see about making arrangements with a college student who would be willing to check your mother a few times a day for room and board." Sometimes it is not enough to spell out alternatives. The physician, when he is in the counseling role, must discuss with his patients the relative merits of each.

On occasion the patient demands a positive statement one way or another from the physician. It is not contrary to good counseling to state a preference, but it should be done with reservation. The physician's preference must not be stated too early because of the possibility that it would influence the way in which subsequent options are considered. It should only be stated after everything has been spelled out and discussed.

Patient: What do you think is best?

Physician: I can't answer that. I can only help you weigh pros and cons.

Patient: We've weighed everything, and I'm still in the dark. Just tell me what you would do if you were me.

Physician: I don't know what I would do if I were you. I can only speak for myself. I would want to keep my own grandmother at home as long as possible, and yet I would not want to tie up my family with nursing care, which can be a full-time job. I guess I would try to get someone else to live at home with her.

FAMILY

It is often difficult to separate family counseling, genetic counseling, environmental counseling, or preventive counseling from one another. They overlap and intertwine. In this chapter they are separated only in the interests of clarity. People usually live with other people, and those that share an individual's bed and table are largely responsible for his emotional well-being. It is imperative that the physician consider the patient's intimate environment as an inseparable part of his life. Physicians do not treat individual patients, they treat social systems. Patients are either involved in family living or came from family living.

If we think of an individual as occupying the center of expanding circles representing other family members, laced together in a web, we see that it is difficult to isolate him from his nexus. Certainly when a patient goes on dialysis, his whole family goes on the machine with him. Everyone's work life, sexual life, vacation life, and choice of residence revolve around the availability of the machine. The quality and quantity of life and leisure must change. Even such things as who will drive the patient back and forth to the hospital are matters of concern. If dialysis is to be done at home, the question is who will remain with the patient to assist him.

The physician who is aware of the involvement of families in the illness of one of its members tries to build in a support system. The family needs to know that the physician understands, is available for counseling, and can direct them to sources of help. Most families have difficulty adjusting to illness and the stresses produced by debilitation, loss of income, loss of services, uncertainty, and general upheaval. The high divorce rate among the chronically ill is a result of these stresses. The physician can help the family adjust to the change by giving the family members an opportunity to ventilate their feelings to him and to each other. They must do this before they can plan on ways to make the transition between health and illness easier.

When the physician counsels the family of a patient who has had a debilitating illness, he feeds out slowly what they can accept at that time, covering the following points:

1. the natural course of what may happen
2. the etiology of illness
3. the need for their help
4. hope

A patient suffering from a CVA will be used as an example. The first encounter with the family may go something like this.

Family: He's had a stroke, hasn't he?
Physician: Yes, your father has had a stroke.
Family: He looks terrible. (cries)
Physician: Even though he does look pretty bad right now, we know that he has the capacity to improve.
Family: How much?
Physician: We don't know yet, but we're going to begin to give him therapy immediately.
Family: How can you give him therapy? The way he looks?
Physician: We have to keep his muscles exercised and supple. The nerves may

come back and the muscles have to be ready to take orders from them as they did before.

Family:　I feel so helpless.

Physician:　There is a lot you can do. More important than anything, your father needs support. He needs to know that you still love him and care about him, no matter what he looks like or what he can do—that you will be there in the months ahead when he needs you more than ever.

Family:　How can he know that? He looks out of it.

Physician:　Your words, your touch. The best guideline is to assume that he hears and understands as well as he did before. Don't say anything in his presence that you wouldn't want him to hear, don't make any signs in front of him you wouldn't want him to see, and don't whisper together in the hall right outside of his door. That can be very frightening to someone who's ill. There is something else you can do that is very important. I need you to help me recognize changes in the way he looks and behaves—changes in things he can do. You'll see many of these things before I will.

Family:　I don't understand how it happened. He was always calm. He never got excited.

Physician:　Your father's stroke had nothing to do with his disposition. In his case, a blood clot left his heart and went to his brain.

Family:　When can he go home?

Physician:　Within a few weeks is my guess. I'm really not sure yet. We'll have an idea fairly early though, most of his gains will be seen very soon. As you know, his left leg and hand are involved in the paralysis. He may have difficulty grasping, difficulty in naming things—some slurring of speech. There may be changes in his mood. One minute he'll be happy, fine; the next, he might be quite sad. His bladder and bowel control may be a problem.

Family:　But you said he would be improving. (a denial to the previous statement. This is a cue to the physician that the family is straw–seizing—taking a previous statement out of context and altering it to serve immediate needs. They are not ready yet for information related to his care at home. This will have to be addressed at a later time.)

There are times when the physician counsels families not in problems of disease but in asspects of normal living. One of these is counseling couples with sexual difficulties. The following is an example of family counseling in which the physician attempts to teach a couple to communicate by communicating effectively with them. They seek help for the husband's secondary impotence. He has had successful intercourse in the past, but he cannot successfully function at present. The husband met with the physician initially, and now the wife has joined them.

Husband:　Well, that's the story. Every time I try, nothing happens.

Physician:　What happens when you try?

Husband:　Well, I worry that I won't be able to do it, it's like I'm watching myself, and darn if I can't do it.

Physician:　How does that make you feel?

Husband:　How would you feel?

Physician:　I don't know how I would feel, bad I guess, but I'm interested in your feelings.

Husband:　Well, I feel like a spectator and I feel bad.

Wife: I told you there was nothing to feel bad about. It doesn't matter.

Husband: Stop saying that, will you? It pisses me off.

Physician: That makes you angry.

Husband: Yeah.

Physician: Why don't you tell your wife.

Wife: I don't know why it should. I just said it to make you feel better.

Husband: Don't try to make me feel better. You sound like my mother when you do that.

(no response)

Physician: Were you aware that your husband didn't want sympathy?

Wife: No.

Physician: What do you want from your wife, Mr. X?

Husband: Just to be patient while I wait this thing out.

Physician: Tell her.

Husband: Just be patient, that's all.

Wife: I thought I was.

Physician: How has this been for you, Mrs. X?

Wife: Well, it's . . . (hesitant)

Physician: Go on.

Wife: I feel like I'm the one to blame. I feel like I did something to, you know, turn him off.

Husband: That's not true.

Wife: Well, I feel it anyhow.

Husband: No, listen. You definitely turn me on!

Physician: You speak of waiting this out. Do you believe it will go away?

Husband: Yes.

Physician: You make it sound like a disease.

Husband: I don't think it's a disease. I mean I don't think I'm sick or anything. I think it's something in my head.

Physician: Well, you're right on both counts. You're not ill. I told you on your last checkup that your body has the capacity to function normally; when you say it's in your head you're right to the degree that the brain can control such things as erection. However, you don't have to wait anything out. There are procedures that you and your wife can do right now, tonight if you want.

Husband: What procedures?

Physician: Techniques that require both your efforts.

Wife: I don't want to do anything mechanical.

Physician: When you say mechanical, what do you mean?

Wife: Special tricks, you know?

Physician: No, I don't, would you explain?

Husband: I know what she means. Nothing, you know, oral. Stuff like that.

GENETIC

Until recently, geneticists have concentrated their efforts on fruit flies and a red mold called neurospora crassa, primarily because of the speed with which those populations reproduced. Since they have turned their attention to the more ponderous multiplication of human beings, they have identified almost 2000 genetic disorders (7, 8, 9).

When considering the complexity of the developing human baby, the surprise is not how frequently abnormalities occur but why they do not occur more frequently. Birth defects have always afflicted man and are reflected in his mythology, his art, and his magic. At one time they were considered omens. Touching a hunchback for good luck is within contemporary recall. An ancient Babylonian tablet dating back to 1700 BC lists a specific prophecy for each kind of malformation, makes such predictions as, "If a woman gives birth and the child has no fingers, the enemy will conquer a famous city."

Congenital defects are a leading cause of death in the first year of life and as a cause of death are outranked only by heart disease. Approximately 250,000 babies each year, one in 16 births, are born with a defect that either causes disfigurement, is a physical or mental handicap, shortens the child's life, or is fatal. It is estimated that 20 percent are due to heredity, 20 percent to mutagenic agents in the environment, and the majority to a combination of both. Statistics do not adequately convey the grief experienced by the family of a child born with a serious defect, the distress of the child, or the cost to the community (33).

For diseases in which genetic factors appear to be the primary causal agent, such as retinitis pigmentosa, progressive muscular distrophies, and Cooley's anemia, the nearest approximation to specific protection seems to lie in a couple's voluntary abstention from parenthood. Decisions in such cases are seldom easy, and there is no neat formula to reach them. They must be made by the persons involved, in consultation with their physician. Sometimes the physician furnishes genetic prognosis to families and individuals when it is past the point of choice. Then the physician's responsibility is to help the patient make the best possible adaptation. He may still offer hope since many serious defects can be repaired. In that case, he spells out treatments required for the safety of such children.

Sometimes parents who might have a child with a defect are identified by screening programs. More often they come to the physician after they have had a deformed or defective child and want to know the chance of having another one. The physician has two tasks: to establish risk and to communicate risk.

The complexities of human genetics that militate against any medical facility being expert in more than a handful of genetic diseases will also limit this writer to a discussion of the method of delivery as opposed to the contents except as illustration.

In order to establish risk, a trained counselor first constructs a pedigree based on the genetic history of at least three generations. He includes data concerning consanguinity, causes of death and ages of the deceased, any apparent familial disease, and any history of spontaneous abortion and stillbirths. Blood samples from both potential parents and from all other members of the family who are likely to be carrying cytogenetic abnormality, buccal smears, and bone marrow studies where indicated, allow the counselor to compute statistical risk. In the chromosomally monitored pregnancy in which fetal diagnosis is made through amniocentesis, the counselor can predict an actual rate of probability of zero to one hundred rather than a theoretical rate.

Besides reviewing family history and blood studies, the identification of a couple likely to produce a child with genetically determined malformation can be made through the examination of embryos, fetuses, and stillborn infants. Autopsies, photographic records, body radiographs, dermatoloyphic patterns, and chromosome studies are invaluable for genetic counseling (42).

Newer methods of detecting asymptomatic carriers provide the physician with genetic information that he did not have before. For example, investigations show that enzyme deficiencies seen in Tay-Sachs disease and Fabry's disease can be detected in human tears (21).

Genetic counseling is one of the most difficult topics a physician discusses with his patient. Presenting a couple with the facts they need to determine whether or not to have children is laced with many communication problems. First, the issue is a sensitive one. What is at stake is, essentially, whether or not the potential parents are fit to be duplicated. Either individually or in combination, who and what they are is in question. No matter how objectively the patient tries to view the situation, these feelings are somewhere in his mind, skirting the periphery of his consciousness. No matter how clinically alleles and loci are presented, they translate into an accusation of defectiveness.

If perceived as a personal assault, the information will elicit defensive communication, which makes a rational decision impossible. The respondents will not hear while seeming to listen passively, will process the information incorrectly or incompletely (10), or will become angry and argumentative.

Wife: You said one in four, that means that since Danny has cystic fibrosis, we have a chance of having three normal children, doesn't it?

Physician: No. It does not. Each pregnancy must be considered separately. Each pregnancy has a one in four chance that the baby will be born with cystic fibrosis.

Husband: How could that be? If we had four kids, and one already had cystic fibrosis, then the odds are that the other three would be O.K.

Physician: I know you are anxious to have more children, and I wish I could tell you otherwise, but the odds are that each baby you have has a 25 percent chance of having cystic fibrosis.

Husband: Doctor, I hate to say this, but you're wrong mathematically, and I think you're being just a little pessimistic.

Physician: You seem pretty annoyed with me.

Husband: Not annoyed, just pissed off that you don't seem to follow what I'm saying.

Physician: That must be frustrating for you.

Husband: Well, yeah.

Physician: This is a difficult decision for both of you.

Wife: Yes it is, Doctor.

Physician: You did very well to come for information.

Husband: Well, we want a family, not that Danny isn't a family, we love Danny —we just want more and we would like them to be healthy.

Physician: I know that you would like healthy children . . . Do you play cards?

Husband: Sometimes.

Physician: Each time the cards are dealt, you have a one in four chance of drawing any suit.

Husband: Right.

Physician: How many times have you been dealt the same suit two or three in a row, or a flush?

Husband: I get your meaning. It's a gamble, but the odds are still in our favor, doctor.

Physician: Let's talk a little more about those odds. Let's assume that the baby is born without cystic fibrosis. That baby has a two-in-three chance of being a carrier. That means that when the baby grows up it can have affected children.

Wife: It's bad blood, isn't it?

One of the most significant psychologic effects in genetic counseling is that of *guilt*. A couple whose genetic structure makes them high-risk parents respond favorably to being told that they are not different from other people, only unlucky. The aspect of fate helps to remove the onus of personal cupability for an existing defective child, or for the potential to produce a defective child (16). The mother who responded, "Bad blood, isn't it?" is helped by the reply, "Not bad blood, just bad luck."

Discussions of genetic ratios may be meaningless to some couples, since considering statistical probability requires a concept of abstraction and mathematics. The physician may find that using visual aids and relating the implications of genetic disease descriptively has more important. Specifying discomforts and complications faced by the affected child, the prognosis for his future, detailing the care that will be required, and the overwhelming changes in the family routine has more relevance (19). Saying there is a *one-in-four chance of cystic fibrosis* is not as graphic as describing the full-time care of the child—insuring postural drainage, putting a medicated mask on the child several times daily, providing a mist tent at night, being alert to symptoms that signal complications—or cataloging the many medical emergencies facing the child, many of which are resolved only with surgery (13).

In giving information, the physician needs to be aware of any misinterpretations and their possibly serious consequences. The difference between trait and disease, for example, must be made clear. A mother who had not understood the difference told her physician that her child had sickle cell anemia (24). The child was treated for sickling crisis instead of acute appendicitis and died. What constitutes consanguinity needs to be clearly defined also. A couple believed that they were unrelated, yet questioning determined that mutual maternal great grandparents were brothers and sisters as a result of the marriage between two sets of identical twins.

The effect of genetic counseling on the parents requires consideration. For example, the time between amniocentesis and completion of the examination of amniotic fluid is hard on the waiting couple (27, 38). Not only is there stress in an undecided outcome, but the longer the pregnancy continues, the more the fetus is regarded as a baby by the mother. The interpersonal relationship between parents may be affected by their concern over reproduction. Fear of pregnancy, the choice of birth control, and the tendency to lay blame whether explicitly stated or covertly expressed can be sources of conflict between them.

Genetic concepts may carry political implications when the affected populations are identified as racial or national in origin. The principle of facilitation underscores all genetic counseling; it is especially important when the respondents are part of a screening survey. Telling someone that he is likely to produce a defective child elicits defensiveness in an optimum setting. Telling someone of a minority culture that he may have to limit his family can be open to misinterpretation. It should be no surprise if suspicion and hostility compound the issue. The manner in which genetic counseling is presented in such circumstances is crucial (32).

There is evidence that when unsolicited counseling is done at the patient's pace, with genetic concepts introduced in repeated and reinforcing sessions, when empathy is part of the process as demonstrated by the physician's interest in the patient's total environment, when neighborhood people with similar concerns are involved in the counseling, and when comfort is enhanced by meeting in his own home, away from the pressures of hospital or clinic, its implications are more likely to be accepted.

INFORMED CONSENT

The controversy over malpractice that involves physicians, hospitals, patients, and lawyers, has the potential to change the delivery of health care. The direction it will take is anybody's guess. It is a major issue and one that will not fold its tent and silently steal away. Nothing happens without a payoff. As long as the patient sees as his only recourse against perceived wrong legal action against his physician, as long as it is his only redress, the issue will continue. The result in the growing dispute is distrust between patient and physician. Physicians feel they have to protect themselves against their patients and potential suit, and patients, alerted that there may be something to sue about, feel they have to protect themselves against their physicians. They face one another like armed conbatants over a debrided area upon which no one wants to step.

Part of the problem in many malpractice suits is that someone thinks he wasn't told something he was supposed to know. Maybe he was, but he doesn't think so. Good communication will not eliminate the malpractice suit, but it will lessen the occurence of the patient who feels he has a grievance against his physician because he feels he did not make an informed decision.

Much of the patient–physician relationship involves a transaction that is made without a written contract. Because of this the courts have recognized an implicit contract which by its very essence is vague. This vagueness creates especially difficult problems in the area of informed consent (18).

The interpretation and application of the doctrine of informed consent, which sets forth means by which the patient is encouraged to take part in making decisions, varies so much from one jurisdiction to the next and is changing so rapidly that the only guidelines are existing law and discernable trends (14, 31, 36, 39, 40, 53).

The basis of the theory of informed consent is that it is the patient's right to be the final judge of what happens to his body. Recent court decisions have held that it is the duty of the treating physician to give his patient sufficient information to make an informed decision (57). Like all social mandates, the concept is cumulative, arising out of the growing public interest in consumer rights which has been extended to medicine, the public wariness of human experimentation, the phenomenal growth of litigation involving physicians and hospitals, the increased concern about quality of care within the patient–physician relationship, and the increased dissemination of medical information to the layman.

DE JURE AND DE FACTO SELF-DETERMINATION

This climate has resulted in other court rulings related to the patient's right to make his own decisions. There have been court decisions on abortion, which protect simultaneously both the right of mother and fetus; on the right to "die with dignity," which allows both patient and physician discretion in terminal cases where life is sustained by extraordinary means (48, 49, 56); and on the right of mental patients to select or decline treatment (15). There is active interest in the right to suicide. (37)

All of these rulings represent an expression of the need for self-determination, that is reflected in other aspects of life seen in such recent social phenomena as the adoption of individualized dress, refusal to accept the military draft, experimentation with alternative living styles, student demands for a voice in academic policy, the growing political awareness of divergent groups within the majority culture, and individual mobility along both latitudinal (geographical) and longitudinal (class) lines.

HISTORICAL PRECEDENT

Ethical principles for medical practice have been expressed for centuries, as in the code of Hammurabi, the Oath of Hippocrates, and Percival's Code of Medical Ethics published in 1803. The legal concept of informed consent, however, did not originate until 1914 in the case of Schloendorf v. Society of New York Hospital, when the classic medical battery was defined as the intentional touching of a patient's body without his consent. After the Schloendorf decision, the courts began to hold that the patient's consent was valid only if his doctor informed him about his treatment. They continued to regard both classic medical battery and the failure to obtain informed consent as batteries. The political and social climate following World War II expedited the decisions which expanded failure to obtain informed consent to include actionable negligence (43).

The testimony of the Nuremburg trials led to the AMA's house of delegates approving a report by its judicial council in 1946, which stated among other points that it is necessary to obtain the voluntary consent of the "person upon whom a new study (involving new drugs or procedures) is to be carried out." The drug law of 1962, enacted after the outbreak of infantile deformity following the use of the drug Thalidomide, and the Declaration of Helsinki in 1964, adopted by the World Medical Association, continued to pave the way for more stringent protection of the consumer. In the following few years three incidents continued to heighten lay and professional concern. The first was in 1964 when 22 elderly patients were injected with live cancer cells as part of a research project. The second was in 1966 when 500 mentally defective children were injected with the hepatitis virus as part of a research program at Willow Brook State School on Staten Island. The third, in 1972, was the Tuskegee study, in which black men with syphilis who were used as experimental controls did not receive antisyphilitic treatment.

CONCEPTS

The central issue underlying these incidents was that of choice, and it is this concept which predicates the recent informed consent decisions. Meaningful consent is considered to be the exercise of *choice*, the opportunity to evaluate knowledgeably the options available and the risks applicable to each (1). It is based on the patient's understanding of the type of procedure or procedures to be performed, the risks and hazards inherent in each, the outcome hoped for, and the available alternatives, if any. It is the prerogative of the patient, after being informed, to determine for himself where his best interests lie.

The impact of the informed consent decisions is that the burden of obtaining informed consent is placed not on the hospital, not on the admitting clerk, and not on the nurse, but squarely on the physician, who has a "fiduciary responsibility," a duty of trust (26a). It has been held that this duty of trust is one of reasonable disclosure, and *reasonable* is the key word in most applications. The general trend of judicial thought is that the patient must be informed of all material risk, and this materiality is determined by the significance a reasonable layman would place on such a risk. The jury must decide what a "prudent person" in the patient's position would have decided, given the picture of all significant dangers. The question is whether the physician gave the patient enough information to make an intelligent decision.

The severity of the risk is a crucial consideration. A very small possibility of death or crippling disability might be very significant to one patient and not to another. Severity is not the only criterion, however. The relationship between the risk and the particular patient involved is also considered of material importance. The likelihood of disability might matter more to a dancer than to a postal clerk.

For liability to be considered, the courts have held that there must be a causal relationship between the physician's failure to inform and the injury to the patient, in that if disclosure had been made, consent to the treatment would not have been given.

EXCEPTIONS

Those occasions when the patient is unconscious or otherwise incapable of consenting and failure to treat is more dangerous than the proposed treatment are exceptions to the rule. (26) Many states have passed Good Samaritan laws to protect the physician from lawsuits as a result of aid rendered in an emergency (stopping and helping). Implied or presumed consent is predicated on the idea that one who cannot give voluntary consent would be willing to do so if he could. An illustration of implied consent is the case of an 84-year-old man whose physician testified before the court asking for an order to authorize medical treatment. Suffering from dehydration, the patient was found to have gangrene and arterial sclerotic peripheral vascular disease, which made him unable to make judgments relative to his health. The court ruled that an emergency condition may justify an implication of consent where emergency conditions threatened the patient's life. Additional ethical concepts of consent include vicarious consent, which may be given by the parent of a young child.

The second exception is when a disclosure of risk poses such a threat to the patient that it is contraindicated from a medical point of view. In the question of disclosure, there is always the danger of precipitating despair, especially in those patients who have strong fears, who deny or minimize the importance of their symptoms, and who do not really want to know their diagnosis. No uniform guidelines can be drawn. Each patient presents new parameters, and it is difficult to apply the same criteria to all. Even the same patient may present a different set of problems at different times, making disclosure dependent upon circumstances.

The critical question is always whether the physician made a sound medical judgment that communication of the risk would threaten the patient's well-being. If the physician can prove facts which would demonstrate to a reasonable man that the disclosure would have seriously upset the patient, the courts have excused him from disclosure.

PSYCHOLOGIC IMPERATIVE

There are other aspects of informing one's patient which are not mandated by legal guidelines. Osler said, "'Tis no idle challenge which we physicians throw out to the world when we claim that our mission is . . . not alone in curing disease but in educating people in the laws of health." Recent studies have presented strong evidence that the patient's response to treatment is directly related to his understanding of that treatment.

Most patients benefit emotionally when they have an understanding of what is being done to them, why it's being done, and what they can reasonably expect. The resulting elimination or reduction of postprocedural anxiety shortens their period of recovery.

In preparing the patient for a decision it is also necessary for the physician to consider some of the psychologic aspects of surgery and procedures. The impact of disease and the resulting image alteration can cause major changes in the patient's occupational, sexual, and social relations, or in his living habits. For example, the colostomy patient whose self–acceptance is based on meticulous cleanliness may spend hours each day irrigating his stoma in a compulsive attempt to obtain a clear rinse. The physician should also be aware of the effect the limited mobility imposed by recovery has on the patient's self–image. Often a loss of self–esteem is seen in the postoperative patient whose lack of mobility, although temporary, causes depression. Although his response may be considered maladaptive, he is reflecting the values of the majority culture, which state that movement typifies good health, vitality, youthfulness, and independence. Both image alteration and lack of mobility may be discussed in advance by a physician who is in touch with feelings regarding these situations and understands the value of their elicitation as part of the agenda of obtaining informed consent.

Past the legal guidelines of informed consent is another vague discretionary area that is the private turf of each physician. In it are myriad decisions he must make concerning what patient to tell what, how much, and when. He follows the direction of no legislation but makes decisions of disclosure based on his knowledge of the patient's ability to handle the information and his understanding of the ways such information can be helpful.

The chief problem of disclosure is that it is often a difficult question of judgment. To chronicle all dangers and list every horror that can affect the patient adversely is impractical, undesirable, and staggering. No procedure or drug is without possible adverse reactions. Aspirin can cause death from edema of the glottis with asphyxia, and any surgical procedure can be followed by pulmonary embolism (25). On the other hand, it is important that the patient be given a good understanding of his own body and how the physician's treatment relates to it. The conflict is between what to tell him and how much he needs to know, both from a legal as well as a psychologic standpoint.

Even if the patient asks to be told everything, the physician should cast a suspicious eye. The patient may be sending a double message, reflecting overtly what health professionals and stoics admire, a brave and uncomplaining patient who is willing to share the burden of responsibility, but expressing covertly, "Don't tell me please!" (28) If the patient is not ready to hear, he can't process information.

Obtaining true informed consent is difficult. There is little parity between the patient's and the physician's medical understanding. In the clinical situation, the perception and the ability of the suffering patient to make decisions are occluded with pain or debility.

The depressed patient may be fulfilling some wish to die when he consents to procedures. In other medical settings, the patient who is eager to please the physician may agree with him, mitigating his own options inherent in informed consent. While ideally and legally it is the patient's decision, the responsibility most often falls upon the physician.

In the process of obtaining informed consent, the physician has three considerations: what he must disclose as mandated by legal guidelines, what he chooses to disclose as suggested by the growing evidence that an informed patient is more cooperative and responds more favorably than an uninformed patient, and the readiness of the individual patient to accept such information.

TRANSLATION

The average patient has little understanding of the medical sciences. It is up to the physician to translate his knowledge into layman's terms so that his patient can understand. The information need not be a medical discourse, but it must provide the patient with sufficient data to make an intelligent choice. It is not enough to rattle off medical information and then ask, "Did you understand?" The onus of educating the patient requires that the physician provide for feedback in which both he and the patient can clarify each other's terms.

In translating for informed consent, the physician covers five points: the type of procedure or procedures to be performed, the risks and hazards inherent in the procedure, the outcome hoped for, the prognosis if the procedure is not performed, and the available alternatives, if any. In other words the physician tells what he plans to do, why, the expected results, the risks, and whether there are other ways of doing business.

Any translation requires that the translator speak clearly and slowly. Language should be as simple as possible, spoken with frequent pauses to allow for questions, and clarified with the use of contextual cues. Analagous references to the patient's experience, referrant gestures where appropriate, and visual aids such as drawings, diagrams, photographs, and models are all helpful. The physician should remember that nothing he says is ever taken lightly by the patient. Often patients will remember verbatim insignificant remarks a physician made years earlier.

While any one method of clarification is effective, at times it may be necessary to use them all. "Your gut is twisted," "This is what it looks like from the inside," "I want to get in there and straighten it out," may be meaningless to a patient who is unable to conceptualize the inner structures of his body. If the physician simultaneously points to a corresponding site on his body, draws an analogy ("It's kinked up like a garden hose."), and relates it to function. ("Your bowel movements get backed up. Nothing can get through."), the patient has additional points of reference.

Disclosure is made optimally when the physician is not rushed and when the patient has time to think, be silent, and to evaluate the new and often anxiety–producing information with which the physician provides him. Intrusions such as telephone calls, knocks, interruptions, or competing gestures of the physician should be minimal. It is easier to make decisions in an atmosphere made as comfortable as possible. The physician's goal is to provide the best possible climate for the reception of new knowledge and its adequate assessment, particularly when anxiety is a concomitant of the interchange. Informed consent cannot be properly given when the patient feels that he must make up his mind quickly.

If the patient is articulate and responsive, his feedback and queries tell the physician how well the patient understands. If the patient is silent or minimally responsive, it is the physician's task to elicit his feedback. When he has made a point, the physician can pause and wait. If the patient says nothing, the physician can say, "Is there anything you would like to ask at this time?" or "What points so far are not clear?" If the patient shakes his head or otherwise indicates a negative response, the physician can specifically request feedback. "Look, you haven't said very much, and I need to know how this is coming across to you." Affirmative leads, expressions of empathy and confrontation, and questions will help the less articulate patient express himself.

Informed consent is an opportunity for the physician to make his patient an active participant in his own care. Encouraging a partnership between patient and doctor has a salutory effect on most patients who then feel that they have an active say in their own well being. In describing some of the risks or side effects of procedures, the physician says in effect, "You will aid me by watching for these consequences." The patient or his family will notice signs before the physician does and will often see things he does not. ("Doctor, he smiled today! There is no question about it. When we brought him his tray, his lip went up.")

Finally, the physician asks the patient to choose the treatment or procedure which he considers best for his own well-being. "The decision is yours; how shall we proceed?" Most often the patient will respond, "Whatever you say, doctor." or "You're the doctor, you decide." If the physician is satisfied that the patient has a clear understanding of all five points, he reiterates his medical opinion, which led to the discussion in the first place.

MUTUAL SAFEGUARDS

While informed consent is a covenant of mutual trust between two persons, the courts were aware that they placed the physician in possible jeopardy by creating a situation in which a disillusioned or bitter patient could claim that he had not been informed or might sincerely believe that he had not. The following suggestions will help to minimize either possibility.

The first is modeled after a psychiatric treatment unit which uses a weekly participatory meeting to provide patients with a forum where their questions concerning research procedures can be explored (12). The value of the forum in which several patients and physicians meet is that it removes the informed consent process from the privacy, inhibition, and possible misunderstanding of the physician–patient dyad. It gives the patient an opportunity to view the physician as a questioning and fallible being, provides support and models for patient questions and refusal, and gives the physician possible insurance against liability in having other people witness the interchange.

Another possible safeguard is a two–part consent form (35). Originally prepared for experimental volunteers, in which the first half contains the signature and the latter half contains questions for the patient to answer. The second half, which also acts as a check against a signature on the first half, covers such topics as benefits ("Do you expect this procedure to benefit you?"), departures from ordinary medical practice ("What other treatments are available to you?"), risks ("Are there any dangers to you?"), inconveniences and tasks ("How long will you be unable to work?"), purposes ("What are they trying to accomplish with this procedure?"), and rights ("What will happen if you decide against it?"). The value of this kind of form is that responding to questions requires more involvement and understanding than signing one's name.

Keeping a record of all discussions pertinent to disclosure with specific notations of time, place, and possible witnesses protects the physician and is helpful to the patient. Detailed notes and tape recordings give the physician an opportunity to review what has been discussed and to discover if he has overlooked a point he wished to make.

In the following examples, the physician covers the five points as set out in the informed consent legal guidelines, including type of procedure, risks, hoped-for outcome, prognosis if the procedure is not performed, and available alternatives. He also discusses with the patient feelings he might have about undergoing surgery, the temporary limitations that he might face immediately after surgery, the permanent limitations he might face, and what he might expect postoperatively in terms of care, treatment, and recovery.

The following illustration of informed consent is an interaction between a physician and a couple discussing a planned vasectomy. After discussing various birth control devices and surgical possibilities for the wife, such as tubal ligation or laparoscopy, the couple concluded that for them the vasectomy presents the least difficulty.

Physician: It's a simple procedure. I can do it in my office in about 30 minutes.

Husband: What about anesthesia?

Physician: I'll use a local—you won't feel anything.

Husband: What is it that you do?

Physician: Well, I make a small incision; then I cut and tie the vasa, the ducts which carry the sperm from the testicles up to where they are stored in the seminal vesicles.

Husband: Cutting off the supply line.

Physician: Exactly. Cutting off the supply line.

Husband: Then I'm safe.

Physician: By safe you mean . . . ?

Husband: Sterile.

Physician: Not yet. Remember that semen is stored in the seminal vesicles, above the ducts. It's still loaded with millions of sperm that may live up to 40 days. Don't consider yourself sterile until you've had a sperm count.

Husband: When you talk about doing it right here in the office, it sounds very simple.

Physician: Compared to other surgical procedures it is simple, but you should still take a few days off from work and stay off your feet as much as possible.

Husband: I sit at a desk; isn't that all right?

Physician: No. Any kind of surgery puts a strain on your body's resources. You have to give it all the help you can in the way of rest and good food. Then after a few days you can resume all your activities.

Husband: I read something about really terrible things happening after a vasectomy, like multiple sclerosis.

Physician: It's possible that your body will form antibodies against sperm; We have no proof that it will or that, if it does, there will be any adverse effects. Any risk of your body's forming antibodies is speculative at this point.

Wife: What if we change our minds, I mean later?

Physician: Once the ducts are cut and tied, it is very difficult to repair them surgically. Even so, your husband will have to have his semen checked and examined in six weeks and at three month intervals until I'm satisfied with the findings. Consider the operation permanent. Once it's done, that's it. On the other side, there are cases that are not successful. We may not get the vas. That's unlikely, but it is a possibility. My point is that there is no guarantee of sterility, but neither is there a sure way to reverse the procedure.

Wife: That's what we want. Three children are enough.

Husband: What will it feel like, afterward?

Physician: You'll be sore for a few days. You might have some minor bleeding, maybe some swelling. If you have bleeding, come to the office. If you have some swelling or pain, a phone call will be enough. I've been doing a lot of talking. Of all the things we have discussed, what would you both consider to be most important?

Husband: That you can do the operation in the office, and that I'm not safe for 40 days.

Physician: Anything else?

Husband: No, that's about it.

In the above, the physician has taken care of the five points in informed consent. The psychologic aspects of vasectomy must also be considered. The physician attempts to elicit the feelings of the wife by using confrontation.

Physician: (to wife) I am interested in something you said earlier.

Wife: What was that?

Physician: You asked what would happen if you changed your minds. Do you see that happening?

Wife: Oh no, we definitely don't want any more children.

Physician: I am curious as to why you asked that question.

Wife: (smiles, shrugs, no verbal response) I don't know what you want me to say.

Physician: You asked what would happen if you changed your mind later. It sounded as if you gave some thought to the possibility.

Wife: Well, it's just that this is so *positive.*

Physician: What do you mean by positive?

Wife: This is it! Once it's done, it's final.

Physician: You might consider it so. How does that make you feel?

Wife: Awed, I guess.

Physician: Does that make you unhappy?

Wife: A little.

Husband: You didn't tell me that.

Another illustration of informed consent is the following case in which a physician gives information to a potential kidney donor. While the risks of nephrectomy and the uncertainty of successful graft have been discussed, the physician is most concerned with the potential donor's freedom of choice, which is determined partly through the patient's clear and persistent expression. The physician's dilemma is the distribution of a supply of healthy tissue between two individuals, assisting one by giving her a transplant and injuring the other by taking a kidney. Although he could take a kidney from a cadaver, it may be second best in terms of match and blood supply. Informed consent in this case must cover two areas: the possibility of rejection by the recipient and what it will be like for the donor with only one remaining kidney.

Physician: The last time we talked we discussed the risks you would face as a donor.

Patient: Yes.

Physician: Do you recall what they were?

Patient: Well, there was a small chance that I could die on the table, I could get an infection, and there was one other, something about a lung problem from anesthesia.

Physician: You're doing fine.

Patient: It doesn't matter, Doctor. I still want to give my sister my kidney.

Physician: You know there are alternatives. We could take a kidney from a cadaver.

Patient: It's not the same.

Physician: No, it's second best in terms of match and blood supply. A biologically close relative, which is what you are, is preferred. A twin is actually the best. I'm not clear why you want to give away a kidney.

Patient: Why? I think that speaks for itself. She's my sister. She would do the same for me. Besides, I owe her a lot.

Physician: Go on.

Patient: My sister is always bailing me out, with money. We're always in debt, now I have a chance to pay her back.

Physician: So you feel that this is a way you can repay your sister for the money she has given you. It's quite a price.

Patient: I don't think so. You said I could get along on one kidney.

Physician: Yes I did. I think it would be a good idea to discuss your sister's chances. You know, after all, the risks you face. The kidney may never work. You sister's body may reject it. She may get an infection or complications of the blood. Also, your sister will receive therapy to prevent her body from fighting off the graft. She may get complications from this therapy and die from them. Last, the success rate declines.

Patient: What do you mean it declines?

Physician: As time goes on, it goes down. If the chances for kidney survival are 70 percent after surgery, they go down about 10 percent each year after, until they level off.

Patient: When do we do it? I want to get it over with.

Physician: This is something you have to give a great deal of thought to. You may even change your mind.

Patient: I'll never do that.

Physician: Well, on the off chance that you do, it's all right. I would understand.

Patient: I can't believe that. You would probably be furious if I came to you and said I wanted out.

Physician: No. I would be very pleased that you believed me and knew you could. Do you?

Patient: What?

Physician: Want out?

The physician facilitates complete freedom of decision by the assurance which he gives the prospective donor that it's perfectly all right if he changes his mind.

Throughout the examples used to illustrate informed consent, self-care, preventive education, and counseling have threads of communication techniques common to all. These are treating the patient as an equal partner, spelling out the information in clear terms, obtaining and giving feedback, displaying empathy, using confrontation when necessary, acknowledging feelings, allowing silence, and answering questions.

Most of information gathering and information giving is done in the ordinary clinical settings of office and hospital; and although many of the illnesses cited are not run-of-the-mill, their occurence is part of medicine—certainly no drama. There are other instances that many people never see in a lifetime, like floods and earthquakes and Mack trucks, that are also a part of medicine. They provide extraordinary circumstances in the practice of medicine, and they present a challenge to the physician in obtaining and giving information. The next chapter will deal with these circumstances.

REFERENCES

1. A patient's bill of rights. J Am Osteopath Assoc 72:667–669, 1973
2. Ad Hoc Committee on Quality Care for Tuberculosis: Standards for Tuberculosis Treatment in the 1970's. New York, National Tuberculosis and Respiratory Disease Association, Dec 1970
3. Ad Hoc Committee on the Treatment of Tuberculosis Patients in General Hospitals: Guidelines for the General Hospital in the Admission and Care of Tuberculous Patients. New York, American Lung Association, Dec 1973
4. Aring CD: Custom approach to patienthood. JAMA 232(7): 743–744, 1975
5. Ball WL: Improving patient compliance with therapeutic regimens. Can Med Assoc J 111:268, 1974
6. Barsky P: Three's C's that spell cure. Can Med Assoc J 112(7): 911–912, 1975
7. Bergsma D (ed): Birth Defects. Original Article Series, Guide to Human Chromosome Defects IV, no 4. New York, National Foundation-March of Dimes, 1968
8. Birth defects and their environmental causes. Medical World News, pp 47–57, Jan 22, 1971
9. Birth Defects: The Tragedy and the Hope. New York, National Foundation-March of Dimes
10. Borkowski JG, Mann T: Effect of anxiety and interference on short-term memory. J Exp Psychol 78:352–354, 1968
11. Bradshaw PW et al.: Recall of medical advice: comprehensibility and specificity, Br J Soc Clin Psychol 14(1):55–62, 1975
12. Carpenter WT Jr: A new setting for informed consent. Lancet 1:500–501, 1974
13. Carter CD: Genetical aspects of cystic fibrosis of the pancreas. Bibl Pediat 86:372, 1969
14. Cheifetz W: Informed consent. Ariz Med 31:437–442, 1974
14a. Dowling HF, Jones T: That the patient may know. Philadelphia, WB Saunders, 1959
15. Ennis B, Siegel L: The Rights of Mental Patients. New York, Avon, 1973
16. Feingold M: Aids to improved genetic counseling. N Engl J Med 290:810–811, 1974
17. Felch WC: Does preventive medicine really work? Prism 1:26–44, 1973
18. Forst BE: Decision analysis and medical malpractice. Operations research 22(1) 1–12, 1974
19. Fraser FC: Genetic counseling. Hosp Practice 6:49–56, 1971
20. Gagne RM: The Conditions of Learning. New York, Holt, 1970
21. Goldberg MF: The use of tears for heterozygote detection and genetic counseling. Invest Ophthalmol 13 (3):159–160, 1974
22. Guthrie ER: The Psychology of Learning. New York, Harper & Row, 1952
23. Hilgard ER, Bower GH: Theories of Learning. New York, Appleton-Century-Crofts, 1966
24. Hilton B: The case against compulsory screening. Laboratory Management No. 2, 11:33–34, 1973
25. Editorial: Informed consent: a tightrope. New York State Journal of Medicine 73:-742–744, 1973
26. Horty JF: When a life is at stake, the court must act quickly. Mod Hosp 121:43–44, 1973

26a. Horty JF (ed) Action Kit for Hospital Law, Pittsburgh, Sept. 1973

27. Intrauterine diagnosis. Birth Defects VII, No. 5. New York, National Foundation—March of Dimes, 1971

28. Korsch BM: The armstrong lecture: physicians, patients, and decisions. Am J Dis Child 127:328–332, 1974

29. Krathwohl DR, Pozne DA: Defining and assessing educational objectives. In Thorndike RJ (ed): Educational Measurement. Washington, American Council on Education, 1970, pp 17–45

30. Lieberman MA: Behavior and impact of leaders. In Solomon LN, Berzon B (eds): New Perspectives in Encounter Groups. San Francisco, Jossey-Bass, 1972, pp 135–170

31. Lieberman M: The physician's duty to disclose risks of treatment. Bull NY Acad Med 50:943–948, 1974

32. Lutcher CL et al.: The role of a sickle cell center in comprehensive screening and counseling for sickle cell and related disorders. South Med J 67 (3): 259–264, 1974

33. Lynch HT, Krush TP, Krush AJ et al.: Psychodynamics of early hereditary deaths. Birth Defects (Reprint Series). New York, National Foundation-March of Dimes, 1964

34. Maslow AH: A theory of human motivation. Psychol Rev 50:370–396, 1943

35. Miller R, Willner HS: The two-part consent form: a suggestion for promoting free and informed consent. N Engl J Med 290:964–966, 1974

36. Monagle JF: Ethical-legal considerations of informed consent. Hosp Prog 55:58–61 passimass, 1974

37. Murphy GE: Suicide and the right to die. Am J Psychiatry 130:472–473, 1973

38. Nadler HL: Indications for amniocentesis in the early prenatal detection of genetic disorders. In Kretchmer N: Whither Birth Defects. New York, National Foundation-March of Dimes, 1964

39. Nick WV: Informed consent–the new decisions. Bull College of Surgeons 59:12–17, 1974

40. O'Donnell TJ: Informed consent. JAMA 227(1):73, 1974

41. Pfungst O: Clever Hans. New York, Holt, Rinehart, and Winston, 1965

42. Poland BJ, Lowry RB: The use of spontaneous abortuses and stillbirths in genetic counseling. Am J Obstet Gynecol 118(3):322–326, 1974

43. Romano J: Reflections on informed consent. Arch Gen Psychiatry 30:129–135, 1974

44. Rosenthal H, Rosenthal J: Diabetic Care in Pictures. Philadelphia, JB Lippincott, 1968

45. Resenthal R: Covert communication in the psychological experiment. Psychol Bull 67:356–367, 1967

46. Rosenthal R, Jacobsen L: Pygmalian in the Classroom. New York, Holt Rinehart, and Winston, 1968

47. Rothenberg RE (ed): The New Illustrated Medical Encyclopedia for Home Use. New York, Abradale Press, 1963

48. Sackett WW Jr: Death with dignity: a legislative necessity. J Fla Med Assoc 61:366–367, 1974

49. Sackett WW Jr: Death with dignity. Ala J Med Sci 10:370–372, 1973

50. Saslow G: Emotional problems of the chronically ill. Minn Med 33:673–682, 1950

51. Shapiro IS: Health education horizons and patient satisfactions. Am J Public Health 62:229–232, 1972

52. Shapiro IS: Health Education and Practice of Medicine, Relating Theory to Practice. Commission in HMO Movement DHEW No. 7313012

53. Simonaitus JE: The law of informed consent. Bull College of Surgeons 59:21–27, 1974

54. Skinner BF: The science of learning and the art of teaching. Harvard Educational Review 24:86–97, 1954

55. Weg JG: Treatment and Control of Tuberculosis. New York, National Tuberculosis and Respiratory Disease Association, 1972

56. Zimring JG: The right to die with dignity. The New Physician 23:52–53, 1974

57. Court Decisions
    Cobbs vs. Grant, 104 Cal. Rptr. 505, 502 P. 2d 1 (1972)
    Canterbury vs. Spence, 464 F.2d 772 (1972)
    The District of Columbia
    Wilkinson vs. Vesey, 295 A.2d 676 (1972)
    Rhode Island
    Schloendorf vs. New York Hospital, 105 N.E.
    92 (N.Y. 1914)

6
Emergency Communication

Here at whatever hour you come, you will find light and help and human kindness.
Albert Schweitzer
Inscribed on the lamp outside his jungle hospital at Lamberéné.

EMERGENCY DEPARTMENT

HOW IT HAS CHANGED

Of all the services a hospital provides, none has changed in recent years as much as the emergency department. The former accident room has changed from a bunker into which the city's wounded were carried into a place with compartmentalized and planned services for all medical problems, emergent or not, dispensing everything from first aid to sophisticated resuscitation. Until recently, the policy in most facilities was to postpone treatment of those less critically ill until the day shift of outpatient services arrived. Now the policy is to treat all who appear with problems involving any medical service, including surgery, medicine, pediatrics, obstetrics, physical medicine, and psychiatry. The Emergency Medical Services Act of 1973, a response to the changing pattern of care, stressed the need for a total emergency care system composed of at least fifteen specific components and most facilities have begun or are contemplating organizational changes to meet it. (18)

While the injured and critically ill still arrive horizontally, victims of major trauma have been estimated at low as only 5 percent of the work of any emergency department (19).

The other patients come with symptoms of recent onset that are of concern to them, or with chronic conditions that, for some reason, appear to them at that moment as emergencies. What characterizes most patients, regardless of their presenting condition, is that they perceive their problem an emergent one, whether in fact it is or not (16).

A slight but continuous nosebleed at 3:00 AM may not be an emergency to the physician, but it is to the patient, especially if the patient is arthritic or bedridden. Remembering that a nurse on the service always keeps a stash of insulin samples, a diabetic who has run out of money and expects to run out of medication considers that he has an emergency. It is an emergency if the patient thinks it is, and it is this perception that determines the policy in most emergency facilities to accept his presence as appropriate.

Between 1968 and 1973 the number of emergency room visits increased 83 percent (21). The approximate number of visits in 1973 of 66,000,000 increased to over 71,000,000 in 1974 (22).

Its bounding popularity can be ascribed to the specialization of physicians, the unavailability of the general practitioner, the public's awareness of newer techniques of medical care, their increasing trust in the hospital, the population increase with no lag in the accident rate, the disappearance of night calls, the trend of the urban poor to consider the emergency department their family physician, and the growing number of hospitals that offer the service (15). What was once the facility designed to handle only trauma is now regarded by the general public as the appropriate source of medical care for a wide variety of problems including colds, headaches, fever, pain, and just anxious concern, making it a new subspecialty of primary care (34). It may even provide like a medical Roseland, a service for the lonely who find comfort in a facility that dispenses care to anyone who appears on a 24-hour basis. Sitting on a bench with a lot of other people who are also waiting to be called is a place to go and a thing to do.

WHO USES IT

Although it is true that the socially disadvantaged use the services of the emergency department more than any other socioeconomic group, it was found that the very young and the very old across class lines use it the most frequently, overshadowing variables of income and education (29). The more affluent regard the emergency department as a medical convenience. People are used to quick service. Even the laundromat is open 24 hours a day. This means that people are less likely to tolerate annoying or frightening symptoms when they are aware that a facility is available to relieve them of their distress. The more affluent turn to the emergency department at night, on the weekends, or during holidays, when it is difficult to locate their own physician, and when most emergencies seem to occur. The emergency department also serves the working patient who cannot come during the day and mobile populations who are less likely to affiliate with a private physician. The mobility rate that places every nuclear family and/or their belongings in a van every four to five years is responsible for those families not seeking a physician in their new location until an emergency occurs. Others who move with even greater frequency, such as travelers and migrants, seek the services of the emergency department almost exclusively. Whatever the reason for the patient seeking its services, the emergency department is now the point of entry into the health care system for greater numbers of people each year. While rural and suburban hospitals feel the increase, the real load is dumped on county hospitals.

In no other area of hospital operation is the quality of care so visible as in the emergency department. The hospital is judged by the emergency department. Prolonged waiting, delays in obtaining x-rays, or the impression that another patient has been treated poorly, create a bad public image for the hospital. This not only affects public relations but may determine the speed with which an individual subsequently seeks the services of that department. A patient who considers an emergency department inadequate will delay going there to get relief for his medical problems.

HOW THEY GET THERE

People arrive at the emergency department in a variety of ways and conditions. They may be ambulatory or nonambulatory; they may be slightly, moderately, or seriously ill, or not ill at all but what has been called the "worried well."

Some patients are dumped. They may be dumped by other hospitals, arriving on a stretcher with an IV still running, with little or no information about the nature of the illness or what the other hospital has done. They may be dumped by family, friends, or strangers; they may be brought in with boxes, with suitcases, or with a paper bag, and left; or they may be dumped by police; who find them in bars, in subways, and on the streets, usually stuperous, with no family and no history. The caring facility is hard put to deal with the "dumps." From a training point of view, no resident enjoys working on a patient whose care has been started by another physician. From a medical point of view, it is almost veterinary medicine to diagnose and provide care for a patient who presents only signs and no history.

Some patients are brought in by working buddies. The problem with many of these cases is that working associates, who may have been the only ones to witness an accident, may leave before a history can be taken. Relatives who know nothing of the accident then arrive to take their place, and it is the relatives who are questioned.

WHAT CONSTITUTES EMERGENCY

Whether consensual or idiosyncratic, emergency involves crisis. Medical crisis is like other crises in that it is time limited. It moves quickly to a positive or negative outcome. Crisis has three requirements: speed, reassurance, and information. There is no time for extraneous considerations in crisis. All efforts need to be sharply focused. This is achieved through expeditious handling, swift and efficient measures of care, and communication. A concomitant to speed is reassurance and information. The patient seen in the emergency department, even the patient suffering cardiac arrest, needs to be reassured and kept informed.

All comers should get prompt attention. According to the Committee on Trauma of the American College of Surgeons, a patient optimally should be seen within 15 minutes after arrival (11). In a busy emergency department, this is often impossible. In the true emergency 15 minutes is too long. If four to six nonemergent patients register in a twenty–minute period, this cluster cannot usually be seen within the prescribed fifteen minutes, even in an adequately staffed emergency department.

All emergency departments expedite treatment with the use of the priority sorting system of triage, which is the responsibility of either a formal triage officer or of anyone who is near the point of entry. This responsibility involves separating the emergent from the nonemergent patients so that those who are not truly emergencies may give priority to those who are more seriously ill or injured.

True emergencies are those of airway obstruction, cardiac arrest, crushing chest injuries, shock, and loss of blood. The presenting condition is rated as emergent when the disorder is acute, when it requires immediate medical attention, and when failure to treat it immediately would be threatening to life or to function. Those conditions that are considered urgent are those that are acute, but not necessarily severe, and require medical attention within a few hours. The last class is those that are nonurgent, including disorders that are nonacute or minor.

PROCEDURE

The first stop for patients, other than those suffering emergencies threatening life or function, is the admitting desk. There clerks get preliminary information and a brief idea of what the patient thinks is wrong with him. It is helpful if whoever mans the desk is not only capable of eliciting necessary information but is also courteous, compassionate, and flexible. The following is an example of an interview with a clerk who was none of these things. A man of about fifty went to the emergency department with his back bent over so sharply that his upper torso was horizontal to the admitting desk.

Clerk: What's wrong?
Patient: Back.
Clerk: What's your last name?
Patient: Givens.
Clerk: What's your address?
(Man groans)
Clerk: Where were you born?
Patient: In a hospital. (This was literal evaluation of the question, not an attempt
            at humor.)
(Expression of annoyance)
Clerk: Are you working?
Patient: Am I working? What kind of question is that? (Begins to turn away
            painfully in despair and annoyance)
Clerk: Are you, yes or no?
Patient: No.
Clerk: What's your religion?
Patient: Don't have any, shit!

When seconds are crucial, demographic data is obtained after treatment. For example, a patient with chemicals in his eye will get prompt irrigation before the clerk finds out if he has coverage.

The triage officer, who sees the patient after the clerk, takes a brief but thorough enough history to assess the seriousness of the complaint and decide how urgently the patient is to be seen and by whom. His sorting procedure will separate the patient with a week's history of sore throat from the patient who needs resuscitation because of an overdose and from the patient in renal failure. The triage officer bases his decisions on the patient's appearance, the description of symptoms, and, most important, the history of the symptoms. A patient with a lower right quadrant abdominal pain would be seen more quickly if he had had this symptom for ten hours than if he had had it for ten days. The general state of the patient sometimes is assessed by the degree of his preoccupation with his illness. If he is introspective, and relates to staff with difficulty, he is usually more seriously ill than if he is able to interact with relative ease.

Occasionally the triage officer sees patients more in need of social than medical services. A dishevelled, malnourished man who came into the emergency department of a large city hospital complaining of a headache revealed when questioned that he always got headaches when he didn't eat. A vomiting child later confided to the examining physician that his distress was caused by his battling parents.

TELEPHONE TREATMENT

In the emergency department the physician's job is to diagnose, initiate treatment, allay the patient's fears, and provide information. Many times he is called to do these things on the telephone. Most emergency departments have a general chart of emergency measures near the telephone so that these measures can be relayed more easily and more swiftly to the frantic caller. Telephone communication for any emergency requires the physician to reflect calm, expertise, and efficiency; to give short simple responses and instructions; and to facilitate mutual feedback so that he and the caller understand one another. All pleasantries and extraneous remarks are replaced by simple, straightforward facts and information, and an opportunity for feedback. All callers should be questioned as to name and telephone number before any other information is obtained because of the danger of panic. Many people call the emergency room, panic, and hang up before the physician can prescribe emergency measures. Then the physician is in the frustrating and unhappy position of knowing that there is a serious situation out there somewhere, and he can do nothing about it.

It is estimated that 65 percent of all poisonings can be handled over the telephone. Symptoms of poisonings are often sufficiently characteristic for a diagnostic estimate to be made through this medium. The following case of poisoning is an example of short and simple questions and instructions, elimination of extraneous matter, reassurance, and an opportunity for feedback to ensure mutual clarity.

Patient: My baby's eaten aspirins.
Physician: Your name and telephone number?
Patient: Mrs. Evans. The number is EV 7–4821.
Physician: How old is your baby?
Patient: Seventeen months.
Physician: How do you know she's eaten aspirins?
Patient: It's in her hands . . . I don't know what to do.
Physician: You're doing just the right thing. In her hands, any place else?
Patient: Her mouth, it's on her teeth . . .
Physician: How many has she taken?
Patient: I can't tell. She's acting so funny.
Physician: Acting funny, how?
Patient: She's just sitting here, and she's breathing strangely.
Physician: O.K. This is what you do. First get her to vomit. Do you have any ipecac in the house?

Patient: What's that?

Physician: Never mind, try to get her to vomit with your finger or a spoon. That should do it. If she doesn't vomit in a few minutes, give her as much milk as you can get her to take, keep her warm, bundle her up in a blanket and bring her in. And bring in the bottle that the aspirins came in. Any questions?

Patient: No—

Physician: Now tell me what you're going to do.

Patient: Make her vomit, if she doesn't, give her milk . . . put a blanket on her.

Physician: Good. Vomit first, then milk, keep her warm. Do you have a way to get here?

Patient: Yes.

Physician: We'll be expecting you.

HISTORY TAKING

While a good history is essential for all patients admitted to the emergency department, it is possible only with certain patients under certain conditions. History taking in the emergency department involves information supplied by the patient, by observers, by family, or it may be purely a patchwork assessment made by physical signs and laboratory tests. Unlike the usual circumstances of history taking, in the emergency department the patient is most likely to have observable or readily detectable pathology.

Urgent

For those patients who visit the emergency department with significant physical complaints, the history should be complete. It should include a systematic and thorough review of systems to rule out complications. A patient who suffered a fractured femur and humerus died in shock 16 hours after admission because it was not known that she was taking large doses of cortisone for arthritis. An injured patient's most obvious injury may not be the most serious one. A patient with a head injury who is in a coma may be dying from a ruptured spleen.

Nonemergent

Histories are easiest to obtain from patients with nonemergent conditions who come to the emergency department to be treated, cared for, and reassured. Most of these patients will either be sitting on the benches in the waiting room for periods up to several hours, depending on the facility, or will wait to be seen in curtained or partitioned cubicles. For the most part they are uncomfortable, worried, and sometimes dazed. Often those in cubicles scout around corners to see who is where, like a spy counting troop movements, and more importantly, to find out if anyone knows that they are waiting behind the curtain. Some may announce their symptoms at the sound of any footstep. Coughs and moans have been known to fluctuate with the arrival and departure of staff. Since a patient's scouting can interfere with more serious business, a helpful technique to use with a patient isolated in a cubicle (the bench person has the corroboration of others around him) is to address him by name and say something like, "Be with you in a little while, Mr. Hicks. There are a few folks who need to be seen in a hurry, but we'll get to you as soon as we can." It is much more alarming to be waiting in solitude than waiting in a room surrounded by other people.

When the staff is ready to examine this patient, the most significant single piece of information is why he believes that he should be seen now. If he has had a fever for a few days, he may go to the emergency department on a Saturday night because he knows he cannot be seen by his own physician until the following Monday, or because he has heard somewhere that fever is a symptom for cancer, or because he lives alone and is afraid that he will get too sick to go to any physician by himself. The interviewer needs to learn what changes have occurred to make the patient think he needs immediate attention. Questions such as "How is it that you are here?", "What is it that brought you to the emergency department to-night?", "How long have you had this problem?", or "What has happened recently to make it worse for you?" give pertinent leads to diagnosis and treatment. While the physician does not have the time in most emergency department settings to investigate nonemergent complaints unrelated to the presenting symptoms, the trivial complaint may mask a medically more significant complaint. The health care professional who interviews this patient is always asking himself, "Why is he here now?" and "What does he need that I can give?"

The reason the patient goes to the emergency department may be simply that he is worried and needs the reassurance and support of someone who touches his arm and says, "I can see that you might be worried about that sore on your lip. Actually it requires no treatment and will take care of itself, but you did the right thing to come in." The physician who is sorting patients as fast as a fruit shipper flipping oranges into crates may feel that he does not have the time for such problems when there are more pressing matters in an emergency department, but the die is already cast. When a worried patient goes to the emergency department, proper reassurance can take less than a minute and is appropriate care under the circumstances. It often serves as preventive medicine. The patient will seek attention for legitimate or more urgent symptoms more quickly in the future if his present concerns are acknowledged than if his complaints are given short shrift.

In the emergency department, unlike the more routine clinical interview, it is appropriate to ask the patient, "What's the trouble?" The context is different from that of the outpatient clinic or the private office. A sense of urgency transmutes a potentially judgmental question into an expeditious one. Because of this sense of urgency, all patients with complaints that appear nonemergent should be questioned for depression. The first question might be "With the troubles you are having, how do you feel?" Questions concerning vital functions such as sex, sleeping or eating, fatigability, and any changes in those areas often uncover depression. If the physician suspects depression, the next step is to question the patient further to find out the depth of his depression and whether he has any idea of suicide(see Chapter 4).

There is less time in the emergency department for the spontaneity in history taking which is sought after in other clinical settings. Yet if the physician were to attempt to ferret information with no patient preparation, he would run the risk of obtaining distorted or incomplete data. There are certain procedures which expedite communication in the emergency setting.

Urgency escalates. A frightened patient who perceives anxiety in his physician really gets scared. Mounting mutual excitement excludes clear communication; therefore, one of the participants must deliberately deescalate. The physician wins this assignment by default, since his professional understanding gives him a tactical advantage. Even if the patient is strafing his sensibilities, his calm and assured manner, expressed in easy movements, unhurried speech, and direct eye contact, will give the patient confidence. [as well as model the behavior which in the emergency interchange is any action that facilitates a clear message.]

In the emergency department credence is given to the presenting complaint immediately. Time spent in challenging it is usually wasted. The presenting complaint is accepted at face value, and the questions of *how* (How did this happen?), *when,* and *where* are asked. Because *how* is more global, the response it generates usually takes the place of both other qualifiers as well as providing significant leads.

Questions that are succinct and well designed work on a sluggish interchange like mineral oil. The nature of succinct questions requires that extraneous and redundant words be pared away, leaving only the bold question, heavy on verbs and qualifying adjectives. This does not mean that feedback and other devices of clarification are absent, only that they, too, are spare. Well designed questions anticipate ambiguity. For example, "Where did you feel this?" could reasonably elicit "While I was lying in bed," or "When I walked across the room." "Where in your body" or "What part of your body" are more suitable alternatives.

The following dialogues demonstrate two levels in efficient communication. Although the first can be considered efficient, the second is more so. In the second the same information is obtained through questions that are pared in syntax and in number. With pared questioning it is essential that the voice convey ease, and the interchange should be interspersed with comments or physical gestures of reassurance.

In this example the patient was told by the student that he saw nothing, which was the case, and that he was going to ask the resident to have a look. The second interview was a deliberate attempt to improve upon the first.

"What's the trouble?"
"I have a fish bone in my throat."
"How do you know it's a fish bone?"
"Cause I was eating fish."
"How do you know it's not just scratched?"
"I can still feel it."
"How did it happen?"
"Tonight."
"Tonight. But *how* did it happen?"
"I was eating fish, and it started to hurt."
"While you were eating fish, you noticed the bone got caught in your throat."
(nods)
"You kept on eating."
(nods)
"Where do you think it is?"
"Right here."
"So you were able to keep eating and drinking with no problem."
"Yes."
"If I press over here does it hurt?"
"I can feel it."
"You can feel it. I'm going to look in your throat."

In this interview, the patient referred to *time* in answering a question concerned with cause. Since he had already given information on *how* it happened, his own presumption reframed the question; he responded, correctly he believed, to a question related to *when.*

"What's the trouble?"
"A fish bone." (points)
"It must be uncomfortable. How did it happen?" (complaint accepted at face value)

"Eating fish at dinner. The bone got stuck."

"Were you able to keep eating and drinking?"

"Yes."

"Where is it?"

"Right here."

"Does this hurt?"

"No."

"I'm going to look in your throat."

Since the physician is going to have a look in his throat anyhow, challenging the patient in an attempt to disprove his hypothesis wastes time. It is more efficient to accept his complaint and check it rather than to challenge it, raise his defenses, and check it anyhow.

CHRONIC COMPLAINTS

The significance of the chronic patient's visit to the emergency department is the same as that of other patients' visits. There is urgency in his perception of his illness. A "chronic" may have other medical problems besides his usual illness, or his sense of urgency may be the result of a perception of a different character of body manifestations. The chronic patient may consider it an emergency if the new symptom he is experiencing is not within his expectations of his illness. He has already made certain adjustments to his known disease, and finds threatening anything which may compound his present illness and make him more sick or more dependent.

An example of a patient with chronic illness with overlay of urgency is a patient with sarcoidosis who presented to the emergency department complaining of breathing difficulty and fever. The resident who interviewed her perceived an urgency in her awareness of her illness. Although she usually visited the outpatient clinic, he admitted her for additional studies, believing that her appearance at the emergency department indicated she was experiencing something different or experiencing familiar symptoms with more difficulty. When he tells her that he is going to admit her to the hospital for a more thorough work-up, he responds to her dismay with empathy. "I know you don't like to go into the hospital, and I'd like to keep you out if I can." "Then why can't you help me here?" "I think you're worried about how you feel. Are you?" "I guess." "I can understand that it worries you not to feel right. There's much more we can do in the hospital. Watch you more closely for one thing." "What's wrong with me?" "You know one problem, and that's sarcoidosis. But we have to check to see if something else is adding to it." "What then?" "Then we'll know what else we can do for you."

The physician acknowledges that she is feeling ill in a new and significant manner, empathizes with her feelings about having to be admitted to the hospital, and ends on a hopeful note.

REASSURANCE

Some conditions in which the patient may cooperate in his history taking are terrifying experiences, and the physician does a neat combination of adroit history taking and reassurance. When a patient is hemorrhaging, for example, it is important to determine the character and origin of blood loss (venous or arterial, in the upper or lower gastrointestinal tract) with a few succinct and tightly framed questions, but it is equally important to calm and reassure this patient. The hemorrhaging patient may be incoherent, in fact, may be semicomatose. If he is alert,

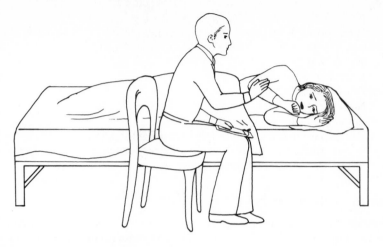

however, the interview may proceed in this manner. First, the questions should be short and to the point. Although he may not be bleeding when he is seen, his story of bleeding should be accepted at face value. The interviewer's voice should be calm and easy, with no tone of urgency. If the questions assume a staccato character, they convey fear on the part of the physician. A laundry list question is helpful with this patient; for, while it doesn't lead the patient as a direct question does, it offers options for someone who may have trouble speaking or understanding. Words or gestures of reassurance should be interspersed in the questioning. A hand on the arm, or a touch on the hand or head may reassure the patient while the physician goes about determining the history of the bleeding. If a relative, a chart, from another service, or the patient's private physician are available, these questions may be unnecessary. In the event that these sources of information are absent, this is the way such an interview might go. The patient is in a weakened state and is lying down.

"Mrs. Jones, where did the blood come from?"

"My mouth, I vomited a lot."

"Your mouth, and it was a lot. (feedback) What color—red, brown?"

"Brown."

"Brown, like coffee?"

"Yes."

"You're doing fine. Did you have a stool today?"

"Yes."

"Was your stool yellow, light brown, dark brown, black?"

"Dark, almost black."

"Black like tar?"

"Yes."

"This ever happen before?"

"No."

"Have you taken any aspirin?"

"No."

"Any other medication?"

"I don't know."

"Are you being treated with medicine for anything by another doctor?"

"No."

"Everything is under control. I'm right here with you, Mrs. Jones, just a few more questions. What have you eaten today?"

"I don't remember. I think a sandwich."

"A sandwich, anything else?"

"No."

"Any alcohol?"

"I don't think so."

"I can't hear you. Any beer, wine, whiskey?"

"No, no booze."

"What about your bowels?"

"O.K."

"Anyone in your family have bleeding problems?"

"No."

"O.K. I want to find out what's going on, and the easiest way is to take a look. I'm going to pass a tube through your nose into your stomach . . . You look a little worried, are you?"

"Yes."

"I can understand that the idea might frighten you, but I'm going to tell you exactly how to handle the tube."

The patient has been reassured, her history has been taken, and she has been informed as to what will happen to her. The entire interaction took less than two minutes.

Another patient who requires reassurance and confidence is the burn victim, for whom supportive care can sometimes do more than pain medication; a true third-degree burn is by itself anesthetized. Treatment of significant burns is generally made in the inpatient service. However, it is in the emergency department the seriousness of the burn is determined. While the staff is computing the depth and area of the burn and considering additional factors of location and age of the patient, he is reassured by softly spoken words that tell him that he is being attended to, that everything is under control, and that he will continue to receive care. He should also be given specific information about staff plans to remove his clothing or prepare lavage.

The patient with a marginal airway who is being supported by oxygen is another patient to be calmed and reassured. Even in the code alert, when everyone flies to their battle stations, someone should be flying near the patient long enough to talk to him, tell him something of what is being done, and leave him with some hopeful thoughts.

Although these patients have been used as examples because of the seriousness of their distress, they are not the only ones deserving and needing reassurance. All patients admitted to the emergency department require reassurance.

UNCOOPERATIVE HISTORY

There are situations in the emergency department in which a nonjudgmental and accepting manner are part of the medical personnel's armamentarium. These include circumstances in which revelation of the true nature of the emergency would likely bring reprisal or censure. Illicit abortion, rape, drug usage, an attempted suicide, alcoholism, suspected child abuse, gunshot, and stabbing incidents are examples of situations likely to elicit defensive communication. Even a hypertensive patient who didn't follow his regimen may be a candidate for this roster.

One of the simplest indications of an invented history is the interruption of normal eye contact. This is not a hard and fast rule, but must be taken in context. Eye contact is minimized in defensive communication. There are some who can maintain uninterrupted eye contact while they improvise fact, but most people find it very difficult to monitor this behavior deliberately. Other nonverbal indications of an invented history are defensive hand to mouth, hand to neck, or hand to head movements. Verbal indications may be interruption of content but most often the delivery of invented history is glib, the result of rehearsal. Any restatement may be verbatim, and exact duplication is seldom a feature of spontaneity.

Illicit Abortion

Because septic abortion is usually accompanied by cardiovascular, respiratory, or gastrointestinal symptoms, it is sometimes missed. Mild vaginal bleeding is insignificant in the presence of tachycardia, vomiting, or dehydration. In most of these cases, questions related to abortion are met with denial. The clandestine nature of extrahospital abortions, which are still being done despite new legislation making it easier to get a legal abortion, make it difficult to obtain an accurate history. Because these surreptitious coat hanger or potassium permanganate improvisations are illegal, the patient may fabricate a history and deny all evidence of pregnancy. The physician who suspects septic abortion must first gain his patient's confidence. This makes him, unlike the con man, responsible for the information. The object is not to trick the patient; it is to proceed in a manner which the patient sees as a limited threat and an optimum help.

A matter-of-fact summary statement of symptoms is helpful. It is the presentation of an objective and value-free list of symptoms. An indirect reference with no labeling is more likely to generate the positive response he needs to make a more precise diagnosis. Not, "You've had an abortion, haven't you?", but "I find signs of an attempt to end a pregnancy." The term "signs" is exchanged for "evidence," which connotes evil doings. If the patient asks what they are, the physician can offer a tally. "Your stomach is swollen, you have a fever, your heart beat is too fast, and your uterus is enlarged." This is not laid on with the triumphant "I gotcha"

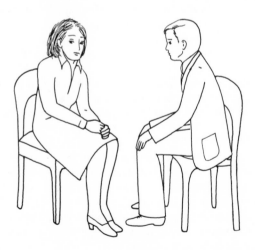

but is also dead-panned and nonjudgmental. This is a crucial moment. If the physician gets no response, he can then add, "You have a serious infection from all this. I need to know much more in order to help you." "Like what?" "Like what was used and what time this was. I'm going to treat you for the infection and admit you for further tests." The patient may perceive that all will be known anyhow. She may ask to go home. "You're not well enough to go home." The physician can then drop the subject of etiology for a moment and get to specifics, such as an assessment of blood loss, which are less threatening.

"You're bleeding. How much blood would you say was lost?"

"I don't know. A lot."

"What did you use on the way to the hospital?"

"Some pads."

"How many?"

"Three, maybe."

"How about at home? What did you use there?"

"Some towels."

"How many?"

"I don't know, I just grabbed some towels."

"Did you spill blood any place else, on the floor, in the toilet, on the bed?"

"I sat on the toilet. It filled up the bowl."

(The patient is praised and reinforced for taking the risk to cooperate.)

"That was very helpful. When did this start?"

"This afternoon."

"How did it start?"

This is where proceedings may break down. If the physician remains silent and doesn't press his advantage, the patient may volunteer specifics of the abortifacient. If the information is not forthcoming, the physician says simply, "You are very ill. What I use to treat you depends on what was used to abort you."

The Rape Victim

The story of the rape victim in the emergency department should be accepted at face value like that of any other patient (3, 4, 20). The purpose of emergency medical personnel is not to disprove the story but to make a clinical evaluation. Contrary to a general idea that many women who claim they have been raped have not really been raped at all but are out to get some guy, most women who charge rape can be assumed to have been attacked. It is usually a very unpleasant experience for any woman to go through the questioning and the physical examination involved in the question of rape.

The burden of proof to the contrary lies on the courts, and not on the physician. His job is only to determine whether or not a sexual act took place and whether there are clinical signs of force. While the physician is checking the patient's clothing for stains and tears and the patient's body for virtually the same thing, his manner should be courteous and matter-of-fact. While a minority of rape charges may be false, the event is laced with enough trauma to warrant making an effort to minimize any additional trauma from the clinical investigation. Attending police officers and other agents of the law are often cavalier, even negative toward the woman who charges rape. Medical personnel can help the patient through a distressing experience by maintaining their objective posture.

Attempted Suicide

To those in medicine who fight to preserve life, there is no problem as frustrating as the would-be suicide (16). It is often difficult for the practicioner to understand this patient's feeling of utter hopelessness (40). Logic does not prevail. Memory does not prevail. The suicidal patient is responding to his own perception of a loss he has suffered or a tragic error he has committed. What is significant in the suicidal patient is that he is suffering. His mind inflicts upon his spirit wounds as corrosive as lye. The physician's task with the suicidal patient is the same as it is with any other patient: to find out where it hurts.

Initially, the best procedure is to question the patient in an open-minded manner in order to find out what he wants, what it is he has done, or who has let him down. The physician's first step is active listening, in which he becomes a sounding board. This is a time when succinct questioning is not appropriate. The physician looks for points of honest agreement and sympathy and listens without arguing or challenging. As the patient ventilates his painful feelings, he dilutes their toxicity to a more tolerable concentration. With the patient who has attempted suicide, the questioning might begin with "Things must have been pretty bad." (not "Why did you do such a stupid thing?"), followed by "Tell me about it."

As the physician listens, he begins to get an idea of what is troubling the patient and can help mobilize the resources that are critical to the patient's survival. These are linkages to the world of people and work. Any person who is close to the patient, and in the absence of any close person, any human link from his past, a minister, working associate, or a former neighbor may help. In their absence, the physician offers himself. It will be necessary to determine whether or not to hospitalize the would-be suicide. If suicide has already been attempted, the patient generally is hospitalized. If the physician's decision is not to hospitalize the patient, whoever undertakes his subsequent care plans frequent initial visits in order to monitor him more closely.

The suicidal patient is unlikely to volunteer a lot of information. In fact, the physician may not even hear many of his responses. Additionally he may make illogical abstractions, which he uses to characterize an entire situation. For example,

Patient: I'm no good.
Physician: What makes you say that?
Patient: I can't do anything right.
Physician: Give me an example.
Patient: I'm still here.
Physician: Give me another.
Patient: When my father needed me the most I wasn't there.
Physician: When was this?
Patient: Two years ago.
Physician: What else have you done since then that wasn't right?
Patient: I dunno, nothing, I guess.
Physician: Tell me how you think you failed your father.

Allowing that a person may have the right to elect death as a solution to overwhelming life events, the cognitive disorder that is present in depression mandates that the person faced with this choice be given every advantage of reason. This means that his choice be the result of logical consideration and not the choice of the kind of distorted thinking represented in the above example.

One last word. The emergency department is very dangerous for any depressed patient. Within easy reach there are many instruments and drugs with which he can kill himself. He needs to be watched closely and not left alone.

Child Abuse

A nonjudgmental manner is crucial to the outcome in the treatment of a child when the physician suspects his parents have abused him (24, 26, 27, 36, 39). It is difficult for those who have been trained to heal not to respond with rage at the sight of a three–month–old infant bleeding from the mouth, with multiple bruises and a fractured femur, when the parents insist the injuries occurred when the child got caught in the crib slats. However, accusatory confrontation scares off the parents, who go on to inflict other injuries, then take their victims to other facilities, or worse, seek no medical attention at all. Although the therapeutic experience with such parents is minimal at this time, all evidence indicates that they can be reached and changed only by professionals who remain nonjudgmental, uncritical, and considerate.

Trauma is the number one killer in the first half of life. It has been estimated that as many as 15 percent of the children who come to an emergency department because of trauma are victims of trauma which is deliberately inflicted. Child abuse statistics show a high rate of repeated assaults on the victim (two-thirds of whom are under three), a 50 percent likelihood of permanent injury, and a 10 percent likelihood of death. Those numbers mandate that the attending emergency department staff marshall their own feelings and behave in a manner that is the most helpful to the child. Although 10 percent of the parents identified as child-abusing may be considered psychotic, the remaining 90 percent fall into that grey area labeled sociopathy, that is, behavior at variance with the views of the majority culture. In the Ik society, whose children are turned out to fend for themselves at the age of three, much of what we consider abuse would be routine behavior. Most child–abusing parents were themselves harshly reared and seem to feel that this was justified. This corroborates studies which indicate that parenting is not instinctive but learned, and that one can learn to be a "good" as well as a "bad" parent.

All fifty states now require physicians to report child abuse cases. New legislation frees the physician from liability, a factor that hindered previous reports. When erroneous charges brought redress in damages, few physicians were willing to risk litigation, patient goodwill, and malpractice insurance. Although approximately 60,000 cases are reported each year, it is estimated that thousands more are overlooked by health care professionals who are unable to identify the case as nonaccidental trauma, or who do not want to get involved. While members of a hospital staff support and corroborate one another, a lone physician in a private office acts reluctantly on a case of child abuse. If is difficult to believe that people whom he knows, perhaps neighbors, can abuse their children. Even if he suspects child abuse, it is part of his own psychological defense system to deny the idea rather than face personal feelings of anger and frustration that accompany such suspicions.

While most emergency departments have prescribed protocol for the handling of these cases, the following is offered as a guideline. All physicians who see children, whether in private practice or in the hospital emergency department, should develop a high index of suspicion in all cases of trauma. The presence of the following factors should arouse suspicion:

1. a marked discrepancy between the injury and the history
2. an unusual amount of soft tissue injury, particularly if in varying stages of healing
3. multiple fractures with various stages of healing
4. subdural hematoma in an infant
5. evidence of sexual abuse
6. previous hospitalization for similar or unexplained injuries
7. evidence of poor nutrition, poor hygiene, and poor skin care
8. a child who is withdrawn and irritable, who does not seek comfort and reassurance from parents, and who is unusually fearful

The physician should also suspect child abuse if the parents:

1. are angry, evasive, contradictory, telling one story to emergency department nurses, and another to pediatrics ward personnel
2. state a history of minor trauma not in keeping with the severity of the child's injury
3. appear self-oriented, with little concern for the child, his injuries, or prognosis
4. seem anxious to get away before making sure child is safe and secure
5. have delayed unduly in bringing the child in for care
6. show evidence of loss of control or fear of losing control

A more extensive list of criteria has been drawn by Kempe and Helfer (27).

In the initial history taking, a confession is not the goal. Even if it were, it would not be the result. These parents have been characterized by Helfer and Kempe as suspicious and defensive. They will deny, lie, and blame a third party, such as a jealous sibling, a neighbor, or a dog if cornered. Besides, the clamor and commotion of the emergency department does not really permit the staff to do anything but get information related to the injury and attempt to establish a therapeutic relationship with the parents, which is more often just detente.

The most effective way for emergency department personnel to obtain any information from suspected child abusers is to present all findings objectively, in a calm and nonjudgmental manner (37). The physician might state honestly that he is confused, that the signs do not match the story, and that he is going to hospitalize the child for further tests. No fingers of blame have been pointed, it is clear fact. He can tell the parents that, in his opinion, the child would not have been injured if he had been properly protected; in order to help them protect the child in the future, he needs all the information he can get. The physician welcomes the whole story. He may get it at this point if his manner conveys interest in the parents.

Empathy is very helpful if he can sincerely muster it. For example, if the family lives in substandard, crowded conditions, in which the parents, especially the mother, have no escape hatches like far-off rooms in which to get a moment's relief, or someone to help with the child, he might say that he can imagine how difficult it is to care for a small child in such conditions. He might even suggest that new parents sometimes lose their tempers and may get a little too rough without meaning to. All conversation should be in tones that are deliberately free from anger or hostility. The more the physician displays empathy to the parents ("I know how hard this must be for you." or "It must be very difficult with three small children.") the more likely he is to gain their cooperation. In fact, in the treatment of these parents, the physician's interest in their welfare plays a crucial part.

If no meaningful information can be obtained, the physician plays out his hand. He is going to hospitalize the child (unless it is against the policy of his hospital or unless the child is of school age and has only minor injuries). He knows that he can get a court order if the parents refuse hospitalization, but he does not play this card. He tells them either that diagnosis is already well established on the basis of clinical findings and laboratory studies, or that it is inconclusive, but in either case, they all have an obligation to see that it doesn't happen again. The physician informs the parents of his plans to hospitalize the child for further studies and observation. He does not ask them; he states firmly but blandly that this is his plan as the physician. He also tells them that he is going to report the incident as he must, but even this can be done noncommittally. "I am obliged to report your child's injuries because there is confusion concerning the details and the injury." Few parents object to their child's hospitalization if it is presented in this manner. It can be presumed that they want help, otherwise they would not have brought the child to the hospital in the first place.

UNCONSCIOUS PATIENT

The greatest challenge to the physician's diagnostic skill is the unconscious patient who is usually brought in from the street by two policemen with no chart and no identification. Physical signs and laboratory studies are all the physician has to go on. After checking the patient's airway, and the basic stability of vital signs the physician is ready to take history; but that history is seldom available. Often in any emergency department, there is one unconscious patient who is the recipient of a lot of escalated shouting. "What happened to you?", "What did you take?", or "Where does it hurt?" As minutes go by and there is no response, the questioners turn up their volume and are yelling at semicomatose patients in a kind of pleading litany. ("Wake up for God's sake and tell me what happened!")

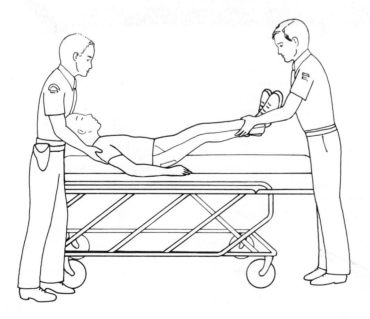

In the absence of family or previous records impressions should be obtained from observers. The observers may state that they don't know what happened, they just found the patient crumpled up on the curb. Appropriate questions are; "When did you find him?", "Did you do anything for him?", "Where did you find him?", "What was he like at the time?" (his position, breathing, speaking, etc.), and "How has he changed, if at all, since then?" In the case of the patient injured at work who is brought in by a coworker, emergency personnel should attempt to learn from the coworker how the patient was injured, the approximate time, the local care given, the condition of the patient at the time, and if he has changed.

Sometimes eyewitnesses will respond to these questions with little or no information. For example, "What was he like when you saw him fall?" "He fell, that's all. He just went down." These clarifying questions can follow: "What part of his body hit first?", "What was his position?", "Did he talk to you?", "Did he speak to you afterwards?", "When was that?", "What did he say?" If the bystander tells the physician that the patient was bleeding a lot, attempts are made to quantify. "When you say a lot, do you mean two cupfuls, two bottles, two spoonfuls?" "Oh, two cupfuls." "How do you know?" "Man, it was all over his shirt. You can see for yourself." In determining change, the physician may have to ask, "How was the breathing then?" "I couldn't tell if he was breathing at all." The next questions would be "Do you see any difference between that time and now?" This question is necessary because the bystander and the physician might have two different points of reference regarding the kind of breathing one "can't tell at all."

The main questions for all witnesses to accidents are: "What happened?", "How did it happen?", "What time?", and "What was done for the patient?", "What was his condition at the time?", "Have you noticed any changes between the time of the episode and the present?"

If members of his family bring in the unconscious patient, they are more likely to give details of what happened and information concerning any previous episodes, the location of the patient's medical records, the names of other physicians, if the patient is under medication, and information regarding his occupation and living habits. For example, a patient was brought into the emergency department by his wife after a week of passing scant urine, becoming more and more drowsy, and noticing that his clothes and shoes were becoming too tight. As the patient drifted in and out of consciousness, his wife was questioned regarding his renal failure, with particular emphasis on his possible contact with nephrotoxic agents. Investigation of his work and hobbies revealed that he had been exposed to mercury.

The unconscious patient sometimes presents what appears to be a clear clinical picture. Because the clear picture may be a double negative compounded by illness or other injuries, every attempt should be made to obtain a full history. The patient with multiple injuries from an auto accident may have become involved in the accident because of a seizure. The patient in an alcoholic stupor may have fallen and struck his head, the blow causing a blood clot. Shock may mask an acute myocardiac infarct.

The unconscious patient, while not a reliable source of information, must still be considered part of the clinical picture. We know that patients in all commonly used planes of surgical anesthetic can hear (5, 6, 7, 8, 9). In all deep levels of unconscious thought, surgical anesthesia, brain trauma, diabetic coma, drug poisoning, insulin shock, or cardiac arrest, the last contact with the external environment seems to be hearing. Evidence indicates that moribund patients are very much in contact with their environment, they just do not have the muscular control to communicate. Even though there is minimal cortical activity, levels of awareness cannot be assessed accurately.

A pseudodeath occurs with many forms of life during periods of stress or privation (33). Cheek postulates that during illness, accident, or surgery human beings escape into a state of suspended animation in which they may be hibernating in fear. Clinical signs are not sure indications of awareness. Patients who have suffered cardiac arrest recall the efforts of the resusitation team who manipulated, squeezed, cut, and jabbed their hearts back into electrical activity (13). These subjective reports also include such remembrances as "He's gone flat," "There's no blood pressure," and sadly, "He's gone." Psychiatric mental status exams which have been made on unconscious patients show that the content of the interviewer's questions can elicit pupillary change. Memories of operating room experiences are preserved at levels so deep that they have to be dynamited out with hypnosis or amytal interviews. Under these altered states of consciousness patients are able to recall facts and events of surgery (30, 31).

During a hypnotic session two years after surgery, one patient was able to recall the surgeon saying, "Look how black that lung is! Have you ever seen anything as black as that?" The patient knew that something was wrong with his lung but could not recall how the thought entered his mind. A depressed patient who was under hypnosis several weeks after surgery, recalled the surgeon saying, "Good gracious, it may not be a cyst at all, it may be cancer." In subsequent studies on patients in a profound depth of anesthesia in which the EEG consisted entirely of irregular, slow high voltage waves comparable to certain comatose states, the patient recalled such statements as "He's saying my color is gray," "It's gangrenous," "He's going to give me some oxygen," "He's saying to get out of here and go home," (common operating room jargon for closing up an abdominal incision).

From all cases reported, it is evident that only meaningful material was remembered. Casual material like golf scores doesn't seem to get recorded. These studies demonstrate that an unconscious patient is sensitive to remarks and to nuances of voice inflection.

Sleep studies show that external events in the sleeper's immediate environment may suggest or affect the low-grade thinking that is dreaming (12, 25, 28). The same principles apply to deeper levels of unconscious states. These patients should be spoken to, reassured, kept posted on their progress, and told what is expected of them. More subtle forms of reassurance such as suggestions and indications of a favorable outcome could also be used by medical personnel attending the unconscious patient.

While it is impossible to monitor everything one says, casual remarks of a negative nature should be guarded against on the chance that they can adversely affect the patient's recovery. The human mind scans environmental stimuli like a radar scope for a guide to what is happening, eagerly assigning literal meaning to every word it hears. Humor or metaphorical statements escape this level of consciousness. Such literal thinking can interpret "Let's get out of here and go home." as a full-scale abandonment.

While hearing seems to play the most significant role in maintaining contact with the unconscious patient, the role of touch should not be overlooked. Since touch is one of the most elemental ways in which one mammal shows interest in another, the patient in a lower level of consciousness may respond favorably to this basic and reassuring action of care-giving behavior.

What we don't know about the human brain and the way it receives and interprets messages exceeds what we do know. When attempting to decipher a brain-print we presently are as equipped to break the code as a chimp with the Rosetta stone. At best we can look at it, turn it over in our hands, recognize enough differences to give them names like alpha and theta, and hand the whole thing over to a computer. While the effect of touch can be traced in brain recordings, the individual's interpretation of the sensation is yet unknown. All that is known is that touch leaves a record.

It is an error to consider the unconscious patient unable to hear or understand just because he has no subsequent memory on a conscious level. Meaningful sounds, silences, and words are registered and may have a profound effect or influence on the patient's recovery and on his life for many years (1).

INSTRUCTIONS

In the emergency department, as with any other service, there comes a time to discharge the patient. He has been diagnosed and given treatment. Now the physician must instruct the patient in his own care. The emergency department setting, which is dramatic and fraught with danger (even if the danger is someone else's), mandates precise instruction. The physician gives all instructions in plain nontechnical language, preferably in words of one syllable. Not exactly, "You go by n' by, take off bandage," but clearly stated. Even if the patient seems to comprehend medical terminology, the physician must make absolutely sure that the patient understands his instructions. The patient who sits nodding attentively, his eyes glued on the physician who tries to tell him what to do with his degloved thumb stuck in his new abdominal flap, may be nodding in disbelief. Frequent pauses between statements give the patient an opportunity to ask questions. In addition, it is helpful to write down all explanations and instructions in clear, readable script.

The following example shows a physician carefully giving instructions. A woman who was treated for hypertension had a pressure reading of 170/105. It had been established that another physician had prescribed medication for her, but she couldn't recall his name or the name of the medication. She subsequently identified the medication from a picture in the *Physician's Desk Reference.* Her presenting complaints were dizziness and headaches. Because of her casual attitude toward her illness and her medication, which was determined by the number of days she missed taking her medication and the amount of time between refills, the attending emergency department physician attempted to impress upon her the seriousness of her condition so that she would comply with his instructions in the future.

Physician: You did right to come in tonight. I'm changing your medication to two pills a day instead of one. When you didn't take your pills often enough, you got worse. That's why you got dizzy and got a headache.

Patient: I stood up too fast.

Physician: No. You got dizzy because your heart has to work too hard to pump your blood. If it has to pump harder, you can have a stroke or die.

Patient: You say I got to take two pills?

Physician: Yes.

Patient: That's a lot of worrying about medicine.

Physician: Yes, it's a lot to think about. Can you think of a way to help you remember to take them?

Patient: Carry them in my purse?

Physician: Yes, that's a good idea. There's something else that will help. I'm going to give you a pill counter. That way you can check every night to see if you took two pills.

(The patient showed interest in the counter. After some discussion about the device, the physician resumed instructions.)

Physician: There are other things you can do just as important as taking your medicine to help you feel better. I want you to watch your salt. Things like pork, ham, potato chips, pickles, pretzels—they have a lot of salt, and they can hurt you. They have already hurt you.

Patient: My folks like a lot of salt.

Physician: That's O.K. Let them salt their food at the table. Make everything without salt. That way your food won't have any. Let your family do what they please. You also have to make a real effort to lose weight. When your weight is up, when you eat salt, when you miss your pills, it's like a runaway train. It takes two of us to stop that train. What can you do to help?

Patient: Something wrong with my heart?

Physician: Not exactly. There is something wrong with the way it has to pump.

Patient: If I don't eat salt, take my pills. . . . then what?

Physician: It's like an extra hand on the pump. No salt, and take your pills. How about losing weight?

Patient: (laughs) Now you know I can't do that.

THEY ALSO SERVE WHO STAND AND WAIT

Many emergency departments now have a special place for anxious friends and relatives (15), segregating the worried from the action for two reasons. The first is for the comfort of those waiting who, while usually distraught, can be reassured and kept reasonably calm in a place where personnel know where to find them. The second reason for a separate place for families and friends is that patients' families often regard the emergency department as open season and left undesignated, they feel free to wander in and out of places they would not dare to venture in other clinical settings. It is as if the "emergency" forgives all, including the indiscretions of entering other cubicles or standing in the nurses' station. Families who are let loose get tangled in IVs, get frightened if they get in the way of a code alert, make odious comparisons between the emergency staff and their own private physician, and may yank indiscriminately on the arms and heads of injured or ill loved ones. Not unlike staff, they may try to shout the patient into consciousness, "It's me, Mike, your brother. Talk to me." or "Wake up, you're in the emergency room."

Often those who wait become hostile. This is especially true if they feel guilty or responsible for the problems suffered by the patient. They may project this hostility onto attendant staff using the same mental gymnastics of someone who barks his shin on a table and then kicks the cat, a mechanism called displacement.

If possible, the waiting room should be attractive and nonclinical, with coffee, ash trays, and vending machines available. The staff should pop in and out and say things like, "We have your uncle/brother/father/daughter in treatment," "The doctor is caring for your . . . he will be ready to leave in about one hour. Why don't you go to the coffee shop and come back?", "He will have to be hospitalized," or "He is ready to go now, the doctor wants to talk to you, too, about how to take care of him at home."

DISASTER

Most people think that disaster is something that happens to someone else. The feeling of personal invulnerability is partly a delusion, a protective mental device similar to our disbelief in personal mortality, and partly the result of our parimutuel approach to life, which always considers the odds. As a result, we ignore or minimize warnings and neglect to protect ourselves, sometimes we have no opportunity to protect ourselves. Whatever the way the wheel dumps the ball on us, we are always dumbfounded to find we could not beat the odds.

ITS FACE

There are all kinds of disasters. Some are man-made such as thermonuclear, biologic, or chemical warfare, fire, and plane and train accidents; some are natural disasters such as epidemics, floods, earthquakes, blizzards, droughts, or tornadoes. Each disaster takes its toll in its own way and leaves its own flotsam in its wake. People are injured and killed; property is damaged and destroyed.

A disaster site resembles a target. The bull's eye is that area of total impact, in which there is full destruction. It is a Boschian scene of wounded lying beneath rubble, with dazed and bewildered survivors picking their way through. The second ring is the fringe area, in which minor damage has occurred. The third is the filter area, an undamaged zone from which rescuers and sightseers enter. Immediately after a disaster, curious onlookers and volunteers begin to converge upon the area. It is sometimes difficult to make a distinction between them since they are often unsure of their purpose and switch from one role to the other. This unofficial convergence results in an unmanageable number of people moving from the periphery into the impact area. Since the line which divides the second and third concentric zones is the entry point of all those who want to get into the area and the exit point for all those who want to get out, this is where service traffic congestion develops.

The common denominator of all disasters is that all available medical professionals are suddenly thrust into caring for mass casualties under circumstances in which the delivery of ideal medical care is impossible (32, 35). The sudden unprecedented demand for large-scale treatment, coupled with inadequate facilities, manpower, and supplies, make disaster medicine not only a different ball game but a different ball park. Disaster medicine in the broadest sense refers to the care of a patient whose needs are critical and urgent, administered under conditions that almost certainly will not be optimal, utilizing whatever facilities are at hand. It is makeshift medicine practiced in a setting of massive disorganization.

PHYSICIAN'S RESPONSIBILITIES

Depending on the likelihood of relief, a few of the basic tenets of medicine may be jettisoned in the face of disaster. The first to go is the usual equal consideration given to all medical problems. In private practice, the individual patient's needs are paramount. Since personnel and supplies are adequate, it is seldom a problem to meet those needs. In disaster medicine, priority treatment for all must be exchanged for a system of triage similar in theory to the triage of the emergency department, in which classification determines priority. The similarity ends with available supports. In the emergency department, the physician is surrounded by other trained personnel and has consultants, supplies, and facilities available. While he identifies those patients needing immediate help, he knows that all will be treated eventually. In disaster medicine, there are no assurances of any supports.

Facilities may be inadequate, and there may be few trained to direct activities. There will not be time to perform necessary technical procedures; essential supplies will be deficient in quality and quantity; those doing surgery will include dentists, nurses, and veterinarians; anesthesia will be lacking or inadequate; contamination will be universal; and postoperative care will be in the hands of untrained personnel. Because of inadequate supports the next to be jettisoned might be procedures. The wiring of a jaw, for example, may be deferred because the after-care task of feeding may be a problem. In disaster medicine, the physician must not make any patient less able to care for himself unless it is lifesaving to do so.

The physician in a disaster is forced to do a little for a great number of people. Individual decisions must be made regarding every patient and his chance of survival. The physician is constantly faced with the questions, "Should I give this patient ten minutes?" or "Should I help ten patients in the same time interval and maybe save six or seven?" The unpalatable job of playing God and deciding who to help is contrary to medicine as it is learned and practiced. Insufficient drugs and surgical materials will constantly force the physician to choose. For example, if there are 100 amebic dysentery cases and just enough drugs for three or four, who gets the drugs? Does the physician make a decision based on the patients' value to the community and the rehabilitation period to come? Based on their age? Based on their chance of survival?

The person who sorts the patients according to need must have an idea of the transportation available, where the patients will be taken, if any place, who will care for them once they get there, and surgical "lag" time (10). Finally, he must have the courage of his convictions. Sorting requires not only good clinical training and sound judgment but the physician's ability to avoid agonizing over a decision and to accept his own limitations. He cannot be all things to all people. If, in the past, he has made promises beyond his ability, has had trouble saying no, or has

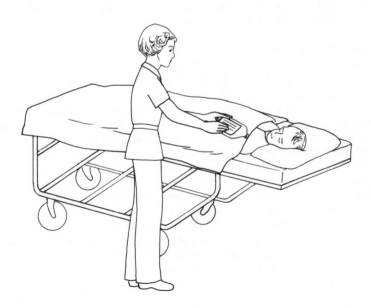

been sensitive to criticism, he might find the demands of a disaster situation very difficult.

In addition to the responsibility of deciding who gets treated, the physician must instruct less qualified personnel in the care of the injured so that he is free to perform surgery, a function of all physicians in emergency situations, regardless of their specialty. He tells families where to put their wounded, he instructs volunteers in the system of duplicate tagging, he shows patients how to staunch their cuts with handkerchiefs, he warns Boy Scouts that if they whack away lumber, they may lessen supports and throw more rubble on the trapped and wounded, and he rounds up the local pharmacist to dispense first aid. Whatever he does, the physician must be prepared to innovate, improvise, substitute, and compromise (38). Casuality management involves creativity, using any materials at hand; for example, a patient's legs may be tied together so that the unbroken leg can serve as a temporary splint for the one that has been broken.

RESPONSE OF SURVIVORS

It is difficult to predict individual response to disaster. Prior to World War II, it was thought that excluding persons of unstable mentality would prevent war neuroses. The emphasis was on the identification and elimination of those considered emotional and intellectual misfits. Despite a rejection rate of three to four times that of World War I, the screening program failed, illustrating the difficulty of predicting response to disaster. The 1943 incidence of psychiatric disorders was three times that of World War I (2).

While individual response cannot be predicted reliably, disaster response follows a general pattern. There is a general misconception of disaster as an event in which most survivors are running amuck while a few responsible people are sharply slapping them into sensibility. The truth is that individual panic is rare. In the first stage, lasting anywhere from a few minutes to a few hours, the survivor may be dazed, stunned, apathetic, and unable to respond to directions. He may putter around the ruins of his home in a disorganized way, looking for some trivial item like a pot holder, while disregarding a dangling broken arm. He may exhibit some trembling, profuse perspiring, feelings of weakness, a constricted manner of speaking, giddiness, pallor, labored respiration, some posture change, or even nausea.

Fifteen to twenty–five percent of the survivors regain their composure fairly soon. These people seem to be able to handle disaster better than their fellows. They are able to grasp relevant details of the situation and can continue effective action. The majority, however, are stunned and bewildered. Some of these may appear depressed, numbed, unable to help themselves without guidance. Others may respond with exaggerated activity. They are easily distracted, jump from one task to another, and are often intolerant of ideas other than their own. They may make inappropriate jokes, be overtalkative, and criticize authority.

Some people regress to a former level of behavior, in which there is a breakdown of self-control and a return to less complex ways of doing things. The temporary backslide of someone with his tie and shoelaces stuffed in his pocket is a way of being taken care of again by "grownups."

Generally, most people respond to disaster with docility and increased suggestibility. They are blank, unemotional, dazed, unresponsive to questions, and oblivious to painful injuries. If they are injured, they are likely to be apathetic and do not seem to want medical attention. When an abrupt and dangerous environmental change occurs, the subsequent alerting action focuses the attention on the threat and narrows perception. This, in turn, inhibits the making of even minor decisions. The reason involves response selection. In normal situations, stimuli are generally perceived, evaluated, and acted upon rapidly and automatically, based on the template of previous learning. What makes them *normal* is that they are *usual.* Normal environmental circumstances generally evoke rapid appropriate responses. New and abrupt changes of catastrophe force an evaluation and a response for which there is no formula, which slows up the process of action. A whole new set of circumstances must be identified and evaluated. If there is no precedent, upon which to assess the new event, identification and reaction is held up while the search goes on for other cues.

The disaster survivor is amenable to suggestion and willing to be helpful, but his efficiency, even in simple and routine tasks, is low. If he is injured, he is likely to minimize his own injuries and ask that others be taken care of first. This rather selfless second stage may last for several days. The survivor may even have guilt feelings because he made it and others did not. In the third stage, a kind of brave new world, which may last for several weeks or several years if the danger is perceived as a continuous threat, there is a euphoric *esprit de corps,* a kind of brotherhood and kinship for all others involved. This period of mutual support typified feelings in Great Britain during World War II.

In the fourth stage, the honeymoon is over. The survivor shows marked annoyance with discomforts, is less tolerant of substitute measures, and begins to criticize agencies and anyone else that is a likely target. These hostilities gradually diminish as things return to normal.

COMMUNICATION UNDER STRESS

Principles of communication under stress have been corroborated by reports of disaster experience. While most physicians will probably never have to practice medicine under catastrophic conditions, these principles are presented as guidelines for the few who will (the presumption being that they will be in the 15–25 percent who can quickly resume responsibility).

The physician's interpersonal skill is a vital function in disaster medicine. In some cases, it will be all he can provide. It consists of providing reassurance, empathy, information, and serving as a leader (2, 14).

Reassurance

In order to give reassurance, contact must be made. When the sick and the wounded surround a physician who is also faced with limited or inadequate facilities, a pat here and a chat there help (23). What must be conveyed essentially is, "I'm here. I am aware of your needs. I will do all I can for you." Sometimes touching may seem like tagging bases, but it provides some reassurance when there is no time for anything else.

Empathy

The physician must accept the patient's limitations as real in order to provide empathy. The patient is not malingering. His inability to follow simple instructions, like staunching his own wound with a gauze pad, is part of his psychologic adjustment to calamity. An impatient "Snap out of it." or "Pull yourself together." are ineffectual and meaningless. He can't. He doesn't have the equipment, because he is busy sorting out what has happened to him. *"It's all in your head."* is a futile statement. It's not all in his head. Something bad really did happen to him. No one chooses to feel bad. If he does or if he responds inappropriately, it is because he *is* psychologically healthy. He is responding to a realistic appraisal of his situation. It is an indication that he has the means to cope, more so than if he appeared unconcerned. The physician does not overwhelm him with pity but indicates a willingness to understand. A word, a gesture, or a simple statement of empathy, "You must be very worried, not knowing where your family is," will do it.

Information

The survivor needs to establish the whereabouts of his family and bring them to safety. Any action on the part of the sorting physician to obtain information as to his identity, the whereabouts of his family, and what has happened to him assure him that people are interested, it is a therapeutic action. It also serves to bind up an enormous network of disrupted and incomplete public information. What is learned from him is passed on to information officers, those people whose job it is to pinpoint the location and condition of survivors.

All information given to patients should be clear and specific. Messages must be repeated frequently to counteract the interference with recall or retention that may be a postdisaster factor. Many patients will assist with or manage entirely their own follow–up care. Instructions to these patients especially must be clear and repeated. Obtaining feedback from them is essential. For example, when a patient who suffered a minor burn is given a fluid preparation of salt, soda, and water to take orally, he must be instructed in the necessity for drinking the entire formula. It may be necessary to add that this replaces the vital ingredients in his body that have been lost. This patient may also be told how to drink it. Instructions may include such specifics as "Go over there where you will be undisturbed, sit down, and sip it slowly."

The exchange of correct information between the physician and members of his work force is essential. All messages that go from one to another must be precise. The physician tells others what he is doing, what he is going to do, and where he's going to do it. He also requests similar information from everyone else. The physician must be prepared to give responsibility to people who would be considered inadequately trained in ordinary circumstances. When he acts as a roving consultant, dispensing advice rapidly to his assistants or his patients, he is providing and receiving valuable information, as well as functioning as a leader.

Leadership

Ordinarily a leader is known by the symbols of his power, or by his actual power. A man behind a desk with an eagle on it or a sumo wrestler are not hard to identify. In a disaster, a leader is anyone who can make sense out of chaos. In disorder, the human being has a limited repertoire. The responses which he makes in answer to new and unexpected demands are untested, and he is ready to follow anyone who can indicate by word or effective action behavior.

The physician can combine his function as role model with the dynamics of the group to counteract the regression in judgment and behavior reflected in others. A group working together for a common purpose has a collective motivation which exerts a powerful influence on an individual member's tolerance for stress. People are better able to tolerate danger when they are with others who are in similar danger. Group members serve each other as verbal or nonverbal sources of information as they scan one another for cues. Everything is taken seriously. Nuances of expression and casual references that would go unchallenged or unnoticed become the cause of careful consideration. The physician can set the tone by his own behavior and his own responses, which should continue to be calm and assured. If he can do this successfully, his responsibilities will be diffused; others who emulate him will share the burden of keeping an even mood and setting an example of effective functioning. The physician can ignite the behavioral mode of the group, which then runs pretty much by itself and may require only an occasional fuel injection.

While few people actually panic in disaster, panic, when it does occur, is contagious. It is caused by the belief in an immediate, severe threat from which there is no escape, and by the lack of effective leadership and correct information. The panicked person must be restrained so that he does not infect anyone else with his "blind flight." He needs to be comforted and reassured. What is most reassuring for the panicked person is the realization that there is a leader. Immobilization followed by simple instruction and reassurance are effective. The panicked person can be directed away from the area for a rest period. After he has rested, it is helpful to give him something to do. Activity is a siphon for anxiety. His potential should be sized up and utilized. Constructive behavior, even if it is counting tongue blades, indeed, any resumption of purposeful activity diminishes fear.

The physician's setting of the group mood should also include an optimistic outlook. Positive expectancy works against any notion of permanent disability. The idea that eventually one will begin to function and feel better has therapeutic value. The importance of nonverbal as well as verbal communication cannot be minimized. If there is a sense of tension or helplessness in the atmosphere, the symptoms and noneffective behavior of the sick, injured, lightly wounded, and psychiatric cases will continue. Even the seriously injured, who are too sick to be capable of any behavior other than the expression of their injuries, benefit from an atmosphere of positive expectancy.

Facilitation

Brief and simple use of facilitation and ventilation are very useful. If the patient can ventilate his experiences, he will experience catharsis, relief in being able to share with someone else the disrupting and horrifying experience. Having an opportunity to part with some of his personal disaster then he can be motivated to participate in an effort which leads to his further recovery.

The leader finally is flexible and inventive, willing to discard previous notions for less desirable ideas that just might work under the circumstances. This and other tasks already set forth as valuable in disaster situations sound like the listing in the Boy Scout Oath. They may seem formidable. Actually, they are just an extension of other techniques made more forceful and more direct by the nature of the situation.

Under disaster conditions it is vital that the health care professional accept his own limitations. It is a source of frustration and anxiety not to be able to help all who need it, particularly when one is trained to do so. If the physician can go about his formidable assignments accepting his own decisions, resting when he needs it, and delegating lesser responsibilities to others wherever he can, he will utilize his own expertise to its best advantage as well as maintain his own sanity.

REFERENCES

1. Beecher HK, Todd DP: A study of the deaths associated with anesthesia and surgery. Ann Surg 140:2–34, 1954

2. Bourne PG: The Psychology and Physiology of Stress, with Reference to Special Studies of the Vietnam War. New York, Academic Press, 1969

3. Burgess AW, Holmstrom LL: Rape trauma syndrome. Am J Psychiatry 131:981–986, 1974

4. Burgess AW, Holstrom LL: The rape victim in the emergency ward. Am J Nurs 73:1740–1745, 1973

5. Cheek DB: Unconscious perception of meaningful sounds during surgical anesthesia as revealed under hypnosis. Am J Clin Hypn 1(3):101–113, 1959

6. Cheek DB: Unconscious reactions and surgical risk: guest editorial. West J Surg Obst Gynec 69:325–328 1961

7. Cheek, DB The meaning of continued hearing sense under general-chemo-anesthesia: a progress report and report of a case. Am J Clin Hypn 8(4):275–280, 1966

8. Cheek DB: Can Surgical Patients React to What They Hear under Anesthesia? Presented to the annual meeting of the Western States Section of Nurse Anesthetists. San Francisco, 1964

9. Cheek DB: Further evidence of persistence of hearing under chemo-anesthesia: a detailed case report. Am J Clin Hypn 7:55–59, 1964

10. Committee on Injuries: Emergency Care and Transportation of the Sick and Injured. Chicago, American Academy of Orthopedic Surgeons, 1971

11. Committee on Trauma, American College of Surgeons: Early Care of the Injured Patient. Philadelphia, Saunders, 1971

12. Dement W, Kleitman N: Cyclic variations in EEG during sleep and their relation to eye movements, body motility, and dreaming. Electroencephalogr Clin Neurophysiol 9:673–690, 1957

13. Dlin BM, Stern A, Poliakoff S: Survivors of cardiac arrest—the first few days. Psychosom 15:61–67, 1974

14. Drayer CS et al.: Psychologic First Aid in Community Disaster. Washington, American Psychiatric Association, Committee on Disaster and Civil Defense, 1954

15. Emergency departments and the non emergency deluge. Medical World News. 11: (52):22–28, 1970

16. Fox RA et al.: The patient in the emergency care unit. Pa Med 76:63–64, 1973

17. French JD: The reticular formation. In Altered States of Awareness (Readings from Scientific American with introductions by Timothy J. Teyler). San Francisco, W H Freeman, 1972, pp 23–29

18. Hamilton WF: Systems analysis in emergency care planning. Med Care 12:152–162, 1974

19. Harvey: The Emergency Medical Services Systems Act of 1973. N Engls Med 292:-529–530, 1975

20. Holleck S: The physician's role in the management of victims of sex offenders. JAMA 180:273–278, 1962

21. Hospital Statistics, Table 5. Chicago, American Hospital Association, 1974, p 34

22. Hospital Statistics, Table 5A. Chicago, American Hospital Association, 1975, p 18

23. Houghton KH: Role of Medical Officers. Presented at the 62nd Annual Convention of the Association of Military Surgeons of the US. Washington, Mass casualties principles involved in Mgmt 1955, pp 408–410. (Reprinted from Milit Med 118, no 4, April 1956)

24. Jacobziner H: Rescuing the battered child. Am J Nurs 64:92–97, 1964

25. Jouvet M: The states of sleep. In Altered States of Awareness (Readings from Scientific American with Introduction by Timothy J. Teyler). San Francisco, W H Freeman, 1972, pp 51–59

26. Kempe CH et al.: The battered-child syndrome. JAMA 181:17–24, 1962

27. Kempe CH, Helfer R: Helping the Battered Child and His Family. Philadelphia, J B Lippincott, 1972

28. Kleitman N: Sleep and Wakefulness. Chicago, University of Chicago Press, 1963

29. Lavenhar M, Ratner R, Weinerman ER: Social class and medical care: indicies of nonurgency in use of hospital emergency service. In Noble JH, Jr (ed): Emergency Medical Services: Behavioral and Planning Perspectives. New York, Behavioral Publications, 1973, pp 181–206

30. LeCron LM: A hypnotic technique for uncovering unconscious material. Experimental Hypnosis 2:76–79, 1954

31. Levinson BW: States of awareness during general anaesthesia. In Lassner J (ed): Hypnosis and Psychosomatic Medicine: Proceedings of the International Congress for Hypnosis and Psychosomatic Medicine. Johannesburg, International Congress for Hypnosis and Psychosomatic Medicine, 1965, pp 200–207

32. Mass casualties—principles involved in management. Milit Med 118, No. 4, 1956

33. Moruzzi G, Magoun HW: Brain stem reticular formation and activation of the EEG. Electroencephalogr Clin Neurophysiol 1:455–473, 1949

34. O'Boyle C: A new era in emergency services. Am J Nurs 72:1392–7, 1972

35. Raker, S.W. et al.: Emergency Medical Care in Disasters: A Summary of Recorded Experience. Washington, National Academy of Science, National Research Council, 1956

36. Sampson P: Medical progress has little effect on an ancient childhood syndrome. JAMA 222(13):1605–1612, 1972

37. Schneider C et al.: Interviewing the parents. In Kempe CH, Helfer R: Helping the Battered Child and His Family. Philadelphia, J B Lippincott, 1972, pp 55–65

38. Spencer JH: Mass casualties in the civilian hospital. Bull Amer Coll of Surgeons 48:-(6):342–344:356–361, 1963

39. Steele BF: Violence in our society. The Pharos of Alpha Omega Alpha 33(2):42–48, 1970

40. Stengel E: Suicide and Attempted Suicide. London, C Nicholls, 1969

7
The Hospitalized Patient

Patients may not swear, curse, get drunk, behave rudely or indecently on pain of expulsion after the first admonition. There shall be no card playing or dicing and such patients as are able shall assist in nursing others, washing and ironing linen and cleaning the rooms and such other services as the matron may require.

Regulations of the Philadelphia General Hospital 1790

THE HOSPITAL EXPERIENCE

Whether through the portal of the emergency room or through the planned admission entering the hospital is a traumatic experience. Hollingshead and Duff found that during hospitalization mental status changed in patients in all accommodations (21). From the minute the celluloid tag is snapped around his wrist, the hospital patient begins to realize that when he checked his body into the hospital, he checked his identity out, the sum total of his worth left somewhere in a little bag marked "valuables." This schizophrenic process goes on every day as hospital staff join forces in the plot to pulverize his ego.

ASSAULT UPON BODY IMAGE

It begins with an assault on body image upon which the compound of self-esteem is predicated. Body image is built upon early tactile sensations and mirror effects, the responses of others who may look up at us, down at us, smile upon us with favor, turn away in disgust, or don't seem to see us at all. It is built by labyrinthine receptors of the inner ear and kinesthetic receptors of muscles, tendons, and joints; by our own view of the world, whether we see it from a vertical, reclining, or wheelchair position; and by how close we can come to the water cooler. Body image makes us at all times conscious of our corporeal self; we may love it or hate it, depending on our conception. Whatever our feelings, it is ours, or so we think. The hospital patient learns otherwise. It is not his. It is the property of anyone who wanders into his room bearing the official trappings which allow him to inspect it, poke it, prod it, and pass sentence on its condition. A janitor in a white coat would have the same privilege; and no doubt there are a few who have taken advantage of this opportunity. Privacy and control over one's spatial integrity are lost somewhere in the papers signed to get in. The hospital patient's body is subject to handling by every technician who wanders in, sometimes without a word, to do his task—every nurse, every aide, even the man who checks the television (if the patient is to have one), who looks at the patient long enough to make some sort of summary judgment as to how long the television figures to be in that room.

Body image is only part of image. Total image is compounded of an external collection of such things as family, friends, job, skills, clothes, and car—the latter four, of course, cannot follow him into the hospital, and the first two usually do (often to his distress). When he checks in, leaving the markings of his status on the outside, he is diminished. The one thing that he does present, his body, is under scrutiny and is getting no awards, since something is wrong with it. That is enough to disturb the self-esteem of any patient, no matter how together he is. There is a close connection between body image and personality. Body image leads to a perception of one's self-worth; and the balance between one's limitations and abilities, often hang by the thread of a urine specimen.

INSTITUTIONAL CUES

Once admitted, the patient gets out of his clothes and into a sterile and formless gown, which fans out from the scapula like a cutaway, a design whose implication is onerous at the least. (Goffman calls it part of the process of institutional mortification which strips the new recruit of his supports in order to make him more amenable to "house rules."(16)

Some patients refuse the hospital vestments and dress in their best pajamas or nightgown and robe, still attempting to present the best foot or the best front. They may discard this facade when they realize that it makes no difference, or if very ill, in pain, or debilitated, may not attempt to put up a fight at all. Whatever his garb, the hospital patient is subject at once to regulations: when he may have visitors, when he may call or be called on the telephone, if he can smoke, and when he eats, sleeps, and rises. He begins to think that coordination and hospital practice are mutually exclusive, and that services work independentaly of each other and of him. The patient sees the hospital not as a city, to which it often has been compared; but as a time warp, a science-fiction curiosity of the prehistoric, the medieval, and the futuristic with their Em² mixed up. When he leans on a call button and begins to think that it is not connected, when he has had two blood samples taken within a half hour by people who cannot find his veins, when the cardiac patient is mistakenly whisked out of bed for a cobalt treatment, and the pre-op patient feels as if the purpose of the enema he is getting is to irrigate his ears he begins to see the hospital as a battlefield, and worries about the crossfire.

Even if the patient were not suffering a sense of self-loss, even if he felt confident about all that was happening to him, the hospital experience would be a frightening one. The alien smells of the halls (no matter how carefully they are scrubbed and sprayed), the strange apparatus, the strange and new language, and the increased tempo of activity are frightening. The patient has seen others carted through the halls with life lines going into or coming out of their bodies, kept fresh in cellophane wrappers; and he hears the sounds and footsteps of urgency, some running, some walking. He hears unfamiliar voices, whispers, the public address system, bells, and carts. Because many sounds are idiosyncratic to the hospital, they evoke a host of ideas about sickness, none of which are good. These associations give the patient cues which help him to make sense out of his environment, but the sense is negative. If he has been in the hospital before, his dread increases.

Even before surgery is an imminent factor, the hospital represents a threat to his body image and his self-esteem. Shame, guilt, anger, and denial all play a part in the patient's response to the threat. In some instances, where hospitalization and surgery are necessary, the patient may inform neither family nor close friends.

ANXIETY

The surgical as well as the medical patient experiences tension because he does not know exactly what is going to happen (30). If he has some ideas, none of them are comforting. Since hospital care is a step up in complexity from home care, the patient considers it inherently more serious. The patient doesn't know how he will feel during procedures, he doesn't know the result of treatment, and he doesn't know if he will walk out feeling better, if he walks out at all. He worries over whether he can ever return to work and if he will remain the person he now knows himself to be. Even hopeful experiences such as childbirth or elective surgery, that offers correction, or the neutral experience of the routine checkup, are enough to arouse anxiety. In the first two, something could go wrong. In the third, "they might find something."

When the human being is under stress, he is like a fish out of water. Flopping on the sand, he seeks to renew his former equilibrium. Anxiety helps him flop a little harder, but sometimes the energy generated is not enough to help him maintain his self-esteem; he resorts to his own particular coping mechanisms (a series or one favorite) to work off anxiety. These include: reassurance of touch, eating and other oral behavior, like chewing off pencil ends; goofing off; laughing, crying, singing, swearing; alcohol and other drugs; sleeping; pointless activity like pacing or scratching; fantasy and daydreaming; boasting, asking questions; and seeking and using new information, the most constructive behavior (12). These usually relate to a mild anxiety, a chronic state that many people feel in varying degrees their whole life.

Anxiety may be described as a feeling of uneasiness from an anticipated threat. All patients feel a mild anxiety upon entering the hospital. Meeting new physicians, the focus upon one's self and relative state of "O.K.ness," and visits of concerned friends and family all will increase anxiety. Severe anxiety, the weak-in-the-knees, butterfly-stomached feeling with increased heart rate, increased rate and depth of respiration, rise in arterial pressure, rapid and extreme shifts in body temperature, and blood pressure diverted from the stomach and intestines to the heart are physiological manifestations which prepare the body for fight or flight. Although few patients actually flee, many would like to. The constant stress from anxiety threatens the patient's ability to cope with illness and procedures, and his well-being (11, 37). The continuous alarm reaction leads to exhaustion and interferes with progress. The thought of hospitalization or treatment may cause a panic and an ennervating state of emotional paralysis. It would be easy to make a case for the reasonableness of feeling *fearful*, especially if one is to undergo surgery or certain treatments. The threat to body integrity is real.

Surgery is a submissive experience, and in the patient's mind close to the nightmare. When one is flat, strapped down, and unconscious, he is helpless, and the surgical experience may be perceived as an attack in which his worst fears of passivity are realized. Other people fear they will tell all during surgery or wake up and feel the knife or lose their inhibitions—particularly dealing with sex, excretion, and aggression. Those who undergo regional anesthesia, especially spinal, fear the loss of motor power (40).

PHYSICIAN'S CONTRIBUTIONS

The very person trained to heal may make matters worse. Many presurgical patients never see their surgeons until after their operations. This can be distressing to a patient who would like to judge the surgeon's competency, or just reassure himself that the surgeon has reasonably good vision, that he seems relatively coordinated, and that he appears to be stable. One 11-year-old presurgical patient refused surgery until the surgeon could win a packaged game called "Operation," the object of which was to insert one's hands through blind entryways and extract objects without touching the sides of the box, that were constructed to flash lights and ring bells if the player made a mistake. The surgeon gamely complied, won, and surgery went as scheduled. Many gifted surgeons can only function in an anonymous relationship. ("Don't tell me how many children he has.") Some need to isolate themselves from their patients in order to protect themselves, especially when surgery carries a high risk.

Many physicians may overemphasize the need for surgery in order to justify it (40). When this happens, the physician transfers his own apprehensions neatly to the patient, who then takes them on in addition to his own. They serve as expert corroboration.

The anxiety of the very sick patient, the one who lifts his head with difficulty, may be seen in another way. He may be too debilitated to display it through facial expressions, words, or characteristic gestures. His subjective concern may be manifest in his eyes and their response to his environment and to what is happening in it. Sometimes this patient is seen watching and listening to those who attend him in a labored and effortful attention, marked only by persistent eye movements, as if he were straining to understand. A 74-year-old dehydrated and weakened patient with signs of acute pneumonia who watched attending staff relentlessly, his eyes darting to all meaningful movement, was able to relax his surveillance only after he was told that the intravenous that was being started and the oxygen tent in preparation were to help him breathe easier. He really seemed to let go when someone advised him to lie on his affected side in order to make coughing less painful.

DEALING WITH ANXIETY

We can assume that all presurgical and preprocedural patients are anxious, and there are communication procedures that are extremely useful in dealing with them (17, 42, 49, 50).

INTRODUCTIONS

While the surgeon cannot personally take the time to take an elaborate history in the hospital and leaves this task to junior staff members, he can take the time to introduce himself to his patient, if to say nothing more than, "I'm Doctor . . . I'll be seeing you tomorrow." A preoperative interchange can be tranquilizing, no matter how brief. The patient can then move from an objective perception of something being done to him to the more subjective perception of a known *person* who will do it.

There is far less danger from one who has *talked to you*, given his name, and perhaps touched you in some way than from an amorphous body of a surgical team. Some physicians make appointments with their patients in the recovery room. This is spelled out clearly as "I'll see you tomorrow morning in the recovery room." That is a very good sign to any patient. He translates it quickly into "He expects me to make it."

VENTILATION

The preprocedural patient needs an opportunity to ventilate his feelings about what he fears. Communication includes ventilation, exploration, explanation, translating medical procedures into layman's terms, obtaining feedback to make sure the patient understands, and empathy.

In getting the preoperative or preprocedural patient to ventilate his fears, the physician should be prepared for wild fears and weird fantasies, although many of the patient's concerns are legitimately founded. He may worry that the technicians will give him the wrong test, that his tests will be mixed up with someone else's, that his tests will hurt and make him more uncomfortable than he already is, that he will wind up more restricted than when he came in, that he will lose body parts or function, that he will look bad when he comes out, that he will lose sexual desire or sexual attractiveness, that the surgeon will have a bad night, that the hospital will suffer a power failure, that some natural disaster will cause him to be left alone on the operating table unplugged, that he will talk during surgery and tell his secret(s), that he will lose other inhibitions (particularly those that relate to sex and excretion), that he will be mistaken for another patient, that he will die, that his wife and children cannot manage without him, that his boss will give his job to someone else, and that the costs will reduce or eliminate his savings. Every patient worries about something different, and it is not safe to anticipate his concerns. Since each patient needs to be heard, as both being heard and being able to admit to emotional difficulties is palliative, it is necessary for the physician to take a few minutes to help him to ventilate (49).

The task is not restricted to the physician, although it is very helpful to have the physician participate in ventilation because so many of the patient's expectations are intricately involved with this one human being. Before a patient is ready to ventilate, however, he needs time to relax. Usually some time after admission, when things quiet down and when his family has gone, a staff member should sit at his side and talk to him. No one has ventilated adequately to a person standing, ready to leave.

Seated at bedside, the physician facilitates the patient's expression. He may lead off by telling the patient about procedures, spelling them out slowly and carefully, and obtaining feedback so that he is assured that the patient understands. Some time during this interchange, the patient may become extremely restless, showing signs of anxiety, or he may appear detached and uninterested. Intervention may be in the form of empathic statements such as "I get the feeling that you are concerned." Or "You seem to be worried." While it is helpful to offer firm reassurance such as "I have every reason to believe that you will respond very well to treatment." or "You will recover quickly." or "Surgery will be helpful," it is important to determine exactly what is bothering him. Not that the physician is in a position to say, "Don't worry, everything is going to be fine."—he has put the patient in the hospital, and he's worried too—but the act of ventilation, of supportive and shared revelation is palliative. If the patient admits that he is worried, either with a nod of his head or with words, the physician can respond with "What is it about surgery/procedures/etc. that worries you?" If the response is "I don't know," the physician can facilitate him further by asking, "Tell me what you think will happen." or "How do you think it's going to be?" or "When you think about surgery/procedures/medication, what is it you think? What is it you feel?"

ACKNOWLEDGMENT

Whatever the patient's responses, it is crucial that the physician acknowledge them either with feedback ("You're concerned that you will not walk again.") or with empathy ("I can understand that you are worried about having tubes in your nose."). The patient may offer an anxious silence. Intervention may be "I know it is hard for you to talk, but it would be helpful if you would try." Touching and direct eye contact can often break an anxious silence. An appropriate statement would be "I can see that it is hard for you to talk. Perhaps another time we can try again." The physician can leave it there, having given an option for renewal of the interaction at a later time of the patient's choosing. What is significant is that the physician has acknowledged the troubled feelings of the patient.

EXPECTATIONS

Patients are helped when they are told what to expect (10, 19, 44, 49). Anyone can handle events better when he has an idea of their sequence and their effect on him. The surgical or medical patient who is prepared for what will be done to and for him and the part that he may play has in fact rehearsed the event, if only in his imagination. This rehearsal acts as a desensitizing agent. In addition, because he is a party to the information, the patient feels that he has some measure of control over his environment (7, 51, 52).

A patient who is privy to some of his own medical information is made a party to a contract, a partnership in which he has a contribution to make, that is, his cooperation. His conception of the future then becomes a finite projection based upon sequential steps. ("First you will sit on the edge of the bed, you may feel a little dizzy; when you are feeling steady, you will stand and maybe walk to the bathroom. In a few days you'll be walking down the hall, maybe sooner.") Studies concluded that keeping a patient informed of his situation rather than simply giving him the directives needed by the staff to do their jobs will gain his cooperation and reduce tension (24).

When preparing patients for coming events, it helps to allow for a time cushion. If things do not go according to schedule, patients panic and assign all sorts of fearful meanings to innocuous situations in which someone simply forgot, got tied up with another patient, or didn't communicate orders. For example, a patient wearing an eye patch because of a corneal abrasion sustained during surgery was informed that the patch would be removed at six o'clock. When six came and went and the eye patch remained, she concluded that something must be seriously wrong with the eye; both the patient and her family panicked.

Elusive answers are sometimes given to patients when the staff believes that they will not understand a direct explanation. Offhand comments which seek to evade rather than elaborate can make a patient suspicious. Most patients interpret evasive answers to mean that something about their condition is being concealed from them. A patient with an inguinal hernia, for example, who is left with unsatisfied questions may conclude that he has a cancerous tumor.

Evasions make some patients angry and resentful, feelings which do not generate cooperation. Even though most hospital patients regard medical information as rightful esoterica ("Doctors have their secrets."), they respond negatively when their questions go unanswered or are met with obvious tangential replies.

In a study patients hospitalized for abdominal surgery who received continued visits fared better postsurgically than the control group who did not. They required half the morphine and went home earlier (9).

NEGATIVE RESPONSE

THE DENYING PATIENT

The anxious patient is easier to deal with than the patient who is so fearful that he denies the threat of hospitalization and extended treatment. Such patients often do more poorly emotionally after surgery than those who do not use denial; therefore, it is essential for the physician to try to help the patient past this distortion of reality.

Denial cannot be erased by forcing the patient to look into a mirror. It won't work. The denying patient is like the earthquake victim who, when asked as he is sifting through the rubble of his house, "How did the earthquake affect you?" responds, "What earthquake?" or "What house?" It can be harmful to force this patient to face reality. He is too well defended. The best tack is to proceed at his pace, which will be a slow one. A tally system, in which the physician lists the patient's assets in a ledger of medical debits and credits, helps him to review all that is positive. The physician can and should comment in this manner: "Your color is very good. I find your heart sound and your blood pressure excellent; you have taken very good care of yourself." The patient can then afford a credit. "These things will help your recovery when you will need to draw upon your own resources."

The physician continues to be supportive and consistent with the denying patient. A patient who uses denial may refuse to admit or discuss his illness or potential procedures. He will talk about everything and anything else and act like someone who has checked into the wrong motel. He may have postponed many previous appointments. He may ascribe an innocuous cause to his symptoms in the same way that the toilet seat takes the rap for VD. Denial may come in the form of increased activity or overindulgences, such as buying a whole new wardrobe.

The main considerations in dealing with a patient who denies his illness are patience, consistent support, not forcing the issue, and listing his assets. If the patient feels that his physician is supportive of him on every meeting, he develops a level of trust. It may happen in the first interchange; it may not happen until the third or fourth. It may not happen until several weeks or months later, although the latter eventuality is rare if the physician actively seeks to help the patient through this difficult time. What must happen is that, on every meeting, the physician indicates concern for the patient's well–being, acknowledges his feelings, and continues to be there.

THE ANGRY PATIENT

Some patients respond to the threat of hospitalization and surgical or extended medical procedures with anger. The anger may be directed to the physician who made the decision, to the world at large, to whatever fateful finger pointed at him, to his wife, or to his dog. It is often hidden, however. The patient who forgets appointments and loses things like his lab requests is suspect. If he suddenly begins to do such things after being informed that he needs to be hospitalized, anger is a good bet.

The attitude of the physician should be friendly but not ingratiating. Feeding this response with conciliatory gestures or speech fuels the fire. It is like saying, "Yes, I know I'm doing something bad, and I feel guilty about it," which would confirm the patient's anger and stamp it with official imprimatur. Silence is very helpful with the patient suspected of sitting on angry feelings. First, the physician can use silence; sitting quietly together for a few moments may encourage the patient to explore his feelings. Empathic statements should come next if silence doesn't elicit a response. "I get the feeling something is troubling you." If the patient does not respond then, a further statement of confrontation might be "It seems to me you are angry." Finally, this can be followed by "Look, we have to work together on this. I can't help you as much as I would like to unless you tell me what's bothering you."

The patient may not deal with any of these questions directly; since our society places a proscription upon anger, especially anger toward an authority figure which his physician represents, he is more likely to respond, "No, I'm not angry. I'm just wondering and doing a lot of thinking." His voice, posture, gesture, and expression will give him away, however. Even a controlled, steady voice coming from a composed body and inscrutable face is a giveaway in its awesome control and punctuated stresses. The physician responds to an objective, rational approach with "When you are doing this thinking, what are you thinking about?" or "What thoughts come to you?"

Primary in this interchange is the patient's exploration of his feelings and the open expression of his anger. If he has gone so far as to say "Why did it have to come at this time?", it is palliative for the physician to offer supportive restatements of empathy or feedback. "You're upset because it is happening to you now." or "You're upset because you have to come into the hospital at this time." Usually the patient will explain why. Whatever happens, when this point has been reached, the physician's most important task with the angry patient has been completed. He has been facilitated in expressing his feelings to the person who is responsible for his care.

THE DEMANDING PATIENT

There are some patients whom nothing will satisfy. They are demanding, harassing the staff and their own families, complaining loudly or in mute and suffering eloquence, annoying other patients, and generally driving everyone crazy. Their behavior is usually the result of lifelong habits of responding to stress and dealing with others. It is unlikely that a hospital stay will change them for the better in any significant degree. What is significant is that these patients will generate anger in the hospital staff, and it is important for those who care for them to be able to identify the feeling and deal with it.

Staff members usually enter the room of the demanding patient armed for battle, expecting the worst and getting it, performing tasks as quickly as possible, and resenting the time spent on him when it could be spent on more pleasant and "cooperative" patients. It is difficult for a staff member to discharge medical responsibilities when angry and frustrated. After facilitative techniques have been tried with no success it is appropriate to express feelings directly in this way: "When you behave in that manner, you make me angry." A matter-of-fact and simple statement does not reinforce irascible behavior. Allowing it to go unchallenged while responding with nonverbal cues of anger does. More importantly, the staff needs the opportunity to ventilate their own feelings and, having expressed themselves, will be more able to interact with this patient.

An aspect of human behavior that is often effective in this situation is shared laughter. If it can be managed, it serves to release tension and divert aggression. The joke and the moment of its delivery is up to the inventiveness and comic style of the physician. The following is offered as an example.

Patient: Doctor, I don't want the operation.

Physician: Very well, then, I'll see what I can do about touching up the x-rays.

THE DEPRESSED PATIENT

The depressed patient may show any or all of the following signs: psychomotor retardation, a tense, determined gait, a reluctance to say much, slowness to respond, listlessness, flat affect, or agitation. He may passively cooperate but display a disturbed sleeping pattern. The more severely depressed patient may refuse food and medication, may have discussed his intentions to commit suicide, or have confided to someone that he doesn't care about the outcome of surgery.

Some milder depressions are helped simply by getting planned surgery over with, but some clinicians believe that a seriously depressed patient may retard or hinder his own recovery and for this reason prefer to defer such cases until the patient has been treated for his depression. Surgery cannot always be deferred; however, there are ways in which depression and suicide intent can be uncovered, estimated, and dealt with by attending staff.

In most depressed hospitalized patients, there have been hints prior to surgery of discouragement and pessimism. This is seen more frequently in middle-aged and elderly people (54). Emotional resonance will often cue the physician into the patient's state. If the physician enters the hospital room and suddenly begins to feel down himself, it is a good bet that he is reflecting the feelings of the patient.

The physician should display quiet optimism in his voice and posture. Any false ebullience will be distrusted and resented. It is not a picnic and everyone knows it. If the patient has lived an active life, surgery threatens to change it to one of inactivity only if temporarily; depression caused by concern for loss of function or activity is a reactive depression, a response to the impending surgery. A reactive depression may be dealt with by talk more easily than an endogenous depression, one that is always more or less present in the personality of the patient. In dealing with presurgical depression it is most important for the physician to help his patient ventilate his feelings and to determine whether or not psychiatric help and/or tranquilization or antidepressant medication is warranted. Since the latter is slower acting, it is usually not chosen as a presurgical medication.

The depth of depression and suicide intent are the two things the physician hopes to determine. They do not necessarily go hand and hand but the presence of depression should always alert the physician to the possibility of suicide. High at risk in suicide is the older male who lives alone, and is physically sick. The patient is most likely to commit suicide when coming out of or going into a deep depression; he is more mobilized and has a higher energy level to carry out his intentions.

The depth of the patient's depression may be determined by questions regarding appetite, sleeping, and sexual activity. If these are altered, which they will be in mild depression, the next step is to determine the level of the patient's ability to enjoy life. For example, the physician may ask, "What do you imagine you'll do in the hospital while you're convalescing?" If the patient replies that he brought a few books, that he will watch TV, or that he expects people to visit him, he has the capacity for some enjoyment. If he replies that he will do nothing or that he looks forward to nothing, he is more seriously depressed. In the more intense depression, the capacity to enjoy life vanishes altogether. Nothing is good, and nothing will be good. To confirm a deep depression, the physician might ask the patient how he expects things to turn out. If he responds negatively, anticipating a bleak outcome, his depression is worse than if he concedes at least some hope.

Talking to a patient about suicide may be unpleasant, but it must be done in his interest. For the sake of safety, all depressed patients should be assumed to be suicidal; but more direct questions regarding it are best asked of the patient who has indicated that he is feeling low. It might begin like this:

Physician: How are things?

(Shrug.)

Physician: Feeling kind of down? You look unhappy to me. (Silence.) Are you?

(Nods.)

Physician: Things look hopeless?

Patient: Yes.

Physician: No point going on?

If these questions are answered in the affirmative, the physician tries to find out if the patient has formulated suicide plans. If plans have been made or thought of and if he has made moves away from other people, the risk is greater than if not. Questions such as "Have you thought of ending it all?" and "Ever think about taking your own life?" are appropriate.

If the patient responds in the negative to the question on taking his own life, the physician's task is to help him ventilate and express his depression. If he lives alone, he might be worried about who will help care for him. He may fear the change in life style that limited function will bring. All of these feelings must be dealt with and encouraged to surface. It will be helpful for this patient to know that his physician is concerned about his feelings as well as his body.

If the patient admits that he has considered suicide, the next question is *how*. "Do you think about how you might do it?" Some patients will admit to a stash of pills or ideas of gas, slashing their wrists, shooting their hearts; and others may say, "Never went that far." When the patient says that he had such thoughts but gave them up, the physician can further question to see if he really did give them up or if he is concealing his intentions. The appropriate question here is "Why did you give them up?" When the patient is able to supply an answer, there is a greater likelihood of sincerity.

HANDICAPPED PATIENT

This category will include patients who suffer limitations of a psychologic or a physical nature. There is a tendency to disregard the feelings and thoughts of the patient who is not playing with a full deck. Whether the patient's is schizophrenic, display symptoms of organicity, retardation, or suffers a sensory impairment, he is often perceived as less aware or less concerned than the "together" patient, who is more in touch with his world. This idea originates from the belief that the brain has room for only one event at a time and that mental disturbance of any kind fills up the convolutions so completely that there is no room for anything else. The truth is that mental dysfunction can coexist with anxiety and depression. The human brain has room for many simultaneous conditions.

ORGANIC BRAIN SYNDROME

The patient whose consciousness resembles alternating current and who exhibits memory impairment, disorientation, and impairment of judgment needs to be continually reoriented and reassured. The hospital, which is confusing to begin with, is even more so for the patient suffering OBS, who may have trouble remembering who he is and why he is there (46). The physician can introduce himself each time. "Hello, Mr. . . . , I'm Doctor . . . , we met yesterday (a few hours ago). Tonight you're going to . . . and tomorrow morning you will go down to surgery. . . . I'll meet you later in the recovery room (in your room). When a patient displays symptoms of OBS, it should be presumed that he does not remember, and every effort should be made to keep him oriented. Many of these patients become particularly confused at night when there is minimal stimuli, such as sounds and lights to cue their environment. It is helpful to keep night lights in their rooms, as well as reminders of time, such as large calendars, clocks, and newspapers.

Some hospital patients, many CVAs for example, have difficulty in comprehension and in communication. They may appear not to understand or they may be aphasic, unable to supply the right word for a thought. The dysarthric patient, with slurred speech and impaired melodic functions of pitch, stress, intonation, inflection, and intensity, may be equally unable to communicate effectively. Any patient who has difficulty expressing himself verbally may be encouraged to use another modality such as gesture, writing, or pointing. There is no magic in maintaining the spoken language; and if pointing is the only game in town, the physician plays it.

THE PARANOID PATIENT

The paranoid patient may be hostile and suspicious, regarding all intended procedures as an organized plot—not an attitude that endears them to medical personnel. Their delusions may make discriminating between a legitimate complaint and an invented one difficult. Swanson cites the case of the paranoid patient who thought the FBI had put something in his stomach and surprised the disbelieving staff with his stool and a real tapeworm (54).

The physician's method of communication with this patient is most safely one of firm and tactful noncommitment. He does not have to pretend to agree with the patient's delusions; but he doesn't have to shoot them down, either. It is tempting to try to pluck out irrational delusions with the tweezers of logic. It won't work. Instead, the patient may become angry and break off the relationship entirely. When the paranoid patient asserts a gross distortion of fact, particularly regarding the surgical staff and their intentions (such as accusing them of wanting his brain for the cyborg they are building in the basement), it is not necessary to appease him or to appear defensive in any way or to buy into his system. Responses should be couched in such a way that they are noncommittal while stating what the physician knows is fact. The physician's fact should not be given like slapping down the trump card (Aha! Got you!) but with gentle assertion. The sounds are as significant as the words.

The following example illustrates how the physician might handle the paranoid patient: "I know you're going to give my heart away." If the physician responds, "What makes you say that?", it would be perceived by this patient as a challenge. Instead, the physician might state, "I'm going to pinch your vein to keep the clot in place." If the patient persists, it is helpful at this point to say, "I know you believe what you are saying." In order to show him that he is not altogether wrong, it also would be helpful to address his anxiety: "It must be very troubling for you to have so many concerns." or "I can understand if you are concerned about surgery. I would like to talk about it with you."

The paranoid patient will not drop his delusions all at once. Like a first–time nudist, he will hold them up like a pair of pants until he is comfortable with those around him. The surgeon may never get to that point. The main thing is to be consistent, firm, supportive, nondefensive, and nonchallenging.

THE SCHIZOPHRENIC

The schizophrenic who is displaying florid symptoms can be worrisome both to the staff and to other patients. Someone who walks around tagging all parts of his body as if he were playing baseball or who makes a turban out of bandages can be distressing on a surgical floor, where everyone has enough to worry about. The problem with the bizarre and unpredictable schizophrenic is that, like any other patient, when he needs treatment, he also needs reassurance. He is generally unable to communicate well; it is part of his problem. For that reason his history will be a confusing one. Talking to this patient may be like trying to catch a mayfly in a fish net. Sometimes he can communicate clearly; and other times he tosses cryptic remarks like smoke bombs, leaving a trail of confusion behind him. That is deliberate. He is not trying to be difficult. He is only protecting himself from having anyone come too close. An effective procedure with the schizophrenic patient is to approach him tangentially and gently, at first perhaps just greeting him by name, giving the names of visiting staff members, and explaining routine examinations simply. He may or may not respond. If he remains mute, the physician can say, "I can see that you don't want to talk now. I'll see you at another time."

The schizophrenic often has a distorted sense of his body. When surgical or medical procedures are explained, they should be clearly stated. Drawings or even the patient's own picture, if one is available, can help to anchor him to reality. He enjoys the use of the metaphor and may say something like "I am dead." Challenging this remark with "If you're dead, how come you're breathing?" will not make him suddenly see the light and realize how crazy he's been. He will simply withdraw further. It would be more helpful for the physician to translate this metaphor into feedback that is a closer approximation of reality, such as "You feel like you are dead."

THE RETARDED PATIENT

Mental retardation is not a clear issue. Retardates cannot be subdivided into well-organized categories, since they differ not only from normals, but from each other. Estimations of an individual retardate's mental age and intellectual capacity are at best informed speculations. Generally, the behavior and speech of a retarded patient will be reminiscent of a similar pattern in children, and this patient or that patient is judged to be like a twelve-, five-, or two-year-old. The difficulty in treating them comes from the fact that they are not children of normal development, so they cannot be expected to behave fully like the developing child. They are not at the brink of the next stage but instead are an incomplete approximation of a single, permanent stage. The retarded patient has not abrogated his rights as a human being and is entitled to the same information and supports as everyone else. The physician should be able to make an approximate assessment of the patient's mental age and arrange his talk so that it is suitable for this age with one major distinction—many of the retarded are acutely aware of their handicap and are sensitive to condescension. When the physician translates, he speaks simply but does not use baby talk. "I am going to listen to your heart now." Body contact is an excellent means of communication. Touching, hugging, and calling him by his name all contribute to his feeling of security. The retarded patient, as all patients do, benefits from attention and encouragement.

The retarded patient can be prepared for surgery in the same way that other patients are. The largest body of retardates fall within the range that would understand an explanation at this level: "When you wake up, you'll have a tube in your arm that is attached to a bottle of sugar water. This is the way we feed people after an operation until they are ready to eat again." Substituting neutral words for more frightening ones, such as substituting "opening" for "cut" and "draining" for "bleeding," will diminish the retarded patient's fear. For example, the physician might say, "I'm going to make an opening so that I can take out some little stones that are hurting you. Then I will sew it up with small stitches, and you will have a bandage over the spot to keep it clean. It may drain a little" (43).

For the more severely retarded, who approximate a child of three or below, the most helpful message is that they will not be abandoned and that all the staff will continue to care for them. This patient has difficulty conceptualizing his internal body, so the physician can simply say, "I'm going to fix your stomach," and he should point to or touch the place. It is difficult to talk to this patient about future projections, so talk should be confined more to the present.

HEARING IMPAIRED

Of all the sensory handicaps, the loss of hearing is considered to be the most significant. Whether the loss is profound or moderate, it affects not only environmental information, but the ability to communicate. Hearing is a primary background sense, used constantly to monitor the landscape. It is so pervasive that it is possible to sit in a quiet house, absorbed in reading, and be startled to attention when the refrigerator shuts off. For those who are losing their hearing, the environment is going flat, like ginger ale that has been left to stand too long. Often the hearing impaired will say, "The world is dead."

What distinguishes the human being from other animals is his language. The more profoundly deaf are handicapped in their ability to communicate with hearing people. Their voice quality and articulation are poor, without melody, and it is difficult for most hearing people not accustomed to the sound of their speech to understand them. The patient who is hard-of-hearing does not have the overwhelming deficit in language skills suffered by the profoundly deaf but he is limited by what he can perceive.

For the hospitalized deaf patient, the loss of hearing does double damage. Because it limits environmental information, it increases his anxiety at the same time it prevents him from obtaining clear information that would alleviate it.

For some reason, the hospitalized deaf patient is often separated from his hearing aid, which is put into his nightstand or even, on occasion, put into an envelope with his watch. Anyone attempting to communicate with the hard-of-hearing patient must first give him back his hearing aid or at least put it within easy reach. The second step is to create the best possible conditions for lip-reading. We all lip-read; the deaf just rely upon it more heavily. (Actually, lip-reading is a misnomer—we read the whole face.) So that the patient can lip-read easily, the physician turns himself squarely in his patient's direction so that they face one another vis-a-vis, making sure that both faces are illuminated and clear of obstructions. It is not necessary to emphasize lip movements. Some people who talk to the deaf look like orangutangs chewing on bananas. If the physician speaks simply and directly to the patient in his normal way, the patient is more likely to understand.

Statements should be made with words that are short and simple. Instead of restating a thought in several different ways it is better to repeat exactly what was said before, especially if the message concerns significant details. Patients with a hearing loss can be cued into topics by pointing to body parts that are being discussed or by using visual aids such as clocks or instruments, in the same way a stewardess gives passengers instructions on how to put on a life vest. "You will have a drain," repeated and accompanied by a visual cue, is less likely to be understood as "You will have a drink."

Those whose hearing loss dates back to their early development have difficulty understanding abstract language. When speaking to a patient with this communication problem, it helps to relate matters to him in specific, concrete terms. For example, if the patient were to ask, "How long will I be sick?", he should not be told, "The disease has to run its course." This response is an abstraction based on metaphorical construction. It is more meaningful to him to respond concretely, "You will be feeling better in about ____ days/weeks."

If the deaf patient is able to speak, it is necessary and helpful to obtain feedback from him, such as "Tell me about tomorrow" and "What is it that I will do?" If the patient is not understood, it is reasonable to tell him so and ask him to repeat what he is trying to say.

When the deaf patient can neither speak nor read lips, someone on the staff who can understand sign language is invaluable. If no such person is available, the physician can esort to drawings and writing. In the latter contingency, the patient should have a slate with an eraser and chalk or a pad and pencil in his room as close–at–hand as his drinking cup.

Finally, because of the lack of background sense, the deaf are sometimes paranoid about what is happening to them, especially what other people are saying. The techniques for dealing with the paranoid patient also apply in this situation.

SIGHT IMPAIRED

While the blind patient does not have the problems of communication experienced by the deaf patient, his disability also limits his environmental stimuli and creates problems peculiar to the blind experience.

Sighted people have a tendency to generalize blindness to other handicaps. They often behave as if the blind were deaf, shouting at them as if noise would influence the optic nerve, or speaking in their presence as if they could not hear. Some confuse sight disability with intellectual function. It is an assault on the integrity of a blind person who has achieved independence to be treated as if he were incompetent. There are many medical aids such as thermometers and insulin syringes for the blind which imply that they are entirely capable of managing self-care. If a blind patient has been successfully caring for himself, the physician may safely assume that he can wrap his own Ace bandage.

When speaking to the blind, the physician will find that he achieves the most satisfactory results by using his normal tone of voice. Since nonverbal cues are missing from the interaction, it is essential to give and obtain constant feedback; there must be more feedback in an interaction with a blind patient than in any other exchange in order to insure clarity.

The lack of eye contact by which human beings stay in touch may be compensated for by physical touching on the hand, arm, or shoulder. Touching is done after verbal contact has been established, however. It can be terrifying for a blind person to be grabbed by someone for whom he is unprepared, much less stabbed in the finger for a blood sample without preparation.

The blind patient orients himself by sound, and the new sounds of the hospital such as carts, hushed voices, running footsteps, public address systems, janitors who mop the floor and don't speak, and the moans of other patients can be frightening. All sounds outside his door should be explained to him. "In the morning we have rounds, and you will hear a lot of people coming through here. Later, lab technicians come through with their carts; and after that, people from the kitchen will come in with trays for lunch."

When orienting this patient to his hospital room, he must be introduced to his new space. It is helpful to describe who may be in the bed or beds next to him and to allow him to explore his space, including the room, the door, the bathroom, the

bedpan, the call button, and the hall. If the blind patient is to be immobilized, the restriction on his already limited perceptual space will be more significant for him than for any other patient. For this reason, he requires a great deal of touch, which represents to him not only care and contact but additional environmental stimuli. Each time the physician enters the room, he introduces himself and reestablishes physical contact.

For the patient who experiences temporary visual impairment such as the patient whose eyes are bandaged after ocular surgery or one whose visual field is cut as a result of a disease process like CVA, the same principles of communication apply: touch, description, orientation, and frequent feedback. Additionally, it helps to place the patient experiencing a visual field cut so that his sighted side faces other people. It does him no good to be placed with his seeing side facing a wall.

PROCEDURAL PREPARATION

EXPECTATIONS

All patients respond well to information. Everyone who talks to the patient has the opportunity to explain procedures to him, including when surgery has been scheduled, medications, food and liquid restrictions, the need to remove nail polish, jewelry, hairpins, dentures, makeup, the possibility of a hypodermic needle before surgery, and how he will wake up in the recovery room.

He should be given thorough explanations of diagnostic procedures. An example is the patient who will have closed kidney biopsy.

Patient: You mean I'll be awake?

Physician: Yes, but you'll be given a local anesthetic so that the area will be numbed. You won't feel any pain, just pressure which may be uncomfortable.

Patient: How much are you taking out?

Physician: Just a small piece, like a grain of rice.

Patient: That sounds small enough.

Physician: Just enough for us to have something to stick under the microscope. When you go back to your room, you'll rest on your back for about 24 hours.

Patient: Twenty-four hours! I'll go crazy!

Physician: I can understand your feeling annoyed about being still for so long, but you'll get a lot of action. They'll be taking your blood pressure, your temperature, and your pulse frequently—they'll be collecting all your urine. You'll have intravenous feeding for a few hours, then you'll be switched to regular meals.

The anesthetist introduces himself and explains what he will do and when. He explains how the patient will feel; and, most important, he reassures the patient that he will not wake up in the middle of everything. Many patients fear that they will feel the knife or that they will awake prematurely. Patients who have been prepared accept anesthetics more easily than those patients who have not.

The patient is prepared for the temporary loss of independence when the anesthetist says, "I will do your breathing for you." The ability to breathe is a primitive and basic accomplishment, being the very first independent thing the newborn does. Disruption of breathing as a result of crying, laughing, coughing, choking, hiccuping, swallowing and getting slammed in the solar plexus can be frightening. When the anesthesiologist reassures the patient that he doesn't have to worry anymore about doing his best rehearsed number, he should be prepared to explain just how he plans to breathe for the patient to alleviate the patient's fears and misunderstandings. The patient knows he has done a good job breathing. He needs a lot of assurances that the anesthesiologist can do it as well as he did.

INCLUDING THE FAMILY

The patient's family should not be left out of presurgical preparation. They tend to get anxious when the operation takes a long time and judge the seriousness of the operation based on some rule of thumb that says one hour, fine, two hours, trouble, and over three hours, big trouble. The family should be told that the patient may be in the operating room for a long time because he is sent there in advance of the actual operation, that the preparations of the anesthesiologist may take from one half to one hour, that a preceding case may upset the surgeon's schedule, and that the patient is kept on the operating floor or in the recovery room until he has come out of the anesthesia and his signs show some stability.

Patient's families also need to be informed of what to expect when they see the patient immediately after surgery. Suction bottles, nasal tubes, airways, oxygen tents, and tracheotomy tubes should be anticipated as well as a groggy patient who doesn't look too good. Unprepared families tend to wail and whisper in hallways and are often heard by the subject in question, who understandably could respond negatively to such hints about his condition.

RECOVERY ROOM

After surgery the patient in the recovery room is remarkably responsive to familiar faces. He can be aroused easily by calling his name, by asking him to wake up, and by reassuring him that it is all over and that everything is all right. This is the time when the surgeon may keep his appointment with the patient. "Remember I said we would meet." or "I see you kept our appointment." or "I'm Doctor. . . . , we said we would meet here in the recovery room. The operation is over. You came through very well." The meeting cannot be more involved than that since the patient, now satisfied, will probably turn over and go back to sleep. If he has been given a local or regional anesthetic, he needs reassurance that sensation and movement will return. The recovery room is also an appropriate time and place to reorient the patient and remind him who he is, where he is, and what time of day it is.

ROUNDS

Teaching rounds are an integral part of traditional medical education. Walking from one bed to the next and reviewing each patient's care and progress provides *in vivo* opportunity to experience the gamut of surgical and medical problems encountered in the hospital. If done with consideration for the patient, they are not only a learning experience for the staff but an opportunity for the patient to receive concerned attention. It may be one of the few times someone who is interested in his condition comes to see him. When the senior house officer or private physician introduces the junior staff to the patient and perhaps indicates in what way they will be interacting with the patient, he is saying in effect that

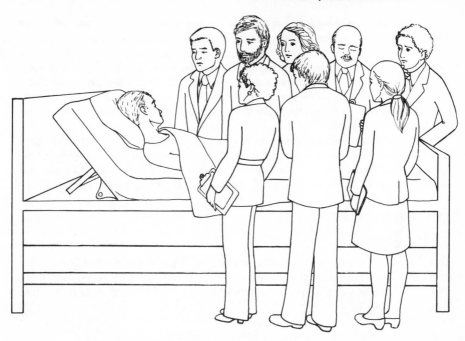

here is a team of professionals interested in his care. This is a significant fact to anyone from a society that measures value in HP and BTU. The manner in which the senior officer interacts with each patient provides the model for the junior staff. Patients look forward to rounds if they are accorded respect and dignity. Each one should be included in rounds by being greeted by name and by having conversation directed to him. All discussions about his case which could be a cause for concern, including treatment options, diagnostic options, and prognosis should be deferred until the tour has left the vicinity.

Everyone thinks of his own case as pretty special. It can be shattering to think that one's suffering, indignities, or discomfort is merely routine. A lofty hand waved at the patient who has had a hemorrhoidectomy with a cursory "Hemorrhoids" tossed in his direction as the group moves on is deflating. The very least the tour guide can say is, "Now *that's* a hemorrhoidectomy!" Rejecting certain patients as uninteresting implies that rounds are intended to deal with diseases, not people.

Some patients who have particularly interesting physical signs may be seen a second time by some group members who return to his bedside. There is a problem inherent in this feature. When attention is called to the pathology of one's body, it says in effect, "Now that you're sick you have something of value." and reinforces in the patient the benefits of infirmity. In order to counteract the disease orientation of rounds, it helps for round members to engage in conversation with patients on some level other than sickness and disease.

The effects of teaching rounds on hospitalized patients have been the object of recent studies (23, 26). The varying ranks and grades who follow the teaching staff from bed to bed are often a depressing flock. Patients scan facial expressions and listen to the remarks of these tour members for cues of any kind—"Are they looking at me? Are they worried about me? Are they puzzled or angry?"—and often don't have to strain too hard to get clear messages, usually distressing ones. One study reports the following interaction which occurred within earshot of a patient: "Have you had experiences with this kind of case, Doctor?" "I've lost one." One young patient who had had cardiac surgery overheard her physician state, "Well, there is nothing more we can do for her." He meant that all diagnostic tests had been carried out, but the youngster interpreted the remark to mean her condition was hopeless.

Patients also respond negatively to disagreement. Indeed, the democratic process of six votes for, two votes against, and two abstaining can be anxiety-provoking. It means that there is a chance that an ill-qualified dark horse can win and determine policy, which may or may not be in the patient's best interest.

INTENSIVE CARE UNIT

ATMOSPHERE

The shiny new intensive care units bristling with the machinery of life for the critically ill and injured, which have proliferated in the past 15 years, have been of unquestionable value to the thousands who have been treated in their facilities.

Organ support systems, monitors, and devices for inobtrusive measurement of a variety of physiological variables function as electronic umbilici, binding the tenuous to his heart beat.

The atmosphere of the intensive care unit is simultaneously highly personal and impersonal. The patient's attachment to technical apparatus which records and regulates every twitch, his constant surveillance under an appraising and evaluating medical team, and the audience of physicians and nurses at his bedside make his care much more personal than that of any other hospital patient. Paradoxically, it is this concentrated focus and the machinery which makes it possible that creates for many intensive care unit patients an impersonal environment in which they experience a host of emotional difficulties, ranging from frank psychotic symptoms to a simple feeling of anonymity. Monitors, respirators, suction devices, and other bedside equipment; glaring lights, beeps and oscillations; the hushed tones and scurrying of personnel; telephones ringing at the central station, the paging intercom; the starkness and sterility of the room; the turmoil of recurring emergency activities; and tubes in every available orifice provide ample ground upon which this variety of feelings can develop (3).

PATIENT RESPONSE

Delirium, hallucinations, paranoia, anxiety and depression, disturbances of orientation, memory, thought, judgment, and perception represent part of the catalogue of symptomatology which is related to the intensive care syndrome (38). They are not seen in all intensive care patients; there are many factors which determine how and if they manifest themselves (27).

The first factor is the patient himself—his age, level of competence, emotional state, characteristic modes of dealing with stress and novelty, his support systems, his family's response to his illness, and his own attitude toward illness. Postanesthetic excitement, for example, is higher in a younger patient, while many elderly patients respond to a minimal degree of sensory disruption with disorientation and hallucinations. Some patients, threatened with the dependency of immobilization, may become irascible and make a behavioral statement that says they are not going to take this lying down!

Patients display two responses to serious illness: passivity or denial. Passivity takes over when denial has failed, when the patient can no longer disavow the oscillation he hears as anything but an electronic translation of his heartbeat.

In no other clinical experience is it so apparent that one is sick. If health can be defined as the lack of awareness of the body, then being in the ICU is the apogee of illness, since one is so acutely aware of his body. The real criterion of illness for most people is being reduced to inactivity, not pain (20). The patient in the ICU does not participate freely, he has no controls, he simply undergoes the experience. This inactivity, that is underscored by the fact that he usually cannot attend his own bodily functions unaided, leads to a change in relations with other people. He is the recipient; he can give nothing. All of the other roles which defined him have vanished, and in their place is the PATIENT.

The world of health is a social world. In the world of illness, the individual is defined not by what he does but by what he doesn't do, his inactivity and his lack of participation in the social world. The inactivity, passivity, dependence, and interruption of social relations in the serious illness experience cause a sense of personal annihilation, which alone is enough to create depression and anxiety.

The illness experience contains other factors which determine who might have emotional difficulties in the ICU and how they will be manifested. The disease process and the mode of treatment are additional variables that affect a patient's response in the ICU. Patients facing pain or disfigurement show a high incidence of postanesthetic excitement. Some patients faced with the monotony of dialysis have behaved in ways that may best be described as self-destructive. Cardiac surgery, being dangerous and elective, has been followed by a high incidence of delirium, memory loss, impaired judgment, disorientation, and hallucinations (5, 29). On the other hand, in coronary units delirium is rarely mentioned; *but* while most patients find the atmosphere reassuring rather than menacing, some may experience depression and distress because of sensory monotony and sleep deprivation. It has been found that postcardiotomy delirium is the result of factors peculiar to heart surgery. The incidence of psychiatric symptoms following lung surgery, for example, is much lower. Additionally, there is a wide spectrum of patients who are threatened in the ICU, including those who suffer organ failure, shock, anemia, toxemia, and fever, all of which could account for differences in cognitive function.

Being isolated in the unfamiliar environment of the ICU, which is usually austere and windowless, followed by lying prone, being under sedation and often deprived of sleep, experiencing pain and discomfort, limited to a visual field of white acoustical ceiling tile, and surrounded by equipment whose function may not be fully understood is at best more than enough to induce perceptual distortion, depression, or anxiety in a patient certain procedures which inhibit communication add to perceptual distortion. After eye surgery, for example if the patient's eyes are bandaged, his ability to communicate his distress is limited to verbal expression. A patient using the artificial ventilation of certain respirators is deprived of the ability to fluently express negative feelings. Inhibition restricts cathartic outlet for the experience, and very often these patients display marked dependence and depression.

Many of the experiences in the ICU resemble the Communist techniques of "brainwashing" seen in the Korean war (13). The techniques produced "debility, dependency, and dread," achieved through a combination of physical pain, disease, sleep deprivation, sensory monotony, isolation, and the inability to satisfy the demands of the interrogators. While the patient does not have to sign any confessions, he is isolated, often in pain, and subject to sensory and sleep disturbance.

Inadequate sensory stimulation, sleep deprivation, and isolation have been the subjects of laboratory experimentation in recent years. It is no secret that under isolated conditions, reduced sensory input, and sleep loss, healthy individuals will develop psychopathological reactions. Hallucinatory experiences may be induced through reduced sensory input without isolation. Sometimes reduction of motor movement alone is sufficient to produce hallucinatory experiences. (29, 41) The immobilized patient may have a reduction in proprioceptive feedback which his reticular activating system, comparable to an alarm, may need to determine how much alertness and orientation he requires.

As far back as the Spanish Inquisition, sleep deprivation was used to impair personality function. Sleep deprivation studies have demonstrated experimentally induced hallucinations, decreases in sensory acuity, impairments in the ability to memorize, behavioral changes such as irritability, feelings of persecution, and periods of disorientation and misperception (14). Sleep deprivation has been found to lead to chemical reactions that may be related to basic processes in schizophrenia. It is believed that certain types of physiologic activity occur during REM sleep, and a deprivation of REM sleep can lead to a hyperresponse state (accelerated heart rate, activity, etc.). Deep sleep deprivation can lead to a hyporesponse state marked by increased physical complaints and withdrawal (57).

The central nervous system, which is responsible for the coordination of other body systems, affects the precarious balance of the severely ill. Data from studies of patients undergoing cardiac surgery suggest that the patient's emotional well-being may be statistically significant to survival rates during the postoperative period. (Blachly reports that anxious, depressed, and paranoid patients have a higher mortality rate [5].) While it may not be possible to eliminate completely the psychopathological manifestations seen in the ICU, it is possible for medical personnel to mitigate them and give the individual fighting for his life a thumb on the scale (1).

COUNTERATTACK

First, the patient must be informed of postoperative phases and of ICU practices in clear and simple terms. He should be told that he may experience some monotony, that he will be in bright lights, and that he will see and hear new sights and sounds. He might be warned that if he experiences some confusion, it is a transitory experience. If his admission to the ICU is planned, he may be introduced to the unit itself, shown the life-supporting equipment such as high humidity oxygen aparatus, the IPPB, drainage tubes, indwelling catheters, and monitoring devices, and perhaps meet with some of the staff that will be caring for him. Additionally, he may be given information on what he will be given to relieve his pain, what he can expect in the way of ambulation, and a demonstration of range of motion and deep breathing exercises. His family should be included in the explanatory procedures, since their fearful response to seeing him connected to and sustained by machinery can be contagious. When a patient is marshaling all his recuperative forces, he doesn't need the negative influence of a terrified and bewildered family.

Brief and frequent mental status assessments should be part of routine care in the ICU. In that way any deterioration in attention, concentration, orientation, and recent memory may be corrected by appropriate therapy. Simple assessment includes asking the patient to name objects and state their function. A more complex examination includes an evaluation of his ability to abstract. Mental status questions are best when they are appropriate to the situation. Asking an intubated patient what is the relationship between apples and pears is enough to make him pull out the tubes. A more relevant question might be what he thinks is the relationship between him and his cannula.

The patient in intensive care should have continual human contact. When carrying out physical tasks, every member of the team can demonstrate "emotional presence," an awareness of the patient as a responsive and valuable human being, by speaking to him while touching him and explaining what is being done, even if the patient appears unaware. This would mean addressing, for example, a patient undergoing dialysis who might display the mental confusion often associated with uremia and seem to be out of touch. Familiar faces, the continued interest of the staff, and reassuring words maintain this emotional presence and assure the patient of his social function. Such interaction should be regular and frequent, even if brief. A physician who suffered cardiac arrest placed special value on contact with other human beings during the first 24 hours after his arrest.

Sensory disruption of light and sound, including the extremes of deprivation and bombardment can be survived if sensory experience of the skin is maintained (60). Not just a protective covering or a thermal regulator, the skin is a panoramic receptor providing continual centripetal information. Touch, which binds and orients one to the immediate, is not only reminiscent of earlier care giving but as a sensory stimulus, can be palliative (18, 22).

The paucity of touch is not a problem in the ICU. Clinical personnel are almost always at the patient's bedside making tactual contact in some way. It is not touch itself but the patient's perception of it which may be important. Lynch and his associates gathered descriptive clinical data in a study on humans which replicated more precisely controlled animal studies of the palliative effects of touch. They found that human contact can have major effects on cardiac function (31, 33, 34, 35, 36). In one study on the effects of human contact on the cardiac responses of patients in a coronary care unit, even the simple act of taking a pulse produced significant change in heart rate and frequency of ectopic beats. In another study of curarized patients in a shock-trauma unit, in whom heart rate change could be observed independently of motor activity, data infer that the heart rate and rhythm were altered by such human interaction as taking the patient's hand (32).

Provisions should be made for increased sensory input. Windows (Wilson demonstrated that delirium was three times higher in windowless rooms than in rooms with windows), clocks, and calendars; familiar bedside objects such as radios and family photos; projected ceiling images if the patient must lie prone; and personalized conversation from attending staff all increase meaningful sensory input to the patient and help him make sense out of his environment (58).

The patient in an ICU will have a host of feelings, including helplessness, dependency, and anger. He may feel superfluous and ineffectual in the management of his vital functions, which indeed he often is. He may even experience anxiety at being transferred out of the ICU (56). Whatever his feeling, he will need an opportunity to express it. It was found that patients in chronic dialysis made a quicker recovery if they were able to verbalize their problems rather than somaticize their feelings (59). Helping the patient express feelings about his experience confirms his value, provides relief from tension, and creates an optimum climate for his recovery.

GENERAL HOSPITAL PATIENT

RECOVERY EXPERIENCE

When the general hospital patient gradually returns to consciousness, he finds that he is not just lying in bed but that he is often attached to all kinds of tubes. He may be ringed by electronic and mechanical gadgets, some of whom beep and make other wierd and rhythmic sounds accompanied by flashing lights. He experiences pain and other discomforts; and if this assault upon his integrity is not enough, he is dependent—forced back into infancy despite his accumulation of marks and rings to indicate his adulthood. Since pain is managed with medication, it is unnecessary to go into a discussion of pain except to say that pain should be anticipated so that the patient does not feel helpless in its path. There is nothing more debilitating to any patient than to feel vulnerable in the face of the pain insult and then have to beg for its alleviation.

Egbert relates how patients were instructed in the management of pain following abdominal surgery (9). They were told that pain was caused by straining the wound and that they had to be careful when they moved the site of surgery. If they had to take a deep breath, they were told to relax their abdominal wall and breathe in slowly. They were also advised to try and turn themselves; some were taught how to pull themselves up with an overhanging bar. Both of these procedures gave the patients control over the circumstance of their pain. Finally, they were told that when they had to cough, they were simply to grit their teeth, hold the dressing, and do it, similar to the instructions given to paratroopers and lake swimmers.

Whether in the surgical, medical, or intensive care service, for the patient the hospital is a subjective experience which reinforces the reality of illness. Illness is differentiated from good health by 4 parameters: special attention, inactivity, changes in relations with other people, and an awareness of one's body. Attentions of staff legitimize the idea of illness. If the patient is inclined to think of himself as a sick person, he adopts the role more easily than one who considers himself healthy (39, 47).

Essential interruption of activities and being reduced to immobility is for most people the real criterion of illness, even more important than pain (20). Being reduced to inactivity causes the patient to see a disintegration of the tasks and responsibilities which constitute his role and define his position in society. He is excluded from the everyday world. The world of health is a social world. The world of illness is the world of the isolated. The person who is ill is relieved of social demands but also risks being excluded from them.

Changes in his relations with other people also determine whether the individual regards himself as healthy or ill. All of the social interactions that define him have been frozen or altered. In their place is a radical shift in the way others respond to him. Some are angry, some are anxious, some are overhearty, some are sad, and some sit on the edge of his bed, eating all his candy and telling him how well he looks.

Finally, there is the patient's overwhelming awareness of his body. Health is having silent organs. Conversely, illness is an attention to the body, its function, and its parts. A hospital patient is constantly made keenly aware of his body and everything that is happening to it through the attentions of others and through his

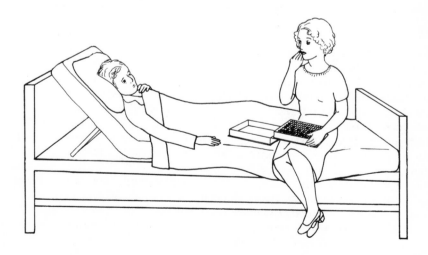

own discomforts. He is concerned with what's going in, what's going out, what works, what hurts, and what his temperature is.

Patients use 4 criteria to gauge the seriousness of their illness: its association with the danger of dying, its duration, its reversibility, and its aftereffects—even minor ones. Therefore, immobility, attention, and changes in social relations, combined with a fresh incision or a decline in function, are enough to cause the patient to consider himself seriously ill.

Inactivity destroys ties with other people. The patient must be assured of the permanence of his social function. One way to do this is to assure him of his individual worth. Talking to him and listening to him, even in brief interchanges, fulfills this need. Anyone who enters his room should call him by name and comment on something about him or on something near him. If there is an option concerning any procedure in which medical opinion is not necessary, his opinion should be sought (55). "I can make a butterfly or a plain bandage, Mr. Cole. Which do you prefer?" When he is feeling better and walking about, he might be encouraged to visit other patients on the floor who have no visitors.

Dependence in the hospital setting may result in feelings of annihilation. The patient must learn that, temporarily, dependence is all right. Our culture has a bias against dependence. We favor stalwart self-reliance for, after all, didn't it cause us to navigate rivers, break through forests, and survive hard winters on the prairies? We heard during childhood, "Don't be a baby." or "Grow up." Illness reverses all of those admonitions. One of the ways to help the patient accept dependence is to accord him dignity and self-esteem through verbal and nonverbal means. This begins early in the game. When orderlies wheel patients through the hospital as if they were handling push carts, it does nothing for the patient's feelings of dignity. During the period of dependence, the physician can focus on near future times when the patient will be less dependent and spell out for him how this present state will change to one of independence. Also, it is helpful to get the patient to ventilate his feelings about being dependent, as well as any previous immobilizations.

The patient must adjust and adapt to the new restraint and restriction of activities. He must reorganize his territory, since his space changes along with self-image, when he sees the world from a hospital bed. He learns the integrity of new space. The physician may suggest that this temporary immobilization is a good time to take a little freedom from the obligations of life and pamper oneself. Illness can be a liberating experience in that now the patient can pursue intellectual activities, enjoy periods of solitude, make the most of the privileges of the invalid, and be just plain irresponsible. This is hard to manage when the work ethic is so prominent a part of our culture. All it really needs is official sanction. "Even if you hadn't come into the hospital, I would have wanted you to take off a few weeks and do nothing." Doctor's orders are as good as a papal dispensation.

Before the patient can participate in his cure through a fight, he must accept his illness. Then his relations with his physician become a form of cooperation or exchange; and strict, passive obedience is rejected in favor of a more equal interchange. To this end, the patient has to be kept informed so that their footing is more equal.

People thrive on hope. It can be symbolized by family pictures; by personal effects of a project such as a sales campaign, blueprints, or a manuscript; or by examples of a hobby such as plants and trophies.

Many people believe that each person has a fixed amount of energy and that the subtraction of any part of the body lessens that energy, which now must be carefully husbanded. The patient needs information. He must be educated daily in what to expect. If orientation is a problem, he should be reminded daily of what to expect, as well as where he is, why he is there, and what is happening to him. Protracted invalidism is caused by a sense of body weakness and fragility, erroneous notions of physiology, and the inhibition of activity (53). The patient believes that his energy is like money, and he doesn't want to overdraw his account.

The general hospital patient, like the patient in the ICU, is suffering from sensory deprivation. Meaningful sensory input from the staff must substitute for the sensory stimulation he lacks. This requires inventiveness and consideration on the part of the staff. Conversation, the loan of a small radio, clocks, calendars, books, newspapers, objects to break up a blank wall, occasionally changed mobiles strung over the patient who must lie prone, the use of overhead projectors for books, pictures, etc. are preferable to counting acoustical tile. Touch is a significant addition to the experience of the bedridden patient. Light touchings, pats, and strokings are part of the care-giving picture—not prolonged massage—just contact. The patient cannot be overwhelmed with touch; he is reorganizing his territory. The physician has to read him for cues. If he pulls away or seems to cringe, then it is not advisable. Taking his pulse may be enough.

Beginning with brushing his own teeth, the patient needs to be returned to activity as soon as possible. He can discuss with the physician how his activity is going to change temporarily but what he *can* do should be emphasized. The more he does, the less likely it is he will regard himself as an invalid. He should be encouraged to do something, if only to keep a daily log of subjective experience, which his physician can share at a later time. These often can be encouraging references if they catalogue improvement.

IMAGE IMPAIRMENT

Problems are not always resolved. Many patients, as a result of surgery, pathology, accident, chemotherapy, or other procedures, experience an impairment of their image. The social creation that is body image, basic to identity, may have been altered. Whether from an arterial shunt, an amputation, the loss of function of a body part, a contracture from a burn, a moon face from steroids, or even from a vasectomy performed in an office the patient who has experienced image impairment requires a good deal more from his attending physicians than physical care. The physician's task with the patient who has had image impairment is to help him go through grief, rage, bewilderment, denial, and shame. Grief and rage are often difficult for the physician, since either interchange can be highly charged emotionally as well as for the patient whose sickness may have reduced his energy for coping with or expressing emotional problems (9, 25).

Our culture places high values upon youth, wholeness, normality, attractiveness, and success. An impaired image may make the patient feel he bears a stigma, with concomitant feelings of shame and guilt at being the marked and the outcast. He may consider himself part of a new minority. Telling the patient that no one will see the new site, that he should be glad to be alive, or that things will look rosier later are useless. They don't deal with the immediate problem, which is the patient's feeling of worthlessness, of being set apart from the others, of being less valued, and of feeling shame.

Characteristic reactions of the patient who is ashamed are: complete or partial withdrawal from visual contact, sudden change in skin color, nervous physical gestures, speech difficulties, or hand to mouth movements. This patient may say things like "I'm all washed up," "I'm no good," or "I don't want to be a burden."

He may not allow anyone to look at the site of external impairment and look away himself when being attended to.

The silent patient may defend against the experience with denial through an outright avoidance of the subject or through depersonalization, in which he feels as if he were floating over the scene, a kind of disembodied spectator. Denial, one of the ways the body attempts to maintain integrity, is seen in the phantom experience, chiefly represented by tactile, thermal, optic, and kinesthetic sensations, of, for example, the amputee who still feels his severed limb. Some patients rebel futiley—they may be demanding, self-centered, child-like, hearing only what they want to hear. Others become falsely cheerful and courageous.

Passivity may replace denial. To be entirely passive is to take no part at all. Denial may be made by the patient's family and friends, who will minimize his symptoms to cheer him up and to make him closer to normal in their own eyes. The passive patient may put forth *no* effort to deny or to affirm anything.

Anger or rage may follow passivity, denial, grief, or may never appear. The angry patient may make such statements as "Why me?" or "It's not fair." He may refuse food and speak rudely to those around him in an impotent rage borne of frustration and a sense of great injustice. If anger is suspected, the physician may confront the patient in this way: "It seems to me you are very angry about all this." He will likely get, "You bet I'm angry!" or "Wouldn't you be angry?" or "What the hell good does it do to be angry?"

Grief is a period of mourning for that which is lost. If we accept that the whole body is beautiful, then it follows that a loss of a part or function of that body is sad. When the patient is creeping through the tunnel of emotional reorganization, one of the way stations he must pass in order to come out the other end is grief. It is the forerunner of coping with the change. Many health professionals feel inadequate when faced with a grieving patient and ask, "What can I possibly tell him?" The important factor is not what to tell the patient but what the patient is allowed to tell the professional. No word can make what was lost reappear or return to function. The patient needs to be able to express his loss and have someone who cares for him respond with empathy. In time, the image change becomes familiar, and he learns to accept it.

COMMUNICATION WITH THE IMAGE IMPAIRED PATIENT

Successful interaction with a patient who has undergone image impairment includes being available, listening, sustaining, facilitating the ventilation of feelings, displaying understanding, discussing the reality of the situation, and offering hope (4, 6, 8, 28, 45).

The patient with image impairment may test significant persons. He seeks to learn how he appears to others and may ask, "How have I changed?" He usually begins with the physician, by asking, "How does it look to you?" The translation may be "I don't know if I'm as attractive as I once was. What do you think?" Another test is to make references to the behavior of others. ("Mrs. Smirley won't do her exercises.") What is sought, is approval by comparison. "I wish Mrs. Smirley took care of herself as well as you do." The questions are designed to elicit positive and hopeful answers. When the patient looks for hope, he is occupied with his cure. This new occupation requires energy, activity, and good spirits and should be reinforced since it makes adjustment possible.

Patient advocacy groups, organizations of former patients with similar surgical or medical experiences, can be very supportive to the disabled patient who is undergoing rehabilitation. People who have had amputations, laryngectomies, mastectomies, or colostomies meet with the patient, discuss experiences, and share in the fight for rehabilitation.

If the patient has been given a realistic appraisal of his condition all along, including expectations, possibilities, and alternatives, discussion of these things prior to his discharge from the hospital will be quite natural. It is similar to all information giving in that the information is given simply, a little at a time, in the patient's language, and with feedback built in.

Patients without a disfiguring external impairment are candidates for chronic invalidism as much as those who have suffered an obvious alteration. An example is the patient who has suffered a myocardial infarction, has had complete rest for several weeks, who may have been told that his disease was similar to a wound in his heart, and who now prepares to go home. Telling him that he may resume normal living does not guarantee that he will do it. He is afraid. The physician needs to increase his confidence so that he does not become a cardiac invalid. Together they analyze his work and home situation, breaking down all he does into components which they will discuss. Walking the distance to the bus, how to take stairs, optimal positions for sexual intercourse, lifting objects, and stopping activities before he becomes fatigued are discussed and explored. The following is an example of this patient ventilating the fact that he is afraid to move.

Patient: I'm afraid to leave the hospital.
Physician: Why is that? What do you think will happen?
Patient: I don't know.
Physician: What do you think of when you get afraid?
Patient: This wound in my heart.
Physician: How do you see it in your mind's eye?
Patient: Like a bullet hole.
Physician: Actually it looks something like this—it's being crisscrossed with scar tissue more and more all the time.
Patient: Like reweaving.
Physician: Something like that.
Patient: But I still have to protect it. . . .
Physician: How do you think you have to protect it?
Patient: Well, I'm very careful, as you know. I'm careful what I do, even what I think about. When my wife comes in, I don't let her aggravate me; and I don't sleep on that side.
Physician: So you've really been protecting it.
Patient: Yeh.
Physician: That must be a heavy responsibility for you, to always have to think about your heart.
Patient: It sure is.
Physician: Well, I think about it too. And I am confident that it is more than strong enough for what you are going to do; and you can sleep on any side you like, you know. Your heart is well protected by your bone structure. You can't hurt it, your ribs act as a shield; it doesn't matter where you sleep.
Patient: What if I turn over suddenly?
Physician: Show me.
Patient: I can't.
Physician: It's O.K. I want to see what you mean.
Patient: All right, like this.

Physician: You can fall on your chest, and you couldn't hurt your heart. Turning over in bed isn't going to make one bit of difference.

Patient: What's going to happen when I get home?

Physician: What do you mean?

Patient: Well, I'm always out of breath. How am I going to climb stairs?

Physician: Like everything else that you do, gradually, in slow, easy stages. If you climb and you get out of breath, you stop and wait till you can breathe easily again. Then you take a few more stairs.

Patient: What about driving my car?

Physician: Are you close to public transportation?

Patient: Yes.

Physician: Why not use that for a while?

Patient: I guess I could.

Physician: How far are you from the bus stop?

Patient: About two blocks.

Physician: How long did it take you to walk two blocks?

Patient: Two minutes. That was before. I could probably do it now in ten. Slow and easy, like a turtle.

Physician: Later you can try again for 2 minutes.

Patient: What if I don't make it?

Physician: What do you mean?

Patient: What if I get out of breath in the middle and can't go on?

Physician: Then you stop. You go into a house or a store, and you say, "I would like to sit down a minute." Then when you're rested, you either go on to the bus stop or you go home.

Patient: What if there's no one to let me in?

Physician: Then you lean against the building or you sit down on the curb, and you wait until you're comfortable. It sounds to me that you're really worried about going home.

Patient: Yes. Everything's changed!

Physician: Yes, there has been a change. You'll never be exactly the same. Each day you are a little different from the day before. But even if you had never had any trouble with your heart, you would change.

The physician has allowed him to ventilate his concerns; has provided empathy, feedback, and confrontation; and has given him a realistic appraisal of his condition.

THE PATIENT'S FAMILY

When a patient is part of a family system, it is imperative to involve the family in plans for his treatment and care after he is discharged from the hospital. Families have the power to make or break the physician's plans. Relatives who are allied with the physician can help sustain treatment when the patient is reluctant to follow a program and can, by their resistance, sabotage a good program. If they have been informed all along, they will naturally be included in plans for the patient's homecoming.

If the health care professional decides to talk to the family apart from the patient, the patient needs to be told. Families have ways of dropping hints and sometimes relish the idea that they are in the know, while the patient is in the dark. Knowing of a secret meeting between his family and his physician can destroy any trust that the patient has in his physician.

If the physician meets with the family alone, he should confine the interview to matters that will help the patient. Often when the family has a shot at the physician, they will launch into an account of their own troubles. He is more likely to gain their cooperation by acknowledging their difficulties, offering them empathy, and then focusing on the patient's needs. The following is an example:

Wife: You know, when he comes home, I don't know what's going to happen.
Physician: What do you mean?
Wife: Well, look. My arm is pretty bad; I used to be able to carry even mattresses around. Now I can't raise it, and I don't know whether it's bursitis or arthritis or whatever.
Physician: And you think that will create problems?
Wife: See, it even hurts to move my shoulder around. Well, what are you gonna do? If there was something I could take . . .
Physician: I can see that not being able to move your arm would concern you. Why don't you make an appointment for yourself so that we can look more carefully into your problem.
Wife: Well, how can I? I mean, if my husband is at home . . .
Physician: It seems to me you are concerned about having to care for your husband.
Wife: Yes.
Physician: Your husband won't need nursing care as much as he will need support and encouragement. You'll certainly be able to leave him to take care of your own needs.

It is not a good idea to assume that families know how to encourage and support each other. Sometimes this needs to be spelled out specifically. The physician can do this best by providing examples: He might say "Whenever your husband tries to do something for himself, praise him. Say, 'That's very good,' or 'I can see you're really trying,' or 'What a difference between today and last week.' "

The patient needs support when he is feeling down or discouraged, and the family should be taught how to provide empathy. Saying "Cheer up!" or "Things will look better tomorrow." does not cheer the depressed and convalescing patient. Families who can say "I can see that you are very upset when you look at your stomach." help him more to recovery than those who pretend that the new opening is really pretty delightful. ("See, the food doesn't have to travel as far!") The patient who is allowed to ventilate his feelings eventually adapts. There is a difference between empathic statements such as "I can see that you are. . . . ," and "Oh my God, it's terrible." The first is an acknowledgment of the patient's feelings. The latter, which is pity, tends to reinforce negative feelings.

In an interview with a family member, the physician should check out the memory of the person who is supposed to help with the patient's aftercare. If he has difficulty remembering names, places, and dates, it is a good bet that he may have difficulty remembering how much medication is needed or when prescriptions run out. If any memory loss is evident, another family member may be included so that the entire responsibility for the patient's care does not fall on this person. If the physician is not sure and simply asks, "How is your memory?", the person who responds, "Well, pretty good. I guess I slip up once in a while," is a better bet than the one who asserts, "Excellent! I'm like an elephant."

Generally, in dealing with a patient's family the best results come from involving both the patient and his family in the discussion of his aftercare. Explanations of the patient's illness, his convalescence, his options, and his expectations can be made to everyone at the same time. This also gives the physician an opportunity to notice any discrepancies in expectations and any attitudes displayed by the family toward their ill member that may hinder his recovery.

Talking to a family is sometimes like refereeing a tennis match. One person may be the spokesman, or a few might compete for the spot. Sometimes families talk about the recovering patient as if he were not present and discuss him in the 3rd person. The patient may be left isolated and uninvolved as the discussion of his disposition passes over his head from member to physician and from member to member. When this happens, the physician should encourage the family members to talk directly to the patient, checking his feelings about the discussion. For example:

Member: He never follows doctor's orders.
Physician: Well, Mr. Brown, what do you think? Is that a fair statement?
Patient: It certainly is not!
Member: He knows that he doesn't.
Physician: Why don't you tell him?
Member: You don't follow doctor's orders. You even forget where you put your
              old medicine bottles. So who can renew prescriptions for you?
Physician: Have you ever misplaced medicine bottles, Mr. Brown?
Patient: Sometimes.
Physician: What can we do about that?
Member: Keep the medicine in the kitchen.

Families differ in personality and in their reaction to illness, just as individual people do. The physician will soon get a feeling of group personality from a family (2, 20a, 43). Do they accept the patient's symptoms or do they pretend they don't exist? Are they defensive, angry, guilty, fearful, denying, adaptive?

The guilty family may feel that in some way, magical or actual, they contributed to the sick member's present condition. They may express this feeling by protecting the patient and giving him everything he wants, but they may be outraged with the staff and berate them for inattention to the patient. Often this guilt is caused by their own fear, below the level of their own awareness, that what happened to him could have happened to them and the relief that it did not. Thus spared, they feel the guilt of the survivor, seeing the patient as a surrogate—a constant reminder that he took "the rap" for them.

Another family may be as a group emotionally labile, playing the heavy drama of illness for all its worth, generating a crisis atmosphere and a worried pall wherever they move, something like Al Capp's little man with the cloud over his head. They carry on bedside and corridor vigils and are alert to every nuance of change including that staff spent two minutes less checking his signs than they usually do.

The denying family may make untrue statements to the patient and withhold information from him. They often hide the truth from themselves and invest a lot of energy in deception, keeping their respective chins up, deep freezing their smiles, becoming very amiable with staff, and likely to report that a patient in deep coma is communicating.

The angry family will regard sickness as a calamity caused by the personal actions of the patient such as neglect to take proper care of himself, or as a punishment, retribution for some wrong that he committed. This family will display hostility toward the patient. They will neglect to visit him, they will berate him for not trying hard enough, they will constantly remind him of how they are affected by costs, extra work, and inconvenience, sometimes in supposedly supportive remarks such as, "We want you to have the best, it doesn't matter that we have to sacrifice."

Some families may have a vested interest in maintaining a sick member and will reinforce a patient who uses his symptoms for attention. Their social esteem may be built upon what martyrs they are and how effective they are as a nursing unit. The responsibilities the sick role places on them may even represent an occupation. One elderly man collared every staff member who came down the hall and occasionally other visitors to demonstrate his skill in getting his wife to eat.

Any physician who has an opportunity to observe his patient's family on a few occasions makes some judgment as to their dynamics. He is in a position to interfere in pathological interaction, if only to call in counseling support from another source. Often it is enough for the physician simply to call negative behavior to their attention. "I notice whenever your father talks about going back to work you change the subject. It would be more helpful to him if he were able to tell you that he feels pretty bad about not working."

Families need to learn not only how to care for their convalescing member physically but how to alter their lifestyle so that they still have good times together. People are not always inventive nor do they realize the need. This must be spelled out, too.

Physician: What kinds of things do you suppose you might plan that would be fun for your wife to do?

Husband: Well, what do you mean? After all, she's pretty limited—she can't do very much with her left side. Like we used to go bowling. . . .

Physician: That's the point. You'll have to plan new activities until she is more able.

Patient: You mean like watching television?

Physician: Well, that's one. Can you think of any others?

Patient: Well, I guess we could visit Mother . . .

Physician: Can you visit anyone else?

Husband: You know, you talk of visit, and she's sick. My wife is sick. I thought she needed to be pretty quiet.

Physician: She needs to get back to a life that is as close to normal as possible. You can help by substituting activities that she can do for activities that she can't do.

Husband: We could visit her sister—

Physician: You're doing fine. Keep going.

THE PATIENT WHO LIVES ALONE

There will be many patients who are ready to leave the hospital who have no family or friends to help them and yet do not require the services of a nursing or convalescent home. Returning to health and the feeling of well-being is a special challenge to the patient who must go it alone. Sometimes, because of his forced independence, he recovers more quickly than the patient who is surrounded by family and friends.

Together with his physician the patient can brainstorm alternative support systems in the absence of family and/or friends. Some patients have been helped by visiting nurses and homemaker services. Others need only an occasional contact with an advocacy group. Sometimes isolated patients are surprised to learn that other tenants in the same building or a next door neighbor are glad to drive them to the physician's office or to buy their groceries until they are able to go to the market alone. These patients can be assured that asking someone to help often fills a need for the other person.

The physician might encourage these patients to write down the telephone numbers of possible sources of help before they leave the hospital. It gives them a greater feeling of security to leave the hospital with such a list in their pocket rather than to construct one on their own once they have been discharged. For the occasional patient returning home alone who does not have a telephone, social service might be able to make arrangements before they leave the hospital. A link to the outside world is essential for someone recently discharged from a hospital who is hobbling around in an isolated apartment. A telephone is not only a good investment; it is preventive medicine.

This patient should be told to take each day as it comes and to plan a little activity for each day, perhaps a little bit more than the day before. He should be taught to plan for a little less activity than he actually thinks he can do so that he will not feel a sense of failure if he does not complete it. As he takes each day successfully, he can cross it off the calendar as one more day toward his goal.

Some days the patient will not feel better, but may feel the same or worse. If he is prepared for occasional bad days, they will not come as a surprise nor will they worry him as much as if he were not prepared at all. He can be told that convalescence is not a straight road but one that backs up occasionally or takes a detour, and that all that is to be expected.

Since his physician is very important to him, this patient may experience some separation anxiety immediately prior to discharge. When the physician makes an appointment for their next meeting and gives him a telephone number to call if he needs help, he reduces some of this anxiety. It is also helpful to discuss it. Any instructions should be given slowly, simply, corrected with feedback, and corroborated with written instructions.

An occasional telephone call to the isolated patient or a written note reminding him of what he can do to help himself and the time of their next appointment maintain a necessary social link with the physician after discharge from the hospital. It is also very comforting to any patient to think that the physician cared enough to remember him between visits.

REFERENCES

1. Abrams HS: Psychological aspects of intensive care units. Med Ann DC 43:59–62, 1974
2. Anthony EJ: The impact of mental and physical illness on family life. Am J Psychiatry 127(1):138–146, 1970
3. Badger TL: The physician–patient in the recovery and intensive care units. Arch Surg 109:359–360, 1974
4. Bilodeau CB et al.: Issues raised in a group session by patients recovering from myocardial infarction. Am J Psychiatry 128:73–78, 1971
5. Blachly PH, Starr A: Postcardiotomy delirium. Am J Psychiatry 121:371–375, 1964
6. Bouchard VC: Hemiplegic exercise and discussion group. Am J Occup Ther 26:330–331, 1972
7. Burgess E: The modification of depressive behavior. In Rubin R, Franks C (eds): Advances in Behavior Therapy. New York, Academic Press, 1968, pp 193–199
8. Drellich MG, Bieber I, Sutherland AM: The psychological impact of cancer and cancer surgery: adaptation to hysterectomy. Cancer 9:1120–1126, 1956

9. Egbert LD: Psychological support for surgical patients. In Abrams HS (ed): Psychological Aspects of Surgery. Boston, Little Brown, 1967, vol 4, no 2, pp 37–51

10. Egbert LD et al.: Reduction of postoperative pain by encouragement and instruction of patients. N Engl J Med 270:825–827, 1964

11. Engel GL: Sudden and rapid death during psychological stress–folklore or folk wisdom? Ann Intern Med 74:771–782, 1971

12. Evans FMC: Psychosocial Nursing. New York, MacMillan, 1971

13. Farber IE, Harlow HF, West LJ: Brain washing, conditioning, and DDD. Sociometry 20:271–285, 1957

14. Fisher C: Psychoanalytic implications of recent research on sleep and dreaming: part I, empirical findings. J Am Psychoanal Assoc 13:197–210, 1965

15. Gantt WH, Newton JEO, Stephens JH: Effect of person. Cond Reflex 1:18–35, 1966

16. Goffman E. Asylums. Garden City, Anchor Books, Doubleday, 1961

17. Hackett TP, Cassem NH, Wishnie H: Detection and treatment of anxiety in the coronary care unit. Am Heart J 78:727–730, 1969

18. Harlow HF: The nature of love. Am Psychol 13:673–685, 1958

19. Healy KM: Does preoperative instruction make a difference? Am J Nurs 68:62–67, 1968

20. Herzlich C: Health and Illness. New York, Academic Press, 1973

20a. Hill R: Generic features of families under stress, crisis intervention: selected readings, Parad HJ (ed): New York, Family Service Association of America, 1965, pp 32–52

21. Duff S, Hollingshead AB: Sickness and Society. New York. Harper & Row, 1968

22. Igel GJ, Calvin AD: The development of affectional responses in infant dogs. J Comp Physiol Psychol 53:302–305, 1960

23. Järvinen KAJ: Can ward rounds be a danger to patients with myocardial infarction? Br Med J 1:318–320, 1955

24. Johnson JE: Approaches to the study of nursing questions and the development of nursing science: effects of structuring patient's expectations on their reactions to threatening events. Nurs Res 21:499–504, 1972

25. Johnson MH: Social and psychological effects of vasectomy. Am J Psychiatry 121:-482–486, 1964

26. Kaufman MR, Franzblau AN, Kairys D: The emotional impact of ward rounds. Journal of Mount Sinai Hospital 23:782–803, 1956

27. Kiely WF: Psychiatric aspects of critical care. Critical Care Medicine 2:139–142, 1974

28. Klein R: Crisis to grow on. Cancer 28:1660–1665, 1971

29. Kornfeld DS: Psychiatric Complications of Cardiac Surgery. In Abrams HS (ed): Psychological Aspects of Surgery. Boston, Little Brown, 1967, vol 4, no 2, pp 115–131

30. Lederer H: How patients view their world. In Jaco EG (ed): Patients, Physicians, and Illness. Glencoe, Free Press, 1958, pp 247–256

31. Lynch JJ: Psychophysiology and development of social attachment. J Nerv Ment Dis 151:(4):231–244, 1970

32. Lynch JJ et al.: Effects of human contact on the heart activity of curarized patients in a shock-trauma unit. Am Heart J 88:(2):160–169, 1974

33. Lynch JJ et al.: Heart rate change in the horse to human contact. Psychophysiology 11:(4):472–478, 1974

34. Lynch JJ et al.: The effects of human contact on cardiac arrythmia in coronary care patients. J Nerv Ment Dis 158(2):88–99, 1974

35. Lynch JJ, Gantt WH: The heart rate component of the social reflex in dogs: the conditional effects of petting and person. Cond Reflex 3:(2):69–80, 1968

36. Lynch JJ, McCarthy JF: The effects of petting on a classically conditioned emotional response. Behav Res Ther 5:55–62, 1967

37. Malik MA: Emotional stress as a precipitating factor in sudden deaths due to coronary insufficiency J Forensic Sci 18:47–52 1973

38. McKegney FP: The intensive care syndrome. Conn Med 30:633, 1966

39. Mechanic, Volkhurst E: Stress, illness behavior and the sick role. Am Sociol Rev 26:-51–58, 1961

40. Meyer BC: Some considerations of the doctor–patient relationship in the practice of surgery. In Abrams HS (ed): Psychological Aspects of Surgery. Boston, Little Brown, 1967 vol 4, no 2, pp. 17–35

41. Meyer BC et al.: A clinical study of psychiatric and psychological aspects of mitral surgery. Psychosom Med 23:94–218, 1961

42. Meyers ME: The effect of types of communication on patient's reaction to stress. Nurs Res 13:126–131, 1964

43. Petrillo M, Sanger S: Emotional Care of Hospitalized Children. Philadelphia J B Lippincott Co, 1972

44. Psychological aspects of intensive care. Nursing Times 70:883, 1974

45. Reach to recovery. J Tenn Med Assoc 66:28–29, 1973

46. Reding GR, Daniels RS: Organic brain syndromes in a general hospital. Am J Psychiatry 120:800–801, 1964

47. Ruesch J: Chronic disease and psychological invalidism. Berkeley, University of California Press, 1951

48. Sand P, Livingston G, Wright RG: Psychological assessment of candidates for a hemodialysis program. Ann Intern Med 64:602–10, 1966

49. Schmitt FE, Wooldridge PJ: Psychological preparation of surgical patients. Nurs Res 22(2):108–116, 1973

50. Schneider DF: Anxiety preceding a heart attack: effect of person. Conditioned Reflex 4:169–180, 1969

51. Seligman ME, Maier SE: Failure to escape traumatic shock. J Exp Psychol 74(1):1–9, 1967

52. Seligman ME, Maier SE, Geer JH: Alleviation of learned helplessness in the dog. J Abnorm Psychol 73:256–262, 1968

53. Sutherland AM, Orbach CE, Dyk RB, Bard M: The psychological impact of cancer and cancer surgery: adaptation to the dry colostomy. Cancer 5:857, 1952

54. Swanson DW: Clinical psychiatric problems associated with general surgery. In Abrams HS (ed): Psychological Aspects of Surgery. Boston, Little Brown, 1967, vol 4, no 2

55. Tryon PA, Leonard NF: Giving the patient an active role. In Skipper JK Jr, Leonard RC (eds): Social Interaction and Patient Care. Philadelphia, J B Lippincott, 1965, pp 120–127

56. Wallace WG, Wallace AG: Transfer from a coronary care unit: some adverse responses. Arch Intern Med 122:104–108, 1968

57. Webb WB: Partial and differential sleep deprivation. In Kales A (ed): Sleep: Physiology and Pathology. Philadelphia, J B Lippincott, 1969, pp 221–231

58. Wilson LM: Intensive care delirium. Arch Intern Med 130:225, 1972

59. Wright RG, Sand P, Livingston G: Psychological stress during hemodialysis for chronic renal failure. Ann Intern Med 64:611–621, 1966

60. Zubek SP et al.: Effect of severe immobilization of the body on intellectual and perceptual processes. Can J Psychol 17:118–133, 1963

8
The Drug and Alcohol Dependent Patient

There can be no doubt that, if tranquilizers could be bought as easily and cheaply as aspirin, they would be consumed not by the billions, as they are at present, but by the scores and hundreds of billions. And a good, cheap, stimulant would be almost as popular.

Aldous Huxley
Brave New World Revisited

DRUG DEPENDENT PATIENT

Man learned very early that there was little he could do to change or stop the forces which caused him to feel bad from time to time. Occasionally something happened to make him happy, like getting a piece of meat to ease his hunger, or discovering that if he heated certain types of earth he got something shiny that he could shape, but the feeling seldom lasted. Other things, like finding no game, or burning his fingers, came along to change it. He did learn that while he could not blink away his anxiety, pain, boredom, or a mate who never smiled, he could, if he got hold of the right stuff, think it away. To this end, he has always chased the perfect soma, the multipurpose, never contraindicated, ultimate substance that would make all reality bearable and beautiful forever. In the finding, obtaining, and experimenting with various substances, however, man has always ended up with more trouble that he had in the first place. What he soon discovers is that these activities dominate him to a degree that often excludes all other behavior.

ADDICTION DEFINED

Any excessive behavior that can dominate human existence can be called an addiction. It is not unusual for an individual to shift from one kind of overwhelming behavior to another. Whether the behavior is called dependence, addiction, habituation, or an obsessive compulsion, the common denominator to all is that they act as a security blanket one can pull over his head to shroud out unpleasantness and to make life acceptable.

The detrimental physiological effects of nicotine, tobacco, and caffeine are well publicized, but physiological damage is not the only criterion of addiction. Excessive eating, sleeping, reading, working, and sitting under a blanket are also quite capable of producing a "drugged" state. There is a deficit in the addict's life that is being filled by the addictive object. If an individual has an overwhelming *need* to do something to the exclusion of alternatives, he is an addict. Although this chapter is addressed primarily to the drug dependent patient, its concerns are of a more global nature and are directed to facilitating the interaction between the

physician and any patient who is so preoccupied with one thing that he neglects his own well-being. Given this definition, a patient who is over committed to his job might be included. To accept such an idea requires considerable stretching of a point, probably with the effect of residual striations, but this author does not consider such an inclusion inappropriate. If a patient is involved in anything to the extent that he finds little or no joy in living without it, if his total existence is threatened by this involvement, many of the principles presented here will apply to him.

PHYSICIAN ACTIONS

The physician's actions with all drug dependent patients are basically the same.

1. He gives facts in terms that can be clearly understood without moralizing.
2. He obtains feedback to make sure those facts are understood, preferrably in the patient's own terms.
3. He offers an ear for listening and facilitates ventilation.
4. He offers support.
5. He deals with the physical effects of the dependence.
6. He deals with the psychologic problems resulting from the problem.
7. He deals with the problems that have led the patient to using the drug in the first place.
8. He does not despair over those who do not want to be helped but realizes that it is impossible to cover all bases.
9. Although he may be told, "You don't understand, you don't use," he knows that it is not necessary to suffer a ruptured appendix in order to understand the techniques of abdominal surgery.

The care of any patient is undertaken with the intention of improving the quality of his being. The physician's goal is to offer the addicted patient alternatives to living which will get him out from under his blanket and let him see that there are some things on the other side of the wool that aren't too bad at all.

There have been many discoveries and inventions which the physician can use to improve the condition of his patient's body: gleaming new instruments, compounds and chemistries unheard of in our philosophy, complicated intubations which screen out the bad and bring in the good, lasers, cryosurgery, and surgery by remote control. None are as therapeutic as the one who prescribes their use. Balint said it "The greatest drug the physician has is himself (3)."

THE DRUG DEPENDENT PATIENT

PHYSICIAN'S ATTITUDES—CURRENT FACTORS

Of all his patients, the one least likely to obtain the sympathy of the physician is the drug abuser (5,9,51). It is usually with annoyance that physicians view the disregard the user displays toward the finely tuned apparatus that is his body. Many factors contribute to the negative and hopeless attitude that often typifies the physician's response to the drug dependent patient.

First, many physicians feel the drug abuser brings upon himself his own misfortune; and since the misery that he reaps is of his own doing, he does not warrant the attentive considerations given to those patients who bear little or no responsibility for their ailments.

Second, the drug abuser challenges the physician's values. Making it through medical school requires arduous application, often at the expense of other more enjoyable aspects of living. The drug abuser is a living refutation of the entire ethic that makes such dedication possible. He says with one gulp, sniff, or needle prick, "None of that means a thing." It is no surprise that the physician may regard the behavior of one who allows such self-indulgence to interfere with other life goals as an outright denial of his own ideals. Not only is the drug abuser not lifting himself up by his own bootstraps, he is cutting off the straps.

Third, the physician may have some personal anxiety concerning drug usage and may avoid this patient in order to protect himself from his own feelings. This may reflect an unconscious attraction to, and fear of, forbidden pleasure—a tug of war to which we are all heir.

Fourth, the physician's authority is challenged by the drug-abusing patient. The medical model in which a cooperative patient seeks help and follows through on the physician's advice does not cover the drug abuser. If the medical model is the round hole, the drug abuser is the square peg.

Finally, the behavior of the drug-abusing patient doesn't help matters. He is usually a reluctant patient who strongly resists treatment. Any relationship with the physician is usually hit or miss. His purpose may not be to quit but to get a prescription for more drugs. If he comes for help voluntarily then he will skirt the issue in such a way as to make a game of history taking, revealing as few details as possible, offering miserly bits of information as if he were feeding a sick chipmunk through an eyedropper. The drug–abusing patient is often self-destructive. Because he becomes quickly disappointed, he may leave a hospital against medical advice, refuse outright to cooperate with out patient treatment plans, or drop out of treatment once begun.

The physician may believe, not entirely without foundation, that he cannot even see an addict, much less treat him, unless he bolts down and locks up everything negotiable in his office; and that includes just about everything but the fingercots.

It is no surprise, therefore, that most physicians, psychiatrists included, are not anxious to participate personally in the care of a drug abuser. Treatment of this patient is an arduous, time consuming, and often unrewarding endeavor made worse by a patient who is unwilling to cooperate or follow advice or even admit that he is ill. And so the patient and the physician stand facing one another, sparring partners who don't want to get into the ring, the patient reluctant to come in for help, the physician reluctant to give it. Cohen et al. pose this question: "How does one move unflinchingly into an arena where he is made to feel unwanted, incompetent, and even malevolent?" (13).

HISTORICAL PRECURSORS

The attitude of the physician has been shaped by historical events as well as by present experiences. Although man has searched throughout history for drugs to make him feel better, he has never made up his mind how he felt about them once they were found. For thousands of years alcohol, peyote, marijuana, hashish, opium, and other substances such as nitrous oxide, ether, and glue solvents have been used to alter consciousness and change the nature of existance. Even if man was not looking to kill his physical pain, he always felt the need to transcend his experience, to plunge more deeply into the matrix of his reality. In almost every culture, someone knew of distillation or of some plant on the hillside that would leave one happily stoned, like the Sumerians who called opium the plant of joy, or murderously assaultive, like the Hashishins, who knocked off crusaders under the influence of hashish. When primitive cultures found ways of altering man's consciousness, there was usually a caretaking member of that society worried enough about the effects of its members lolling about sipping, popping, dropping, and snorting to restrict their use. Often the distiller and the caretaker were one and the same.

In the nineteenth century opiates were generally available and widely used. Physicians dispensed them, drug stores sold them over the counter, grocery stores stocked them, and if one was housebound, they could be ordered by mail. Patent medicines like Ayers Cherry Pectoral or Mrs. Winslow's Soothing Syrup included liberal dosages of opiates in their formulas and were advertised as a cure for every ailment from warts to mysterious and nameless female disturbances. While no one was getting better, no one noticed. Physicians unwittingly addicted patients to opium and morphine because of an incomplete understanding of the addictive liability of these drugs. When this liability became known, the medical profession reacted strongly by condemning heroin, by vigorously supporting legal control of drugs, and by criticizing strongly those physicians called "script doctors," who prescribed narcotics without attempting to treat addiction.

When the Harrison Act was passed in 1914, medical societies advised physicians not to attempt to treat addicts; and the use of narcotics in medical school was often taught in a way that encouraged a phobic response in students (36). Originally designed to control the sale of opiates, the Harrison Act was later used to close medical treatment facilities and to prosecute and imprison any physicians who attempted to treat narcotics addicts with opiates. Federal inpatient facilities were built such as the large prison hospitals at Lexington and Fort Worth, and treatment was no longer a responsibility of physicians in private practice.

The brush with fire was too close. The medical profession had to stand further back from a conflagration about whose combustible qualities it knew very little. The physician's attitude toward the narcotics addict has remained negative to this day. Negative attitudes have been reinforced by two other considerations. Isbell suggested that prejudice against minority groups may have reinforced prejudice against drug addicts (28). Although narcotics users in the last century were largely middle-aged, middle class white women, addiction occurred with noticeable frequency among the minority groups with which it became associated (35). Aunt Sally May, stoned while fluting her pie crust, didn't take the rap. The opium dens of the Chinese did. In this century, narcotics addiction has become associated with criminality. Addicts automatically become law breakers when they obtain their supply, many have to resort to illegal activities to support their habits, and people connected to the criminal underworld have greater access to illicit drugs, since that is where the traffic originates.

DRUG DEPENDENCE DEFINED

Drug dependence is a behavior pattern of compulsive drug use. It is generally characterized by an overwhelming preoccupation with using the drug and securing a continuous supply; by a strong tendency to relapse after withdrawal: and by an increasing tolerance level seen in the diminished returns experienced by the chronic user who must get larger and larger doses to obtain the same effect. Dependence may range from mild desire to wild craving.

A user may have a physical dependence resulting in a withdrawal syndrome, which is not the same as tolerance, and a psychologic dependence, a condition in which the effects of the drug have become necessary to keeping the individual feeling good. It is possible to be psychologically dependent on a drug without being physically dependent, and conversely to be physically dependent without being psychologically dependent, as for example, an infant born to a drug dependent mother. Because difficulty with abstinence is not determined solely by the drug, because drugs are often used in doses so low that the degree of physical dependence is questionable, and because drug dependence is the result of psychological conditioning to psychopharmacologic reinforcement, experts concerned with drug abuse have begun to blur the conceptual edges between physical and psychologic dependence (16, 46).

THE PAYOFF

The drug abuser takes drugs to feel good. Life has its ups and downs. The drug abuser likes to be able to call his. Fashion has something to do with drug use, giving it a contagious endemic factor. In some circles, particularly among the young, experience with drugs has become a social currency. This is the reason why most drug abusers are introduced to the drug by other users, often their friends. Drug abuse also solves the problem of having nothing to do, particularly for the user from urban poverty areas. The addict who is part of a drug taking milieu gets three things out of his involvement. He gains an identity, he gains a place in a society which is accepting and not too demanding; and third and most important, he acquires a career at which he can be reasonably competent. If an individual uses drugs steadily, his life is devoted to maintaining and securing his supply, to avoiding arrest, and to performing the rituals of taking the drug. "Taking care of business" is a full-time job.

In addition to the reinforcement in the drug, dependence among the urban poor is perpetuated by social support from the drug using community and fear or not making it in the straight world (40). This last point is significant. An important prognostic consideration in treating the addict is how much of a life he had before the addiction began. Someone approaching 30 who dropped out of school at 15 has legitimate reason to be concerned about survival in the straight world (25).

Another population of the drug dependent do not use drugs to expand their awareness, as an act of social custom, or as an occupation. They are the millions of middle aged and elderly people who self-prescribe psychoactive drugs as a way of coping with the tensions of living. Many of these users consider their dependence valid because it is therapeutic rather than pleasure seeking, and would be offended at the label of addict (54).

The drug dependent patient comes for help when he has encounters with the law, if his health is bad, because a friend convinces him to get help, if he no longer gets any kicks out of his habit, if he cannot afford it, or if he wants a prescription (40).

If he has been dependent for a long time, his request for help suggests desperation. He has a lot invested in his habit including time, money, effort, and his well-being. He may have wanted to give it up, he may have tried to give it up, he may have succeeded for a while only to find himself right back where he started. The point is that when he does see a physician, a major investment no longer yields sufficient returns. He is bankrupt. It's frightening and humbling to have one's supports kicked out. Since the drug dependent patient may regard the physician essentially as an antagonist, his appearance in the physician's office is indicative not only of personal defeat but of a cry for help.

If any patient is deserving of a nonjudgmental attitude, it is the patient who is drug dependent. His presence in the physician's office, while not guaranteeing capitulation, is a truce. The physician has a better chance of achieving an armistice if he allows his patient integrity. General Grant gave General Lee back his sword. The physician who regards the drug dependent patient as another appropriate recipient of his knowledge and his skills lets him keep his sword.

NARCOTICS

The User

The narcotics user seeks not oblivion nor the clouding of consciousness, but detachment. What is known of this patient indicates that he is most likely to live in a densely populated urban area. He is usually underprivileged, not only in the economic sense but in the emotional sense; his family may have lacked affection, shown little or no respect for one another, and generally provided an inadequate environment for a growing child. Chein draws a picture of the chronic addict as one who suffers from a low frustration threshold, is unequal to the demands of an enduring intimate relationship or a time consuming responsible activity, functions less capably under conditions of anxiety and frustration, and distrusts others (11). His characteristic mood is colored by a sense of futility and general deep seated depression.

This composite description is based on the limited known addict population. There are many businessmen, students, housewives, medical personnel, and rural users who do not fit the template of the urban slum addict (15, 43). Not all addicts come to the attention of those who tally their numbers. Many can afford to support their habit, consequently do not get arrested, or are comfortable in their use and therefore don't seek treatment, the two ways besides death that an addict comes to the attention of the authorities. Some work out a method of spacing injections so that they never become really hooked even though they use the drug regularly. This measure of control means that they often lead stable lives and remain fairly hidden. The development of tolerance and physical dependence is common to the use of all narcotics. The withdrawal syndrome which varies with the user and the habit includes the following symptoms: yawning, perspiration, dilated pupils, sneezing, fever, chills, runny nose, anxiety, restlessness, tremors, diarrhea, cramps, vomiting, flushing, pains in the muscles and bone, and waves of gooseflesh (12).

What Happens

Heroin is the drug most often abused. It can be administered orally, by inhalation, by subcutaneous injection, or by intravenous injection (57). The latter is preferred because it gives the quickest effect, known as a rush, which is described as a warm flushing of the skin and a feeling like an orgasm. The user then drifts into a euphoric state which can last for a few hours. If he is mainlining, he is shooting the stuff a few times a day.

Morgan writes that drug addicts inject any conceivable injectible substance when they cannot get their hands on drugs. They like to see the blood come back into the syringe or eyedropper; they like to see their veins stand up (40). Some addicts report that their craving for the drug is not as bad as their craving for the needle. Others report that the "bang" from the needle is as good as that from the drug. The mechanics of drug abuse, putting in the needle, seeing blood in the syringe, and pushing the plunger down, are as integral to the high as the substance.

Treatment

The narcotic addict may be treated by maintenance or planned withdrawal with a synthetic narcotic agent such as methadone, by detoxification, by outpatient abstinence, or by an attempt to modify personal and social factors through a therapeutic community such as Synanon, which relies upon peer pressure, shared experience, and a sense of belonging to help the addict become drug free (17, 23, 26). Therapeutic communities provide their inhabitants with a drug free social setting in which all social pressures are directed toward abstinence. Gut level confrontations and stringent and continual proof of intention weed out all but the dedicated.

The problem with rehabilitation in the substitute community is that when the patient is no longer in that setting, he is under pressure from another peer group to return to drugs. Among most known narcotics users there is a language, a dress, a code, and a life style that clearly establishes a separate and distinctive subculture. The conversation of addicts revolves around where to buy drugs, what big users they were or are, and how great it is to be a member of the club. It is a better than odds on bet that even if the addict has been treated successfully outside of his community, if he returns to his former environment, other forces of peer pressure may operate on him with equal success. In addition the use of narcotics is functional. It helps the user live his life in some way. If he has not learned other adaptive behavior, he may resume his habit by default.

Current investigations of the mechanics of opiate action sparked by the discovery of opiate receptors in the brain and a more accurate idea of who else is using narcotics will yield a better understanding of the problem and hopefully more effective treatment modalities (38).

THE ONLY GAME IN TOWN

When addicted patients come to the physician seeking to break their habits, it is important that he find out how long they have been using, what they are using, how often they use it, what it does for them, how it has affected their lives, and something of their life style (48). He should be well acquainted with facilities such as treatment centers, halfway houses, hospital programs, and aftercare community programs that are available to his patients. Certain patients may require, for example, the cushioning that the halfway house provides. Whether he recommends a methadone maintenance program, a methadone withdrawal program, a therapeutic community, detoxification, or outpatient abstinence, the physician must know if the patient has tried to break the habit before, how often, with what results, and if so, what caused him to resume the habit. There are no hard and fast rules. Addicts and reasons for addiction vary; it is necessary for the physician to know the background, pressures, and life style of the patient before making plans for treatment. For example, if a patient has tried several times to kick his habit, he is considered a more likely candidate for maintenance than the patient who has never attempted to become drug free.

The biggest problem faced by the physician in terms of mutual goals is that the narcotics user has a sure way to feel good. What the physician offers him is chancy. Maybe it will work out, maybe it won't. Besides, the physician is a representative of the establishment. He lives and works in a straight world, and the addict, who may not, believes that the physician cannot possibly understand him or what it's like to use.

The physician may not know what it's like to use, but his clinical background gives him a broader picture than the narrow perspective of the addict. His interest in the drug addict is one of the best things he can offer him. If the physician accepts the addict's request for help at face value, he will find less resistance in questioning and make himself seem less like an antagonist. An extensive glossary of drug terms has been compiled by Keup to which the reader is referred (31). However, unless he is familiar and comfortable with street talk, it is better to stay away from the jargon of the junkie. He may know that *skag* or *horse* or *H* are heroin, but unless he is comfortable with that usage, the official term will come off with more conviction. As with any patient, the drug user's terms must be mutually understood. The physician does not ruin his professional credibility if he asks, "What do you mean by copping a bag?" There is no merit in attempting to persuade a drug user that one is "with it," nor does being "with it" guarantee understanding. Good faith and good feeling are demonstrated by a physician who is not afraid to admit that he does not understand but is willing to learn (40).

Questioning should be directed to finding out whether the patient is currently using or if he has quit and for how long. If he is using, it is necessary to know how often and with what effect? As with all patients, his spontaneity will be encouraged if the interview is begun with indirect questions such as "What brings you to see me?", "How did all this happen," or, "You say that drugs have messed you up. Tell me about it." These can be followed by direct questions related to feelings such as, "What do you worry about most?", "Why do you want to quit?", "What changes in your life would make you feel better?" and questions related to specifics of use such as "When was your last fix?", "How long have you been shooting?", "Have you ever been clean?", "What made you start shooting again?", and because the chances are good that he is using other drugs, "What other things have you gotten into?"

Supportive statements of empathy such as "I can see that this has been very difficult for you." may be met with "Man, you don't know what it's been like." A helpful response then would be "I guess I don't. Why don't you explain it to me?" Gradually, the physician may gain an understanding of why the patient turns to drugs and may develop some tentative ideas of how the patient can be made less trouble to himself his family, and his community.

The major goal of any therapeutic measures with the narcotics addict is to transfer his interest from drugs to reality. Often his behavior and his habit are neatly tied together. If part of the pattern is broken, his supports may also be yanked away. Before taking away his supports, the physician must offer an alternative way of holding him up. Struts for the addict may be guidance in problems of daily living and a physician who cares about him.

SEDATIVE-HYPNOTICS

Some that are drug dependent obtain drugs through acceptable channels, and because their life style is no different from the majority culture, they are able to remain undetected almost indefinitely. One of these is the user of barbiturates, although not all barbiturate users obtain their supply through licit channels.

What started out and continues to be an enormously useful drug, a sedative, a sleeping pill, and a mainstay in such diseases as epilepsy, became by the end of the 1940s a new way to get drunk without the odor and the taste of alcohol. Since that time illicit barbiturate use has increased in alarming quantum leaps (39).

Relatively inexpensive, they are commonly abused in combination with other drugs, usually amphetamines, in a malevolent seesaw. Accidental overdose is common because of the narrow margin between dose and overdose and because the development of tolerance does not markedly elevate the lethal dose (57).

Barbiturates, most commonly taken orally, cause an intoxication similar to al-cohol—impairing judgment, coordination, and reaction time—and may produce tolerance and physical dependence. Physical dependence is related to the dose, frequency, and duration of use. Abrupt withdrawal from high doses of barbiturates can cause tremulousness, anxiety, weakness, and insomnia, followed by grand mal convulsive seizures. While withdrawal from narcotics can be unpleasant, it is not as life threatening as withdrawal from barbiturates, which is similar to the dangers of the the delirium tremens syndrome.

It is estimated that 10–50 percent of the primary physician's workload is made up of patients who ask for something to calm their nerves. Keniston states that 60% of today's prescriptions are for medication primarily intended as psycho-active (30). These patients present a continual dilemma. Prescribing medication seems most in line with medical practice, which essentially is introducing things into the organism to provide relief. In this situation, however, the patient's toler-ance of the medication will increase while his problem will not have changed. In responding to this patient's need with medication, the physician reinforces the common behavioral pattern of reaching into the medicine cabinet to solve all problems (50). Yet the physician may not have the time to listen to this patient's problems, and the patient, who expects quick relief, may go on to the next physi-cian and the next until he finds someone who will prescribe the necessary pill. Since referral may be perceived as rejection, many physicians opt for the tempo-rary treatment of anxiety with medication while acknowledging the existence of a problem. If the patient has already stated a problem, the physician can acknowl-edge in this manner: "This is really quite a problem and will take time to resolve. In the meantime, this drug will make you feel less anxious and may help you to deal with the problem more effectively." Some physicians give this kind of medica-tion only in the presence of overwhelming anxiety believing that some anxiety is necessary to work through problems. The patient is better able to handle the pressures of everyday living if he feels the normal tensions, anxieties, depressions, and dissatisfactions of life which help to generate alternatives.

The barbituate user often does not recognize the fact that he is a drug addict, nor is he as visible to the physician as most narcotics addicts who know they are addicted and have already relinquished their place in middle class society. When coming for treatment to help him break his habit, the barbiturate user may feel out the physician by asking questions such as "Do you think pills are dangerous?" or by saying "I have some sleeping medication and wonder what would happen if I got sleepy and accidentally took more than I should" (57). These kinds of questions, which are not only information seeking but which imply a request for help, require tactful answers. "What kinds of pills are you talking about?" The answer will cue the physician into the patient's relative sophistication about what he is doing. If he responds, "Reds, barbs, downs, goofballs," the chances are good that he already knows they are dangerous, for he has discussed them with other users and learned the language. If he responds with the name of a trade barbitu-rate, he may have discovered only recently that he can get a high with them and that, better than alcohol, they leave no trace of liquor on his breath. When either patient asks if the pills are dangerous, answering with "Yes they are, and if you keep taking them in the way that you are, there is a good chance you will either become addicted or die of an overdose," while straight and matter-of-fact, is like a premature ejaculation. Both patients must first confirm that they are users.

The patient who asks bluntly about the dangers of barbituates may be answered with a gentle confrontation. You seem to be quite concerned," or "Do *you* think they are dangerous?", or "I get the feeling you already know the answer to that." If the physician's manner is accepting and nonpunitive, the patient is more likely to respond that he is pretty worried because downs are screwing his head up.

The patient who refers to his sleeping medication is less likely to confirm confrontation since he has already troubled to legitimize his use. His question may be accepted at face value, but it is more helpful to both patient and physician if the patient can admit to use. Before the physician responds with straight facts, he can ask, "What do you think would happen?" or "When you say dangerous do you mean addicting?" "Are you asking if they're addicting?" If the patient answers in the affirmative, he should be praised for his intelligent concern. "You are right to be concerned." or "I'm glad that you asked me." or anything else that demonstrates the physician's *approval* of the question.

If this patient were to respond negatively, "No, I'm not concerned about addiction at all," the physician may still praise him for intelligent concern for whatever he claims, and answer his expressed question. "Yes, it would be dangerous if you took more than your prescribed dosage. The consequences are. . . ."

Early diagnosis of barbiturate dependence often only occurs after the patient has been hospitalized for some other reason. Often the onset of withdrawal is the first finding (18). At the first signs of the withdrawal syndrome, the physician may state his objective findings. If presented in a matter of fact manner, the patient is more likely to cooperate in giving vital information. For example, "Your headache, your nervousness, and the difficulty you are having when you try to stand are signs of barbiturate withdrawal which can be very dangerous if untreated. It is important that you help me to help you now. I need to know what you take, how much, and how often."

The barbiturate dependent patient seen may give misleading data. Instead of acknowledging that he takes several pills daily, he may concede only one or two for sleep. Someone who reveals nightly barbiturate use may be asked, "Do you ever feel the need at other times for something to calm your nerves or bring you down?" The answer may be "Sometimes." It's like flushing grouse. If the physician remains nonjudgmental, accepting, and even quiet at this point, the patient may come out and say something like, "I get a little edgy in the afternoon. I may take something then."

In treatment of barbiturate addiction, the patient is usually given a combination of supported withdrawal under a carefully supervised medical regimen in an in patient setting and counseling to alleviate the personal factors that have contributed to abuse. In the two patients used earlier in this section as illustrations, the former has the additional problem of a life style which sustains and perpetuates use, where it is easy to obtain drugs, and where most friends use something or other.

Counseling of that patient would be different from counseling the patient who became dependent primarily because taking drugs enabled him to cope. Both are faced with different reinforcements, and it is these reinforcements which the physician considers.

AMPHETAMINES

Frequently used in combination with barbituates or alcohol, amphetamines and cocaine are the most commonly used stimulant drugs (14, 20). Amphetamines, which were first used clinically in the treatment of narcolepsy, were expanded to include certain hyperactive children, and overweight adults (45).

Characteristically, amphetamines are first used to create euphoria, to combat fatigue, or as a diet aid. Students take them to get through periods of intensive study, businessmen take them to help them get through rough schedules, and truck drivers use them to stay awake over long hauls, the longest one known as the "Los Angeles turn around" in which the driver takes enough amphetamines to make it from coast to coast and back without sleeping. The early misuse of amphetamines is reflected in a song of the 40's titled, "Who put the benzedrine in Mrs. Murphy's ovaltine?" While most abusers take them orally many graduate to the needle after other users persuade them that the high is better (57). The intravenous use of amphetamines is very dangerous, involving all of the complications of the needle as well as the risk of a toxic psychosis of paranoid character with delusions of persecution and with auditory or visual hallucinations. Ellinwood believes that a "hypervigilance" may be required by the paranoid amphetamine user who must maintain his use in order to protect himself (20). This paranoid personality may make the user fearful of hospitalization. (Refer to chapter on hospitalization for suggestions relevant to the hospitalized paranoid patient.)

Amphetamines produce sleeplessness, anorexia, loquacity, and increased motor activity. "Speed" is an appropriate name, because the user feels as if he were in a 1920s movie. The user feels competent and decisive and may experience feelings such as a warm glow, tension, and irritability. Although amphetamines are more addicting than heroin, the abrupt cessation of their use produces no dramatic withdrawal syndrome; however, psychologic changes such as fatigue, lassitude and depression, and a marked craving will probably create another cycle of repetitive use.

The subjective effects of cocaines are so similar to those of amphetamines that even experienced users may be unable to distinguish between them. Cocaine may be sniffed as a powder, or injected intravenously, either alone or in combination with heroin. A "speed freak" may shoot in runs of 3–6 days interrupted by 1 or 2 days of deep sleep called "crashing." Not only does he turn his circadian rhythm inside out but he often neglects to eat. The chief causes of death among amphetamine abusers are violence as a result of their frenetic state and malnutrition and debilitation due to lack of food and sleep. Tolerance to amphetamines varies widely between users, and it is characteristically difficult to obtain an accurate picture of dosage. For example, a patient may relate that he "takes them like candy."

The amphetamine user, like the barbiturate user, may be invisible. He may say in an ordinary visit to the physician that he would like not to be so tired or he may say that he would like to have a little something on hand to "pep him up" especially when extra physical or mental endurance is required of him.

Patients taking amphetamines may relate sleep difficulties, weight loss, and irritability. He will often relate depression; and if he admits to use, they may have a sense of futility in attempting to control the use. Such a patient may say, "I'm doing speed again and I can't stop." Amphetamine users may be restless, agitated, and preoccupied with guilt feelings over their increased dependency upon the drug.

Patients who use amphetamines develop an overpowering need to continue their use and to obtain them at any means, a tendency to increase the dose, and generally both a psychologic and a physical dependence.

Appropriate information is more important for the amphetamine user than advice. He must be armed with information. Later in the interview the physician may want to indicate that he is prepared to discuss the patient's problems with him and that he is willing to prepare the patient to make decisions.

The biggest problem with amphetamines is that they, like the barbiturates, are so available. The market in "bennies" is phenomenal, and even drug companies cannot make reasonable estimates because so many are manufactured illicitly.

HALLUCINOGENS

In the past most users of illegal drugs have had deprived socioeconomic backgrounds, poor social and educational records, and easy access to narcotics. The user of hallucinogens is more often from the middle class and has had good educational experiences whose general pattern of use appears to be periodic rather than continuous (22).

The most common hallucinogen is LSD, sometimes called psychodelic because of its mind-altering effect. Usually taken orally it produces psychologic effects which can be euphoric or disphoric depending on the personality of the user, his predrug emotional state, the dose, the surroundings, succeeding events, and unknown factors, possibly including genetic constitution. It is difficult to predict the outcome of a trip, although it has been estimated that less than ten percent have negative outcomes.

The LSD state is characterized by vivid awareness, altered perception, and intense clarity. As a consequence, the user's experiences may range from isolated awe to a change in values. Freedman states that the most striking aspect of the use of LSD is the contrast between the LSD experience and the ordinary experience; the former is boundless (22). During the first three hours, laughing or crying is common. A striking self-centeredness is noticed. There is a heightened sensitivity to nuances and to nonverbal sensory-motor cues. It is an intense experience without clouded consciousness in which users commonly report that they can "hear" colors and "see" sound (55).

One ill effect of LSD is the possibility of unexplained recurrences (flashbacks). No one knows why they happen, but recurrences are usually associated with the taking of another drug, such as marijuana or alcohol. Patients who have experienced flashbacks may need to be reassured that this is not uncommon, that they are not a sign of impending insanity, and that they are often triggered by other drugs.

Talking Him Down

The LSD user may be first seen when his friends bring him into the office or the emergency room. It is not unusual for him to display behavior seen in acute schizophrenia. They will only bring him in if he is experiencing a *bummer*, a bad trip. The majority of bummers are panic reactions, and a patient experiencing one responds well to gentling (27). He needs to be told that he is experiencing a drug effect that will wear off and that he is not going crazy. Someone may have to spend hours with him providing *structure* and *attention*. Most users can be brought safely through bummers just by attention and soothing, steady talking. It is like giving him a map to guide him home. The map consists of signposts such as "You're doing fine.", "We're with you and everything is all right.", "This will wear off soon.", etc. One of the dangers in the use of LSD is misrepresentation by the seller. Sometimes it has been cut with other chemicals, creating an unfortunate combination when added to the therapeutic drugs used to bring a patient down (10).

Some patients who have taken LSD may be anxious about what they have experienced and may need to discuss it in order to come to terms with the sharp contrasts of drugged and real life. Some talk about their experience as if they were trying to put it together. Ventilation of the experience and discussion are usually all the patient needs. In order to handle the staggering remembrances, the patient may want to think through the experience and talk to the physician as a concerned listener.

Usually one trip produces psychologic satiation, and, as an experiment in awareness, is sufficient for some people forever and for others for a few days, months, or years. The attraction is understandable when with a simple act of ingestion one can create a mental state that hardly anyone achieves after a lifetime of yoga and meditations. While not a drug that causes physical dependence, the hallucinogens rate mention in this context because of the danger they pose to an individual, whether he uses acid once a month or has had one bad trip. Dangerous and tragic psychologic consequences are now confirmed, and the habitual long–term use of LSD may result in serious depression, paranoid behavior, and prolonged psychotic episodes.

SNIFFING

The practice of sniffing the fumes of commercial solvents, model airplane cements, certain cleaning agents, gasoline, lighter fluid, and paint-thinner has become widespread enough among school children to be considered a problem by school and law enforcement agencies as well as by organized medicine (1, 4, 8). The general effects of sniffing are similar to those produced by alcoholic intoxication. A period of excitement is followed by a period of depression.

The majority of children report that during their jags they feel invulnerable and imbued with feelings of amazing capabilities. Some lacerate or bang themselves in order to test their insensitivity to pain. A common feeling is being able to fly. Among the long-term effects are fatigue, reduced physical activity, depression, anorexia, weight loss, irritability, inattentiveness, and a myriad of organ function disturbance.

The child who is dependent normally uses one to two tubes of glue to produce a jag. The glue may be squeezed onto a rag and then inhaled nasally or orally. Intoxication may be expedited by putting the glue in a plastic bag, which is pressed to the face. At first, a few breaths are enough. Then, as tolerance increases, the glue

may be heated in a pan or taken by alternating sniffs with drinks of wine or beer. The euphoric stage may last 30–45 minutes; then it is followed by a let down or hangover period which can last anywhere from a few hours to several days. There may be headache, gastrointestinal upsets, difficulty in concentration, tremors, lethargy, a depressive feeling, and other symptoms. Intoxication has also been responsible for suffocation from the plastic bags, suicide, and acute pulmonary edema.

Gasoline sniffers *huff* directly from the source, such as an automobile tank or a lawn mower. Some spray the material directly into their mouths. Often they simply take deep breaths from gasoline cans after which they feel "tingling all over," "drifting in space," or hear an "eerie sound."

Glue sniffing, which has been seen in youngsters as young as six, may be done individually or in groups, perhaps in the rest rooms of schools or in someone's backyard. Boys have been found to sniff more than girls. The child is usually introduced to it by others, often on a dare. They buy the glue with lunch money, allowances, or money stolen from others.

Glue sniffing can be considered addictive in that one develops tolerance and can become psychologically dependent upon it. It has been reported that, although abstinence does not bring on a true withdrawal syndrome, it does cause irritability, severe restlessness, anxiety, headache, and stomach pains.

Treating a patient who sniffs glue is not too much different from treating any other drug dependent patient. Symptomatic relief, if it is warranted, is combined with finding and correcting the factors which made this youngster turn to inhaling a noxious chemical. A young child's use of drugs often does not have the permanency of dependence seen in later adolescence or adulthood. His behavior may be nonverbalized demands for attention that will stop when his needs are met.

Asking a child *why* he sniffs will most likely elicit an eloquent shoulder shrug. He has probably been put through a wringer of why's unless the physician is treating him for intoxication. The *why* can be more easily determined by asking when he uses, who he uses with, how often he uses, what substance he uses, and what effect it has. For example, "I know you are pretty busy between going to school and helping your mother around the house. I wonder when you get the time to sniff?" or "When is the best time to do it?" "Are you by yourself or do you sniff with friends?" is less dangerous for him to answer than "Who sniffs with you?", since the answer to the latter question involves getting some buddies in trouble. "How does it make you feel?" will complete a picture of a child who sniffs because of peer pressure, because there's nothing else to do, because he likes the feeling he gets when he's intoxicated, or because things are bad in his house.

Several states have enacted legislation to restrict the purchase of glue and other solvents that are intoxicating when sniffed. Substituting nontoxic solvents in glues or incorporating an irritant odorant or a nauseant in their formulas while easing the problem of glue sniffing, do not alter the fundamental need for the individual, whether child or adult, to find something that will change his reality for the moment.

MARIJUANA

The physical effects of smoking marijuana include tachycardia and conjunctivitis. In contrast to alcohol, hypnotics, and tranquilizers, marijuana affects motor function only in high doses. The effect of low doses is primarily in the realm of feeling and thought. The psychologic effects depend on the user, his experience with the drug, his personality, how he administers it, the dose, and the circumstances surrounding drug use. The major difference between marijuana and the hallucinogens is that the marijuana user is able to remain objective if he wishes. The inexperienced user will describe the effect as a weird dizziness or say that he felt nothing at all. The experienced user will find it pleasurable; he will have increased appetite and thirst and describe heightened awareness. The effect of the drug is largely dependent on the setting in which it is taken. In one setting the user may feel tranquility, apathy, and euphoria. In another, although less likely, he may experience fear, aggression, and hilarity. Because of the lethargy and mental inertia seen among heavy users, marijuana can be considered a potentially toxic substance capable of causing the user to become a social or intellectual zero.

Under the influence of marijuana, the user may develop an impaired time sense and be unable to estimate the passage of time as well as spatial distortion. The effects of marijuana reach their maximum intensity in a half hour, diminish within an hour, and usually disappear three to 5 hours after smoking. There is little evidence of physical dependence and the effects are less intense than those associated with alcohol, hypnotics, and tranquilizers. Adverse emotional reactions occur only infrequently. More commonly they are a simple depression. It has the unusual property of reverse tolerance in that regular users are more sensitive to its effects than first timers (33). There is evidence that its chronic use may cause tracheobronchitis (34).

Questions related to the use of marijuana will most often be asked when a patient's general history is being taken. Usually, questions should be tailored to the patient. With a young patient it is more productive to ask "how much do you" rather than "do you." "Do you" may be construed as judgmental or may elicit a negative response in someone 27, who a few years ago smoked daily. If the response is "Oh, about average, I guess," the physician should find out exactly what the patient considers average. In one neighborhood *average* is every morning; in another it's every weekend. Some times questions seeking reassurance will be asked by an older experimenter who has tried the drug at a party and is now concerned that he has rearranged his chromosomes. He may say something like, "I hear they're doing all kinds of studies on grass and LSD." "Why do you ask?" might cause this patient to deny concern ("No reason, just curious."), and eliminate the opportunity for drug education. A better response would be, "What would you like to know?" which still affords a shield of anonymity to the tentative.

THE ALCOHOL DEPENDENT PATIENT

Narcotics have passed through two stages, one of widespread use followed by one of stringent prohibition. The history of alcohol is a close parallel, but alcohol is now in a third stage in which its use is again allowed. It is because of this evolution that those who suffer from alcoholism enjoy a slight edge in professional attention over other drug addicts. Alcoholics are not subject to the same stigma and punitive measures as other drug addicts. Unlike the narcotic abuser, he has been granted an imprimatur of helplessness; ipso facto, he deserves help, although he still ranks low on the totem pole of preferred patients.

The process by which someone discards everything and everyone, alienates himself from society, and in many cases, jeopardizes his existence through a compulsive need to drink ethyl alcohol is inexplicable. Although there have been a few attempts to portray this process compassionately in films and in the theater, beginning in the late 19th century with "The Drunkard" in which the protagonist loses all to demon rum, the picture of the alcoholic in our society is a funny one. Most characterizations show him clutching a lamp post, falling down a lot, slurring his words, and looking past the capillary flush on his nose at a world that puzzles him. Sometimes this image is printed on red and black cocktail napkins which are passed around with the martinis. Whoopee cushion humor is oddly inappropriate to the problem. There is nothing funny about alcoholism.

THE COSTS

Alcoholism ranks among the major diseases by both incidence and gravity. Excessive drinking is involved in over one-half of the motor vehicle associated fatalities in the United States (42). Crimes of physical violence have a ten to one chance of being committed under the influence of alcohol. The National Council on Alcoholism has found that the estimated five percent of alcoholic employees in the United States "cost business and government in excess of six billion dollars a year in absenteeism, poor work, wasted material, and replacement training" (19). Twenty-five to thirty percent of all patients in the medical and surgical wards of a general hospital are estimated to suffer the effects of an alcohol related problem (32).

The Statistical Bulletin of Metropolitan Life adds motor vehicle accidents and medical expenses and comes up with a formidable tally of 26 billion lost yearly to the nation (2).

Although limited and moderate consumption is considered relatively harmless, its chronic use can lead to a formidable catalogue of disturbances. These include gastrointestinal problems (one-third of all alcoholics suffer from gastritis), damage to the endocrine glands, cardiovascular and hepatic disease, vitamin deficiencies, peripheral neuropathies, Wernicke's encephalopathy, Korsakoff's psychosis, and complications such as pneumonia and head injuries due to falls. A withdrawal syndrome results when the alcoholic stops using alcohol; it ranges from the "shakes" to convulsive seizures (rum fits) and delirium tremens, a serious life threatening complication. The life expectancy of an alcoholic is 12 years less than his nonalcoholic counterpart (37). If a car doesn't get him, his liver will.

It has been estimated that four to six million people in the United States are alcoholics. Since the disease has a ripple effect, including four to five additional people who suffer its consequences tangentially, it is a safe guess that ten percent of the population is involved in some way. The heavy cost to industry, to medicine, to the individual, to his family and community, gives the alcoholic a legitimate, high-priority claim to medical services.

ALCOHOLISM DEFINED

Jellinek defines alcoholism as any damage to the individual, to society, or both brought about by the use of alcohol (29). A chronic, progressive, and addictive disease, alcoholism is the result of complicated etiology. One view is that it satisfies oral craving; another is that the alcoholic is the offspring of a dominant mother and a weak or absent father, a parental twosome that have taken the rap for other malfunctioning offspring, such as the homosexual and the schizophrenic. The hypothesis that it is the organism's way to correct a chemical imbalance is under investigation. The commonly accepted view is that alcoholism is a maladaptive behavioral adjustment, a learned pattern of coping with feelings through intoxication. Why one learns to handle his problems by drinking rather than thinking them through depends on a combination of cultural, social, personal, and physical factors.

WHY DRINK?

In our society alcohol is not only permitted by law but encouraged by social tradition. The ability to take and hold alcohol is often a measure of worth. A father was heard to remark with pride how his seventeen year old son could down "five scotches and still call his uncle *sir*". At most social gatherings the first thing any guest is greeted with is "What are you drinking?" If he says he's drinking nothing he's cajoled to confess that he is on a.) a diet, b.) the wagon, or c.) prescribed medication (40).

Social factors which influence the use of alcohol include marital, economic, or interpersonal problems and demographic determinants such as sex, age, ethnic background, and occupation.

One may drink, yet in the absence of social or other factors, not become an alcoholic. Physical factors involve organic variables such as whether a biochemical need is satisfied by the pharmacologic action of alcohol in depressing the brain. Psychologic or personal factors include the effects of the alcohol on the user, does it relieve anxiety and does it make him feel that he can cope? Temporary moods as well as long–term personality traits influence the individual's response to alcohol. The alcoholic will experience different effects if he drinks when depressed than if he drinks when he is feeling happy.

While psychologic factors do not provide all the answers, they seem to be the most significant in the case of the alcoholic. If the effects of alcohol help the user to resolve conflict and dissipate tension, the act becomes rewarding; he *learns* to drink.

The alcoholic drinks to feel good. Alcohol relieves psychic and physical pain, reduces tension, and seems to make conflict go away. It fulfills many functions. It is a bolsterer ("I can't see the boss unless I'm oiled up first."), a releaser of inhibitions ("I have to get half-crocked before I can let him touch me."), a neutralizer of anxiety (for anyone who cannot board a plane without a few belts), an escape from guilt (for the person who got yelled at by his boss for goofing off), a hostility surrogate (for the person who gets drunk and yells at the man on the next stool instead of his brother-in-law), and an acceptable regression, a state in which one can cry and maybe get a little mothering.

Alcohol also provides an excuse for irresponsible behavior, an outlet that many societies have built-in, such as the *Pibloctoq* of the Eskimos, in which one can lose control, throw off his skins, roll naked in the snow, generally act crazy, and still maintain social approval (21). ("Boy, was I bombed last night. What did I do?" "Man, you were really wild." "No kidding!")

CHARACTERISTICS OF THE ALCOHOLIC

The image of the alcoholic conjures up a skid row bum, a derelict who skitters about the city streets clutching a bottle in a paper bag against a coat padded with newspapers. While this is the highly visible alcoholic, he makes up less than five percent of the alcoholic population. Other less visible alcoholics derive from all segments of the general population. Although studies have shown the alcoholic to be preponderantly white, Catholic, urban, middle–aged, of Irish descent, and male, the ranks of alcoholics have increasingly come to include younger people, women, and diverse ethnic groups. The alcoholic is as likely to be a suburban housewife lacing her orange juice with Smirnoff before her children go off to school or a young steelworker who has just begun to get tanked up nightly on his way home from work. Little retrospective information is helpful in predicting which members of the population are likely candidates for alcoholism. While there is no one alcoholic personality, alcoholics have been found to display general characteristics.

The alcoholic is often dependent, impatient, sensitive, easily offended, passive, unable to assert himself appropriately or to express hostility (when sober). Work done by Plutchik and DiScipio suggests that the personality profile of chronic alcoholics may reflect a lifetime of heavy drinking rather than the heavy drinking occuring as a result of the personality (44).

Whether the chicken or the egg, the alcoholic deals with his feelings in immature ways. Self-control appears to be missing. His personal relations are tenuous and difficult. Interpersonal relationships never crystallize, and he moves on a periphery of social communication. It is difficult for him to project into the future, to anticipate eventualities and consequences. This makes detailing matters of medical significance to him of little value, since he cannot relate such long-term consequences to himself. He is easily discouraged and cannot deal with inner conflicts. He often finds minor frustrations hard to accept and may react to disappointments with extreme hurt and depression.

Once in the body, alcohol has several roles. It is a food, a tranquilizer, a poison (in high enough dosage alcohol can cause death by respiratory paralysis), and an addicting agent if consumed in sufficient quantities over a long period of time. There is a line between the social drinker and the addicted drinker. The major difference between the recreational drinker and the dependent drinker is the latter's compulsion to drink.

A more precise definition of the addicted alcoholic considers somatic and personality changes and is plotted through the lines of tolerance and dependency. The alcoholic can be identified by the following criteria: loss of control over when and how he drinks, change in tolerance, a withdrawal syndrome, and the relinquishing of other interests in favor of a preoccupation with alcohol. The manual on Alcoholism prepared by the AMA states that the key factor in alcoholism is control or its lack (37).

STAGES OF ALCOHOLISM

It is possible for an alcoholic to go for years before he is recognized or before he seeks help. The alcoholic usually does not become an addicted drinker overnight but moves through progressive stages. The physician's major goal with the alcoholic may be to identify the individual in the intermediary stages, the transitional period when he changes from a social drinker to an alcoholic.

It is estimated that no more than ten percent of the alcoholic population receives treatment, and those that are treated are considered the most difficult to treat. They are characterized by severe social, psychologic, and physical features typical of the late stages of alcoholism. They are often in middle or old age, they show evidence of marital or occupational instability, and they may have been arrested and imprisoned. At this advanced stage an alcoholic ignores the needs of his family, has shown destructive behavior at work, has lost his sense of ethics, and displays impaired reality testing.

The National Council on Alcoholism lists 13 gradual steps to alcoholism, 12 of which are listed here (53). Not every alcoholic follows them exactly; often some steps are taken in a different order, overlap, or are omitted entirely.

1. He begins to drink, takes an occasional cocktail, and once in a while drinks too much.
2. He starts having blackouts, getting drunk with regularity; sometimes after getting tanked up, he recalls nothing after a certain point in the evening. This is not because he drinks until he passes out; it is a kind of chemical amnesia.
3. He finds liquor means more to him than to others; he changes from sipping to gulping; he begins to sneak drinks and doesn't want to discuss drinking. (A danger line is drawn under this point.)
4. He consistently drinks more than he planned; this comes about two years after the first blackout. Drinking behavior is getting out of hand; the effect of drinking shows on his everyday conduct: This is marked by a loss of control, shown in extravagant spending.
5. He starts excusing himself for drinking, erecting a rationale, a defensive structure of alibis and excuses.
6. He starts taking eye openers, drinks in the morning to start the day.
7. He begins to drink alone, a serious step because the solitary drinker is considered a social misfit. Solitary drinking does not refer to any drink taken alone; the definition applies to drinking in which the fantasy world is too pleasurable to share with another.
8. He gets antisocial when he drinks; hostility and violent acting out become part of his behavioral repertoire. (The pamphlet draws a second danger line beneath this step.)
9. He begins the acute stage of compulsive drinking, considered the stage of the true alcoholic, by going on benders which last for several days. During this time he drinks blindly with one goal: to get and stay drunk. At step 4 he lost control of how much he drinks; now he loses control of *when*.
10. He feels deep remorse and deeper resentment; he feels personal guilt first, then projects it outward—the fault is someone else's.
11. He feels deep, nameless anxiety—trembling hands, vacant stare, the

shakes; he becomes clever and persistent about getting and protecting his liquor supply.
12. He might wake up in the hospital after the DTs and realize drinking has him licked.

Jellinek lists four stages of alcoholism (29). First is the *prealcoholic symptomatic phase*. Lasting several months to two years; it is characterized by occasional or constant drinking to obtain relief from tension. At the end of this stage, the individual develops an increased tolerance for alcohol and finds that he needs a larger amount to reach the same stage of feeling good. The *prodromal phase* is characterized by sudden blackouts during some of the periods of drinking, surreptitious rather than open drinking; a preoccupation with alcohol; and gulping rather than sipping alcohol when in conversation. The third phase of addiction, called the *crucial phase*, begins with a loss of behavioral control which makes the alcoholic's drinking conspicuous; and earns for him censure and warning, to which he responds with alibis or remorse and limited periods of total abstinence. He loses his outside interests, is concerned over protecting his supply, forgets to eat, displays self-pity, may move to a new environment, is likely to be hospitalized for the first time, and shows metabolic changes and a decrease in his sex drive. If he is married, he becomes paranoid about the activities of his spouse and begins to drink regularly in the morning. The fourth phase, which is the *chronic phase* of alcohol addiction, is seen in prolonged benders which often lead to ethical deterioration, impairment of thinking, and in ten percent of the cases, alcoholic psychosis. The individual in this stage drinks anything with anyone, although he may lose his tolerance of alcohol when his liver loses the ability to oxidize it.

Although some alcoholics quickly make the jump between first and last steps, the pattern is usually gradual. The individual who is becoming an alcoholic, concerned with when he drinks and where he can drink, undergoes a change in drinking pattern. He may go on the wagon for a while in the beginning and engage in other self-imposed restraints in order to maintain control of his drinking; for example, he may drink only at certain times on Saturday night in order to sober up for work on Monday, or he may drink only wine or beer. The alcoholic who will not drink alone or early in the morning may point to his drinking pattern as proof that he not an alcoholic. The artificial controls of drinking usually dissolve in the need to simply drink. While drunk, he may experience either euphoria or depression. The effect doesn't matter because the behavioral pattern has already been learned. When sober he may feel guilt and shame, but that doesn't matter either because he also feels the original emotional stress that caused him to drink in the first place.

EARLY DETECTION

Since it is impossible to predict who will become an alcoholic through personality factors, the physician has to rely on physical signs and observer reports of behavior for the clues necessary to detect potential alcoholism in the absence of a voluntary admission. Chief complaints of the unrecognized alcoholic may be epigastric burning and distress, nausea, anorexia, vomiting, hangover, diarrhea, sleep and appetite disturbances, and depression. Since these complaints are shared by the general population (approximately ten percent of the United States male population show symptoms of gastritis), they are not enough to make a case but are only alerting sign posts.

Besides bloodshot eyes, hand tremors, and pants held up by grocery string, factors which might corroborate the physician's suspicions would include observations from those with whom he works such as a decline in job performance, lack of job interest, frequent absences on Monday and Friday, and the use of personal or family problems as an excuse for excessive absenteeism. Those with whom he lives could add information by revealing that he is becoming a loner, is very sensitive to advice, is alternatively sullen and talkative, and has begun to run up serious debts.

Following a general questioning about the use of all drugs, the physician can lead into drinking history by pointing out that alcohol is a commonly used drug (56). "O.K., now I'm clear about the amount of coffee you drink and how many cigarettes you smoke. How about alcohol?"

The alcoholic is notoriously inaccurate when discussing amounts. One who may be consuming a quart of hard liquor daily may state that he takes a few nips. Questioning of all patients, suspected alcoholics or not, should cover, "How much and how often do you drink?", "With whom?", "Where?", "Under what circumstances?", "With what effect?", "Have you always drunk in this way?", "How have your drinking habits changed?" or "How does your alcohol consumption compare with a year ago?" Knott et al (32). point out that determining the amount, frequency, and type of alcohol use is not as important as determining the extent to which alcohol figures in the daily life of the patient. For example, there is a difference between a daily drink at lunch, and a nightcap that is essential for sleep. The next question would be "why?" and "How long has this been necessary?"

A significant clue to the potential alcoholic is his tendency to construct alibis (49). He is more likely to defend or deny his drinking than other patients and will minimize usage. If he appears uneasy or glibly supplies a reasonable excuse for a tear now and then, he is a more likely candidate than the patient who freely and openly discusses usage.

When alcoholism is suspected, the whole range of questions about the sequelae to the disease must be explored, such as binges, blackouts, amnesia, DTs, morning drinking, solitary drinking, effect on work, arrests, dietary habits, and secret drinking.

It may be customary for someone to have a cocktail at lunch and another one or two before dinner. If this person began to stash a thermos in his locker and organize his time around when he could pop his head in and sneak a few, he is crossing the line. One question the physician may ask to elicit this key behavior is "What is the attitude of others to your drinking?" or "Do others seem to understand why you drink?" The patient may reply, "There's nothing to understand." He may reply in the negative or he may not reply at all. If he is in transition, he is more likely to state that they do not.

Swenson and Morse (52) and Seltzer (47) have devised screening tests to be used by the physician in diagnosing the alcoholic. Swenson and Morse's instrument which is designed to be self administered, built upon many of the questions in Seltzer's test is intended for the physician to use as a guide to the interview. It includes, such questions as "Have you ever been told by a doctor to stop drinking?", "Have you ever felt the need to cut down?", and "Have you ever been told you have liver trouble?"

Once the physician has formed a tentative diagnosis of this patient as an alcoholic who is crossing the line between social drinking and the compulsive drinking of alcoholism, he does not play out his hand. Accusation will only create denial or rationalization. Using euphemisms such as *problem drinking, compulsive drinking, secret drinking,* or *alcohol addiction* are more palatable, the physician can state clearly that he is concerned because there are strong indications that the patient's drinking habits are changing and are leading to more serious drinking behavior. The patient may be shown how his drinking differs from that of the social drinker. The physician can help this patient by counseling him on his problems of daily living, referring him to outside counsel, and teaching him *how* to drink.

Alcohol does not affect behavior until it is in the bloodstream. As the level of blood alcohol rises, behavior increasingly is impaired. The concentration of alcohol in the blood depends on the rate of drinking, the rate of absorption, the size of the person, and the ability of the person's liver to metabolize the alcohol. By teaching this patient his own approximate rate of metabolism, ("You can handle a glass of beer or a shot of rye every hour") to space his drinks, to eat before he drinks, to eat while he drinks, to plan in advance how many drinks he will have to sip instead of gulping, and to drink drinks that are absorbed more slowly, the physician creates a situation in which the effects of drinking are minimized. The result may be that his drinking is under greater control, partially because he perceives that the control is his. Additionally the drinking itself loses some of its magic because it has been planned in the physician's office. This renders it the same excitement as drinking from the sterilizer jar.

Not all alcoholics in the early stages of alcoholism reject aid. Some seek it. Some may see a physician because of their concern about blackouts, benders that they have gone on with lapses of memory, or other signs of serious trouble. They may or may not relate the experience to their drinking habits and can be helped only if they will put the two together. A helpful question at this point would be "What do you think has caused this?" or "What do you think about your drinking habits?" If the patient answers, "I drink too much." or "When I drink I can't seem to stop," the concession that he has made allows the physician to make an objective connection.

THE CROSSED LINE

The alcoholic who has crossed the line has probably put in 8–10 years of heavy drinking before he appears for treatment for his alcoholism. These years have been marked by deteriorating social relations and an increased preoccupation with getting a drink. Although he previously may have sought medical attention for an alcohol related illness, he seeks help for his addiction because of an emergency in his life. In most cases the emergency is identified by others and not by the patient himself. There is usually some external pressure to change his behavior. A spouse or an employer will call and ask, "Please talk to John about his drinking." Sometimes a spouse will threaten to leave, or an employer will threaten to fire him if he does not get help. The alcoholic may be motivated to see a physician if he learns that alcohol is turning his liver into a sponge, but more likely it is after a serious drinking crisis that he seeks help on his own. Some alcoholics have to reach "low bottom," a point when they are without home, family, friends, job, funds, and in poor health before they look for assistance.

FIRST VISIT

It has been found that patients admitted to the emergency service of a general hospital with alcohol problems could be motivated to seek subsequent treatment for their alcoholism if they were made to feel that their physician was interested in them (6, 7). The initial encounter with the physician, when complaints second-ary to alcoholism were managed, was considered a crucial variable. If the patient received his care in a nonpunitive, nonjudgmental climate from a caretaker who showed concern, he was more likely to become a willing participant in voluntary treatment.

Estimates suggest that the primary care physician sees five to ten patients weekly who are already alcoholic or on their way to becoming alcoholic. When this patient first walks into the physician's office, he must be met with complete accept-ance. The physician neither endorses nor censures. The patient may be in the midst of a drinking spree, he may be in the midst of withdrawal, or he may be in a period of abstinence. Whatever his condition, the first visit is crucial, for it is then that possibilities for a therapeutic relationship are decided.

The physician may be knocked over by the fumes; but if he hopes to treat this patient, his best bet is to toss him a few Life Savers, lean backwards, and conduct a smooth and low key interview, something like a Rolls Royce salesman, who doesn't care if you buy or not but who enjoys talking to you.

PHYSICIAN'S APPROACH

A detached and objective approach by itself is too devoid of feeling to create rapport. An authoritarian physician who scolds and forecasts doom will also not do well, especially so because the alcoholic needs to defy authority. His lack of cooper-ation may be his way of testing the physician. Any harsh or critical attitude will bring about more denial.

The physician attempting to find a happy ground on which to communicate with his alcoholic patient is like a mountain climber trying to get purchase on a moss–slick ledge. Fortunately, the physician has a toe hold. When the alcoholic comes to the physician's office, the physician may assume that if he asks for help for his immediate problems, he is also seeking help for the broader problem.

The best attitude for the physician to adopt is a combination of objectivity and sympathy. If the physician is empathic ("I can understand how your boss's attitude would upset you."), he conveys an interest and an understanding of his patient's daily problems. If he is consistent in his attitude, not judgmental one moment and supportive the next, he has a shot at earning the patient's trust. The main thing the physician can do is become a concerned and patient listener who encourages ventilation. Because this patient may go into considerable detail over grievances, the physician may find it necessary to interrupt diplomatically and tactfully. "I have a good understanding of what it's like at home for you, and we can go into greater detail later; but now I'd like to hear about how you sleep nights."

HISTORY TAKING

When giving his medical history, the alcoholic uses two mechanisms and uses them well. The first is denial. This is usually very strong, well–developed, and not easily disturbed by mirroring reality for him. Because of the strong denial system, in-teraction with the alcoholic will not usually be facilitated by confrontation. Even when he is intoxicated, if the physician were to say, "Look at you, you can't even stand," the alcoholic will argue, "I know exactly what I'm doing; I'm in perfect control." The power of denial is so strong that many patients who must be hospital-ized for cirrhosis as salient as an illuminated text, yellowed skin and eyes, swollen body and all, will not acknowledge the connection to alcohol. Unless the patient

is generally concerned about his physical well-being, telling him that he will die in a few years if he does not curb his alcohol intake will not help. His denial system has not allowed him to see the deterioration of his body.

The second defense mechanism used well by the alcoholic is rationalization. He justifies his actions; he has learned neat mind tricks that help him fix the reason for his drinking on causes perfectly acceptable to him. He was fine except that his boss yelled at him, unfairly, of course; he was at a party and the host insisted that he drink; he had a fight with his wife; etc.

These two systems of denial and rationalization make the alcoholic what has been called a lukewarm participant in the clinical interaction at best (41).

Two problems in the clinical setting are that the alcoholic is notoriously uncooperative and the physician is notoriously short of time. It is a strong temptation to treat the patient's existing physical disorders and send him on his way.

When taking the alcoholic's history, the physician's initial questions should revolve around his marital status, the kind of work he does, the state of his health, what he feels are his main problems and worries, how he lives, and where he lives. The idea is to get a picture of the individual, not just another alcoholic. If questions about his drinking habits are fitted into a general framework of investigation regarding all drug use, the topic is part of a flow and loses its intrusive quality. Inquiry into prescribed medication, drugs suggested by the pharmacist, and drugs he selects for himself provides a natural backdrop against which alcohol plays only a cameo part. (32)

Questions related to the patient's drinking history seek to determine when his drinking first became a problem to him or to anyone else. He might deny that it has ever been a problem for him, but the physician can determine when others began to hassle or annoy him about drinking. If he is able to answer when it first became a problem, the next question is under what circumstances? What is his concept of the disease? Where, when, how much, and with whom does he drink? What is the effect of alcohol on his personality and his feelings about himself?

While it facilitates the interchange to accept his statements at face value, excessive understanding may reduce the physician's effectiveness (37). The patient may not want to believe that the contusions on his head are the result of falls while drunk, but the physician, while listening to his explanation that he bangs his head while he sleeps, does well not to appear to support statements that are obviously at variance with probability. How does it affect his behavior toward his friends, coworkers, and family? What previous efforts has he made to overcome his problems with alcohol? Does he want to stop drinking?

AA asks these 11 questions, which might be useful to the physician.

1. Do you crave a drink at a definite time daily?
2. Do you gulp your drinks and sneak extras?
3. Do you drink to relieve feelings of inadequacy?
4. Do you drink to escape worry and to dispel the blues?
5. Do you drink when overtired, to "brace up?"
6. Is it affecting your peace of mind?
7. Is it making your home life unhappy?
8. Do you prefer to drink alone?
9. Do you require a drink the next morning?
10. Do you lose time from work due to drinking?
11. Do you organize your life around drinking?

The patient should be questioned about his pattern of sobriety. Does he go two months between bouts or is two weeks his usual "dry" period? Establishing a pattern is necessary to focus on those periods when he does not drink, even if it's only between four and seven in the morning. Identifying a dry period means that the alcoholic is not a total washout; he still has a shred of behavior upon which both he and the physician can hang their hopes. It's like hoping a plug of skin graft will stretch to the next graft. A pattern that can be identified also provides a picture of the circumstances that promote or provoke his alcoholism.

THE EYEWITNESS

On one visit to the physician, the patient may bring a spouse to complete the picture. If so, it is helpful to see the patient alone first. Usually the spouse will relate a family history of disaster and destruction in which the alcoholic shows increasing irresponsibility and preoccupation with alcohol, and decreasing concern for family and job. When the patient presents his story, the physician may believe he is listening to members of two different families. Everything is usually accounted for with plausible and reasonable explanations, and the physician may wonder if something is wrong with the spouse.

There are others besides one's husband or wife or could contribute observations to a clinical picture. It is necessary that before the physician requests their help, he get the consent of his patient.

TREATMENT—LIVING PROBLEMS

Besides restoring the patient to a physiologically normal state, the physician helps the alcoholic by listening to his difficulties, by giving him feedback in the way of observations, by making suggestions, and by helping him to deal with his day–to–day problems on a practical, common sense level. The primary care physician does not usually have the time or the training to probe for underlying conflicts, but he can use the clinical setting as a suitable place in which to teach the alcoholic patient how to handle social pressures. This may include the discussion of drinking and related problems, teaching him to anticipate difficulties, to plan for short periods in advance, to head problems off at the pass, to balance his options, to seek help when he feels he cannot handle things by himself or when he is anxious or depressed, to live with a decision once made, and to make no promises that cannot be kept.

Discussing how to handle daily problems involves the language of the present. Terms should stress here and now. "I used to. . . ." and "She always . . ." are statements that do not help today. The alcoholic should be made *present* oriented with an increasing emphasis on future planning. For example, an alcoholic patient with a strong attachment to the last child remaining at home can anticipate difficulties when that child makes marriage plans. Anticipatory guidance would involve discussing the matter, airing feelings that the alcoholic will have, and discussing alternative ways of living when an important person has gone from the home.

The physician can also attempt to strengthen the alcoholic's motivation to enter therapy and should be prepared to make appropriate referrals. Social agencies or outpatient clinics and supportive counseling services may undertake his therapy. Agencies such as AA or the Salvation Army operate on the principle of total abstinence and work to achieve and maintain sobriety. Religious in base, they act as peer support.

Family and environment play a major role in planning for this patient. Often the patient's life style has to be completely changed. The family will also need the physician's guidance, and the physician may decide that he can only restore family balance by seeing them together. An alert physician may see that certain family members have vested interests in maintaining the status quo and act in ways that promote drinking. A wife, for example, may enjoy the role of martyr or saddened and dependent spouse. The physician can help the family understand how members reinforce one another.

In the families of most alcoholics, there seems to be a chronic battle of control centering around who does what, at what time, and by whose authority (24). It has been noted that the interaction between husband and wife is a cooperative one, but one in which *one up* or competitive messages are exchanged. Often, when an alcoholic stops drinking, his wife will fight with him over when he is going to start again.

The physician may want to enlist the aid of a family counselor, or he may attempt to work with the family himself. In treating couples there are certain guidelines. The first is get out of the line of fire. The remaining principles of conflict mediation allow both sides to state their case without interruption, followed by each responding to the other in a straight feedback statement. Couples usually have to be taught to respond not with anger but with "I hear you say. . . . is that what you mean?" When each person has the other's message fairly straight, each is allowed to respond. They are taught how to resolve conflicts by mutually seeking acknowledging common ground as a starting place. They also have to learn how to express their feelings directly to each other. Most alcoholics cannot do this. Their communication is tangential, and they must be taught to make direct statements. "When you say that, it makes me feel . . ." This is not always a negative statement, but can be a positive one. "It makes me feel good that you . . ."

The major problem in establishing a therapeutic relationship with the alcoholic is that many times he will come in drunk, or he will miss appointments and not come in at all. Many will assert that they are in control and can stop whenever they want—even when they are intoxicated.

Both patient and physician should be prepared for occasional setbacks. The course is not a steady one. The patient who is moving toward independence might become anxious, for example, when his physician goes on vacation.

Just as in preparing the presurgical patient for the after effects of surgery, it is helpful to prepare this patient for times when he is feeling that he is getting nowhere or that he's slipping backwards. The physician in the above example might say something like, "I'll be leaving town for a few weeks vacation. You might begin to get a little anxious about not being able to reach me. If you do it's a natural feeling and to be expected."

Even in therapy the alcoholic is not going to cling firmly to his decision to accept help. If the physician can offer the alcoholic the same care and concern as patients suffering from somatic illness, the alcoholic's chances for recovery are enhanced. However, the addictive qualities of his disease make his resistance to change greater, and chances for his recovery are less than optimal. Since no patient is accepted on the basis of his chances for recovery, the alcoholic must be viewed strictly as another patient with a serious disease.

THE PATIENT WHO DOES NOT SEEK HELP

Whatever treatment is used—supported withdrawal psychotherapy, or deterrent and suppressive measures such as aversive conditioning or the use of antabuse, the physician should be aware of all the causes that contribute to this particular alcoholic's dependence in order to intervene in as many ways as he can.

Some patients cannot be helped. That is difficult for any health care professional to accept. The physician may treat his patient for medical problems and then be stopped cold. When the patient who harms himself or his family through the use of alcohol cannot be made to realize it, or when he no longer has the will or strength to overcome it, there is little that can be done. A patient who comes in reluctantly at the insistence of her husband, denies drinking, and says that her husband's behavior and attitude are the source of all their problems cannot be helped against her will (56). The physician is in a bind. Although he can say that she is ruining her life and making her family miserable, she already knows this and is probably feeling guilty about it, which speeds up the drinking spiral a bit. Telling her that she is an alcoholic and should go to AA is no help. They will accept only those who admit to the problem, and this woman denies it. Advising her to stop drinking for health reasons will not help. Her strong denial system suggests that her problems are emotional and not easily amenable to logical persuasion.

The only thing that the physician can do for this patient is to state that if she has any problem stopping her drinking, she can always come to him for help.

REFERENCES

1. A-huffin' and a-puffin', a-sniffin' and a-suckin'. Lancet 2(7885): 876–877, 1974
2. Alcholism in the United States. Stat Bull, 55:3–5, 1974
3. Balint M: The Doctor, His Patient & the Illness. New York, International Universities Press, 1957

4. Bauer M et al.: Volatile solvent addiction and traffic safety. Act Nerv Super (Praha) 16:178–179, 1974

5. Blane H: Attitudes, treatment, and prevention. In Mendelson JH (ed): Alcoholism. Boston, Little Brown, 1966, vol 3, no 2, pp 103–125

6. Chafetz ME et al.: Establishing treatment relations with alcoholics. J Nerv Ment Dis 134:395–409, 1962

7. Chafetz ME et al.: Establishing treatment relations with alcoholics: a supplementary report. J Nerv Ment Dis 138:390–393, 1964

8. Chapel JL, Taylor DW: Glue sniffing. Mis Medicine 65:288–292, 1968

9. Chappel JN: Attitudinal barriers to physicians involvement with drug abusers. JAMA 224:1011–1013, 1973

10. Cheek FE, Newell S, Joffe M: Deceptions in the illicit drug market. Science 167(1):276, 1970

11. Chein I: Psychological, social, and epidemiological factors in drug addiction. In Rehabilitating the Narcotics Addict. Washington, Vocational Rehabilitation Administration of HEW, 1966, pp 53–72

12. Cherubin CE: The medical sequelae of narcotic addiction. Ann Intern Med 67:23–33, 1967

13. Cohen CP, White EH, Schoolar JC: Interpersonal patterns of personality for drug-abusing patients and their therapeutic implications. Arch Gen Psychiatry 24:353–358, 1971

14. Cohen S: Amphetamine abuse. JAMA 231:414–415, 1975

15. Crowther B: The college opiate user. Int J Addict 9:241–253, 1974

16. Delong JV: The drugs and their effects. In Dealing With Drug Abuse, a Report to the Ford Foundation. New York, Praeger, 1973

17. Dole VP, Nyswanger ME, Warner A: Successful treatment of 750 criminal addicts. JAMA 206:2708–2711, 1968

18. Dependence on barbiturates and other sedative drugs. Drug Dependence. Chicago, AMA, 1970, pp 97–109

19. Eaton MT: Alcohol, drugs and personnel practices. Personnel Journal 50 (10):757–758, 1971

20. Ellinwood EH: Amphetamine psychosis: individuals, settings, and sequences. Cohn S (eds): Current Concepts on Amphetamine Abuse. Rockville, NIMH, 1972, pp 143–156

21. Foulks E: The Arctic Hysterias of the North Alaskan Eskimoo. Anthropological studies No. 10. Washington, American Anthropological Association, 1972

22. Freedman DX: On the use and abuse of LSD. Arch Gen Psychiatry 18:330–347, 1968

23. Gay G et al: Short term heroin detoxification on an outpatient basis. Int J Addictions 6(2):241, 259–60, 1971

24. Gorad SL et al.: A communications approach to alcoholism. Q U Stud Alcohol 32:-651–668, 1971

25. Henry MJ: Society's misfits: the drug problem. Practitioner 213(1275):373–374, 1974

26. Holcenberg JS: Drug abuse . . . after acute management, supportive care. Postgrad Med 54:114, 1973

27. Irwin S: Drugs of abuse: An introduction to their actions and potential hazards. Student Association for the Study of the Hallucinogens, 1970

28. Isbell H: Historical development of attitudes toward opiate addiction in the United States. In Faiber SM, Wilson RHL (eds): Conflict and Creativity. New York, McGraw Hill, 1963, pp 154–170

29. Jellinek EM: Phases of alcohol addiction. Q J Stud Alcohol 13:673–684, 1952

30. Keniston K: Search and Rebellion Among the Advantaged. Drug Dependence. Chicago, AMA, 1970, pp 42–52

31. Keup W: The vocabulary of the drug user and alcoholic: a glossary. Int J Addict 6:347–73, 1971

32. Knott DH, Fink RD, Beard JD: Unmasking alcohol abuse. Am Fam Physician 10(4):123–126

33. Lemberger L et al: Marijuana: studies on the disposition and metabolism of delta 9-tetrahydrocannabinol in man. Science 170:1320–1322, 1970

34. Lieff J et al.: Attitudes of the medical profession toward drug abuse. Am J Public Health 63:1035–1039, 1973

35. Lindesmith A: The Addict and the Law. New York, Random, 1967, pp 105–6, 124

36. Maddux JF: Treatment of narcotic addiction: issues and problems. In Rehabilitating the Narcotics Addict. Washington, Vocational Rehabilitation Administration of HEW, 1966, pp 11–21

37. Manual on Alcoholism. Chicago, AMA, 1968

38. Marx JL: Opiate Receptors: Implications and Applications. Science 189:708–710, 1975

39. May E: Drugs without crime. Harper's Magazine 243:60–65, 1971

40. Morgan AJ, Moreno JW: The Practice of Mental Health Nursing. Philadelphia, J B Lippincott, 1973

41. Mullen H, Sangiuliano I: Alcoholism. Boston, Little Brown, 1966

42. 1968 Alcohol and Highway Safety Report: A Study Transmitted by the Secretary of the Department of Transportation to the Congress. Washington, U S Government Printing Office, 1968

43. O'Donnell JA: Narcotics Addiction in Kentucky. Rockville, NIMH, 1969

44. Plutchik R, Di Scipio WJ: Personality patterns in chronic alcoholism (Korsakoff's syndrome) chronic schizophrenia and geriatric patients with chronic brain syndrome. J Am Geriatr Soc 22:514–516, 1974

45. Prinzmetal M, Bloomberg W: The use of benzedrine for treatment of narcolepsy. JAMA 105:2051, 1935

46. Seevers MH: Etiological considerations in drug abuse and dependence. Drug Dependence, Chicago, AMA, 1970

47. Seltzer ML: The Michigan alcoholic screening test: The quest for a new diagnostic instruement. Am J Psychiatry 128:1565–69, 1972

48. Shader RI et al: Suggestions for treating drug abusers in a family practice. Med Times 102:91–92, 1974

49. Smith JA: Difficult Patients. Chicago, Year Book Medical, 1963, pp 199–211

50. Society overmedicated? Lancet 1:1325–1326, 1974

51. Sowa PA et al.: Attitudes of hospital staff toward alcoholics and drug addicts. Q J Stud Alcohol 35:210–214, 1974

52. Swenson WM, Morse RM: The use of a self administered alcoholism screening test (SAAST) in a medical center. Mayo Clin Proc 50(4):204–208, 1975

53. 13 Steps to Alcoholism. New York, The National Council on Alcoholism, March, 1974

54. Wald PM, Hutt PB: The drug abuse survey project: Summary of findings, conclusions, and recommendations. In Dealing with Drug Abuse, A Report to the Ford Foundation. New York, Praeger, 1973

55. Weil AT: Altered states of consciousness. In Dealing with Drug Abuse, A Report to the Ford Foundation, New York, Praeger, 1973

56. Weinberg JR: Interview technique for diagnosing alcoholism. Am Fam Physician 9:-107–115, 1974

57. Weisman T: Drug Abuse and Drug Counseling: A Case Approach. Cleveland, The Press of Case Western Reserve University, 1972

9
Death and Dying

In a little while I will be gone from you, my people, and whither I cannot tell. From nowhere we come, into nowhere we go. What is life? It is the flash of a firefly in the night. It is the breath of a buffalo in the wintertime. It is the shadow that runs across the grass and loses itself in the sunset.

Chief Crowfoot

DEATH—A TABOO SUBJECT

ESTRANGEMENT

Somehow the subject of death has replaced sex as a fundamental, powerful, and universal experience which is shrouded in spectacular taboo (23). Death has been relegated to our dark corners, those places in hospitals, homes for the aged, and mortuaries where an anonymous army who attend the dying and the dead pump in infusions, hook up machinery, and plug up the orifices with cotton when the infusions and the machinery fail. Those of us who are not part of this army meet death only accidentally, probably seeing more dead and dying animals on the side of the road in one year than we see of human beings in a lifetime.

Advances in medicine and preventive care and changes in social structure which have altered the nature and place of death are responsible for the estrangement. The most significant change in the cause of death has been the increase of the so-called chronic degenerative diseases which occur later in life and are thought to be associated with the aging process.

Until a few decades ago, high infant mortality, obstetrical complications, infectious diseases, famine, and congenital malformations made death familiar. Now the experience of death is limited in most families to their aged, so much so that when anyone of less than retirement age dies, the response of friends and relatives is generally one of outrage similar to that displayed to an umpire who called the play incorrectly. That's not the way the game is played; it's not fair; it wasn't supposed to happen.

Although most Americans died at home at the turn of the century, it is estimated that death now takes place in institutions nearly 80 percent of the time (27). One reason for the change in the location of dying is our high mobility. We have become a nation of back packers, living like snails in mobile homes, or shipping our nautilus chambers ahead of us in huge vans that barrel down the nation's highways, averaging one move for each nuclear family every five years. One can't travel fast saddled with large houses or with aging family members who move a little too slowly. As a consequence, many elderly are left behind to live alone in small apartments or in single rooms. Even if they do have relatives nearby who could help them, those that are available do not always feel they are responsible for giving help.

222

Very few relatives are at the bedside of a dying family member at the moment of his death (28). Young children especially are shielded from the event and are hustled out of the house or restricted from the hospital by regulation. Thus our sociology insulates us from dying and from death, clouding it with mystery that is reflected throughout our culture.

SUBTERFUGE

The taboo is the reason for using all manner of euphemisms when referring to the dead. Someone has passed away, gone on, departed, or is lost. "I understand you lost your father." is a commonplace condolence, spoken as if the father were an aged Hansel who couldn't find his way out of the forest. When we kill our pets, supposedly with mercy, we put them to sleep. We use the same analogy for humans who have died. "He looked so peaceful he could've been sleeping," "Grandpa's gone to sleep," and "The big sleep" are other common statements spoken as if to reassure the living that when they experience this nameless event, they too will be simply sleeping. There is nothing final about sleeping. It is a rest period, a transition period. We have slept through thousands of nights and have always awakened. There is no reason to think that this sleep will be any different.

Funeral directors go to great lengths to sustain the myth of sleep. They have sleeping or dreaming rooms in which bodies are placed before burial. They also go to great pains to take the sting from death, which is its look, and substitute the face of sleep (26). They remove adhesive tape marks from medical and surgical dressings, clean the fingernails (which is advised before arterial injection which plumps the tips of the fingers), drain blisters, remove loose facial blisters, correct skin slip, bleach areas where ecchymosis and purpura exist, correct buck teeth, straighten nostrils, align ear lobes, support sagging tissues (particularly of the eye and cheek regions), set features, cosmetically remove tissue gas, subcutaneous emphysema, or decomposition, and dress the dead in flowing, sleep-like garments that produce an ethereal effect.

Small wonder that it often comes as a surprise to those who encounter an accidental death in their work, police officers, the military, firemen, rescue squads, and whoever helps clean away the rubble, to see that the dead don't always close their mouths or eyes, their bodies often swell up, and sometimes their skin slips down.

DEATH DENYING

Denial is a coping mechanism so powerful that many Americans do not believe in their own death. Intellectually they will agree that everyone dies. The fact of death is posted everywhere, in whole pages of the daily newspaper, in actuary tables, and in one of the first syllogisms we learn, "Man is Mortal." However, people secretly believe that they will be exceptions. Some act, some talisman, or some piece of kryptonite will make them impervious and grant them protection, like the red "X" on the door of the ancient Hebrews that was a signal to the Angel of Death not to come in. This feeling of invulnerability may be the result of all the narrow brushes with death most of us have had: near misses in an automobile, in an airplane, or on a bicycle; with the chicken pox; or on a battlefield. Having escaped relatively unharmed, we are somehow innoculated.

The feeling of immortality usually lasts until some time after the first physical signs of aging occur, like grey hair, wrinkles, sagging bellies, aches and pains, menopause, or a cholesterol warning. The first inkling that one might be finite after all brings a sense of time wasted and time lost, of not having accomplished what one would have wished, of missed opportunities, and of a rush to complete whatever it is one is doing. This accelerates as each one moves past an invisible time zone of his own in which he begins to have strong intimations of his own death.

Certainly it is not contrary to human motivation to fear death and try to prevent it. Self-preservation is a fundamental human motive. Life, even with its bad moments, is a seductive event for most people. We live for the next breath, the next taste, the next corner, the next breeze to caress our skin, and the next sun to warm us. Even in depression we live for the next sob, otherwise everyone would only cry once. We ingest life with all of our senses, even when those senses become limited. Young people marvel at the old and the infirm, many of whom, in spite of having lost significant body function, cling as tenaciously to life as a barnacle on the hull of a ship.

DEATH DEFYING

Death denying extends to death defying (34). We challenge death in order to prove that we are immune. Evel Knievel vaulting the Snake River Canyon with his SkyCycle 2, demolition derbies, bronco busting, free–falling from airplanes, skiing, soaring over cliffs with flimsy kites like polyester pterodactyls, shooting rapids in a canoe, and climbing sheer faces of rock are games against death. If one wins the game, it means that death's power has been diminished. For the moment at least, man has triumphed over nature. At the core of this defiance is part of the American value system, that part which prizes man's ability to master nature. This attitude has been responsible for taming vast expanses of the continent and has motivated the remarkable technological progress which we now enjoy. We defy death when we suspend dead people in thermos bottles filled with liquid nitrogen, hoping that the future medical professionals will be able to thaw them out and repair the damage and that not too many cells will be destroyed in the process. Despite this challenge to dying, death is still the ultimate thwart to man's attempts to control nature.

DEATH'S REALITIES

The seriously ill are usually introduced to their own dying with a rush in a wailing ambulance to a place of fearsome smells that they make out as the hospital. There they lie under a glare of lights, the object of attention of anonymous hands and faces all swinging into the practiced and coordinated action of acute care, barking words like *morphine, IPPB, digitalis,* and *tourniquet.* No one has the time to listen to or answer questions. Kubler-Ross describes this experience (21):

"He (the patient) slowly but surely is beginning to be treated like a thing. He is no longer a person. Decisions are made often without his opinion. If he tries to rebel, he will be sedated, and after hours of waiting and wondering whether he has the strength, he will be wheeled into the operating room or intensive treatment unit and become an object of great concern and great financial investment."

ISOLATION AND DEPERSONALIZATION

Despite the often valiant battle that is being waged for this patient's life, two unfortunate processes have begun. These are isolation and depersonalization. The care that is being given him not only demands his separation from the outside

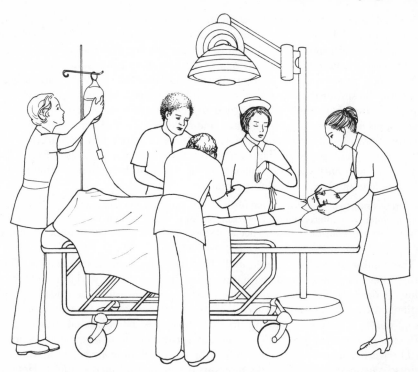

world, but subjects him to an interhospital insulation. The function of medical personnel is to make the patient's systems work as well and as long as they can (7, 36). To this end they will often labor past their rounds and past their endurance, maintaining intimacy with his body, but separating themselves from his person, especially withdrawing when their labors seem to fail (1). Family and friends may now visit only for short periods of time unless he is considered close to death. Other patients are shielded from his struggles with curtains that don't close all the way, screens that block everyone's light and air, and stellar performances by the staff, who talk to him or keep his IV running after he dies while they hustle his body past the living. Sometimes the charade is unnecessary, since it is frequent practice to transfer a dying patient to a private room.

The separation and isolation we associate with death and dying we also equate with punishment. Our society isolates to punish, as illustrated by the seclusion rooms in our correctional and psychiatric facilities, the social deprivation enforced on prisoners of war, the social ostracism that faces offenders of custom, the physical removal of criminal offenders to the literal outskirts of society, the practice of sending misbehaving children out of sight, and the "silent treatment" we give someone who has wounded us.

Most hospital staff members avoid the issue of death by avoiding the patient, popping in and out of his room long enough to keep an eye on him and give him treatment, but moving and talking too fast to answer any questions or to listen to any woeful comments. Although their efforts to sustain his life may be of heroic proportions they find talk with him too painful, too awkward, and too fruitless.

In dealing with the seriously ill, many physicians and nurses rely on objectivity, which translates to disinterest in anything that cannot be palpated, drained, or infused. They find it easier to maintain composure if they concentrate on solving the problems of disease. There is less risk of personal investment in connecting a respirator or performing a tracheotomy than in dealing with the patient on the receiving end who may want someone to tell him what is happening to him.

In a study on response to call lights, it was found that the closer the patient was to death, the slower the nurse was to respond to his light. Nurses do not take the rap alone, but share their attitudes and behavior with interns, residents, house officers, private physicians, technicians, and orderlies, most of whom are uncomfortable with the interpersonal aspects of dying and respond by withdrawal.

In an eloquent paper on his own dying, an anonymous professor from the University of Pennsylvania described how the actions of hospital personnel made him feel like an object. His illness seemed

"to demonstrate to people that I'm not really people anymore, I'm something else. I'm a body that has some very interesting characteristics about it, which include twitching of the muscles, rather symptomatic of this particular disease . . . I felt treated as an object. Being a patient is one thing, but being an object is even less than being a patient (30)."

The combination of separation and objectivity create depersonalization. The patient becomes then "a body with interesting characteristics" and ironically that which is denied, death or its possibility, has in some measure been dealt to the patient. Although he may not have suffered a biologic death, he experiences a social death, a state of nonbeing. In some instances, he is treated as a corpse although he is clinically alive. The staff may speak in front of a comatose patient as if he were dead or insert dentures into the mouth of someone whose imminent demise is expected (46). Social death grants the patient peculiar visibility. He is a body to be done to, no longer a person to be reckoned with. Medical personnel alone do not create a social death. The family shares the responsibility when they taper off their visits or begin to talk of the distribution of property and effects in his presence.

CULTURAL ATTITUDES

During the 1950s, Feifel, who was investigating death and dying, initially encountered strong resistance from physicians and hospital directors when he asked for permission to talk with terminally ill patients about their own deaths (11). The rationale with which he was dismissed was that it was cruel, sadistic, and traumatic to discuss death with the seriously ill. Oken's investigations revealed similar attitudes (33). Even after the impact of the work of Kubler-Ross, it is still standard medical practice to keep a dying patient in the dark concerning his condition (4, 27, 34, 39). Although it may be called benign protection, most of the credit for the dissembling goes to denial. When physicians do not discuss death with their patients, they reflect the attitudes of society which places limits on what can be freely discussed.

Physicians keep information on death not only from the patient involved but from other personnel. Although a nurse prefers to hear about a patient's condition from the physician, he often does not tell her, perhaps because he does not know himself. It is difficult to know which coma is the last. Often the nurse must gather cues about the patient's condition from other sources, such as the patient's chart, the physician's mood, the physician's actions (stopped blood transfusions, moved the patient nearer the nurse's station, ordered the patient screened off from other patients, placed him in a single room or in the intensive care unit), or from physical signs she observes herself.

ORIENTATION

There are reasons other than denial for the reluctance of medical personnel to involve themselves in the feelings of the dying. One of them is the matter of orientation. Health care professionals are trained to treat the living, not to bury the dead. They are more concerned with the techniques and procedures of life maintenance than with the psychologic and sociologic effects of life termination. Medical professionals may regard death as defeat (6). What more blatant affront to medical practice than a patient who died despite or because of treatment? Nurses and physicians express frustration and anger over patients who die unexpectedly after "everything possible had been done for them." If a patient takes a sudden, unexpected turn for the worse, the staff reexamine his symptoms and search their consciences in an attempt to determine if it could have been foreseen or if they were negligent in any way. There is also a feeling of helplessness. When the end comes, rationalization deals with the finality. "He is better off," "He would have been left with half a brain," "He lived a full life," "He was in pain," are given as reasons to support de   as the only logical course.

Krant notes that (17):

> "Medical students, house officers, and staff physicians, especially in universities and large teaching hospitals, are held accountable to senior staff . . . for a vigorous biologic model of disease . . . The knowledge of disease, of dying and death is defined in terms of physical and chemical faltering and deficit. Mortality conferences are directed toward a search for potential deficit or default . . . the medical student, the house officer, or the staff physician is not accountable for the human dimension of living and dying . . . therefore the question at a staff conference or at mortality rounds is not directed toward whether a patient died peacefully or in control of his limited options."

The dying threaten the health professional in another way. They offer irrefutable evidence of mortality, despite the elaborate denial system of the culture. If the physician has not come to terms with his own death, he adds a third dimension to the disengagement from the dying.

PERSONAL ATTITUDES

Unresolved feelings which the physician may have about his own death act as a barrier, preventing him from relating successfully to his dying patient. Repressed guilt, anger, disbelief, fear, and sorrow generate anxiety. He seeks relief from the unpleasantness of anxiety by avoiding the subject that seems to cause it. When Dylan Thomas exhorts his father not to "go gentle into that good night," he expresses his own needs of denial, not his father's. If the physician is to work successfully with the dying, he has to consider what his own death means to him. This may never be completely resolved, but by dealing with it honestly and by being aware of his own responses, he is more able to listen to his patient without insulating himself with distractions, such as checking every inch of intubation for air bubbles.

Physicians know the patient less well than in the past. House staff are often interchangeable, and attachment to any one patient is a thing of the moment. Discontinuous care giving as a result of a succession of specialists increases the likelihood of leaving the discussion of death to someone else, particularly if the physician is not accountable for that aspect of the patient's care. Physicians are often reluctant to talk to the dying because they are uncertain. They cannot answer when death will take place. Like an airport in a desert principality, schedules can only be estimated. Many physicians underestimate the patient's understanding of the seriousness of his illness and feel it is cruel to discuss death with him. Finally, they are reluctant to talk to the dying patient because they don't know what to say.

COMMUNICATING WITH THE DYING

To tell or not to tell is not the issue of this chapter. Many fine papers document an eloquent case for truth (2, 16, 29, 37, 39). Psychotherapy is predicated upon facing and dealing with truth as a prerequisite for mental health. We will assume it is appropriate in treating the dying if it is their need (8).

WHAT THE PATIENT NEEDS TO TELL

The dying patient requires something very simple from those who care for him. He needs to know that he can count on them (49). When he asks, "What do I have?", he is really saying, "Will you be here?" He needs to be able to talk about his death if he wants to, to tell what it means to him, what his feelings are, and what he fears. He needs to be able to complain that he is being robbed (3, 5, 31).

There is a qualitative difference in the dying experience of patients who are allowed to examine their feelings about death. They become more relaxed, experience less pain, and accept it more quickly than those who are denied an outlet. These patients are very often grateful when they are allowed to express themselves, as if they had been granted some special favor (22, 43).

The dying patient also needs to feel that he can, to some measure, control his destiny by making some decisions regarding his care even if nothing more than to plan his menus, select his TV channel, or state a preference for the sun or the shade. Not all patients want to talk about their dying. Some need to rail against the process until the end; and if that is the case, those around such a patient need to support his defenses. If, however, the patient wishes to express his feelings, he particularly needs to be able to talk about these matters with those who give him medical care and be assured that their support will continue until the end. He will not feel isolated or depersonalized if the attending staff will listen to him, stop long enough to talk to him, answer his questions, ask his opinion, and are not so afraid, embarrassed, or angry about death that they cannot talk about it.

Truth does not have to be harsh. Truth can be revealed in a gentle, merciful, and supportive manner, as slowly as a baby sparrow is fed through an eyedropper. The emphasis here will not only be on what the physician needs to tell the patient, but what the patient needs to tell the physician. The short-term goal of supportive truth is the welfare of patients now under the physician's care. The long-term goal is a reversal of the way in which society views death. When it filters down to those who are not in the process of dying that death can be less traumatic than the projectile experience of birth, cultural attitudes may change.

The physician has three concerns in dealing with the dying patient. These are the illness and its symptoms, the patient's awareness and his psychologic responses, and the patient's interpersonal relations with his family and members of the staff.

In the very beginning, before cognition, the central nervous system receives subliminal sensory input on a cellular or organic level. Some patients respond to metabolic variations and are very sensitive to subtle changes in their own bodies that cannot be measured or detected by others. They may have a vague sense of uneasiness. When symptoms become clearly defined, they begin to be registered on a conscious level. At this stage, weak stimuli and fleeting sensations are acknowledged, but brushed aside. The individual then may experience disturbance of homeostasis a little more strongly, and this produces anxiety. Cognition becomes more pronounced when the symptoms become more pronounced and when fleeting sensations can no longer be easily ascribed to a cold, fatigue, heavy yard work, or simply age. At this point the patient is forced to acknowledge that all is not well with him.

This brings about the decision to tell someone else that he thinks something is wrong, although he won't put it quite that strongly. When he tentatively shares information with another, he will stack all the cards in his favor by presenting the symptoms in their most innocuous light. He wants corroboration that, of course, it's nothing. He may tell a friend that he has trouble swallowing and that he feels like pieces of food are sticking in his throat, but omit the fact that he experiences occasional pain. He may wonder out loud if there could be a connection to his new dentures. If his friend responds that he's probably not chewing as finely as he did before he got the new dentures, he is satisfied for the time being. This disclosure is a crucial step because the patient gives up his freedom to interpret his symptoms. He abrogates his right to rationalize when he asks another person's opinion, especially if that person were to say, "I don't like the sound of that. Why don't you check it out with your doctor?" At this point, if he refuses to take action that would confirm his suspicions, he displays denial.

By the time the patient makes his first visit to the physician, he is aware that something is wrong. He is hopeful that the physician will tell him it is nothing, it can be fixed with a pill, a shot, or a week in the country. Even at this juncture, however, he is aware on some level that he has a problem.

In the initial interview the physician is more oriented to the illness per se than to its implications. Symptoms, signs, and medical history take his immediate attention. The physician may have suspicions, but they are usually unconfirmed and require the corroboration of diagnostic studies. If pressed for an opinion, he can tell the truth which is simply, "I don't have enough information at this time to make a complete diagnosis." or "The trouble you are having is with your blood." If the patient asks, "What's wrong with it?", a truthful answer is "You have an anemia—that means that your blood is weak, it doesn't have enough red cells to do its job." Most physicians who deal with the dying patient find it more helpful to approach the patient gradually, with facts instead of interpretations (18). "You have to build up your strength for treatment. Now may be a good time to give up some of your responsibilities."

WHAT THE PHYSICIAN NEEDS TO TELL

When the physician has reached a diagnosis, he begins to think of when he will share the information with his patient. In the very beginning, while establishing a therapeutic relationship, it is helpful if the patient is kept advised of the physician's findings and the treatment he plans. The patient at this point need know only the facts of the illness. It is easier to begin to tell the patient about his condition in natural starting places such as after tests are completed, after therapy has been recommended, and after surgery.

Before the physician tells the patient anything regarding the seriousness of his illness, he needs to know how much the patient is ready to know, how much the patient already knows, and how much the patient wants to know. This will depend on the individual patient. Each one presents a different clinical picture and a different personality.

The first thing the physician should consider before giving any information is his patient's emotional reserves. An assessment of emotional reserves is a guide to how much the patient is ready to know. A patient with a high degree of emotional stability could reasonably be expected to handle more distressing information than one with less, to whom information must proceed more slowly. There are two criteria to help the physician make this determination: his patient's ego strength and his philosophy. His ego strength is measured in the way he has handled other crises in the past. If he has demonstrated maturity and strength through previous distressful situations, he will be more likely to handle this crisis than the patient who goes to pieces when the water heater breaks. Consistent life-long faith or adherence to a philosophy is an additional resource that will help to sustain the dying patient. Philosophy is a democratic commodity. Some find it in stones, some find it in a lifetime of poverty and failure. Two men on a bench whose only comment to one another is a shrug of the shoulders and a shared "What are you gonna do?" have a philosophy. They may think epistomology is an incision made on their wives, but in their corroboration of powerlessness they demonstrate a fatalistic philosophy. The ability to comprehend, judge, plan, gain insight, and formulate a rationale, which the physician can determine through the patient's previous function and through the clinical interchange, will add the resource of reason.

The physician next needs to determine how much his patient already knows. The patient's previous contact with other physicians and the information he may have gained from them; the medical setting, for example, a cancer clinic as opposed to a suite in a general office building; the nature of the illness (some diseases give themselves away more readily than others); the family medical history, which may yield a family member who died of a similar illness; and the patient's comments indicate what he already knows.

The patient's comments may indicate how much he knows but do not necessarily reflect how much he wants to know. Careful observation of his communication revealed in lexical, kinesic, and somatic expressions and the way in which they complement or contradict one another will tell the physician how much the patient wants to know. The patient who demands to know what is wrong with him

but adopts a closed protected posture, the patient who forces a grim smile and a staccato laugh and chirps to her physician that she has every confidence in him, or the patient who asks as either he or the physician are walking out the door, "Am I dying?", need to be dealt with cautiously. The physician listens for questions with built-in answers.

If the patient asks no questions or does not seem curious, it is a cue that he is not yet ready. Even if he says, "Tell me what is wrong." with congruent messages, the physician should feel him out first. "The trouble you are having is affecting your colon. It might be advisable to do more tests." If the patient responds, "I thought of cancer, but I knew it couldn't be that." or "I don't have cancer, do I?", he is giving the message that he is not ready for more information.

The feelers can be ambiguous yet truthful prognostic statements. For example, to "What is wrong with me?", the physician may respond, "You have a serious illness." or "It is life threatening." Most patients will not push any further at this point. That is devastating information as it stands. If, however, the patient were to follow with "Can you do anything for it?", ambiguous but truthful responses might be "I can treat it for awhile," "I can relieve your symptoms," or "There are several treatments that keep it under control." These statements are invitations to further discussion, and the patient's reaction will clue the physician to his readiness for additional information. A careful assessment of the patient's response will determine the physician's next move. A patient who indicates readiness may be told, "It's what you expected." Time must be allowed for the facts to sink in and for questions to arise. If patients are told more than they can handle, they will screen out the information; it will not be processed.

The physician releases facts gradually, using understatements that increase in force and carefully monitoring the patient's cues that signal he is ready for the next piece of information. Telling can be nonverbal. Changes in staff pattern or staff behavior, such as frequency of care and attention, oversolicitous behavior from someone who before was quite matter-of-fact, the physician's serious demeanor, withdrawal, the staff's reluctance to speak of anything but the most surface events ("Your flowers need water"), and hurried whispers in the corridor all clue the patient. The physician's use of the nonverbal as a means for telling his patients the seriousness of their illness is often much less traumatic than the verbal. Silence or a shrug of the shoulders following an earnest "Am I going to die?" are more eloquent than any verbal response.

Few patients persist in talking about dying. They accomodate to the awareness of death in slow stages and sometimes intersperse the telling with other, less threatening topics. Timing is a crucial factor in revealing to a patient that his illness is terminal. Rapport should be established between patient and physician before disclosure. All discussion optimally occurs when both are on the same physical level. The quality of sharing is enhanced when the physician is seated by his patient's side, more so than when the patient is recumbent and the physician is standing.

Sometimes the use of analogies is effective in preparing the patient for the seriousness of his illness. For example, "It's like a car that's beginning to run down, occasionally you can put in new parts, you can give it gas, but eventually it just wears out." or "You're not producing the defenses that are needed. It's like fighting a battle with no army."

Respect and tact should color every communication. The patient should not be discussed if he is within hearing. It would be an equal breach of tact to be seen in conversation with another, obviously discussing him as determined by glances in his direction, if he cannot hear.

Whatever is told, the physician must convey that "No matter what happens, I will be with you doing what I can." The patient needs to know that their relation-

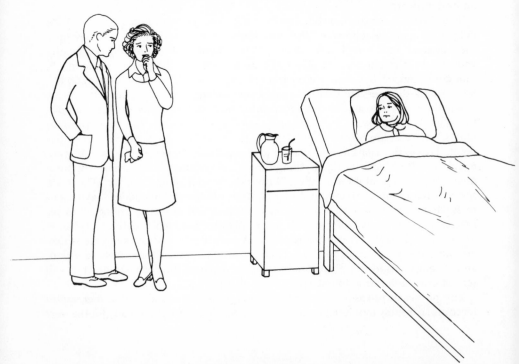

ship will continue to the end and that the physician will not abandon him once he has made a diagnosis of a fatal disease. When the physician indicates, "We will fight this thing together," he has made himself an ally in the crisis of dying. His task is to emphasize hope but to give no false reassurance. Reassurance can be given simply as "I'm not sure I can help you as much as I would like, but I will do all within my power." or "It looks that way now but there are still things we can do." The physician avoids, if he can, stating flatly, "Nothing more can be done."

Most dying patients retain hope. Even though it is statistically unlikely, there is the possibility that in a laboratory somewhere some research chemist has found the answer in mice, that his new treatment is ready for human trial, and that his physician will come to him and ask if he will agree to an experimental drug. That's how the first transplant patient must have experienced what is, in essence, a reprieve. Hope is what sustains the dying patient through pain, loneliness, disability, and fatiguing procedures. Emily Dickinson calls it the "thing with feathers." It is often the sudden absence of hope that tells the attending physician death is near. Many investigators report that once the dying patient has given up hope and has expressed it verbally or nonverbally, death will occur within days or hours (38).

Miracles are all around us. It is the nature of the human spirit to entertain them, and no physician tells a patient that for him they will not exist. He can say it is unlikely, or that he doesn't expect a miracle, but he leaves the door open a crack when he says truthfully, "We don't know."

Telling the patient is not the end but the beginning of the relationship. The physician's goal is to help the patient face death, go about the problem of dying, and make it a period as meaningful as the rest of his life. If the object is to prolong life, the concomitant should be to enhance what can be prolonged. The earlier the patient is prepared, the better chance the relationship has. If the patient learns the truth about his condition from someone other than his physician, an opportunity for closeness has been lost. On the other hand, if disclosure is made by the physician, sympathetic candor will make it easier for the physician to discuss new symptoms and treatment with the patient.

CONCERNS OF THE DYING

For the physician to be able to lend meaning to his dying patient, he needs some idea of what dying means to him. The dying have many concerns (18, 34).

DISTINCTION BETWEEN DEATH AND DYING

First it is necessary to make a distinction between death and dying. Dying is feared for isolation, pain, and the gradual loss of ability, function, will, self, and loved ones. The fear of dying appears to be universal.

Death is feared not for physical reasons as in the fear of dying, but for ceasing to be, for the loss of consciousness, and for the end of all meaningful existence. The fear of death is not universal. It is not expiring that is so frightening, but the slow erosion of self. Many people accept their impending death with equanimity. In Osis' interviews with over 300 dying patients, he discovered that anxiety seemed to disappear almost completely from one to three hours before death (32). "Extinction is less feared than the process that brings about the progressive dissolution of the things that have been considered to be the act of living." The experience of dying seems to be influenced by age, and the relative importance of concerns for one who is dying is determined by his life stage. For the child, the experience of dying is primarily a separation from his parents and the fear of pain, punishment, or mutilation (12, 13, 44). For the active adult, dying means loss of one's healthy body, of one's work, and of one's involvement with children, mate, family, friends, and colleagues. In the aged there is more likely to be an acceptance of death. Many friends and relatives have already died. There is often the feeling that one has lived past his "time."

Many of the aged have prepared for their death by writing wills, buying burial plots, thinking about who will show up at their funeral (much the same as checking off a guest list), and working through a life review, mulling over what one has done, where one has been, and what one would like to do if given the chance to do it all over again. This patient shows more of a willingness to "let go."

FEAR OF THE UNKNOWN

The dying fear the unknown. The act of dying is strange and new, and like birth, only happens once. Because most of us have been shielded from death, we are not sure how the scene is played. Are we going to fling our head suddenly to the side like they do in the movies, are we going to have time for a last important word, will our eyes be open and staring, will we have an astral experience and be able to watch the whole event, will it be like sleep, will they make fun of us, will we be in the middle of a thought, do we go out with a whimper or a bang, and will it hurt?

FEAR OF LONELINESS

The dying next fear loneliness (25). Separation and isolation are associated with death and with reason. Attending staff, family, and friends are not known for their constancy to those suffering a lingering illness. The dying wonder if they will be left alone and abandoned in some back ward for incurables, if someone will be at their side to turn them from a bed sore or to change a saturated dressing, if someone will be there to hold their hand and hear about their childhood in Minnesota. What if that someone has to go for lunch or to the bathroom? Or worse, what if they don't come back till after it's all over? [There is a Jewish burial society that for a fee keeps a 24-hour vigil over the corpse until it is interred. Why not a society that keeps the same watch over the dying, spelling busy medical personnel, and taking the place of family or friends if there are none.]

LOSS OF FAMILY AND FRIENDS

The dying fear the loss of family and friends. At some point in the patient's awareness of his own death is the realization that he will have to leave loved ones who will go on living. In a sense his family and friends are dying, too. It is a solopsistic view but one that has meaning for the dying. When he dies and his consciousness ceases to exist, persons, as that consciousness perceives them, also cease to exist. The patient has to work through a double grief, mourning his own death and mourning the loss of his loved ones.

LOSS OF SELF-IMAGE

Self-image determines how well or poorly someone does in school, his choice of occupation, mate, dwelling place, dress, life style, his relative comfort with his place in the world, and whether or not he likes himself. Self-image can be so firmly fixed that even after such positive radical changes as plastic surgery or weight loss, an individual thinks of himself as he was prior to the change. Negative changes in self-image through aging, disease, accident, and surgery, which conflict with prized values of the culture such as youth, beauty, and good health, succeed where positive changes fail; and the individual thinks of himself as he now is.

Our self–image is directly related to our bodies. Anything that disturbs the self–image of the dying patient causes him great concern; he fears the loss of his body or its parts. Yet even with the heavy investment people have in maintaining a positive self–image, it has been found that patients are better able to tolerate external disfigurement than internal disease whose processes they cannot see and monitor for themselves (10a). For this reason, a failing heart may provoke more anxiety than visible tumors or lesions of the skin.

LOSS OF FUNCTION AND CONTROL

The dying patient fears not only the loss of his body or its parts, but loss of function. Loss of function implies limited activity, limited ability to do the things one did in health, and the need to make new and often difficult adaptations.

Loss of function leads to loss of control, a fear of particular significance. Our society places high value on control of oneself, both physical and mental. A debilitating disease makes control more difficult, if not impossible, since it affects the functions of mobility, ingestion, excretion, sleeping, and the ability to bear stress. Of particular concern is the loss of one's mental faculties. That is why cardiovascular disease and diseases of cerebral degeneration which may lead to senility produce great fear and anxiety. Often patients say, "I don't mind what else goes as long as my mind is O.K." Loss of control means that one's independence is threatened. If *stalwart self-reliance* has been like a lifelong bumper sticker to a patient, he may find it humiliating to have a stoma irrigated, or to have to ask for something to relieve the pain that is chewing at his belly.

LOSS OF IDENTITY

All the things which the dying patient is afraid to lose—the familiar, human contact, his body, his possessions, function, control, and independence—are tied in with his sense of who he is. These things reaffirm us and give us our identity. The dying patient fears the loss of identity, of the particular qualities and events that make him unique and separate from other individuals. He fears that the erosion caused by disease will make him just another dying patient threaded to life by a battery of wires and tubes.

PAIN

Lastly, the dying fear pain. Everyone has heard grisly tales, some true, some exaggerated, some fabricated, of someone who died in intractable pain begging to be put out of his misery. These are things the dying remember. They have no assurance that the same fate does not wait for them. They may already be in some kind of chronic pain, not a surrounding, enveloping pain that becomes their whole existence, but just nagging enough and strong enough so that they can't forget it or concentrate too long on anything or anyone else. They fear its exacerbation and its permanence. They become acutely aware that they are dependent upon others for the relief of the pain and wonder if they will get relief on time, whether they should ask for medication before they really need it just in case, whether they should secure medication on their own, like a squirrel storing nuts for the winter, how they would get it, and where they would keep it. Later they are too sick and too weak to make such elaborate plans.

COPING MECHANISMS

The human being does not take his fears lying down even if he happens to be in that position. He has a battery of coping mechanisms and mind tricks which he uses to deal with reality that is too painful to process directly. They figure more or less in the five stages Kubler-Ross has identified as the sequence of emotions through which most dying patients pass (21, 22).

DENIAL

The first is denial, a complete disavowal, a numbed bewilderment which acts as a buffer and gives the patient time to collect himself. This is usually a temporary stage of shock where the patient reacts with "No, not me." Most patients use it at one time or another, and some come back to it, even though they may have passed through it into another stage. During this period the patient will shop for other physicians who will give him a better diagnosis, will insist that errors have been made, will refuse to discuss the illness or allude to it directly, or will spontaneously volunteer negative statements (41). The patient will give clear cues when he is going back into the denial stage. He will talk one minute about making a will and the next about needing new teeth, a moment-to-moment, seesaw between death and life which he springs with a thrust of future plans.

Often denial occurs when the patient has been told before he is ready, and the key for its resolution is flexibility. If the physician is ready to go where the patient leads him, he will find the patient's psychologic management easier. Denial may take the form of excessive talking, like seeding bare spots on a lawn with rye grass, —a frantic attempt to fill up all pauses, or joke telling as the patient plays the role of the genial and entertaining host. It may take the form of facile invention as the patient creates a plausible reason for everything.

ANGER

The second stage is anger, which replaces denial. Anger may be displaced, projected onto the environment at random, but most often onto staff members. As sickness worsens, the patient lashes out at the healthy with increasing complaints. The service is poor, the food is lousy, the nurse is clumsy, the physician didn't do what he promised. The patient who is angry needs to be listened to, he needs to feel that he has some control over what is happening to him. For example: "You seem to be pretty upset." "You bet I am. You could ring that thing for hours, but no one would come." No attempt at logic helps: "You know it was only a few minutes." A supportive statement does: "It must be frustrating to lie here and wait for someone else." Often the concept of justice intrudes as the patient questions, "Why me? Why not that other evil/nonproductive/defective person?" A supportive statement in this case would be "You feel singled out." or "You feel it's not fair."

BARGAINING

Kubler–Ross lists the third stage as bargaining, a kind of reasonable but childlike approach to the problem, where the patient attempts to postpone the inevitable by offering to make a deal with the physician or God. The deal can be simply, "If you let me live another six months, I will . . . or I will not . . ." It reminds the attending staff of the patient's obligations and responsibilities. "You know my oldest girl graduates this June. If you keep me in good shape till then, I'll do whatever you want."

DEPRESSION

The fourth stage is depression. When the patient becomes weaker and cannot hide his symptoms, he experiences a great sense of loss. Financial burdens are added. One coping mechanism seen in the depressed patient is simply giving up. Anyone who has had to swim a very long distance, reaching the point where the effort of the next stroke is physically painful, experiences the temptation to let go. The dying patient in the stage of depression throws in the towel and becomes apathetic. The physician can prevent depression, or at least lessen it, by finding out the patient's private fears. For example, many patients are afraid of nighttime. If a patient expresses such a fear, it would be wise to plan his time span from one morning to the next, structuring his activities on a continuum rather than a finite block that ends with darkness.

A similar coping mechanism is depersonalization, an estrangement from reality in which the patient is an objective and detached viewer of the scene about him. All of his defenses are aimed at mastery and control. He should be encouraged to ventilate his sorrow, since it is necessary to work through depression before reaching the stage of acceptance.

REGRESSION

Some patients regress into former patterns of behavior such as demanding attention, becoming dependent, or pulling the covers over their heads in full retreat to a preverbal level of being. Touch and silence are important, especially in the latter case since they match the patient's communication mode. Unlike denial, which excludes the threat of dying, regression is a retreat from the threat. The physician helps this patient by accepting his need to retreat and by slowly reestablishing contact through familiar activity. The patient who becomes self-centered and overly concerned with his body may display exasperating behavior. Dependent upon others to satisfy his needs, he becomes demanding. This patient should be handled with gentleness and firmness. Brief, frequent visits by different members of the medical team help lessen the patient's dependence upon one person. It is often a heavy responsibility for one person to be the patient's sole emotional support. The medical team, although sharing information in a slightly different contextual framework, develops a common objective of supporting the patient. Some regression is harmless and is actually encouraged by focusing on day-to-day living.

ACCEPTANCE

The last stage is acceptance. The patient is no longer denying, angry, bargaining, or depressed. He is simply tired, and in most cases, weak. Kubler-Ross reports that this is not a happy stage but one devoid of feelings. The patient wishes to be left alone; he has insulated himself by rejecting outside stimuli. Communication with this patient is best when it is nonverbal. Holding his hand, patting his arm, stroking his forehead, sitting on or at the side of his bed, and being silent with him for a few moments convey the physician's concern. Saunders writes of the value of short visits to patients in this approximate stage and the need to make some contact with them when entering the room (42). Even if they are sleeping on and off, they are waiting for the physician or nurse to come in. Contact of some kind, even a touch, prevents them from feeling isolated and depersonalized. Some patients close to death experience transcendence, an almost out-of-body experience in which they face death peacefully and even joyfully. There have been subjective reports of these feelings from those who have been revived from a near death. Observers sometimes note the peaceful countenance of some of the dying, which seems to corroborate the experience.

WHEN THE PATIENT NEEDS TO SHARE

CUES

The patient will send cues when he is ready and willing to talk. He may need to express anxiety, grief, anger, hostility, fear, guilt, sadness, or he may just want to reminisce. He may feel guilt about burdening others and fear he may be abandoned if he does burden them, so, like the physician, he is sending out feelers. They face each other, physician and patient, like praying manti pawing at the air, each afraid to land the first punch.

PHYSICIAN'S APPROACH

Many patients express the fear of being a burden to those who care for them. The physician's first move is to assure his patient that he is not burdening him and that he is ready and willing to listen (15). Patients know that the physician making hospital rounds is in a hurry. They will never open proceedings with "I want to talk to you about dying." Instead, the first feeler may be a sigh. If the physician ignores the sigh, communication has been stopped at the pass. If he responds, communication has begun. Response can be an empathetic statement such as "That was a heavy sigh." The physician should stop what he is doing and perhaps sit on the edge of the bed. At that moment, that may be all that is necessary. If the patient does not pursue it at that moment, negotiations have been opened up, and the patient will feel free at a later time to talk to his physician. Sometimes the patient's feeler may be a cry. If the physician can remain there with him, perhaps holding his hand or simply engaging him in eye contact, he has demonstrated his willingness to listen, and the patient will feel closer to someone he can cry in front of.

Bursting into tears and spending several days in depression may be a necessary reaction. The patient with no apparent reaction may have little regard for himself or may place an extremely high value on self-control as displayed by a stiff upper lip or a similarly rigid backbone. If his value system prizes a rigid check on his feelings, he may need to discuss the situation. The physician should make no attempt to unmask him but should allow him his defenses. The patient will find it increasingly difficult to hold onto them. He should know that the attending staff will not snow him with barbiturates to hide his grief and that they are ready to sit with him and take whatever he can dish out (43). Telling any patient who has indicated sadness that "You have nothing to feel sad about, you're doing so well." is a rejection.

Some patients feel guilt and shame about their illness, it is a source of embarrassment to them. This patient may defend against embarrassment by displaying hostility. The patient still needs to feel wanted, however. If the physician were to respond angrily to his hostility, he would feel abandoned. Hostility can be addressed by feedback statements of confrontation or empathy: "You seem to be very angry." or "It must annoy you to have people poking in here at all hours." Usually, the hostility is a feeler, a test. If the physician passes, then the patient knows it is safe to display other emotions.

The patient may need to reminisce. He should be encouraged in constructive reminiscing in which he reviews his relations with others, a process similar to the review by those who are mourning the death of another. It is a necessary process for the dying patient and prepares him to let go and to say good-bye. There will be many occasions when the dying can say good-bye. It is a feature of closure that is needed by most people. Very often the survivors express sorrow at not having had the opportunity to bid farewell. This can be prevented by encouraging the dying patient to reflect, reminisce, and prepare to leave.

When distressing symptoms and disfigurements are part of the prognosis, the physician gives unhurried verbal and nonverbal support. The physician may think, "What can I possibly say that will make the loss of a body part or the erosion of cartilage or soft tissue acceptable?" Actually what he says is unimportant. It is what the patient tells him that is significant, the opportunity to express feelings to someone who will listen that is important (40).

The most difficult aspect of listening to the terminally ill patient is to be able to *take it*, to hear what he has to say without flinching. Talking about death does not always relate to the philosophical question of ceasing to be, but includes everyday realities of the dying. The patient may say that he feels dirty or that he smells bad. There seems to be more dignity in discussing death as an abstraction, as the unseen one on our left, as a capricious lottery organizer, or as nature's plan (the leaves fall, too) than in describing the insults of pain, debilitation, and incontinence.

In the presence of incurable disease the physician has nothing to offer but himself. This is no small gift. By voluntarily sharing the colossal effrontery of much of the dying experience, the professional affirms his own vulnerability and helplessness. Oddly it is this that lends to the interchange its humanity, its tenderness, and its heroics.

The health care professional may be concerned about formulating clever responses that work like an eraser on a blackboard and make everything all right. If this is a goal, it is an awesome challenge and one of unnecessary imposition. Few speakers are endowed with a supply of rejoinders that have both the wit and wisdom to "patch grief with proverbs." The dying require neither as much as a listener who consistently displays interest, concern, and empathy. It may be enough to reflect simply, "You think you smell bad." An empathic statement would be "I can see how an odor would upset someone as fastidious as you." Taking the remark a step further would involve the simple question, "What does smelling bad mean to you?" The answer might be "That no one wants to come near me." There is little that can be said to mitigate the reality of a foul smelling patient whom members of both staff and family keep at arm's length. What *can* be said illustrates the depth of the listener's understanding and enhances the quality of the moment. For example, "I guess that's a pretty lonely feeling." Many professionals have said, "But I feel so inane. How can that possibly help?" It helps because it demonstrates to the patient that, although he may be physically disabled, what he thinks and feels is of sufficient merit to be communicated and shared.

Care for a patient confronting a life–threatening illness should be aimed at helping the patient *live* as deeply and meaningfully as possible. All corollary goals such as facilitating the patient's self-esteem and self-acceptance, helping to alleviate loneliness by making continual human contact available, and encouraging the patient to share his feelings are directed toward this ultimate goal (48).

HELPFUL QUESTIONS

Some patients will be reluctant to reveal their feelings, which may be demonstrated by previous remarks and behavior or by their responses to the first two questions below. For example, "How sick are you?" may elicit "Well, things looked bad for a while there, but now everything is under control." This response indicates less willingness than the patient who answers, *"Pretty sick."* If the patient demonstrates reluctance, no attempt should be made to continue the discussion to the point where his defenses are attacked.

While the patient will always signal his readiness and his willingness to discuss his condition, he or his physician may not be sure how to initiate proceedings. It may be helpful to use questions to keep things moving. The questions listed which have been prepared by Vashtyan are offered only as a bridge and not a wedge. (47)

Communication Between the Patient and the Staff

1. How sick are you?
2. What kind of illness do you have?
3. How did you come to know this?
4. When did you find out what was wrong with you?
5. How were you told this?
6. What was said?
7. What was your reaction?
8. Do you feel the doctors have been open in answering your questions?
9. How satisfied are you with the way your illness has been diagnosed and treated?
10. How long have you been in the hospital this time?
11. How long do you think you will stay in the hospital?
12. Do you think you are getting better?
13. Are there some problems that it is difficult to talk about?
14. Are there certain staff members with whom you find it easier to talk?

The Patient's Communication with His Family.

1. Whom do you feel closest to in your family?
2. Whom do you find it easiest to talk with in your family?
3. Do you ever talk to your family about your illness?
4. Is it difficult to do so? In what way?
5. Do you ever talk with them about their worries or fears about your illness?
6. How sick does your family think you are?
7. How often do you have visitors? Would you like visitors to come more frequently or less frequently?
8. Which visitors have been most helpful to you? What do you talk to them about?
9. What kinds of problems has your illness caused?
10. Which are the most difficult for you? How are you managing to cope with them?
11. How have these problems affected your family?
12. What kinds of things does your family have most trouble with?

Coping Patterns

1. What kinds of things do you find upsetting about your illness?
2. What do you do when you get upset? lonely? low?
3. What kinds of things do you find helpful when you feel this way?
4. Do you find it helpful to talk to other people about problems? With whom do you talk most?
5. Whom do you lean on when the going gets rough?
6. Does your clergyman (pastor, rabbi, priest) help?
7. Does your doctor help?
8. What helps you most in keeping you going?
9. What kinds of problems do you see in the future?

These questions are not to be used as rapid fire ammunition. Only a few at a time may be used, or none may be used. They are only offered as a guide to help the physician get started in what is generally considered difficult communication.

PATIENT'S FAMILY

The dying may be surrounded by family and friends, many of whom they haven't seen in a long time. The sudden appearance of anxious family members at one's bedside is a major cue card to the seriously ill, particularly if those members have traveled great distances or maintain a vigil around the clock. It's encouraging to see a favorite relative at three in the afternoon. At three in the morning it's terrifying.

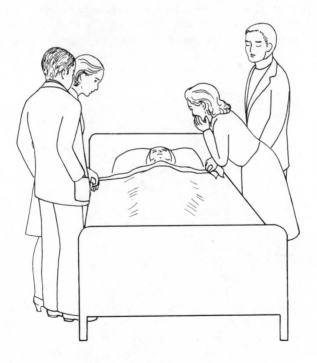

SAME SUPPORTS NECESSARY

It is imperative that the physician communicate with the family in the same manner as he does the patient and offer them the same supports (9, 16, 20). Life-threatening illness is a family crisis of major proportions. A lengthy disease process not only debilitates the patient but places an intolerable strain on his family. Unfortunately, the role of the family in terminal illness has usually been one of collusion with the physician—the object being to keep the truth from the patient (45). The patient then is forced to play a role for which he did not audition. If he tries to bring up the subject, family members will hush him with "You're getting better." or "He's looking great, isn't he?", or worse, "Don't talk like that." Patients feel in this situation that they are not even allowed to say good–bye.

At a time when they are most in need of close and sustained human relationships, the restrictions forced upon them by an imposed role drive a wedge between them and those to whom they have been closest. For this reason the family should be encouraged to communicate openly with their dying member in order to reduce the tensions generated by evasiveness, avoidance, and secrecy.

When the patient is being told of his illness, it is helpful if the entire family is included in the information process. The truth should be divulged at the same rate as it is to the patient. Families have idiosyncratic signal systems, whose cues even the youngest understand. When the family knows that the patient is fatally ill, the patient is sure to pick up this information if only from their oversolicitous or suddenly extra cheerful demeanor.

Families should be discouraged from hallway conferences and from signaling to one another in the presence of the patient. Frantic eye messages, issued while holding the patient's drinking cup to his lips, will be revealed to him in other ways. The cup may not be held as steadily, or the quality of the bearer's voice will communicate very clearly to the patient that others are communicating about him surreptitiously.

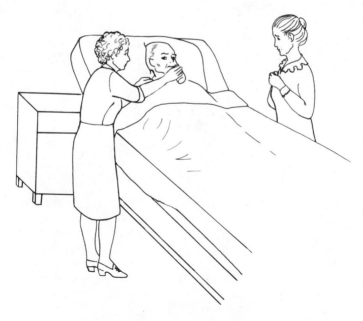

The family, like the patient, should be encouraged to ventilate their feelings. This includes helping family members to see common feelings as normal and acceptable. Shock, denial, ambivalence, rejection, anger, guilt, and exhaustion are to be expected. They are called upon to marshall physical, financial, and emotional support and are soon exhausted by the demands. To protect their eroding resources, family members often withdraw, claiming pressing needs such as businesses to run, children to care for, or neglected personal health needs to attend to. The family may feel guilty for doing normal things and may react by giving up all normal pursuits and adopting what they consider a properly serious attitude.

Family members often resist and resent the patient moving out of his usual role. A 30-year-old married son, who must not only share the expenses for his 55-year-old father's illness but assume his responsibilities, may resent his father's helplessness and may express this with fewer visits, expressed annoyance at his father's lack of cooperation in his recovery ("Why don't you get up and move around like they tell you?"), or anger directed at the attending staff. If this hostility is directed at the physician, it may be a complaint about a specific technique or about the management of the patient in general. For example, "I was here all day yesterday and didn't see you once," "It seems to me that my father should be doing better," or "I don't think you're doing all you could. I'm bringing in someone else." The best response is to remain calm, sidestep attacks, not adopt a defensive posture. The family, like the patient, should be encouraged to express their anger and frustration; ventilation will be reflected positively in the relationship between them and the patient. The physician in this case might stop long enough to sit down with this man and quietly empathize. "It must be very hard on you to see your father in this condition." This should be tried before confrontation such as "You seem very angry."

The family needs help in understanding the needs of the terminal patient. A husband may not understand that his wife's refusal to undergo additional surgery that would prolong her life is not a rejection of him. Many terminal patients desire to be left in quiet, although they do want to know that someone is there. They may be tired and sleepy and may not be up to lengthy or emotionally laden visits. When the physician conveys this, he helps the family achieve a real picture of terminal illness.

The family should be encouraged to continue their normal relationship with their dying member and not take any action that would isolate him. A patient with a radical neck dissection and laryngectomy got into the habit, by mutual agreement, of eating separately from his family (14). His wife would leave his nasogastric tube feeding on the dining room table, and his family would dish out their own meal on the kitchen table. The pattern of separate eating understandably increased his feeling of isolation and diminished his feeling of self-worth.

Families are usually in a double bind. Disease places both an economic and an emotional strain on the resources of a family. The family, often from guilt, want no expense spared, even though it continues to sap their own reserves and may be of questionable merit. They will need the physician's help to make decisions: how much nursing is necessary, what treatments are necessary, how much hospitalization, and so forth. The physician can help enlist social support such as homemaker services, child care, visiting nurses, and sources of funding, both private and public.

PREDEATH QUESTIONS

The following questions are useful in eliciting feelings and helping family members ventilate their concerns (47).

Communication Within the Family

1. How sick is (the patient)?
2. What kind of illness does (the patient) have?
3. Is there anyone in the family who doesn't know what (the patient's) illness is?
4. How did you find out about his illness?
5. What did they say to you?
6. How did you feel when you found out?
7. Did you talk with other family members when you found out?
8. Do you talk about his illness in the family now? Often?
9. Can you talk with (the patient's) doctor?
10. How long do you think (the patient) will stay in the hospital?

Communication Between Patient and Family

1. How often do you visit (the patient) in the hospital?
2. Do you feel comfortable visiting (the patient)?
3. What do you talk about with (the patient)?
4. Does (the patient) know why he's in the hospital now?
5. How sick does he think he is?
6. How do you talk with (the patient) about his illness?
7. Is it difficult to talk wtih (the patient) about his illness? What makes it so?
8. Do you ever talk to him about your fears concerning his illness or its outcome? In what ways?
10. Does (the patient) ever seem to withdraw and not want to talk to you? How do you handle this?

Communication Concerning Care of the Patient

1. Who takes care of (the patient) when he is at home?
2. How much do you help take care of (the patient)?
3. What problems are there in taking care of (the patient)?
4. Do you find it helpful to talk to other people about it?
5. Whom do you talk with?
6. Whom do you lean on when the going gets rough?
7. What kinds of problems do you see in the future?
8. Does your clergyman help you?
9. Does your doctor help you?

GRIEVING

Grief runs a constant course, modified by the nature of the loss, its significance to the bereaved, the nature of any preparation for the loss, and the abruptness with which it comes. Engel divides the process of grief into three stages: numbness and disbelief; developing awareness in which feelings of anguish and despair are the strongest; and restitution, the period of recovery in which one begins to cope with the loss (10). At first, there is a tendency to idealize the dead loved one, but this yields to a more realistic remembrance in which the mourner can handle both negative and positive feelings about the deceased. This period is the one of return to normal life.

Lindemann describes the symptoms that can be observed in the common grief reaction as a syndrome characterized by sensations of somatic distress occurring in repeated waves lasting from 20 minutes to an hour, a feeling of tightness in the throat, choking with shortness of breath, sighing, an empty feeling in the abdomen, and feelings of tension and mental pain (24). There is strong preoccupation with guilt and a need to cry, especially in the second stage described by Engel. Mourners will show a lack of warmth in relationships with other people. They will become restless, self-centered, and irritable, exhibiting a sense of futility, sometimes confusion, disorganization, and apprehension.

The grief syndrome, like the railroads, is unreliable. It may be delayed, exaggerated, absent, or replaced by distorted representations of one special aspect. Normal grief consists of a constellation of responses. The duration, expression, and appearance of these responses depends on *grief work*, readjustment to an environment that is missing a piece and psychologic release from bondage to the deceased. Although overt linkages have been severed with burial, more insidious invisible lines remain. The role played by the dead person in the mourner's life needs to be replaced by another role, by another player, or written out of the script. Until this happens, the mourner remains immolated in a symbolic suttee.

One of the big stumbling blocks to grief work is the mourner's reluctance to express his distress. Grief cannot be swept under the rug. It will foment if not ventilated. Like an agitated and overheated Coke bottle, it will explode into the delayed reaction of someone who feels responsible for maintaining the morale of others, the distorted reaction of zestful overactivity, a display of symptoms belonging to the last illness of the deceased, an avoidance of social activities, actions detrimental to the mourner, or profound depression.

Effective management of a family's grief reactions may prevent psychopathologic reactions as well as somatic diseases. The physician needs to facilitate, actively listen to, support, acknowledge, and empathize with grief work (19, 35). White and Gathman have recommended that the physician explain the grief process to reassure the bereaved that what they are experiencing is normal (50). In this way someone who may be experiencing numbness or an abundance of mental images will not be faced with the additional burden of worrying that he is going crazy.

If he has encouraged open communication among the patient, the patient's family, and the attending staff all through the illness, and if he has been supportive of the family before their death experience, the physician can facilitate the process of grief. If family problems and issues can be settled before the patient's death, the family will be spared the overwhelming guilt of unresolved conflicts. When a family member is dying, it is appropriate to conduct family counseling. This does not mean that a moribund and debilitated patient should be subjected to a rigorous session in which his family airs their grievances; such a session can be traumatic for a well person. It does mean that those who are concerned with the patient's care should be alert to moments when he is feeling strong enough or receptive enough to hear an overdue apology from one who wants to give it or even take part in an involved interaction in which he and his wife mediate discrepancies in their handling of their adolescent son.

After death, families should be encouraged to express their feelings openly. Anger, ambivalence, guilt, helplessness, dependency, and a sense of abandonment may be added to sorrow. The physician may deal with such issues as social support, legal counseling, insurance settlements, job training, foster care, and ways to encourage new relationships. He may find himself in the role of interpreter as he explains the needs of survivors to each other. A woman's need to rely heavily upon her grown daughter for solace may conflict with the daughter's need to express anger at her father for putting her in that position.

POSTDEATH QUESTIONS

The following questions may be helpful guidelines in facilitating a family's expression of grief (47).

The Patient's Last Days

1. Did you expect (the deceased) to die when he did, or were you surprised?
2. Where was (the patient) when he died?
3. Who was there with him?
4. Were you able to say good–bye to each other at any point?
5. During the latter stages of (the patient's) illness, was there anything you felt you should be doing for him, but weren't doing?
6. Are you satisfied with the care (the patient) got in his last days?
7. Was there anything that any doctor or nurse did which was particularly disturbing?

Feelings and Defenses

1. How much sadness are you experiencing now?
2. To what extent do you try to keep from crying if you feel sad?
3. How often do you find yourself crying now?
4. How angry are you feeling now?
5. What do you feel angry about now?
6. Do you find yourself sometimes having outbursts of anger you are sorry for later?
7. How nervous or anxious do you feel now?
8. How often do you experience a sense of "numbness" or lack of feeling?
9. Do you still find it hard to believe that (the deceased) is dead?

Memories

1. How frequently do you find yourself going over memories of (the deceased)?
2. Do they tend to be good or bad memories?
3. Do you ever feel that you see (the deceased) or hear his voice?
4. Do you sometimes feel the "presence" of (the deceased)?
5. How often do you find yourself having dreams about (the deceased)?
6. Do your dreams tend to be pleasant or unpleasant?
7. Do you find yourself avoiding places that you associate with (the deceased)? How does this happen?
9. To what extent do you find yourself thinking like (the deceased)? Under what circumstances?

Debits and Credits

1. Do other people try to keep you from crying if you feel sad? How?
2. Do other people try to keep you from talking about (the deceased)? How?

3. Do you feel that other people have tried to push you into too many activities? In what ways?
4. In what ways have people been helpful to you?
5. What things have people done that have made you feel worse?
6. What kinds of problems do people in your family seem to be having?
7. What kinds of problems are you having?
8. What kinds of things have you found helpful in getting back on your feet?

We go through grief stages all the time beginning with the first time we realized that our mother could leave the room. The more we have lost and sorrowed, the more experienced with the sequence we are, and the less strange it becomes. Death then becomes another event in a series of good–byes. It has not lost its sting, it's just that we know the sting will hurt less as the day wears on and even less if we can put some ammonia on it. Each one of us prepares for his own death dozens of times in a lifetime of helloes and good–byes. The elderly are better at it, not so much because they are close to death themselves, but because they are old hands at saying good–bye.

REFERENCES

1. Aldrich CK: The dying patients' grief. JAMA 184:329–331, 1963
2. Becker AH, Weisman AD: The patient with a fatal illness—to tell or not to tell. JAMA 201 (8):153–154, 1967
3. Biörck G: How do you want to die? answers to a questionnaire and their implications for medicine. Arch Intern Med 132:605–606, 1973
4. Bok S: Euthanasia and the care of the dying. BioScience 23(8):461–465, 1973
5. Bowers MK et al.: Counseling the Dying. New York, Nelson, 1964
6. Brim OG Jr et al.: The Dying Patient. New York, Russell Sage Foundation, 1970
7. Caroline NL: Dying in academe. New Physician 21:655–657, 1972
8. Dying must be told truth, hospital staff told. Hosp Prog 54:25, 1973
9. Easson WM: The family of the dying child. Pediatr Clin North Am 19(4):1157–1165, 1972
10. Engel GL: Grief and grieving. Am J of Nurs 64:93–98, 1964
10a. Feder SL: Death and Dying: Attitudes of Patient and Doctor, 3. Attitude of patients with advanced malignany. Group Advance Psychiatry (Sympos) 5:614–622, Oct 1965
11. Feifel H: Death. In Farberow NL (ed): Taboo Topics. New York, Athertor, Press, 1963, pp 8–21
12. Gould RK et al.: The chronically ill child facing death–how can the pediatrician help? Clin Pediatr (Phila) 12:447–449, 1973
13. Hardgrove C et al.: How shall we tell the children? Am J Nurs 74:448–450, 1974
14. Hershberger PA: Waiting with a dying man and his family. In Hall & Weaver (eds.): Nursing of Families in crisis. Philadelphia, JB Lippincott Company, 1974
15. Heymann DA: Discussions meet needs of dying patients. Hospital 48:57–62, 1974
16. Hodge JR: How to help your patients approach the inevitable. Medical Times 102(11):-123–133, 1974
17. Krant MJ: The organized care of the dying patient. Hospital Practice 7:101–108, 1972
18. Krant MJ: Dying and Dignity: The Meaning and Control of a Personal Death. Springfield, CC Thomas, 1974
19. Krant MJ: Grief and bereavement: an unmet medical need. Del Med J 45:282–290, 1973
20. Krant MJ: A Death in the family. JAMA 231 (2):195–196, 1975

21. Kubler-Ross E: On Death and Dying. New York, MacMillan, 1969
22. Kubler-Ross E: Questions and Answers on Death and Dying. New York, MacMillan, 1974
23. Lifton RJ: The sense of immortality: on death and the continuity of life. Am J Psychoanal 33:3–15, 1973
24. Lindemann E: Symptomatology and management of acute grief. Am J Psychiatry 101:141–148, 1944
25. May WF: On not facing death alone: the trauma of dying need not mean the eclipse of the human. Hastings Cent Rep 1(1):6–7, 1971
26. Mayer RG: Restorative procedures may precede embalming. Casket and Sunnyside 104 (2):19, 1974
27. Dealing with Death. Med World News 12(20):30, 1971
28. McNeil D: A death at home. Can Nurse 70:17–19, 1974
29. Muslin HL et al.: Partners in dying. Am J Psychiatry 131:308–310, 1974
30. Notes of a dying professor. Pennsylvania Gazette 70(5):18–24, 1972
31. Noyes R Jr: The care and management of the dying. Arch Intern Med 128:299–303, 1971
32. Osis, K: Deathbed observations by physicians and nurses. New York, Parapsychological Foundation, 1961, p 23
33. Oken D: What to tell cancer patients: a study of medical attitudes. JAMA 175:1120–1128, 1961
34. Pattison EM: The experience of dying. Am J Psychother 21:32–43, 1967
35. Paul N: The use of empathy in resolution of grief. Perspect Biol Med 11:153–169, 1967
36. Potter G: The death of Elizabeth Meinders: 1878–1971. The Washington Post, Feb 6, 1972, no 65
37. Raft D: How to help the patient who is dying. Am Fam Physician 7:112–115, 1973
38. Richter CP: The phenomenon of unexplained sudden death in animals and man. In Feifel H (ed): The Meaning of Death. New York, McGraw–Hill, 1959, pp 302–313
39. Robinson JA: The patient's right to know the truth. Proc R Soc Med 66:536–537, 1973
40. Rogers CR: The characteristics of a helping relationship. Personnel and Guidance Journal 37:6–16, 1958
41. Saul LJ: Reactions of a man to natural death. Psychoanal Q 28:383–386, 1959
42. Saunders C: The last stages of life. Am J Nurs 65:70–75, 1965
43. Saunders C: A therapeutic community: St. Christopher's hospice. In Schoenberg B et al. (eds): Psychosocial Aspects of Terminal Care. New York, Columbia University Press, 1972
44. Spiretta JJ: The dying child's awareness of death: a review. Psychol Bull 81:256–260, 1974
45. Strauss AL: Awareness of dying. In Pearson L (ed): Death and Dying. Cleveland, The Press of Case Western Reserve University, 1969, pp 108–132
46. Sudnow D: Passing On. Englewood Cliffs, NJ, Prentice Hall, 1974
47. Vashtyan EA: Unpublished Material, Hershey College of Medicine, Department of Humanities, 1974
48. Verwoerdt A: Communication with the Fatally Ill. Springfield, C Thomas, 1966
49. Weisman AD: On Dying and Denying. New York, Behavioral Publications, 1972
50. White RB, Gathman LT: The syndrome of ordinary grief. Am Fam Physician 8 (2):-97–104, 1973

10
The Aged Patient

*For I have known them all already, known them all—Have known the evenings,
mornings, afternoons, I have measured out my life with coffee spoons;*

T.S. Eliot
The Love Song of J. Alfred Prufrock
The Waste Land and Other Poems

Imagine that you wake up one morning to find that it hurts to get out of bed
and instead of swinging your legs over you have to ease them out one at a time.
Your teeth are sitting in a glass instead of in your mouth. When you go to the
bathroom, your urine dribbles, you're constipated, and the mirror reflects someone who looks like an apple that was left too long on the windowsill.

When you look in your wallet to check how much cash you have, you discover
your hand shakes a little and you cannot read the denominations easily, which
doesn't seem to be a problem since there aren't too many anyway; then suddenly
you forget why you're standing there holding your wallet. You don't have a car so
you take the bus to work. It takes you a little longer than you would have expected
to get to the bus stop; you don't seem to hear the traffic as well as you usually do;
in fact, when you crossed one street, the light changed too fast and a driver, for
some reason, shook his fist at you. At the bus stop other people shouldered past
you, and you are the last to get on the bus. When you ask the driver for directions,
he rolls his eyes in impatience and jerks a thumb toward the rear; that's the end
of the conversation. Once you get to your job, you're told that you have been
replaced by someone younger who can do your work faster and better. When you
go to telephone a friend to tell them what has happened, the operator tells you
that the phone has been disconnected.

EXPERIENCE OF AGING

In our society every period of life has a dangling carrot in front of it but the last.
A 7-year-old looks forward to a two-wheeler, an 18-year-old looks forward to being
on his own, a 30-year-old looks forward to the benefits an increasing income might
bring, a 40-year-old looks forward to greater status on the job, and a 55-year-old
looks forward to retirement when he can travel and maybe grow orchids in a
urethane hothouse.

The 65-year-old has nothing in front of him but disaster and disintegration. He
sees it all around him. Threaded through his life are constant losses of loved ones,
objects, status, respect, role, and income. A younger fighter will rally from the
punch and stand to take the next blow; but an aged fighter is a little punchy and
takes longer to recover from trauma. The aging individual sees no compensations
for this new role, and it is difficult to convince him that he has anything to look

forward to except falling down on the sidewalk and breaking his hip. Indeed, it is difficult for those who offer the aged services and care to think of anything positive about aging except perhaps the opportunity to reflect on a job well done in a kind of total life review. That only applies to those who have handled their lives to their satisfaction, however. How about all the rest who have not? This leaves all a little puzzled and wondering what Browning had in mind when he wrote, "Come grow old with me, the best is yet to be."

PHYSICAL EROSION

The aged individual faces not only constant losses but the slow and steady erosion of his body. Data issued by the United States Public Health Service indicates that approximately five and one half million Americans are incapacitated each year by chronic illness defined as illness lasting more than 3 months. Almost one half (45%) are over 65, a population in whom the incidence of chronic disease is estimated at 17%. It has been found that chronic conditions tend to accumulate with age (14).

Many disabilities occur as a result of degenerative vascular disease. The frequency of cardiovascular disease and cerebrovascular accidents increases with age (25). Cardiac disorders may limit an individual's capacity for physical exercise, and cerebrovascular accidents may cause permanent incapacity in varying degrees. Occlusive vascular disease from arteriosclerosis may cause pain in the lower extremities and sometimes leads to amputation. Multiple occlusions of the arteries in the cerebral cortex are responsible for the mental deterioration of the "senile" patient, resulting in increasing irritability, impairment of memory, and an inability to integrate thoughts and observations. Impairment of sensory and motor function are common, and the combined effects of muscular weakness and loss of pain perception may result in burns. Disequilibrium and uncertainty of gait may cause falls. Additionally, the aged patient is subject to gastrointestinal disturbances, softening of the bones, degernative arthritis, skin problems, cancer, mental illness, and conditions affecting the locomotor system, hearing, and vision (29).

While all this is going on, he lives in a society that places high premiums on youth, health, good looks, and productivity. He finds he is stuck with devalued currency. Age is a stigma, one is not supposed to grow older. In a kind of madness, we increase the percentage of our superannuated then deny them full citizenship while we also deny aging (16). A dictum from our advertising industry, "You're not getting older, you're getting better," is representative of our collective madness. The Chinese, who used to be a model to the contrary, no longer revere age either and didn't as soon as they discovered productivity. The only place where longevity appears to be a valuable commodity is in geographically obscure parts of Russia where oldsters who credit their astounding years to things like bean kurd soup get special awards.

SOCIAL EROSION

While our nation venerates youth, the percentage of those over 65 is growing (6, 24). Statistics indicate that in 1980 over nine million Americans will be over 65 (32). They have no function, they are often sick, and many are without money. They compose a growing minority that has been listed among our invisible poor (15). Around half their number have that dubious distinction. Enormous strides in medicine, a decreasing fertility rate, and no new waves of young immigrants result in an older society. As their membership expands, there is an inverse correlation to their opportunity since they are forced from productivity at increasingly earlier

retirement age. Some industries consider a factory worker obsolete at the age of 40. Some aged come to poverty from a working life that yielded them fixed retirement incomes that shrink in the face of inflation. Many are poor because they were young and poor and forced into a cycle which guaranteed their continued poverty. Society has little to give them except a social worker who is their link to goods and services.

While the majority of the aged live with family members, the rest live out their days in small apartments, in rooming houses, in public housing, and in nursing homes. These residences represent a forced relocation and separation from friends and familiar people (20). Many live in transitional neighborhoods whose rapid change they are ill–equipped to handle (7). If they live in a large city, they may live in a section of rooming houses with their most constant companion a hot plate in a ghetto of the aged. While there is certain street life for other ghetto people, the aged are usually cut off from each other. It is not as easy to stand on street corners, the city equivalent of the village square, when one's vision is likely to be poor nor is it comfortable to sit on the front steps with thinning haunches. In addition they enter the life of urban isolates with no expectations of social access. Generally, their area has a high crime rate. Their mailboxes are robbed, they are often the victims of muggings and petty thefts, and their social highlight may be a midday walk to the corner in good weather. It is difficult for the aged to obtain redress against the wrongs which they suffer because the bureaucracy is frightening to them, and they have difficulty establishing the credentials necessary for assistance. Only between four and five percent of the aged live in nursing homes. Once custodial care has begun, however, they rarely regain their independence. Since custodial care is seldom rehabilitative, the effects are usually irreversible.

The social isolation experienced by the aged is compounded by the loss of spouses, friends, and other relatives. Usually their own children are in middle age and are beginning to have some problems of their own which prevent them from being much help. This leaves the aged spinning like solitary tops, occasionally getting jarred out of revolution and slowly coming to a stop.

Loneliness, isolation, and sickness are usually part of the aged person's picture. This becomes a worse picture when the aged are poor. As Mae West said, "I've been rich and I've been poor, and rich is better." Health is preconditioned by social factors.

Those who were always poor were more likely to be born of mothers who had little or no prenatal care. Coupled with poor nutrition, less visits to a physician's office for prophylaxis or remedy, and less educational attainment which correlates with their degree of medical information, they are likely candidate for inadequate health which may leave them with some chronic illness (33). The illness forces them into a state of physical dependency which is compounded by the social, psychologic and economic dependency that they already face. Our society reveres independence and self reliance, and we are ashamed having to have another aid us because we are incapable. For the aged, needing and getting help from others often increases their sense of being in the way; for this reason many cling tenaciously and stubbornly to independent action. A woman in her late seventies or maybe older (with the look of fine parchment) was laboriously crossing a four lane highway with the aid of three-pronged hand walkers. She was only able to move a few inches at a time. Traffic was backed up to the point that drivers were stepping out of their cars to see what the trouble was, horns were honking, and a man, anxious to facilitate her torturous journey and eager to end his own, leaped out of his car to help her. When she took her elbow, she lifted one of her walkers, hit him with it, and yelled, "Go away, I can do it by myself." A few of us cheered.

MEDICINE'S TASK

Many societies are on record for disposing of those who were born defective or who have outlived their productivity. The ancient Spartans placed defective infants on hillsides to die. The Eskimoes had a reputation for placing those who could no longer chew hides on ice floes and supposedly watched them drift into the sunset. Other societies delegated the eldest son to dispatch his parents while they were still in their prime to insure their going into the next world in the best possible condition.

What marks civilization is not that there will be those who need care but the manner in which this care is given. Neanderthal, that much maligned early forebear who might cause us to move if he sat down beside us today, cared for those who were injured and maimed. Eisley relates evidence of a Neanderthal who lost an arm 40,000 years ago, yet who lived and was cared for by others in a hard and stony world (12). The onus of production in a time when glaciers winked on the horizon and food was scarce was great, possibly higher than it is in our own time; yet this maimed individual from whom the scathing "low brow" derives was cherished by his fellows.

Those of us who offer medical care and other services to the aged feel that we discharge our responsibility by being there in the first place. If we don't want to take a back seat to Neanderthal, we should understand that it is not the care that is significant but the manner in which we give it.

BASE TOUCHING

Medical care of the aged begins with getting them to come in for periodic visits (27). While over 80% may have no limits on their mobility, there may be some limits on their transportation (6). It is simple to say to an aged patient, "See you in two months." It is also necessary to find out if he has a way to get to the office. Many have difficulty traveling to their physicians. The more fortunate ones can arrive on their own or have family members take them. Some cities have programs where health care teams travel the city in vans and visit the aged in their own homes. Other communities have minibuses, volunteer drivers, and other services that will pick up the aged patient on request, take him to his physician, and return him to his home (23). Some of the aged may need to be referred to a facility that is more accessible.

Getting the aged patient to come in for checkups when he is feeling relatively well involves educating him and providing incentives by making the experience as pleasant as possible. Not all elderly people are aware that frequent medical checkups, while not an absolute assurance of a healthier old age, are odds-on favorites to help. It would seem to be a self-evident piece of information, but it is not. Most people need to be reminded by their physician that he expects to see them again soon, even if nothing (new) is wrong. Appointments made in advance, cards given out, and a telephone call or a note as a reminder helps.

The elderly patient should be taught that he is not ill because he is old but because of a disease process (3). That way he will be less likely to slough off distressing symptoms as merely another bit of evidence that he is growing older. So-called "common complaints" may be wrongly regarded as natural consequences of aging.

The aged patient fears incapacitation; it is important to him that he remain independent as long as possible. The physician can tell him that frequent checkups will keep him independent much longer than if he were to let something go that could have been corrected earlier. Also, the aged patient should be told that coming in for frequent checkups is the mark of an independent person. It is an action he takes in his own behalf for his own protection. Someone who is dependent does not have that option.

If their clinical experiences are rewarding, the aged will be more likely to come in for frequent checkups. Many aged patients see a different physician at each visit, and they have to recite their ailments over and over again. A sense of continuity is particularly important for this segment of the population, since the aged lack

social organization. Any changes in the essential people in their lives, a role which health care professionals fulfill, is more difficult for them to accept. When they had others to provide a fairly stable social environment, these changes mattered less. For this reason, every effort should be made to insure that the same physician sees the patient or that another bridging professional has been with the patient on enough occasions to provide an interface. Whoever treats the elderly patient should demonstrate interest and reinforce him for seeking medical help.

Constancy of personnel and programs designed with a maximum of personal care insure against the bewilderment many aged experience in the staggering bureaucracy under which certain types of health care are delivered. Antagonisms common to office visits should be dealt with before they develop into fixed attitudes (8). The aged patient often has long office delays in which he has to sit a long time on hard seats; a hurried physician who rushes through answers, cuts him short, refuses to make house calls, and is not the same one he had before. It helps to give him a soft chair while he waits if he wants one, a number so that his wait seems finite, a complaint box in which he places his suggestions, and an opportunity to discuss these antagonisms with the physician.

It is also helpful if he tells his physician that he is annoyed because the physician could not come to his home that he get an empathic reply. "Yes, I can see that taking two buses must be difficult. I wish I could come to your home, but I'm afraid that's just not possible. I can see how it could upset you."

Some older people, out of the mainstream of social congress, tend to think of everyone as potential listeners. They perceive anyone with ears as an appropriate recipient of their message. To be such a listener is a passive and colorless role, and most people don't want it—least of all busy health care professionals. The aged patient can be taught to notice the interests of their listener so that they don't buttonhole and bore a captive audience. No one does a garrulous aged patient a favor by pretending interest.

As the aged person launches into his talk, the physician should be direct and give him the kind of feedback that will help him in his dealings with others. Humoring him only reinforces ineffective behavior. Getting up unceremoniously and leaving his words dangling, cuts him off further and also antagonizes him. It is not too late for him to learn to read his listener.

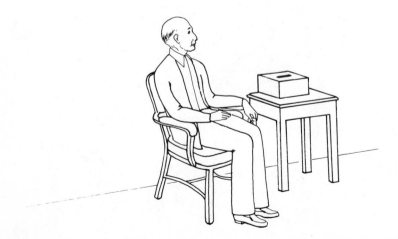

The technique is to give honest but gentle feedback and to acknowledge his needs. When the elderly patient says, "Did I ever tell you about the time . . . ," the physician can reply, "I know you are anxious to tell that story and I wish I could hear it, but I have a lot of things on my mind. I turned my head away from you just now. I didn't do it on purpose; it's just that I was thinking of other things that I must do very soon. When I stopped looking at you that should tell you that I am not interested in hearing that story at this time."

HISTORY TAKING

When taking history from an aged patient, it is good to keep in mind that as a lot the aged are rather spectacular. Through tenacity and dumb luck they are the survivors of many changes, including significantly different orientations. Toffler has suggested that the rate and growth of changes from 1900 to the present is as great as that of all recorded history to 1900 (31). It's no big deal for a redwood to have survived in Muir Forest, where conditions are ideal for the acquisition of a lot of rings; but if the redwood achieved its stature and girth in the hurricane zone of south Florida, that really would be an achievement.

In speaking to the aged, it helps to speak slowly and to face them in the event they have a hearing problem and need to read lips. If a hearing problem is known, the physician should speak face to face at their level and use simple phrases. Some elderly deaf patients, as a result of their hearing loss, become paranoid and suspicious. The physician should not be seen talking about them with another when they are not close enough to hear.

The physician can come fairly close to the patient, since there may be a sight problem. He states his name and perhaps gives them a card at the end of the interview to help them recall the name at a later time. Most aged people do not have impaired memory; but on the off chance that a patient suffers its loss, it is helpful to be prepared.

The aged patient responds well to touch from the health professional. It is especially helpful to shake hands with him at the beginning and the end of a meeting. His spatial integrity is not as rigid as a younger person's, and he invites

its invasion. If the physician will warm his hands first, rubbing them together or putting them under his jacket or armpits, he will find the response a happier one. This writer roused a semicomatose aunt into full consciousness by touching her with cold hands. In this case it proved helpful, but generally cold hands can be a jarring and aversive experience to an aged patient.

The chief complaint of the aged patient may not be his most important medical problem. He may complain of the beginning of a decubitus ulcer from sitting, but questioning may reveal that he sits because his legs hurt him and that the difficulty is due to circulatory insufficiencies that may require more serious measures.

He may be a poor observer of his own functions; and for that reason and others, he may not be a good historian. Sometimes it is necessary to supplement a clinical picture with evidence from medicine bottles, other records, landlords, and family members. Hotel managers are emerging as an excellent source of information as well as an important medical ally. They can often be called regarding the patient's activities, diet, and medication. It is not unusual for their information to complete a clinical puzzle. Often they are a major link between the isolated aged residents of their hotels and the rest of the world.

The elderly patient is often part of the chronic "nuisance" patient population who never feel good, are always waiting to be seen, and are usually left unhappy to wander to the next clinic (5, 18). Any medical investigation of these patients is more helpful when holistic. Besides checking their cardiovascular, metabolic, and endocrinal status, the physician needs to know what changes have occurred in their lives as a result of aging—what do they do with their time, whom do they see, how well oriented are they, are they surviving on Spam, do their teeth fit, do they wear comfortable shoes, and do they feel they need a champion (5). If the practitioner in geriatrics considers the total patient, he will be better able to foresee, forestall, discover, and treat any difficulties that the aged patient might face.

INFORMATION GIVING

The aged patient needs to be told of medical procedures and plans just as he did when he was younger. Information may have to be given in minute details, slowly, and repeated often; but it is necessary that the procedures be understood. If the physician obtains feedback, he will have a better idea of the patient's understanding. Older people sometimes anticipate difficulty in learning. Because of this, they will ask detailed questions, tend to be overcautious, appear fearful of making mistakes, and will cling to what they are familiar with. The physician can help the aged to learn more easily by reinforcing them for their efforts, by teaching them in small steps, and by giving them opportunities to succeed. For example, if the physician is trying to teach a patient how to care for his varicose veins, one of the objectives is to teach him to elevate his legs above heart level periodically. Breaking this down into smaller steps involves determining where and when these periods of elevation might take place. The patient is reinforced for his suggestions if the physician says, "That's a fine idea," "That would help," "Excellent," etc. When the patient demonstrates how he would do this, his achievement is acknowledged. The physician is then ready to tackle other points such as elastic stockings, avoiding prolonged standing or sitting, etc.

Nutritional inadequacies are a problem with the aged (26). Poor dentition is one factor (4). It is easier to grab two doughnuts and dunk them in some instant coffee than it is to prepare a table with good food. Many people don't like to eat alone, and food is costly. The aged need instruction in the value of eating small but frequent meals high in protein, alternative sources of protein such as soy and peanut butter and certain vegetables, how to make food last longer, how to store and cook it properly, and how to use vitamins judiciously. The older patient should be made aware that, because he is older, he expends less energy and does not have the same caloric requirements he had as a younger person with greater muscle mass. The value of fresh air and drinking lots of water should also be stressed. If the physician takes the time to explain all this to his aged patients, providing them with large print charts and logs to record what they eat, he will find that they cooperate more fully.

Eating in isolation may be as much a deterrent to good nutrition as the selection and preparation of food. For this reason, *where* to eat should have equal billing with *what* to eat. There are some community programs that encourage its geriatric citizens to eat at school cafeterias. This provides not only one nutritious daily meal but gives youngsters a chance to mingle with the aged, an opportunity they do not often have. There are other community agencies that offer a daily meal for the aged so that they can eat with each other. In the absence of either opportunity, the physician can suggest that in good weather the patient take his lunch in a paper bag and go sit on a park bench (with a few crusts of bread for the birds).

The aged patient should be prepared for a normal loss of taste, smell, sight, and hearing. Any current problems will be discovered through such questions as "What do you like to eat best?", "Do your eyes give you any trouble?", "Do you ever/always wear glasses?", "Do you ever smell anything unusual?", "Do your ears ever ache?", "Do you have trouble hearing?", "Do other people mumble?" (His loss of consonant sounds makes it difficult to understand speech), "Do they make print too small today?", "Does food taste different than it used to?" This patient needs to ventilate his feelings about his fading abilities and to plan how he may compensate for their loss. He may be taught to do things slowly and surely; for example, if he falls a lot for no apparent reason, he should learn to avoid changing posture suddenly. His limited or absent sense of smell may require the installation of safety taps on gas apparatus. His decreased ability to feel pain may require that he give particular attention to whatever he is doing. For example, if his problem is one of circulatory insufficiency, he may need to avoid crowds so that he is not stepped on, to sit without crossing his knees, or to wear circular garters. A decreased ability to perceive discomfort would prevent him from receiving warning signals of any of these events (2). Regarding skin care, the elderly should be taught that bathing too frequently may be harmful to them since their skin has been depleted of oils. Rubbing in lotions and wearing clothing that does not chafe are helpful.

Some of the aged, although not the majority, have difficulty remembering to take medications. In this case it is helpful to use a pill counter or to teach the patient to place a large chart in some conspicuous and convenient place and to record daily what he takes. If he is reinforced with praise after bringing in the chart to his physician, he is more likely to continue taking notes than if his efforts are hastily addressed or not addressed at all.

Preventive patient education of the elderly is directed to safety care. The aged figure high statistically in accidents (22). Almost 90 percent of fractures suffered by the elderly are the result of falls.

For those over 65, falls are the most prevalent fatal home accident. In New York state boxing rings have floors made of an energy–absorbing plastic foam to reduce the chance of injury to falling contestants. While it would be impractical to line

the streets with foam, installing handrails or cushioning the floors where the elderly walk would help.

The aged are less able to perceive danger because of failing sensory abilities and an inability to organize and interpret warning signals. If they do perceive danger, they are handicapped in dealing with it by an inability to move in a rapid, coordinated manner and a reluctance to compensate for physical impairment by asking for help because they do not wish to burden others or even admit that they are growing older. Discussions of safety should include the use of hand rails around the home, tub mats, rails around the bathtub, wearing laced shoes instead of loose slippers, avoiding flowing garments that could trip the wearer, checking flooring and carpeting periodically, checking electrical appliances and outlets, checking foodstuffs to prevent the ingestion of noxious substances, checking gas ranges, the need to ventilate living areas, etc. The physician might emphasize that forgetfulness and smoking do not go hand in hand but often result in disaster—for example, when a smoldering cigarette reignites after the smoker has fallen asleep. It might be done in this way:

Physician: I know that you are a smoker, Mr. P., and that concerns me.

Patient: How is that? Hasn't hurt me yet. I'm the living proof of that.

Physician: I'm not concerned about the harmful effects of smoking as much as I am about the danger of fire.

Patient: I'm very careful. Don't you worry about that, Doctor—always have an ashtray right at my side.

Physician: I'm concerned about your falling asleep or forgetting that you have a cigarette burning . . .

Patient: What do you think I am, dotty? My memory is as sharp as it ever was —I can remember things as clear . . . did I ever . . .

Physician: Mr. P., I know you to believe that you don't forget, but the truth is, you don't remember everything. The other day you forgot to bring in your medicine for a refill. The last time we met, you had trouble remembering the name of the doctor who took care of your foot. And that is to be expected—it is not unusual to be 73 and forget things from time to time. That doesn't mean that you aren't intelligent and very able and that you didn't do some really great things in your time . . . but it does mean that you are capable of forgetting.

Patient: So? What does that prove? That I have to give up smoking?

Physician: Not entirely. It means you have to be fully awake when you sit down to smoke. You should make your own smoking rules. Let's see if we can get some together . . .

UNCOVERING DEPRESSION

Depression in the elderly is frequently undetected. Many professionals mistake the psychomotor retardation and despondency of depression for the normal affect of aging and do not believe the situation is pathologic or requires remedy. Any of the losses incurred in aging can be responsible for triggering depression, but it is a condition which can and should be treated. Since the elderly, particularly those who live alone, are high suicide risks, the depth of depression and the possibility of suicide should be explored (30). Sleep disturbance such as early morning wakening (to be checked against the time they fell asleep), tossing, turning, a sense of hopelessness and futility, loss of appetite, and chronic fatigue should be regarded with suspicion and not as a usual clinical syndrome of the aged. Questioning may begin with a suggestion of possibility rather than fact. The back door approach is helpful; for example, "Do you get blue or sad?" rather than "Are you blue or sad?" The aged patient is particularly anxious to have his physician approve of him and may avoid showing a side of himself that he believes is unattractive. *Are* you is more likely to elicit a negative than the question of possibility. On the other hand, *feeling blue* may have been a normal state of affairs for such a long time that the aged patient is unable to make a distinction between that condition and a happier one. He may respond negatively to "Do you get . . . etc." and still show signs of depression. A helpful question then would be "Does life seem worthwhile?" If the response is negative, it can be explored." What would make it better?" The response may be a shrug followed by "At my age, what's the difference?", "I don't know what you mean, worthwhile.", or "Who has any say in the matter?" These are all typical parry responses of aged patients who will not respond directly to questions related to psychic intimacy.

Many elderly, because of the value system in which they grew up, are unwilling to talk about gynecologic, urologic, rectal or mental problems. It is often necessary to handle all related questions slowly, matter-of-factly, and with great tact. An elderly woman may be more comfortable discussing itching "down there" than itching of her genitals, a hard word for her to hear much less articulate. The physician may have to approach mental difficulties with similar delicacy. This may be handled by first stating, "Everyone has their ups and downs. For each person it's a little different. What do you think about when you're down?" Since expressions of *thinking* are often more acceptable to the elderly patient than expressions of *feeling*, the approach is more fruitful.

It is well within the province of preventive medical care to see that aged patients have an opportunity to learn new skills and hobbies. One of the best deterrents to depression brought on by a depleted and defeated sense of self is an involvement with something or someone new (17). Those of the aged population who are involved in some activities are less liable to mental illness than those who are not. Since the aged figure prominently in suicide statistics (attempts among elderly males are frequent and usually successful), it is imperative that all health care professionals who treat the aged be concerned with helping them achieve new good feelings in life.

It is possible for the aged patient who is becoming deaf to learn sign language or to read lips, which he is probably learning by himself anyway. It is possible for those with diminishing eyesight to be taught braille. It is possible for the elderly to learn a foreign language or a new hobby such as growing vegetables on the windowsill or teaching children how to read by first telling them stories, a skill in which aged people are adept. First it is necessary to convince the elderly that change is possible. The aged face feelings and ideas of futility, and many believe that who they are is indelibly traced. This is not true. Behavioral studies indicate otherwise and dispute the shibboleth that you can't teach an old dog new tricks. Human beings can learn at any time, although they learn more slowly in advanced age. Health care personnel must indicate their own belief in change before the patient will buy it.

COUNTING MARBLES

Senility is neither usual nor inevitable (21). Most elderly patients do business just as they always have, except perhaps more slowly. Anyone who addresses an older patient might reasonably presume that he is as tightly wrapped as he always was. As it is in our legal system, the burden of proof to the contrary rests upon the investigator. A patient who suffers a diminished sense of self to begin with will be further diminished if he believes the physician is speaking down to him.

If altered brain function is part of the clinical picture of an elderly patient, he will show evidence of any or all of the following: impairment of cognition, orientation, judgment, and affect. There are impairment tests of a perceptual and neurological nature such as the Bender hand-face in which one who is suspected of organicity may be specifically evaluated to determine if brain syndrome is mild, moderate, or severe.

The patient may display a chronic cognitive impairment in which his memory (both recent and remote), orientation, judgment, and ability to concentrate and calculate are diminished. He may also display disturbed affect. If he is aware of his problems, he may be anxious as he searches for a name or date, may even shake his head and reject a response, and may often recognize the right response if given several choices. If the physician suspects cognitive impairment, he may investigate further with such questions as "When and where were you born?", "How old are you?" "How many jobs have you held?", "Where did you attend school?", all pertaining to remote memory. "What time did you get up today?" and "What did you have to eat today?" pertain to recent memory. Questions formulated to test the patient's ability to retain new information will also give the physician an idea of the impairment of his short–term memory, an important piece of information if he is to handle his own medication. The physician may give the patient three items and ask him to recall them a few minutes later. The patient should be told the purpose of the exercise. ("I'm going to give you a little memory test.") The three items may be the name of a medication, its color, and the time it is to be taken. Finally, the patient may be asked directly, "Have you any trouble with your memory?" A patient with impaired memory may have difficulty listing the three items at the time they are given, as well as recalling what they were at a later time in the interview.

A disoriented patient may be unconcerned about his inability to keep tabs on where, who, or when he is, and in what time. ("What day is today?" "What month is it?") This will usually come out in the interview. Certain organic diseases result in the patient confabulating replies, inventing them on the spot to supply missing data that he perceives the interviewer searches for. Confabulation is seen in the patient with a history of alcoholism. The disoriented patient may misname where he is, a usual form of place disorientation, or he may reduplicate, asserting that there are two hospitals with the same name and staff, only the other one takes the more serious cases. He may state that there are two people with the same name and characteristics. The physician or nurse, for example, may be identified as someone he has known before. The elderly patient may give an incorrect future date. Because the bland, disoriented patient is more cooperative, he may be assumed incorrectly to be in better condition than one who is agitated.

Kahn defines an additional category which is neither cognitive impairment nor disorientation but is more a function of the institutionalization process (19). He calls it unorientation, a condition in which the patient shows no interest in his environment or its stimuli. If questioned as to where he is, the unoriented patient may respond, "I don't know. Ask my daughter."

Judgment may be assessed by examining how the patient manages his life. If he handles his day-to-day affairs with relative success, his judgment may be presumed to be intact. If he doesn't pay the electric bill so that he can play the numbers, goes out on a cold day without a coat, stops to talk to anybody on the street who will listen, there *might* be an impairment of judgment. Not always. Someone sitting on a park bench talking to chipmunks may be addressing the only audience that will stick around. No one of these actions alone is enough to make a case for impaired judgment. A judgment made on judgment is best if it is a composite one, a picture put together from many smaller pieces.

Judgment is also determined by how well the patient is able to make reasonable projections. Questions such as "What are you going to do today?" or "What are your plans for the future?" will help complete the composite.

The patient's ability to concentrate will have been seen throughout the interaction. If he looks up from time to time, appears bewildered or is unable to follow through with an idea or a train of thought, his concentration may be impaired. If he has evidence of disturbed concentration the physician can check by asking, "Do you have similar trouble concentrating on people's names or keeping track of meals or of where you are?" The patient's ability to calculate can be tested by giving him numerical tasks relevant to his life. ("If you have three dollars for bus fare and must make three trips here, how much will you have left over?")

Affect is the mood the patient presents and the manner in which he presents it. If he is emotionally labile, flowing from one mood to the next with relative ease, if his affect does not match what is being said or what he professes to feel, if he is blunted or agitated, it might be a feature of organic brain syndrome. A problem with determining affect in the elderly is that affect can be blunted by disuse and not always as a function of disease process. Expressions of communication are continually reinforced by what we perceive as our effect upon others and our observations of the manner in which they formulate an expression. When social contacts are limited, as they may be with the aged, and with their diminishing visual, auditory, and kinesthetic receptors, the mirror effect of someone else's responses and the ability to model after another decrease. The result is an atrophied repertoire. Questions related to affect may be quite direct. "How do you feel now?", "How long have you felt that way?", "What is it like to feel that?" help to corroborate the physician's impressions of the patient's affect.

Relatives and staff may be questioned for recent changes in the patient's behavior. It must be made clear to family that what is sought are changes noticed within months or weeks as opposed to gradual changes which occur over the years. Some 'changes' turn out to be nothing more than the altered perception of the witness who might report that he has noticed his father appears vulnerable instead of impervious and has become shorter.

PHYSICIAN AS INTIMATE AND CHAMPION

The physician fills three psychosocial functions for the elderly. First, as care giver for a patient of limited social contacts, he occupies the role of a significant intimate. The physician's role in the life of a younger person is proportionately one of less prominence.

The one who cares for the physical well-being of the aged, however, takes up the slack in a natural succession as meaningful others depart from his world. The second function is that of champion. The patient perceives that his physician stands between him and incapacity or death. As the physician uses his medical armamentarium, he fights off all the invisible pathological processes that have gathered in growing numbers to threaten the patient like Huns camping outside Rome. The third function, a result of the first, is his ability to affect the patient's behavior, especially sexual behavior.

The physician's attitude toward sexual activity in his elderly patient can have a profound effect on that activity. If he displays disapproval, the patient may diminish or cease activity altogether. On the other hand, if he offers psychologic support and technical advice, many of his patients will respond to his encouragement (28).

Some people, not all of them laymen, believe that sexual activity in declining years is somehow indecorous. One may curtail his sexual activity because he believes that it is improper "at his age." Influences of family, friends, and community usually reinforce this attitude. It is not unusual for an elderly widower to abandon his pursuit of some woman when he has been informed (usually by his children) that the neighborhood disapproves of such activity from someone his age. Others believe that each person is allotted so much sexuality and that unhusbanded and injudicious use will cause one to "burn out" his supply. If they have any left, they're spending it wisely. Actually, it is known that one who maintains an active sexual life throughout his adult years is more likely to continue into advanced age than those who do not.

The sexual activity of the aged declines for reasons other than the negative attitudes of society. The first is reduced incentive. The available partners can't compete with the billboards. The aged may forget that they, too, with perhaps varicosities and pendulosities, are winning no prizes, but that doesn't seem to matter. Diminished eyesight may be seen as a blessing in this circumstance. If they are retired, they may see a lot of their partners, which further dulls interest.

The aged usually have reduced opportunity. Since sex is generally not considered appropriate behavior, and since they are no longer as active socially as they once were, their contacts with prospective sexual partners decrease. Younger people have many more opportunities available than the elderly.

The third reason is a reduced capacity due to alcohol, certain medications such as barbiturates or some hypertensive agents, and the fear that illnesses such as mild heart conditions or inguinal hernias could be worsened by intercourse. Many of the aged who believe in a finite energy level prefer to put their figurative eggs into activities that yield a bigger payoff.

Finally, the elderly accept the decline in their sexual activity as natural. This resignation is perhaps the most significant reason for the decline. They expect it, then honor the prophecy. By contrast some of the aged have adapted to social rejection, loss of intimates, loneliness, loss of esteem, and loss of financial resources by moving in with other oldsters. Cohabitation serves two purposes. Each retains personal social security benefits; and while they usually assure their respective families that it is only for companionship, the word is leaking out that something else is going on. These aged, among others, are changing our ideas of human sexuality.

Recent studies involving the sexual habits of the elderly indicate that the maintenance of sexual activity contributes to their general physical well-being (11).

By two major actions the physician can help the elderly patient enjoy the natural and continuing function of sex (9). The first is to take the time to question his elderly patients regarding their sexual activities in a way that suggests that he expects such activities. A cursory or judgmental questioning may reinforce the patient's idea that somehow it is not expected. Since elderly patients may be reluctant to discuss sexual activity, the approach should be gentle and matter-of-fact, tangential if necessary. For example, "How often do you engage in sex?" might be preferred to "Do you engage in sex?", and both would be preferred to "You don't still have sex, do you?" "Is it satisfactory?" is a necessary follow-up question. This leads to the second major action the physician can take to help his patients enjoy sexual activity in their declining years—technical advice. The elderly patient can be taught sexual techniques to enhance the event, such as prolonged precoital play, how to set up the event in an unhurried and pleasant atmosphere, and the positions indicated for certain physical limitations with which they might be faced.

HOSPITALIZATION

Although they remain in the hospital twice as long and require hospitalization twice as often, the elderly tolerate elective surgery as well as younger patients (10). Since age has become less of a reason to limit surgical procedures, they will figure even more prominently as hospital patients.

The elderly patient who requires surgery sometimes believes that if he goes into the hospital, he will come out feet first. That and other ideas about medicine are usually holdovers from impressions made in his youth. He needs to be assured that the operation is less hazardous than the disease it is intended to remedy and that he is often more resilient, contrary to popular opinion, than a younger person. Like the younger patient, he will adjust more easily to new situations and be able to handle them if he is properly prepared.

Initial history taking is repetitive and often more intense than that involving a younger patient. The chronicle of disease, surgery, and medication has more chapters and takes longer to tell. The storyteller may get bogged down by the legend, something like trying to recall all the characters in *Dr. Zhivago*. To preserve the major story, he may jettison a few details. In any case, the staff will probably find it necessary to go over his history with greater care. The patient will have to answer the questions of interns, residents, and his own physician. He may become annoyed at the repetition and if so should be told that it is because the hospital staff want to be very careful and not miss anything important. If he understands that they are cautious because they care about him, he will accept the repetition more readily. The elderly patient may be subjected to complex tests that require days to perform. This is likely to irritate him and make him short–tempered with those around him, earning him the label of "crotchety." Anyone who scorns such an attitude need only wait interminably in a drafty hospital gown that won't close for procedures which are seldom explained by technicians who seldom speak except to give explicit orders such as "Turn," "No," or "Off." All this is made worse by the fact that the elderly patient is a little stiffer, a little slower, can't see as well, and probably has less muscle mass to put between himself and a metal table.

Once in the hospital, disorientation may become a problem for the elderly patient. Even though he managed well at home, adjusting to the hospital environment might cause some temporary confusion. His reduced sensory input, compounded by immobilization, has the same effect on his ability to understand his environment as a rainstorm has on highway signs. The guideposts to the landscape are clouded.

It is helpful if the elderly patient has clocks, access to T.V., radios, large calendars, photographs, night lights, and newspapers in his hospital room. Some papers, the *New York Times* for example, print a large type edition that give synopses of top stories for those with a sight disability. Printing menus and patient information pamphlets in larger type is also helpful if diminished sight is a problem.

The physician can help to orient the aged patient in the cues he gives as they speak. He covers all three bases, person, place, and time, if he says something like, "Good morning, Mr. Reed. I'm Dr. Forster. How's the hospital treating you?" Follow-up statements which continue to orient would be "Today is Wednesday, and I think it's time for you to walk down the hall." The physician may sound like a railroad conductor, but it's better than having a patient who doesn't know what he's doing there.

Many facilities insist on a regular and rigid schedule for aged patients. While a fixed routine contributes to their orientation, rigid insistence on following nonessential routines is not helpful. For example, if wants to brush his teeth at night, then he should be allowed to do it that way. If he still has his teeth, he's doing something right.

The aged patient should be introduced to other patients in beds near him and in nearby rooms. Many aged patients don't interact as easily with other aged patients as they do with those still reflecting youth and vitality. This is a good sign. It means that they gravitate towards life. Not too many people prefer the company of someone who sits with his head hanging down, least of all a person who thinks he might be in the same category and judiciously avoids contamination by association. Sometimes it helps to introduce the aged patient to patients on the pediatric floor if arrangements can be made for their safe passage. Most hospitals frown on interfloor exchanges; others–more permissive–allow it. The geriatric patient is often good with children and can be asked to tell stories and to play with bed-bound youngsters. He is also good company for those who have infrequent visitors. A double purpose is served, not the least of which is making the elderly patient feel useful, a powerful weapon in fighting the effects of feeling shelved.

There will be differences among the aged in the way they respond to hospitalization. Some will be philosophical and accepting; others will be despondent. The elderly patient may not express his wants as well as a younger patient. Determining his needs may require inventive investigation. One postoperative patient, for example, did not drink water because his glass was too full, and that frightened him. Staff discovered that a half–filled glass was less overwhelming. Another did not get out of bed because it was cranked too high.

In both cases, the information had to be dredged up, it was not volunteered. The attending staff should consider the quiesecent patient more likely to be in a self–made protective cocoon than content or having all his needs met. A useful question is to ask simply, "What can we do to make you more comfortable?", stated in an unhurried and relaxed manner. This patient is more likely to respond if he is not rushed.

Not all aged patients are reluctant to state their needs and complaints. Others state them a lot, in a kind of wearisome litany. Many times this patient is appeased if those who care for him simply acknowledge that they hear him. It is not necessary for them to try to undo irrevocable situations or to make promises that they cannot keep. It does help when they listen and indicate that they have heard either in flat feedback, "You say the food has been terrible.", or empathic feedback, "I can understand that you miss your wife's stuffed peppers."

When ambulation is appropriate, the aged patient should be encouraged to walk about the halls. The aged were taught in their youth that bed rest was beneficial and must unlearn this idea. Sometimes the hospital staff prefers that they sit in their rooms, for that makes less trouble all around. Since social worth is a factor in the elderly patient's care, however, he will recover more quickly if he is encouraged to walk and meet with other people. The staff needs to decide if they want clear corridors or convalescing patients. Rocking chairs are good investments for hospitals who expect geriatric patients, and that means every hospital except those specific to pediatrics and obstetrics. The use of calf and forearm muscles encourages venous return and increases cardiac output; besides, it feels good.

Any instructions to the elderly patient should be especially clear and repeated often followed by pauses for response. He should be given reasons for his having to do things for himself, since he may feel that it is the staff's way of dodging responsibility. The elderly patient may have to be persuaded to sleep less during the day so that he will sleep during the night. Often he goes to sleep at seven, after having had a few naps during the day, and then complains that he has lain awake all night. While he has more likely been sleeping on and off, he will be more rested if his daytime sleeping is discouraged. It should be explained to him that he requires less sleep than he once did. When he is told to exercise, he should not only have a reason, but an incentive. It is one thing to tell an aged patient that he must walk a little every day. It is something else to tell him to walk down to the pay phone and call someone daily, to water the plants in the waiting room, or to walk down the hall to cheer a patient who is bed-bound and has no visitors.

Often the cost of efficient professional care is depersonalization, insecurity, loss of dignity, and may even impair recovery. Increased anxiety in the aged patient has a detrimental effect on his performance and on his recovery. He responds well, as everyone does, to hope and optimism. Short successful exchanges are best with the elderly. They afford a sense of continuity and security. The physician should question the aged patient about his current status, listen to him, and discuss with him what he will do that day that perhaps he was unable to do the day before.

When talking to the aged, it is helpful to talk of something in the past, for their past occupies the largest percentage of their identity, something of the present, which is not only an assessment of current status but a way to orient, and something of the future to give them hope (13a). Something of the past might be "I understand you were an auto mechanic. I'll bet it was a lot different then than it is today."; something of the present, "Miss Feingold tells me you were trying to turn yourself yesterday."; and something of the future, "It looks like you'll be able to visit your children this summer."

DEALING WITH EROSION

Integrity means wholeness. How do we help an individual maintain integrity in the face of the continual erosion of himself? It involves first a willingness to entertain the idea that the self is subject to the same sculpting given to sea cliffs who face not only time, but sea and wind. Given that construct, there is no diminishing of self, only physical change. Second, while both man and cliff must brave the elements, man is distinguished by choice. He can turn and take the wind at his back if he chooses.

One way to maintain ego strength in the aged is to confront them continually with problems requiring solutions (1). Their cooperation in their own behalf should be elicited concerning decisions about their care, convalescence, and daily living. Not a rhetorical, "How would you like to go in the sun with Miss Williams?", as Miss Williams has the handlebars of the wheelchair in a death grip and is firmly propelling the patient toward the porch, but a real choice. They don't have to be major decisions. All that is required is that the patient gets to *pick*, which puts him in a prime position. For example, "When you go home you'll have trouble going up stairs for a few days. You'll have to decide whether to set up camp upstairs or downstairs. What do you think?", "I want to see you in two weeks. Would you rather come in the morning or the afternoon?", "Do you want the blinds lowered or raised?"

A second way to maintain integrity is to help him make plans. Plans mean a belief in the future and if one is involved in making them he then considers that he is going to be around to carry them out. It means that all the returns aren't in yet, and that he is still somebody with something to do. Some people have never made plans of any sort and must be taught how to take a realistic goal and break it down into smaller pieces. When teaching an older patient to make plans, it is a great temptation for the health care professional to chuck the whole idea.

It is like a jab with an ice pick on a balloon to hear, "Doctor, I know you mean well . . .", or "That's a nice idea, but . . .", or worse, "I'm too old for that." To reduce some of this, the plans must first be of the patient's choice. Even if the options are presented to him, it should be something he picks. A plan might be to start a plant from seed, read a book, take a course in something, learn a new recipe every week, learn to care for a pet, or volunteer to do something for someone else. The purpose of the plan is to give him a link to tomorrow. A plan is better when you can share it and for that reason it helps if other people are involved. In the absence of other people, the physician can say that he wants a weekly progress report on a post card (the physician may have to provide) of the plan that the patient is to make.

A third way to help the aged patient maintain ego strength is to review his past successes. The aged are involved in a life review. In a series of flashbacks they sift and sort through past successes and failures to arrive at some sort of balance sheet. The crisis of age is the acceptance of this balance sheet (13).

REFERENCES

1. Amster LE et al.: The relationship between life crises and mental deterioration in old age. Int J Aging Hum Dev 5:51–5, 1974
2. Anderson WF: Practical Management of the Elderly. Philadelphia, F A Davis, 1967
3. Anderson WF: Geriatric medicine: diagnosis is the key word. Geriatrics 29:132–136, 1974
4. Banting DW: Dental care for the aged. Can J Public Health 62 (6):503–508, 1971
5. Bonner, CD: Medical care and Rehabilitation of the Aged and Chronically Ill. Boston, Little Brown, 1974
6. Brotman HB: The fastest growing minority: the aging. Am J Public Health 64(3):-249–252, 1974
7. Chevan A, O'Rourke JF: Aging regions of the United States. J Gerontol 27 (1):119–126, 1972
8. Cowdry EV (ed): The Care of the Geriatric Patient. St Louis, C V Mosby, 1968
9. Dean SR: Geriatric sexuality: normal, needed, and neglected. Geriatrics 29:134–70, 1974
10. Deaver JM: The abdomen: surgery. In Freeman JT (ed): Clinical Features of the Older Patient. Springfield, C Thomas, 1965, pp 228–232
11. DeNicola P et al.: Sex in the aged. J Am Geriatr Soc 22:380–382, 1974
12. Eisely L: The Firmament of Time. New York, Atheneum, 1972
13. Erikson E: Identity and the life cycle. Psychological Issues, Monograph 1. New York, International Universities Press, 1959, vol 1, no 1
13a. Evans FMC: Psychosocial nursing. New York, Macmillan, 1971
14. Haber LD: Disabling effects of chronic disease and impairment. J Chronic Dis 24 (7): 469–487, 1971
15. Harrington M: The Other America. Baltimore, Penguin Books, 1972
16. Henry J: Human Obsolescence. In Culture Against Man. New York, Random House, 1963
17. Hiemstra RP: Educational planning for older adults: a survey of "expressive vs instrumental preferences." Int J Aging Human Dev 4 (2):147–156, 1973
18. Hodkinson HM: Non–specific presentation of illness. Br Med J 4:94–96, 1973
19. Kahn RL: Psychological aspects of aging. In Rossman I (ed): Clinical Geriatrics. Philadelphia, J B Lippincott, 1971, pp 107–113
20. Kasl SV: Physical and mental health effects of involuntary relocation and institutionalization on the elderly–a review. Am J Public Health 62 (3):377–384, 1972
21. Landsberg G, Taylor S: Evaluating a center's multiservice program for the self-sufficient elderly. Hosp Community Psychiatry 24(11): 747, 1973, passim
22. Mortality from home accidents. Stat Bull Metropl Life Ins 54:2–5, 1973
23. Nisbet G: Community services to the aged in Great Britain. Am J Public Health 61 (10):2018–2022, 1971
24. Number of elders growing nationwide. Stat Bull Metropl Life Ins Co 54:4–8, 1973
25. Old age–a problem for society as a whole. WHO Chron 28 (11):487–494, 1974
26. Pelcovits J: Nutrition to meet the human needs of older americans. J Am Diet Assoc 60 (4):297–300, 1972
27. Ramcharan S et al.: Multiphasic checkup evaluation study-2-disability and chronic disease after seven years of multiphasic health checkups. Prev Med 2(2):207–220, 1973
28. Finkle AL: Sexual function during advancing age. In Rossman I (ed): Clinical Geriatrics. Philadelphia, J B Lippincott, 1971, pp 473–478
29. Shanas E: Health status of older people. Am J Public Health 63(3):261–264, 1974

30. Spalt L, Weisbuch JB: Suicide: an epidemiologic study. Dis Nerv Syst 33(1):23–29, 1972
31. Toffler, A: Future Shock. New York, Random House, 1970
32. United States Bureau of the Census Illustrative Pop Projections of the United States: The demographic effects of alternate paths to zero growth. Current Population Reports, Series P-25, no 480, Washington, DC, US Government Printing Office.
33. Wan T: Social differentials in selected work–limiting chronic conditions. J Chronic Dis 25 (6):365–374, 1972

11
Pediatric Communication

O.K. Let's get our signals straight, then ... one finger will mean a fast ball, two fingers a curve, and three fingers a slow ball.

Peanuts
Charles M. Schultz

Early Flemish masters depicted children as miniature adults, scale replicas of their elders telescoped in size, faithfully duplicated in every detail, including some nasolabial folds that don't usually appear until middle age. Children are not homunculi, needing only the thimbleful of "drink me" to spring to full size. They reach maturity through Chinese boxes of developmental phases, each one having its own unique characteristics, its own goals, its own communication techniques, and its own ticket of admission to the next phase.

The genetically prescribed sequence of stages by which a child develops is by no means a smooth and orderly process. There are overlaps as earlier behavior patterns recede to admit later ones into prominence. It is common for a child to regress temporarily to a former developmental stage when threatened by some new task. A five-year-old entering kindergarten, who has been meeting strangers with aplomb for a year or so, at the sight of his teacher may suddenly glue himself next to his mother as if they were contenders in a three-legged race.

The communication procedures in this chapter are not meant to be hard and fast rules. They are general guidelines roughly following techniques described in earlier chapters. Their use will be tempered by the variance in individual development of each child, by his immediate need, by cultural determinants, and by the nature of the medical interaction.

NEONATE

CHARACTERISTICS

A neonate is capable of sharing in the communication process. His inexperienced and underdeveloped transmission system may prevent him from enjoying full rights and privileges, but he is a receptive and responsive being nonetheless. The major shift in physiological functioning of the newborn from intrauterine to extrauterine life, an event which is similar to being shot from a cannon, is one of irregular adjustments and extends from two to eight weeks after birth. Despite his projectile experience and his unfinished state, he has a vague but intense perception of his inner needs, such as hunger, thirst, and thermal stability. He can also perceive changes in his environment, although he has no real sense of self and cannot distinguish himself from that environment. There is evidence to support the idea that a neonate who is nursed considers himself and the breast one and the same.

The neonate will be heedful of sounds and will often stop postural activities to attempt an auditory "fix" in their direction. Within his visual range he will give faces brief regard, but being egalitarian, will extend this courtesy to the ceiling and the window. He is tactilely responsive and can be stimulated by fondling.

COMMUNICATION CUES

The newborn has communication cues of his own. His vocalizations signal distress and a need for help (2). This stage has been characterized as one of "omnipotence," since those needs are quickly met. The intensity and manner of the cry will vary with cause and circumstance. He will make sounds similar to those of a mewing kitten; these are not signals of distress but precursors of later babbling behavior. He will present early indications of a smile, which later will be developed and reinforced by his mother or major care person into a bona fide social response. Initially, the vaguely perceptible upturnings of his mouth, usually noticed just after feeding or when he is drowsy, cannot be taken too seriously as signs of approbation. He may or may not think you are a handsome fellow. With a neonate, the value of the smile in terms of communication is academic.

Much of the neonate's time will be spent sleeping. Up to 50 percent of his sleep is similar to that identified in the adult as dreaming sleep. During this time he will display the same increased eye and body movements, absence of muscle tone, and irregular respiration that the adult dreamer does. A major characteristic of this twilight period of neonatal existence is instability. The newborn will sneeze, choke, vomit, grimace, twitch, and suddenly be galvanized by a mass reflex response if startled (16). He has a low autonomic threshold which will be responsible for reddened skin or irregular respiration. This instability, which is normal for the neonate, is often the cause for trepidation in his handling. Sometimes a sudden and unexpected startle response can trigger a matching startle response in a first–time handler.

PHYSICIAN'S APPROACH

The best approach to the newborn is a gentle but firm one (1). Since he is neurologically unable to support himself, whoever handles him must provide body and head support. It helps if the practitioner's movements are slow and deliberate. In response to an easy, sure approach the neonate will make subtle adaptations of his own, imperceptible accomodations to the change in his environment, in this case, someone's arms. A well held baby is not a unilateral action but a mutual effort that is simply a good fit. It is a good idea to avoid sudden noises or sudden and intense pressure, except when it is necessary to test response as in the Moro reflex. The hesitation of some medical personnel to handle the newborn is often compounded by the fear of appearing clumsy or inept in the eyes of a supervisor or some charge nurse who has been running the nursery for 30 years. There is nothing so discomforting for a physician as conducting an examination on a howling, red-faced infant and attempting to juggle a mental checklist of femoral pulse, head circumference and Apgar data while someone is watching over his shoulder. The physician's thoughts usually follow this line: "This baby is telling me something and I'm not getting it," or "I'm doing something wrong and everyone knows what it is except me." The chances are good that the physician is doing nothing seriously wrong and

that the baby would be crying anyway, whether he was being examined or not. If he is saying anything, it is simply "Don't drop me!" or "Don't startle me!" It is helpful to keep in mind that the neonate is not Steubenware and the physician is not King Kong. The physician's leverage in handling the neonate is his medical expertise, his interest in the baby's well–being, and his body temperature.

Gentle sounds and gentle strokings link up sensory modalities of touch and hearing, which, together with that of sight tie a neat bow on his environment. Some clinicians conduct a large part of the examination while cradling the newborn in their arms. As can be imagined, this requires some dexterity and skill, and like a juggling act, takes practice. The physician can prepare for this kind of examination by using a doll surrogate to learn how to go about examining the umbilicus of an infant snuggled against his chest. Although this may seem at first like twirling a plate on top of a stick, with practice it becomes a neat way to do business. The temptation for some, flush with success, is to take on another plate.

Most physicians prefer to examine a newborn in his crib or on a table, and at times this is the only convenient method. If the neonate is examined on a table, the examining physician can be seated on the table with him. This allows for direct

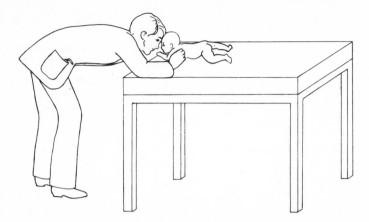

eye contact, which with a neonate lying on his back, falls within a narrow visual field of approximately 90 degrees (5, 6, 9, 10). The physician can sometimes engage the attention of a neonate with a gently swinging stethoscope. When he provides the neonate patient with visual as well as tactile and auditory stimuli, he increases the parameters of the interaction.

Gentle whispers in the baby's ear have a calming as well as an arresting effect. Placing one's forehead against that of the neonate patient when he is either on his stomach or on his back allows for continued body contact. Body contact is important, since all communication with the neonate makes use of the rich and powerful nonverbal signals which human beings use to conciliate, affiliate, and reassure (25).

INFANCY

COMMUNICATION PATTERNS

The neonate could not distinguish between himself and his environment. During the period of infancy, the baby will learn to make this distinction as well as to make the distinction between his mother and other people. Physiologically he will grow in quantum leaps, changing from a passive recipient of external stimuli to an aggressive seeker of new experiences. He will develop motor skills and specific listening and sighting skills which will aid him in his attempt to grasp or "incorporate" his environment.

As a neonate his needs were quickly met by his mother. To obtain satisfaction he had merely to express a need. Often his needs were anticipated. This pattern of expression and virtually immediate gratification gave him a feeling of omnipotence. As his mother returns to her conjugal role, other responsibilities and possibly a new pregnancy also require her attention. Since the infant is no longer the object of his mother's constant attention, he loses his feelings of omnipotence. His behavior at this time is not too different from that of any deposed monarch who is left with a straw empire. He adapts. He attempts a comeback. He looks for new countries. In the case of the infant, the new country is his increasing actual power, his mastery of his own body, and his ability to manipulate and "get at" his environment. An abrupt or precipitate loss of mother in either attention or breast feeding can lead to infantile depression, similar to the depression of the monarch who said after the coup, "I don't understand it. The people loved me" (26).

As the infant recognizes his mother's face, so is he beginning to recognize her mood. Often he shares her feelings and reflects them in a kind of emotional resonance. He is beginning to comprehend tones, inflections, and in later infancy, words. At about four months he begins to pay particular attention to the human voice as opposed to other sounds around him. To his responsiveness to nonverbal language he begins to add his increasing ability to transmit nonverbal gestural language of his own. This is in addition to the language of somatic manifestations of which he has been capable all along.

The infant is becoming a social being, capable of flashing appropriate smile display and adjusting it quickly at the sight of someone unfamiliar (3, 12). Even before head balance is mastered, he will delight in being held upright so that he can participate more advantageously in social orientation.

At about midinfancy, playing games such as peek-a-boo back and forth with his mother, repeating them over and over, paves the way for dialogue, the give and take of verbal communication. The mewing and crowing he did as a neonate, which yielded to cooing, now becomes babbling. Babbling at first is accidental. The infant produces sounds, likes them, gradually connects the sound to the origin, and tries to make them again. He is rewarded by the *feedback aspect* of sound production, as evidenced by the fact that the deaf baby gives up babbling. At about this time he begins to display strong anxiety towards strangers. He is particularly afraid of faces and has the tendency to see facial expressions in objects (17).

PHYSICIAN'S APPROACH

Except in early infancy when the fear of strangers is not yet developed, the physician's best approach to an infant is an indirect one, a casual yet artful circumnavigation like Magellan sneaking past his Straights.

The indirect approach to an infant is no different in principle from the technique of indirect questioning used with older children and adults. Both circuitous and tangential, the object is to create a climate of comfort, familiarity, acceptance, and independence in which the older patient can express himself spontaneously and the infant can experience security.

To relieve the anxiety created by the physician's intrusion, at first the physician might stand with his back to the infant while addressing remarks to his mother or anyone else in attendance. His attitude should be one of nonchalant unconcern, which might be reinforced with a brief glance at the infant that says, "What? You here?" The physician will find this gives the baby an opportunity to look him over first, a decided edge in any contest. After a few minutes the physician might extend a finger or hand for the baby to grasp. The maneuver, like that of a counterboxer, allows the other fellow to make the first move.

An interesting aspect of human communication is the mugging behavior used to attract the very young. These often grotesque caricatures of human facial expression and the clacking and snorting sounds associated with them may be delightful to a happy baby. To a sick or anxious baby, however, they can be terrifying. The best facial expression to use with an infant is a smile (8). He has learned to associate this facial configuration with pleasant things and pleasant people, and its absence may be enough to formulate an infantile equivalent of "oh oh." A constant smile makes the smiler feel as if his face were cast in concrete and is wearying to boot. An occasional smile, with a relaxed pleasant expression, is enough to do the job.

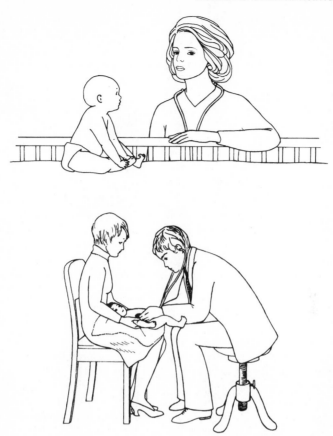

In middle infancy, unlike earlier stages, a child may be frightened by direct eye contact. A preventive measure is to keep eyes averted either altogether or occasionally, dependent upon the response of the infant. This is a situation in which oblique facing, helpful with some older patients, might be used.

Many physicians prefer to handle a child of this age in his mother's lap, mother and physician making a table out of their combined knees. If it becomes necessary for the physician to hold the infant, the physician's movements should be swift and sure. A faltering "Would you like to come to me?" will only make him clutch his mother more desperately. The physician should remember that the infant is beginning to have a good understanding of non-verbal signals. He can read hesitancy as clearly as an adult can read a fluorescent exit sign. He translates what he feels as, "He who hesitates doesn't know what he is doing, might drop me, take me away from my mother, or do some other dumb thing and is clearly not to be trusted."

Every infant has a favorite way to be held (4). The way his mother holds him will indicate his preferred position, and the physician should try to duplicate what she does. Is her grip loose or firm? Does she hold him face up, face down, seated, or upright? If, like most babies, the infant prefers to be held firmly upright, the physician should stand with his back to the mother so that the infant, with his head resting on the physician's shoulder, can face her.

In middle and late infancy, it is probable he understands some words. Since comprehension precedes the ability to express, it is best not to say anything in his presence that one would not want him to hear if he were a speaking child. Infants do respond to the physician's tone of voice. Some physicians keep up a steady cheerful chatter. One pediatrician "explains" things to his infant patients. He tells them what he is doing and what he is going to do. His explanations have a calming effect, although it is less likely the result of understanding the words as the matter-of-fact and lulling sound of them.

THE TODDLER

Establishing a therapeutic relationship with a toddler is as hazardous as signing an agreement with Attila. Just when you think you are making headway, events may suddenly reverse. The physician and the toddler are something like goose fat wrestlers who slip in and out of each other's grasp. This phase of the child's development, roughly between the ages of one and two and a half years is marked by incessant and tireless energy. He will go until he drops, like a wind-up toy churning out that last arm thrust.

PHYSICAL AND VERBAL GROWTH

He experiences increasing autonomy as his developing ability to walk, run, climb, and manipulate take him to where the action is; and with him it is everywhere: in cupboards, up on shelves, and under beds. He has more solid stool formation as well as greater sphincter control that gives him some say in what goes when. His negations, at first expressed by postural protest, will become verbal "No's." 'No' as a refusal will come to include even positive responses on occasion, with the result that most of the time he can be counted on to say no, regardless of what he means. His play, which to an observer may appear repetitive and monotonous, can be all engrossing, the intensity of his efforts often causing beads of sweat to form on his forehead. Mastery of play objects, in which he takes great pleasure, increases his sense of autonomy.

The toddler is beginning to have a better defined personal identity. He will change from referring to himself by name at the age of two to referring to himself by pronoun at the age of two and a half. As he is learning who he is, so is he learning that how he responds to situations often depend on circumstances, leading the way to different roles of interpersonal demands. He will begin to respond differently according to the context of the situation, his responses to the physician in his office being quite different from his responses to his mother in their home.

Learning acceptable social control of bowel and bladder sphincters can be an emotionally charged event and is believed to be significant in regard to personality development. It is here that the toddler's new feeling of autonomy comes in direct conflict with his mother. Toilet training plays a major part in Western acculturation of the young. Acting as society's agent, his mother, who previously was with him all the way, even applauding some of his actions, now tells him that he must release those sphincters at special places and at special times, and that any improvisation on his part will be looked upon with disfavor.

The developing speech of the toddler is one of his major accomplishments. His early communication needs are met by gesture and vocalizations. These vocalizations, early lexical activities that are a remarkably faithful imitation of the inflection, stress, and cadence of the language of his culture, peak between the ages of 15 and 18 months. They will be replaced by intelligible verbalizations at the age of two. The toddler will be able to verbalize immediate experience but will still have difficulty answering even simple questions about nonpresent events when he is as old as two and a half or three. Recalling implies the ability to observe ourselves and to call back the experience intentionally. Simultaneous experience of living in the present and recalling experiences of even the immediate past require language to form conceptual organizations of the experience and to tease them out of storage neurons by exchanging them for efficient and transportable symbols. Later language development of the child will enable him to recall and relate nonimmediate events (13).

PHYSICIAN'S APPROACH

When examining the toddler, as opposed to the infant, the physician can take advantage of his developing speech. At fifteen months of age the toddler will respond to a few key and catch words. By eighteen months he will respond to simple commands. From there, the intimate revelations which the physician offers him are limited only by his discretion.

The physician's attitude toward the toddler should be a firm but tolerant one. If the meeting takes place in an office, the furniture and equipment should be arranged so that the child doesn't face too many restrictions. The physician might give some warning of his approach. Footsteps, a voice, or a knock will do. He enters, ignores the child, and smiles at the mother. If there is time, he should sit down while addressing the mother, since a seated adult is less of a threat to a toddler. No attempts should be made to separate the child from the mother, and she should be allowed to place him on the examining table.

If the examination takes place in the hospital or beside his bed at home, the physician should try to sit next to his bed. Then he can give the child a brief smile, a few words, and become occupied with something else for a moment. His chart

will do. In the absence of a chart, the physician might check his book for the next appointment.

Once the physician opens communication negotiations with the toddler, he should be direct. Any false heartiness will be met with suspicion. The toddler knows the situation is not funny, and he will wonder why the physician thinks it is.

In this period, the child has begun to develop specific fears of the physician. While the physician is highly respected in some circles, in the toddler's world he occupies a spot on the bottom of the totem pole. The physician is associated with needles that stick, tongue depressors that choke, and other insults. It is necessary to secure his cooperation, however, in order to conduct any reasonable examination. One of the ways to do this is to allow him time to handle and explore any

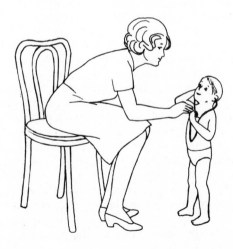

expendable instruments. Another way is to ask him to help: "Help me look in your throat." or "Help me hold the bandage." He will be proud of his ability to identify body parts. The physician should allow him to demonstrate this. "Show me your tummy" will go further toward establishing any relationship than an imperious inspection of his abdomen.

The physician should remember that the toddler is struggling for autonomy. He can be assured that "Do you want to sit on the table?" will elicit "No," even if the child means "Yes." The physician can give him a choice: "Shall I begin by looking at your head or your feet?", "Shall I listen first to your back or your chest?", or "Do you want to stand up or sit down on the table?" He might respond negatively to both options. In that case, the physician can make a decision for him with a firm stand. "You will sit on the table."

The physician can reinforce the toddler's cooperation by positive statements similar to affirmative leads—"Good.", "Fine.", "Thank you.", and "Yes." should punctuate steps along the way. They are similar to the statements of encouragement the physician uses to foster spontaneity in adult patients.

There are times when the toddler will simply not feel like cooperating. Maybe there is a new baby at his house that he would like to get rid of. Maybe he has been waiting a long while to see the physician and is hungry (or thirsty or sleepy). The physician does not have to throw in his hand; there are still cards up his sleeve.

First, limits for the toddler should be explicit. The physician will find it wise not to give the toddler an opportunity to improvise on a theme. "You may not hit me." is preferred to "Do not hit me with my stethoscope." (Maybe he can hit the physician with something else.) Likewise, "You may not throw anything on the floor." is preferred to "You can throw your shoes on the floor but not my ophthalmoscope." Second, the physician can divert the toddler to another activity by taking advantage of his short attention span. Some physicians keep hand toys in their pockets for just such emergencies. Third, if he is crying, the physician can stress the positive aspects of the clinical interaction. "I am going to help you," said in a firm and steady voice and followed by reinforcing positive statements for any abatement, is sometimes sufficient. Last, if all else fails, he can immobilize the toddler by holding him firmly or call in the mother as the heavy. A hammer lock is a last ditch measure and should be used only if absolutely necessary.

PRESCHOOL CHILD

The preschool stage of development, roughly between the ages of two and a half to five and a half years, is one in which the child acquires strength, ease, and facility of movement. His increasing manual dexterity and precision can be seen in his handling of drawing materials and in the way he ties his shoelaces, which will change from haphazard spaghetti-like agglomerations to neat little bows. This is a period of chrysallis in which the child will change from a clumsy awkward being into one of remarkable coordination and balance.

LANGUAGE ABILITY

The language ability of the preschooler increases along with his motor skills. At the age of three he can express limitations with such remarks as "I can't." His developing interest in social approbation will be expressed in such statements as "Is this right?" His refusals change from "No" to "I don't want to." At four he can carry on long conversations and will often ask "why" until the target of his interrogation, backed into a dialectic corner, will answer in desperation, "Because! That's why!"

The preschool child uses words politically and will boss, criticize, and call people by names, particularly those with scatologic reference. He does not like to admit failure or inability and will often confabulate on such occasions, changing from the three-year-old's "I can't" to "I could do that but I don't feel like it." "I don't want to" changes to "I won't." At five, his increasing social awareness is manifest in his often polite cooperation. "May I listen to your heart?" will elicit "Sure," perhaps even a tactful suppression of breathing. He may ask how things work and what they are for. The preschooler freely expresses his feelings and is able to relate events not of the immediate present.

One of the characteristics of cognition at this stage is concrete conceptualization and interpretation. Piaget designates it as the age of preoperational thought (20). The preschooler attaches literal meaning to words. Thus, a two-faced person is imagined as having two faces, and someone "over the hill" is doing some mountain climbing. For the preschooler there is no such thing as an analogy, an abstraction, or a joke. Meanwhile, his developing locomotion and language permit him to expand his imagination, and he will engage in a kind of magical thinking that endows objects or anything active with life. He might see medical instruments as malevolent living devices quite capable on their own of jumping, biting, or cutting (4). The inability to distinguish the animate from the inanimate allows him to give a toy the same respect he might give a person.

The preschooler is developing as a social being with a newly emerging conscience and an ability to place limited restrictions on himself. The greatest portion of his energy is devoted to his play, alone and with other children. It is his major occupation, and one in which he learns through experiment and planning to master reality.

He begins to develop sexual curiosity and to form gender identification, an awareness of his own gender. There is a natural tendency beginning in this stage to explore and manipulate the genitals in preliminary masturbation activity. This universal and normal phenomenon of children, more common when the child is anxious or insecure, is seen in the sick or hospitalized child who often reduces tension through masturbation.

In the latter part of this stage, the child begins to develop anxiety and pride in his body, its parts, and his prowess. All parts, including his genitals, become impor-

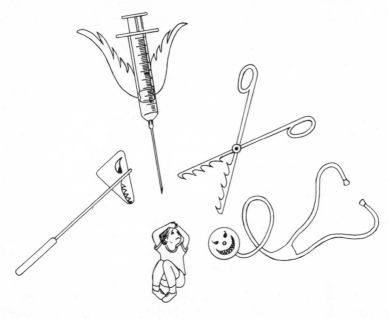

tant possessions to him. He places a high value on his body, which makes him especially fearful of loss, injury, or impairment of powers. This concern with image will cause conflict with anyone seen as potentially interfering, especially the physician, who, in the child's own experience, is quick to probe and spy upon the parts of his body. Apart from this anxiety, the child has additional reason to fear the physician, which has nothing to do with the fear of strangers present in his earlier years. It has to do with his new sense of parental identity.

Parents are models for their children and the preschooler will imitate them by reflecting their cues and their attitudes. If his parents are anxious or fearful in the presence of the physician, the child will consider this the normal way to behave. If they spell D-O-C-T-O-R in the context of "It doesn't look too good. We'll have to put him in the car and run him to the _____.", he will be able to extrapolate DOCTOR and figure out that it means the guy with the needle. He will then reason that meaning was deliberately hidden. That fact, added to the tone of voice, portends nothing good.

PHYSICIAN'S APPROACH

The preschooler will construe as potentially dangerous direct questions about the state of his health. "I'm here to find out what's wrong with you." will elicit a predictable and defensive "There's nothing wrong with me." Bird suggests that the physician's goal in this case is to create a medical debit/credit ledger by tallying all the child's commendable and functional aspects so that by their sheer weight he can afford a few on the negative side (4). For example, "You are getting big and strong.", "I notice you jumped up all by yourself.", and "Your eyes are perfect. I bet you can see very far." followed by "I understand you threw up." From the vantage point of all his successes, the child can afford a gratuitous acknowledgment of malfunction.

The preschooler has no notion of gradation, relativity, or the nuances of comparison. Everything is the worst or the best. "How bad does it hurt you?" might be a difficult question to answer. In his world there are simply good guys and bad guys, bad hurts or no hurts, a shrug at a scrape ("It doesn't hurt at all") or screams of pain. A physician looking for shades of gray is unlikely to get them.

Once he is engaged in dialogue with the physician, open-ended questioning may be used to facilitate response. The preschooler can now relate to events that occurred in the nonpresent situation. "You went into the bathroom, you stood up on the stool, and you . . ." Leading the witness has its pitfalls; he may supply answers that he believes the physician wishes to hear. Further questioning is necessary to separate fact from fiction and fact from elaboration. For example, a child who is particularly good at improvisation might say in response to the above, "Flied around." The physician's intent is not so much to discredit the story but to elicit relevant information. Further questioning might be "You flied around. O.K. Did you fly near the medicine cabinet?" "Sure." "Then what happened?" "I opened it and I took out a bottle."

Another way to elicit information from a preschool patient is to use an inanimate surrogate. This technique, used by Oriental practitioners in the not too distant past, was originally designed to allow modest and reticent ladies to participate indirectly in the medical examination. The use of dolls, puppets, and stuffed animals allows the physician to ask the child, "Where does it hurt?" The child will very often point to a spot coincidentally corresponding to his own site of pain.

The physician should reflect the child's expressions, both verbal and nonverbal. To the child shrinking back at his approach, the physician might say, "You don't want me to touch your bandage." If this matter-of-fact statement does not obtain response from him, the physician verbalizes his nonverbal gestures in order to help him express himself. "When you see someone coming near your bandage, you worry that he might hurt you." Where or when his dressing will be changed is not as crucial as getting the child to express how he feels about it.

When the child expresses feelings, the physician should acknowledge them. The child faced with the snout of an x-ray machine who volunteers, "I'm afraid," needs *ventilation* before explanation. Thus, "You're afraid of the x-ray machine." should precede "It's a big camera." As with an adult patient, the physician should avoid hurried reassurance. "There's nothing to be afraid of." terminates meaningful communication. In addition to his original fear, the child is now afraid to be afraid.

It is a big burden to act like a big man if you are a little one. The physician's major tasks in eliciting a child's expression of feelings are the same as those he performs with an adult patient: active listening, rephrasing, feedback, and clarification. Long silences are to be avoided as they are especially anxiety provoking to a child.

The physician should respect the feelings of the preschool patient. Denial of his feelings is a punitive action and one that discourages future response. "Now that didn't hurt a bit." is a negation of the child's feelings. "I know that must have hurt." or "Yes, I know it hurt, and I'm sorry." are preferred.

A note about mothers at this point. Mothers sometimes spell what they consider crucial words during examinations. The physician should discourage this if he can. Besides interrupting the relationship that may be developing between him and his patient, the child can probably comprehend meaning from context. One physician reports an incident involving the mother of a four-year-old who said, "Doctor, he seems to be concerned about his P-E-N-I-S," whereupon the child immediately gripped his crotch in a death lock which he maintained throughout the balance of the visit.

The child must be prepared for medical procedures. If not, the result will be a sense of betrayal and years of resistance to future medical care. He should be told what is necessary over and over, even if he is crying, does not appear to hear, says he understands, or looks perfectly happy. The explanation, which need not be too detailed, should give him some idea of what to expect. Words should be carefully chosen, remembering that the child takes things literally. An explanation of the dye injected in an intravenous pyelogram will surely be heard as "die." The physician can obtain feedback from the child by having him repeat what he has been told. Simple pictures, where possible, can be drawn. Since the child ascribes animation to objects, the physician should explain the functions of instruments in simple terms, emphasizing that their energy and direction come from him. "This is made of aluminum, and it does what I want it to."

This is where the preschool patient will ask why. "Why" is a holding action. It keeps the physician, his instruments, and his own fears at the end of a question mark. An inordinate string of "why's" (a subjective evaluation) may be followed by the physician's reflection: "You are asking a lot of questions about. . . ." If no response is forthcoming, he can add, "Sometimes when people ask a lot of questions, it is because they are worried."

When discussing anesthesia, the physician should try to avoid the analogy of putting him to sleep. He may have fears about sleep–loss of control being primary. He may worry about wetting himself, telling some shameful secret, or worse, never waking up. Many children have had a pet, who, after being "put to sleep," never showed up again.

The crying preschooler should be handled as an older patient. He should be encouraged to express his distress. The physician should try to reflect and acknowledge the child's feelings: "You are upset.", "You are unhappy.", or "You are worried." Unless there is pain and suffering involved, the child should be asked what worries him. This technique sometimes requires time, the one commodity (together with concern), that separates the physician from a gum ball machine.

There will be times, arising from excesses of one sort or another, that the preschool patient will demonstrate disregard for the physician, his office, or his instruments. Depending on the severity of the destruction, the physician might feel anger or annoyance. He should *not* remember that the patient is only a child. He has the same right to feelings as the child does. Anger is a reality and the physician's professional image will not suffer if it is expressed. When the physician is angry, he should address himself to the situation and not to the character or personality of his patient. He can use what Ginott calls "I" messages: "I see my office in shambles.", "Instruments belong in the sterilizer. I get angry when I see instruments on the floor.", "Tongue depressors belong in the jar. I am annoyed.", or "Doctors' offices are not for playing. I am upset at this mess" (11a). These statements reflect the physician's feelings. They are not an attack on the child as "You are a bad boy and a rotten patient." would be.

The expression of the physician's own feelings in this situation has several positive effects. First, it relieves some tension, allowing an easier resumption of medical interaction. Second, the likelihood of the situation recurring is reduced. Third, appropriate expression of feeling is modeled for the child. Last, *trust is established*. Twitching mandibles can be eloquent, and the child will know that the physician is angry whether he tells him so or not. It is difficult for a child to trust someone who pretends one thing to him while he feels another.

THE GRADE–SCHOOL CHILD

Grade–school age, sometimes referred to as the period of latency, includes the child from age six to eleven. This stage, which extends to the boundaries of puberty, snaps back and forth like a rubber band to accomodate individual variances in development, particularly at the end when there can be up to three years normal developmental difference.

CHARACTERISTICS

Physically, the school-aged child is growing like crabgrass. His clothing and shoes shrink as they are taken out of the box. He will attain 90 percent of his height by the time he is 12 and, unlike the preschooler, will find compliments on his continued rise offensive (15). Like yeast, he would prefer to do this in the dark. He also sees a remark such as "You've gotten so big I hardly know you." as one of many stupid clichés that adults seem to drop as fast as pigeons spatter a statue.

The grade–school child is learning physical skills necessary for games which will enable him to compete, as well as fundamental skills of reading, writing, and calculating that will lay the groundwork for more sophisticated scholarship. He is getting a lot of information about his ever-widening world, with particular attention to human behavior, rules, taboos, jokes, his body, his peers, his nation, and totems of his society. In some cultures the child will learn from adults who become teachers by acclamation rather than by appointment. This learning will most likely emphasize and promulgate values of the particular cultures. In this country, for example, "street–wise" has come to refer to the inner-city child who learns to count by determining how many blocks are safe and to read by which street sign spells for him, "Danger, you're on enemy turf." In the same mode, which is part of an adaptive-protective process, he also learns that to reveal anything to "the man" is not in his best interests.

The grade-school child learns to build and to complete what he is building, unlike the cavalier preschooler who doesn't mind knocking everything down. He develops what Erikson refers to as a "sense of industry." Reinforcement of accomplishment, together with pleasure in mastery, teaches him to win recognition by producing things (7). There is a danger at this age, however, that the child will develop feelings of inadequacy and inferiority. If the child fails at enough tasks and if enough of his projects never reach fruition, he will accumulate a deficit of esteem. The school-aged child needs successes to succeed.

With his growing desire for independence, he begins to think in terms of community. My house, my parents, my toys become our teacher, our team, our town. His world expands from family and neighboring children to include schoolmates from other neighborhoods, teachers, and community adults. Not all children happily enter the larger social network of school. The phenomenon of school phobia, most commonly seen in the early grades, is found in those instances in which the mother and child, usually from an achievement oriented home, are excessively dependent upon one another. It is distinguished from truancy, which usually involves children who come from homes in which there is general indifference to school.

The decreasing sex drive and sex interest of the grade-school child make the preschool period lascivious by comparison. Actually, he is not going to forget sex, he is just going to put it on a back burner while he addresses himself to more immediate and important issues. Sometime later, at about puberty, he will remember it with a start. The greatest concern of the school-aged child is his peer group —their approbation, acceptance, and activities. He regards members of the opposite sex with apparent disdain carrying this to extremes such as refusing to eat Girl Scout cookies.

The school-aged child, as a result of his new community role, learns to compromise and to negotiate. This is the time when the child will develop his own characteristic ways of coping and his concepts of morality. This is the age when he really is "father to the man."

PHYSICIAN'S APPROACH

Many of the communication techniques discussed in regard to the preschool patient will also be applicable to the school-aged patient. In addition, because of the child's increased vocabulary and understanding, verbal communication will be easier. Explanations of procedures, however, should still be simple and to the point. Beware the child who responds to an explanation with apparent stoicism and bravery. The physician shouldn't buy it. Instead, it would help if he were to encourage his young patient's expression of anxiety by requesting feedback and restatement.

If the interaction is with a child from a socioeconomically disadvantage background and the physician is a member of the dominant culture, there might be an additional communication stumbling block. The child, depending on his experience, may perceive the physician as potentially hostile. The physician's major task is to create an atmosphere of acceptance in which the youngster learns to trust. This child's clinical experience, which is limited compared to that of the middle-class child, has most likely been with a succession of physicians who don't seem to remember him from one time to the next. The physician is also a representative of a body of people whom he is beginning to perceive as members of an alien group (14, 21).

As with an adult patient from a minority culture, there should be no attempt by the physician to imitate the child's vernacular in order to form common ground. He will regard the physician's use of his language with suspicion; he will consider it a skillful mimicry used to infiltrate behind the lines. The physician has another more valuable common ground, which is mutual interest in the child's welfare. Moderate and even pacing of speech is important. The physician's own anxiety may cause him to fill in silences and dispatch the preliminaries hastily. This is one of those occasions when the allotment of time to the clinical interchange is crucial. Finally, this child will respond to an easy and tactful approach which the physician displays in an open posture, by minimal intrusion and by soft-sell encouraging leads.

In communication with any child, the physician should avoid the use of "why." "Why" is judgmental. It infers that the child's conduct and his ability to make decisions are under question. "How did this happen?" is preferred to "Why did you do that?" The school-aged child needs success, and the physician is in a position to give it to him. Initial inquiries into his hobbies and activities give the physician an opportunity to praise the child's efforts. Medically, the physician can dispense success along with treatment by congratulating the child for cooperation. "You have helped me a great deal by holding still while I was stitching your knee. That required patience and courage."

The child's new sense of community permits the use of inclusive phrasing. This is not the same as "We are going to have our tonsils out," but rather "Girls your age often wonder about their bodies." or "Most people find it helps to chew on an ice cube." Inclusive phrasing is distinguished from generalities such as "everyone," which is used to minimize expression. For example, "I'm afraid you are going to give me a shot." "Everyone is afraid of needles."

The school-aged child will be seen for elective medical and surgical procedures that, because of the previous high premium he had placed on his body, were postponed. He still cares very much about his body parts, but his maturing self-image teaches him that he is larger than their sum.

Many children feel guilty about their illnesses. In some households it is impossible for a child to become ill without being made to feel that in some way he caused it. He might have gone out without his sweater, stayed up too late, left his vegetables on his plate, or worse, played in the rain. Some of his anxiety might stem from feelings that his parents are angry with him for his neglectful actions.

If the child must be hospitalized, the separation from his parents adds to his anxiety. It is important to note that even when he is not crying, he is probably anxious. There are three nonverbal cues to his anxiety that will lead the physician to further investigation: if the child is unnaturally quiet; if he is tense and jumpy; or if, when he thinks he is not being observed, he takes off his "on face," the mask that conceals the doleful expression beneath.

Some children will feel anger toward a parent who has left them alone in the hospital and will displace this anger with irrascible behavior directed at everyone else. This patient may snarl at the dietician, or worse, tell the "play lady" and her games to get lost. He may be so angry with his mother that he will ignore her entirely or turn his head away at her approach.

Just as the adult hospital patient, the hospitalized child needs explanations of medical procedures (19). They are especially important for the child because they correct false expectations. A child who experienced a death in the family preceded by hospitalization may be panicked at the approach of his own hospitalization. He may even expect magical changes such as "You'll be bigger than your brother" implanted by zealous parents anxious to have a cooperative and uneventful admission. Explanations prevent distortions. If they are given no clear explanations, children fantasize conclusions often more frightening than the real thing. For example, a seven-year-old with visual disturbance who was admitted for diagnostic studies confided to a nurse that he knew he was going to have his eyes removed. Inadequate preparation retards aftercare. The child cooperates in his recovery when he can trust those who care for him, and trust is a result of shared and corroborated realistic expectations.

Explaining anticipated procedures and situations to a child is enhanced by visual aids. Pictures, models, dolls, and instruments which he can handle help the child visualize coming events. The physician will also find it helpful if he encourages the child to ask questions and offers no assurances until he has a good idea what the child thinks is wrong. A preschool child or an immature school child may be preoccupied with mutilation, especially of his sexual organs. It is helpful to emphasize that no body part will be touched but the one already planned on. "We are removing your tonsils, not your belly, not your heart, not your penis." Explanations, as with the adult, should cover all hospital procedures including rounds, tests, and postsurgical measures. Being told "You'll be on your belly so you can spit up old blood. Some of it may still be in your nose." is far less frightening to a child than waking up on a strange high bed with a sore throat and thinking the inside of his head is coming out (19).

The feelings of the patient of any age can enhance or detract from the effectiveness of medical procedures. The two actually fold in upon each other like a Johnson and Johnson Möbius strip. This inseparability mandates the physician's attention to those feelings and to the manner in which he can elicit them. The angry or anxious child needs an opportunity for ventilation. He can do this with a direct statement of fact such as "Miss Lake tells me you threw your tray on the floor." He can offer interpretation: "People who throw their trays on the floor are usually angry." Humor should be used cautiously. "You training for the Mets?" may make him laugh, but the goal is not so much to jolly him out of his feelings as it is to get him to verbalize what they are.

The importance of expressing feelings is not limited to the hospitalized child. When an individual's hostility cannot be expressed outwardly, it has a way of turning inward and results in an attempted or actual self–destruction.

Children rarely commit suicide or make overt suicide attempts; they express their self-destructive feelings in suicide equivalents such as depression, "accidental injuries," or antisocial acts. These suicide equivalents are distinguished from the common childhood fantasy of punishing parents by "eating worms until I die" (23, 24). Mildly depressive states occur in a lesser degree frequently during childhood, although there appears to be a gap in their clinical recognition between Spitz's "anaclitic" depression seen in infancy and after the age of five (26). The child will respond to these ordinary affective displays with his own characteristic defense and coping mechanisms.

The depression of "suicide equivalence" occurs when these coping mechanisms fail. It is seen in a constellation of behaviors such as despondence, withdrawal, frequent crying, expressions of feeling unloved or rejected, insomnia, and autoerotic activities. It is characterized by a negative self–image. These children feel worthless, inadequate, or "bad." Frequently they are reflecting their parents' inability to support them when they failed or had difficulty in mastering a situation. They are unable to conceive of "good" and "bad" living in peaceful coexistence within the same body. The parents' inability to support may be interpreted as actual or threatened loss, and the child's actions may be seen as an attempt to recoup this loss. Severe childhood depression requires psychotherapeutic intervention.

ADOLESCENCE

CHARACTERISTICS

Adolescence is the time when the child remembers sex with a start. The rapid physiological development of his genitals and reproductive organs, which will stimulate him to initially awkward hereterosexual activities, make his gonads and not his feet primarily responsible for tripping over wastebaskets, walking into walls, and turning roseate like litmus paper sprinkled with lemon juice. New and powerful sexual urges, slapped awake by tantalizing expressions of society, produce a fantasy life that is in paradoxical conflict with the prohibitions of society. Those youngsters who realize their sexual fantasy life usually do so within the smaller counterculture enclave, still in conflict with predominant social values.

The adolescent rebels against authority. One of his purposes at this stage is to free himself from childhood ties and establish his independence. He resents unsolicited attention and advice and will strut and slink in an effort to appear aggressive, cynical, grown-up, and self-sufficient. He vacillates between wanting independence and running from it, like a tightrope walker who takes a few steps, beats his chest, yells yoo-hoo, then races back to the safety of the platform.

This vacillation of the adolescent reflects a normal lack of stability. He is in constant disequilibrium, an obvious handicap for a tightrope walker. The constant flux which characterizes adolescence is responsible for making it a vulnerable phase for mental disorder. This is the time of turmoil and stress, a period of shifting moods. Behavior that would be poorly regarded in the younger child or in the adult is somehow accepted in adolescence.

The adolescent is concerned with how he appears to his peer group. His dress, which at first glance may appear carelessly and hastily conceived, is actually artfully contrived. His object is to look like his friends, and their object, in turn, is to avoid looking like the grown–ups. Everything the adolescent does, the way he dresses, dances, speaks, and behaves, is executed with an eye to peer approbation.

When he is in love, he frequently seeks to bolster his own self-esteem by finding who he is reflected in the eyes of his loved one and probably would, if he could, proliferate his reflection by exchanging them for the multifaceted omnatidiae of the lobster.

All of the pursuits which occupy the adolescent are designed to find and establish an identity. As early as junior high level he will have to make decisions affecting major career interests and an eventual choice of occupation by choosing high school curriculum. The distress caused by the variety of possible choices and the necessity to settle on an occupational identity is resolved temporarily by the adolescent blending so well into his peer group that he loses individual distinction. Marin describes the adolescent deeply involved in peer culture. "Community and collective wisdom have vanished, and the young seem forced in the vacuum to improvise, to find their own ways back to wisdom and joy" (18).

PHYSICIAN'S APPROACH

The physician who is primarily concerned with health care delivery cannot hope to lead his adolescent patient back to "wisdom and joy." He can, however, by means of his interpersonal skills facilitate that delivery and provide an acceptable pontoon to the adult world.

Adolescents speak their own language, which changes as rapidly as the seasons. Words suddenly appear, are "in," then just as suddenly disappear, like memories of Stalin. Even if the physician is in his internship, unless he has younger brothers and sisters at home, he is already hopelessly out of touch with current usage. The physician should speak his own language with an adolescent, who will consider anything else a "put on." (At the time of this writing, "put on" has probably been put out.)

The disequilibrium which is the natural state of the adolescent will make things uncertain for the physician, who will never be sure whether he is opening the door to the lady or the tiger. One way to approach this uncertainty is to address it directly.

When speaking to an adolescent, the principles that apply to adult and child apply to him. He is both. It is common to be lulled into a false security by the arrogance of a few whiskers and then be surprised at a show of tears that the adolescent manages to hold back like stagnant water. It helps to take him seriously, to expect that his language understanding is that of most adults, but that his understanding of *how* and *who* he is is still developing. So that while he may sound and look like a grown-up, he's more often a little kid in disguise.

By recognizing the adolescent's dual possibilities, the physician demonstrates acceptance of him as he is with no unreasonable expectations for constancy.

The physician should not expect wisdom and control from his teen–aged patient. The adolescent, in spite his insistence to the contrary, wants some guidelines. The physician's position on the adolescent's totem pole is now somewhat higher than the adolescent's parents (a spot shared with just about everyone else who is not his parent) and possibly higher than most adults because of professional expertise. The physician is in a favorable position to provide guidelines and a sense of security by clear statements of how he stands on certain matters and his own feelings. For example, the teen–ager may respond to all questions, whether direct or indirect, with short grunts. Obviously, more than grunts are needed to form a clinical judgment. The physician's response can be "I am feeling frustrated and annoyed by your refusal to talk to me." The adolescent patient may indicate that this is entirely the physician's problem. The physician can then face him directly in an expectant silence that demands response. Finally, cooperation can be facilitated by offering the patient autonomy, since dependency breeds hostility. The adolescent may or may not recognize his dependence on his parents; but if he is ill, he clearly depends on the physician. The physician can offer the patient autonomy by presenting him with choices: "I can guess about what is troubling you and treat you accordingly, or you can provide me with the information that will help me make a better judgment. The choice is yours."

The physician shouldn't be too understanding. The adolescent, for all his camouflage to the contrary, wants to be unique. He does not want to be transparent. It is not a good idea to say things like "I understand. I felt the same way when I was your age." That was eons ago. The ice age and the space age have nothing in common.

The adolescent is very concerned about his body and has had plenty of opportunity to make comparisons in gym, with particular attention to height, muscular development, genitalia, and body hair. Because of the physician's familiarity with bodies of all shapes and sizes, his comments in this area assume tremendous importance. A caveat, then, to be given serious consideration: no teasing, no jesting. The teen–ager needs to be reassured about the great developmental variance in adolescence, as well as the variance in the finished product of adulthood. Remarks like "I smelled the Phisohex and knew it was you." are more than a stumbling block to communication; they are a brick wall.

When he does open up, it is important not to belittle his fears but to acknowledge and reflect them. For example, "That little thing is worrying a big girl like you?" would be better expressed as "You are concerned about the mole on your leg." A follow-up question might be "In what way?", or specifically, "What worries you about the mole on your leg?" Elicitations of expressed fear should precede explanations of what it is or how it may be dealt with.

When the physician praises the adolescent patient, the focus should be on his efforts rather than on his character (11). The communication goal should be description rather than evaluation. "That was very helpful." is preferred to "You are very helpful." The latter creates an onus of continual performance which may be hard for the adolescent to live up to.

The majority of adolescents seek medical aid for headache, menstrual dysfunction, acne, or excessive weight. Once they get inside the office, many of these presenting complaints while valid, turn into are red herrings, designed to throw the receptionist and the parents off the scent. What they really come for are questions concerning sexual activity, drugs, and running away from home (27).

When the physician addresses the adolescent's complaint his patient may throw out a cue about the issue that to him is more significant to which the physician should be alert. It goes something like this.

Physician: O.K. Now you know that fried foods, greasy foods are out, so is seafood, chocolate . . .
Patient: Right.
Physician: I'm not sure which one is the biggest trouble maker in your case, but let's stop everything suspicious for the time being.
Patient: Could anything beside food make my face break out?
Physician: What did you have in mind?
Patient: I dunno, things like sex.
Physician: Are you worried that sex can give you acne?

Patient: Can it?
Physician: No.
Patient: What about a lot of sex?
Physician: What's a lot of sex?

Most of the adolescent's problems will in some way be connected to sexual development. When offered an opportunity to discuss sex seriously, he will usually talk quite freely. Masturbation is high on his list of concerns. His easily triggered desire is constantly at odds with a society that says no, and masturbation will probably be his major outlet. He will have all sorts of feelings about this activity and needs to ventilate them. Approach to the subject might be general rather than specific, not "How often do you masturbate?" but "Usually people your age find relief in masturbation." He will need information about venereal disease, contraception, and abortion. He will need to be sure that the physician will not violate his confidences and his privacy. Values are given at home; the physician's task is to provide him with information necessary for his well-being. The physician shouldn't expect the adolescent to be terribly knowledgeable in the specifics of conception. Many teen-agers, for example, are surprised to learn that withdrawal or intracrural intercourse can still result in pregnancy.

The adolescent patient will be exposed to drugs. Both alcohol and narcotics are as accessible to him as ice cream from a truck. The simple truth is that any young person can get his hands on anything he wants. No community can claim immunity from this phenomenon of our current scene. Even if the adolescent is not using, he probably knows what it looks like, what it's called, how much it costs, and who he can get it from.

Even when parents, school officials, and the adolescent himself say that he is not using drugs, the physician's best approach is a wary, if not prophylactic one. If the patient displays characteristic signs or behavior of drug abuse, the physician can obtain information by honest confrontation. "There is a peculiar odor on your breath." This will probably be met with denial. The physician can continue with "That is the breath of someone who is sniffing glue." Further, "Tell me about it." If response is negative, the physician plays his final card. "The evidence tells me that you are using/taking. . . ." This should be said in a flat, nonjudgmental manner. The adolescent drug abuser needs information from the physician at this moment, not criticism. The physician should spell out the dangers of overdose, a major cause of death among young addicts; the problems and consequences of addiction in terms of function, possibilities of infection, genetic damage (this will concern the adolescent the least, since he considers parenthood in the far distant future if at all); and local statutes regarding arrest and incarceration. The physician needs to know what the adolescent takes, under what circumstances he takes it, when he takes it, how often, who he is getting it from, and how it makes him feel. Last, since success of treatment involves the cooperation of his parents, the physician discusses with him the ways in which he would like to enlist their help. The conversation may go something like this:

Physician: I would like to tell your parents.
Patient: Why?
Physician: You can be treated better with their help.
Patient: Don't tell them. I'll do whatever you say.
Physician: I believe you mean to, and that is very important; but the success of
             your treatment depends on their help. How can we get this help if they
             are not informed?

Patient: I knew you would tell them.
Physician: Would you rather tell them yourself?
Patient: No, you tell them. Boy, are they going to be mad.
Physician: You feel they will be angry?
Patient: You better believe it.
Physician: They might be. They might be angry, but then, they may not.
          (Pause.)
Patient: How would they help?

When a child feels that his environment restricts him too tightly from personal expression or when his parents use coercive procedures to mold him into some vague ideal, he may want to run away. In the past this was done by token actions such as truancy, staying out all night, or withdrawing into an unapproachable shell. Today's young have the added option of really running away. Transportation is no problem, they can hitchhike with ease across the United States and back if they want to. Places to sleep are also no problem, since other young people willingly share a corner of the bed or a spot on the floor where one can "crash" for a day, a week, or a month.

While the great majority never act on these feelings, many youngsters consider that the only viable solution to the problem of continual parental strife is to quit the scene of combat. The physician may hear, "I can't make it there anymore.", "I'm thinking of getting my own place." or, "How much does an apartment cost?"

Ventilation may be elicited by asking, "Tell me about it." or "What's it like at home?" If he replies, "It's a bummer.", he should be asked to described just what makes it a bummer. He may list a catalogue of grievances that all pretty much fold under the same umbrella. He's straining for independence. That's what he's pro-grammed to do. His parents, who are faced with rapid change themselves, may not be familiar with the forms his independence takes. Hence the problem.

More and more the courts are honoring the adolescent's right to the privi-leged professional relationship. The physician must make his own decision re-garding disclosure which is seldom the solution in any case. What helps is counseling of the youngster in ways to help him tolerate what he considers re-straints, or family counseling with him and his parents which is effected pretty much as conflict mediation. In the latter, points of contention are expressed by both sides followed by a chance to respond to each issue. Both sides are then led by the counselor to acknowledge a common ground, an overlap in which opposing issues meet. Sometimes getting opposing sides to agree on points of similarity is like trying to get two horses, straining in opposite directions, to drink from the same water hole.

What helps is to realize that they are thirsty. The adolescent doesn't really want to go. He would just like his parents to hassle him a little less. His parents don't really want him to go. They would just like him to shape up. Solution usually involves a contractual arrangement where each side agrees to do something in exchange for something they want.

Sometimes in the absence of, or in spite of help, the adolescent leaves.

Runaway children, if seen by a physician at all, are seen usually on an isolated, one–shot basis, since their fear of recognition and discovery will decrease the likelihood of return units. Their presenting complaints, if not emergencies, are maladies exacerbated by neglect. They will be seen for drug abuse, hepatitis, viral infections, pregnancy (and its complications), venereal disease, dermatological problems, dental problems, and general problems of malnutrition and neglect.

The major problems in the medical management of such children are misinformation and inadequate follow-up. The physician's initial task is to support these young patients and to encourage their continual cooperation in their own health care. Support is offered by acknowledgement of their predicament, encouragement of their self–expression, and acceptance of their ventilation. Their friends may or may not want to hear about their worries. It is necessary to give such a patient an opportunity to express what he feels. The physician should make no judgment and no initial attempt to put the patient in touch with his parents, unless he indicates that this is what he wants. If the physician has any hope at all of establishing a therapeutic relationship, it is necessary for the patient to feel that a visit to the physician offers more than relief from physical discomfort. Any sudden moves in the direction of uniting him with his family will send him scurrying into some new hiding place.

By scheduling appointments at short intervals, the physician can check on his progress and continue to dispense health care education. Hopefully, in time he can persuade the patient to return home or to some agency that will take an interest in his care. The high mobility of runaway children is a source of frustration for the physician who treats them, similar to that felt for any patient who suffers from his own neglect.

If the reader has gathered that adolescents are to be handled with kid gloves, bravo! That is precisely the message. As with all patients, empathy and tact are crucial to communication. With adolescent patients, it helps if the physician can remember when inadequacies, real or imagined, kept him a prisoner, a frog prince struggling to shed his ugly skin to show the world how beautiful he really is.

REFERENCES

1. Ader R: The basic variable in the early handling phenomenon. Science 136:580–583, 1962

2. Aldrich A, Sung C, Knop C: The crying of newly born babies. J Pediatr 27:95, 1945

3. Ambrose JA: The development of the smiling response in early infancy. In Foss BM (ed): Determinants of Infant Behaviuor. London, Methuen, 1961, Vol 1, pp 179–196

4. Bird B: Talking With Patients. Philadelphia, J B Lippincott, 1955

5. Bower TGR: The visual world of infants. Sci Am 215:80–92, 1966

6. Bronson GW: Vision in infancy: structure and function relationships. In Robinson RJ (ed): Brain and Early Behaviour—Development in the Foetus and Infant. New York, Academic Press, 1969, pp 207–210

7. Erikson EH: Childhood and Society, 2nd ed. New York, W W Norton, 1963, pp 247–274

8. Etzel BC, Gewirtz JL: Experimental modification of caretaker–maintained high–rate operant crying in a 6– and 20–week old infant (infans tyrannotearus): extinction of crying with reinforcement of eye–contact and smiling. J Exp Child Psychol 3:303–317, 1967

9. Fantz RL: Visual perception from birth as shown by pattern selectivity. Ann NY Acad Sci 118:793–814, 1965

10. Friedman S et al.: Newborn attention: differential response decrement to visual stimuli. J Exp Child Psychol 10:44–51, 1970

11. Ginott HG: Teacher and Child. New York, MacMillan, 1972

11a. Ginott HG: Between Parent and Child. New York, Macmillan, 1965

12. Goodenough FL: The Expression of the emotions in infancy. Child Dev 2:96–101, 1931

13. Harrison ML: The nature and development of concepts of time among young children. Elementary School Journal 34:507–514, 1934

14. Irelan L (ed): Low–Income Life Styles. Washington, Department of HEW, 1966

15. Kohler E: A single sheet pediatric growth chart. Clin Pediatr (Phila) 12(8):497–500, 1973

16. Korner AF: Neonatal startles, smiles, erections, and reflex sucks as related to state, sex, and individuality. Child Dev 40:1039–1053, 1969

17. Lewis M: Infants' responses to facial stimuli during the first year of life. Dev Psychology 1:75–86, 1969.

18. Marin P: The Free People. New York, Outerbridge & Dienstfrey, 1969

19. Petrillo M: Preventing hospital trauma in pediatric patients. Am J Nurs 68:1468, 1968

20. Piaget J, Inhelder B: The Psychology of the Child. New York, Basic Books, 1969

21. Reissman F: The Culturally Deprived Child. New York, Harper & Row, 1962, pp 36–48

22. Robson KS: The role of eye-to-eye contact in maternal-infant attachment. J Child Psychol Psychiatry 8:13–26, 1967

23. Salk L: Emotional factors in pediatric practice. Pediatric Annals (1):66–71, 1973

24. Schechter MD: The Recognition and Treatment of Suicide in Children. In Schneidman ES, Farberow NL (eds): Clues To Suicide. New York, McGraw Hill, 1957

25. Sokoloff, N. et al.: Effects of handling on the subsequent development of premature infants. Devel Psych 1(6):765–68, 1969

26. Spitz RA: The First Year of Life. New York, International Universities Press, 1965

27. Teenage Patients–Their Legal Rights and yours. Med World News 12 (19): 49–57, 1971

Bibliography

COMMUNICATION: ITS MEANING TO THE PHYSICIAN

Chomsky N: Language and Mind. New York, Harcourt Brace and Jovanovich, 1972
Fromm E: The Sane Society. New York, Rinehart, 1955
Hayakawa SI: Language in Thought and Action: New York, Harcourt Brace, 1949
Hymes DH (ed): Language in Culture and Society: A reader in linguistics and anthropology. New York, Harper & Row, 1964
Korzybski A: Science and Sanity: An Introduction to Non-Aristotelian Systems and General Semantics. Lakeville, International Non-Aristotelian Library, 1958

CRITICAL OBSERVATION

Beatty J, Kahneman D: Pupillary changes in two memory tasks. Psychon Sci 5:371–372, 1966
Birdwhistell RL: Body signals: normal and pathological. Presented at the Proceedings of the American Psychological Association, 1963
Black P (ed): Physiological Correlates of Emotion. New York, Academic Press, 1970
Blurton-Jones NG (ed): Criteria for the use in describing facial expressions in children. Hum Biol 43:365–413, 1971
Bradshaw JL: Pupil size and problem solving. Q J Exp Psychol 20:116–122, 1968
Brannigan CR, Humphries D: Human nonverbal behaviour: a means of communication. In Blurton-Jones NG (ed): Ethological Studies of Infant Behavior. London, Cambridge University Press, 1972 pp 37–64
Eiseley L: The Firmament of Time. New York, Atheneum, 1972
Ekman P, Sorenson ER, Friesen WV: Pan-cultural elements in facial displays of emotion. Science 164:86–88, 1969
Ellsworth P et al.: Eye contact and gaze aversion in an aggressive encounter. J Pers Soc Psychol 28:280–292, 1973
Elshtain EL, Schaefer TS: Effects of storage load and word frequency on pupillary responses during short-term memory. Psychon Sci 12:143–144, 1968
Exline RV, Winters LC: Affective relations and mutual glances in dyads. In Tomkins SS, Izard C (eds): Affect, Cognition and Personality. New York, Springer, 1965, pp 319–350
Fridja NH, Van de Geer JP: Codeability and facial expressions. Acta Psychologica 18:360–367, 1961
Garvey C, Dickstein E: Levels of analysis and social class differences. Language and Speech 15:378–384, 1972
Goodenough FL: Expression of the emotions in a blind-deaf child. J Abnorm Soc Psychol 27:328–333, 1932
Greenberg D, Vzgiris IC, Hunt JMcV: Attentional preference and experience: III. Visual familiarity and looking time. Genet Psychol 117:123–135, 1970
Hall ET: The Hidden Dimension. Garden City, Doubleday, 1966
Hayakawa SI: Language in Action. New York, Harcourt, 1951
Hinde RA (ed): Non-Verbal Communication. London, Cambridge University Press, 1972
Hobson GN et al.: Anxiety and gaze aversion in dyadic encounters. Br J Soc Clin Psychol 12:122–129, 1973
Knopp PH: Expression of Emotions in Man. New York, International University Press, 1963
Lorenz K: King Solomon's Ring. New York, Crowell, 1952
Lorenz K: On Aggression. New York, Harcourt Brace & World, 1966
Lowen A: The Betrayal of the Body. New York, Collier Books, 1969
Miller L: Personal Communication. Philadelphia, Temple University, 1975
Montagu A: Man: His First Two Million Years. New York, Delta, 1969
Pey M: The Story of Language. New York, Columbia University Press, 1950
Pfeiffer JE: The Emergence of Man. New York, Harper & Row, 1972
Reusch J: Disturbed Communication: The Clinical Assessment of Normal and Pathological Communicative Behavior, rev. New York, W W Norton, 1972
Schaefer TJ, Ferguson B, Klein JA, Rawson EB: Pupillary responses during mental activities. Psychon Sci 12:137–138, 1968
Scheflen AE: Human communication: behavioral programs and their integration in interaction. Behav Sci 13:44–55, 1968
Scheflen AE: Behavioral programs in human communication. In Gray W, Duhl FJ, Rizzo ND (eds): General Systems Theory and Psychiatry. Boston, Little Brown, 1969
Scheflen AE: Stream and structure of communication behavior. Behavioral Studies Monograph No 1. Philadelphia, Eastern Pennsylvania Psychiatric Institute, 1966
Scheflen AE: Communicational Structure of a Psychotherapy Transaction. Bloomington,

Indiana University Press, 1973
Spitz RA: The smiling response: a contribution to the ontogenesis of social relations. Genet Psychol Monogr 34:57–125, 1946
Thompson J: Development of facial expression of emotion in blind and seeing children. Arch Psychol (NY) a monograph, 47 pgs. Columbia, N.Y. 264:47, 1941
Tinbergen N: Social Behaviour in Animals. London, Metheun, 1953
Tinbergen N: Animal Behavior. New York, Time–Life Books, 1965
von Cranach M, Vine I: Social Communication and Movement: Studies of Interaction and Expression in Man and Chimpanzee. New York, Academic Press, 1973

FACILITATION

Balint M, Balint E: Psychotherapeutic Techniques in Medicine. London, Travistock, 1961
Bird B: Talking with Patients. Philadelphia, JB Lippincott, 1955
Blum LH: Reading Between the Lines. New York, International Universities Press, 1972
Blum RH: The Management of the Doctor–Patient Relationship. New York, McGraw Hill, 1960
Enelow AJ, Wexler M: Psychiatry in the Practice of Medicine. New York, Oxford University Press, 1966, pp 35–97
Meares A: The Medical Interview. Springfield, Charles C Thomas, 1958
Neal H (ed): Better Communication for Better Health. New York, Columbia University Press, 1962
Parsons T: The Social System. New York, Free Press, 1951, pp 428–473
Stevenson I: The Diagnostic Interview. New York, Harper & Row, 1971
Sullivan HS: The Psychiatric Interview. New York, WW Norton, 1954

INFORMATION GATHERING

Aring, CD: The clinical method. Med Arts Sci 28:5–16, 1974
Balint E, Norell JS (eds): Six Minutes for the Patient: Interactions in General Practice Consultation. London, Tavistock Publicatons, 1973
Browne J, Freeling P: The Doctor-Patient Relationship. London, E and S Livingstone, 1967
Bursten B: Family dynamics and illness behavior. GP 29(5):142–145, 1964
Enelow AJ, Swisher S: Interviewing and Patient Care. New York, Oxford University Press, 1972
Feinstein AR: Clinical Judgement. Baltimore, Williams & Wilkins, 1967
Lusted L: Introduction to Medical Decision Making. Springfield, C Thomas, 1968
McGraw RM: Ferment in Medicine. Philadelphia, W B Saunders, 1966
Schwarz K: Preventive Medicine in Medical Care. London, H K Lewis, 1970
Taylor RB: A Primer of Clinical Symptoms. New York, Harper & Row, 1973

INFORMATION GIVING

Alsobrook HB, Jr: Informed consent: a right to know. J La State Med Soc 126:189–200, 1974
Centerwall WR, Centerwall SA: Phenylketonoria. Washington, US Department of HEW, 1965
Chusid EL, Siltzbach LE: Sarcoidosis of the pleura. Ann Intern Med 81:190–194, 1974
Conger CB, Karafin L, Kendall AR: Preliminary Information Concerning Bilateral Vasectomy. Department of Urology at Temple University Medical Center, personal communication, Philadelphia, March 1975
Duff RS, Campbell AGM: Moral and ethical dilemmas in the special-care nursery. N Engl J Med 289:890–894, 1973
Freeman MVR, Miles PA: Cytogenic evaluation: luxury or necessity? Milit Med 136:851–54, 1971
Gordis L: Epidemiology of Chronic Lung Disease in Children. Baltimore, The Johns Hopkins University Press, 1973
Green LW, Figa-Talmamanica I: Suggested designs for evaluation of patient education programs. Health Education Monographs, SOPHE 2:54–71, 1974
Holder AR: Voluntary sterilization. JAMA 225(13):1743–1744, 1973
Human Genetics and Public Health. Second report of the WHO expert committee on human genetics (subtitle) Geneva, WHO 1964
Hurley, L. Nutrients and genes: interactions in development. Nutr Rev 27:3–6, 1969
Isaac R: Defining death. Can Med Assoc J 108:1102, 1973
Kennedy WP: Epidemiologic Aspects of the Problem of Congenital Malformations, 111, no 2, New York, National Foundation-March of Dimes, 1967
Kimball CP: Emotional and psychosocial aspects of diabetes mellitus. Med Clin North Am 55 (4): 1971
Kretchmer N: Heredity, development, and disease. Stanford Medical Bulletin 18:25–28,

1960
Lieberman JE: Psycholocial aspects of selective abortion. Birth Defects. Intrauterine Diagnosis, vii, no. 5, 1971
Lin-Fu JS: Neonatal Narcotic Addiction. Washington, US Department of HEW, 1969
Malpractice: M.D.'s Revolt. Newsweek. June 9, 1975, p 59
Merritt AD et al.: Incidence and mode of inheritance of cystic fibrosis. J Lab Clin Med 60:998, 1962
Modell W: A "will" to live. N Engl J. Med 290(16):907–908, 1974
Orten JM, Orten AU: DNA and inborn errors of metabolism. J Am Diet Assoc 59:331–41, 1971
Penrose LS: Memorandum on dermatoglyphic nomenclature In Birth Defects IV, no 3. New York, National Foundation-March of Dimes, 1968
Obrien D: Rare inborn errors of metabolism in children with mental retardation. Washington, US Department of HEW, 1965
Schowalter JE, Ferholt JB, Mann NM: The adolescent patient's decision to die. Pediatrics 51:97–103, 1973
Schroeder E: The birth of a defective child: a cause for grieving. In Hall JE, Weaver BR (eds): Nursing of Family in Crisis. Philadelphia, Lippincott, 1974
Shaw A: Dilemmas of "informed consent" in children. N Engl J Med 289:885–890, 1973
Simonaitus JE: More about informed consent. Part 2. JAMA 225(1):95–96, 1973
Siltzbach LE et al.: Course and prognosis of sarcoidosis around the world. Am J Med 57:-847–852, 1974
Smoller M, Hsia DT: Studies on the genetic mechanism of cystic fibrosis of the pancreas. Am J Dis Child 98:277, 1959
Stone SV Jr: Informed consent–Texas supreme court update. Tex Med 70:86–87, 1974
Curran WJ: The Tuskegee syphilis study. N Engl J Med 289:730–731, 1973
Tips RL, Smith GS et al.: The Whole Family" Concept in Clinical Genetics. Birth Defects (Reprint Series). New York, National Foundation-March of Dimes, 1964
Woodruff MFA: Ethical problems in organ transplantation. Br Med J 1:1457, 1964

EMERGENCY COMMUNICATION

Browning CH, Tyson RL, Miller SI: A Study of Psychiatric Emergencies. II. Suicide. Psychiatr Med 1(4):359–66, 1970
Cole WH, Pestow CB: Emergency Care. New York, Appleton-Century-Crofts, 1972
Eckert C (ed): Emergency Room Care. Boston, Little Brown, 1971
Garb S, Eng E: Disaster Handbook. New York, Springer, 1969
Mahoney RF: Emergency and Disaster Nursing. Toronto, MacMillan, 1969
Noble JH: Emergency Medical Services: Behavioral and Planning Perspectives. New York, Behavioral Publications, 1973
Oaks W, Spitzer S: Emergency Room Care. New York, Grune and Stratton, 1970
Ohio Trade and Industrial Education Service: Emergency Victim Care. Columbus, Instructional Materials Laboratory, 1971

THE HOSPITALIZED PATIENT

Abrams HS (ed): Psychological Aspects of Surgery. Boston, Little
Beal JM, Eckenhoff JE (eds): Intensive and Recovery Room Care. New York, MacMillan, 1969
Herzlich C: Health and Illness. London and New York, Academic Press, 1973
Hollingshead AB, Duff RS: Sickness and Society. New York, Harper & Row, 1968
Reeves RBJ: What is it like to be a patient? Del Med J 45:12–15, 1973
Skipper JK, Leonard RC (eds): Social Interaction and Patient Care. Philadelphia, J B Lippincott, 1965
Talbot NB: The need for behavioral and social sciences in medicine. In Knowles JH (ed): View of Medical Education and Medical Care. Cambridge, Harvard University Press, 1968, pp 19–49

THE DRUG AND ALCOHOL DEPENDENT

Alcohol: a growing danger. WHO Chronicle 29(3):102–105, 1975
Benforado JM: The treatment of drug abuse: update for the physician. Wis Med J 73 10:-133–136, 1974
Braceland F, Freedman K, Rickels K et al.: Drug Abuse: Medical and Criminal Aspects. New York, MSS Information Corporation, 1972
Brecher EM et al.: Licit and Illicit Drugs. Boston, Little Brown, 1972
Byrd OE: Medical Readings on Drug Abuse. Reading, Addison-Wesley, 1970
Campbell RS et al.: Patterns of drug abuse. Int J Addict 9(2):289–300, 1974
Cole JO, Wittenborn JR (eds): Drug Abuse: Social and Psychopharmacological Aspects.

Springfield, Charles C Thomas, 1969
Drug Dependence: A Guide for Physicians. Chicago, American Medical Association, 1970
Edwards JG: Doctors, drugs and drug abuse. Practitioner 212(1272):815–822, 1974
Epstein SS (ed): Drugs of Abuse. Cambridge, Massachusetts Institute of Technology, 1971
If you're asked to talk to school children on drug abuse. Med Times 102:178–179 passimass, 1974
Larson TG: Alcoholism and drugs: addiction. Minn Med 55:1144–1146, 1972
Manual on Alcoholism. AMA Chicago, 1968
Medical Times. A drug abuse manual, vol 102, no 9, Sept 1974
Mendelson JH (ed): Alcoholism. Boston, Little Brown, 1966
Weisman T: Drug Abuse and Drug Counseling: A Case Approach. Cleveland, The Press of Case Western Reserve University, 1972

DEATH AND DYING

Langone J: Vital Signs: The Way We Die in America. Boston, Little Brown, 1974
Kapleau P (ed): The Wheel of Death; a Collection of Writings from Zen Buddhist and Other Sources on Death-Rebirth-Dying. New York, Harper & Row, 1971
Maeterlinck M: Before the Great Silence. New York, FA Stokes, 1937
Neale RE: The Art of Dying. New York, Harper & Row, 1973
Perkins W: A Salve for a Sicke Man, or, A Treatise Containing the Nature, Differences, and Kindes of Death: as Also the Right Manner of Dying Well. Cambridge, Printed by John Legate, 1595. Microfilm, Temple University Library.
Thielicke H: Death and Life. Philadelphia, Fortress Press, 1970
Toynbee A: Man's Concern With Death. St. Louis, McGraw Hill, 1969
Williams WC: The Collected Later Poems. New York, New Directions, 1963
Zandee J: Death as an Enemy, According to Ancient Egyptian Conceptions. Leiden, Brill, 1965

THE AGED PATIENT

Beauvoir S de: The Coming of Age. New York, Putnam, 1972
Busse EW (ed.): Behavior and Adaptation in Late Life. Boston, Little Brown, 1969
Clague E, Palli B, Kramer L: The Aging Worker and the Union; Employment and Retirement of Middle Aged and Older Workers. New York, Prager, 1971
Curtin SR: Nobody Ever Died of Old Age. Boston, Little Brown, 1972
Field M: The Aged, The Family, and the Community. New York, Columbia University Press, 1972
Hoffman AM (ed): The Daily Needs and Interests of Older People. Springfield, Illinois, CC Thomas, 1970
Jaeger D, Simmons LW: The Aged Ill. New York, Appleton-Century-Crofts, 1970
Stout, Rex: A Family Affair. New York, Viking Press, 1975

PEDIATRIC COMMUNICATION

Bird B: Talking with Patients. Philadelphia, J B Lippincott Company, 1955
Bridger WH, Birns B: Experience and temperament in human neonates. In Newton G, Levine S (eds): Early Experience and Behaviour. Springfield, C Thomas, 1968, 83–101
Douvan E, Gold M: Modal patterns in american adolescents. In Hoffman L, Hoffman M (eds): Review of Child Development Research, Vol 2. New York, Russell Sage Foundation, 1966, pp 469–528
Fagan JF III: Memory in the infant. J Exp Child Psychol 9:217–226, 1970
Farb P: The language of children. In Word Play. New York, Bantam, 1974, pp 270–288
Finch SM, McDermott JF Jr: Psychiatry for the Pediatrician. New York, W W Norton, 1970
Schulman J I (ed): Management of Emotional Disorders in Pediatric Practice: with a Focus on Techniques of Interviewing. Chicago, Yearbook Medical Publishers, 1967
Freud A: Emotional and social development of young children. In Feelings and Learning. Washington, Association for Childhood Education, 1965, pp 41–47
Gardner RA: Therapeutic Communication with Children. New York, Science House, 1971
Gesell A: The First Five Years of Life. New York, Harper & Row, 1940
Gesell A et al.: Youth: The Years from Ten to Sixteen. New York, Harper & Row, 1956
Greenman GW: Visual behaviour of newborn infants. In Solnit A, Provence S (eds): Modern Perspectives in Child Development. New York, International Universities Press, 1963
Havighurst RJ, and Hilda T. Adolescent Character and Personality. New York, John Wiley & Sons, 1949
Ilg F, Ames LB: Child Behavior. New York, Harper & Row, 1951
Krakowski AJ, Santora DA: Child Psychology and the General Practitioner. Springfield, CC Thomas, 1962

Lidz T: The Person: His Development Throughout the Life Cycle. New York, Basic Books, 1968

Provence SA, Lipton R: Infants in Institutions. New York, International Universities Press, 1962

Ribble M: The Rights of Infants. New York, Columbia University Press, 1953

Richards MPM: The Child from Five to Ten. New York, Harper & Row, 1946

Richards MPM: Social interaction in the first weeks of human life. Psychiatr Neurol Neurochir 74:35–42 1971

Simmons JE: Psychiatric Examiniation of Children. Philadelphia, Lea and Febiger, 1969

Spitz RA: No and Yes. New York, International Universities Press, 1957

Index

W9-CGQ-361

CITIES AND AGRICULTURE

As people increasingly migrate to urban settings and more than half of the world's population now lives in cities, it is vital to plan and provide for sustainable and resilient food systems which reflect this challenge. This volume presents experience and evidence-based "state of the art" chapters on the key dimensions of urban food challenges and types of intra- and peri-urban agriculture.

The book provides urban planners, local policy makers and urban development practitioners with an overview of crucial aspects of urban food systems based on an up-to-date review of research results and practical experiences in both developed and developing countries. By doing so, the international team of authors provides a balanced textbook for students of the growing number of courses on sustainable agriculture and food and urban studies, as well as a solid basis for well-informed policy making, planning and implementation regarding the development of sustainable, resilient and just urban food systems.

Henk de Zeeuw is Senior Advisor at the RUAF Foundation, based in Leusden, the Netherlands. The RUAF Foundation (Resource Centres on Urban Agriculture and Food Security) is a global network and a leading centre of expertise in the fields of (intra- and peri-) Urban Agriculture and City Region Food Strategies.

Pay Drechsel is Principal Researcher at the International Water Management Institute, based in Colombo, Sri Lanka, and Leader of the Flagship on Recovering and Reusing Resources in Urbanized Ecosystems of the CGIAR Water, Land and Ecosystems Research Program.

Other books in the Earthscan Food and Agriculture Series

For further details please visit the series page on the Routledge website:
http://www.routledge.com/books/series/ECEFA/

CITIES AND AGRICULTURE

Developing resilient urban
food systems

Edited by Henk de Zeeuw and Pay Drechsel

Routledge
Taylor & Francis Group

LONDON AND NEW YORK

from Routledge

First published 2015
by Routledge
2 Park Square, Milton Park, Abingdon, Oxon OX14 4RN

and by Routledge
711 Third Avenue, New York, NY 10017

Routledge is an imprint of the Taylor & Francis Group, an informa business

© 2015 RUAF Foundation and International Water Management Institute

All rights reserved. No part of this book may be reprinted or reproduced or
utilised in any form or by any electronic, mechanical, or other means, now
known or hereafter invented, including photocopying and recording, or in
any information storage or retrieval system, without permission in writing
from the publishers.

Trademark notice: Product or corporate names may be trademarks or registered
trademarks, and are used only for identification and explanation without
intent to infringe.

British Library Cataloguing in Publication Data
A catalogue record for this book is available from the British Library

Library of Congress Cataloging-in-Publication Data
   Cities and agriculture : developing resilient urban food systems / edited
by Henk de Zeeuw and Pay Drechsel.
      pages cm.—(Earthscan food and agriculture series)
   Includes bibliographical references and index.
   1. Urban agriculture.   2. Sustainable agriculture.   3. Food
supply.   4. Food security.   I. Zeeuw, Henk de.   II. Drechsel, Pay.
   S494.5.U72C566 2015
   338.1—dc23
   2015007324

ISBN: 978-1-138-86058-2 (hbk)
ISBN: 978-1-138-86059-9 (pbk)
ISBN: 978-1-315-71631-2 (ebk)

Typeset in Bembo
by Apex CoVantage, LLC

MIX
Paper from
responsible sources
FSC   FSC® C013056
www.fsc.org

Printed and bound in Great Britain by
TJ International Ltd, Padstow, Cornwall

CONTENTS

PREFACE

Urban agriculture – both inside the built-up city and in the peri-urban area – has various functions in the urban system. It plays, for example, an important role in feeding the increasing urban populations, often with highly nutritious food; a role that is specific and complimentary to food supply from rural areas. This context has often been underestimated, but the latest data point at a global farm area of more than 60 million ha within urban agglomerations,[1] which is a larger area than what we see, for example, under rice in South Asia, and if we include all farms up to 20 km from a city, the area is larger than the one of the European Union.

Next to the specific role in urban food supply, urban agriculture also plays other important functions in the urban system including the provision of eco-services, offering opportunities for recreation and enabling synergies (water, energy, CO2, organic wastes) with other urban sectors.

Given the increasing recognition of urban food demand and other opportunities and challenges for agriculture in the urban context, the RUAF Foundation decided that it is timely to produce an up-to-date overview of the "state of the art" on agriculture in the urban context.

The developments in this innovative field of work in the last decade have been manifold, including amongst others:

- A growing interest of local governments and citizens in the Global North and Global South in food and agriculture and urban-rural linkages.
- The emergence of new drivers steering attention to urban agriculture and urban food systems.

For decades, many local governments have supported urban farming as a strategy for poverty alleviation, social inclusion and enhancing food security and nutrition of the urban poor. Also, the role of (intra- and peri-) urban agriculture and forestry in urban greening and providing recreational opportunities for the urban citizens has been recognized for quite some time. However, more recently:

- Local governments started to support urban agriculture for the eco-services it provides (e.g., urban heat reduction, storm water management, biodiversity management) and its role in disaster risk management and city adaptation to climate change.
- Other cities have set out to shorten the food supply chains and promote the consumption of food produced in the city region in order to enhance the resilience of the urban food system and stimulate the local economy.
- There is also an increasing consciousness for a stronger water-energy-food nexus and closed-loop processes (circular economy, ecosanitation) through resource recovery and reuse, turning, for example, organic wastes and wastewater and excess energy, heat or CO_2 from industry, into valuable resources for urban food production.
- A broadening of the research and planning focus from urban agriculture to urban (or city-region) food systems, including (intra- and peri-) urban food production as well as the processing of the local produce, its marketing/distribution, food waste management (including resource recovery and reuse), and related inputs supply and support services.
- And as a consequence, a quickly growing body of evidence and experience-based knowledge.

With this publication we attempt not only to update earlier benchmark publications by the RUAF Foundation (*Growing Cities, Growing Food* with DSE, 2000; *Cities Farming for the Future* with IIRR, 2006; and *Cities, Poverty and Food* with Practical Action, 2011), but also to bridge between urban food and agriculture research and planning in the South and North. We hope that this publication will contribute to the intensified sharing of research results and policy and planning experiences between different regions and countries and to facilitate innovation and more effective urban food system research, policy planning and implementation. However, urban food systems, and the socio-economic, cultural and political factors shaping these systems, may differ substantially from region to region and even country to country, and lessons learned in one country or region might not fit another.

We expect that this publication will be of use for policy advisors, researchers, urban planners, specialists, practitioners and others involved in urban food system assessments and the design of urban food strategies and/or specific policies on urban agriculture or other components of the urban food system and that it will find its way to educational institutes that provide training in this field.

We want to thank all the authors that contributed to the various chapters: We are very grateful.

We also like to thank our chapter reviewers, Kingsley Kurukulasuryia for the language editing, Desiree Dirkzwager (RUAF Foundation) for the text editing and layout, and Ashley Wright (Earthscan) for coordinating the production and distribution of this book.

The editors,
Ir. Henk de Zeeuw *(RUAF Foundation, Leusden, the Netherlands)*
Dr. Pay Drechsel *(IMWI, Colombo, Sri Lanka)*

Note

1   Thebo, A. L.; Drechsel, P.; Lambin, E. F. 2014. Global assessment of urban and peri-urban agriculture: irrigated and rainfed croplands. *Environmental Research Letters* 9: 114002.

CLARENCE HOUSE

With so many challenges and pressures evident on the road to sustainability, it is easy to feel overwhelmed by the magnitude and diversity of barriers that must be passed in reaching the kinds of outcomes that the scientific community tell us are evermore urgently required. Anyone seeking solutions to the loss of biological diversity, depletion of critical resources, such as soils and water, or who is dealing with the causes and consequences of climate change will know what I mean.

One thing that I have learned during the four decades or so that I have paid close attention to these questions is that our lack of progress is not so much due to our inability to address individual parts of the sustainability challenge, but more to do with our inability to come up with truly integrated, systemic approaches that can tackle multiple facets of what are ultimately different expressions of common, underlying problems. Perhaps nowhere is this more evident than in relation to the rather important matter of how we feed ourselves.

This has been a key challenge for people down the ages, revolving around the conundrum of how to secure enough food to supply rising demand while at the same time keeping prices affordable. When one looks at the various indices of nutrition and how we have more or less managed to keep pace with recent explosive population growth, a record of apparent success is revealed. Despite a four-fold increase in human numbers during the 20th century, the supply of more and more food has meant that forecasts of epic famines affecting hundreds of millions of people have been largely avoided. There is, however, good reason to pause before declaring an unqualified triumph.

Our ever more globalized and high-input food systems have delivered massive increases in the supply of calories, but it is now becoming clear that not only has this performance not been enjoyed by all, it has also been bought largely at the expense of the overall health of the food system. Indeed, what we have seen is a kind of mining of the food system's key assets; ranging from the loss of farmers, soils and biodiversity to massive greenhouse gas emissions that are affecting the stability of our climate, and to changes in diets that are not only harmful to the health of our environment, but to people's health as well. This parlous situation is more and more widely recognized and a growing chorus of voices is now asking if there might be ways of doing things better, not only to ensure affordable nutrition, but also to sustain the healthy ecosystems that are an essential prerequisite for healthy people and to foster the healthy social systems that might enable societies to adapt better to the inevitable shocks that will come with changing conditions, not least shifts in climate.

The big question, of course, is how? One encouraging trend is the way that people in different contexts around the world are taking the opportunity to improve their food systems. This is being done through actions at the city level, and strengthening the linkages between urban areas and their rural hinterlands in ways that help reduce some of the negative consequences arising from the current conventional approach. Such actions can help to increase the resilience of farming in the face of the pressures that during the coming years we can only expect to grow. The potential benefits are manifold. They include improved security in nutrition, increased availability of healthier food, opportunities to secure the livelihoods of small producers and their businesses, increased local participation in decision-making and engagement with food culture, improved scope for the more sustainable management of landscapes and the natural assets they sustain, and increased opportunity for synergy in meeting other key priorities, for example in relation to energy, waste and water security. All this, and more, can be achieved from a more integrated and socially inclusive approach at the city level. Experience from different parts of the world is beginning to reveal the scale of the positive opportunities at hand, if only we can adopt the strategies to seize them.

One important way to render these benefits more transparent is to undertake what might be called true cost accounting. The negative impacts that come in the wake of our ever-more industrialized food system are often justified in the name of 'cheap' food. Stepping back, however, and taking a more comprehensive view reveals that our food is actually very far from cheap; it is just that the costs are cropping up elsewhere. The effects of soil damage are, for example, reflected in increased water bills as technology has to be installed to remove pesticides, chemicals and nitrates. Soil degradation also creates costs in protecting people and property from flooding, which can increase due to the silting up of watercourses. There are mammoth hidden costs in "dead zones" in the oceans caused by the run-off of agri-industrial pollutants. There are costs reflected in public health trends too, for example arising from diets dominated by cheap processed food and so called 'empty calories' with too few fresh fruits and vegetables. Then there are the costly social impacts arising from rural unemployment. Crucially, these and other costs often resonate more loudly at the city level than at the national level which is often more focussed on short term macroeconomic concerns. The true costs of cheap food can also often be more effectively minimized at a city-region level than they can globally, thus offering prospects not only for more resilient outcomes but, in the end, more cost-effective ones too.

Fortunately, and in large part due to the leadership of organizations such as R.U.A.F., there is now real interest and engagement with the question of how to re-embed the historic relationship that existed for thousands of years between cities and the countryside surrounding them. For example, a range of international processes have recently considered the different steps that might be taken. These include an agreement reached at the World Urban Forum in 2014, amongst key U.N. and other international organizations, to share knowledge and to improve the coordination of their actions under the City Region Food Systems Collaborative. Cities themselves have also begun to act together, generating and exchanging knowledge in order to develop frameworks for action such as the Global Urban Food Policy Pact that has been catalysed by the city of Milan in 2015.

This is why I am so pleased to see the publication of *Cities and Agriculture – towards resilient urban food systems*. This timely and thorough overview about the opportunities for enabling city regions to drive a transformation towards much more sustainable, resilient and healthy food systems will, I hope, raise awareness as to the potential for a different direction of travel to the one we are presently embarked upon. Such a transformation would be based on using our increased knowledge to empower partnerships and develop the kind of integrated approaches to policy and planning that take us beyond the simple trade-offs which place faith in 'cheap food' and toward seeing the wider picture.

I can only congratulate the many scientists and practitioners for their valuable contributions to this important publication and very much hope it will find its way to national and local policy-makers, urban planners, academia, non-governmental groups, producers and consumers organizations, private sector companies and others that can make a contribution to building more resilient food systems through concerted and far-sighted action at the level of the city region.

HRH The Prince of Wales

ABBREVIATIONS AND ACRONYMS

AAA	Atelier d'Architecture Autogérée
AB Bank	AB Bank Limited (Bangladesh)
ADB	Asian Development Bank
AESOP	Association of European Schools of Planning
AFSUN	African Food Security Urban Network
AMAP	Associations pour le Maintien de l'Agriculture Paysanne (Associations for the Maintenance of Peasant Agriculture)
APA	American Planning Association
AR5	Fifth Assessment Report of the IPCC
As	arsenic
ASF	animal source food
AVRDC	the World Vegetable Center (formerly: "Asian Vegetable Research Centre")
BMI	body mass index
BSE	bovine spongiform encephalopathy, commonly known as mad cow disease
CAP	Common Agricultural Policy of the European Union
CBA	cost benefit analysis
CBD	Convention on Biological Diversity (UN)
Cd	cadmium
CDKN	Climate Change and Development Knowledge Network (UK)
CFF	Cities Farming for the Future (a RUAF programme)
CFS	Committee on World Food Security
CGIAR	Consortium of 15 international agricultural research organisations (originally founded as the "Consultative Group on International Agricultural Research")
CIRAD	Centre de coopération Internationale en Recherche Agronomique pour le Développement

CLT	community land trusts
C/N	carbon/nitrogen ratio
CO_2	carbon dioxide
CPULs	continuous productive urban landscapes
Cr	chromium
CSA	Community Supported Agriculture
Cu	copper
CWP	Center for Watershed Protection (USA)
DEP	Department of Environmental Protection (New York City)
DPSIR	Driving forces, Pressures, State, Impacts, Responses (an assessment framework)
DPU	Bartlett Development Planning Unit, University College London
DRR	disaster risk reduction
ECHO	European Commission's Humanitarian Aid and Civil Protection Department
EKW	East Kolkata Wetlands
EKWMA	East Kolkata Wetlands Management Authority
EMPs	environmental management plans
ENPHO	Environment and Public Health Organization (NGO, Nepal) Top of Form
EPA	Environmental Protection Organization (USA)
FAO	Food and Agriculture Organisation of the United Nations
FEU	family economical unit
FStT	From Seed to Table (a RUAF programme)
GAP	good agricultural practices
GBH	gravel bed hydroponic system
GHG	greenhouse gas (emissions)
GIS	geographical information systems
HACCP	hazard analysis and critical control points
HighARCS	Highland Aquatic Resources Conservation and Sustainable development project (EU)
HIV	human immunodeficiency virus
HOPSCOM	Horticulture Cooperative Horticulture Marketing Society (India)
IAP	integrated action plan
ICLEI	ICLEI-Local Governments for Sustainability (founded as the International Council for Local Environmental Initiatives; an international association of local governments)
ICM	impervious cover model
ICRC	the International Committee of the Red Cross (Switzerland)
ICRISAT	International Crops Research Institute for the Semi-Arid Tropics
IDPs	internally displaced persons
IDRC	International Development Research Centre (Canada)
IFA	International Federation of Landscape Architects
IICA	Inter-American Institute for Cooperation on Agriculture

IIED	International Institute for Environment and Development (UK)
ILRI	International Livestock Research Institute
INRA	L'Institut National de la Recherche Agronomique (French National Institute for Agricultural Research)
IPCC	Intergovernmental Panel on Climate Change
IPES	IPES-Promotion for Sustainable Development (NGO, Peru)
IPGRI	International Plant Genetic Resources Institute (now Bioversity International)
IPM	Integrated Pest and Disease Management
IRC	International Water and Sanitation Centre (the Netherlands)
IRRIGASC	an NGO based in Senegal working on sustainable development in the Sahel region, especially small-scale irrigation
ISA	International Society for Arboriculture
ISDR	International Strategy for Disaster Reduction (United Nations)
IUFRO	International Union of Forest Research Organizations
IWMI	International Water Management Institute
JEV	Japanese Encephalitis Virus
LAC	Latin America and the Caribbean
LEGS	livestock emergency guidelines and standards
LMR	limit maximal residues
LPI	lived poverty index
LRRD	linking relief, rehabilitation and development
LST	land surface temperatures
MAMC	Maulana Azad Medical College (India)
MDG	Millennium Development Goal
MENA	Middle East and North Africa
MFI	micro-finance institution
MOISA	The Markets, Organisations, Institutions and Actors' Strategies Unit of CIRAD
MPAP	multi-stakeholder policy formulation and action planning
MPSACCO	Mahila Prayas Savings and Credit Co-operative Ltd. (Nepal)
MSc	Master of Science
MSW	municipal solid waste
N	nitrogen
NBO Bank	National Bank of Oman
NFIs	national forest inventories
NGO	non-governmental organization
Ni	nickel
NO_2	nitrogen dioxide
NUFU	National Urban Forestry Unit (UK)
NYC	New York City
O_3	ozone
O&M	operation and maintenance
OECD	Organisation for Economic Co-operation and Development

OPV	open-pollinated varieties
P	phosphorus
PAPUSSA	Production in Aquatic Peri-Urban Systems in Southeast Asia project (Stirling University)
Pb	lead
PB	participatory budgeting
PhD	Doctor of Philosophy
PROVE	Programa de Verticalisão da Produção (Verticalisation of Production Programme, Brazil)
PTE	potentially toxic element
PYMV	potato yellow mosaic virus
RCZI	Roadmap to Zoonosis Initiative
RGB image	digital aerial maps that are made by a special processing of perpendicular camera axis aerial images
RS	remote sensing
RUAF	RUAF Foundation (International network of Resource centres on Urban Agriculture and Food security)
SAD-APT	The joint interdisciplinary research team formed by INRA-SAD and AgroParisTech (France)
SDGs	Sustainable Development Goals (UN)
SFSC	short food supply chain
SISEF	Italian Society of Silviculture and Forest Ecology
SO_2	sulfur dioxide
SSHRC	Social Sciences and Humanities Research Council (Canada)
STEPS	Social, Technical, Environmental, Political, Sustainability (a planning framework)
SWOT	Strengths, Weaknesses, Opportunities, Threats (an assessment method)
T4P	training for performance
TFPC	Toronto Food Policy Council
TIPA	techno-agricultural innovations for poverty alleviation
TLVs	traditional leafy vegetables
ToF	trees out of forests
TYLCV	tomato yellow leaf curl virus
UAV	unmanned aerial vehicles
UCLG	United Cities and Local Governments
UHI	urban heat island
UK	United Kingdom
UMP	Urban Management Programme (UN-Habitat/UNDP)
UN	United Nations
UNEP	United Nations Environmental Programme
UNHCR	United Nations High Commission for Refugees
UNU	United Nations University
USA	United Sates of America
USDA	United States Department of Agriculture

VSLA	village savings and loans associations
WASH	water, sanitation and hygiene
WISDOM	Wood Fuel Integrated Supply and Demand Review Mapping
WHO	World Health Organization
WRAP	Wetland Resources Action Planning (a toolkit)
WTP	willingness to pay
WWF	World Wildlife Fund
Zn	Zinc

1

URBAN FOOD SYSTEMS

Johannes S. C. Wiskerke

RURAL SOCIOLOGY GROUP, WAGENINGEN UNIVERSITY, THE NETHERLANDS

Introduction

An important milestone occurred in mid-2009, when the world's population, at that time about 6.8 billion, became more urban than rural. By 2050, when the world population is expected to have increased to 9.5 billion, approximately 66% of the world's population will be living in urban areas (UN 2014). Levels of urbanization differ when one looks at different continents. As Cohen (2006: 70) states: "There are enormous differences in patterns of urbanization between regions and even greater variation in the level and speed with which individual countries or indeed individual cities within regions are growing". Currently, Asia and Africa still have a predominantly rural population, while Europe, North America and Oceania were already urbanized regions before 1950. By 2050, however, all major areas will be urbanized (see Table 1.1).

TABLE 1.1 Urbanization trends by major regions (1950–2050)

Major region	Percentage urban				
	1950	*1970*	*2014*	*2030*	*2050*
Africa	14.4	23.5	40.0	47.7	56.0
Asia	17.5	23.7	47.5	55.5	64.4
Europe	51.3	62.8	73.4	77.4	82.2
Latin America and the Caribbean	41.4	57.1	79.5	83.4	86.0
Northern America	63.9	73.8	81.5	85.8	87.3
Oceania	62.4	71.2	70.8	71.4	74.0

Source: UN 2014.

Urbanization is and will partially be taking place through the growth of mega cities, cities with a population of more than 10 million (Sorensen and Okata 2010). However, the vast majority of urban population growth will occur in smaller cities and towns (i.e., urban settlements with a population of less than 1 million residents), followed by medium-sized cities (1–5 million residents). According to Cohen (2006), about 10% of the world's urban population will be living in mega cities, while just over half of the total urban population will reside in the smaller cities and towns.

Both mega cities and smaller cities face several development, governance and sustainability challenges, albeit that in some cases the kind of challenges differ substantially between the two. According to Sorensen and Okata (2010: 7–8), the increasing speed of urbanization has major consequences for mega cities: "building infrastructure takes time as well as money, and rapid growth often means that there is not enough of either to keep up with needs. Perhaps more fundamentally, political processes and governance institutions take time to evolve and generate effective frameworks to manage complex systems that make giant cities more liveable". The governance capacity is also mentioned as a challenge for the smaller cities and towns: "many small cities lack the necessary institutional capacity to be able to manage their rapidly growing populations" (Cohen 2006: 74). The increasing governance complexity is not only due to the rapid urban population growth, but is also a result of the decentralization of regulatory responsibilities and policy implementation: "In the areas of health, education, and poverty alleviation, many national governments have begun to allow hitherto untested local governments to operate the levers of policy and programs" (ibid.: 74–75).

In addition to shifting governance responsibilities and growing governance complexities for cities, urbanization also poses a number of other challenges. One of these challenges is resource use (Madlener and Sunak 2011). Cities consume 75% of the world's resources, while covering only 2% of the world's surface (Pacione 2009), which means that the vast majority of resources used by a city are taken from, and produced in, places outside cities' borders. This is often referred to as the urban ecological footprint: "the total area of productive land and water required continuously to produce all the resources consumed and to assimilate all the wastes produced, by a defined population, wherever on Earth that land is located" (Rees and Wackernagel 1996: 228–229). Hence, the ecological footprint is "a land-based surrogate measure of the population's demands on natural capital" (ibid.: 229). In the process of urbanization, the urban ecological footprint, expressed in the annual demand for land and water per capita, has increased, particularly due to the growing energy demand for mobility, for cooling and heating of houses and offices, for all sorts of equipment for domestic use, and for long-distance transport, processing, packaging, cooling and storage of food (Lang 2010, Madlener and Sunak 2011). The growing ecological footprint of cities has also resulted in a characterization of cities as "parasites", exploiting the resources of its rural hinterland while simultaneously polluting land, water and air (Broto et al. 2012). A shortcoming of the urban ecological footprint approach is that it is based on the average annual resource use per capita, thereby obscuring differences between urban dwellers within cities.

This brings us to another urbanization challenge: growing inequalities in wealth, health, access to resources and availability and affordability of services (Cohen 2006, Broto et al. 2012). Historically, cities developed in places that had a natural advantage in resource supply or transport and that hence offered opportunities for social and economic development: "cities have always been focal points for economic growth, innovation and employment" (Cohen 2006: 64). In most major regions of the world urbanization has gone hand in hand with economic development. This does not hold true for Africa, where current urbanization seems to occur despite economic development: "cities in Africa are not serving as engines of growth and structural transformation" (World Bank 2000 cited in Cohen 2006). Rather, these cities serve as a magnet for those seeking a better quality of life. However, the structural investments to provide this are largely lacking or at least insufficient. Urban growth generally means that cities become culturally and socioeconomically more diverse. Typical for many cities in developing countries, regardless of whether these cities are small, medium-sized or very large, is the significant difference between the upper- and middle-class and the low-income class with regard to access to clean drinking water and electricity and presence of adequate sewerage and solid waste disposal facilities (Cohen 2006, Broto et al. 2012). The reproduction, or perhaps even acceleration, of urban inequalities is often attributed to poor urban governance – i.e., municipal authorities unable to keep up with the speed of urban growth and/or with the increasing complexity of urban governance as a result of decentralization of policies – and neo-liberal reforms of urban services, which tend to exclude the urban poor from access to these services (Broto et al. 2012).

A fourth challenge of urbanization often mentioned in the domain of urban studies is environmental pollution, like water pollution across the developing world and air pollution, in particular when it comes to mega cities (Mage et al. 1996, Cohen et al. 2005). The images of cities full of smog and pedestrians wearing face masks to protect themselves from air pollution are telling examples of the problem of urban air pollution. Traffic congestion is considered to be a major source of air pollution in developing countries: "Over 90% of air pollution in cities in these countries is attributed to vehicle emissions brought about by high number of older vehicles coupled with poor vehicle maintenance, inadequate infrastructure and low fuel quality" (www.unep.org/urban_environment/issues/urban_air.asp). The greatest environmental health concerns caused by air pollution are exposure to fine matter particles and lead. This contributes to learning disability in young children, increase in premature deaths and an overall decrease in quality of life (Cohen et al. 2005, Cohen 2006). As "vegetation can be an important component of pollution control strategies in dense urban areas" (Pugh et al. 2012: 7693), the prevalence of air pollution in cities worsens due to the disappearance of the urban green (Pataki et al. 2011). The lack of urban green also contributes to urban heat islands, an urban environmental health challenge that is aggravated by climate change (Susca et al. 2011). Heat islands "intensify the energy problem of cities, deteriorate comfort conditions, put in danger the vulnerable population and amplify the pollution problems" (Santamouris 2014: 682). Recent research indicates that green roofs can play an important role in mitigating urban heat islands and hence in reducing the urban environmental health problems resulting from climate change (Susca et al. 2011, Santamouris 2014).

An urban challenge that is gaining attention, but which was ignored for a long time in urban studies as well as in urban policies and planning, is food provisioning. Neglecting the dynamics and sustainability of food provisioning in scientific research on sustainable urban development is a serious omission, because, as Steel (2008) argues, "feeding cities arguably has a greater social and physical impact on us and our planet than anything else we do". Like Steel in her much acclaimed book *Hungry City: How Food Shapes Our Lives,* the founders of food planning in the USA, Pothukuchi and Kaufman (1999: 216) state that in urban policy "food issues are hardly given a second thought" because urban policies are usually associated with issues such as "the loss of manufacturing jobs, rising crime rates, downtown revitalization, maintaining the viability of ageing neighbourhoods, and coping with rising city government expenditures". This is also reflected in the names of municipal departments and the domains for which municipalities usually bear political responsibility (although this may differ between countries): planning and spatial development, finances, waste management, health, public transport, education, parks and recreation, and community development.

One reason why food has never been a prominent issue on the urban agenda is rooted in the persistent dichotomy between urban and rural policy. Food is often seen as part of the realm of agriculture and hence as belonging to rural policy. According to Sonnino (2009), this urban–rural policy divide is responsible for three shortcomings in urban food research, policy and planning:

a) The study of food provisioning is confined to rural and regional development, missing the fact that the city is the space, place and scale where demand is greatest for food products.
b) Urban food security failure is seen as a production failure instead of a distribution, access and affordability failure, constraining interventions in the realm of urban food security.
c) It has promoted the view of food policy as a non-urban strategy, delaying research on the role of cities as food system innovators.

Linked to the urban–rural policy dichotomy is ignorance among many urban dwellers and policy officials about the significance of food for sustainable urban development and quality of urban life (Pothukuchi and Kaufman 1999), although this is more likely to be the case in cities where the availability of food has never been a real issue of concern for the "average" urban dweller. According to Pothukuchi and Kaufman (1999: 217), food should be understood as an important urban issue as it is "affecting the local economy, the environment, public health, and quality of neighbourhoods".

In this chapter, I want to elaborate on this by presenting and discussing the conditions that are shaping urban food systems. An urban food system encompasses the different modes of urban food provisioning, in other words, the different ways in which locations where food eaten in cities is produced, processed, distributed and sold. This may range from green leafy vegetables produced on urban farms, to rice produced in the countryside surrounding the city, up to breakfast cereals produced, industrially processed and packaged thousands of kilometres away from the place of consumption. The food provisioning system of any city, whether small or large, in Europe, sub-Saharan Africa or Latin America, is always a hybrid food system, i.e., combining different modes of food provisioning. Some cities are mainly, though not exclusively, fed by intra-urban, peri-urban and nearby rural farms and food processors, while other cities are largely dependent, though not entirely, on food produced and processed in other countries or continents. Hence an urban food system is not only shaped by the dynamics characteristic for that particular city-region (i.e., the city and its urban fringe and rural hinterland), but also, and sometimes even predominantly, by dynamics at a distance. This is why the elaboration of the conditions shaping urban food systems is somewhat of a global and generic nature, introducing and explaining the main trends influencing urban food system dynamics. I will introduce some examples to highlight more concretely how and to what extent a city's food system is influenced by these conditions. However, the primary aim of this chapter is to introduce the different topics and themes related to urban food systems, and more in particular to (intra- and peri-) urban agriculture, elaborated upon in the following chapters in the book.

Building on these conditions, I want to conclude this chapter by proposing and discussing several guiding principles for designing and planning future urban food systems. Also this will touch upon issues that are further developed, discussed and illustrated in the following chapters.

The conditions shaping urban food systems

Living and eating in cities have increasingly become inextricably linked to globalized chains of food provisioning (Murdoch et al. 2000, Steel 2008). This is particularly true for industrialized economies, but also in many developing economies, processed foods, long-distance food transport and supermarkets as important food outlets for domestic consumption are on the rise (Reardon and Timmer 2007, Popkin et al. 2012). This globalized food system has brought many benefits to the urban population: food is usually constantly available at relatively low prices and many food products have a year-round supply. However, these benefits have also come at a series of costs (Wiskerke 2009, Lang 2010, De Schutter 2014), which are undermining a continuation of business as usual. Together with several current trends and dynamics that are impacting upon food provisioning activities, these costs inherent in the globalized industrial food system shape the conditions for current and future urban food systems. I will present and discuss below these trends, dynamics and costs.

Population growth, urbanization and changing diets

The first condition shaping current and future urban food systems is the combined process of population growth, urbanization and changing diets. As mentioned in the introduction to this chapter, the world population is expected to grow from 7 billion at present to 9.5 billion in 2050, of which 6.2 billion will be living in urban areas. Concomitant with population growth and urbanization, a change in diet is occurring, regularly referred to as the nutrition transition (Popkin 1999). The nutrition transition consists of two aspects: 1) an increase in energy intake and 2) a change in the composition of diets. The energy intake per capita per day has been increasing in the past decades and is expected to increase in the forthcoming decades (see Table 1.2).

TABLE 1.2 Global and regional food consumption patterns (in kcal per capita per day)

Region	1964–1966	1974–1976	1984–1986	1995–1997	2006–2008	2030
World	2,358	2,435	2,655	2,680	2,790	3,050
Developing countries	2,054	2,152	2,450	2,540	2,570	2,980
Near East and North Africa	2,290	2,591	2,953	3,100	3,150	3,170
Sub-Saharan Africa	2,058	2,079	2,057	2,150	2,270	2,540
Latin America and the Caribbean	2,393	2,546	2,689	2,740	2,920	3,140
East Asia	1,957	2,105	2,559	2,830	2,980	3,190
South Asia	2,017	1,986	2,205	2,300	2,360	2,900
Industrialized countries	2,947	3,065	3,206	3,250	3,430	3,500

Sources: Joint WHO/FAO Expert Consultation on Diet, Nutrition and the Prevention of Chronic Diseases 2003 (1995–1997 data) and www.fao.org/fileadmin/templates/ess/documents/food_security_statistics/FoodConsumptionNutrients_en.xls (2006–2008 data).

Diet composition is also changing with the transition from a rural to an urban diet as, for instance, illustrated by trends in the consumption of animal proteins (see Table 1.3). Popkin (1999) states:

> Urban residents obtain a much higher proportion of energy from fats and sweeteners than do rural residents, even in the poorest areas of very low-income countries. Most urban dwellers also eat greater amounts of animal products than their rural counterparts. Urbanites consume a more diversified diet and more micronutrients and animal proteins than rural residents but with considerably higher intakes of refined carbohydrates, processed foods, and saturated and total fat and lower intakes of fiber.

TABLE 1.3 Per capita consumption of livestock products

Region	Meat (kg per year)			Milk (kg per year)		
	1964–1966	1997–1999	2030	1964–1966	1997–1999	2030
World	24.2	36.4	45.3	73.9	78.1	89.5
Developing countries	10.2	25.5	36.7	28.0	44.6	65.8
Near East and North Africa	11.9	21.2	35.0	68.6	72.3	89.9
Sub-Saharan Africa	9.9	9.4	13.4	28.5	29.1	33.8
Latin America and the Caribbean	31.7	53.8	76.6	80.1	110.2	139.8
East Asia	8.7	37.7	58.5	3.6	10.0	17.8
South Asia	3.9	5.3	11.7	37.0	67.5	106.9
Industrialized countries	61.5	88.2	100.1	185.5	212.2	221.0

Sources: Joint WHO/FAO Expert Consultation on Diet, Nutrition and the Prevention of Chronic Diseases 2003.

Hence the combined process of population growth, urbanization and nutrition transition implies that one of the grand societal challenges for the decades to come is how to feed the growing and urbanizing world population. An often heard slogan is that we "need to double food production to feed 9 billion" (Godfray et al. 2010, Foley 2011, Herrero 2013). This need to double food production is, however, criticized by different scholars (e.g., Holt-Giménez et al. 2012, Tomlinson 2013) for several reasons.

The first critique regards the production bias in the food security discussion. By focusing on food production as the means to address global food and nutrition insecurity, the real cause of food and nutrition insecurity is neglected. Food insecurity is first and foremost a problem of availability, accessibility, affordability and adequacy (De Schutter 2014). At the global level there are significant inequalities between countries and within countries in the availability of food; in some parts of the world there is an abundance of food available for consumption while in other parts there is insufficient food available, in terms of energy needs and/or nutritional needs. But even in places where there is sufficient food available, not everyone has equal access to nutritious food. The notion of "food deserts" (Wrigley 2002, Wrigley et al. 2002, Cummins and Macintyre 2006), i.e., impoverished urban neighbourhoods that lack supermarkets and grocery stores, but boast dozens of fast food and snack shops – has been introduced to highlight the problem of unequal access to food in cities in industrialized economies. With supermarkets and grocery stores moving to the outskirts of cities for logistical reasons, ownership of a car becomes more or less a prerequisite to have access to fresh food for home preparation and consumption (Pothukuchi and Kaufman 1999). If public transport facilities to these outskirts are underdeveloped or simply lacking, then disadvantaged people are deprived of access, or at least easy access, to nutritious foodstuffs.

A third aspect of food security is affordability, referring to the price of food and the amount of money a person or a household has to purchase food. This implies that poverty is an important, if not the major, cause of food and nutrition insecurity (De Schutter 2014, Wegerif 2014). There is no reason to assume that doubling world food production will change anything in the affordability of food. A final aspect of food and nutrition security that is quite often neglected in international debates is the adequacy of food (De Schutter 2014). Adequacy refers not only to safety and nutritional value, but also to cultural appropriateness. What is considered to be a normal food item or even a delicacy for one person may be too sweet, too heavy or a taboo for another one. This means that food and nutrition security cannot be reduced to having access to sufficient calories and micronutrients. Also the kinds of food products that are available, accessible, safe, nutritious and affordable define food security.

An illustrative example of the availability, accessibility and affordability side of the food security equation is Wegerif's study of patterns of food provisioning in Dar es Salaam, Tanzania's largest city and among the top ten fastest-growing cities in sub-Saharan Africa. In Dar es Salaam only 10% of the households have motorized transport, 16% of the households live under the basic needs poverty line, 41% of the households have only one room in a house they share with other households, 74% of the households have three or more members and 23% of the city's population has a refrigerator (Wegerif 2014). This implies that for the vast majority of the population food outlets at walking distance are crucial due to limited or no possibilities to travel far to purchase food. Furthermore, the statistics indicate that a large percentage of the population has little to no space to store food and no possibility for cool storage of food. Using eggs as a case study, Wegerif shows the importance of the egg-provisioning network consisting of (intra- and peri-) urban farmers and *dukas* (street shops). The farmers often not only produce the eggs but also transport them by bicycle to the *dukas*. According to Wegerif (2014) this network has four main strengths for the urban poor compared to the supermarket system:

1   The price of eggs in a *duka* is lower than in supermarkets.
2   *Dukas* are found in any street in the city, while there are only a few supermarket stores in Dar es Salaam. Hence, a *duka* is always within walking distance.
3   *Dukas* offer the flexibility of being able to buy fewer eggs from one upwards compared to the 6, 10 or 30 egg trays available in the supermarket.
4   *Duka* owners offer access to short-term interest-free credit, something that the supermarkets are unable to do.

Lower prices, proximity, flexibility and the possibility of interest-free credit are "crucial for people surviving on limited and sporadic incomes. In addition, these factors do away with the need for storage space, something not to be taken for granted by people who live in cramped spaces, often sharing, with uncertain tenure and with limited or no assets such as fridges or other furniture" (ibid.: 3768).

A second argument for criticizing the production-bias in the food security debate is that the perceived need to double food production is based on the assumption that food consumption trends in the past decade can be extrapolated to the future (see Tables 1.2 and 1.3). Recent figures show, however, that, in Europe and North America, consumption levels of red meat, in particular beef, are declining (Kearney 2010). Poultry consumption levels are increasing, which seems to indicate that red meat is replaced by white meat. Feed conversion efficiencies for poultry are much higher than for beef, implying that poultry consumption is less resource demanding than beef consumption (Cronje 2011, Mekonnen and Hoekstra 2012). Although the overall meat consumption levels in Europe and North America are not yet declining, the increase in recent years has been much more modest than in the second half of the 20th century (Kearney 2010).

The third argument to question the need to double food production is that, at the global level, enough food is currently produced to feed 10 billion, yet approximately 40% of the food produced is not consumed due to harvest losses on the farm and post-harvest losses further up the food chain, including post-consumer waste. According to Smil (2000) and Lundqvist et al. (2008), current agricultural production levels are equal to about 4,600 kcal per capita per day, of which 1,400 kcal per capita per day are lost in different stages of the food chain. Reducing harvest and post-harvest losses could therefore be as important as increasing yields (Herren 2011). Obviously, this does not mean that reducing food waste in Europe and North America will help to reduce the problem of food insecurity in sub-Saharan Africa and South Asia. In industrialized economies food losses primarily occur in the latter stages of the food chain: in supermarkets and restaurants and at home. Food is removed from supermarket shelves or is not bought or consumed because it is close to or past expiry date, because people buy too much or because the portions served are too large to consume (Steel 2008).

According to Lang (2010), approximately 33% of all food purchased in the United Kingdom is thrown away. Reducing food waste in the last stages of the food chain, in particular the still good and safe food that supermarkets dispose of, only contributes to reducing food security insofar as this food goes to nearby food banks and charities. For many developing countries, food waste primarily occurs in the first stages of the food chain, i.e., during harvest, storage and transport (Aulekh and Ragmi 2013). Especially for perishable products such as fruits and vegetables, harvest and post-harvest losses are high. In an emerging economy like India, which is the world's second-largest producer of fruits and vegetables, up to 30% of all food produced is lost during harvest, post-harvest storage and distribution. Poor transport infrastructure between city and countryside, together with a lack of cool storage, are the main causes of these food losses. Hence, improving rural–urban distribution connections and creating and preserving space for intra- and peri-urban production of fruits and vegetables are key means to enhance urban food security (Renting and Dubbeling 2013), as studies about urban agriculture in different cities in the Global South show that up to 40% of the urban demand for fruits and up to 90% of the urban demand for leafy vegetables are met by intra-urban and peri-urban agriculture (De Zeeuw and Dubbeling 2009). The contributions of (intra- and peri-) urban agriculture to safeguarding and enhancing urban food security and nutrition are further explored in Chapter 6.

Scarcity and depletion of resources

Food provision activities – referring to the whole range of activities from agricultural production to eating – depend on the availability and quality of a variety of natural and human resources, such as energy, nutrients, seeds, water, land and labour. The ways in which resources are used and the amounts of resources needed to produce food differ according to the system of urban food provisioning, but generally speaking, many of the crucial resources for food provisioning are depleting at a rate in which they are likely to become scarce. Changes in the use of resources – both in the way they are used and in the amounts needed – are therefore inevitable to safeguard urban food provisioning in the long term. The most important resource constraints for urban food provisioning are:

a) *Fossil fuel*. Food production, processing, distribution, storing and sales have become heavily dependent on fossil fuels and as a result the globalized food system contributes significantly to greenhouse gas (GHG) emissions and hence to climate change (Carlsson-Kanyama et al. 2003, Carlsson-Kanyama and Gonzalez 2009, Lang 2010). Life cycle analyses of Western diets indicate that it takes an average of seven calories of fossil fuel energy to produce one calorie of food energy (Heller and Keoleain 2000). Although different elements of the global food supply chain contribute to this energy inefficiency, the "heavy fossil fuel users" are pesticides and chemical fertilizer, food processing and packaging, food transport (depending on the means of transport) and cooling (during transport, storage and sales) (Pimentel et al. 2008). Regarding the type of food product, animal protein supply chains require more fossil fuels than do crop supply chains. This implies that the expected dietary changes occurring as a result of urbanization (more processed food and more animal protein) will lead to an increased demand for fossil fuel if nothing changes in the energy input-output ratio of food provisioning. The second implication is that the price of food will be strongly influenced by the price of oil – as actually happened during the food price hikes in 2008 – and this may worsen the food security situation for the urban poor in developing economies, who spend up to 80% of their income on food (De Schutter 2014).

b) *Water*. Most of the world's surface water and groundwater is used for the production of food. In the UK, the average use of tap water is 150 litres per person per day. If the amount of water embedded in the products that are used is included, the daily water consumption amounts to 3,400 litres per day. Of this, 65% is embedded in the food that is consumed: "A tomato has about 13 litres of water embedded in it; an apple has about 70 litres; a pint of beer about 170 litres; a glass of milk about 200 litres; and a hamburger about 2,400 litres" (www.waterwise.org.uk/pages/embedded-water.html).

Mekonnen and Hoekstra (2011: 1578) make a distinction between blue, green and grey water to calculate the water footprint of food products: "The blue water footprint refers to the volume of surface and ground-water consumed (evaporated) as a result of the production of a good; the green water footprint refers to the rainwater consumed. The grey water footprint of a product refers to the volume of freshwater that is required to assimilate the load of pollutants based on existing ambient water quality standards".

Mekonnen and Hoekstra (2011) conclude that 78% of the water used for crop production is green water and 12% is blue water, but that the fraction of blue water increases for crops produced in arid and semiarid regions. For the production of animal protein (meat, dairy and eggs) the water footprint is (much) higher. Beef cattle have the highest contribution to the global water footprint, followed by dairy cattle, pigs and chickens. Industrial forms of live-stock husbandry have a higher water footprint than grazing systems. Also the share of blue water in the overall water footprint is higher for industrialized forms of animal husbandry. Mekonnen and Hoekstra (2012) conclude that "from a freshwater resource perspective, it is more efficient to obtain calories, protein and fat through crop products than animal products". A similar con-clusion was already drawn for the use of fossil fuels. It has been estimated that if the entire world population were to adopt a Western-style diet, 75% more water would be necessary for agriculture and this could imply that the world runs out of freshwater (Lang 2010).

c)   *Land.* At a global scale land is becoming a scarce resource (Lambin and May-froidt 2011), which implies that the competition over land use is becoming increasingly fierce (Lang 2010). Agricultural land is needed for the expansion of cities (or construction of new cities), for industrial development and for infrastructure. As many cities, though not all, have developed in areas that were (and often still are) very suitable for agricultural production, the expansion of cities usually goes at the expense of land for agricultural production, triggering deforestation to maintain sufficient amounts of land for agricultural produc-tion. In many countries we also witness a growing demand for other forms of land use in rural areas, such as land for recreation, nature and rural dwelling (Van Dam et al. 2006). Another competing claim regarding agricultural land use is the competition between food production and the production of biofuels (Matondi et al. 2011). With an increase in the price of oil, the production of biofuels becomes an economically interesting alternative for food production. Finally, there is also competition over land use for food production, especially in Africa and South East Asia, with foreign governments and transnational corporations buying large areas of land ("land grabbing") that can serve as sites for fuel and food production in the event of future price spikes (Borras et al. 2011).

These three resource constraints – energy, water and land – have for example been identified by New York's City Council as potential threats to New York City's food supply. To improve the resilience of New York City's food system its City Council has developed a food strategy that promotes agricultural production methods that are less energy demanding, supports regional food production to reduce food transport, encourages the development of urban agriculture and preserves farmland in the city's rural hinterland. New York City's food strategy entitled "FoodWorks: a vision to improve NYC's food system" is a perfect example of a City Council's understanding of the relations between these general and global trends like resource depletion and the future resilience of its urban food system:

> Although many of these problems are national and global in nature, there are immediate steps that can be taken within New York City to strengthen our food system. The city can facilitate urban-rural linkages, support a market for regional products, and use its institutional purchasing power to support small and local producers. Moreover, by helping green the city's landscape, assisting companies with adopting new technologies, and exploring better distribution networks, we can begin to address the high energy usage and greenhouse gas emissions characteristic of our food system.
>
> *(Quinn 2012: 8)*

Climate change

Climate change is another condition that will impact on the dynamics and resilience of urban food systems in a twofold way. First of all, climate change already has and will have a tremendous impact on the productive capacity of agriculture across the globe (Garnett 2008). Some regions are expected to benefit from global warming, as this will create a more productive environment (longer growing season, sufficient rainfall), while many other regions are likely to suffer from global warming due to severe droughts and floods and will hence be confronted with food shortages. In particular, some of the currently most food-insecure regions in the world (sub-Saharan Africa, the Middle East and South Asia), which are also the regions with the highest population growth and urbanization rates, are expected to face significant declines in agricultural production. This is partly due to the long-term average temperature increase; but particularly for the most food-insecure regions in the world the frequency and severity of extreme climate events will have the highest negative consequences for food production and food insecurity (Easterling et al. 2007), affecting food availability, food accessibility, food utilization and food systems stability (FAO 2008). The relation between agricultural production and climate change is a dualistic one. On the one hand, agricultural production is largely negatively affected by climate change but, on the other hand, it also contributes to climate change by emitting GHG. This implies that agriculture can also "contribute to climate change mitigation through reducing greenhouse gas emissions by changing agricultural practices" (FAO 2008).

This brings us to the second relation between climate change and urban food systems. As mentioned in the introduction to this chapter, urban heat islands are the result of the combined effect of global warming and the decline in the urban green. Urban agriculture is increasingly recognized for its role in climate change adaptation and mitigation (Dubbeling 2014, see also Chapter 8 in this volume) by creating and maintaining green open spaces and increasing vegetation cover in the city. This can help to reduce urban heat islands by providing shade and increasing evapotranspiration. Preliminary analyses of the impact of (intra- and peri-) urban agriculture on climate change mitigation and adaptation in the municipality of Rosaria in Argentina show that average temperatures in the urban gardens are 2.4 °C lower than in the centrally built environment (Piacentini et al. 2014). Furthermore, green productive urban spaces can help to store excess rainfall and thus reduce flood risks in cities. Urban agriculture can also help to reduce food transport and cool storage of perishable products, which are food-provisioning activities that contribute to GHG emissions. Finally, urban agriculture can play a role in the productive reuse of urban organic waste and wastewater, which may help to reduce energy use in fertilizer production and in organic waste collection and disposal (Dubbeling 2014, Piacentini et al. 2014) and in lowering emissions from wastewater treatment (see also Chapter 7 in this volume).

Public health

Of the 7 billion people on the planet more than 2 billion suffer from diet-related ill-health: obesity, malnutrition and hunger (Lang 2010, De Schutter 2014). According to the *European Strategy for Child and Adolescent Health and Development* of the World Health Organization, "the growing obesity epidemic is one of the most worrying emerging health concerns in many European countries" (WHO 2005: 5). Obesity rates in Europe range from 10 to 38% of the population. In particular, the rapidly rising prevalence of overweight children is alarming (Lobstein et al. 2005). Obesity costs society tens to hundreds of Euros per person per year (Van Baal et al. 2006) and is responsible for approximately 25% of the annual increase in medical spending (Thorpe et al. 2004). Simultaneously, malnutrition is also a growing health concern which, like obesity, is more prevalent among the socially and economically disadvantaged sections of the urban population. Surveys in the United States in the 1990s revealed that up to 80% of elderly people in homes were suffering from malnutrition (Pothukuchi and Kaufman 1999). Research carried out by the charity Age Concern in the UK shows that 40% of people aged over 65 admitted to a National Health Service hospital are malnourished, while an additional 20% may develop malnutrition during their hospital stay (Age Concern 2006).

Child malnutrition is a major concern in many developing countries. Although the overall percentage of child malnutrition is decreasing worldwide, the prevalence of stunting among young children remains high in Africa (in particular western and eastern Africa) and South-Central Asia (De Onis et al. 2012). Particularly in Africa the slow decline in the percentage of malnourished children combined with the rapid population growth leads to an increase in the numbers of stunted children: from 44.9 million stunted pre-school children in 1990 to an expected 64.1 million stunted pre-school children in 2020 (ibid.: 4). Hunger in its most extreme form has decreased globally from over 1 billion people in 1990–1992 (18.9% of the world's population) to 842 million in 2011–2013 (12% of the world's population). According to De Schutter (2014: 4), these figures are an underestimation of the global hunger problem as "these figures do not capture short-term undernourishment, because of their focus on year-long averages; they neglect inequalities in intra-household distribution of food; and the calculations are based on a low threshold of daily energy requirements that assume a sedentary lifestyle, whereas many of the poor perform physically demanding activities".

In many cities, diet-related ill-health is increasingly becoming a driver of change in urban food systems. The origin of the Toronto Food Policy Council (TFPC) can be traced back to the city's Department of Health incorporating food and nutrition in its health policy in the 1980s (Blay-Palmer 2009). The TFPC, established in 1990, has been an advisory body for the Toronto Department of Health for a long time. Similarly, the London Food Strategy developed by Mayor Ken Livingstone was largely inspired by his public health agenda (Reynolds 2009). An example of public health concerns driving urban food system reforms in the Global South is Belo Horizonte's policy to increase the access to healthy food for all urban dwellers along three action lines (Rocha and Lessa 2009):

1   Preventing and reducing malnutrition by assisting poor families and individuals at risk to supplement their food consumption needs, and promoting healthy eating habits throughout the metropolitan region.
2   Bringing food to areas of the city previously neglected by commercial outlets, through partnerships with private food vendors, and regulating prices and controlling quality of basic staples, fruits and vegetables.
3   Increasing food production and supply by providing support to small producers, creating direct links between rural producers and urban consumers, and promoting different forms of urban agriculture.

Belo Horizonte has received national and international recognition for its successful approach in reducing hunger and malnutrition and has been the prime source of inspiration for Brazil's national Zero Hunger *(Fome Zero)* campaign initiated by the Lula administration.

Guiding principles for resilient urban food systems

The variety and complexity of the conditions shaping current and future urban food systems, combined with the interdependency of these conditions, indicate that it is an enormous challenge to create resilient urban food systems. To quote Lang (2010), these conditions "cannot be addressed singly, but must be addressed comprehensively and collectively" as "there is the danger of unintended consequences in single solutions". I will therefore not present solutions but limit myself to a set of guiding principles for designing and developing resilient urban food systems which provide stepping stones for addressing the aforementioned conditions in a comprehensive way.

Adopt a city region perspective

The 2007/2008 food crisis has made municipal authorities more aware of the need to strengthen the resilience of the urban food system. As a result, intra- and peri-urban agriculture have been taken up in municipal and sometimes also in national policies (Blay-Palmer 2009, Rocha and Lessa 2009, De Zeeuw et al. 2011, Moragues-Faus et al. 2013) in many developing countries, initially with a strong focus on enhancing food security and reducing poverty. With climate change becoming a more prominent urban challenge in recent years, strategies to reduce the urban ecological footprint and urban heat islands and to mitigate climate change have been incorporated as additional goals for intra-urban and peri-urban food production programmes in cities in developing countries. In Europe and North America public health concerns (obesity and malnutrition) together with concerns about the ecological footprint of urban food systems, have been the main reasons for municipal and regional authorities to place food on the urban agenda (Moragues-Faus et al. 2013). According to De Zeeuw et al. (2011), these trends in both developing and developed countries "fit with concepts in urban development that stress the regionality of city space", which indicates "a spatial and economic urban development model that focuses on a regional urban system in which various nodes interact with each other and with the open spaces included in such a functional urban region".

Hence, the first guiding principle is to adopt a city region perspective on urban food systems, implying that the city region is the most appropriate level of scale to develop and implement an integrated and comprehensive solution for a future-proof urban food system. Due to the diversity in the characteristics, problems and challenges of urban food provisioning systems, it is impossible to develop an integrated comprehensive set of solutions that can work in all city regions. Each city region has its specific characteristics, challenges and solutions and hence it is vital that city regions "assess their food dependencies, identify weaknesses and potential pressure points and, where possible, develop a variety of channels through which they can procure their food" (De Schutter 2014: 15). The Zero Hunger policy of the Brazilian city of Belo Horizonte (Rocha and Lessa 2009) and New

York City's food vision FoodWorks (Quinn 2012) are both based on a thorough analysis of the strengths and weaknesses of the city's food system, including the city's relation with its rural hinterland through its different food provisioning channels. As weaknesses and opportunities are context specific, the programmes developed by Belo Horizonte and New York City differ greatly: in Belo Horizonte the focus has been on reducing hunger and malnutrition among the urban poor and on creating direct access to food markets for peri-urban family farmers (Rocha and Lessa 2009), while in New York City the emphasis has been on fighting obesity, preserving farmland and supporting urban agriculture to create a green infrastructure to mitigate climate change (Cohen and Wijsman 2014).

Furthermore, the city region is increasingly becoming the appropriate level of action as a result of the aforementioned decentralization of policy responsibilities (Cohen 2006). Many of the conditions shaping urban food systems refer to policy domains for which many local governments bear responsibility (e.g., waste management, transport, spatial planning, environmental health) or are expected to develop programmes and strategies (e.g., biodiversity, climate change, public health).

Connect flows

A second guiding principle is to connect different urban flows, allowing resources in waste to be recovered for flows creating value. Due to the sanitary-environmental approach to urban waste management (Geels 2006), different urban flows that were once interdependent (e.g., pigs in cities fed on organic waste) have become disconnected from one another. In most cities in developed countries and in (parts of) some cities in developing countries, domestic wastewater and urban rainwater disappear from the urban scenery through sewage systems. In many cities in developing countries the lack of sewage systems and floods resulting from heavy rainfall pose an enormous challenge. Solid waste (organic and non-organic) is put into a landfill or is being incinerated. The collection and disposal of urban waste generally take up a large percentage of municipal budgets and contribute to GHG emissions. However, urban waste can be used for other purposes as well, that may have a higher rather than lower value (up-cycling rather than down-cycling).

When it comes to food waste there is a systematic approach developed in the Netherlands, called Moerman's ladder, which starts with preventing food waste, followed by a range of possibilities for optimizing residual food waste streams (Van der Schans et al. 2014):

- Use for human food (e.g., food banks).
- Conversion to human food (processing).
- Use as animal feed.
- Raw material for the industry (bio-based economy).
- Transforming into fertilizer through cofermentation (+ energy generation).
- Transforming into fertilizer through composting.

- Input for sustainable energy (goal is provision of energy).
- Incineration (goal is destruction, with potential benefit of providing energy).

Using food waste as animal feed not only reduces the amount of food gone to waste but also reduces the amount of water needed for the production of animal protein: "Animal farming puts the lowest pressure on freshwater systems when dominantly based on crop residues, waste and roughages" (Mekonnen and Hoekstra 2012: 413). In Europe it is, however, not allowed to feed kitchen waste to pigs, as this has been restricted after the Boviene Spongiforme Encefalopathie (BSE, also known as mad cow disease) crisis.

Another waste flow that could be converted into a valuable resource is that of human excrements (Cofie and Jackson 2013), which are rich in nutrients, in particular phosphate, which is one of the resources that may become scarce in the future. From a sanitary hygiene perspective there are quite a few legal and cultural barriers to use human excrements as a resource for food production (Geels 2006, Jewitt 2011). Pilot studies about collecting and co-composting faecal sludge and solid organic waste are, however, promising (Cofie and Jackson 2013) and may create both sanitary and economic solutions for cities in developing countries where sewage systems are lacking in large parts of the city. The potential of intra- and peri-urban agriculture in the productive reuse of urban organic waste and wastewater is further explained in Chapter 7.

Using the waste generated by one flow as the input for another flow implies that the approach to waste management should shift from reducing something harmful to adding something useful. This is, for instance, central to the Cradle-to-Cradle approach of McDonough and Braungart (2002) in which waste equals food. Circular metabolism is a similar concept increasingly featuring in the academic debates about creating more sustainable cities: "the long-term viability and sustainability of cities is reliant on them shifting from a linear model to a circular model of metabolism in which outputs are recycled back into the system to become inputs" (Broto et al. 2012: 853).

There are many different ways in which flows can be (re-)connected, ranging from decentralized low-tech systems to more centralized high-tech systems. Within agro-ecological production systems the production of compost from household waste and the use of human urine as liquid fertilizer in agriculture or urban wastewater-fed aquaculture are examples of decentralized low-tech systems of connecting flows (Cofie and Jackson 2013). Within agro-industrial production systems, metropolitan food clusters and agroparks based on the concept of industrial ecology are examples of spatially clustered and connected chains of food production, in which the waste or by-product of one chain can serve as a resource for another chain (Smeets 2011). Which kind of system or combination of systems works best will depend on the specific characteristics of a city region. Agroparks may be the best solution for mega cities with a small or poor productive rural hinterland and/or with a small percentage of the population working in agriculture, while other systems may perform better in cities that lack sewage systems, in which a large part of the population earns a living from intra- or and peri-urban agriculture.

Create synergies

A third guiding principle in the design of resilient urban food systems is to create synergies. The aforementioned guiding principle of connecting flows can also be seen as an example of creating synergies by constructing urban food systems in which waste can be used as, or converted into, a valuable resource. In this section the emphasis will be more on spatial synergies by achieving multiple benefits from the same place and on creating synergies by using food as a medium to link different urban policy objectives. Developing multifunctional urban and peri-urban agriculture and agroforestry spaces in city-regions may serve different purposes simultaneously. For instance, the cultivation of rice in the floodplains in Antananarivo (Madagascar) provides a staple crop for a large part of the urban population, mitigates floods during the rainy season, contributes to income generation and job creation for farmers and reuses urban wastewater that flows onto (intra- and peri-) urban agricultural land (Renting et al. 2013).

Another example is rooftop farming, which can contribute to greening of cities, reduce energy consumption for heating and cooling buildings, help to combat urban heat islands, be used for storm water containment and generate biodiversity in cities (Mandel 2013, Ackerman et al. 2014). Other examples of creating spatial synergies through intra- and peri-urban agriculture are, for instance, the synergies between food supply, leisure and education in agro-recreational parks in different Chinese cities, the synergies between food production, climate change adaptation and water management in Amman (Jordan), and the synergies between food provisioning, green urban infrastructure and biodiversity conservation in Cape Town (South Africa) (Renting et al. 2013).

By rethinking and redesigning systems of urban food provisioning, several urban policy domains can be addressed simultaneously, for instance enhancing environmental quality, alleviating poverty, reducing nutrition insecurity and generating jobs. In the Introduction, the problem of air pollution caused by vehicle emissions was mentioned. As a significant percentage of vehicle movements in cities is related to food delivery and food purchase (Pothukuchi and Kaufman 1999), measures to reduce food transport and to use modes of transport that emit less GHG, fewer fine particles and less lead may help to improve air quality. The aforementioned case of egg supply in Dar es Salaam by bicycle from intra- and peri-urban farms to street shops and wet markets is an interesting example in this respect. This system of food provisioning is not only one without GHG emissions during transport and little to no waste as egg trays are being reused, it also outperforms the more corporate system of industrialized agriculture and supermarkets with regard to the accessibility and affordability of eggs (Wegerif 2014).

Protecting land for urban farming, developing people's markets within walking distance of as many people as possible and better designed cycle paths to increase safety and extend the effective range of bicycles would be important measures to reduce air pollution caused by food transport, enhance food and nutrition security for the urban poor and safeguard jobs and income generation in the urban food economy (ibid.: 3775). Other urban policy domains that can be addressed by redesigning the urban food systems are, for instance, public health, community building and education (Pothukuchi and Kaufman 1999, Brown and Jameton 2000, Mikkelsen 2011). Creating synergies between urban sustainable development goals through rethinking and redesigning the way food is produced, transported, sold and eaten requires the support from governments by including food as a topic in urban policy and planning (Pothukuchi and Kaufman 1999, Viljoen and Wiskerke 2012).

Plan for resilient urban food systems

This brings us to the fourth and final guiding principle, i.e., to plan for resilient urban food systems. As discussed in the introduction to this chapter, food has been absent on the urban policy and planning agenda for many decades. Urbanization, combined with decentralization of policies and a growing understanding that many urban challenges are either directly related to, or influenced by, the system of food provisioning, makes food a suitable vehicle to integrate the economic, social and environmental dimensions of sustainability, as well as addressing justice and health issues.

In recent years, a rapidly growing number of cities in Europe and North America are developing food policies or strategies (Moragues-Faus et al. 2013, Morgan 2013) in which food provisioning challenges are addressed simultaneously with concerns and problems related to public health, quality of neighbourhoods, climate change, biodiversity, energy and transport. But cities in developing countries and emerging economies are also developing or have already well-developed programmes and policies in support of resilient urban food systems. Examples are Rosario (Argentina), Lima (Peru), Belo Horizonte (Brazil), Kesbewa (Sri Lanka), Antananarivo (Madagascar), Casablanca (Morocco) and Bogota (Colombia) (De Zeeuw et al. 2011, Renting and Dubbeling 2013). Urban food strategies, described as "a process consisting of how a city envisions change in its food system, and how it strives toward this change" (Moragues Faus et al. 2013: 6), differ tremendously between cities as they are shaped by the particular characteristics and circumstances of a city, like historical and cultural factors, strength and basis of the local economy, geographical setting, access to food sources and infrastructure, the political and democratic system, and strength of the state and of civil society (ibid.: 5). Developing comprehensive urban food strategies capable of, or at least enabling, the aforementioned connection of flows and creation of synergies are difficult, but not impossible, as the cases of Belo Horizonte (Rocha and Lessa 2009) and Toronto (Blay-Palmer 2009) show.

As the food policies and strategies of many cities are relatively new, it is difficult to assess if, and to what extent, these integrated comprehensive approaches are capable of successfully addressing the challenges that urban food systems are facing. However, the few city regions that began developing and implementing a food strategy about two decades ago, such as Belo Horizonte and Toronto, show that significant progress can be made in different domains simultaneously (Rocha and Lessa 2009, Blay-Palmer 2009). The importance of developing such integrated and comprehensive strategies at city-region level is increasingly understood by local authorities in all regions of the world, as for instance symbolized by the 2013 Bonn Declaration of Mayors at the 4th Global Forum on Urban Resilience and Adaptation: "We invite local governments to develop and implement a holistic ecosystems-based approach for developing city-region food systems that ensure food security, contribute to urban poverty eradication, protect and enhance local biodiversity and that are integrated in development plans that strengthen urban resilience and adaptation" (http://resilient-cities.iclei.org/fileadmin/sites/resilient-cities/files/ Resilient_Cities_2013/ MAF_2013_Bonn Declaration_of_Mayors. pdf.).

As integrated urban food strategies cross different policy domains, one of the key challenges is to organize the administrative and political responsibility for an urban food strategy. Pothukuchi and Kaufman (1999) propose three different options: a municipal department of food, food as the responsibility of the planning department or a food policy council. A department of food might offer a new focal point for urban food issues but which has the danger of becoming a department in itself, and thereby losing the possibility of using food as a vehicle to link different urban policy domains and goals. In that respect it would be better to have an interdepartmental body linked to, and governed by, the different municipal departments that are responsible for food-related issues. The success of Belo Horizonte's food strategy is largely attributed to the Secretariat for Food Policy and Supply (Secretaria Municipal Adjunta de Abastecimento – SMAAB), an example of such an interdepartmental body (Rocha and Lessa 2009). Food as the responsibility of the planning department can bring a more holistic understanding of the food system by putting food in the centre of urban and regional planning.

A food policy council, which can also be complementary to a food department, the planning department, or any other relevant municipal department or even the city council or the mayor's office, is a steering group or network of actors from public, civil society and private sectors involved in the formulation and implementation of a food strategy (Moragues Faus et al. 2013). Having stakeholders from the public, private and the civic sphere involved in a food policy council or another kind of partnership has proven to be extremely important for the development of a long-term food strategy and to be less vulnerable to political change (Wiskerke 2009). To what extent this could work in cities and city-regions where the institutional capacity is still weak remains to be seen. The many inspiring cases of urban food policy and planning around the globe are promising and encouraging examples of cities having the energy and capacity to design and construct more resilient urban food systems, capable of addressing the urban challenges of food security, resource depletion, environmental pollution, climate change and public health.

References

Ackerman, K.; Conard, M.; Culligan, P.; Plunz, R.; Sutto, M.P.; Whittinghill, L. 2014. Sustainable food systems for future cities: The potential of urban agriculture. *The Economic and Social Review* 45(2): 189–206.

Age Concern 2006. Hungry to be heard: The scandal of malnourished older people in hospital. London: Age Concern.

Aulakh, J.; Regmi, A. 2013. Post-harvest food losses estimation: Development of consistent methodology. Available from: www.fao.org/fileadmin/templates/ess/documents/ meetings_and_workshops/GS_SAC_2013/Improving_methods_for_estimating_post_ harvest_losses/Final_PHLs_Estimation_6–13–13.pdf.

Baal, P.H.M. van; Heijink, R.; Hoogenveen, R.T.; Polder, J.J. van. 2006. Zorgkosten van ongezond gedrag, Zorg voor Euro's 3. Bilthoven: Rijksinstituut voor Volksgezondheid en Milieuhygiëne.

Blay-Palmer, A. 2009. The Canadian pioneer: The genesis of urban food policy in Toronto. *International Planning Studies* 14(4): 401–416.

Borras Jr., S.M.; Hall, R.; Scoones, I.; White, B.; Wolford, W. 2011. Towards a better understanding of global land grabbing: An editorial introduction. *The Journal of Peasant Studies* 38(2): 209–216.

Broto, V.C.; Allen, A.; Rapoport, E. 2012. Interdisciplinary perspectives on urban metabolism. *Journal of Industrial Ecology* 16(6): 851–861.

Brown, K.H.; Jameton, A.L. 2000. Public health implications of urban agriculture. *Journal of Public Health Policy* 21(1): 20–39.

Carlsson-Kanyama, A.; Ekström, M.P.; Shanahan, H. 2003. Food and life cycle energy inputs: Consequences of diet and ways to increase efficiency. *Ecological Economics* 44: 293–307.

Carlsson-Kanyama, A.; González, A.D. 2009. Potential contributions of food consumption patterns to climate change. *American Journal of Clinical Nutrition* 89: 1704S–1709S.

Cofie, A.; Jackson, L. 2013. Innovative experiences with the reuse of organic wastes and wastewater in (peri-) urban agriculture in the global South. SUPURBFOOD deliverable 3.1. Leusden: RUAF Foundation.

Cohen, A.J.H.; Anderson, R.; Ostro, B.; Pandey, K.D.; Krzyzanowski, M.; Künzli, N.; Gutschmidt, K.; Pope, A.; Romieu, I.; Samet, J.M.; Smith, K. 2005. The global burden of disease due to outdoor air pollution. *Journal of Toxicology and Environmental Health, Part A: Current Issues* 68(13–14): 1301–1307.

Cohen, B. 2006. Urbanization in developing countries: Current trends, future projections, and key challenges for sustainability. *Technology in Society* 28: 63–80.

Cohen, N.; Wijsman, K. 2014. Urban agriculture as green infrastructure: The case of New York City. *Urban Agriculture Magazine* 27: 16–19.

Cronje, P.B. (ed.) 2011. Recent advances in animal nutrition – Australia 18. Armidale, NSW: University of New England.

Cummins, S.; Macintyre, S. 2006. Food environments and obesity: Neighbourhood or nation? *International Journal of Epidemiology* 35: 100–104.

Dam, F. van; de Groot, C.; Verwest, F. 2006. Krimp en Ruimte: Bevolkingsafname, ruimtelijke gevolgen en beleid. Rotterdam: NAI Publishers.

Dubbeling, M. 2014. Urban agriculture as a climate change and disaster risk reduction strategy. *Urban Agriculture Magazine* 27: 3–7.

Easterling, W. E.; Aggarwal, P. K.; Batima, P.; Brander, K. M.; Erda, L.; Howden, S. M.; Kirilenko, A.; Morton, J.; Soussana, J .F.; Schmidhuber, J.; Tubiello, F. N. 2007. Food, fibre and forest products. In: *Climate change 2007: Impacts, adaptation and vulnerability. Contribution of Working Group II to the Fourth Assessment Report of the Intergovernmental Panel on Climate Change.* (Eds.) Parry, M. K.; Canziani, O. F.; Palutikof, J. P.; Linden, P. J. van der; Hanson, C. E. Cambridge and New York: Cambridge University Press, pp. 273–314.

FAO 2008. Climate change and food security: A framework document. Rome: Food and Agriculture Organization of the United Nations (FAO).

Foley, J. A. 2011. Can we feed the world & sustain the planet? *Scientific American* 305(5): 60–65.

Garnett, T. 2008. Cooking up a storm: Food, greenhouse gas emissions and our changing climate. Guildford: Food Climate Research Network, Centre for Environmental Strategy, University of Surrey.

Geels, F. W. 2006. The hygienic transition from cesspools to sewer systems (1840–1930): The dynamics of regime transformation. *Research Policy* 35(7): 1069–1082.

Godfray, H.C. J.; Beddington, J. R.; Crute, I. R.; Haddad, L.; Lawrence, D.; Muir, J. F.; Pretty, J.; Robinson, S.; Thomas, S. M.; Toulmin, C. 2010. Food security: The challenge of feeding 9 billion people. *Science* 327(5967): 812–818.

Heller, M. C.; Keoleian, G. A. 2000. Life cycle-based sustainability indicators for assessment of the U.S. food system. Ann Arbor: Center for Sustainable Systems, University of Michigan.

Herren, H. 2011. 'Agriculture at a Crossroads' Lecture for the All Party Parliamentary Group on Agroecology. Tuesday, March 15th, 2011. London, United Kingdom: House of Commons.

Herrero, M. 2013. Feeding the planet: Key challenges. In: *Energy and protein metabolism and nutrition in sustainable animal production.* (Eds.) Oltjen, J. W.; Kebreab, E.; Lapierre, H. Wageningen: Wageningen Academic Publishers, pp. 27–34.

Holt-Giménez, E.; Shattuck, A.; Altieri, M.; Herren, H.; Gliessman, S. 2012. We already grow enough food for 10 billion people . . . and still can't end hunger. *Journal of Sustainable Agriculture* 36(6): 595–598.

Jewitt, S. 2011. Geographies of shit: Spatial and temporal variations in attitudes towards human waste. *Progress in Human Geography* 35(5): 608–626.

Joint WHO/FAO Expert Consultation on Diet, Nutrition and the Prevention of Chronic Diseases 2003. *Diet, nutrition and the prevention of chronic diseases: Report of a joint WHO/ FAO expert consultation, Geneva, 28 January–1 February 2002.* WHO Technical Report Series 916. Geneva: World Health Organization.

Kearney, J. 2010. Food consumption trends and drivers. *Philosophical Transactions of the Royal Society B: Biological Sciences* 365(1554): 2793–2807.

Lambin, E. F.; Meyfroidt, P. 2011. Global land use change, economic globalization, and the looming land scarcity. *Proceedings of the National Academy of Sciences of the USA* 108: 3465–3472.

Lang, T. 2010. Crisis? What crisis? The normality of the current food crisis. *Journal of Agrarian Change* 10(1): 87–97.

Lobstein, T.; Rigby, N.; Leach, R. 2005. Obesity in Europe: Briefing paper for the EU Platform on Diet, Physical Activity and Health. London: International Obesity Task Force.

Lundqvist, J.; de Fraiture, C.; Molden, D. 2008. Saving water: From field to fork. Curbing losses and wastage in the food chain. SIWI Policy Brief. Stockholm: Stockholm International Water Institute (SIWI).

Madlener, R.; Sunak, Y. 2011. Impacts of urbanization on urban structures and energy demand: What can we learn for urban energy planning and urbanization management? *Sustainable Cities and Society* 1(1): 45–53.

Mage, D.; Ozolins, G.; Peterson, P.; Webster, A.; Orthofer, R.; Vandeweerd, V.; Gwynne, M. 1996. Urban air pollution in megacities of the world. *Atmospheric Environment* 30(5): 681–686.

Mandel, L. 2013. Eat up: The inside scoop on rooftop agriculture. Gabriola Island: New Society Publishers.

Matondi, P. B.; Havnevik, K.; Beyene, A. 2011. Biofuels, land grabbing and food security in Africa. London: Zed Books.

McDonough, W.; Braungart, M. 2002. Cradle to cradle: Remaking the way we make things. New York: North Point Press.

Mekonnen, M. M.; Hoekstra, A. Y. 2011. The green, blue and grey water footprint of crops and derived crop products. *Hydrology and Earth System Sciences* 15: 1577–1600.

Mekonnen, M. M.; Hoekstra, A. Y. 2012. A global assessment of the water footprint of farm animal products. *Ecosystems* 15(3): 401–415.

Mikkelsen, B. E. 2011. Images of foodscapes: Introduction to foodscape studies and their application in the study of healthy eating out-of-home environments. *Perspectives in Public Health* 131(5): 209–216.

Moragues-Faus, A.; Morgan, K.; Moschitz, H.; Neimane, I.; Nilsson, H.; Pinto, M.; Rohracher, H.; Ruiz, R.; Thuswald, M.; Tisenkopfs, T.; Halliday, J. 2013. Urban food strategies: The rough guide to sustainable food systems. FOODLINKS report. Available from: www.foodlinkscommunity.net/fileadmin/documents_organicresearch/foodlinks/publications/Urban_food_strategies.pdf.

Morgan, K. 2013. The rise of urban food planning. *International Planning Studies* 18(1): 1–4.

Murdoch, J.; Marsden, T. K.; Banks, J. 2000. Quality, nature and embeddedness: Some theoretical considerations in the context of the food sector. *Economic Geography* 76: 107–125.

Onis, M. de; Blössner, M.; Borghi, E. 2012. Prevalence and trends of stunting among pre-school children, 1990–2020. *Public Health Nutrition* 15(1): 142–148.

Pacione, M. 2009. Urban geography: A global perspective. New York: Routledge.

Pataki, D. E.; Carreiro, M. M.; Cherrier, J.; Grulke, N. E.; Jennings, V.; Pincetl, S.; Pouyat, R. V.; Whitlow, T. H.; Zipperer, W. C. 2011. Coupling biogeochemical cycles in urban environments: Ecosystem services, green solutions, and misconceptions. *Frontiers in Ecology and the Environment* 9(1): 27–36.

Piacentini, R. D.; Bracalenti, L.; Salum, G.; Zimmerman, E.; Lattuca, A.; Terrile, R.; Bartolomé, S.; Vega M.; Tosello, L.; Di Leo, N.; Feldman, S.; Coronel, A. 2014. Monitoring the climate change impacts of urban agriculture in Rosario, Argentina. *Urban Agriculture Magazine* 27: 50–53.

Pimentel, D.; Williamson, S.; Alexander, C. E.; Gonzalez-Pagan, O.; Kontak, C.; Mulkey, S. E. 2008. Reducing energy inputs in the US food system. *Human Ecology* 36: 459–471.

Popkin, B. M. 1999. Urbanization, lifestyle changes and the nutrition transition. *World Development* 27(11): 1905–1916.

Popkin, B. M.; Adair, L. S.; Ng, S. W. 2012. Global nutrition transition and the pandemic of obesity in developing countries. *Nutrition Reviews* 70(1): 3–21.

Pothukuchi, K.; Kaufman, J. L. 1999. Placing the food system on the urban agenda: The role of municipal institutions in food systems planning. *Agriculture and Human Values* 16: 213–224.

Pugh, T. A.; MacKenzie, A. R.; Whyatt, J. D.; Hewitt, C. N. 2012. Effectiveness of green infrastructure for improvement of air quality in urban street canyons. *Environmental Science & Technology* 46(14): 7692–7699.

Quinn, C. C. 2012. FoodWorks: A vision to improve NYC's food system. New York: The New York City Council. Available from: http://council.nyc.gov/downloads/pdf/foodworks_fullreport_11_22_10.pdf.

Reardon, T.; Timmer, C. P. 2007. Transformation of markets for agricultural output in developing countries since 1950: How has thinking changed? *Handbook of Agricultural Economics* 3: 2807–2855.

Rees, W.; Wackernagel, M. 1996. Urban ecological footprints: Why cities cannot be sustainable – And why they are a key to sustainability. *Environmental Impact Assessment Review* 16(4): 223–248.

Renting, H.; Dubbeling, M. 2013. Innovative experiences with (peri-) urban agriculture and urban food provisioning: Lessons to be learned from the global South. SUPURB-FOOD deliverable 3.5. Leusden: RUAF Foundation.

Renting, H.; Naneix, C.; Dubbeling, M.; Cai, J. 2013. Innovative experiences with multifunctional (peri-) urban agriculture in city regions in the global South. SUPURBFOOD deliverable 3.4. Leusden: RUAF Foundation.

Reynolds, B. 2009. Feeding a world city: The London food strategy. *International Planning Studies* 14(4): 417–424.

Rocha, C.; Lessa, I. 2009. Urban governance for food security: The alternative food system in Belo Horizonte, Brazil. *International Planning Studies* 14(4): 389–400.

Santamouris, M. 2014. Cooling the cities: A review of reflective and green roof mitigation technologies to fight heat island and improve comfort in urban environments. *Solar Energy* 103: 682–703.

Schans, J. W. van der; Ge, L.; Schmid, O.; Dominguez Garcia, M. D.; Simón Fernández, X.; Swagemakers, P. 2014. Closing of nutrient, water and urban waste cycles in urban and peri-urban agriculture: Results of the exploration stage. Wageningen: Wageningen University and Research Centre.

Schutter, O. de. 2014. The transformative potential of the right to food. New York: UN Human Rights Council.

Smeets, P. J. 2011. Expedition Agroparks: Research by design into sustainable development and agriculture in the network industry. Wageningen: Wageningen Academic Publishers.

Smil, V. 2000. Feeding the world: A challenge for the 21st century. Cambridge, MA: MIT Press.

Sonnino, R. 2009. Feeding the city: Towards a new research and planning agenda. *International Planning Studies* 14: 425–435.

Sorensen, A.; Okata, J. 2010. Introduction: Megacities, urban form, and sustainability. In: *Megacities: Urban form, governance and sustainability*. (Eds.) Sorensen, A.; Okata, J. Tokyo and New York: Springer, pp. 1–11.

Steel, C. 2008. Hungry city: How food shapes our lives. London: Random House.

Susca, T.; Gaffin, S. R.; Dell'Osso, G. R. 2011. Positive effects of vegetation: Urban heat island and green roofs. *Environmental Pollution* 159(8–9): 2119–2126.

Thorpe, K. E.; Florence, C. S.; Howard, D. H.; Joski, P. 2004. The impact of obesity on rising medical spending. *Health Affairs* W4: 480–486.

Tomlinson, I. 2013. Doubling food production to feed the 9 billion: A critical perspective on a key discourse of food security in the UK. *Journal of Rural Studies* 29: 81–90.

UN 2014. World urbanization prospects: The 2014 revision. Washington, DC: United Nations, Department of Economic and Social Affairs, Population Division. Available from: http://esa.un.org/unpd/wup/Highlights/WUP2014-Highlights.pdf

Viljoen, A.; Wiskerke, J.S.C. 2012. Sustainable food planning: Evolving theory and practice. Wageningen: Wageningen Academic Publishers.

Wegerif, M.C.A. 2014. Exploring sustainable urban food provisioning: The case of eggs in Dar es Salaam. *Sustainability* 6(6): 3747–3779.

WHO 2005. European strategy for child and adolescent health and development. Copenhagen: World Health Organization (WHO) – Regional Office for Europe.

Wiskerke, J.S.C. 2009. On places lost and places regained: Reflections on the alternative food geography and sustainable regional development. *International Planning Studies* 14: 369–387.

World Bank 2000. World development report 1999/2000: Entering the 21st century. New York: Oxford University Press.

Wrigley, N. 2002. Food deserts in British cities: Policy context and research priorities. *Urban Studies* 39: 2029–2040.

Wrigley, N.; Warm, D.; Margetts, B.; Whelan, A. 2002. Assessing the impact of improved retail access on diet in a 'Food Desert': A preliminary report. *Urban Studies* 39: 2061–2082.

Zeeuw, H. de; Dubbeling, M. 2009. Cities, food and agriculture: Challenges and the way forward. *RUAF Working Paper 3*. Leusden: RUAF Foundation.

Zeeuw, H. de; Veenhuizen, R. van; Dubbeling, M. 2011. The role of urban agriculture in building resilient cities in developing countries. *The Journal of Agricultural Science* 149(S1): 153–163.

2

URBAN FOOD POLICIES AND PROGRAMMES

An overview

Lauren Baker¹ and Henk de Zeeuw²

1 CITY OF TORONTO/PUBLIC HEALTH, TORONTO FOOD POLICY COUNCIL, CANADA

2 RUAF FOUNDATION, THE NETHERLANDS

Introduction

Historically, the development of cities was intimately intertwined with the development of food and agriculture in the city region. Over the past 65 years this connection has been increasingly lost due to the industrialization and globalization of food systems. Urban policy development and planning increasingly got separated from policy development regarding food and agriculture – and the planning and management of the ecosystem and natural resources – in the hinterland of the cities.

As a consequence, with the exception of land use planning, municipal authorities usually have little influence on defining agricultural and food policies and mainly play roles related to the delivery of national or provincial programmes (Steel 2008; Friedmann 2011; Crush and Frayne 2011).

Many local governments, not only in the Global North but also increasingly in developing countries, have started to acknowledge and reclaim jurisdictional responsibility for food systems activities that directly impact the health and well-being of their residents. Cities and citizens increasingly recognize that local authorities and governments have a role to play to address problems related to urban food insecurity, hunger, the increase of diet-related chronic diseases, the growing dependency on global food markets and large-scale supermarket chains, and the growing vulnerability of the urban food system (distortions in globalized food supply chains, impacts of climate change). For example, over the last 30 years across Toronto a vibrant food movement has sprung up to confront this situation, developing alternatives to the corporate food retail format such as farmers markets, food box programmes, coops, etc. Toronto's food movement is linked directly to the municipal government through the Toronto Food Policy Council, a multi-stakeholder citizen's advisory committee created by Toronto City Council in the early 1990s when it recognized that the city had a role to play to address the food security of its residents (MacRae et al. 2011; Mah and Baker 2012).

To date, hundreds of cities in the USA, Canada, China, Brazil, South Africa, UK, the Netherlands, Germany, and other countries have developed, often in collaboration with civil society and private sector stakeholders in the food system, policies and programmes on urban food security, nutrition, urban agriculture, etc.

The scope and focus of these policies and/or programmes vary widely, ranging from single-issue policies and plans that address one or more specific elements of the food system (e.g., policies to support residential and community gardening, municipal local food procurement policies, policies to improve the food distribution network in underserved areas of the city, food waste reduction and management plans) to comprehensive approaches that seek to assess and plan the urban (or city region) agro-food system including the complex interactions between its various components (production, transport, processing, distribution, consumption and waste-management) and the social, ecological and economic interactions between the agro-food system and other urban systems (see also Chapter 3 of this volume). The spatial scope of these policies and programmes varies (from neighbourhood level to a wide geographic area including various urban centres and substantial peri-urban or even rural areas).

Below we provide an overview of the variety of policies and programmes that cities apply related to the urban and regional food system. To identify these policies and programmes we have drawn on a number of inventories that have been published over the last several years, as well as literature on individual cases. For the USA and Canada the main sources used are Hatfield (2012), MacRae and Donahue (2013) and Hodgson (2014). For Europe the main sources have been the articles on various European cities included in the book *Sustainable Food Planning* (Viljoen and Wiskerke 2012) and the inventory prepared by the Food Links project (Moragues et al. 2013). For urban food and agriculture policies and plans of cities in developing countries we mainly relied on RUAF working paper #2, "Key Issues and Courses of Action for Municipal Policy Making on Urban Agriculture" (de Zeeuw et al. 2007) and the Growing Greener Cities publications by the UN Food and Agriculture Organization (FAO) (FAO 2012; Thomas 2014). From a global perspective, these inventories are incomplete, but do provide a sense of how various municipalities in the North and South are acting on food systems issues. The municipal documents in which these policies and programmes are mentioned include city development plans, sustainability plans, food policy strategies and plans, etc. We could not always determine if these documents were formally adopted by the municipality/council or still had the status of a plan or proposal.

BOX 2.1 TORONTO, CANADA: FOOD POLICY COUNCIL

Toronto's focus on food policy began with the creation of the Toronto Food Policy Council (TFPC) in 1991. Toronto City Council was concerned about the institutionalization of emergency food programmes (food banks) and created the TFPC to look at the systemic causes of hunger and food insecurity. The TFPC is a subcommittee of the Board of Health and advises Toronto City Council on policies and programmes that will increase food security for Torontonians.

In 2001 Toronto City Council endorsed a Food Charter that recognizes Toronto's commitment to realizing the United Nations Covenant on Social, Economic and Cultural Rights, which include "the fundamental right of everyone to be free from hunger" and outlines a series of actions for the city to improve food security. Food security is also embedded in the city's Official Plan that recognizes the importance of rural–urban linkages, and in the city's Environmental Action Plan, which acknowledges that urban agriculture and local food procurement can help the city achieve its environmental goals. In 2010 Toronto Public Health endorsed a food strategy for the City of Toronto, and created a new team to implement the priorities articulated in the strategy. Current initiatives include a food retail analysis, a healthy corner store pilot project, a community food sector procurement pilot and an urban agriculture action plan. The TFPC now has an expanded mandate to act as the community reference group for the food strategy.

The City of Toronto has passed numerous policies and developed programmes related to improving the food system over the past 20 years. These include:

- A community gardens policy with the goal of creating a garden for every ward in the city and a programme in the Parks and Recreation Department that supports community garden development.
- Supporting the establishment of farmers markets in city parks and at civic centres.
- Food and beverage sector specialist on staff to support new and existing food businesses.
- Creating and providing financial support to a student nutrition programme.
- Local food procurement policy with the goal of 50% local food purchased by City Divisions.
- Toronto Food Strategy endorsed with financial support dedicated for implementation.
- Food truck policy.
- Regional Food and Farm Action Plan endorsed with financial support dedicated for implementation.

- Toronto Agriculture Programme created to support scaling up of urban agriculture.

The TFPC continues to bring new policy ideas forward to the city, most recently illustrated by its advocacy for increased city support for urban agriculture that resulted in the creation of the Toronto Agriculture Program and an urban agriculture steering committee chaired by the Deputy City Manager. The City of Toronto also endorsed and contributes staff time and financial resources to a regional economic development strategy for the food and agriculture sector: The Golden Horseshoe Food and Farm Action Plan.

A number of factors contribute to the success of Toronto's food policy activities: 1. Toronto Public Health's ongoing staff support and resources for the TFPC and Food Strategy implementation; 2. embedding responsibility for programmes and activities across various City Divisions including Parks, Forestry and Recreation, Environment and Energy Division, Social Development, Administration and Finance, etc.; and 3. drawing on the expertise of food system stakeholders to provide strategic advice and support for policy and programme implementation.

More information about Toronto's food policy development can be found at www.tfpc.to.

Sources: Blay-Palmer 2009; Mah and Baker 2012; Roberts 2014.

Main objectives of urban food policies and programmes

Our review suggests that the various food and agricultural policies and programmes developed by cities can be grouped under four main objectives:

1 *Realize equitable (physical and economic) access for all citizens* to safe, healthy, affordable, culturally appropriate food and reduce hunger and dependency on food aid/charity.
2 *Secure adequate nutrition and public health,* especially for people at risk of (under or over) malnutrition and related health problems.
3 Promote (sustainable) food production, processing and distribution within the city region (especially by small-scale producers) in order to *stimulate the local/regional economy and enhance urban food security.*
4 Optimize the contributions of the urban food system to *urban environmental sustainability, diversity and resilience.*

The first and second objectives focus on the social and health dimensions of the urban food system, while the third and fourth objectives focus on the contributions of the urban food system to the local/city-regional economy and ecology, respectively.

Many of the documents reviewed contain specific policies and programmes that relate to only one or two of the above four objectives. Only the few comprehensive urban food strategies or plans cover several or all of these objectives.

Municipal policies and programmes regarding the urban food system

We provide below an overview of the (planned or ongoing) municipal policies and programmes regarding the urban (or city-region) food system. We grouped these policies around the above-mentioned four main objectives. Some policies are mentioned more than once since such a policy might be used to realize different objectives. In such cases, we provide details about the policy only once.

For each policy identified, we give one or more examples to illustrate the variation in the way cities implement a certain food policy. For several policies it was easy to find many examples (e.g., creation of farmers markets, preferential food procurement, supporting community gardening or school food programmes), of which we include only a few. For other policies (like policy measures aiming to enhance access of the urban poor to food by means of regulating food prices, raising minimum wages or creating job/income opportunities for poor or disadvantaged households) it was more difficult to find examples of application by municipalities.

This overview is by no way exhaustive and is only meant to provide insight into the diversity of policies and programmes cities have developed – often in close interaction with other local stakeholders in the urban food system – in order to strengthen the urban food system, or certain component(s) of that system.

BOX 2.2   BELO HORIZONTE (BRAZIL): ENHANCING FOOD SECURITY, EMPLOYMENT AND INCOME FOR THE URBAN POOR

In 1993 the City of Belo Horizonte created the Municipal Secretariat of Food Supplies (Secretaria Municipal de Abastecimento, SMAB) to address food security ("that all citizens have the right to adequate quantity and quality of food throughout their lives"), recognizing that it is the duty of governments to guarantee this right. The creation of the SMAB, with a separate administrative structure and budget, mainstreamed food security into the municipal public policy (Rocha 2001). The programme is advised by COMASA (Conselho Municipal de Abastecimento e Segurança Alimentar), a 20-member council with representatives from other governmental orders and institutions, labour unions (agricultural and industrial workers), food producers and distributers, and civil society organizations.

The municipal programme implemented by SMAB includes three parallel and interconnected programmes (Rocha 2001). The first provides supplementary food assistance to food-insecure households. The second addresses equitable food access by regulating the price of basic healthy staples and linking the private sector to areas with poor food access. The third programme provides technical and financial incentives to local and small-scale food producers to grow, distribute and market their products by creating supply-chain connections between rural producers and urban consumers and promoting (intra- and peri-) urban food production.

The municipal programme is embedded within the national "Fome Zero" (Zero Hunger) Strategy that aims to reduce hunger and address food insecurity across Brazil. "Fome Zero" includes measures to create jobs for the urban poor and increase the minimum wage in order to enhance their food security, links healthy food access to family farming in the city region, and recognizes the importance of partnerships between the public, private and civil society sectors.

The World Future Council notes the following achievements and results of the Belo Horizonte policy and associated programmes:

- A reduction of child mortality by 60% in the first 12 years.
- A reduction of malnourishment among children under the age of five by 75%.
- An increase of fruit and vegetable consumption by 25%.

Sources: Rocha and Lessa 2009; World Future Council 2013.

Objective 1. Enhance equitable (physical and economic) access to safe, healthy, affordable, culturally appropriate food especially of the urban poor and disadvantaged households and reduce hunger and dependency on food aid/charity

Policies applied in relation to this objective are the following:

1.1 Policy measures to generate job and income for the urban poor

- Belo Horizonte (Brazil) adopted measures to increase the minimum wage and stimulates commercial food production projects to employ urban poor and disadvantaged (see Box 2.2 and Rocha and Lessa 2009).

1.2 Policy measures to regulate prices and control quality of basic staples, fruits and vegetables

- Belo Horizonte: see Box 2.2 and Rocha and Lessa 2009.
- Toronto (Canada) supported the creation of – and provides funding for – FoodShare Toronto's Good Food Box, a non-profit food access and distribution

programme that makes healthy, good-quality fruit and vegetables (sourced directly from local farmers when possible) available for the wholesale price (www.foodshare.net).

1.3 Policy measures to improve food distribution within the city

1.3.1 Protection of shops in low-income neighbourhoods that provide day-to-day food needs (especially fresh and healthy food)

- United Kingdom: the "Town first" policy protects inner-city shops from superstores in the city fringe (DC&LG 2012).
- Portland (USA) supports the viability of grocery stores in neighbourhood centres (especially sole shops), e.g., by abatement of property taxes (Portland Council 2012).

1.3.2 Support for the establishment of (healthy) food outlets in underserved areas

- Chicago (USA): The Chicago Retail Programme provides incentives (e.g., property tax abatements and low-interest loans) to private food vendors (supermarkets and other grocery stores) who invest them in underserved areas (Pothukuchi 2005).
- Belo Horizonte supports the establishment of ABC-markets ("food at low prices") and People's Restaurants in low-income neighbourhoods (Rocha and Lessa 2009).
- Baltimore (USA): The City Health Department operates a Virtual Supermarket Program (VSP) that increases access to healthy foods for low-income residents with low vehicle and low internet access by allowing them to place and receive grocery orders at their local library, elementary school, or senior/disabled housing site without paying a delivery fee (see: http://archive.baltimorecity.gov/Government/AgenciesDepartments/Planning/BaltimoreFoodPolicyInitiative/VirtualSupermarket.aspx).

1.3.3 Facilitating the establishment of farmers markets especially in or close to neighbourhoods that lack access to fresh and healthy produce

- Philadelphia (USA) identifies potential farmers market sites on public property (including streets, parks, bus stations, schools, institutions) and on private property (e.g., hospitals and commercial centres) and incorporates spaces suitable for new farmers markets into larger development projects (DVRPC 2011).
- Sacramento (USA) provides incentives for street and farmers markets (e.g., low market fees and stall costs) (City of Sacramento 2009).
- Bristol (UK) seeks to maintain independent retailers – especially in underserved areas – by promoting to buy (preferably locally produced food) in independent retail shops (http://bristolindependents.co.uk/).

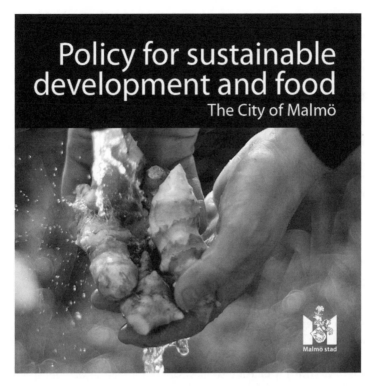

FIGURE 2.1 Malmö sustainable development and food policy
Source: City of Malmö.

1.3.4 Support for the establishment of consumers' food-buying cooperatives by low-income groups

- Manchester (UK): The Manchester Food Futures funding scheme supports consumers' food-buying cooperatives (Manchester City Council 2007).
- Brighton and Hove Food Partnership (UK) promotes the creation of buying groups and food cooperatives by provisioning information on suppliers and creation process (www.bhfood.org.uk/food-buying-groups).

1.4 Policy measures to facilitate home and community gardening and small-scale livestock keeping especially by low-income and disadvantaged categories of the urban population

1.4.1 Accommodation of zoning regulations to allow front and back yard gardening/small livestock keeping and community gardening in residential areas

- London (UK) incorporated urban agriculture in the London Development Plan which commits the city to support urban agriculture especially in locations near food-insecure and vulnerable urban communities, and obliges local authorities to include space for urban agriculture in local spatial planning (London Assembly 2010).

1.4.2 Provision of access to vacant municipal land (especially close to low-income areas) and facilitate access to semi-public spaces (like the grounds of schools, hospitals, community centres) for community and school gardens

- Cape Town (South Africa) leases out underutilized land around public facilities, road verges, etc., to groups of urban poor households and to prospective individual urban farmers and gardeners (City of Cape Town 2007).
- Pretoria (South Africa) entered into a partnership with low-income citizens to manage municipal open spaces that combine community gardening with other functions (park or recreational area) (de Zeeuw et al. 2007).
- Baltimore maintains a land bank of available vacant city-owned land and provides such land to commercial small-scale urban farmers in five-year leases (2 years' notice) (BCPC 2013).

1.4.3 Facilitating access of poor urban producers to private vacant land (e.g., land bank, tax incentives)

- Rosario (Argentina) created a Municipal Agricultural Land Bank (a cadastral-based land registry) and brings those in need of agricultural land in contact with the owners of vacant land. The city also leases vacant land from private landowners to sub-lease it to community groups interested in using the land productively. A third effective instrument used in Rosario is the increase of municipal taxes on idle urban land and reduction of taxes for landowners who make idle land available for farming (temporary or permanent) (Dubbeling 2004).
- Minneapolis (USA) is creating an online web "match-making" service to connect public and private landowners with people and organizations looking for land to grow food and to establish tax incentives for private landowners who lease land to urban farmers (Minneapolis-DHFS 2009).

1.4.4 Integration of permanent garden space in block and neighbourhood planning and upgrading projects

- Kampala (Uganda) integrates space for home and community gardening in new public housing projects and slum-upgrading schemes (Wolfe and McCans 2009).
- Toronto's policy to establish one community garden in every city ward has resulted in over 100 community gardens in city parks (Toronto Food Policy Council 2012).

1.4.5 Enhancing security of land use for community gardens

- Chicago established NeighborSpace, a land trust to acquire (hitherto vacant) land on which local community groups developed community gardens, in order to ensure their survival and preserve these gardens as a valuable community asset (see the NeighborSpace website: http://neighbor-space.org/about/history-of-neighborspace).

- Amsterdam (the Netherlands) provides longer-term leases to urban gardeners' associations (that rent out plots on an annual renewable basis to individuals) under the agreement that if these areas are needed for other planned uses, the municipality will provide an alternative location and assist with basic infrastructural development (Agenda Proeftuin Amsterdam 2007).

1.4.6 Provision of training, technical assistance and (funds for) inputs, equipment and basic infrastructure to food growing initiatives by the urban poor

- Cape Town provides technical assistance, fencing, basic infrastructure (water connection, storage room), vegetable seeds and seedlings, compost and hand tools to community gardening groups in low-income neighbourhoods (City of Cape Town 2007).
- Brighton and Hove (UK) provides grants for school and community gardening projects (Brighton and Hove Food Partnership 2012).
- London: The Capital Growth programme provides grants, technical assistance and training to growers in new community-based urban food growing initiatives (Reynolds 2009).
- Cleveland (USA) provides infrastructure to collect rainwater runoff from adjacent building roofs to community and school gardens (City of Cleveland 2008).
- Toronto provides grants under the Live Green programme to community groups for training, infrastructure, etc.

BOX 2.3 ROTTERDAM, THE NETHERLANDS: URBAN AGRICULTURE FOR IMPROVED HEALTH AND SUSTAINABLE REGIONAL ECONOMIC DEVELOPMENT

The City of Rotterdam adopted in 2012 the strategic policy document "Food and the City" as part of its "Agenda for Sustainable Rotterdam" (2011).

The main focus in the Rotterdam policy is on three main targets:

1 Improve health of citizens

The main actions in this area undertaken are:

- Public education programmes on healthy food and gardening.
- Stimulation of the creation of new community gardens and rooftop food gardens in dense urban districts.

- Promoting the establishment of school gardens and food education.

2 Reinforce sustainable economic development

The main actions undertaken in this area are:

- Abolishment of land use regulations that hinder initiatives for (including commercial) urban agriculture.
- Provision of municipal land for creating (intra- and peri-) urban farms; inventory of vacant open spaces.
- Support for the establishment of farmers' shops and markets in the city.
- Organize "regional trade missions" to shorten the food chains: Connect local producers with potential urban customers (consumers, restaurants, hospitals, supermarkets, agribusinesses, etc.).
- Preferential procurement of regional food products for municipal catering. Yearly competition for best initiative for urban agriculture by citizens.

3 Improve quality of public spaces

This is implemented as component of the above-mentioned actions (e.g., community- and school-gardens, urban farms) as well as green roofs, cleaning up/greening of vacant open spaces, etc.

Source: van Oorschot 2014.

Objective 2. Improve nutrition and public health especially of people under risk of malnutrition and related health risks

Policies applied in relation to this objective are the following:

2.1 Enhancing access to home and community gardening by the urban poor and disadvantaged

- (See 1.4 above for more details.)

2.2 Prevention of over-concentration of hot food takeaway shops, fast food eateries, liquor and convenience stores in residential areas and around schools and youth facilities

- Tower Hamlets (a municipality of Greater London, UK) adopted a policy regarding fast-food takeaways (A5 restaurants), regulating that applications for new establishments of an A5 are only approved if the A5 is located in a city centre, where A5s are not surpassing 5% of the total number of shops, at least two non-food shops are on both sides of the new A5 and the A5 is not within a 200-metre zone of a school (200–400 metres: approved with restrictions) (Tower Hamlets 2012). Greater London developed a toolkit to guide local councils on this issue: www.london.gov.uk/sites/default/files/TakeawaysToolkit_0.pdf.

2.3 Policy measures that enhance supply of fresh and nutritious food and reduce the supply of unhealthy food

2.3.1 Promoting that healthier food is provided at municipal buildings, schools, business and sports canteens, care centres and hospitals and that the supply of carbonated beverages, processed foods and foods containing trans fat or with high sugar contents are reduced

- Marin County (USA) provides reliable information, training and technical assistance on food and nutrition (and its connections with health and environment) to municipal catering staff, teachers, community organizations and other facilities (MCCDA 2007).
- Malmö (Sweden) established a food procurement scheme for restaurants at schools, nurseries and service centres that is applying the SMART concept (smaller amount of meat, minimize intake of junk food, increase in organic food: right sort of meat and vegetables, transport efficient) (City of Malmö 2010).

2.3.2 Promoting provision of healthy foods at super markets, small grocery stores and restaurants

- Philadelphia requires: a. neighbourhood corner stores and markets to stock a certain amount of fresh and locally grown fruits and vegetables, and b. nutritional information on the labels of food products and menus (DVRPC 2011).
- Portland (USA) supports the viability of grocery stores and local markets in neighbourhood centres that supply healthy, affordable food in underserved areas (Portland Council 2012).
- Toronto Public Health has supported a mobile good food market to travel to underserved communities to sell fresh fruit and vegetables.

2.3.3 Stimulating agro-enterprises in the region to improve the nutritious quality of the food products they provide

- Amsterdam (the Netherlands) stimulates agro-processing industry in the city region that participate in the "Proeftuin Food Centre Amsterdam" to process food produced within the city region and to enhance the nutritious quality of their products (Vermeulen 2008).

2.3.4 Assisting households and individuals at risk to supplement their food consumption needs

- The US Department of Agriculture (USDA) provides supplemental nutritional assistance in the form of food vouchers/stamps to vulnerable households and has made these also exchangeable at farmers markets and similar outlets in order to enhance their access to fresh and nutritious vegetables and fruits (see www.fns.usda.gov/ebt/learn-about-snap-benefits-farmers-markets). In Philadelphia, 31% of the urban households receive such nutritional support.
- Chicago supports food banks collecting surplus food from grocery stores, farms and manufacturers and redistributing it to urban households in underserved areas of the city (Chicago Council on Global Affairs 2013).
- Toronto has committed to a five-year plan to increase investments for the student nutrition programme from US$5 million in 2013/14 to US$9.5 million in 2017/18 (City of Toronto 2014).

2.4 Support for healthy food and nutrition education (especially in low-income areas)

- Philadelphia promotes the integration of training on nutrition, gardening and sustainable food systems into existing school curricula (DVRPC 2011).
- Quito (Ecuador) supports the establishment of school gardens and food education (some 128 to date) (Thomas 2014).
- Manchester (UK) organizes public awareness campaigns about the importance of locally produced and organic food and agricultural products (Manchester City Council 2007).
- Marin County supports local food banks and other organizations providing nutrition education and healthy cooking classes to vulnerable households (MCCDA 2007).
- Brighton and Hove delivers advice on how to shop and cook healthy nutritious food with a low budget (www.bhfood.org.uk).

BOX 2.4 LONDON, UK: IMPROVING FOOD SECURITY, FOOD(T) PRINT, FOOD ECONOMY AND FOOD CULTURE

In 2006, the Greater London Authority Food Team, under the leadership of then-mayor, Ken Livingstone, developed the London Food Strategy: a ten-year timeframe to reform London's food system towards health, sustainability and economic viability, and to:

1 Improve Londoners' health and reduce health inequalities via the food they eat.

2 Reduce the negative environmental impacts of London's food system.
3 Support a vibrant food economy.
4 Celebrate and promote London's food culture.
5 Develop London's food security.

The London Food Board was created to support the implementation of the Food Strategy, and continues to meet and coordinate initiatives with policy and staff support from the Greater London Authority (London Development Agency 2006).

Initially, the Food Strategy has focused on public procurement of school meals and increasing green spaces to grow food. With a change in mayoral leadership, the "Capital Growth Initiative" was launched and created 2012 food garden spaces before the 2012 Olympics and continues to provide support to London's food growing community.

Other initiatives include support for small food enterprises, a food waste project with the goal of preventing food waste and diverting surplus food, and the creation of an apprenticeship programme to attract workers and link them to the food sector (see: www.london.gov.uk/priorities/business-economy/working-in-partnership/london-food-board).

Factors that have led to success for the London Food Strategy are the dynamic food community and multiple partnerships to enable implementation of key priorities, as well as the ability to adapt to the shifting political context and climate. Challenges include a limited budget and fragmented local governance across broader London.

Sources: Reynolds 2009; Morgan and Sonnino 2010.

Objective 3. Enhance sustainable food production in the city region (especially by small-scale producers) in order to stimulate the local/ regional economy and enhance urban food security and resilience of the urban food system

Policies applied in relation to this objective are the following:

3.1 Policy measures that facilitate access to land and land use security for commercial (intra- and peri-) urban agriculture

3.1.1 Modification of spatial planning and land-use zoning codes and norms to accommodate commercial farming in (certain parts of) the city

- Dar es Salaam (Tanzania) accepted urban agriculture (crop and livestock) as a major urban land use and included urban agriculture in land use zoning and the Strategic Urban Development Plan (IDRC 2006a).

- Kampala (Uganda) changed its land use regulations and developed a new set of ordinances on urban horticulture, fish culture and livestock rearing, each including sections on production, processing and sales (IDRC 2006b).
- Baltimore adapted its zoning regulations and included commercial urban agriculture as a conditional permanent land use category (urban agriculture defined as the cultivation, processing and marketing of food within the city: horticulture, animal husbandry, aquaculture, agro forestry, vineyards and wineries) (BCPC 2013).

3.1.2 Enabling access to municipal and private land for commercial urban agriculture

- See the policies mentioned under 1.4.2–6 above, but now applied to commercial agriculture.

3.1.3 Preserving and sustaining best and most versatile land in the city region and reserve for agricultural or multi-functional use (e.g., in green belts and corridors)

- Marin County (neighbouring San Francisco) prohibits non-agricultural buildings, impermeable surfaces, or other non-agricultural uses on soils classified as prime or normal farmland soils of state-wide importance (MCCDA 2007).

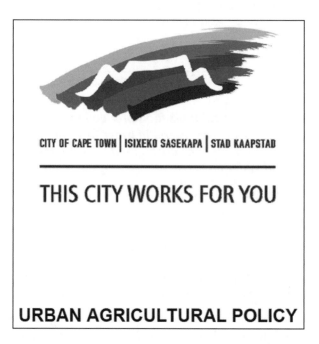

CITY OF CAPE TOWN | ISIXEKO SASEKAPA | STAD KAAPSTAD

THIS CITY WORKS FOR YOU

URBAN AGRICULTURAL POLICY

FIGURE 2.2 Cape Town urban agriculture policy 2007
Source: City of Cape Town.

- Mexico City (Mexico) established a legally protected "conservation area" (organic agriculture + eco-services) (Thomas 2014).
- Allegheny County (USA) encourages infill- and re-development within the existing urban areas of the city (e.g., recycling of an 178-acre former steel factory site in Hazelwood into residential housing areas) in order to minimize the pressure for premature conversion of productive agricultural lands into other uses (Allegheny County 2008).
- Philadelphia maintains affordable land for farmers through a range of potential innovations and new business models, including identification of opportunities for transition of preserved land into food production, and creating investment vehicles for long-term agricultural production on preserved land (DVRPC 2011).
- Minneapolis supports affordable land ownership and/or affordable long-term leases for small enterprise urban agriculture on various types of land and rooftops (Minneapolis-DHFS 2009).

3.1.4 Adaptation of building regulations and zoning codes to enable commercial rooftop gardening and green houses and other building-integrated forms of commercial agriculture

- Seattle (USA) adapted its building regulations to enable rooftop gardening and runs a municipal green roof programme that also promotes rooftop farms (City of Seattle 2012).
- Tilburg (the Netherlands) provides incentives to promote green roofs at residential and non-residential buildings (Plantinga and Derksen 2014).

3.2 Policy measures to enhance the viability of small-scale agricultural producers in the city region

3.2.1 Provision of access to information sources, training, technical advice and business development services to (actual and starting) entrepreneurs in small- and medium-scale urban agriculture

- Minneapolis enhances access to information on new market opportunities, technologies, available sources of financing, technical and business development services, city policies and regulations (Minneapolis-DHFS 2009).
- Tilburg stimulates technological and organizational innovation in commercial urban agriculture (Plantinga and Derksen 2014).
- Chicago (USA) provides job training on food production and processing (CMAP 2010).

3.2.2 Providing access to financing opportunities for agricultural producers in the city region

- Philadelphia incorporates farming and food into its economic development policies and funding programmes and, amongst others, supports farm-to-buyers marketing schemes for nutritious and affordable food with finance for inventory and capital items, technical assistance and advertising support (DVRPC 2011).

- Minneapolis is expanding city-sponsored small business financing opportunities to agricultural producers in the city region (Minneapolis-DHFS 2009).
- Sacramento (USA) is reducing property taxes for agricultural producers within the city administrative boundaries (City of Sacramento 2014).

3.2.3 Defining municipal procurement norms that give preference to buying food from small farmers in the city region to enhance their viability and stimulate the regional economy

- Malmö adopted SMART food procurement regulations (see 2.4.2 above).
- Amsterdam signed a covenant with caterers to purchase organic and regional products for cafeteria services in local government buildings and in organizations and at events sponsored by the municipality (Brand et al. 2010).
- Paris (France) is establishing a local supply chain for school restaurants, procuring organic school meals from local producers (fresh foods within 20 km; bread and beef within 100 km) and subsidizing related extra costs plus technical assistance to involved local organic farmers (Darly 2012).

3.2.4 Promote supermarket chains and other agro-food businesses in the city region to make their products more locally/regionally based

- Amsterdam stimulates agro-processing industry in the city region that participate in the "Proeftuin Food Centre Amsterdam" to preferably process food that is produced within the city region (Vermeulen 2008).

3.3 Policy measures to stimulate the processing and distribution of food produced in the region

3.3.1 Support to collective value adding and direct marketing initiatives by local farmers and social enterprises creating green jobs for the urban poor (e.g., farmers markets, e-marketing, box schemes, crop share schemes, etc.) with land, infrastructure, training, technical support and funding

- Brasilia FD (Brazil) operated the PROVE programme that assisted urban producer groups to establish value adding enterprises by providing organizational and legal support, land, infrastructure, technical and business development advice and marketing support (e.g., establishing brands, farmers markets) (Homem de Carvalho 2005).
- Detroit (USA): The Recovery Park programme provides US$25 million of mixed funding and 100 acres of reclaimed land to support food-related entrepreneurs and community projects to create jobs for people with low access to employment and improve the local economy and neighbourhood (FWP 2013).

FIGURE 2.3 Good food policy London

Source: Sustain.

- Minneapolis established a food business development centre that provides start-up funds, such as low-interest matching loans, and access to technical assistance tailored to starting entrepreneurs and cooperative food initiatives (see: www.minneapolismn.gov/cped/ba/cped_homegrown_business_center).
- Manchester: The Food Futures scheme provides funding to collective process-ing and marketing initiatives like farmers markets, box schemes, food hubs and other forms (Manchester City Council 2007).
- New York: The Green Thumbs programme supports the establishment and functioning of farmers markets (now over 600) (see: www.greenthumbnyc.org/about.html).
- Northumberland County (Ontario, Canada) is building a processing facil-ity with flash freezing capacity and a commercial kitchen to support local farmers.

3.3.2 Revision of city regulations in order to provide a hospitable but safe regulatory environment for networks aggregating, processing, packing and distributing (healthy, ecologically produced, regional) food to urban consumers

- Minneapolis revised the city regulations in order to provide a hospitable regula-tory environment for local foods operations including year-round food pro-duction, processing, aggregation and distribution and on site and industrial composting efforts (Minneapolis-DHFS 2009).
- Kampala (Uganda): health and agricultural and town planning specialists closely cooperated in the development of a series of evidence-based ordinances on urban agriculture livestock and fisheries, replacing old regulations containing a lot of ungrounded restrictions for urban horticulturists and livestock keepers (IDRC 2006b).

3.3.3 Promotion of networking and cooperation among local/regional producers and facilitate their communication and cooperation with other actors in the regional food system

- Rosario: The Municipal Urban Agriculture Programme supports the development of the Network of Urban Producers and has assisted the network to establish working relations with strategic governmental and private organizations (Lattuca et al. 2005).
- Mexico City: The Federal District established a Rural Council, representing producer organizations, traders and service providers, to guide its policies and programmes for sustainable sub-urban and peri-urban agriculture (Thomas 2014).
- Amsterdam established a regional food network "Proeftuin Food Centre Amsterdam-Alkmaar" (Tuin = garden; Proef = "experiment" as well as "tasting"), including agricultural producers, agro-processing industries, consumers' organizations and local food initiatives in the city region that promotes regional products amongst others through establishing a regional brand, culinary festivals and fairs of regional products, and organizing "fruit and vegetables" car and biking routes in the city region (Vermeulen 2008).

BOX 2.5   QUITO, ECUADOR: URBAN AGRICULTURE AS A DRIVER OF SOCIAL INCLUSION AND COMPETITIVE LOCAL ECONOMIC DEVELOPMENT

Quito's Participatory Urban Agriculture Programme (AGRUPAR), implemented by the municipality's Economic Development Agency, ConQuito, aims at improving the employment, income and food security of vulnerable populations in the urban and peri-urban areas of Metropolitan Quito. The programme was launched in 2002 and today brings together some 12,250 intra- and peri-urban farmers and 380 community-based organizations, supported by local and national government departments, universities, NGOs and the private sector.

AGRUPAR's primary focus is on enhancing food security and promoting food processing, access to microcredit, microenterprise management and marketing. At the last count, the project had helped establish 140 community gardens, 800 (semi-) commercial gardeners and 314 livestock keepers, and 128 school gardens. Between 2004 and 2012, the project provided training for more than 7,350 people, most of them women, including recent migrants to the city and underemployed workers. The staff of AGRUPAR provide fencing, seeds and seedlings, equipment, animals (such as poultry, guinea pigs and bees), and half of the investment in productive infrastructure such as drip irrigation, small greenhouses and sheds for animal husbandry to groups of at least six persons. The groups also receive technical training on (organic) agricultural production, nutrition and management skills. For those urban famers who lack the capital to invest in productive infrastructure for the agricultural production and/or for the processing and packaging of produce, the project helped to establish 35 grassroots investment societies, to which each member contributes between US$10 and US$20 in start-up capital.

About half of the production is sold; the rest is kept for home consumption. AGRUPAR assists the producer groups with the certification of their products. Certified organic vegetables are sold through farmers markets as well as through home delivery of organic food baskets including vegetables, fruits, herbs, pickles, jams and bread.

AGRUPAR also encourages the participating groups to form microenterprises in food processing and the production of organic inputs, trains them in business planning, marketing and accounting, and has introduced improved processing technologies and the use of packaging and labels. Certified organic chilli and tomato paste are also sold to local food processing companies, free-range chicken meat to restaurants, and jams and pickles through the home delivery scheme. In fact, adding value to surplus production has recently become one of the most prominent features of Quito's urban agriculture, generating revenue and providing full- or part-time employment for half of the project participants.

The average income of households joining the project is around US$350 per month. They make a further saving of at least US$72 a month on food purchases by consuming what they grow. Total savings are 2.5 times the value of the government's human development voucher, which provides US$50 a month to vulnerable households. Urban agriculture has helped diversify the diet of urban farmers and their families. Among the environmental benefits of urban agriculture is the conservation of biodiversity (some 50 edible plant species are maintained in Quito's urban gardens) and the recycling of kitchen wastes as compost. An estimated 1,820 tonnes of organic wastes are recycled each year by AGRUPAR project participants. The increased availability of fresh produce also means less need to transport it from rural areas, which generates fuel savings and reduces air pollution.

A notable AGRUPAR innovation has been the opening of organic produce markets – or *bioferias* – that have become sources of healthy food for Quito residents and a practical example of Ecuador's solidarity economy. The city now has 14 one-day *bioferias,* open weekly between Thursday and Sunday. To ensure the widest possible availability and consumption of organic food produced in urban gardens, *bioferias* are located in low-income neighbourhoods and peri-urban zones, as well as in better-off parts of the city. In 2012, the *bioferias* of Quito sold more than 100 tonnes of organic produce (valued at US$176,000), which amounts to one-quarter of the programme's total estimated garden production.

Quito's experience has shown that intensive agriculture is feasible in an urban environment, and that it helps reduce malnutrition in poor households, strengthens household food security, and generates employment and income. For the municipal government, AGRUPAR is a flagship programme of its social inclusion policy and its vision of competitive economic development. The programme's challenges relate to the lack of a facilitating legal framework for urban agriculture and the need to integrate urban agriculture further into the municipal spatial planning.

Source: Thomas 2014.

Objective 4. Enhancing environmental sustainability, diversity and resilience of the city region

Policies applied in relation to this objective are the following:

4.1 Inclusion of sustainability criteria in the norms for municipal food procurement

- Malmö established SMART norms for municipal food procurement for restaurants at schools, nurseries and service centres: organic food, smaller amount and right sort of meat, minimize intake of junk food, right sort of vegetables, food preferably produced and prepared close to consumers with low GHG emissions and efficient transport, food wastes to be minimized, food wastes to be used in biogas production (City of Malmö 2010).

4.2 Promotion of sustainable eco-friendly agricultural production/processing/distribution methods in the city region

- Montreal (Canada): The municipal community gardening programme promotes ecological gardening methods and only environmentally friendly methods to control bugs, plant diseases and weed infestation are allowed in the city's community garden parks (Reid and Pedneault 2006).
- Havana: The urban agriculture programme in Havana prohibits the use of agrochemicals in the city and supports the establishment of decentralized low-cost facilities for compost production and the production and supply of bio-fertilizers and bio-pesticides (packaged in small quantities) to urban farmers through a network of 52 agricultural stores that also provide technical services, advice and training to the city's farmers. The Havana urban agriculture programme has calculated that producing 1 million tonnes of vegetables applying

agro–ecological production methods saves over US$41 million in the costs of fertilization and pest control as compared to conventional agriculture (Thomas 2014).

- King County provides incentives for agricultural practices that maintain water quality, protect public health, fish and wildlife habitat and historic resources, maintain flood conveyance and storage, reduce greenhouse gas emissions, control noxious weeds, and prevent erosion of valuable agricultural soils while maintaining the functions needed for agricultural production (King County 2011).
- Governador Valadares (Brazil) stimulates the use of ecological techniques in urban agriculture production, processing and marketing by organizing training courses and providing technical assistance to urban farmers' groups (Lovo and Pereira Costa 2006).

4.3 Supporting decrease of GHG emissions related to food production, processing, distribution, consumption and food waste management in the city region

- Amman (Jordan) included urban agriculture/forestry in its plan to mitigate and adapt to climate change and enhance urban resilience (Dubbeling 2013).
- Antananarivo (Madagascar) is protecting agriculture in flood zones to prevent construction of houses and enhance urban resilience (Aubry et al. 2012).
- Philadelphia pays farmers for the ecosystem services they provide, such as carbon sequestration and groundwater recharge (DVRPC 2011).
- Ghent (Belgium) operates a meat consumption moderation campaign (one meat/fish free day/week): maps indicating restaurants serving vegetarian meals (Leenaert 2014).
- Brighton and Howe (UK) supports the set up and running of community compost projects by providing advice, resources and training (www.bhfood.org.uk).

4.4 Providing regulations and incentives to stimulate recovery and agricultural reuse of nutrients and irrigation water from urban organic wastes and wastewater

- Bulawayo (Zimbabwe) provides treated wastewater to poor urban farmers in community gardens (Mubvami and Toriro 2008).
- Amman is actively promoting the recovery, treatment of wastewater and its reuse in peri-urban agriculture, fruticulture and (agro-) forestry (Kfouri et al. 2009).
- Mexico City promotes systems for rainwater collection and storage, construction of wells and the establishment of localized water-efficient irrigation systems (e.g., drip irrigation) in urban agriculture to stimulate production and to reduce the demand for potable water (Thomas 2014).

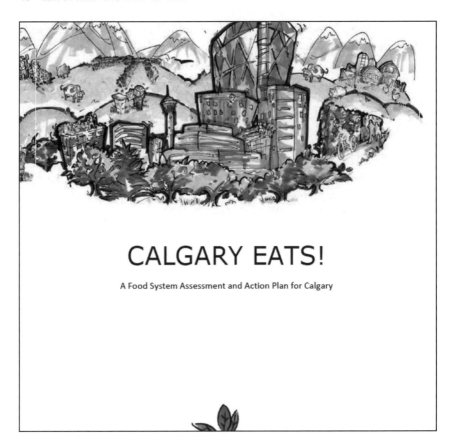

FIGURE 2.4 Calgary eats

Source: City of Calgary.

- King County supports the development and use of innovative technologies to process dairy and other livestock wastes to reduce wastes and create energy and compost. King County also operates a municipal food recovery programme and provision of this food to organizations that distribute food to low-income groups (King County 2011).
- Portland is developing efficient systems for the separation and collection of organic wastes from households and vegetable markets (Portland Council 2012).
- Minneapolis supports the establishment and expansion of composting infrastructure in the city region (Minneapolis-DHFS 2009).

4.5 Facilitating protection and conservation of agricultural land and water resources

- See 3.1.3 but now with the emphasis on management of natural resources, biodiversity, and land- and water-conservation.

4.6 Adoption of new productive and environmentally friendly approaches to neighbourhood planning

- Tilburg developed "De Groene Kamer" (the Green Room, an estate combining retail, nature, agricultural production and recreation) and "De Nieuwe Waranda" (a residential area integrating housing, retail, agriculture and eco-education/agro-recreation) (Plantinga and Derksen 2014).
- Almere developed the Oosterwold area (4000 ha) as a "rurban" area: a continuous productive landscape including housing, food production, water management and biodiversity and recreational services; in 2030 the area should produce 10% of locally consumed fruit and vegetables, which would reduce food-related GHG emissions in Almere with an equivalent of about 5,000 households (if organic production methods are applied) (Jansma et al. 2014).
- Chicago includes space for urban agriculture in several neighbourhood plans (CMAP 2010).
- Detroit is adapting neighbourhood plans to include mixed use zones and facilitating the transformation of vacant properties to urban green spaces by local actors (gardening, forestry, etc.) with joint planning and technical advice (FWP 2013).
- Minneapolis established norms and provides incentives to require/encourage developers to include space for food production and distribution and composting in new developments (Minneapolis-DHFS 2009).

BOX 2.6 MEXICO CITY, MEXICO: ORGANIC AGRICULTURE PRESERVING THE PERI-URBAN ENVIRONMENT

Since 2000, Mexico City's government has increased its support to agriculture in the Federal District, with the main objective of protecting the ecosystem services that suburban and peri-urban areas provide to the city and, to a lesser extent, to ensure a local food supply. The Federal Environmental Law promotes organic farming systems and prohibits the use of agrochemicals and synthetic fertilizers in the demarcated conservation zone. Training, technology development, agro-processing and marketing support are provided to the producers and the amounts spent between 2007 and 2012 were some US$24.6 million in horticulture, floriculture, and crop and livestock production, US$37 million in the conservation and sustainable use of natural resources in primary production, and US$1.8 million in emergency assistance to farmers affected by extreme weather events, such as drought and flooding. Another programme, for the promotion of traditional food culture, helps rural farmers to enter local, national and international markets, and organizes trade fairs and exhibitions in the Federal District and

provides subsidies to farmers who preserve local maize varieties under traditional production systems with low environmental impact. Meanwhile, the
city's Secretariat for the Environment has instituted Mexico's first system of
organic certification of produce, known as the Green Seal, and has set standards for organic agriculture in the conservation zone.

Source: Thomas 2014.

Final observations and recommendations

This chapter reviewed the specific policies and programmes developed by municipalities related to the urban – or city-region – food system. We observe a trend to link
specific policies and programmes through comprehensive urban food system strategies
or plans. We also observe a gradual shift from food planning at the neighbourhood-
city level to the city-region level (or more correctly: the city-region level is added).

Governance is critical for both the development of these policies, as well as
their implementation. Many jurisdictions are engaging multi-stakeholder groups
to support this policy development. This is discussed in Chapter 3.

In urban food policies and plans prepared by cities in the Global South, more
attention is often given to social inclusion, employment creation and income
generation for/by the urban poor through (intra- and peri-) urban agriculture,
providing access to urban markets for small-scale producers in the city region and
more recently the role of urban agriculture in city climate change mitigation and
adaptation strategies.

In urban food policies and plans formulated in the Global North, often the
focus has been on improving physical access to (healthy, nutritious) food, support
for community gardens, urban agriculture and farmers markets, and local food
linkages. More recently, strengthening the regional food production, processing
and distribution system is getting attention.

Many food policies or programmes do not contain measurable goals, which
makes it difficult to monitor to what extent the expected changes in the urban
food system are realized. Hodgson (2014) also observed this and recommended
to include aspirational goals (indicating the longer term perspective) and specific
measurable goals (to be attained in a certain period of time along the route indicated by the aspirational goals). There is a strong need for comparative evaluation
of the impacts of urban and city-region food policies, strategies, plans or programmes in order to get a better understanding of the effectiveness of the various
policy measures applied and results obtained in relation to the investments in such
programmes. Such information will be of great importance for the planning and
decision making on future food policies.

In many cities the ambitions of the food policy or strategy are not in balance with
the funding made available for implementation. Bock and Caraher (2014), reviewing

a number of European experiences, come to the conclusion that the activities implemented in the context of an urban food policy, plan or strategy are mainly rather small scale and dispersed and that these will not lead to structural system change. However, examples of more mature implementation of an urban food policy implementation suggest the potential for transformative reform (i.e., Belo Horizonte).

Many food policies and programmes and plans also face complex jurisdictional problems. Urban food planning requires alignment across various orders of government, as well as the involvement of various departments/disciplines and a range of civil society and private actors. There is a clear need for linked and supportive policy across orders of government and across government departments. The urban food system does not neatly coincide with the municipal area. Moreover, few municipalities will have the human and financial resources to analyse the food system, develop food policy and make significant investments without support and incentives from other orders of government and pioneering funders. This creates the need for food and agriculture planning beyond the municipal administrative boundaries (OECD 2013; Harrison and Hoyler 2014). National governments should support, encourage and incentivize municipal food policy development as a way of realizing their own policy goals and meeting international commitments related to a broad range of food systems issues.

Sharing of experiences across countries and continents should be enabled. Emerging international urban food policy and practice networks, such as the CityFood Network under development by ICLEI (Local Governments for Sustainability) and the RUAF Foundation, may provide essential avenues for sharing urban food policy experiences and could provide capacity building opportunities for municipal staff and officials (see www.ruaf.org/sites/default/files/CITYFOOD%20 brochure%20final.pdf).

References

Agenda Proeftuin Amsterdam. 2007. Agenda Proeftuin Amsterdam: Voor gezonde en duurzame voeding in stad en regio. Amsterdam: Dienst Ruimtelijke Ordening.

Allegheny County. 2008. Allegheny Places: The Allegheny County comprehensive plan. Pittsburgh. Available from: www.alleghenyplaces.com/comprehensive_plan/comprehensive_ plan.aspx.

Aubry, C.; Ramamonjisoa, J.; Dabat, M. H.; Rakotoarisoa, J.; Rakotondraibe, J.; Rabeharisoa, L. 2012. Urban agriculture and land use in cities: An approach with the multi-functionality and sustainability concepts in the case of Antananarivo (Madagascar). *Land Use Policy* 29: 429–43.

BCPC. 2013. Homegrown Baltimore: Grow local, buy local, eat local: Baltimore's city urban agriculture plan. Baltimore: Baltimore City Planning Commission (BCPC).

Blay-Palmer, A. 2009. The Canadian pioneer: The birth generics of urban food policy in Toronto. *Journal of International Planning Studies* 14(4): 401–416.

Bock, B.; Caraher, M. 2014. Integrating health, environment and society: Introducing a new arena. In: *Sustainable food planning: Evolving theory and practice.* (Eds.) Viljoen, A.; Wiskerke, J.S.C. Wageningen: Wageningen Academic Publishers, pp. 173–180.

Brand, L.; Schendelen, M. van; Vermeulen, P. 2010. Naar een metropolitane voedselstrategie: Proeftuin Amsterdam. Amsterdam: Dienst Ruimtelijke Ordening.

Brighton and Hove Food Partnership. 2012. Spade to spoon: Making the connection; a food strategy and action plan for Brighton and Hove. Available from: http://bhfood.org.uk/downloads/downloads-publications/20-spade-to-spoon-strategy-2012-interactive-pdf/fil.

Chicago Council on Global Affairs. 2013. Feeding an urban world: A call to action. Available from: www.thechicagocouncil.org/publication/feeding-urban-world-call-action.

City of Cape Town. 2007. Urban agriculture policy for the City of Cape Town. Available from: www.capetown.gov.za/en/ehd/Documents/EHD_-_Urban_Agricultural_Policy_2007_8102007113120_.pdf.

City of Cleveland. 2008. Re-imagining a more sustainable Cleveland: Citywide strategies for reuse of vacant land. Cleveland: Cleveland City Planning Commission and Neighborhood Progress, Inc. Available from: www.reconnectingamerica.org/assets/Uploads/20090303ReImaginingMoreSustainableCleveland.pdf.

City of Malmö. 2010. Policy for sustainable development and food. Malmö. Available from: http://malmo.se/download/18.d8bc6b31373089f7d9800018573/1383649558411/Foodpolicy_Malmo.pdf.

City of Sacramento. 2009. Sacramento 2030 General Plan. Sacramento. Available from: http://portal.cityofsacramento.org/Community-Development/Resources/Online-Library/General%20Plan.

City of Sacramento. 2014. Planned urban agriculture ordinance. Sacramento. Available from: http://portal.cityofsacramento.org/Community-Development/Planning/Long-Range/Urban-Agriculture.

City of Seattle. 2012. Seattle local food action plan. Seattle Office of Sustainability and Environment. Available from: www.seattle.gov/Documents/Departments/OSE/Seattle_Food_Action_Plan_10–24–12.pdf.

City of Toronto. 2014. Student Nutrition Program: Five-year plan status update and 2015 operating budget request. Available from: www.toronto.ca/legdocs/mmis/2014/hl/bgrd/backgroundfile-72514.pdf.

CMAP. 2010. GO to 2040 comprehensive regional plan, part 4: Promote sustainable local food. Chicago: Chicago Metropolitan Agency for Planning (MCAP). Available from: www.cmap.illinois.gov/documents/10180/18727/Local-Food_10–6–2010.pdf/2050e22d-57eb-40c4-8666-eeb4646a507d.

Crush, J.; Frayne, B. 2011. Urban food insecurity and the new international food security agenda. *Development Southern Africa* 28(4): 527–44.

Darly, S. 2012. Urban food procurement governance: A new playground for farm development networks in the peri-urban area of greater Paris region. In: *Sustainable food planning: Evolving theory and practice.* (Eds.) Viljoen, A.; Wiskerke, J.S.C. Wageningen: Wageningen Academic Publishers, pp. 115–126.

DC&LG. 2012. National planning policy framework. London: Department for Communities and Local Government. Available from: http://planningguidance.planningportal.gov.uk/wp-content/themes/planning-guidance/assets/NPPF.pdf.

Dubbeling, M. 2004. Optimization of use of vacant land for urban agriculture in the municipality of Rosario, Argentina. Paper presented at the workshop IDRC-Supported Initiatives on Urban Agriculture and Food Security, 26 August–3 September at Ryerson University, Toronto, Canada. Available from: www.ruaf.org/sites/default/files/econf4_casestudies_rosario_en.pdf.

Dubbeling, M. 2013. Urban and peri-urban agriculture as a means to advance disaster risk reduction and adaptation to climate change. *Regional Development Dialogue* 34(1): 139–149.

DVRPC. 2011. Eating here: Greater Philadelphia's food system plan. Philadelphia: Delaware Valley Regional Planning Commission.

FAO. 2012. Growing greener cities. Rome: Food and Agriculture Organization of the United Nations (FAO). Available from: www.fao.org/ag/agp/greenercities/en/whyuph/index.html.

Friedmann, H. 2011. Food sovereignty in the Golden Horseshoe Region of Ontario. In: *Food sovereignty in Canada: Creating just and sustainable food systems.* (Eds.) Wittman, H.; Desmarais A. A.; Wiebe, N. Winnipeg: Fernwood Publishing, pp. 169–189.

FWP. 2013. Detroit future city: 2012 Detroit strategic framework pan. Detroit: Food Works Project – Economic Growth Commission. Available from: www.DetroitFutureCity.com.

Harrison, J.; Hoyler, M. 2014. Governing the new metropolis. *Urban Studies* 51: 2249–2266.

Hatfield, M. M. 2012. City food policy and programmes: Lessons harvested from an emerging field. Portland: City of Portland–Bureau of Planning and Sustainability.

Hodgson, K. 2014. Planning for food access and community-based food systems: A national scan and evaluation of local comprehensive and sustainability plans. Washington, DC: American Planning Association.

Homem de Carvalho, J. L. 2005. PROVE – Small scale agricultural production verticalisation programme. In: *Cities farming for the future: Urban agriculture for green and productive cities.* (Ed.) Veenhuizen, R. van. Manila: IIRR; Leusden: RUAF Foundation. Available from: www.ruaf.org/publications/cities-farming-future-urban-agriculture-green-and-productive-cities.

IDRC. 2006a. Building the food secure city: Incremental progress brings about change in Dar es Salaam. Case study #1. In: *Cities, urban agriculture for sustainable development.* Ottawa: International Development Research Centre (IDRC). Available from: www.idrc.ca/EN/Documents/builing-the-food-secure-city.pdf.

IDRC. 2006b. From the ground up: Urban agriculture takes root in Kampala. Case study #2. In: *Cities, urban agriculture for sustainable development.* Ottawa: International Development Research Centre (IDRC). Available from: www.idrc.ca/EN/Documents/from-the-ground-up.pdf.

Jansma, J. E.; Wijnand, S.; Stilma, E.S.C.; Oost, A. C. van; Visser, A. J. 2014. The impact of local food procurement on food miles, fossil energy use and greenhouse gas emissions: The case of the Dutch city of Almere. In: *Sustainable food planning: Evolving theory and practice.* (Eds.) Viljoen, A.; Wiskerke, J.S.C. Wageningen: Wageningen Academic Publishers, 307–322.

Kfouri, C.; Mantovani, P.; Jeuland, M. 2009. Water reuse in the MNA Region: Constraints, experiences, and policy recommendations. In: *Water in the Arab world: Management perspectives and innovations.* (Eds.) Jaganathan, V. J.; Mohamed, A. S.; Kremer, A. Washington, DC: World Bank, pp. 447–477.

King County. 2011. King County Comprehensive Plan 2008 with 2010 update. Available from: file:///C:/Users/Henk.Henk-HP/Downloads/Cover_adopted10.pdf.

Lattuca, A.; Terrile, R.; Bracalenti, L.; Lagorio, L.; Ramos, G.; Moreira, F. 2005. Building food secure neighbourhoods in Rosario. *Urban Agriculture Magazine* 15: 23–24.

Leenaert, T. 2014. Meat moderation for government and civil society: The Thursday Veggie Day campaign in Ghent, Belgium. In: *Sustainable food planning: Evolving theory and practice.* (Eds.) Viljoen, A.; Wiskerke, J.S.C. Wageningen: Wageningen Academic Publishers, pp. 189–196.

London Assembly. 2010. Cultivating the capital: Food growing and planning system in London. London: Greater London Authority. Available from: http://legacy.london.gov.uk/assembly/reports/plansd/growing-food.pdf.

London Development Agency. 2006. Healthy and sustainable food for London. The Mayor's food strategy. London: London Development Agency.

Lovo, I. C.; Pereira Costa, Z. R. 2006. Making laws for urban agriculture: The experience of Governador Valadares, Brazil. *Urban Agriculture Magazine* 16: 45–47.

MacRae, R.; Donahue, K. 2013. Municipal food policy entrepreneurs: A preliminary analysis of how Canadian cities and regional districts are involved in food system change. Ottawa: Canadian Agri-Food Policy Institute (CAPI). Available from: http://tfpc.to/wordpress/wp-content/uploads/2013/05/Report-May30-FINAL.pdf.

MacRae, R. J.; Szabo, M.; Anderson, K.; Louden, F. N.; Trillo, S. 2011. Could Toronto provide 10% of its fresh vegetable requirements from within its own boundary? *Journal of Agriculture, Food Systems and Community Development* 2(2): 147–169.

Mah, C.; Baker, L. 2012. The Toronto Food Policy Council: Twenty years of citizen leadership for a healthy and sustainable food system. In: *CHIR's citizen engagement in health casebook*. Ottawa: Canadian Institutes of Health Research, pp. 79–82.

Manchester City Council 2007. Food Futures: A food strategy for Manchester. Manchester: Food Futures Partnership. Available from: www.foodfutures.info/www/images/stories/pdf/food-futures-strateg-2007.pdf.

MCCDA. 2007. Marin Countywide Plan. San Rafael: Marin County Community Development Agency. Available from: www.marincounty.org/~/media/files/departments/cd/planning/currentplanning/publications/county-wide-plan/countywideplan.pdf.

Minneapolis-DHFS 2009. Homegrown Minneapolis. Minneapolis: Department of Health and Family Support (DHFS). Available from: www.minneapolismn.gov/www/groups/public/@health/documents/webcontent/convert_273062.pdf.

Moragues, A.; Morgan, K.; Moschitz, H.; Neimane, I.; Nilsson, H.; Pinto, M.; Rohracher, H.; Ruiz, R.; Thuswald, M.; Tisenkopfs, T.; Halliday, J. 2013. Urban food strategies: The rough guide to sustainable food systems sustainable food systems. Document developed in the framework of the FP7 project FOODLINKS (GA No. 265287).

Morgan, K.; Sonnino, R. 2010. The urban foodscape: World cities and the new food equation. *Cambridge Journal of Regions, Economy and Society* 3(2): 209–224.

Mubvami, T.; Toriro, P. 2008. Water supply and urban agriculture in Bulawayo. *Urban Agriculture Magazine* 20: 31–32.

OECD. 2013. Rural-Urban Partnerships: An integrated approach to economic development. OECD rural policy reviews. Paris: OECD publishing. DOI:10.1787/9789264204812-en.

Oorschot, K. van. 2014. Urban agriculture: Sustainable economic development of the city and its region. Presentation, Municipality of Rotterdam, March 26th 2014. Available from: www.innoviris.be/fr/documents/food-the-city_rotterdam.

Plantinga, S.; Derksen, P. 2014. How food travels to the public agenda. In: *Sustainable food planning: Evolving theory and practice*. (Eds.) Viljoen, A.; Wiskerke, J.S.C. Wageningen: Wageningen Academic Publishers, pp. 79–90.

Portland Council. 2012. The Portland Plan. Portland. Available from: www.portlandonline.com/portlandplan/index.cfm?c=58776&a=405753.

Pothukuchi, K. 2005. Attracting supermarkets to inner-city neighbourhoods. *Economic Development Quarterly* 19(2): 232–244.

Reid, D.; Pedneault, A. 2006. Montreal's community gardening programme. Montreal: City of Montreal. Available from: www.montreal.qc.ca.

Reynolds, B. 2009. Feeding a world city: The London food strategy. *International Journal of Planning Studies* 14(4): 417–424.

Roberts, W. 2014. Food for city building: A field guide for planners, actionists and entrepreneurs. Toronto: Hypenotic.

Rocha, C. 2001. Urban food security policy: The case of Belo Horizonte. *Brazilian Journal for the Study of Food and Society* 5(1): 36–47.

Rocha, C.; Lessa, I. 2009. Urban governance for food security: The alternative. *International Planning Studies* 14(4): 389–400.

Steel, C. 2008. Hungry city: How food shapes our lives. London: Random House.

Thomas, G. (ed.) 2014. Growing greener cities in Latin America and the Caribbean: A FAO report on urban and peri-urban agriculture in the region. Rome: Food and Agriculture Organization of the United Nations (FAO). Available from: www.fao.org/ag/agp/greenercities/en/GGCLAC.

Toronto Food Policy Council. 2012. GrowTO: An urban agriculture action plan for Toronto. Toronto: Toronto Food Policy Council.

Tower Hamlets. 2012. Tackling the take-aways: A new policy to address fast food outlets in Tower Hamlets, London. Tower Hamlets: Tower Hamlets Healthy Spatial Planning Project.

Vermeulen, P. 2008. Amsterdam Food Strategy the Netherlands: Urban-rural linkages enhancing European territorial competitiveness: Mini case-study on food chains. Bonn: ICLEI Europe. Available from: http://ec.europa.eu/regional_policy/archive/conferences/urban_rural/2008/doc/pdf/6a_iclei_amsterdam.pdf.

Viljoen, A.; Wiskerke, J.S.C. (eds.) 2012. Sustainable food planning: Evolving theory and practice. Wageningen: Wageningen Academic Publishers.

Wolfe, J.M.; McCans, S. 2009. Designing for urban agriculture in an African City. *Open House International* 34(2): 25–35.

World Future Council. 2013. Sharing the experience of the food security system of Belo Horizonte. Available from: www.fao.org/fileadmin/templates/FCIT/Meetings/Africites/presentations/WorldFutureCouncil_experience-Belo-Horizonte.pdf.

Zeeuw, H. de; Dubbeling, M.; Veenhuizen, R. van; Wilbers, J. 2007. Key issues and courses of action for municipal policy making on urban agriculture. Leusden: RUAF Foundation. Available from: www.ruaf.org/publications/key-issues-and-courses-action-municipal-policy-making-urban-agriculture.

3

PROCESS AND TOOLS FOR MULTI-STAKEHOLDER PLANNING OF THE URBAN AGRO-FOOD SYSTEM

Henk de Zeeuw and Marielle Dubbeling

RUAF FOUNDATION, THE NETHERLANDS

Introduction

The foregoing chapter focused on the policies and programmes certain cities apply in order to strengthen the agro-food system in their city region. In this chapter we will discuss the experiences gained regarding the *process* of multi-stakeholder planning of the agro-food system in a community, city or city region in countries of the global North or South and *tools* that may be used in that process.

Our point of departure will be the experiences gained in the "Cities Farming for the Future" (CFF) and "From Seed to Table (FStT)" programmes implemented by the RUAF Foundation in close cooperation with international, regional and local partners in 20 cities in 17 developing countries during the years 2004–2011 (Dubbeling et al. 2010; Dubbeling et al. 2011; Amerasinghe et al. 2013) and the experiences gained in a large number of cities in the USA/Canada and Europe as summarized in a number of recent international publications (including Harper 2009; Freedgood et al. 2011; White and Natelson 2011; Viljoen and Wiskerke 2012; MacRae and Donahue 2013; Moragues et al. 2013).

Before discussing the various phases in the process of multi-stakeholder planning of the urban agro-food system and assessment and planning tools that may be applied in that process, some general considerations have to be made:

City-region agro-food system

The UN Food and Agriculture Organization (FAO) and partners defined at the World Urban Forum "City-region food systems" as follows: "the complex relation of actors, relations and processes related to food production, processing, marketing, and consumption, and related wastes and nutrient management and support services (technical assistance, credit, quality control) in a given geographical region that includes one main or several smaller urban centres and surrounding peri-urban and rural areas that exchange people, goods and services across the urban rural continuum" (FAO 2014).

Although in the literature it has become widespread to speak of the urban or city-region "food system," we prefer the term "*agro*-food system" to indicate that the planning does not relate to food alone. Most urban food planning exercises in Western countries initially focused mainly on enhancing the food security of the urban population especially by improving access of the urban poor to (healthy) food and later also by enhancing food production in the city region (Harper 2009; Freegood et al. 2011). But in recent years such exercises are also undertaken to enhance the resilience of the urban region against the impacts of climate change, reduce food-related greenhouse gas (GHG) emissions, reclaim nutrients and irrigation water from urban wastes and wastewater, stimulate the regional economy and support local farmers also by broadening to non-agro services: e.g., recreational and eco-services they supply (see Chapter 1 by Wiskerke; Morgan, 2009). That is the reason why we prefer to use "agro-food system" (with multiple functions) rather than "food system."

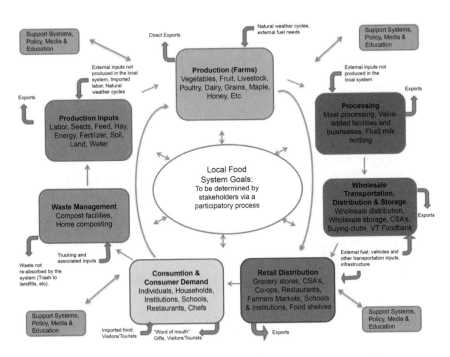

FIGURE 3.1 A model of the city-region food system

Source: Koliba et al. 2011; figure reprinted with permission of the Center for Rural Studies, University of Vermont.

Multi-stakeholder planning

Multi-stakeholder planning approaches are characterized by the following (Dubbeling and de Zeeuw 2007):

- The participation of various stakeholders in the agro-food system in the city region including local government authorities, civil society actors and private enterprises.
- In a transparent and open strategic planning process: situation analysis/problem diagnosis, formulation of vision and objectives, identification of development strategies, etc.
- In these, the final (political) decisions take honour – to the greatest extent possible – of the contributions of all participants.

In, especially, the case of the urban agro-food system, it is highly recommended to apply a multi-stakeholder approach (by now a common practice in several countries): the agro-food system is complex in itself and links with so many sectors (including urban development and spatial planning, health, social development, local economic development, environmental management) it is only by involving the various stakeholders directly in the planning process that a sustainable result may be obtained.

Multi-stakeholder planning has a number of advantages/benefits as compared to more conventional approaches (Hemmati 2002; Dubbeling et al. 2010; Amerasinghe 2013):

- Contributes to more participatory governance and public–private partnerships.
- Allows better situation analysis and quality of decision making through a better understanding of (the complex relations between) the various components of the urban agro-food system by linking the knowledge and views of the various actors who have a stake in that system.
- Enhances the likelihood of implementation success and sustainability through improved coordination, mobilization of scarce human, technical and financial resources, and enhanced acceptance and ownership of the resulting strategic plan or policies.
- Improves the problem solving and innovation capacity of the participating actors.

But it has also a number of disadvantages/costs (Dubbeling and de Zeeuw 2007):

- It often takes more time.
- It adds complexity to the planning process and is more difficult to manage/facilitate.
- In certain cases it may not lead to satisfactory results due to this complexity, difficulties to overcome tensions between contrasting views/interests and problems to arrive at a joint vision at the desired development of the agro-food system in the city region.

Policy vs action; top-down vs bottom-up; mainstream vs alternative

Agro-food system planning in a city region has a number of built-in tensions that the organizers have to deal with:

Top-down versus bottom-up

In some cities the planning process is led by the local or regional government and their departments and/or researchers hired and controlled by them. In this case the risk is high that certain stakeholders in the regional agro-food system do not see their problems and potentials taken into account and do not develop a sense of ownership and thus the social acceptability of the resulting agro-food plan and the active participation of the various stakeholders in the realization thereof will be low.

In other cities the initiative for the agro-food planning process was taken by civil society actors; participation of local/regional government in the exercise in these processes might be low (e.g., at technical level only). In this case, the risks are high that the results of the planning process are not sufficiently incorporated by local/regional government in the local policies, laws, budgets and programmes, which will limit the impact of the agro-food plan.

MacRae and Donahue (2013), when reviewing municipal food policy initiatives in Canada, observe that the hybrid organizational model with direct participation of civil society organizations *and* local government departments and created with formal municipal endorsement have better results (effectivity and continuity) due to the blending of local government interests, expertise, procedures and the interests and expertise of private and civil society actors, better access to financing and supportive staff during diagnosis and planning (allowing a more systemic and integrative approach) as well as for the implementation.

Policy framework versus direct actions

A dilemma closely related to the former is whether the emphasis in the planning process should be on identification and implementation of actions to tackle certain key problems and that can be implemented in the short term and within the actual institutional and financial conditions, or whether the emphasis should be on the development of a longer-term strategy to transform the agro-food system in the city region that may require new policies, new laws and regulations, new institutional arrangements and acquisition of additional resources, and thus take more time to result in concrete actions.

In the practice of the RUAF-CFF programme we learned that the emphasis should be on strategic mid-term planning and careful embedding of the strategic agro-food plan in the actual policies, budgets and programmes *combined with* early implementation of priority actions at the local level while the diagnosis and strategic planning process is still ongoing (Dubbeling et al. 2011). Also Scherb et al. (2012), when reviewing local food planning initiatives in the USA, conclude that successful food policy initiatives (surviving for three years or longer) had undertaken early actions that provided a solution to a pressing problem that might not have been addressed otherwise.

Mainstream versus alternative

Also closely related is the potential conflict of interest between certain stakeholders, e.g., between those that defend vested interests in the urban agro-food system and actors that want to transform that system and seek to reduce the power of certain dominant actors in the food system, or seek to force them to accept new norms and adapt their practices, or that are building up "alternative" food chains and undermine the market position of the dominant actors.

The basic principle of multi-stakeholder planning is that the various stakeholders in the agro-food system enter into exchange and dialogue, develop a better understanding of each other's viewpoints, practices and needs, and identify joint strategies to strengthen the local agro-food system. However, in practice it may be difficult to make the voice of the less-powerful stakeholders heard, to harmonize the various viewpoints and to come to a shared view on the policies to be applied. Those who manage the multi-stakeholder planning process should be aware of the differences in policy influencing and market power of the various stakeholders in the food system, detect potential conflict areas and have the ability to manage (potential) conflicts. Multi-stakeholder planning is often (also) a negotiating process between the various actors and it is an advantage when the facilitators of the process understand that and have experience in managing such a negotiating process.

In our view it is important to keep both "mainstream" actors, "informal" and "alternative" food chain actors involved in the planning process. The resulting plan to strengthen the urban agro-food system might contain measures to adapt and improve the mainstream food chains (e.g., reduce the ecological footprint of the local food system, improve access to food by the urban poor, enhance product nutritive quality) as well as to support the development and sustainability (especially economic) of "alternative" producers-to-consumers local food chains and link mainstream and alternative systems whenever possible and meaningful.

MacRae and Donahue (2013) observe that in Canada conventional mainstream food chain actors (e.g., food processing firms, larger traders, supermarket chains, agricultural input providers) are far under-represented in most food policy councils and other local/city-region food-planning initiatives, which may result in a low impact of the local/regional food-planning efforts on changing the local/regional food system.

The process of planning the local or city-region food system

Introduction

Non-linear process; flexible work planning/approach

Although the planning process is described below in a linear stepwise way, in practice the process will be (and even must be) more "chaotic," with certain steps advancing already while earlier steps are still developing, will need to repeat certain activities from earlier steps during later steps (e.g., awareness-raising, collecting additional data, sharing viewpoints on the desired development of the agro-food system, etc.) or change the order of certain steps (e.g., the moment to create the broader forum for dialogue and joint planning). There are many (hampering and facilitating) factors that influence the planning process and that cannot be known in advance. Therefore, it is important that the organizers of the planning process periodically adapt their work planning and approach in order to adapt to emerging new insights/demands and changing conditions during the process.

Adaptation to local conditions and priorities

Although we will describe below the planning process in the form of "a best practice," a main lesson learned in the RUAF-CFF programme and in other urban agro-food planning initiatives is that no two cities are alike and in each city region those who lead the planning process have to develop their own approach that fits best local conditions, needs and political priorities.

TABLE 3.1 Overview of the multi-stakeholder agro-food planning process

	Phase	Main actions
1	Getting started	The initiative
		Stakeholder inventory; raising awareness
		Inter-institutional cooperation agreement; establishment of working group
2	Assessment of the current agro-food system in the city region	The vertical dimension
		The horizontal dimension
		The policy and institutional dimension
3	Multi-stakeholder dialogue and strategic planning	Stakeholder consultations
		Establishment of a Multi-stakeholder Forum on Urban Food and Agriculture
		Identification of key issues (problems and potentials) to be attended
		Joint visioning; objective setting
		Identification of policies to be applied to transform the agro-food system in the city region
		Drafting the strategic agro-food plan

(Continued)

TABLE 3.1 (Continued)

Phase		Main actions
4	Formalization, operationalization and institutionalization of the proposed food and agriculture policies	Formalization of the strategic plan Operationalization Creating an institutional home for urban food and agriculture
5	Implementation, monitoring and renewal of the strategic agro-food plan in the city region	Implementation; monitoring progress and impacts; renewal of the strategic plan (start at 1)

Source: authors.

Phase 1: Getting started

The initiative

The initiative for the urban food planning process may be taken by civil society actors, commercial actors in the food chains or a local or regional governmental organization. It is important that those who take the initiative have a good capacity to establish linkages with a variety of stakeholders in the agro-food system and to cross existing gaps and barriers between those stakeholders, especially between government-civil society actors and private commercial actors, and the capacity to initiate and facilitate a multi-stakeholder strategic action planning process (Amerasinghe et al. 2013).

Stakeholder inventory; raising awareness

A good starting point is to make a quick review of the main actors involved in each of the components of the food system in the city region (production/farmer types, transport/storage, processing, distribution, consumer categories, and support services).

Such an inventory normally involves telephone calls and visits to the various institutions and organizations, a review of recent publications (research and project reports, articles in the local media) and chamber of commerce registry, in order to identify the policy and public actors, businesses and civil society organizations that should be approached in order to motivate them to participate in the intended process of joint planning and realization of the necessary changes in the food system. When making this inventory also try to find out what may facilitate or hamper the engagement of certain categories of actors in the planning process so that such barriers may be taken into account when planning the next steps in the process.

Once the main stakeholders have been identified, a series of actions have to be organized to enhance the awareness of the stakeholders of the importance of building a resilient and equitable food system in the city region and to obtain their active participation. Various strategies may be applied: visits to key persons in the various institutions and organizations, or preparation and distribution of short memos on some key issues in the local food system to local decision makers, journalists, networks of local retailers, agro-businesses and farmers, consumer organizations and other civil society organizations. Also organizing public debates in face-to-face seminars and/or electronic discussion platforms, food festivals, awards for innovative ideas for food activities, visits to other cities or local successful initiatives, and other events rousing interest and debate are helpful to raise interest and involvement.

Establishing an inter-institutional cooperation agreement and working group

Once the key actors in shaping the regional agro-food system have been identified and motivated to participate, these actors are brought together in order to agree to undertake a process of joint analysis, action planning and implementation to transform the local food system.

In RUAF's experience, it was important for a successful start of the planning process that:

- A working group is established comprising a core group of committed key actors including minimally one or more municipal departments (e.g., city planning, health, parks/agriculture, . . .), one or more local universities, one or more non-government organizations (NGOs) or other civil society organization active in the field of urban food and agriculture, and representatives of main food-chain actors: urban farmers, organizations of local retailers and agro-businesses, and consumers groups.
- The partners in the core group sign a formal cooperation agreement. The agreement makes the cooperation less informal, clarifies the intended contributions by each of the partners to the joint process (e.g., provision of staff time, transport, office space, supply of data and research support) and the arrangements for work planning, coordination and progress monitoring) during the first stages of the process. Formalizing agreements to work together through carefully structured work plans stimulates concrete results, and generally results in a good buy-in from the stakeholders. However, compliance may, in part, be jeopardized, for example, due to rapid staff turnover or conflicts with government directives (Amerasinghe et al. 2013).
- The chair of the core group is occupied by a person with strong organizational and facilitation skills and made available by an organization with sufficient

invitation and coordination power, in most cases the mayor's office, the city planning department or a municipal department that was given a coordinating role in this field.

- The strategic planning is organized as an interchange of preparations by the working group (where the work might be divided between several task groups) and consultations of the various stakeholders and regular meetings of the Multi-stakeholder Forum (see below) to discuss proposals and arrive at conclusions.

- There is an application of a systematic, stepwise approach, maintaining sufficient intensity and speed of the process and to further build up institutional commitments during the process. In each phase of the process a matrix may be used to provide all partners with an overview of all activities agreed upon, the agreed timeline for implementation, the expected outputs, the responsible actor(s) and related commitment of resources, and to enable joint monitoring of the realization of the commitments.

- Concrete development actions are implemented during the planning process with means available in the participating organizations. Early implementation of activities on the ground with high visibility of tangible results is very important to maintain the motivation and active participation of urban farmers, community groups and other civil society actors during the often lengthy process of assessment, planning and formal approval of the strategic plan, and acquiring the required resources for its implementation. Experiences gained in these small projects were reported to the Multi-stakeholder Forum (see below) to stimulate inter-institutional learning among the participating organizations and presented in the media to gain wider public support and stimulate similar actions by other local actors.

Phase 2. Assessment of the current agro-food system in the city region

Transforming the urban agro-food system should start with a thorough assessment of the agro-food system in the city region and ongoing trends. The assessment will provide appropriate information to the various stakeholders to enter into dialogue, facilitate joint goal setting and strategic action planning and establish baseline data and indicators for monitoring and evaluation.

Assessments of the agro-food system are undertaken in various ways (e.g., rapid mainly qualitative appraisal versus more systematic data gathering including statistically representative quantitative data), using a variety of methods (e.g., review of available research data and available statistics, GIS [Geographic Information Systems] mapping, key informants, focus group interviews, community food mapping, *sondeos* [short focused surveys], and more extensive surveys; see also the next paragraph on tools) and with varying focus (e.g., focusing on food security of the urban poor and disadvantaged groups, or just on the environmental sustainability of the local agro-food system) and width (narrower or more comprehensive/ systemic).

FIGURE 3.2 Cover of the Bristol food system assessment
Source: Bristol City Council.

According to Moragues et al. (2013), the assessment should be methodologi-
cally rigorous, consult a variety of stakeholders and look at a diversity of food
system issues, considering vertical (stages of the food chains), horizontal (action
fields) and institutional dimensions of the agro-food system. They listed the following elements that may be included in the assessment (which we further elaborated based on the experiences gained in RUAF programmes):

Assessing the vertical dimension of the food agro-system

This refers to the collection of data and the application of a SWOT (Strengths,
Weaknesses, Opportunities, Threats) analysis on each main component of the
regional food system (using economical, ecological, food security/nutrition/health
and sociocultural lenses):

- **Food production:** What food is produced in the city region, by whom, where
  and under what working conditions, and using which production techniques?
  What types of inputs are used and by whom are these produced and delivered?
  Which are the main types of producers in the city region, their characteristics,
  the main constraints encountered by each type of producers, their potential for
  development and related support needs? Where is agricultural land use threatened by city extension? Where is suitable space available in the city, with which

agro-ecological characteristics, and what obstacles hamper their use for food production? How do the different types of producers market their products? What innovative marketing initiatives exist in the city region? What are the main critical issues related to food production and marketing for the development of a sustainable agro-food system in the city region? What per cent of urban food consumption (of total nutrients/calories consumed and for specific food groups) is actually covered by production in the city region? What are the main current food deficiencies? What could be potentially grown locally, e.g., to replace products with high food miles and enhance urban food resilience?

- *Processing:* Which processing companies and other food processors (e.g., informal) operate in the city region? How do their input and output relate to the local economy and society? What is the nutritive quality of their products? What are the related GHG emissions? What are the new initiatives by existing companies and other actors? What are the main constraints encountered by the various types of food processors and what is the development potential of each type in the city region and related support needs? What are the main critical issues related to food processing for the development of a sustainable agro-food system in the city region?

- *Distribution and storage:* How is food distribution organized in the city region: the retail and other food distribution structures (conventional, alternative, informal); location of food distribution points (food hubs, open markets, supermarkets, small retail shops, street/mobile vending, etc.)? Where do the main access problems occur (especially of poor and vulnerable people to fresh and nutritious food) and what are the main causing factors? What is the actual role and importance of short food supply chains within the agro-food system in the city region?

- *Consumption:* Who is consuming what kinds of food, in what context and in what amounts? How is the affordability of food for various socioeconomic classes? Which groups are already at risk of food insecurity and where are they located? What is the impact of actual food consumption habits and trends on health-related issues, such as obesity? What is the effectivity of actual food and nutrition programmes?

- *Wastes/nutrients management:* What are the sources and volumes of urban organic wastes and wastewater and their actual disposal/recycling routes? What are the food wastes, energy use and GHG emissions in all components of the current agro-food system? What are the main options and constraints for resource recovery and productive reuse of organic wastes and wastewater (and related nutrients) and reduction of food wastes in various parts of the agro-food system?

Assessing the horizontal dimension of the agro-food system

This refers to bringing the results of the analysis of the various elements of the food system (the vertical dimension) together around certain areas of concern and themes related to the objectives of such a policy or strategy. In other words: the desired changes in the local agro-food system one wants to realize:

- **Public health:** Critical health issues related to the actual agro-food system; food safety regulating bodies and laws, labelling practices; presence or lack of promotion and support of healthy lifestyles and nutrition; and assessment and management of health risks associated with urban agriculture.
- **Social justice/food security:** Access to healthy food/main food-insecure and vulnerable households, flaws in actual retail system (e.g., underserved categories of the population and/or areas of the city); presence or lack of assistance measures for food-insecure and vulnerable households; role of urban agriculture in urban poverty alleviation, social inclusion and neighbourhood renovation and in enhancing the resilience of the urban food system.
- **Environment:** Food miles; GHG emissions related to food production, processing, packaging, distribution, and waste management practices; actual and potential GHG reduction through short(ening) supply chains; contributions of local agriculture to disaster prevention, urban climate management (heat, dust, storm water management, CO_2); actual and potential productive reuse of urban wastes and wastewater in urban agriculture.
- **Economic:** Impact on the regional economy and local livelihoods (income and jobs) implicated in all stages of the urban agro-food system; emergence of new business models in the area of local food economies.
- **Sociocultural:** Food-related social and cultural meanings, diversity of foods and cuisines consumed in the city region, food preferences of immigrants and minority groups, valorization of traditional foods and practices including local breeds, varieties and farming systems.

As indicated earlier, the planning process might be more comprehensive/systemic or focused on one or two of the above-mentioned elements (e.g., on the food security/health/social inclusion elements, or on the environmental/resilience element). This means that when preparing the assessment of the local or regional agro-food system, one already has to make conscious choices regarding the main objectives of the diagnosis and the – to be formulated – urban food plan or strategy. A more comprehensive assessment is preferable since the various elements are strongly interlinked and understanding the food system in a systemic way helps to arrive at effective intervention strategies. However, this will also be more complex, time-consuming and costly.

In cities where the awareness of the importance of the urban agro-food system is still rather low, or where available means for the assessment are rather low, in RUAF's experience it is recommendable to focus the diagnosis initially on those elements of the system that actually attract most attention from the policy makers and that seem to mobilize the stakeholders best. In most cases, during the process (or later, when preparing an update of the plan) the interest in other elements of the agro-food system will grow and new resources may become available to broaden/deepen the assessment.

Assessing the policy and institutional dimension of the agro-food system in the city region

This refers to a further exploration of the policy and institutional context:

- *Policies, instruments and programmes* at city, regional and national levels that influence the agro-food system in the city region (agricultural policies, health regulations, land use norms and zoning, environmental policies, city development plans, poverty alleviation strategies, food security schemes, nutrition education and food supply programmes, economic development and marketing policies, etc.).
- *Institutions:* Mandates and values that influence their views on urban food and agriculture and their related actions and regulations; community and civic values related to food system functioning and management; relevant bodies implicated in agro-food system policy and management. Current integration of agro-food system issues in municipal programmes, plans and budgets.
- *Participation structures:* Approaches and norms that encourage or limit stakeholder participation; existing and potential opportunities for civil society to participate in defining, planning and implementing food policies and interventions; existing levels of participation by various stakeholders; measures taken to ensure involvement of various stakeholders.
- *Knowledge, learning and empowerment opportunities and practices* that might be valorized and developed further (e.g., ongoing food community projects; sustainable production and processing pioneers and innovators; short chain initiatives; good food ambassadors; and sustainable and healthy food consumption educational programmes).

It is crucial that the core group develops a clear work plan for the assessment, indicating clearly what kinds of information will be collected and how, what will be the role and contributions of each of the partners in the core group and other actors to be involved, and what are the timeline and coordination mechanisms. In RUAF's experience best results are obtained when one organization experienced in this field (e.g., a local university or research institute) is assigned to coordinate the assessment, with clear supporting roles of each of the partners regarding specific sets of data/themes/research or support activities like provision of staff, transport or funding (Dubbeling et al. 2011). Needless to say, sufficient financial means need to be secured timely for the realization of the assessment according to plan. Especially when larger amounts are needed to assign a substantial part of the assessment to a university or consultancy organization, acquiring these funds (from the municipality and/or other sources) may be a lengthy process, which needs to be started early and pursued with sufficient energy and mobilization of support.

In a later section of this chapter we will discuss a number of assessment methods (each with a different focus) that may be applied in assessments of the agro-food system at local or city regional level.

FIGURE 3.3 RUAF-CFF city teams preparing for the planning process
Source: RUAF Foundation.

Phase 3. Multi-stakeholder dialogue and strategic planning

Stakeholder consultations

The various actors that shape the agro-food system in the city region have different positions and interests. It is important to clarify and understand the differences in motivations, interests and goals of the various categories of stakeholders in the city agro-food system and related views on the actual problems and visions on the desired development of the agro-food system in an early stage of the joint planning process. Some stakeholders are well organized and have well-established linkages with policy circles and can influence the political decision making in the city, while others are hardly organized (e.g., small farmers and gardeners in the city region, concerned consumer groups, urban poor and disadvantaged) and their voice may be rarely heard at policy levels.

The interests and views of the stronger stakeholders may be obtained through interviews with senior staff in the various institutions and organizations as well as by analysis of their reports and statements in the media. It is of value to collect information on their institutional mandate and priorities; past, ongoing and planned activities in the field of urban food and agriculture; available resources for such activities, their linkages with other key actors, their views on the actual situation and the desired changes in the actual agro-food system and what should be done to realize these changes.

The views of the weaker stakeholder categories can be obtained through consultations/focus group interviews (often as part of the assessment of the agro-food system) with one or a few groups of people considered representative for this stakeholder category (e.g., different types of local farmers and gardeners, consumers, retailers) seeking to understand their present position in the agro-food system, problems encountered, their views on how these problems could be resolved and the direction to which the agro-food should be transformed.

Although presented here as a separate "step" in the process, in practice these consultations will be organized mainly together with, and as part of, the assessment of the local agro-food system. These consultations also have an important role in (further) raising the awareness and involvement of the various stakeholders. Where practically possible and scientifically sound, the involvement of stakeholders in the data-gathering process may go beyond consultations, e.g., involvement of community organizations in mapping the retail system and food insecurity/vulnerability in their neighbourhood, or the involvement of local agro-industry in collecting data on the water, energy and inputs use in their processing activities and related GHG emissions. In other cases, such direct involvement will be minimal (e.g., mapping actual agricultural land use and available open spaces in the city with the help of GIS by a municipal department).

Establishment of a multi-stakeholder forum on urban food and agriculture

Once the local stakeholders show a strong interest to engage in a joint planning process and the basic information is on the table, the time is ripe to establish a Multi-stakeholder Forum on Food and Agriculture in the city region or a Municipal (or City-region) Food Policy Council or similar platform where the various stakeholders can meet, engage in dialogue and joint planning with other stakeholders in the urban agro-food system and, in a later stage, coordinate the implementation and monitoring of concerted policies to transform the agro-food system in the city region and stimulate their institutionalization (e.g., inclusion in municipal and institutional policies, budgets, establishment of a coordinating urban agricultural office or department, etc.).

In the RUAF-CFF programme the composition of the Multi-stakeholder Forum varied from city to city. In most cases, the partners in the core team were complemented by representatives of 15 to 50 other organizations (farmers groups, community organizations, NGOs, agro-enterprises, food retailers, educational centres, health programmes, media, etc.).

Special efforts may have to be taken to engage informal and less-organized stakeholder groups, as, for example, the many small-scale producers in and around cities in developing countries. It may take time to build relationships of trust and find effective ways to include their voice in the Multi-stakeholder Forum.

In developing countries, to obtain the active involvement of certain stakeholders (especially governmental organizations) often requires not only the official commitment to engage in the process but also some incentives for the persons who represent their organization like remuneration, training or travel opportunities (Amerasinghe et al. 2013).

In the RUAF-CFF experience it turned out to be of great importance that the Multi-stakeholder Forum has close links with local government, is recognized as the main advisory body in the field of urban food and agricultural issues and that municipal departments participate in and support the Forum. The Forum, however, should have an independent position and should not be dominated by local political parties or depend on municipal funding only. The Multi-stakeholder Forum should also develop strategies that enable to continue functioning after elections and related changes in political priorities.

Discussion of the draft report on the situation analysis; identification of key issues (problems and potentials) to be attended

In order to initiate and feed the dialogue in the Multi-stakeholder Forum, the results of the assessment of the actual agro-food system have to be made available to all stakeholders in a concise and clear way. The report should present key facts and trends on the urban food and agriculture situation, the views of the various stakeholders on the actual situation and the remedial or development actions proposed by them.

In the RUAF-CFF programme this discussion document was distributed to councillors, senior staff of several city departments, NGOs, universities, farmer groups, local agro-food businesses and other relevant local actors identified in the stakeholder analysis in order to enhance their understanding of the present situation of the agro-food system and its effects on urban food security and social inclusion, local economy and the urban environment, and in the preparation of the dialogue with other stakeholders about this situation.

The core group will prepare the draft report and present it for discussion in the Multi-stakeholder Forum. The main elements of the assessment presented above can be used as the structure for this presentation and related discussions.

In this step and the following ones, there is an interchange between the preparatory and follow-up activities by the core group and the sharing, dialogue and decision making in the Multi-stakeholder Forum meetings.

All members of the Forum are informed before the Forum meeting about the preparatory activities implemented by the core group and the issues to be discussed in the Platform, allowing them to consult their peers before the meeting if desired. Also important is to inform all members on the results of the Forum meeting and the follow-up given by the core group.

Joint visioning; objective setting

The discussions on the actual situation and related key issues will be followed by the development of a joint vision on the desired development of the agro-food system in the city region: How should the agro-food system in the city region look like in five or ten years from now? What role(s) should it fulfil in sustainable and equitable city development? What changes in the actual agro-food system in the city region would that imply? Which indicators should we use to measure such changes and what is our aspiration level for each indicator (e.g., reduction in the number of food-insecure households and/or obese people in the city; reduction in GHG emissions or food miles related to urban food consumption; increase in per cent of urban organic wastes and wastewater that are reused in agriculture in the city region or reduction in the amount of urban organic wastes that end up in the landfill; number of farmers in the city region that apply ecological farming practices, etc.)?

This is a very crucial phase in the strategic planning process and sufficient time should be taken to arrive at a coherent joint vision on the desirable development of the agro-food system in the city region and seeking win–win solutions to existing conflicts of interests. Assistance of an experienced facilitator of negotiations might be needed. The development of the vision and associated goals constitute a negotiation and learning process: actors have different interests but the process also allows the different actors to learn from each other's knowledge and experience, building a common cause. Different knowledge brokerage activities and facilitation techniques can be applied that help in advancing the process of joint vision building and related goal setting.

It is often debated what comes first: the assessment of the actual situation of the agro-food system or the joint vision building and objective setting in the Multi-stakeholder Forum. In RUAF's experience, the vision building should build on a well-informed dialogue on the problems (and assets/potentials) in the actual situation. That is why we prefer that the assessment is implemented first (the core group could select some preliminary broad objectives to focus the assessment).

Eventually, after the joint vision and development objectives have been defined by the Multi-stakeholder Forum, some additional data-gathering might be needed to fill some information gaps identified during that process.

Identification of policies to be applied to transform the agro-food system in the city region

For each of the key issues identified, the policies are selected that may be applied to realize the required changes regarding this issue. The joint vision and related objectives will orient the identification of alternative policies. Each of the alternative policies identified will be jointly analyzed, especially the related costs/benefits (how effective and efficient is this policy in realizing the desired changes?) and the applicability of this policy (how likely is it that we will have the means and tools to apply this policy with success? Will policy circles and stakeholders support this strategy sufficiently?). Evaluation of the alternative policies will lead to selection of the preferred policies to tackle the key issues and bring about the desired changes in the agro-food system. An overview of policies that are frequently applied in city agriculture and food policies is provided in Chapter 2 of this book.

Drafting the strategic agro-food plan

The selected policies will be included in a (draft) city food and agriculture strategy or plan that should preferably include:

- A concise description of the actual situation of the agro-food system in the city region, its main elements and actors and the key issues identified (problems, potentials; threads, opportunities).
- The joint vision on the desired transformation of the agro-food system and the changes to be realized and related indicators and time horizons.
- The policies to be undertaken to tackle each of the main issues identified and realize the desired changes indicated by the joint vision, including:

FIGURE 3.4 Cover of the Seattle Food Action Plan

Source: Neighborhood Farmers Market Alliance.

- The actions to be implemented under each policy included in the plan and related implementation targets, the priority of each of these actions and the ease of implementation of each action.
- The main actors that will/should be involved in the implementation of each of the strategies.
- The resources required for each of the strategies, the resources that can be contributed by the implementing partners themselves and potential sources of additional resources.
- Proposals regarding the institutional arrangements needed for the implementation of the strategic plan.

Phase 4. Formalization, operationalization and institutionalization of the proposed food and agriculture policies

Once the strategic plan for the transformation of the agro-food system in the city region has been finalized by the Multi-stakeholder Forum, a process starts to get this strategic plan accepted by the local policy makers and included in municipal and/or regional policies and laws, in city spatial and development plans, in the municipal budget and in the budgets and programmes of relevant institutions and organizations. However, to be successful this process of linking up with and influencing decision makers should start right from the very beginning (during stakeholder identification and awareness raising) and is continued throughout the diagnosis and planning stages, but is intensified and is the main challenge during this stage.

In this process, actions like the following may be helpful:

- **Preparation of a policy brief** that briefly describes the actual situation of the agro-food system in the city region and the reasons why the urban food system should be transformed, the vision of the multi-stakeholder forum on the desired changes and a summary of the proposed policies to realize these changes.
- **Organization of a policy seminar** for councillors and their advisors/senior local government officers, where the strategic plan is presented and discussed.
- **Presentation of the food and agriculture strategic plan to the most relevant council committee** for discussion and approval (eventually after making changes and/or further elaboration) and subsequent forwarding of the strategic plan to the Municipal Council for its formal approval.
- **Dissemination** of the strategic plan and media outreach.

In the formalization and institutionalization process attention needs to be given to:

- **Formalization:** Translation of the strategic food and agriculture plan into city development (master) plans and land use plans, in municipal by-laws, standards and regulations, and inclusion in municipal budgets. The American Planning

Association (Raja et al. 2007) stresses in its "policy guideline" that local and regional food planning includes much more than the assessment and drafting of the food plan or strategy, and that ample attention should be given to creating standards and guidelines, regulating and codifying, targeting public investments, etc.

This is often a lengthy process that is largely done within the various local and/ or regional government departments. This uptake of these tasks in most cases is faster and substantive when local government actors (sector specialists, legal advisors, urban planners, councillors, etc.) have been involved actively in the planning stage.

It is very important that the Multi-stakeholder Forum closely monitors the progress of this process, enables inputs by non-government actors and – whenever needed – puts pressure on local government to perform these activities with more urgency.

- *Operationalization of the strategic plan:* In order to be able to implement the strategic plan, the various stakeholders have to include the actions in which they will be involved in their own (multi-) annual plans and budgets and programmes and to work out operational plans for the implementation of their own contributions to certain components of the strategic plan (what to do, when, how, by whom, with what means/tools, expected results, how to monitor). Too often, commitments made in the strategic planning phase by certain actors are not realized in the implementation phase (or only in a very late stage) due to lack of timely operationalization of the promised contributions and inclusion in institutional work plans and budgets.

Also here, the Multi-stakeholder Forum has an important encouraging and monitoring role. Kingdon (2010) observes that if local food planning initiatives and the opening of a new policy window (problem recognition, policy formulation) is not followed by legislation, funding and implementation, the opportunity passes and politicians will move on to another issue (or are replaced by others after elections with other priorities) and the momentum is lost.

- *Creating an institutional home for urban food and agriculture:* If not yet existing, the establishment of an interdepartmental committee on urban food and agriculture and providing one department with the mandate and staff to coordinate the operationalization, implementation and monitoring of the city food and agriculture strategy is of great importance for the continuity and implementation. Also, formal recognition of the Multi-stakeholder Forum on Food and Agriculture (or City Food Policy Council or similar platform) as a policy advisory body and main mechanism for the coordination and monitoring of the implementation of the city strategic plan on food and agriculture is of strategic importance. The Multi-stakeholder Forum creates a balance between top-down and bottom-up elements and increases the resilience against short-term political changes and slowing down of public or civil engagement.

Phase 5. Implementation, monitoring and renewal of the strategic agro-food plan in the city region

As indicated above, it is of crucial importance that the Multi-stakeholder Forum continues to function after the initial planning process. First to monitor and support the formalization, institutionalization and operationalization of the strategic food and agriculture plan and thereafter to function as the platform to coordinate public-private-civic cooperation during implementation, to facilitate exchange and learning of experiences gained and to monitor progress and impacts.

The above is more complicated than it looks at first sight. Most of the actors are not used to reporting to other stakeholders on their activities and results obtained, and when they do they are tempted to stress the positive results and leave out the disappointments and failures or use their institutional templates to report to the Multi-stakeholder Forum, which might not be suited to monitor the impact of their actions on the realization of the desired changes indicated in the joint vision. It requires continuous attention by the core group to motivate the partners in the Multi-stakeholder Forum to share their experiences in a meaningful way in order to facilitate joint learning and to enable the evaluation and future adaptation of the policies of the strategic plan.

The monitoring should relate to the implementation process (approach/ methods applied, inter-institutional cooperation, civic participation, etc.), progress (activities implemented and outputs realized), as well as the impacts obtained: the degree of realization of the desired changes in the regional agro-food system as a result of the interventions, as well as unintended impacts. Since this is a complex task (e.g., How to filter out other influences on the regional agro-food system?) and to get a more objective view on the effects of the actions undertaken in the context of the implementation of the strategic food and agriculture plan, it may be necessary to ask an independent research institute to periodically assess the changes in the regional agro-food system applying the indicators established in the strategic plan.

Reflection on the experiences gained and the monitoring results can be used by the individual partners to improve their programmes and by the core group to prepare periodic upgrades of the strategic food and agriculture plan (every three to five years) for discussion in the Multi-stakeholder Forum followed by formal political approval.

Moreover, local/regional food planning should not be undertaken as a one-time exercise but promoted as an area of continuous attention of urban planners/planning departments built into the urban planning processes.

FIGURE 3.5 Cover of the Melbourne Food Policy

Source: City of Melbourne.

Methods for the assessment of the local or city regional agro-food system

Introduction

As Freedgood et al. (2011) indicated, the development of local/regional food assessment and planning methods is quite recent and there have been few systematic efforts to classify the various methods applied, their main differences and similarities and their results and effectivity. Moreover, methods that are quite similar may have been given different names, while methods that yield quite different results may have been given similar names: local food system assessment, community food security assessment, community food mapping, foodshed analysis, etc.

Rather than reviewing all these concepts/methods one by one and seeking to explain the differences/overlaps between these methods, we will briefly list and discuss below some methods that analyze the food system with a specific focus and yield specific results. Depending on the local conditions and priorities in each city, certain methods will be selected and combined in a locally specific approach for the assessment of the local or city regional agro-food system.

The selection of methods has to be done very carefully since this has a strong influence on both the development of the process and its results. When selecting the methods/tools to be used one has to consider the following:

- The main objectives of the food system planning exercise and its focus (more integrated/systemic assessment and planning, or focused on one or two main dimensions of that system, e.g., its food security/nutrition or environmental dimension).
- The planning level (metropolitan area, city/district, neighbourhood).
- Financial means available.
- The available human resources/areas of expertise.
- The intended time frame.
- Sources and types of information that are already available and main gaps in the actual information base.
- The types of stakeholders one wants to involve in the process and the forms and degree of participation in data gathering and/or planning one has in mind.

Food asset-mapping

Food asset-mapping (as, for example, applied in the Greater Philadelphia Food System Assessment Study: DVRPC 2010) is one specific type of assessment that identifies and maps the main stakeholders in the local or regional food system, their locations and related assets (access to land, water, staff, infrastructure, etc.): agricultural producers by type, providers of agricultural inputs, food processors, wholesale traders, transportation and warehousing, sites of food access (formal and informal food retailers and markets), actors in waste and nutrients management, and related infrastructure, support actors (technical assistance, quality control, licenses, financial assistance, assistance to food-insecure households, etc., by governmental institutions, private commercial and civil-society organizations).

The stakeholder/assets inventory is preferably combined with an inventory of the views/needs of each key stakeholder category in the food system on the actual problems and opportunities for the development of a sustainable, fair and safe food system in the city region.

Food asset maps can inform the planning process about the actors to be involved in the diagnosis and planning of the local/regional food system, the available human and other resources that may be mobilized to transform the local/regional food system and the views of the various stakeholders on the needed transformation of the food system.

Mapping actual and potential agricultural land use in the city region

In this approach the following activities are undertaken:

- Inventories of *land currently used for agricultural production* in the city region (by type and scale; formal and informal, commercial and non-commercial).
- Identification of available *vacant or underused open spaces* (publicly and privately held) in the city region (and other spaces like rooftops) that can be potentially used for food production in the city region (e.g., Mendes et al. 2008).

The available land inventory is usually combined with the following:

- An assessment of the production capacity ("local foodshed carrying capacity") of the potentially available spaces for (intra- and peri-) urban agriculture, taking into account factors like location, size of the plots, soil quality, access to irrigation water, accessibility of the plots and other limiting factors; see, e.g., Peters et al. (2009, 2013) and Kremer and DeLiberty (2011). Hu et al. (2012) used a systems optimization modelling approach to assess how alternative policy measures would affect the foodshed carrying capacity in Iowa. A key problem in this kind of calculations is often the definition of the border of the "foodshed" (municipal borders, city region up to 50, 100, 150 km?), which strongly influences the results.
- An analysis of barriers and opportunities for transitioning vacant or underused land into cultivated spaces and how the available potential production capacity can be fully developed in practice.

Land-use mapping exercises provide – amongst others – a basis for policies that enable access to land for agricultural production and more secure lease agreements, the integration of intra- and peri-urban agriculture in urban land-use planning and zoning and to determine the extent to which local/regional food production may cover the total urban food needs.

Community food assessment

Community food assessments (see, e.g., Zahilay 2010 for Bedford-Stuyvesant and Isles Inc. 2005 for Trenton) focus on engaging community members and other local stakeholders in assessing the local food system – with an emphasis on local food distribution and access to (nutritious) food, especially of urban poor and disadvantaged households – and framing action initiatives. The needs assessment compiles information on maps on a cross-section of issues in the local food situation – including who/where the food-insecure householders are, their access to food, food availability/prices/quality in the community; spatial distribution of retail shops; eating and shopping habits, diet-related health trends; local food production and processing activities and trends – by interviewing food purveyors, conducting focus group interviews with residents, local school students keeping diaries on the quality and quantity of food, etc., making inventories and price comparisons at food stores, mapping locations of retail shops and markets, etc.

The collected information can be used to identify locations in a given community where residents have limited access to healthy food sources ("food deserts"), as a basis for policy advocacy (showing the problems encountered by the urban poor to access healthy food at affordable prices in their communities) and to identify policy measures that may improve the local food situation. The participatory process also mobilizes local food initiatives and enhances community building and empowerment. Several guides for local community food assessments have been developed and are widely applied nowadays (Hugh 1997; Cohen 2002; Siedenberg and Pothukuchi 2002).

SWOT analysis of different types of intra- and peri-urban farming

While local community food system assessments mainly focus on the consumer side (analysis of access of urban producers to healthy food and food distribution issues), the urban agriculture assessments undertaken in the context of the RUAF-CFF sought to understand the actual constraints and development opportunities for different types of intra- and peri-urban agriculture. The interests and production conditions of the various types of intra- and peri-urban producers vary with their main aims (for subsistence, commercial, social), scale/technology, main products (horticulture, livestock, aquaculture, etc.,), organizational form (family based, cooperative, SME [small or medium enterprise], larger enterprise), location, etc. In order to be able to strengthen food production in the city region, it is important to understand the specific interests, constraints and development opportunities of each of these types of producers in the city region.

In the RUAF-CFF and RUAF-FStT programmes, first an inventory and classification were made of the main types of (intra- and peri-) urban agriculture present in the city region. Subsequently, focus group workshops were held with representatives of each main type to jointly make an analysis of their main strengths and weaknesses, opportunities and threats (de Zeeuw et al. 2011).

The results of the differentiated SWOT analysis of the intra- and peri-urban producers provide valuable information for urban planners and decision makers and local agricultural support institutions regarding main development constraints and perspectives for different types of urban producers and related support needs/opportunities.

Food chain analysis

This type of analysis focuses on the analysis of the relations between the various actors in a specific food chain (either a mainstream conventional food chain or an "alternative" short food chain) with the aim to analyze key problems in the functioning of this food chain (e.g., for fresh green vegetables) and to identify opportunities to improve its functioning by concerted actions of the stakeholders involved.

The chain analysis includes the tracing of the flow of a certain (type of) food product(s) from its origin on a farm to its ultimate point of consumption and the mapping of all flows related to this specific food chain: flows of inputs (manure, water, seeds, fodder, etc.) and services (finance, advice, quality control, etc.), raw and processed food products and related wastes (water, excrements, refuse and the nutrients and pollutants these contain) and to measure different costs of producing and transporting these products through the chain and the value added at each stage in the food chain.

CIAT developed a guide for participatory analysis of, and intervention in, rural–urban food chains with a focus on Latin America (Lundy et al. 2007). Folke et al. (2010) present various cases of food chain analyses and interventions in Asia.

The chain/flows analysis helps to understand the economic, ecological, socio-cultural and health impacts of certain food chains and to identify building blocks for the development of a more sustainable, effective and fair food chain. When a participatory approach is applied, it also mobilizes the chain actors and creates mechanisms to plan and implement concerted actions to improve the functioning of this specific food chain.

Ecological food footprint analysis

Food(t)print analysis refers to the quantification of the energy use and greenhouse gas (GHG) emissions of the food consumed by the population in a particular city region.

Food print analysis builds on the chain/flows analysis for specific food products but the following are added:

a. The quantification of the energy use and GHG emissions involved in the pro-duction/transport/processing/distribution/consumption/waste management of each main food product. See, e.g., Denny (2012) who provides a lifecycle analysis of tomato production and consumption in the UK.

b. Combining the data on individual products (often food products that are representative of certain food groups are selected) in an analysis of the actual energy use and GHG emissions of the total food consumed in that city region.

c. The analysis of the options to reduce the urban food footprint (total energy use/GHG emissions related to food consumption in the city region): changing production and/or processing practices (e.g., reduced use of industrial agro-chemicals and reuse of urban organic wastes and wastewater), change in pro-duction location (close to the city rather than imported into the city region), changes in food consumption patterns (e.g., more fresh, unprocessed or pack-aged food).

For an example of activities b and c mentioned above see, e.g., Jansma et al. (2012), who calculated the GHG emission reduction due to (two scenarios for) integrating agriculture (horticulture and livestock) in a planned residential area.

Such an analysis is valuable for determining the vulnerability of populations to disruptions in their food supplies, to estimate the capacity for population centres to supply more of their food from local sources, to plan policy measures that can reduce the energy use and GHG emissions related to the city region food system and to reduce dependence on fossil energy.

Economic assessment of local food systems

In various cities, especially in the USA, studies (often local or city regional inputs/outputs modelling) have been undertaken to assess the economic impacts of enhancing local/regional food production for the urban markets in the city region (e.g., Conner et al. 2008; Enshayan 2008; Swenson 2009): to assess new (additional) labour income and jobs (that may be expected to be) generated as a result of different scenarios for enhanced production of certain food products (e.g., vegetables and fruits, meat products) and their processing/distribution through alternative marketing channels (conventional vs alternative).

Such studies help planners to identify ways in which the local food economy can be strengthened most effectively (e.g., establishment of supporting infrastructure like food hubs, farmers' markets, preferential government food procurement, etc.) and provide policy makers with information on the potential impacts of certain plans or policy measures on the local/regional economy (enabling decisions on related investments).

A quick but much more restricted approach is to calculate the fiscal contribution (revenues/costs ratios) of different types of intra- and peri-urban agriculture and forestry farms, urban forests, and other green, open urban spaces in comparison to alternative uses such as residential or commercial use (see, e.g., the studies implemented by the American Farmland Trust, the Brandywine Conservancy and the Heritage Conservancy in the Delaware region; cited in DVRPC 2010).

Gómez-Baggethun and Barton (2013) provide an overview of valuation methods that can be applied to assess the economic value of eco-services provided by agriculture and forestry in the city region, including the "avoided expenditures" method (what would be the costs if urban agriculture and forestry would not provide these eco-services, e.g., more energy use due to increasing food miles and higher temperatures, more damage due to floods and landslides, etc.?), the "replacement costs" method (what would it cost to provide similar eco-services in another way?) and contingency valuation (e.g., hedonic pricing, stated preferences, willingness to pay).

Such methods make the economic value of productive green open (intra- and peri-) urban spaces visible, which is very important for awareness-making among urban planners and decision makers, to include "green infrastructure" in municipal budgets/asset accounting, decision making on the location of new residential, industrial and office areas, and the forward urban development and land use planning.

Such methods may also be applied to assess the economic value of other potential impacts of enhanced local/regional food production (e.g., social benefits, health benefits).

Comprehensive agro-food system assessments

Comprehensive agro-food system assessments combine most of the above and other methods in an integrated approach (including system modelling) to evaluate the performance of the local or regional agro-food system in a systemic way, including the complex interactions between the various components of the agro-food system: to determine the actual performance of the agro-food system with the help of a number of selected indicators (social, economic, ecological) and to assess the expected changes in such indicators as a consequence of certain proposed policies and plans in relation to the local/regional agro-food system. Often, metropolitan or regional planning authorities take a leading role in such exercises.

Examples of more comprehensive city region agro-food assessments are Bristol, UK (Carey 2013) and Vermont, USA (Koliba et al. 2011).

Conclusions and the way forward

We have shown that choices made in the initial phases of the planning process will strongly influence the scope of the exercise and the type of results that may be achieved:

a. Choice for a specific geographical scope: Is the focus on neighbourhood, city or city-region level? Each level is bringing its own demands (and limitations) for information, policy orientation, stakeholder involvement, etc.
b. Choice for a specific focus: Is the attention mainly at improving health/nutrition, enhancing food security and access to food of the urban poor, strengthening the local economy and resilience of the agro-food system in the city region, on reduction of the urban food(t)print, on improving the urban green infrastructure with recreational and eco-services next to food production, or a combination thereof? Such choice will – amongst others – lead to other data requirements, stakeholders and selection of other assessment methods, and finally to identification of a different set of priority food strategies.
c. Choice for a specific approach: Is the process mainly focused on mobilizing and supporting innovative and alternative local initiatives in the field of food and agriculture (e.g., Amsterdam: Vermeulen 2010), or rather on the realization of a systematic assessment and planning of the local or city regional agro-food system as, e.g., in Bristol (Carey 2013).
d. Choice of the position viz. local authorities: Is the process managed by local or regional authorities or by a group of concerned civil society actors, or

characterized by an intermediate position (independent from government but with more- or less-developed linkages). This strongly influences policy uptake, access to financing and sustainability (also amidst political and institutional changes). Also the degree of awareness among urban planners and decision makers strongly influences the planning process (crucial role of "champions" in the process, more time and efforts needed for awareness-raising and engagement and search for funds to implement the process).

The review of the assessment and planning methods applied in urban agro-food planning indicates a number of challenges for the practitioners and scientists involved in such exercises:

- There is a strong need for comparative assessments of the efficacy of different approaches to local/regional food system planning: Which approaches have more effects on local policies and planning, lead to better participation of the less powerful actors in the local food system, lead to a better systemic understanding of the functioning of the food system and are more effective in leading to concrete changes in the urban food system (in terms of access to food, nutritive quality of food, ecological footprint of urban food consumption, resilience of the urban food system, etc.)?
- In that perspective, there is a need to include in reports on local/regional food system assessment and planning studies detailed information on the methods used and their implementation (process applied, participating actors/how/ in what, hampering and facilitating factors, lessons learned) and related costs (financial means, human resources) and time horizon. Especially the resources used in urban food planning processes so far are hardly documented and analyzed.
- There is a need for stronger integration of the more participatory community-based local food system approaches and the more planning-led comprehensive city region food system planning approaches.
- Also the adaptation of the methodology for less endowed cities (in terms of available data and information management systems, staff, financial means), e.g., medium and smaller size cities, especially in developing countries.
- The development of a (minimum) package of indicators to monitor the functioning and development of the city region agro-food systems is much needed.

References

Amerasinghe, P.; Cofie, O.; Larbi, T. O.; Drechsel, P. 2013. Facilitating outcomes: Multi-stakeholder processes for influencing policy change on urban agriculture in selected West African and South Asian cities. IWMI Research Report 153. Colombo: International Water Management Institute (IWMI).

Carey, J. 2013. Urban and community food strategies: The case of Bristol. *International Planning Studies* 18(1): 111–128.

Cohen, B. 2002. USDA community food security assessment toolkit. USDA Food Assistance and Nutrition Programme. E-publication available from: http://ers.usda.gov/media/327699/efan02013_1.pdf.

Conner, D. S.; Knudson, W. A.; Hamm, M. W.; Peterson, H. C. 2008. The food system as an economic driver: Strategies and applications for Michigan. *Journal of Hunger and Environmental Nutrition* 3(4): 371–383.

Denny, G. M. 2012. Urban agriculture and seasonal food prints: An LCA study of tomato production and consumption in the UK. In: *Sustainable food planning: Evolving theory and practice.* (Eds.) Viljoen, A.; Wiskerke, J.S.C. Wageningen: Wageningen Academic Publishers.

Dubbeling, M.; Zeeuw, H. de. 2007. Multi-stakeholder policy formulation and action planning on urban agriculture for sustainable urban development. RUAF Working Paper 1. Leusden: RUAF Foundation. Available from: www.ruaf.org/sites/default/files/WP_01_1.pdf.

Dubbeling, M.; Merzthal, G.; Soto, M. 2010. Multi-stakeholder policy formulation and action planning for urban agriculture in Lima, Peru. *Journal of Agriculture, Food Systems and Community Development* 1(2): 145–154.

Dubbeling, M.; Zeeuw, H. de; Veenhuizen, R. van. 2011. Cities, poverty and food: Multi-stakeholder policy and planning in urban agriculture. Rugby: Practical Action Publishing.

DVRPC. 2010. Greater Philadelphia food system assessment study. Philadelphia: Delaware Valley Regional Planning Commission (DVRPC).

Enshayan, K. 2008. Community economic impact assessment for a multi-county local food system in Northeast Iowa. Ames: Leopold Center for Sustainable Agriculture, Iowa State University.

FAO and partners. 2014. City region food systems and sustainable urbanisation: A call for action. Conference on City Region Food systems and sustainable urbanization at the World Urban Forum, Medellin, Colombia. Available from: www.fao.org/fileadmin/templates/FCIT/Meetings/WUF_7_City_Region_Food_Systems_2014_05_09_Call_to_Action.pdf.

Folke, L.; Riisgaard, L.; Ponte, S.; Hartwich, F.; Kormawa, P. 2010. Agro-food value chain interventions in Asia: A review and analysis of case studies. Vienna: United Nations Industrial Development Organization (UNIDO).

Freedgood, J.; Pierce-Quiñonez, M.; Meter, K. A. 2011. Emerging assessment tools to inform food system planning. *Journal of Agriculture, Food Systems, and Community Development* 2(1): 83–104.

Gómez-Baggethun, E.; Barton, D. 2013. Classifying and valuing ecosystem services for urban planning. *Ecological Economy* 86: 235–245.

Harper, A.; Shattuck, A.; Holt-Giménez, E.; Alkon, A.; Lambrick, F. 2009. *Food policy councils: Lessons learned.* New York: Food First/Community Food Security Coalition.

Hemmati, M. 2002. Multi-stakeholder processes for governance and sustainability: Beyond deadlock and conflict. London: Earthscan.

Hu, G.; Boeckenstedt, R.; Wang, L.; Wohlsdorft-Arendt, S. 2012. Mapping potential food-sheds in Iowa: A systems optimization modelling approach. Ames: Leopold Center for Sustainable Agriculture, Iowa State University.

Hugh, J. (ed.) 1997. Community food security: A quick guide to concept design and implementation. Venice, CA: Community Food Security Coalition (CFSC).

Isles Inc. 2005. Trenton community food assessment. New Jersey: Rutgers Community Development Studio.

Jansma, J. E.; Sukkel, W.; Stilma, E.S.C.; Oost, A.C. van; Visser, A. 2012. The impact of local food production on food miles, fossil energy use and greenhouse gas emissions: The case of the Dutch city of Almere. In: *Sustainable food planning: Evolving theory and practice.* (Eds.) Viljoen, A.; Wiskerke, J.S.C. Wageningen: Wageningen Publishers

Kingdon, J. 2010. Agendas, alternatives and public policies. 2nd edition. New York: Longman

Koliba, C.; Campbell, E.; Davis, H. 2011. Regional food systems planning: A case study from Vermont's Northeast Kingdom. Opportunities for Agriculture Working Paper Series 2(2). Burlington: Center for Rural Studies, University of Vermont.

Kremer, P.; De Liberty, T. L. 2011. Local food practices and growing potential: Mapping the case of Philadelphia. *Journal of Applied Geography* 1(10): 1252–1261.

Lundy, M.; Gottret, M. V.; Ostertag, C.; Best, R.; Fertris, S. 2007. Participatory market chain analysis for smallholder producers. Cali: International Centre of Tropical Agriculture (CIAT).

MacRae, R.; Donahue, K. 2013. Municipal food policy entrepreneurs: A preliminary analysis of how Canadian cities and regional districts are involved in food system change. Ottawa: Canadian Agri-Food Policy Agency.

Mendes, W.; Balmer, K.; Kaethler, T.; Rhoads, A. 2008. Using land inventories to plan for urban agriculture: Experiences from Portland and Vancouver. *Journal of the American Planning Association* 74(4): 435–449.

Moragues, A.; Morgan, K.; Moschitz, H.; Neimane, I.; Nilsson, H.; Pinto, M.; Rohracher, H.; Ruiz, R.; Thuswald, M.; Tisenkopfs, T.; Halliday, J. 2013. Urban food strategies: The rough guide to sustainable food systems. FP7-FOODLINKS project. Available from: www.foodlinkscommunity.net/fileadmin/documents_organicresearch/foodlinks/publications/Urban_food_strategies.pdf.

Morgan, K. 2009. Feeding the city: The challenge of urban food planning. *International Planning Studies* 14(4): 341–348.

Peters, C. J.; Bills, N. L.; Lembo, A. J.; Wilkins, J. L.; Fick, G. W. 2009. Mapping potential foodsheds in New York State: A spatial model for evaluating the capacity to localize food production. *Renewable Agriculture and Food Systems* 24(1): 72–84.

Peters, C. J.; Bills, N. L.; Lembo, A. J.; Wilkins, J. L.; Fick, G. W. 2013. Mapping potential foodsheds in New York State by food group: An approach for prioritizing which foods to grow locally. *Renewable Agriculture and Food Systems* 27(2): 125–137.

Raja, S.; Born, B.; Russell, J. 2007. A planner's guide to community and regional food planning: Transforming food environments, facilitating healthy eating. Washington, DC: American Planning Association.

Scherb, A.; Palmer, A.; Frattaroli, S.; Pollack, K. 2012. Exploring food system policy: A survey of food policy councils in the United States. *Journal of Agriculture, Food Systems and Community Development* 2(4): 3–14.

Siedenberg, K.; Pothukuchi, K. (eds.) 2002. What's cooking in your food system? A guide to community food assessment. Venice, CA: Community Food Security Coalition (CFSC).

Swenson, D. 2009. Investigating the potential economic impacts of local foods for Southeast Iowa. Ames: Leopold Center for Sustainable Agriculture, Iowa State University.

Vermeulen, P. 2010. Towards an Amsterdam food strategy. Presentation held at Eating City Workshop, April 13, Rome, Italy. Available from: www.ecomeal.info/documents/eating_city_Amsterdam.pdf.

Viljoen, A.; Wiskerke, J.S.C. 2012. Sustainable food planning: Evolving theory and practice. Wageningen: Wageningen Academic Publishers.

White, H.; Natelson, S. 2011. Good planning for good food: How the planning system in England can support healthy and sustainable food. London: Sustain. Available from: www.sustainweb.org/publications/?id=192.

Zahilay, G. 2010. Bedford-Stuyvesant community food assessment. New York: City Harvest.

Zeeuw, H. de; Dubbeling, M.; Veenhuizen, R. van; Wilbers, J. 2009. Key issues and courses of action for municipal policy making on urban agriculture. RUAF Working Paper 2. Leusden: RUAF Foundation.

Zeeuw, H. de; Veenhuizen, R. van; Dubbeling, M. 2011. The role of urban agriculture in building resilient cities in developing countries. *Journal of Agricultural Science* 149: 153–163. doi:10.1017/S0021859610001279.

4

AGRICULTURE IN URBAN DESIGN AND SPATIAL PLANNING

André Viljoen,[1] *Johannes Schlesinger,*[2] *Katrin Bohn*[1] *and Axel Drescher*[2]

1 UNIVERSITY OF BRIGHTON, ENGLAND, AND BOHN&VILJOEN ARCHITECTS

2 UNIVERSITY OF FREIBURG, GERMANY

Introduction

This chapter will focus on particular issues, driven by increasing urbanization worldwide, that are affecting the planning for (intra- and peri-) urban agriculture in the Global North and South. The attitudes taken in the future towards the position of urban agriculture within design and planning theory and practice will have a profound effect on the spatial qualities of the urban and rural sectors. The chapter aims to draw out design and planning opportunities presented by, in the main, intra-urban agriculture referring to a repertory of state-of-the-art examples from around the world.

Planning and design

Developments regarding agriculture in urban design and planning

Since the publication of RUAF's "state of the art" in 2006 (van Veenhuizen 2006), the most significant planning document within a developed country has been the *Policy Guide on Community and Regional Food Planning* adopted nationally by the US American Planning Association (APA) in 2007. Most memorably it notes that

> Food is a sustaining and enduring necessity. Yet among the basic essentials for life – air, water, shelter, and food – only food has been absent over the years as a focus of serious professional planning interest. This is a puzzling omission because, as a discipline, planning marks its distinctiveness by being comprehensive in scope and attentive to the temporal dimensions and spatial interconnections among important facets of community life.
>
> *(APA 2007: 1)*

This policy guide followed on from the paper by Pothukuchi and Kaufman (2000) "The food system: A stranger to urban planning", as well as from other related writing, but none that dates back further than 20 or so years.

In developing countries, both at the planning and design level, important progress has also been made since 2000. On the planning side, for example in the context of the RUAF programme "Cities Farming for the Future", 17 municipalities – working with other local stakeholders – developed a *Strategic Agenda on Urban Agriculture* as a basis for local policies and programmes to include urban agriculture into local land-use plans and regulations. Such global policies and strategies have then to be translated into concrete action plans and designs at the local level, such as house, site, cluster and neighbourhood.

In cities like Colombo (Sri Lanka) and Rosario (Argentina), McGill University's School of Architecture (Canada) and the RUAF Foundation collaborated with local architects and stakeholders to elaborate lane, housing and neighbourhood designs that included urban agriculture. In Rosario, for example, local government, neighbourhood groups, local producers and invited experts jointly designed multifunctional "productive parks" in poor neighbourhoods, combining urban greening with community gardens, children's playgrounds, food-producing school gardens, and facilities to capture and store excess storm water and grey household water (see: www.ruaf.org/projects/making-edible-landscape-integrating-urban-agriculture-urban-development-and-design).

In parallel with practical action on the ground, research publications and programmes have continued since the start of the new millennium. EC-funded projects were undertaken, for example, by the *SWAPUA* programme in five Eastern European countries implemented by RUAF and ICLEI in 1999 and 2000. Programmes like PUREFOOD, FOODLINKS, COMFOOD, Eating City/Risteco, SUBURBFOOD, SUSCHAIN, RURURBAL and others followed in later years (see: http://publications.jrc.ec.europa.eu/repository). The outcomes of these programmes are directed towards high-level research and policy agendas and do not easily or quickly reach or inform practitioners in a way that addresses their day-to-day concerns. In part as a response to this, in 2009, a number of active European researchers undertaking work in this field established the Sustainable Food Planning Group under the umbrella of the Association of European Schools of Planning (AESOP). The aim of this group is to further cross-disciplinary dialogue, research and practice and to disseminate findings within schools of planning and design as well as within practice. An annual *European Sustainable Food Planning Conference* has been held since the group's inception (see: www.aesop-planning.eu/blogs/en_GB/sustainable-food-planning).

Another strand of development has occurred within the field of design, often led by architects, and resulted in several publications, exhibitions and events aimed at envisioning and visualizing how, in the main, urban agriculture could contribute to the urban realm. For example, in Europe, 2005 saw, as far as we know, the publication of the first book advocating a comprehensive design strategy for the integration of urban agriculture into cities (Viljoen 2005), and in 2007, the

Netherlands Architecture Institute in Maastricht hosted the first major exhibition on the subject, titled *De Eetbare Stad/The Edible City* (see: http://culiblog. org/2007/02/the-edible-city). A further publication with a significant public impact in the English-speaking world was Carolyn Steel's (2008) book *Hungry Cities: How Food Shapes Our Lives*. Since 2009, the *Carrot City* project, consisting of a travelling exhibition, a website (see: www.ryerson.ca/carrotcity) and a book (Gorgolewski et al. 2011), has been providing an important international overview of current urban agricultural design.

All these publicly accessible initiatives complement long-established resources like the online *City Farmer News* (see: www.cityfarmer.info) and RUAF's extensive international policy and practice-focused archive and journal (see: www.ruaf.org). The recent emergence of Food Policy Councils, especially in North America, highlights the start of a transition of the debate about urban agriculture and urban food within the wider population towards food systems planning. Figure 4.1 reflects the emergence of urban agriculture as a design subject and the increasing international attention paid to it, as evidenced by major design-related outputs (note: *this chart is not exhaustive, but reflects trends evident to the authors Bohn and Viljoen in their practice*).

Intra- and especially peri-urban agriculture has been encouraged in the Global South for a considerable period of time within the broad field of development initiatives, both as an area for practical implementation and academic investigation. Receiving ever more attention in the recent past, it has been – implicitly rather than explicitly – incorporated in urbanization studies as well as in urban planning initiatives. Von Braun (1987), for example, broached the issue of developmental potentials of urban agriculture in the late 1980s.

Comparing the world's situation in summary: Within developing nations, peri-urban agriculture remains a significant food-supplying land use, but one which is threatened by rapid urbanization and the consequent loss of land to building activities. Within developed nations, and especially evident in Europe, farms in peri-urban areas are diversifying their commercial activities towards recreation and health in order to remain financially viable (EU 2008).

Green infrastructure and multifunctional landscapes

Today, intra- and peri-urban agriculture can be theorized in relation to regional planning and the concept of multifunctional landscapes (Kasper et al. 2012). Multifunctional landscapes are often equated with the larger concept of *Green Infrastructure,* as in the case of the UK-based Landscape Institute advocating green infrastructure as a connected and multifunctional landscape (Landscape Institute 2009).

Four guides issued in 2012 by UN Habitat under the general heading *Urban Patterns for a Green Economy* are significant for explicitly linking calls for urban compaction, increased biodiversity and economic competitiveness within a context of environmental sustainability. Each guide focuses on a theme, namely i) Working

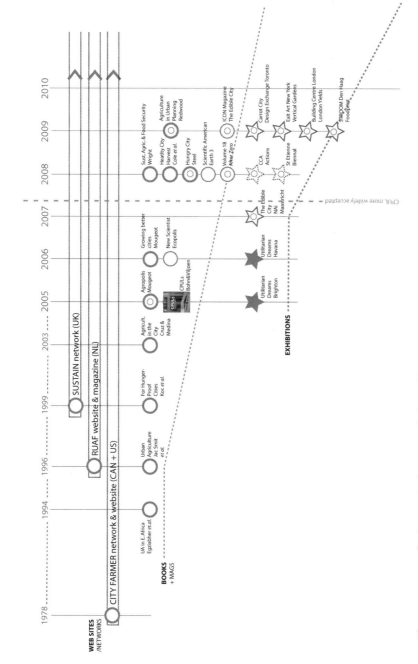

FIGURE 4.1 The emergence of urban agriculture as a design subject

Source: Bohn&Viljoen.

with Nature, ii) Levering Density, iii) Clustering for Competitiveness, and iv) Optimizing Infrastructure. Intra- and peri-urban agriculture is dealt with most explicitly in *Working with Nature* (UN Habitat 2012a) and *Optimizing Infrastructure* (UN Habitat 2012b).

Issues affecting space for urban agriculture

The high cost of urban land is common to all dynamic cities, whether in developing or developed nations, and poses very real challenges for the implementation of intra-urban agriculture, as does a general lack of policy to support it within planning documents. This is exacerbated by increasing levels of urbanization, which puts pressure on intra- and peri-urban agriculture. On the other hand, recognition of the need for enhanced urban biodiversity and access to open urban spaces for social interaction supports the importance of multifunctional landscapes including agriculture. Furthermore, agricultural production can facilitate local cradle-to-cradle systems, for example by utilizing organic waste to produce soil for growing food.

As a starting point for the rest of this discussion, we accept the rationale and desirability for thinking about intra- and peri-urban agriculture as part of an urban–rural continuum embodying multiple interdependencies, as most recently set out in the document *City Regions as Landscapes for People, Food and Nature* (Forster and Getz Escudero 2014). If this rationale is employed and if it includes urban (i.e. spatial) design – which, surprisingly, is missing from the mentioned document – then there is potential to improve qualitative and quantifiable aspects of daily life, while simultaneously creating a shift towards smaller ecological footprints and more enjoyable places to live.

Urbanization and political-administrative challenges

Actual and projected population growth and urbanization in developed and developing nations are having a major impact on the access to potential land for intra- and peri-urban agriculture. Dar es Salaam (Tanzania), for example, has quadrupled in size within just over 20 years (UN Habitat 2010; UN 2012), and Ouagadougou (Burkina Faso) show similar growth (Figure 4.2). Population growth and the respective rapid expansion of urban agglomerations – such as Lagos (Nigeria), Nairobi (Kenya) and Mumbai (India) – are the most severe challenges to urban planning institutions.

In many countries of the developing world, similar issues also arise in small and medium-sized cities. This particularly applies to smaller settlements in the vicinity of major settlements or along important rural–urban corridors, e.g. from Ouagadougou (Burkina Faso) to Accra (Ghana). Spatial growth of these cities is therefore usually understood as a threat to arable land in and around cities and to those farmers whose livelihoods depend on it.

Urban growth of Ouagadougou 1986–2013

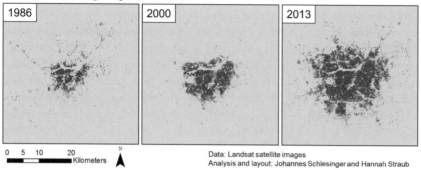

FIGURE 4.2 Rapid urban growth in the developing world – the example of Ouagadougou (Burkina Faso)

Source: Schlesinger and Straub.

As cities in the Global South grow, they can spread into territories over which the city authorities have no control, and there are manifold examples of repeated adjustments of municipal boundaries over time. The consequences for intra- and peri-urban farmers can be dramatic. As boundary changes are usually conducted following a political or administrative top-down approach without consulting the affected farming communities (Tinker 1994), they can appear arbitrary to the farmers. Peri-urban farmers are especially confronted with a lack of predictability about future development (Mougeot 2006). Sometimes without knowing about these changes, their farming activities might suddenly become illegal when territories are newly defined as urban and fall under municipal jurisdiction (van Veenhuizen and Danso 2007). As municipal by-laws tend to prohibit agricultural activities within areas classified as urban, farmers might be forced to stop their activities or shift to other areas. Additionally and regardless of its importance for many urban dwellers, agriculture is still often looked at as a traditional, old-fashioned form of securing livelihoods, which should be kept out of the administratively defined cities (Smit et al. 2001).

But there is cause for optimism too, as the UN Habitat's *Working with Nature* report shows in the following very important work that is underway in Africa: "The Sustainable Cities International Network's Africa Program is assisting the municipalities in Dar es Salaam to lobby for secure land tenure by requesting the government to allocate land for urban agriculture in the same way that land is allocated to residential developers" (UN Habitat 2012a: 35). Similarly, in its recent *State of African Cities* report, UN Habitat (2010: 20) emphasizes that "expanding the urban administrative territory is an option that should be considered by African governments and city managers, particularly in rapidly growing intermediate-size cities." If such strategies are achieved and spread more widely, they will represent a quantum leap in the progress of integrating urban agriculture into urban planning in the Global South.

Consequently, urban growth poses new challenges to planning institutions in the Global South. Planning in the Global North also deals with new challenges due to urbanization, especially as population numbers grow without cities being able to expand proportionally. Compared to developing nations, however, settlement patterns in cities of the Global North are largely consolidated, as their natural increase in population and rural-urban migration rates are rather low. To deal with population growth, city councils apply the planning tool of "secondary densification" through in-fill and redevelopment by which existing underutilized open urban space is used for construction of infrastructure and housing. Outlining long-term strategies for the (temporal) use of underutilized land still remains crucial for minimizing the city's ecological footprint through the productive use of that land.

The environmental need for (food) productive spaces

Environmentally, urban agriculture can impact on cities of the Global South and North in various ways at a micro and macro scale (Smit et al. 2001; Rakodi et al. 2002). For example, keeping green areas in the cities can cushion the impact of an increasing number of heavy precipitation events (Smit et al. 2001; Freshwater Society 2013). And by lowering average temperatures in the "urban concrete jungle", as another example, agriculturally used surfaces can improve the urban micro climate and hence the well-being of the urban population (van Veenhuizen 2006; Lovell 2010; de Zeeuw et al. 2011). However, whilst "planting" is beginning to be specified in urban planning documents as a way to mitigate climate change and reduce climate-related stress, "edible planting" is still specified much less. Furthermore, including food waste as a source of compost as, for example, advocated in the cradle-to-cradle system by Braungart and McDonough (2002), would not only reduce environmental footprints, but the quantity of compost thus generated would also provide a measure of the amount of urban agriculture that a city could support (Viljoen and Bohn 2014).

The urgency with which the loss of urban and regional biodiversity needs to be reversed to achieve environmental and economic resilience has been articulated in the UN Habitat's (2012a) publication *Urban Patterns for a Green Economy – Working with Nature*. This document makes the case for "landscape mosaic patterns" as defined by Richard Forman (2008), consisting of different-sized patches of open space connected by green corridors of small "stepping stone spaces". These are ideally suited to organic agriculture, which enables the maintenance of diverse ecosystems. In 2010, the United Nations' University Institute for Advanced Studies made an even more explicit connection to urban agriculture when they noted that "as the rule of interdependent adjacencies in urban ecology has it: the more diversity, and the more collaboration between unlikely partners, the better the chances for biodiversity, sustainability, and resilience. Linked to this idea is the concept of Continuous Productive Urban Landscapes (CPULs), which represents a powerful urban design instrument for achieving local sustainability while reducing cities' ecological footprints (Viljoen 2005)" (UNU 2010: 31–32).

With respect to planning, Bohn and Viljoen have long argued that, if land is to be provided for intra- and peri-urban agriculture, a conceptual leap is required by which it becomes considered "essential infrastructure" (Viljoen and Bohn 2005). The many-faceted arguments in favour of urban agriculture, beyond yields, allied to the recognized needs for changing consumer behaviour and enhancing urban biodiversity, are all advancing this argument. Detroit (USA), for example, which is well known as a shrinking city facing multiple challenges, has concluded in its 2012 *Strategic Framework Plan* to "utilize productive landscapes as the basis for a sustainable city" (Detroit Future City 2012).

Spatial opportunities for agriculture in and around cities

According to Mougeot, manifold types of locations can be identified "respective to residence (on-plot or off-plot), development status (built-up or open space), modality of tenure/usufruct (cession, lease, sharing, authorised or unauthorised – through personal agreement, customary law or commercial transaction) and the official land-use category of the sector where [urban agriculture] is practised (residential, industrial, institutional, etc.)" (Mougeot 2000: 7–8). This can include cultivation on private land, such as backyards and around houses, or on community and other public lands, such as parks, along roads, railways, under power lines and alongside streams, or in areas that are too steep for construction (Bryld 2003; Viljoen et al. 2004; Drescher and Gerold 2010; de Zeeuw et al. 2011).

The economic use of these sites can be increased, "since income is generated from temporarily available land and lands not suitable for building" (Bryld 2003). Thus, urban agriculture can take place in a broad range of settings, often transforming vacant or under-utilized land into productive areas (de Zeeuw et al. 2000). Accordingly, the areas where urban agriculture is conducted are as diverse as the farmers cultivating the land, and despite the increasing pressure on (intra- and peri-) urban arable land, farmers manage to find locations to pursue agricultural production. The locations where agriculture occurs are important because "this points to specific constraints and opportunities such as the degree of land access, the land tenure situation, costs and time related to travelling to and from the production site, closeness to markets and risks" (van Veenhuizen and Danso 2007).

The importance of tenure

The lack of formal land titles appears as one of the key obstacles to increasing the access to finance for urban farmers in the developing world (Drescher and Iaquinta 1999). In general terms, lack of secure tenure is a major disincentive for farmers because it restricts their access to land or becomes a barrier to financial investment. A programme developed in Freetown (Sierra Leone) provides a promising example of how to address this problem:

The Freetown Urban and Peri-Urban Agriculture Forum, involving key political institutions, credit institutions and farmers, have designed an innovative financing mechanism in 2010. The new program relies on authorities for the permanent allocation of valleys, slopes and low lands for urban and peri-urban agricultural use. Land is allocated to registered and functioning farmers' groups for a period of 5 years for a token rent provided that they abide by the agreement regulations. The groups receive technical training and monitoring, and four credit institutions (First International Bank, Access Bank, Luma Micro Finance Trust Limited, Salone Micro Finance Trust) have agreed to accept such land agreement together with the groups' existing savings or current accounts as a collateral for two purposively designed credit products (personal comment, Marco Serena 2011). The first is a micro credit of between 100 and 400 EUR (repayment period 1 year); the second is a loan between 1,000 and 2,000 EUR (repayment period 2 years) with a yearly interest rate of 24%. The number of households who could potentially benefit from the scheme once fully established is estimated at 2,500.

(Cabannes 2011)

If planning policies can be agreed and enforced in developing countries, as in the example above, a tremendous opportunity exists to incorporate designated spaces for urban agriculture within their cities' future urban expansion areas. By contrast, cities in developed countries, even dynamic ones like London (UK), Rotterdam (The Netherlands) and New York (USA) are seeking the evidence for supporting planning policies to retrofit or reintroduce productive spaces within their current boundaries.

Integration of agriculture into urban and city-region land-use planning

Planning tools

The most commonly used planning tools include master plans, strategic plans and structure plans (Dowall and Giles 1997). Different zoning measures are part of those plans. Experience has shown that general and master plans tend to be static, prescriptive or assume slow-growing cities. They also tend to ignore how households and the commercial sector alter their demand for land as prices change. Even when such master plans have taken substantial time and effort to make, they could be of limited relevance to real developments on the ground, unless the most powerful stakeholders are willing to adhere to them. In other words, the authority of a master plan can vary a great deal (van den Berg 2000).

A more appropriate and dynamic planning tool is "structure planning". It provides a broad framework for local decision making and involves public participation. The structure plan sets out a framework for the development of a community. Being more indicative than master plans, it requires not only projections of future demands and needs of the community, such as housing, infrastructure, employment, transport, local markets, etc., but also environmental aspects like waste management. We can see this approach being applied more formally in developing and developed countries where elected city authorities are increasingly cash-strapped and aim to facilitate development rather than lead it as was often the case during the second half of the last century. To facilitate *structure planning*, participatory processes are required as described in Chapter 3 of this volume.

The increasing use of remote sensing tools for urban land-use planning

The use of remote sensing (RS) for mapping and monitoring (intra- and peri-) urban green spaces facilitates the mapping process, but needs to be combined with actual ground data evaluation if it is to be of practical use. Although urban planning has made wide use of geographical information systems (GIS) for decades, this hardly ever included the management of open spaces. The experience of applying GIS to urban food production activities has, however, rapidly increased in recent years in many cities in the Global North and South. GIS is not only used for urban planning and open space mapping, but also for monitoring the loss of agricultural land within city boundaries, to visualize food security indicators or for measuring urban greening indicators (Idbamerica 1998; American Forests 2000; Fazal 2000). It also has the potential to foster the preparation of urban food policies and strategies by providing detailed analyses of food flows from the production sites to the different locations within cities, as exemplified by the US *Foodprints and Foodsheds* project (see: www.foodprintsandfoodsheds.org).

In a situation where cities continue to undergo rapid changes, GIS allows planners to more easily monitor changing urban food production trends by applying this tool to the entire urban food system (Dongus and Drescher 2000; Drescher et al. 2013; Schlesinger and Drescher 2013; Schlesinger 2013). Innovations in the field of "unmanned aerial vehicles" (UAV) further reduce costs for GIS data collection. The significant comparative advantages of these systems typically include: very high ground resolutions (ca. 3 cm/pixel), flexibility in terms of payload (e.g. RGB-, Infrared- or Laser-systems) and applications (e.g. crop mapping, site monitoring, digital surface models). UAVs were already successfully applied in the quantification of crop production areas in West Africa by Schlesinger (2014) (Figure 4.3).

Nevertheless, the use of RS reveals institutional difficulties in planning. Planning can only be carried out efficiently if the different data on space, infrastructure, markets, nutrition, health, soils, water, waste, socioeconomy, agriculture, etc., amassed by different departments is linked together. Furthermore, the technical equipment (data, computers, plotters, computer networks) and the skills needed in applying RS are often missing. Traditionally, GIS has been used in a rather centralized way, in that one institution takes the lead in the planning process with little or no participation from other units. GIS does not automatically facilitate the dialogue

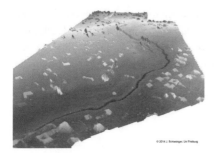

FIGURE 4.3 Digital surface model (left) and high-resolution RGB ortho image (right) of an agricultural site in Tamale (Ghana)

Source: Schlesinger.

with the decision makers, but it needs to be used innovatively. Community building is a prerequisite for enabling participatory planning, and the successful application of GIS for participatory urban planning has been demonstrated in Cagayan de Oro (The Philippines) (Holmer and Drescher 2005).

Planning and access to land

Once sites for urban agriculture have been identified, whether they are plots on the ground or building-integrated agriculture, we come back to the question of tenure, which remains critical because of the significant investments of time and infrastructure required to raise crops. As regards the protection of existing agricultural land, the lessons learnt from a radical "zero-loss policy" being applied in India will be relevant to the future of urban agriculture: "As proposed by the Indian National Planning Commission, new development activities should be carried out with zero loss of agricultural productivity; if agriculture land has to be used, innovations should be included to introduce new forms of agriculture in the same premises" (NAAS 2013).

Protecting spaces for (intra- and peri-) urban agriculture by securing tenure

Experiences from site-and-service schemes, whereby areas are designated for self-help housing and provision of basic services such as roads and water to upgraded squatter settlements, have shown that the poor tend to gradually improve their housing, provided they have land security. Similar observations are true for urban agricultural activities, as shown in South African townships (Small 2001). On the other hand, experience shows that the poor, because of high costs, often tend to sublet or sell these sites and move back to the original squatter settlement (Dowall and Giles 1997). Also, increasing population density of squatter sites reduces agricultural land in these areas. Sometimes in-town or rural-urban chain migration is the cause of this, but often the owner of the plot sublets part of the plot to strangers to make money. With respect to the public interest in the conservation of open spaces in cities, this is a strong argument to lease and not to sell urban agricultural land.

Leasehold provides a limited right to use land for a specific time and for a specific purpose often including protected tenure with rights for prolongation and of transfer (Österberg 1998). Contrary to outright landownership, leasehold (from public bodies) prevents land speculation, thus protecting public interest in open spaces. Proper leasehold is closely related to customary tenure, which, for example in Africa, often includes land use for specific purposes. Another model is community leasehold whereby land is given to a community or association to use it for specific purposes. The European allotment systems work along this line. Nevertheless, this requires the establishment of management associations, garden clubs or similar community-based groups (Drescher 2001).

Within Europe and North America, Community Land Trusts (CLTs) are emerging as a new way of providing tenure for urban producers. Urban agriculture is not usually the primary driver behind the establishment of CLTs, but they can, through cross-subsidy or because of community concern support UPA practitioners. A 2012 study by the US-based Lincoln Institute of Land Policy usefully explored this potential in greater detail:

> Community Land Trusts (CLTs) are non-profit, community-based land organizations with a place-based membership, a democratically elected board, and a charitable commitment to the use and stewardship of land on behalf of local communities. In most cases, CLTs retain permanent ownership of land, which is then leased – through a system of inheritable leases – to various users that own the improvements upon the land, such as residential homes, recreational facilities or, more recently, also urban agriculture. Such ground leases have different benefits: (1) they secure occupancy rights for land users; (2) they preserve affordability by restricting the resale price of improvements; (3) they prevent undesirable uses and improvements of the land; (4) they prohibit predatory lending and reduce foreclosures; and (5) they create a source of income through monthly lease fees to support CLT activities.
>
> *(Rosenberg and Yeun 2012)*

Planning and practical action

Municipalities, professional bodies and enterprising individuals still have the power to make forward-looking interventions and are increasingly doing so. However, the picture is uneven, for example in former British colonies the category of farming or agriculture did not exist in urban master plans and this has still not changed in many of these countries (personal communication, Pay Drechsel 2014). Furthermore, local authorities are often overwhelmed by the dimension of urban development. In the few cases where the planning institutions are willing to support urban agricultural schemes, it is often the sheer lack of human resources in the respective administrative bodies that hinders locally adjusted urban development measures that take into account the importance of urban agriculture. As pointed out by Allen et al. (2014) for the example of Accra (Ghana), unsolved land tenure conflicts and increasing land speculation – especially in the peri-urban areas – often hamper long-term planning for agricultural activities in African cities. Even proper institutionalization of urban vegetable farming was, in the case in Accra, not leading to long-term sustainability. For example, the revision of Accra's bylaws lost its dynamic when external funding expired (Drechsel et al. 2014).

In India, by contrast, the role of urban food production is increasingly recognized not only by the scientific community but also by policy makers and urban planners. The Indian government developed a vegetable production scheme, and the Planning Commission for the *12th Five Year Plan* (2012–2017) has emphasized the potential of urban agriculture with regard to environmental services and health care (NAAS 2013). Similar trends can be observed in some cities in Latin America. In Rosario (Argentina), for example, urban planners start recognizing the importance of including the local population in urban design and development measures, to enhance the local food production (Dubbeling et al. 2009). The support by the municipal Urban Agriculture Office led to the development of more than 700 community gardens as well as four large parks located in the vicinity of marginalized communities (POLIS 2010).

Looking to North America and Europe, we can identify concrete initiatives in support of urban food planning. In 2011, for example, the American Planning Association followed up their *Policy Guide on Community and Regional Food Planning* (APA 2007) with a substantial advisory report specifically addressing urban agriculture (Hodgson et al. 2011).

Although policy in support of urban agriculture within municipal legislation is still by no means the norm, it is beginning to appear, and precedents continue to be set since about the last ten years. In addition to those cases described above, notable examples at the municipal level include Brighton & Hove (UK) Council's adoption, in 2011, of a non-binding planning advisory document titled *Food Growing and Development,* advocating the integration of food-growing spaces within urban development proposals. This advisory notice, the first of its kind in the UK, has resulted in a measurable increase in the integration of food-growing spaces within subsequent planning applications. Similarly, US cities like New York City have relaxed restrictions on the construction of rooftop greenhouses to remove barriers to the implementation of rooftop gardens as well as greenhouses. Furthermore, cities are beginning to promote productive urban landscapes within development plans, e.g. Berlin (Germany) (SenStadt 2012) and, as already mentioned, Detroit (USA) (Detroit Future City 2012).

Designing urban spaces for and with agriculture

Urban design and agriculture

Due to its relatively large and visible presence, urban agriculture has a very significant impact on urban space. It is apparent that these spaces have the potential not only to be unique spaces, but also to contribute to a new evolution within thinking about urban space. An early design study titled *Cuba Laboratory for Urban Agriculture* (Viljoen and Howe 2005) took the approach that the pragmatic positioning of extensive "organoponicos" (commercial urban market gardens applying large amounts of organic materials in raised beds and eventually established on paved and concreted areas) in Cuba provided an opportunity to speculate on their design potential. The fact that "organoponicos" had been positioned using a set of clearly defined horticultural criteria, but had not consciously been planned as part of an urban design strategy, meant that these provided an ideal vehicle for examining how they could be designed to contribute beneficially to their surrounding environment. This study, published in 2005, was so far as we know the first attempt to apply design criteria to agricultural sites. From this a set of principles were proposed related, for example, to the design of edges, paths, topography and uses in addition to food growing. The subsequent expansion of urban agriculture has reinforced these and we refer readers to the original document for further elaboration. Another major ongoing and accessible resource, making the case for understanding the design potential of urban agriculture and documenting international projects, is the *Carrot City* (2009) repository that has been referred to at the start of this chapter.

Other significant and recent pieces of work led by architects and landscape architects are the *Edible Rotterdam* project (Graaf 2012) and the Swiss research programme titled *Food Urbanism Initiative* (see: www.Foodurbanism.org). The former develops design strategies based on spatial opportunities identified within Rotterdam (The Netherlands), whilst the latter produced an online definition of particular *Food Urbanism* typologies of use to planners and designers and categorized under the headings *"Site"*, *"Cultivators"*, *"Motivation"* and *"Production Entity"*.

From the body of work that the above examples belong to, we can extract a number of key ideas with which a designer can work, which will be briefly discussed in the next section.

Key design ideas

Programme and place

It is when additional programmes of use are added to food production that spaces require the most design input. And where intra-urban agriculture is not self-evidently required on conventional economic grounds (e.g. in much of Europe), it is often the multiprogramming of space that makes agriculture economically viable by providing opportunities to meet social needs. A number of ambitious projects like this are underway in Europe.

For example: R-Urban is a neighbourhood project in the Paris suburb of Colombes (France) led by Atelier d'Architecture Autogérée (AAA), which includes agriculture as a major spatial and social component using co-design principles (Figure 4.4). Edible Landscape projects are being integrated in the Dutch neighbourhoods of Rotterdam, Den Haag and Amsterdam by Urbaniahoeve's Social Design Laboratory for Urban Agriculture, using arts-based practice as a way of engaging in dialogues with city authorities and local stakeholders (Figure 4.5). Multifunctional communal food gardens have been developed by the Department of City and Nutrition within the Technical University of Berlin's Landscape Architecture programme for the Berlin suburb of Marzahn (Germany) (Figure 4.6). As well as food production, they have various functions for different age groups, such as children's playground, environmental and food education, and recreation for the elderly.

FIGURE 4.4 Agrocité: the agricultural site designed by the R-Urban neighbourhood project in Colombes near Paris (France)

Source: Bohn&Viljoen.

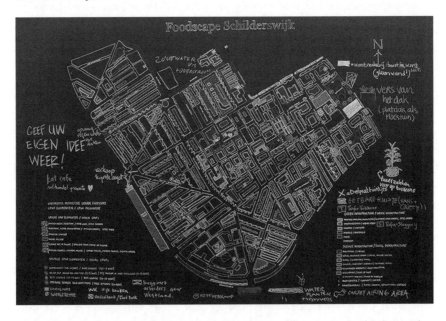

FIGURE 4.5 The borough Schilderswijk in The Hague (The Netherlands) designed as a Continuous Productive Urban Foodscape by Urbaniahoeve

Source: Urbaniahoeve.

FIGURE 4.6 View of the Marzahn multifunctional community garden project in Berlin (Germany)

Source: Bohn&Viljoen.

Importance of scale – urban or architectural scale

Intra-urban agriculture spaces can be thought of as "urban rooms", "floors" or "corridors" within the city. Without understanding that these spaces can be made part of a wider network, they will remain disconnected from the wider urban structure even if by themselves they create attractive individual spaces. Concepts like *CPUL City* or *Food Urbanism* aim to offer design solutions for knitting agriculture into the urban fabric.

Recent strategic city-scale urban designs from Bobo Dioulasso (Burkina Faso) and Detroit (USA) provide good examples for this approach. As part of an overall climate change adaptation strategy, the city of Bobo Dioulasso, with a population of 800,000, plans to implement a series of productive and "climate smart" land-use strategies within green corridors (Figure 4.7). A demonstration project has been constructed along a 1.65 km long, 50 m wide green corridor which previously existed as a long dusty void in the city. In design terms, this project exemplifies the multifunctional planning and design of open urban

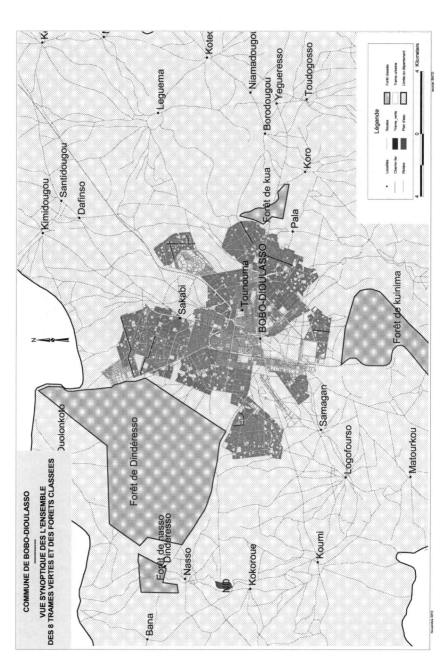

FIGURE 4.7 Mulifunctional greenways (Trames vertes) in Bobo Dioulasso, Burkina Faso.

Source: Sy.

space. The site has been divided up into a sequence of four zones, dealing respectively with forestry, food growing, recreation and education. This intelligent mix of uses creates a place with different attractions for different groups, and, by facilitating these uses, has transformed a void from a space into a place. The material means by which this transformation has occurred are minimal: paths, planting beds and fields are demarcated by small changes in level and surface texture (in this case due to compaction or the breaking open of soil) (Sy et al. 2014).

In certain respects, the ambition and scale of Bobo Dioulasso's productive landscapes echo one of the earliest and most ambitious examples of a "place making" productive landscape, namely that developed in conjunction with RUAF by residents of Rosario (Argentina) (Dubbeling et al. 2009).

In a very different climatic and demographic context, Detroit (USA), well known for its severe financial problems and loss of population, has used a comprehensive multi-stakeholder planning methodology to develop a strategic framework plan titled *Detroit Future City* to guide future development. The plan includes the intention to "utilize productive landscapes as the basis for a sustainable city" (Detroit Future City 2012). It specifically defines "innovative productive" as a new land-use category, including food growing, greenhouses, fields of flowers, aquaponics and ecological services. Detroit has so much partially occupied former suburban territory that its condition is not such that agricultural space is under obvious pressure from urbanization. Rather it has developed a scenario for intensively cultivated modern smallholdings alternating with large-scale horticultural production, resulting in an extensive mosaic of differently sized productive territories around and between which inhabited areas occur and between which inhabited areas occur (Figure 4.8). The productive territories are analogous to lakes in a landscape, and in many respects offer citizens similar benefits as a health-improving recreational landscape, without detracting from the critical densities required to create a vibrant and desirable urban culture. So-called carbon forests have been designed to run as long avenues leading towards the city center from the periphery, demarcating territory while also giving directionality and presence to ecological and personal corridors. Detroit's strategic framework plan demonstrates how essential infrastructure can create desirable territorial identity as well as climate-sensitive landscapes. The scale and process by which Detroit has developed its framework plan provides a working model for large expanding cites, such as those found in China or Africa, where, despite many challenges, the current and future prospects, including human capital, are far more optimistic than for Detroit.

Programme, place, architectural and urban scale operate at a strategic level. The following section aims to extract more site-specific ideas which help to determine particular components of a design.

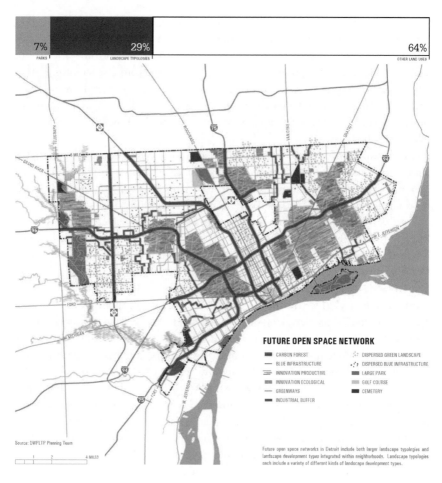

FIGURE 4.8 A leading spatial design from the *Detroit Future City* framework plan including various types of urban agriculture

Source: Detroit Future City.

Site-specific ideas and components

Strongly demarcated horizontal or vertical surfaces

Horizontal topographies tend to create a sense of openness and public conviviality in dense cities. Within horizontal territories small-level changes can create powerful demarcations of space. Vertical surfaces for agriculture are usually created by vegetation, either by means of traditional planting or technologically intensive systems such as hydroponics or aquaponics. The vertical surfaces so created are usually screen-like and visually permeable and well suited to subdividing space to create more private areas for small groups of people.

Public, open-air rooftop gardening, which has become increasingly prevalent within the USA in recent years, as for example in New York's well-publicized *Eagle Street Rooftop Farm* (Figure 4.9), accentuates many of the qualities associated with horizontality. Rooftop farms also have an additional and enormously powerful characteristic conferred by being isolated and elevated. Jerry Caldari, architect for New York's *Brooklyn Grange Farm,* particularly commented on the "universal, childlike amazement of everyone who come to see it, whoever these people are" (personal communication, Aug 2011).

A more subtle form of building-integrated urban agriculture, including vertical elements, is evident in projects where intensive, but low technology and low-cost techniques are used to improve low-income informal housing areas as for example applied in Wanathamulla, Colombo (Sri Lanka), where improvement of the sanitation was combined with mainly vertical greening turning a rundown alleyway into an attractive space (Figure 4.10).

FIGURE 4.9 Eagle Street Rooftop Farm, Queens, New York (USA): one of several rooftop farming initiatives in North America

Source: Bohn&Viljoen.

FIGURE 4.10 Wanathamulla, Colombo (Sri Lanka): lane improvement incorporating vertical greening

Source: Dubbeling.

A more high-tech version of this, but in design terms using a conceptually similar approach, is evident in the designs for prototype *Growing Balconies* proposed for use in high-density dwellings in London (Figure 4.11).

FIGURE 4.11 *Growing Balconies*: prototype developed by Bohn&Viljoen in 2009 as part of an exhibition in London

Source: Bohn&Viljoen.

Inclined planes/slopes

In addition to solar aspect and opportunities for some forms of irrigation, inclined surfaces enable agricultural sites to be seen from below, and in so doing they provide for a visual connection with a large number of inhabitants, for whom, if located in dense urban environments, this can offer an essential connection with the natural seasonal cycles. To exploit effects like this, alignments with streets, the disposition of tall buildings and distance are all important design considerations. An interesting example exists in Villa Maria del Triunfo in Lima (Peru) (Figure 4.12), where a sloped site over which power cables run has been used to establish a highly productive site. Because the site is on a slope it is visible from buildings within the valley, providing a register of seasonal change for residents. The bottom of the sloped field, where it meets the settlement, provides a great opportunity for establishing a market, much in the same way as at the new Parc Agro Urbain de Bernex et Confignon (Switzerland), referred to below.

FIGURE 4.12 Small garden (on steep hill, in dune sand) in Villa Maria del Triunfo (Lima, Peru)

Source: IPES.

Paths and bridging elements

Paths are extremely significant within the design of agricultural spaces. Their requirement for cultivation is self-evident, but it is in their use as access routes to sites for the public where much design occurs. The interface/edge between cultivation areas and the public, where a formal separation will often be required, is significant in design terms, even if this is in practice mainly to provide a symbolic measure of security. Level changes, fences, streams and planting are all typical tools for achieving this. Often public paths will be structured so as to provide a fast route (following a so-called desire line), off which a series of branching or forking paths are set, configured to minimize disruption to the sites of cultivation. The integration of well-used existing public paths as spatial dividers that also enable views of crops under cultivation is a particular feature of the Marzahn project in Berlin (Germany) (Figure 4.6). Here paths also define a space for gathering in what would otherwise be a space used only for circulation (Figure 4.13).

In Switzerland on the outskirts of Geneva, a new nine-hectare "agro park" (Figure 4.14) designed by Verzone Woods Architects is, at the time of writing, scheduled to go on site, having been selected following an architectural competition. This park, named Parc Agro Urbain de Bernex et Confignon, is of note for several reasons: strategically, the city authorities have been far-sighted in deciding to implement this project on a site that is currently on the edge of the city, but that will shortly become a "green finger" due to planned development beyond the existing municipal boundary. The site will be one of Europe's first productive

FIGURE 4.13 Marzahn community garden, Berlin (Germany): raised beds for food growing intersect with footpaths and spaces for public gathering, sightseeing and playing

Source: Bohn&Viljoen.

FIGURE 4.14 The Parc Agro Urbain de Bernex et Confignon, Geneva (Switzerland)

Source: Verzone Woods Architects.

parks and will integrate crop fields, a market space and leisure space. The design accommodates several different users and has adopted a highly refined and controlled system of paths that give structure to the site and define territories for sport, gatherings, a market, picnics and walking, in addition to growing food.

In many cases, entire linear agricultural sites operate as urban bridges, connecting otherwise separated parts of a city or settlement; this is a powerful element of urban design, supporting biodiversity and ourselves as residents. This bridging could possibility be explored at the Villa Maria del Triunfo site by, for example, connecting different parts of the city, or by directing people to viewing platforms as a destination for walkers or families. Here, developing a path with stopping-off points along the way, combined with a footpath and cycle way, would add a whole new layer of significance to this site.

Edges – thick, thin and topographical

Edges can have a thickness and support particular uses, such as markets, restaurants, sports areas, and sitting, picnicking and viewing spaces. The material and architectural language of the structures required by these uses will have a major impact on how they are perceived and valued, as evidenced by New York's *High Line* (USA) (Figure 4.15), which, although not an urban agricultural project, embodies many of the design considerations referred to here. Vantage points along this regenerated former

FIGURE 4.15 The High Line, New York (USA)

Source: Beyond My Ken, http://en.wikipedia.org/wiki/File:High_Line_20th_Street_looking_downtown.jpg.

railway line provide spaces accommodating individuals and groups, allowing for sitting and lying, looking out and beyond, over and into planted areas. The popularity of New York's High Line demonstrates the desire for coherently designed urban landscapes combining paths, planting and spaces for stopping.

Materiality

The choice of materials for use in a design has a huge impact on its appearance, durability and public acceptability, but until (intra- and peri-) urban agriculture is recognized as having an important contribution to make to wider concerns about the city and public well-being, cost will have a large bearing on what is available and accessible. In some instances the temporary nature of a project can be its strength, allowing for changeable and responsive solutions that are capable of accommodating a multitude of programmes in addition to food growing. Berlin's Prinzessinnengärten (Figure 4.16) is an exemplary case for the extremely successful and popular transformation of an abandoned urban space through the development of a "nomadic food garden".

FIGURE 4.16 Prinzessinnengärten, Berlin (Germany): a food garden on derelict urban space
Source: Bohn&Viljoen 2011.

Building-integrated agriculture

Although rooftop urban agriculture has been practised at a domestic scale for a number of years within developing countries, a quantum leap has occurred with respect to scale and publicity of this new type. In design terms the questions and opportunities they raise depend very much on the degree to which they are enclosed by a glass house and are typically private working concerns, or if they are open fields, typically operating with a number of sub-programmes in addition to growing food. Enclosed rooftop greenhouses do act as markers for developments, as for example, in the case of *Arbor House* New York City (USA); here a municipal housing project including a commercial rooftop greenhouse is expected to yield 80,000 to 100,000 pounds of fresh produce per year (Figure 4.17). Furthermore, rooftop greenhouses have the potential to be integrated into the building's heating and cooling system as thermal buffer zones, by means of utilizing heat pumps to transfer heat from one part of a building to another.

FIGURE 4.17 Arbor House, New York City (USA) with green houses on top
Source: Bernstein Associated.

The concept of vertical city farming, developed by Dickson Despommier, who proposes multistorey food-producing buildings (Despommier 2010), has generated a great deal of interest within the popular press and resulted in a number of dramatic and speculative proposals by architects and designers. With more design work aimed at facilitating multi-use strategies and the optimization of natural energy systems, such as designing vertical thermal buffer spaces operating symbiotically between spaces for people and for planting, it is likely that the future will see the emergence of vertical farms as one of a diverse set of urban agriculture types.

That rooftop gardening can also take place at small scale and at low cost is shown by the rooftop gardens in Kathmandu (Nepal) (Figure 4.18) established by the project *Monitoring the impacts of urban agriculture on climate change adaptation*

FIGURE 4.18 Rooftop garden in Kathmandu (Nepal)
Source: ENPHO.

and mitigation implemented by the NGO ENPHO and the Kathmandu Metropolitan City Authority with support from CDKN (UK) and the RUAF Foundation (The Netherlands) (Dubbeling and Massonneau 2014).

Layered-growing for small spaces

Techniques for maximizing the growing capacity and yield of urban agriculture, either by physically stacking planting containers, or by using hybrid systems such as aquaponics that combine hydroponic and fish farming techniques, are closely related to building integrated urban agriculture. The relationship comes about because these systems require structures for support, are frequently enclosed by a protecting structure for climatic control, and due to their three-dimensional forms are inherently architectural. This space-making potential has yet to be fully realized, and prototypes that exist tend to be experimental, as found in Skygreen's prototype constructed in Singapore, or they are more modest but probably more resilient, as found for example in El Alto (La Paz, Bolivia) (Figure 4.19).

Incremental architecture and urbanism

Perhaps the most important strategy for designers and planners to adopt is one that accommodates an incremental approach to implementing urban agriculture. Planning and design strategies should accommodate the potential for the incremental development of local food projects (like the many community gardens in Cape

FIGURE 4.19 Low-space, low-cost horticulture using tables and racks in El Alto (La Paz, Bolivia)

Source: IPES.

FIGURE 4.20 A community food garden in Cape Town (South Africa)

Source: Abalimi Bezekhaya.

Town, South Africa), enabling growth and refinement as the community itself develops, and would enable the demarcation of space for future use (Figure 4.20).

Community food gardens are often established with the minimum of resources, either driven by the needs of food security or community cohesion; but as the communities become more stable and prosperous, the site's potential with respect to the wider use and design potential can be realized. Without a long-term plan, it is all too easy for sites to be built on, at precisely the time when, due to densification and urbanization, open space needs to be protected.

Conclusions

During the past ten years, intra- and peri-urban agriculture has moved from a peripheral position on planning and design agendas to one that is now being taken seriously in developed and developing nations. A rich and mutually beneficial dialogue and knowledge-sharing is emerging between practitioners and academics in developed and developing countries.

Urban agriculture is beginning to be understood as part of wider urban and ecological planning and design strategies, operating at a regional scale. Typologies and design strategies are beginning to be defined. For example, spatial network concepts, such as Green Infrastructure, support design strategies that specifically include intra- and peri-urban agriculture, such as *Food Urbanism* or the *CPUL City* concept. Cradle-to-cradle strategies can also enable multiple benefits. Design research and knowledge transfer, such as exemplified in the *Carrot City* project, help build new online design-based repositories of best practice that are of value to designers and planners.

The increasing density of building in cities and unprecedented levels of urbanization, especially in developing countries, pose great challenges for the coherent planning of urban agriculture.

Planning methods therefore need to be adaptive and include participation by active and relevant stakeholders. Emerging Food Policy Councils are likely to help shift thinking towards a food systems approach capable of integrating intra- and peri-urban agriculture into the wider urban food system (see Chapter 2). Technological inventions, such as GIS systems, utilizing remote sensing and data from direct observation on the ground can, if dynamic and current, offer a powerful tool to aid decision making.

The rural–urban relationship in the future is likely to be seen as a continuum, rather than as a relationship between discreet entities. Equally, future farming practices will most likely happen on a spectrum, combining social and economic benefits and utilizing a range of technological approaches.

Regardless of the type and location of farming, it is evident that appropriate tenure agreements for farmers will be critical for long-term success, especially when involving livelihoods. Where food security is not a major driver, specific ways of adding value to intra- and peri-urban enterprises are required, especially where land is scarce and expensive.

Urban policy is being developed by some cities to support and remove barriers to the implementation of intra- and peri-urban agriculture. But the speed at which intra-urban projects are being established, for example in Europe and North America, or peri-urban agriculture is being lost, for example due to urban expansion in Africa, is outstripping the speed at which supportive policy is being developed. Successful pathways to policy need to be found urgently. If this shift is to be consolidated, then the next step is to collect and disseminate metrics to encourage its further integration into intra- and peri-urban design.

Summing up: During the last decade a lot has happened enabling and supporting the integration of urban agriculture into cities in the Global South and North, but a conceptual shift is still required, if agriculture is to become and remain valued as an essential element of urban infrastructure.

References

Allen, A.; Apsan Frediani, A.; Wood-Hill, M. 2014. Land and planning for urban agriculture in Accra: Sustained urban agriculture or sustainable urbanization? In: *Irrigated urban vegetable production in Ghana. Characteristics, benefits and risk mitigation.* (Eds.) Drechsel, P.; Keraita, B. Colombo: International Water Management Institute (IWMI), 2nd edition, pp. 161–179.

American Forests. 2000. CITYgreen software. Available from: www.americanforests.org/garden/treescities_sprawl/citygreen/index.html.

APA (American Planning Association). 2007. Policy guide on community and regional food planning. Washington, DC: American Planning Association (APA). Available from: www.planning.org/policy/guides/adopted/food.htm.

Berg, L. van den. 2000. Peri-urban agriculture and urban planning. Paper for the CGIAR SIUPA Action Plan Development Workshop South East Asia Pilot Site, Hanoi, 6–9 June 2000. Wageningen: ALTERRA.

Braun, J. von. 1987. Food security policies for the urban poor. In: *Scientific positions to meet the challenge of rural and urban poverty in developing countries. Proceedings of a conference organized by the German Foundation for International Development and the Centre for Regional Development Research at the Justus-Liebig-University Giessen, held June 22–26, 1987.* (Ed.) Kopp, A. Hamburg: Verlag Weltarchiv GMBH, pp. 305–328.

Braungart, M.; McDonough, W. 2002. Cradle to cradle: Remaking the way we make things. New York: North Point Press.

Bryld, E. 2003. Potentials, problems, and policy implications for urban agriculture in developing countries. *Agriculture and Human Values* 20(1): 79–86.

Cabannes, Y. 2011. Financing urban agriculture. Current challenges and innovations. *Urban Agriculture Magazine* 25: 32–35.

Despommier, D. 2010. The vertical farm: Feeding the world in the 21st century. New York: St Martin's Press.

Detroit Future City. 2012. Detroit Future City-Detroit strategic framework plan December 2012. Available from: http://detroitfuturecity.com/framework/.

Dongus, S.; Drescher, A. W. 2000. La aplicación de Sistemas de Información Geográficos (SIG) y Sistemas de Posición Global (SPG) para trazar un mapa de actividades agrícolas urbanas y el espacio abierto en ciudades. Presentation to the workshop La Agricultura Urbana en las Ciudades del Siglo XXI, Quito, Ecuador, 16–21 April 2000.

Dowall, D.; Giles, C. 1997. Urban land policies for the uninitiated. Bangkok: United Nations Economic and Social Commission for Asia and the Pacific (UN-ESCAP).

Drechsel, P.; Obuobie, E.; Adam-Bradford, A.; Cofie, O. O. 2014. Governmental and regulatory aspects of irrigated urban vegetable farming in Ghana and options for its institutionalization. In: *Irrigated urban vegetable production in Ghana. Characteristics, benefits and risk mitigation*. (Eds.) Drechsel, P.; Keraita, B. Colombo: International Water Management Institute (IWMI), 2nd edition, pp. 161–179.

Drescher, A. W. 2001. The German allotment system – A model for food security and poverty alleviation for the Southern African situation? Proceedings of the Expert Meeting on Urban and Peri-urban Horticulture in Southern Africa, Stellenbosch, January 2001. Rome: FAO, pp. 159–167. Available from: www.cityfarmer.org/germanAllot.html.

Drescher, A. W.; Gerold J. 2010. Urbane ernährungssicherung: Kreative landwirtschaftliche nutzung städtischer räume. *Geographische Rundschau* 12(2010): 28–33.

Drescher, A. W.; Hoschek, M.; Glaser, R.; Holmer, R. J.; Pariyanuj, C. 2013. VegGIS – a web-based collaborative research environment: Pilot application in research on vegetable production in Greater Bangkok, Thailand. 2013. Presentation at Tropentag 2013: Agricultural Development within the Rural-Urban Continuum, Stuttgart-Hohenheim. Available from: www.tropentag.de/2013//abstracts/full/414.pdf.

Drescher, A. W.; Iaquinta, D. 1999. Urban and peri-urban food production: A new challenge for the FAO. Internal Report. Rome: The Food and Agriculture Organization of the United Nations (FAO).

Dubbeling, M.; Bracalenti, L.; Lagorio, L. 2009. Participatory design of public spaces for urban agriculture, Rosario, Argentina. *Open House International* 34(2): 36–49.

Dubbeling, M.; Massonneau, E. 2014. Rooftop agriculture in a climate change perspective. *Urban Agriculture Magazine* 27: 28–32.

EU 2008. Other gainful activities: Pluriactivity and farm diversification in EU-27. Brussels: European Union (EU)-Directorate G. Economic analysis, perspectives and evaluation. Available from: http://ec.europe.eu/agriculture/rural-area-economics/ more-deports/ pdf/other-gainful-activities-text_en.pdf.

Fazal, S. 2000. Urban expansion and loss of agricultural land: A GIS-based study of Saharanpur, India. *Environment and Urbanization* 12(2): 133–150.

Forman, R.T.T. 2008. Urban regions: Ecology and planning beyond the city. Cambridge: Cambridge University Press.

Forster, T.; Getz Escudero, A. 2014. City regions as landscapes for people, food and nature. Washington, DC: Landscapes for People, Food and Nature Initiative.

Freshwater Society. 2013. Urban agriculture as a green stormwater management strategy. Minneapolis: Mississippi Watershed Management Organization.

Gorgolewski, M.; Komisar, J.; Nasr, J. 2011. Carrot city: Creating places for urban agriculture. New York: Monacelli Press.

Graaf, P.A. de. 2012. Room for urban agriculture in Rotterdam: Defining the spatial opportunities for urban agriculture within the industrialised city. In: *Sustainable food planning: Evolving theory and practice*. (Eds.) Viljoen, A.; Wiskerke, J.S.C. Wageningen: Wageningen Academic Publishers, pp. 533–546.

Hodgson, K.; Caton Campbell, M.; Bailkey, M. 2011. Urban agriculture: Growing healthy, sustainable places. Planning Advisory Service Report No. 563. Chicago: American Planning Association.

Holmer, R. J.; Drescher, A. W. 2005. Building food-secure neighbourhoods: The role of allotment gardens. *Urban Agriculture Magazine* 15:19–20.

Idbamerica. 1998. Who owns this lot? *Idbamerica* Sept.–Oct.: 13.

Kasper, C.; Giseke, U.; Martin Han, S. 2012. Designing multifunctional spatial systems through urban agriculture: The Casablanca case study. In: *Sustainable food planning: Evolving theory and practice*. (Eds.) Viljoen, A.; Wiskerke, J.S.C. Wageningen: Wageningen Academic Publishers, pp. 495–506.

Landscape Institute 2009. Green infrastructure. Connected and multifunctional landscapes. Position Statement. London: Landscape Institute.

Lovell, S. T. 2010. Multifunctional urban agriculture for sustainable land use planning in the United States. *Sustainability* 2(8): 2499–2522.

Mougeot, L. J. A. 2000. Urban agriculture: Definition, presence, potentials and risks. In: *Growing cities, growing food: Urban agriculture on the policy agenda.* (Eds.) Bakker, N.; Dubbeling, M.; Gündel, S.; Sabel-Koschella, U.; Zeeuw, H. de. Feldafing: German Foundation for International Development (DSE), pp. 1–42.

Mougeot, L. J. A. 2006. Growing better cities: Urban agriculture for sustainable development. Ottawa: International Development Research Centre (IDRC).

NAAS (National Academy of Agricultural Sciences). 2013. Urban and peri-urban agriculture. Policy Paper No. 67. New Delhi: NAAS.

Österberg, T. 1998. Cadastral systems in developing countries – Legal options. Copenhagen: International Federation of Surveyors.

POLIS. 2010. The right to urban agriculture in Rosario, Argentina. Available online: www.thepolisblog.org/2010/09/right-to-urban-agriculture-in-rosario.html.

Pothukuchi, K.; Kaufman, J. 2000. The food system: A stranger to urban planning. *Journal of the American Planning Association* 66(2): 113–124.

Rakodi, C.; McCallum, D.; Nunan, F. 2002. Sustainable urbanization: Achieving agenda 21. Nairobi: UN-Habitat.

Rosenberg, G.; Yeun, J. 2012. Beyond housing: Urban agriculture and commercial development by community land trusts. Lincoln: Lincoln Institute of Land Policy.

Schlesinger, J. 2013. A transect approach: An interdisciplinary method for understanding agricultural dynamics in and around cities 2013. Paper presented at the Annual Meeting of the Association of American Geographers, Los Angeles, 9–13 April 2013.

Schlesinger, J. 2014. The use of UAVs for high-resolution crop mapping in urban contexts. Unpublished presentation.

Schlesinger, J.; Drescher, A. W. 2013. Spatio-temporal dynamics along the urban-rural continuum: A GIS-based analysis of two African cities. Paper presented at the Tropentag 2013: Agricultural Development within the Rural-Urban continuum, 17–19 September 2013, Hohenheim. Available from: www.tropentag.de/ 2013/proceedings/ proceedings.pdf.

SenStadt Berlin. 2012. Strategie stadtlandschaft Berlin: Natürlich – urban – produktiv. Berlin: Senatsverwaltung für Stadtentwicklung und Umwelt. Available from: www.stadtentwicklung. berlin.de/umwelt/ landschaftsplanung/strategie_stadtlandschaft/download/Strategie-Stadtlandschaft-Berlin.pdf.

Small, R. 2001. Slide show on urban agricultural activities in Cape Town townships. Presented to the Subregional Expert Consultation on urban horticulture, FAO/University of Stellenbosch, January 2001.

Smit, J.; Nasr, J.; Ratta, A. 2001. Urban agriculture: Food, jobs and sustainable cities. New York: United Nations Development Programme (UNDP). 2nd edition.

Steel, C. 2008. Hungry city: How food shapes our lives. London: Chatto and Windus.

Sy, M.; Baguian, H.; Gahi, M. 2014. Multiple use of green spaces in Bobo-Dioulasso, Burkina Faso. *Urban Agriculture Magazine* 27: 33–35.

Tinker, I. 1994. Urban agriculture is already feeding cities. In: *Cities feeding people: An examination of urban agriculture in east Africa.* (Eds.) Egziabher, A .G.; Lee-Smith, D.; Maxwell, D. G.; Memon, P. A.; Mougeot, L. J. A.; Sawio, C. J. Ottawa: International Development Research Centre (IDRC), pp. vii–xi.

UN (The United Nations). 2012. World urbanization prospects. The 2011 revision. New York: United Nations.

UN Habitat. 2010. State of the world's cities 2010/11 – Cities for all: Bridging the urban divide. Nairobi: UN Habitat.

UN Habitat. 2012a. Urban patterns for a green economy: Working with nature. Nairobi: UN Habitat. Available from: http://mirror.unhabitat.org/pmss/listItemDetails.aspx?publicationID=3341.

UN Habitat. 2012b. Urban patterns for a green economy: Optimizing infrastructure. Nairobi: UN Habitat. Available from: http://mirror.unhabitat.org/pmss/listItemDetails.aspx?publicationID=3343.

UNU. 2010. Cities, biodiversity and governance: Perspectives and challenges of the implementation of the convention on biological diversity at the city level: Policy report. Yokohama: Institute for Advanced Studies, United Nations University (UNU).

Veenhuizen, R. van. (ed.) 2006. Cities farming for the future: Urban agriculture for green and productive cities. Leusden: RUAF Foundation; Manila: International Institute for Rural Reconstruction (IIRR).

Veenhuizen, R. van; Danso, G. 2007. Profitability and sustainability of urban and peri-urban agriculture. FAO Agricultural Management, Marketing and Finance Occasional paper no 19. Rome: Food and Agriculture Organization of the United Nations (FAO). Available from: ftp://ftp.fao.org/docrep/fao/010/a1472e/a14713OO/.pdf.

Viljoen, A. (ed.) 2005. Continuous productive urban landscape: Designing urban agriculture for sustainable cities. Oxford: The Architectural Press.

Viljoen, A.; Bohn, K. 2005. Continuous productive urban landscapes: Urban agriculture as an essential infrastructure. *Urban Agriculture Magazine* 15: 34–36.

Viljoen, A.; Bohn, K. (eds.) 2014. Second nature urban agriculture: Designing productive cities. Oxford: Routledge.

Viljoen, A., Bohn, K.; Pena Diaz, J. 2004. London Thames Gateway: Proposals for implementing CPULs in London Riverside and the Lower Lea Valley. Brighton: University of Brighton.

Viljoen, A.; Howe, J. 2005. Cuba: Laboratory for urban agriculture. In: *Continuous productive urban landscapes: Designing urban agriculture for sustainable cities.* (Ed.) Viljoen, A. Oxford: Architectural Press, pp. 146–191.

Zeeuw, H. de; Guendel, S.; Waibel, H. 2000. The integration of agriculture in urban policies. In: *Growing cities, growing food: Urban agriculture on the policy agenda.* (Eds.) Bakker, N.; Dubbeling, M.; Gündel, S.; Sabel-Koschella, U.; Zeeuw, H. de. Feldafing: German Foundation for International Development (DSE), pp. 161–183.

Zeeuw, H. de; Veenhuizen, R. van; Dubbeling, M. 2011. The role of urban agriculture in building resilient cities in developing countries. *Journal of Agricultural Science* 149/S1: 153–163.

5

URBAN AGRICULTURE AND SHORT CHAIN FOOD MARKETING IN DEVELOPING COUNTRIES

Paule Moustier[1] and Henk Renting[2]

1 CIRAD-UMR-MOISA, FRANCE

2 RUAF FOUNDATION, THE NETHERLANDS

Introduction

In this chapter, we focus on the specific role of urban agriculture and short marketing chains in urban food supply and distribution, with an emphasis on developing countries. Markets in the context of urban agriculture are often characterised by short supply chains and social relations based on proximity in which we may distinguish the traditional, mainly informal forms of short marketing chains and innovative new forms of more direct producer-to-consumer food supply that are developing more recently.

To sketch the context, we will first briefly discuss presence and economic performance of urban agriculture in cities of the Global South and subsequently discuss the specific and complementary role of urban agriculture in total food supply and related ways of marketing locally produced food. In the following section a number of innovative types of short chain food supply and distribution are discussed. We will conclude with listing a number of consequences for policy development on urban food supply and distribution and some challenges for research.

Presence and economic performance of urban agriculture in developing countries

Presence

Numbers on involvement of urban residents in agriculture in countries in developing countries are substantial, although the percentage of participation in urban agriculture is highly variable from one city to another. A recent study of the FAO confirms that in Latin America and the Caribbean the practices of (intra- and peri-) urban agriculture are widespread. Urban agriculture activities include a wide range of activities, varying from backyard and school gardening, to intensive production of flowers and small animals. It is practised, for example, by 40% of households in Cuba, and 20% in Guatemala and Saint Lucia. In Bolivia's main cities and municipalities, 50,000 families are (also) food producers. In Bogotá, 8,500 households produce food for home consumption. In Haiti, 260 hectares of land in and around Port-au-Prince and other towns are cultivated by 25,500 families (FAO 2014).

Similarly, for Africa another FAO study (FAO 2012) estimates that 40% of households in sub-Saharan cities are involved in intra- and peri-urban horti-culture, either in "grow-your-own" schemes or as in market-oriented gardening. Ten countries provided estimates of the extent of horticulture practised in their principal cities and towns. The data indicate that horticulture was practised by almost half of urban households in Cameroon, one-third in Malawi, one-quarter in Ghana, and one in ten in Nigeria. In others – Botswana, Cape Verde, Gabon, The Gambia, Namibia and Senegal – participation was less than 10%. For capital cities, highest shares were reported for Lilongwe and Yaoundé, with 35% of households engaged in horticulture, followed by Nairobi (36%) and Accra (25%).

In a survey conducted in 2008–2009 in 11 Southern African countries, representing a total of 6,453 households in poor urban neighbourhoods, the authors concluded that 22% of them grow some food (Crush et al. 2011). The percentages are the highest (between 30 and 64%) in four cities with a high level of food insecurity and a local government with a positive or neutral attitude towards agriculture (Harare, Blantyre, Maseru, and Misunduzi). How-ever poorer areas in some other cities were well below the average such as Johannesburg (9%), Gaborone and Cape Town (5%), and Windhoek and Lusaka (3%). This implies that poverty per se does not adequately explain the resort to household production as a source of food. On the other hand, the extremely low rates of participation by poor households in some neighbourhoods of Cape Town and Johannesburg may not be typical of the city or country as a whole.

While the above given figures mainly relate to participation of urban citizens in agriculture, a recent study, based on global data on croplands and urban extents using spatial overlay analysis, indicated that 60% and 35% of, respectively, all irri-gated and rainfed croplands fall within a distance of 20 kilometres of a city (Thebo et al. 2014). Croplands *within* urban extents constitute a small, but not negligible portion at 67.4 million hectares (5.9%) of the sum of the maximum monthly irrigated and rainfed cropland area. A greater proportion of croplands *within* city extents are irrigated (35.0%) than their non-urban counterparts (17.7% irrigated). Urban croplands also proved to be extremely prevalent globally, with 87% of all urban extents with populations of over 50,000 people containing at least some area of irrigated urban cropland and 98% containing at least some area of rainfed urban cropland.

Economic performance

The economic performance of (intra- and peri-) urban agriculture builds on a number of complementary mechanisms that are differentiated according to specific geographical settings and types of socio-economic profiles of involved social actors. Depending on the specific combination of mechanisms, urban agriculture in different degrees may contribute to poverty alleviation and/or generating monetary income.

Subsistence-oriented urban agriculture activities enhance dietary improvement especially by including more fresh vegetables and livestock products and reducing food expenditures. Dubbeling (2013) discusses the role played by urban agriculture in reducing the vulnerability of the urban poor and vulnerable groups and enhancing their coping capacity by diversifying their food and income sources and increasing the stability of household food consumption and savings on food expenditures against seasonality, disturbances in food supply from rural areas or imports, increases in food prices and (temporary) losses of income from other sources. Also Zezza and Tasciotti (2010), on the basis of a review of various studies, indicate that there is a correlation between income derived from agriculture (mostly from livestock) and household dietary diversity. In addition, the self-production of food (e.g., vegetables, poultry) results in cash savings on food expenditures that otherwise would have to be purchased (Prain and Dubbeling 2011).

Urban agriculture activities with a semi- or full market orientation contribute to the generation of (complementary or main) monetary family income and the creation of employment opportunities in the city. The provision of monetary income by urban agriculture appears to be related to the nature of products and the amount of invested capital (in particular irrigation, value of animals, input use). Monetary income tends to increase from staple food (e.g., rice, maize or cassava) to horticultural crops and more so: aquaculture and livestock; and from seasonal-dry to all-year irrigated crops (Moustier and Danso 2006, van Veenhuizen 2007).

A systematic assessment of intra- and peri-urban agriculture activities in four cities (Accra, Ghana; Bangalore, India; Lima, Peru; and Nairobi, Kenya), implemented by RUAF Foundation for the World Bank between March 2010 and May 2011, demonstrated the role of urban agriculture as an economic livelihood strategy (stable occupation and income) for low-income urban households (Prain and Dubbeling 2011). The same study found that urban agriculture is better rewarding than petty trading and casual labouring. Moreover, urban agriculture is highly compatible with several other kinds of employment and allows combining multiple income sources, which – for resource poor and vulnerable households – is a very important risk-reduction and adaptation strategy.

Mougeot summarised the research on the contributions of urban agriculture to urban employment and income as follows (Mougeot 2013):

- Urban agriculture contributes to considerable low-cost job creation in periods of crisis; and has the ability to grow in periods of recovery (as in Cuba after the oil crisis, in Argentina after the 2001 monetary crisis and in many other countries after the 2007–2008 food price hikes).
- The higher the market value of the produce, the larger its contribution to household income.
- Incomes and wages in market urban agriculture compare favourably to those of unskilled construction workers, even of mid-level civil servants (up to five times higher than national per capita income in Dakar and Nairobi and four times higher than the national poverty line in Maputo; FAO 2012).
- Annual savings on food expenditures can add up to several months of a minimum wage;
- Savings and incomes from home-based urban agriculture allow re-investing in other income-generating home business to improve household well-being.
- Market oriented urban agriculture provides a relatively accessible entry on job market for youth (with beneficial impacts on income, food, trade learning, own small business, and self-esteem).

The specific role of urban agriculture in urban food supply

Though it is recognised that (intra- and peri-) urban agriculture will by itself not be able to feed entire cities (Cofie et al. 2003, Moustier 2007), it provides important and specific contributions to urban food supply and nutrition especially in the provision of perishable food commodities. For fresh perishable vegetables the relative contribution of urban agriculture in total urban food supply in many cities is around 60–70% (and during the dry season even higher), whereas for other fresh vegetables, eggs, milk, poultry meat, and pork these percentages may reach levels of 40% or even higher with large variations between the cities (see Chapter 6 for more details).

The specific role of urban agriculture in the urban food supply is characterised by complementarity of food supply flows and advantages of proximity in market organisation.

Complementarity of food supply flows

A growing body of evidence supports the complementarity between urban food supply from within the city region and from outside the city region including rural areas and imports (Moustier 2007).

Perishable food products

Basic food products (cereals or tubers) and dry vegetables (onions) come mostly from rural areas in the country or are imported from abroad, whereas urban agriculture in the provision of fresh perishable vegetables, mainly leafy vegetables, poultry and dairy products come mostly from peri-urban areas.

Fresh vegetables in this category are mainly leafy vegetables such as amaranth, water convolvulus, sorrel, okra, morel, cabbage, lettuce and chives and related leafy plants. These vegetables top the list of vegetables consumed in Africa and in Asia. These vegetables are well known for their short shelf life: after one day they are no longer fresh – and in many countries, freshness is an important criterion for consumers, most of whom do not own refrigerators. These leafy vegetables are mostly brought into town from distances of less than 30 kilometres from the city centres. The (intra- and/or peri-) urban percentage of supply in most cities in Africa and Asia is above 70%, depending on the administrative city boundary.

In the case of less-perishable vegetables, such as tomatoes and cabbage, which can stay fresh for a few days, supply varies from peri-urban to rural production and the peri-urban percentage of supply is highly variable according to the city under study and season. Dry onion, which is even less perishable, originates only from rural areas or was imported in the investigated cities of Africa and Asia.

Improved broiler chicken, milk and eggs come from city farms or from the sub-urbs. These farms are run by city dwellers, whereas local beef comes from traditional pastoral or agro-pastoral farms. Urban animal food products are also imported from lower-end European production facilities and pose strong competition to certain local products, such as chicken, despite differences in quality (Laroche-Dupraz et al. 2009).

Most fresh milk found in Kumasi is produced in the urban area at the local university. In the peri-urban areas of Kumasi, large poultry farms produce 80% of the eggs consumed in the city, while these farms suffer increasingly from cheap poultry meat imports, especially from Brazil (Cofie et al. 2003).

Complementarities in time

A comparative advantage of (intra- and peri-) urban agriculture is lying in the continuity of product supply, either because of specific natural conditions, or because urban farmers are able to sustain continuous production due to more specialised and irrigated systems – characteristics they may share with some specialised rural areas. This comparative advantage is observed especially in the dry season and for temperate vegetables (Moustier and Danso 2006).

The seasonal advantage of intra- and peri-urban agriculture is further enhanced by access of intra- and peri-urban producers to piped and recycled urban waste-water, which allows (part of) the urban producers to produce year round (Raschid-Sally and Yayakody 2008).

The advantage of proximity in market organisation

Short marketing chains

Food produced in and around cities in Africa and Asia is normally distributed through very short marketing chains. More often than not, the producers sell their produce to retailers/collectors at their farm field (often many of these collectors are producers themselves) or at night at wholesale markets (e.g., 100 to 200 kg/day^{-1} brought to the markets on overloaded bicycles, scooters or in minibuses). Another (smaller) part of the production is traditionally sold directly by the producers to consumers living nearby.

The short chain in the marketing of their products has a positive impact on the reduction of transaction costs in the marketing of perishable products of varying quality standards. The small-scale of production and low market prices make it attractive for producers to spend some hours in transportation to get as much as possible of the final price. Yet these characteristics contribute to further fragmentation of the final supply, while economies of scale could be reached by collective marketing. Experiences of collective marketing, until recently, are hardly developed in urban- and peri-urban areas though, or have had little success, given the variability of production in quantity and quality that makes farmers reluctant to "put their eggs in the same basket" as other farmers. Well-known success stories include the Horticulture Cooperative Horticulture Marketing Society (HOPSCOM) established in 1959. HOPSCOM buys vegetables and fruits from their members (over 16,000 horticulture producers in/around Bangalore and Mysore) in 13 procurement centres (direct cash payment) and sells these to consumers through a network of over 230 outlets located near bus stations and other easily accessible locations in the city (Chandrashekar 2011). Another success story is the AMUL Kaira District Dairy Co-operative Union, established in 1944, that buys milk from 231 primary cooperatives and sells fresh and packaged milk to consumers through its own distribution network (Laidlaw 1977). More recently, new innovative initiatives are found where intra- and peri-urban producers have identified reliable collective ways to market their products directly to urban buyers (consumers, restaurants, social food distribution programmes, etc.), as will be discussed in more detail in a later section of this chapter.

Geographical proximity is still important in the supply of perishable food commodities in Africa and Southeast Asia, especially for leafy vegetables, which play a strong role in the livelihoods of the poor, be they farmers or consumers. This situation can change with the development of transportation, cooling/storage facilities and increased pressure on urban land. For example, the comparison of areas supplying Hanoi between 2002 and 2011 (Sautier et al. 2012) shows that Hanoi province (which has been extended) supplies 75% of water convolvulus (rather than 89% in 2002), and nearby provinces have increased their share of supply. Cucumber is no longer supplied by Hanoi province, but is sourced in nearby provinces.

Next to geographical proximity, relational proximity plays an important role: the opportunities that urban producers have to establish direct linkages with consumers and other urban market parties especially to trade perishable products, as well as with urban sources of water and nutrients, or to gain direct access to information on market demand and consumer preferences.

FIGURE 5.1 Direct sales to consumers in Hanoi by a vegetable producer
Source: Moustier.

Low price differential

Short marketing chains contribute to a low price differential for products between farm and final consumption: in Hanoi these account for 30% on leafy vegetables, 35 to 50% for cabbage, and 75% for tomato (Gia 1999). In rural chains, wholesalers' incomes may be up to ten times higher than that of farmers, but the risks of bankruptcies are higher. Price differentials are higher for rural products due to higher transportation costs and higher wholesalers' margins. The references indicate the need for an update on the comparison of food price generation between rural and urban areas for a same commodity. Actually this kind of comparison is not easy because it is difficult to find the commodity with the same quality characteristics being available at the same time of the year, and with two possible origins, urban and rural. Simulations could be made on different scales of urban and rural production and transportation, and on their consequences on the final price formation.

Information on quality and control

The proximity of production areas to consumers and other urban market parties (e.g., restaurants, hotels, hospitals, school food programmes, supermarkets) makes it easier for consumers and other actors in the short chain to control quality, and at the same time, keeps producers from cheating on product quality. Proximity enables frequent contacts between farmers, traders, and consumers and checks on the production process. Proximity between farmers and consumers is not a perfect substitute for independent public control, which is still deficient in many countries, but it does reinforce the incentive for farmers not to deceive their customers. A survey of 356 consumers in Senegal showed that the first two factors influencing purchase decisions are: (i) trust in the vendor; and (ii) safety of food. They complain about illnesses having increased, one possible source being the growing use of pesticides by farmers. Half of those interviewed worry about food safety (Badj 2008).

Freshness

In situations of limited access to fridges, freshness of produce is especially valued by urban consumers. In Thiès (Senegal), more than 90% of 150 interviewed housewives thought that vegetables should be grown nearby, for freshness and quick access (Broutin et al. 2005). In Hanoi, freshness is the advantage of peri-urban vegetable production cited by 74% of the respondents (out of 500) (Figuié 2004). However, production in urban proximity can also affect produce quality negatively where, for example, polluted irrigation water is used (see Chapter 7 for more details).

The development of innovative collective short food chains in city regions of the Global South

During the last two decades several important changes have been taking place in developing countries regarding the urban food supply and distribution system, including – amongst others – the rapid rise of supermarket chains and the rise of new types of short food chains in the city region.

The impacts of the supermarket revolution

The rapid spread of supermarket chains in developing countries started in Latin America in the second half of the nineties, followed by Asia some years later and most recently in Africa. A crucial factor was the liberalisation of retail foreign direct investment in the early nineties, while domestic policies have often included tax incentives for supermarkets. The spread was further accelerated by intense competition, consolidation and multi-nationalisation in the supermarket sector seeking to improve their competitive positioning. The supermarkets first established in the larger cities serviced the higher-income groups but over time gradually also spread into the food markets of the middle- and lower-income sections of the population and into smaller towns (Reardon and Gulati 2008).

The description that Reardon and Gulati give of the impacts of the quick spread of supermarket chains in developing countries may be summarised as

FIGURE 5.2 Supermarket selling fresh vegetables, Vietnam
Source: Moustier.

follows: Supermarkets – due to their economies of scale and efficient procurement systems – tend to charge consumers lower prices (first only in the processed and semi-processed food segments) and offer more diverse products of constant and good quality. However, the food security and nutrition impacts on poor consumers may be limited where price savings may accrue to the middle class, mainly due to uneven physical access to supermarkets for the urban poor and/or because the offer of the supermarkets does not include fresh vegetables and fruits or only at higher prices.

As supermarkets modernise the procurement of fresh produce (some 10–15% of supermarkets' food sales in developing countries), they increasingly source through wholesalers that are specialised in certain product lines from larger, more reliable and better-equipped farmers (land, irrigation, etc.) and good access to infrastructure (like roads and cold chain facilities). Where supermarkets cannot source from medium- or large-scale farmers, supermarket chains may – in partnerships with other organisations – provide assistance to local small producers with training, credit, and other needs in order to secure sufficient supply of required quality. Such assistance is not likely to become generalised, however, and so over time asset-poor small farmers will face increasing challenges surviving in the market since they can't make the higher up-front investments, nor meet the greater demands for quality, consistency, and volume.

They recommend developing-country governments to put in place policies to help both traditional retailers and small farmers to pursue "competitiveness with inclusiveness" in the era of the supermarket revolution. "Some countries are already taking such steps, and their experiences offer lessons for others" (Reardon and Gulati 2008).

Innovative short food chain initiatives

Especially during the last decade, in cities in developing countries, more and more initiatives with several types of innovative collective businesses for the direct sales of food products to consumers and other urban markets parties could be observed. Such innovative short supply chains include, amongst others:

- Box schemes (e.g., Harvest of Hope in Cape Town, pooling vegetables grown ecologically by community gardeners in low-income neighbourhoods and delivering these weekly in boxes to their clients in better-off areas of the city; Hoekstra and Small 2010).
- Door-to-door delivery (e.g., by fresh mushrooms producers in Accra; Danso et al. 2002).
- Farmer shops (e.g., the Dang Xa Cooperative in Gia Lam (peri-urban Hanoi, Vietnam) selling "safe" vegetables directly to consumers in their own shops in Hanoi; Moustier and Nguyen 2010).
- Farmers' markets (e.g., in Rosario where the municipality supported the establishment of seven farmers' markets in different parts of the city where urban producers can sell their produce directly to interested customers; Mazzuca et al. 2009).
- Online food shops (e.g., the Jinghe online store in Beijing that delivers seasonal vegetables, fruits, eggs, milk, oil, poultry meat, etc., produced by several cooperatives of peri-urban producers to staff of government offices and universities in Beijing that order these food products through the Jinghe website; Renting and Dubbeling 2013).
- Producers cooperatives directly delivering to restaurants, hotels, schools, institutions (such as, for example, the Van Noi Cooperative in Hanoi) that deliver fresh vegetables directly to vegetable shops and food stalls at markets as well as directly to METRO Cash and Carry Supermarkets (Ho Than Son and Dao The Anh, 2006, Moustier and Nguyen 2010).
- Food buyers cooperatives (for example, the Canastas Comunitarias in Ecuador: groups of urban poor that bi-weekly collectively buy a basket of ca. 15 food items from ecological producers in the city region; Sherwood et al. 2013).
- Mobile food carts (for example, the Kedai Balitaku social business in Djakarta that buys food from ecologically producing small-scale producers in the city region and provides "healthy and affordable menus" to mobile food vendors that sell these menus to children in underserved areas of the city; Rosenberg 2011).

A recent analysis of 26 innovative short food chain initiatives in developing countries (Renting and Dubbeling 2013) and of eight cases in Asia, Africa and Brazil (Moustier 2013) showed that these initiatives have a wide diversity in various characteristics: the products marketed, the ways in which the products are distributed to the clients, the quality attributes that are brought to the fore in the marketing (ecologically grown, fresh, produced within the city region, by small-scale farmers, fair prices for farmer and consumer, safe, . . .), the degree and type of certification, the degree of external support received and the degree and speed of growth.

Yet also some common characteristics can be identified:

- These new short food supply chain (SFSC) initiatives use in their marketing often specific attributes of their products and process of production which address consumer concerns (e.g., reduction in use of agro-chemicals, food safety, solidarity with poor small-scale producers in the city region) and in this way create a special market niche for their products, generating better price margins by excluding intermediaries in the value chain and by valorising distinctive product qualities.
- Many SFSCs mainly concern fresh foods (vegetables, fruits, eggs, and exceptionally dairy) and often focus on a limited number of products. SFSC initiatives are often crucial in developing markets for local and organic food where these did not exist yet.
- Even when there is expansion of the SFSC, its share in the total food supply is in general rather low. In general there is a considerable demand for the food products produced by intra- and peri-urban producers that often is exceeding the production by the producers associated with the SFSC. Urban consumers appear to be increasingly interested in urban, locally produced and healthy food, especially when they receive reliable information about where, by whom and how (food safety, ecological practices) these products are produced.
- Many SFSC initiatives are "social enterprises" in which profit maximisation is not the main driver, but the realisation of certain social goals (e.g., to enable marketing against fair prices for small-scale urban producers and/or create jobs for jobless youth and/or facilitate access to healthy food from known sources) although – of course – also social enterprises need to – at least – break even. Eventual surpluses are reserved for future investments rather than distributed to owners/shareholders.
- Many of these new SFSC initiatives are supported by some external organisation, be it an NGO or governmental organisation, during their establishment and early development. The degree and length of this support varies a lot. SFSC initiatives which build on a well-balanced mix of governance (public, market and civic) mechanisms appear to be relatively successful and more sustainable in the longer term.

FIGURE 5.3 An organic farmers' market in Laos
Source: Moustier.

Main drivers for the development of such innovative short food chains include:

- On the producer side: new channels for selling products, obtaining higher margins, more security of sale, more working capital (advance payments by consumers).
- On the consumers side: obtain healthier and/or safer food, solidarity with small farmers, strengthening the regional economy, facilitate ecological/responsible production and nature conservation in the city region.
- Local authorities may value also other benefits, e.g., reduction of urban food(t) print, or enhancing the resilience of the urban food system, or improving food security/nutrition of the urban poor.

The above-mentioned study by Renting and Dubbeling also observed that the development of innovative short food supply chains often reinforces the development of multi-functional (intra- and peri-) urban agriculture, and that the latter reinforces urban agriculture. The direct contact between producers and consumers during the food-selling activities in the city (at farmers' markets, in home delivery schemes, cooperative shops, etc.) leads to involvement of the citizens in activities in the surrounding agricultural areas, e.g., for recreational activities, or – the other way around – increased recreational visits by citizens to the surrounding countryside may lead to more direct food sales (on farm or through participation in direct marketing schemes).

Moreover, local authorities start to value eco-services provided by urban producers (such as management of flood zones, city greening, capturing CO_2 and reduction of urban food(t) print and reuse of recycled urban organic wastes and wastewater). Services that may lead to cost savings for public goods compared to state provisioning (e.g., waste disposal, green space management) and cost avoidance (e.g., health costs due to floods and rising temperatures due to climate change). This may result in more local government support for urban agriculture producers and their marketing efforts through various measures like preferential procurement of ecological food produced in the city region by small farmers, support for the establishment of farmers' markets and other direct marketing enterprises, and other measures (Renting and Dubbeling 2013).

Some lessons learnt by SFSCs in the South

Collective marketing schemes by small-scale urban producers often have limited access to mainstream food trading and distribution systems due to the requirements of supermarkets (demanding large volumes, uniform and high quality of the products, secured delivery throughout the year, timely delivery, etc.) and public administrations (product safety regulations, etc.), as well as their limited scale of production that make it difficult to compete with other suppliers due to economies of scale in production and transport and resource limitations that make it difficult to make larger up-front investments.

Market-diversification appears to be an important factor to reach scale. Two or more marketing channels may be combined: e.g., an outlet at farmers' markets with an arrangement with local institutions or restaurants and/or an online food shop.

In order to ensure stable consumer demand, it turns out to be important that food safety is secured and that the origin of the products is traceable by the consumers, that product quality is guaranteed and standardised, and that attention is paid to the presentation of products (branding, packaging, barcode, etc.). Also accreditation with local government or establishing a participatory quality control/ guarantee scheme helped SFSCs to enhance consumer confidence and outreach.

Building stable relations with specific consumer groups is instrumental for the creation of stable demand and the articulation of consumer preferences. Various of the SFSC initiatives involve the consumers in one way or other in the planning of production and market organisation (consumer supported agriculture), e.g., farmers inviting consumers to the farms to get to know how the food is produced, consumers making orders in advance (allowing the farmer to plan the production better and secure sales) and jointly defining quality criteria for the products and production practices to ensure safe, healthy and sustainable production.

Customer convenience plays another important role in generating demand. Enabling ordering by mobile phone or internet and home delivery of fresh food saves the consumers time and money (transport costs) and widens the group of clientele of the SFSC substantially.

Also product differentiation plays an important role in enhancing the customer satisfaction of SFSCs. Many SFSCs still mainly market a limited number of products, often starting with basic seasonal fresh vegetables and fruits only. In order to enhance sustainability of the SFSC it is important to broaden the product offer to a broader range of vegetables and fruits, and also include eggs, vegetable oil, kitchen herbs, etc., as well as transformed and conserved food products (produced by cooperative agro-enterprises in the city region).

Consequences for local policies and key issues for research

Consequences for local policies

Local governments can play an important role in the development of SFSCs in the city region by facilitating public–private linkages, especially by creating a facilitating legal framework and enabling conditions for SFSCs and specific support for new SFSC business, especially small and medium and social agro-enterprises involving small-scale producers from the city region.

Such facilitating policies might include the following:

- Promote networking and cooperation among ecologically producing small-scale producers in the city region and between them and urban consumer groups and service providers.
- Establish a city region SFSC development centre that provides start-up funds, such as low-interest matching loans, and training, technical assistance and business development services to new SFSC initiatives and during their first phase of development: support in-business planning, assisting in establishing quality control/certification schemes and commercial brands, start-up matching funds and soft loans, access to information on processing and packaging technologies and relevant policies and regulations (e.g., on food safety, waste management, etc.).
- Address the infrastructure needs of SFSCs for procurement, processing, warehousing, and distribution (establishment of farmers' markets or shops, regional food hubs/food procurement centres, provision of land/buildings for processing, storage and packaging).
- Adopt legislation and establish programmes regarding preferential local government food procurement of (nutritious, ecologically and fairly produced) food from small farmers in the city region (for canteens in offices, schools, hospitals, jails, food aid programmes, community centres, etc.).
- Organise and support campaigns to enhance consumer awareness about the need to eat healthy food and the importance of supporting ecologically produced fresh foods from the city region.

Box 5.1 provides an example of the many municipal or metropolitan programmes that support the development of short food supply chains in Latin America, Asia, the Middle East and Africa.

BOX 5.1   URBAN AGRICULTURE PROGRAMME ROSARIO, ARGENTINA: PROMOTING URBAN PRODUCTION, PROCESSING AND MARKETING

In response to the economic crisis of 2002, the municipal government of Rosario established the Municipal Urban Agriculture Programme with a very clear vision of establishing urban agriculture as a permanent and commercial activity in the city.

Vacant land in the city was mapped and areas that could not be built on and were suitable for farming were provided to citizens for gardening and agriculture. Basic equipment, training, seed, tools and compost were supplied. Within two years, some 10,000 low-income families were producing (organically grown) vegetables, earning from sales up to US$150 a month, well above the poverty line. To enhance security of tenure and facilitate permanent urban agricultural cultivation, in 2004 an ordinance was adopted that formalised grants of vacant urban land to residents for agriculture, and the Municipal Planning Secretariat integrated agriculture into Rosario's urban development plan.

A key part of its long-term strategy was the establishment of a system for the direct marketing of gardeners' produce amongst others by providing space, funding and technical support for the establishment of farmers' markets and associative agro-enterprises for the processing of vegetables, fruit, and medicinal and aromatic plants.

Also the city's commercial gardeners were supported to organise themselves in the Rosario Gardeners' Network and have been enrolled in the National Registry of Family Farmers, which entitles them to apply for municipal funding for their own investment projects, technical assistance and social benefits.

Source: FAO 2014.

Emerging themes for future research

On-going research in the context of the EU funded SUPURBFOOD programme (www.supurbfood.eu) shows that information on the business models applied by SFSCs in the Global South and their costs-benefits, their organisational and logistical setup, customer segments and market demand is still very scarce. Especially very few quantitative data can be found on costs and profits made and the economic margins realised by SFSC initiatives. This can be because of a real lack of data available, or, in other cases, the information is available but restricted because it is considered market-sensitive information or of poor quality. This constitutes an important bottleneck for the further analysis and development of business models for urban agriculture-based short chain enterprises.

Another research gap identified is the need to better understand the specific roles of governmental organisations, private entrepreneurs and civil society groups play in the organisation and development of SFSCs, and how these roles influences the sustainability of the SFSCs. What should be specific roles played by each of these sectors? What specific mix works best? This includes facilitating and supporting roles as well as taking part as a partner in the constitution and implementation of the SFSCs and their governance mechanisms.

Moreover, existing concepts and methods for business analyses are not always well-suited for application within the framework of SFSCs indicating a need for conceptual and methodological development, e.g., adaptation of the "business model canvas" approach to urban food procurement, processing and distribution in SFSCs in the context of countries in the Global South.

More research is needed into specific constraints encountered by SFSC initiatives in developing countries and through which strategies these might be tackled best. Issues related to enhancing scale and economic sustainability need special attention as well as issues related to access to (soft) financing and technical, marketing and management support services.

Also the value of urban agriculture and short food chains to the urban economy needs to be better estimated. This is first in terms of updated data on the contribution of short food chains to urban food consumption through self-consumption and market access, which requires rigorous consumer and market survey. This is also in terms of jobs and income generated. But also the economic value of the social benefits and eco-services provided by urban food systems should be estimated. A related challenging question to be further explored is how these social benefits and public costs savings provided by urban agriculture can be translated into economic opportunities for the urban producers and related SMEs in the city region.

References

Badj, S. 2008. Promoting organic and IPM market in Senegal. *Pesticidesnews* 79 (March). Available from: www.pan-uk.org/pestnews/Issue/pn79/pn79pp10-11.pdf.

Broutin, C.; Commeat, P.G.; Sokona, K. 2005. Le maraichage face aux contraintes de l'expansion urbaine. Le cas de Thiès/Fandène (Sénégal). Dakar: GRET/ENDA-GRAF.

Chandrashekar, H.M. 2011. Role of HOPCOMS in socio-economic change of farmer members in Mysore City. *International NGO Journal* 6(5): 122–132. Available from: http://eprints.uni-mysore.ac.in/14475/.

Cofie, O.; Veenhuizen, R. van; Drechsel, P. 2003. Contribution of urban and peri-urban agriculture to food security in sub-Saharan Africa. Paper presented at the Africa session of 3rd WWF, Kyoto, 17 March 2003.

Crush, J.; Hovorka, A.; Tevera, D. 2011. Food security in Southern African cities: The place of urban agriculture. *Progress in Development Studies* 11(4): 285–305.

Danso, G.; Keraita, B.; Afrane, Y. 2002. Farming systems in urban agriculture, Accra, Ghana. With special focus on its profitability, wastewater use and added malaria risk. Consultancy report submitted to FAO-Ghana office. Accra: International Water Management Institute, Ghana-office.

Dubbeling, M. 2013. Scoping paper feeding into the development of UNEP's position on urban and peri-urban agriculture. Leusden: RUAF Foundation. Available from: www.ruaf.org/sites/default/files/UNEP%20RUAF%20Scoping%20paper%20on%20Urban%20Agriculture%20FINAL.pdf.

FAO. 2012. Growing greener cities in Africa. First status report on urban and peri-urban horticulture in Africa. Rome: Food and Agriculture Organization of the United Nations.

FAO. 2014. Growing greener cities in Latin America and the Caribbean. A FAO report on urban and peri-urban agriculture in the region. Rome: Food and Agriculture Organization of the United Nations.

Figuié, M. 2004. Consumers' perception of tomato and water convolvulus quality in Hanoi. Hanoi: AVRDC (SUSPER project).

Gia, B. T. 1999. Vegetable production and marketing in Hanoi. In: *Agricultural products marketing in Japan and Vietnam: Proceedings of the first joint workshop at faculty of economics and rural development.* Hanoi: Agricultural University and HAU-JICA ERCB project, pp. 37–47.

Hoekstra, F.; Small, R. 2010. Harvest of Hope: Vegetable box scheme in Cape Town, South Africa. Leusden: RUAF Foundation.

Ho Than Son; Dao The Anh. 2006. Analysis of safe vegetable chain in Hanoi Province. Hanoi: Vietnam Agricultural Science Institute, CASRAD.

Laidlaw, A. 1977. Cooperatives and the poor. Ottawa: Canadian International Development Agency (IDRC).

Laroche-Dupraz, C.; Awono, C.; Vermersch, D. 2009. Impact des politiques commerciales sur le marché du poulet au Cameroun. Intérêts et limites d'un modèle d'équilibre partiel. *Économie rurale* (5): 67–84.

Mazucca, A.; Ponce, M.; Terrile, R. 2009. La agricultura urbana en Rosario: balance y perspectivas. Lima: IPES-Promoción del Desarrollo Sostenible.

Mougeot, L.J.A. 2013. Urban agriculture: Our logics of integration. Presentation made to the Canadian International Development Agency, Ottawa, March 2013.

Moustier, P. 2007. Urban horticulture in Africa and Asia: An efficient corner food supplier. *Acta Horticulturae* 762: 239–247.

Moustier, P. 2013. Short urban food chains in developing and emerging countries: Signs of the past or of the future? Presented in the 5th AESOP Conference on Sustainable Food Planning, Montpellier, 28–29 October 2013. Revised version forthcoming in: *Food territories: Essays on environmental and social impacts of the short chain delivery* (provisional title). (Ed.) Traversac, J. B. Heidelberg: Springer Verlag.

Moustier, P.; Danso, G. 2006. Local economic development and marketing of urban produced food. In: *Cities farming for the future: Urban agriculture for green and productive cities.* (Ed.) Veenhuizen, R. van. Leusden: RUAF Foundation and Manila: International Institute of Rural Reconstruction, pp. 173–208.

Moustier, P.; Nguyen, T.T.L. 2010. The role of farmer organisations in marketing peri-urban "safe vegetables" in Vietnam. *Urban Agriculture Magazine* 24: 50–52.

Prain, G.; Dubbeling, M. 2011.Urban agriculture: A sustainable solution to alleviating urban poverty, addressing the food crisis and adapting to climate change. Synthesis report on five case studies prepared for the World Bank. Leusden: RUAF Foundation.

Raschid-Sally, L.; Jayakody, P. 2008. Drivers and characteristics of wastewater agriculture in developing countries: Results from a global assessment. IWMI Research Report 127. Colombo: International Water Management Institute (IWMI). Available from: www.iwmi.cgiar.org/Publications/IWMI_Research_Reports/PDF/PUB127/RR127.pdf.

Reardon, T.; Gulati, A. 2008. The supermarket revolution in developing countries: Policies for "Competitiveness with Inclusiveness". IFPRI Policy Brief 2. Washington, DC: International Food Policy Research Institute (IFPRI).

Renting, H.; Dubbeling, M. 2013. Synthesis report: Innovative experiences with (peri-) urban agriculture and urban food provisioning: Lessons to be learned from the global South. Study for the EC-SUPURBFOOD project. Leusden: RUAF Foundation.

Rosenberg, T. 2011. Food deserts, Oases of nutrition. *New York Times* May 23. Available from: http://opinionator.blogs.nytimes.com/2011/05/23/in-food-deserts-oases-of-nutrition/?_r=0.

Sautier, D.; Anh, D. T.; Pham, C. N.; Nguyen, N. M. 2012. Agriculture et croissance urbaine à Hanoi. Hanoi: Adetef.

Sherwood, S.; Arce, A.; Berti, P.; Borja, R.; Oyarzun, P.; Bekkering, E. 2013. Tackling the new modernities: Modern food and counter movements in Ecuador. *Food Policy* 41: 1–10.

Thebo, A.; Drechsel, P.; Lambin, E. F. 2014. Global assessment of urban and peri-urban agriculture: Irrigated and rainfed croplands. *Environmental Research Letters* 9(11). Available from: http://iopscience.iop.org/1748-9326/9/11/114002/article.

Veenhuizen, R. van. 2007. Profitability and sustainability of urban and peri-urban agriculture. FAO-Agricultural Management, Marketing and Finance Paper No. 19. Rome: Food and Agriculture Organisation of the United Nations (FAO).

Zezza, A.; Tasciotti, L. 2010. Urban agriculture, poverty and food security: Empirical evidence from a sample of developing countries. *Food Policy* 35: 265–273.

6

URBAN AGRICULTURE'S CONTRIBUTIONS TO URBAN FOOD SECURITY AND NUTRITION

Maria Gerster-Bentaya

RURAL SOCIOLOGY DEPARTMENT, UNIVERSITY OF HOHENHEIM, GERMANY

Introduction

Urban food security is a growing concern, and the number of food-insecure people in the cities is approaching the number of rural food-insecure people (FAO 2013). Urbanization, specifically in Africa, goes hand in hand with urban poverty and thus urban food insecurity (e.g. Sen 1981; IFPRI 2002; Burton et al. 2013). Satterthwaite et al. (2010) report that from six out of ten African cities under study, even a higher percentage of the urban population than rural population was energy deficient despite their more sedentary lifestyle and lower energy requirements than in rural areas. Population growth and urbanization in Latin America as well puts pressure on food production and the distribution systems and cannot be covered by national production (Piñeiro et al. 2010). The rise of food prices in 2007–2008 and consequent hunger problems particularly affecting cities (e.g. Cohen and Garrett 2009; Prain and de Zeeuw 2010) revealed the problem of urban food and nutrition security. Food prices are expected to remain at a relative high level (IIED 2013), with an increase in food insecurity for certain groups of the urban population. Food insecurity and malnutrition occur in various forms, such as undernutrition, micronutrient deficiency and overnutrition, with negative health implications.

In the first part of this chapter, the complex nature of urban food security is discussed. Subsequently, the literature regarding the potential of urban agriculture for addressing various dimensions of urban food security, nutrition and health is reviewed. Both direct and indirect effects will be looked into. Direct effects relate to the potentials of urban agriculture in facilitating access to fresh and nutritious food products, as well as risks associated with urban agriculture that might negatively influence the health of urban citizens. Indirect effects of urban agriculture relate to the contributions urban agriculture and forestry make to the urban environment (e.g. reduction of urban heat) and risk reduction (e.g. improved urban water management). The final part of the article discusses challenges to be addressed in order to promote urban agriculture and as an important element of a city's food system for its contributions to urban food security, nutrition and health.

The dimensions of urban food security and nutrition

This chapter is based on a holistic understanding of food and nutrition security as worded by FAO/AGN:

> Food and nutrition security exists when all people at all times have physical, social and economic access to food, which is safe and consumed in sufficient quantity and quality to meet their dietary needs and food preferences, and is supported by an environment of adequate sanitation, health services and care, allowing for a healthy and active life.
>
> *(cited in CFS 2012: 7)*

Urban food security needs to consider the peculiarities of the urban context, specifically concerning the households' sources of food, accessibility and reliability (see Figure 6.1). Food must be available and accessible for the urban

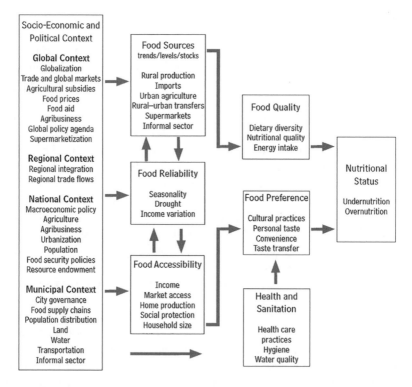

FIGURE 6.1 Dimensions of urban food security

Source: Dodson et al. 2012.

population at places they can reach, and it must be affordable. At household level, food must be prepared and consumed according to the individuals' dietary needs and preferences in the best possible quality. Health status, care for children and other weak household members, sanitation and hygiene aspects, as well as socio-cultural issues (specifically food preferences) all influence food intake at the household level and thus the nutritional status of the individual household member.

Looking at food and nutrition security from a rights-based approach (the right to adequate food) and the obligation of the states to respect, protect and fulfil that right, states should adopt measures to ensure that no individuals are deprived of their access to adequate food, and that they should proactively engage in activities to strengthen people's access to and use of resources, including means to ensure their livelihood and food security (McClain-Nhlapo 2004).

The key: access to food

The core of urban food (and nutrition) security is *access* to food (economically and physically). Economical access refers to the capacity of households to purchase food (Weingärtner 2009a) and, therefore, income is the decisive factor. Since food expenses for urban low-income households in cities in developing countries often make up 50–70% of their cash income, changes in income or food prices have tremendous impact on a household's food security (Zingel et al. 2011). The rapid increase of the number of food banks in cities in the USA, Canada and Europe indicates that problems related to economically restricted access to food are not restricted to developing countries (see, e.g., Riches and Silvasti 2014).

Physical access to food may be limited in cases where low-income areas lack grocery shops, supermarkets or fresh markets to obtain their day-to-day food nearby or have trouble reaching such outlets further away due to lack of, or costly, transport, fear of crime or other limitations (e.g. old age, physical handicaps). Especially, access to fresh and nutritious food may be a problem in certain parts of the city (and especially low-income areas) when neighbourhood shops are getting fewer in number (and/or tend to concentrate on food items with a longer shelf life) due to competition with large supermarkets at city or district margins, or where hot food takeaways and fast food eateries are becoming more frequent (offering food at affordable prices but also containing more trans fats and saturated fats and refined sugar and additives and less vitamins, minerals and fibres) (Pereira 2005). Literature on the urban food system, especially from the USA and the UK, often discuss the issue of the limited physical access of low-income urban households to food (especially healthy and nutritious food) due to flaws in the distribution system. Underserved low-income areas are often named "food deserts" (e.g. Wrighley 2002).

Battersby's (2011) research in two (densely build, inner-city, low-income) areas of Cape Town showed a diversity of food sources (Figure 6.2). The graph clearly

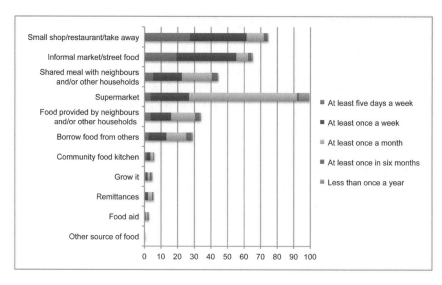

FIGURE 6.2 Sources of food and frequency of use in two low-income areas of Cape Town

Source: Battersby 2011.

shows the important role of the informal sector for the day-to-day provision of food to urban citizens, especially the low- and middle-income households.

Change in eating habits and dietary patterns

Globalization, economic growth and urbanization lead to important changes in the diets of urban consumers – specifically in the South – where populations especially shift towards processed foods richer in salt, sugar and saturated fats, foods that have a long shelf life and are attractive to urban populations and younger generations, but are often less nutritious and less healthy (Pinstrup-Andersen 2012). The drastic changes in food procurement and diets of urban households is related to the establishment of supermarkets and the increasing dominance of supermarket chains in the urban food provisioning as well as the increased reliance on food imports (de Schutter 2014).

Research in Asia (Anderson and Strutt 2012; IIED 2013), and specifically the two biggest growing countries, India and China (Gandhi and Zhou 2014), and also in megacities like Casablanca (Gerster-Bentaya et al. 2015) and other cities in southern Africa (Crush and Frayne 2010), have shown that food demand is undergoing a huge transformation and will undergo further change. The urban citizens consume more refined products (e.g. white bread instead of full-grain products), more fast food and more convenience food, such as meals and take-home food, and more sugar and fat/oil. Better-off households are also increasing their consumption of animal products, vegetables and fruits, and reducing their consumption of cereals.

Also people cook less at home. Due to the daily "migration" between living and working places, as well the lack of alternative choices and lack of means to prepare food at home, an increase of extra-household food consumption can be observed: meals in schools, canteens, street food, fast food restaurants in the inner cities, etc. The negative effect of fast food consumption on obesity (children and adults) is widely researched (e.g. Bowman et al. 2004; Schröder et al. 2007, Hollands et al. 2012).

The influence of health on nutrition and vice versa

The health status influences the body's capacity of using the food. Sick people can use good quality food less efficiently than a healthy person. In return, the quality and quantity of food influence the nutritional status and well-being of a person.

Negative health consequences of bad nutrition are various forms of malnutrition, such as stunting (low height for age, caused by long-term insufficient nutrient intake at young age; effects are largely irreversible), wasting (low weight for height of children under five, the result of acute significant food shortage and/or disease indicating a serious mortality risk) and overweight and obesity (excessive fat accumulation that presents a health risk. A body mass index [BMI] of more than 25 is considered overweight and obese if BMI is 30 or more).

Higher consumption of animal products, processed foods and eating-out-of-home in combination with less physical work can result in overweight and obesity. The health risks associated with obesity include type 2 diabetes, coronary artery disease, and stroke, cancers, osteoarthritis, liver and gall bladder disease (Kopelman 2007). Overweight may lead not only to obesity and influence physical health but also determines a person's well-being as a whole.

If the body lacks micronutrients, minerals and vitamins, these deficiencies may also cause health problems (such as anaemia, goiter, night blindness) (Weingärtner 2009b).

Undernutrition and overweight co-exist in many cities, leading to a double burden of malnutrition (see, e.g., Prain and Dubbeling 2011).

Who is food insecure in cities – or at risk of being so?

The food and nutrition security of urban household members is determined within the context of their livelihoods. Other than in rural areas, urban dwellers' livelihoods predominantly depend on cash economy: what urban people eat, they must buy. The food price hikes in the years 2007–2009 have clearly demonstrated that these strongly affect urban food security (e.g. Cohen and Garrett 2009; Tacoli et al. 2013), and that rising food prices (and economic crisis) especially affect the food security of households with a low and/or insecure or irregular income, because – as mentioned – already a large part of their income is spent on food items and the capacities of poor food insecure households to recover from stress and shocks (e.g. low food prices, economic crisis) is limited.

Research undertaken by RUAF Foundation in Rosario, Bogota, Accra, Kitwe and Colombo during the second half of 2009 (Prain and de Zeeuw 2010) – including household surveys, 24-hour food recall, and anthropometry of under-five-year-olds and women from 15 to 49 – showed that:

- In the large majority of households in low-income neighbourhoods, food accounted for half or more of all expenditures.
- In reaction to economic crisis and food price hikes, the low-income households reduced substantially the quantity of food intake and the quality of food purchased.
- This substantially further increased the already high levels of stunting and wasting, especially in Kitwe, Colombo and Accra, but less so in Rosario due to the presence of a strong urban agricultural programme in this city since the Argentinian economic crisis in 2002.
- Remedial actions taken in the other cities during the crisis had little effect on lessening food insecurity (too little, too late and not well directed).
- Together with underweight, there is also high incidence of overweight and obesity, especially among women, and also in some populations of children, indicating the earlier indicated "double burden" due to malnutrition.

IIED (2013) predicts stable but relatively high-level food prices for prospering economies and in the increasingly urban and non-agricultural Asian countries. In South America, food inflation has been constantly higher than in other sub-regions. Inflation of food price is expected to increase more significantly in Europe and in Asia, remain stable in Africa, and decrease in Latin America (FAO 2014). In the long run, food prices will rise again if agricultural productivity cannot keep up with the increasing demand and will have adverse effects on economic growth, "particularly to the detriment of the poor as higher prices make it more difficult to get out of poverty" (IIED 2013: vii).

Malnutrition in urban areas is often concentrated in poor neighbourhoods and associated with low income and unmet basic needs. Research carried out by the Food and Agriculture Organisation of the United Nations (FAO) shows that the poor consume fewer calories and nutrients than higher-income families, although they spend a greater share of their income on food (Argenti 1998). Moreover, the urban poor often live in slums, squatter and resettlement areas in unhealthy conditions due to poor access to clean and safe water, and poor sanitary conditions; exposure to HIV/AIDS, crime, violence, alcohol and other drug abuse; limited food choices and poor access to health and social support systems (Mercato et al. 2007). As indicated above, poor health and poor nutrition mutually reinforce each other.

At special risk are children. They show signs of malnutrition first. If young children do not get adequate nutrition over a longer period of time, some negative effects are irreversible (including the risk of becoming obese at adulthood

(Sawaya et al. 2004)). Another risk group are old and sick people in general, and people living with HIV/AIDS specifically.

Coping strategies of urban households in case of food insecurity

When urban households experience food insecurity, a range of coping strategies are activated by the household members, including both immediate actions like – amongst others – changes in diets/food intake (quality and quantity), shifts in the household budgets, using alternative food sources (e.g. food aid, food banks), taking up local food production and maintaining urban–rural linkages through multi-locational households. These strategies will be explained further in the following paragraphs.

Change in diets/food consumption

Consumption-related reactions to food (and income) shortages as reported, e.g., by Cohen and Garrett (2009), Prain and de Zeeuw (2010), Battersby (2011) and Owino et al. (2013), include reduction of the number of meals per day, reduction of portions per meal and eating cheaper/less quality food. Additional strategies reported by Hoisington et al. (2001) are mothers depriving themselves of nourishment to feed their children, and specifically their daughters.

Alternative food sources

Part of the coping strategies of food-insecure households include the participation in early childhood nutrition and school meals programmes, food aid programmes (in kind, stamps and vouchers, cash), soup kitchens and food banks and other ad hoc institutional arrangements to address emergency food needs (Mitchell and Heynen 2013); to borrow money from neighbours and relatives, share meals with neighbours or relatives (or send children to eat there) and other community based mechanisms (Gerster-Bentaya et al. 2011); and to scavenge food from restaurant dumpsters and waste left at fresh markets (Miewald and McCann 2014).

Shifts in household budget

If money is scarce and needs to be spent on food, other expenses are reduced or stopped, such as postponing buying needed medicines or clothes, delaying paying bills (e.g. house rent, water/electricity services, and school), and buying food on credit. The latter is rather possible with informal retail stores (Ligthelm 2005 in Battersby 2011; Knight et al. 2014). Also removing children temporally or permanently (especially girls) from school (if school meals are not provided) to save expenses for school fees, school material and uniforms is often practiced in emergencies (Prain and de Zeeuw 2010).

Socially marginalized strategies

Socially critical strategies are mentioned by Owino et al. (2013) who report about strategies of the urban poor to cope with food insecurity by arranging early marriages, engaging daughters in prostitution and sending children on streets to beg.

Local food production for self-consumption

Engaging in local food production for self-consumption and additional income (or exchange for other goods) is another coping strategy to enhance household food security (e.g. FAO 2009; Tambwe et al. 2011; Corbould 2013). We will discuss the role of urban agriculture (including market-oriented urban agriculture) in urban food supply and nutrition in the next section of this chapter in more detail.

Urban–rural linkages for (urban) food security

Tacoli (2000) points out that maintaining strong linkages between urban and rural households and between members of the same household located in both urban and rural areas is an important strategy to ensure their food security: sending food to urban relatives in need and temporary migration of some family members to rural relatives may contribute to the food security of urban households.

Schmidt-Kallert and Kreibich (2004) explain the phenomena of multi-locational households whereby one part of the household members stays in the countryside (mostly the elderly people and very young children) and the other part lives in the city (the adults and elder children for education). They describe the sharing of tasks as follows:

> The rural section of the household has the function of looking after the small children, taking care of the elderly and the sick, and producing surplus food for the urban household members. The urban members earn the cash income and take on a mentoring role for new migrants. They also organize the exchange of goods, services and information.
>
> *(Schmidt-Kallert and Kreibich 2004: 466)*

Such arrangements can work out for many years and exist in the North and the South equally (Dick and Schmidt-Kallert 2011).

The potential of (intra- and peri-) urban agriculture for urban food security, nutrition and health

According to Mougeot (2013), research shows that intra- and especially peri–urban agriculture contributes to a non-negligible share of all food consumed in the city, with high shares for all fresh and perishable products, and that food production in and around the cities contributes to enhancing household food security, especially of the poorer sections of the urban population and improving nutrition (more meals, more balanced diet year-round, savings for other food, less stunting and wasting) (Yeudall 2007; Zezza and Tasciotti 2010).

The contribution of urban agriculture in total urban food supply

Though it is recognized that (intra- and peri-) urban agriculture will by itself not be able to feed entire cities, nor will it provide all food that households need, it may constitute a relevant and needed food source to meet urban food demand. The available data confirm the importance of (especially peri-) urban agriculture in the provision of perishable food commodities, including fresh vegetables (e.g. amaranth, okra, cabbages, lettuces, tomatoes), fruits, eggs, milk, pork and other products. A compilation of available research data by Van Veenhuizen (2007) indicated that in many cities in the Global South a large part of the fresh vegetables consumed in the city are supplied from within the city region (see Table 6.1).

TABLE 6.1 Food provided by (intra- and peri-) urban agriculture

City (source)	Percentage of urban demand met by (intra- and peri-) urban agriculture						
	Leafy vegetables	All vegetables	Eggs	Poultry	Milk	Pork	Fruit
Havana (Gonzalez Novo and Murphy 2000)		58					39*
La Paz (Kreinecker 2000)		30					
Dakar (Mbaye and Moustier 2000)		70–80		65–70			
Dar es Salaam (Jacobi et al. 2000)		90			60		
Addis Ababa (Tegegne et al. 2000)					70		
Nairobi (Foeken and Mwangi 2000)							
Accra (Cofie et al. 2003)		90					
Brazzaville (Moustier 1999)	80						
Bangui (David 1992)	80						
Yaoundé (Dongmo 1990)	80						
Bissau (David and Moustier 1993)	90						
Nouakshott (Laurent 1999)	90						
Jakarta (Purnomohadi 2000)		10					16
Shanghai (Cai and Zhang 2000)		60	90	50	90–100	50	
Hong Kong (Smit et al. 1996)		45		68		15	
Singapore (Smit et al. 1996)		25					
Hanoi (GTZ 2000; Phuong Anh et al. 2004)	70–80	0–75 seasonal variation	40	50		50	
Vientiane (Kethongsa et al. 2004)	100	20–100 seasonal variation					

Note: * non-citrus.

Source: Van Veenhuizen 2007 (further elaboration of a table in Moustier and Danso 2006).

It is quite probable that due to ongoing urbanization and new developments in the food supply and distribution system during the last few years (e.g. improved road structure and cold storage facilities, the growing role of supermarkets) these percentages have undergone changes during the last decade, changes that are still under-researched.

The contribution of urban agriculture to enhancing access of the urban poor to nutritious and healthy food

For the households involved in local food production

Fresh, nutritious food is often relatively expensive and lower-income households tend to buy fewer such foods (Beaulac et al. 2009 cited in Gordon et al. 2011; Larson et al. 2009 cited in Hartline-Grafton 2011). Moreover, as discussed earlier, the offer of fresh and nutritious foods by groceries in their own neighbourhood might be limited. Moreover, good-quality food, especially fruits and perishable vegetables, imported from the rural areas or abroad, lose part of their nutritional value during transport and storage (Kader 2005).

Self-produced nutritious food

Local food production by the urban poor (in home and community gardens, and on temporally vacant plots, on the grounds of hospitals, schools and community centres, along highways and railways, below power lines and in flood zones) enhances local availability of fresh and nutritious foods (especially leafy vegetables, and also eggs and meat of small livestock) that are consumed by its producers and surpluses are sold at reasonable prices mainly in the same neighbourhoods.

The participation of the urban poor in urban agriculture is substantial in many cities, especially in sub-Saharan Africa, with considerable variation between cities (from 5 to 64% with an estimated average of about 20–25% of urban households involved in local food production in one way or another [Crush and Frayne 2010; Prain and Lee-Smith 2010]. However, the self-produced food is often only part of the total household food needs, although important to diversify the diets and adding essential vitamins and minerals to the diet. This is because the spaces available for intra-urban food production are often very small, land use insecure, and production practices and conditions far from optimal.

Savings and income to purchase more/better food

Next to consuming their self-produced fresh food, the producing urban households also save money on the purchase of vegetables and other self-produced products. The systematic assessment of the socio-economic impacts of (mainly intra-) urban agriculture undertaken by the RUAF Foundation for the World Bank in four major cities (Accra, Bangalore, Lima and Nairobi) showed that high percentages of respondents in most cities (Bangalore 56%; Nairobi 70%; Lima 73%; Accra 80%) report that savings coming from own food production enabled them to purchase other types of food (either local staple foods like rice or floor) or higher-value items in the diet like fish, eggs, dairy, meat, sugar, oil) or essential other non-food household needs (e.g. house rent or health care) (Prain and Dubbeling 2011).

A third route to improved nutrition for the urban poor who are involved in local food production is through income generated from the sales of (the surpluses) of their produce. As stated earlier, economic access to food is a key factor in urban food security. Local market-oriented food production, processing and selling can help the urban poor to gain an additional, or the only, income needed to obtain food they could not afford otherwise.

The above-mentioned RUAF study demonstrated the role of urban agriculture as an economic livelihood strategy (stable occupation and income) for vulnerable urban households, especially women-headed households and households with elderly or less-educated people. The same study found that urban agriculture is highly compatible with several other kinds of employment and better rewarding than petty trading and casual labouring. Urban agricultural activities can also be combined relatively easily with other occupations and thus allows combining multiple income sources, which – for resource poor and vulnerable households – is a very important risk-reduction and adaptation strategy. Most of the interviewed households considered the income generation from urban agriculture of greater importance than access to additional food. The study also found that an important part of the income from their agricultural production (e.g. vegetables, poultry) consisted of cash savings on food expenditures that otherwise would have to be purchased (Prain and Dubbeling 2011).

Zezza and Tasciotti (2010) compiled data from various reports worldwide published between 1998 and 2005 on the contribution of (intra- and peri-) urban agriculture to household income. The greatest was in African countries (18–24%) and Asia (3–13%) while, in other regions, the contribution was below 5%. These values are averages for all urban producers (for subsistence-oriented and market-oriented producers). For specific categories of the urban producers, especially for the livestock keepers, (mainly peri-urban) irrigated vegetable producers, and fish or mushroom producers, the percentages of income derived from agriculture are often quite higher as well as the level of incomes derived by them.

The provision of monetary income by urban agriculture appears to be related to the nature of produced products and the amount of invested capital (in particular in irrigation, animals and inputs). Monetary income tends to increase from staple food (e.g. rice, maize or cassava) to horticultural crops, aquaculture and livestock; and from seasonal-dry to all-year irrigated crops (Moustier and Danso 2006). Studies by Danso et al. (2002a, 2002b) indicate that irrigated mixed vegetable farming in Ghanaian cities generates incomes close to gross national income per capita. In Bangkok the activity generating the highest income and also requiring the most capital is shrimp farming (Vagneron 2007). Omore et al. (2004) calculate that the number of jobs (mobile collectors, assemblers, small-scale processors and distributors) generated in (mainly urban and peri-urban) small scale dairy per 100 litres of milk was 13.4 in Bangladesh, 13.7 in Kenya and 17.2 in Bangladesh, and that the wage of the workers ranged between US$20 in Bangladesh and US$67 in Kenya. Knowing that, e.g., in Kenya over 1 million litres of milk were collected, processed and marketed, these values indicate substantial incomes and jobs generated.

Zezza and Tasciotti (2010) conclude that there is a correlation between income derived from urban agriculture and household dietary diversity. They also report a correlation between participation in agriculture and poverty, with participation in the poorest quintiles being higher than 50% in eight out of fifteen countries.

However, Frayne et al. (2014) report from the comparison between 11 African cities in southern Africa that rather relatively "richer" households can benefit more from urban agriculture than poor ones, because poorer households have less means of production (access to land and water, capital to buy seeds and other inputs, and to invest in animals, irrigation, etc.).

So while the urban poor are participating more in (often intra-) urban agriculture to secure their food security and livelihood, the higher incomes from agriculture are obtained by the less-poor and middle-income producers (often small-scale commercial and mainly peri-urban producers).

According to FAO (2010), urban households that engage in farming activities tend to consume greater quantities of food (sometimes up to 30% more) and have a more diversified diet, as indicated by an increase in the number of food groups consumed. Vegetable, fruit and meat products are consumed in greater quantities, which translate into an overall higher intake of energy as well as higher calorie availability (see also Alaimo et al. 2008; Davis et al. 2011). Positive effects of self-production activities on the nutritional balance and micronutrient intake of the households are enhanced if the participants receive assistance in crop choice and nutrition education (HKI 2012).

Davies et al. (2011) observed positive health benefits of the physical gardening activities.

For non-producing urban poor households

The earlier section on the role of urban agriculture in total urban food supply indicates that urban agriculture makes substantial, specific and complementary contributions to urban food supply, especially of perishable goods. But do these products produced within the city region also end up being consumed by the (non-producing) urban poor?

Figure 6.1 on the food distribution sources used by the urban lower-income groups in Cape Town underlined the importance of the informal sector in the urban food distribution to the urban poor. According to FAO (2003), the informal sector participates in urban food supply and distribution at three levels: (1) maintaining urban–rural links via exchanges of food items and services within or outside the family or through direct sale by urban producers; (2) serving as an intermediary in the supply and distribution of unprocessed products (transporters and retailers, including mobile fresh food vendors; also generating jobs and income for these informal workers); and (3) the processing and sale of ready-to-eat food: street food and small catering, mainly performed by low- and middle-income households.

FAO specifically recognizes the significant role of street food for millions of low- and middle-income consumers in urban areas on a daily basis. Street foods (e.g. mobile carts selling hot food, open air hot food shops at markets) may be the least expensive and most accessible means of obtaining a nutritionally balanced meal outside the home for many low- and middle-income people, provided that the consumer is informed and able to choose the proper combination of foods. But at the same time, street food includes a number of challenges regarding food safety, sanitation, traffic congestion and accidents (FAO 2009; Chakravarty 2011).

Next to the traditional informal channels, products from market-oriented (intra- and peri-) urban producers also reach the consumers through innovative short food chains (farmers markets, box schemes, virtual shops, buyers' cooperatives, etc.). However, only a part of these new distribution channels reach the urban poor, while other parts are more directed towards the higher income groups in order to enlarge their margins (see Chapter 5 for more details).

When low-income households can purchase food directly from urban producers, this enhances their access to fresh and nutritious food and probably at lower prices (fewer intermediaries, less transport and storage costs) than in longer food chains, although supermarkets nowadays may have such advantages of scale that it may be more difficult to compete on price (e.g. Mkwambisi et al. 2011; Prain and Dubbeling 2011). Because of lengthy transport and the related deterioration of quality, the nutritive quality of products in the short food chains can be better (FAO 2011).

The contribution of urban agriculture to the resilience of the urban food system

Urban food supply can be heavily affected by distortions in food imports due to price hikes and other distortions in the global food markets, droughts and other natural disasters that reduce rural agricultural production, and floods and armed conflicts that interrupt the transport of food to the cities from harbours and rural areas.

As discussed earlier, it is quite probable that international food prices will continue to increase. The climate change will affect rural production and transport to the city. Also the risk that food supply from distant or global sources will be interrupted due to armed conflicts has recently increased substantially in large parts of Africa and the Middle East.

Producing more in and around the cities will enhance the resilience of the urban food system by reducing the reliance on more distant and global supply chains and creating a buffer against shocks in affecting the supply from rural and global sources (FAO 2011; Burton et al. 2013).

UN Habitat (2014) considers urban agriculture as an important strategy for mitigating the negative effects of climate change in cities. Indirectly, urban agriculture reduces the negative effects of floods by keeping flood zones free from construction, reducing run off and facilitating prevention of infiltration. It also reduces urban heat in providing more shade and evapotranspiration. In both cases important health costs and deaths are prevented. For a more extensive discussion on urban agriculture and climate change, see Chapter 8.

Change in nutrition habits – specifically in children – occur best if knowledge of nutrition and dietary intake is coupled with information about the food chain (including production, storage, processing and transport) (see Heim et al. 2009; Guitart et al. 2014), especially when they are actively involved in this process themselves or at least can see how food is produced. This also creates enhanced understanding of the food system and thus an awareness and willingness to pay for healthy food, as some public health programmes have shown (Bellows et al. 2004).

Health risks associated with urban agriculture

There are a number of health risks for human health related to producing food close to many human beings. A number of factors may affect the quality of the food produced in urban areas and have a negative influence on the consumer's health. The production and processing itself also includes some risks for human health of the workers. Lock and de Zeeuw (2001), Gerster-Bentaya (2013) and others have provided overviews of such risks and on how these can be reduced or prevented, which we briefly summarize below.

Most of the health risks associated with urban agriculture can be well managed if these risks are well assessed and taken into account during planning (e.g. appropriate selection of sites and production systems), appropriate preventive measures are taken, and people involved in local production, processing and marketing are well instructed on health aspects related to their activities and how to reduce/prevent health risks through adequate practices.

Main health issues related to urban agriculture include the following:

Uptake of heavy metals and other toxic residues from polluted soils, irrigation water and air

The heavy metals contained in contaminated soils and irrigation may accumulate in the edible parts of crops that are consumed by people or fed to animals and may provoke – after a long period – carcinogenic effects on human health (Birley and Lock 2000). However, Puschenreiter et al. (1999) conclude that, after considering the several available pathways of heavy metals to the human food chain, that soils with slight heavy metal contamination can be used safely for gardening and agriculture if proper precautions are followed.

Specifically when growing on brownfields, special caution is needed (e.g. Heinegg et al. 2002; Egwu and Agbenin 2013). Where soil contamination is likely, soil testing is highly recommended, also to know what measures have to be taken (von Hoffen and Säumel 2014). Such measures may include removal of certain layers, biological remediation, application of lime or farmyard to immobilize the heavy metals, and crop restrictions (excluding crops that take up heavy metals easily like spinach). See, for example, the guidelines developed by the EPA (2011).

Contamination of irrigation water by industry has to be prevented by regulations and programmes to promote treatment at the source and reduce disposal of toxic residues in streams and rivers and in the air. The quality of sources of irrigation water should be regularly tested and, if needed, preventive measures taken (e.g. crop restriction and changes in the irrigation practices, application of lime and farmyard). Where air pollution is above critical level, e.g. downwind of heavy industry and within 50–100 meters of main highways, buffer areas with trees could be created and/or crop choice restricted and washing crops before marketing required (Birley and Lock 2000).

Contamination of crops with pathogenic organisms due to re-use of urban wastewater and organic solid wastes

Irrigation with water from rivers and streams contaminated with human and animal excreta and improperly treated wastewater may contain various bacteria, protozoan parasites, enteric viruses and helminths, which may cause a variety of negative health effects in human beings. Urban farmers in developing countries use these water sources because it may be the only water source available to them and/or for the nutrients this water contains (Huibers and van Lier 2005; Drechsel et al. 2006).

Also, the re-use of urban organic solid wastes (household wastes, market refuse, night soil, manure, and agro-industrial wastes) as a soil improver in urban agriculture (and as an ingredient for livestock and fish feed) may contaminate crops with pathogens if the compost is not properly prepared (too-low temperature).

The World Health Organisation (WHO) published in 2006 revised guidelines for the use of wastewater and excreta in agriculture, indicating various risk management strategies, including establishment of adequate wastewater treatment facilities and improved functioning of existing ones; waste separation at source and application of proper composting methods; restriction of crop choice in areas where water quality cannot be guaranteed; farmer education on adequate crop choice and proper irrigation techniques; education of food traders and retailers and consumers (hygiene, washing, etc.) (WHO 2006). For more details, see Chapter 7.

Unhygienic handling of food

Food safety does not end with production. Frequently, food is contaminated during processing, storing or distribution. Frequent sources of contamination are, for example, vegetable markets, slaughterhouses and small-scale processing units (e.g. of dairy products) that lack clean water, good standards of hygiene and/or adequate equipment (Gerster-Bentaya 2013). Risk management strategies include proper education of the entrepreneurs involved in processing, transport and storage of food produced in the city region on safety issues, regular control of processing businesses and assistance in improving the infrastructure.

Residues of agrochemicals

Intensive use of agrochemicals (fertilizers, pesticides, fungicides) in agriculture may lead to residues of agrochemicals in crops, especially vegetables, as well as in meat, milk or eggs (FAO 1988). Especially after many years of intensive commercial horticulture, residues of noxious chemicals may accumulate in the crops. However, most small-scale urban producers do not use large amounts of agrochemicals due to lack of means to buy these inputs or because they use compost and apply Integrated Pest and Disease Management (IPM) and other sustainable farming principles (Lee-Smith and Prain 2006).

Among the many risk management strategies, the following items figure amongst others: farmer education on the proper management of agrochemicals; promotion of ecological farming practices and IPM; better control of sales of banned pesticides; introduction of cheap protective clothing and equipment; and monitoring of product quality especially in areas of intensive production. See also Chapter 9.

Zoonotic diseases and diseases transferred to humans by rodents and flies attracted by agriculture

Zoonotic diseases are infectious diseases transmitted through direct contact of human beings with animals during production, processing or consumption of contaminated animal products (bovine tuberculosis and brucellosis mainly from ingestion of contaminated unpasteurised milk; tapeworms and trichinosis mainly by consumption of infected meat; Leptospirosis mainly through contact of humans with infected animal urine; and Salmonella and campylobacter through contamination of animal feed). Malaria occurs in many environments but particularly in areas where irrigation is practiced mainly in relatively clean water. The mosquitos that spread filiarsis and dengue breed in standing water containing much organic matter. Farms attract rodents and flies that may be carriers of diseases (e.g. plague). Scavenging by pigs is associated with food-borne diseases such as amoebic and bacillary dysentery.

Risk management strategies include, amongst others: farmer education on proper waste management practices in livestock; restriction of uncontrolled movement of livestock in urban areas and promotion of stall feeding; proper design of water tanks and irrigation systems in peri-urban areas; strict slaughterhouse regulations; consumer education regarding heating of milk and proper cooking or freezing of meat products; and composting of manure before application. See also Chapter 10.

Conclusion

Many cities have recognized the urgent need to place food on the policy agenda and to develop adequate policies and programmes to secure urban food security and create favourable conditions for the development of an urban food system that provides safe and nutritious and affordable food to all categories of the urban population.

The above sections show that urban food security and nutrition are influenced by a variety of factors that vary from city to city and even within cities. This implies that urban food security and nutrition policies need to be comprehensive and integrate a variety of policy measures and programmes.

Such policies and programmes need to be based on thorough knowledge about food insecure groups, their localities, the magnitude, type of food insecurity, times and duration as well as the reasons for food insecurity and the likelihood of occurrence of these factors, and these basic aspects need to be explored prior to any action. Food security situation analysis including risk assessments to prevent food insecurity situations need to be conducted specifically in poverty pocket areas of the cities.

Important challenges that need to be tackled are, amongst others:

- Lack of awareness and knowledge among consumers as well as planners and decision makers about the links between food, adequate nutrition and health as well as insufficient insight into the complexity of the urban food system with its variety of actors, channels, linkages, drivers and trends and how this effects urban food security, nutrition and health.
- Ongoing city expansion: Urban centres often expand on the most productive land because cities are historically built on fertile soils (Satterthwaite et al. 2010). In addition, urbanization causes environmental perturbations in the surrounding agricultural ecosystems (e.g. landscape fragmentation, changes in the water cycle and reduced habitats) (Gardi et al. 2014). City planners for a long time have not given much attention to safeguarding the food production and eco-services of productive open spaces in and around the city and have to develop new ways of incorporating such functions in the urban system and preserve the green and productive spaces (see also Chapter 4).
- Need for inter-institutional collaboration: Food and nutrition issues are normally dealt with by Departments of Health mainly. However, as seen above, enhancing urban food security and nutrition have as much to do with other departments too: economic development, planning, urban agriculture, to mention a few, which need to collaborate closely in situation analysis and food system planning.

References

Alaimo, K.; Packnett, E.; Miles, R. A.; Kruger, D. J. 2008. Fruit and vegetable intake among urban community gardeners. *Journal of Nutrition, Education and Behaviour* 2008(40): 94–101.

Anderson, K.; Strutt, A. 2012. Agriculture and food security in Asia by 2030. ADBI Working Paper Series No. 368. Tokyo: Asian Development Bank Institute.

Argenti, O. (ed.) 1998. Food into cities. Food into Cities Collection, Vol. 09/98. Rome: Food and Agriculture Organization of the United Nations (FAO).

Battersby, J. 2011. The state of urban food insecurity in Cape Town. Urban Food Security Series No. 11. Kingston: Queen's University; Cape Town: AFSUN.

Bellows, A.; Brown, K.; Smit J. 2004. Health benefits of urban agriculture. Available from: www.community-wealth.org/sites/clone.community-wealth.org/files/downloads/paper-bellows-brown-smit.pdf.

Birley, M. H.; Lock, K. 2000. The health impacts of peri-urban natural resource development. London: Cromwell Press.

Bowman, S. A.; Gortmaker, S. L.; Ebbeling, C. B.; Pereira, M. A.; Ludwig, D. S. 2004. Effects of fast-food consumption on energy intake and diet quality among children in a national household survey. *Paediatrics* 113(1 Pt. 1): 112–118.

Burton P.; Lyons, K.; Richards, C.; Amati, M.; Rose, N.; Des Fours, L.; Pires, V.; Barclay, R. 2013. Urban food security, urban resilience and climate change. Gold Coast: National Climate Change Adaptation Research Facility.

Cai, Y.; Zhang, Z. 2000. Shanghai: Trends towards specialized and capital-intensive urban agriculture. In: *Growing cities, growing food: Urban agriculture on the policy agenda.* (Eds.) Bakker, N; Dubbeling, M.; Guendel, S.; Sabel-Koschella, U.; Zeeuw, H. de. Leusden: RUAF Foundation, pp. 467–475.

Chakravarty, I. 2011. Role of informal sector in urban food supply: Traditional markets and street vendors. Presentation at FAO Regional workshop Ensuring Resilient Food Systems in Asian Cities, Bangkok, 17–18 November 2011.

CFS. 2012. Coming to terms with terminology. FAO United Nations Food and Agriculture Organization (FAO) – Committee on World Food Security (CFS). Available from: www.fao.org/fsnforum/sites/default/files/file/Terminology/MD776%28CFS___Coming_to_terms_with_Terminology%29.pdf.

Cofie, O. O; Veenhuizen, R. van; Drechsel, P. 2003. Contribution of urban and peri-urban agriculture to food security in Sub-Saharan Africa. Paper presented at the Water and Food Session, Africa Day, 3rd World Water Forum, Kyoto, 17 March 2003.

Cohen, M. J.; Garrett, J. L. 2009. The food price crisis and urban food (in)security. Human Settlements Working Paper Series. Urbanization and Emerging Population Issue 2. London: International Institute for Environment and Development (IIED).

Corbould, C. 2013. Feeding the Cities: Is urban agriculture the future of food security? Strategic Analysis Paper. Future Directions International. Available from: www.future-directions.org.au.

Crush, J.; Frayne B. 2010. The invisible crisis: Urban food security in southern Africa. Urban Food Security Series No. 1. Cape Town: African Food Security and Urban Network (AFSUN).

Danso, G.; Keraita, B.; Afrane, Y. 2002a. Farming systems in urban agriculture, Accra, Ghana. Consultancy report for FAO. Accra: International Water Management Institute (IWMI).

Danso, G.; Drechsel, P.; Wiafe-Antui, T.; Gyiele, L. 2002b. Income of farming systems around Kumasi, Ghana. *Urban Agriculture Magazine* 7: 5–6.

David, O. 1992. Diagnostic de lápprovisionnement de Bangui en legumes. Memoire de stage de l'ESAT. Montpellier: CNEARC.

David, O.; Moustier, P.; 1993. Systèmes maraîchers approvisionnant Bissau: résultats des enquêtes. Montpellier: CIRAD.

Davis, J.; Ventura, E. M.; Cook, L. T.; Gyllenhammer, L. E.; Gatto, N. M. 2011. LA sprouts: A gardening, nutrition, and cooking intervention for Latino youth improves diet and reduces obesity. *Journal of the American Dieticians Association* 2011(111): 1224–1230.

Dick, E.; Schmidt-Kallert, E. 2011. Understanding the (mega-)urban from the rural: Non-permanent migration and multi-locational households. Editorial to *DIE ERDE* 143(3): 173–176.

Dodson, B.; Chiweza, A.; Riley, L. 2012. Gender and food insecurity in Southern African cities. Urban Food Security Series No. 10. Kingston: Queen's University and Cape Town: AFSUN.

Dongmo, J. L. 1990. l'Approvisionnement alimentaire de Yaoundé. Yaoundé: CEPER/ Université de Yaoundé.

Drechsel, P.; Graefe, S.; Sonou, M.; Cofie, O. O. 2006. Informal irrigation in urban West Africa: An overview. IWMI Research Report 102. Colombo: International Water Management Institute (IWMI).

Egwu, G. N.; Agbenin, J. O. 2013. Field assessment of cadmium, lead and zinc contamination of soils and leaf vegetables under urban and peri-urban agriculture in northern Nigeria. *Archives of Agronomy and Soil Science* 59(6): 875–887.

EPA. 2011. Brownfields and urban agriculture: Interim guidelines for safe gardening practices. Chicago: United States Environmental Protection Agency (EPA).

FAO. 1988. Pesticide residues in food. Report of the joint meeting of the FAO Panel of Experts on Pesticide Residues in Food and the Environment and a WHO Expert Group on Pesticide Residues, Geneva, 19–28 September 1988. Available from: http://apps.who. int/iris/handle/10665/38219#sthash.WIkbPmZC.dpuf.

FAO. 2003. The informal food sector. Municipal support policies for operators. A briefing guide for mayors, city executives and urban planners in developing countries and countries in transition. Food in Cities Collection No. 4. Rome: Food and Agriculture Organization of the United Nations (FAO).

FAO. 2009. Food for the city. Rome: Food and Agriculture Organization of the United Nations (FAO).

FAO. 2010. Fighting Poverty and hunger. What role for urban agriculture? Policy Brief No. 10. Rome: Food and Agriculture Organization of the United Nations (FAO).

FAO. 2011. Food, agriculture and cities. Challenges of food and nutrition security, agriculture and ecosystem management in an urbanizing world. Position paper of the Food for the Cities Multi-Disciplinary Initiative. Rome: Food and Agriculture Organization of the United Nations (FAO).

FAO. 2013. The state of food insecurity in the world: The multiple dimensions of food security. Rome: Food and Agriculture Organization of the United Nations (FAO).

FAO. 2014. Global and regional food consumer price inflation monitoring. Issue 4 – April 2014. Available from: www.fao.org/fileadmin/templates/ess/documents/consumer/ NewsReleaseApr14_EN.pdf.

Foeken, D. W. J.; Mwangi, A. M. 2000. Increasing food security through urban farming in Nairobi. In: *Growing cities, growing food: Urban agriculture on the policy agenda.* (Eds.) Bakker, N.; Dubbeling, M.; Gündel, S.; Sabel-Koschella, U.; Zeeuw, H. de. Feldafing: German Foundation for International Development, pp. 303–327.

Frayne, B.; Crush, J.; McLahlan, M. 2014. Urbanization, nutrition and development in Southern African cities, *Food Security* 2014(6): 101–112.

Gandhi, V.; Zhou, Z. 2014. Food demand and the food security challenge with rapid economic growth in the emerging economies of India and China. *Food Research International* 2014(65): 108–124.

Gardi, C.; Panagos, P.; Liedekerke, M. van; Bosco, C.; Brogniez, D. de 2014. Land take and food security: Assessment of land take on the agricultural production in Europe. *Journal of Environmental Planning and Management* 4(1): 1–15.

Gerster-Bentaya, M. 2013. Nutrition-sensitive urban agriculture. *Food Security* 2013(5): 723–737.

Gerster-Bentaya, M.; Giseke, U.; Dérouiche, A. 2015. Food and nutrition. In: *Urban agriculture for growing city regions: Connecting urban-rural spheres in Casablanca.* (Eds.) Giseke, U.; Gerster-Bentaya, M.; Helten, F.; Kraume, M.; Scherer, D.; Spars, G.; Amraoui F.; Adidi A.; Berdouz, S.; Chlaida, M.; Mansour, M.; Mdafai, M. Abingdon: Taylor & Francis (forthcoming).

Gerster-Bentaya, M.; Rocha C.; Barth, G. 2011. The food security system of Belo Horizonte – A model for Cape Town? Report of a fact finding mission to specify the needs for an urban food and nutrition security system in Cape Town based on the system of Belo Horizonte realised from 19th of April to 8th of June, 2011. Feldafing: InWent.

Gonzalez Novo, M.; Murphy, C. 2000. Urban agriculture in the city of Havana: A popular response to a crisis. In: *Growing cities, growing food: Urban agriculture on the policy agenda.* (Eds.) Bakker, N; Dubbeling, M.; Guendel, S.; Sabel-Koschella, U.; Zeeuw, H. de. Leusden: RUAF Foundation, pp. 329–347.

Gordon, C.; Purciel-Hill, M.; Ghai, N. P.; Kaufman, L.; Graham, R.; Wyea, G. van 2011. Measuring food deserts in New York City's low-income neighbourhoods. *Health and Place* 17: 696–700.

GTZ. 2000. Fact sheets on urban agriculture. Eschborn: Deutsche Gesellschaft fuer Technische Zusammenarbeit (GTZ).

Guitart, D. A.; Pickering, C. M.; Byrne, J. A. 2014. Color me healthy: Food diversity in school community gardens in two rapidly urbanising Australian cities. *Health and Place* 26: 110–117.

Hartline-Grafton, H. 2011. Food insecurity and obesity: Understanding the connections. Washington, DC: Food Research and Action Center (FRAC).

Heim, S.; Stang J.; Ireland, M. 2009. A garden pilot project enhances fruit and vegetable consumption among children. *Journal of American Dieticians Association* 109: 1220–1226.

Heinegg, A.; Maragos, P.; Mason, E.; Rabinowicz, J.; Straccini, G.; Walsh, H. 2002. Brownfield remediation: Solutions for urban agriculture. Montreal: McGill School of Environment of McGill University.

HKI. 2012. Homestead food production. Dhaka: Hellen Keller International (HKI). Available from: www.hki.org/reducing-malnutrition/homestead-food-production.

Hoffen, L. P. von; Säumel, I. 2014. Orchards for edible cities: Cadmium and lead content in nuts, berries, pome and stone fruits harvested within the inner city neighbourhoods in Berlin, Germany. *Ecotoxicology and Environmental Safety* 101: 233–239.

Hoisington, A.; Butkus, S. N.; Garrett, S.; Beerman, K. 2001. Field gleaning as a tool for addressing food security at the local level: Case study. *Journal of Nutrition Education and Behaviour* 33(1): 43–48.

Hollands, S.; Campbell, M. K.; Gilliland, J.; Sarma, S. 2012. Association between neighbourhood fast-food and full-service restaurant density and body mass index: A cross-sectional study of Canadian adults. *Canadian Journal of Public Health* 105(3): e172–e178.

Huibers, F. P.; Lier, J. B. van. 2005. Use of wastewater in agriculture: The water chain approach. *Irrigation and Drainage* 2005(54): S3–S9.

IFPRI. 2002. Living in the city: Challenges and options for the urban poor. Washington, DC: International Food Policy and Research Institute (IFPRI).

IIED. 2013. Food security challenges in Asia. Working Paper. Manila: Asian Development Bank (ADB).

Jacobi, P.; Amend, J.; Kiango, S. 2000. Urban agriculture in Dar es Salaam: Providing an indispensable part of the diet. In: *Growing cities, growing food: Urban agriculture on the policy agenda.* (Eds.) Bakker, N; Dubbeling, M.; Guendel, S.; Sabel-Koschella, U.; Zeeuw, H. de. Leusden: RUAF Foundation, pp. 257–283.

Kader A. 2005. Increasing food availability by reducing postharvest losses of fresh produce. *Acta Hort* 682: 2169–2176.

Kethongsa, S.; Khamtanh, T.; Moustier, P. 2004. Vegetable marketing in Vientiane (Lao PDR). Montpellier: CIRAD.

Knight, L.; Roberts, B. J.; Aber, J.L.; Richter, L. 2014. Household shocks and coping strategies in rural and peri-urban South Africa: Baseline data from the size study in Kwazulu-Natal, South Africa. *Journal of International Development* 2014(4): 213–233.

Kopelman P. 2007. Health risks associated with overweight and obesity. *Obesity Reviews* 2007(8 Suppl. 1): 13–17.

Kreinecker, P. 2000. La Paz: Urban agriculture in harsh ecological conditions. In: *Growing cities, growing food: Urban agriculture on the policy agenda.* (Eds.) Bakker, N; Dubbeling, M.; Guendel, S.; Sabel-Koschella, U.; Zeeuw, H. de. Leusden: RUAF Foundation, pp. 391–411.

Laurent, M. 1999. L'approvisionnement de Nouakshott en légumes. Mémoire de master. Montpellier: CNEARC.

Lee-Smith, D.; Prain, G. 2006. Urban agriculture and health. IFPRI 2020 Vision for Food, Agriculture and the Environment. Brief 13 of Focus 13: Understanding the links between agriculture and health. Washington, DC: International Food Policy and Research Institute (IFPRI).

Ligthelm, A. A. 2005. Informal retailing through home-based micro-enterprises: The role of spaza shops. *Development Southern Africa* 22(2): 199–214.

Lock, K.; Zeeuw, H. de. 2001. Health risks associated with urban agriculture. Discussion paper for the Electronic conference Urban Agriculture at the Policy Agenda, organized by RUAF Foundation and Food and Agriculture Organization of the United Nations (FAO). Available from: www.ruaf.org/sites/default/files/Health_risks_ua.pdf.

Mbaye, A.; Moustier, P. 2000. Market-oriented agricultural production in Dakar. In: *Growing cities, growing food: Urban agriculture on the policy agenda.* (Eds.) Bakker, N; Dubbeling, M.; Guendel, S.; Sabel-Koschella, U.; Zeeuw, H. de. Leusden: RUAF Foundation, pp. 235–256.

McClain-Nhlapo, C. 2004. Implementing a human rights approach to food security. 2020 Africa Conference Brief 13. Washington, DC: International Food Policy and Research Institute (IFPRI).

Mercato, S.; Havemann, K.; Sami, M.; Ueda, H. 2007. Urban poverty: An urgent public health issue. *Journal of Urban Health* 84(1): i7–i15.

Miewald, C.; McCann, E. 2014. Foodscapes and the geographies of poverty: Sustenance, strategy and politics in an urban neighbourhood. *Antipode* 46(2): 537–556.

Mitchell, D.; Heynen, N. 2013. The geography of survival and the right to the city: Speculations on surveillance, legal innovation, and the criminalization of intervention. *Urban Geography* 30(6): 611–632.

Mkwambisi, D.; Fraser, E.D.G.; Dougill, A. J. 2011. Urban agriculture and poverty reduction: Evaluating how food production in cities contributes to food security, employment and income in Malawi. *Journal of International Development* 2011(23): 181–203.

Mougeot, L. J.A. 2013. Urban agriculture: Our logics of integration. Presentation made to the Canadian International Development Agency, Ottawa, March 2013.

Moustier, P. 1999. Complémentarité entre agriculture urbaine et agriculture rurale. In: *Agriculture urbaine en Afrique de Ouest.* (Ed.) Smith O. B. Ottawa: International Development Research Centre, pp. 41–54.

Moustier, P.; Danso, G. 2006. Local economic development and marketing of urban produced food. In: *Cities farming for the future: Urban agriculture for green and productive cities*. (Ed.) Veenhuizen, R. van. Manila: IRRR Publishers; Leusden: RUAF Foundation, pp. 173–208.

Omore, A.; Cheng'ole Mulindo, J.; Fakhrul Islam, S. M.; Nurah, G.; Khan, M. I.; Staal, S. J.; Dugdill, B. T. 2004. Employment generation through small-scale dairy marketing and processing: Experiences from Kenya, Bangladesh and Ghana. Rome: Food and Agriculture Organization of the United Nations (FAO).

Owino, J. O.; Cheserek, G. J.; Saina, C. K.; Murgor, F. A. 2013. The coping strategies adapted by urban poor to food insecurity in Eldoret Municipality, Kenya. *Journal of Emerging Trends in Economics and Management Sciences* 4(2): 196–202.

Pereira, M. A.; Kartashov, A.; Ebbeling, C. B.; Horn, L. van; Slattery, M. L.; Jacobs D. R.; Ludwig, D. S. 2005. Fast-food habits, weight gain, and insulin resistance (the CARDIA study): 15-year prospective analysis. *The Lancet* 365 (9453): 36–42.

Phuong Anh, M. T.; Ali, M.; Lan Ahn, H.; Thu Ha, T. T. 2004. Urban and peri-urban agriculture in Hanoi: Opportunities and constraints for safe and sustainable food production. Technical Bulletin No. 32. Shanhuan: AVRDC–World Vegetable Center.

Piñeiro, M.; Bianchi, E.; Uzquiza, L.; Trucco, M. 2010. Food security policies in Latin America: New trends with uncertain results. IISD Series on Trade and Food Security – Policy Report 4. Winnipeg: IISD.

Pinstrup-Andersen, P. 2012. Food systems and human health and nutrition: An economic policy perspective with a focus on Africa. Stanford: The Center on Food Security and the Environment (FSE), Stanford University. Available from: http://fsi.stanford.edu/sites/default/files/Pinstrup-Andersen_final.pdf.

Prain, G.; Dubbeling, M. 2011. Urban agriculture: A sustainable solution to alleviating urban poverty, addressing the food crisis, and adapting to climate change. Leusden: RUAF Foundation. Available from: www.ruaf.org/sites/default/files/Synthesis%20report%20 Worldbank%20case%20studies%20UA-a%20solution%20to%20alleviating%20urban%20 poverty%20and%20the%20food%20crisis.pdf.

Prain, G.; Lee-Smith, D. 2010. Urban agriculture in Africa: What has been learnt? In: *African urban harvest: Agriculture in the cities of Cameroon, Uganda and Kenya*. (Eds.) Prain, G.; Karanja, N.; Lee-Smith, D. 2010. New York: Springer Publishers; Ottawa: International Development Research Centre (IDRC); Lima: International Potato Centre (CIP)/ Urban Harvest, pp. 13–35.

Prain, G.; Zeeuw, H. de. 2010. Effects of the global financial crisis on the food security of poor urban households: Synthesis report to the World Bank on five city case studies. Leusden: RUAF Foundation. Available from: www.ruaf.org/sites/default/files/Synthesis%20report%20Food%20security%20and%20Nutrition%20study%20for%20UN%20 Habitat%20%26%20IDRC.pdf.

Purnomohadi, N. 2000. Urban agriculture as an alternative strategy to face the economic crisis. In: *Growing cities, growing food: Urban agriculture on the policy agenda*. (Eds.) Bakker, N; Dubbeling, M.; Guendel, S.; Sabel-Koschella, U.; Zeeuw, H. de. Leusden: RUAF Foundation, pp. 453–465.

Puschenreiter, M.; Hartl, W.; Horak, O. 1999. Urban agriculture on heavy metal contaminated soils in Eastern Europe. Vienna: Ludwig Boltzmann Institute for Organic Agriculture and Applied Ecology.

Riches G.; Silavasti, T. 2014. First world hunger revisited. Food charity or the right to food? London: Palgrave Macmillan.

Satterthwaite, D.; McGranahan, G.; Tacoli, C. 2010. Urbanization and its implications for food and farming. *Philosophical Transactions* 365(1554): 2809–2820.

Sawaya, L. A.; Martins, P. A.; Grillo, L. P.; Florencio, P. P. 2004. Long-term effects of early malnutrition on body weight regulation. *Nutrition Reviews* 62: 127–133.

Schmidt-Kallert, E.; Kreibich V. 2004. Split households. *Development and Cooperation* 2004(12): s464–s467.

Schröder, H.; Fito, M.; Covas, M. I. 2007. Association of fast food consumption with energy intake, diet quality, body mass index and the risk of obesity in a representative Mediterranean population. *British Journal of Nutrition* 2007(98): 1274–1280.

Schutter, O. de. 2014. The transformative potential of the right to food: Final report of the Special Rapporteur on the right to food. Geneva: Human Rights Council.

Sen, A. 1981. Ingredients of famine analysis: Availability and entitlements. *The Quarterly Journal of Economics* 96(3): 433–464.

Smit, J.; Ratta, A.; Nasr, J. 1996. Urban agriculture: Food, jobs and sustainable cities. New York: United Nations Development Programme.

Tacoli, C. 2000. Rural-urban interdependence. In: *Achieving urban food and nutrition security in the developing world – A 2020 vision for food, agriculture, and the environment – Focus 3*. Washington, DC: International Food Policy Research (IFPRI), 4–6.

Tacoli, C.; Bukhari, B.; Fisher, S. 2013. Urban poverty, food security and climate change. Human Settlements Working Paper No. 37. London: International Institute for Environment and Development (IIED).

Tambwe, N.; Rudolph, M.; Greenstein, R. 2011. 'Instead of begging, I farm to feed my children': Urban agriculture: An alternative to copper and cobalt in Lubumbashi. *Africa* 81(3): 391–412.

Tegegne, A.; Tadess, M.; Yami, A.; Mekasha, Y. 2000. Market oriented urban and peri-urban dairy systems. *Urban Agriculture Magazine* 1 (2): 23–24.

UN Habitat. 2014. Integrating urban and peri-urban agriculture into city-level climate change strategies. *Cities and Climate Change Initiative Newsletter,* June 2014.

Vagneron, I. 2007. Economic appraisal of profitability and sustainability of peri-urban agriculture in Bangkok. *Ecological Economics* 61: 516–529.

Veenhuizen, R. van. 2007. Profitability and sustainability of urban and peri-urban agriculture. FAO-Agricultural Management, Marketing and Finance Occasional Paper No. 19. Rome: Food and Agriculture Organisation of the United Nations (FAO).

Weingärtner, L. 2009a. The concept of food and nutrition security. In: *Achieving food and nutrition security. Actions to meet the global challenge.* (Ed.) Klennert, K. Feldafing: InWent (3rd updated edition), pp. 21–52.

Weingärtner, L. 2009b. The food and nutrition security situation in 2009. In: *Achieving food and nutrition security. Actions to meet the global challenge.* (Ed.) Klennert, K. Feldafing: InWent (3rd updated edition), pp. 53–68.

WHO. 2006. Guidelines for the safe use of wastewater, excreta and greywater. Geneva: World Health Organization (WHO).

Wrigley, N. 2002. Food deserts' in British cities: Policy context and research priorities. *Urban Studies* 2002(39): 2029–2040.

Yeudall, F.; Sebastian, R.; Cole, D. C.; Ibrahim, S.; Lubowa, A.; Kikafunda, J. 2007. Food and nutritional security of children of urban farmers in Kampala, Uganda. *Food and Nutrition Bulletin* 28(2): S237–S246.

Zezza, A.; Tasciotti Z. 2010. Urban agriculture, poverty, and food security: Empirical evidence from a sample of developing countries. *Food Policy* 35: 265–273.

Zingel, W. P.; Keck, M.; Etzold, B.; Bohle, H. G. 2011. Urban food security and health status of the poor in Dhaka, Bangladesh. In: *Health in megacities and urban areas.* (Eds.) Krämer, A.; Khan, M. H.; Kraas, F. Heidelberg: Springer, pp. 301–319.

7

PRODUCTIVE AND SAFE USE OF URBAN ORGANIC WASTES AND WASTEWATER IN URBAN FOOD PRODUCTION SYSTEMS IN LOW-INCOME COUNTRIES

Pay Drechsel,[1] *Bernard Keraita,*[1,2]
Olufunke O. Cofie[1] *and Josiane Nikiema*[1]

1 INTERNATIONAL WATER MANAGEMENT INSTITUTE (IWMI), ACCRA,
GHANA AND COLOMBO, SRI LANKA

2 GLOBAL HEALTH SECTION, DEPARTMENT OF PUBLIC HEALTH,
UNIVERSITY OF COPENHAGEN, DENMARK

Introduction

Rapid urbanization in developing countries raises the challenges of urban food supplies and management of the waste flows from urban households and markets. Large amounts of municipal solid waste, human excreta and wastewater are produced, which mostly end up in non-engineered landfills or polluting the urban environment, especially in low-income countries where sanitation infrastructure is less developed. Wastewater and many organic wastes are nutrient rich and can be productively used in intra- and peri-urban agricultural systems, enhancing the resilience of the urban metabolism.

However, productive reuse of waste faces a variety of challenges. These range from securing cost recovery for up- and out-scaling successful examples of planned reuse to the acceptance of safety practices within the informal reuse sector in urban and peri-urban areas. Opportunities for addressing the first challenge include more attention to business models which can build on different value propositions beyond 'water' or normal 'composting', and for the second challenge they include more attention to social marketing options, private-sector engagement and incentive systems for catalysing behaviour change towards the adoption of safety practices.

A shift in thinking about solid and liquid waste

Cities are hungry and thirsty and there are enormous hubs of consumption of all kinds of goods including food. This in turn makes them major centres of generation of food waste. If this waste remains in the urban environment or its landfills,

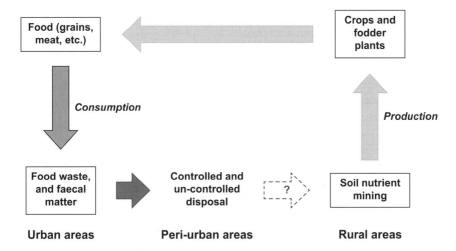

FIGURE 7.1 Urban and peri-urban areas as vast nutrient sinks
Source: authors.

cities will also become vast sinks for the resources, like crop nutrients, while rural production areas face degradation of soil fertility (Figure 7.1). The same applies to nutrient-rich wastewater discharged from households (excreta, urine and grey water), and commercial and industrial establishments, which could also be mixed with storm water as may be present.

Given the value of the resources hidden in waste, and the environmental burden of a business-as-usual scenario in growing cities, there is need for a paradigm shift. For example, in solid waste management, there is increasing advocacy to a shift in the behaviour of the public towards the 'three Rs', i.e., 'Reduce, Reuse and Recycle' (UNEP 2011). Social science research is re-conceptualizing waste from 'risk, hazard or dirt' towards 'resources, values, assets and potentials' (Moore 2012). In wastewater management, a clear shift from nutrient removal to nutrient recovery is taking place with treatment facilities shifting from waste disposal to resource conservation (Murray and Buckley 2010). This conceptual thinking of 'design for reuse' or a 'reverse water chain approach' considers the ultimate fate of the water as the design base for the urban water chain, including treatment and upstream issues (Huibers and van Lier 2005).

This thinking has been strengthened through an increasing focus on dry sanitation systems, especially ecological sanitation systems, in regard to the managing of human faecal matter. Ecological sanitation is based on three principals: (i) preventing pollution rather than attempting to control it afterwards, (ii) sanitizing urine and faeces (excreta), and (iii) using safe products for agricultural purposes (Winblad and Simposon-Herbert 2004). There is also increasing efforts for using faecal waste and other organic waste in energy production through biogas schemes.

The modern dry sanitation systems facilitate the transport of faeces and potential resource recovery through the 'drop-store-sanitize-and-reuse' approach in a controlled environment which conventional approaches like 'drop-and-flush' or 'drop-and-forget' of sewered systems or pit latrines, respectively, do not support (Rautanen and Viskari 2006). These newer approaches incorporate the 'three Rs' thinking across scales for increasing the resilience of urban areas, and society at large. A change in thinking is not only a possibility but, in many cases, a 'must' as limited water resources do not allow flush sewer systems while some resources like phosphorus are non-renewable, and especially poorer countries will be the first to feel increasing fertilizer prices (Mihelcic et al. 2011).

Resource recovery ideally starts at the household level. Supported by public awareness, households reduce their waste collection fees by separating, for example, old glass, used paper, plastic waste and organic kitchen residues into dedicated collection systems. Where space and regulations allow, backyard composting of kitchen residues for urban farming is encouraged. For grey water from kitchens and bathrooms and black water from toilets, local reuse options, e.g., via urine diverting toilets, are being explored, although for the large majority of urban households the conventional target remains the removal of faecal matter from household premises through the sewer system.

In most developing countries, collection of wastewater and solid waste and the separation of different solid waste streams are still a major challenge, resulting in severe pollution of water bodies. Less than 10% of the urban population in sub-Saharan Africa, about 3% in South-East Asia and 31% in South Asia are connected to any wastewater collection system (Lautze et al. 2014). Collection of solid waste does not require expensive infrastructure but shows a similar picture with South Asia and Africa ranking lowest with 65% and 46% collection rates, respectively (Hoornweg and Bhada-Tata 2012). The remaining waste is a severe public health hazard. As most households are poor, waste management cannot rely on fees and taxes to finance its operations. In fact, expenditure on waste management often takes up to half of the municipal budget and even then is seldom enough to cope with waste generation, especially in the low-income high-density parts of the city which are difficult to access. The possibility of increasing household fees is not only limited by poverty, but also due to low education, resulting in limited environmental awareness and responsibility. If collection fees are raised, households are likely to start dumping their waste in the street or drains.

In low-income countries, increasing collection coverage is the highest priority in most local authorities, much more so than introducing resource recovery activities, which often remain at pilot scale. However, recycling takes place, but is more poverty-driven than done for environmental reasons, with landfill scavenging and e-waste burning for metal recovery being popular examples. However, an increasing number of entrepreneurs are engaged in activities such as commercial plastic recycling, and the reuse of organic residues for various purposes.

While urban and peri-urban food production and especially food safety clearly suffer from poor sanitation, urban farmers do often take advantage of underutilized solid and liquid waste resources. This may be food waste from agro-industrial production, such as cotton husks or poultry manure, composted market-waste, domestic wastewater or faecal matter.

In this context, we need to consider two waste 'streams': the waste that is managed and on its way to treatment or disposal; and the waste that bypasses formal systems, leaking out or never getting there in the first place (Drechsel et al. 2011). This chapter will focus on both streams in developing-country contexts (though there are many similarities with developed countries), and the related challenges and opportunities for the productive and safe use of urban organic wastes and wastewater. While there are several reuse options, from industrial reuse to the production of potable water, in the context of this publication, agricultural reuse, especially in intra- and peri-urban farming, will be the focus.

With the emergence of intensive – high input, high output – urban and peri-urban food production systems, which are often a direct response to changing diets in urban areas, we see an increasing interest in water reuse and alternative fertilizer making use of different types of waste (Box 7.1).

BOX 7.1   FORMS OF URBAN WASTE OF VALUE IN AGRICULTURE

Urban waste can be solid, partially solid (e.g., manure, sludge) or liquid (grey water), organic or inorganic, recyclable or non-recyclable. Of interest to urban agriculture as a source of nutrient and organic matter is the organic fraction of municipal solid waste (MSW) and agro-industrial waste, and as a source of water and nutrients also domestic wastewater. For example, at least 50% of urban solid waste is biodegradable and hence of immediate interest in recycling. Wastewater on the other hand is often already used, directly where water is scarce or indirectly if mixed with other water sources. Typical types of waste commonly used in urban farming are:

1   **Solid waste:** Domestic and market wastes, food waste including vegetable and fruit peelings, and charcoal ash. This also includes waste from institutions and commercial centres.

2   **Horticultural and agricultural waste:** Common especially in high-income areas: garden refuse, leaf litter, cut grass, tree cuttings, weeds, animal dung, crop residues, waste from public parks, etc.

3   **Agro-industrial waste:** Waste generated by abattoirs, breweries, timber mills, poultry farms, food processing and agro-based industries.

4   **Sludge and biosolids:** Human faecal matter from septic tanks and treatment plants.

5   **Wastewater:** Typically, it is estimated that 70–80% of total water supplied for domestic use leaves the household as wastewater. However, high wastewater collection is not always successful because of the low coverage of sewer.

Source: Cofie et al. 2006; modified.

Resources in urban organic waste and wastewater

Municipal solid waste (MSW)

Current global MSW generation levels are approximately 1.3 billion tons per year (Btyr⁻¹), and are expected to increase to approximately 2.2 Btyr⁻¹ by 2025. This represents a significant increase in per capita waste generation rates, from 1.2 to 1.42 kg person⁻¹day⁻¹ in the next 15 years (Hoornweg and Bhada-Tata 2012). In sub-Saharan Africa, approximately 62 million tons of MSW are generated per year. Per capita waste generation is generally low in this region, but spans a wide range, from 0.09 to 3.0 kg person⁻¹day⁻¹, with an average of 0.65 kg capita⁻¹ day⁻¹. In the MSW stream, waste can be organic and inorganic, and generally categorized organic, paper/cardboards, plastics, glass, metals, textiles and other materials (see Figure 7.2).

Of most relevance to urban food production systems is the organic waste, which is most commonly used to improve soil productivity. In general, the organic fraction is the largest one within domestic waste (Figure 7.2). According to Hoornweg and Bhada-Tata (2012), low-income countries have an organic fraction of 64% compared to 28% in high-income countries. The potential benefits of organic waste recycling are particularly in reducing the environmental impact of disposal sites, in extending existing landfill capacity, in replenishing the soil humus layer and in minimizing waste quantity (Zurbruegg and Drescher 2002).

In a comprehensive review on MSW use in agriculture, Hargreaves et al. (2008) described the positive effects of MSW on the biological, physical and chemical soil properties. The review showed that MSW has high organic matter

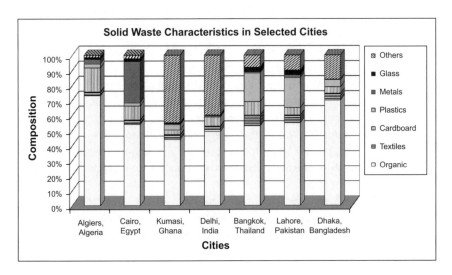

FIGURE 7.2 MSW characteristics in selected cities

Source: Cofie et al. 2006.

content, limited amounts of nutrients and low bulk density. Once composted, these characteristics can influence, in particular, the physical properties of soils by increasing the soil C/N ratio, water-holding capacity, etc. In view of biological properties, the review showed a general improvement on soil microbial health through increasing organic biomass, increasing soil aeration and accelerating the activities of enzymes which help in the transformation of nutrients. Reduced soil acidity and – depending on the type of waste or supplements – the addition of nutrients was identified as a possible beneficial effect on soil chemical properties.

Other benefits adapted and summarized from Hoornweg et al. (1999), with particular reference to organic waste composting, are that it:

- Reduces overall waste volume, transport costs and landfill lifetime.
- Enhances recycling and incineration operations by removing moist organic matter from the waste stream.
- Promotes environmentally sound practices, such as the reduction of methane generation at landfills.
- Is flexible for implementation at different levels, from household efforts to large-scale centralized facilities; i.e., can also be started with very little capital and operating costs.
- Addresses possible health impacts from faecal matter due to the composting (sanitizing) process.
- Can integrate existing informal sectors involved in the collection, separation and recycling of wastes, and contributes to the 'green economy' of a city.

However, despite these benefits, current MSW management practices show very small proportions of MSW being recycled and/or composted. This ranges from over 30% in some high-income countries to as low as less than 2% in low-income countries (see Table 7.1). On average, only 1.5% of MSW is

TABLE 7.1 Global MSW disposal practices (by income levels of the countries)

	High income (%) Total = 588.05 million tons	Upper middle income (%) Total = 135.78 million tons	Lower middle income (%) Total = 55.32 million tons	Low income (%) Total = 3.76 million tons
Dumps	0	33	49*	13
Landfills	43	59	11	59
Compost	11	1	2	1
Recycled	22	1	5	1
Incinerated	21	0	0	1
Other	3	6	33	25

Note: * including China.

Source: adapted from Hoornweg and Bhada-Tata 2012.

composted in low- and middle-income countries. The reasons for these low shares are as various as the theoretical benefits. More than a decade ago, Hoornweg et al. (1999) had already identified six common challenges preventing compost initiatives from going to scale: (i) inadequate attention to the biological process requirements like under tropical climates; (ii) over-emphasis placed on electricity-demanding and often fragile mechanized processes rather than labour-intensive operations; (iii) lack of vision and marketing plans for the final product – compost; (iv) poor feed stock which yields poor-quality finished compost, for example, when contaminated by heavy metals; (v) poor accounting practices which neglect the fact that the economics of composting rely on externalities, such as reduced water contamination, avoided transport and disposal costs, etc.; and (vi) difficulties in securing finances since the revenue generated from the sale of compost will rarely cover processing, transportation and application costs.

Although there are an increasing number of success stories, as documented for example in the *Urban Agriculture Magazine* Vol. 23 (www.ruaf.org), an over-reliance on technical approaches and lack of business thinking was reconfirmed also in more recent studies. Based on experiences from composting projects in Africa, Drechsel et al. (2010) identified as a key constraint that the composting gains in terms of reduced transport volumes and cost are seldom made available to (run) the composting unit due to poor coordination among involved institutions and the lack of an enabling institutional (e.g., private–public partnership) framework. While, for example, city authorities stress that composting is most welcome as a means to reduce waste volume and transport costs, the savings remain inaccessible to the private compost plant operator. However, in many situations, and especially for larger cities, these 'savings' would be a higher benefit (revenue stream) than the actual compost sales. The situation might be very different for smaller towns where agricultural demand might surpass waste supply.

The importance of transport costs derives from the increasing problems of city authorities to find community-supported landfill sites in the city vicinity, while local communities are less reluctant to accept a compost station (Drechsel et al. 2010). From this point of view, compost stations should be planned as close as possible to the points of waste generation, and from the sales perspective as decentralized as possible to support farmers' access to the product. Knowing customers' locations and demand, the corresponding daily production of compost, transport and operation and maintenance (O&M) costs, it is possible to determine the optimal number of decentralized compost (and transfer) stations to minimize costs.

Possible market segments go beyond intra- and peri-urban crop production and include landscaping, housing sector, coffee and tea plantations, forestry, etc. As long as the reuse market is not fully assessed, cost recovery for compost

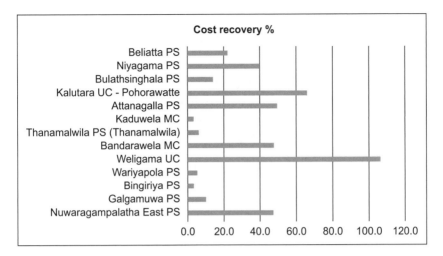

FIGURE 7.3 Range of O&M cost recovery among selected compost plants in Sri Lanka

Source: Fernando et al. 2014.

production will remain small, and any compost business will have to be based on subsidies based on transport and landfill cost saving.

Based only on compost sales, cost recovery can vary in wide margins, as the Pilisaru project in Sri Lanka has shown. More than 110 compost plants were set up under the first project phase, with an average cost recovery of less than one-third of the O&M costs (Figure 7.3). The average value hides the fact that several compost plants produced far less compost than planned (reducing also the O&M cost), although several accepted more waste than they were designed for, targeting more volume reduction than the production of a marketable product (Fernando et al. 2014). However, some plants in Sri Lanka performed well and even achieved profits (Otoo and Drechsel 2015). This was interesting, as almost all MSW compost plants in the country are owned by the public sector. Thus the differences between poor- and well-performing stations could not be easily attributed to management, technology or regulatory differences, allowing cross-case analysis. A typical reason for difference in performance related to different expertise and knowledge about local markets and the emergence of private–public partnerships.

Human excreta

Human excreta are the final 'food waste' and a key component of domestic waste production. Like animal manure, they are an excellent fertilizer, and richer in organic matter with essential plant nutrients such as nitrogen, phosphorus and potassium than the average organic MSW. The use of human excreta as a fertilizer dates back to many centuries. For example, Chinese were aware of the benefits of using excreta in crop production more than 2,500 years ago, enabling them to sustain more people at a higher density than any other system of agriculture (Lüthi et al. 2011). Even in many European cities, fertilization of farm lands continued into the middle of the 19th century as farmers took advantage of the value of nutrients in excreta to increase production, and urban sanitation benefited as they used farming lands as a way of treatment and disposal (Lüthi et al. 2011). The practice only stopped due to the need to manage possible health risks within increasingly dense human settlements.

It has been shown that the nutrient content of human waste collected in a year is approximately equal to what has been eaten during the year (Drangert 1998). Each year, a human excretes up to 500 litres of urine and 50 to 180 kg (wet weight) of faeces, depending on water and food intake (Drangert 1998). These contain about 4 kg of nitrogen, 0.6 kg of phosphorus and 1 kg of potassium, with variations depending on protein intake (Drangert 1998; Jönsson et al. 2004). Phosphorus (P) recovery from excreta is of particular importance due to the fast depletion of phosphorus reserves (see Box 7.2).

BOX 7.2 THE NEXT INCONVENIENT TRUTH – PEAK PHOSPHORUS

Phosphorus is an essential nutrient for all plants and animals. About 80% of mined phosphate rock, the main source of phosphorus, is used in fertilizers, thus making it very vital for the world's agriculture sector. Today, about 90% of phosphate rock reserves are found in only five countries and the largest commercially recoverable reserves are found in three countries – China, United States and Morocco/Western Sahara. The US Geological Survey reports that phosphate rock reserves are running out and that phosphate rock extraction will peak around the year 2030. The extraction rate of phosphate rock in the United States (US) peaked 15 years ago and present forecasts show that the US will deplete its reserves within 30 years. Globally, phosphate rock reserves are estimated to be depleted within 75–100 years. Being a non-renewable resource, phosphorus cannot be manufactured from alternative sources. Therefore, there is need for agricultural reforms and innovative and sustainable strategies to recover phosphorus from human, animal and other organic wastes for use in agriculture.

Source: Rosemarin et al. 2009.

While most of the organic matter is contained in faecal matter, most of the nutrients (88% of the nitrogen, 67% of the phosphorus and 71% of the potassium) are found in urine (Heinonen-Tanski and van Wijk-Sijbesma 2005) in forms that are readily available for crops. Organic matter from decomposed faeces can also serve as a soil conditioner, improve soil structure, increase water-holding capacity, and can reduce pests and diseases while neutralizing certain soil toxins like heavy metals (Esrey et al. 2001). An important benefit from recycling excreta is the reduction of environmental pollution and degradation of water quality from uncontrolled dumping of faecal sludge.

Following the promotion of urine-diverting toilets, extensive field trials conducted both in tropical and temperate climates have shown increase in yields from using human excreta compared to when the soils are unfertilized. Jönsson et al. (2004) reviewed various field experiences regarding agricultural yields on using human excreta in agricultural production. Despite very promising agronomic results, the reuse of faecal matter (excreta and urine) is facing various challenges from the cost of toilets separating the resources, to limitations based on perception or health regulations, or the logistics of transportation where households do not have the opportunity of on-site reuse. More progress has been achieved in view of urine and its high phosphorus content. Modern technologies allow the recovery of high percentages of P before it starts damaging pipes and valves in wastewater treatment systems through unwanted precipitation. This results in significant savings for treatment operators by reducing the use of chemicals otherwise needed to remove the crystals. Enterprises specialized in P recovery thrive on these savings while the generated P fertilizer (struvite) is still struggling to move beyond selected niche markets given the lower price of natural rock phosphate (Otoo et al. 2015).

Wastewater

For reasons of simplicity, and in comparison with safe freshwater sources, the term 'wastewater' is commonly used in the literature on urban and peri-urban agriculture, although the water quality varies in very wide margins from raw wastewater to diluted wastewater to grey water and polluted stream water. These differences might even be larger than between treated and untreated wastewater, as what is called treated in one country might still be considered unsafe in another one. In general, treated wastewater reuse is more common in developed countries while a ten-time larger area is irrigated with diluted or raw wastewater in developing countries and emerging economies (Scott et al. 2010). The most direct benefits of wastewater use in urban food production systems can be the nutrients in the water, especially in raw wastewater, but otherwise it is the water itself, or more precisely the reliable and low/no cost supply of water where and when freshwater is not available. A typology of different common reuse scenarios is attempted in Table 7.2.

TABLE 7.2 Typology of water reuse

Type	Value addition to the resource	Farmer pays?	Commonly seen in (examples)	Reuse-based business model
1. **Direct** use of **untreated** wastewater	None, except for facilitation of water access (canals). Water use can be considered a land treatment	Seldom as usually illegal, but if then, e.g. for land near wastewater channel	Pakistan Mexico Vietnam Peru	Where resources are scarce, farmers might pay for access to land or wastewater (which could support wastewater collection, basic treatment or health care)
2. **Indirect** use of **untreated** wastewater	Dilution and natural treatment depending on distance between source and use	Wastewater is diluted and not perceived as wastewater	India Ghana Mexico China	Water perceived as natural water with low willingness to pay. Business model could request for safety measures against market or tenure incentives
3. **Direct** use of **treated** wastewater	Provision of water safe for agricultural use through treatment	For provision of treated wastewater (but see right for inverse cash flow)	Tunisia Egypt USA Australia Chile Israel	Several revenue options: Payment for access to safe wastewater, or farmers are paid for swapping freshwater with wastewater, or savings in freshwater use pay for reuse system
4. **Indirect** use of **treated** wastewater	Provision of safe water through treatment before mixing with surface water or for groundwater recharge	As above, if water users know about treatment and appreciate it	Jordan Spain Mexico USA	Water often perceived as natural water limiting farmers' willingness to pay. Otherwise also water swap models are possible exchanging freshwater against treated wastewater

Source: Evans et al. 2013; modified.

Undiluted wastewater has nutrients that can significantly contribute to crop growth and improving soil fertility. It is estimated that 1,000 m^3 of municipal wastewater for irrigating one hectare can contribute 16–62 kg total nitrogen, 4–24 kg phosphorus, 2–69 kg potassium, 18–208 kg calcium, 9–110 kg magnesium and 27–182 kg sodium (Qadir et al. 2007). In Mexico's Mezquital (Tula) Valley, wastewater irrigation provides 2,400 kg of organic matter, 195 kg of nitrogen and 81 kg of phosphorus ha^{-1} yr^{-1}, contributing significantly to crop yields (Jimenez 2005). Larger crops and reduced growth periods in wastewater irrigated fields are also reported from Dakar, Senegal, which is attributed to the nutrients in wastewater (Faruqui et al. 2004).

Wastewater not only adds nutrients to soil, but can also amend soils through its organic matter content (biosolids or stabilized sludge) (Christie et al. 2001). Compared to freshwater, there is a significant body of literature showing advantages for soils and yields under wastewater irrigation, although many comparative assessments are not free from shortcomings (Drechsel, Danso and Qadir 2015). In Guanajuato, Mexico, the estimated cost for farmers for replacing the nitrogen and phosphorus loss through wastewater treatment was estimated at US$900 ha^{-1} (Scott et al. 2000).

Making an asset out of wastewater appears as a necessity especially where farming faces increasing water competition from the urban and industrial sectors. Other than availability and its low price, many farmers use wastewater because it is reliable, allowing year-round production, hence giving a strong competitive advantage during the dry season. Studies conducted in Hubli–Dharwad showed that wastewater allowed farming to be done in the dry season when farmers could sell their produce at 3–5 times the kharif (monsoon) season prices (Bradford et al. 2002). Reliability of wastewater also allows for multiple cultivation cycles and flexibility of crops planted (Raschid-Sally et al. 2005). In Haroonabad, Pakistan, the reliability and flexibility of untreated wastewater supply allow farmers to cultivate even-priced, high-value and short-duration crops (van der Hoek et al. 2002). In Ghana, the reliability of free wastewater allows urban farmers to intensify vegetable production to multiple cycles year-round. Similarly in Dakar, Senegal, untreated wastewater allows 8–12 harvests per year, compared to 5–6 harvests per year when farmers had no access to wastewater (Gaye and Niang 2002).

Where wastewater reuse is formally promoted and culturally acceptable, a critical question concerns the viability of the wastewater treatment facility and reuse scheme. The main challenges in this regard are the commonly low revenues from the sale of treated wastewater especially where already freshwater is subsidized. In this situation not only the financial gains but also economic benefits for the society should be considered as well as other possible value propositions and revenue streams from wastewater treatment, which might benefit farming or other sectors (Figure 7.4).

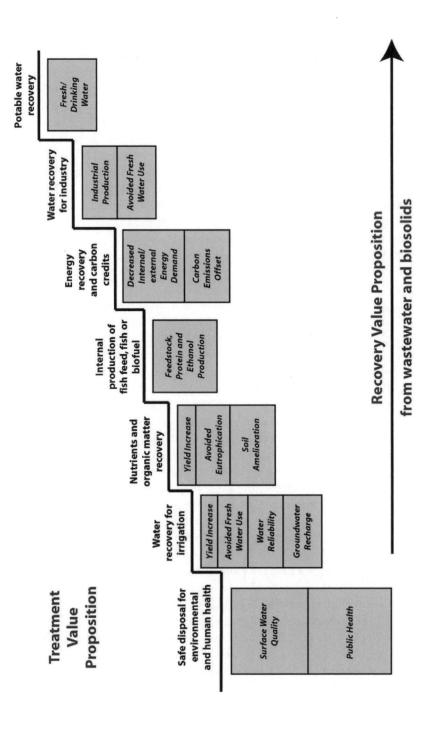

FIGURE 7.4 Value propositions related to water, nutrient and energy recovery from wastewater

Source: Rao et al. 2015.

Concerns of using solid and liquid waste in urban food production systems

Productive use of urban waste and wastewater faces a number of challenges from institutional and technical obstacles like the required treatment capacity, to the distance between waste/water generation and the agricultural market, as intra-urban farming can usually only absorb a small amount of the waste generated, making this farming sector not the major target for effective volume reduction or cost recovery. However, the largest concerns resource recovery, and reuse is facing possible risks for human and environmental health, especially where waste products are used in food production (Table 7.3). Depending on their origin, solid and liquid wastes can carry harmful chemicals and, when mixed with human faecal matter, also pathogens, potentially causing various diseases. In low-income countries, with only emerging industrial production, emphasis is laid on pathogens, since people in these countries are most affected by diseases caused by poor sanitation such as diarrhoeal diseases and helminth infections (Prüss-Ustün and Corvalan 2006). The situation changes in transitional economies with increasing industrialization and is again different in high-income countries, where infections from pathogens are largely under control while chemical pollution like heavy metals, and so-called emerging pollutants (e.g., residues of antibiotics) are of significant public concern.

While data on pathogens and heavy metals are frequently reported from irrigated urban agriculture, emerging contaminants are so far more difficult to analyse in low-income countries and data are rare (e.g., Asem-Hiablie et al. 2013; Amoah et al. 2014; Keraita et al. 2014).

TABLE 7.3 Common uses of different types of waste and related concerns

Type of waste	Common use in low-income countries by farmers in urban and peri-urban areas	General concerns/risks
MSW – Food waste	• Food waste fed to animals, deposited on nearby dumps, used in community composting and vermicomposting	• Direct feeding of household livestock is probably rather low-risk compared to livestock roaming streets • Low chemical risk as farmers know contents but community compost heaps could be harmful to children when playing around the heaps and attract rodents and other disease vectors

(Continued)

TABLE 7.3 (Continued)

Type of waste	Common use in low-income countries by farmers in urban and peri-urban areas	General concerns/risks
MSW – Mixed waste	• Farmers collect formally or naturally composted waste from decentralized dumping sites and apply it to fields; other stakeholders might use formally composted waste in parks or for landscaping	• Pathogens – when insufficiently composted which pose health risks to waste handlers, farmers, produce consumers and children playing near or on dumping sites • Toxic substances – such as heavy metals could cause soil and crop contamination • Glass splinters, plastics – cause physical harm to handlers
Human excreta – faeces, urine and faecal sludge	• Normally disposed of via toilets or latrines, but in some regions also used raw or after storage in farming • In urine diversion toilets, urine can be separated from faeces and used after storage, often diluted	• High risk from pathogens, especially in faeces and faecal sludge if not well handled and treated before use or use on low-growing crops • If sludge derives from treatment plants (sewage sludge) also high probability of chemical contaminants. This is significantly less the case for sludge of on-site systems like septic tanks (septage) • Foul smell and flies • Negative public and authority perceptions on using excreta for crop production and aquaculture
Wastewater	• In water-scarce countries, used formally as a source of irrigation water (often after some level of treatment) or informally without treatment • In more humid countries with poor sanitation, wastewater is disposed to drains and urban water streams which farmers might use in crop production	• High risk of exposed groups (farmers, produce traders and consumers, children playing in wastewater irrigated sites) from pollutants if not well-managed. • These pollutants can include pathogens, salts, metals/metalloids, residual drugs and other organic contaminants, also dependent on the water source • Smell (concern is lower than that of excreta) • High concentration of chemicals can also affect crop growth and productivity • Negative public and authority perceptions on using especially untreated wastewater for irrigating vegetables

Source: adapted from Keraita et al. 2006.

Safe and productive use of solid and liquid waste

While composting has, across many cultures, a long tradition, awareness, perceptions and acceptance of the use of treated wastewater, urine or faecal matter vary with the development stage of the society, and can be a very dynamic process which makes social feasibility studies, close participation of target groups, and trust-building essential components of successful reuse programmes (Drechsel, Mahjoub and Keraita 2015).

On the other hand, where reuse already takes place in the informal sector, a favourable economic benefit and limited risk awareness can jeopardize the introduction of risk-mitigation measures (Karg and Drechsel 2011). However, where markets or farmers are aware of risks, the range of technical options for conventional and/or farm-based treatment has been established (e.g., Koné et al. 2010; Libhaber and Orozco-Jaramillo 2013; Keraita et al. 2015).

The following sections will discuss experiences, challenges and opportunities for resource recovery from MSW and wastewater.

Increasing the value of composting and co-composting

Composting the organic fraction of MSW is seen as one of the most successful methods of preventing organic waste materials to end on landfills, while creating a valuable product at relatively low cost that is suitable for agricultural purposes (Wolkowski 2003). The benefits are not only attributed to increased soil fertility, but as mentioned above also to economic and environmental factors, such as costs associated with landfilling and transportation, decreasing use of commercial fertilizer imports, etc. (Hargreaves et al. 2008).

Success stories of MSW composting range from community-level projects to large-scale composting (Otoo and Drechsel 2015). An often-cited example is the 1995 established 'Waste Concern' which, since 2009, has managed to treat in Dhaka city more than 100,000 tons of waste, is tapping into carbon credits as an additional revenue stream and which, between 2001 and 2006, has produced compost in the larger Bangladesh area worth more than USD 1 million in local currency (www.wasteconcern.org).

These success stories on compost do not, however, rely only on urban farming, especially in larger cities, for reasons concerning compost quality and quantity (Danso et al. 2008), such as quality and quantity, as follows:

a) **Quality:** Urban farmers with a sufficiently high willingness to pay for compost (allowing compost stations to break even) are those producing for the urban market, not subsistence farmers. Commercial crops are often of short rotation, like exotic vegetables, which need most of all a nitrogen fertilizer, less an organic soil ameliorant. Even on sandy soils where compost can help retain soil water, farmers complained about additional labour as the compost first of all absorbed the water and required more irrigation. In addition, these premium customers often have poor tenure security and seek a more short-term fertilizer supply than a long-term soil ameliorant.

b) **Quantity:** Urban waste management is usually only interested in embarking on composting if this can reduce a significant volume of the waste. To start a compost station for saving, for example 3% of its transport volume, is usually not worth the effort. However, most intra- and peri-urban farming systems can hardly absorb any larger amounts of compost. A detailed market assessment by IWMI in Kumasi and Accra (both in Ghana) found that, of the organic waste which is collected and not otherwise used, if composted, less than 1% could be absorbed across all intra- and peri-urban farming systems if the willingness to pay should cover compost operational production costs. It was only in smaller cities with less waste generation, like in Tamale (also Ghana), that up to 5% was possible, and higher percentages can be expected from towns. But also in a city like Accra, the percentage can increase up to 20% if, for example, the non-agricultural demand, like from the housing sector, is considered.

If resource recovery is the target, and not only waste-volume reduction, then it is important to produce a high-quality product which can be attractive and competitive for different market segments. One possibility is to 'boost' the fertilizer value and attractiveness of the MSW compost (Figure 7.5), for example, through (i) co-composting organic MSW with dewatered but nutrient-rich urban faecal sludge or other nutrient-rich waste products; (ii) further enriching the compost with inorganic fertilizer, rock phosphate or urine to create a 'fortified' organo-mineral material tailored to market needs; and (iii) pelletizing the compost to reduce its bulkiness and to create a product similar in its appearance and handling to an inorganic fertilizer (Adamtey et al. 2009; Nikiema et al. 2014; Figure 7.6).

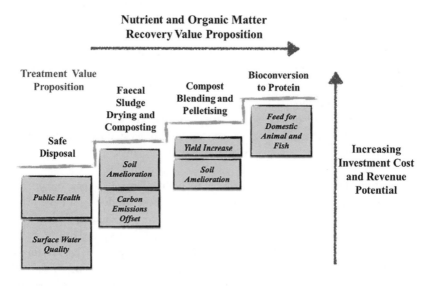

FIGURE 7.5 Value propositions for nutrient and organic matter recovery and reuse from septage from household-based sanitation systems

Source: Otoo et al. 2015.

FIGURE 7.6 Pellets of MSW-faecal sludge co-compost
Source: IWMI.

These options can also be combined with due care that any related increase in production costs is matched by the willingness to pay of the targeted customer segments, and remains competitive to alternative (and sometimes subsidized industrial) fertilizer.

Pelletized and un-pelletized co-compost is being tested for its safety for selected soils and crops, including vegetables and cereals in field and greenhouse trials. In most cases, the product proved to be competitive to inorganic fertilizer as for maize and cabbage[1] (Figure 7.7). While long-term trials are still needed to match more soils and crops with different types of pellets, farmers' interest and willingness to pay (WTP) for the product has been confirmed in very different cultural contexts, like Vietnam, Uganda, India, Bangladesh, Ghana and Sri Lanka (IWMI, unpublished). A market survey conducted, for example, in Kurunegala (Sri Lanka), where a co-composting pilot station started in 2014 its operations, showed a high WTP for nutrient-rich pelletized co-compost with a common WTP of Rs.17–20 per kg, which is 70–100% higher than what is normally paid for MSW compost (Fernando et al. 2014).

However, although the concepts of co-composting and compost pelletizing do not require any technical proof of concept anymore, related advanced compost stations remain few and research continues to be needed to capture customer feedback to adjust the technical process for market satisfaction.

Another option for increasing the value of organic waste as shown in Figure 7.5 is the use of the Black Soldier fly larvae *(Hermetia illucens)*, which feeds on organic matter, such as faecal sludge and organic wastes, and leapfrogs the

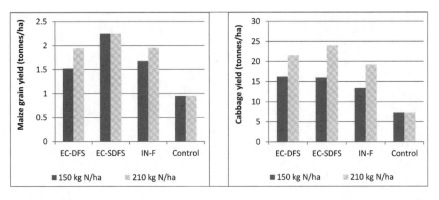

FIGURE 7.7 Maize and cabbage yields with different nitrogen (N) rates

Source: after Impraim et al. 2014.

nutrient extraction via crops by directly generating high-value protein and fat, which can be marketed for poultry, duck, pig and fish feed (Diener et al. 2014).

Increasing the safety of wastewater use

For wastewater irrigation, the focus has always been on reduction of health risk. This applies to the introduction of formal reuse schemes as well as to the challenges of already ongoing informal reuse. For formal schemes the additional challenge is cost recovery.

Due to the common shortfall in wastewater collection and treatment, WHO (2006) recommends a multi-barrier approach which decentralizes the responsibility of safeguarding public health along the food chain from production to consumption (see Figure 7.8). This approach is similar to the Hazard Analysis and Critical Control Points (HACCP) concept for food safety, which has been adopted in many developed countries. The advantage of multiple barriers is the additional security if one barrier fails. A typical example is 'crop restriction', which was successfully introduced, e.g., in Chile, Jordan or Mauritius, while farmers in other countries might ignore them due to market demand and their need to generate profits for sustaining their livelihood.

To determine how much safety is needed, WHO guidelines recommend the so-called health-based targets. These targets need to be realistic, measurable, based on scientific data and feasible within local conditions. Examples of health-based targets can be:

- Health-outcome targets (e.g., tolerable burdens of disease).
- Water-quality targets (e.g., guideline values for chemical hazards).

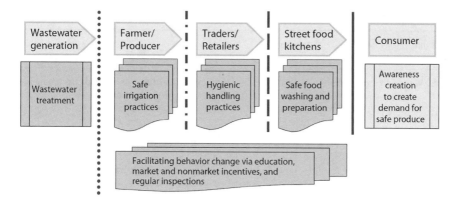

FIGURE 7.8 The multiple-barrier approach for consumption-related risks along the food chain as applied in wastewater irrigation

Source: Amoah et al. 2011.

- Performance targets (e.g., reductions of specific pathogen levels).
- Specified technology targets (e.g., application of defined treatment processes).

Looking at a risk scale from 1 to 7 with 1 being safe and 7 presenting the worst-case scenario, then a common management option is to assume the worst case and aim at maximum risk reduction of 6 units down to 1, which can be cumulative from one barrier to the other.

Table 7.4 shows some examples of the strength of some risk reduction. Some options, like cooking irrigated crops, are very powerful on their own, and can achieve 6 units, but do not fit every crop and diet. It might thus be safer to support several alternative barriers which in combination can achieve the targeted 6 units, like through combining (i) a minimal (farm-based) wastewater treatment (1–2 units pathogen reduction), (ii) drip irrigation (2–4 units pathogen reduction), and (iii) washing vegetables after harvesting, which can reduce in addition 2–3 units (Amoah et al. 2011; Drechsel and Keraita 2014).

Compared with other options for health risk reduction, including the construction of wastewater treatment plants, these on-farm or off-farm-based interventions are highly cost effective (Drechsel and Seidu 2011).

The advantage of the multi-barrier approach became obvious through the disastrous earthquake that afflicted Chile in early 2010. It affected, according to WHO, the only chlorine-producing plant in Chile, and two weeks later 30,000–40,000 cases of diarrhoea were reported from the North where chlorine is used as a single safeguard in agricultural production systems based on wastewater irrigation (R. Bos, pers. communication).

TABLE 7.4 Examples of risk–reduction barriers and effectiveness in pathogen removal

Control measure	Units* (max = 7)	Notes
A. Wastewater treatment	6–7	Reduction of pathogens depends on type and degree of treatment selected
B. On-farm options		
Crop restriction (i.e. no food crops eaten uncooked)	6–7	Depends on (a) effectiveness of local enforcement of crop restriction, and (b) comparative profit margin of the alternative crop(s)
On-farm treatment:		
(a) Three-tank system	1–2	One pond is being filled by the farmer, one is settling and the settled water from the third is being used
(b) Simple sedimentation	0.5–1	Sedimentation for ~18 hours.
(c) Simple filtration	1–3	Value depends on filtration system used
Method of wastewater application:		
(a) Furrow irrigation	1–2	Crop density and yield may be reduced
(b) Low-cost drip irrigation	2–4	Lower value for low-growing crops, higher value for high-growing crops
(c) Reduction of splashing	1–2	Splashing adds contaminated soil particles on to crop surfaces, which can be minimized
Pathogen die-off per day	0.5–2	Die-off between last irrigation and harvest (value depends on climate, crop type, etc.)
C. Post-harvest options at local markets		
Overnight storage in baskets	0.5–1	Selling produce after overnight storage in baskets (rather than overnight storage in sacks or selling fresh produce without overnight storage)
Produce preparation prior to sale	1–2	(a) Washing salad crops, vegetables and fruits with clean water.
	2–3	(b) Washing salad crops, vegetables and fruits with running tap water
	1–3	(c) Removing the outer leaves on cabbages, lettuce, etc.
D. In-kitchen produce-preparation options		
Produce disinfection	2–3	Washing salad crops, vegetables and fruits with an appropriate disinfectant and rinsing with clean water
Produce peeling	2	Fruits, root crops
Produce cooking	5–6	Option depends on local diet and preference for cooked food

Note: * log units of pathogen reduction

Sources: EPHC-NRMMC-AHMC 2006; WHO 2006; Amoah et al. 2011.

Influencing perceptions and behaviour on the use of urban waste

With respect to the promotion of waste reuse, two common situations prevail: (i) the introduction of reuse as a coping strategy to water shortage and (ii) the trajectory of already ongoing informal reuse to formal reuse to facilitate the adoption of safety measures. Both situations require social acceptance and behaviour change. While the informal use of waste products is a common practice in low-income countries, the largest challenge is the transformation of the practice into one that does not put public health in jeopardy. This concerns especially the production for urban markets, where along the food chain the number of people at risk is continuously increasing. For urban Ghana, for example, it was estimated that up to 2,000 urban vegetable farmers produce salad greens consumed eventually by up to 800,000 urban dwellers every day (Table 7.5).

TABLE 7.5 Estimated number of urban farmers, street food kitchens, and urban consumers along the lettuce and cabbage value chain in Ghana based on survey and sector data

Urban farmers producing lettuce and cabbage	Street restaurants offering salad side dishes	Daily consumers of salad side dishes in Ghana cities
Ca. 1,700–2,000	Ca. 3,600–5,300	Ca. 500,000–800,000

Source: Drechsel et al. 2014.

The situation where *treated wastewater* is being introduced as an alternative water source is more common in countries with established treatment capacity and freshwater shortage, like in the MENA region, Australia or USA. In these cases, negative perceptions can be a key constraint, while cost recovery is a key challenge. Where public perception is positive, the right business plan can, however, combine several revenue streams for a high cost-recovery rate as the example of the Drarga plant near Agadir in Morocco shows. The municipality collects sewage fees to recover its O&M costs and designed the plant to generate additional revenue from the sale of (i) treated wastewater to crop farmers, (ii) reed grass from the constructed wetlands, (iii) sludge compost, and (iv) methane gas from energy recovery (Rao et al. 2015). Although not all of these components have been implemented so far, a noteworthy innovation in this case is that all sales revenues and revenues from the water and sewage tariff and connection fee are deposited into a special account, independent of the main community account to serve solely the wastewater treatment plant. This special arrangement is a response to common bottlenecks in public financing of O&M costs like spare parts which contributed to the breakdown of about 70% of the wastewater treatment plants in the country (Choukr-Allah et al. 2005).

The compliance with food safety measures is a common reality in more developed countries where the HACCP approach has been adopted. In low-income countries where *untreated wastewater* use dominates, the adoption of farm or off-farm based safety measures still requires its proof of concept as so far the WHO

2006 Guidelines have not been implemented in any low-income country. Feasibility studies for such an implementation showed that the likely success will depend on a number of internal and external factors such as risk awareness and risk perceptions (not only of producers but also of the market), peer pressure, incentives, or the possible need for investments in terms of additional space, labour or capital which could affect, e.g., time allocation or the profit margin (Drechsel, Mahjoub and Keraita 2015). As behavioural change is a complex subject and often underestimated as an 'educational' challenge, it can be slow or of short duration (Karg and Drechsel 2011).

Another potential shortcoming in addressing behavioural change is an underestimation of the wider system within which key actors operate, like institutions, regulatory bodies, media and in- and output-market agents, which can have a significant influence on key actors' decision making (Figure 7.9):

FIGURE 7.9 Behaviour change support factors
Source: authors.

- ***Awareness creation:*** It is important to understand that behavioural change can hardly be achieved through educational means and awareness creation alone, while both have, however, an important supporting role. A pilot social marketing study in Kumasi showed that it is more likely that safe practices spread from farmer to farmer through social networks than through external facilitation, although the reason was not the absence of contact with extension officers. Farmers preferred, however, field demonstrations and/or learning by doing.

A particular communication challenge in countries with limited public-risk awareness is the invisible nature of most risk carriers, like pathogens (Amoah et al. 2009; Keraita et al. 2007, 2010).

- *Incentives:* Studies show that people are most likely to adopt innovations for direct economic returns on investments (Frewer et al. 1998). However, this will only happen if consumers are willing to pay more for safer products. But, in low-income countries, where risk awareness might be low and no dedicated marketing channels for safe produce exists, economic incentives from the public sector (subsidies, credit access, tax reductions, etc.) based on likely savings in the health sector, or indirect economic incentives like tenure security, could be considered. For public support, a quantification of costs and benefits would help justify the intervention (FAO 2010). A particular incentive for compliance is fear of going out of business. In Ghana, for example, farmers experienced significant pressure from media when using wastewater (Drechsel and Keraita 2014).
- *Social responsibility:* Private-sector involvement can facilitate a shift towards safety. Out-grower schemes supplying wholesale or supermarkets might be urged to comply with, e.g., a 'responsible sourcing policy' or any other type of 'sustainable agricultural code of conduct' which the private-sector demands from its own policy perspective and/or reasons of international competiveness and branding.
- *Social marketing:* Where economic incentives might not work due to low risk awareness, social marketing strategies could help identify valuable benefits in support of behaviour change, similar to hand-wash campaigns. Studies must identify positive core values that can trigger the target audience to voluntarily accept, modify or abandon behaviour for the benefit of personal and or public health (Drechsel and Karg 2013).
- *Laws and regulations:* Regulations are an important external factor to institutionalize safe and productive reuse practices for compliance monitoring, and to provide the legal framework for both incentives (for example, certificates, tenure arrangements) and disincentives (such as fees). However, regulations should not be based on imported standards, but rather on locally feasible standards that are viewed as practical and are not prone to corruption. In this way, regulation and institutionalization may contribute to ensuring the long-term sustainability of behaviour change, whereas promotional and educational activities are usually limited to a specific time frame.

Conclusion

There are many good reasons, including financial and economic gains, for the recovery of resources from liquid and solid waste. In this regard, it is no surprise that the productive use, especially of wastewater in urban agricultural systems, is already a common reality. However, the reason is not only water scarcity but also, especially in low-income countries, water pollution, making it difficult for farmers to find clean water sources. The resulting use of polluted water is mostly charged in the informal sector, resulting potentially in significant health risks for farmers and consumers.

Wastewater treatment to reduce the volume of polluted water discharged into water bodies will remain the most powerful means to address this concern. However, the costs of comprehensive wastewater collection and treatment are often prohibitive in developing countries where, so far, most investments are more 'upstream', targeting water supply. As a result, the generation of untreated wastewater will continue to increase and it is essential that authorities give attention to the food safety along those food chains, depending on irrigated urban and peri-urban agriculture.

The multi-barrier approach recommended by WHO (2006) is addressing this situation in low-income countries. However, the approach is relying on behaviour change, which is not without challenges, and the implementation of related concepts, like HACCP, is so far limited to more-developed countries with treatment capacity, risk awareness and regulations which allow compliance monitoring. Moreover, in such countries, public health relies significantly on wastewater treatment and the institutional capacities and incentives to maintain its technical functionality. In low-income countries with limited treatment capacity, public health will have to rely solely on the adoption of safety practices by farmers and food traders, which requires significant efforts to increase public risk awareness to eventually create market incentives for safer food production. Till this is achieved, officials must determine the best ways to motivate and/or regulate farmers, food vendors and consumers to buy into the multi-barrier approach. Successful strategies will probably include combinations of financial and non-financial incentives, as well as regulations and awareness campaigns that enhance understanding of the potential harm involved when safe practices are not adopted. Supporting policies and related education will be milestones in this process, but might not be sufficient on their own to trigger behaviour change (Drechsel and Karg 2013).

Where treatment plants are in place and reuse is formally organized, the ideal situation is that farmers pay for the water to contribute to the recovery of the operational costs of the treatment facility. In most situations, the direct revenues from selling treated wastewater are, however, very small, given that freshwater prices are usually subsidized and the wastewater has to be sold even cheaper. However, there are options to increase the value of the wastewater and also business models to maximize cost recovery, or to reverse the cash flow and pay farmers for accepting treated urban wastewater while renouncing their freshwater rights for urban development (Otoo and Drechsel 2015).

In view of organic waste and faecal sludge, especially from on-site sanitation facilities, composting and co-composting offer low-cost means for pathogen destruction and risk minimization. The resulting organic product is a well-accepted soil input with a long tradition of use. An important benefit is reduced transport costs through the reduction of the waste volume. If in addition, revenues from compost reuse are targeted, then a professional business approach will be needed to move with customer-specific value propositions' organic waste recycling from the traditional appearance of a household- or community-based initiative to scale. The customers will certainly include urban and peri-urban farmers but, even more so, other sectors interested in organic matter, if the target is to effectively reduce the urban waste volume.

Note

1   EC-DFS: Enriched compost of dewatered faecal sludge; EC-SDFS: Enriched co-compost with sawdust faecal sludge; IN-F: inorganic fertilizer (i.e., ammonium nitrate, supplemented with muriate of potash and triple super phosphate); Control: soil only. Application rates: 150 and 210 kg of nitrogen per hectare.

References

Adamtey, N.; Cofie, O.; Ofosu-Budu, G. K.; Danso, S. K.; Forster, D. 2009. Production and storage of N-enriched co-compost. *Waste Management* 29(9): 2429–2436.

Amoah, P.; Drechsel, P.; Schuetz, T.; Kranjac-Berisavjevic, G.; Manning-Thomas, N. 2009. From world cafés to road shows: Using a mix of knowledge sharing approaches to improve wastewater use in urban agriculture. *Knowledge Management for Development Journal* 5(3): 246–262.

Amoah, P.; Keraita, B.; Akple, M.; Drechsel, P.; Abaidoo, R. C.; Konradsen, F. 2011. Low cost options for health risk reduction where crops are irrigated with polluted water in West Africa. IWMI Research Report Series 141. Colombo: International Water Management Institute (IWMI).

Amoah, P.; Lente, I.; Asem-Hiablie, S.; Abaidoo, R. C. 2014. Quality of vegetables in Ghanaian urban farms and markets. In: *Irrigated urban vegetable production in Ghana: Characteristics, benefits and risk mitigation.* (Eds.) Drechsel, P.; Keraita, B. Colombo: International Water Management Institute (IWMI), 2nd edition, pp. 89–103.

Asem-Hiablie, S.; Church, C. D.; Elliott, H. A.; Shappell, N. W.; Schoenfuss, H. L.; Drechsel, P.; Williams, C. F.; Knopf, A. L.; Dabie, M. Y. 2013. Serum estrogenicity and biological responses in African catfish raised in wastewater ponds in Ghana. *Science of the Total Environment* 463 & 464: 1182–1191.

Bradford, A.; Brook, R.; Hunshal, C. S. 2002. Crop selection and wastewater irrigation, Hubli–Dharwad, India. *Urban Agriculture Magazine* 8: 31–32.

Choukr-Allah, R.; Thor, A.; Young, P. E. 2005. Domestic wastewater treatment and agricultural reuse in Drarga, Morocco. In: *The use of non-conventional water resources.* (Ed.) Hamdy, A. Options Méditerranéennes: Série A. Séminaires Méditerraéens: no. 66. Bari: CIHEAM/EU DG Research, pp. 147–155.

Christie, P.; Easson, D. L.; Picton, J. R.; Love, S.C.P. 2001. Agronomic value of alkaline-stabilized sewage biosolids for Spring Barley. *Agronomy Journal* 93: 144–151.

Cofie, O.; Bradford, A.; Drechsel, P. 2006. Recycling of urban organic waste for urban agriculture. In: *Cities farming for the future: Urban agriculture for green and productive cities.* (Ed.) Veenhuizen, R. van. Leusden: RUAF Foundation; Manila: IIRR Publishers, pp. 210–242.

Danso, G.; Drechsel, P.; Cofie, O. 2008. Large-scale urban waste composting for urban and peri-urban agriculture in West Africa: An integrated approach to provide decision support to municipal authorities. In: *Agricultures et développement urbain en Afrique subsaharienne: environnement et enjeux sanitaires.* (Eds.) Parrot, L.; Njoya, A.; Temple, L.; Assogba-Komlan, F.; Kahane, R.; Ba Diao, M.; Havard, M. Paris: L'Harmattan, pp. 51–62.

Diener, S.; Semiyaga, S.; Niwagaba, C. B.; Murray Muspratt, A.; Gning, J. B.; Mbéguéré, M.; Ennin, J. E.; Zurbrugg, C.; Strande, L. 2014. A value proposition: Resource recovery from faecal sludge: Can it be the driver for improved sanitation? *Resources, Conservation and Recycling* 88: 32–38.

Drangert, J. O. 1998. Fighting the urine blindness to provide more sanitation options. *Water (South Africa)* 24(2): 157–164.

Drechsel, P.; Adam-Bradford A.; Raschid-Sally, L. 2014. Irrigated vegetable farming in urban Ghana: A farming system between challenges and resilience. In: *Irrigated urban vegetable production in Ghana: Characteristics, benefits and risk mitigation.* (Eds.) Drechsel, P.; Keraita, B. Colombo: International Water Management Institute (IWMI), 2nd edition, pp. 1–6.

Drechsel, P.; Cofie, O.; Danso, G. 2010. Closing the rural-urban food and nutrient loops in West Africa: A reality check. *Urban Agriculture Magazine* 23: 8–10. Available from: www.ruaf.org/sites/default/files/UAM23%20west%20africa%20pag8–10.pdf.

Drechsel, P.; Cofie, O. O.; Keraita, B.; Amoah, P.; Evans, A.; Amerasinghe, P. 2011. Recovery and reuse of resources: Enhancing urban resilience in low-income countries. *Urban Agriculture Magazine* 25: 66–69.

Drechsel, P.; Danso, G.; Qadir, M. 2015. Wastewater use in agriculture: Challenges in assessing costs and benefits. In: *Wastewater: Economic asset in an urbanizing world.* (Eds.) Drechsel, P.; Qadir, M.; Wichelns, D. New York: Springer, pp. 39–152.

Drechsel, P.; Keraita, B. (eds.) 2014. Irrigated urban vegetable production in Ghana: Characteristics, benefits and risk mitigation. Colombo: International Water Management Institute (IWMI), 2nd edition. Available from: www.iwmi.cgiar.org/Publications/Books/PDF/irrigated_urban_vegetable_production_in_ghana.pdf.

Drechsel, P.; Karg, H. 2013. Motivating behaviour change for safe wastewater irrigation in urban and peri-urban Ghana. *Sustainable Sanitation Practice* 16:10–20.

Drechsel, P.; Mahjoub, O.; Keraita, B. 2015. Social and cultural dimensions in wastewater use. In: *Wastewater: Economic asset in an urbanizing world.* (Eds.) Drechsel, P.; Qadir, M.; Wichelns, D. New York: Springer, pp. 75–92.

Drechsel, P.; Seidu, R. 2011. Cost-effectiveness of options for reducing health risks in areas where food crops are irrigated with wastewater. *Water International* 36(4): 535–548.

EPHC – NRMMC – AHMC. 2006. Australian guidelines for water recycling: Managing health and environmental risks (Phase 1). Environment Protection and Heritage Council (EPHC), Natural Resource Management Ministerial Council (NHRMMC) and Australian Health Ministers' Conference (AHMC). Available from: www.susana.org/en/resources/library/details/1533.

Esrey, S. A.; Andersson, I.; Hillers, A.; Sawyer, R. 2001. Closing the loop: Ecological sanitation for food security. Mexico: Sarar Transformación SC. UNDP-SIDA (United Nations Development Program – Swedish International Development Agency).

Evans, A.; Otoo, M.; Drechsel, P.; Danso, G. 2013. Developing typologies for resource recovery businesses. *Urban Agriculture Magazine* 26: 24–30.

FAO. 2010. The wealth of waste: The economics of wastewater use in agriculture. FAO Water Reports 35. Rome: Food and Agriculture Organization of the United Nations (FAO).

Faruqui, N.; Niang, S.; Redwood, M. 2004. Untreated wastewater reuse in market gardens: A case study of Dakar, Senegal. In: *Wastewater use in irrigated agriculture: Confronting the livelihood and environmental realities.* (Eds.) Scott, C. A.; Faruqui, N. I.; Raschid-Sally, L. Wallingford: CABI Publication, pp. 113–125.

Fernando, S.; Drechsel, P.; Amirova, I.; Jayathilake, N.; Semasinghe, C. 2014. Solid waste and septage co-composting as a pathway to cost and resource recovery in Sri Lanka. Paper presented at 1st Specialist Conference on Municipal Water Management and

Sanitation in Developing Countries, 2–4 December 2014, Asian Institute of Technology, Bangkok, Thailand.

Frewer, L. J.; Howard, C.; Shepherd, R. 1998. Understanding public attitudes to technology. *Journal of Risk Research* 1(3): 221–235.

Gaye, M.; Niang, S. 2002. Epuration des eaux useés et l'agriculture urbaine. Etudes et Recherches. Dakar: ENDA-TM.

Hargreaves, J. C.; Adl, M. S.; Warman, P. R. 2008. A review of the use of composted municipal solid waste in agriculture. *Agriculture, Ecosystems and Environment* 123: 1–14.

Heinonen-Tanski, H.; Wijk-Sijbesma, C. van. 2005. Human excreta for plant production. *Bioresour Technol* 96(4): 403–411.

Hoornweg, D.; Bhada-Tata, P. 2012. What a waste: A global view of waste management. Urban Development Series Knowledge Papers, Paper No. 15. Washington, DC: World Bank.

Hoornweg, D.; Thomas, L.; Otten, L. 1999. Composting and its applicability in developing countries, urban waste management. Working Paper Series No. 8. Washington, DC: The World Bank.

Huibers, F. P.; van Lier, J. B. 2005. Use of wastewater in agriculture: The water chain approach. *Irrigation and Drainage* 54: 3–10.

Impraim, R.; Nikiema, J.; Cofie, O.; Rao, K. 2014. Value from faecal sludge and municipal organic waste fertilizer cum soil conditioner in Ghana. Paper No. 2035 presented at the 37th WEDC International Conference, 15–19 September 2014, Hanoi, Vietnam.

Jimenez, B. 2005. Treatment technology and standards for agricultural wastewater reuse: A case study in Mexico. *Irrigation and Drainage* 54 (Suppl. 1): S22–S33.

Jönsson, H.; Richert Stintzing, A.; Vinnerås, B.; Salomon, E. 2004. Guidelines on the use of urine and faeces in crop production. Report 2004–2. EcoSanRes Publications Series. Stockholm: Stockholm Environment Institute.

Karg, H.; Drechsel, P. 2011. Motivating behaviour change to reduce pathogenic risk where unsafe water is used for irrigation. *Water International* 36(4): 476–490.

Keraita, B.; Drechsel, P.; Amoah, P.; Cofie, O. 2006. Assessment of health risks from urban wastewater and solid waste reuse in agriculture. In: *Health risks and benefits of urban and peri-urban agriculture and livestock in sub-Saharan Africa.* (Eds.) Boichio, A.; Clegg, A.; Mwagore, D. UPE Series Report #1. Ottawa: International Development Research Centre (IDRC), pp. 55–73.

Keraita, B.; Drechsel, P.; Konradsen, F. 2007. Safer options for wastewater irrigated urban vegetable farming in Ghana. *Leisa Magazine* 23(3): 26–28.

Keraita, B.; Drechsel, P.; Seidu, R.; Amerasinghe, P.; Cofie, O.; Konradsen, F. 2010. Harnessing farmers' knowledge and perceptions for health-risk reduction in wastewater-irrigated agriculture. In: *Wastewater irrigation and health: Assessing and mitigating risks in low-income countries.* (Eds.) Drechsel, P.; Scott, C. A.; Raschid-Sally, L.; Redwood, M.; Bahri, A. London: Earthscan-IDRC-IWMI, pp. 189–207.

Keraita, B.; Mateo-Sagasta Dávila, J.; Drechsel, P.; Winkler, M.; Medlicott, K. 2015. Risk mitigation for wastewater irrigation systems in low-income countries: Opportunities and limitations of the WHO guidelines. In: *Alternative Water Supply Systems.* (Eds.) Memon, F. A.; Ward, S. London: IWA Publishing, pp. 267–389.

Keraita, B.; Silverman, A.; Amoah, P.; Asem-Hiablie, S. 2014. Quality of irrigation water used for urban vegetable production. In: *Irrigated urban vegetable production in Ghana: Characteristics, benefits and risk mitigation.* (Eds.) Drechsel, P.; Keraita, B. Colombo: International Water Management Institute (IWMI), 2nd edition, pp. 62–73.

Koné, D.; Cofie, O. O.; Nelson, K. 2010. Low-cost options for pathogen reduction and nutrient recovery from faecal sludge. In: *Wastewater irrigation and health: Assessing and mitigating risk in low-income countries.* (Eds.), Drechsel, P.; Scott, C. A.; Raschid-Sally, L.; Redwood, M.; Bahri, A. London: Earthscan-IDRC-IWMI, pp. 171–188.

Lautze, J.; Stander, E.; Drechsel, P.; da Silva, A. K.; Keraita, B. 2014. Global experiences in water reuse. CGIAR Research Program on Water, Land and Ecosystems (WLE). Resource Recovery and Reuse Series 4. Colombo: Sri Lanka: International Water Management Institute (IWMI).

Libhaber, M.; Orozco-Jaramillo, A. 2013. Sustainable treatment of municipal wastewater. *Water* 21 (October 2013): 25–28.

Lüthi, C.; Panesar, A.; Schütze, T.; Norström, A.; McConville, J.; Parkinson, J.; Saywell, D.; Ingle, R. 2011. Sustainable sanitation in cities: A framework for action. Sustainable Sanitation Alliance (SuSanA), International Forum on Urbanism (IFoU). Rijswijk: Papiroz Publishing House.

Mihelcic, J. R.; Fry, L. M.; Shaw, R. 2011. Global potential of phosphorus recovery from human urine and feces. *Chemosphere* 84: 832–839.

Moore, S. A. 2012. Garbage matters: Concepts in new geographies of waste. *Progress in Human Geography* 36(6): 780–799.

Murray, A.; Buckley, C. 2010. Designing reuse-oriented sanitation infrastructure: The design for service planning approach. In: *Wastewater irrigation and health: Assessing and mitigating risks in low-income countries.* (Eds.) Drechsel, P.; Scott, C. A.; Raschid-Sally, L.; Redwood, M.; Bahri, A. London: Earthscan-IDRC-IWMI, pp. 303–318.

Nikiema, J.; Cofie, O.; Impraim, R. 2014. Technological options for safe resource recovery from fecal sludge. CGIAR Research Program on Water, Land and Ecosystems (WLE). Resource Recovery and Reuse Series 2. Colombo: International Water Management Institute (IWMI).

Otoo, M.; Drechsel, P. 2015. Resource recovery from waste: Business models for energy, nutrients and water reuse. London: Earthscan; Colombo: IWMI. (In press).

Otoo, M.; Drechsel, P.; Hanjra, M. A. 2015. Business models and economic approaches for nutrient recovery from wastewater and fecal sludge. In: *Wastewater: Economic asset in an urbanizing world.* (Eds.) Drechsel, P.; Qadir, M.; Wichelns, D. New York: Springer, pp. 217–245.

Prüss-Ustün, A.; Corvalan, C. 2006. Preventing disease through healthy environments, towards an estimate of the environmental burden of disease. Geneva: WHO.

Qadir, M.; Wichelns, D.; Raschid-Sally, L.; Singh Minhas, P.; Drechsel, P.; Bahri, A.; McCornick, P. 2007. Agricultural use of marginal-quality water: Opportunities and challenges. In: *Water for food, water for life. A comprehensive assessment of water management in agriculture.* (Ed.) Molden, D. London: Earthscan; Colombo: International Water Management Institute, pp. 425–457.

Rao, K.; Hanjra, M. H.; Drechsel, P.; Danso, G. 2015. Business models and economic approaches supporting water reuse. In: *Wastewater: Economic asset in an urbanizing world.* (Eds.) Drechsel, P.; Qadir, M.; Wichelns, D. New York: Springer, pp. 195–216.

Raschid-Sally, L.; Carr, R.; Buechler, S. 2005. Managing wastewater agriculture to improve livelihoods and environmental quality in poor countries. *Irrigation and Drainage* 54 (Suppl. 1): 11–22.

Rautanen, S.; Viskari, E. 2006. In search of drivers for dry sanitation. *Land Use and Water Resources Research* 6: 4.1–4.9.

Rosemarin, A.; Bruijne, G. D.; Caldwell, I. 2009. The next inconvenient truth, peak phosphorus. *The Broker* 15: 6–9.

Scott, C. A.; Zarazua, J. A.; Levine, G. 2000. Urban wastewater reuse for crop production in the water-short Guanajuato River Basin, Mexico. Research Report 41. Colombo: International Water Management Institute (IWMI).

Scott, C.; Drechsel, P.; Raschid-Sally, L.; Bahri, A.; Mara, D. D.; Redwood, M.; Jiménez, B. 2010. Wastewater irrigation and health: Challenges and outlook for mitigating risks in low-income countries. In: *Wastewater irrigation and health: Assessing and mitigating risks in low-income countries.* (Eds.). Drechsel, P.; Scott, C. A.; Raschid-Sally, L.; Redwood, M.; Bahri, A. London: Earthscan-IDRC-IWMI, pp. 189–207.

UNEP. 2011. Towards a green economy: Pathways to sustainable development and poverty eradication. United Nations Environment Programme (UNEP). Available from: www. unep.org/greeneconomy.

Van der Hoek, W.; Ul-Hassan, M.; Ensink, J.H. J.; Feenstra, S.; Raschid-Sally, L.; Munir, S.; Aslam, R.; Ali, N.; Hussain, R.; Matsuno Y. 2002. Urban wastewater: A valuable resource for agriculture. Research Report 63. Colombo: International Water Management Institute (IWMI).

WHO. 2006. Guidelines for the safe use of wastewater, greywater and excreta in agriculture and aquaculture. Geneva: World Health Organization (WHO).

Winblad, U.; Simpson-Hebert, M. 2004. Ecological sanitation. Stockholm: Stockholm Environment Institute, 2nd edition.

Wolkowski, R. 2003. Nitrogen management considerations for landspreading municipal solid waste compost. *J. Environ. Qual.* 32: 1844–1850.

Zurbruegg, C.; Drescher, S. 2002. Solid waste management: Biological treatment of municipal solid waste. *SANDEC News* 5. Duebendorf: SANDEC.

8

URBAN AGRICULTURE AND CLIMATE CHANGE

Shuaib Lwasa[1] and Marielle Dubbeling[2]

1 DEPARTMENT OF GEOGRAPHY GEO-INFORMATICS AND CLIMATIC SCIENCES, MAKERERE UNIVERSITY, UGANDA

2 RUAF FOUNDATION, THE NETHERLANDS

Introduction

Communities in many cities around the world have practised (intra- and peri-) urban agriculture for various reasons (Dubbeling et al. 2010; FAO 2012 and 2014). Urban agriculture is considered as a holistic set of activities that involve production systems such as horticulture, livestock, forestry and agroforestry and aquaculture, as well as related input supply, processing and marketing activities contributing to regional food systems (Mougeot 2001).

For several years urban agriculture has been analyzed for its potential to contribute to poverty alleviation and social inclusion, enhanced food security and nutrient recycling, income and employment generation, and productive reuse of organic wastes and wastewater (de Zeeuw et al. 2011). More recently urban agriculture has also been identified as a strategy for mitigating the impacts of climate change and reduction of climate related risks (Dubbeling 2013a; Lwasa et al. 2013; Lwasa 2014). Urban agriculture has a potential for the provision of micro-level ecosystem services, with a cumulative impact at the macro-scale, next to delivering a number of developmental benefits such as poverty reduction and social inclusion (Grimm et al. 2008; Padoch et al. 2008; Swalheim and Dodman 2008; Lwasa et al. 2009).

At the same time, urban agriculture is affected by climate variability and change, posing risks to the sustenance of city regional food systems (Dubbeling 2013a; Lwasa et al. 2013). Urban agriculture systems and practices have to be adapted to the changing climatological conditions in order to continue fulfilling the role in sustainable and smart urban development.

This chapter analyzes the opportunities and limitations for urban agriculture in the context of climate change mitigation and adaptation, and provides information on some first-city projects, monitoring data and policies in this field, and using examples from different cities and climatic conditions. It also outlines innovations needed to make urban agriculture more resilient to climate change. The chapter concludes with the identification of challenges for research and policy development regarding the potential for urban agriculture as a city climate change and disaster risk-reduction strategy.

The chapter is based on a recent global literature review on urban agriculture and climate change. It also draws on studies regarding the potential of (intra- and peri-) urban agriculture and forestry for city climate change mitigation and adaptation undertaken by RUAF Foundation with Climate Change and Development Knowledge Network (CDKN) (Dubbeling 2014a) and UN Habitat (Dubbeling 2014b), respectively,[1] and on synthesis studies conducted in various cities across Africa that analyzed grey and peer-reviewed literature for urban resilience building (Lwasa et al. 2013).

Cities and climate change

Climate change and climate-related disasters are recognized as key challenges facing cities today. Impacts of variable and extreme climate events are reported in many cities (Lwasa et al. 2013). The *Fifth Assessment Report* (AR5) of the Intergovernmental Panel on Climate Change (IPCC) (University of Cambridge and ICLEI 2014) reports that many emerging climate change risks are concentrated in urban areas and these impacts are increasing. The climate risks faced by cities include storm surges, sea level rise, droughts and water scarcity, excessive rainfall, floods and landslides, heat waves and cold waves leading to infrastructure damage, disrupted food systems, pollution of water, and ultimately negative health impacts with associated economic losses (UN-Habitat 2011). Moreover, urban poor are particularly vulnerable to variations in food prices and income since food makes up a large part of the household expenses. Variations in income or food prices have a significant and direct impact on their diets (lower food intake, turning to cheaper/less-nutritious food), leading to a further reduction of health care and schooling expenditures or to the sale of productive assets (FAO 2008; Prain 2010). The World Bank estimated that the rise in food prices between 2007 and 2008 increased the number of people living in extreme poverty in urban areas in East and South Asia, the Middle East and sub-Saharan Africa by at least 1.5% (Baker 2008). Reduced food supply to the cities due to climate change distortions will result in further increases in food prices affecting the urban poor.

Climate change may also be aggravating the urban heat island effect (characterized by higher mean temperatures and less variation in night-time and day-time temperatures in built-up areas). This relates to human and industrial activities that absorb heat, which leads to an increase in the amount of energy used for cooling and refrigeration purposes (Grimm et al. 2008; Rosenzweig et al. 2011; University of Cambridge and ICLEI 2014). The levels of exposure and vulnerability to the impacts of climate change vary from city to city. Within cities, there is even more marked differentiated vulnerability associated with socio-economic and spatial structures of the cities (Action Aid 2006; Douglas et al. 2008; Frayne et al. 2012). As noted by Adelekan (2010), the urban poor may be disproportionally affected by the impacts of climate change. This is because the urban poor largely live in informal settlements often located on marginal land such as low-lying and flood-prone areas or steep slopes. In addition, the limited resources of the urban poor hamper their ability to respond to the changing climatic conditions (Satterthwaite 2008).

BOX 8.1 FLOODING DUE TO CONVERSION OF FLOOD PLAINS TO RESIDENTIAL AREAS AND INCREASING RAINFALL AND EXTREMES

A vulnerability assessment implemented in the city of Kesbewa (Sri Lanka) indicated highest risks on former rice or paddy fields converted into other uses and their surrounding areas. In the ancient land use system in Sri Lanka, low-lying lands were kept free from construction for drainage of rainwater and paddy cultivation. However, the rapid filling and conversion of these lands to residential and commercial lands has significantly altered the natural water flow and drainage in the area. This, coupled with increases in rainfall, has made recurrent flooding a common sight in these and surrounding areas, leading to damages to infrastructure and lower agricultural production.

Source: Mohamed and Gunasekera 2014.

Cities are increasingly called upon to address the vulnerability of people, places and sectors that may be affected by a changing climate, but they also have a responsibility to mitigate their greenhouse gas emissions to avoid unmanageable climate change. At the same time, cities have the responsibility to ensure access to food, water and energy for their growing population (Tuts 2014). Cities are therefore at the centre not only of climate change mitigation but also of adaptation.

According to the World Bank (IBRD 2010), building resilience in a city requires an integrated approach "that considers mitigation, adaptation and development." Such an integrated approach brings together strategies that reduce greenhouse gas emissions and also reduce the vulnerability of settlements to climate change while addressing developmental needs. The latter involves reducing urban poverty, promoting social inclusion, and the provision of health, water and sanitation services. In that perspective, the World Bank recommends orienting urban climate change programmes towards realization of the Millennium Development Goals (or the new Sustainable Development Goals (SDGs)), and asks for priority attention to the inclusion of measures that reduce the vulnerability of the urban poor, enhance the resilience of community organizations, improve settlements to reduce slums, improve building quality and ensure local food security by encouraging local food production as important key components of climate change strategies (see: http://sustainabledevelopment.un.org/?menu=1300). The Communitas Coalition specifically calls for more attention for urban climate change, sustainable urbanization in the SDGs, as well as linkages with rural development, food security and eco-systems resources (Forster 2014).

In 2010, the World Bank (IBRD 2010) has also already made a plea for "innovative solutions" to climate change adaptation. It points out that environmentally sustainable solutions for food, water, energy and transport should be integrated components of a city climate change adaptation and disaster risk-management plan. The recent IPCC AR5 report indeed indicates that adaptation options exist in the areas such as water, food, energy and transport in urban areas (University of Cambridge and ICLEI 2014).

The effects of climate variability and change on urban agriculture; required innovation

Climate variability and change are affecting urban agricultural systems, with varying effects to the urban agriculture systems across spatial and temporal scales. Depending on the specific local context, climate change, as an intervening factor influencing production, may present risks such as droughts, flooding or increased temperatures that would affect the production systems negatively as well as opportunities mainly in terms of water resource availability or prolonged growing seasons (Atkinson 2000; Abdulsalam-Saghir and Oshijo 2009; Mkwambisi et al. 2011; Brownlee et al. 2013). The latter has so far not received much attention in the climate change discourse, although the uncertainty about variability of climate may offset potential opportunities.

Enhancing the resilience of the urban agricultural production systems to a variable climate, to mitigate the negative effects of climate change on urban agriculture and to facilitate the optimal use of the new opportunities require (preferably participatory) technology development and innovation of urban agricultural systems and practices. Response strategies could include adjustment of production systems, cropping patterns, selection of adapted crop varieties, diversification of farming systems, improved water management and rezoning of urban agriculture. For example, in cities where fresh water is relatively scarce, such as Dakar (Senegal) and Addis Ababa (Ethiopia), technologies using trapezoidal water collection ponds at the household level have been used in mountainous regions to provide water during the drier part of the year (Van Rooijen et al. 2010). This kind of technology is appropriate with high-value and low-water-consuming enterprises, some of which include leafy vegetables, poultry and medicinal plants.

Rainfall harvesting from roof and road runoff has been promoted in Beijing (China) since 2000, as climate change trends also project increasing water scarcity in that region. Harvested water is collected in water ponds for primary treatment (sedimentation) and later used for irrigation of parks and gardens, aquifer recharge and maintaining water levels in small ponds and lakes in the city. Capacity for collecting rainwater can reach up to 40 million cubic meters (m^3). Capturing rainwater from greenhouses has been propagated since 2005. On average, 200–300 m^3 of rainwater can be annually collected from greenhouses with roofs covering

667 m², allowing to irrigate 2–3 times this area of crops if efficient irrigation methods (drip irrigation) are used (personal communication, Yang 26–04–2012).

Also reuse of organic wastes and wastewater is a key element for enhanced resource efficiency in urban agricultural production systems where producers adapt to more irregular rainfall or periods of drought (see also Chapter 7 of this volume). Because of (perceived) health risks, there is generally a hesitation to take advantage of the great potential of wastewater reuse in urban agriculture. Low-cost technologies for decentralized wastewater treatment and reuse in urban and peri-urban agriculture are available (including, amongst others, natural infiltration and oxidation ponds or reed bed systems), but their further development and larger-scale implementation are needed (RUAF Foundation 2013).

In the context of climate change, there is also a need to further investigate production systems and technologies that are resource efficient and use more renewable energy in areas of irrigation and pumping of water, soil preparation and plant management, drying, processing, storing and transport of food.

Pest and (zoonotic) disease management (including potential livestock mortality due to heat waves) may become even more crucial as a result of changing climate (Magnusson and Follis Bergman 2014), and further farmer training on the subject is required. Local innovation funds are interesting mechanisms by which farmers can not only fund testing of new technical innovations, but also social and organizational innovations (Dubbeling 2013b). Also, more research is needed to improve the understanding of the interactions between climate stressors and non-climate stressors and their impacts on urban agriculture.

BOX 8.2   INNOVATING FOOD PRODUCTION IN VIEW OF CLIMATE CHANGE IN DUMANGAS (THE PHILIPPINES)

Being a flood and drought-prone area, Dumangas organizes Climate Field Schools that seek to combine indigenous knowledge with scientific methods. It helps local communities to strengthen their food security and livelihoods by teaching farmers to read weather forecasts, interpret satellite photos, set up their own weather stations, and to decide what and when to plant based on this timely information. Its overall goal is to reduce disaster risks and enhance the capacities of local institutions and communities. Dumangas recognizes the role of peri-urban and rural farmers in the long-term resilience of the city-region food system, and the need to enhance their capacity and production systems. This results in reduced damages to infrastructure, which lessens reconstruction and rehabilitation expenses for the government. In addition, the livelihoods of both producers and inhabitants are protected and local production is preserved and increased, contributing to a more resilient urban food supply system.

Source: ICLEI and RUAF Foundation 2013.

Potential of urban agriculture for city adaptation to climate change

The climate projections in the IPCC AR5 indicate that there is likely to be a loss of food production and productive arable lands due to storms, floods, shifting seasonal patterns, droughts or water scarcity (University of Cambridge and ICLEI 2014). For example, changing rainfall patterns are expected to affect rural agricultural productivity and threaten yields in many developing countries (Lotsch 2007; Nellemann et al. 2009). Cities with a heavy reliance on food imports would be more significantly affected (University of Cambridge and ICLEI 2014). Related adaptation options for, and local responses to, climate change include, next to other strategies in the field of water, transport and energy, support for intra- and peri-urban agriculture, green roofs, local markets and enhanced social safety nets and development of alternative food sources, including inland aquaculture (University of Cambridge and ICLEI 2014). Intra-urban and peri-urban agriculture also involves the growing of trees and the raising of livestock (including fisheries) within the built-up area or on the fringe of cities.

Diversifying food and income sources

Urban agriculture can help cities to become more resilient through enhancing access to nutritious food, diversifying food sources, reducing the impacts of disturbances in food supply from rural areas or imports and reducing shocks of food prices. Urban agriculture can support the urban poor to enhance adaptation through diversifying income opportunities, creating "green jobs" and functioning as a safety net in times of economic crises (Dubbeling 2013b).

Reducing the urban heat island effect

Urban areas are also associated with local climate effects of high temperature due to impervious surfaces and reduced vegetation. The urban heat island (UHI) effect is moderated by urban agriculture when land cover by crops and trees offsets UHI effects by increasing the amount of green space in urban areas and peri-urban zones (Tidball and Krasny 2007). The urban gardens, agricultural lands, street and fruit trees, parks and forests decrease solar radiation, increase evapotranspiration and lower temperatures through evaporative cooling and by providing shade and facilitating faster cooling at night-time (Simon 2012).

Reduced UHI is assessed highest for specific types of urban agriculture, such as intra- and peri-urban forestry and green productive rooftops, that help regulate temperatures of buildings. For this reason, cities such as Kathmandu Metropolitan City (Nepal) promote rooftop gardening as part of its environmental policy (Dubbeling 2013a). The city of Bobo-Dioulasso (Burkina Faso) promotes intra-urban green way (by promoting agroforestry types of activities in open urban lots) and peri-urban forestry management to reduce increasing urban temperatures. Satellite images and remote sensing data were used to quantify the effect of land uses on land surface temperatures (LST) in Bobo-Dioulasso. A comparison of 1991–2013 data showed that LST differences between urban and peri-urban areas increased approximately 6% a year. The study also showed that mean LST over a ten-year period were consistently cooler (0.3 °C) in the three specific green infrastructural areas analyzed than in adjacent urbanized areas (Di Leo et al. forthcoming 2015). Where tree density is higher, the UHI reduction capacity will be higher.

Windstorm control benefits

Along with changes in local temperatures, urban environments are subject to increasing wind intensities, partially due to loss of vegetation. Areas of vegetation can provide windbreaks that absorb the energy of strong gusts, and provide buffers between large structures. Nonetheless, urbanization often simplifies landscapes and removes such features along with their storm-mitigating benefits. Cities such as Ibadan (Nigeria) and Makati (the Philippines) have started using urban forestry to reduce effects of windstorm events and also for city beautification and prevention of landslides (Adelekan 2012; Dubbeling 2013a). Increasing tree cover through urban (agro-) forestry provides breaks between built-up areas. Storm mitigation is an adaptation measure that cities can integrate into the climate change plans.

Runoff and flood-risk reduction

Increases in impervious surfaces associated with urbanization reduce soil infiltration and increase surface runoff during rainstorms. As a result, flooding is common in dense urban developments that lack adequate drainage systems. In cities including Kampala (Uganda), Ibadan (Nigeria), Addis Ababa (Ethiopia) and Dar es Salaam (Tanzania), increased runoff has caused greater frequency of flooding associated with building in retention swamps and hill slopes and the increase of impervious surfaces (Matagi 2002). Shifting rainfall patterns, coupled with expanding urban settlements have similarly increased flooding hazards (Mbow et al. 2008).

Urban agriculture may provide one economical approach to address this climate impact by reducing flood hazards through the control and reduction of surface runoff. Urban agriculture can reduce the impacts of higher rainfall (average/ extremes) by keeping low-lying zones free from construction so that floods have less impact, storm water runoff is reduced, and excess water is stored and infiltrated in the green open spaces. A range of sustainable urban drainage designs solutions are under validation in some cities to assess the cumulative reduction of floods through proper drainage design, grassing, infiltration ponds and urban agriculture (Ellis et al. 2011). Several cities that are increasingly confronted with floods are considering the role of urban agriculture as alternative options for flood-risk management. In Sri Lanka, rehabilitation of former paddy fields and drainage channels has proven to be an effective strategy for the reduction of flood risks (Dubbeling 2014a).

The city of Freetown (Sierra Leone) has zoned all wetlands and low-lying valleys for urban agriculture. Next to promoting local food production, this measure is expected to help keep flood-zones free from construction and improve water infiltration, resulting in reduced flooding incidences and related damage. Other positive effects may be reduction of costs associated with maintenance of such areas (Dubbeling 2013a). The city of Rosario (Argentina) promotes the preservation and protection of green and productive areas on stream banks to reduce flood risks (Hardoy and Ruete 2013). Agricultural use of lowlands in Antananarivo (Madagascar) is reported to prevent flooding as the lowland rice and watercress systems can store large amounts of water. It has been calculated that one of the city's low-lying valleys with a total area of 287 ha can store up to 850,000 m³ of water, corresponding to three successive days of heavy rains (Aubry et al. 2012).

Under the Sustainable Urban Drainage Systems framework (Ellis et al. 2011), a combination of upstream and downstream measures aimed at increasing infiltration and retention of water in urban systems is now a new principle for design of such drainage systems. Permaculture and agroforestry are particularly well-suited to reduce flooding and landslides by creating extensive root structures that stabilize soils and enhance infiltration, and by providing permanent soil cover.

Coastal flooding hazards result from different conditions, but may benefit from some similar solutions. For example, Mangrove forests play a particularly important role for suppressing coastal inundation during extreme events (Badola et al. 2005). In cities, including Douala (Cameroon), Dakar (Senegal) and Dar es Salaam

FIGURE 8.1 Productive use of flood zones in Rosario, Argentina

Source: Dubbeling.

(Tanzania), where coastal flooding is projected to constitute an increasing climate hazard, mangrove restoration is now a key component of the climate change adaptation strategies (Din et al. 2008). Efforts to improve coastal flood control have taken into account the economic incentives and provisioning services provided by coastal ecosystems.

While reducing runoff, more porous land surfaces also support recharge of groundwater flows. The steady recharge of water tables and surface water supplies through infiltration plays a critical role in supporting urban water supplies. Natural movement through the water cycle helps to purify water supplies and reduces contamination from surface runoff in urban areas.

The value of ecosystems, particularly urban wetlands, for purifying water supplies has become increasingly recognized, and the restoration of wetlands is now considered as an economical alternative to traditional industrial water-treatment solutions (Chichilnisky and Heal 1998). Several studies have demonstrated the effectiveness of wastewater treatment using wetland systems and, if coupled with aquaculture, the effect would be a double win. Ecological management of water purification may provide a useful strategy to address the challenges of water purification in many cities.

In some cities, runoff capture in ponds for use as irrigation water has utilized relatively simple techniques of water plants to fight breeding of vectors responsible for certain diseases. When designed to enhance flood regulation, agriculture may actually provide a second-order service of disease regulation by reducing the extent of breeding grounds of flood waters for disease vectors.

BOX 8.3   URBAN AGRICULTURE AS A STORM WATER MANAGEMENT STRATEGY IN NEW YORK CITY (USA)

In the past years, many cities have suffered from extreme weather events – which may occur more frequently due to climate change – with heavy rains that cannot be absorbed by the storm water drainage system and flooding roads and properties. A conventional strategy to address this is to invest in "grey infrastructure": such as increased-diameter sewage pipes that hold larger volumes of storm water. This is, however, quite costly and politically unpopular in communities faced with the prospect of road break up and disturbances. A potentially more cost-effective option is to increase the permeability of the cityscape through diverse forms of "green infrastructure": parks, green corridors, agricultural sites, permeable pavement, and green multifunctional spaces.

Since 2011, New York City has provided funding to various urban agriculture projects through its Green Infrastructure Grant Program. New York's experience suggests that if productive landscapes are integrated into storm water management planning, cities may be able to reduce storm water flow and at the same time support the creation of farms and edible gardens, with their respective social and other benefits, at a lower cost than traditional storm water adaptation measures would require.

In developing its strategy, the city evaluated the costs and benefits of grey and green infrastructure and found that investing in a green scenario that includes some grey infrastructure was significantly more cost-effective than a conventional approach. New York City's Department of Environmental Protection (DEP) is committed to investing USD 192 million in green infrastructure by 2015, including "blue roofs" that hold rainwater and release it to the sewage system slowly, extra-large street tree planters, landscaped storm water "green streets", parking lots paved with porous concrete, and vacant paved lots and asphalt rooftops turned into gardens. Over 20 years, the green scenario would cost USD 5.3 billion, including the USD 2.4 billion for this green infrastructure. In contrast, an estimated USD 6.8 billion would be required for a scenario based solely on grey infrastructure. The green infrastructure scenario thus saves the city and the property owners who pay water and sewer fees USD 1.5 billion in costs over a 20-year period. Beyond initial saving, there are also the lower maintenance fees, which would be considerably higher for grey infrastructure over the years.

Nevertheless, there are obstacles to expanding urban agriculture's role as green infrastructure. Administrative agencies in charge of water pollution control, like New York City's DEP, focus primarily on the absorptive capacity of green infrastructure. This is also because the agency mandates do not include supporting urban agriculture. Nutritional, education and other benefits are valued, but are subsidiary to water retention capacity. A second challenge is that farms require active management to produce storm water retention benefits year-round, including a cover crop outside of the growing season, as bare soil retains less storm water than plant-covered soil and is also subject to erosion. Though this management is often provided by for-profit farming businesses like Brooklyn Grange or non-profit community organizations, thus lowering public management costs, public agencies need assurances that these entities are financially viable or, in the case of a non-profit, well-established within the community, and therefore likely to maintain site management over the long run.

Source: Cohen and Wijsman 2014.

Enhancing resource efficiency

Urban agriculture has potential to close nutrient cycle and resource flows. Nutrient cycles are more open in urban systems with nutrients imported (as food and other commercial products) and then often exported as wastes (disposed of in rivers, streams and in disposal sites resulting in river pollution and methane emissions). Urban agriculture and (agro-) forestry have demonstrated capability for nutrient uptake by recycling urban organic waste and wastewater (Smit et al. 1996; Drechsel and Kunze 2001; Troschinetz and Mihelcic 2009). Agricultural lands can benefit from the nutrients contained in (preferably composted) organic wastes, while providing an important service to the city (Asomani-Boateng 2007). Organic waste use in agriculture additionally improves water-holding capacity. It reduces the need for chemical fertilizers and related greenhouse gas emissions (NO_2 and CO_2) during their production and reduces nitrate leaching and sequesters carbon in the soil (Jansma et al. 2012).

Biodiversity conservation

Urban biodiversity is now recognized as important in maintaining ecosystem services. Studies have shown and highly agree that different urban surfaces are rich in agro-biodiversity, including genetic, functional and species diversity, that can serve to diversify household nutritional and livelihoods portfolios under changing conditions. Such diversity may be particularly important for adaptation of agricultural practices under climate change. Urban agriculture can support in situ conservation of plant genetic diversity, particularly of indigenous varieties (Trinh et al. 2003; Eyzaguirre and Linares 2004).

Potential of urban agriculture for climate change mitigation

Carbon storage and sequestration

In respect to mitigation of climate change, urban agriculture (Stoffberg et al. 2010) can contribute to reducing emissions, particularly if permanent soil cover and no-till production systems are applied. Permanent soil cover has low carbon emissions because the soil is left intact, and also stores carbon in the structure of the trees. Properly managed trees have carbon sequestration benefits (Havstad et al. 2007), though the scale of production may not be feasible for many urban settings due to high density of buildings and limited land area, although even trees planted along roads have a potential to increase carbon storage. Studies illustrate that CO_2 stocking by street trees and the urban green surfaces covered with multiple functional plants and trees is potentially high in cities. The structure of the landscape mosaic is thus important; canopy cover in agroforestry plots and the relatively less-intensive uses of field crops can shape climate resilient urban landscapes (Perfecto and Vandermeer 2010).

Carbon storage (the total current carbon stocks as a function of plant biomass) can be around 30 and 80 metric tons of carbon per hectare of forest, depending on the tree species, size, climate and planting area. Existing trees in Toronto are estimated to store about 61.1 metric tons of carbon per hectare, equalling 1.1 million metric tons of carbon given total tree cover area. If these trees were to be removed, the loss or emission of carbon that was stored by these trees would be equivalent to the annual carbon emissions from 733,000 automobiles or 367,900 single-family houses (Nowak et al. 2010).

Carbon sequestration by urban forests in Hangzhou (China) is calculated to add up 1.66 metric tons of carbon per hectare per year. This offsets 18.57% of the amount of carbon emitted by industrial enterprises in the city region (Zhao et al. 2010). Although urban and peri–urban forestry does not represent a major sink for global greenhouse gases, it can help offset a city's greenhouse gas (GHG) emissions to a certain extent (IBRD 2010).

Reducing energy use and emissions

Urban agriculture may furthermore contributes to the reduction of urban energy use and GHG emissions as it produces fresh food close to the city. This can reduce energy use for transport, cooling, storage, and less packaging. Reuse of composted organic wastes that otherwise would be disposed of in landfills and reduces the emission of methane and other GHGs at the landfill (Jansma et al. 2012). Furthermore, reuse of organic wastes in urban agriculture can be combined with controlled fermentation and production of bio–gas as a renewable energy source. Resource efficient technologies of urban agriculture have both adaptation benefits and climate mitigation potential. Reuse of urban wastewater in urban agriculture has a potential to free fresh water for higher value uses and reduce emissions from wastewater treatment.

Seattle's (USA) goal of reducing fossil fuel emissions is one of the reasons behind their Local Food Action Initiative that promotes community gardening, local food sourcing and increased food waste recycling (Dubbeling 2013a).

BOX 8.4   PRESERVATION OF AGRICULTURE IN FLOOD PLAINS AND PERI-URBAN AREAS IN ROSARIO (ARGENTINA)

Rosario (Argentina) is currently monitoring impacts of different (productive) green areas on runoff and flooding, and calculating energy and GHG reductions in different scenarios of local urban food production. Different land-use scenarios were developed with varying models of urbanization with different degrees/ways of protection/promotion of productive green areas.

Based on expert consultations on the role that urban agriculture can play in reducing runoff and flood risks, the first results of measurements in test sites and scenario development (indicating that substantial increase in built-up area would lead to tripled flood risks), a policy proposal on inclusion of intra- and peri-urban agriculture and forestry in watershed management was developed by a group of local researchers and presented to the Urban Agriculture Programme of the Municipality of Rosario for their review.

The proposal advises that public policy for highly urbanized watersheds and sub-watersheds should aim (1) to reduce the risk of flooding and water-logging by optimizing urban vegetation; (2) to increase the area of green roofs on new and existing buildings through ordinances that define where they should be built, and specifying technical characteristics; (3) to integrate urban agriculture in public parks, squares, walkways, side of motorways, railways, institutional green spaces, and public woodland; and (4) to increase urban agriculture surface in flood areas by means of land use ordinances and intersectoral strategies and preserve existing urban agriculture production zones in peri-urban areas.

Similarly, different scenarios for local food production were developed in order to understand their impacts on local food production, energy use and GHG emissions. The traditional horticulture zone in Rosario's peri-urban area is under threat by urbanization and conversion of agricultural land to soybean production. Horticulture production from the greenbelt used to supply most of the fruits and vegetables to the city. The number of horticulture farms has, however, steadily decreased, while remaining farms generally apply high levels of chemicals and pesticides, constituting a potential human health risk (increasing incidences of diseases have been observed among households living in or close to the area). Preliminary results of the urban food systems scenario study led to increased awareness of policy makers at city and provincial levels of the need to protect and preserve the horticulture greenbelt around Rosario and promote more agro-ecological production technologies. In order to preserve agricultural production in peri-urban areas, the municipality has included a new land use category on "land used for primary production" in their urban development plan. They have currently doubled the peri-urban agricultural protection zone from 400 to 800 ha. A first group of producers in the peri-urban area of Rosario are now receiving technical and financial support to convert to more agro-ecological practices. Together with marketing support and buyer agreements, this will allow increasing producer income, while reducing environmental contamination, which on its turn will contribute to preserving agricultural zones around the city.

Source: Piacentini et al. 2014.

The amount of food that can be actually produced in intra- and peri–urban areas was more recently a subject of study in Almere (the Netherlands). A scenario study found that 20% of total food demand (in terms of potatoes, vegetables, fruits, milk and eggs) projected for a future population of 350,000 can be produced locally in a radius of 20 km around the city (with more than 50% of the area destined to animal production: grass and fodder). When replacing 20% of the food basket by local production in Almere, while at the same time promoting fossil fuel reduction in production, processing and cooling by renewable energy sources, energy savings (363 TJ) would add up to the equivalent of the energy used by 11,000 Dutch households. Savings in GHG emissions (27.1 Kt CO_2 equivalent) would equal carbon sequestration of about 1,360 ha of forest or the emission of 2,000 Dutch households. The largest savings are due to: (a) reduction in transport, (b) replacing fossil fuel use by renewable energy sources (solar, wind energy; use of excess heat from greenhouses), and (c) replacing conventional production by organic production (Jansma et al. 2012).

Urban agriculture is also a source of GHG emissions. Emissions depend on production intensity, management aspects such as degree of external inputs (such as chemical fertilizers and pesticides; fuel); materials used and their related energy costs/GHG emissions; seasonality (production per unit of energy); and energy costs of setting up the system (for example, for rooftop gardens). Emissions will be highest for more mechanized (fuel costs), input-intensive systems and specific production systems such as livestock. Especially for livestock, waste management practices will be key for reducing emissions.

The specific type of urban agricultural systems to be promoted will depend on local socio-economic, climatic and spatial conditions. Each agricultural system varies in its suitability and relevancy for certain urban areas and the kind of climate change-relevant impacts they may have (see Table 8.1). Other variables influencing the extent to which certain impacts can be achieved include total surface area, product choices, type of food distribution network, and type of water and waste management.

BOX 8.5 PROMOTING GREEN AND PRODUCTIVE ROOFTOPS IN DURBAN, SOUTH AFRICA

Integrating food production with building infrastructure (rooftops, balcony gardening, growing walls, greenhouses) may contribute to reducing the urban heat island effect, reducing/slowing down storm water runoff and regulating temperature (heating and cooling requirements), depending on the type of production system and local climatic conditions. Studies in Durban (South Africa) showed that the average ambient air temperature above a green roof was substantially lower (on average 18°C) than above a blank roof (22°C and 41°C respectively). The daily temperature fluctuations are also smaller: 2.7°C fluctuation above the green roof as against 9.8°C fluctuation above the blank roof (Van Niekerk et al. 2011). See also Figure 8.2.

Reductions in energy savings and emissions may, however, be offset against energy use and GHG emissions related to maintenance of the green roof and to production activities and related transport of inputs and products. Effects on heating and cooling will also depend on degree of (permanent) cover of the rooftop, local climatic conditions, building insulation, building types, and heating and cooling behaviour of the owners (are homes or buildings cooled/heated using energy intensive equipment?).

Green rooftops may also contribute to storm water drainage and reducing runoff, depending on the depth of soil or type of substrate used and type of vegetation cover. According to eThekwini Municipality's Environmental Planning and Climate Protection Department studies on Durban, the amount of the storm water runoff from green roofs is eight times less as the amount from blank roofs (Van Niekerk et al. 2011). The efficiency to reduce rainwater runoff from green roofs depends on several factors especially the soil depth, type of plants grown, degree of green cover and seasonality of production.

The climate mitigation impact of green roofs also depends on the extent to which "building integrated agriculture" enables synergic and cyclical processes between urban agriculture and other industrial sectors (e.g., agricultural use of excess heat or cooling water produced by the block heating facility or by industry in a neighbouring area).

Significant barriers to using rooftop space for agricultural production are: structural requirements, existing building codes, access (e.g., transport of inputs/outputs and customers) and insurance issues.

Source: authors.

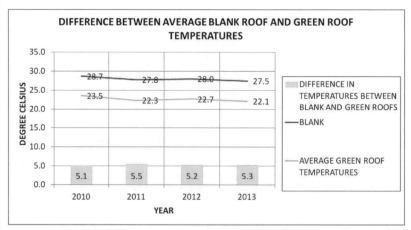

FIGURE 8.2 Difference between average blank roofs and green roofs in Durban 2010–2013

Source: Clive Greenstone, PHD student UKZN School of Built Environment & Development Studies.

The extent to which urban agriculture may mitigate climate change, contribute to city adaptation to climate change and enhance city resilience will depend also on the level of urban development, the status and quality of infrastructure and degree of integration of urban agriculture into urban policies. Often, the latter has been obstructed or slowed down as a result of (perceived and potential) environmental and health risks related to urban agricultural production (de Zeeuw et al. 2011). Use of organic municipal waste, sewage and market refuse in crop production has been found to cause microbial and heavy metal contamination of produce (Keraita and Drechsel 2004; Amoah et al. 2005). Production in sensitive areas can also result in soil or water contamination with heavy metals such as cadmium (Cd) and lead (Pb) (Nabulo 2002; Amoah et al. 2005). Additionally, inappropriate usage of contaminated water supplied from rivers or canals to irrigate crops is a concern, particularly in cities where treatment is unavailable. Access to, and availability of, land are other limiting factors for many urban agricultural enterprises. In densely urbanized areas, food production can be limited by space and conflicts on land, while extensive institutional land may remain largely unutilized in many cities, creating complex challenges for urban planners when considering sustainability at various scales (Aubry et al. 2012).

FIGURE 8.3 Peri-urban agricultural land use in Mbale Town, Uganda

Source: Lwasa.

TABLE 8.1 Potential impacts of selected urban agriculture production systems on climate change mitigation, adaptation and developmental benefits

City zone	Urban agriculture production system	Impacts on climate change		Development benefits	Variables that determine the extent to which such impacts on climate change can be achieved
		Mitigation benefits	Adaptation benefits		
A	**Backyard and community gardening**	++ Less energy use and GHG emission due to reduced food miles Reduction of waste volumes due to on-the-spot composting/reuse Minor carbon storage and sequestration	+++ Less vulnerable to an increase in food prices and disturbances in food imports to city due to enhanced local production and diversification of food (and income) sources Positive effects on urban biodiversity (especially niche species)	Enhanced food security and nutrition (especially for the urban poor and women) due to improved access to nutritious food close to consumer Positive effect on urban biodiversity and liveabilityEducational and recreational opportunities	Food import and consumer transport distances for buying food Degree of external inputs and materials used in UPAF and related energy costs/GHG emissions (ecological vs. conventional production; degree of recycling and use of organic waste, use of rainwater harvesting and water-saving production techniques; crop choice: use of drought-resistant species)
A	**Green productive rooftops**	++ Less energy use and GHG emission due to reduced urban temperatures and insulation: less energy use for acclimatization of homes and offices Minor carbon storage and sequestration	+++ Minor: less vulnerable due to enhanced local production and diversification of food (and income) sources Enhanced water retention capacity and reduced runoff Reduced urban heat island effect Positive effects on urban biodiversity (e.g., migratory stops)	Enhanced food security and nutrition due to improved access to nutritious food close to consumer Educational and recreational opportunities Multifunctional use Enhanced city liveability	Degree of external inputs and materials used in UPAF and related energy costs/GHG emissions (degree of recycling and use of organic waste, use of rainwater harvesting and water-saving production techniques; crop choice: use of drought-resistant species; choice of production technologies and inputs required, (energy-costs of setting up the system)

A–B	**Food and biomass production (e.g., agroforestry) in flood zones and other urban open spaces needing conservation**	+++	Less energy use and GHG emissions due to reduced transport, cooling, refrigeration, storage and packaging Carbon storage and sequestration	+++	Less vulnerable due to enhanced local production and diversification of food (and income) sources Enhanced water storage and retention capacity Reduced flooding incidences/ lower water peaks; lower impacts of floods due to prevention of housing in flood plains Positive effects on urban biodiversity	+++	Food production (volumes) Enhanced food security and nutrition due to improved access to nutritious food close to consumer Employment Positive effect on urban biodiversity and liveability Multifunctional use	Seasonality of production Degree of external inputs and materials used in UPAF and related energy costs/GHG emissions (ecological vs. conventional production; degree of recycling and use of organic waste, use of rainwater harvesting and water-saving production techniques; crop choice: use of drought-resistant species)
B–C	**Forestry and agroforestry (especially on steep slopes and other areas susceptible to erosion and landslides)**	+++	Carbon storage and sequestration Less energy use for cooling/refrigeration/ acclimatization due to reduction of urban temperature (in warmer climates) Reduction of air pollution	+++	Less incidence of floods and landslides due to reduced runoff and enhanced water storage and retention capacityPositive effect on biodiversity conservation	+++	Production of food (crops, fruit, nuts)/fuel/woodLiveability enhanced (shade, aesthetics, temperature, air quality)Less health problems due to less heat stress (heat stroke, skin diseases, and heart problems) and air pollution	% under high-/low-density productionDegree of combination with food productionChoice of tree species (growth rate; water needs, maintenance requirements; retaining leaves year-round or not, long- or short-living, etc.)Degree of maintenance and maintenance techniques applied and related energy costs and GHG emissionsForest fires and other causes of reduction of tree coverage

(Continued)

TABLE 8.1 (Continued)

City zone	Urban agriculture production system	Impacts on climate change		Development benefits	Variables that determine the extent to which such impacts on climate change can be achieved
		Mitigation benefits	Adaptation benefits		
B-C	**Agriculture in city fringes/peri-urban areas, including wetlands (where appropriate)**	+++ Less energy and GHG emissions due to reduced food miles and more locally produced fresh food: less transport, cooling/refrigeration, storage and packaging. Less cost in maintaining infrastructure for transport, storage and cooling. Carbon storage and sequestration	+++ Improved health of biodiversity for appropriate habitats and species, especially in conjunction with organic, low-till agriculture. Enhancing food resilience for city (especially during disasters and political/financial crisis periods); less vulnerability due to enhanced local production and diversification of food (and income) sources	Enhanced food security and nutrition due to improved access to nutritious food close to consumers. Employment. Positive effect on urban biodiversity and liveability	Seasonality/lower production per unit of energy. Degree of external inputs and materials used in UPAF and related energy costs/GHG emissions (ecological vs. conventional production; degree of recycling and use of organic waste; use of rainwater harvesting and water-saving production techniques; crop choice: use of drought resistant species)

Notes:

City zone: A = Inner city; B = Suburban (less densely built up); C = Peri-urban (mainly open spaces).

Mitigation benefits: the mitigation effects expected to be obtained from each urban agriculture production system. The number of plusses indicates the expectations regarding the magnitude of these impacts at city level.

Adaptation benefits: the adaptation effects expected to be obtained from each urban agriculture production system. The number of plusses indicates the expectations regarding the magnitude of these impacts at city level.

Developmental benefits: the expected developmental benefits of each urban agriculture production system measure (on food security, on income and employment creation, on city liveability, etc.).

Scale used: + to +++ indicating low to high level of potential impact.

Source: adapted from RUAF Foundation 2014.

Research and policy challenges

Urban policies need to incorporate food-security considerations and focus on building cities that are more resilient to crises. There is growing recognition of intra- and peri-urban agriculture and forestry as an important strategy for climate change adaptation and disaster-risk reduction. But there are research and policy challenges that require attention.

More research is needed to assess thresholds for mitigation of climate change (such as reduction of GHG emissions) that may be expected to be realized by different urban food production scenarios and pathways. City-specific scenarios and thresholds will be useful in informing policy and integration of urban agriculture into climate change strategies and urban development plans and translating the potential into actions. Testing and quantification of the adaptation potential of urban agriculture under different climate risks also require further research and identification of actions for adaptation that can be integrated into policy.

With regard to policy, it will also be important to enhance the awareness of local authorities and other pertinent stakeholders involved in urban climate change and other programmes (land department, agriculture and green spaces) of the potentials (and limitations) of urban agriculture and forestry for climate change adaptation and mitigation. Metropolitan, municipal and other local government institutions can play a proactive and coordinating role in enhancing urban food security and city resilience by the following:

1 Integrating urban food security and urban agriculture into climate change adaptation and disaster management strategies.
2 Maintaining and managing agricultural projects as part of the urban and peri-urban green infrastructure.
3 Identifying open urban spaces prone to floods and landslides, and protecting or developing these as permanent agricultural and multifunctional areas.
4 Integrating urban agriculture and forestry into comprehensive city watershed management plans, and in social housing and slum upgrading programmes.
5 Developing a municipal urban agriculture and food security policy and programme (Dubbeling 2013a).

As the impacts of specific types of urban agriculture and forestry on climate change vary, policies and strategies should specify which types of urban agriculture will be promoted, where and why.

If intra- and peri-urban agriculture are to be further promoted as integral strategies for climate change adaptation, mitigation and disaster risk reduction, respective indicators and monitoring frameworks are needed to better understand its actual contributions. It was in response to this request that the RUAF Foundation, with support from UN-Habitat and CDKN, designed a framework for indicators and tools to monitor the actual adaptation and risk-reduction impacts and development benefits of urban agricultural activities in different cities and for different urban agricultural models. The monitoring framework is currently being tested and improved upon in various partner cities. Application of this model at wider scale, and in different contexts, will enhance availability of data and evidence-based policy-making.

Conclusion

Urban agriculture interfaces with climate change in various ways. Though challenges and risks of urban agriculture exist, if well managed and innovated, its activities have a potential to be a low-cost and locally adaptable strategy for adaptation as well as mitigation of climate change. Research to generate more evidence-based data and examples about the mitigation potential of various urban agricultural systems is needed to inform policy that can be implemented at various scales of the city. This will need to be supported through sharing of knowledge and other resources that can help scale out and scale up best practices. Policy interventions needed include integrated urban development, with special attention to productive green infrastructure, access to water and innovation of production systems.

Building urban resilience will require broad strategies from micro- to city-region scales. Finally, for climate change and urban food systems planning to be meaningful, it is important to consider planning along the urban–rural gradient at the city-region level – beyond the boundaries of the urban centre itself, including towns, semi-urban areas, and outlying rural hinterlands. At this level, there are key opportunities to plan for landscape mosaic patterns that protect valuable ecosystems and biodiversity hotspots; preserve natural corridors that prevent flooding and landslides; optimize and expand existing transportation network infrastructure; construct a built environment that uses water and energy efficiently; and promote compact cities and planned extensions. In terms of urban management, special attention needs to be paid to health standards, storage and processing, land zoning, land tenure systems, use of vacant land and access to water. In terms of urban governance, it is important for vulnerable groups, producers and other actors in the food chain, particularly women, youth and migrant workers, to have a voice in a transparent decision-making process (Tuts 2014).

Note

1   The projects by RUAF Foundation with CDKN (Dubbeling 2014a) and UN Habitat (Dubbeling 2014b), respectively, were implemented in Kesbewa (Sri Lanka), Bobo Dioulasso (Burkina Faso), Rosario (Argentina) and Kathmandu (Nepal). The projects designed and tested a methodological framework and tools for the assessment of main potential contributions of urban productive green infrastructure to city mitigating of, and adaptation to, climate change. Also different urban food scenarios were developed and their respective impacts on energy use and greenhouse gas emissions were calculated. Pilot projects on potential urban agriculture models with highest expected climate change impacts were implemented and monitored in each of the cities. Finally the integration of types of urban agriculture that contribute most to climate change

mitigation and adaptation into city climate change plans or strategies was facilitated. For more details, see: www.ruaf.org/projects/monitoring-impacts-urban-agriculture-climate-change-adaptation-and-mitigation-cities, and www.ruaf.org/projects/integrating-urban-agriculture-and-forestry-climate-change-adaptation-and-mitigation.

References

Abdulsalam-Saghir, P. B.; Oshijo, A. O. 2009. Integrated urban micro farming strategy mitigation against food crises in Odeda Local Government Area, Ogun State, Nigeria. *Journal of Agricultural Extension* 13: 35–44.

Action Aid. 2006. Climate change, urban flooding and the rights of the urban poor in Africa: Key findings from six African countries. London: Action Aid.

Adelekan, I. O. 2010. Urbanization and extreme weather: Vulnerability of indigenous populations to windstorms in Ibadan, Nigeria. Paper presented at the International Conference on Urbanization and Global Environmental Change, Arizona State University, Tempe, Arizona, October 15–17, 2010.

Adelekan, I. O. 2012. Vulnerability to wind hazards in the traditional city of Ibadan, Nigeria. *Environment and Urbanization* 24(2): 597–617.

Amoah, P.; Drechsel, P.; Abaidoo, R. C. 2005. Irrigated urban vegetable production in Ghana: Sources of pathogen contamination and health risk elimination. *Irrigation and Drainage* 54: S49–S61.

Asomani-Boateng, R. 2007. Closing the loop: Community-based organic solid waste recycling, urban gardening, and land use planning in Ghana, West Africa. *Journal of Planning Education and Research* 27: 132–145.

Atkinson, S. 2000. Approaches and actors in urban food security in developing countries. *Habitat International* 19(2): 151–163.

Aubry, C.; Dabat, M. H.; Ramamonjisoa, J.; Rakotoarisoa, J.; Rakotondraibe, J.; Rabeharisoa, L. 2012. Urban agriculture and land use in cities: An approach with the multi-functionality and sustainability concepts in the case of Antananarivo (Madagascar). *Land Use Policy* 29: 429–439.

Badola, R.; Hussain, S. A. 2005. Valuing ecosystem functions: An empirical study on the storm protection function of Bhitarkanika mangrove ecosystem, India. *Environmental Conservation* 32(1): 85–92.

Baker, J. 2008. Impacts of financial, food and fuel crisis on the urban poor. *Directions in urban development. World Bank.* Washington, DC: World Bank-Urban Development Unit.

Brownlee, M. T.; Powell, R. B.; Hallo, J. C. 2013. A review of the foundational processes that influence beliefs in climate change: Opportunities for environmental education research. *Environmental Education Research* 19:1–20.

Chichilnisky, G.; Heal, G. 1998. Managing unknown risks: The future of global reinsurance. In: *Sustainability: Dynamics and uncertainty.* (Eds.) Chichilnisky, G; Heal, G. A.; Vercelli, A. Alphen aan den Rijn: Wolters Kluwer

Cohen, N.; Wijsman, K. 2014. Urban agriculture as green infrastructure. *Urban Agriculture Magazine* 27: 16–19.

Di Leo, N.; Escobedo, F.; Dubbeling, M. (forthcoming). The role of urban green infra-structure in mitigating land surface temperatures in Bobo-Dioulasso, Burkina Faso. Submitted to Springer publication.

Din, N.; Saenger, P.; Priso, R. J.; Dibong, D. S.; Blasco, F. 2008. Logging activities in mangrove forests: A case study of Douala Cameroon. *African Journal of Environmental Science and Technology* 2(2): 22–30.

Douglas, I.; Alam, K.; Maghenda, M.; Mcdonnell, Y.; Mclean, L.; Campbell, J. 2008. Unjust waters: Climate change, flooding and the urban poor in Africa. *Environment and Urbanization* 20: 187–205.

Drechsel, P.; Kunze, D. 2001. Waste composting for urban and peri-urban agriculture: Closing the rural-urban nutrient cycle in sub-Saharan Africa. Wageningen: CABI.

Dubbeling, M. 2013a. Urban and peri-urban agriculture as a means to advance disaster risk reduction and climate change. *Regional Development Dialogue* 34(1): 134–149.

Dubbeling, M. 2013b. Scoping paper feeding into the development of UNEP's position on urban and peri-urban agriculture. Leusden: RUAF Foundation.

Dubbeling, M. 2014a. Integrating urban and peri-urban agriculture and forestry in city climate change strategies: Lessons from Sri Lanka. *Inside stories on climate compatible development.* London: Climate Development Knowledge Network. Available from: http:// cdkn.org/cdkn_series/inside-story/?loclang=en_gb.

Dubbeling, M. 2014b. A first framework for monitoring the impacts of urban agriculture on climate change. *Urban Agriculture Magazine* 27: 44–49.

Dubbeling, M.; Zeeuw, H. de; Veenhuizen, R. van. 2010. Cities, poverty and food: Multi-stakeholder policy and planning in urban agriculture. Leusden: RUAF Foundation and Rugby: Practical Action.

Ellis, J. B.; Lundy, L.; Revitt, D. M. 2011. An integrated decision support approach to the selection of Sustainable Urban Drainage Systems (SUDS). Presented at the SWITCH Conference: The Future of Urban Water: Solutions for Liveable and Resilient Cities, Paris, January 24–26, 2011.

Eyzaguirre, P. B.; Linares, O. F. 2004. Home gardens and agrobiodiversity. Washington, DC: Smithsonian Books.

Forster, T. 2014. Linkages with rural development, including food security and ecosystem resources. Final Issues Paper. Communitas Coalition, Working Group 5. Available from: http://communitascoalition.org/wg5.html#wg5.

Frayne, B.; Moser, C.; Ziervogel, G. 2012. Constructing the climate change-asset adaptation-food insecurity nexus for pro-poor urban development. In: *Climate change, assets and food security in African cities.* (Eds.) Frayne, B.; Moser, C.; Ziervogel, G. New York: Earthscan, pp. 186–197.

Grimm, N. B.; Faeth, S. H.; Golubiewski, N. E.; Redman, C. L.; Wu, J.; Bai, X.; Briggs, J. M. 2008. Global change and the ecology of cities. *Science* 319: 756–760.

Hardoy J.; Ruete, R. 2013. Incorporating climate change adaptation planning for a liveable city in Rosario, Argentina. *Environment and Urbanisation* 25: 339–360.

Havstad, K. M.; Peters, D. C.; Skaggs, R.; Brown, J.; Bestelmeyer, B. T.; Fredrickson, E. L.; Herrick, J. E.; Wright, J. 2007. Ecological services to and from rangelands of the United States. *Ecological Economics* 61: 261–268.

IBRD. 2010. Cities and climate change: An urgent agenda. Urban Development Series – Knowledge Papers 10. Washington, DC: International Bank for Reconstruction and Development (IBRD).

ICLEI and RUAF Foundation. 2013. CITYFOOD: Linking cities on urban agriculture and food systems. Bonn: ICLEI.

Jansma, J. E.; Sukkel, W.; Stilma, E.S.C.; Oost, van A.C.J.; Visser, A. J. 2012. The impact of local food production on food miles, fossil energy use and greenhouse gas (GHG) emission: The case of the Dutch city of Almere. In: *Sustainable food planning: Evolving theory and practice.* (Eds.) Viljoen, A.; Wiskerke, J.S.C. Wageningen: Wageningen Academic Publishers, pp. 307–321.

Keraita, B.; Drechsel, P. 2004. Agricultural use of untreated urban wastewater in Ghana. In: *Wastewater use in irrigated agriculture: Confronting the livelihood and environmental realities.*

(Eds.) Scott, C. A.; Faruqui, N. I.; Raschid-Sally, L. Cambridge: CABI International, pp. 101–112.

Lotsch, A. 2007. Sensitivity of cropping patterns in Africa to transient climate change. Policy Research Working Paper 4289. Washington, DC: World Bank.

Lwasa, S. 2014. Managing African urbanization in the context of environmental change. *INTERdisciplina* 2: 263–280.

Lwasa, S.; Mugagga, F.; Wahab, B.; Simon, D.; Connors, J.; Griffith, C. 2013. Urban and peri-urban agriculture and forestry: Transcending poverty alleviation to climate change mitigation and adaptation. *Urban Climate* 7: 92–106.

Lwasa, S.; Tenywa, M.; Majaliwa Mwanjalolo, G. J.; Prain, G.; Sengendo, H. 2009. Enhancing adaptation of poor urban dwellers to the effects of climate variability and change. IOP Conference Series, Earth and Environmental Science no. 6. p. 332002.

Magnusson, U.; Follis Bergman, K. 2014. Urban and peri-urban agriculture for food security in low-income countries: Challenges and knowledge gaps. Series: SLU-Global Report 2014: 4. Uppsala: Swedish University of Agricultural Sciences (SLU).

Matagi, S. V. 2002. Some issues of environmental concern in Kampala, the capital city of Uganda. *Environmental Monitoring and Assessment* 77: 121–138.

Mbow, C.; Diop, A.; Diaw, A. T.; Niang, C. I. 2008. Urban sprawl development and flooding at Yeumbeul suburb (Dakar-Senegal). *African Journal of Environmental Science and Technology* 2: 75–88.

Mkwambisi, D. D.; Fraser, E.D.G.; Dougill, A. J. 2011. Urban agriculture and poverty reduction: Evaluating how food production in cities contributes to food security, employment and income in Malawi. *Journal of International Development* 23: 181–203.

Mohamed, L. S.; Gunasekera, J. 2014. Promoting urban agriculture as a climate change strategy in Kesbewa, Sri Lanka. *Urban Agriculture Magazine* 27: 20–23.

Mougeot, L. J.A. 2001. Urban agriculture: Definition, presence, potentials and risks. In: *Growing cities, growing food: Urban agriculture on the policy agenda.* (Eds.) Bakker, N.; Dubbeling, M.; Gündel, S.; Sabel-Koschella, U.; Zeeuw, H. de. Feldafing: DSE, pp. 1–42.

Nabulo, G. 2002. Assessment of heavy metal uptake by selected food crops and vegetables around Kampala city area, Uganda. Ottawa: International Development Research Centre (IDRC).

Nellemann C.; MacDevette, M.; Manders, T.; Eickhout, B.; Svihus, B.; Prins, A. G.; Kaltenborn, B. P. (eds.) 2009. The environmental food crisis: The environment's role in averting future food crises: A UNEP rapid response assessment. Norway: Birkeland Trykkeri AS and United Nations Environment Programme (UNEP).

Niekerk, M. van; Greenstone, C.; Hickman M. 2011. Creating space for biodiversity in Durban: Guideline for designing green roof habitats. eThekwini Municipality – Environmental Planning and Climate Protection Department. Available from: www. durban.gov.za/City_Services/development_planning_management/environmental_ planning_climate_protection/Publications/Documents/Guideline%20for%20Designing% 20Green%20Roof%20Habitats1.pdf.

Nowak D. J.; Hoehn, R. E.; Greenfield, E.; Sorrentino, C.; O'Neil-Dunne, J.; Pelletier, K. 2010. Every tree counts: A portrait of Toronto's urban forest. Toronto: City of Toronto, Urban Forestry Services.

Padoch, C.; Brondizio, E.; Costa, S.; Pinedo-Vasquez, M.; Sears, R. R.; Siqueira, A. 2008. Urban forest and rural cities: Multi-sited households, consumption patterns, and forest resources in Amazonia. *Ecology and Society* 13(2): 2. Available from: www.ecologyandsociety.org/vol13/iss2/.

Perfecto, I.; Vandermeer, J. 2010. The agro ecological matrix as alternative to the land-sparing/agriculture intensification model. *Proceedings of the National Academy of Sciences* 107: 5786–5791.

Piacentini, R. D.; Bracalenti, L.; Salum, G.; Zimmerman, E.; Lattuca, A.; Terrile, R.; Bartolomé, S.; Vega M.; Tosello, L.; Di Leo, N.; Feldman, S.; Coronel A. 2014. Monitoring the climate change impacts of urban agriculture in Rosario, Argentina. *Urban Agriculture Magazine* 27: 50–53.

Prain, G. 2010. Effects of the global financial crisis on the food security of poor urban households: Synthesis report on five city case studies. Leusden: RUAF Foundation.

Rooijen, D. J. van; Biggs, T. W.; Smout, I.; Drechsel, P. 2010. Urban growth, wastewater production and use in irrigated agriculture: A comparative study of Accra, Addis Ababa and Hyderabad. *Irrigation and Drainage Systems* 24(1): 53–64.

Rosenzweig, C.; Solecki, W.; Hammer, S. A.; Mehrotra, S. (eds.) 2011. Climate change and cities: First assessment report of the Urban Climate Change Research Network. Cambridge: Cambridge University Press.

RUAF Foundation 2013. Sustainable financing for WASH and urban agriculture. *Urban Agriculture Magazine* 26.

RUAF Foundation 2014. A first framework for monitoring the impacts of urban agriculture on climate change. *Urban Agriculture Magazine* 27: 44–49.

Satterthwaite, D. 2008. Climate change and cities. ID 21 Insight no. 71. Brighton: IDS. Available from: www.eldis.org/id21ext/publications/insights71.pdf.

Simon, D. 2012. Climate and environmental change and the potential for greening African cities. *Local Economy* 28: 203–217.

Smit, J.; Ratta, A.; Nasr, J. 1996. Urban agriculture: Food, jobs and sustainable cities. Washington, DC: United Nations Development Programme (UNDP).

Stoffberg, G. H.; Rooyen, M. W. van, Linde, M. J. van der; Groeneveld, H. T. 2010. Carbon sequestration estimates of indigenous street trees in the City of Tshwane, South Africa. *Urban Forestry and Urban Greening* 9(1): 9–14.

Swalheim S.; Dodman, D. 2008. Building resilience: How the urban poor can drive climate adaptation. In: *OPINION sustainable development November 2008.* IIED UK. Available from: http://pubs.iied.org/pdfs/17043IIED.pdf.

Tidball, K. G.; Krasny, M. E. 2007. From risk to resilience: What role for community greening and civic ecology in cities? In: *Social learning towards a sustainable world: Principles, perspectives.* (Ed.) Wals, A. Wageningen: Wageningen Academic Publishers, pp. 149–164.

Trinh, L. N.; Watson, J. W.; Hue, N. N.; De, N. N.; Minh, N. V.; Chu, P.; Sthapit, B. R.; Eyzaguirre, P. B. 2003. Agrobiodiversity conservation and development in Vietnamese home gardens. *Agriculture Ecosystems and Environment* 97(1–3): 317–344.

Troschinetz, A. M.; Mihelcic, J. R. 2009. Sustainable recycling of municipal solid waste in developing countries. *Waste Management* 29(2): 915–923.

Tuts, R. 2014. Cities as key actors to act on food, water and energy security in the context of climate change. *Urban Agriculture Magazine* 27: 8–9.

UN-FAO. 2008. State of food insecurity in the world 2008: High food prices and food security: Threats and opportunities. Rome: Food and Agriculture Organization of the United Nations.

UN-FAO. 2012. Growing greener cities in Africa. First status report on urban and peri-urban horticulture in Africa. Rome: Food and Agriculture Organization of the United Nations.

UN-FAO. 2014. Growing greener cities in Latin America and the Caribbean. A FAO report on urban and peri-urban agriculture in the region. Rome: Food and Agriculture Organization of the United Nations.

UN-Habitat. 2011. Cities and climate change. Global report on human settlements. Nairobi: United National Human Settlements Programme.

University of Cambridge; ICLEI. 2014. Climate change: Implications for cities. Key Find-
ings from the Intergovernmental Panel on Climate Change Fifth Assessment Report.
Available from: www.iclei.org/fileadmin/PUBLICATIONS/Brochures/IPCC_AR5_
Cities_Summary_FINAL_Web.pdf.

Zeeuw, H. de; Veenhuizen, R. van; Dubbeling, M. 2011. The role of urban agriculture in
building resilient cities in developing countries. Paper for the DFID foresight project
on global food and farming futures. *Journal of Agricultural Science.* doi: 10.1017/
S0021859610001279.

Zhao M.; Kong Z. H.; Escobedo, F. J.; Gao, J. 2010. Impacts of urban forests on offsetting
carbon emissions from industrial energy use in Hangzhou, China. *Journal of Environmental
Management* 91: 807–813.

9

URBAN HORTICULTURE

Hubert de Bon,[1] Robert J. Holmer[2] and Christine Aubry[3]

1 HORTSYS RESEARCH UNIT OF CENTRE DE COOPÉRATION INTERNATIONALE EN RECHERCHE AGRONOMIQUE POUR LE DÉVELOPPEMENT (CIRAD), FRANCE

2 REGIONAL SCHOOL HEALTH PROGRAMME "FIT FOR SCHOOL" OF THE DEUTSCHE GESELLSCHAFT FÜR INTERNATIONALE ZUSAMMENARBEIT (GIZ), THE PHILIPPINES

3 SADAPT RESEARCH UNIT OF THE INSTITUT NATIONAL DE LA RECHERCHE AGRONOMIQUE (INRA), FRANCE

Introduction

Intra- and peri-urban horticulture includes all horticultural crops grown for human consumption and ornamental use within, and in the immediate vicinity of, cities. Although crops have always been grown inside the city, the practice is expanding and gaining more attention. The products of urban horticulture include a large variety of vegetables, cereals, flowers, ornamental trees, aromatic vegetables and mushrooms. Table 9.1 presents the main species cultivated in urban horticultural systems and more specifically those presented in this chapter.

Generally, the types of crops cultivated vary according to the area, influenced by culture and tradition. In cities, short-cycle crops are preferred, while in the vicinity of the city crops with longer cycles are cultivated, for example in orchards.

Crops are grown in small gardens or larger fields, using traditional or high-tech and innovative practices. The major plant production systems and practices of urban horticulture are described in this chapter, together with the major constraints. Some new techniques that have been adapted to the urban situation and tackle the main city restrictions are also documented. These include horticultural production on built-up land using various types of substrates (e.g., rooftop, organic production and hydroponic production), water saving in highly populated areas, and the production of pesticide-free vegetables year-round with control of wastes and leaching (fertilizers, pesticides, organic matter, water) in the urban environment. The aspects of waste recycling, local consumers and producers' links will be always taken into account.

Urban horticulture also contributes to strengthening social sustainability and increasing ecological sustainability by transforming wastes, conserving natural resources, preventing soil erosion, and reducing pollution. Urban horticulture, like urban agriculture in general, has multiple functions. The main function is supplying fresh food, but emerging functions that are becoming more and more

TABLE 9.1 Horticultural and other plants cultivated in urban areas

Vegetables	*Aromatic and flowering plants*
Amaranth, Genius *Amaranthus*	Agati, *Sesbania grandiflora*
Beans, *Vigna radiata* & *Phaseolus vulgaris*	Basil, *Ocimum basilicum*
Beetroot, *Beta vulgaris* var. *Esculenta*	Chives, *Allium schoenoprasum*
Bitterleaf, *Vernonia amygdalina*	Horseradish tree, *Armoracia rusticana*
Broccoli, *Brassica oleracea* var. *italic*	Indian borage, *Plectranthus amboinicus*
Cabbage, *Brassica oleracea* var. *Capitata*	Kohlrabi, *Brassica oleracea* var. *gongylodes*
Cardoon, *Cynara cardunculus*	Lemon grass, *Cymbopogon citratus*
Cassava leaves, *Manihot esculenta*	Mustard, *Brassica compestris*
Cauliflower, *Brassica oleracea*	Pakchoy, *Brassica camperstris* var *chinensis*
Chinese cabbage, *Brassica rapa* var. *Pekinensis*	Parsley, *Petroselinum crispum*
Chinese mustard, *Brassica juncea* var. *Rugosa*	Peppers, Genius *Schinus*
Choy sum, *Brassica rapa* var. *Parachinensis*	Perilla, *Perilla frutescens*
Cucumber, *Cucumis sativus*	Roselle, *Hibiscus sabdariffa*
Eggplant, *Solanum melongena*	Tuberose, *Polianthes tuberosa*
French bean, *Phaseolus vulgaris*	
Garlic, *Allium sativum*	*Fruits*
Gourd, Genius *Cucurbita*	
Indian mustard, *Brassica juncea*	Banana, Genius *Musa*
Jaxatu, *Solanum aethiopicum*	Melon, *Cucumis melo*
Kangkong (water convolvulus), *Ipomoea aquatica*	Orange, *Citrus sinensis*
Leek, *Allium ampeloprasum*	Papaya, *Carica papaya*
Lettuce, *Lactuca sativa*	Peach, *Prunus persica*
Lotus, *Nelumbo nucifera*	Pineapple, *Ananas comosus*
Melindjo, *Gnetum gnemon*	Strawberry, Genius *Fragaria*
Mizuna, *Brassica rapa* var. *Japónica*	Drumstick, *Moringa oleifera*
Mungo bean, *Vigna radiata*	
Okra, *Hibiscus esculentus*	*Ornemental plants*
Onion, *Allium cepa*	
Palak, *Beta vulgaris*	*Bougainvillea (Genius)*
Pea, *Pisum sativum*	*Chrysanthemum (Genius)*
Potato, *Solanum tuberosum*	Kumquat, Genius *Fortunella*
Squash, *Cucurbita máxima*	Rose, Genius *Rosa*
Sweet pea, *Lathyrus odoratus*	
Sweet pepper, *Capsicum annuum*	
Snow pea, *Pisum sativum*	
Tomato, *Lycopersicon esculentum*	
Wheat, *Triticum aestivum*	
Yardlong bean, *Vigna unguiculata sesquipedalis*	

essential are economic (income generation), social (labour), cultural, living environment (open spaces and greening), environmental (recycling wastes and wastewater) and security (food and natural risks).

Policy makers around the world are showing an increased interest in urban horticulture, although their major focus is still on the temporary use of peri-urban lands. Peri-urban agriculture is "encouraged" in poor countries, mainly because it improves food security of poor households and the urban population's nutritional status (freshness of products and better access to fruits and vegetables, considered as a major source of vitamins and micronutrients), especially in view of the inefficient transportation and storage facilities in these countries. Policy makers also encourage urban horticulture because it provides jobs and incomes to poor and landless urban dwellers and because it is well adapted to the urban environment where water and land are scarce.

Urban demand, crop diversification and sustainability

Urban demands for horticulture

The proximity to urban markets often defines the production of specific fruits or vegetables, while there are also seasonal differences between rural and urban areas in terms of supply to the urban market. The case study from Hanoi, Vietnam, is an interesting example of how the horticultural market has evolved dynamically over the years in relation to social, climatic and cultural factors. Fruits and vegetables for city markets are supplied from different areas: rural, peri-urban and intra-urban, from within the country or from foreign countries. There is complementarity between the supply flows from the various origins, which may change over time. Products from urban horticulture make up a very large part of the supply of vegetables to urban markets, such as in the capital city Hanoi (with a population of 2.7 million). Here, 80% of the vegetables (118,628 tonnes) comes from the Province of Hanoi, an area of 7,095 ha of urban gardens (Mai Thi Phuong Anh 2000).

Factors such as climate, soil, access to water, insects and diseases, costs of production and, most importantly, the shelf life of the crop itself influence the location of vegetable production. The last factor explains why, for most urban markets, leafy vegetables are produced in urban and peri-urban areas. Some leafy vegetables are well adapted to a hot wet season. The very short shelf life of cut flowers such as roses and chrysanthemums explains the development of these horticultural crops around Hanoi, where they are grown on 1,000 ha. The season also influences the distribution of supply to the urban market from rural/urban areas. In Bangui, the share of tomatoes from rural areas increases from 40 to 50% in the wet season. In Bissau, the share of tomatoes from urban areas increases from 10 to 20% in the wet season. Urban horticultural areas may also supply the urban market more regularly than the rural areas. In Nouakchott, urban horticulture supplies the urban market during nine months of the year, whereas the rural areas provide vegetables to the city only during three months

(Margiotta 1997). Around Hanoi, *choysum* and leafy mustard are grown year-round. In Dar-es-Salaam, amaranth is grown throughout the year. This tendency to crop year-round is increased by the urban producers' need to derive an income from various high-value crops throughout the year. This bias towards urban horticulture may also be due to production constraints and access to transportation infrastructure during the rainy seasons or to socio-economic causes. In some countries, however, where flooding of urban areas increases every year, it is easier to find suitable spaces to grow vegetables in rural areas (Phnom Penh, Dacca).

Even if the consumption of vegetables per person is relatively low, consumer demand remains the major driving force behind urban horticulture. In developing countries, the consumption of vegetables is generally lower than the FAO recommendation of 75 kg/year/inhabitant (205 g/capita/day). The importance of vegetable consumption depends on the population group. Over the period 1994–1998, consumption in Vietnam was higher in urban areas (182 g/capita/day) than in rural areas (122 g/capita/day), but lower than in mountainous areas (196 g/capita/day) (Nguyen Thi Lam and Ha Huy Khoi 1999). As shown in Table 9.2, the consumption of vegetables in Bangladesh was higher in urban areas than in rural areas (Ali 2000). The same observation has been made in developed countries (Dean and Sharkey 2011).

TABLE 9.2 Monthly per capita consumption of vegetables (kg) in Bangladesh

	Total vegetables	Leafy vegetables	Potato	Banana, papaya, eggplant	Other vegetables
Urban	6.20	1.42	1.67	0.82	2.29
Rural	5.13	1.08	1.13	0.80	2.12

Source: Ali 2000.

Urban consumption is related to the size of households, income and socio-cultural characteristics (Bricas 1998). In Africa, the most popular vegetables are tomatoes, onion and leafy vegetables, but there are location-specific variations. In Brazzaville, for instance, the importance of vegetables varies from one socio-economic group to another (Moustier 1999b; see Table 9.3).

Culture and festivals also have a very strong influence on consumer demand for specific products. In many countries, the main demand for flowers occurs on Mother's Day, Valentine's Day and during the Christmas period. In Vietnam, the Tet celebration is the opportunity to offer two ornamental trees: kumquats bearing mature orange fruits and peach trees in blossom. In urban and peri-urban areas in Hanoi, ornamental fruit tree specialists have set up production to meet this demand, which means that they nurture young trees for a period of one year to prepare them for sale.

TABLE 9.3 Most-frequently eaten vegetables per socio-economic group in Brazzaville (Congo) (in order of importance per group)

Socio-economic groups	Vegetables eaten most frequently
Congolese households	Cassava leaves, cherry tomato, pakchoy, roselle, melinjo, dry kidney bean
Non-Congolese African households	Potato, cassava leaves, cherry tomato, dry kidney bean, amaranth, lettuce
Expatriates	Potato, "European-type" vegetables

Source: Moustier 1999b.

Crop diversification and biodiversity

Through the large variety of crops that are produced, urban horticulture makes a major contribution to the food and economic security (see Chapters 5 and 6).

Although most of these species are not specific to peri-urban horticultural systems and can also be grown elsewhere, horticulture in urban areas minimizes the transportation time for the supply of fresh produce to city dwellers. The cropping system in urban and peri-urban areas is usually adapted to the specific circumstances. Many traditional crops have been adapted to better respond to the needs of city consumers. Horticulture is practised for home consumption and for the market as high-value cash crops. In such a competitive environment, a focus on profitability may lead to improper management, such as the intensive use of water, land and other (chemical) inputs, and thereby pose threats to humans and the environment. This issue will be discussed later in this chapter.

The urban horticultural farms present a high diversification of the fruits and vegetables produced. In Africa, Maundu et al. (2009) mentioned that about 1,000 species are used as vegetables, the majority of which (about 800) are leafy vegetables. They include very diverse forms including annual and perennial crops and some trees such as *Moringa oleifera*. Large areas of vegetable production with market-gardeners specialized in one or two crops have been developed in various parts of the world with long supply chains, for instance: melon in the Languedoc region of France; tomatoes in the Senegal River valley; and onions in the valleys of Maggia, Tarka and Aïr in Niger.

In other areas, like the peri-urban area of Montpellier (France), a large number of market-gardeners have highly diversified their crops, in terms of species and varieties, to fit the consumers' demands. Small vegetable farmers, with one to ten hectares (ha), might produce more than 30 different vegetables (Lenoble 2013) and we note the same phenomenon in the peri-urban area of Paris (Pourias 2010).

Urban home gardens also show a large crop diversity (Keatinge et al. 2012). Such diversity can be considered as a repository of rarer plant varieties or land races, thus acting as areas of *in situ* germplasm preservation (Oluoch et al. 2009; Galluzi et al. 2010). Moreover, the Community Supported Agriculture (CSA) movement pushed for the (re)discovery of old species and varieties. We observe

TABLE 9.4 Daily fruit and vegetable intake in 2006, Brazos Valley (Texas)

Servings (mean+/−SD)	Combined	Urban	Rural
Fruits	1.4+/−0.99	1.6+/−0.99	1.3+/−0.9
Vegetables	2.0+/−0.92	2.0+/−0.94	2.0+/−0.92
Total fruits and vegetables	3.4+/−1.61	3.6+/−1.63	3.3+/−1.59

Source: Dean and Skarkey 2011.

nowadays a renewal of forgotten vegetables like parsnip (*Pastinaca sativa* L.) and Jerusalem artichoke *(Helianthemum tuberosus),* or of old tomato varieties like "Coeur de boeuf". This phenomenon contributes to a real cultivated biodiversity near the cities (Lovell 2010).

The diversity of crops and the diversity of the farming activities (producing, transporting, selling, managing the communication with customers, etc.) lead to a more complex farm management in comparison with the more specialized farm with a few crops. This complexity sometimes leads to a difficult sustainability of the farm system, not because of economic or ecological aspects, but because of a lack of "liveability" (Petit et al. 2013): too much workload and economic and practical difficulties to employ new workers lead some of these farms to have no successor inside the farmer's family. In the Paris region, for example, around 37% of market-gardeners in short supply chains ceased their activities and their farms generally contributed to the growing size of arable crop farms in around ten years. Around Montpellier (France), the small vegetable farmers (with around 1.3 ha) have difficulty in paying a second full-time worker, so they turn to trainees or familial support. They grow 15 different species per year. If short supply chains are an opportunity for peri-urban horticulture, very often it is not at all sufficient to ensure the survival of peri-urban horticultural farms. The combination of different ways of marketing is a solution to improve its sustainability.

Statistics and research about these peri-urban horticultural farms are dramatically failing, especially in European countries: since horticulture is not an activity that is supported by the Common Agricultural Policy (CAP), it is poorly informed at statistical level, and if research about short supply chains at economic and sociological levels is increasing, their consequences on technical management and work organizations are scarcely studied. Nevertheless, data seem to show that the above-mentioned points could be critical ones for the sustainability of such forms of urban horticulture.

Factors influencing urban horticulture

The development of horticultural systems in urban and peri-urban areas is determined by specific opportunities and constraints in the city. The constraints are mainly related to resource scarcity (water, land, labour and access to other inputs) and pollution.

Access to natural resources and labour

Access to suitable land is a key factor in urban agricultural development. Land-ownership and tenure arrangements are important. In the large and fast-growing cities of developing countries, land pressure is high and often leads to rising prices. In this context, access to land by intra- and peri-urban producers is difficult and poses a major constraint to their activities. As they are usually not landowners, they are obliged to rent from others or to squat on public land in order to have a small plot to cultivate. This uncertainty of land tenure has a strong influence on land-use strategy and maintenance. Producers may select fast-growing plants (such as leafy vegetables) rather than perennials (such as fruit trees), and may use places regarded as unsuitable for dwellings (such as swamps), which limit the range of crops that can be grown.

Insecurity of land tenure is a major problem that often leads to two types of responses by producers: they might choose inputs with strong and quick effects, such as chemical fertilizers and pesticides, rather than improving the soil using long-acting fertilizers and integrated production techniques, or urban producers may turn to soilless production systems on diverse substrata. But sometimes short land leases also create some flexibility that could be an advantage. For instance, around Montpellier (France), the peri-urban growers prefer to rent land for melons (2 years) and potatoes (1 year) to avoid damages due to the soil-borne diseases such as *Fusarium spp.* or nematodes (Lenoble 2013).

The size of plots is also a constraint. In the inner cities or peri-urban areas, horticultural crops are grown on very small parcels of land. This leads to the development of specific systems: intensive, high-yielding and year-round production with the same or different crops. High yields require high use of inputs – water and fertilizer – combined with good light. As will be discussed later, different techniques have been developed for situations with land scarcity or poor soil quality, such as hydroponics or organoponics (to be discussed later in this chapter).

Different sources of water are available in urban and peri-urban areas: potable water, wastewater, rivers, lakes and ponds. The specificity of horticultural systems is their adaptability in using these different sources, particularly the use of waste-water (see Chapter 7). In all cases, this scarce source needs to be used efficiently and with precaution. Drip irrigation with different systems of micro-irrigation is possible. Use of a watering tank is more popular and is also one of the most efficient systems. The advantage of using wastewater is that it provides nutrients together with the water. This saves the cost of fertilizers and labour to apply the fertilizer.

In urban areas, there is fierce competition for the use of land and water between horticultural and other economic activities. In a context of high economical competition, horticulture can be maintained if it generates more benefits than any other use of the resources (see also Chapter 5). Yet, even without intensification of production and even if it is less profitable, horticulture continues to exist, if its other functions (i.e., social, greening, water management) are valued by city stakeholders.

Another aspect of this competition comes from the many other human economic activities that occupy urban producers. In Hanoi, for instance, peri-urban gardeners seek jobs in industry, business and administration. Most often urban horticulture is a part-time job in this city, and different activities are combined in order to maintain livelihoods. The household members also divide their activities between production, sales and employment. The multiple economic activities of most urban gardeners may lead to a lack of sufficient labour during certain cropping periods, such as planting or harvesting or for irrigation.

Environmental pollution

Industry, services, traffic and high population density in urban areas are known to cause pollution to water, soil and air and reduce light intensity. A major challenge for urban horticulture is to supply safe products in this often-polluted environment. In urban or peri-urban areas, the main pollutants of horticultural crops are heavy metals, pesticide residues, and biological contaminants. Such pollution presents a risk not only to the consumers, but also to the producers who come in contact with contaminated materials, for instance in wastewater. Additionally, these forms of pollution can be major factors in limiting crop growth. The source of human parasites is wastewater or animal wastes that are not composted (see Chapter 7).

Heavy metals

The causes of soil pollution from heavy metals (including lead, cadmium, chromium, zinc, copper, nickel, mercury, manganese, selenium and arsenic) are diverse: irrigation with water from streams and wastewater contaminated by industry, application of contaminated solid wastes and the use of former industrial land contaminated by spilled oil and industrial wastes, or inorganic fertilizers that may contain relatively some proportions of heavy metals. If the concentration of these elements in human food increases, it may cause toxic symptoms and cause damage to health (carcinogenic and mutagenic effects). The soils of urban gardens are very often more polluted by heavy metals than are rural ones (Chenot et al. 2013). Toxicity from heavy metals can directly affect plant physiology and growth, and many cases of toxicity from heavy metals have been reported. For example, Jørgensen et al. (2005) show that intensive horticultural systems (particularly in greenhouses) in urban areas may be threatened by soil toxicity through trace elements such as Zn, Cu, As and Pb.

The health effects and the heavy metal threshold concentration under which it is possible to practise safe agriculture have been subjects of much discussion. Puschenreiter et al. (1999) conclude that, having considered the several available pathways to reduce the transfer of heavy metals to the human food chain, urban soils with slight contamination by heavy metals can be used safely for gardening and agriculture if proper precautions are taken. However, Birley and Lock (2000) argue that little is known of the chronic health effects of consuming tiny amounts of heavy metals over long periods of time and that further research is needed. Mapanda et al. (2005) show that, in vegetable gardens of Harare (Zimbabwe), irrigation by wastewater may lead to significant heavy metal (Cu, Zn, Cd, Ni, Cr and Pb) enrichment in the soils. On the other hand, studies have shown that production in urban and peri-urban areas does not produce lower-quality vegetables than in rural areas (Midmore 1998).

Depending on the species and the plant parts, accumulation of heavy metals varies. Leaves can reach a high level while seeds are often less affected. It is possible to adapt the choice of crops in relation to the degree and type of contamination. Some horticultural crops such as bean, pea, melon, tomato and pepper show very low uptake of heavy metals.

The risk of pollution depends directly on the location of the fields. The rate of absorption of heavy metals by vegetables seems to be linked with their levels in the soil. Lead is taken up by the plant roots and is then transported to the leaves. Lead from traffic fumes in the air settles on the leaves. It can be washed away by watering the leaves, especially when the leaf surface is waxy (cruciferous plants, Alliums). Cadmium can be taken up by plants through roots and leaves. For these two very poisonous heavy metals with no positive biological functions, their presence in plants is controlled by respecting the soil standards. The location of vegetable production, with regard to roads and polluting industries, should be selected carefully.

In European countries, risks of heavy metal pollution are scarcely measured in peri–urban areas. Some studies show the possibility of pollutant deposition for fields located at the very proximity of roads – within around 50 m (Petit et al. 2013). Recent research showed that crop samples from inner-city sites had higher metal traces than the samples from the supermarket that are supposed to have come from rural areas (Saümel et al. 2012).

The conquest of urban rooftops for market vegetable production is maybe one of the possible answers to reduce soil contamination in urban gardens. But the level of pollution on the roofs is for the moment poorly informed, although some experiments show that it could be very low (Grard et al. 2013).

In addition to heavy metals, air pollution too can contribute to crop toxicity. For instance, Agrawal et al. (2003) show that, in the polluted environment of Varnasi, India, some physiological characteristics of bean, palak, wheat and mustard are significantly affected by the SO_2, NO_2 and O_3 concentrations. These gases are very common in large cities in developing countries, especially with the fast growth of personal transport.

Pesticide residues

As in many forms of crop production, horticulture is confronted with pesticide residues in the plants and pesticide exportation to the environment. This can lead to major health problems for producers and/or consumers. The residues of pesticides and fertilizers originate not from agricultural inputs used by the producers alone. Cultivation in contaminated areas or irrigation with contaminated wastewater also contributes to increasing the residual levels in plants above the allowed limit. In Bangkok, a survey has shown residues of organo-chlorine and organo-phosphate in irrigation water (Eiumnoh and Parkpian 1998); these contaminants are adsorbed in soil and are characterized by a very long half-life. Most belong to families of products that are banned worldwide.

All levels of cropping intensity are encountered in urban areas, from the most extensive in developing countries and in allotment gardens, to the very intensive agriculture using large amounts of agrochemicals and expensive equipment.

Vegetables containing pesticide residues above the maximum residue limit have been identified in markets for more than 20 years (Midmore 1998; Moustier 2000; Diop Gueye and Sy 2001). A review (de Bon et al. 2014) and some recent works confirmed this trend. Bempah et al. (2012) have shown that the percentage of higher pesticides residues (over the LMR) in plants is 31.5% of the samples in Accra Region, Ghana. In France the samples show a rate of around 2.8% pesticide residues over the LMR. This occurs often, in spite of the fact that regulations for the use of pesticides and recommendations for the protection of human health are in place.

Awareness of the risks caused by excessive use of chemical pesticides exists among all stakeholders, ranging from producers, consumers and public authorities to agrochemical companies. The urban horticulture sector is more sensitive to this problem because of the proximity of consumer and producer. More negotiation between all players in the commodity chain might be one solution. The development of new technologies, such as integrated pest management, agroecology and biological control, can help in reducing pesticide use.

Nitrates

Nitrates deserve mention in pollution related to agricultural inputs. They can cause health problems in very young babies and pregnant women. Nitrates are also an indicator of good or bad agricultural practices. Nitrates cause eutrophication of water in combination with phosphorus. Nitrates are brought by organic and inorganic fertilizers. In African cities, the quantities brought in the gardens are higher than in the fields (Abdulkadir et al. 2014). The over-fertilizations of the crops seem to be rather frequent (Sangare et al. 2012), but in some cases N and P leakages are low as in Niamey (Predotova et al. 2011). In Europe there are standards regulating the nitrate content in crops and water. In urban horticulture systems, nitrates stem from fertilization and from irrigation water. Some quick tests, such as Nitracheck®, appear to help producers manage nitrogen. Still, many of the methods available need to be validated for the specific intra- and peri-urban leafy vegetables grown in developing countries. Moreover, with the aim of making better use of organic matter obtained from urban wastes in mind, specific tools need to be developed that take into account the problem of the irregular and slow release of nitrogen. If the source of pollution is close to the water resource, as is often the case with urban horticulture, the risk of pollution of water by nitrates is enhanced. This is particularly true in developing countries that do not have a good network of water supply and where many people depend on the local water resources for their supply.

Biological contaminants

In horticultural systems, solid wastes are mainly used to improve the soil (household wastes, market refuse, sewerage, night soil, manure, fish wastes and agro-industrial wastes). Urban organic wastes are mainly composted; this process significantly reduces health risks. However, if the compost is not properly prepared (i.e., at too low temperatures), the organic wastes may still contain disease-causing pathogens such as bacteria and helminth eggs, particularly if organic materials are mixed with human excreta (Holmer and Itchon 2008). The use of domestic sewage for irrigating and fertilizing field crops, perennials and trees is widespread. A large part of the wastewater used is untreated or poorly treated and contains various bacteria, protozoan parasites, enteric viruses and helminths. Coliform bacteria are mainly transmitted to humans from wastewater via the contamination of crops irrigated with wastewater or through consumption of contaminated meat from domestic animals that have ingested tapeworm eggs from faeces in untreated sewage.

The contamination of crops with pathogenic organisms by reuse of urban wastewater and organic solid wastes is an important issue associated with food safety, especially in the context of urban horticulture (Karanja et al. 2010; see Chapter 7). These diseases may affect the producers who handle the contaminated material, as well as the consumers who may eat contaminated fruits or vegetables. This is particularly a health risk in case the crops will not be cooked before consumption such as salads and herbs that may be eaten raw (Petterson et al. 2001). In Antananarivo (Madagascar), the watercress supply of more than 90% of the urban consumers is coming from intra-urban specialized farms cultivating mostly with urban wastewater. The watercress produced presents high levels of bacteria like *Escherichia coli*. Knowing this risk, the consumers adapted to this situation by cooking watercress (Dabat et al. 2010).

Based on a scientific consensus of the best available evidence, the World Health Organization has established guidelines for the safe use of wastewater, excreta and grey water in agriculture, including minimum procedures and specific health-based targets, and how those requirements are intended to be used (WHO 2007). However, there is still a dire need to translate these guidelines into local protocols that best suit the agronomic requirements of the crops grown as well as the specific socio-economic, cultural and environmental realities of many developing countries (Seidu et al. 2008). See Chapter 7 for more details.

Pollution by horticultural practices

Horticultural systems may also pose a risk to their environments, and especially so in an urban context because of the proximity to people. Additional conflicts may arise between urban gardeners and city dwellers, especially when horticultural systems cause odours or improperly use large amounts of pesticides or fertilizers – artificial or otherwise – that urban dwellers fear may cause pollution. Although it is a general rule that inputs that affect human and environmental health must be used with care, this is more so in urban areas. The intensive use of agrochemicals (fertilizers, pesticides) may lead to residues in crops, surface water or groundwater, and cause negative effects to the health of agricultural workers.

Recommendations for safe urban horticulture

De Zeeuw and Lock (2000) suggest a number of prevention and control measures that can be applied in urban horticulture systems to help produce safe and healthy products. Such measures should help reduce risk of pollution of crops by heavy metals, agrochemical residues, pathogens and diseases. The general principle of these "good practices" is often based on good communication between health sector actors and urban farmers, ensuring the latter is educated to respect rules to limit/stop contamination of the horticultural products. A summary of the major recommendations is presented below (see Box 9.1).

BOX 9.1 MAJOR RECOMMENDATIONS FOR REDUCING RISKS IN URBAN HORTICULTURE

Heavy metals

- Define norms regarding crop restrictions according to type and level of contamination of agricultural soils; test agricultural soils and irrigation water for heavy metals.
- Establish minimum distance between fields and main roads and/or boundary crops to be planted beside them.
- Treat soil to immobilize heavy metals: application of lime increases pH and thus decreases the availability of metals, except for selenium; application of farmyard manure reduces the heavy metal content of nickel, zinc and copper (but may increase cadmium levels); iron oxides (like red mud) and zeolites are also known to absorb heavy metals such as cadmium and arsenic.
- Wash and process contaminated crops to effectively reduce heavy metal content.

Agrochemical residues

- Train gardeners in proper management of agrochemicals.

- Promote ecological farming practices and replacement of chemical control of pests and diseases by integrated pest and disease management techniques.
- Establish better control on sales of banned pesticides.
- Introduce cheap protective clothing and equipment.
- Monitor residues of agrochemicals in groundwater.

Use of organic wastes and wastewater

- Improve inter-sectoral linkages between health, agriculture, waste and environmental management.
- Separate waste at source; collect organic refuse regularly; establish decentralised composting sites; ensure the application of proper composting methods (temperature, duration) to kill pathogens; identify quality standards for municipal waste streams and composts produced from them.
- Monitor quality of composts and irrigation water from rivers and wastewater outlets; certify safe production areas; restrict crop choice in areas where wastewater is used but water quality cannot be guaranteed.
- Establish adequate wastewater-treatment facilities with appropriate technologies.
- Train gardeners in managing health risks (for workers and consumers) associated with reuse of waste in agriculture.
- Educate consumers (scraping and washing of fresh salads; eating only well-cooked food).

Diseases

- Maintain cooperation between the health sector and the natural resource management sector (solid waste management, water storage, sewerage, agriculture and irrigation).
- Ensure water tanks and irrigation systems (especially in peri-urban areas) properly designed to prevent malaria.
- Apply slow-release floating formulations to control the malarial vector; use expanded polystyrene balls to effectively control mosquito breeding in latrines and stagnant polluted water.

Source: based on De Zeeuw and Lock 2000.

Agronomic techniques

Greenhouses and plastic tunnels

Horticulture in urban areas will continue to be adapted to specific circumstances, as determined by the opportunities and constraints, and specific techniques will be developed, including combinations of practices from traditional horticulture and more modern, innovative practices (see later). Horticulture is practised in various agro-ecological and climatic zones, from dry areas to tropical and equatorial climates, in areas with cold seasons and in those without. Urban producers strive to grow crops year-round, to be able to better regulate delivery. However, in different parts of the world, certain periods of the year are too cold or too hot to produce crops. The producer may also face drought in arid zones and excess of water in wet tropical areas, mainly in the rainy season. Temperatures and water can be regulated by using greenhouses and plastic covers. In developing countries, the two main difficulties encountered are excess and lack of water.

In tropical areas, the distribution of rainfall often varies greatly between the dry and the wet season. In the wet season, heavy rains, often in combination with strong winds, may stop horticultural activities even though the consumer demand is high. In addressing this problem, producers in some areas, such as Martinique (French West Indies) and Mayotte, use shelters as "umbrellas" to prevent excess of water for the crops. In some areas, despite the tropical location (e.g., Réunion, Vietnam, Kenya), closed shelters have to be used during winter when the temperatures are low.

In some other cases, an insect-proof greenhouse has to be used to protect the crops (at least in their early stage of growth) from a virus frequently transmitted by insects. This is the case of tomatoes, which can be infected by Potato Yellow

FIGURE 9.1 Horticulture in low plastic tunnels near Beijing, China

Source: IGSNRR.

Mosaic Virus (PYMV) and Tomato Yellow Leaf Curl Virus (TYLCV) through the white fly *(Bemisia tabaci)*. These shelters help increase yields but require significant investment and may lead to side effects, such as the soil becoming too poor to further sustain production. Producers may need to turn to new techniques as described in the next section (organoponics or hydroponics). Producers, whether rural or urban, are often willing to adapt and improve their practices based on their own experiences and new information. Most of the new techniques, however, require access to capital for investments and to specific knowledge.

Low tunnel nets

Low tunnel nets can be applied as physical barriers against pest species (Weintraub 2009). This technique has been applied for cabbage production in Africa against *Plutella xylostella* (Martin et al. 2006). A combination of a visual barrier with a repellent product would reduce the rate of *Bemisia tabaci* crossing through the net, thereby reducing the risk of virus transmission such as the TYLCV. Thus, the protection of vegetables with nets seems to be an economically viable method because it can be reused several times, in addition to its environmental benefits (Martin et al. 2014). The only difficulty with this is that the resource-poor farmers in Benin (and possibly elsewhere) will have to face the initial investment in material. Using nets to protect vegetables has the additional advantage that this technique can be easily combined with other integrated pest management (IPM) techniques.

Irrigation systems

Water requirements are related to climatic conditions and plant species. Generally, water availability in cities has been showing a decreasing trend and the forecasts predict it will continue at least in the next 30 years. In most capital cities of developing countries located in tropical and subtropical areas, the quantities needed vary from 0.1 to 8–10 $l/m^2/day$ in very dry and hot weather. For a crop of 30 days, the quantity of water needed by a leafy vegetable during the dry season is around 15–90 l/m^2. Depending on the climate and the yields, producing 1 kg of a crop such as tomato requires 60–140 litres of water. Table 9.5 presents the water consumption of some horticultural crops observed in Bobo-Dioulasso.

TABLE 9.5 Water consumption of some horticultural crops in Bobo-Dioulasso (Burkina Faso)

	Cycle length without nursery	Yield (fresh weight, kg/m^2)	Water consumption (l/m^2)
Tomato	2.1–3.5	2.8–5.8	5.0–8.9
Cabbage	2.3–2.9	4.9–5.2	4.5–8.6
Carrot	2.6–3.1	4.6–5.0	4.1–4.8
Lettuce	1.0–1.5	3.6–7.7	2.4–7.2

Source: Sangaré et al. 2012.

Different techniques are used for irrigation. Water is applied by overhead irrigation using watering cans, and also through sprinklers or perforated pipes from wells, ponds or the sewer.

Vegetables, especially leafy ones such as lettuce and cabbage, need to be watered twice a day, every day or at least every other day to obtain a good quality (freshness, tenderness) for marketing. There are three steps in watering: (1) lifting the water from the well or the irrigation canal, (2) bringing it to the plots, and (3) applying the water to the plants. These steps may be merged or kept separate. For urban horticulture in developing countries, the watering can is the most commonly used system. Each can holds 8–15 litres; one worker usually carries two cans. The water is taken from shallow wells, deep wells, "céanes" in Senegal, small cement reservoirs, drums (Ghana), etc. Reservoirs are filled by hand using small buckets, or with treadle, electric or motorised pumps. Crops could also be irrigated by submersing of the field. The manual system is efficient because, most of the time, the gardener applies the exact quantity of water needed by the crop. It is, however, labour intensive, and in Senegal this operation takes 60% of the total labour requirement for vegetable production.

Drip or trickle irrigation is another irrigation technique that has been promoted for nearly 30 years (Holmer and Schnitzler 1997). It saves water by 20–30% compared with overhead irrigation, but requires clean water in order to avoid blocking of the emitters. The fully-fledged system includes filters, pumps, a pressure regulator and plastic tubes, which low-income vegetable growers cannot usually afford. The advantage of this technique is that water is not in contact with the fruits and leaves. It will not, however, avoid contamination of the soil and roots of vegetables with biological pathogens.

Some simple drip-irrigation systems have been developed, in different locations, functioning with low gravity, e.g., Niger (ICRISAT TIPA), Vietnam (International Development Enterprises) and in South Africa. This system consists of a 210-litre drum, which is connected via a tap to a set of five polyethylene dripper lines, each with a length of 6 m. The drippers are constructed by perforating the polyethylene pipe with a heated nail. A piece of string is threaded through these perforations by means of a bag-needle. Knots on both ends of the string prevent it from slipping out of the pipe. When the perforations get clogged, pulling the string from side to side usually unblocks the openings. Clogging of the drippers is reduced by placing a stone and sand filter at the bottom of the drum. The filter prevents coarse particles, which may be present in the irrigation water, from entering the pipes and blocking the drippers (Khosa et al. 2003). Such a system of micro-irrigation is particularly suitable for small farms in urban areas, because it does not require a high capital investment and because it uses rainwater collected from roofs.

Underground irrigation provides water to the plant by capillary action. Such an underground system can limit the transmission of pathogens to the vegetables thanks to the filtrating effect of the soil. A simple system based on a vertical plastic tube filled with soil has been developed in Senegal (IRRIGASC).

Fertilization

Crops require nutrients: macro-elements such as nitrogen, phosphorus, potassium, calcium; and micro-elements such as manganese, copper, etc. Intensive cropping systems on very small areas, using only solid and liquid urban wastes, are not always optimal for crops.

Two main groups of fertilizers are used: organic fertilizers and chemical (or inorganic) fertilizers. There has always been a heavy use of organic fertilizers in intensive production such as vegetables and ornamental flowers. The quantity varies from a few tons/ha/year to 50 or even 100 tons/ha/year. Organic fertilizers provide most of the micronutrients and, in addition, improve the structure of the soil. Organic fertilizers can be manure from livestock or poultry, compost from vegetable wastes or wastes from urban activities including sewage sludge, night soils, and household wastes. Over many centuries, intra- and peri-urban farmers have managed and recycled urban wastes (Fleury and Moustier 1999). In South-East Asia, use of fresh night soil is a common practice even though it disseminates human pathogens. These practices may cause some risks to the environment – pollution of soils with heavy metals from sewage sludge, pollution of water with nitrates due to large quantities of organic manure – and also to the health of the consumer.

Solid organic fertilizers have the disadvantage that they release nutrients, especially nitrogen, slowly. Liquid fertilizers act faster. This explains why liquid organic fertilizers are often used on short-cycle leafy vegetables like amaranth and mustard. In Hanoi (Vietnam), liquid organic fertilizer, e.g., pig urine, is used to supply nitrogen during crop growth. Research has often focused on combining organic and inorganic fertilizers to enhance their efficacy. The use of organic wastes as fertilizer can lead to a different form of pollution as discussed earlier. This problem is strongly linked to recycling of wastes in the cities (see also Chapter 7).

Inorganic fertilizers are easier to use and allow for application of the right dose of nutrients. However, there are risks of over-application and contamination of soils and water by nitrates and phosphates, which is especially relevant in the city. Also, they could be a source of heavy metals. In Thailand, it has been shown that ammonium phosphate can release cadmium, zinc and chromium into the environment in excessive quantities (Tran Khac Thi 1999). Urea is the main inorganic fertilizer used in horticulture, especially for vegetables. There is often a lack of phosphorus and potash, and this can lead to an imbalance in the proportion of nutrients in the soil. However, the physical and financial access to fertilizers in general and inorganic fertilizers in particular is still a challenge for farmers in most developing countries.

Pesticides

Chemical pesticides have contributed to yield increases in agriculture in general for more than 50 years. Especially in peri-urban horticulture, easy access to pesticides (via national and international companies, retailers and wholesalers) and technical information has increased its use. However, this has also increased the negative perception of agricultural production in and around the cities. There are three major risks involved: (1) health risks for consumers; (2) risks of polluting the environment (mainly water sources); and (3) risks for users. Surveys have been conducted regularly on the use of chemicals, their rate of application and the period between the last application and the harvest for marketing. The application of pesticides on crops also endangers workers if little information is available on how to use them and when no protective measures are taken. This mainly affects low-income gardeners who cannot afford to buy proper protective clothing and equipment or are not aware of the importance of doing so.

In Vietnam, low-cost pesticides (organo-phosphates, pyrethroids, carbamates) with high toxicity (classes I and II) are very commonly used with little information about how to use them. Surveys show that application rates are much higher than the recommended rates for most of the pesticides used. This and the high spraying frequency are the causes for high pesticide residues in the marketed vegetables. But, in Hanoi districts, Huong et al. (2013) have shown that pesticide use was positively related to growth duration and profit. We must therefore continually insist on the application of Good Agricultural Practices (GAP) or compliance with current standards, and that research should find solutions as effective and less polluting for horticulture, especially in urban systems.

New trends in urban horticultural systems

Rural horticulture adapted to urban situations

Horticulture in urban areas requires some specific adaptations, as discussed in the previous sections. In this section we present some discussion on general cropping systems and their adaptation to the urban context.

Kessler (2002) describes the different farming systems in four West Africa capitals (Lomé, Cotonou, Bamako and Ouagadougou). In this study, the farming systems are characterized by the crops grown by farmers. The study reveals that differences in crops and inputs of the different farming systems are due to different economic strategies adopted by the farmers. Mixed vegetable farming with watering cans and/or with pumps to cultivate short- and long-cycle vegetables like lettuce, cabbage, carrots, onions, etc. is an example. Robineau (2013) in Bobo-Dioulasso described four types of farmers growing vegetables: small-scale urban gardeners with high diversification of crops, specialists in two vegetable crops; gardeners on public urban allotments and peri-urban vegetable farmers. Differences are based on number of crops, marketing and irrigation systems.

Similar systems are also described in Asia. Farming systems in the peri-urban areas of Hubli-Dharward (India) comprise vegetable production, agroforestry systems, Napier grass (fodder) production and small-scale livestock production (Bradford et al. 2002). In Hyderabad (India), the predominant system is paragrass production, which like Napier grass is used as fodder (especially in intra-urban zero-grazing dairy production). Green leafy vegetables are grown here on small sections for subsistence needs and for sale. Other crops include rice, fruit trees and flowers. There is also coconut and banana as well as livestock (water buffalo) keeping (Buechler et al. 2002). In Cagayan de Oro (Philippines), urban types of agriculture are characterized by home gardens as well as aquaculture and other specialized food crops (banana, cereals, vegetables, etc.). Production can be for home consumption as well as for market sale. Peri-urban agriculture is often dominated by irrigated vegetable production, as is the case in Vietnam or Malaysia. Other systems that can be encountered are commercial and domestic livestock production, flowers and seldom agroforestry (Potutan et al. 2000; own observations). Major systems mentioned for Shanghai are cereals, vegetable and livestock production (Yi-Zhang and Zhangen 2000).

Many additional types could be named using the major crops grown or animals raised as a criterion. A study under the Urban Harvest Programme in Cameroon identified three major types of cropping systems:

1   Mixed crop systems dominated by open-pollinated varieties (OPVs) of improved maize in the upland areas (vacant lots, unused municipal lands).
2   Mono-cropping systems of OPVs of improved maize grown in valley bottoms.
3   Intensive horticultural systems in valley bottoms, primarily for the production of traditional leafy vegetables (TLVs).

In addition, they observed that there is widespread use of small home garden plots for growing leafy vegetables and stands of banana, plantain, avocado, African

FIGURE 9.2 Watering plants close to Accra, Ghana

Source: IWMI (Image: Nana Kofi Acquah).

plum and other fruit trees around homesteads. Within these cropping systems, the research identified two types of agricultural units: "commercial" and "household food" producers based on the criterion of producing for sale, at least, half of the output from one of their products. The study found that women are the main producers of both household food and food for sale, accounting for 87% of the total sample (see also the case of Yaoundé).

Moustier (1999a) summarized the different descriptions found in literature of cropping and farming systems in five major types of urban agriculture based on a few traits: subsistence, family-based commercial or entrepreneurs activities; intra- or peri-urban locations; and number of crops grown. In Montpellier, Lenoble (2013) added the trait: cultivated area. In some cases, animal production may be associated with vegetables production as dairy in Meknes (Morocco), fishing in the Philippines or piggery around Bobo-Dioulasso.

So we observe in all these typologies a large diversity of systems that represent a continuum between rural and urban areas, including or not, plant and animal production, with different crops of different types as mentioned above.

Impact of food sanitary crisis

In Europe, food sanitary crises (dioxin, BSE, avian influenza, *Escherichia coli*) at the end of the 20th century had a lot of consequences for consumers and producers, and the "globalized agri-food system" is being considered as the main causing agent. As a consequence, different food movements and new forms of short supply chains between producers and consumers have emerged to redevelop the trust in the food supply: from Community Supported Agriculture (CSA) in North America, their French version being the AMAP (Associations for the maintenance of peasant agriculture), to Internet sales, going through different box schemes, direct selling on the farm, urban market places, and even direct selling to the large food distributors. In Europe these movements relate mainly, but not exclusively, with peri-urban market-gardeners that – due to the decreasing of vegetable prices in the wholesale market – were encouraged to change their production and marketing systems and to engage themselves in short supply chains to urban consumers in the region (see Chapter 5 for more details).

The interaction with the consumers involved in these short chain systems results in a trend to more environmental-friendly production practices and an increase in the number of horticulture farms producing organically or applying similar practices, such as biodynamic horticulture or permaculture, while many other horticulture farms seek to reduce the use of pesticides and agrochemicals.

In the city environment, new horticultural practices, such as organoponics, hydroponics, and permaculture, have emerged that maximize the use of space, optimize the use of inputs and minimize the impacts of horticulture on human and environmental health. Such practices will be described below. Crops are also grown on vacant open spaces of the city, such as brownfields, overgrown lots, abandoned properties and rooftops. The social organization of the horticultural use of these spaces can be individual, communal or mixed forms.

Community gardens

Community gardens have emerged in many cities in response to urban poverty and food insecurity, as a way to get access to culturally preferred, fresh and healthy food products and/or as a recreational and social activity. Community gardens may be worked collectively or split up in small plots that are assigned to individual households (then in Europe called "allotment gardens"), or a combination of both. Community gardens are established on land leased by the community group or association of allotment gardeners from the municipality, a school, church or hospital, from a private owner, or on vacant public or private land that is informally occupied.

Allotment gardens have been very popular in Europe for more than 150 years, although their functions have shifted over the years. The history of the allotment gardens is closely connected with the period of industrialization and urbanization during the 19th century, when a large number of people migrated from the rural areas to the cities to find employment and a better life. Very often, these families were living under extremely poor conditions, suffering from inappropriate housing, malnutrition and other forms of social neglect. To improve their overall situation and to allow them to grow their own food, the city administrations, the churches or their employers provided open spaces for garden purposes.

At the beginning of this century community gardens have re-emerged as a phenomenon of urban horticulture in different cities of North America and Europe, as well as in Latin America, Africa and Asia.

FIGURE 9.3 Eora Summerhill Community Garden, Ashfield

Source: Ashfield Council.

In developing countries this was mainly in response to the growing urban poverty and urban food insecurity and malnutrition. Many cities in the South run programmes nowadays providing (often temporal) access to vacant public land to groups of urban poor and underprivileged as well as basic training, seed and tools for community gardening. Next to access to nutritious food, generation of complimentary income and group- and self-confidence building are often also important impacts of the community gardens (see also Chapter 6).

The functions of community and allotment gardens in USA and Europe have gradually shifted from enhancing food security to semi-public green spaces with recreational, social, environmental and educational functions (Holmer and Drescher 2005; PUVeP 2008; Holmer 2010). Duchemin and Wegmuller (2010) have underlined their multifunctionality to reconnect social links, to have more nature in the city, to contribute to education as well as to a healthier urban life. However, Alaimo et al. (2008) and Litt et al. (2011) have showed that also in Europe and USA, participating in a community garden significantly increased intake of fruits and vegetables compared to non-gardeners and even to home-garden owners, even if the production in itself is low. A recent work underlines the variability of the food supply function among other ones in Paris and Montréal (Pourias 2014). In Eastern European countries community gardens still have an important weight in the urban food supply (Boukharaeva and Marloie 2010). The economic and financial crisis in south-western European countries leads to a new interest for these forms of self-made horticulture.

Permaculture

Due to the limited area for cultivation and the constraints this poses, agricultural activities within the city have to be efficient and have minimal impacts on the environment. Some integrated systems called "permaculture" have been developed to meet these requirements. They combine growing fruits, vegetables or grains with keeping livestock by creating a symbiotic ecosystem, with an ethical foundation in sustainability and copying nature, and a scientific basis in ecology. Permaculture (for permanent agriculture) is particularly relevant in the context of urban horticulture because it is a flexible option that suits city conditions due to the local recycling of energy and resources. The variety of production limits the risk and gives financial security. It is well suited to the developing countries because external inputs (chemical fertilizers, pesticides, etc.) are limited or absent.

Permaculture can be considered as one ultimate cropping system concept that uses a wide range of techniques and concepts: rainwater collection, excrement composting, reusing and recycling of wastewater and organic wastes, saving energy, green building and planning, and developing the local economy. For Holmgren (2013), who developed the principles of permaculture, urban agriculture will be a possibility to integrate the human material construction (the city) and the agriculture by renewing the place of the man in the

FIGURE 9.4 Permaculture garden
Source: Chriss Southall.

ecosystems. For example, in London (UK), Becontree Organic Growers in Dagenham develop the local economy through a local exchange trading scheme (Sherriff and Howe, pers. comm.). In Havana (Cuba), permaculture has been encouraged (Lazo and Barada, pers. comm.), where it has not only permitted the production of food, medicinal plants, spices and ornamental plants, but also resulted in a knowledge network by including a range of interested actors through periodic workshops, courses and conferences in environmental education and other related topics.

Organoponics

The term "organoponics" had its origin in Cuba where so-called *organopónicos* were organized as a response to the oil crisis in Cuba after the collapse of the Soviet Union in 1991. A shift to urban agriculture applying ecological principles seemed an appropriate response with minimized transportation costs and reduced need for machinery and petrochemical-based fertilizers and pesticides, which were no longer available (Bourque and Cañizares 2000). The organoponics are a labour-intensive form of urban gardens that often consist of low-level concrete walls filled with organic matter (e.g., wastes from the sugar plantations, composted household organic wastes) and soil, with lines of drip irrigation laid on the surface of the growing media and crops being sown or transplanted in holes or furrows (Novo 2003).

Organoponics can be constructed on all types of surfaces (even contaminated soils or former parking places) and as such it is well suited for vegetable production in intra-urban and peri-urban areas because it maximizes the use of space and water. Linking horticultural organoponic systems with ecological sanitation, as discussed by Arroyo (2003), may be an option appropriate to increase the productivity of organoponic systems if acceptability of the produce by the consumers can be assured.

FIGURE 9.5 Organopics Havana

Source: RUAF, courtesy of Martin Bourke.

Hydroponics

Hydroponics (or water culture) is a technology characterized by the absence of soil: roots suspended in moving water absorb food and oxygen. It needs less space, labour, external inputs and time, but needs proper management and often higher investments. As mentioned earlier, it is often difficult to control or quantify nutrient availability in the soil. Hydroponic systems provide a convenient means to control plant uptake of nutrients. An additional advantage of water culture is that the accumulation of soil toxins and some soil-borne diseases are likely to be reduced (Lissner et al. 2003).

When oxygen in the water is insufficient, plant growth will be retarded. This is a point to look carefully in warm climates. The grower's task is to balance the combination of water, nutrients and oxygen with the plants' needs in order to maximize yield and quality. The use of water and inputs is optimized: the exact amount needed by the plants is provided. For the best results, a few important parameters need to be taken into account: temperature, humidity, CO_2 levels, light intensity, ventilation and the plant's genetic make-up. In order to fix the crop roots in the required position, some inert substrata may be used (sponges, artificial mineral marbles, rock wool, etc.).

Hydroponics allows production in abundance of healthy fresh vegetables, ornamentals, and aromatic and medicinal plants, and suits the requirements of poor urban farmers. When the technique is well controlled, the productivity generated by hydroponic systems is greater than that from traditional gardening systems. It is

FIGURE 9.6 Hydroponic production of tomatoes in greenhouse, Gabon
Source: Hubert de Bon.

a technology adapted to the conditions where the soil is poor or polluted. In many countries of South America, hydroponics is a technique that is fast gaining importance (Tabares 2003).

Small hydroponic units can be operated by families. This may help in meeting their food needs and in getting an additional income. Some special hydroponic techniques have been developed, especially for limited spaces and to suit people in developing countries. Such simplified hydroponic systems often use recycled materials and are easier to understand, learn and implement (Caldeyro-Stajano 2004; Fecondini et al. 2009). Simplified hydroponics is a technology incorporating soilless culture techniques without using mechanical devices or testing equipment. This technology was developed in the early 1980s in Colombia and is propagated by FAO. It is accessible to people with limited resources and is optimized to use minimal inputs of land space, water, nutrients and grower infrastructure (see Box 9.2). A Family Economical Unit (FEU) of 20 bed-growers of 2 m² each (40 m²) is designed to produce crops that bring an income estimated at USD 3.33 per day in Colombia (year 2000 figures). Simplified hydroponics is well suited for fresh vegetables and fruits (with a high water content) such as lettuces, tomato, bell pepper, basil, celery and radish.

BOX 9.2 COST ESTIMATION OF A SIMPLIFIED HYDROPONIC SYSTEM

In data gathered from the Colombia project, the results of garden productivity were averaged and the commercial values were estimated. The cost of building 20 bed-growers for the FEU from recycled wood is estimated to be USD 12.84 (6.42 m^2). The annual costs for operating a garden, using the same crops as in the Colombia project, will average about USD 355. This includes costs for medium replacement, seeds, nutrients and water. The annual net income from this garden is estimated to be about USD 1,210.00 (USD 101/month). Water is applied to the bed-growers and the excess water is collected underneath them and recycled to the growers the next day. The average water use for a grower is 2–4 litres/day/m^2 or at most 160 litres per day. The annual water requirement for each garden is estimated to be 60,000–120,000 litres.

Source: Bradley and Marulanda 2001.

Another interesting process is hydroponics with floaters, where plants are fixed on polystyrene beds that float over a tank. The water surface is completely covered by the floating bed, which permits a very limited growth of algae. The tank's nutritive solution is oxygenated, e.g. by a pump. This hydroponic system is characterized by a large volume of nutritive solution, no losses of water, minimal evaporation and the possibility to use the solution for many crop cycles. It is a low-cost method needing little maintenance. It is used in Martinique (French West Indies), an island with high constraints of space in peri-urban areas, for production of lettuce or onion (Langlais, CIRAD, pers. comm.). Hydroponic systems also present interesting solutions in combination with the recycling of water, and has been studied in water hyacinth, reed and flower (roses) production systems. Another possible future development of hydroponics is the production of bioenergy crops using wastewater as a nutrient solution (Mavrogianopoulos et al. 2002).

Water quantity and quality are key factors in hydroponic systems. Water quality depends mainly on the source used. Growers use water from different sources, such as surface water (lakes, natural and artificial ponds), groundwater (wells), municipal tap water, rainwater and combinations of these. Rainwater has a low ionic strength and usually low micro-organism and algal densities; it conforms to water-quality guidelines and is often better than other sources. A common practice is to collect rainwater from greenhouse roofs into ponds. However, as these ponds are fed by atmospheric precipitation, they are vulnerable to changes in the environment, e.g., eutrophication and acidification. Rainwater is not always available for use in irrigation because of technical problems in collection and storage. Therefore, the grower must find other water sources, e.g. rivers or lakes, but, in many cases, such sources are polluted (Schwarz et al. 2005).

The Gravel Bed Hydroponic (GBH) system developed by the University of Portsmouth, UK, includes a rock filter in gabions for primary treatment, GBH beds for secondary treatment and a pond for tertiary treatment. It reduced the biochemical oxygen demand (from 350 to less than 20 mg/l) of the output water in a bed planted with narrow-leaf cattail *(Typha angustifolia)* in Colombia (Stott et al. 1999). The use of plants is also a technique to improve the quality of the water for hydroponics (Vymazal 2011).

Urban horticulture in or on top of buildings

Will urban horticulture in the future be inside the cities, in and on urban buildings? This question is not at all an imaginary one, while urban agriculture, and chiefly (but not exclusively) urban horticulture is reaching the heart of the cities, with the conquest of indoors and more frequently of rooftops and walls. The "Z-farming" (for Zero Acreage farming) is now studied in its interests and functions to produce food and also for other non-food and non-market functions (Calkins 2005; Specht et al. 2014).

Some commercial farms, for the moment chiefly in North America (Brooklyn Grange or Eagle Farm in New York, Lufa farm in Montréal) and Asia (Sky Greens in Singapore) were born some years ago, with different technical systems: open-air rooftop production (with substrates like translated soils and/or organic ones), or on-the-roof greenhouses, generally with hydroponic production systems.

FIGURE 9.7 Rooftop greenhouse Arbor House in New York, USA

Source: Nexus.

In developing countries, horticulture on rooftops using either hydroponics or organoponics (often in containers, boxes, pots or other containers) is gaining in importance and allows production of various leafy vegetables and aromatics, often tomatoes, but could also be more diverse and include tubers and small fruits. For instance, in Senegal, rooftop gardening, based on bricks or wooden box beds filled with compost, allows growing a wide variety of crops, including fibrous roots crops, tomato, hot pepper, eggplant, etc. (Deesohu Saydee and Ujereh 2003). Such cultivation is characterized by its high level of intensity due to the small spaces available on the roof of buildings. Due to being located outdoors, these systems face natural attacks, e.g., of insects and birds, and some crops would therefore need protection, e.g., with nets.

Some forms of rooftop gardening are not commercial or not commercial alone. Rooftop gardens may be established to reduce storm water runoff and energy use of the buildings and/or to increase urban green spaces with various social, environmental and/or educational functions (like is promoted in New York and Singapore; the "Santropol Roulant" project in Montréal).

Another variation comprises the so-called vertical gardens or "green walls", which is a system where plants can be grown on, up or against the wall of a building such as a vine, as part of a window shade or in a vertical hydroponic system. Typically, they consist of indoor/outdoor modular planters with multiple levels of vertically spaced pots or planters. Using the vertical space instead of

FIGURE 9.8 Rooftop garden, Uncommon Ground Restaurant, Chicago

Source: Lauren Mandel, EAT UP.

horizontal space is an important feature for urban dwellers that lack space for growing horticultural crops, such as those living in apartments with small balconies. The system is also water saving, since it flows from the top plants, passing to all the lower pots.

A more artificial system that is proposed now is the plant factory (Kozai 2013): a closed space in a closed insulated building or other structure where plants are grown on tiered shelves under artificial light. In the factory, the concentration of CO_2, temperature, humidity, light intensity, light-versus-dark hours, and other conditions are controlled to help the plants grow faster. Plant factories vary in scale from large ones for commercial use, extending over 1,000 to 2,000 m^2 with 10 to 20 tiers of shelving, to smaller ones for households that can fit on a table top. Mainly leafy vegetables (lettuce, mizuna) are grown but experiments are ongoing with various other crops (including dwarf varieties of rice). The irrigation water of the hydroponic systems is recycled. Hypotheses are that in such an environment the risks due to pest and diseases will be almost zero, the contents in biological contaminants and heavy metals will disappear, and the development time of the plants will be shorter. This system could be used also for nursery, aromatic plants, herbs and all plants with short life cycles. Some large industrial companies have invested in these prototypes.

FIGURE 9.9 Plant factory at Chiba University Kashiwa-no-ha Campus, Chiba, Japan, operated by Mirai Co. Ltd.

Source: Prof. Toyoki Kozai.

As rooftop open-air farms, green houses and indoor plant factories are new forms of urban horticulture, a lot of research questions are emerging. Some are technical: What is the productivity of the open-air rooftop systems? How to apply urban organic wastes as crop substrates?

Are the available references for production in classic greenhouses valuable for these new intra-urban ones (Sanyé-Mengual et al. 2012)? What adaptations are needed in the design of buildings to integrate well rooftop green houses or indoor plant factories (strength of floors, dimensions/number of elevators, etc.? How to reduce the energy use in plant factories (improved LED lighting, solar panels, use of excess CO_2/heat/energy/water of neighbouring industry or bio-digesters at landfills; interactions with the zero or plus energy building programmes will be required). Will these "ultra short" supply chains permit to improve the taste and nutritive qualities of fruits and vegetables as they can be harvested at maturity, or will these qualities deteriorate (due to industrial production in plant factories)?

The issue of the movement of inputs, crops and crop residues produced by rooftop systems is also a consideration in the urban context and could be a limiting factor in the development of this form of agriculture if not accounted for in urban planning.

The environmental effects of cultivated rooftops on reduction of "urban heat islands", on reducing and slowing down of storm water runoff, and on urban biodiversity began to be studied sometime back (Eumorphopoulos and Aravantinos 1998; Bass et al. 2003; Oberndofer et al. 2007; Hitchmough 2010; Kowarik 2011). The effect of rooftop gardens on reducing the energy consumption of commercial buildings was measured to be up to 14.5% in Singapore (Wong et al. 2003; see also Chapter 8).

Some work also has started on the question of investments in relation to the energy cost and the value of the production, which raise the necessity of further technical improvements (Wilson 2002; Oberndofer et al. 2007; Bojaca and Schrevens 2010).

Conclusion

In many expanding cities in developing countries, urban horticulture is already a large contributor in supplying fresh produce to city markets and is expected to remain so in the near future. On the one hand, the available land will decrease because of the need for industrial development and urban housing. On the other, the demand for fruit, vegetables and flowers will increase with rising standards of living and growing populations. Horticultural production units will evolve and adapt to new environments as cities continue to develop. In the future, vegetable production will remain essential as a source of high income and healthy food for growing cities.

To answer consumers' demand and to produce healthy fruits and vegetable in a manner that respects the environment and producers, it will be necessary to combine agro-technical solutions with urban planning. In urban agriculture there will be a choice between (or combination of?): (1) anthropised agro-systems as proposed by permaculture with a "natural" use of some parts of the intra- and peri-urban lands, or (2) totally artificial city plant and animal production in buildings (plant factories). It is therefore important to undertake agro-technical studies that could provide more in-depth information on the conditions required for obtaining good-quality vegetables. Urban planning should help to provide optimal conditions for urban gardeners. Supply of inputs and materials, management of crop residues and linkage between activities are key points that need to be taken into account early in the urban planning process. It involves all aspects of a city's organization and requires commitment to provide goods and services to agricultural activities and people (Pinderhughes 2004).

Urban horticulture is nowadays in a state of deep, rapid and multiform renewal. Some cities like New York are facing a real boom of different forms of urban agriculture chiefly concerning vegetables and fruit productions (Cohen et al. 2012). Non-professional, professional and hybrid systems are emerging generally without real urban planning, or at the best with a partial one (Mansfield and Mendes 2012), changing directly or indirectly the way urban dwellers may have access to food production.

A lot of technical systems are also emerging in a double objective to produce tastier and more diversified vegetables than before, and to produce them in more environmental-friendly ways than "traditional" long chain supplying and industrial forms of horticulture. Research is needed to have more information on the advantages, possible disadvantages, complementarities and eventually competitions of these multiple forms or urban horticulture.

Various functions of urban horticulture have been mentioned in this chapter. The food supply function remains the most important, even though economic, social (labour), cultural, living environmental, environmental (recycling) and security (food and natural risks) functions appear to be essential too. More than any other agricultural system, urban horticulture has a multifunctional role that should be taken into account by researchers and policy makers. Implementation of an urban planning policy that includes the sustainability of this form of agriculture is a necessity for well-balanced urban development. Urban horticulture plays a substantial role in the development of local (micro)enterprises, including input supply, processing and marketing. It also reduces the distance that fresh food needs to travel from producer to consumer.

If well managed, urban horticulture can play an important role in reducing socio-economic and environmental problems in cities. Planners and policy makers should develop and support community-wide plans to improve poor people's incomes using urban organic waste, to improve urban food safety and to create sustainable food systems.

References

Abdulkadir, A.; Dossa, L. H.; Lompo, D. J.P.; Abdu, N.; Keulen, H. van. 2014. Characterization of urban and peri-urban agro-ecosystems in three West African cities. *International Journal of Agricultural Sustainability* 10(4): 289–314.

Agrawal, M.; Singh, B.; Rajput, M.; Marshall, F.; Bell, J. 2003. Effect of air pollution on peri-urban agriculture: A case study. *Environmental Pollution* 126: 323–329.

Alaimo, K.; Packnett, E.; Miles, R. A.; Kruger, D. J. 2008. Fruit and vegetable intake among urban community gardeners. *Journal of Nutrition Education and Behaviour* 40: 94–101.

Ali, M. 2000. Dynamics of vegetable production, distribution and consumption in Asia. Taiwan: AVRDC-World Vegetable Center.

Arroyo, F. 2003. Organoponics: The use of human urine in composting. *Urban Agriculture Magazine* 10: 29.

Bass, B.; Liu, K.K.Y.; Baskaran, B. A. 2003. Evaluating rooftop and vertical gardens as an adaptation strategy for urban areas. CCAF Report #B1046. Ottawa: National Research Council Canada, Institute for Research Canada.

Bempah, C.K.; Kwofie, A. B.; Enimil, E.; Blewu, B.; Martey, G. A. 2012. Residues of organochlorine pesticides in vegetables marketed in Greater Accra region of Ghana. *Food Control* 25: 537–542.

Birley, M.; Lock, K. 2000. The health aspects of peri-urban natural resource development. Trowbridge: Cromwell Press.

Bojaca, C. R.; Schrevens, E. 2010. Energy assessment of peri-urban horticulture and its uncertainty: Case study for Bogota, Colombia. *Energy* 35: 2109–2118.

Bon, H. de; Huat, J.; Parrot, L.; Sinzogan, A.; Martin, T.; Malézieux E.; Vayssières, J.F. 2014. Pesticide risks from fruit and vegetable pest management by small farmers in sub-Saharan African. A review. *Agronomy for Sustainable Development* 34(4): 723–736.

Boukharaeva, L.; Marloie, M. 2010. L'apport du jardinage urbain de Russie à la théorisation de l'agriculture urbaine. *VertigO: La revue électronique en sciences de l'environnement* 10(2). Available from: http://vertigo.revues.org.

Bourque, M.; Cañizares, K. 2000. Urban agriculture in Havana (Cuba). Food production in the community by the community and for the community. *Urban Agriculture Magazine* 1: 27–29.

Bradford, A.; Brook, R.; Hunshal, C. 2002. Risk reduction in sewage irrigated farming systems in Hubli-Dharwad, India. *Urban Agriculture Magazine* 6: 40–41.

Bradley, P.; Marulanda, C. 2001. Simplified hydroponics to reduce global hunger. *Acta Horticulturae* 554: 289–296.

Bricas, N. 1998. Cadre conceptuel et méthodologique pour l'analyse de la consommation alimentaire urbaine en Afrique. *Série Urbanisation, alimentation des filières vivrières* 1: 48. Montpellier: CIRAD; Rome: FAO.

Buechler, S.; Hertog, W.; Veenhuizen, R. van. 2002. Editorial: Wastewater use for urban agriculture. *Urban Agriculture Magazine* 8: 1–4.

Caldeyro-Stajano, M. 2004. Simplified hydroponics as an appropriate technology to implement food security in urban agriculture. *Practical Hydroponics and Greenhouses* 76: 1–6.

Calkins, M. 2005. Strategy use and challenges of ecological design in landscape architecture. *Landscape and Urban Planning* 73: 29–48.

Chenot, E. D.; Douay, F.; Dumat, C.; Pernin, C.; Pourrut, B.; Scwartz, C. 2013. Les sols de jardins. In: *Jardins potagers: Terres inconnues?* (Ed.) Swartz, C. Les Ulis: EDP-Sciences, pp. 47–56.

Cohen, N. 2012. SF urban agriculture ordinance: NYC should follow suit. Available from: http://urbanfoodpolicy.com/2012/08/02/sf-urban-agriculture-ordinance-nyc-should-follow-suit.

Dabat, M.H.; Andrianarisoa, B.; Aubry, C.; Ravoniarisoa, E. F.; Randrianasolo, H.; Rakoto, N.; Sarter, S.; Trèche, S. 2010. Production de cresson à haut risque dans les bas-fonds d'Antananarivo? *VertigO: La revue électronique en sciences de l'environnement* 10(2). Available from: http://vertigo.revues.org.

Dean, W.R.; Sharkey, J.R. 2011. Rural and urban differences in the associations between characteristics of the community food environment and fruit and vegetable intake. *Journal of Nutrition Education and Behavior* 43(6): 426–433.

Deesohu Saydee, G.; Ujereh, S. 2003. Rooftop gardening in Senegal. *Urban Agriculture Magazine* 10: 16–17.

Duchemin, E.; Wegmuller F. 2010. Multifonctionnalité de l'agriculture urbaine à Montréal: étude des discours au sein du programme des jardins communautaires. *VertigO: La revue electronique en sciences de l'environnement* 10(2). Available from: http://vertigo.revues.org.

Eiumnoh, A.; Parkpian, P. 1998. Impact of peri-urban vegetable production on soils and water: A case of Bangkok plain, Thailand. Paper presented at the conference Peri-urban Vegetable Production in the Asia-Pacific Region for the 21st Century, 29 September–1 October 1998, Kasetsart University, Bangkok, Thailand.

Eumorphopoulos, E.; Aravantinos, D. 1998. The contribution of a planted roof to the thermal protection of buildings in Greece. *Energy and Buildings* 27: 20–36.

Fatou Diop Gueye, N.; Sy, M. 2001. The use of wastewater for urban agriculture. *Urban Agriculture Magazine* 1(3): 30–32.

Fecondini, M.; Casati, M.; Dimech, M.; Michelon, N.; Orsini, F.; Gianquito, G. 2009. Improved cultivation of lettuce with a low cost soilless system in indigent areas of Northeast Brazil. *Acta Horticulturae* 807: 501–507.

Fleury, A.; Moustier, P. 1999. L'agriculture périurbaine, infrastructure de la ville durable. *Cahiers Agricultures* 8: 281–287.

Galluzi, G.; Eyzaguirre, P.; Negri, V. 2010. Home gardens: Neglected hotspots of agrobio-diversity and cultural diversity. *Biodiversity Conservation* 19: 3635–3654.

Grard, B.; Madre, F.; Jeanneteau, C.; Cambier, P.; Castell, J.F.; Manoucheri, N.; Besançon, S.; Houot, S.; Barot, S.; Bel, N.; Aubry, C. 2013. Assessment of trace element contamination in vegetables and in growing substrates made from recycled organic wastes for an experiment on a rooftop in Paris, France. Poster at the Urban Environmental Pollution Conference, 17–20 November 2013, Beijing, China.

Hitchmough, J. 2010. Applying an ecological approach: The future of urban horticulture? Proceedings of the second International Conference on Landscape and Urban Horticulture. *Acta Horticulturae* 881: 193–200.

Holmer, R. J. 2010. Community-based vegetable production systems: An answer to the food and sanitation crisis of urban poor in the Philippines? *Acta Horticulturae* 881: 125–130.

Holmer, R. J.; Drescher, A. W. 2005. Building food secure neighbourhoods: The role of allotment gardens. *Urban Agriculture Magazine* 15: 19–20.

Holmer, R. J.; Itchon, G.S. 2008. Is human excreta an answer to the food & fertilizer crisis? *Appropriate Technology* 35 (4): 31–33.

Holmer, R. J.; Schnitzler, W.H. 1997. Drip irrigation for small-scale tomato production in the tropics. *Kasetsart Journal (Natural Sciences)* 32(5): 56–60.

Holmgren, M. 2013. Urban agriculture as a way to develop a holistic client centred community. Presentation at Alberta Land Use Knowledge Centre, 12 November 2013. Available at: www.youtube.com/watch?v=HZpMnfkSpmA.

Huong, P.T.T.; Erveraarts, A. P.; Neeteson, J. J.; Struik, P. C. 2013. Vegetable production in the Red River Delta of Vietnam II. Profitability, labour requirement and pesticide use. *Journal of Life Sciences* 67: 37–46.

Jørgensen, N.; Laursen, J.; Viksna, A.; Pind, N.; Holm, P. 2005. Multi-elemental EDXRF mapping of polluted soil from former horticultural land. *Environment International* 31: 43–52.

Karanja, N.; Njenga, N.; Prain, G.; Kang'ethe, E.; Kironchi, G.; Githuku, C.; Kinyai, P.; Mutua, G. K. 2010. Assessment of environmental and public health hazards in wastewater used for urban agriculture in Nairobi, Kenya. *Tropical and Subtropical Agroecosystems* 12: 85–97.

Keatinge, J.D.H.; Chadha, M. L.; Hughes, J. d'A.; Easdown, W. J.; Holmer, R. J.; Tenkouano, A.; Yang, R. Y.; Mavlyanova, R.; Neave, S.; Afari-Sefa, V.; Luther, G.; Ravishankar, M.; Ojiewo, C.; Belarmino, M.; Ebert, A. W.; Wang, J. F.; Lin, L. J. 2012. Vegetable gardens and their impact on the attainment of the millennium development goals. *Biological Agriculture & Horticulture* 28(2): 1–15.

Kessler, A. 2002. Economic strategies of different plant production farming systems of urban and peri-urban agriculture in West Africa. *Urban Agriculture Magazine* 9: 30–31.

Khosa, T.; Averbeke, W. van; Böhringer, R.; Maswikaneng, J.; Albertse, E. 2003. The 'Drum and drip' micro-irrigation system, tested in South Africa. *Urban Agriculture Magazine* 10: 4–5.

Kowarik, I. 2011. Novel urban ecosystems, biodiversity, and conservation. *Environmental Pollution* 159: 1973–1984.

Kozai, T. 2013. Resource use efficiency of closed plant production system with artificial light: Concept, estimation and application to plant factory. *Proceedings of Japan Academy; Series B: Physical and Biological Sciences* 89(10): 447–461.

Lenoble, R. 2013. Analyse du fonctionnement technique des exploitations maraîchères en circuits courts en zone urbain été périurbaine de Montpellier: Quelle durabilité? *Montpellier Sup'Agro, Mémoire de fin d'études*. Montpellier: UMR Innovation.

Lissner, J.; Mendelssohn, I.; Anastasiou, C. 2003. A method for cultivating plants under controlled redox intensities in hydroponics. *Aquatic Botany* 76: 93–108.

Litt, J.; Soobader, M. J.; Turbin, M. S.; Hale, J. W.; Buchenau, M.; Marshall, J. A. 2011. The influence of social involvement, neighborhood aesthetics, and community garden participation on fruit and vegetable consumption. *American Journal of Public Health* 101 (8): 1466–1473.

Lovell, S. T. 2010. Multi-functional urban agriculture for sustainable land use planning in the United States. *Sustainability* 2: 2499–2522.

Mai Thi Phuong Anh. 2000. Current status and prospective planning upon agricultural development in Hanoi. Paper presented during the CG Strategic Initiative of Urban and Peri-Urban Agriculture Workshop, 5–9 June 2000, Hanoi, Vietnam.

Mansfield, B.; Mendes, W. 2012. Municipal food strategies and integrated approaches to urban agriculture: Exploring three cases from the Global North. *International Planning Studies* 18(1): 37–60.

Mapanda, F.; Mangwayana, E.; Nyamangara, J.; Giller, K. 2005. The effect of long-term irrigation using wastewater on heavy metal contents of soils under vegetables in Harare, Zimbabwe. *Agriculture, Ecosystems and Environment* 107: 151–165.

Margiotta, M. 1997. Développement de la production maraîchère dans les périmètres urbains et péri-urbains de Nouakchott. République Islamique de Mauritanie: Ministère du Développement Rural et de l'Environnement.

Martin, T.; Assogba-Komlan, F.; Houndete, T.; Hougard, J. M. and Chandre, F. 2006. Efficacy of mosquito netting for sustainable small holders' cabbage production in Africa. *Journal of Economic Entomology* 99: 450–454.

Martin, T.; Kamal, A.; Gogo, E.; Saidi, M.; Deletré, E.; Bonafos, R.; Simon, S.; Ngouajio, M. 2014. Repellent effect of alphacypermetrine-treated netting against Bemisia tabaci (Hempitera: Aleyrodidae). *Journal of Economic Entomology* 107(2): 684–690.

Maundu, P.; Achigan-Dako, E.; Morimoto, Y. 2009. Biodiversity of African vegetables. In: *African indigenous vegetables in urban agriculture.* (Eds.) Shackleton, C. M.; Pasquini, M. W.; Drescher, A. London: Earthscan, pp. 65–101.

Mavrogianopoulos, G.; Vogli, V.; Kyritsis, S. 2002. Use of wastewater as a nutrient solution in a closed gravel hydroponic culture of giant reed (*Arundo donax*). *Bioresource Technology* 82: 103–107.

Midmore, D. J. 1998. Importance of peri-urban vegetables to Asian cities. Paper presented at Meeting on Peri-urban Vegetable Production in the Asia-Pacific Region for the 21st Century, 29 September–1 October 1998, Kasetsart University, Bangkok, Thailand.

Moustier, P. 1999a. Définitions et contours de l'agriculture périurbaine en Afrique subsaharienne. In: *Agriculture périurbaine en Afrique subsaharienne.* (Eds.) Moustier, P.; Mbaye, A.; de Bon, H.; Guérin, H.; Pagès, J. Montpellier: CIRAD, pp. 17–29.

Moustier, P. 1999b. Filières maraîchères à Brazzaville. Quantification et observatoire pour l'action. Montpellier: CIRAD et Agrisud-Agricongo.

Moustier, P. 2000. Urban and peri-urban agriculture in West and Central Africa: An overview. Provisional paper (30/10/00) for SIUPA Stakeholder Meeting and Strategic Workshop, sub-Saharan region, 1–4 November 2000, Nairobi, Kenya.

Nguyen Thi Lam; Ha Huy Khoi. 1999. Daily nutrient requirements and vegetable consumption by Vietnamese people. In: *National workshop on safe and year-round vegetable production in peri-urban areas.* 15–16 December 1999, Hanoi, Vietnam. Hanoi: RIFAV, CIRAD, pp. 65–74.

Novo, M. G. 2003. Organoponics, a productive option. *Urban Agriculture Magazine* 10: 29.

Oberndorfer, E.; Lundholm, J.; Bass, B.; Coffla, R. R.; Doshi, H.; Dunnett, N.; Gaffin, S.; Kolher, M.; Liu, K.K.L.; Rowe, B. 2007. Green roofs as urban ecosystems: Ecological structures, functions and services. *BioScience* 27(10): 823–833.

Oluoch, M. O.; Pichop, G. N.; Silue, D.; Abukutsa-Onyango, M. O.; Diouf, M.; Shackelton, C. M. 2009. Production and harvesting systems for African indigenous vegetables. In: *African indigenous vegetables in urban agriculture.* (Eds.) Shackleton, C. M.; Pasquini, M. W.; Drescher, A. W. London: Earthscan, pp. 145–175.

Petit, C.; Loubet, B.; Rémy, E.; Aubry, C. 2013. Dépôt de polluants sur les espaces agricoles à proximité des voies de transport en Île-de-France. In: *Pollutions atmosphériques, transport et agriculture.* (Eds.) Petit, C.; Rémy, E. Special Issue 15 of *VertigO: La revue électronique en sciences de l'environnement.* Available from: https://vertigo.revues.org/12865.

Petterson, S. R.; Ashbolt, N.; Sharma, A. 2001. Microbial risks from wastewater irrigation of salad crops: A screening-level risk assessment. *Water Environment Research* 72: 667–672.

Pinderhughes, R. 2004. Urban food production. In: *Alternative urban futures: Planning for sustainable development in cities throughout the world.* (Ed.) Pinderhughes, R. Boulder: Rowman & Littlefield Publishers; Oxford: Lanham, pp. 185–218.

Potutan, G. E.; Schnitzler, W. H.; Arnado, J. M.; Janubas, L. G.; Holmer, R. J. 2000. Urban agriculture in Cagayan de Oro: A favourable response of city government and NGOs. In: *Growing cities growing food: Urban agriculture on the policy agenda.* (Eds.) Bakker, M.; Dubbeling, M.; Sabel-Koschella, U.; Zeeuw, H. de. Feldafing: DSE, pp. 413–428.

Pourias, J. 2010. Approche par la gestion technique des liens entre système de culture et système de vente: Exemple des exploitations maraichères dans la plaine de Versailles. Mémoire de fin d'études présenté pour l'obtention du diplôme d'ingénieur en horticulture, spécialisation Production végétale durable. MSc thesis, Montpellier: Agro Campus Ouest-Sup Agro Montpellier.

Pourias, J. 2014. Production alimentaire et pratiques culturales en agriculture urbaine: Analyse agronomique de la fonction alimentaire des jardins associatifs urbains à Paris et Montréal. Doctoral thesis, Paris: AgroParisTech and UQAM (University of Quebec at Montreal, Canada).

Predotova, M.; Bischoff, W.-A.; Buerkert, A. 2011. Mineral-nitrogen and phosphorus leaching from vegetable gardens in Niamey, Niger. *Journal of Plant Nutrition and Soil Science* 174: 47–55.

Puschenreiter, M.; Hartl, W.; Othmar, H. 1999. Urban agriculture on heavy metal contaminated soils in Eastern Europe. Vienna: Ludwig Boltzmann Institute for Organic Agriculture and Applied Ecology.

PUVeP 2008. Philippine allotment garden manual with an introduction to ecological sanitation. Periurban Vegetable Project (PUVeP). Cagayan de Oro City: Xavier University College of Agriculture.

Robineau, O. 2013. Vivre de l'agriculture dans la ville africaine. Une géographie des arrangements entre acteurs à Bobo-Dioulasso, Burkina Faso. Doctoral thesis in Geography and Land Use Management, UMR 951 Innovation. Montpellier: Université de Montpellier.

Sangare, S. K.; Compaore, E.; Buerkert, A.; Vanclooster, M.; Sedogo, M. P.; Bielders, C. L. 2012. Field-scale analysis of water and nutrient use efficiency for vegetable production in a West African urban agricultural system. *Nutrient Cycling in Agroecosystems* 92: 207–224.

Sanyé-Mengual, E.; Ceron-Palma, I.; Oliver-Sol, J.; Montero, J.I.; Rieradevall, J. 2012. Environmental analysis of the logistics of agricultural products from roof top greenhouses in Mediterranean urban areas. *Journal of the Science of Food and Agriculture*. 2013(93): 100–109.

Säumel, I.; Kotsyuk, I.; Hölscher, M.; Lenkereit, C.; Weber, F.; Kowarik, I. 2012. How healthy is urban horticulture in high traffic areas? Trace metal concentrations in vegetable crops from plantings within inner city neighbourhoods in Berlin, Germany. *Environmental Pollution* 165: 124–132.

Schwarz, D.; Grosch, R.; Gross, W.; Hoffmann-Hergarten, S. 2005. Water quality assessment of different reservoir types in relation to nutrient solution use in hydroponics. *Agricultural Water Management* 71: 145–166.

Seidu, R.; Heistad, A.; Amoah, P.; Drechsel, P.; Jenssen, P. D.; Stenström, T. A. 2008. Quantification of the health risk associated with wastewater reuse in Accra, Ghana: A contribution toward local guidelines. *Journal of Water Health* 6: 461–471.

Specht, K.; Siebert, R.; Hartmann, I.; Freisinger, U. B.; Sawicka, M.; Werner, A.; Thomaier, S.; Henckels, D.; Walk, H.; Dietrich, A. 2014. Urban agriculture of the future: An overview of sustainability aspects of food production in and on buildings. *Agriculture and Human Values* 31(1): 33–51.

Stott, R.; Jenkins, T.; Bahgat, M.; Shalaby, I. 1999. Capacity of constructed wetlands to remove parasite eggs from wastewaters in Egypt. *Water Science and Technology* 40: 117–123.

Tabares, C. M. 2003. Hydroponics in Latin America. *Urban Agriculture Magazine* 10: 8.

Tran Khac Thi. 1999. *Cultivated techniques of safe vegetables.* Hanoi: Agricultural Publishing House.

Vymazal, J. 2011. Plants used in constructed wetlands with horizontal subsurface flow: A review. *Hydrobiologia* 674(1): 133–156.

Weintraub, P. G. 2009. Physical control: An important tool in pest management programs. In: *Biorational control of arthropod pests.* (Eds.) Ishaaya, I.; Horowitz, A. R. New York: Springer Science+Business Media, pp. 317–327.

WHO 2007. Guidelines for the safe use of wastewater, excreta and greywater: Wastewater use in agriculture (Volume 2). Geneva: World Health Organization (WHO).

Wilson, G. 2002. Can urban rooftop microfarms be profitable? *Urban Agriculture Magazine* 7: 22–24.

Wong, N.; Cheong, D.; Yan, H.; Soh, J.; Ong, C.; Sia, A. 2003. The effect of rooftop garden on energy consumption of a commercial building in Singapore. *Energy and Buildings* 35: 353–364.

Yi-Zhang, C.; Zhangen, Z. 2000. Shanghai: Trends towards specialised and capital-intensive urban agriculture. In: *Growing cities, growing food: Urban agriculture on the policy agenda.* (Eds.) Bakker, N.; Dubbeling, M.; Guendel, S.; Sabel-Koschella, U.; Zeeuw, H. de. Feldafing: DSE, pp. 467–476.

Zeeuw, H. de; Lock, K. 2000. Urban and peri-urban agriculture, health and environment. Discussion paper for FAO-ETC/RUAF electronic conference Urban and Peri-Urban Agriculture on the Policy Agenda, 21 August–30 September 2000.

10

URBAN LIVESTOCK KEEPING

Delia Grace,[1] *Johanna Lindahl,*[1,2] *Maria Correa*[3]
and Manish Kakkar[4]

1 INTERNATIONAL LIVESTOCK RESEARCH INSTITUTE, NAIROBI, KENYA

2 SWEDISH UNIVERSITY OF AGRICULTURAL SCIENCES, UPPSALA, SWEDEN

3 NORTH CAROLINA STATE UNIVERSITY COLLEGE OF VETERINARY MEDICINE, USA

4 PUBLIC HEALTH FOUNDATION OF INDIA, DELHI, INDIA

Introduction

For the first time in history, more people are living in towns and cities than in the countryside and at least one billion intra- and peri-urban dwellers are estimated to practise agriculture. Their farming varies from growing herbs on a windowsill, to cultivating a vegetable allotment, to raising poultry under their bed, to running a dairy.

Urban livestock keeping is an interesting aspect of urban agriculture. Compared to crops, livestock produce foods that bring more profits and have a higher nutrient content, but that are more expensive to produce and buy. Livestock products are highly perishable, a strong driver for producing them around cities; also, livestock products are more prone to spoilage and contamination with disease-causing organisms. Livestock require little room and can better share spaces with human beings, but they also create more nuisance, waste and injuries than plants. Hence maintaining livestock in ways that minimize risks and maximize benefits is a powerful indicator that urban agriculture is thriving.

This chapter considers the past, present and future of urban livestock keeping and discusses the benefits and risks and their management. We first review keeping of livestock in cities: nearly ubiquitous in historical times, gradually evicted from 'modern cities' over the last century, and their comeback in recent decades. The second section discusses the different types of livestock keeping in cities and provides up-to-date information on the extent of livestock keeping and its motivation. We then discuss benefits and risks of livestock keeping in cities and suggest ways to maximize the former while reducing the latter. Finally, conclusions are drawn and a way forward offered. The chapter as a whole revisits the earlier synthesis by Schiere et al. (2007).

History of livestock and cities

In the beginning was livestock, and then came cities

Livestock are older than cities. Bezoars, ancestral to goats, were probably the first animals to be domesticated around 11,000 years ago (Pereira and Amorim 2010), followed by cattle, whose ancestors were so large and savage they were almost not domesticated at all; the world's 1.3 billion head of cattle are descendants from an original population of just 80 aurochs (Bollongino et al. 2012). More peaceable jungle fowl have been domesticated on multiple occasions, starting at least 5,400 years ago (Miao et al. 2013).

Cities probably arose after the invention of agriculture (although some argue the other way round). Ancient cities often had only modest populations and archaeology suggests livestock mingled with citizens. With time, cities and civilizations grew, and by the year AD 100 the world's three most populous cities (Rome, Luoyang and Seleucia) had more than a million human inhabitants among them, and likely many more productive animals and peri-domestic pests. Animals were kept in biblical towns, in ancient and medieval European cities, in Mayan and Aztec city-states, as well as in Chinese civilizations (Schiere et al. 2007). In pre-colonial Nigeria, the edges of cities consisted of intensively farmed land where the majority of the urban population worked each day (Winters 1983), while in eastern and central African cities, the quarters of these cities were separated and the spaces between them used for farming. As one observer said of Kampala, "it was less of a city than an immense garden" (Gutkind 1963).

Up to the last century, equids, camelids, ruminants and canids transported people and goods into, out of and around cities. As late as the 1960s, citizens in Europe and America got dairy products delivered to their door by horse and wagon. In England, rag and bone carts did rounds to buy sellable discards, while dustcarts removed refuse for a fee. In America, urban dairying grew rapidly after the 1850s when breast-feeding fell out of favour for cultural reasons (Du Puis 2002). In the mid-nineteenth century New York, many dairies were attached to breweries and distilleries where as many as 2,000 cows could be maintained in one giant stable feeding on brewers' wastes, hot from the still.

Some cities owe their origins to livestock. The American stockyard cities such as Chicago, Kansas City, Fort Worth and "Porkopolis" (Cincinnati) depended on the livestock and meat-packing trade during their establishment and growth. By 1900, the Chicago stockyards employed more than 25,000 people and produced 82% of the meat consumed in the United States. They also provided the backdrop for Upton Sinclair's novel *The Jungle*. This book was intended to draw attention to appalling workers' conditions, but ended up becoming a *cause celebre* for food safety, eventually leading to the establishment of the US Food and Drug Administration.

> All day long the blazing midsummer sun beat down upon that square mile of abominations: upon tens of thousands of cattle crowded into pens whose

wooden floors stank and steamed contagion; upon bare, blistering, cinder-strewn railroad tracks and huge blocks of dingy meat factories, whose labyrinthine passages defied a breath of fresh air to penetrate them; and there are not merely rivers of hot blood and carloads of moist flesh, and rendering-vats and soup cauldrons, glue-factories and fertilizer tanks, that smelt like the craters of hell – there are also tons of garbage festering in the sun, and the greasy laundry of the workers hung out to dry and dining rooms littered with food black with flies, and toilet rooms that are open sewers.

(Sinclair 1906: 8)

Livestock leave (some) cities

The first half of the last century saw a striking decline in the number of productive animals in cities in North America, Europe and Australia. Some authors trace this de-urbanization of animals to attitudes emerging in the nineteenth century whereby animals were increasingly seen as "impure, polluting, disruptive, and discomforting occupants of city spaces" (Philo 1995). A belief which the quotation from Upton Sinclair suggests was not wholly unwarranted.

These developed country cities could throw off their agriculture because of the invention of fertilizers, refrigeration, and steam and motorized transport, which together created the modern food system. Agriculture became increasingly industrialized, large-scale, dependent on specialized and expensive inputs, and located far from urban consumers. In parallel, urban areas stopped being seen as spaces for food production (Bellows 2010), at least in the countries where agriculture intensified first.

Several well-documented case studies show how livestock left cities. Perhaps surprisingly, the temperance (no alcohol) movement had a major role in the de-urbanization of livestock in the United States. Feed has always been the most expensive input for intensive livestock keeping, and at the time, urban dairies were heavily dependent on by-products of city breweries and distilleries. Temperance leagues joined with physicians to campaign against filthy conditions of urban dairies and the resultant "white poison"; instead, they called for "pure country milk" to replace beer and gin (Shaftel 1978). These campaigns, along with the decline of the distillery industry, rising land values and 'standards of propriety', led to the expulsion of dairies from Brooklyn by the twentieth century (Tremante 2000).

Gaynor (2007) describes how livestock went from ever-present to almost-absent in Australia's cities. In 1895 metropolitan Sydney recorded no less than 8,246 sheep and goats, 7,318 dairy cows and 5,560 swine. By the late twentieth century, almost no productive animals remained. The decline resulted from an increasing intolerance to animals in residential areas, leading to zoning restrictions, prohibitive license fees and regulations that made keeping of livestock increasingly difficult. This was not an uncontested eviction and many people, especially women and the working class, resisted the re-imagining of cities as livestock free.

Many of the regulatory mechanisms to exclude livestock from cities were adopted by cities in Africa and Asia but their application was generally much less successful. A review of laws of southern Africa published in 1999 found that regulations on land use in urban areas were present in most countries but little enforced and corruption was regularly reported (Briscoe 1999). Although livestock were kept out of some residential and commercial areas, their presence was widely visible and indeed has been considered a characteristic of developing-country cities.

Livestock comeback

The eviction of livestock from cities, never total, was soon to prove transitory. The last 50 years have witnessed a remarkable resurgence of interest in urban agriculture, and with this keeping of livestock in cities. In Africa and Asia, where urban agriculture remained an important subsistence and economic activity, it was the focus for sporadic civic action and research from the 1960s on, but this failed to persuade international organizations or governments to take urban agriculture seriously (Lee-Smith 2010). But, around the same time, there was a blossoming of community farms in the UK, Europe, USA and Australia, probably linked to increasing environmental concerns and more leisure, and these movements had more influence in the policy arena.

As urban agriculture became popular, it started to attract the attention of development agencies and donors. In 1991 the United Nations Development Programme commissioned an assessment of the relatively unknown field of urban agriculture. Canada's International Development Research Centre (IDRC) later played a leading role in forging this new discipline. IDRC and other partners supported the creation of a key global network, the RUAF Foundation (International network of Resource centres on Urban Agriculture and Food security) (Mougeot 2011). The CGIAR launched a decade-long program on health and resource recovery dimensions of urban agriculture in selected cities.

In developed countries, attitudes and policies have gradually become more positive to urban agriculture. A survey of urban agriculture regulation in 16 US cities, including Washington, DC, Detroit and Boston found that most cities supported community gardens. Keeping chickens was permitted in many cities but fewer allowed keeping of other livestock or bees. Moreover, regulations regarding the keeping of animals were stricter than those for gardens and restrictions on where animals were kept and the number that could be kept were nearly always in place (Goldstein et al. 2011). In the UK, up to 50 household chickens can be kept without the need to register.

The same trends are seen in developing countries. The Food and Agriculture Organization of the United Nations (FAO) reports that in the past decade, governments in 20 countries have sought their assistance in removing barriers and providing incentives, inputs and training to low-income city farmers (FAO 2010).

But paradoxically, although developing-country cities were slower to eject livestock from cities, they have also been slower to accept them. A case study on urban policy-makers in Dharwad, India, observed that there was no official recognition of urban agriculture or policies to support it. Especially, urban livestock keeping was viewed by city officials as a major obstacle to fulfilling their responsibility of providing water and sanitation and the apex court had adopted regressive laws which ban 'stray' cattle and aims to phase out all cattle within cities of a population larger than 500,000 (Nunan 2000b).

Livestock in cities today

Why are livestock kept in and around cities?

In 2008, for the first time the majority of the world's population lived in cities, around one-third of them in informal settlements or slums. Over 90% of urbanization is occurring in poor countries and the urban population is expected to double from 3.3 billion in 2007 to 6.4 billion in 2050. Increasing urban populations create increasing demands for food products (Yeung 1988), as urbanization

FIGURE 10.1 Transporting live pigs by motorbike in Vietnam
Source: ILRI.

is associated with higher consumption of meat and other animal-source food products (Rae 1998; Delgado 2003) and greater reliance on ready-to-eat foods.

The massive increase in demand for livestock products over the past few decades has created equally significant opportunities for smallholders who raise animals to meet that demand (Herrero et al. 2010). In urbanized economies, there may be fewer opportunities for smallholder provision of livestock commodities; but this also varies, with smallholders being far more competitive, for example, in the dairy sector, but far less likely to prosper for monogastric production (Tarawali et al. 2011).

In many developing countries, transport infrastructure is inadequate and expensive and it is difficult or impossible to maintain a cold chain. Hence, growing demands for perishable products can best be met by nearby production: it is most efficient to produce milk and eggs and slaughter livestock for food as near to the point of consumption as possible (Schiere and Hoek 2001; Veenhuizen and Danso 2007). Figure 10.1 shows some of the challenges of transporting pigs without a cold chain in Vietnam and, partly as a result, 97% of the pork consumed in Vietnam is sold in wet markets. By bringing live pigs to cities, and reducing times between slaughter, sale and consumption, large amounts of pork can be cheaply delivered to millions of urban consumers (Fahrion et al. 2014).

In some countries, policy-makers have actively encouraged farming within city limits. In China, making cities self-sufficient in food is a policy objective. Within Beijing, intra-urban agriculture supplies 70% of non-staple food to city inhabitants (consisting mainly of milk and vegetables) (FAO 2011). In developed countries, livestock are often kept for reasons other than production or work: mainly leisure and community development.

Where are livestock kept in cities?

Animals can be kept almost anywhere in and around cities and towns. There is a tendency for livestock density to decrease as human density increases, and for livestock to be less present in slum and central business areas (Lindahl et al. 2012). However, this is not absolute. For example, a study in a Vietnamese city found that pig-farming can persist at even high human density and in many cities livestock may pass through highly populated areas, either providing transport or looking for food. In densely populated slums, livestock are less common and small stock, such as poultry and rabbits, which have minimal space requirement, predominate (Figure 10.2).

The suburbs and outer areas of cities typically have more space and available biomass for feeding animals. In these areas, dairies are common (Figure 10.3) and so are multi-species enterprises, which may include poultry, dogs, cats and rabbits. The specialized sheep- and goat-fattening systems, which are a feature of semiarid systems, are also typical of suburban farming.

Outside the city bounds there are often fewer regulations that restrict livestock keeping while access to the large city markets is still good. Unsurprisingly, peri-urban production is characterized by larger farms, more animals and a greater

FIGURE 10.2 Pigeons in Burkina Faso require little space or housing costs
Source: ILRI.

FIGURE 10.3 Peri-urban dairy in Bamako, Mali
Source: ILRI.

business orientation. Peri-urban production is predominantly based on pigs and poultry because these are most suited to intensive production. Commercial peri-urban production of livestock is an extremely fast-growing sector, representing 34% of total meat production and nearly 70% of egg production worldwide (FAO 1999).

The importance and character of urban livestock also vary by region:

- **Asia:** More than half of the world's urban population live in Asia, and more than 60% of them are estimated as poor (Mougeot 2005; Satterthwaite 2010). Urban livestock keeping includes rearing of dairy cattle and buffaloes, small ruminants (sheep, goat), pigs, poultry (chicken, ducks, turkey) and small animals like guinea pigs, rabbits and pigeons. They are reared in intensive systems or backyard, scavenging systems. As in other parts of the world, the species present in the urban livestock keeping are reflections of the species commonly kept and consumed in the area. Whereas India has a large number of urban dairy cows, Vietnam and China have higher proportions of urban pigs and Indonesia of poultry.
- **Africa:** Today, about 40% of the African population live in urban areas. Over the next four decades, Africa's urban population is likely to triple in size. In many cities of sub-Saharan Africa, slums account for three-quarters of urban residents. Studies show that livestock keeping is common in African cities and that smaller livestock (poultry, rabbits) are most common, but keeping of sheep and goats (called shoats in East Africa) and dairy cattle is also prevalent (Kang'ethe et al. 2007). Cities in South Africa have tended to have fewer livestock and those of West Africa the most (Heilig 2012).
- **South America:** Three-quarters of the population and half of the poor in Latin America live in cities (Fay 2005). Swine and poultry are the two more common species raised in urban areas in Latin America, although rabbits are becoming more popular. Guinea pigs have been historically domesticated and raised for food in the Andean region of South America. In the periphery of the cities, small ruminants in small to medium-size herds are common. These animals are walked to public lands for foraging during the day and brought back at night to be housed in patios adjacent to houses (Correa and Grace 2014).
- **Europe and North America:** In developed countries, livestock are often kept as part of community development or as a leisure enterprise. Livestock are kept in petting zoos, children's farms, rare breed farms, science museums and residential care homes for the disabled (LeJeune and Davis 2004). Currently, there are around 136 million international migrants living in developed countries, with numbers continuing to rise (OECD 2013). Many immigrants come from a rural background or developing-country cities where livestock keeping is ubiquitous and they often choose to keep city livestock in their new home.

Who keeps livestock in cities?

The rapid growth of cities has led to previously rural areas being incorporated in cities. Many of the original inhabitants were farmers, and have continued their occupation as cities engulfed them. At the same time, many poor people have left the countryside to seek new opportunities in cities, and brought their livestock or their habits of livestock keeping with them. Livestock keeping is widespread among poor people. Recent estimates suggest nearly 1 billion people living on less than two dollars a day are dependent to some extent on livestock (Staal et al. 2009), so it is not surprising that the influx of poor people to cities has led to increases in urban livestock keeping.

Livestock keeping in cities can be very profitable and has attracted entrepreneurs, sometimes with no background in livestock keeping. Many of these are young people with tertiary education but who cannot find jobs in the formal sector.

How common is livestock keeping in cities?

Obtaining accurate information about the extent of urban livestock keeping is not easy. The largest urban populations live in the informal settlements of rapidly growing cities in developing countries. But in these areas there is little reliable information on human demography, let alone animal populations; additionally, the ambiguous legal position of livestock keeping also hinders reporting.

Schiere et al. (2007) summarized some earlier studies and reports on livestock in cities: over one-third of households surveyed in Harare, Zimbabwe, kept chickens, rabbits, pigeons, ducks and turkeys. In Cairo, Egypt, 5% of households kept small animals like chickens and pigeons. Some 41% of the households in Hue City, Vietnam, had livestock and 80% of Dhaka's (Bangladesh) inhabitants kept animals. However, many of these earlier reports lacked sufficient rigour to accurately estimate livestock populations. Moreover, as livestock keeping in cities has long been controversial, estimates by interest groups are prone to an upwards or downwards bias. Box 10.1 describes a study, which overcame the challenges of gaining information of livestock in cities to develop an accurate estimate of actual numbers along with an estimate of uncertainty.

BOX 10.1   ESTIMATING THE NUMBER OF LIVESTOCK KEEPERS IN CITIES

As part of an IDRC supported study, the International Livestock Research Institute (ILRI) undertook the first statistically rigorous survey of livestock keeping in two cities in Nigeria. As there was no reliable census for households or livestock keepers, households were selected by random sampling from a spatial grid. Nearly 2,000 households were involved with 985 detailed questionnaires. In Ibadan and Kaduna, with a combined human population of approximately 1.7 million, around 2 million livestock are kept. Chicken predominated (1.7 million), and sheep and goats (shoats) were also common (200,000). Cattle were comparably infrequent (15,000), but around 200,000 from a wide range of niche species were kept (turkey, guinea fowl, quail, snail, grass-cutter, camel, etc.) Two-thirds of households reported keeping livestock on the compound in the last year. Poultry keeping was most common (46% of households), followed by small ruminants (31% of households), while cattle and pig keeping was rare (2% and 1%, respectively). Herd size was generally small, but a small number of households kept substantial numbers of animals (3% of households had more than 100 animals on the compound). Livestock contributed most to food (purchase or direct consumption) and to a lesser extent to general expenses, school fees and medical fees.

Source: ILRI project report.

In 2007, in India, the Ministry of Agriculture estimated there were 67 million livestock in Indian cities (6% of the total livestock in India) or one livestock for every five persons in cities (Singh et al. 2013). Numbers were dominated by poultry but cattle made up 85% of the livestock biomass. Numbers of poultry and cross-bred cattle were increasing rapidly and goats slowly: sheep, pigs, equids and indigenous cattle were declining. This implies the dairy and poultry, which can best supply rapidly increasing demand, are increasing while less-productive animals are declining and transport animals are being replaced by motor vehicles.

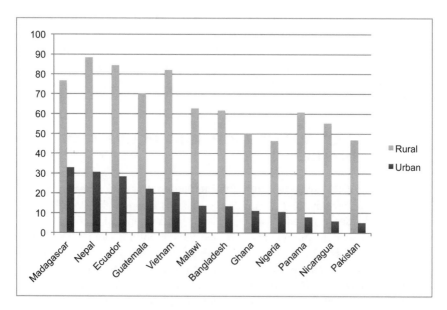

FIGURE 10.4 Livestock keeping by rural and urban households in 12 developing countries

Source: Data from Pica Ciamarra et al. 2011 (Image: ILRI).

A recent study provides solid information on livestock keeping in 12 other developing countries between the years 1995 and 2004 (Pica-ciamarra et al. 2011). Across the 12 countries, 65% of rural households and 17% of urban households kept livestock. If this proportion is extrapolated across the 2.5 billion people who currently live in developing-country cities, it implies there are 450 million people in urban livestock keeping households in poor countries. The study also found that, in cities, poor people were much more likely to keep livestock, whereas in rural areas, it was often the rich who had more and higher-value livestock. Although little information is available, it is probable that in developed countries a much lower proportion of households keep livestock. In developed countries, a far lower proportion of households keep livestock, although the trend has been upwards, probably less than 5%.

How are livestock kept in cities?

Livestock keeping in cities is highly diverse (Table 10.1). Systems may be categorized according to location (slum, urban, suburban, peri-urban); species (from guinea pigs to camels); farming system (intensive or semi-intensive predominate); production objective (food, money, draft power, financial services, assets and psychosocial well-being); and stage in the value chain (supplying young stock, males for breeding, livestock products).

Livestock as well as other animals are often kept for production or work. Most common are dogs and geese for guarding houses and compounds, and cats for pest control. In South East Asia, songbirds and fighting cocks are also common. In West and Central Africa, wild-caught deer and monkeys may be kept as curiosities. Table 10.1 summarizes some of the characteristics of urban livestock diversity.

In developing countries, the most common urban livestock keeping systems are backyard poultry, urban dairying, pig-keeping and fattening of sheep and goats.

Backyard poultry: Poultry are probably the most common type of livestock kept in urban areas. It is likely that poultry are present in all developing-country cities and towns in Africa, South Asia and South East Asia. A study from Kampala reveals a typical system. The household contained on average 8 persons and 17 local chickens. Women were most commonly in charge of chickens. The main reason for keeping poultry was income, and additional reasons were for food for the household and manure. Neighbours were positive about urban chicken production, 70% saying they benefited directly. One respondent stated, "Friendship is formed because chickens scavenge on my land" (Dimoulas et al. 2008). In India, large-scale poultry farms exist near every big city. In North America, poultry are the most commonly kept backyard livestock and seem to be increasing. A 2010 US Department of Agriculture study in four urban areas (Los Angeles, Denver, Miami and New York) found that 4% of the households planned to get chickens within the next five years, compared to less than 1% who had backyard poultry at the time of the survey (USDA 2013).

TABLE 10.1 Typologies of urban livestock keeping diversity

Diversity in scale	Diversity in species	Diversity in management
Small-scale predominates but medium- and even large-scale are found. In Nairobi, a crowded city with a population of 2 million, there are 1,350 commercial pig and poultry farms linked to national chains. Farmers with 3,000 birds or 50 breeding sows can earn USD $1,000 per month.	Small stock (poultry, sheep and goats) predominate but dairying and feedlots are found in most cities. Niche and unusual species are common. These include rabbits, snails, grass–cutters (greater cane rat), cattle, dogs and even camels. Often, a mix of species is kept.	Backyard systems where animals are confined to premises but allowed to roam freely for part of the day are most common. Permanent housing (zero-grazing) is a high input, high output system. The poorest often let animals scavenge freely or illegally use common spaces (roadsides, open areas, rubbish heaps).
Diversity in production objective	Diversity in input level and capitalization	Diversity in farmers
Unlike other urban agricultural activities, production for sale is usually the most important objective. Self-consumption usually ranks second. Other functions are: - Financial - Converting by-products - Social (status, presents) - Pleasure (the enjoyment of living things, hobby)	Businesses generating high profits such as dairying and fattening male sheep for Ramadan and Eid are usually high input. Most livestock kept by the poor are in low external input systems.	Women have a high involvement in livestock keeping. The poor have a high involvement. The poor generally keep a wider mix of lower-value animals (indigenous species and small stock) than do richer farmers.

Sources: based on UNDP 1996; Waters-Bayer 1996; Schiere and van der Hoek 2001; Schiere et al. 2007.

Dairying: Dairying is probably the second most important urban livestock system. It is common in cities and towns inhabited by milk-drinking cultures. These are mainly found in East Africa (especially Kenya and Ethiopia), Sahelian cities of West Africa and South Asia. Studies in Nairobi and Addis found one in 100 urban households kept cattle and in Indian cities there was one bovine for every 20 persons. These cultures have rich traditions around cattle.

There are also emerging dairies in cities without a tradition of milk-drinking, such as South East Asia. These are much less numerous and, in some cases, interesting new systems have evolved. A study in Greater Beijing found that approximately one-quarter (26%) of farmers checked into cow hotels after the Milk Scandal, increasing from 2% before the crisis (Mo et al. 2012).

Pig-keeping: Urban pig-keeping is most common in South East Asia and North East India. Pork-China is often compared to Dairy-India, because pork has the same central role in China as dairy products do in India. Pigs are reared near and inside every city of China. Estimates suggest around 500 million pigs are kept, with 60% in intensive systems which are generally urban or peri-urban. In the Philippines, 30% of pigs are kept in commercial herds and 65% of these are near the major urban market of Metro Manila (one pig per three persons).

Small ruminant-fattening: Sheep- and goat-fattening is common in towns and cities of arid and semiarid regions of West and East Africa and the Middle East. In these systems, sheep and goats are born in rural areas and reared in extensive, low-input systems and then taken to cities for intensive fattening before slaughter. However, free range sheep and goats are found at lower densities in Asia and southern Africa. In the Sahel and Middle East, fattening is linked to the Islamic festival of Eid-al-Kabir (Tabas ki) (Ayantunde et al. 2008). In Ethiopia, it is common to see sheep and goats in urban areas, including the capital, Addis Ababa. Feed resources are usually household wastes, market area wastes, mill leftovers, by-products and roadside grazing (particularly in the peri-urban system (Abegaz et al. 2002)).

What other activities do urban livestock keeping necessitate?

The entire livestock value chain is compressed into urban areas. Figure 10.5 shows some of the different stakeholders involved in the urban livestock chain. These include:

- Input suppliers: Feed, fodder, housing material, equipment, drugs, animals, utilities.
- Service suppliers: Extension, health and breeding advice.
- Producers: Ranging from small to large scale.
- Transporters: Inputs, animals, livestock products.
- Processors: Abattoirs, dairy cooperatives, food processing.
- Retail: Door-to-door hawkers, street sellers, kiosks, milk bars, restaurants, shops, supermarkets.
- Consumers: household, institutions (schools, hospitals), restaurant consumers.

All of these stakeholders are present in many or most developing-country cities. In the developed world, large-scale processing operations (abattoirs, dairy cooperatives) and larger farms have been mainly moved outside cities. In some developing countries there has been a dramatic increase in farmers' markets. According to USDA-AMS-Marketing Services Division, in the USA, the number of markets nearly doubled from 5,000 in 2008 to 8,144 in 2013. These typically sell livestock products, but not live animals.

Live animal markets: Live animal markets for cattle, sheep and goat are often found in, or close to, cities. These are often referred to as terminal or tertiary markets, as large numbers of animals are brought from smaller markets or other countries for distribution or sale. In many cases animals are sold to butchers for slaughter, but other animals may be bought for fattening, breeding or work. For example, the Niamana market in Bamako, Mali, is the largest in the country. Around 25,000 animals are sold each month. Live markets are dominated by cattle,

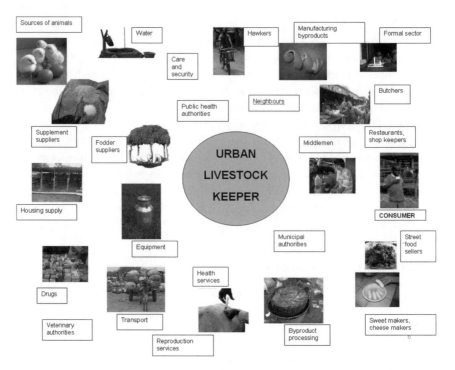

FIGURE 10.5 Different stakeholders involved in providing inputs to and taking up products from urban livestock keepers
Source: ILRI.

sheep and goats. Pigs are typically sold from the farm to the butcher or slaughterhouse, and poultry and eggs are sold alongside other perishable products in wet markets.

Slaughterhouses: Many of the cattle, goats and sheep bought in terminal markets will be slaughtered in urban abattoirs. Urban slaughterhouses have typically poor conditions but the lack of a cold chain makes it imperative that animals are killed close to the point of consumption. For example, a typical abattoir in a West African city may kill 300–400 animals a day. Slaughter is done without stunning on a concrete slab. The lack of infrastructure leads to filthy and unpleasant conditions. Many animals are not inspected and even when problems are found veterinarians find it difficult to ensure condemned meat is discarded. If an animal is condemned by veterinarians as unfit for human consumption, middlemen lose their entire days' earnings, so they strongly resist attempts to condemn meat.

Wet markets: Most of the livestock products produced in and outside developing-country cities is sold in wet markets. These exist in many different forms across Africa and Asia but have common characteristics: food escapes effective health and safety regulation; many retailers do not pay tax and some are not licensed;

traditional processing, products and retail practices predominate; infrastructure, including water, electricity, sanitation and refrigeration, is lacking; and little support is provided from the public or the non-governmental sector. Unsurprisingly, women and the poor have much greater involvement in informal markets. In addition to their meat and eggs, poultry and rabbits, animals are most commonly sold live to be slaughtered in the household or by the producer of ready-to-eat food.

Hawkers and retailers: Eggs and dairy products are often sold directly to neighbours: a very short value chain. In addition, traders may buy eggs and milk to sell directly to consumers or to other users. Especially in India, hawkers often have an established round whereby they deliver milk direct to the doorstep. Figure 10.5 illustrates some of the different ways peri-urban milk makes its way to consumers in India.

Street food: Many livestock products end up as street food (FAO/WHO 2005). Street food is a source of inexpensive, convenient and nutritious food and is especially important for the poor, who lack resources to prepare meals at home (Riet et al. 2001). In Ghana, for example, a study found that among the poorest quintile almost 40% of the total food budget goes to purchasing street food, compared to just 2% in high-income households (Maxwell et al. 2000). Lower-cost livestock products are popular types of street food. In Kenya, vendors sell sausages as a franchise business. In South Africa, 'walky talkies' are chicken feet and heads sold ready cooked. In most African countries, the majority of street-food processors and vendors are women (Canet and N'Diaye 1996), while the majority of customers are men (Nago 2005), and animal source food is often sold alongside alcohol in roadside eateries (the pork joints of Uganda, pubs in Tanzania and dietaries in Senegal).

Benefits and risks associated with urban livestock keeping

Food and nutrition security

Urban livestock keeping contributes directly to food security by providing food for consumption and contributes indirectly to food security by providing income to buy food. Animal-source foods (ASF) are nutritionally dense sources of energy, protein and essential micronutrients. Micronutrients tend to be more bio-available in animal-source foods, and some, such as vitamin B12, are found naturally only in animal-source foods (Smith et al. 2013).

Cross-country evidence consistently shows children in urban areas are better nourished than those in rural areas. For example, in 82 out of 95 developing countries for which evidence is available, the proportion of underweight children is less in urban areas (UNICEF 2013). Moreover, livestock products benefit not just the poor but also middle-income households, who prefer fresh products and pay a premium for fresh milk (Nunan 2000b).

Yet, despite the obvious connection between producing food and consuming food, recent reviews agree that there is little evidence that farming benefits nutrition (Leroy et al. 2008; Webb et al. 2008). This is partly because many evaluations of agricultural interventions have not looked at nutritional outcomes, but it is also possible that direct access to livestock products is offset by the need to obtain income. For example, experience from India shows that poorer households keeping buffaloes sell more of the milk produced and keep back less for home consumption (Nunan 2000b).

Income, assets and financial instruments

Production and processing of livestock may be the main or a subsidiary source of livelihood. Animals contribute to income sources in a household and, therefore, agriculture improves the ability to spread livelihood risks in a largely informal economy where the majority of the urban poor are daily-wage earners (Lupindu et al. 2012). Employment in intensive urban-rearing systems also forms a ready poverty alleviation pathway for those who are recently migrated from rural agricultural systems.

In countries with poor performing financial markets and weak credit systems, livestock act as savings, insurance and collateral. They are critical assets available even to disadvantaged groups that are not entertained by the formal credit suppliers. They reduce vulnerability of households to unplanned expenditures and act as collateral for quick loans (Randolph et al. 2007).

There are few formal studies on the economics of urban livestock keeping, with most studies on nutrition and livelihood benefits or health impacts.

Health impacts

By providing nutritious foods and by generating income that can be used for health care, urban livestock keeping makes important although indirect contributions to health. Negative impacts of overconsumption of ASF are increasingly contributing to chronic diseases, such as cardiac disease, even in developing nations plagued by malnutrition (Randolph et al. 2007).

A direct health advantage of urban livestock keeping is zooprophylaxis, or the reduction of transmission of diseases by using animals to attract disease-transmitting insects away from people. Recommended by the WHO as a management strategy for malaria since 1982, it has been found to be effective if (but only if) epidemiological factors are favourable. For example, pigs have been associated with a greater risk of Japanese encephalitis viral transmission in urban areas, but the presence of livestock like cattle may be a protection as they divert mosquitoes away from human beings or pigs by providing alternative food sources (Lindahl et al. 2012).

However, urban livestock keeping is also an important source of health risks in the urban environment. These may be categorized as occupational risks encountered by people working in livestock value chains and public health risks that affect the wider urban population.

Occupational hazards include:

- Mechanical injuries and ergonomic morbidity resulting from close proximity to animals as well as repetitive tasks associated with urban livestock keeping often carried out in confined spaces.
- Bio aerosols include biological agents, endotoxins, gaseous irritants as well as allergenic factors like dust, fungi and mites. This increases the risk for immunotoxic occupational diseases of the respiratory organ (bronchitis, occupational asthma and inflammation of the mucous membrane), especially in vulnerable groups such as children and the elderly, as well as manure handlers and poultry farm workers (Myers 2011).
- Biological agents include viruses, bacteria, fungi, microbial toxins and various particles of plant and animal origin. Many of these include zoonotic diseases. Value chain actors other than farmers are also susceptible, especially abattoir workers. Exposure to *Brucella* was found to be 22% among abattoir workers in Abbottabad, Pakistan, and as high as 35% in endemic regions in Saudi Arabia (Mukhtar and Kokab 2008).
- Bacterial resistance factors may be more common in the micro-flora of urban animals as antimicrobial agents are more accessible, and may be more used. These can transfer to humans. It is also interesting to note study findings that have identified resistant bacteria in the nasal, throat and faecal microflora of pig farmers (Aubry-Damon et al. 2004).
- Chemicals are often used in urban livestock keeping including pesticides, fungicides, antibiotics, and cleaning and disinfection agents. In addition, water used in urban livestock keeping may include agricultural or industrial chemicals.
- Allergens produced by microscopic fungi pose an occupational hazard (Dutkiewicz et al. 2011).

Close proximity to livestock and waste management practices create not only zoonotic risk to livestock keepers but also public health risk to urban populations. These diseases can be categorized by their transmission routes:

- **Direct transmission:** Crowding and high density of population constitute a contributing factor in direct transmission of pathogens where pigs, poultry and livestock act as intermediary hosts (De Haan 2013).
- **Vector-borne:** Cities without a proper sewage and waste disposal system favour vectors such as mosquitoes and rodents that transmit malaria, and viral diseases like dengue, Rift Valley fever, Hanta virus and West Nile Virus (Baumgartner and Belevi 2001). A study in Can Tho City, Vietnam, showed that urban pig-rearing increased the number of mosquitoes competent as vectors for JEV (Lindahl et al. 2012).
- **Water-borne:** In addition to vector-borne diseases, open sewage and untreated urban waste also aid in transmission of zoonotic parasitism. Important waterborne zoonoses include salmonellosis and cryptosporidiosis.

- **Urine-borne:** Diseases like leptospirosis are re-emerging as a public health problem in urban centres. This is attributed to increased exposure of humans, especially children to playgrounds, and recreational spaces contaminated with the urine of reservoir hosts (Dutkiewicz et al. 2011).
- **Food-borne:** There is evidence from major cities in Nigeria, India, Brazil and Saudi Arabia on human brucellosis infection and echinococcosis transmitted by domestic livestock through food (Satterthwaite et al. 2010). Brucellosis can spread to humans by drinking unpasteurized milk. Food-borne pathogens not only cause active infections or toxin-related symptoms, but also endanger intrauterine foetuses (Listeria and Toxoplasma) causing death or serious malformations (Birley and Lock 1998).

In addition to zoonotic diseases, urban livestock keeping can threaten human health by antibiotic resistance and exposing people to agro-chemicals and livestock waste.

- Emergence of antibiotic resistance has been linked to the higher disease burden and higher production costs in urban farms. These drive farmers to over-use antibiotics. Leaching, improper waste disposal and contaminated animal faeces can introduce these antibiotic-resistant pathogens into the food chain. Antibiotic resistance in human pathogens may also result when people eat products that contain high residues (Birley and Lock 1998).
- Chronic illness has also been associated with agro-chemicals in the food chain in urban ecosystems (Birley and Lock 1998).
- Livestock waste generates as many as 60 volatile and non-volatile compounds. This can cause nausea, headaches, breathing problems, sleep interruption, appetite loss and irritation of the eyes, ears and throat. The urban poor, residing closer to open dumps, appear to be more exposed to this environment.

Increased animal transportation increases the spread and distribution of disease pathogens. This transitioning epidemiology is further influenced by persisting rural and pastoral practices in urban areas (Flynn 1999). As mentioned earlier, pastoral practices like open grazing, and scavenging practised for ruminants, poultry and pigs magnify the zoonotic risk in crowded urban and peri-urban spaces. One example is the increased prevalence of echinococcosis. What was essentially a rural disease is fast establishing itself as an urban menace. Despite a lower prevalence in urban canine population when compared to rural population, risk of transmission to humans is higher in urban areas due to greater human–animal contact. This situation is further aggravated in policy environments where food security takes precedence over food safety (Randolph et al. 2007). The non-adaptation of husbandry practices in response to urbanization and related changes increases the risk of urban population to zoonoses.

FIGURE 10.6 Urban food is often prepared under unsanitary conditions
Source: ILRI.

Direct environmental impacts

Urban livestock keeping can contribute to the reuse of urban solid and liquid waste. Easy and cheap access to by-products of the food processing industry (bran, oilseed cakes), hotel refuse and kitchen waste in urban spaces is one of the main reasons why urban livestock keeping flourishes and remains profitable in urban ecosystems. Along with better management of urban waste, organic manure from the livestock industry helps in maintaining soil fertility for gardens and recreational spaces (Randolph et al. 2007).

However, urban waste is considered one of the most serious and pressing urban environmental problems, and urban livestock keeping contributes to this. Abattoir effluent containing blood, fat, solid waste (intestines, hair, horns, etc.) and rumen content are often discharged into nearby rivers and reused for crop irrigation and as drinking water for cattle. Dumping solid wastes from livestock production or abattoirs is common. Nitrates from feedlots percolate to groundwater, and runoff into water sources is said to contribute to water contamination. Urban livestock keeping increases the competition for resources such as water and land. This can exacerbate prevailing shortages for household and industrial use.

Environmental impacts can be mitigated if farms in peri-urban spaces can develop better waste management practices. Some farmers generate a substantial part of their income from the sale of organic waste. Other farmers install biogas plants or dry manure for direct usage as cooking fuel (Ishagi et al. 2002). The latter use is less beneficial as biomass fuels form the largest source of indoor air pollution, causing acute respiratory disease in children and chronic obstructive lung disease in adults (Birley and Lock 1998).

Greenhouse gases and contribution to global warming

Ruminant livestock are a major contributor (18%) of global anthropogenic green-house gas emissions (Gill et al. 2010), and may cause up to 2% of global warming in the next 50 to 100 years (Johnson and Johnson 1995). The negative impact of global warming is also felt by peri-urban farmers through major floods and landslides as well as degradation of grazing land (Deka et al. 2009).

However, intensification of livestock can reduce the emission of methane and other greenhouse gases per unit weight of livestock product produced, as intensive agriculture produces more outputs per animal. In developing countries, most intensive livestock systems are urban or peri-urban. For example, 80% of the Chinese operations related to large intensive livestock are located around Beijing and Shanghai. Similarly, almost all intensive pig farms in Kenya are located around Nairobi (Burney et al. 2010; De Haan 2013; Havlík et al. 2014). Urban agriculture also reduces carbon footprint of cities by reducing the traffic flow of food and manure from distant rural areas and by substituting non-renewable fuels with biogas or biomass (Nunan 2000b).

Equity

Overall, men have more ownership of livestock and their products. Typically, men have ownership and responsibility for larger and more valuable animals, and as farms become more intensive and highly capitalized, male participation tends to increase. In backyard farms, women and children are often responsible for care-giving tasks (feeding and cleaning), thus making them more prone to health risks from occupational exposure. However, smaller ruminants and poultry are women's most important assets and income (Niamir–Fuller 1994; Deka et al. 2009; Smith et al. 2013). In addition, women are often involved in dairying, traditional processing of foods, and foods in wet markets and streets.

In rural areas, livestock keeping tends to increase with wealth but in cities the reverse is the case and the poor keep more livestock. In general, urbanization is often associated with worsening equity. For example, poor children in urban areas are at up to ten times higher risk for childhood stunting than the wealthiest group, differences which are not so marked in rural areas (Menon et al. 2000; Smith and Aduayom 2003). Urban livestock keeping could help improve nutritional and income equity in urban areas.

Social impacts

Urban livestock keeping also aids in increasing social cohesion and improving the social position of farmers in urban communities. Urban farmers in India sell milk directly to hotels and households in exchange for kitchen waste. Some farmers milk their cows in front of consumers to assure clean and unadulterated produce (Nunan 2000a). Trust in the community improves social security of farmers and aids social cohesion. In low-income urban districts of Bissau, urban farmers contribute to community welfare and funeral groups and gift their home produce as a reciprocation of social support, especially in times of distress and natural calamity (Mougeot 2000).

However, urban livestock value chain actors can be in conflict amongst themselves as well as with other groups such as non-rearing neighbours and civic authorities. In cities with shortage of water resources, livestock farmers compete with other industries for these resources and thus may face a hostile neighbourhood. Livestock farmers have been in conflict with non-rearing neighbours on the detrimental effect of the surrounding aesthetics caused by organic waste and pests. While farmers following the intensive system of rearing have conflicts regarding waste disposal, those involved in backyard farming and scavenging system can have conflicts associated with damage to neighbourhood gardens, theft, accidents on road traffic as well as injury from aggressive livestock (Ishagi et al. 2002). A study in Nigeria found that urban farmers suffered higher losses from pilfering of livestock than from rural farmers. Moreover, they were more likely to report emotional distress and discouragement as a result of pilfering (Anongoku et al. 2008).

Municipal authorities and public health researchers often see urban livestock keeping as a public health risk, pollution hazard and an impingement on urban aesthetics. Since urban agriculture is taken up usually by the urban poor and vulnerable groups, they lack a supporter or champion for urban agriculture in the policy space. Legislation and law enforcement therefore work against urban and peri-urban livestock keeping (Flynn 1999; Ishagi et al. 2002; De Haan 2013).

Maximizing the benefits and minimizing the risks of urban livestock keeping

The fact that most studies of hazards in urban livestock keeping find the presence of high levels of hazards demonstrates that current risk management is not very effective. Indeed command- and control-based regulation may actually make things worse. A study in Kampala found that dairy farmers who had more harassment from public authorities had fewer good practices (Grace et al. 2012).

When tackling hazards in urban livestock keeping, the best way can be the enemy of the good. For example, in Lusaka, Zambia, street sellers were moved to a new ultra–modern market funded by a USD $3 million grant from the European Union. The process involved careful consultation with vendors and other stake-holders. Yet many vendors returned to selling on the streets as they found they made more money by being closer to consumers (Ndhlovu 2011). During the bird flu epidemic, there were many attempts to close or upgrade wet markets. However, most were unsuccessful in improving hygiene or they covered only a tiny proportion of birds sold.

Approaches based on working with the existing situation and gradually improv-ing it have been more successful. A well-documented initiative working with butchers in wet markets of Ibadan used positive deviants and peer-to-peer training. This led to 20% more meat samples meeting standards and cost USD $9 per butcher but resulted in saving USD $780 per butcher per year from reduced cost of human illness (Grace et al. 2012). This resulted in a very attractive benefit cost ratio of $87 benefit for every $1 invested.

In Kenya, authorities moved from harassing the informal milk vendors who distributed more than 80% of the milk consumed in Kenya, to supporting them. This included training on hygienic milk production and business management; provision of better technologies such as milk cans; and providing a license and certificate. The change in policy is shown to have improved the safety of milk and saved the Kenyan economy USD $26 million a year by lowering the cost of providing milk to consumers.

Effective strategies for risk mitigation include: education of farmers on hazards and prevention; quality labelling of products (Fall et al. 2001); education of con-sumers on hygiene (Sheth and Obrah 2004); animal health programmes to reduce the double burden of zoonoses (Lopetegui 2004); pollution assessment and zoning of areas (Kucharski et al. 1994); monitoring of fresh urban solid–waste treated soil and crops (Rao and Shantaram 1995); composting methods and variable sorting to control chemical and microbiological agents ('t Hart and Pluimers 1996); and programmes to eliminate schistosomiasis and occupational risks in freshwater fish farming (McCollough 1990). A project on the risks of livestock keeping in Nai-robi, Kenya (Box 10.2), provides an example of a rational and effective approach to health risks associated with urban livestock.

BOX 10.2 SYSTEMATIC AND RISK-BASED APPROACHES TO MANAGING HEALTH HAZARDS IN URBAN DAIRYING IN NAIROBI.

With the objective of assessing and minimizing the risks of diseases spread from urban dairies, the project team applied an 'ecohealth' approach to its study. A multidisciplinary team was formed, which started by surveying and understanding dairying in Dagoretti, a district of Nairobi. Next, a systematic risk assessment was undertaken which covered a range of hazards: aflatoxins, brucellosis, cryptosporidiosis, brucellosis, coliosis, tuberculosis and antimicrobial residues. The study also looked at social and gender determinants of health. This identified cryptosporidiosis as the issue of greatest concern to be tackled first (on the grounds of its unexpectedly high prevalence, its emerging nature, and its riskiness to children and people living with HIV). The team of professionals, policy-makers and Dagoretti residents developed targeted messages for each high-risk group. They identified practices that were both good and uncommon and so had high potential for being more widely adopted. They incorporated social incentives (such as the desire to be seen as good parents) to help motivate behaviour change. The communication strategy included workshops, community champions, brochures and a television episode, and it involved policy-makers. Surveys showed a significant improvement in knowledge and practice and a reduction in the risk of cryptosporidiosis and other pathogens transmitted through the faecal route. The research findings were published in 17 multidisciplinary papers in two special editions (*East African Medical Journal* and *Tropical Animal Health and Production*).

Source: Kang'ethe et al. 2012.

Conclusions

Much attention has been paid to the role of urban livestock keeping in maintaining and transmitting diseases and contaminating the environment but little to the role of urban livestock keeping in supporting livelihoods and nutrition. Urban livestock keeping supplies livestock products for household consumption and sale. The informal markets where most urban farmers sell their products offer benefits to poor farmers, traders and consumers. They often sell food at lower prices than the formal sector and the food sold often has other desired attributes including freshness, preferred taste and convenience, and the food originates from local breeds.

Because of the perishable nature of livestock products, there are strong incentives to produce livestock for city markets in cities and their surroundings. However, city farming is often banned or restricted by city by-laws. Considered to be dirty, smelly, noisy, disruptive, disease-ridden and a symptom of backwardness, city livestock are ignored or underestimated in official records. In Mexico City, authorities denied that pigs were kept on urban rooftops until they were dislodged by an earthquake and found walking the streets. By-laws are often based on precedent or on arbitrary decisions and rarely on evidence or logic. For example, in Tanzania it is legal to keep four cows in urban areas but illegal to keep five. Much of the opposition to keeping livestock in cities and selling livestock products in informal markets is based on the strongly held but poorly evidenced belief that city livestock and their products are a risk to human health.

Undoubtedly hazards can be found in urban livestock and their products, but this is also true for the rural counterparts. As a rule of thumb, most studies that look for hazards find them. Food-borne illnesses and animal diseases are of growing concern to consumers and policy-makers alike. Consumers respond to scares by stopping or reducing purchases with knock-on effects on smallholder production and wet market retail. Policy-makers often respond to perceived health risks by favouring industrialization and reducing smallholder access to markets. These changes are often based on fear and not on facts. Without evidence of the risk to human health posed by informally marketed foods or the best way to manage risks while retaining benefits, the food eaten in poor countries is neither safe nor fair (Grace 2011).

Urban and peri-urban livestock also plays an important, and in some cases increasing, role in supporting livelihoods and nutrition. Recent studies suggest there are 450 million people in urban livestock keeping homes and most of the 2.5 billion people who live in developing-country cities depend on urban live animal markets, wet markets, slaughterhouses and vendors to obtain their animal sources of food.

Although the potential harm of urban livestock keeping is well documented, there is surprisingly little evidence on quantified impacts (e.g., the number of people who fall sick from eating street food) or the relative importance of the risks versus the benefits of urban livestock keeping (which have been much less well documented). Better evidence is needed on the costs and benefits of urban livestock keeping to help decision makers and others to identify its most appropriate role. Encouragingly, the last decade has given many examples of how risks can be mitigated and livestock can contribute to a green and resilient urban environment. This offers a roadmap for future development of urban livestock keeping.

Keeping of animals has always been part of the city, and a link between the countryside and cities. After decades of neglect, urban livestock keeping is back on the development and political agendas. Urban livestock keeping has always been vulnerable to fears around disease and environmental contamination; fortunately, we now have the evidence and tools to ensure that it is not only productive and profitable but can be safe, fair and environmentally friendly.

Note

This work was carried out with the aid of a grant from the International Development Research Centre, Ottawa, Canada.

References

Abegaz, K.; Beyene, F.; Langsrud, T.; Narvhus, J. A. 2002. Parameters of processing and microbial changes during fermentation of borde, a traditional Ethiopian beverage. *The Journal of Food Technology in Africa* 7(3): 85–92.

Anongoku, C. P.; Obinne, O.; Daudu, S. 2008. A socio-economic analysis of livestock pilferage in rural and urban areas of Benue State, Nigeria. *Journal of Social Sciences* 17(2): 169–172.

Aubry-Damon, H.; Grenet, K.; Sall-Ndiaye, P.; Che, D.; Cordeiro, E.; Bougnoux, M. E.; Rigaud, E.; Le Strat, Y.; Lemanissier, V.; Armand-Lefèvre, L.; Delzescaux, D.; Desenclos, J. C.; Liénard, M.; Andremont, A. 2004. Antimicrobial resistance in commensal flora of pig farmers. *Emerging Infectous Diseases* 10(5): 873–879.

Ayantunde, A. A.; Fernandez-Rivera, S.; Hiernaux, P. H.; Tabo, R. 2008. Botanical knowledge and its differentiation by age, gender and ethnicity in south-western Niger. *Human Ecology* 36(6): 881–889.

Baumgartner, B.; Belevi, H. 2001. A systematic overview of urban agriculture in developing countries. Dubendorf: EAWAG-SANDEC.

Bellows, A. C. 2010. On the past and the future of the urban agriculture movement: Reflections in tribute to Jac Smit A. *Journal of Agriculture, Food Systems, and Community Development* 1(2): 17–39.

Birley, M. H.; Lock, K. 1998. Health and peri-urban natural resource production. *Environment and Urbanization* 10(1): 89–106.

Bollongino, R.; Burger, J.; Powell, J.; Mashkour, M.; Vigne, J.-D.; Thomas, M. G. 2012. Modern taurine cattle descended from small number of near-eastern founders. *Molecular Biology and Evolution* 29(9): 2101–2104.

Briscoe, A. 1999. Review of business licensing laws of Southern Africa: Report prepared for the SEPAC Working Group Policy Issues. Gaborone: Friedrich Ebert Stiftung.

Burney, J. A.; Davis, S. J.; Lobell, D. B. 2010. Greenhouse gas mitigation by agricultural intensification. *Proceedings of the National Academy of Sciences of the United States of America* 107(26): 12052–12057.

Canet, C.; N'Diaye, C. 1996. Street foods in Africa. *Food Nutrition and Agriculture* 17(18): 4–13.

Correa, R. G.; Tergaonkar, V.; Ng, J. K.; Dubova, I.; Izpisua-Belmonte, J. C.; Verma, I. M. 2004. Characterization of NF-kappa B/I kappa B proteins in zebra fish and their involvement in notochord development. *Molecular and Cellular Biology* 24(12): 5257–5268.

Deka, R.; Bin Qutub, A.; Barburah, I.; Omore, A.; Staal, A.; Grace, D. 2009. Mission impossible? Pro-poor innovation that is socially equitable, gender fair, and environment-friendly. Paper presented at the Innovation Asia-Pacific Symposium held at Kathmandu, Nepal, 4–7 May 2009. Nairobi: ILRI. Available from: www.prolinnova.net/iaps/media/21.

Delgado, C. L. 2003. Rising consumption of meat and milk in developing countries has created a new food revolution. *The Journal of Nutrition* 133(11): 3907S–3910S.

Dimoulas, P.; Waltner-Toews, D.; Humphries, S.; Nasinyama, G. 2008. Household risk factors associated with chicken rearing and food consumption in Kampala. In: *Healthy City Harvests: Generating Evidence to Guide Policy on Urban Agriculture.* (Eds.) Cole, D.; Lee-Smith, D.; Nasinyama, P. Lima: CIP and Makarere University Press, pp. 177–191.

Dutkiewicz, J.; Cisak, E.; Sroka, J.; Wójcik-Fatla, A.; Zając, V. 2011. Biological agents as occupational hazards: Selected issues. *Annals of Agricultural and Environmental Medicine* 18(2): 286–293.

Fahrion, A. S.; Jamir, J.; Richa, K.; Begum, S.; Rutsa, V.; Ao, S.; Padmakumar, V. P.; Pratim Deka, R., Grace, D. 2014. Food-safety hazards in the pork chain in Nagaland, North East India: Implications for human health. *International Journal of Environmental Research and Public Health* 11(1): 403–17.

Fall, A.; Guèye, O.; Ba, E.H.M. 2001. The network approach: The production consumption chain in Senegal. *Urban Agriculture Magazine* 5: 36.

FAO. 1999. Spotlight issues in urban agriculture: Studies suggest that up to two-thirds of city and peri-urban households are involved in farming. Rome: Food and Agriculture Organization of the United Nations (FAO). Available from: www.fao.org/ag/magazine/9901sp2.htm.

FAO. 2010. Growing greener cities. Rome: Food and Agriculture Organisation of the United Nations (FAO). Available at: www.fao.org/ag/agp/greenercities/pdf/ggc-en.pdf.

FAO. 2011. Livestock and global food security. Rome: Food and Agriculture Organisation of the United Nations.

FAO/WHO. 2005. FAO/WHO guidance to governments on the application of HACCP in small and less-developed food businesses. Rome: Food and Agriculture Organization of the United Nations (FAO).

Fay, M. 2005. The urban poor in Latin America. Washington, DC: The World Bank.

Flynn, K. 1999. Overview of public health and urban agriculture: Water, soil and crop contamination and emerging urban zoonoses. Ottawa: International Development Research Centre (IDRC). Available from: http://idl-bnc.idrc.ca/dspace/handle/10625/32952.

Gaynor, A. 2007. Animal agendas: Conflict over productive animals in twentieth-century Australian cities. *Society & Animals* 15(1): 29–42.

Gill, M.; Smith, P.; Wilkinson, J. M. 2010. Mitigating climate change: The role of domestic livestock. *Animal* 4(3): 323–333.

Goldstein, A. L.; Wekerle, C.; Tonmyr, L.; Thornton, T.; Waechter, R.; Pereira, J.; Chung, R. 2011. The relationship between post-traumatic stress symptoms and substance use among adolescents involved with child welfare: Implications for emerging adulthood. *International Journal of Mental Health and Addiction* 9(5): 507–524.

Grace, D. 2011. Agriculture-associated diseases research at ILRI: Safe foods in informal markets. Livestock Exchange Issue Brief 11. Nairobi: International Livestock Research Institute (ILRI). Available from: http://cgspace.cgiar.org/handle/10568/10626.

Grace, D.; Mutua, F.; Ochungo, P.; Kruska, R.; Jones, K.; Brierley, L.; Lapar, L.; Said, M.; Herrero, M.; Phuc, P. M.; Thao, N. B.; Akuku, I.; Ogutu, F. 2012. Mapping of poverty and likely zoonoses hotspots. Report to the UK Department for International Development. Nairobi: ILRI. Available from: http://dspacetest.cgiar.org/handle/10568/21161.

Gutkind, P.C.W. 1963. The royal capital of Buganda: A study of internal conflict and external ambiguity. The Hague: Mouton.

De Haan, C. 2013. Urbanization and farm size changes in Africa and Asia: Implications for livestock research. Paper prepared for the Foresight study on Urbanization and Farm Size by the Independent Science and Partnership Council (ISCP). Available from: www.sciencecouncil.cgiar.org/fileadmin/templates/ispc/documents/Strategy_and_Trends/2013/Foresight.deHaan.pdf.

't Hart, D.; Pluimers, J. 1996. Wasted agriculture: The use of compost in urban agriculture. Gouda: WASTE. Available from: www.globenet.org/preceup/pages/fr/chapitre/reflreco/reflex/asptech/a.htm.

Havlík, P.; Valin, H.; Herrero, M.; Obersteiner, M.; Schmid, E.; Rufino, M. C.; Mosnier, A.; Thornton, P. K.; Böttcher, H.; Conant, R. T.; Frank, S.; Fritz, S.; Fuss, S.; Kraxner, F.; Notenbaert, A. 2014. Climate change mitigation through livestock system transitions. *Proceedings of the National Academy of Sciences of the United States of America* 111(10): 3709–3714.

Heilig, G. 2012. World urbanization prospects the 2011 revision. Presentation at the Center for Strategic and International Studies (CSIS), Washington, DC, 7 June 2012. Available from: http://esa.un.org/unpd/wpp/ppt/CSIS/WUP_2011_CSIS_4.pdf.

Herrero, M.; Thornton, P.K.; Notenbaert, A. M.;Wood, S.; Msangi, S.; Freeman, H. A.; Bossio, D.; Dixon, J.; Peters, J.; Steeg, J. van der; Lynam, J.; Parthasarathy Rao, P.; Macmillan, S.; Gerard, B.; McDermott, J.; Seré, C.; Rosegrant, M. 2010. Smart investments in sustainable food production: Revisiting mixed crop-livestock systems. *Science* 327(5967): 822–825.

Ishagi, N.; Ossiya, S.; Aliguma, L.; Aisu, C. 2002. Urban and peri-urban livestock keeping among the poor in Kampala City. Kampala: Karen Consultants.

Johnson, K. A.; Johnson, D. E. 1995. Methane emissions from cattle. *Journal of Animal Science* 73(8): 2483–2492.

Kang'ethe, E. K.; Grace, D.; Randolph, T. F. 2007. Overview on urban and peri-urban agriculture: Definition, impact on human health, constraints and policy issues. *East African Medical Journal* 84 (11 Suppl): S48–S56.

Kang'ethe, E. K.; Kimani, V. N.; McDermott, B.; Grace, D.; Lang'at, A. K.; Kiragu, M. W.; Karanja, N.; Njehu, A. N.; Randolph, T.; Mbugua, G.; Irungu, T. W.; Ombutu, P. 2012. A trans-disciplinary study on the health risks of cryptosporidiosis from dairy systems in Dagoretti, Nairobi, Kenya: Study background and farming system characteristics. *Tropical Animal Health and Production* 44 (Suppl 1): 3–10.

Kucharski, R.; Marchwińska, E.; Gzyl, J. 1994. Agricultural policy in polluted areas. *Ecological Engineering* 3(3): 299–312.

Lee-Smith, D. 2010. Cities feeding people: An update on urban agriculture in equatorial Africa. *Environment and Urbanization* 22(2): 483–499.

LeJeune, J. T.; Davis, M. A. 2004. Outbreaks of zoonotic enteric disease associated with animal exhibits. *Journal of the American Veterinary Medical Association* 224(9): 1440–1445.

Leroy, J.; Ruel, M.; Verhofstadt, E. 2008. Micronutrient impact of multisectoral programs focusing on nutrition: Examples from conditional cash transfer, microcredit with education, and agricultural programs. Paper presented at the Micronutrient Forum, Florence, 22–25 September 2008. Available from: https://lirias.kuleuven.be/handle/123456789/445950.

Lindahl, J. F.; Chirico, J.; Boqvist, S.; Thu, H.T.V.; Magnusson, U. 2012. Occurrence of Japanese encephalitis virus mosquito vectors in relation to urban pig holdings. *American Journal of Tropical Medicine and Hygiene* 87: 1076–1082.

Lopetegui, P. 2004. Bovine brucellosis control and eradication programme in Chile: Vaccine use as a tool within the programme. *Developments in Biologicals* 119: 473–479.

Lupindu, A. M.; Ngowi, H. A.; Dalsgaard, A.; Olsen, J. E.; Msoffe, P.L.M. 2012. Current manure management practices and hygiene aspects of urban and peri-urban livestock farming in Tanzania. *Livestock Research for Rural Development* 24(9): Article #167. Available from: www.lrrd.org/lrrd24/9/lupi24167.htm.

Maxwell, D.; Levin, C.; Armer-Klemesu, M.; Ruel, M.; Morris, S.; Ahiadeke, C. 2000. Urban livelihoods and food and nutrition security in Greater Accra, Ghana. Research Report 112. Washington, DC: International Food Policy Research Institute (IFPRI).

McCollough, F. S. 1990. Schistosomiasis and aquaculture. In: *Wastewater-Fed Aquaculture: Proceedings of the International Seminar on Wastewater Reclamation and Reuse for Aquaculture.* Calcutta: Environmental and Sanitation Center, Asian Institute of Technology.

Menon, P.; Ruel, M. T.; Morris, S. 2000. Socio-economic differentials in child stunting are considerably larger in urban than rural areas: Analysis of 10 DHS data sets. *Food and Nutrition Bulletin* 21: 282–289.

Miao, Y. W.; Peng, M. S.; Wu, G. S.; Ouyang, Y. N.; Yang, Z. Y.; Yu, N.; Liang, J. P.; Pianchou, G.; Beja-Pereira, A.; Mitra, B.; Palanichamy, M. G.; Baig, M.; Chaudhuri, T. K.; Shen, Y.Y.; Kong, Q. P.; Murphy, R. W.; Yao, Y. G.; Zhang, Y. P. 2013. Chicken domestication: An updated perspective based on mitochondrial genomes. *Heredity* 110(3): 277–282.

Mo, D.; Huang, J.; Jia, X.; Luan, H.; Rozelle, S.; Swinnen, J. 2012. Checking into China's cow hotels: Have policies following the milk scandal changed the structure of the dairy sector? *Journal of Dairy Science* 95(5): 2282–2298.

Mougeot, L. 2000. Urban agriculture: Definition, presence, potentials and risks and policy challenges. Ottawa: International Development Research Center (IDRC). Available from: www.ruaf.org/sites/default/files/Theme1_1_1.PDF.

Mougeot, L. 2005. Agropolis: The social, political and environmental dimensions of urban agriculture. London: Bath Press.

Mougeot, L. 2011. International support to research and policy on urban agriculture (1996–2010): Achievements and challenges. *Urban Agriculture Magazine* 25: 12–17. Available from: www.ruaf.org/sites/default/files/UAM 25-International Support 12–17. pdf.

Mukhtar, F.; Kokab, F. 2008. Brucella serology in abattoir workers. *Journal of Ayub Medical College Abbottabad* 20(3): 57–61.

Myers, M. L. 2011. Livestock rearing. In: *Encyclopedia of Occupational Health and Safety*. (Ed.) Stellman, J. M. Geneva: International Labour Organisation (ILO). Available at: www. iloencyclopaedia.org/component/k2/116-70-livestock-rearing/livestock-rearing-its-extent-and-health-effects.

Nago, C. 2005. Experiences on street foods in West Africa. Paper presented at an FAO/ Consumers International Workshop on Street-Vended Foods in Eastern and Southern Africa: Balancing Safety and Livelihood, Lilongwe, Malawi, 15–17 June 2005.

Ndhlovu, P. 2011. Street vending in Zambia: A case of Lusaka District. The Hague: International Institute of Social Studies (ISS). Available from: http://thesis.eur.nl/pub/10844/ RP_Final_Pity_Ndhlovu.pdf.

Niamir-Fuller, M. 1994. Women livestock managers in the Third World: A focus on technical knowledge. Rome: International Fund for Agricultural Development (IFAD).

Nunan, F. 2000a. Livestock and livelihoods in Hubli-Dharwad. *Urban Agriculture Magazine* 2: 10–12. Available from: www.ruaf.org/livestock-and-livelihoods-hubli-dharwad.

Nunan, F. 2000b. Waste recycling through urban farming in Hubli-Dharwad. In: *Growing Cities, Growing Food*. (Eds.) Bakker, N.; Dubbeling, M.; Gündel, S.; Sabel-Koschella, U.; Zeeuw, H. de. Feldafing: German Foundation for International Developmen (DSE), pp. 429–452. Available from: www.ruaf.org/sites/default/files/Hubli-Dharwad_1.PDF.

OECD. 2013. International migration outlook 2013. Paris: Organisation for Economic Co-operation and Development Publishing. Available from: http://dx.doi.org/10.1787/ migr_outlook-2013-en.

Pereira, F.; Amorim, A. 2010. Origin and spread of goat pastoralism. New York: John Wiley & Sons, Ltd (ELS). Available from: http://doi.wiley.com/10.1002/9780470015902.

Philo, C. 1995. Animals, geography, and the city: Notes on inclusions and exclusions. *International Journal of Urban and Regional Research* 13(6): 655–682.

Pica-Ciamarra, U.; Tasciotti, L.; Otte, J.; Zezza, A. 2011. Livestock assets, livestock income and rural households: Cross-country evidence from household surveys. Rome: Food and Agriculture Organisation of the United Nations (FAO). Available from: https:// openknowledge.worldbank.com/handle/10986/17890.

Du Puis, E. 2002. Nature's perfect food: How milk became America's drink. New York: New York University Press.

Rae, A. 1998. The effects of expenditure growth and urbanisation on food consumption in East Asia: A note on animal products. *Agricultural Economics* 18(3): 291–299.

Randolph, T. F.; Schelling, E.; Grace, D.; Nicholson, C. F.; Leroy, J. L.; Cole, D. C.; Demment, M. W.; Omore, A.; Zinsstag, J.; Ruel, M. 2007. Invited review: Role of livestock in human nutrition and health for poverty reduction in developing countries. *Journal of Animal Science* 85(11): 2788–2800.

Rao, J. K.; Shantaram, M. 1995. Contents of heavy metals in crops treated with urban solid wastes. *Journal of Environmental Biology* 16(3): 225–232.

't Riet, H. van; Hartog, A. P. den; Mwangi, A. M.; Mwadime, R.K.N.; Foeken, D.W.J.; Staveren, W. A. van. 2001. The role of street foods in the dietary pattern of two low-income groups in Nairobi. *European Journal of Clinical Nutrition* 55(7): 562–570.

Satterthwaite, D. 2010. *Urban myths and the mis-use of data that underpin them.* Working Paper No. 2010.28. Helsinki: United Nations University – World Institute for Development Economics Research. Available from: www.econstor.eu/handle/10419/54031.

Satterthwaite, D.; McGranahan, G.; Tacoli, C. 2010. Urbanization and its implications for food and farming. *Philosophical Transactions of the Royal Society of London. Series B, Biological Sciences* 365(1554): 2809–2820.

Schiere, H.; Hoek, R. van der. 2001. Livestock keeping in urban areas: A review of traditional technologies based on literature and field experiences. Rome: Food and Agriculture Organization of the United Nations (FAO).

Schiere, J. B.; Zhang, X.; Koning, K. de; Hengsdijk, H.; Wang, H. 2007. China's dairy chains: Towards qualities for the future. Lelystad: Animal Sciences Group – Wageningen University and Research Centre. Available from: http://library.wur.nl/WebQuery/groenekennis/1870756.

Shaftel, N. 1978. A history of the purification of milk in New York or how now brown cow. *New York State Journal of Medicine* 58(6): 911–928.

Sheth, M.; Obrah, M. 2004. Diarrhea prevention through food safety education. *Indian Journal of Pediatrics* 71(10): 879–882.

Sinclair, U. 1906. The jungle. Auckland: The Floating Press.

Singh, S. V.; Singh, A. V.; Singh, P. V.; Gupta, S.; Singh, H.; Singh, B.; Kumar, O.R.V.; Rajendiran, A. S.; Swain, N. N.; Sohal, J. S. 2013. Evaluation of "Indigenous Vaccine" developed using "indian bison type" genotype of Mycobacterium avium subspecies paratuberculosis strain "S5" of goat origin in a sheep flock endemic for Johne's disease: A three years trial in India. *World Journal of Vaccines* 3(02): 52–59.

Smith, J.; Sones, K.; Grace, D.; MacMillan, S.; Tarawali, S.; Herrero, M. 2013. Beyond milk, meat, and eggs: Role of livestock in food and nutrition security. *The Review Magazine of Animal Agriculture* 3(1): 6–13.

Smith, L.; Aduayom, D. 2003. Measuring food insecurity using household expenditures surveys: New estimates from Sub-Saharan Africa. Paper presented at Workshop on Food security Measurement in a Developing World Context with a Focus on Africa. Available from: http://scholar.google.com/scholar?hl=en&btnG=Search&q=intitle:Measuring+food+insecurity+using+household+expenditure+surveys:+new+estimates+from+Sub-Saharan+Africa.#7.

Staal, S.; Poole, J.; Baltenweck, I.; Mwacharo, J.; Notenbaert, A.; Randolph, T.; Thorpe, W.; Nzuma, J.; Herrero, M. 2009. Targeting strategic investment in livestock development as a vehicle for rural livelihoods. Bill and Melinda Gates Foundation – ILRI Knowledge Generation Project Report. Nairobi, Kenya: International Livestock Research Institute (ILRI). Available from: http://cgspace.cgiar.org/handle/10568/35206.

Tarawali, S.; Herrero, M.; Descheemaeker, K.; Grings, E.; Blümmel, M. 2011. Pathways for sustainable development of mixed crop livestock systems: Taking a livestock and pro-poor approach. *Livestock Science* 139: 11–21.

Tremante, L. 2000. Livestock in nineteenth-century New York City. *Urban Agriculture Magazine* 2: 5–7. Available from: www.ruaf.org/livestock-nineteenth-century-new-york-city.

UNDP. 1996. Human development report. New York: United Nations Development Programme (UNDP). Available from: www.economics-ejournal.org/economics/journalarticles/2010-11/references/@@export.

UNICEF. 2013. UNICEF data: Monitoring the situation of children and women. United Nations Children's Fund (UNICEF). Nutrition database available at: www.childinfo.org/malnutrition_weightbackground.php.

USDA. 2013. Urban chicken ownership in 4 U.S. cities. Washington, DC: United States Department of Agriculture – National Animal Health Monitoring System.

Veenhuizen, R. van; Danso, G. 2007. Profitability and sustainability of urban and periurban agriculture. Rome: Food and Agriculture Organization (FAO). Available from: www.ruaf.org/sites/default/files/Profitability%20and%20Sustainability.pdf.

Waters-Bayer, A. 1996. Animal farming in African cities. *African Urban Quarterly* 11: 218–226.

Webb, A. L.; Schiff, A.; Currivan, D.; Villamor, E. 2008. Food stamp program participation but not food insecurity is associated with higher adult BMI in Massachusetts residents living in low-income neighbourhoods. *Public Health Nutrition* 11(12): 1248–1255.

Winters, C. 1983. The classification of traditional African cities. *Journal of Urban History* 10(1): 3–31.

Yeung, Y. 1988. Agricultural land use in Asian cities. *Land Use Policy* 5: 79–82.

11

URBAN FORESTRY AND AGROFORESTRY

Fabio Salbitano,[1] Simone Borelli[2] and Giovanni Sanesi[3]

1 UNIVERSITY OF FLORENCE, ITALY — DEPARTMENT FOR THE DEVELOPMENT OF AGRICULTURAL, FOOD AND FORESTRY SYSTEMS

2 FOOD AND AGRICULTURE ORGANIZATION OF THE UNITED NATIONS (FAO)

3 UNIVERSITY OF BARI, ITALY — DEPARTMENT OF AGRICULTURAL AND ENVIRONMENTAL SCIENCE

Introduction

Today, cities already house almost 4 billion people (United Nations 2014). As the world continues to urbanize, sustainable development challenges will be increasingly concentrated in cities, particularly in lower- and middle-income countries where urbanization is faster.

While cities occupy less than 4% of the global terrestrial surface, they account for 80% of carbon emissions, 60% of residential water use and over 75% of wood use for industrial and domestic purposes. Urbanization is increasingly regarded as a critical process in the frame of global change and integrated policies to improve the lives of both urban and rural dwellers, which are urgently needed.

The expansion of cities leads to the "urbanization of poverty" (Baker 2008). Twenty-five percent of the world's total poor live in cities (Ravallion et al. 2007). Many of them live in small cities and towns where the incidence of poverty tends to be higher than in big cities (Baker 2008). Urban poverty and vulnerability, i.e., the risk of falling into poverty, is related to three characteristics of urban life: access to resources and commodities, environmental hazards and social fragmentation (Alkire et al. 2014).

This urbanization of poverty is an increasing concern for decision-makers: *nutrition, water* and *energy security* are essential for the livelihood and quality of life of citizens: urban (agro-) foresters are looking for new solutions and more efficient actions. However, urban forestry can also contribute to the quality of life and environment of existing and future cities by addressing other challenges that have emerged during the last decade: *climate change, soil sealing, human health* and *well-being* and *integrated environmental governance*.

In 2005, Konijnendijk and Gauthier (2006) prepared an overview of the status of urban forestry research and development, policy-making, implementation and education. This chapter provides an overview of the developments in the last decade and the current status of (intra- and peri-) urban forestry research and development, policy-making, implementation and education, and aims to demonstrate the dynamic status of the discipline and highlight emerging experiences and issues.

Growing attention for urban forestry

One of the most interesting facts of the 2005–2014 decade concerning urban forestry and agroforestry issues is the exponential growth of knowledge, action research and practice on *green infrastructure* and *ecosystem services* approaches as means to enhance the quality of life in cities and towns. A lot of work has gone into methodologies, technical issues, communication and education, multidisciplinary approaches and synergies.

The volume of studies focusing on urban forestry has grown substantially: over the past 15 years (1998 to 2014), the scientific contributions containing the keyword *urban forest* have increased more than four times (Figure 11.1) and include studies from all continents.

Three international journals mainly cover urban forestry: *Urban Forestry and Urban Greening; Arboricultural Journal;* and *Arboriculture and Urban Forestry.* Research findings are also published in other journals, e.g., *Landscape and Urban Planning.*

The International Union of Forestry Research Organisation (IUFRO) promotes conferences and sessions on urban forestry. At the last IUFRO World Conference in October 2014 in Salt Lake City, 38 papers and posters on urban landscape and

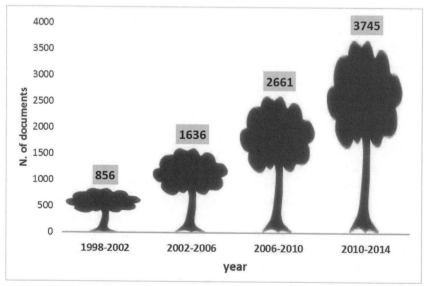

FIGURE 11.1 Number of documents on urban forestry and related issues in scientific publications from 1998 to 2014

Source: www.scopus.com.

urban forest issues were presented. Many other conferences, workshops and research projects at different levels refer to urban forests and urban green infrastructure.

Indeed, urban forestry and agroforestry are no longer only domains for experts but are now well rooted in the knowledge of many urban communities and in the capacity of technical and institutional boards. In the last ten years, urban forestry has become more and more attractive for investments and for urban policy and strategic frameworks.

The 2007 *State of the World Forests* (FAO 2007) selected urban forestry as one of the key issues related to restoration of the forest landscape and reported that 46 countries have stepped up afforestation efforts around towns with the primary objective of environmental protection, to a level of nearly 400,000 hectares per year.

The *State of the World Cities* 2013 report (UN-Habitat 2013) on "Sustainability and the Prosperity of Cities" clearly points out the important role of urban green spaces as a provider of ecosystem services and a fundamental resource for the citizens' livelihoods.

The World Health Report of 2013 (WHO 2013) highlights the positive role of green economy and green investments on the status of health in urban contexts. Since 1960, the World Health Organization (WHO) has promoted the adoption of a set of indicators and guidelines for Healthy Urban Environments. The WHO Note of Secretariat of 1967 on "The challenge to public health of urbanization" reports the need of setting minimum standards for healthy urban environments. Among them is the need of indicators for the density of, and accessibility to, urban green spaces. Although no official records of WHO ever mention a minimum green space area per resident, the figure of 9 m^2 per resident is generally accepted as being proposed by WHO (Singh et al. 2010 quoting Kuchelmeister 1998), and many national laws have adopted the square meters per urban resident as a criterion for urban development. That is the case of the Italian law on new urban development (D.M. 2 April 1968, n. 1444), which adopted 9 m^2 of green space as a standard.

Several international institutions, such as FAO, UN-HABITAT and UNEP, have promoted and sustained institutional as well as informal partnership and networking on urban forestry at global, regional and national levels. The FAO Multidisciplinary Action Group "Food for the Cities" also includes an action area on "Forests and trees – improving livelihoods through healthy green cities".

Since the late nineties, the RUAF Foundation (the International network of Resource centres on Urban Agriculture and Food security) is actively promoting and sustaining actions and guidelines for development at global (www.ruaf.org/topics/urban-agro-forestry) and regional levels.

ICLEI-Local Governments for Sustainability and United Cities and Local Governments (UCLG) have been very active at regional and local levels to support the dialogue and the partnerships on urban forestry and green infrastructure. ICLEI and UCLG-Africa supported UN-Habitat in the preparation of the *State of African Cities 2014* (UN-Habitat 2014), which included various aspects of urban forests and green infrastructure. According to this review, there is a strong need for building solid partnerships among African cities to build capacity and exchange knowledge as well as to attract financial support for the implementation of urban forestry.

The European Forum of Urban Forestry, launched in 1998, constitutes a robust example of regional networking and partnership. There are proposals to build similar experiences in Asia (FAO 2014b) and Latin America (FAO 2014a).

In 2012, Silva Mediterranea, FAO's statutory body on the forests of the Mediterranean, launched a working group on Urban and Peri-urban Forest (www.fao. org/forestry/80480/en/) that now is operating to create networking, partnership, knowledge and research/education opportunities in the region.

City twinning programmes, implemented in many different contexts, are other tools for networking and capacity building. The Lombardy Region (Italy), one of the most urbanized areas in Europe, and the Osrednjeslovenska – Ljubljana urban region in Slovenia – twinned their efforts and experiences to monitor intra- and peri-urban forests and the goods and services they provide (www.emonfur.eu/). In May 2014, the "50 Municipal Climate Partnerships by 2015" project was launched. Fifty German municipalities and their partner municipalities in the Global South will develop joint action programmes on climate change mitigation and adaptation in city regions including resilience, biodiversity, reforestation, energy supply, solid waste management, water management, awareness raising and education (www.service-eine-welt.de/en/climatepartnerships/climatepartnerships-start.html).

The development and institutionalization of urban forestry in the United States gained force as a result of major lobbying efforts by NGOs such as American Forests, Tree Link and ICLEI-USA. The "Urban Forests Create Vibrant Cities" programme (www.icleiusa.org/blog/urban-forests-make-vibrant-cities) was a very successful initiative towards creating partnership around urban forest issues. Great Britain's National Urban Forestry Unit (NUFU), an independent organization, has provided assistance to many local and regional urban forestry initiatives.

Several guidelines on urban forestry and agroforestry at global, regional and national levels were recently produced to support decision-makers and practitioners (FAO 2013; de Foresta et al. 2013) in improving urban life and environmental conditions through urban forestry strategies. In the last decade, indicators and approaches have been designed to assess the contribution of urban forestry in terms of ecosystem services (Nowak et al. 2007, 2008). Natural England, an advisory body to the British government that provides practical scientific advice on how to preserve England's landscapes, has developed *Green Infrastructure Guidance* (http://publications.naturalengland.org.uk/publication/35033).

ICLEI developed a technical guide for practitioners and decision-makers, *Talking Trees, an Urban Forestry Toolkit for Local Governments* (ICLEI 2006), aimed at supporting local environmental governance of resilient cities and strengthening integrated technical, institutional and community capacities.

Assessment of urban forest resources

In order to promote and develop urban forests, it is essential to know their status and understand the challenges they face as well as their potential contribution in term of ecosystem services. The characterization of the urban forest and the assessment of their condition are challenging tasks (Pauleit et al. 2005; Konijnendijk and Gauthier 2006).

Singh et al. (2010) provided a synthetic overview on the global extent of urban forests in the world. According to their analysis, cities in developed countries, in general, have more trees compared to cities in developing countries, which often fall below 9 m² of green open space per city dweller.

Large-scale international and national inventories and monitoring of urban forests are still scarce or fragmentary (Corona et al. 2011). However, there are a number of cases where National Forest Inventories (NFIs) also include urban forests (Table 11.1).

TABLE 11.1 Urban forests in National Forest Inventories

Data collected/methods applied	*Source*
USA: Urban tree canopy and impervious surface cover maps for 48 States by US Forest Service (2007) from 2001 Landsat satellite imagery to assess urban forest data including carbon storage and sequestration rates and air pollution removal estimates	Nowak and Greenfield 2010
Europe: An outlook study on the status of urban forests in 26 countries in Europe	EU COST action FP1204 GreeninUrbs
France: Data on the extent and characteristics of the forest in and around towns since 2006	National Forest Inventory of France
England: a survey of urban trees and their condition and management	Britt and Johnston 2008
Germany (Berlin): combining airborne LiDAR and QuickBird derived data to assess carbon stored in urban trees and to identify differences between urban structure types	Schreyer et al. 2014
Morocco: Basic inventory of 154 intra- and peri-urban forests (2006): location, area and status	HCEFLD 2010
China: application of airborne LiDAR data and hyperspectral imagery to generate species-level maps of urban forests with high spatial heterogeneity	Zhang and Qi 2012
China: Information on the average green cover of 439 cities	Wang 2009
Turkey: General Directorate of Forestry (OGM) collected information on the status of 112 urban forests: physical aspects of the forests, management issues, functions and ecosystem services	Atmiş et al. 2012
India: No national inventory but case studies on Chadingarh and Delhi using satellite imageries	Nagendra and Gopal 2010; FSI 2009 respectively
West and Central Asia: Basic information on urban forests	Åkerlund (2006)
Mapping the extents of urban tree canopy using aerial or satellite imagery	MacFaden et al. 2012; McGee et al. 2012
Use of airborne LiDar for measuring and mapping urban forest and trees	MacFaden et al. 2012; McGee et al. 2012; He et al. 2013; Alonzo et al. 2014

Source: authors.

Urban forest inventories are numerous. The case studies on Bogota (Tovar-Corzo 2013) and Montpellier (Besse et al. 2014) are excellent examples of two different approaches on the assessment of urban forests and green areas in cities.

The issue of "trees outside forests" (ToF) is also an important challenge for urban forest assessment. The ToF assessment by de Foresta et al. (2013) includes a specific chapter on the sound assessment of trees in cities.

Finally, an emerging aspect in implementing inventories of urban forests and trees is related to communication and involvement of the public. In the last few years, the use of information technologies was decisive in the implementation of community-based surveys and interactive inventory tools (Abd-Elrahman et al. 2010).

Green infrastructure and ecosystem services for future sustainable cities

Green infrastructure

Urban green infrastructure is the interconnected network of green spaces that conserves natural ecosystem values and functions and provides associated benefits to human populations. Urban and peri-urban forests and trees, together with agroforestry

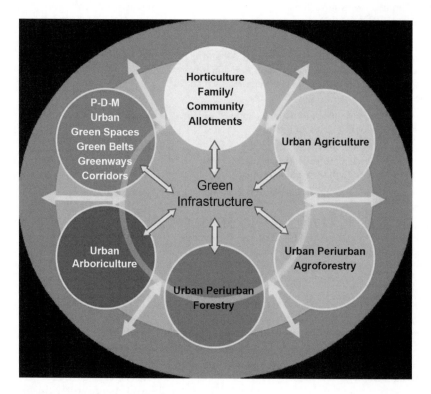

FIGURE 11.2 The green infrastructural framework

Source: authors.

systems, urban horticulture, green spaces, tree lines and hedges, parks, green roofs and walls, and riparian corridors form the physical and functional *green infrastructure* of the city region. They constitute the critical dynamic elements of urban and peri-urban landscapes, providing benefits as the structural component of the watershed, woodshed, foodshed, ecological network and nature protection areas.

Over the last decade, green infrastructure has developed as an approach to landscape planning that addresses the fragmented thinking associated with urban development. Green infrastructure is often viewed as an alternative to the so-called grey infrastructure, i.e., human-engineered solutions that often involve concrete and steel. The assumption of urban economists and town planners is that infrastructure is essential for economic growth. People often do not think of forests, wetlands, coral reefs and other natural ecosystems as forms of infrastructure. But they are. As such, "green infrastructure" can have an equivalent economic interest as "grey infrastructure".

Green infrastructure serves the interests of both people and nature, as quoted in the European Green Infrastructure Strategy (European Commission 2013). Green infrastructure enables citizens to benefit from the multiple services of the natural and semi-natural features of the landscape (Davies et al. 2006). This definition completely reverses the urban-centric vision of the 20th century by assuming that human activities and cities are hosted in the nature and not the opposite.

The green infrastructure planning agenda has brought together planners, ecologists, architects and developers, and proposed a holistic and functional understanding of the ecology of urban environments by proposing that natural resources should form the fundamental building blocks for landscape management and meeting a number of planning issues (Benedict and McMahon 2006; Mell 2007, 2010). In green infrastructural planning, local communities, landowners and organizations work together to identify, design and conserve the land cover diversity required for the maintenance of a healthy ecological functioning of the urban landscape (Benedict and McMahon 2006).

In the last decade, planning of strategic green infrastructure has been gaining momentum. In Europe, a multi-scale planning approach, ranging from the local community level through to regional, national and international platforms, is emerging. The European Green Belt (www.europeangreenbelt.org/), the Pan-European Ecological Network (Council of Europe 2000) and the European Green Infrastructure Strategy (European Commission 2013) are good examples of integrated directives, tools and actions oriented to implement multiple planning agreements and national/local legislation about urban forests and green infrastructure.

Ecosystem services

Urban forests and agroforestry systems are primary sources of *goods* and *ecosystem services* that are directly enjoyed, consumed, or used to produce specific, measurable environmental and human benefits, e.g., contributions to nutrition security as well as to health, well-being and quality of life of the citizens and particularly of the poor who need easily accessible resources and opportunities at low cost (Chen and Jim 2008; Dobbs et al. 2011). Intra- and peri-urban forests can buffer human settlements from extreme heat and cold, rain and wind, and provide fruit, timber, fuel and employment for a growing population.

Services provided by urban forestry and agroforestry can be categorized in four main types:

a   *Provisioning* services are the products obtained from ecosystems such as food, freshwater, wood, fibre, genetic resources and medicines.
b   *Regulating* services are defined as the benefits obtained from the regulation of ecosystem processes such as climate regulation, natural hazard regulation, water purification and waste management, pollination or pest control.
c   *Habitat* services highlight the importance of ecosystems to provide habitat for migratory species and to maintain the viability of gene-pools.
d   *Cultural* services include non-material benefits that people obtain from eco-systems such as spiritual enrichment, intellectual development, recreation and aesthetic values.

Understanding and quantifying these benefits can raise citizen awareness of the value of their public resources, such as urban trees on publicly owned lands, as well as provide a basis for management to maximize benefits while controlling costs. As the amount, distribution and composition of urban forests vary from city to city, so do ecosystem functions and services and the resulting economic, social and ecological benefits.

Design, implementation, management and maintenance of urban forests, trees and public green spaces have always been seen as a cost to the community. However, during the last decade the awareness of the economic role of urban forest and green infrastructure has increased rapidly. Investing in urban forests can directly contribute to city revenues and citizens' incomes as well as being an affordable tool for savings and indirect economic benefits.

For instance, where there is an efficient green infrastructure in place, the impacts of extreme weather events (e.g., winds, floods, landslides and sand encroachment) are mitigated. Likewise, a well-managed watershed produces and supplies good-quality water and reduces the need for costly engineering works. The high and recurrent cost of rebuilding roads, housing and commercial infrastructure is greatly reduced, creating savings, while the maintenance of woodlands and trees generates green jobs and income through multipurpose management. Well-designed green infrastructure enhances physical activity and psychological restoration, contributing to save expenditures in the health system. Finally, farming and landscape systems that incorporate agroforestry and high-yielding plantations can supply nearby markets at competitive prices (FAO 2009).

The example of Toronto (Table 11.2) shows that urban forests provide the city with over USD80 million worth of environmental benefits. For the average single-family household, this works out to USD125 of savings per annum.

TABLE 11.2 Annual benefits provided by Toronto's forests

Benefit	Quantity	Economic value	
		(Millions Can $)	*Can $/tree*
Reduced wet-weather flow (less strain on water transportation and processing infrastructure)	25,112,500 m3	53.95	5.28
Absorbed air pollutants	1,905 tonnes	19.09	1.87
Energy savings (through shading and climate moderation)	41,200 MWH	6.42	0.63
Carbon sequestration	36,500 tonnes	1.24	0.12
Carbon emission avoided by climate moderation	17,000 tonnes	0.58	0.06
Total benefit		81.29	7.95
Benefits per $ investment in maintenance of urban forests: Can $ 1.35–3.20.			

Source: Alexander and McDonald 2014.

Cities and towns of different size, character, culture, income (e.g., Toronto, Canada; London, UK; Singapore; Curitiba, Brazil; Montpellier, France; Stara Zagora, Bulgaria) have decided to invest in green infrastructure for their future. For example, Bogotá, Colombia, is pursuing upstream landscape conservation and restoration as an alternative to more conventional water treatment technologies. Ho Chi Minh City, Vietnam, restored mangroves instead of building dikes in order to protect shorelines from storm damage. And a chemical facility in Texas, USA, built a wetland instead of using deep well injection to treat wastewater (www.greenbiz.com/blog/2012/06/22/green-vs-gray-infrastructure-when-nature-trumps-concrete).

The "Million Trees" programmes, started in the USA (e.g., New York City, Los Angeles, Miami) and then adopted in many other cities of the world, from Santa Cruz de la Sierra (Bolivia) to London (www.milliontrees.ca/), are excellent examples of merging the different potential ecosystem services provided by urban forests and getting back economic benefits as an added value for the future of the cities. The programme "ReForest London: Planting the Future Today" (http://reforestlondon.ca/) is emblematic of this approach.

Studies on specific ecosystem services provided by urban forestry are available for a number of cities around the world, e.g., on biodiversity (e.g., Sandström 2008), carbon storage (e.g., Escobedo et al. 2010; Schreyer et al. 2014) and wood energy supply (Drigo and Salbitano 2008; FAO 2009, 2012a). Chen and Jim (2008) provided a valuation of ecosystem services at the global level and Jim and Chen (2009) for Chinese urban forests identifying the emerging benefits and the regulating, provisional and social values.

However, the assessment of ecosystem services requires well-defined procedures and further development of a comprehensive set of good indicators for urban forest ecosystem services and the provision of goods (Dobbs et al. 2011, 2014). In the last decade, the *iTree* suite of software tools (www.itreetools.org) has been increasingly used as a ground-based method of assessing urban forest structure and ecosystem services and enabling scenario planning and land cover classification for planning purposes (Nowak et al. 2007, 2008).

Urban and peri-urban forestry: emerging issues

Nutrition, water and energy security: the contribution of urban and peri-urban forestry and agroforestry

Maintaining food and nutrition security for rapidly growing urban populations is one of the greatest challenges of the 21st century (Camhis 2006; Tanumihardjo et al. 2007; FAO 2011). The contribution of agroforestry systems to urban food security is one of the key issues highlighted in the global agroforestry guidelines prepared by FAO (FAO 2013). Intra- and peri-urban forests and trees are a source of fruits, seeds, leaves, mushrooms, berries, medicinal herbs, rattan, and fodder (leaves, sprouts, young shoots and seeds) for animal husbandry, while bush meat and edible insects are valuable sources of proteins in many areas of the world. In West Africa, for example, urban forestry practices such as the collection of wild edible plants, planting of fruit-bearing street trees and establishment of multifunctional public parks have contributed to an improvement in food security (Fuwape and Onyekwelu 2011; Dubbeling 2014). Also in Pacific Islands, the contribution of fruit and fodder urban trees is decisive for the daily consumption and the improvement of the nutritional values in vitamins and other key nutrients. Reliable estimates of the contribution of urban forestry and agroforestry to food and nutrition security of urban dwellers are still scarce. Income from forests and trees in urban farms can increase the food security of peri-urban households. A large number of women in West Africa earn a substantial income from the collection, processing and marketing of nuts harvested from naturally occurring shea trees, like for example the 300 women from the Alaffia Shea Butter Cooperative in Sokodé, Togo (Olowo-n'djo Tchala 2011). In India, *Jamun* trees alongside roads of Delhi yield about 500 MT of fruit each year (Singh et al. 2010), which is harvested and sold to pedestrians and motorists passing by these roads during the monsoonal season, when fruits are ripe. "A food-secure city" foresees productive tree systems for food production, as well as has an awareness of the environmental services that these systems also produce (Kyle and Kimberly 2013).

Forests and trees within and around cities and towns also help to maintain clean water supplies and to improve watershed health by decreasing the quantity of storm-water runoff, recharging groundwater, decreasing flooding and erosion and reducing the pollutants that are washed into streams from impervious surfaces (Gash et al. 2008; Brown and Farrelly 2009; Pearson et al. 2009). As forests are cleared for development in urbanizing watersheds, they are replaced with paved or compacted surfaces such as roads, driveways, parking lots and sidewalks that, together with rooftops, make up an impervious cover. In Rhode Island, the 14%

of land of the Narragansett Bay watershed is under impervious cover. The value ranges from 3 to 40% by municipality, with only 17 of 39 towns having less than 10% of the impervious cover. Impervious cover increased 43% between 1972 and 1999, six times faster than population growth in the area (Zhou and Wang 2007). Nowak and Greenfield (2010) analyzed the relationships between tree cover and impervious surface in 20 cities in the USA. All the sample cities had a reduction of tree cover and an increase in impervious cover from 2003 to 2009, excepting Syracuse, where the tree cover slightly increased while the impervious surfaces decreased.

The watershed of the valley of Mexico City has an area of 9,600 km². The conurbation area (60 municipalities) covers 7,815 km², i.e., 81% of the watershed. The urban sprawl of Mexico City in the last century is impressive (see Table 11.3). The water supply for the city has been in crisis for 20 years. The major problem is the inability of the watershed to meet the demands of drinking water (Breña Puyol and Breña Naranjo 2009).

TABLE 11.3 Urban growth in Mexico City and urban cover of Mexico Valley watershed

Year	Dense urban area (km²)	Urban population (million)
1910	27	0.5
1960	382	5.6
1990	1209	15.6
2000	1350	18.4
2010	1475	20.1

Source: Breña Puyol and Breña Naranjo 2009.

The Impervious Cover Model (ICM) developed by the Center for Watershed Protection (CWP) predicts that most stream quality indicators decline when the watershed impervious cover exceeds 10%, with severe degradation expected beyond 25% (Cappiella et al. 2005). The CWP developed an *Urban Forestry Watershed Manual* (Cappiella et al. 2005, 2006a, 2006b), a working tool to plan, design and manage trees and forests to protect watersheds from floods and runoff, as well as to enhance the quality of water in hydrological systems serving cities. They introduced the concept of *urban watershed forestry* as an integration of urban and community forestry and watershed planning.

Urban watershed forestry sets watershed-based goals for managing urban forests as a whole rather than managing them on a site-by-site or jurisdictional basis, and provides strategies for incorporating forests into urban watershed management. Reforestation programmes constitute the pillars of integrated strategies and alliances oriented to reduce the devastating effects of floods caused by extreme climate events. The example of the Marikina Watershed Integrated Resource Development Alliance (Box 11.1) in the Manila region represents a way of incorporating urban forestry actions in the strategic watershed plan devoted to reduce future dramatic floods.

BOX 11.1 THE MARIKINA WATERSHED INTEGRATED RESOURCE DEVELOPMENT ALLIANCE: BUILDING PARTNERSHIPS FOR DISASTER RISK REDUCTION IN URBAN CENTRES OF METRO MANILA (THE PHILIPPINES)

The Marikina Watershed, located in the wider metropolitan area of Manila, the city capital, spans 28,000 hectares of what used to be rainforests and cuts across three main townships (Antipolo, San Mateo and Rodriguez). Only roughly 20% of the rainforest remains.

Late in 2009, the Philippines was battered by tropical storm Ondoy and typhoon Pepeng, leaving nearly a thousand dead and thousands homeless, with total damage and losses estimated at USD4.38 billion. The intensity of flash floods that devastated the Metro Manila region was attributed to the degradation of the Marikina Watershed.

Local government leaders – led by Marikina city mayor and the mayors of Pasig City, Antipolo City, Cainta City, Quezon City, Rodriguez and San Mateo – also known as the "Alliance of Seven" – signed a Memorandum of Agreement, in September 2010, and committed to work together to rehabilitate and sustainably develop the Marikina Watershed under the framework of disaster risk reduction and enhancing urban resilience. Proposed actions include rehabilitation and reforestation of the Marikina Watershed, including a review of existing policies, resettlement plan for high-risk communities and possible in-city relocation and livelihood assistance, as well as the development of harmonized mechanisms within a sustainable and climate-sensitive plan for the Marikina Watershed. Emphasis is also placed on building partnerships not only between the seven city governments but also with other key stakeholders across the seven municipalities, including civil society and the private sector. The Alliance of Seven is working with citizens' groups and local NGOs, and will also build on previous reforestation efforts by the United Coconut Planters Bank, a private bank, which started in the 1990s to rehabilitate the Marikina Watershed.

Source: Tuaño and Sescon 2013.

In many parts of the world, wood is by far the most affordable source of energy, very often the only one available to the urban poor. Timber and non-timber products are considered the first and very likely the most important tangible benefits that urban forests can provide to African citizens: wood for energy, among them, plays a leading role (Fuwape and Onyekwelu 2011). Marien prepared a complete outlook study on the interconnected urban forestry-wood fuel system for African cities (Marien 2009; FAO 2012d) as part of a series of studies and actions promoted by FAO in Central Africa to establish and improve the use of urban forestry as a strategic tool for the future of the cities.

In Bangui, Central African Republic (FAO 2009), wood fuel was one of the main issues around which an urban forestry action plan was developed. In N'Djaména, Tchad (FAO 2012a, 2012b, 2012c), and Kinshasa, Democratic Republic of the Congo (Schure et al. 2011), the wood energy component was studied and planned not only as part of urban forestry programmes but as a key determinant of strategic town planning.

A recurrent criticism to the wood fuel sector is that the unsustainable harvesting of wood fuel supplying large urban and industrial markets significantly contributes to forest degradation and to deforestation when coupled with other land-use changes (IPCC 2014). Sustainable harvesting and transformation techniques are almost well known in the traditional wood fuel supply rural zones while the intra- and peri-urban chain of production is informal and very often illegal. There is no recognition of the wood fuel harvesting needs and very little is done to grant these activities even in technical terms. However, recent technological advances suggest that energy production from biomass can also be an opportunity for facing the carbon sequestration challenge (Zeng et al. 2007; Fargione et al. 2008; Hoekman 2009; Azar et al. 2010). Especially in OECD (Organisation for Economic Co-operation and Development) countries, wood-efficient applications for wood energy are increasingly being used to produce cost-effective, high-quality energy services at various scales (Abd'razack et al. 2013).

The urban forest and trees as sources of bioenergy are mainly used by the urban poor. Urban trees can provide up to the 80% of their needs but the access is uncertain and risky (Drigo and Salbitano 2008). The major blockings are the lack of visibility, the absence of norms and regulations, and the failure of any investment on the sector of wood fuel and charcoal production and marketing in urban and peri-urban areas. In this sense, the contribution of intra- and peri-urban forestry can be decisive, at least for some component of the urban poor.

Therefore, the projections of significant growth in wood fuel demand, particularly in developing countries (Mwampamba 2007; Drigo and Salbitano 2008; Zulu 2010; Agyeman et al. 2012) make it vital that this sector is overhauled and modernized using new technologies and approaches, and that governance mechanisms, such as "WISDOM for cities", are highlighted (Drigo and Salbitano 2008).

Even if, from a strictly quantitative point of view, they cover only part of the urban wood fuel demand, urban forests play a fundamental role in planning a sustainable urban wood energy system. In collaboration with urban development agencies, (intra- and peri-) urban forestry may trigger a virtuous planning process and provide good management practices aimed at meeting urban needs through sustainable and responsible interaction with rural areas and communities well beyond the city boundaries.

In this perspective, urban planning should extend its responsibility to extra urban resources and socio-economic processes influenced by the urban footprint. The first task in this expanded role would be to disclose the nature, in terms of environmental and socio-economic sustainability and impacts, of the relation between growing urban needs, on the one hand, and the resources and processes that provide commodities and services, on the other.

In their study, Drigo and Salbitano (2008) called this expanded area of influence *urban woodshed* and adapted the WISDOM (Wood fuel Integrated Supply and Demand Overview Mapping) platform to the city scale, highlighting the proactive relationships with urban forestry.

Climate change and urban forestry

The fact that the Earth's climate has changed as a result of human activities has become increasingly clear over the last years, and there is strong evidence that we can expect further dramatic changes in the next decades. The 2014 report of the Intergovernmental Panel on Climate Change (IPCC 2014) refers to urban greening and green infrastructure as one of the major tools to reduce the effects of climate change at the urban scale, particularly in view of their potential to mitigate the urban warming and its associated effects.

The warming of the atmosphere leads to long-term changes in rain and snowfall patterns, wind and ocean currents, ice and snow accumulation, and other climatic aspects. It can increase the frequency of droughts, heat waves, heavy rainfall and snowfall, and other extreme weather events (Duryea et al. 2007). It is associated with a wide set of environmental and economic risks which, depending on the geographical context, can be desertification, floods, erosion, landslides and avalanches that could affect urban regions (Seppälä et al. 2009).

Trees and forests adjacent to cities and towns provide important ecosystem services by reducing the direct or indirect risks associated with climate change. Urban forests and agroforestry systems, especially if planned according to a green infrastructure approach, can substantially contribute to sequestering and storing greenhouse gases (Schreyer et al. 2014; Timilsina et al. 2014).

One of the most important characteristics of urban climate is the Urban Heat Island effect (UHI) that causes urban temperature to be higher in the city centre than in the peri-urban areas. Normally, heat island intensity is proportional to the population size and density of a city. Urban trees reduce UHI effects through shading and cooling through evapotranspiration (the evaporation of water trough foliage) thus reducing demand for air-conditioning in summer and the associated demand for fossil fuel energy and water. Joint studies by the Lawrence Berkeley National Laboratory (LBNL) and the Sacramento Municipal Utility District (SMUD) placed varying numbers of trees around houses to shade windows and then measured the buildings' energy use. The cooling energy savings ranged between 7% and 47% and were greatest when trees were planted to the west and southwest of buildings (www.epa.gov/heatislands/resources/pdf/TreesandVegCompendium.pdf). According to McPherson et al. (2005), the benefits of urban forestry in energy saving can vary considerably by community and tree species, but they are always higher than the costs. The five-city study found that, on a per-tree basis, the cities accrued benefits ranging from about USD1.50–USD3.00 for every dollar invested. These cities spent roughly USD15–USD65 annually per tree, with net annual benefits ranging from approximately USD30–USD90 per tree. The impacts of specific greening interventions on the wider urban area, and whether the effects are due to greening alone, have yet to be demonstrated. Nevertheless, the positive effects of urban forestry on UHI and thermal profiles have been assessed in several cities (Ruth and Cohelo 2007; Seppälä et al. 2009). The cooling effect of green areas is related to a range of variables, such as local urban morphology around the parks, land use around the parks, wind-flow, types of pavements, types of trees and landscape design (Tsiros 2010; Tuaño and Sescon 2013).

However, the climate change and urban forest literature has mostly focused on environmental services and climate mitigation (e.g., Lundholm and Marlin 2006; McPherson et al. 2008; Lawrence and Escobedo 2012) but little work has been done so far in the adaptive side. Urban forests and green spaces make important contributions to the cities in term of building resilience and adaptiveness to climate change stressors. The green infrastructure approach is considered a very promising conceptual framework in emphasizing the individual contribution of the different types of green spaces towards adaptive cities (Gill et al. 2007).

Climate change also affects the urban forests and these need to be adapted to an increase in stress variables including higher temperatures, precipitation changes (in both quantity and quality; i.e., snow to rain), air pollution increases, soil habitat alterations, among other stress variables (Li et al. 2007; Seppälä et al. 2009; Arnbjerg-Nielsen and Fleischer 2009).

While scientific knowledge, technical tools and guides to cope with urban forest adaptation to climate change have been developed in North America and Europe (Cullington and Gye 2010; Natural England and RSPB 2014) such contributions are almost absent in tropical regions and in low-income countries.

Urban soil sealing: new discussions on old problems

Soils provide a number of ecosystem services which make them environmentally, economically and socially crucial for human societies (Scalenghe and Marsan 2009). Soil sealing by impervious materials is, normally, detrimental to its ecological functions. Exchanges of energy, water and gases are restricted or hampered and increasing pressure is being exerted on adjacent, non-sealed areas. The negative effects range from loss of plant production and natural habitats to increased floods, pollution and health risks, and, consequently, higher social costs.

In the last century, urban sprawl has been the driving process of soil sealing. Unplanned or poorly planned urban development has transformed agricultural and forest land into the impervious, harsh cover of industrial, residential and commercial structures and infrastructures.

Well-designed green infrastructure can indeed avoid or reduce soil sealing but requires sound policies and a strategic commitment. The *European Green Infrastructure Strategy* (European Commission 2013), adopted at the beginning of 2014, is the first official document calling for strategic actions to limit soil sealing derived by urban sprawl. Understanding the relationships between soil sealing, urban forestry and green infrastructure in scientific and in policy terms is highly challenging, and researchers, practitioners and decision-makers in urban forestry and related issues will need to provide answers in the near future.

Urban forests, green spaces and human health and well-being

The WHO (1998) defines a healthy city as "the one that is continually creating and improving those physical and social environments and expanding those community resources which enable people to mutually support each other in performing all the functions of life and developing to their maximum potential." A green city, with a high availability of trees and forest, green and open spaces, is the best urban environment to meet these requirements and provide three types of functions related to health processes: prevention, therapy and recovery/restorativeness.

Urban forests and green spaces can be designed and managed to assist therapies for very different type of diseases (Weldon et al. 2007). Urban trees and forests provide shade and help cool the atmosphere and the soil. Thus, longer and more frequent visits to green spaces generate significant improvements in the real and perceived well-being of users (Guite et al. 2006; Lafortezza et al. 2009; de Vries et al. 2011) and alleviate discomfort from extreme heat (Shashua-Bar et al. 2010).

The contribution of urban forests to the reduction of pollution and contamination of atmosphere, water and soil is also the object of various studies (Escobedo et al. 2008; Escobedo et al. 2010; Escobedo et al. 2011). Urban forest and trees are excellent filters. They reduce harmful ultraviolet radiation and air pollution, noise and negative sensorial perception. This filtering function contributes to drastically decreasing some direct and indirect causes of non-communicable disease and urban stressors (Tiwary et al. 2009).

A sedentary lifestyle increases the overall risk of early mortality, cardiovascular diseases, obesity and some forms of cancer, including colon and breast cancer. The presence and access to open green spaces can also help promote more active lifestyles (Tzoulas et al. 2007), and it is well established that regular exercise, including walking, can reduce the negative effects of many major health threats (Bird 2015).

Another benefit of urban forests is the positive effect of green spaces on psychological well-being, including stress reduction and mental health improvements. Surgery patients who could see a grove of deciduous trees recuperated faster and required less pain-killing medicine than matched patients who viewed only brick walls (Ulrich 2002; Berto 2007; Heerwagen 2009; Grahn and Stigsdotter 2010).

In parallel, there are forests designed and managed to serve specific programmes of convalescence and restorativeness. The sense of well-being induced by relaxing or carrying out activities in urban forests and greening has deep significance in the restorativeness needs of urban populations (Carrus et al. 2013, 2014). The number of healing gardens is increasing and design styles emphasizing the psychological restorativeness potential of urban forests and parks are currently taught in landscape architecture and urban forestry courses worldwide. Indeed, informal activities in green spaces also have a positive effect on the treatment of depression (Townsend 2006).

On the other hand, it is necessary to be aware of the fact that urban trees and forests can cause problems to human health and well-being. Some tree species are allergogenic and urban forests can provide habitat for fungi and insects that are potential vectors of either epidemic or non-communicable diseases (Cariñanos et al. 2014).

Integrated environmental governance to achieve long-term sustainability

The need to integrate environmental concerns into city governance and planning represents a major shift in urban policy thinking in the last decades. The prevailing focus on built infrastructure of the 1970s moved gradually towards a landscape and territorial approach. Urban forest in its larger meaning (Konijnendijk and Gauthier 2006) is a public asset that must be protected, maintained and also improved over time. To achieve this, elected officials and planning agencies must balance regional and community growth with environmental quality. Urban forestry requires innovative approaches to working together with a range of stakeholders to plan and manage all the resources that constitute the "urban forest", so it is important to find clearer ways to learn from innovation and experience (Lawrence et al. 2013).

Over the last decade there has been an increasing interest in urban green space, trees and forests but it has focused largely on the benefits (social, environmental and economic), the distribution of those benefits, and technical aspects of tree and green space management (Lawrence and Carter 2009). Much less attention has been paid to the processes, interactions, organizations, and decisions which lead to the establishment and maintenance of such resources and the resulting benefits. This complex area of human organization and behaviour is referred to as governance (Lawrence and Ambrose-Oji 2010).

Urban forest governance is still a new concept, particularly in Europe (Bentsen et al. 2010). In the USA, individual aspects of urban forest governance have been widely discussed but the term *governance* has rarely been used. In other parts of the world it is virtually unknown.

Compared with traditional rural forest governance, urban forest governance involves a much wider range of stakeholders, interacting with state and non-governmental organizations operating at multiple scales. All levels of government can impact on urban forests, from national level (administrations and policies relating not only to forestry, environmental protection, natural resources, nature conservation, but also to transport or road works), to various scales of local government (Van Herzele et al. 2005; Trefon et al. 2007). Urban forests are intensively used for a wide range of purposes and to obtain a number of benefits and services.

As a result, interest groups and user demands play an important role in urban forest governance but differ from city to city, depending on which benefits and services are dominating.

One of the main difficulties in applying an integrated approach to urban forest policy at the local level is that in many countries the local authorities' responsibilities for trees and woodlands are split between different departments with different visions and mandates.

Urban forests are still frequently an afterthought in the process of developing comprehensive plans at local and national scales. Often, there is a fundamental disconnect between the community's vision of environmental quality and the ecosystem functions and services that constitute the cornerstone for achieving environmental quality and sustainable development (Schwab 2009). Good data and inclusive dialogue across disciplines, sectors and institutions are necessary components of any successful planning process. Both are currently lacking in nearly all regions and countries, but many local entities are compiling good data and instituting progressive practices to engage affected landowners and interest groups, and to develop a sustainable green vision for their communities.

The results of more comprehensive research on urban forestry are driving planners towards new models of urban management where social inclusion, cultural integration, water and food security and well-being are being adopted as core objectives. An integrated management style (Randrup 2006) is recommended as the best way to harmonize urban forests and green infrastructure in the frame of urban governance. The Urban Forest Management Plan of the city of Gresham, Oregon (USA), is one of the best examples of a working application of new concepts of integrated environmental governance (https://greshamoregon.gov/urbanforestryplan/).

An important development in recent years concerns the ongoing attempts to link urban forestry to wider urban development: the *urbanscape* approach and the policies based on *green infrastructure* represent a short medium–term perspective for city decision-making and planning and for urban environmental programmes.

Needs and perspectives: designing the future of urban forests and green infrastructure

Policy

The institutionalization of urban forestry has further progressed in North America, where the concept of urban forestry has become an integral part of policy and legislation. Asian countries and particularly China are rapidly developing policy and planning tools for urban forests. European countries refer to urban green space and peri-urban afforestation in their policies and legislation (Bentsen et al. 2010), but the concept of urban forestry is seldom used explicitly. This is particularly true in Mediterranean Europe as well as in northern African countries. Networking and exchange of experiences and ideas is growing and there is a promising perspective for a more effective policy approach to urban forestry in this region of the world.

Africa is still lacking specific policies on urban forestry except in a few cities. A policy framework is lacking (Conigliaro et al. 2014) and there is a concrete need to develop tools and reference experiences in a continent that has the fastest urban growth in the world.

In order to be successful, urban forestry requires a strategic perspective and the development of targeted, specific policies as well as of sufficient capacities. Guidelines and scientific/technical solutions are already available to some extent but there is a need to produce more effective as well as clear and simple tools to support the decision-making processes at various levels (from local to global).

Although positive perceptions are dominant, the potential negative aspects of forests and trees in urban and peri-urban contexts such as wildfires, diseases, crime (Sreetheran et al. 2014) and increased allergies still need to be properly explained and placed in the framework of active policies on urban forests and trees (Cariñanos et al. 2014).

Local communities should benefit from urban forests, and legal, economic and institutional arrangements should be in place to ensure this. In many countries, land tenure is still a major constraint to proactive community involvement in urban forestry and related activities. Moreover, planning, design and management of urban forest resources is even more complex than in the previous decade (Carreiro et al. 2008). In fact, the effects of urban forestry actions are becoming significant to a wider set of actors, while the number of individuals and groups involved is growing.

The perspective of integrated governance and collaborative programmes oriented towards involving an increasing number of stakeholders requires collaborative efforts among decision-makers, experts, researchers and the civil society.

Research needs and perspectives

Ongoing research on urban forestry shows a complex pattern of research lines and it is rather difficult to capture gaps in knowledge and the research needs within urban forestry.

Priority topics for research mentioned in different fora and publications include species selection, managing pests, diseases and abiotic stress caused, for instance, by air pollution, adaptation mechanisms to climate changes and eco-physiological constraints of trees growing in the urban environment. There is also a need for additional knowledge on the relationship between green infrastructure and soil sealing.

Other research needs relate to the development of environmentally sound adaptive management methods, studies of public preferences and changing demands for urban forest benefits, assessment of these ecosystem services and related payments, strategies for sustainable development, and the development of better information and public participation tools. Performance indicators for ecosystem services and the methods of balancing the payments of ecosystem services (PES) also need to be explored more in depth.

The development of expert systems to support planning and management has improved in the last decade but research is still needed on methodologies for capacity building and user-friendly solutions. Applied research to support decision-making processes and collaborative and public involvement processes is still rather poor. Efforts are required in activating multidisciplinary research to strengthen the knowledge base on green infrastructure at various levels, from the pattern and processes of urban ecosystems to inter-sectoral dialogue.

Research on urban forestry and green infrastructure needs to be supported and improved in several regions of the world. Africa, some countries of Latin America and the Caribbean, and southern and western Asia have huge gaps in basic knowledge in almost all the research sectors referring to urban forestry and green infrastructure. The need for technology transfer and information-sharing exists not only within countries, but also between countries and the world's regions. Calls for research networking, identification of centres of research excellence, and the establishment of demonstration urban forests and landscape laboratories are some of the potential tools for applied research in the domain of urban forestry and green infrastructure. In order to meet these calls and make sure that developing countries are not excluded, sustainable donor and other funding options need to be explored, as already pointed out by Konijnendijk and Gauthier (2006).

Educational needs and perspectives

In the last decade, the inclusion of urban forestry in education has advanced substantially in Europe, North America, central northern Asia and the Pacific. It is still in its early stages of development, or completely neglected in other parts of the world. One of the major challenges is to develop integrated educational programmes on green infrastructure. Programmes and courses should make an effort to focus on the strengths not only of urban forestry concepts and practices, but also of incorporating multiple perspectives and disciplines, and take a comprehensive view of the green infrastructure resources.

Initiatives taken in the direction of international cooperation in education should be encouraged. Life-long learning opportunities should be activated and promoted to update professionals on the current knowledge on urban forestry and green infrastructure. The work of the International Society of Arboriculture (ISA), the International Federation of Landscape Architects (IFA) and other organizations to enhance the professionalism of green space practitioners, for example through international certification and accreditation, should be supported and further developed. In parallel, there is a clear need for enhancing higher-education opportunities for designers, planners and policy advisors of green infrastructure and integrated environmental governance.

Urban forestry for development, and green infrastructure for the future cities

The experiences described above show the significant potential of urban forestry and green infrastructure for any city and town of the world, in low-income countries as well as in the so-called developed world. The concept of green infrastructure promotes inclusiveness in terms of involving experts, policy-makers and stakeholders from all walks of life. The need to join forces with other initiatives aimed at sustainable urban development is therefore crucial. Green infrastructure needs to dialogue and to find synergies with other comprehensive approaches for natural resource management and land use in intra-urban areas, at the urban fringe, and at the urban–rural interface, such as urban greening, green structure planning and landscape planning, nature conservation, forestry, agroforestry and agriculture. Green infrastructure is definitely a place where it is possible to provide urban livelihoods and help cities "farm for the future". The same piece of land should not have to accommodate conflicts between urban forestry, urban agriculture, urban agroforestry, and urban recreation but should host an integrated opportunity for providing significant benefits to urban dwellers.

References

Abd-Elrahman, A. H.; Thornhill, M. E.; Andreu, M. G. and Escobedo, F. 2010. A community-based urban forest inventory using online mapping services and consumer-grade digital images. *International Journal of Applied Earth Observation and Geoinformation* 12 (4): 249–260.

Abd'razack, N.T.A.; Nazir bin M. A. 2013. Wood fuel consumption and ecological footprint of African cities. *International Journal of Education and Research* 1 (2): 129–146.

Agyeman, K. O.; Amponsah, O.; Braimah, I.; Lurumuah, S. 2012. Commercial charcoal production and sustainable community development of the Upper West Region, Ghana. *Journal of Sustainable Development* 5 (4): 149–163.

Åkerlund, U. 2006. Urban and peri-urban forestry and greening in west and Central Asia Experiences, constraints and prospects. LSP Working Paper 36. Rome: FAO.

Alexander, C.; McDonald, C. 2014. Urban forests: The value of trees in the city of Toronto. Toronto: TD Economics.

Alkire, S.; Chatterjee, M.; Conconi, A.; Seth, S.; Vaz, A. 2014. Poverty in rural and urban areas: Direct comparisons using the global MPI. Oxford: Poverty and Human Development Initiative, University of Oxford. Available from: www.ophi.org.uk.

Alonzo, M.; Bookhagen, B.; Roberts, D. A. 2014. Urban tree species mapping using hyperspectral and lidar data fusion. *Remote Sensing of Environment* 148: 70–83.

Arnbjerg-Nielsen, K.; Fleischer, H. S. 2009. Feasible adaptation strategies for increased risk of flooding in cities due to climate change. *Water Science and Technology* 60 (2): 273–281.

Atmiş, E.; Günşen, H. B.; Yücedağ, C.; Lise, W. 2012. Status, use and management of urban forests in Turkey. *South East European Forestry (SEEFOR)* 3 (2): 69–78.

Azar, C.; Lindgren, K.; Obersteiner, M.; Riahi, K.; Vuuren, D. P. van; Elzen, K.M.G. J. den; Möllersten, K.; Larson, E. D. 2010. The feasibility of low CO_2 concentration targets and the role of bio-energy with carbon capture and storage (BECCS). *Climatic Change* 100: 195–202.

Baker, J. L. 2008. Urban poverty: A global view. Washington, DC: World Bank.

Benedict, M. A.; McMahon, E. T. 2006. Green infrastructure: Linking landscapes and communities. Washington, DC: Island Press.

Bentsen, P.; Lindholst, A. C.; Konijnendijk, C. C. 2010. Reviewing eight years of urban forestry and urban greening: Taking stock, looking ahead. *Urban Forestry and Urban Greening* 9: 273–280.

Berto, R. 2007. Assessing the restorative value of the environment: A study on the elderly in comparison with young adults and adolescents. *International Journal of Psychology* 42 (5): 331–341.

Besse, F.; Conigliaro, M.; Fages, B.; Gauthier, M.; Mille, G.; Salbitano, F.; Sanesi, G. 2014. Montpellier, green city. *Unasylva* 65 (242): 23–28.

Bird, W.; Bosch, M. van den (eds.) 2015. Nature and public health: The role of nature in improving the health of a population. Oxford: Oxford University Press.

Breña Puyol, A.; Breña Naranjo, J. 2009. Problemática del recurso agua en grandes ciudades: zona Metropolitana del valle de Mexico. *Contacto S.* 74: 10–18.

Britt, C.; Johnston, M. 2008. Trees in towns II: A new survey of urban trees in England and their condition and management. London: Department for Communities and Local Government (CLG).

Brown, R. R.; Farrelly, M. A. 2009. Delivering sustainable urban water management: A review of the hurdles we face. *Water Science and Technology* 59: 839–846.

Camhis, M. 2006. Sustainable development and urbanization. In: *The future of sustainability.* (Ed.) Marco, K. Netherlands: Springer, pp. 69–98.

Cappiella, K.; Schueler, T.; Wright, T. 2005. Urban watershed forestry manual. Part 1: Methods for increasing forest cover in a watershed. Washington, DC: United States Department of Agriculture (USDA).

Cappiella, K.; Schueler, T.; Wright, T. 2006a. Urban watershed forestry manual. Part 2: Conserving and planting trees at development sites. Washington, DC: United States Department of Agriculture (USDA).

Cappiella, K.; Schueler, T.; Wright, T. 2006b. Urban watershed forestry manual. Part 3: Urban tree planting guide. Washington, DC: United States Department of Agriculture (USDA).

Cariñanos, P.; Casares-Porcel, M.; Quesada-Rubio, J.-M. 2014. Estimating the allergenic potential of urban green spaces: A case-study in Granada, Spain. *Landscape and Urban Planning* 123: 134–144.

Carreiro, M. M; Song, Y. C.; Wu, J. (eds.) 2008. Ecology, planning and management of urban forests: International perspectives. New York: Springer Science.

Carrus, G.; Lafortezza, R.; Colangelo, G.; Dentamaro I.; Scopelliti, M.; Sanesi, G. 2013. Relations between naturalness and perceived restorativeness of different urban green spaces. *Psychology* 4: 227–244.

Carrus, G.; Scopelliti, M.; Lafortezza, R.; Colangelo, G.; Ferrini, F.; Salbitano, F.; Agrimi, M.; Portoghesi, L.; Semenzato, P.; Sanesi, G. 2014. Go greener, feel better? The positive effects of biodiversity on the well-being of individuals visiting urban and peri-urban green areas. *Landscape and Urban Planning* 134: 221–228.

Chen, W.Y.; Jim, C.Y. 2008. Assessment and valuation of the ecosystem services provided by urban forests. In: *Ecology, planning and management of urban forests: International perspectives.* (Eds.) Carreiro, M. M.; Song. Y. C.; Wu, J. New York: Springer Science, pp. 53–83.

Conigliaro, M.; Borelli, S.; Salbitano, F. 2014. Urban and peri-urban forestry as a valuable strategy towards African urban sustainable development. *Nature and Fauna* 28 (2): 21–26.

Corona, P.; Agrimi, M.; Baffetta, F.; Barbati, A.; Chiriacò, M. V.; Fattorini, L.; Pompei, E.; Valentini, R.; Mattioli, W. 2011. Extending large-scale forest inventories to assess urban forests. *Environmental Monitoring and Assessment* 184 (3): 1409–1422.

Council of Europe 2000. General guidelines for the development of the Pan-European Ecological Network. Nature and Environment Series No. 107. Strasbourg: Council of Europe.

Cullington, J.; Gye, J. 2010. Urban forests: A climate adaptation guide. British Columbia: Ministry of Community, Sport and Cultural Development. Available from: www.retooling. ca/_Library/docs/Urban_Forests_Guide.pdf.

Davies, C.; McGloin, C.; MacFarlane, R.; Roe, M. 2006. Green infrastructure planning guide project: Final report. Annfield Plain: North East Community Forests.

Dobbs, C.; Escobedo, F. J.; Zipperer, W. C. 2011. A framework for developing urban forest ecosystem services and goods indicators. *Landscape and Urban Planning* 99: 196–206.

Dobbs, C.; Kendal, D.; Nitschke, C. R. 2014. Multiple ecosystem services and disservices of the urban forest establishing their connections with landscape structure and sociodemographics. *Ecological Indicators* 43: 44–55.

Drigo, R.; Salbitano, F. 2008. WISDOM for cities: Analysis of wood energy and urbanization using WISDOM methodology. Rome: FAO Forestry Department.

Dubbeling, M. 2014. Integrating urban and peri-urban agriculture and forestry (UPAF) in city climate change strategies. Final project report. Nairobi: UN-Habitat; Leusden: RUAF Foundation.

Duryea, M. L.; Kampf, E.; Littell, R. C.; Rodríguez-Pedraza, C. D. 2007. Hurricanes and the urban forest: II. Effects on tropical and subtropical tree species. *Journal of Arboriculture and Urban Forestry* 33 (2): 98–112.

Escobedo, F. J.; Kroeger, T.; Wagner, J. E. 2011. Urban forests and pollution mitigation: Analyzing ecosystem services and disservices. *Environmental Pollution* 159: 2078–2087.

Escobedo, F. J.; Varela, S.; Zhao, M.; Wagner, J. E.; Zipperer, W. 2010. Analyzing the efficacy of subtropical urban forests in offsetting carbon emissions from cities. *Environmental Science and Policy* 13: 362–372.

Escobedo, F. J.; Wagner J. E.; Nowak D. J.; De la Maza, C. L.; Rodriguez, M.; Crane, D. E. 2008. Analyzing the cost effectiveness of Santiago: Chile's policy of using urban forests to improve air quality. *Journal of Environmental Management* 86: 148–157.

European Commission 2013. Green infrastructure (GI): Enhancing Europe's natural capital. Communication from the Commission to the European Parliament, the Council, the European Economic and Social Committee and the Committee of the Regions. Bruxelles: European Commission.

FAO 2007. State of the world's forests 2007. Rome: Food and Agriculture Organization of the United Nations (FAO).

FAO 2009. Stratégie de développement et plan d'action pour la promotion de la foresterie urbaine et périurbaine de la ville de Bangui. Urban and Peri-urban Forestry Working Paper 3. Rome: FAO.

FAO 2011. State of the world's forests 2011. Rome: FAO.

FAO 2012a. Plateforme WISDOM pour N'Djaména, Tchad. Diagnostic et cartographie de l'offre et de la demande en combustible ligneux. Urban and Peri-urban Forestry Working Paper 8. Rome: FAO.

FAO 2012b. Proposition de fiches-projets prioritaires pour la phase 1 de la stratégie de foresterie urbaine et périurbaine de la ville de N'Djaména, Tchad. Appui à la formulation d'une stratégie nationale et d'un plan d'action de foresterie urbaine et périurbaine à N'Djaména, République du Tchad. Document de travail. Rome: FAO.

FAO 2012c. Synthèse des études thématiques sur la foresterie urbaine et périurbaine de N'Djaména, Tchad. Urban and Peri-urban Forestry Working Paper 7. Rome: FAO.

FAO 2012d. Urban and peri-urban forestry in Africa: The outlook for wood fuel. Urban and Peri-urban Forestry Working Paper 4. Rome: FAO.

FAO 2013. Advancing agroforestry on the policy agenda: A guide for decision-makers. (Ed.) Buttoud, G. Agroforestry Working Paper 1. Rome: FAO.

FAO 2014a. FAO trees connecting people in action together. Developing guidelines for decision and policy makers: Trees and forests for healthy cities. Meeting proceedings Glasgow, United Kingdom, 30–31 May 2011. Urban and Periurban Forestry Working Paper No. 9. Rome: FAO.

FAO 2014b. FAO international workshop: Developing guidelines for decision and policy makers: Optimizing trees and forests for healthy cities. Meeting Proceedings, New Delhi, India, 7 March 2012. Urban and Periurban Forestry Working Paper No. 10. Rome: FAO.

Fargione, J.; Hill, J.; Tilman, D.; Polasky, S.; Hawthorne, P. 2008. Land clearing and the biofuel carbon debt. *Science* 319: 1235–1238.

Foresta, H. de; Somarriba, E.; Temu, A.; Boulanger, D.; Feuilly, H.; Gauthier, M. 2013. Towards the assessment of trees outside forests. Resources Assessment Working Paper 183. Rome: FAO.

FSI 2009. State of forest report 2009. Forest survey of India. Dehradun: Ministry of Environment and Forests.

Fuwape, J. A.; Onyekwelu, J. C. 2011. Urban forest development in West Africa: Benefits and challenges. *Journal of Biodiversity and Ecological Sciences* 1 (1): 77–94.

Gash, J.H.C.; Rosier, P.T.W.; Ragab, R. 2008. A note on estimating urban roof runoff with a forest evaporation model. *Hydrological Processes* 22: 1230–1233.

Gill, S. E.; Handley, J. F.; Ennos, A. R.; Pauleit, S. 2007. Adapting cities for climate change: The role of green infrastructure. *Climate Change and Cities* 33 (1): 115–133.

Grahn, P.; Stigsdotter, U. K. 2010. The relation between perceived sensory dimensions of urban green space and stress restoration. *Landscape and Urban Planning* 94 (3–4): 264–27.

Guite, H. F.; Clark, C.; Ackrill, G. 2006. The impact of the physical and urban environment on mental well-being. *Public Health* 120: 1117–1126.

HCEFLD 2010. Guide des forêts urbaines et périurbaines du Maroc. Maroc: Haut Commissaire aux Eaux et Forêts et à la Lutte Contre la Désertification (HCEFLD).

He, C.; Convertino, M.; Feng, Z.; Zhang, S. 2013. Using LiDAR data to measure the 3D green biomass of Beijing urban forest in China. *PLoS ONE* 8 (10): e75920. doi:10.1371/journal.pone.0075920.

Heerwagen, J. 2009. Biophilia, health, and well-being. In: *Restorative commons: Creating health and well-being through urban landscapes.* (Eds.) Campbell, L.; Wiesen, A. Newtown Square, PA: U.S. Department of Agriculture, Forest Service, Northern Research Station, pp. 38–57.

Herzele, A. van; Clercq, E. M. de; Wiedemann, T. 2005. Strategic planning for new woodlands in the urban periphery: Through the lens of social inclusiveness. *Urban Forestry and Urban Greening* 3: 177–188.

Hoekman, S. K. 2009. Biofuels in the U.S.: Challenges and opportunities. *Renewable Energy* 34: 14–22.

ICLEI 2006. Talking trees. An urban forestry toolkit for local governments. Available from: www.milliontreesnyc.org/downloads/pdf/talking_trees_urban_forestry_toolkit.pdf.

IPCC 2014. Climate change 2014: Mitigation of climate change. Contribution of Working Group III to the Fifth Assessment Report of the Intergovernmental Panel on Climate Change (IPCC). Cambridge: Cambridge University Press.

Jim, C. Y.; Chen, W. Y. 2009. Ecosystem services and valuation of urban forests in China. *Cities* 26 (4): 187–194.

Konijnendijk, C. C.; Gauthier, M. 2006. Urban forestry for multifunctional urban land use. In: *Cities farming for the future: Urban agriculture for green and productive cities.* (Ed.) Veenhuizen, R. van. Leusden: RUAF Foundation; Ottawa: International Development Research Centre; Manila: International Institute for Rural Reconstruction Publishing, pp. 411–442.

Kuchelmeister, G. 1998. Urban forestry: Present situation and prospects in the Asia and Pacific region. FAO Asia-Pacific Forestry Sector Outlook Study, FAO Working Paper No. APFSOS/WP/44. Rome: FAO.

Kyle, H. C.; Kimberly, A. N. 2013. Introducing urban food forestry: A multifunctional approach to increase food security and provide ecosystem services. *Landscape Ecology* 28: 1649–1669.

Lafortezza, R.; Carrus, G.; Sanesi, G.; Davies, C. 2009. Benefits and well-being perceived by people visiting green spaces in periods of heat stress. *Urban Forestry and Urban Greening* 8: 97–108.

Lawrence, A.; Ambrose-Oji, B. 2010. Understanding the effects of community woodlands and forests in Great Britain. In: *Proceedings of the 18th Commonwealth Forestry Conference, Edinburgh, UK, 28 June–2 July 2010.* Edinburgh: Conference Ltd.

Lawrence, A.; Carter, C. 2009. Human behavioural and institutional change. In: *Combating climate change: A role for UK forests: Main report. An assessment of the potential of the UK's trees and woodlands to mitigate and adapt to climate change.* (Eds.) Read, D. J.; Freer-Smith, P.H.; Morison, J.I.L.; Hanley, N.; West, C. C.; Snowdon, P. London: The Stationery Office, pp. 209–214.

Lawrence, A.B.; Escobedo, F. J. 2012. Analyzing growth and mortality in a subtropical urban forest ecosystem. *Landscape and Urban Planning* 104 (1): 85–94.

Lawrence, A.; Vreese, R. de; Johnston, M.; Konijnendijk, C. C.; Sanesi, G. 2013. Urban forest governance: Towards a framework for comparing approaches. *Urban Forestry and Urban Greening* 12 (4): 464–473.

Li, W.; Wang, F.; Bell, S. 2007. Simulating the sheltering effects of windbreaks in urban outdoor space. *Journal of Wind Engineering and Industrial Aerodynamics* 95 (7): 533–549.

Lundholm, J. T.; Marlin, A. 2006. Habitat origins and microhabitat preferences of urban plant species. *Urban Ecosystems* 9: 139–159.

MacFaden, S. W.; O'Neil-Dunne, J.P.; Royar, A.R.; Lu, J. W.; Rundle, A.G. 2012. High resolution tree canopy mapping for New York City using LIDAR and object-based image analysis. *Journal of Applied Remote Sensing* 6 (1): 70–83.

Marien, J. N. 2009. Peri-urban forests and wood energy: What are the perspectives for Central Africa? In: *The forests of the Congo Basin: State of the forest 2009.* (Eds.) Wasseige, C. de; Devers, D.; Marcken, P. de; Eba'a Atyi, R; Mayaux, P. Luxembourg: Publications Office of the European Union.

McGee, J. A.; Day, S. D.; Wynne, R. H.; White, M. B. 2012. Using geospatial tools to assess the urban tree canopy: Decision support for local governments. *Journal of Forestry* 110 (5): 275–286.

McPherson, E.G.; Simpson, J. R.; Peper, P. J.; Maco, S. E.; Xiao, Q. 2005. Municipal forest benefits and costs in five US cities. *Journal of Forestry* 103 (8): 411–416.

McPherson, E.G.; Simpson, J. R.; Xiao, Q.; Wu, C. 2008. Million trees: Los Angeles canopy cover and benefit assessment. *Landscape and Urban Planning* 99 (1): 40–50.

Mell, I. C. 2007. Green infrastructure planning: What are the costs for health and well-being? *Journal of Environment, Culture, Economic and Social Sustainability* 3 (5): 117–124.

Mell, I. C. 2010. Green infrastructure: Concepts, perceptions and its use in spatial planning. Doctoral dissertation, Newcastle: School of Architecture, Planning and Landscape, Newcastle University.

Mwampamba, T. H. 2007. Has the wood fuel crisis returned? Urban charcoal consumption in Tanzania and its implications to present and future forest availability. *Energy Policy* 35: 4221–4234.

Nagendra, H.; Gopal, D. 2010. Street trees in Bangalore: Density, diversity, composition and distribution. *Urban Forestry and Urban Greening* 9: 129–137.

Natural England; Royal Society for the Protection of Birds. 2014. Climate change adaptation manual. Available from: www.naturalengland.org.uk

Nowak, D. J.; Crane, D.; Stevens, J.; Hoehn, R.; Walton, J.; Bond, J. 2008. A ground-based method of assessing urban forest structure and ecosystem services. *Arboriculture and Urban Forestry* 34 (6): 347–358.

Nowak, D. J.; Greenfield, E. J. 2010. Urban and community forests of the North Central East region: Illinois, Indiana, Michigan, Ohio, Wisconsin. Newtown Square, PA: U.S. Department of Agriculture, Forest Service, Northern Research Station.

Nowak, D. J.; Hoehn III, R. E.; Crane, D. E.; Stevens, J. C.; Walton, J. T. 2007. Assessing urban forest effects and values. Resource Bulletin NRS-6. Newtown Square, PA: U.S. Department of Agriculture, Forest Service, Northern Research Station.

Olowo-n'djo Tchala. 2011. African self-empowerment through fair trade. Shea butter. Available from: www.fairworldproject.org.

Pauleit, S.; Jones, N.; Nyhuus, S.; Pirnat, J.; Salbitano, F. 2005. Urban forest resources in European Cities. In: *Urban forests and trees.* (Eds.) Konijnendijk, C. C.; Nilsson, K.; Randrup, T. B.; Schipperijn, J. Berlin: Springer; New York: Heidelberg, pp. 49–80.

Pearson, L. J.; Coggan, A.; Proctor, W.; Smith, T. F. 2009. A sustainable decision support framework for urban water management. *Water Resources Management* 24: 363–376.

Randrup, T. B. 2006. Editorial: Integrated green-space planning and management. *Urban Forestry and Urban Greening* 4: 91.

Ravallion, M.; Chen, S.; Sangraula, P. 2007. New evidence on the urbanization of global poverty. Policy Research Working Paper 4199. Washington, DC: World Bank.

Ruth, M.; Coelho, D. 2007. Understanding and managing the complexity of urban systems under climate change. *Climate Policy* 7: 317–336.

Sandström, U. G. 2008. Biodiversity and green infrastructure in urban landscapes: The importance of urban green spaces. Saarbrücken: VDM Verlag Dr. Muller.

Scalenghe, R.; Marsan, F. A. 2009. The anthropogenic sealing of soils in urban areas. *Landscape and Urban Planning* 90 (1–2): 1–10.

Schreyer, J., Tigges, J., Lakes, T., Churkina, G. 2014. Using airborne LiDAR and QuickBird data for modelling urban tree carbon storage and its distribution. A case study of Berlin. *Remote Sensing* 6: 10636–10655.

Schure, J.; Ingram, V.; Marien, J.-N.; Nasi, R.; Dubiez, E. 2011. Wood fuel for urban centres in the Democratic Republic of Congo. The number one energy and forest product returns to the policy agenda. CIFOR Briefs. No. 7. Bogor: Centre for International Forestry Research (CIFOR). Available from: www.cifor.org.

Schwab, J. (ed.) 2009. Planning the urban forest, ecology, economy, and community development. Chicago: APA Planning Association.

Seppälä, R.; Buck, A.; Katila, P. (eds.). 2009. Adaptation of forests and people to climate change. A global assessment report. IUFRO World Series Volume 22. Helsinki: International Urban Forestry Research Organisation (IUFRO).

Shashua-Bar, L.; Pearlmutter, D.; Evyatar, E. 2010. The influence of trees and grass on outdoor thermal comfort in a hot-arid environment. *International Journal of Climatology* 31 (10): 1498–1506.

Singh, V. S.; Pandey, D. N.; Chaudhry, P. 2010. Urban forests and open green spaces: Lessons for Jaipur, Rajasthan, India. Jaipur: Rajasthan State Pollution Control Board (RSCP).

Sreetheran, M.; Konijnendijk van den Bosch, C. C. 2014. A socio-ecological exploration of fear of crime in urban green spaces: A systematic review. *Urban Forestry and Urban Greening* 13 (1): 1–18.

Tanumihardjo, A.; Anderson, C.; Kaufer-Horwitz, M.; Bode, L.; Linden, D.; Emenaker, N. J.; Haqq, A. M.; Satia, J. A.; Silver, H. J.; Stadler, D. D. 2007. Poverty, obesity, and malnutrition: An international perspective recognizing the paradox. *Journal of the American Dietetic Association* 107 (11): 1966–1972.

Timilsina, N.; Escobedo, F. J.; Staudhammer, C. L.; Brandeis, T. 2014. Analyzing the causal factors of carbon stores in a subtropical urban forest. *Ecological Complexity* 20: 23–32.

Tiwary, A.; Sinnet, D.; Peachey, C.; Chalabi, Z.; Vardoulakis, S.; Fletcher, T.; Leonardi, G.; Grundy, C.; Azapagic, A.; Hutchings, T. 2009. An integrated tool to assess the role of new planting in PM10 capture and human health benefits: A case study in London. *Environmental Pollution* 157: 2645–2653.

Tovar-Corzo, G. 2013. Aproximación a la silvicultura urbana en Colombia. *Revista Bitácora Urbano Territorial* 22 (1): 119–136.

Townsend, M. 2006. Feel blue? Touch green! Participation in forest/woodland management as a treatment for depression. *Urban Forestry and Urban Greening* 5: 111–120.

Trefon, T.; Cogels, S.; Mutambwe, S. 2007. Espaces périurbains d'Afrique centrale et gouvernance environnementale. Brussels: Université Libre.

Tsiros, I. T. 2010. Assessment and energy implications of street air temperature cooling by shade trees in Athens (Greece) under extremely hot weather conditions. *Renewable Energy* 35: 1866–1869.

Tuaño, P. A.; Sescon, J. 2013. The "Alliance of 7": Climate change adaptation in the Greater Metro Manila Region. *Philippine Human Development Reports* 2012/2013 (13): 1–31. Available from: http://hdn.org.ph/wp-content/uploads/DP_13_Tuano_Sescon.pdf.

Tzoulas, K.; Korpela, K.; Venn, S.; Yli-Pelkonen, V.; Ka´zmierczak, A.; Niemela J.; James P. 2007. Promoting ecosystem and human health in urban areas using green infrastructure: A literature review. *Landscape and Urban Planning* 81: 167–178.

Ulrich, R. S. 2002. Health benefits of gardens in hospitals. Paper for the Conference Plants for People, International Exhibition Floriade, Venlo, The Netherlands, 5 April–7 October 2002. Available from: http://plantsolutions.com/documents/HealthSettingsUlrich.pdf.

UN-Habitat 2013. State of the world's cities. Prosperity of cities. New York: Earthscan.

UN-Habitat 2014. The state of African cities 2014: Re-imagining sustainable urban transitions. Nairobi: UN-Habitat.

United Nations 2014. World urbanization prospects: The 2014 revision, highlights. New York: UN – Department of Economic and Social Affairs, Population Division.

Vries, S. de; Classen, T.; Eigenheer-Hug, S.; Korpela, K.; Maas, J.; Mitchell, R.; Schantz, P. 2011. Contributions of natural environments to physical activity. Theory and evidence base. In: *Forests, trees and human health.* (Eds.) Nillson, K.; Sangster, M.; Gallis, C.; Hartig, T.; de Vries, S.; Seeland, K.; Schipperijn, J. Berlin: Springer, pp. 205–243.

Wang, X. J. 2009. Analysis of problems in urban green space system planning in China. *Journal of Forestry Research* 20 (1): 79–82.

Weldon, S.; Bailey, C.; O'Brien, L. 2007. New pathways to health and well-being: Summary of research to understand and overcome barriers to accessing woodland. Edinburgh: Forestry Commission Scotland.

WHO 1998. Health promotion glossary. Geneva: World Health Organization (WHO).

WHO 2013. Research for universal health coverage: World health report 2013. Geneva: World Health Organization (WHO).

Zeng, X.; Ma, Y.; Ma, L. 2007. Utilization of straw in biomass energy in China. *Renewable and Sustainable Energy Reviews* 11: 976–987.

Zhang, C.; Qiu, F. 2012. Mapping individual tree species in an urban forest using airborne Lidar data and hyperspectral imagery. *Photogrammetric Engineering and Remote Sensing* 78 (10): 1079–1087.

Zhou, Y.; Wang, Y. Q. 2007. An assessment of impervious surface areas in Rhode Island. *Northeastern Naturalist* 14 (4): 643–650.

Zulu, L. C. 2010. The forbidden fuel: Charcoal, urban wood fuel demand and supply dynamics, community forest management and wood fuel policy in Malawi. *Energy Policy* 38: 3717–3730.

12

URBAN AQUACULTURE FOR RESILIENT FOOD SYSTEMS

Stuart W. Bunting[1] and David C. Little[2]

1 BUNTING AQUACULTURE, AGRICULTURE AND AQUATIC CONSERVATION SERVICES', ENGLAND

2 INSTITUTE OF AQUACULTURE, UNIVERSITY OF STIRLING, SCOTLAND

Introduction

Urban aquaculture has been defined in several ways. Clearly the location of aquacultural production within built-up areas of cities or within municipal administrative boundaries can be classified as such but the definition 'urban' has been attached to aquaculture outside this strictly literal definition (Little et al. 2012). Aquacultural practices established in conjunction with commercial, industrial and infrastructural developments – for example, power stations and dams for hydro-electric power generation – have previously been categorized as urban (Bunting and Little 2003, 2005; Leschen et al. 2005; Bunting et al. 2006). Aquaculture located on the edge of towns and cities *(peri-urban)* that makes use of nutrient-enriched drainage and sewerage water for producing food and at the same time treats the waste is often termed urban (Edwards 2003). The city as a source of nutrients and other key inputs, as well as being the major demand driver for the outputs, explains the location of much traditional or emergent aquaculture being located close to urban settlements. The very nature of 'urban' in densely populated, dynamic economies that are increasingly well networked is subject to redefinition (Leschen et al. 2005; Little and Bunting 2005). Aquacultural practices developed in rural areas but inspired by examples operated in urban areas or based on knowledge derived from urban-rural migrants and returning students or intended to supply demand from urban markets may be regarded as urban from a socio-cultural or social-psychological perspective (Iaquinta and Drescher 2000; Bunting and Little 2005).

A range of physical systems with different technical attributes are used in urban aquaculture. These range from shallow irrigated ricefields modified to allow alternate or continuous production of aquatic vegetables, fish or crustacea through, to adapted natural lakes or man-made reservoirs, to extensive natural or modified wetlands. A key requirement is that water quality is maintained through balancing inputs (feeds, fertilizers) with management to ensure adequate dissolved oxygen and other water quality parameters (e.g., low concentrations of toxic compounds and optimal nutrient levels for in situ primary production). In *extensive* systems, in which productivity is based solely on natural run-off, this is mainly achieved through maintaining a low stocking density with regular stocking and harvesting of multiple species, whereas *intensive* systems such as tanks and cages usually involve a monoculture and require provision of complete formulated diets and careful water exchange. Compared to aquaculture in general, which is globally still dominated by *semi-intensive* aquaculture, urban production is more likely to be either *extensive* or *intensive,* reflecting the different risk and opportunity cost profiles (Table 12.1).

TABLE 12.1 Urban aquaculture systems, prevailing management regimes and production risks

Aquaculture system	Prevailing management regime	Production risks
Tanks	Tanks can be constructed from brickwork and concrete or preformed from plastic and corrugated metal sheets. Aeration and filtration can be used to condition the culture water and water exchange used to remove waste.	Poor water quality and the accumulation of waste can impact on production and in severe cases cause mass mortalities. High stocking densities can lead to the rapid spread of diseases.
Ponds	Ponds ranging from tens of square meters to several hectares can be made by digging and forming embankments to make the best use of cut-and-fill options. Ponds can be static or flow-through depending on the prevailing hydrology and access to water sources.	Poorly designed and constructed ponds can suffer from erosion and collapse of embankments. Ponds sited on inappropriate soil types can be difficult to seal to avoid leaks. Optimizing the productive potential of ponds by stimulating in situ primary production and feed use is difficult.
Ponds in converted ricefields[1]	Peripheral areas of ricefields might be excavated to permit the combined culture of fish and rice, or ricefields might be excavated completely for the sole purpose of aquaculture.	Maintenance of combined ricefield-pond systems can be difficult depending on the prevailing soil type and hydrology. Production in ponds created in rice growing areas may suffer from pesticide drift and run-off.
Borrow pits	Borrow pits are formed as a result of extracting aggregates, clay and soil. The excavations are often deep to maximize the amount of material extracted. The depth of water may make it difficult to promote primary production through fertilizer application and feeding may be needed. Cages can be used in borrow pits to avoid problems with them being too deep.	Borrow pits are often much deeper than might be desirable for fish culture, making it difficult to catch the fish or drain completely for maintenance and pre-stocking preparations. Borrow pits in low-lying areas are prone to flooding.

(Continued)

TABLE 12.1 (Continued)

Aquaculture system	Prevailing management regime	Production risks
Lakes and reservoirs	Fish can be stocked in lakes and reservoirs and supplementary feed given to increase production but catching them requires a significant effort. Cages can be used to contain the stocked fish and enhance feed conversion and husbandry.	Problems with poaching and harvesting fish from large water bodies can mean that financial returns are insufficient to cover associated costs. Fish released into lakes and reservoirs or stocked in cages are susceptible to pollution and poor water quality; excessive cage culture development can cause self-pollution.
Multifunctional wetlands[2]	Aquatic plants are often cultivated in peri-urban wetlands in southeast Asia and fertilizer and pesticides may be used to enhance production. Ponds can be constructed within wetlands and are typically managed semi-intensively.	Wetlands are prone to drying and flooding and rapid changes in water depth can cause problems for cultured animals and plants. Construction of ponds on acid-sulphate soils can lead to water quality problems affecting cultured animals.
Cages	Cages constructed with wood, plastic or steel frames and covered in netting typically range in size from 1–50 m^3 in freshwater situations and production depends on the provision of feed.	Free movement of water through cages can present problems when pollution is present if the prevailing quality is poor. Accidental or deliberate damage to cages can cause major stock losses.

Notes:

1 Areas of low-lying ricefields within peri-urban areas are often converted to ponds for aquaculture to enhance financial returns, but prevailing physical and hydrological conditions may not be ideal for pond culture.

2 Multifunctional wetlands are defined here as areas that are inundated with water for most of the year, dominated by emergent aquatic macrophytes and used for several purposes including food production, storm water discharge and wastewater treatment.

Source: authors.

Here we consider urban aquaculture from a geographical perspective as practices occurring within larger towns and cities (intra-urban) and at their edges in peri-urban areas. Aquaculture includes the production of any plant or animal in water and embraces finfish, shellfish (crustacea and molluscs) and a range of less orthodox species. Aquaculture production is globally centred on Asia and in freshwaters is dominated by finfish production; however, a very common type of aquaculture in Asia is the production of aquatic vegetables. Producers located in urban environments face similar challenges in terms of a) accessing space for production, often with insecure tenure arrangements and property rights, b) sourcing water of sufficient quality and quantity throughout the year to carry out aquaculture, and c) having limited access to institutional support, input and service providers and credit facilities.

An overview is provided below, regarding the different urban aquacultural production strategies that meet our geographical criteria, and the relevance of each to pro-poor and food security imperatives and sustainable urban development is described (Table 12.2). Risks associated with each, such as pollution and theft,

TABLE 12.2 Relevance of urban aquaculture to pro-poor action, food security and sustainable urban development and associated risks

Urban aquaculture production strategy	Relevance to pro-poor and food security	Relevance to sustainable urban development	Risks
Land-based culture systems	Market demand for cultured catfish presented new opportunities for underemployed youth to engage in rewarding livelihoods; small tank-based systems can provide homestead-based income generating opportunities for women.	Fish farming opportunities prompted investment in human capital that has contributed to social-economic development; aquaculture can facilitate integrated production of agricultural crops; visits to fish farms by school children foster learning and understanding amongst their families.	Institutional capacity is often lacking, especially the limited capacity of government extension services to support commercial aquaculture development; access to credit also presents a barrier to expansion and new entrants.
Ponds, borrow pits and lakes	Numerous ponds within larger towns and peri-urban areas of secondary cities and borrow pits left following clay and soil extraction for construction can make a notable but often overlooked contribution to supplying fish to urban markets. Multifunctional urban lakes can alleviate flooding in low-lying areas housing poor and marginal groups; fish produced in urban water-bodies can provide an affordable protein source.	Ponds in larger towns and peri-urban areas often receive combined flows of domestic wastewater and surface run-off and facilitate treatment processes that contribute towards environmental protection. Retaining urban lakes can provide capacity for storm water discharge to mitigate flooding and open spaces that are beneficial for psychological well-being and an environment to capitalize on recreation and tourist economies. Aquatic production can be a good functional bio-indicator of environmental health.	Stagnant water bodies can suffer from intermittent poor water quality leading to fish kills; standing water can harbour disease vectors and parasites; it is difficult for operators to monitor their ponds and therefore they are vulnerable to thefts. Urban lakes can be regarded as prime areas for commercial and residential development and appropriate controls are needed.
Multifunctional wetlands	Foraging in urban wetlands can yield animals and plants for human consumption or livestock feed; women engage in cultivating aquatic plants with minimal costs and risks. Large areas of fish and shrimp ponds downstream of cities in the tropics provide employment and income opportunities, both directly and in associated value chains.	Wetlands within urban and peri-urban areas provide storage for storm water, whilst observable food production increases the pressure on authorities to eliminate pollution. Nutrients discharged from urban areas are assimilated in extensively managed ponds and production of valuable fish and shrimp contributes to economic development.	Agrochemical use to combat plant diseases can raise public health risks and surface water pollution can constitute a hazard for producers, local communities and consumers. Mangrove removal and suppression of regeneration makes urban coastal communities vulnerable to storms and tidal surges and disrupts other vital ecosystem services.
Cages and culture-based fisheries	Cage culture can provide employment for poor and marginal groups; small cages can allow households to culture and fatten fish in common property water bodies. Action to increase fish stocks can enhance incomes for poor fishers and bolster food security locally.	Fortunes of cage culture can be a good functional bio-indicator of prevailing environmental health, which can be a proxy for the effectiveness of urban planning and governance. Increased surveillance by concerned authorities can help eliminate pollution, resulting in general public health benefits.	Excessive numbers of cages can overwhelm the capacity of the environment to support cage culture, resulting in self-pollution and environmental degradation. Stocking invasive non-native or native fish outside their range could damage indigenous fish populations and aquatic ecosystems.

Source: authors.

are summarized and recent research to address constraints is reviewed and opportunities to put research findings into use to capitalize on the potential of aquaculture to contribute to sustainable urban develop are discussed. As with other contributions to this volume, the focus is on cases from developing countries.

Land-based culture systems

Aquaculture in concrete tanks in peri-urban settings in Nigeria has emerged as a novel production practice able to generate employment for underemployed youth and produce fish for consumption locally (Miller and Atanda 2011). These systems are used to produce African catfish *(Clarias gariepinus)* to meet rapidly expanding market demand. Serviced by intensively managed hatcheries and with access to good-quality formulated feeds, investors are able to make a positive return on their money within one year of commencing production.

Cooperative management of several hundred tanks located together in fish farming villages or fish farm estates within peri-urban areas has become established as an effective production strategy. Trained staff employed to maintain and watch over the estates ensure that individual tanks are well managed and that poaching is reduced (Miller and Atanda 2011). The scale of production also means operators are able to secure credit based on professional business plans and credible documentation.

FIGURE 12.1 Fish growing in concrete tanks Azemor, Ibadan, Nigeria
Source: SARNISSA project, courtesy of V. Poumogne, 2009.

Aquaculture to produce ornamental fish was reported from Bhubaneswar, Odisha, and Kolkata, West Bengal in India, and it was noted that fish culture in small brick-built tanks within peri-urban settlements offered important livelihoods opportunities, especially for women (Mukherjee et al. 2004). Aquaponics[1] production systems have been established in peri-urban locations in Phnom Penh, Cambodia, and Kathmandu, Nepal, with the dual intention of producing fish and salad crops for food and income and of providing an educational resource (Mallapaty 2012; *Khmer Aquaponics* 2014). It is not clear, however, whether such systems would be financially viable based purely on the sale of crops produced, or to what extent their establishment depended upon external interventions and financial support.

Research into use

Calls to establish urban and peri-urban land-based aquacultural systems for enhanced food security and livelihoods and as a resource for learning and teaching and human capacity-building have come from authorities and social organizations in countries including Cuba, England and the United States (Bunting and Little 2005; Frederick 2005; Prain 2005; Roy 2005; The Able Project 2014). Proponents have developed technology packages, such as the 'fish farm in a container', a series of tanks in a modified shipping container that can enable the intensive production of fish in a small, secure space (Crone 2013). Discussing the evolution of peri-urban aquaculture in Nigeria, Miller and Atanda (2011: 281) noted that 'the industry was led by the establishment of intensive fish hatcheries and delivery of quality fish feeds through imports or greatly improved local production'. It was noted, however, that veterinary provision and disease and parasite identification and treatment were inadequate, as was environmental management. These authors also cautioned that continued expansion of the sector may be constrained by the availability of locations with 'adequate environmental capacity' to sustain production (281). Although clustering of enterprises close together and shared water use and effluent disposal can exacerbate the spread of pathogens, the co-location of hatchery and nursery enterprises undoubtedly results in faster social knowledge generation and exchange (Little et al. 2002).

Ponds, borrow pits and lakes

Farm and village ponds are often retained in peri-urban areas as a source of water and as part of the drainage system. As the population density increases, the water draining into these ponds can contain a significant proportion of domestic wastewater and the ponds can become important in treating this, although bathing and washing in such ponds would constitute a public health hazard. Elevated nutrient levels in peri-urban ponds as a result of waste inputs can enhance fish production, but excessive nutrient levels can cause water quality problems and affect the health and survival of the fish being cultured. Where towns and cities in Asia are

FIGURE 12.2 Fishponds Kakamega, Kenya
Source: SARNISSA project.

expanding into agricultural areas and in predominantly rice-growing regions in particular, conversion of land to growing aquatic vegetables and fish is a common strategy to generate higher financial returns. Such a transition has been reported in the cases of Mymensingh in Bangladesh and Hai Duong, Vietnam.

Rapidly expanding urban areas in many developing counties demand large amounts of soil or dredged material to fill low-lying areas and sand and bricks for construction. Borrow pits dug to extract clay and soil usually fill with water and although not ideal for fish culture as they are difficult to drain and maintain, entrepreneurs often commence aquaculture as the potential returns outweigh the challenges (Little et al. 2007). Both ponds and borrow pits in peri-urban areas are vulnerable to theft and contamination and it may be difficult for producers to monitor their ponds to counter such problems.

Large lakes in built-up areas are often protected from urban encroachment as they are considered important in enhancing the capacity of urban environments to absorb surge floodwaters, a key attribute in climate change mitigation. They also provide an open area for amenity and recreation and can be used to supply water and fish. Construction of multifunctional lakes can be included in urban development plans to avoid the problems of reclaiming and building on low-lying areas and to create green infrastructure to sustain the urban economy. Hoan Kiem Lake and West Lake in Hanoi, Vietnam, are managed principally for storm water drainage, amenity and fish production; they have particular cultural significance as the location for pagodas and the setting for mythical tales. New lakes have been constructed as part of the urban development projects in Thanh Tri District, Hanoi, Vietnam, and Rajarhat New Town, West Bengal, India, with the intention of creating multifunctional green spaces where fish culture is an intrinsic component.

Research into use

Retaining and creating lakes within urban and peri-urban areas can serve a number of purposes (Table 12.2), but an integrated urban landscape planning approach is needed to adequately value the benefits of large water bodies within built-up areas. Similarly, there may be tensions between stakeholders owing to economic returns that might be realized through filling in old borrow pits for redevelopment versus their continued use for urban floodwater mitigation and other uses including aquaculture. Ponds within peri-urban areas can perform multiple functions but fish culture may be regarded as vulnerable owing to fears over poaching and the composition of wastewater draining from local residential and commercial areas. Management strategies such as sharing a proportion of the fish harvest with local residents can foster community cohesion and lead to greater vigilance. Risks associated with wastewater entering ponds may not necessarily constitute a major health hazard if viewed from the perspective of a holistic risk assessment (WHO 2006a).

Multifunctional wetlands

Several cities in Southeast Asia have low-lying areas within their boundaries or at their periphery that are inundated with water for large parts of the year. Often, the seasonal nature of these wetlands and limited scope to establish perennial deep water areas or regulate water exchange mean they are only suited to cultivating aquatic plants. Extensive areas of aquatic plant production were noted in peri-urban areas such as Bin Chanh District and Thu Duc District, Ho Chi Minh City, Vietnam; Boeng Cheung Ek, Phnom Penh, Cambodia; Gia Lam and Thanh Tri, Hanoi, Vietnam; and Pathumthani, Bangkok, Thailand (Hung and Huy 2005; Khov et al. 2005; Nguyen and Pham 2005; Yoonpundh et al. 2005). Aquatic plants cultivated included water cress *(Rorippa nasturtium-aquaticum)*, water dropwort *(Oenanthe stolonifera)*, water mimosa *(Neptunia oleracea)* and water spinach *(Ipomoea aquatica)*, and they were often harvested daily and sold at local markets. Frequent pesticide applications were found to be a major public health hazard.

Samples of water spinach analyzed from Boeng Cheung Ek contained thermo-tolerant coliforms (ranging from 10^5 to 10^7 g^{-1}), protozoan parasite (*Cryptosporidium* spp., *Cyclospora* oocysts and *Giardia* spp.) cysts (9.2 g^{-1}) and helminth (*Ascaris lumbricoides, Trichuris trichura* and hookworm) eggs (0.1 g^{-1}) (Vuong et al. 2007). Thermotolerant coliform concentration in the water used to cultivate the plants was 10^4–10^7 100 ml^{-1} and exceeded the World Health Organization guideline level of $\leq 10^3$ 100 ml^{-1} for water used for unrestricted irrigation of crops that are likely to

FIGURE 12.3 Fish grown in the East Kolkata Wetlands, India, going to market
Source: Bunting.

be consumed raw (WHO 2006a). These findings indicate that the cultivation and sale of aquatic plants grown in Boeng Cheung Ek constituted a public health hazard to both growers and consumers. A separate study noted that levels of potentially toxic elements (PTEs) were low and it was concluded that water spinach from the lake presented a low food safety risk with respect to PTEs (Marcussen et al. 2009).

Intra-urban and peri-urban aquaculture in wetlands has emerged in sub-Saharan Africa with examples described from Dar es Salaam, Tanzania, and Harare, Zimbabwe (Rana et al. 2005; Aquaculture Zimbabwe 2011). Tilapia culture dominated in Dar es Salaam and was practised in ponds ranging 10–10,000 m^2 and covered 50 ha in total. Urban aquaculture was promoted as part of the Aquaculture Zimbabwe initiative and focused on the sustainable use of peri-urban wetlands and integrated gardening activities for enhanced livelihoods outcomes and nutrition.

Extensive peri-urban wetlands were widely exploited for wastewater disposal and, in some cases, these wetlands were modified to optimize wastewater treatment and produce valuable fish, rice and vegetable crops. Extensive ponds stocked with fish in the East Kolkata Wetlands (EKW) occupy 3,900 ha, although a much larger area was designated a wetland of international importance in 2002 under the United Nations Ramsar Convention in respect of historical land-use practices and to establish a buffer to further urban encroachment. The Government of West Bengal made a significant commitment to safeguarding and enhancing the wise-use of these wetlands, passing 'The EKW (Conservation and Management) Act (2006)' and constituting the 'East Kolkata Wetlands Management Authority' (EKWMA). The EKW provides a living and working example of an alternative paradigm for solid and liquid waste management for towns and cities in India and worldwide.

The concept of wise-use embodied by the EKW and its associated environmental and biodiversity attributes was instrumental in the designation of this wetland area as a Ramsar Site. Research has demonstrated that farming fish, rice and vegetables in the EKW benefits local people and Kolkata residents in several ways:

- Direct employment for thousands of men and women, catching fish, weeding and harvesting and as casual labourers.
- Indirect employment in supply and distribution networks, e.g., seed traders and market vendors.
- Payment-in-kind for work undertaken on farms, e.g., weed clearing or carrying fish to market.
- Supplying affordable and fresh fish and vegetables to markets serving poor communities.
- Low-cost and natural wastewater treatment.
- Managed solid organic waste and wastewater use, mitigating environmental degradation and reducing health risks.
- Ecosystems services, including provisioning, regulatory, cultural and supporting services.
- Overall improvement in environmental quality due to the existence of peri-urban farming and wetlands.

Practices devised by farmers in the EKW to optimize production and the financial returns generated by the lakes under their jurisdiction were combined with engineering principles to formulate rational design criteria for wastewater reuse through aquaculture (Mara et al. 1993). Comparative benefits of adopting this rational design approach as opposed to a conventional one for lagoon-based wastewater treatment and use in the context of the EKW demonstrated that production could be potentially increased from 11,560 t to 45,500 t.yr^{-1}, but that this would require extensive reconfiguration of the existing system and modification of management practices (Bunting 2007). Use of wastewater and excreta in aquaculture was recognized as a legitimate means to achieve incremental improvements in sanitation provisions with the publication of the World Health Organization guidelines for such practices (WHO 2006b). Cities now constitute major driving forces leading to the relocation of significant water resources within river catchments and the concentration of nutrients in anthropogenic waste streams. Ecological processes within wetland agroecosystems constitute a low-cost and environmentally sound means to recover valuable nutrients entrained in waste streams and rehabilitate water resources for other purposes and to safeguard environmental flows that sustain receiving aquatic ecosystems (Bunting et al. 2010; Finlayson et al. 2013).

Cities have been traditionally located close to perennial water, usually on floodplains or close to estuaries, and consequently many cities have encroached into coastal wetlands. The EKW was initially a series of salt lakes, and further downstream where the main drainage canals discharge into the Kulti River estuary a vast area of fish and shrimp ponds has been constructed. Water used to fill these ponds contains wastewater from the city and this has been cited as benefiting producers as it stimulates primary production in the ponds. The animal, environmental and public health risks associated with this have yet to be assessed. Similar aggregations of shrimp ponds can be observed to the south of Bangkok, Thailand, and to the north of Jakarta, Indonesia.

Research into use

Research findings from the European Commission-sponsored PAPUSSA (Production in Aquatic Peri-Urban Systems in Southeast Asia) project were used to produce better management practices for aquatic plant growers to optimize production and minimize health risks for producers and consumers. The guidelines noted that in many cities 'aquatic vegetable growers have an almost non-existent voice in the urban planning process' and that national and local governments should 'target and incorporate aquatic production systems in their city development and land use plans' (PAPUSSA 2006). Considering the multifunctional wetlands observed in cities such as Bangkok and Phnom Penh, rapid economic growth and urban development have, however, resulted in wholesale programmes of in-filling and reclamation for construction purposes. The plight of families growing morning glory and living in Boeng Tompun, Phnom Penh, was covered in a national newspaper (*The Cambodia Daily* 2014) and described how in-filling 80% of this wetland with sand threatened the dual role of this area in treating wastewater from the city and producing aquatic vegetables.

Despite the benefits derived from the EKW, a number of problems threaten the system and the communities that depend upon its continued operation (Edwards 2005), including: deficiencies in managing and maintaining the system, notably siltation of canals and fish ponds; inadequate quantity and distribution of waste-water to farms; changing quality of waste resources; perceived threat of urban encroachment; limited access to alternative livelihoods and economic activities; and uneven and incomplete service and infrastructural coverage. Provisions within 'The East Kolkata Wetlands (Conservation and Management) Act, 2006' addressed the 'conservation and management of the East Kolkata wetlands' and a schedule of landholdings within the EKW was presented specifying their character and mode of use. Furthermore, the Act set out the functions and powers of the East Kolkata Wetlands Management Authority (EKWMA) and one of these functions was to prepare action plans and another to implement and monitor activities specified in the action plans.

Formulation of Environmental Management Plans (EMPs) addressing aquaculture management, wastewater management, waste recycling and best practices was carried out in consultation with various stakeholders associated with the EKW as part of an Asian Development Bank (ADB) sponsored programme of Technical Assistance (Bunting et al. 2011). Based on a wealth of knowledge derived from various studies and surveys in the EKW over the past 20 years, it was possible to prepare preliminary EMPs that addressed the major problems faced by different stakeholder groups associated with the system and highlighted some of the main ways in which management of the EKW could be improved. It was deemed essential that stakeholder groups associated with the EKW should have the opportunity to participate in jointly assessing the preliminary plans and suggesting amendments and additions making the plans more likely to find widespread support, contain important and worthwhile objectives, and lead to the desired enhancements in wise-use practices, environmental protection, biodiversity conservation and livelihoods. Following this review phase, the preliminary plans were amended where appropriate.

EMPs included several sections, covering management objectives, compliance to regulations, environmental and ecological objectives, social and economic objectives, educational objectives, principles of operational management, research objectives, monitoring controls and surveillance, consultation with stakeholders, post-harvest sector assessment, triggers for periodic review of the plans, institutional assessment, and legislative and regulatory assessment. Furthermore, there was provision within the EMPs for any stakeholders to propose new areas for inclusion in the plans, thus helping to guide an ongoing process of management plan review and improvement. The agreed plans were published in the *Environmental Management Manual East Kolkata Wetlands* (Bunting et al. 2011) along with a historical account of the systems development and contemporary challenges to support the EKWMA in formulating and implementing a comprehensive environmental management system.

The concept of exploiting wastewater flows to realize employment and income was adopted under the Ganges Action Plan and a series of lagoon-based treatment systems incorporating fish culture were constructed at several places in West Bengal (Mara 1997). It was envisaged that cooperatives would produce fish using these systems and the revenue generated would help pay for the operation and maintenance of the wastewater treatment lagoons. Use of wastewater for catfish culture in Ghana for income generation and to support wastewater treatment was described by Murray and Yeboah-Agyepong (2012), who extolled the virtues of a public-private business model to foster the adoption of this approach elsewhere in sub-Saharan Africa. Related and other 'Business Models for Resource Recovery & Reuse' were conceived as part of the CGIAR Research Programme on Water, Land and Ecosystems (IWMI 2014).

Cages and culture-based fisheries

Cage culture is a well-established practice that offers huge potential in terms of producing fish in water bodies where the capture of stocked fish would be difficult or in open-water areas such as large lakes and marine areas where securing exclusive rights to benefits associated with enhanced fish stocks and catches are problematic. Cages for the culture of tilapia were observed in rivers in peri-urban areas of Ho Chi Minh City, Vietnam. These cages were constructed from wood and incorporated accommodation and storage space at one end, reminiscent of traditional fish cage designs (Beveridge 2006). Cage culture is widely practised in peri-urban lakes

FIGURE 12.4 Cages in river downstream Ho Chi Minh, Vietnam

Source: Bunting.

and reservoirs in Southeast Asia but there is a tendency for the number of cages installed by multiple operators to exceed the carrying capacity of the ecosystem (Hart et al. 2002). Accumulation of wastes below cages and deteriorating water quality can result in self-pollution, leading to mass fish kills, meaning that the water is not fit for other purposes, for example, as a source of drinking water.

Widespread pollution from industrial and residential development and agricultural intensification had a severe impact on water quality in the Beijiang River running through Shaoguan City, Guangdong Province, China (Cai et al. 2010). This situation was compounded by the extensive construction of dams for hydroelectric power generation and to divert water for irrigation. Dredging of aggregates that accumulated on the bed of the impounded river has caused extensive damage to aquatic habitats. Consequently, the abundance and diversity of fish species declined significantly and households that engaged in fishing became more impoverished, with the younger generation forced to move away to seek urban-based employment (Punch and Sugden 2013).

Overfishing was implicated in the decline of wild fish stocks throughout the Pearl River Basin and consequently a no-fishing season was instigated to reduce this source of pressure. Declining catches combined with limited alternative livelihood opportunities for aging fishers on the Beijiang River has had negative impacts on their health and well-being. Subsidized fuel supplies helped fishers to a limited extent, but the authorities instigated a more drastic programme to relocate the fishers from living on their boats on the river to living in flats in urban areas. Authorities in Shaoguan City tried to control pollution and established a number of aquatic conservation zones in an attempt to regenerate aquatic habitats. Stocking of cultivated fish species was initiated to bolster fish stocks and supplement the catches of fishing households. Fish species stocked in the river included bighead carp *(Aristichthys nobillis)*, black amur bream *(Megalobrama terminalis)*, common carp *(Cyprinus carpio)*, crucian carp *(Carassius auratus)*, grass carp *(Ctenopharyngodon idellus)*, silver carp *(Hypophthalmichthys molitrix)* and *Spinibarbus denticulatus*. Releases commenced in 1995 and by 2012 the estimated number of fry stocked was 8 million.yr^{-1}. Records from boats in a stretch of river 50 km downstream of the stocking point indicated that cultured fish accounted for 12–38% of the catch (Luo et al. 2013). Such programmes can be cost-effective if the ecological benefits of bolstering wild fish stocks and socioeconomic benefits of sustaining the livelihoods of poor fishers are considered.

Research into use

Considering the need to enhance the conservation of aquatic resources in Shaoguan City, integrated action planning was facilitated with stakeholders to better characterize the problems faced by resource users and threats to biodiversity. A number of short-, medium- and long-term actions were identified to enhance biodiversity conservation whilst ensuring that wise-use of aquatic resources was regarded as legitimate and actually beneficial in increasing the importance ascribed to conserving and restoring urban aquatic ecosystems. Activities included in the Integrated Action Plan (IAP) developed for the Beijiang River passing through Shaoguan City included changes to ongoing measures and new short- and long-term actions.

Formulation of IAPs jointly with authorities and other stakeholders led to improvements in the regulation of sand mining in the river and the establishment of clearer communication channels between fishers and the operators of the hydroelectricity dams. The interactive participation of multiple stakeholder groups in the integrated action planning process can be regarded as a notable outcome in its own right. Specific interventions proposed within the IAP for the Beijiang River included 'Improved regulations regarding water pollution', 'Compensation received from sand mining and hydropower to be used for conservation of aquatic resources', 'Setting up Aquatic Conservation Zone offices' and 'Increased numbers of fish fry released.' The potential impact of these was evaluated with bioeconomic modelling and indicated that stricter pollution control could increase net benefits accruing to fishers by 15.9% as well as benefiting other user groups and local communities and enhancing biodiversity and stocks and flows of ecosystem services. Adoption of an ecosystems approach to fisheries management is effective at balancing the capacity of the environment to supply ecosystem services that sustain social and economic activity. Pertinently, it was concluded that such an approach would be critical to rehabilitating the ecosystems and fisheries of the Old Brahmaputra River running through Mymensingh city in central Bangladesh (Ahmed et al. 2013). The evidence in Bangladesh is that the governance required to conserve such ecosystems is complex and unlikely to be effective in a context of such open access fisheries in which large numbers of poor people remain dependent. Concomitantly, there has been a large increase in dependence on farmed fish by poorer consumers (Tofique and Belton 2014).

Tools and approaches devised for integrated action planning were compiled in the Wetland Resources Action Planning (WRAP) toolkit (Bunting et al. 2013) to enable similarly integrated and multidisciplinary joint assessments with stakeholders. Integrated action planning to achieve biodiversity conservation founded on the wise-use of aquatic resources could make a significant contribution to achieving the United Nations' Convention on Biodiversity (CBD) Strategic Plan for Biodiversity, which included 20 targets, known as the Aichi Targets,[2] notably Targets 2 and 4 under Strategic Goal A: 'Address the underlying causes of biodiversity loss by mainstreaming biodiversity across government and society', and Target 6 under Strategic Goal B: 'Reduce the direct pressures on biodiversity and promote sustainable use.'

Opportunities and challenges

Opportunities for (intra- and peri-) urban aquaculture development as a response to adverse conditions experienced by poor and marginal groups in urban areas were identified using the version of the DPSIR (Driving forces, Pressures, State, Impacts, Responses) (Maxim et al. 2009; Spangenberg et al. 2009) framework conceived within the EU-project HighARCS (Highland Aquatic Resources Conservation and Sustainable Development) (Bunting et al. 2013) (Table 12.3).

TABLE 12.3 DPSIR assessment of urban aquaculture in developing countries from a systems perspective

DPSIR elements	Description
Driving forces	- economic growth and industrialization - population growth and rapid urbanization - rural–urban migration - rapid expansion in physical extent of urban areas
Pressures	- population pressure results in in-filling of vacant land with buildings and informal settlements on any accessible areas - lakes, pond, wetlands and other low-lying areas in-filled, making them suitable for urban development - population growth and urban and industrial activities result in greater untreated wastewater flows and pollution
State	- proportion of global population living in urban areas surpassed 50% in 2007 and continues to grow - number of poor people living in urban areas is expected to reach 5 billion in 2030 - 750 million people in urban areas in developing countries in 2002 were living below the poverty line of $2 per day - several factors conspire making the urban poor particularly vulnerable (insecure living conditions, limited employment and income, inadequate infrastructure and services, insecure food supplies and lack of social-ecological resilience) - air and surface water quality in many urban environments is below acceptable international standards and extent of open and green spaces has declined significantly
Impacts	- poor and marginal urban populations suffer as a result of comparatively high food prices, compounded by the lack of access to health care and sanitation - pollution and untreated wastewater flows result in livestock, environmental and public health problems - residents suffer owing to the absence of urban ecosystem services, i.e., flooding due to limited infiltration; extreme temperatures owing to urban heat island effects; denial of psychological benefits associated with accessing green (and blue) spaces - participation in urban farmed seafood value chains appears a complementary component of livelihood portfolios for a proportion of poor people - urban areas disrupt ecological processes in rivers and their catchments and present insurmountable barriers in the migratory routes for several fish species, affecting food-chains and capture and recreational fisheries - urban food systems and populations are increasingly vulnerable to social-ecological shocks, notably civil unrest, global commodity price surges and worsening climate change impacts
Responses	- aquaculture as one element of multifunctional lakes and reservoirs in urban areas - culture-based fisheries enhancement to restore stocks decimated by pollution and habitat destruction - processes of urbanization enclose ponds and wetlands or transform peri-urban areas making them suitable for aquaculture but unsuited to other uses owing to water-logging or costs of reclaiming land for construction - entrepreneurs initiate intensive aquaculture in urban areas to capitalize on market access, transport links, access to services or other business opportunities - specialist activity such as seed production for restocking, holding seed at key distribution points or ornamental fish production

Source: authors.

Urban centres in many developing countries have undergone rapid change over the past decade with many of the more widely known examples of large urban and peri-urban aquaculture systems having been lost. The rapid pace of change has resulted in large numbers of poor people living in substandard accommodation with inadequate water supplies and sanitation coverage. Environmental conditions are bad as a result of air and surface water pollution and this situation is compounded by limited employment opportunities, elevated food prices, limited access to health care and insecure living conditions.

Where large lakes and remnants of extensive peri-urban wetlands remain, these can sustain a range of urban ecosystem services that can improve the environment, with notable benefits for poor and marginal groups (reduction of flood risks, improved quality of surface water, moderation of extreme heat events and enhanced psychological well-being). Cultured fish might also be used to supply local markets, and, depending on the quality and size of fish, these might be purchased by poor families contributing to their food security and nutrition.

Current and emerging challenges and opportunities to the development of urban aquaculture were critically reviewed using the SWOT (Strengths, Weaknesses, Opportunities, Threats) assessment framework (Table 12.4). Intra- and peri-urban aquaculture is an established practice in many larger towns and cities in Asian countries and this has demonstrated the potential range of benefits that could contribute to sustainable urban development. Compared to volumes of regional and national aquacultural production, those from urban and peri-urban systems may be modest. This may mean the demand for support services does not warrant

TABLE 12.4 SWOT assessment of urban aquaculture in developing countries

Strengths: existing or potential resources or capability	Weaknesses: existing or potential internal force that could be a barrier to achieving objectives/results
- strong demand for aquaculture products - broad range of aquaculture production systems and strategies suited to niches found in urban environments - urban aquaculture recognized in national and international policy and supported by donors and development agencies - aquaculture in urban areas can be a good indicator of environmental health and help restore degraded urban ecosystems - urban aquaculture provides income and employment opportunities in production phase and across associated value chains and produces fish and plants that can be an affordable and important source of protein and nutrients for the poor	- deficiencies with urban environmental management lead to widespread pollution of surface waters - insecurity of tenure constrains investment in urban aquaculture - difficulties in monitoring aquaculture systems in urban settings can lead to thefts and indiscriminate dumping and in-filling - dispersed and often transient nature of small-scale urban aquaculture means support from government institutions and access to service providers is lacking- urban authorities may not recognize aquaculture as a legitimate land-use practice - lack of information on extent of peri-urban aquaculture means its contribution to livelihoods, economic development and food security is overlooked

Opportunities: existing or potential factors in the external environment that, if exploited, could provide a competitive advantage	Threats: existing or potential forces in the external environment that could inhibit maintenance or attainment of unique advantage
- opportunities to access markets locally with fresh produce on a timely basis - increasing demand for high value aquatic products amongst burgeoning middle classes in many urban areas in developing countries - rising demand for affordable aquatic products for nutrition and food security amongst poor urban communities - underutilized resources (low-lying areas, nutrients in organic waste streams, wastewater flows) that urban aquaculture could exploit - international agreements and guidelines that support responsible aquaculture development and the use of waste resources - national policies that advocate and recognize urban agriculture (encompassing aquaculture) as a legitimate urban activity	- access to land and inputs (water and nutrient sources) denied or disrupted owing to competition or development plans that do not consider or recognize the claims of aquaculture producers - improved transport links and communications mean urban aquaculture must compete with production in rural areas with lower capital and operating costs - demand for fish from urban aquaculture systems declines owing to negative media coverage resulting from animal, environmental or public health concerns - inappropriate urban aquaculture development results in conflict with other resource users or local residents - excessive urban aquaculture development overwhelms capacity of supporting ecosystem areas, resulting in self-pollution and environmental degradation

Source: authors.

government attention and that the number of input suppliers is limited and producers do not benefit from competition for their custom. Broader benefits associated with urban and peri-urban aquaculture may be overlooked by authorities faced with more immediate and potentially controversial issues such as pollution, transport and waste disposal.

Deficiencies with pollution control and inadequate wastewater treatment can impact severely on aquacultural production, causing widespread fish-kills and resulting in public health risks for consumers. Aquaculture producers could garner broader support by highlighting their potential role as a component in integrated wastewater management and nutrient recovery strategies. This could reduce the costs for wastewater treatment that must be met from squeezed public spending budgets and alleviate environmental degradation caused by untreated discharges. Despite potential benefits, a number of threats must be considered; the pace of peri-urban land-use change means aquaculture producers with insecure tenure, minimal institutional support or contemplating more lucrative investment opportunities may only continue for a limited time.

With better transport links, increased access to formulated feed supplies and lower capital and operating costs, aquaculture producers in rural areas can out-compete urban and peri-urban producers. Despite this, urban and peri-urban aquaculture occurs in developed and developing counties and it is necessary to take account of the full range of values associated with such practices to explain why they persist and continue to be established.

Creating an enabling environment for development of urban aquaculture

Conditions required to enable and sustain development of urban aquaculture as part of resilient food systems were defined using the STEPS (Social, Technical, Environmental, Political, Sustainability) framework (Bunting et al. 2005; Lewins et al. 2007) (Table 12.5).

A critical issue for policy-makers, urban planners and implementing authorities is to prevent toxic compounds and those causing off-flavours from entering the aquatic environment. This constitutes a tall order, requiring the upgrade of urban waste management generally; otherwise the fish produced will only have distant, poor markets as an outlet and local urban people will buy 'imports'. An added benefit of modest and dispersed aquacultural systems operating in urban and peri-urban areas is that they could constitute functional bio-indicators of urban environmental health.

The role of burgeoning urban markets in many developing countries in governing development of aquaculture nationally is increasing (Toufique and Belton 2014) and arguably they constitute the main driving force for expansion of urban and peri-urban aquaculture. Proximity to markets is only one consideration, however, and an assessment of the needs, logistics and impacts of aquacultural production across the value chain, including input and service provision and marketing, consumption and waste disposal, is required.

As with the production of both urban agriculture and livestock (Ellis and Sumberg 1998) it is important not to overstate the current or potential future contribution of (intra- and peri-) urban aquaculture to supplying affordable fish to poor and marginal groups. Local initiatives, where circumstances permit, may be able to produce modest volumes of good-quality fish, but for the substantial amounts of affordable fish needed to meet the demand for burgeoning urban populations this requires large land areas that are not available in urban areas and would not be cost-effective to develop in peri-urban areas.

Peri-urban land prices are comparatively high as a consequence of the proximity to build up areas and expectations that such land will increase in value as development for commercial or residential purposes becomes more likely. Larger aquacultural systems that might make a notable contribution to fish supplies are more likely in low-lying and coastal peri-urban areas where the risk of flooding prohibits urban development and in areas where drainage and sewerage water from urban areas is discharged. Such hazardous situations may, however, require producers to adopt culture systems and practices that minimize the risks they face and the likelihood of damage and financial losses.

TABLE 12.5 STEPS assessment of conditions needed to support and promote urban aquaculture

STEPS elements	Conditions
Social	- acceptance and support for aquaculture as a legitimate and worthwhile urban activity - demand for products from urban aquaculture continues and grows - urban aquaculture is able to generate sufficient financial returns to make it viable and a continued and novel employment and income-generating activity
Technical	- access to appropriate spaces within urban environments is possible and sufficient periods of tenure guaranteed to safeguard investments made by producers - inputs to establish and sustain aquaculture are readily available - haulage providers and processing and marketing facilities willing and able to accept products from urban aquaculture - transaction costs and overheads are reasonable given the production volumes and financial returns generated by urban aquaculture systems
Environmental	- responsible authorities implement and enforce policies and laws that prevent pollution and environmental degradation in urban areas - city planning and infrastructure development (including green infrastructure) safeguards areas where urban aquaculture can be practiced against encroachment and shocks (floods, drought, disruption to electricity and water supplies) and includes provisions for aquaculture as potential element of multifunction urban water management plans - wastewater aquaculture included as a legitimate element in establishing and upgrading sewage treatment systems in accordance with WHO (2006b) guidelines to help protect receiving water bodies and facilitate productive reuse of waste resources
Political	- national and international polices explicitly support urban aquaculture for employment and income generation and associated ecosystem services and food security benefits - municipal authorities recognize and encourage aquaculture as a legitimate urban activity - land-use policy and tenure agreements provide sufficient security so as to encourage prospective producers and reassure investors and credit providers - government and private sector aquaculture support services cover aquaculture in urban environments
Sustainable (long-term viability)	- policies supporting urban aquaculture and production system management strategies are adaptable given the rapidly changing urban environment - urban aquaculture producers join forces to promote knowledge sharing, raise awareness and lobby for greater support, negotiate for cheaper inputs and coordinate sales and marketing - producers develop links with business advisors, development agencies and researchers to enhance efficiency and capitalize on accessible resources and income-generating opportunists

Source: authors.

Enabling policies and institutions are needed that recognize and support aquaculture as a legitimate and beneficial activity within urban and peri-urban environments (IWMI 2002). Policy-makers may call for evidence concerning the likely benefits associated with the development of urban and peri-urban aquaculture. Cost Benefit Analysis (CBA) carried out to evaluate the potential of the development of aquaculture should include the valuation of the full range of ecosystem services that it can sustain in urban and peri-urban environments. Similarly, application of CBA and complementary efficiency indicators (Murray et al. 2011) could demonstrate the advantages of urban and peri-urban aquacultural practices that incorporate the use and upgrading of wastewater as compared with conventional treatment plants. Regulatory authorities and practitioners may require appropriate hazard assessment and control frameworks to ensure that practices adopted locally do not pose unacceptable animal, environmental or public health risks.

Notes

1 Aquaponics is the integrated production of terrestrial plants (flowers, salad crops and vegetables) in an aquatic growing medium; also used to culture fish in unit where the water is recirculated to optimize nutrient uptake.

2 Aichi Target 2: By 2020, at the latest, biodiversity values have been integrated into national and local development and poverty reduction strategies and planning processes and are being incorporated into national accounting, as appropriate, and reporting systems.

Aichi Target 4: By 2020, at the latest, governments, business and stakeholders at all levels have taken steps to achieve or have implemented plans for sustainable production and consumption and have kept the impacts of use of natural resources well within safe ecological limits.

Aichi Target 6: By 2020 all fish and invertebrate stocks and aquatic plants are managed and harvested sustainably, legally and applying ecosystem based approaches, so that overfishing is avoided, recovery plans and measures are in place for all depleted species, fisheries have no significant adverse impacts on threatened species, and vulnerable ecosystems and the impacts of fisheries on stocks, species and ecosystems are within safe ecological limits.

References

Ahmed, N.; Rahman, S.; and Bunting, S. W. 2013. An ecosystem approach to analyse the livelihood of fishers of the Old Brahmaputra River in Mymensingh region, Bangladesh. *Local Environment* 18: 36–52.

Aquaculture Zimbabwe. 2011. Urban aquaculture: Sustaining Zimbabwe's urban livelihoods. *Fish Tidings* 2(2): 1–6.

Beveridge, M.C.M. 2006. Cage aquaculture. Oxford: Blackwell Publishing.

Bunting, S. W. 2007. Confronting the realities of wastewater aquaculture in peri-urban Kolkata with bioeconomic modelling. *Water Research* 41(2): 499–505.

Bunting, S. W.; Kundu, N.; Edwards, P. 2011. Environmental management manual East Kolkata Wetlands, New Delhi: MANAK Publishers.

Bunting, S. W.; Kundu, N.; Saha, S.; Lewins, R.; Pal, M. 2005. EKW water management action plan and preliminary development activities. Report to be submitted to the EKW Management Committee. Stirling: Institute of Aquaculture; Kolkata: Institute of Environmental Studies and Wetland Management.

Bunting, S. W.; Little, D. C. 2003. Urban aquaculture. In: *Annotated bibliography on urban agriculture*. Leusden: ETC-RUAF Foundation.

Bunting, S. W.; Little, D. C. 2005. The emergence of urban aquaculture in Europe. In: *Urban aquaculture* (Eds.) Costa-Pierce, B. A.; Edwards, P.; Baker, D.; Desbonnet, A. Wallingford: CAB International.

Bunting, S. W.; Little, D.; Leschen, W. 2006. Urban aquatic production. In: *Cities farming for the future: Urban agriculture for green and productive cities*. (Ed.) Veenhuizen, R. van. Leusden: RUAF Foundation; Manila: IIRR.

Bunting, S. W.; Pretty, J.; Edwards, P. 2010. Wastewater-fed aquaculture in the East Kolkata Wetlands: Anachronism or archetype for resilient ecocultures? *Reviews in Aquaculture* 2: 138–153.

Bunting, S. W.; Smith, K. G.; Lund, S.; Punch, S.; Bimbao, M. P. 2013. Wetland resources action planning (WRAP) toolkit: An integrated action planning toolkit to conserve aquatic resources and biodiversity by promoting sustainable use. Philippines: FishBase Information and Research Group Inc. (FIN). Available from: www.wraptoolkit.org.

Cai, K.; Chen, F.; Cui, K.; Gao, M.; Fu, J.; Gan, L. 2010. HighARCS situation analysis report: China site. China: South China Agricultural University.

Crone, A. 2013. Fish farm in a container in the running for global award. South Africa: Bright Continent. Available from: www.brightcontinent.co.za/2013/09/24/fish-farm-container-running-global-award/.

Edwards, P. 2003. Peri-urban aquaculture in Kolkata. *Aquaculture Asia* 8(2): 4–6.

Edwards, P. 2005. Demise of periurban wastewater-fed aquaculture? *Urban Agriculture Magazine* 14:27–29.

Ellis, F.; Sumberg, J. 1998. Food production, urban areas and policy responses. *World Development* 26: 213–225.

Finlayson, M.; Bunting, S. W.; Beveridge, M.; Tharme, R.; Nguyen-Khoa, S. 2013. Wetlands. In: *Managing water and agroecosystems for food security*. Comprehensive Assessment of Water Management in Agriculture Series. (Ed.) Boelee, E. Wallingford: CABI Publishing.

Frederick, J. A. 2005. Science in action: Tools for teaching urban aquaculture concepts. In: *Urban aquaculture*. (Eds.) Costa-Pierce, B. A.; Edwards, P.; Baker, D.; Desbonnet, A. Wallingford: CAB International.

Hart, B. T.; Dok, W. van; Djuangsih, N. 2002. Nutrient budget for Saguling Reservoir, West Java, Indonesia. *Water Research* 36: 2152–2160.

Hung, L. T.; Huy, H.P.V. 2005. Production and marketing systems of aquatic products in Ho Chi Minh City. *Urban Agriculture Magazine* 14:16–19.

Iaquinta, D. L.; Drescher, A. W. 2000. Defining periurban: Understanding rural-urban linkages and their connection to institutional contexts. Paper presented at the Tenth World Congress of the International Rural Sociology Association, 1 August 2000, Rio de Janeiro, Brazil.

IWMI. 2002. The Hyderabad declaration on wastewater use in agriculture, Hyderabad, India, 14 November 2002. India: International Water Management Institute (IWMI).

IWMI. 2014. Business models: Where there's muck, there's money. Colombo: International Water Management Institute (IWMI). Available from: www.iwmi.cgiar.org/issues/wastewater/business-models/.

Khmer Aquaponics. 2014. *Khmer Aquaponics*. Available from: www.facebook.com/pages/Khmer-Aquaponics/.

Khov, K.; Daream, S.; Borin, C. 2005. Periurban aquatic food production systems in Phnom Penh. *Urban Agriculture Magazine* 14: 13–15.

Leschen, W.; Little, D.; Bunting, S.; Veenhuizen, R. van. 2005. Urban aquatic production. *Urban Agriculture Magazine* 14: 1–7.

Lewins, R.; Coupe, S.; Murray, F. 2007. Voices from the margins: Consensus building and planning with the poor in Bangladesh. Rugby: Practical Action Publishing.

Little, D. C.; Barman, B. K.; Belton, B.; Beveridge, M. C.; Bush, S. J.; Dabaddie, L.; Demaine, H.; Edwards, P.; Haque, M. M.; Kibria, G.; Morales, E.; Murray, F. J.; Leschen, W. A.; Nandeesha, M. C.; Sukadi, F. 2012. Alleviating poverty through aquaculture: Progress, opportunities and improvements. In: *Farming the waters for people and food.* Proceedings of the Global Conference on Aquaculture 2010, Phuket, Thailand. 22–25 September 2010. (Eds.) Subasinghe, R. P.; Arthur, J. R.; Bartley, D. M.; De Silva, S. S.; Halwart, M.; Hishamunda, N.; Mohan, C. V.; Sorgeloos, P. Rome: FAO and Bangkok: NACA.

Little, D. C.; Bunting, S. W. 2005. Opportunities and constraints to urban aquaculture, with a focus on south and Southeast Asia. In: *Urban aquaculture.* (Eds.) Costa-Pierce, B. A.; Edwards, P.; Baker, D.; Desbonnet, A. Wallingford: CAB International.

Little, D. C.; Karim, M.; Turongruang, D.; Morales, E. J.; Murray, F. J.; Barman, B. K.; Haque, M. M.; Kundu, N.; Belton, B.; Faruque, G.; Azim, E. M.; Islam, F. U.; Pollock, L.; Verdegem, M. J.; Leschen, W.; Wahab, M. A. 2007. Livelihood impacts of ponds in Asia: Opportunities and constraints. In: *Fishponds in farming systems.* (Eds.) Zijpp, A. J. van der; Verreth, J. A. J.; Le Quang Tri; Mensvoort, M. E. F. van; Bosma, R. H.; Beveridge, M. C. M. Wageningen: Wageningen Academic Publishers.

Little, D. C.; Tuan, P. A.; Barman, B. 2002. Health management issues in freshwater fish hatcheries, nurseries and fry distribution, with emphasis on experiences in Vietnam and Bangladesh. In: *Primary aquatic animal health care in rural, small-scale, aquaculture development.* FAO Fisheries Technical Paper No. 406. (Eds.) Arthur, J. R.; Phillips, J. M.; Subasinghe, R. P.; Reantaso, M. B.; MacRae, I. H. Rome: FAO.

Luo, S. M.; Cai, K. Z.; Liu, Y. M.; Zhao H. H.; Li H. S.; Jiang B. G. 2013. Report on the implementation and assessment results of actions for Beijing river watershed, Shaoguan, China. Report for the European Commission Funded HighARCS Project. China: South China Agricultural University.

Mallapaty, S. 2012. Nepal sees potential in aquaponics. London: SciDevNet. Available from: www.scidev.net/global/biotechnology/news/nepal-sees-potential-in-aquaponics.

Mara, D. 1997. Design manual for waste stabilization ponds in India. Leeds: Lagoon Technology International.

Mara, D. D.; Edwards, P.; Clark, D.; Mills, S. W. 1993. A rational approach to the design of wastewater-fed fishponds. *Water Research* 27: 1797–1799.

Marcussen, H.; Dalsgaard, A.; Holm, P. E. 2009. Element concentrations in water spinach (Ipomoea aquatic Forssk.), fish and sediment from a wetland production system that receives wastewater from Phnom Penh, Cambodia. *Journal of Environmental Science and Health* 44 (part A): 67–77.

Maxim, L.; Spangenberg, J. H.; O'Connor, M. 2009. An analysis of risks for biodiversity under the DPSIR framework. *Ecological Economics* 69: 12–23.

Miller, J. W.; Atanda, T. 2011. The rise of peri-urban aquaculture in Nigeria. *International Journal of Agricultural Sustainability* 9: 274–281.

Mukherjee, M.; Banerjee, R.; Datta, A.; Sen, S.; Chatterjee, B. 2004. Women fishers in peri-urban Kolkata. *Urban Agriculture Magazine* 12: 40.

Murray, A.; Cofie, O.; Drechsel, P. 2011. Efficiency indicators for waste-based business models: Fostering private-sector participation in wastewater and faecal-sludge management. *Water International* 36: 505–521.

Murray, A.; Yeboah-Agyepong, M. 2012. Waste enterprisers' wastewater-fed aquaculture business. Accra: WASTE Enterprisers.

Nguyen, T.D.P.; Pham, A. T. 2005. Current status of periurban aquatic production in Hanoi. *Urban Agriculture Magazine* 14: 10–12.

PAPUSSA. 2006. Integrating aquaculture into urban planning and development. Available from: www.ruaf.org/publications/urban-aquaculture-policy-briefs-s-e-asia-papussa.

Prain, G. 2005. Integrated urban management of local agricultural development: The policy arena in Cuba. In: *Cities farming for the future: Urban agriculture for green and productive cities*. (Ed.) Veenhuizen, R. van. Leusden: RUAF Foundation; Manila: IIRR.

Punch, S.; Sugden, F. 2013. Work, education and out-migration among children and youth in upland Asia: Changing patterns of labour and ecological knowledge in an era of globalisation. *Local Environment* 18: 255–270.

Rana, K.; Anyila, J.; Salie, K.; Mahika, C.; Heck, S.; Young, J. 2005. Aquafarming in urban and peri-urban zones in Sub Saharan Africa. *Aquaculture News* 32: 6–8.

Roy, J. J. 2005. Growing a future crop of aquaculturists: Creating an urban aquaculture education programme in New Haven, Connecticut, USA. In: *Urban aquaculture*. (Eds.) Costa-Pierce, B. A.; Edwards, P.; Baker, D.; Desbonnet, A. Wallingford: CAB International.

Spangenberg, J. H.; Martinez-Alier, J.; Omann, I.; Monterroso, I.; Binimelis, R. 2009. The DPSIR scheme for analysing biodiversity loss and developing preservation strategies. *Ecological Economics* 69: 9–11.

The Able Project. 2014. ABLE matters: Fish farming & sales. Wakefield: The Able Project. Available from: www.theableproject.org.uk/able/shop/fish-farming.

The Cambodia Daily. 2014. Drying up: As Boeng Tompun Lake is filled in, Phnom Penh faces a development dilemma. *The Cambodia Daily* June 28–29.

Toufique, K. A.; Belton, B. 2014. Is aquaculture pro-poor? Empirical evidence of impacts on fish consumption in Bangladesh. *World Development* 64: 609–620.

Vuong, T. A.; Nguyen, T. T.; Klank, L. T.; Phung, D. C.; Dalsgaard, A. 2007. Faecal and protozoan parasite contamination of water spinach (Ipomoea aquatic) cultivated in urban wastewater in Phnom Penh, Cambodia. *Tropical Medicine and International Health* 12: 73–81.

WHO. 2006a. Guidelines for the safe use of wastewater, excreta and greywater: Volume 1: Policy and regulatory aspects. Geneva: World Health Organization (WHO).

WHO. 2006b. Guidelines for the safe use of wastewater, excreta and greywater: Volume 3: Wastewater and excreta use in aquaculture. Geneva: World Health Organization.

Yoonpundh, R.; Dulyapurk, V.; Srithong, C. 2005. Aquatic food production systems in Bangkok. *Urban Agriculture Magazine* 14: 8–9.

13

GENDERING URBAN FOOD STRATEGIES ACROSS MULTIPLE SCALES

Liam Riley[1] and Alice Hovorka[2]

1 BALSILLIE SCHOOL OF INTERNATIONAL AFFAIRS, WATERLOO, CANADA

2 QUEEN'S UNIVERSITY, KINGSTON, CANADA

Introduction

Gender provides a powerful lens for analysing and addressing urban food insecurity (Hovorka et al. 2009). This chapter examines gender-related issues in urban food systems across multiple scales and offers strategies to integrate gender analysis in practice. The chapter builds on Hovorka and Lee-Smith's (2006) review of gender and urban agriculture literature in *Cities Farming for the Future: Urban Agriculture for Green and Productive Cities,* with two key differences in focal point. First, whereas the 2006 contribution focused on food production in urban areas, this chapter encompasses multiple aspects of urban food systems including food distribution, consumption, and livelihoods. Second, whereas the 2006 chapter was focused on cities in developing areas, this chapter draws together research from cities of the Global North and the Global South, using gender as a unifying concept to connect extremely diverse case studies.

In adopting a comprehensive and interdisciplinary scope, this chapter draws on the concept of a 'feminist foodscapes framework' (Hovorka 2013) to emphasise the social justice questions at the heart of urban food security. The feminist foodscapes framework highlights the power imbalances that create and sustain food insecurity in urban areas. These power imbalances are evident in the structural disadvantages faced by women relative to men at multiple scales, including: the distribution of resources at the household level, access to employment, education and health care, and the protection of women's human rights. These structural issues shape men's and women's food security status differently, while also intersecting with disempowering social categories and identities based on race, class, age, religion, and sexuality. The precise causes and effects of these differences differ by context, but the feminist perspective reveals the resonance of each case with a bigger picture of inequality and injustice. Hovorka (2013) argues that the ubiquity of food and gender difference in all societies makes the overlapping of food and gender studies particularly constructive for a social progress agenda.

The literature review provided in this chapter illuminates the ways in which gender is necessarily embedded within and across various scales of urban life: individual, household, neighbourhood, city, nation, and globe. Indeed, it exposes the ways in which gender roles, responsibilities, and expectations are normalised and often the root of inequality in terms of food access and security. In foregrounding the political economic dimensions of urban food systems, the feminist foodscapes framework resonates with the growing literature of critical food studies related to urban agriculture (McClintock 2014; Tornaghi 2014), urban food marketing and distribution (Lerner and Eakin 2011; Riley 2014), and the role of the global food system (Ruel et al. 2010). These increasingly prominent critical approaches draw on earlier work on the political economy of food (Sen 1981; Watts 1983), applied to the 'new food equation' of an increasingly integrated global food system, climate change, land grabs, and rapid urbanisation in the Global South (Morgan 2009).

The use of the feminist foodscapes framework as an analytical framework draws the chapter's examination of urban food systems in line with important literature on gender, poverty, and development. Feminists have been very influential in debates on how to address global poverty, particularly in the context of a post-2015 agenda to replace the Millennium Development Goals (MDGs) (Fukuda-Parr and Orr 2014; Sen and Mukherjee 2014). Feminist development scholars have long argued the need to approach research, policies, and development projects in a way that simultaneously targets practical (e.g., jobs, educational opportunities, and access to health care) and strategic (e.g., legal reforms, social protection, and recognition of human rights) needs (Moser 1993; Kabeer 1994). The feminist foodscapes framework applies this duality to the analysis of food security, recognising that the practical need for people to have food in the immediate term and the strategic need to ensure that the human right to food are equally important.

This chapter seeks to contribute to academic and policy-oriented discussions about urban food systems by connecting issues at multiple scales to provide a snapshot of the complex relationship between gender and urban food systems. The following section provides an overview of issues that tie together gender and urban food security. The examples mainly draw from literature published in the past decade and serve as an update to Hovorka and Lee-Smith's (2006) contribution to *Cities Farming for the Future: Urban Agriculture for Green and Productive Cities*. The following section discusses challenges in integrating these insights into policies, research programmes, and development interventions aimed at improving the food security benefits of urban food systems generally. Gender mainstreaming has been increasingly central to food security interventions in cities (Hovorka et al. 2009), and this chapter concludes with reflections on the practical benefits to food security programming, particularly in the longer term, that can result from a broad conceptualisation of the links between gender inequality and food insecurity in cities.

Gender and urban food systems at multiple scales of analysis

Food insecurity is increasingly widespread in cities of the Global North and South. It is a manifestation of urban poverty that links problems of income inequality, under employment, environmental degradation, and rights to urban space. In seeking to understand this problem in general terms, and from a feminist perspective, this section provides a multi-scaled examination of diverse issues drawn from interdisciplinary perspectives that convey the richness of gender-based analyses of urban food systems. Table 13.1 summarises the issues examined at each scale and provides a road map for the discussion in this section. The multi-scaled analysis facilitates the integration of women's and men's daily experiences of urban food systems with the broader structures and processes that shape ideas about urban food security as a global development issue.

TABLE 13.1 Gender and urban food system topics examined at multiple scales

Scale	Topics
Individuals	Gendered cultures of consumption
	Men and women as economic actors
	The mobility of women's and men's bodies in relation to food access
Households	Household livelihoods
	Urban household food security in southern Africa
	Gender relations within urban farming households
Cities	Food deserts
	Informal economies and informal food systems
	The provisioning of municipal services
States	National social protection schemes
	National agricultural and urbanisation policies
	Rural–urban connections and urban food security
Global	International trade and the global food system
	The effects of global climate change
	The Millennium Development Goals for 2015

Source: authors.

Individuals

At the smallest scale, that of individual men and women, many issues related to gender and urban food security are apparent. The body is a common scale of analysis in feminist scholarship because physiological difference is the starting point for the constellation of cultural, social, political, and economic implications of gender difference. Bodies are also at the core of food studies and the universal experience of eating to nourish and sustain bodies is at the core of food studies. This first of five scalar subsections examines three issues that elucidate the link between gender and urban food security at the scale of bodies: (1) gendered cultures of consumption, (2) men and women as economic actors, and (3) the mobility of women's and men's bodies in urban spaces.

The growing rates of obesity in cities in all parts of the world is evidence that food consumption choices are not purely practical, but situated within a cultural context that generates desire for certain types of food based on its meaning (Allen and Sachs 2007). Gender identities shape what foods are desirable and considered culturally appropriate for different people. Research in Blantyre, Malawi, for example, found that people associated some foods such as clay *(dothi)* and baobab fruit with maternity, and men's fertility was associated with other food such as fresh cassava and soaked rice (Riley 2013). These findings resonated with Hovorka's (2012) research in Botswana, where the association of men with cattle and women with chickens shaped food security strategies, including production and consumption.

Research in the Global North into gender consumption choices has shown that women's dominance in food purchasing and preparation has given them a prominent role in shaping alternative food networks (Little et al. 2009). Identification with a female ethic of care and community building was also reported in research on women food producers in American cities (Jarosz 2011; White 2011). These cultural dimensions of why urban women choose to produce food and why they choose to consume certain foods is less prevalent in studies based in the Global South, where economic necessity is presumed to be the main motivation. This perspective presents an exciting avenue for future research in more diverse settings.

Individual men and women have different economic opportunities and face different livelihood constraints in cities, which shape gendered outcomes for food security. In the Global South and the Global North, women face structural constraints in achieving the same economic status as men (Kabeer 2003). Women are more likely to be employed informally, which raises problems of income regularity and security, in addition to the higher likelihood that women's incomes will be insufficient to meet an urban household's basic needs. Interventions such as micro-finance projects are often targeted at women because of the structural impediments they face as independent economic actors, including: difficulty in accessing credit, lower rates of literacy, and time constraints due to domestic responsibilities (Kabeer 2003; Hovorka et al. 2009). An important structural barrier for women in many places is the gender discrimination embedded in property rights. While the issue of property could also be considered at the national scale of analysis where property laws are formulated and enforced, the differential *effects* of these laws and practices shape food security outcomes differently for men and women. Research on gender and urban agriculture has consistently found that tenure of farmland is more often a barrier face by women than by men (Hovorka et al. 2009). Additionally, lack of secure housing tenure constrains women's options for economic independence or to generate income through rentals.

The scale of individual bodies also raises the issue of mobility for food security, an issue increasingly recognised as part of the 'mobilities turn' in social sciences (Cresswell 2010; Hanson 2010). Accessing food entails going to places where nutritious and affordable food is available (Frayne 2010). In some places, this entails going to markets on the outskirts of cities where urban residents are buying directly from rural producers (Tacoli 2007). Mobility is gendered in that women

FIGURE 13.1 Ana Huamani is a single mother in Mala (near Lima) growing organic vegetables and fruits, which she sells in her own stall at a weekly farmers' market
Source: MESA-program.

are often less mobile than men for several contextually various reasons (Uteng and Cresswell 2008; Uteng 2011). Women's responsibilities in the home are oner- ous and time-consuming in many low-income urban households, which restricts the time they can spend to travel for work or food procurement (Riley and Dodson 2014). In some places, women's mobility is directly constricted by laws or customs that proscribe their presence in public spaces (Robson 2006). Public safety concerns also gender mobility, for example in places where urban violence can make it unsafe for women to travel at night. Women's movements in public space can also be the result of domestic violence in cases of husbands seeking to control their wives' movements (Uteng 2011). A focus on gendered mobilities and food security demonstrates the overlapping forces within and beyond households that influence the different possibilities for movement of women's and men's bodies in space.

Households

The household is the main social unit used in urban food security research. The household is a small social and economic unit that lends itself to comparisons across time and space. Most studies of household food security infer from the supply of food in the household and the needs of its members if the household is food secure or food insecure. Yet feminist scholars have argued that this inference is based on a false assumption that food is shared equitably within households (Agarwal 1997; Devereux 2001). A variety of context-specific factors shape the way in which resources (including food and the means to buy and produce it) and responsibilities (including the responsibility for feeding household members) are divided among household members according to gender. This subsection examines three topics of relevance to gender and urban food security at the household scale: (1) household livelihoods, (2) household food strategies, and (3) gender relations within urban farming households.

The question of how households, especially low-income households, function economically has been taken up by the literature on livelihoods framework (Rakodi and Lloyd-Jones 2002; Foeken and Owuor 2008). The livelihoods framework highlights the full range of contributions by household members, which may be in the form of labour, money, or other resources. In a household in which the husband is employed and is the primary income earner, his wife might also be producing food in the garden, earning income through petty trading, and providing labour in food preparation, cleaning, and childcare. Income-based models often obscure non-financial contributions and focus solely on income through formal employment, which in this scenario would overemphasise the husband's contribution. Notably, research on urban livelihoods has also shown that children also contribute to households in various ways (Porter et al. 2010). The livelihoods framework offers a fuller picture than income-focused measures of urban household economic status. It is crucial for capturing the value of subsistence food production, casual employment, informal training, and domestic labour within the household.

The food security status of different household types reflects the important role of gender in shaping urban food systems. The African Food Security Urban Network (AFSUN) survey of 6,453 households in eleven cities compared four household types: female-centred, male-centred, nuclear, and extended (Crush and Frayne 2010). A gender-focused analysis of the survey findings demonstrated that female-centred households were over-represented in the severely food insecure category relative to other types of households. Poverty was an important factor determining food security status, and while female-centred households were the most likely type to be poor and to be food insecure, the effect of poverty on food security status was less pronounced among female-centred households. This finding suggests that at lower levels of income, female-centred households are doing better at feeding their households. The explanation for this finding is unclear, but it is possible that female household heads dedicate a greater proportion of household resources to food relative to male household heads. This explanation aligns with research that has identified gendered differences in priorities for the use of household resources whereby women's greater control over the use of household resources can lead to greater food security status (Kennedy and Peters 1992; Haddad et al. 1997).

The household scale of analysis has been used extensively in research on food production in cities, particularly subsistence production (Hovorka et al. 2009;

Mkwambisi et al. 2011; Shillington 2013; Simiyu and Foeken 2013). In most urban food producing households, men and women are both highly engaged in farming-related activities, but in most households men make the final decision on what to produce and how to deploy women's labour. Simiyu and Foeken (2013) found that some women subverted this control by taking advantage of their husbands' frequent absences from home and hiding proceeds from the sale of farm products from their husbands. Shillington (2013) argued that gendered labour in backyard fruit tree cultivation in Managua, Nicaragua, was not only economic, but also served a cultural purpose of making a home in the city. Mkwambisi et al. (2011) identified many women household heads who were also farmers in their study of urban Malawi, but female-headed farming households produced less food per hectare than male-headed farming households. Reasons included relative lack of money for inputs like seeds and fertiliser, relatively less household labour, and less capacity to develop agricultural skills because of illiteracy. Household scale case studies provide a rich resource for understanding the nexus of power, culture, and food in cities.

Cities

At the city scale, questions about planning, governance, and the effects of different built environments on people's ability to access food come into focus. Urban food security is often discussed with reference to sustainability, which can refer to overlapping objectives, including: the long-term viability of the city's economy, the vulnerability of city structures to natural hazards, the health of the city's population, and the social cohesiveness of the city (Pieterse 2011). Until recently, food has been an invisible issue for urban planners thinking about sustainability (Morgan 2009). This is partly a result of the mainstream assumption that food was primarily an agricultural, and hence a rural issue. The past decade has seen a proliferation of interest among planners, municipalities, and researchers on the issue of urban food security. Box 13.1 further illustrates the importance of the city scale in practical terms, as it illustrates the important contributions municipal governments can make to food security programmes focused on gender equality. This subsection examines three issues pertinent to understanding gender and urban food security at the city scale: (1) food deserts, (2) informal economies and food systems, and (3) the provisioning of municipal services.

The concept of food deserts encapsulates widespread injustice in many post-industrial cities where the supermarket-based food distribution system does not adequately serve the needs of low-income communities (Shannon 2014). Food deserts are areas where safe and nutritious food is not readily available. As an issue arising primarily from research in cities in the Global North, it dovetails neatly with the nexus of mobilities, livelihoods, and food excess emerging from research in cities of the Global South. Its framing of urban food security as a social justice issue evident in the urban geography of the city offers lessons for understanding urban food security research in the Global South, just as the livelihoods approach offers insights that can enrich the understanding of urban food security in cities of the Global North (Battersby 2012). A focus on gender equality has the potential to serve as a connective thread between these lines of theorising urban food systems because of its unifying reference to gender difference as a core cause of hunger and poverty.

In many cities of the Global South, most work, services, trade, and production takes place informally. In spite of the near ubiquity of informality in cities in developing countries, planners, urban managers, and politicians often seek to put an end to these practices (Potts 2008; Riley 2014). Formality is associated with development because it is better suited to government regulation and taxation, as well as global trade and investment, and therefore to a particular ideal of urban development and urban food system (Riley and Legwegoh 2014). Yet from the perspective of many low-income urban residents and the needs of their household members, informal economies are critical for survival. This is particularly true of informal food systems, which provide flexibility and convenience to millions of consumers who are unable to access formal food sources (Porter et al. 2007). They also provide a vital source of livelihoods and income for people who cannot secure sufficient employment in the formal economic sector, the majority of whom are women (Roever 2014).

Municipal authorities can be partners rather than adversaries of informal economic actors (Tinker 1997). The construction of market facilities with piped water, sanitation facilities, and security services is one way of investing in informal sector workers and consumers (Porter et al. 2007). Partnering with traders and consumers, and ensuring that the women among them have a voice, can be an important step towards empowering low-income men and women economically and politically

FIGURE 13.2 Market on the outskirts of Blantyre, Malawi, where urban consumers buy low-cost food directly from producers

Source: Riley.

and promoting gender equity. A similar approach is needed to address problems associated with informal food production in cities. The benefits of using urban space for food production are increasingly recognised, and the idea of a city as an agricultural site is less alien to planners and urban managers now than it was a decade ago (Hovorka et al. 2009). The 13 case studies of gender-focused urban agriculture projects featured in *Women Feeding Cities* (Hovorka et al. 2009) attest to the multiple possibilities for improving urban livelihoods by building on diverse experiences of implementing gender-mainstreamed urban agriculture projects. Nonetheless, challenges remain in how to best 'mainstream' gender into urban agricultural projects, especially in regards to achieving the strategic goals related to gender equality in the long term (Hovorka 2006; Lessa and Rocha 2012).

A final point on the city scale of analysis is to note the importance of equitable provision of other urban services and amenities such as clean water, adequate housing, electricity, intra-urban transit, sanitation, schools, and hospitals. These basic necessities are increasingly difficult to provide in part because population growth usually outstrips municipal resources, but the stress on natural resources in and around cities means that environmental concerns at the city scale are central to understanding urban food systems. Inadequate or unaffordable provisioning of services and amenities can impact household food security in several ways, such as:

- Lack of affordable housing can divert scarce income to housing costs rather than food.
- Lack of clean water can compromise food safety and health.
- Inadequate transit can increase the time expense of livelihood activities.
- Poorly resourced schools and hospitals have long-term impacts on public health, economic development, and social cohesion.
- Poor environmental stewardship reduces the productivity of agriculture in and around cities.

These issues often have a greater impact on women than men, in some cases making domestic tasks more onerous and in other instances removing opportunities to close the gender gaps in health, education, and economic participation. The de-prioritisation of services and amenities that could make food provisioning and preparation less onerous for women often reflects women's lack of political influence in municipal decision-making.

Nations

At the national scale (or in some cases state or provincial scale), the ideals for the recognition of human rights and gender equality formulated in international agreements are translated into the local context and government action plans. The goal of representing women's voices equally in legislatures is a key feminist goal, which is also intrinsic to democratic values. Progress has been made worldwide and the proportion of parliamentary seats held by women increased from

14% in 2000 to 22% in 2014 (UN 2014: 23). While this value is nowhere near parity, and there are vast differences among countries, it suggests that women are having a greater influence in political affairs than they did in the past. This progress potentially bodes well for the formulation and implementation of laws, policies, and development objectives that prioritise social justice and gender equity. Box 13.2 illustrates the importance of these reforms based on direct experiences implementing gender-mainstreamed urban food security programmes in Kenya. This subsection examines three national scale topics related to the gendering of urban food systems: (1) national social protection schemes; (2) national agricultural and urbanisation policies, and (3) rural–urban connections and food security.

One area of direct relevance to gender and urban food security has been the policy of social protection schemes in low-income countries (Miller et al. 2011; Nino-Zarazua et al. 2012). The AFSUN survey finding that female-centred households benefited more than other types of households from South Africa's social grants scheme is strong evidence that social protection has a gender-positive effect on urban food security (Dodson et al. 2012). The comparison between the three South African cities surveyed, where social grants were available, and the eight cities in other countries without social grants is striking:

> The three South African cities tend to have lower LPI [Lived Poverty Index] scores than the other eight cities in the survey. The biggest gap is amongst female-centred households: in South African cities their LPI is 0.8, whereas in cities outside South Africa it is nearly double at 1.5. This almost certainly reflects the impact of social grants, and especially child grants, in South Africa.
>
> *(Dodson et al. 2012: 21)*

In targeting dependents including children and retired people, the social grants are able to support households with the highest ratio of mouths to feed relative to economically productive members, which are most likely to be households headed by women. For these economically marginalised households, the stability and reliability of the income source can be as critical as the sum itself, facilitating budgeting for household needs on a monthly basis.

In their study of the gendered effects of social protection schemes in eight diverse countries (Ghana, Peru, Bangladesh, Ethiopia, India, Indonesia, Mexico, Vietnam), Holmes and Jones (2010) demonstrated that social protection schemes are not a panacea for reducing women's poverty relative to men. Gender equality was not a primary objective of most programmes, and even in cases where gender was mainstreamed into the project, problems with implementation (including gender biases and stereotypes held by officials and participants) negated the effectiveness of the schemes for addressing gender needs. By failing to include an objective of transforming gender relations at all scales, most programmes operate with a 'narrow conceptualisation of gender vulnerabilities and focus on supporting

FIGURE 13.3 Women producers associated with the Harvest of Hope box home delivery scheme of Abalimi Bezekhaya in Cape Town ready to deliver their vegetables

Source: Abalimi Bezekhaya, courtesy Patrick West.

women's care and domestic roles and responsibilities in the household' (Holmes and Jones 2010: vii). In supporting women's care and domestic roles, gender inequality was often reinforced and the gendered division of labour at the heart of inequality was perpetuated rather than transformed.

The design and implementation of gender sensitive social protection programmes, whether they take the form of cash or asset transfers, public works, or food subsidies, hold the potential for national or state governments to directly intervene in urban poverty and food insecurity by setting a minimum standard of living. These programmes can simultaneously address gender inequality by lightening the burden of responsibility for feeding households from women's shoulders.

In the Global North, food and agricultural policies are increasingly central in debates over public health, environmental justice, and the nutritional appropriateness of food (Shannon 2014). Policies and development objectives formulated at the national level shape how cities are built, with consequences for gender relations and urban food systems. Urban policies in North America after World War II promoted the suburban sprawl of cities and the spatial division of male/urban/production from female/suburban/reproduction (Domosh and Seager 2001). The spread of suburban sprawl distanced people from food sources and created a new reliance on cars to access food. Doubts about the environmental sustainability of industrial agriculture and the corporate-dominated food distribution system have influenced the governments of major countries, including the US, to (slowly) start supporting alternative food networks through policies and investment (McClintock 2014). Eco-feminists have contributed to the debates by emphasising the social and cultural costs of urban consumers being alienated from the social and environmental processes of food production (White 2011). Their experiences of urban food systems are expressed in terms that link the personal need for healthy bodies and communities with the political need to re-envision the policy frameworks that create food deserts and perpetuate class and gender-based health inequalities.

National urbanisation policies in developing countries can play a key role in shaping settlement patterns, urban built environments, and the standard of living in cities (Parnell and Pieterse 2010). Many developing countries that experienced rapid population growth in the twentieth century also experienced rapid internal migration into cities at a pace that outstripped their governments' capacity to provide basic housing and municipal services (Davis 2006), such that the development of cohesive national urban food strategies was not feasible. The response by some governments was to attempt to curtail rural to urban migration, or to reserve the right to fully participate in urban civic life. China's *hukou* system, for example, prevents rural to urban migrants from accessing government services in the cities, thus preserving their 'rural' status and promoting temporary or circular migration (Fan 2008). Such policies preclude the political question of urban food security by *de jure* marginalising many of the would-be urban poor, particularly women who are more likely to face legal and economic barriers to establishing themselves formally in cities.

Circular forms of migration between rural and urban places are increasingly recognised as the norm in many developing countries (Lynch 2005). Rural–urban social and economic linkages that facilitate access to a variety of resources and opportunities at different times of the year are vital for livelihoods and urban food security (Tacoli 2007; Lerner and Eakin 2011; Agergaard et al. 2010). Progress on the re-theorisation of urban livelihoods as transgressing the rural–urban divide ties into the aforementioned benefits of personal mobilities, which facilitate 'straddling' multiple places and often benefit women disproportionally in giving them opportunities to diversify their informal economic activities in reaction to their marginalisation within urban formal economies (Flynn 2005; Riley and Dodson 2014). This research is instructive for planners, researchers, and development workers to broaden their geographical frame of reference when developing urban food system improvements.

Global

Political, economic, and environmental structures and processes functioning at the global scale shape urban food systems and vulnerability to hunger. It is increasingly important to integrate the global scale in studies of food security and gender equality because of the increasing role of international economic transactions, political agreements, and social development priorities on everyday life. This subsection examines three global scale topics in relation to the feminist foodscapes framework: (1) the role of international trade, (2) the effects of global climate change, and (3) the Millennium Development Goals for 2015.

The 2007–08 global price shocks of basic food commodities exposed the vulnerability of millions of urban residents to become food insecure as a result of global scaled events (Clapp 2009; Ruel et al. 2010; Hadley et al. 2012). In many countries, urban markets rely on geographically dispersed supply chains to make food available in cities. Households that rely on their incomes to purchase food for survival (rather than drawing on a variety of livelihood strategies) were the most directly impacted when financial speculation, droughts in key food producing areas, and a rapid rise in demand for biofuels caused food prices to spike (UN 2011). The hyper integration of the food system also impacts on rural (and urban) producers, many of whom fail to compete with the economies of scale and subsidies provided to the agriculture and food industries in the Global North (Weis 2007). The consequential decline of rural agricultural economies can lead to increases in rural to urban migration and more dependence on global markets for survival as domestic production declines. This trend can be particularly deleterious for women, many of whom are responsible for feeding their households even when food becomes suddenly unaffordable or unavailable. The challenges faced by migrants themselves are also gendered, and in most cases female migrants are more vulnerable to the economic marginalisation and social alienation that causes urban food insecurity.

The increasingly distantiated integration of consumers and producers in the global food system is fundamental to why the impact of global climate change is expected to be extremely profound and widespread. Local changes in temperature, water availability, the frequency of extreme weather events, and seasonality will not only have local impacts on food supplies: global integration means that production shortfalls in specific areas can reshape global supplies and trade patterns, with price shocks such as that experienced in 2007–08 becoming more frequent. In general, the negative consequences of global climate change will most severely impact people in the poorest and least developed countries. Urban residents in these countries will be among the most vulnerable to hunger in most climate change scenarios. These processes create new forms of environmental injustice that are starkly evident at the global scale where the people most severely affected are the least likely to have benefitted from industrialisation that caused global warming. The need for analysis that can support adaptive strategies for urban households is urgent (Frayne et al. 2012). Integrating strategic gender needs will be key to developing and implementing durable strategies for on-going livelihood adaptation as climate change leads to unpredictable and unprecedented new circumstances.

The MDGs represent a global consensus among governments and global civil society organisations on the priorities for social development. Hunger figures prominently in the first MDG, with the target of 'halving, between 1990 and

2015, the proportion of people who suffer from hunger' (UN 2014: 8). The prevalence of undernourishment has been reduced from 23.6% in 1990–92 to 14.3% in 2011–13, but with rapid population growth the absolute number of hungry people remains high at 842 million (UN 2014: 12). Furthermore, the most rapidly urbanising regions, sub-Saharan Africa (25%) and southern Asia (17%), have the highest portions of hungry people. Fukuda-Parr and Orr (2014) argued that the MDG hunger target has reduced the problem of hunger from one of food as a human right, as expressed in the 1996 FAO declaration, to food as a nutritional problem amenable to technological solutions of production and supply. Urban issues are under-represented in the MDGs, reduced to a conservative target for slum improvement (Cohen 2014). In light of the prolific body of research on urban food security produced in the past decade, and the rapidly growing urban populations in the Global South, the post-2015 agenda should recognise the distinct needs of urban food systems to meet the needs of urban residents. The goals for gender equality are also notably weak in the MDGs and key structural issues such as reproductive freedom and economic empowerment for women are understated relative to their importance for social development (Sen and Mukherjee 2014). Within a feminist foodscapes framework there is a discernible connection between the depoliticisation of food security and the depoliticisation of gender in the MDGs that needs to be redressed to make progress on both fronts. The global scale of analysis brings important discursive trends to the surface and highlights the pressing need to bring discourses and policies in line with the values associated with gender equality and the human right to food.

Action for gender-equitable urban food systems

The feminist foodscapes framework not only illuminates the ways in which gender is necessarily embedded within and across various scales of urban life, it also opens up exciting possibilities for action to improve the gender equity of urban foods systems. In reiterating the central importance of strategic goals related to achieving gender equality, the feminist foodscapes framework reinvigorates the political dimensions of food activism. Hunger continues to be a serious problem for nearly a billion people in their daily lives, while millions more are highly vulnerable. Furthermore, millions of people who are not at risk of hunger are unhealthy because the food they consume does not meet their nutritional or cultural needs. The people who have the least opportunities to influence the broad social, economic, and political structures that shape their urban food systems are mostly women constrained by economic marginalisation, access to fewer resources for their livelihoods, patriarchy within their households and communities, and unjust laws. Empowerment for women and men in urban communities can be conceived in terms of expanding these opportunities to change urban food systems at multiple scales.

BOX 13.1 THE ROLE OF MUNICIPAL GOVERNMENT IN THE MUSIKAVANHU URBAN AGRICULTURE PROJECT IN HARARE, ZIMBABWE

Development practitioners in the Global South have observed that gender inequality is a consistent challenge to implementing urban food security programmes that promote food production by urban households (Hovorka et al. 2009). The Musikavanhu Project in Harare, Zimbabwe, granted the use of vacant urban land to low-income households 'in order to maintain their food security, save money on food expenditures, and generate complementary income from regular sales' (Toriro 2009: 94). Although the project was not intended to target women farmers, 90% of farmers were women during the 2008 survey. The popularity of urban farming among women in Harare was partly a reflection of the gendered burden to feed household members during the political economic crisis taking place at the time of the survey.

An analysis of the challenges for the Musikavanhu Project to promote sustainable social change toward gender equality led Toriro (2009: 102–3) to list six ways in which the municipal government in Harare could support the project:

1   Creating a facilitating legal framework that recognises the economic and social contributions of urban farmers and provides rights and protections to male and female urban farmers equally.
2   Raising awareness of gender and urban agriculture through gender sensitivity training and public awareness campaigns.
3   Improving land tenure through the designation of zones for urban agriculture and giving ownership or leasehold lands to women rather than granting it only to their husbands.
4   Stimulating adequate support services by co-funding programmes with Non-Governmental Organisations to support female farmers and by implementing tax incentives for private enterprises to donate resources to such programmes.
5   Providing protection against theft of crops that women are not normally equipped to protect at night because of obligations at home and safety concerns.
6   Giving access to free medical support to reduce the burden of caring for relatives suffering from HIV/AIDS and other health problems, thus freeing up more of women's time for agricultural activities.

These lessons for the municipal government in Harare can be transferred to other cities as they implement policies aimed at achieving food security that also enhances gender equality. It emphasises the important role of politics at the 'city' scale.

Source: Toriro 2009.

The 'five elements of mainstreaming' presented in Hovorka and Lee-Smith (2006: 131–33) warrants repeating in this chapter in light of the multiple scales approach to gendering urban food systems. The five elements are: (1) conceptual clarity, (2) identifying practical and strategic needs, (3) political will and commitment, (4) capacity building and resource allocation, and (5) scientific research.

The first element speaks to the narrow understanding of gender among actors across multiple scales, from project participants and managers to World Bank and UN employees. The overuse and oversimplification of 'gender' in policy documents and strategic frameworks can reinforce the false impression that it is relevant only to women (Hovorka and Lee-Smith 2006: 131). The research above demonstrates the need to develop gender capacity at multiple scales in order to make the necessary connections between the power-laden fields of food and gender. For grassroots project implementation, this is a matter of engaging in critical dialogue with participants about the meaning of gender in their social context in order to make the core concept of gender equality accessible and relevant to their daily challenges. While the particular obstacles in this process will be different in different settings, for example in places with low literacy rates, different means of communication will be required (Cornwall and Scoones 2011), there is a perennial need to build and reinforce capacity in this regard and it should not be overlooked in projects based in the Global North. In like manner, reinforcement of the meaning of gender and its role in shaping hunger and vulnerability is consistently required among policymakers at all scales.

The second element, to identify practical and strategic needs, has been a major theme of this chapter. The process of articulating these needs in the local context should be allotted time in the planning process, and ideally be conducted using participative approaches that include participants. Hovorka and Lee-Smith (2006: 132) note that 'identifying the type and scale of intervention (be it through programmes, planning or policies) should rely on a solid understanding of the local context and structural factors that delineate opportunities and constraints for individual producers'. The feminist foodscapes framework highlights the interconnectedness of the 'local context' with structures and processes at multiple scales, such that 'understanding the local context' goes far beyond the spaces in which project participants' daily lives take place. The process of articulating practical and strategic needs should involve a dialogue between facilitators, who are more likely to be able to comment on big picture dynamics that shape gender and urban food systems, and participants, who have vital knowledge of urban food systems based on their daily experiences living in the city. Applying a feminist foodscapes framework therefore requires a balance between these types of needs, and their related action plans and objectives, to be at the forefront of planning, implementation, and assessment of project outcomes.

The third element is 'political will and commitment amongst key stakeholders at all scales' (Hovorka and Lee-Smith 2006: 132). This element emphasises the need for leadership in forging a cohesive commitment to the goal of gender equality as a central goal of efforts to ensure urban food security. In the policy realm, gender inequity should be addressed by first seeking to understand the particular effects of existing policies on men and women. This awareness of gender difference should guide policy responses at all levels of government and actors operating at the global scale. For development projects aimed at improving urban food systems, maintaining a political will and commitment to gender equality will overlap with the integration of practical and strategic needs. Addressing structural causes of urban poverty and hunger will be key to the sustainability of these projects over the long term.

BOX 13.2 THE ROLE OF THE NATIONAL GOVERNMENT IN CREATING THE CONDITIONS FOR WOMEN AND MEN TO BENEFIT FROM URBAN LIVESTOCK KEEPING IN KISUMU, KENYA

Development practitioners in the Global South have observed that gender inequality is a consistent challenge to implementing urban food security pro- grammes that promote livestock keeping by urban households (Hovorka et al. 2009). Urban livestock, which in the case of Kisumu, Kenya, included chickens, goats, pigs, ducks, and cattle in significant numbers, is a source of food and livelihood security in many households (Ishani 2009). Ishani (2009) reported on a survey conducted as part of a project aimed at improving urban household food security by supporting urban livestock keeping. The project included men and women, including many women who were also the heads of their house- holds. Gender mainstreaming throughout the project cycle led to an increase in the sharing of household responsibilities between men and women and 'a mea- sure of self-esteem and confidence which did not exist before' among partici- pants (Ishani 2009: 118). Women, previously excluded from decision-making at all scales, often experienced a dramatic change in outlook: 'Women in particu- lar have become the "push" factors for change, and they now take the lead in the household to ensure that these changes do take place' (Ishani 2009: 119).

The project adopted a multi-stakeholder approach and the report on expe- riences highlighted the importance of support from the central government. In the first instance, there is a need for financial, technical, and institutional resources to extend the benefits of this programme. The state plays a unique role in potentially providing a funding source available in the longer term and not vulnerable to project funding cycles. In her conclusions, Ishani (2009: 119) also argues for a scaling-up of the gender mainstreaming focus dem- onstrated in the project and the importance of policy reforms at local and national levels aimed at improving gender equality:

> Gender equity, however, cannot be achieved at the project level if there is a disparity in policies benefitting one sex and not the other.

> All policies, at the local level and at the central government level, have to be formulated in a gender-sensitive manner. Issues such as inheritance and succession, especially for women, should be of paramount importance in order for the whole of the household to benefit.
>
> Implementing a gender-mainstreamed urban food security programme around urban livestock revealed the importance of policies and resources at multiple scales, particularly the national scale where sustainable financial resources can be mobilised and key policy reforms can be made.
>
> *Source:* Ishani 2009.

The fourth element is capacity building and resource allocation. It is related to the first element in that resources need to be devoted to achieving conceptual clarity, and these actions constitute capacity building. Hovorka and Lee-Smith (2006: 132) identify a danger of losing the focus on gender *because* of its ubiquitous relevance at multiple scales and to multiple dimensions of any project or policy, summed up in the statement: 'By making gender everybody's job, it can easily become nobody's job'. The investment of substantive resources into the gender elements of a project will demonstrate the leadership and commitment noted in the third element of political will and commitment. Investing resources into mainstreaming gender will help stakeholders at multiple scales to 'look beyond' the conceptual conflation of gender with women and to engage in the kind of self-reflexive and critical thinking needed to overcome ingrained stereotypes and biases (Cornwall and Molyneux 2007).

The fifth element is 'scientific research on gender dynamics' (Hovorka and Lee-Smith 2006: 133). Within a project or policy formulation cycle, this research element can provide a virtuous cycle of monitoring and adjusting action plans when gender-related objectives are not being met. The ubiquity and complexity of gender difference means that even the most rigorous gender planning can have unforeseen consequences. With regular monitoring and mechanisms for on-going communication among stakeholders, developments that reinforce gender inequality (for example, by adding onerously to women's labour or disproportionally enriching men) can be re-conceived. The focus on scientific research also speaks to the important role of the wider research community to contribute to policy formulation and programme/project development to address urban food insecurity. As the examples in this chapter demonstrate, academic researchers play central roles in identifying problems, linking issues at multiple scales, and identifying connections between practical and structural causes of gender inequality and food insecurity. In an increasingly urban world, with an increasingly integrated global food system and a persistent correlation of being female and being poor, the integration of perspectives rooted in multiple scales will play an increasingly instrumental role in understanding and overcoming global poverty.

Concluding thoughts

A gendered lens of analysis is fundamental to understanding food security: gender identities and social categories shape the meaning of food, how and by whom it is consumed, and the systems of production and distribution. This chapter's gender analysis of urban food systems draws from feminist understandings of how to bring about gender equality by addressing practical and strategic needs to understand simultaneously the immediate needs of urban residents to have access to safe, nutritious, and culturally appropriate food while also recognising the bigger picture of long-term sustainability of urban food systems to realise the human right to food. The chapter demonstrates that challenges and opportunities for urban food systems exist at multiple scales, and that they consistently intersect with problems related to gender inequality. Future action to improve urban food systems can refer to the five elements of gender mainstreaming for guidance. Policymakers, development workers, and researchers should also integrate into their projects an understanding of the multiple layers of policies, discourses, and social relations that contribute to shaping urban food systems. This will help to bring a balance of practical and strategic objectives of gender equality and food security in cities.

References

Agarwal, B. 1997. 'Bargaining' and gender relations: Within and beyond the household. *Feminist Economics* 3(1): 1–51.

Agergaard, J.; Fold, N.; Gough, K. (eds.) 2010. Rural–urban dynamics: Livelihoods, mobility and markets in African and Asian frontiers. New York: Routledge.

Allen, P.; Sachs, C. 2007. Women and food chains: The gendered politics of food. *International Journal of Sociology of Food and Agriculture* 15(1): 1–23.

Battersby, J. 2012. Beyond the food desert: Finding ways to talk about urban food security in South Africa. *Geografiska Annaler: Series B, Human Geography* 94(2): 141–159.

Clapp, J. 2009. Food price volatility and vulnerability in the Global South: Considering the global economic context. *Third World Quarterly* 30(6): 1183–1196.

Cohen, M. 2014. The city is missing in the Millennium Development Goals. *Journal of Human Development and Capabilities: A Multi-Disciplinary Journal for People-Centred Development* 15(2–3): 261–274.

Cornwall, A.; Molyneux, M. (eds.) 2007. The politics of rights: Dilemmas for feminist praxis. London: Routledge.

Cornwall, A.; Scoones, I. (eds.) 2011. Revolutionizing development: Reflections on the work of Robert Chambers. London: Earthscan.

Cresswell, T. 2010. Towards a politics of mobility. *Environment and Planning D: Society and Space* 28(1): 17–31.

Crush, J.; Frayne, B. 2010. The invisible crisis: Urban food security in Southern Africa. Cape Town: African Food Security Urban Network (AFSUN).

Davis, M. 2006. Planet of slums. London: Verso.

Devereux, S. 2001. Sen's entitlement approach: Critiques and counter-critiques. *Oxford Development Studies* 29(3): 245–263.

Dodson, B.; Chiweza, A.; Riley, L. 2012. Gender and food insecurity in Southern African cities. Cape Town: African Food Security Urban Network (AFSUN).

Domosh, M.; Seager, J. 2001. Putting women in place: Feminist geographers making sense of the world. New York: The Guilford Press.

Fan, C. 2008. China on the move: Migration, the state, and the household. London: Routledge.

Flynn, K. 2005. Food, culture, and survival in an African city. New York: Palgrave.

Foeken, D.; Owuor, S. 2008. Farming as a livelihood source for the urban poor of Nakuru, Kenya. *Geoforum* 39: 1978–1990.

Frayne, B. 2010. Pathways of food: Mobility and food transfers in southern African cities. *IDPR,* 32(3–4): 291–310.

Frayne, B.; Moser, C.; Ziervogel, G. (eds.) 2012. Climate change, assets and food security in Southern African cities. New York: Earthscan.

Fukuda-Parr, S.; Orr, A. 2014. The MDG hunger target and the competing frameworks of food security. *Journal of Human Development and Capabilities: A Multi-Disciplinary Journal for People-Centred Development* 15(2–3): 147–160.

Haddad, L.; Hoddinott, J.; Alderman, H. (eds.) 1997. Intrahousehold resource allocation in developing countries: Models, methods, and policy. Baltimore: The Johns Hopkins University Press.

Hadley, C.; Stevenson, E.; Tadesse, Y.; Belachew, T. 2012. Rapidly rising food prices and the experience of food insecurity in urban Ethiopia: Impacts on health and well-being. *Social Science & Medicine* 75: 2412–2419.

Hanson, S. 2010. Gender and mobility: New approaches for informing sustainability. *Gender, Place and Culture* 17(1): 5–23.

Holmes, R.; Jones, N. 2010. Rethinking social protection using a gender lens. London: Overseas Development Institute.

Hovorka, A. 2006. Urban agriculture: Addressing practical and strategic gender needs. *Development in Practice* 16: 51–61.

Hovorka, A. 2012. Women/chicken vs. men/cattle: Insights on gender-species intersectionality. *Geoforum* 43: 875–884.

Hovorka, A. 2013. The case for a feminist foodscapes framework: Lessons from research in urban Botswana. *Development* 56(1): 123–128.

Hovorka, A.; Lee-Smith, D. 2006. Gendering the urban agriculture agenda. In: *Cities farming for the future: Urban agriculture for green and productive cities.* (Ed.) Veenhuizen, R. van. Ottawa: International Development Research Centre (IDRC).

Hovorka, A.; Zeeuw, H. de; Njenga, M. (eds.) 2009. Women feeding cities: Mainstreaming gender in urban agriculture and food security. Rugby: Practical Action; Leusden: RUAF Foundation Publishing.

Ishani, Z. 2009. Key gender issues in urban livestock keeping and food security in Kisumu, Kenya. In: *Women feeding cities: Mainstreaming gender in urban agriculture and food security.* (Eds.) Hovorka, A.; Zeeuw, H. de; Njenga, M. Rugby: Practical Action; Leusden: RUAF Foundation.

Jarosz, L. 2011. Nourishing women: Toward a feminist political ecology of community supported agriculture in the United States. *Gender, Place and Culture* 18(3): 307–326.

Kabeer, N. 1994. Reversed realities: Gender hierarchies in development thought. London: Verso.

Kabeer, N. 2003. Gender mainstreaming in poverty eradication and the Millennium Development Goals: A handbook for policy-makers and other stakeholders. Ottawa: Canadian International Development Agency (CIDA).

Kennedy, E.; Peters, P. 1992. Household food security and child nutrition: The interaction of income and gender of household head. *World Development* 20(8): 1077–1085.

Lerner, A.; Eakin, H. 2011. An obsolete dichotomy? Rethinking the rural-urban interface in terms of food security and production in the global south. *The Geographic Journal* 177: 311–320.

Lessa, I.; Rocha, C. 2012. Food security and gender mainstreaming: Possibilities for social transformation in Brazil. *International Social Work* 55(3): 337–352.

Little, J.; Ilbery, B.; Watts, D. 2009. Gender, consumption and the relocalisation of food: A research agenda. *Sociologica Ruralis* 49(3): 201–217.

Lynch, K. 2005 Rural-urban interaction in the developing world. London: Routledge.

McClintock, N. 2014. Radical, reformist, and garden-variety neoliberal: Coming to terms with urban agriculture's contradictions. *Local Environment* 19(2): 147–171.

Miller, C.; Tsoka, M.; Reichert, K. 2011. The impact of the social cash transfer scheme on food security in Malawi. *Food Policy* 36: 230–238.

Mkwambisi, D.; Fraser, E.; Dougill, A. 2011. Urban agriculture and poverty reduction: Evaluating how food production in cities contributes to food security, employment and income in Malawi. *Journal of International Development* 23: 181–203.

Morgan, K. 2009. Feeding the city: The challenge of urban food planning. *International Planning Studies* 14(4): 341–348.

Moser, C. 1993. Gender planning and development: Theory, practice and training. London: Routledge.

Nino-Zarazua, M.; Barrientos, A.; Hickey, S.; Hulme, D. 2012. Social protection in sub-Saharan Africa: Getting the politics right. *World Development* 40: 163–176.

Parnell, S.; Pieterse, E. 2010. The 'right to the city': Institutional imperatives of a developmental state. *International Journal of Urban and Regional Research* 34(1): 146–162.

Pieterse, E. 2011. Recasting urban sustainability in the South. *Development* 54(3): 309–316.

Porter, G.; Hampshire, K.; Abane, A.; Robson, E.; Munthali, A.; Mashiri, M.; Tanle, A. 2010. Moving young lives: Mobility, immobility and inter-generational tensions in urban Africa. *Geoforum* 41: 796–804.

Porter, G.; Lyon, F.; Potts, D. 2007. Market institutions and urban food supply in West and Southern Africa: A review. *Progress in Development Studies* 7(2): 115–134.

Potts, D. 2008. The urban informal sector in sub-Saharan Africa: From bad to good (and back again?). *Development Southern Africa* 25(2): 151–167.

Rakodi, C.; Lloyd-Jones, T. (eds.) 2002. Urban livelihoods: A people-centred approach to reducing poverty. London: Earthscan.

Riley, L. 2013. Gendered geographies of food security in Blantyre, Malawi. University of Western Ontario – Electronic Thesis and Dissertation Repository. Paper 1223. Available from: http://ir.lib.uwo.ca/etd/1223.

Riley, L. 2014. Operation *Dongosolo* and the geographies of urban poverty in Malawi. *Journal of Southern African Studies* 40(3): 443–458.

Riley, L.; Dodson, B. 2014, Gendered mobilities and food access in Blantyre, Malawi. *Urban Forum* 25(2): 227–239.

Riley, L.; Legwegoh, A. 2014. Comparative urban food geographies in Blantyre and Gaborone. *African Geographical Review* 33(1): 52–66.

Robson, E. 2006. The 'kitchen' as women's space in rural Hausaland, northern Nigeria. *Gender, Place and Culture* 13(6): 669–676.

Roever, S. 2014. Informal economy monitoring study sector report: Street vendors. Cambridge, MA: Women in Informal Employment: Globalizing Organization.

Ruel, M.; Garrett, J.; Hawkes, C.; Cohen, M. 2010. The food, fuel, and financial crises affect the urban and rural poor disproportionately: A review of the evidence. *The Journal of Nutrition* 140: 170S–176S.

Sen, A. 1981. Poverty and famines: An essay on entitlement and deprivation. Oxford: Oxford University Press.

Sen, G.; Mukherjee, A. 2014. No empowerment without rights, no rights without politics: Gender-equality, MDGs and the post-2015 development agenda. *Journal of Human Development and Capabilities: A Multi-Disciplinary Journal for People-Centred Development* 15(2–3): 188–202.

Shannon, J. 2014. Food deserts: Governing obesity in the neoliberal city. *Progress in Human Geography* 38(2): 248–266.

Shillington, L. 2013. Right to food, right to the city: Household urban agriculture, and socionatural metabolism in Managua, Nicaragua. *Geoforum* 44: 103–111.

Simiyu, R.; Foeken, D. 2013. Gendered divisions of labour in urban crop cultivation in a Kenyan town: Implications for livelihood outcomes. *Gender, Place & Culture* 21(6): 768–784.

Tacoli, C. 2007. Poverty, inequality and the underestimation of rural-urban linkages. *Development* 50(2): 90–95.

Tinker, I. 1997. Street foods: Urban food and employment in developing countries. Oxford: Oxford University Press.

Toriro, P. 2009. Gender dynamics in the Musikavanhu urban agriculture movement, Harare, Zimbabwe. In: *Women feeding cities: Mainstreaming gender in urban agriculture and food security.* (Eds.) Hovorka, A.; Zeeuw, H. de; Njenga, M. Rugby: Practical Action; Leusden: RUAF Foundation.

Tornaghi, C. 2014. Critical geography of urban agriculture. *Progress in Human Geography* 38(4): 551–567.

UN. 2011. The global social crisis: Report on the world social situation 2011. New York: The United Nations (UN).

UN. 2014. The Millennium Development Goals report 2014. New York: The United Nations (UN).

Uteng, T. 2011. Gender and mobility in the developing world. Available from: http://siteresources.worldbank.org/INTWDR2012/Resources/7778105–1299699968583/7786210–1322671773271/uteng.pdf.

Uteng, T.; Cresswell, T. (eds.) 2008. Gendered mobilities. Aldershot: Ashgate.

Watts, M. 1983. Silent violence: Food, famine & peasantry in northern Nigeria. Berkeley: University of California Press.

Weis, T. 2007. The global food economy: The battle for the future of farming. London: Zed Books.

White, M. 2011. Sisters of the soil: Urban gardening as resistance in Detroit. *Race/Ethnicity: Multidisciplinary Global Contexts* 5(1): 13–28.

14

FINANCING URBAN AGRICULTURE

What do we know and what should we know

Yves Cabannes

BARTLETT DEVELOPMENT PLANNING UNIT (DPU), UNIVERSITY COLLEGE LONDON

Introduction

In cities around the world, urban agriculture, considered here as both intra-urban and peri-urban agriculture, plays an increasingly important role in making cities more sustainable and better fed. By growing food, the urban poor can reduce household food expenses and generate additional income, thereby enhancing food security and reducing poverty. However, urban agriculture requires increased financial and political legitimacy if it is to continue developing as a productive force. While political support for urban agriculture has been steadily increasing, financial support for urban growers has been more limited. Most urban agricultural producers lack access to credit and, at the same time, the few financial systems in place do not fit well into urban farmers' needs, expectations and capabilities. Information about such schemes is also scarce. Little is known about how urban producers fund their activities and about how credit and investment interventions around the world could benefit large numbers of producers. Existing literature on financing urban agriculture is scarce, and refers essentially to credit systems for market-orientated urban agriculture in North America and, to a lesser extent, Europe.

This chapter thus examines how different types of urban agriculture are financed, a concept that encompasses credit but is not limited to it, as will be discussed further down.[1] It draws from direct exposure to a large number of local processes in Latin America and the Caribbean region from 1994 to 2004 and to others from 2004 to 2014. It draws as well primarily from findings from three programmes spanning from 1988 to 2014:

- Research on, and development of, urban agriculture in the Fortaleza metropolitan region of Brazil from 1988 to 1997 (Maranguape, Maracanaú, Eusebio, Fortaleza) with special attention to their economic and financial dimensions (Cabannes 1997a).

- Survey on credit and investments for urban agriculture was carried out with 13 cities – from Asia, Latin America and Europe. It was commissioned in 2002 and 2003 by UN-HABITAT, UMP-LAC, IPES, IDRC and RUAF Foundation (Cabannes 2006).[2]
- Applied research programme coordinated by RUAF Foundation (2008–2011) carried out with 17 cities from the "Global South" on financing of small-scale urban and peri-urban agriculture (Cabannes 2012; Cabannes 2013).

As a result, this chapter reflects the collective work and contributions of a wide array of actors, both academics and practitioners. It addresses the following central question "What kind of financial system is best suited to each different type of urban agriculture?"

First, some key concepts used are clarified and in particular what we mean by "financing urban agriculture", a notion far from access to credit, as it is commonly understood. The following two sections summarize key lessons from the first survey in 13 cities and for the most recent one in 17 cities. Then we will explore if there is a right mix between savings, resource mobilization, credits and subsidy. The next section makes a balance of what we know better than 20 years ago, and what we should know better. The final section concludes with recommendations for an action-research agenda on urban agricultural finance.

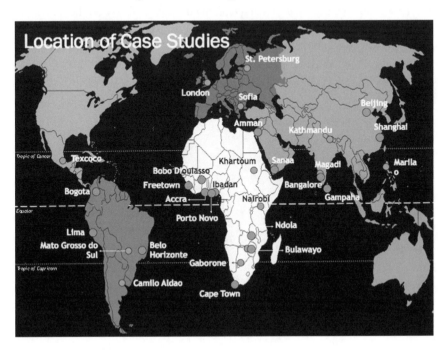

FIGURE 14.1 Location of case studies

Source: Cabannes 2012.

Key concepts

Different financing practices for different types of urban agriculture

Currently, urban agriculture is being practised for meeting subsistence needs, as a market-oriented activity, for recreation, or as a combination of these, each of which requires a different financing instrument or mechanism. For instance, micro-credit may not be the best form of financing for a poor family that undertakes urban agriculture at subsistence level and is not capable of repaying a formal loan. And a small cooperative composed of farmers aiming for expansion of their urban agricultural activities would need forms of financial support that go beyond the provision of free access to seeds or other equipment. Thus it is necessary to get an in-depth conceptual understanding of these types of urban agriculture in order to select the appropriate financing mechanisms of these interventions (see also Figure 14.2).

The first type of urban agriculture, and probably the most common, refers to urban agriculture as a way by which the urban poor and, to a lesser extent, the middle class, support their livelihoods. In this case, urban agriculture plays a part in a subsistence economy, generally family-based, and is seldom monetary. This activity does not generate a cash surplus but provides food or medicinal plants that reduce the expenses of the family, improves their diet and provides them with medicine (Cabannes 1997a).

The second type is related to market-oriented activities. They can be individual or family-based enterprises stretching from small to large or activities undertaken through larger cooperatives or producer associations. They refer to the whole food chain, from the production of vegetables, milk, fruit and other products, to agro-processing and marketing. As part of these market-oriented activities, the products

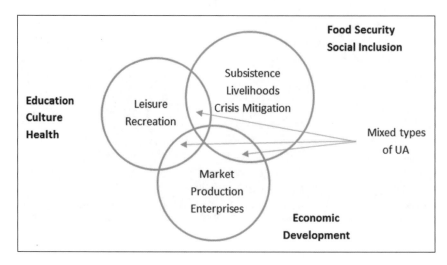

FIGURE 14.2 Various types of urban agriculture

Source: author.

are sold directly by the producers at markets or through intermediaries. To a lesser extent, these products are distributed through formal distribution channels such as supermarkets and greengrocers.

The third type refers to urban agriculture that is undertaken as a part of leisure and recreational activities, occasionally or regularly. This type is more common in the developed rather than the developing countries. In some cities, this type of urban agriculture is seen as a way to maintain or restore the relationship between urban citizens and nature, raise awareness on environmental issues and allow children to experience food production cycles.

Mixed forms are a combination of two or three of the previously described types. For instance, a family involved in urban agriculture for its own food consumption can also sell the surplus locally, providing extra, occasional cash. Similarly, European farmers practising urban agriculture primarily as a recreational or health-related activity use some of the produce for food, thus reducing their home expenses occasionally. The choice of the most appropriate financing mechanisms for urban agriculture should be guided by the type of urban agriculture type that is looked for: (a) subsistence-oriented, (b) market-oriented, (c) leisure and recreation or a combination of them.

Financing as a highly complex and changing combination of four ingredients

The concept of financing is not limited to micro-credit or credits delivered by banks and Micro Finance Institutions (MFIs), as in most of the scarce existing literature. Financing is considered here as a highly complex and changing combination of: Resource Mobilization (both monetary and non-monetary) + Savings + Subsidies + Credits. One central argument is that this equation needs to be taken into account and serve as a base for any consolidation of the financing system for urban agriculture. Approaches only focusing on credit usually show their limits and might be useful for a thin slice of the variety of producers.

Most studies from the 2002–2003 survey have indicated that financial support for urban agriculture is best based on a combination of those mechanisms: savings, subsidies and (micro-) credit. Savings could, for example, work as collateral for receiving credit. Tax incentives or other subsidies could motivate people to become involved, and complement credit systems with training and assistance, and in this way better guarantee success and sustainability of urban farming.

Learning from field experience: credits and investments in urban agriculture

The first global survey on diverse modalities of credit and investment provision to urban agriculture that took place in 2002 and 2003 highlighted how local financial systems for urban agriculture work, identified the myriad of actors involved, the origin of resources, the financial intermediaries and the "financial products" proposed to develop urban agriculture. Some studies went one step further and identified major bottlenecks of local financial systems for urban agriculture.

Understanding the credit cycle: from financial sources to financial products

In general terms, a credit cycle can be summarized in three successive steps. The first refers to the financial sources, which can be international, national or local, from public, private or institutional sectors or from private savings. The second refers to the transformation of these resources into financial products by specific financial intermediaries, and the third to the wide array of financial products offered to potential loan takers. The case of St. Petersburg, based on information from 2002 with some level of complexity, illustrates how a system works at local level – see Figure 14.3.

Financial flows and products for urban farmers from the study case of St. Petersburg, Russia (Moldakov 2002), illustrate the complexity and the richness of financing urban agriculture. The sources of finance are of different origins:

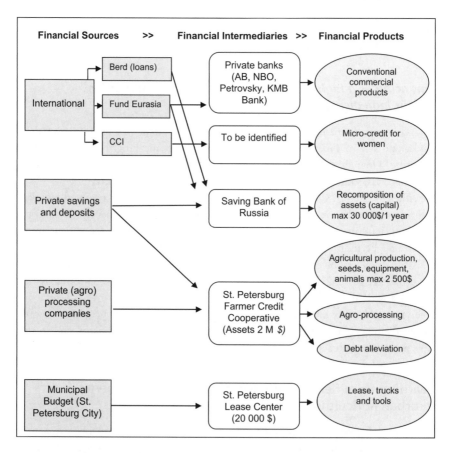

FIGURE 14.3 The St. Petersburg urban agricultural credit cycle: an example of complexity
Source: Cabannes 2004a based on Moldakov 2002.

(a) international, being loans and grants through the European Bank for Reconstruction and Development or the Eurasia Fund; (b) private (agro-) processing companies; (c) private savings and deposits from individuals; and (d) public resources coming from the municipal budget. These sources have different time horizons: the savings and deposits are on a monthly or occasional basis, whereas the municipal budget is annual; the international resources are usually made on a project-by-project basis, stipulating a number of years for disbursement. Transforming financial resources from diverse origins into strong, reliable and steady credit flows is a key issue in any financial system. A good answer lies essentially in the quality and the nature of the financial intermediaries that will transform these resources into financial products.

The case of St. Petersburg is typical of the multiplicity and different characteristics of the financial intermediaries, some of them being local and others being a branch of a national bank. Some of these institutions have a unique source of financing, whereas others have the capacity to draw on from multiple sources. The main institutions identified in this particular case are: (a) St. Petersburg Lease Centre, having a limited volume of resources, drawn mainly from the municipal budget; (b) St. Petersburg Farmer Credit Cooperation, fed by both private agroprocessing companies and private savings; (c) Saving Bank of Russia that is channelling international credit and grants to various Russian cities, including St. Petersburg; and (d) some private banks, such as the Petrovsky Bank, AB Bank or NBO Bank who, in their turn, receive funds from national and international sources.

These multiple sources and the variety of financial intermediaries explain the wide variety of products that an urban farmer can access, in theory. They cover the following kind of credits and grants: leases for trucks and tools, debt alleviation; micro-credits for agro-processing or for agricultural production, seeds and animals; short-term loans (less than one year) for composition of assets; and micro-credits, especially for women or conventional commercial loans, open to clients able to provide a high level of guarantee.

Central role and diversity of financial intermediaries

One crucial finding is that financial intermediaries play a central role in transforming a great diversity of financial sources into multiple "financial products" with specific interest rates, maturity period, level of collaterals, grace period, eligible destination and beneficiaries, minimum and maximum levels of loans, etc. Understanding these intermediaries, who they are, how they operate and their comparative advantages and limits was crucial simply because, by and large, they have a vast power to decide on the financial products that will be offered to urban farmers and which types of urban farmers can be eligible for both subsidies, soft loans or conventional loans. Figure 14.4 introduces the tool that allows unpacking a financial system at local level by organizing existing

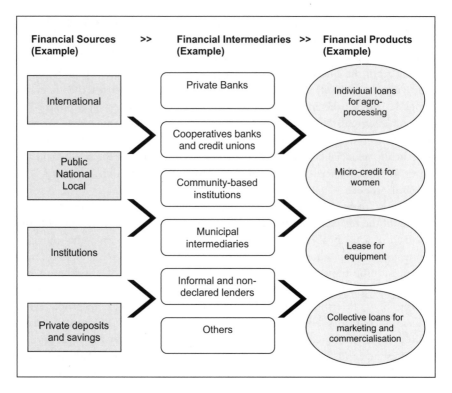

FIGURE 14.4 Financial intermediaries in the urban agricultural financial cycle
Source: Cabannes 2004a.

information and measuring the importance of the flows and the role of intermediaries.

The city surveys clearly pointed out the large number of actors providing financial sources and managing funds (intermediaries) for urban agriculture. A more detailed analysis is needed to define which system(s) is(are) best adapted to the specific local circumstances. Funding sources are found in the context of programmes for poverty alleviation, food security (Argentina), employment and income generation (Brazil, Botswana), or integrated environmental management. Funds stem from, for example, the "Fund for Social Municipal Infrastructure" in Mexico (Ramirez Garcia 2002), "Fund for Social Investment" in Brazil (Araújo 2002), within general "Financial Assistance or Entrepreneurial Programmes" in Botswana (Mosha 2002) or through specific "Agricultural or Horticultural Programmes" as, for instance, in Bangalore, India (Premchander 2002).

However, in most of the surveys, there is confusion and overlap between the source of funds – private, public, institutional, international – and their transformation into credit or subsidies. These two aspects and the role different actors play in each of them should be distinguished and clarified.

Various financial intermediaries that transform resources into loans directed to urban farmers will be presented in the next sections and illustrate the three most common types found in the cities surveyed:

a. Local government intermediaries will be illustrated with the cases of Texcoco in Mexico and Rosario in Argentina.
b. Private and community-based intermediaries illustrated by the experience of a savings and credit cooperative from Nepal.
c. Private banking system with the case of PROVE Pantanal Programme in Brazil.

a. Local governments and public sector intermediaries

The case of Texcoco, Mexico

The local government of Texcoco, in the Mexico metropolitan region, set up an innovative urban agricultural loans programme in the early 2000s that obtained significant results both in financial and social terms (Ramirez-Garcia 2002).

Resources from the central governments were transferred to local governments as part of a vast national social programme. The Texcoco municipality decided to transform these resources into a limited and innovative set of loans to agricultural cooperatives (in particular for flower production) and to small solidarity groups of producers that had not yet formed cooperatives, as was the case with a group of rabbit keepers. A third line of loans was specifically tailored to women urban farmers. No specific institution was set up and the resources were simply earmarked and deposited in a bank that was managing the municipal resources.

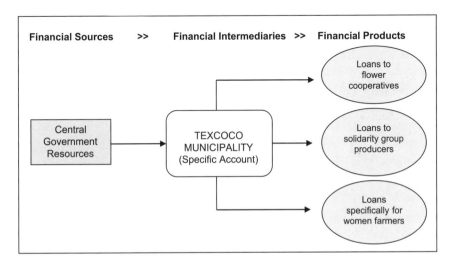

FIGURE 14.5 Financial flow for urban agriculture, Texcoco, Mexico

Source: Cabannes 2004a based on Ramirez-Garcia 2002.

After a couple of years, this successful programme received less attention from the newly elected local senior officials and the mayor. Despite requests from the producers, the technicians in charge and the university that was technically supporting the activities, the programme was left to die out slowly.

Participatory budgeting (PB) in Rosario

The experience of the city of Rosario, a city of one million inhabitants in Argentina, shows under which conditions municipal earmarked resources can meet the needs and the expectations of urban producers. As shown in Figure 14.6 the financial resources for urban agriculture are managed in two different ways: on the one hand, the Municipal Secretariat for Social Promotion develops a set of support activities to assist local urban farmers (input supply, technical assistance and training). In addition, since 2002, Rosario Municipality leads every year a Participatory Budgeting process through which citizens – whether organized or not – define the destination of part of the public resources of their city (Mazzuca et al. 2009).

Interestingly enough, in two out of the six districts of Rosario where the approach was introduced, organized urban farmers proposed projects related to

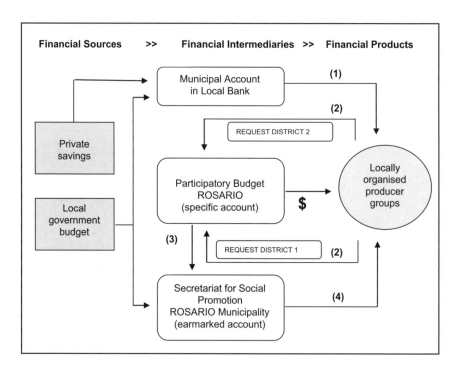

FIGURE 14.6 Financing of urban agriculture with participatory budgeting in Rosario, Argentina

Source: Cabannes 2004a based on Municipality of Rosario (oral communication).

the production and processing of vegetables and transformation of medicinal plants. These two projects were eventually prioritized and were integrated into the municipal budget allocations. The corresponding resources were then earmarked within the Municipal Secretariat for Social Promotion. Financially speaking, they were included in the budgetary allocation and specific funds were deposited in the bank managing the budget of the city.

Comparison of Texcoco and Rosario financial intermediaries

The key element that differentiates the experience in Texcoco from that of Rosario lies in the control of resources. In Rosario, the producers have direct control of public resources (bottom-up approach), whereas in Texcoco, decision-making over the resources always remained in the hands of the local government. However, even though participatory budgeting allows for better adaptation of public resources to the needs of the population, it is not a full guarantee of continuity as the process could be interrupted by circumstances such as a change of government.

Public resources and subsidies have been a crucial source of funds for facilitating the access to credit of small urban farmers, and for leveraging and channelling additional resources. However, the dependence on public money has the risk of a sudden interruption to, or closing of, excellent and economically successful urban agricultural activities. The case of Texcoco shows the risk of depending on public resources as the urban agriculture programme was halted after a change of local government. The extent of independence of a financial intermediary and its ability to survive political or policy changes should be given close consideration. In order to reduce the dependency of a credit system on political will, it is necessary to build strong intermediary financial institutions that can lend and work with public money, but that will not depend on political orientation for their continuity. This is probably one of the key issues to be dealt with as far as financing of urban agriculture is concerned.

b. Private and community-based intermediaries

The experience of a savings and credit cooperative in Nepal

The Mahila Prayas Savings and Credit Co-operative Ltd. (MPSACCO) was established in Nepal in 1998 (CMF 2002). This relatively young institution offers both individual and peer lending for agricultural activities, for setting up shops and for dairy farming.

The financial resources of the cooperative's members are generated through various types of savings such as regular compulsory (monthly), voluntary, marriage and festival savings. This variety indicates how a community-based banking facility is tailored to cultural and local practices and substantially different from conventional banking systems for the poor in which savings is simply a compulsory activity that is a precondition for getting a loan.

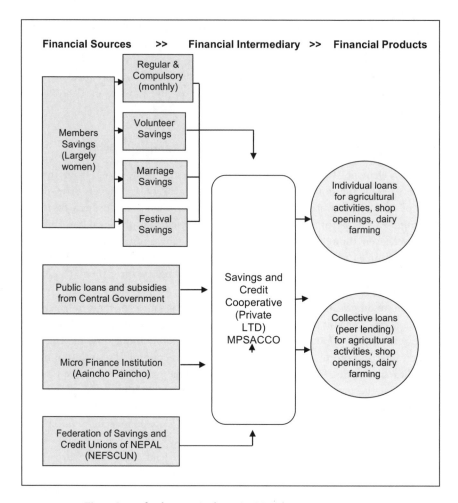

FIGURE 14.7 Financing of urban agriculture in Nepal
Source: Cabannes 2004a based on CMF 2002.

In addition, the central government provides loans and (limited) grants. Various "Social Economy" institutions have provided loans, occasional subsidies and technical assistance to MPSACCO and its members (i.e., Cooperative Development Board, Federation of Savings and Credit Unions of Nepal and Aaincho Paaincho, a Micro-Finance Institution).

c. Private and banking sector as financial intermediaries

The PROVE experience in the state of Mato Grosso do Sul, Brazil

The PROVE programme is based on a similar successful experience carried out in Brasilia, in the mid-90s (Homen de Carvalho 2001; Araújo 2002). Its basic

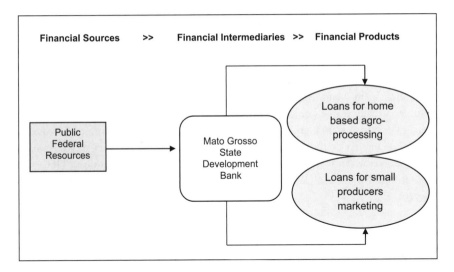

Financial Sources >> **Financial Intermediaries** >> **Financial Products**

Public Federal Resources

Mato Grosso State Development Bank

Loans for home based agro-processing

Loans for small producers marketing

FIGURE 14.8 The case of PROVE Pantanal, Mato Grosso do Sul State, Brazil

Source: Cabannes 2004a based on Araújo 2002.

principle is to provide credits and technical assistance to home-based producers, so that they can add value to their agricultural family-based production by processing primary produce and selling it to supermarkets.

The credit that PROVE provides at state level was funded through central government resources, while the technical assistance comes from the state government budget. Interestingly, the state government separated the technical assistance component from the management of the credits, and delegated the financial management to a development bank operating through its branches at state level. The bank authorizes the various loans and the borrowers repay at this same bank, in a fairly conventional way.

Such a model raises again the issue of what might happen in the case that the federal government stops feeding the current credit line. Two answers might be given. For one, the loans are paid back to the State Development Bank that does not have to pay back to the federal government. The budget allocation from the federal government to the State Bank is used as a starter for generating a revolving fund. The money paid back by the clients can be given out again as loans. However, currency devaluation and possible reimbursement defaults will cause the lending capacity to shrink.

Secondly, this financial setup has had the opportunity to open the doors of the bank, in most cases for the first time ever, to family-based urban farmers. If they pay their first loans back and thus gain credibility, they will be in a better position to apply for future loans from the bank, beyond the specific, subsidized PROVE credit line. In this sense, the PROVE programme acts as a bridge between informal producers and the formal banking system, and this makes it especially attractive.

*Lesson learned: urban farmers should be involved in
financial intermediation*

A thorough understanding of the best adapted financial intermediaries – either a
private cooperative such as in Nepal; a public/private one in Bangalore; a public
bank such as in Mato Grosso do Sul; or a private bank – is crucial in order to
optimize usually scarce or at least limited financial sources. In this context, involvement of producers/user groups in fund management such as is often the case in
credit cooperatives, credit unions and community-based financial organizations
appear as viable and important mechanisms that necessitate attention. The cases
of London (Mbiba and Wiltshire 2002) and St. Petersburg are also particularly
relevant.

Financial practices of small-scale urban farmers, banks and public actors: lessons learned from 17 cities

From 2008 to 2011, 17 cities from the Global South carried out an applied research
which focused primarily on practices and innovative ways that small-scale urban
farmers, producers' organizations, local governments, MFIs, banks or NGOS were
putting into place to finance activities related to urban agriculture. In connection
with this the following three key issues were examined:

- What are the practices of public and private institutions that finance, or could
  possibly finance, urban agriculture?
- Needs and demands for finance from urban poor engaged in urban agriculture,
  agro-processing or marketing. A central objective was to understand how and
  through which mechanisms these urban farmers all along the value chains are
  financing their activities and expanding them.
- The third broad issue explored was to identify a way to bridge the gap between
  existing and potential financial resources (the offer side) and the needs and
  demands from small-scale urban farmers (the demand side).

The cities studied are a selective sample of primarily large cities where some
form of urban- and peri-urban agriculture is being practised. Most of the cities
(see Figure 14.1) have a population above one million (Bulawayo, Accra, Ibadan,
Amman, Sanaa, Cape Town, Belo Horizonte and Freetown); four of them (Bogota,
Lima, Shanghai, Beijing) are megacities. Apart from the small municipality of
Magadi, at the periphery of Bangalore, the remaining ones have between 500,000
and one million inhabitants (Ndola, Bobo Dioulasso, Porto Novo, Gampaha). Most
of them are either national capitals (Accra, Amman, Sana'a, Porto Novo, Bogota,
Lima, Freetown, Beijing) or regional ones (Ibadan, Bulawayo, Ndola, Cape Town,
Bobo Dioulasso, Belo Horizonte and Gampaha). Districts from Shanghai (Minhang), Beijing (Huairou, Tangzhou) and Magadi were chosen for being positioned
at the periphery of large metropolises, offering a more peri-urban perspective.

Credits and subsidies practices from public and private financing institutions

One of the assumptions that resulted from the 2001–2003 city survey on credit and investment was that credits for urban agriculture were the exception and not the rule. The second batch of observations suggested a different conclusion as credits for small-scale urban farmers do exist in various cities even if they are generally limited in scope and number. Moreover, they are more frequently for commercially oriented activities such as raising animals, agro-processing or marketing. These loans are relatively common, for instance, in cities such as Lima, Ibadan or Amman. The number of credits and their volume has reached such a critical mass that these practices deserve further research and understanding.

A second finding is that despite the volume and reasonable number of loans in some cities, most credit institutions interviewed expressed reluctance to give loans to urban farmers for a long list of (good and bad) reasons. The most frequently mentioned in most studies that underlie their position are relatively few: (i) a high rate of default; (ii) too high risk because of possible crop failure, essentially for climatic reasons as, for instance, in Gampaha, Sri Lanka (Jayasinghe-Mugalide 2009); (iii) limited financial management capacities of farmers (e.g., Ndola, Zambia); and (iv) lack of proper title deeds or collaterals from urban farmers.

A third conclusion common to various cases is that high interests loans practised by MFIs and conventional banks have had limited positive impacts for improving the situation of poor farmers to shift from a subsistence practice and venture into more market-oriented activities.

Another lesson learned is that central and local governments play a major role in the success and failure of city-level financing systems for urban agriculture. Their role is primarily to deliver subsidies and in some cases, such as in Cape Town, with significant value (Mangaliso 2010). One key finding relates to the creative range of ways through which local governments are using their scarce resources. In addition, they tend to play a role in setting up public finance strategies covering a wide range of financial interventions that complement the banking and micro-finance system. Some of these interventions are presented later.

The first survey on 13 cities had already given some preliminary clues on different forms of subsidies designed locally:

- Financial subsidies to the banking system, such as those related to "soft conditions" for credit.
- Direct subsidies to the farmer, for main agricultural inputs (land, water, seeds etc.), or subsidies in the form of free technical assistance and training or support to obtain inputs (Botswana, Nairobi-Kenya).
- Subsidies to generate a facilitating environment, such as in St. Petersburg, where transport to agricultural plots outside the city was subsidized. Private-sector subsidies such as grants and charities from NGOs and other civil society

groups (as in the London case), and from public subsidies coming from local and national governments, such as the case of the HOPCOMS cooperative in Bangalore, are other forms of subsidies.

Urban farmers' financing practices; priority to self-financing and non-monetary resource mobilization

Poor urban farmers usually self-finance their activities

One of the key conclusions of the 2002–2003 research was that urban farmers rely heavily and primarily on the mobilization of their own resources, either monetary or non-monetary. Generally speaking, resource mobilization and savings occur in very different ways: (a) individual, (b) family-based, (c) collective savings of small groups of producers, or (d) community-based. In some cases, voluntary and organized savings are more formalized as in the case of the Nepalese savings and credit union cooperatives. These results were enriched through the second applied research that concluded most poor urban farmers stand outside the formal institutional landscape. They usually self-finance their activities through a rich array of solutions that exist across the board and in various continents, such as the following:

- Loans from families and friends, or (less commonly) from remittances sent by some members of the family working abroad.
- Rotating savings systems are present under different names in different cities: called *tontines* in Porto Novo, Osusu in Ibadan, groups savings in Bulawayo, or *banquitos* ("tiny banks") in Lima; they share the same basic principles with some local variations: small groups of persons saving; voluntary adhesion; and each member receives the sums saved on a weekly, fortnightly or monthly basis.
- Cross subsidies from one item that at a specific period is highly valued, for instance, raising and selling goats in the Sana'a case, that allows taking risks on less profitable or risky products (Al Jundi 2010). These forms of multiple commodities produced at the same time on a family-based perspective recall the quite resilient and traditional poly-cultivation and animal breeding of family-based rural farming systems.
- Informal credits from input suppliers of seeds, pesticides or fertilizers, or market traders as seen across urban Ghana, who accept being paid back once the products are sold (Drechsel et al. 2013).

High level of needs and reluctance to ask for loans or even subsidies

A second key finding is that urban farmers, in most cities, express a high level of needs but at the same time are quite reluctant to ask for loans or even subsidies. There are many reasons for this expressed by the urban farmers; the key reasons are briefly mentioned below:

- The loans offered are generally not adapted to agricultural and animal-raising cycles: the loans to be paid back in one year are not sufficient for livestock (Beijing); timing is too short for reimbursement, too long to be made available (Bobo Dioulasso) while referring to the need of resources at a specific sowing time in the year, usually at the beginning of the rainy season (Ouattara 2009).
- "Too much bureaucracy"... "the process is onerous"... "lots of paperwork"... "no clear procedures" are opinions expressed in cities as different as Porto Novo, Ndola, Sana'a or Bobo Dioulasso, highlighting the difficulties encountered with financial institutions.
- The impossibility to get loans for not having formal land titles required by banks as collateral or guarantee is expressed by urban farmers in a large number of cities such as Magadi, India. As a result, they do not want to apply for "impossible loans" or even subsidies that might require a proof of ownership of the land cultivated that poor farmers usually do not possess (Ramalingegowda et al. 2010).
- Much too high interest rates, primarily those imposed by MFIs is a recurrent argument, even if some of the loan takers accept them for a lack of other options. Interest rates as high as 60% per year are offered in Accra, making it quite difficult for a poor urban farmer to reimburse (Egyir 2010), which forces them to continue seeking informal credits, e.g., in West Africa from market women with all related disadvantages.
- Loans are not small enough: for instance in Bulawayo, urban farmers are reporting that the loans offered are 1,000 dollars as a minimum, and therefore beyond the repayment capacities (Chaibva 2010). This opinion echoes another one, stating that the financial products offered are not related to the (limited) income of urban farmers.
- A low capacity to prepare funding applications, either to obtain subsidies or to get a loan, is expressed under different forms by the interviewed farmers who explain their reluctance to engage: for instance, the Freetown reports summarize, "there is a lack of knowledge on how to obtain credits" (Konneh 2010).

Innovative ways of bridging the gap between a limited demand and a restricted offer

In several of the 17 studied cities and in various cities much beyond the study, quite innovative solutions significantly improve the access of poor urban farmers to finance understood in its broader sense summarized in the following equation:

Urban agriculture finance = monetary and non-monetary resources mobilization + individual and collective savings + subsidies under different forms + micro credits and conventional loans.

These innovative experiments relate fundamentally either to the improvement of the financial sector itself or to generating a more enabling environment.

Improving the financial sector and its volume of resources

Four innovative mechanisms were identified through the research for improving the financial sector itself:

- Diverting or channelling financial resources to urban agriculture primarily from (a) rural agriculture loans; (b) housing loans and subsidies, to be used for the development of "productive" housing, encompassing the house itself and at the same time its immediate productive surroundings, such as a garden to cultivate vegetables, sheds to raise animals or develop home-base agro-processing activities; (c) income-generating and job-creation loans and subsidies that are marginally benefiting the urban farmers; and (d) slum improvement resources and programmes that again rarely consider urban agriculture.
- Evolutionary loans with decreasing levels of subsidies that allow the loan taker to pass through a couple of lending cycles from a high level of subsidy to a conventional banking loan. This system was massively put into place in Fortaleza, Brazil, for the Better Home (Casa Melhor) programme that considered housing as a productive asset (Cabannes 1997b).
- Creation of community banks and creation of local and regional currencies, such as the Banco Palmas, in Fortaleza, Brazil (www.bancopalmas.org.br/).
- Credits for consumption (in local currencies) of locally produced or transformed food, such as in the case of the Banco Palmas. They were crucial to generate a locally sustainable financial system and are unfortunately very rare.

Generating an enabling financial environment

The following innovations emerging from the research differ from the previous ones, as they are not properly speaking of financial nature but contribute to generating a positive environment that in turn impacts the performance of the sector. Five of them seem particularly important:

Creating or strengthening of formal organizations and confederations of producers

One of the challenges faced by urban farmers and producers is that they are often not legalized and are considered informal. As a result they are not eligible for most of the formal banking systems and public institutions.

Agrosilves, an organization that gathers a couple of hundreds of pig raisers in Metropolitan Lima, has been successful in attracting the attention of two banking institutions and negotiating individual loans as a result of a collective approach. The credit institutions see their benefit in getting a critical mass of clients already "pre-selected" by Agrosilves. One of the most difficult obstacles to obtaining a mortgage is to get a proper land title that will guarantee the loan. It could be by-passed in this case as Agrosilves emits a certificate of residence that is accepted as a proxy by the banks (Saénz 2010).

In the city of Ibadan, Nigeria, the urban farmers are locally organized in 21 "commodity associations" out of the 28 sectors that compose the All Farmers Association of Nigeria, resulting in increased legitimacy of the farmers (Adeoti 2010), while at the same time singling out specific risks and financial specific needs of the different producers in terms of amount of loans, possible guarantees offered, and grace period or duration of the repayment in relation to the cycle of the production. Getting organized is not only proposed by urban farmers but also by public and finance institutions.

Increase security of tenure and access to urban land for farming

The lack of formal land titles appears as one of the key obstacles to increasing the accessibility of urban farmers to finance. An ongoing experience developed in Freetown, Sierra Leone, is a good example of how to promisingly address this bottleneck:

> The Freetown Urban and Peri Urban Agriculture Forum, involving key political institutions, credit institutions and farmers, have designed an innovative financing mechanism in 2010. The new programme relies on authorities for the permanent allocation of valleys, slopes and low lands for use in intra- and peri-urban agriculture. Land is allocated to registered and functioning farmers groups for a period of 5 years for a token rent provided that they abide by the Agreement regulations. The group receives technical training and monitoring and, for farmer groups participating in the scheme, four credit institutions (First International Bank, Access Bank, Luma Micro Finance Trust Limited, Salone Micro Finance Trust) have agreed to accept such land agreement together with the group's existing savings or current account as a collateral for two purposively designed credit products. The first is a micro credit of between 100 and 400 EUR (repayment period 1 year); the second is a loan between 1,000 and 2,000 EUR (repayment by 2 years) with a yearly interest rate of 24%. The number of households that could potentially benefit from the scheme once it is fully established is estimated at 2,500.
>
> *(Personal comment Marco Serena 2011)*

Positive impact of technical support to urban farmers for formulation of business plans

One of the main reasons why urban farmers are reluctant to try to get loans is their limited capacity to put together an application and more importantly a business plan that does not go against their own interest. At the same time, the financing institutions repeatedly express the limited capacities of urban farmers at that level. The RUAF FStT programme, such as in Porto Novo, Benin, gives support to farmers to get a proper business plan. As a result, a first batch of 19 loans was approved by a locally established MFI to around 130 tomato growers (Glele 2009).

Participatory budgeting

As referred to already through the experience of Rosario, Participatory Budgeting is a mechanism (or a process) by which the population defines the destination of part, or the totality of, public resources (Cabannes 2004b). Participatory Budgeting emerged in 1989 in Brazilian municipalities, and Porto Alegre became the most emblematic of them all. Twenty-five years later, in 2014, at least 1,700 municipalities in more than 40 countries in all regions in the world have adopted Participatory Budgeting as a means to decide upon their financial priorities, with a great deal of difference between them. Some cities, such as Seville in Spain, Rosario in Argentina or Porto Alegre in Brazil, have included urban agriculture projects as part of eligible priorities by the population. Results have deserved, and would deserve, much greater attention. The most interesting aspect is that Participatory Budgeting offers a permanent and endogenous source of funding to organized urban farmers to finance what they exactly want and need.

Urban agriculture insurance system

Both Beijing and Shanghai have been setting up insurance and security systems for urban farmers (Cai and Guo 2010; Cai et al. 2010). Limited information gathered so far through the research, and that would deserve a more in-depth examination, already suggest that opening up insurance mechanisms to urban farmers could be one of the most interesting mechanisms for consolidating urban farming activities. In Minhang district (Shanghai), Anxin Insurance Cooperation Ltd., a public finance institution, provides insurance to urban farmers, subsidized in 2009 to the value of 4.5 million Yuan (about USD470,000). Fifteen types of insurance are tailored to different equipment and crops: greenhouses, vegetable plants, fruit and wheat, pig, cow and fowl breeding, seed production, agricultural implements and property insurance.

The insurance system is one of the ten pillars of a comprehensive subsidy policy. Information to date is insufficient to calculate what proportion of the insurance is devoted to small-scale urban agriculture, as it seems earmarked essentially for what in China is called "upper end" urban agriculture. In Huairou and Tongzhou districts in Beijing, a similar system started in 2007, and so far 18 kinds of plants and breeds are insured for around 1,600 households; 30% of the total cost is subsidized.

Is there a right mix between savings, subsidies, credits and resource mobilization?[3]

Two subsequent and challenging questions remained unanswered thus far: Is there a right or best mix among these various components that would increase the chances of long-term sustainability of urban and peri-urban agriculture? And if there is, how can it be made operational? Instead of giving a general answer, four specific and quite innovative cases summarized below were analyzed in order to bring to light their local mix and combination of savings, subsidies, credits and resource mobilization for business-oriented and self-consumption practices:

- Village Savings and Loans Associations (VSLA) have been expanding since 2009 in Liberia. In 2013, around 3,000 VSLA members belonged to these associations. VSLA improved access to credit for urban and peri-urban farmers, and even bridged community-based finance with micro-credit and central government banking (RUAF Foundation 2013).
- Community Land Trusts (CLTs), as non-profit, community-based institutions, retain permanent ownership of land on behalf of their members and have been expanding swiftly, primarily in the United States, since the early 1980s, in order to provide affordable housing for lower- and lower-middle-class citizens. Interestingly enough, an increasing number of CLTs have non-residential components and support urban agriculture in diverse forms (Davis 2010).
- SANASA Development Bank, a cooperative Bank in the city of Gampaha, Sri Lanka, recently set up an innovative revolving fund, operating partially as a fixed deposit account bringing financial resources to urban farmers, and partially as a savings and short-term loan device opened up to small groups (RUAF Foundation 2013).
- As briefly introduced before, both Beijing and Shanghai have been setting up insurance and security systems for urban farmers, introducing what could become one of the most interesting mechanisms for consolidating urban farming activities.

Based on this limited number of cases, and referring back to the 30 cities that were part of the research programmes mentioned previously, it seems that there is not one right mix: successful combinations are country- and city-specific. Accordingly, no standard recipe is proposed here. However – and this is important – successful local cocktails tend to use the same four basic ingredients: monetary and non-monetary resource mobilization by farmers + savings + credits + subsidies. Even if some local financial systems might be initially based essentially on one or two components (for example, credit or subsidies only), the systems that last and grow through time are precisely the ones that gradually integrate the missing elements. For instance, even if Community Land Trusts, as their name denotes, are community-based organizations drawing on the community's own resources, their resilience through time goes hand-in-hand with their capacity to obtain financial subsidies from a wide array of sources in order to acquire "free" land and, at the same time, access low-cost credits from cooperative or commercial banks.

Another remarkable common thread between the cases that were not highlighted during the study is the subtle combination of individual and collective dimensions for both savings and loans. Each one of the four cases sheds some light on this issue. For instance, VSLA in Liberia are certainly collective saving groups, composed usually of 15 to 30 members who voluntarily get together to save in order to allow one or more member of the group to take a loan from the fund. These associations share common features with *sou-sou, tandas, banquitos* or *tontines,* sometimes called rotatory saving systems that exist often among urban farmers. They share features in the sense that saving amounts, number of members and frequency of deposits are fixed by the members, and collected resources are highly controlled and managed by the community. The essential difference in the case of VLSA is that the collective saving group authorizes individual loans to its members, with interest rates decided collectively. Discussions between SANASA Development Bank, urban farmers and their advisors at Gampaha, Sri Lanka, led to the setting up of a collective saving scheme with a unique account. However, each individual who deposits his or her saving has a passbook clearly indicating the amount of savings.

A third common thread is that each one of the cases presented includes an amount of subsidies of various origins; these subsidies were largely underestimated, or at least kept quiet in the first drafts on the four cases, as if a key for success for financing urban agriculture was that they could function without a certain level of subsidy. Making these subsidies explicit is key in order to make the best use of them, as is having their destination defined by the urban farmers. Why should NGOs, international aid, researchers, local or the central government decide on the destination of subsidies? One lesson learned from Participatory Budgeting experiences open to urban farmers, in cities such as Seville in Spain or Porto Alegre in Brazil, is precisely that the farmers themselves decided the best way to optimize scarce public resources that were made available, and in both cases they were quite successful.

Quite interestingly, subsidy for training, and for technical assistance to urban and peri-urban producers, appear as a common feature in the cases presented: CARE Liberia is supporting the training modules and one year of a technical officer for VSLA in Liberia; CLT provides information and training courses to any candidate, for instance, on banking conditions and affordability; and at Gampaha, training workshops and services are offered free of charge to participants (first by RUAF, now by Gampaha Agricultural Department). Specific subsidies to each case and situation, such as subsidized insurance premiums in China or limited ground lease permitting affordability in CLTs, are referred to in the dossier cases.

Our last observation refers to the credit component. A surprising aspect is the limited role of MFIs and micro-credit institutions in spearheading innovations in finance related to urban agriculture. They are largely absent, as noticed in the conclusions of the research on 17 cities. Quite remarkable and counter-intuitive is the fact that public banks such as those in Beijing or Shanghai, or cooperative commercial banks such as those in Sri Lanka, or the Central Bank of Liberia, through its micro-finance unit are introducing innovative solutions and also taking some risks. One could have expected private MFIs to play that role as well.

Examining the financial products offered and the loan conditions is quite revealing and inspiring. First, they tend to be customized and tailored to specific needs, as the financial needs of an individual starting with small-scale agro-processing are quite different from those of a farmer needing to buy seeds and equipment before a rainy season, or those of a family who would like to expand its production of chickens. Each one of them needs different amounts, for different reimbursement periods – depending on when they will sell their vegetables, chickens or transformed products – and at quite a different period in the year. Second, the intricate individual/collective dimension is maintained, even if different from what was observed in savings: peer pressure for reimbursement, mixed with solidarity in case of proven hardship, seems to be a recurrent feature, associated with collective guarantee and individual responsibility.

These findings have a direct consequence on the way business plans are formulated. Once they are formulated and the cost of the operation is defined, the next exercise is to establish a financial plan that would indicate the specific contribution of the four ingredients: credit, subsidy, savings and resources mobilized. As the combination might vary over time, a systematic exercise that any business plan should consider is to anticipate how the mix of components could and should vary. For instance, the proportion of subsidies (e.g., for training) might go down when, in parallel, credit might increase, and the proportion of own resources mobilized by farmers might increase as well.

Conclusions and balance: what do we know better and what should we know better?

Good progress has been made since the first research in the 1990s on financing urban agriculture. The analytical tools designed to unpack local monetary flows going to urban agriculture allowed to identify bottlenecks and design proper financial products. In parallel, better understanding of the informal and non-monetary side of urban agriculture was probably one of the major items of progress achieved over the last ten years, notwithstanding the need to process available primary data collected during both applied research programmes.

Optimization of public subsidies

Research in the early 2000s pointed out the empowering and leveraging impact of subsidies for urban agriculture. Some progress has been achieved over the last ten years in widening our knowledge on subsidy mechanisms for urban agriculture along the value chain and their quick positive impact. However, much research still needs to be done to identify the comparative advantages of these mechanisms, primarily processing the information available in the 17 cities from the second research. This should help in setting up strong and clear subsidy components within national and municipal urban agricultural policies that should unlock the key bottlenecks of the finance system.

Fiscal and financial municipal policies

Progress has been made on increasing knowledge on issues such as Participatory Budgeting and its impact on urban agriculture. However a lot remains to be done still on partnerships with banks and micro-finance institutions, mixed municipal funds, innovative institutional financial setups, and fiscal policies, which are keys to increase the access of urban producers to financial products.

Comparative advantage of financial intermediaries

Several types of institutions of financial intermediation have been identified and described such as public bodies, private agencies and banks or community-based institutes. A comparative study of their advantages and their limits remains to be done to further strengthen the ongoing experiments.

Combined local mix of resource mobilization, savings, subsidies and credits

Urban agricultural finance offers unconventional and quite innovative solutions that are not standardized, and this is probably one key of their – as yet – limited, but expanding, success. However, they tend, as described above, to gain strength gradually through relying on the same combined local mix of resource mobilization, savings, subsidies and credits.

Financing urban agriculture as part of urban metabolisms

Progress has been made over the last ten years on conceptualizing (intra- and peri-) urban agriculture as part of an urban metabolism and on showing how urban agriculture is a unique possibility to make cities work better and at the same time produce nutritious food: for instance in making good use of grey waters for irrigation, or in being a solution to treat used waters. What we know very little still is what should be financed and how should be financed a better integration of urban agriculture within urban metabolism, primarily to improve the links between urban agriculture and the transformation of organic waste into compost in order to reclaim existing soils, or between used water networks and cultivated urban lands.

Financing which type of urban agriculture?

One lesson learned is that different financial mechanisms and a specific balance of credit/subsidy/savings/monetary and non-monetary resource mobilization are needed for each specific type of urban agriculture, e.g., market-oriented activities, subsistence ones for domestic consumption, or leisure and education in urban agriculture. Lessons from the field suggest that a right balance between all three types is probably the best way to turn urban agriculture more resilient at city level. Specific financial mechanisms and a facilitating financial environment probably play a crucial role in urban agriculture.

Financing access to secure land through collective, cooperative and communal forms of tenure

Financing access to intra- and peri-urban land remains probably one of the least studied and most needed topics in relation to urban agricultural finance. How do small-scale urban farmers resist against evictions and land grabbing? What are the financial mechanisms they use to stay in place, or expand farming or breeding land? Putting into light financial mechanisms that increase secure tenure is particularly important in front of massive land grabbing in rural and peri-urban areas and speculative land markets in cities. In this context, financial mechanisms and practices that facilitate or strengthen collective, communal or cooperative forms of farming and land tenure are crucial for years to come. These non-individual forms of tenure tend to indicate, as in the case of Community Land Trusts, that they increase security on land for the poor and for small-scale producers.

Recommendations for an action-research agenda on urban agricultural finance

Financing remains a major bottleneck for expansion of urban agriculture

Findings from research on the 17 cities, which confirm and expand the early research in the 2000s, strongly suggest that, despite some progress in a limited number of cities, the financing of urban and peri-urban agriculture is a major bottleneck in maintaining, expanding and scaling up the production of affordable, nutritious and accessible food in cities.

Therefore, strategic decisions with a strong financial significance should be taken.

Support from a broad scope of public and private institutions is needed

Governments, banks and international aid agencies need to support urban farmers all along the value chain. National and municipal urban agricultural policies should have a strong, clear subsidy component aimed at removing the key bottlenecks in the financial system. Governments and finance organizations could concentrate on supporting, consolidating and transferring innovations currently taking place in various cities and that are quite promising for the future. This is the price to pay if we want to be serious about expanding intra- and peri-urban agriculture and increase the capacity of cities to produce affordable nutritious food, not only for the better-off but for the poor and the most vulnerable.

Innovative ideas that need to be further developed

In several participating cities, innovative proposals were formulated and some were partially implemented. Their aim is to improve the access of poor urban farmers to finance, understood in its broader sense. The first recommendation is that these proposals that result from deeply grounded practices and research should be given a strong support locally, nationally and internationally. Proposals include the following:

- Local revolving funds for urban farmers with an insurance component in Amman (Samir El-Habbab 2010). Experiments in Beijing and Shanghai mentioned in this chapter could be useful.

- Involvement of leasing companies in Ndola, for instance for acquiring tractors or watering cans (Phiri 2009). The experience in the capital city Lusaka with leasing of bicycles proved positive and could serve as a source of inspiration.
- Mutual saving funds for urban farmers in Bogotá and support from the Banca Capital municipal programme that would match each peso saved by farmers (Figueroa et al. 2010).
- Introduction of the Islamic law principle of *reba* by some banks, such as Al Amal Bank (Sana'a), to address the prohibitive interest rates practised by MFIs. Two modalities co-exist: first, *murabaha,* whereby the institution buys the product that is needed by the borrower who, in turn, repays the price of the product plus the transaction expenses; and second, *mudarabah,* whereby the institution gives a loan to start a specific business and claims a percentage of the profit for itself (Al Jundi 2010).

Creation of a powerful international funding facility and of municipal local funds for urban agriculture

Support at all levels to generate a funding facility for urban agriculture is urgently required. It could channel a mix of funding and subsidies to the sector through, for instance, small grants to subsistence agriculture; revolving local funds; grants for technical advice and support to business plans; and guarantee funds and insurance facilities. RUAF Foundation, along with the vast numbers of actors it works with, could spearhead such an initiative.

Mixed municipal funds are not yet very common in the field of urban agriculture, but they exist in other sectors such as home improvement and/or

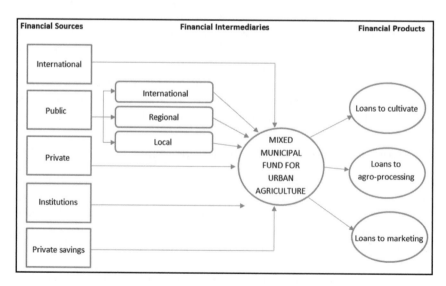

FIGURE 14.9 Mixed municipal fund for urban agriculture
Source: Cabannes 2004a.

generation of income. They were largely discussed and introduced as a result of the 2002–2004 survey on financial intermediaries (Cabannes 2004a). A central element of these funds would be the diversity of their financial sources to include international donations or loans, public resources and private savings, particularly of urban farmers.

"Resource cities" on financing mechanisms for urban agriculture

In addition to consolidating experiences at city level, it is suggested to build the capacities of the actors of these cities, in order for them to become the international and national advocates of their experience. Such consolidated cities could become "resource cities", capable of exporting their knowledge and advising interested cities that would become their associates and become "on-the-job training centres". The situation is ripe to select a limited number of cities and contribute to build their capacities.

Urban agriculture needs a broader urban scope: 21st century Garden Cities of To-Morrow

Over one hundred years ago, Ebenezer Howard launched Garden Cities of To-Morrow, and soon after Letchworth Garden City started to be built. It introduced two major innovations: land was commonly held in trust and half of it was cultivated. In 2014, this land is still cultivated and the Heritage Foundation still manages most of the city land. The financial mechanism was resilient enough to resist speculation and allows for substantial resources for the benefit of the community.

There is a need to posit urban agriculture within a broader framework of principles adapted to the constraints and opportunities of the 21st century cities. This is the challenge that the manifesto on Garden Cities for the 21st century addresses, embedding urban agriculture within a renovated urban vision (Cabannes and Ross 2014). Financing urban agriculture has to be part of the broader city-region financial mechanism that must, and can, be beneficial for family-based, community-based, and small- and medium-scale agriculture.

Notes

1   This paper draws on the major RUAF research programme and on analysis carried out in cooperation with Marielle Dubbeling, RUAF Foundation. Her invaluable contribution is duly acknowledged. We would like to thank as well each of the authors of the 30 case studies for their unique contribution and goodwill. For a more comprehensive research synthesis, see Cabannes, Y. 2012. Financing urban agriculture. *Environment & Urbanization* 24(2): 665–683.
2   A summarized description of these 13 cases is available in the ninth issue of the *Urban Agriculture Magazine* (RUAF, April 2003).
3   This section is adapted from a text from the author: Financing urban agriculture: Seeking the right mix of subsidies, credit, savings, and resource mobilization, published in *Urban Agriculture Magazine* 26, 2013.

References

Adeoti, A.I. 2010. Current practices of finance institutions and programmes for urban agriculture in Ibadan (Nigeria): Opportunities, difficulties and bottlenecks in financing small-scale urban agriculture. Study for RUAF Foundation. Ibadan: Department of Agricultural Economics, University of Ibadan. Available from: www.ruaf.org/sites/ default/files/Practices%20of%20finance%20institutions%20for%20urban%20agriculture% 20in%20Ibadan%20Nigeria.pdf.

Al Jundi, R. 2010. Applied study on local finance and credit for poor urban and peri-urban producers, Sana'a (Yemen). Study for RUAF Foundation. Beirut: Environmental and Sustainable Development Unit, University of Beirut. Available from: www.ruaf.org/sites/ default/files/Local%20finance%20and%20credit%20for%20urban%20producers%20 in%20Sanaa%20Yemen.pdf.

Araújo, P.S.S. 2002. Programa Prove Pantanal. Paper prepared for UN HABITAT, UMP-LAC, IPES and IDRC. Quito: Urban Management Program.

Cabannes, Y. 1997a. Agriculture urbaine et création de revenus. In: *Agriculture urbaine pour l'assainissement et la creation de revenues dans l'agglomération de Fortaleza, Etat de Ceará, Brésil: Rapport technique final.* Grupo de Pesquisa e Intercambios Tecnológicos. Ottawa: International Development Research Centre (IDRC).

Cabannes, Y. 1997b. From community development to housing finance: From mutirões to Casa Melhor in Fortaleza, Brazil. *Environment and Urbanization* 9(1): 31–58.

Cabannes, Y. 2004a. Public financing and investments for urban agriculture. Paper prepared for the World Urban Forum 2004, 13–17 September, Barcelona, Spain.

Cabannes, Y. 2004b. 72 frequently asked questions about participatory budgeting. Quito: Urban Management Programme in Latin America (UMP-LAC). Available from: http:// ww2.unhabitat.org/campaigns/ governance/ documents/FAQPP.pdf.

Cabannes, Y. 2006. Financing and investment for urban agriculture. In: *Cities farming for the future: Urban agriculture for green and productive cities.* (Ed.) Veenhuizen, R. van. Manila: IIRR Publishers.

Cabannes, Y. 2012. Financing urban agriculture. *Environment & Urbanization* 24(2): 665–683.

Cabannes, Y. 2013. Financing urban agriculture: Seeking the right mix of subsidies, credit, savings, and resource mobilization. *Urban Agriculture Magazine* 26: 13–17.

Cabannes, Y.; Ross, P. 2014. 21st century garden cities of tomorrow. A manifesto. London: New Garden City Movement.

Cai, J.; Guo, H. 2010. Financing for urban agriculture in Tongzhou and Huairou districts, Beijing (China). Study for RUAF Foundation. Beijing: IGSNRR-Chinese Academy of Sciences.

Cai, J.; Yin, Z.; Liu, M. 2010. Urban agricultural financing in Minhang district, Shanghai (China). Study for RUAF Foundation. Beijing: IGSNRR-Chinese Academy of Sciences.

Chaibva, C.N. 2010. Local finance for small-scale urban and peri-urban agricultural producers in Bulawayo (Zimbabwe). Study for RUAF Foundation. Harare: Municipal Development Partners. Available from: www.ruaf.org/sites/default/files/Local%20 finance%20for%20small%20urban%20agriculture%20producers%20in%20Bulawayo%20 Zimbabwe.pdf.

CMF. 2002. Managing credit and investment schemes for urban/peri-urban agricultural activities: A case study of two urban based cooperatives in Nepal. Paper prepared for UN HABITAT, UMP-LAC, IPES and IDRC. Kathmandu: Centre for Micro Finance (CMF).

Davis, J.E. 2010. The community land trust reader. Cambridge: Lincoln Institute of Land Policy.

Drechsel, P.; Hope, L.; Cofie, O. 2013. Gender mainstreaming: Who wins? Gender and irrigated urban vegetable production in West Africa. *Journal of Gender and Water (H₂O)* 2: 15–17.

Egyir, I. S. 2010. Applied study on local finance for poor urban and peri-urban producers in Accra (Ghana). Study for RUAF Foundation. Legon: Department of Agricultural Economics and Agribusiness, University of Ghana. Available from: www.ruaf.org/sites/default/files/Applied%20study%20on%20local%20finance%20for%20urban%20producers%20in%20Accra%20Ghana.pdf.

Figueroa, M.; Huertas J.; López I.; Mesa S.; Ramírez L.; Sarria, A. 2010. Estudio aplicado de finanzas locales para agricultores urbanos y periurbanos en condición de pobreza en Bogotá (Colombia). RUAF Foundation, Leusden, The Netherlands.

Glele, E. K. A. 2009. Accés au crédit et financement de l'agriculture urbaine et péri-urbaine à Porto Novo (Benin). RUAF Foundation, Leusden, The Netherlands.

Homen de Carvalho, J. L. 2001. O Prove-Programa de verticalização da pequena produção familiar, Brasilia, Brasil. APROVE, PGU, IDRC, IPES, Cuaderno de Trabajo N° 83, Urban Management Programme in Latin America (UMP-LAC). Available from: www.agriculturaurbana.org.br/RAU/AU05/AU5prove.html.

Jayasinghe-Mugalide, U. 2009. Study on local finance for urban and peri-urban producers. Study for RUAF Foundation. Gampaha: Dept. of Agribusiness Management, Wayamba University of Sri Lanka. Available from: www.ruaf.org/sites/default/files/Local%20finance%20for%20urban%20and%20periurban%20producers%20in%20Gampaha%20Sri%20Lanka.pdf.

Konneh, P. 2010. Applied study of credit and financing opportunities for farmers in urban and peri-urban Freetown (Sierra Leone). Study for COOPI and RUAF Foundation. Freetown: Ministry of Agriculture Forestry and Food Security Sierra Leone. Available from: www.ruaf.org/sites/default/files/Credit%20and%20finance%20opportunities%20for%20UPA%20households%20in%20Freetown%20Sierra%20Leone_1.pdf.

Mangaliso, M. 2010. Study on financing of small-scale urban and peri-urban agricultural producers in Cape Town (South Africa). RUAF Foundation, Leusden, The Netherlands.

Mazzuca, A.; Ponce, M.; Terrile, R. 2009. La agricultura urbana en Rosario: balance y perspectivas. Lima: IPES-Promoción del Desarrollo Sostenible.

Mbiba, B.; Wiltshire, R. J. 2002. Resources and financing of urban agriculture interventions in London: The Woodlands Farm and Vauxhall City Farm Experience. Paper prepared for UN HABITAT, UMP-LAC, IPES and IDRC. London: Urban and Peri-urban Research Network at South Bank University.

Moldakov, O. 2002. Micro credit and investment for urban agriculture in Russia, St. Petersburg. Paper prepared for UN HABITAT, UMP-LAC, IPES and IDRC. St. Petersburg: Urban Gardening Club.

Mosha, A. C. 2002. Credit an investment for urban agricultural interventions: Case study Gaborone City. Paper prepared for UN HABITAT, UMP-LAC, IPES and IDRC. Gaborone: University of Botswana.

Ouattara, H. 2009. Etude sur l'accès au credit et le financement de l'agriculture urbaine et péri-urbaine à Bobo Dioulasso (Burkina Faso). RUAF Foundation, Leusden, The Netherlands.

Phiri, O. Y. Z. 2009. Applied study on local finance for poor urban and peri-urban producers, Ndola (Zambia). Study prepared for RUAF Foundation. Ndola: School of Natural Resources, Copperbelt University. Available from: www.ruaf.org/sites/default/files/Applied%20study%20on%20local%20finance%20for%20urban%20producers%20in%20Ndola%20Zambia.pdf.

Premchander, S. 2002. Cooperative for sale of fruits and vegetables: A success story of urban horticultural marketing: Horticultural Produce Cooperative Marketing Society,

Sampark, Bangalore. Paper prepared for UN HABITAT, UMP-LAC, IPES and IDRC. Bangalore.

Ramalingegowda, U. C.; Srikanthamurthy, P. S.; Nagaraj, N.; Chandrakanth, M. G. 2010. Credit and financing study, Magadi–Bangalore (India). RUAF Foundation, Leusden, The Netherlands.

Ramirez-Garcia, G. 2002. Estudios de micro crédito e inversión para la agricultura urbana. El caso de Texcoco, Mexico. Paper prepared for UN HABITAT, UMP-LAC, IPES and IDRC. Mexico: Centro Operacional de Vivienda y Poblamiento A.C.

RUAF Foundation. 2013. Sustainable financing for WASH and urban agriculture. *Urban Agriculture Magazine* 26.

Saénz, H. E. 2010. Estudio: Mejorando el acceso a capital de los agricultores urbanos. Estudio aplicado de finanzas locales para agricultores urbanos y periurbanos en condición de pobreza en Lima (Peru). Estudio preparado para Fondacion RUAF. Lima: PRISMA. Available from: www.ruaf.org/sites/default/files/Mejorando%20el%20acceso%20a%20 capital%20de%20los%20agricultores%20urbanos%20en%20Lima%20Peru.pdf.

Samir El-Habbab, M. 2010. Local finance for poor urban and peri-urban producers, Amman (Jordan). Study prepared for RUAF Foundation. Amman: Department of Agricultural Economics and Agribusiness, University of Jordan. Available from: www.ruaf.org/sites/ default/files/Local%20finance%20for%20poor%20urban%20and%20periurban%20 producers%20in%20Amman%20Jordan.pdf.

15

ROLE OF URBAN AGRICULTURE IN DISASTERS AND EMERGENCIES

Andrew Adam-Bradford[1] and René van Veenhuizen[2]

1 CENTRE FOR AGROECOLOGY, WATER AND RESILIENCE, COVENTRY UNIVERSITY, ENGLAND

2 RUAF FOUNDATION, THE NETHERLANDS

Introduction

> More than 1 billion people live in unsafe and unhealthy conditions in slums, refugee camps and informal settlements. And these numbers are growing. Over 50 million of them are refugees living in camps or temporary illegal settlements. If these forcibly displaced people had their own nation, it would be the world's 26th largest country.
>
> *(Buscher 2011)*

Natural hazards, civil conflicts, wars and economic crises can all have a profound impact on generating unstable and unsafe conditions, and placing immense pressures on communities and local support mechanisms. These emergency scenarios often result in people fleeing their homes to safe areas or crossing borders to other countries, thereby creating mass refugee situations. Many of these refugees or internally displaced persons (IDPs) not only remain in refugee camps for extended periods but also increasingly in and around urban areas (often illegally). Consequently, many people living under the harsh conditions of refugee life will try to improve their livelihoods, including improving their access to food by establishing some form of agriculture, such as small-scale gardening or livestock husbandry.

In this chapter the linkages between urban agriculture and disasters and emergencies are explored, by providing a broad illustration of the potential role that urban agriculture can play in "disaster risk management". Disaster risk management is an overarching term that covers all aspects of disaster management, including *pre-disaster* activities such as "disaster risk reduction" (DRR) programmes that aim to build resilience, as well as *post-disaster* activities such as working with refugees in camps or urban areas, linking relief, rehabilitation and development (LRRD). The pre-disaster and post-disaster phases are commonly referred to as the "disaster management cycle". The core message is that enhancing the role of urban agriculture, both in pre- and post-disaster situations, may assist in increasing the resilience of communities, prevent (some) disasters from happening in the first place, and improve effective responses at local, national, regional and international levels when disasters do strike.

Increasingly, refugees seek their refuge in cities, and many camps gradually develop into settlements. Urban agriculture has been identified by many organizations as a component of that response, illustrated by a number of guidelines seeking to mainstream local food production into disaster and emergency programmes. The Humanitarian Charter and Minimum Standards in Humanitarian Response, for example, recommends the protection of local food production systems while also promoting kitchen gardens and agroforestry in refugee camp settings (The Sphere Project 2011).

The chapter starts with looking at different disaster and refugee situations, finding that there is an increasing need to look (differently) at urban areas to find solutions. It then continues by describing the role of urban agriculture in different settings, and the existence of guidelines on the issue. It ends by looking at disaster risk reduction, and concluding that urban agriculture can play a role in all aspects of disaster management, which increasingly is urban and hence should take an urban focus.

Disasters and emergencies and the immediate demand for food

There is no shortage of examples that illustrate the graphic and often horrifying impacts that disasters and emergencies can have. Despite the different hazards and geographical settings, many of the impacts at the location where the disaster strikes, and where people seek refuge, are similar, such as food and water shortages, insecurity and a collapse of the normal (urban) functions. The level of vulnerability determines the actual impact of a hazard, and the disaster risk is a function of the intensity of the hazard and the level of vulnerability, often expressed as: *risk = hazard* x *vulnerability* (Wisner et al. 2004).

Environmental and natural disasters impact upon millions of people globally in the form of drought, flooding, hurricanes and earthquakes. Unlike natural disasters, many *man-made emergencies* are deliberate and intentional acts that cause significant population movements (internal and cross border). These situations involve an intricate web of volatile and often hostile military and political forces. Disasters can be rapid-onset, such as the 2004 tsunami in South Asia, or slow-onset, the latter building up over a period of months, such as the Ebola outbreak in West Africa, or even years as was the case with the global spread of HIV (human immunodeficiency virus). If the crisis is characterized by conflict, political instability or high levels of violence, it is often referred to as a complex emergency, as is occurring in Iraq and Syria.

In the first decade of this second millennium, *economic crises* have resulted in rising food prices, declining real wages, redundancies in the formal labour market, and cuts in food subsidies, affecting vulnerable people. Reduced public expenditure also has its impact on basic services and infrastructure. As a result, a mix of IDPs, refugees and migrants adds up to the urban poor and resort to non-market (informal sector) livelihood activities, including urban agriculture. Economic crises often have a social or political origin. Probably the best known example of a country adopting a national urban agricultural policy in response to such economic and political constraints is Cuba. Other examples of cities that have promoted backyard gardening, rooftop gardens, institutional and school gardens as a standard component of emergency agricultural response include Harare, Zimbabwe; Jakarta, Indonesia; Lagos, Nigeria; Rosario, Argentina; and Gaza in Palestine.

BOX 15.1: CIENFUEGOS, CUBA

Cuba is often presented as an example of effectively supportive government policies that encouraged urban agriculture. Major national measures were taken in response to the economic crisis in the 1990s affecting the agriculture and food sector, like the conversion of large state-owned farms into new cooperatives, or Basic Cooperative Production Units, and the granting of land to people and organizations to produce food. The National Urban Agriculture Programme started in 1993, and proposed to stimulate food production in available urban and peri-urban spaces, taking advantage of the opportunities offered by the availability of labour and the close proximity between producer and consumer. Within 15 years of implementation, the National Urban Agriculture Programme led the municipality of Cienfuegos to unprecedented levels of production, along with other favourable results.

Source: Socorro Castro 2009.

Global food prices increased over 80% in the period 2006–2008 (RUAF Foundation 2008). Net food-importing countries – such as most countries in Africa – were hit hardest by these rising prices. Although the prices of main commodities have come down, the prices of most food items are still high and often double what they were before the increase. Tackling the complex causes of the food and agriculture crisis requires a comprehensive approach (Hovland 2009), at international, national and local levels. Urban agriculture has a clear role to play in contributing to urban food security. Agricultural production in and around cities reduces food transportation costs, and can improve access to (cheaper) fresh food, thus reducing vulnerability in the poorer sections of the city, while also improving the general urban ecology and environment.

Complex emergencies are frequently found in fragile states. Many of the fragile states, a group of 30 to 50 countries depending on the definition used, are low-income countries characterized by weak state institutions that are largely ineffective, leading to bad governance and corruption. Their economic, social and political institutions have a diminished capacity to absorb shocks and they are therefore more susceptible to conflict and crisis. As the level of vulnerability determines the actual impact of a hazard, the impact will be more extensive in these countries than in countries characterized by security and stability, thus highlighting the increased attention needed for these fragile states.

Refugee camps and settlements

Insecurity in specific regions can continue for many years resulting in refugee camps gradually converting into "shanty towns" or becoming permanent settlements (Adam-Bradford et al. 2009). Many of these "camps" are difficult to distinguish from surrounding towns. Many displaced people will never return to their original "home" areas for a variety of reasons, and would rather seek new livelihood opportunities in and around nearby cities. While displaced people are entitled to support themselves in obtaining food and other basic needs (for instance, in Kenya and Jordan), they are often not allowed to work or fully integrate with the host society, a constraint that is often compounded by a lack of access to land for productive uses. Although displaced people have a certain protective status, the reality on the ground often shows that they do not have the right to use land or undertake productive activities. Refugees are initially completely dependent on aid from the international community. In addition, land is scarce and not always of good quality, hampering the development of gardens.

Dispersed refugees in urban areas

Although camps are clearly different, similarities exist between agriculture in camp settings and in urban (slum) areas. Many refugees become "urbanized" by the experience in these refugee camps, or because they seek refuge in urban areas (Buscher 2011; UNHCR 2012 and 2014) and when they return they do not want to go back to the rural areas. Consequently, an increasing number of refugees live in urban areas, usually in slum areas, or otherwise face similar challenges as the urban poor. More than 50% of the refugees live in urban areas, and at greater distances than before. The majority of these people stay unemployed, live in poor and overcrowded areas, and depend on international and/or non-governmental organizations. The growth of these urban refugees is much larger than the growth in humanitarian financial assistance, and as the average length of displacement is 17 years (Buscher 2011), continued feeding and providing direct services to these populations is not possible. This is increasingly recognized, although still many refugee organizations are not equipped to work in the highly complex urban areas.

Refugees, who migrate to urban areas, are looking for access to better housing, health care, education and economic opportunities, sometimes after having been in camps. They are, on the whole, higher educated and more resourceful, and under the right conditions would be able to become self-sufficient. In Kampala, for example, a study found that most of the urban refugees are educated and self-selection often brings the most entrepreneurial and educated to the cities (Buscher 2011). Most countries and cities, though, are ill equipped to host this large number of refugees. And when the large number of refugees that arrive in urban areas exceeds the ability of local urban authorities to effectively manage their integration, then pressures on services and local resources soon emerge, bringing tensions between the refugees and the host communities.

Furthermore, most host governments are reluctant to allow refugees to work. They fear competition and worry that with jobs and income, refugees will de facto locally integrate, never to return to their countries of origin. It appeared that refugees with cash in pocket and marketable skills are more likely to return home, as was the case with the Liberian Buduburam camp in Ghana (Crowell and Nutsugah 2013). Hence, refugees residing in cities are often very vulnerable as most of them are single women heads of households. This is due to the consequences of the international food crisis, which results in increased unemployment, rising food prices, increasing difficulties in paying rent and lack of access to education and healthcare. But also due to the fact that in some areas, like East Africa, and in countries like Jordan and Lebanon, there are simply too many refugees and the cities cannot cope. An increasing number of them are requesting to be moved to the camp as they are unable to pay rent, or send their children to school.

BOX 15.2: SOMALI REFUGEES IN NAIROBI

Mark Yarnell of Refugees International illustrates the precarious situation of urban refugees as he describes the situation of Somali refugees in Nairobi *(adapted text by the authors):*

> Tens of thousands of refugees from Somalia and elsewhere live in urban centres throughout Kenya, where they are able to provide for themselves, send their children to local schools, and access health facilities. Over the years, Nairobi's Eastleigh developed into one of the most dynamic parts of Nairobi's economy, with shoppers going there from all over the city to take advantage of the competitive prices and range of goods available there. It is a far cry from life in the sprawling Dadaab refugee camp in arid north-eastern Kenya, where over 350,000 Somalis live in tents provided by the United Nations High Commission for Refugees (UNHCR) and remain dependent on monthly food rations. However these days,

the streets of Eastleigh are unusually quiet. In March, Kenya's Cabinet Secretary for Interior ordered, on the grounds of 'emerging security challenges in our urban centres,' all refugees to report to the Dadaab and Kakuma refugee camps.

Source: Mark Yarnell at http://urban-refugees.org/debate/category/non-classe/.

Crisis situations therefore have a higher impact in vulnerable areas and a disproportionate impact on the urban poor, especially women, children and the elderly. Building resilience, or reducing this vulnerability, is paramount. Urban agriculture can play an important role and hence needs to be integrated in disaster mitigation strategies. Mitigation is a collective term for all actions taken prior to the occurrence of a disaster (pre-disaster measures), including preparedness and long-term risk reduction measures. New insights in the field of disaster risk reduction have demonstrated the strong connection between resilience and the sustainability of socio-ecological systems. The costs of restoring communities back to something resembling their original states are much greater than the costs of investing in a community or urban disaster risk reduction programme and increasing its resilience before a disaster strikes.

The role of urban agriculture

Urban agriculture has always been used as a food security strategy during economic and emergency situations. Examples include the extensive "Dig for Victory" campaign in Britain during the Second World War, and more recently "Operation Feed Yourself" in Ghana during the 1970s. Similarly, in many other countries, backyard farming, and institutional and school gardening have all been encouraged during times of food instability.

Urban agriculture, with its emphasis on space-confined technologies, use of composted organic waste and recycling of grey wastewater, offers good options for the provision of fresh vegetables, eggs, dairy products and other perishables to the population of these "new settlements" in addition to generating some income, and other benefits. Growing nutritious crops requires a limited growing period and low investments, and the use (often available) of traditional knowledge and skills and local resources (minimal land of low quality, recycled organic waste and wastewater, local seed, etc.).

Increasingly these potentials of vegetable gardening and other agricultural production activities (e.g., eggs, mushrooms, medicinal herbs, etc.) in protracted refugee situations are being recognized, in addition to the need for higher calorie intake (The Sphere Project 2011). In addition to food, becoming involved in constructive activities may help people regain dignity, hope and self-respect and enhance overall well-being. Home or community gardening activities help increase self-reliance, allowing people to grow their preferred crops and varieties, and can improve their skills and knowledge, while additionally reducing operational costs for humanitarian agencies and potentially contributing to restoring the social fabric of disaster-affected communities. Urban agriculture can play multiple roles in different phases of the disaster management cycle. Instructions for developing and protecting primary food production are given in a number of guidelines, which also contain planning and design recommendations for allocating small plots of land for use as kitchen gardens.

FIGURE 15.1 Cultivation tower (India)

However, in reality NGOs seldom provide such technical assistance but rather resort to the provision of food aid which is often implemented with no exit strategy and thus in the long-term building dependency on food aid.

When developing agriculture-based interventions and projects in urban refugee settings, the following issues should be taken into consideration:

- Physical characteristics of the local setting, such as infrastructural capacities, basic social services (water, sanitation, waste use, health), land availability and energy supply (wood, kerosene).
- Social characteristics, such as IDP/refugee rights, security, social fabric and cohesion (race, tribe, gender), uncertainty, traumas, labour supply (abundant but weakened), and possibility of conflict among refugees and IDPs.
- Food availability, food quality, balanced food basket, culture, income, etc.
- Political issues that can inhibit interventions.

The development of livelihood strategies, including agriculture and animal husbandry, will depend not only on the availability of, and access to, land, irrigation water, seeds and natural resources, but also on freedom of movement. Humanitarian agencies may provide refugees with seeds, tools and, when necessary, technical support, but access to land and common resources is often constrained by the policies implemented by the host country, which may restrict their freedom and mobility. In particular, access to land is limited by the traditional land tenure system and laws concerning landownership and rights of usufruct. Hence the host governments need to take a more positive attitude to the planning and management of refugee camps and settlements as in the case of Uganda (van Rooij and Liem 2009; Betts et al. 2014). Likewise in the process of slum development, attention to increased self-reliance is important. Protecting and supporting livelihoods can be instrumental in safeguarding food security and minimizing relief aid dependency among beneficiaries.

Beneficiaries' interest in agricultural activities may evolve over time, as their immediate needs start to be met. But some may not wish to start growing vegetables as this might trigger the impression that they have to settle at that location for an extended period of time. For many, agriculture still has a permanent character. During the first period of emergency relief, agricultural production is unlikely, but the planning of future production sites must be taken into account in the camp layout or the housing reconstruction plans. We will discuss here the importance of food production versus solely distribution, the role of urban gardening in refugee camps, and the role of urban agriculture for urban refugees.

Food distribution versus food production

Despite some successful examples of small-scale food production in refugee camps, many relief aid strategies still focus on food distribution as the main response mechanism (Adam–Bradford et al. 2009). In a disaster aftermath the emphasis is on fast and effective food distribution. But when food distribution programmes are viewed over the long-term, secondary issues such as food dependency, corruption, and programme costs come into play. Despite being effective for its purpose, i.e., saving life, food distribution remains a highly inefficient food security tool due to high food and fuel prices and often extensive logistical costs. Of course, there are situations when food production is not a viable option, for example when agricultural land is contaminated or mined. Food distribution with no or minor attention for gardening initiatives (not as part of the longer-term strategy) would result in major lost opportunities, as the implementation of food production can play an important role in mobilizing and rehabilitating communities following the impacts of a disaster or emergency.

Therefore, food distribution, as part of immediate relief, should be planned in conjunction with food-producing options, as part of the rehabilitation and development strategies, so that transitions from food dependency to food security can be made at the earliest opportunity and with minimum risk to the beneficiaries. The reasons to support agriculture-related activities in the early stages of the post-disaster phase are numerous, such as the need for fresh and diverse food (in addition to the supply of staple foods).

Refugee camps and settlements

Despite many ongoing conflicts, in some countries there are opportunities to rebuild communities and to facilitate the return of refugees and other displaced populations. This is also still the basic assumption in the political standpoints and hence of refugee strategies (Adam-Bradford et al. 2009). Due to prolonged stay in camps, humanitarian aid is often not enough to sustain basic needs, and refugees are forced to find other ways to support themselves. Refugees make a living through (illegal) trade, small businesses and agricultural production. A typical refugee camp will, after some years, have several visible activities of this nature (Jansen 2009). However, refugees face restrictions that ordinary citizens do not face in conducting business, which makes earning a livelihood difficult. Examples are the restriction of free movement, work permits, and high costs of all kinds of services, especially market information (although many black markets develop). Land is not always of good quality, hampering the development of gardens, while access to this land and water of good quality, as well as seeds, construction material, etc., is also restricted. The United Nations High Commissioner for Refugees (UNHCR) estimates that more than half of the refugee camps in the world are unable to provide the recommended daily water minimum of 20 litres of water per person per day (UNHCR 2012 and 2014). The application of micro-finance in refugee camps is difficult, since many refugees are reluctant to start a business, and repayment is low.

Most refugee camps do not have sufficient food to provide for their populations, and refugees are frequently dependent entirely on humanitarian aid. Besides, the quantity of food is often insufficient and the lack of calorie-rich and nutritious food causes many refugees to suffer from deficiencies in essential vitamins and minerals, which can lead to a variety of diseases. Guidelines do exist and refugees are encouraged to grow their own food in small gardens or sacks (Corbett 2009), ensuring the consumption of some vegetables. These gardens serve as a supplement to food rations, though in most cases refugees are not allowed to sell surplus. For over two decades the official government policy in Uganda is that refugee settlements are designed and planned around agricultural livelihoods. Once a refugee is registered in a settlement, they are allocated a plot of land and issued seeds and tools to farm their plots. In addition, they also receive extension and support in the rearing of chickens and pigs, and the planting of home gardens. Many of the settlements, such as Nakivale, have become so productive they now export crops to local and regional markets (Betts et al. 2014).

BOX 15.3   GUIDANCE ON AGRICULTURAL INTERVENTIONS IN THE SPHERE GUIDELINES

The minimum requirement of surface area per person in a planned settlement is 45 m^2, so a camp for 1,000 refuges would have to be 4.5 hectares (ha). This includes space for household plots, roads, footpaths, sanitation, and other infrastructural inputs, but moreover it also allows for "limited kitchen gardens for individual households" (page 257). On a 4.5 ha site and using an average household plot size of six persons, this would result in the implementation of 166 small kitchen gardens. The Minimum Standards in Food Security and Nutrition provide the bulk of practical guidance for practical agricultural interventions with key aspects being addressed in Chapter 4 Food Security (page 175), which includes three components: 4.1 Food security – food transfers; 4.2 Food security – cash and voucher transfers; and 4.3 Food security – livelihoods. For example, primary production mechanisms should be protected and supported through local capacity building measures and, where appropriate, with the distribution of seeds, tools, fertilizers, livestock, fishing equipment, hunting implements, credit and loan facilities, market information, transport facilities, etc.

Source: The Sphere Project 2011.

During the prolonged period, these micro-gardens, provide livelihood and even income-generating opportunities, but may also contribute to wider social and economic rehabilitation, in protracted camps, and in and around cities, where levels of unemployment and urban poverty may be particularly high.

Refugees may also arrive at a camp or settlement with their own livestock and seeds and, once settled, start their own agricultural activities. Examples include IDP camps in Iraq where Kurdish refugees were keeping goats and sheep in livestock pens built from scrap materials, and growing vegetables and even small plots of wheat which were processed on site and then used for traditional bread-making (Adam-Bradford et al. 2009). In Banda Aceh, many of the survivors from the 2004 tsunami have planted home gardens around their temporary shelters; two years later, these gardens had matured into highly bio-diverse home gardens with multiple layers and, in some cases, with over 30 different crops being grown on small plots of land measuring just 3x5 metres (Adam-Bradford and Osman 2009).

Stimulating small-scale gardens for groups, or community gardening, can also help build different forms of capital (social, human, financial, economic, physical, natural, etc.), and contribute to longer-term resilience. To be able to build sustainable, shock-resistant communities, the active engagement of people themselves throughout the process is crucial. In cases where food growing systems are introduced as project activities, it is important to use participatory processes to ensure the technologies are appropriate to the local context and to the culture of the beneficiaries themselves. Rather than implementing what may become complicated technical solutions, such as hydroponics or even rearing livestock, efforts should be directed at building the foundations first, such as developing compost-production plants utilizing camp organic waste that will then feed into horticultural projects or planting fodder trees as camp windbreaks, which will then increase availability of fodder before livestock are introduced (SAFIRE and UNHCR 2001).

Also the use of grey water is propagated, although this needs to be done with care, needs risk minimization strategies and proper management (Dalahmeh and Almoayed 2009). These initial activities can also be used to galvanize community-based groups, share knowledge and identify early innovators or experienced farmers who can then serve as community role models using demonstration garden and livestock sites.

Insecurity in specific regions can continue for many years. Refugee camps tend to gradually convert into "shanty towns" or become permanent settlements. Many of these "camps" are difficult to distinguish from surrounding towns. Many displaced people will never return to their original "home" areas for a variety of reasons, and would rather seek new livelihood opportunities in and around nearby cities. More than 50 million people live in camps or temporary settlements. The average lifespan of a refugee camp is close to 20 years, and the average stay of a refugee in such a camp is up to 12 years (UNHCR 2012 and 2014). It is clear that a new and integrated approach to designing and managing these camps is required. Consequently, the status of refugees and IDPs needs to be improved and implementing agencies need to give adequate attention to human rights and entitlements, such as access to land for gardening and farming.

BOX 15.4   REFUGEE CAMPS IN JORDAN

More than 50 million people in the world live in camps or temporary settlements. The average lifespan of a refugee camp is close to 20 years, and the average stay of a refugee in such a camp is up to 12 years. Various organizations are discussing and working on a change in humanitarian aid, and are stimulating innovation, and developing an integrated approach in designing, managing and financing refugee camps.

The Al Za'atari camp in northern Jordan opened in mid-2012, and it is unknown how long the community will have to live here. Currently there are around 100,000 refugees, more than 50% children, who live in close to 30,000 tents and caravans. Its envisaged lifespan is five years, costing overall 14 million Euros a month (already half a million on electricity). Infrastructure is already deteriorating, for instance the WASH (water, sanitation and hygiene) centres that did not meet cultural contexts were destroyed and need rehabilitation.

The refugee community is making the best of available opportunities, innovating while trying to find solutions to their day-to-day struggle. Governance structures are emerging, childcare and theatre are organized, and informal commerce has started: the market of Al Za'Atari is the fastest growing in the region.

More efficient, effective and sustainable planning is required, based on the local situation and a vision on (urban) development of the entire Mafraq Region. Linkages need to be made between the ever-increasing urban refugees of the region of Mafraq and the huge impact this has on the host communities. The efforts of the many relief organizations and private initiatives need to be coordinated and formed into multi-stakeholder planning processes with longer-term perspectives, with the objectives of building resilient settlements.

The former UNHCR camp commander of Za'Atari invited many key experts in the world to bring innovative solutions for the transition from emergency aid into development. The Dutch Government asked VNG-International and the City of Amsterdam to step in. The Dutch mission operates via the Jordan Government and UNHCR. With integrated planning as an overarching theme, the project focuses on solutions in key aspects as transport, WASH, waste, ambulance, food and governance. Planning is addressing and connecting three levels of scale: *Region, Camp and Shelter*. This is based on the philosophy that any confrontation between refugees and host communities causes problems but this can also lead to local solutions. The aim is to deliver flexible planning instruments, supporting expertise and design assistance, with process-driven participation and implementation that ensures project activities are connected with local procedures and social cultural patterns, and facilitate community building and self-reliance.

Planning investigates scenarios which both the area of Mafraq and the camp might overcome in the near future. At any scale, key drivers are resources, production, connectivity and existence. Key design principles are synergy, adaptability and prototype. Solutions and interventions are developed together with stakeholders for the short-, middle- and long-term: direct interventions, development and empowerment.

Sources: Oral information by AlZaatariWorks, City of Amsterdam and RUAF Foundation.

Dispersed refugees in urban areas

An increasing number of refugees live in urban areas, usually in slum areas, or otherwise face similar challenges as the urban poor. More than 50% of the refugees live in urban areas, and at greater distances than before (UNHCR 2014). The majority of these people stay unemployed, live in poor and overcrowded areas, and depend on international and/or non-governmental organizations. And many refugees become "urbanized" by their experience in camps (Buscher 2011).

Organizations like UNHCR and the International Committee of the Red Cross (ICRC) are changing their policies, but host government legislation and NGO services are slowly adapting to the ensuing situation (and restrictions of movement, access to land and developing businesses still occur). Creating economic opportunities for refugees in urban areas is a challenging and complex undertaking. There are many similarities in working with urban refugees and the urban poor, but as mentioned, also differences. In addition, hostilities may arise between refugees and the local community.

A first step is bringing parties together and to lobby and advocate for recognition of refugee rights in local policy and practice. Support is required to empower vulnerable refugee groups to build small businesses to support themselves and other vulnerable refugees in the community. For this, (short-term) financial assistance is required, until they become more self-reliant. Identification of, and facilitating access to, existing business development services could build refugees' financial literacy and entrepreneurial skills (Betts et al. 2014).

While economic programming in urban environments is complex and local markets and opportunities are often limited, starting with and building on what exists both within the refugee populations and with the local economic service providers would facilitate better practices and ultimately should lead to better outcomes (Buscher 2011). The ability to provide for themselves allows urban refugees to address their own needs without substantive further assistance from the humanitarian community, and thereby also restore some of the refugees' dignity. Thinking in urban development would use humanitarian assistance more effectively and sustainably – supporting local economic development or improving government health and education facilities.

BOX 15.5   ENHANCING URBAN AGRICULTURE IN THE GAZA STRIP

Gaza Strip is a physical, social and economic environment that is almost unique in the world and that is determined by a political deadlock where access to land, sea, water, markets, and human resources is restricted by an intransigent Israeli blockade and isolation politics. Since the second Intifada (2000–2001), access and mobility restrictions have been imposed on Gazans. Since 2007, the Gaza Strip has been even more tightly closed off, resulting in exceptional conditions where both imports and exports of goods are very restricted and irregular. Coupled to the closure and destruction of the tunnels that allowed the traffic of goods to and from Egypt, and a high population growth, the resulting complex socioeconomic situation has dramatically increased poverty and unemployment in the Gaza Strip.

As 90% of all agriculture in Gaza can be considered urban or semi-urban, there is increasing national recognition for urban agriculture to be promoted as a complementary strategy for enhancing urban food security and nutrition, income and employment generation to improve the market. There are production opportunities and demands for locally produced, good-quality produce. However, urban agriculture and especially more market-oriented urban agriculture in Gaza is challenged by various constraints, such as limited access to land and low quality of service providers.

Source: authors.

Guidelines and frameworks

Several frameworks and guidelines have been developed to integrate food productions systems in the planning and design of urban agricultural intentions in post-disaster and emergency situations.

The Livestock Emergency Guidelines and Standards (LEGS) provide a set of international guidelines and standards for the design, implementation and assessment of livestock interventions to assist people affected by humanitarian crises. The guidelines aim to improve the quality of emergency response by increasing the appropriateness, timeliness and feasibility of livelihoods-based interventions and can be found at: www.livestock-emergency.net/.

Instructions for developing and protecting primary food production are given in the Sphere Project Guidelines (The Sphere Project 2011), which also contain the planning and design recommendations for allocating small plots of land for use as kitchen gardens. These Sphere Project Guidelines are often used by donors to indicate the minimum required standards in the development of humanitarian inventions and programmes and have become an important and influential tool for the justification of programme funding. In addition, some UNHRC handbooks

FIGURE 15.2 Rooftop garden, Gaza Strip

have been developed that address the environmental management of refugee camps and settlements with additional livelihood guidelines addressing agriculture, forestry and livestock (UNHCR and CARE 2002 and 2005; UNHCR 2012).

In addition, various organizations like ICRC, the UN Food and Agriculture Organization (FAO), the International Water and Sanitation Centre (IRC), etc., have developed manuals. Applying a combination of these frameworks and guidelines would ensure the participatory design and implementation of appropriate interventions that maximize the benefits of integrating urban food production in emergency responses while minimizing the associated environmental risks. However, the implementation in the harsh reality of refugee situations is a different ball game altogether.

BOX 15.6 THE SPHERE PROJECT GUIDELINES

The Sphere Project guidelines consist of a Humanitarian Charter and Minimum Standards in Disaster Response that are presented in a book format aimed to assist humanitarian relief workers in delivering high-quality and an accountable disaster response (The Sphere Project 2011). The initiative was launched in 1997 through an international collaboration that includes the Red Cross and Red Crescent movements. The collaboration currently consists of over 400 organizations in over 80 countries which have all adopted the Sphere consensus, including donor organizations which now request that emergency funding proposals be written in the context of the Sphere Guidelines.

The combination of food production with food distribution is clearly advocated in The Sphere Project guidelines, which is a handbook designed for use in disaster response situations but has an equal role in disaster pre-paredness and broader disaster risk reduction programmes, applicable in a range of scenarios, including natural disasters as well as armed conflict in both slow-onset and rapid-onset situations, and urban refugee situations. The Sphere Handbook provides appropriate guidance for agricultural interven-tions in a range of the key sectors from food security to physical planning of settlements. Important guidance notes are also provided on the viability of primary production, technological development, improving choice, timeli-ness and acceptability of primary production, seeds, local purchase of inputs, monitoring usage and unforeseen or negative effects of inputs. The guidance notes also address complex issues to ensure programmes are well designed, appropriate to local conditions and sustainable.

Source: The Sphere Project 2011.

The Sphere Handbook highlights that food security responses should aim to meet short-term needs, "do no harm", reduce the need for the affected popula-tion to adopt potentially damaging coping strategies, and contribute to restoring longer-term food security. Thus in urban areas a priority may be the re-estab-lishment of normal market conditions, but equally important are small kitchen gardens and primary production methods: such strategies may be more appropriate than food distribution because they uphold dignity, support livelihoods and thereby reduce future vulnerability (The Sphere Project 2011).

Integrating gardening in slum upgrading or in the design and development of new neighbourhoods will support the development of more food-secure and inclusive human settlements. Even in a slum or a densely built settlement, there is space for, and presence of, food growing. Agriculture can be integrated in lane upgrading by leaving small stretches of soil for growing on either side of the road or by applying vertical growing and container gardening along lanes.

Agriculture can also be integrated in housing improvements and design. For instance, housing should cover no more than 50% of a lot area to provide adequate space for growing food. Exterior house walls can be used for agriculture and all windows could have a shelf or window box to accommodate container gardens. Fencing could support growing and rooftops can be designed for water harvesting. Furthermore, the productive use of public areas (multifunctional parks, roadsides, flood zones, waterfront/canal areas) within slums can also be utilized. Urban agriculture can also be integrated in the sanitation systems of a settlement through wastewater recycling for gardening or organic solid waste recycling for growing vegetables.

In the longer-term, gardening also generates income and improves associations and linkages with other refugees or local communities, while contributing to the broader development of the area and building resilient cities, where refugees are hosted by stimulating local markets and trade. In addition, natural resources can be conserved and protected by promoting sound agricultural practices and introducing waste-recycling systems appropriate to the local conditions. In this context the project aims may start initially as conflict-prevention, with secondary objectives including improvements in environmental sanitation and food production. Generating livelihoods and youth employment has been identified as a key strategy to prevent the radicalization of the youth and this is not only important in refugee camps but also with refuge and host populations in many urban centres, particularly in North and East Africa and in the Middle East.

Despite the above-mentioned guidelines and calls for innovative local food production solutions, the mainstreaming of urban agriculture in disaster and emergency response settings is still woefully inadequate, thus resulting in lost opportunities to protect and promote, and when necessary rehabilitate, local food production systems, thus building resilience at a wider local level.

Integrating urban agriculture and planning for resilience

Insecurity in specific regions can continue for many years. Refugee camps gradually convert into "shanty towns" and are better seen as becoming permanent settlements, allowing planning and using resources accordingly. Many displaced people will never return to their original "home" areas for a variety of reasons, and would rather seek new livelihood opportunities in and around nearby cities. Urban agriculture can play an important role in all aspects of the disaster management cycle and is a multifunctional policy instrument and tool for practical application; it is valid for integrated design and management of refugee camps, as well as in creating resilience in urban areas.

Various approaches in preventing and coping with disasters have developed in the course of time. In the text below two project-based disaster risk management approaches are briefly discussed, which are already applied to urban and peri-urban areas and are including urban agriculture in planning for resilience and disaster risk management programmes.

Linking relief, rehabilitation and development

As illustrated in the disaster management cycle (see Figure 15.3), emergency interventions are still too often delivered in isolation and fail to address longer-term development goals. The need to fill the gap between humanitarian aid and development is frequently debated and is addressed in an approach called Linking Relief, Rehabilitation and Development. The European Union (in its European

Commission Humanitarian Aid (ECHO) programme) emphasizes the importance of this linkage. The primary objective of LRRD is to address the gaps between emergency relief and longer-term development aims and objectives. In this LRRD process attention to self-reliance is also important: this is the capacity of a community to produce, exchange or claim resources which are necessary to ensure its sustainability and resilience against future disasters.

The introduction of the concept of sustainable livelihoods also moves away from perceiving disaster victims and/or refugees as vulnerable people entirely dependent on external relief aid. For example, a livelihoods approach in emergency settlement camps focuses on strategies that facilitate beneficiaries to meet their basic needs, while also identifying the constraints that prevent them from enjoying their (human) rights and thus developing their livelihoods. The concept of human security finally promotes a shift from focusing on state security (i.e., mainly on the protection of state territory), to focusing on human issues and rights (e.g., the right to food, and the right to shelter).

In doing so, it widens the scope of interventions from governments and international organizations and addresses issues such as increasing access rights of displaced people to land, rather than just addressing food security and human protection. Human security further pays attention to the array of issues behind the complex international causes of population movements, explaining the causes and linking them to development and poverty. Increasingly, there is an emphasis on preventive strategies, such as the development of good governance.

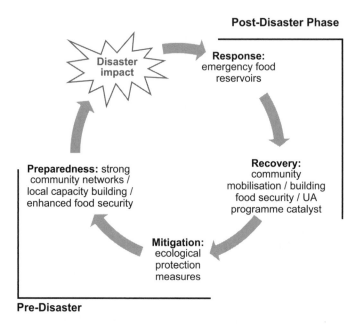

FIGURE 15.3 Disaster management cycle with linkages to urban agriculture

Source: authors.

The LRRD process involves a thorough context and political analysis with the objectives of identifying the root causes of vulnerability and poverty. The process also works directly with local institutions to build capacity so that inequality and access to resources can be addressed through continued programming and intentions. Then the linkages between relief and long-term development can be made. For urban agriculture this starts by recognizing the practice as a formal urban process and identifying the positive role it can play; this can then lead not only to policies to promote safe practices but also to practices that incorporate risk reduction measures.

BOX 15.7   THE ROLE OF URBAN AGRICULTURE IN REBUILDING LIBERIA

Since the end of the war that raged from 1989 to 2003, Liberia has suffered from chronic food insecurity. With much of its agricultural sector destroyed, over 40% of Liberians are still estimated to be food insecure. As the economy slowly recovers, the urban population is growing quickly, but a generation without education is struggling to survive and prosper amidst the wreckage of devastated infrastructure. Access to local food is paramount. This need has been aggravated by the 2014 Ebola crisis.

In Greater Monrovia, over 5,000 households are engaged in urban and peri-urban agriculture, mostly for domestic consumption (WHH/RUAF 2012). Urban farmers (75% of whom are women) generally produce vegetables and fruits, with staple crops such as rice and cassava produced on larger open spaces and swamps in peri-urban areas. But there are no clearly defined areas for urban agriculture and land rights are uncertain. Restaurants, hotels, mining companies, supermarkets and hospitals are increasingly sourcing urban agricultural produce, but improved storage facilities and post-harvest technologies are needed. Farmers also lack reliable access to proper tools, good seeds and formal credit systems.

Urban agriculture provides a strategy to help reduce urban poverty, improve food security and enhance waste management. But urban agriculture also plays a wider role in developing the city of Greater Monrovia, as well as in smaller towns like Gbarnga and Tubmanburg. Women play a critical role in the production and processing sectors and are often dynamic entrepreneurs. Therefore improving women's involvement in and access to credit, farming inputs, extension services and business opportunities must be prioritized.

RUAF Foundation, with Welthungerhilfe, collaborated with Monrovia Municipality and other stakeholders to promote urban agriculture, to develop and strengthen linkages and to support policy change, by facilitating a multi-stakeholder policy formation and action planning (MPAP) process and supporting urban farmers and processors.

Source: RUAF Foundation.

Disaster risk reduction (DRR)

Disaster risk reduction (DRR) is a systematic approach to identifying, assessing and reducing the risks of disaster. A DRR programme can be implemented at any time so that it differs from LRRD in that it may not be making strong linkages to any relief programme, although DRR programmes are also sometimes implemented in the aftermath of a disaster or emergency. DRR is a planning and implementation tool that addresses the practical issues of vulnerability through the building of resilience and local capacity to respond to natural hazards and anthropogenic disasters (Pelling and Wisner 2009). The United Nations International Strategy for Disaster Reduction (ISDR 2004) defines disaster risk reduction follows:

> The conceptual framework of elements considered with the possibilities to minimize vulnerabilities and disaster risks throughout a society, to avoid (prevention) or to limit (mitigation and preparedness) the adverse impacts of hazards, within the broad context of sustainable development. The disaster risk reduction framework is composed of the following fields of action:
>
> - Risk awareness and assessment including hazard analysis and vulnerability/capacity analysis.
> - Knowledge development including education, training, research and information.
> - Public commitment and institutional frameworks, including organizational, policy, legislation and community action.
> - Application of measures including environmental management, land use and urban planning, protection of critical facilities, application of science and technology, partnership and networking, and financial instruments.
> - Early warning systems including forecasting, dissemination of warnings, preparedness measures and reaction capacities.
>
> *(ISDR 2004: 23)*

Resilience is a measure of a household, city or nation's ability to absorb shocks and stresses. Enhancing the role of urban agriculture includes not only improving linkages to food security but also income and environmental management (see other chapters on the linkages to urban planning and climate change). Urban agriculture itself is characterized by innovation and adaptation to specific urban needs. Examples are micro-gardens, which can provide an emergency food source in the context of disaster risk management; green rooftops, which represent a built environment adaptation to climate change impacts; planting of trees, which serve as green "lungs" contributing to improved air quality; and rainwater harvesting systems, which can help lessen the effects of flooding. Urban agriculture can keep environmentally sensitive and dangerous urban lands from being used for illegal residential development. It mitigates the adverse effects on the urban poor of financial and food crises through job creation; offers opportunities for small-scale income generation; increases food security and enables self-sufficiency; and improves nutrition and health.

DRR programmes can build capacity of urban farmers to take risk reduction measures that are integrated into their urban farming-based livelihoods, and building of local resilience in vulnerable urban communities. However, urban agriculture, in addition to other green urban infrastructures, can make wider contributions to disaster risk reduction at the landscape level through urban land-use planning and zoning. This would include the allocation of marginal land, such as steep slopes, riverbanks and flood-prone areas to agricultural land use. It is also proven that once secure land tenure is issued to urban farmers, then they become excellent land stewards who prevent urban encroachment from informal settlements and commercial enterprises. Thus marginal land such as steep slopes and flood-prone areas remain free from settlement. In addition farmers can then be supported to adopt specific land management techniques that then reduce the risk of landslides and floods through the adoption of risk reduction measures such as the planting of trees on contours, etc.

Enhancing the role of urban agriculture in building resilience

Experiences show that agriculture is not only a survival strategy for displaced people to obtain food on a temporary basis, but also a valuable livelihood strategy for those who settle permanently, and for those who eventually return to their home cities or countries. Many displaced people, both in camps and in and around cities, engage in agriculture for subsistence and market production. Increasingly, international organizations and relief agencies include agricultural production as part of their development strategies, as expressed in various guidelines. And although there are still various obstacles for refugees in terms rights and access, local and national authorities are not only increasingly allowing it but also, intentionally, supporting it.

Urban agriculture can play an important role in all aspects of the disaster management cycle and is a multifunctional policy instrument and tool for practical application. It is also valid for integrated design and management of refugee camps, as well as in creating resilience in urban areas.

Policies and interventions to promote agriculture by refugees need to be included in planning and design. At the camp level this should include the following:

a. Adequate camp and slum arrangements (such as the Sphere Project guidelines).
b. Promotion of low-space crops and animal production and water saving technologies.
c. Organizational support and training, both in technology and marketing, as well as in reintegration and rehabilitation activities.
d. Provision of inputs and financial support (which becomes especially important in longer-term settings, and when farmers move towards producing for the market) when displaced persons want to move from self-consumption to market production.

e. Maximize the safe utilization of organic wastes for compost production and grey water for the irrigation of gardens and trees.

Income generation from agriculture-based livelihoods will play an increasingly important role in developing economic self-reliance amongst refugee populations, and will help create an effective transition between emergency relief and longer-term development. It is likely that the availability of capital equipment or loan capital for small businesses will improve the ability of displaced people to pursue livelihoods and food security, and it is likely that the benefits will eventually also reach the host community.

The choice of food relief strategy must be made to suit the conditions on the ground rather than external factors such as donor influence, NGO technical expertise or lack of access to basic, appropriate food aid. Food distribution must be planned in conjunction with food-producing options so that transitions from food dependency to food security can be made at the earliest opportunity and with minimum risk to the beneficiaries that the food distribution supposedly serves.

Facilitating the change from emergency relief operations towards rehabilitation, sustainable development (by building resilience) requires innovative approaches and changes in current rules and legislation. It requires putting in place participatory mechanisms, such as farmer or gardening groups and farmer field schools, bringing refugees and host communities together, and enhancing a sense of community. Multi-stakeholder processes involving public and/or non-government actors can help build governance, which is especially important in fragile states that lack government capacity and willingness to perform key functions and services.

Growing food in camps and cities, when appropriate to the local conditions, reduces dependency on external food supplies, improves the availability and access to more nutritious food, and in the longer term may increase the resilience of people and cities. Both refugee camps and urban refugee settlements and slums require integrated planning approaches with a long-term perspective, and doing so would make humanitarian assistance more effectively and sustainably.

References

Adam-Bradford, A.; Hoekstra, F.; Veenhuizen, R. van. 2009. Linking relief, rehabilitation and development: A role for urban agriculture? *Urban Agriculture Magazine* 21: 3–10.

Adam-Bradford, A.; Osman, M. 2009. Tsunami aftermath: Development of an indigenous home garden in Banda Aceh. *Urban Agriculture Magazine* 21: 29–30.

Betts, A.; Bloom, L.; Kaplan, J.; Omata, N. 2014. Refugee economies: Rethinking popular assumptions. Humanitarian Innovation Project. Oxford: Refugee Studies Centre, University of Oxford.

Buscher, D. 2011. New approaches to urban refugee livelihoods. Women's Refugee Commission. Available from: http://womensrefugeecommission.org/press-room/journal-articles/1614-new-approaches-to-urban-refugee-livelihoods.

Corbett, M. 2009. Multi-storey gardens to support food security. *Urban Agriculture Magazine* 21: 34–35.

Crowell, M.; Nutsugah, E. 2013. Status of the Liberian refugees: The leftovers of Buduburam. *Modern Ghana* 12 August 2013. Available from: www.modernghana.com/news/481422/1/status-of-the-liberian-refugees-the-leftovers-of-b.html.

Dalahmeh, S.; Almoayed, A. 2009. Health risk assessment of children exposed to greywater in Jerash Refugee Camp in Jordan. *Urban Agriculture Magazine* 21: 41–42.

Hovland, I. 2009. The food crisis of 2008. Impact assessment of IFPRI's communication strategy. Washington, DC: International Food Policy Research Institute (IFPRI).

ISDR. 2004. Living with risk. A global review of disaster reduction initiatives. Volume I. International Strategy for Disaster Reduction. Geneva: United Nations International Strategy for Disaster Reduction (ISDR).

Jansen, B. J. 2009. The accidental city: Urbanisation in an East-African refugee camp. *Urban Agriculture Magazine* 21: 11–12.

Pelling, M.; Wisner, B. (eds.) 2009. Disaster risk reduction: Cases from urban Africa. London: Earthscan.

Rooij, A. van; Liem, L. 2009. From dependence to self-reliance: Experiences from northern Uganda. *Urban Agriculture Magazine* 21: 13–15.

RUAF Foundation. 2008. Urban agriculture for resilient cities: Green, productive and socially inclusive. DVD distributed at the World Urban Forum in Nanjing, China, November 2008. Leusden: RUAF Foundation.

SAFIRE and UNHCR. 2001. Permaculture in refugee situations: A refugee handbook for sustainable land management. Harare: Southern Alliance for Indigenous Resources (SAFIRE); Geneva: United Nations High Commissioner for Refugees (UNHCR).

Socorro Castro, A. R. 2009. Addressing the crisis in Cienfuegos, Cuba. *Urban Agriculture Magazine* 21: 4.

The Sphere Project. 2011. Humanitarian charter and minimum standards in humanitarian response. Rugby: Practical Action Publishing.

UNHCR. 2012. Livelihood programming in UNHCR: Operational guidelines. Geneva: UNCHR. Available from: www.unhcr.org/4fbdf17c9.pdf.

UNHCR. 2014. Statistics database. Geneva: UNHCR Operation Data Section. Available from: http://data.unhcr.org/.

UNHCR and CARE. 2002. Livelihood options in refugee situations: A handbook for promoting sound agricultural practices. Geneva: United Nations High Commissioner for Refugees (UNHCR); Washington, DC: CARE International. Available from: www.unhcr.org/406c2fae7.html.

UNHCR and CARE. 2005. Livestock-keeping and animal husbandry in refugee and returnee situations. Available from: www.unhcr.org/4385e3432.html.

WHH/RUAF. 2012. Enhancing urban and peri-urban agriculture in Liberia: City strategic agenda on urban and peri-urban agriculture in Greater Monrovia. Monrovia: Welt Hunger Hilfe and RUAF Foundation.

Wisner, B.; Blaikie, P.; Cannon, T.; Davis, I. 2004. At risk: Natural hazards, people's vulnerability and disasters. Second Edition. London: Routledge.

CONTRIBUTORS

The editors

Henk de Zeeuw holds a BSc in Land and Water Management (Larenstein College, Arnhem, the Netherlands, 1968) and an MSc in Rural Sociology and Planning (Agricultural University, Wageningen, the Netherlands, 1975). Henk has wide experience as a Senior Advisor in agricultural development in Europe and several developing countries in Latin America, sub-Saharan Africa and Asia, focusing on participatory research and extension, farmer organizations, capacity development and institutional strengthening. In 1999 he initiated the International Network of Resource centres on Urban Agriculture and Food security (RUAF) and in 2004 he was appointed as the first Director of the RUAF Foundation, when the RUAF network evolved from a network into an international institution specializing in urban food systems. He handed over the directorship in 2012.

Pay Drechsel holds an MSc in Soil Fertility and Plant Nutrition (University of Bayreuth, Germany, 1987) and a PhD in Environmental Sciences (University of Bayreuth, 1992). Pay has more than 25 years of working experience on biophysical, social and economic aspects of safe wastewater use and the recovery of nutrients from solid and liquid waste for intra- and peri-urban farming systems. In 2001, Pay joined the International Water Management Institute (IWMI) where he is currently leading the global Theme on "Resource Recovery, Water Quality and Health". He is working closely with WHO and FAO and has authored or edited several books and over 250 publications. After working extensively in West and East Africa, Pay is now based in South Asia. He served many years on the board of the RUAF Foundation.

The authors

Chapter 1. Urban food systems

Johannes S.C. (Han) Wiskerke has been Chair and Professor of Rural Sociology at Wageningen University, the Netherlands, since 2004 and Professor in Foodscape Studies & Design at the Amsterdam Academy of Architecture, the Netherlands, since 2013. He holds an MSc in Agronomy (1992) and a PhD in Rural Sociology (1997), both from Wageningen University. He worked as project manager at the Centre for Agriculture and Environment (Utrecht, the Netherlands) and as postdoctoral researcher at the Centre for Studies of Science, Technology & Society of Twente University (the Netherlands). He has coordinated several international research programmes on rural development, short food supply chains and city-region food systems funded by the European Commission and is supervising PhD projects in the fields of food sociology, food policy and rural and regional development.

Chapter 2. Urban food policies and programmes: an overview

Lauren Baker a PhD in Environmental Studies from York University, Canada, is a Policy Specialist with the Toronto Food Policy Council who is working with community and business partners, Toronto Public Health's food strategy team and across city divisions to promote a healthy, sustainable food system. She has consulted widely on municipal food policy development and has been involved in many "farm to fork" initiatives. Lauren was the founding director of Sustain Ontario – the Alliance for Healthy Food and Farming. She teaches at the University of Toronto, Canada, and is a Research Associate with Ryerson University's Centre for Studies in Food Security. She is the author of the book *Corn Meets Maize: Food Movements and Markets in Mexico* (2013).

Henk de Zeeuw See editors.

Chapter 3. Process and tools for multi-stakeholder planning of the urban agro-food system

Henk de Zeeuw See editors.

Marielle Dubbeling (MSc Agronomy, Wageningen University, the Netherlands) is the Director of the RUAF Foundation (www.ruaf.org). Marielle has coordinated several policy-oriented research, planning and development programmes on urban agriculture and climate change. She has over tens years of experience in multistakeholder planning and policy formulation on urban agriculture and is supporting the development of sustainable short food-value chains in more than 20 cities around the world. Before joining RUAF Foundation, Marielle worked with the Urban Management Programme in Latin America (UN HABITAT-UNDP), where she supported the development of municipal programmes on urban agriculture and food security in several cities in Latin America. Marielle has published several articles, working papers and books on urban agriculture.

Chapter 4. Agriculture in urban design and spatial planning

André Viljoen is an Architect and a Principal Lecturer in Architecture at the University of Brighton, England, and with Katrin Bohn contributes to the work of Bohn&Viljoen Architects. He is Chair of the Association of European Schools of Planning (AESOP) Food Planning Group. With Katrin Bohn he developed the concept of Continuous Productive Urban Landscapes (CPULs), which advocates the coherent introduction of urban agriculture into cities. Significant publications include Bohn&Viljoen's book *CPULs Continuous Productive Urban Landscapes: Designing Urban Agriculture for Sustainable Cities* (2005) and its sequel, *Second Nature Urban Agriculture: Designing Productive Cities* (2014).

Johannes Schlesinger is a Postdoctoral Research Fellow at the Institute of Environmental Social Sciences and Geography at the University of Freiburg, Germany. His current research focus is on the use of natural resources, specifically in – but not limited to – an urban context, matters of food security, as well as the linkages between urban and rural areas in the developing world. The methodological focus thereby lies on the application of remote sensing based analyses and the use of Geographic Information Systems (GIS).

Katrin Bohn is an Architect and Senior Lecturer in Architecture at the University of Brighton, England. Between 2010 and 2014, she held a guest professorship at the Technical University in Berlin, Germany, where she headed the Department of City & Nutrition. Together with André Viljoen, she runs Bohn&Viljoen Architects, an architectural practice and environmental consultancy based in London. Bohn&Viljoen Architects have taught, lectured, published and exhibited widely on the design concept of CPUL (Continuous Productive Urban Landscape) with which they contributed to the international urban design discourse in 2004. Their projects on productive landscapes include feasibility and design studies as well as food-growing installations and events for clients in the UK and Germany as well other European countries.

Axel Drescher is Professor (apl.) of Applied Geography of the Tropics and Subtropics and Head of the working group Geographic Development Research at the Institute of Environmental Social Sciences and Geography University of Freiburg, Germany. His research interests are on water and land resource management; application of geographic information systems (GIS) and remote sensing (RS) in development research; intra- and peri-urban agriculture with a main focus on small-scale production systems (home gardens, school gardens, allotment gardens); and food security and livelihood analysis in Africa and Asia.

Chapter 5. Urban agriculture and short chain food marketing in developing countries

Paule Moustier is an Agricultural Economist at the Centre de coopération Internationale en Recherche Agronomique pour le Développement (CIRAD), Montpellier, France. She is the Director of the research unit MOISA on agricultural markets and stakeholders' strategies. Her research work is about the organization and performance of food chains supplying cities of Africa and Asia. From 2002 to 2009, she was appointed in Hanoi, Vietnam. Previously she was in charge of research on the organization of vegetable supply of cities of West and Central Africa, with a focus on the role of geographical and relational proximity in market transactions.

Henk Renting is Senior Programme Officer at the RUAF Foundation. He holds MSc degrees in Rural Sociology and Environmental Sciences. He participated in international research projects on sustainable food systems, short food supply chains, and collective marketing. For over ten years he was connected to the Rural Sociology Group of Wageningen University, the Netherlands. He also was a visiting professor at the International University of Andalusia and Córdoba University, both in Spain, and Innsbruck University in Austria. His current research interests include urban agriculture, city-region food systems, and new forms of food governance.

Chapter 6. Urban agriculture's contributions to urban food security and nutrition

Maria Gerster-Bentaya has a PhD in Social Sciences, and is Senior Researcher and Lecturer at the Department of Rural Sociology, University of Hohenheim, Germany, in the field of communication and extension, knowledge and innovation management. Further areas of expertise are: food and nutrition security, urban agriculture, food systems and capacity development and stakeholder involvement in development processes. Between 2006 and 2014 she was a partner in the collaborate research project on "Urban agriculture as integrative factor of climate optimized urban development" in Casablanca (Morocco), resulting amongst others in the publication of Giseke, U., et al. (eds) 2014, *Urban Agriculture for Growing City Regions. Connecting Urban-Rural Spheres in Casablanca* (New York: Routledge).

Chapter 7. Productive and safe use of urban organic wastes and wastewater in urban food production systems in low-income countries

Pay Drechsel See editors.

Bernard Keraita is an International Researcher at the Global Health Section of the Department of Public Health, University of Copenhagen, Denmark. Bernard holds an

MSc in Soil and Water (Irrigation) at Wageningen University, the Netherlands, and a PhD at the University of Copenhagen, Denmark. He formerly worked as an irrigation and water engineer at IWMI, Regional Office for Africa, in Ghana, with a focus on environmental and human health, informal wastewater irrigation and agricultural water management. Bernard has worked extensively in West and East Africa.

Olufunke O. Cofie is a Senior Researcher with a background in soil science. She is Head of IWMI's West Africa Office in Ghana, and worked over the past 14 years in the interface of sanitation and agriculture. Since 2001, Funke has been with IWMI, focusing on formulation and implementation of development-oriented projects using multi-stakeholder processes. She also pioneered co-composting of solid and liquid waste in Ghana which led, among others, to the development of compost-fertilizer mixtures appropriate for intensive agriculture in and around cities. Funke also worked as the Regional Coordinator for the RUAF Foundation.

Josiane Nikiema holds an MSc and a PhD in Chemical Engineering for design and optimization of processes. She is adjunct Professor in Chemical and Civil Engineering at the Université de Sherbrooke in Canada and is a researcher in environmental sciences, based at IWMI's West Africa Office. Josiane's core technological interests are in environmentally friendly (bio-)technologies that can be applied at minimal cost to limit pollution impacts on humans and the environment. She worked on biofuels and pioneered the development of low-cost pelletized co-compost using faecal sludge and municipal organic waste.

Chapter 8. Urban agriculture and climate change

Shuaib Lwasa (PhD) is a researcher and academic at Makerere University, Uganda in the Department of Geography. He has taught for over 14 years at this university and undertaken research on various topics including urban poverty, urban environment, urban agriculture, urban planning and most recently on issues of landscape ecology within East and West Africa. Publication topics include adaptation to urban agriculture and climate change, mitigation strategies, land and property rights, urban poverty and innovative alternative urban development strategies. He was a lead author of the IPCC Working Group III for the Fifth Assessment Report chapter 12 on Human Settlements.

Marielle Dubbeling See Chapter 3.

Chapter 9. Urban horticulture

Hubert de Bon is Agronomist and Specialist in vegetable management in tropical areas at CIRAD, Montpellier, France, based in the research Unit HortSys. He has worked as a researcher and project leader in tropical areas of Mauritania, Senegal,

Martinique, Réunion, Vietnam and Taiwan. Hubert has implemented research projects on intra- and peri-urban agriculture for more than 15 years in cities like Dakar, Hanoi, Vientiane and Phnom Penh. Hubert has wide expertise in agricultural training, research, project evaluation and vegetable management, and runs projects on organic fruit and vegetable production, agroecology in West Africa and an innovation network in French territories.

Robert J. Holmer has a PhD in Agriculture from the TU München, Germany, and is presently holding the position of Senior Advisor for School Nutrition and Sanitation of GIZ for its Regional School Health Program "Fit for School". His areas of expertise are in sustainable vegetable production, post-harvest and marketing in urban and rural settings of Southeast Asia, with a particular focus on the nexus between agriculture, nutrition and health. He served as Regional Director of AVRDC – The World Vegetable Center in East and Southeast Asia, in Bangkok, Thailand, from 2010 to 2014. In the years before he coordinated a research and development programme for urban and peri-urban vegetable production at Xavier University, Philippines, funded by the European Union and the German government.

Christine Aubry is a Senior Agronomist and is in charge of the "Urban Agricultures" team in the INRA research unit SADAPT in Paris (France). After finishing her PhD on farmers' decision rules for technical management, she managed research projects about urban agriculture in Madagascar and in France for more than ten years. The new research team "Urban Agricultures" includes various scientific fields: agronomy, bioclimatology, geography, urbanism and sociology. Various projects are in course such as the T4P Project about rooftop gardening in France and the collective gardening project in France and Canada.

Chapter 10. Urban livestock keeping

Delia Grace is a Senior Researcher at the International Livestock Research Institute, Kenya, and Programme Leader of the Food Safety and Zoonoses Programme. She also leads the Agriculture Associated Diseases Theme in the new CGIAR Research Program on Agriculture for Human Nutrition and Health. Delia is an epidemiologist and veterinarian with more than 15 years of experience in developing countries. Her career has spanned the private sector, field-level community development and aid management, as well as research. She has lived and worked in Asia, West Africa and East Africa. Her research focuses on the design and promotion of risk-based approaches to food safety in livestock products, emerging diseases, participatory epidemiology, gender in development and animal welfare. She has authored more than 70 peer-reviewed publications.

Johanna Lindahl is a Veterinary Epidemiologist working on a joint appointment between Swedish University of Agricultural Sciences and the International Livestock Research Institute. Johanna graduated from Swedish University of Agricultural

Sciences and has been focusing her research on zoonotic and emerging infectious diseases in developing countries. Many projects related to her work have been addressing urban livestock keeping and the associated risks, both in Asia and Africa.

Maria Correa is Professor of Epidemiology and Public Health at the College of Veterinary Medicine at North Carolina State University, USA, where she has been a member of the faculty for 20 years. She specializes in programme development for zoonotic disease control and risk communication. Maria has collaborated with the Organization of American States Inter-American Institute for Cooperation on Agriculture (IICA) on global health and international trade issues and has been a member of many review panels. Her work on animal agriculture on city slums will be featured in a forthcoming book. She has more than 70 peer-reviewed and proceedings publications and developed many training courses.

Manish Kakkar is Professor of Communicable Diseases at the Public Health Foundation of India (PHFI), New Delhi since 2006. He is a Senior Public Health Specialist and provides technical support for research and training to national and state governments on priority communicable disease issues. Manish has done niche work in incorporating surveillance, training and research aimed at crystallizing and integrating a strong public health approach to emerging and zoonotic infections and launched the Roadmap to Zoonoses Initiative (RCZI) in 2008 as a national initiative on research, capacity building and health promotion for prevention and control of zoonotic infections in India. He started his career as a senior resident doctor in the Department of Microbiology in MAMC, India, and later moved to WHO's India Office as a national professional officer.

Chapter 11. Urban forestry and agroforestry

Fabio Salbitano is Professor at the University of Florence, Italy, teaching Urban Forestry, Silviculture and Landscape Ecology. He holds a PhD in Forest Ecology from the University of Padua, Italy. His main research skills refer to urban forestry (design and strategic planning, urban ecology, collaborative tools), landscape ecology, and ecological history. He is member of the Editorial Board of *Urban Forestry and Urban Greening*. He has participated in the Food and Agriculture Organization of the United Nations (FAO) activities concerning urban forestry since 2001 as an advisor or consultant. Currently, he is coordinating the working group on Urban and Peri-urban Forestry of FAO-SILVA MEDITERRANEA statutory body.

Simone Borelli is currently working as Agroforestry and Urban Periurban Forestry Officer in the Forestry Department of the FAO. He holds a degree in Forest Science from the University of Viterbo (Italy), an MSc in Watershed Management from the University of Arizona (USA) and a Postgraduate Diploma on Public Management from the University of London (UK). He has worked for FAO in various capacities for over 15 years and has also worked for WWF, IPGRI (now Bioversity) and as an independent forestry consultant.

Giovanni Sanesi is Professor in Forestry, Urban Forestry and Wildfires Prevention at the University of Bari, Italy. He held lectures also at Bari Polytechnic, University of Tuscia, University of Bologna, University of Catania and University of Napoli. He is a member of the Board of Directors of the Italian Society of Silviculture and Forestry Ecology (SISEF) and member of the Editorial Board of the *Urban Forest and Urban Greening* (Elsevier) and *Italian Journal of Forest and Mountain Environments*. He is active in the Urban Forestry unit and the Landscape Ecology unit of the International Union of Forest Research Organizations (IUFRO).

Chapter 12. Urban aquaculture for resilient food systems

Stuart W. Bunting holds a PhD from the University of Stirling, Scotland, in 2001. Stuart coordinated a series of research projects concerning the sustainability of peri-urban aquatic production systems in Asia. Between 2005 and 2015 he was based at the University of Essex, England, and conducted research, capacity-building and conservation projects focused on climate change, food security and livelihoods. He is now an independent researcher and consultant at Bunting Aquaculture, Agriculture and Aquatic Resources Conservation Services providing expertise in: bio-economic modelling of agricultural and aquaculture systems and alternative land-use management practices; stakeholder Delphi assessments for building and evaluating consensus for natural resources management; integrated action planning for wise-use and conservation of wetlands (see www.wraptoolkit.org); carbon footprint assessments of farming systems and product value chains to mitigate GHG emissions.

David C. Little is Professor of Aquatic Resource Development at the Institute of Aquaculture, University of Stirling, Scotland. He has over 30 years' experience in tropical aquaculture. He is Editor of the Society and Sustainability section of the journal *Aquaculture* and is active in both research and teaching at undergraduate and postgraduate level on livelihoods and aquatic resource management, sustainable aquaculture, aquatic pathobiology and other subjects.

Chapter 13. Gendering urban food strategies across multiple scales

Liam Riley is an SSHRC Postdoctoral Fellow at the Balsillie School of International Affairs in Canada. His research interests are global development, urbanization, food security, gender, and childhoods. His regional research focus is in southern Africa, particularly Malawi, where he has conducted extensive qualitative fieldwork and published original research on the lives of orphans, the politics of urban street vending, and the gendered dimensions of urban household food security. He is currently exploring the linkages between urban informality and urban food security in a global comparative perspective.

Alice Hovorka is a Professor of Geography and Environmental Studies at Queen's University in Canada. Her research focuses on contemporary human–environment relations in southern Africa. She has published widely on the gendered dimensions of urban agriculture and urban food security in the region, with a particular focus on urban Botswana. Her research is broadly concerned with the lives of animals and species relations of power in Botswana, both in terms of how animal–human interactions shape urban food security and in broader terms of culture and social development.

Chapter 14. Financing urban agriculture: what do we know and what should we know

Yves Cabannes is Professor and Chair of Development Planning at Bartlett Development Planning Unit (DPU), University College, London. He was previously lecturer at Harvard University Graduate School of Design and Coordinator of UN Urban Management Programme for Latin America and the Caribbean. Yves is an urban specialist with experience in various regions of the world and an interest in urban agriculture and food sovereignty, land rights, local currencies, participatory planning and budgeting, low-cost housing, community-based financial systems and appropriate technologies for local development. He is currently Secretary of the board of directors of the RUAF Foundation. He published several articles and books on planning, legal, institutional and financial aspects of urban and peri-urban agriculture.

Chapter 15. Role of urban agriculture in disasters and emergencies

Andrew Adam-Bradford is a geographer, specializing in agroecology, stabilization agriculture and urban agriculture. His practice and research interests include the application of agriculture in post-disasters and conflict situations and agriculture in refugee camps and settlements. He is a Technical Advisor at the Human Relief Foundation, a British-registered humanitarian relief international non-government organization, a Senior Research Fellow in Stabilization Agriculture at the Centre for Agroecology, Water and Resilience, Coventry University (England), an Associate Member of the RUAF Foundation and a Fellow of the Royal Geographical Society.

René van Veenhuizen holds an MSc in Land and Water Management from Wageningen University, the Netherlands. Since 1999 he has been Senior Programme Officer with the RUAF Foundation, Editor of the *Urban Agriculture Magazine* and co-author of several books published by RUAF. Previously he has worked with

Wageningen University, the Dutch Open University, the Food and Agriculture Organization of the United Nations (FAO) and ETC Foundation on sustainable agricultural development. He has over 25 years of professional experience and is currently involved in projects related to urban agriculture and water and sanitation (WASH), in Nepal, Bangladesh, Ethiopia, Kenya, Ghana, Burkina Faso, Mali, Benin, Liberia, Sierra Leone, Gaza, Jordan and the Netherlands.

ABOUT THE RUAF FOUNDATION

The RUAF Foundation (Resource centres on Urban Agriculture and Food security) is an international network with member organizations in Africa, Asia, the Middle East, Latin America and Europe, together constituting a leading centre of expertise in the field of (intra- and peri-) urban/city region food and agriculture systems research, planning and development. The RUAF Foundation is a not-for-profit organization legally registered in the Netherlands and in operation since 1999.

The RUAF Foundation seeks to contribute to the development of resilient, equitable and healthy urban/city region food systems, in the global South and North, by facilitating awareness raising, knowledge generation and dissemination, capacity development, policy design and action planning.

The RUAF Foundation has assisted local governments, urban producers and consumers organizations, local entrepreneurs and social enterprises, non-governmental development organizations (NGDOs), local universities and other stakeholders in the urban food system in over 30 countries.

In addition, we support advocacy, sharing and learning activities at national and international levels. The RUAF Foundation has implemented international projects in cooperation with the EU, FAO, UN Habitat, World Bank, ICLEI, DGIS, IDRC, Sida, GTZ and other international and national organizations as well as with NGOs like CARE, Welthungerhilfe, Action contra la Faim and Cordaid.

The RUAF is publishing the *Urban Agriculture Magazine,* books, technical and methodological guidelines and working papers on urban agriculture and city region food systems reaching about 800,000 readers globally today.

More information on the activities of the RUAF Foundation is available on the website: www.ruaf.org. The website also provides access to all RUAF publications, an online bibliographic database on urban agriculture and various other resources (manuals, policy documents, etc.).

ABOUT THE INTERNATIONAL WATER MANAGEMENT INSTITUTE (IWMI)

IWMI is a non-profit, scientific research organization focusing on the sustainable use of water and land resources in developing countries. It is headquartered in Colombo, Sri Lanka, with regional offices across Asia and Africa. IWMI is a member of CGIAR, a global research partnership for a food secure future and a long-term partner in the RUAF network.

IWMI's Mission is to provide evidence-based solutions to sustainably manage water and land resources for food security, people's livelihoods and the environment.

Most of IWMI's research on urban and peri-urban agriculture takes place within its research division on "Resource Recovery, Water Quality and Health", which aims at a better understanding of rural-urban resource flows and competition, the safe recovery of water, nutrients and energy from domestic and agro-industrial waste streams, related drivers and business models, and the support of ecosystem services under urban pressure.

IWMI works through collaborative research with many partners in the North and South. The research division on Resource Recovery works under the CGIAR programme on Water, Land and Ecosystems closely with the World Health Organization (WHO), Food and Agriculture Organization of the United Nations (FAO), United Nations Environment Programme (UNEP), United Nations University (UNU), the Water and Sanitation Program of the World Bank, and many national and international partners across the globe, ultimately targeting development experts, investors and other stakeholders in the research for development continuum.

IWMI staff authored or co-authored only in the domain of urban agriculture and/or wastewater use nearly 400 publications from peer-reviewed journal articles to textbooks, videos and reuse manuals.

More information on the work of IWMI is available at www.iwmi.cgiar.org.

INDEX

Note: page numbers in *italics* indicate figures and tables.